Y0-BTD-537

# The World of Children

# The World of Children

Claire Etaugh
Bradley University

Spencer A. Rathus
St. John's University

Harcourt Brace College Publishers
Fort Worth Philadelphia San Diego New York Orlando Austin San Antonio
Toronto Montreal London Sydney Tokyo

*Publisher* TED BUCHHOLZ
*Executive Editor* CHRISTOPHER P. KLEIN
*Acquisitions Editor* TINA OLDHAM
*Senior Developmental Editor* MEERA DASH
*Project Editor* JEFF BECKHAM
*Senior Production Manager* KATHLEEN FERGUSON
*Art Director* NICK WELCH
*Picture Development Editor* GREG MEADORS
*Literary Permissions Editor* SHEILA SHUTTER

COVER IMAGE: © DAVID BROWNELL / THE IMAGE BANK



ADDRESS FOR EDITORIAL CORRESPONDENCE: HARCOURT BRACE COLLEGE PUBLISHERS, 301 COMMERCE STREET, SUITE 3700, FORT WORTH, TX 76102.

ADDRESS FOR ORDERS: HARCOURT BRACE & COMPANY, 6277 SEA HARBOR DRIVE, ORLANDO, FLORIDA 32887. 1-800-782-4479, OR 1-800-433-0001 (IN FLORIDA).

ACKNOWLEDGMENTS AND PERMISSIONS APPEAR FOLLOWING THE REFERENCES AND CONSTITUTE A CONTINUATION OF THIS COPYRIGHT PAGE.

PRINTED IN THE UNITED STATES OF AMERICA

ISBN: 0-15-500147-7

LIBRARY OF CONGRESS CATALOG CARD NUMBER: 93-61402

4 5 6 7 8 9 0 1 2 3 032 9 8 7 6 5 4 3 2 1

# Dedication

*To my children Andi and Adam, who taught me more about child development than any book, and to my grandson Anthony, who continues to teach me.*
*C. E.*

*To my daughters Jill, Allyn, Jordan, and Taylor, whose worlds have overlapped with mine yet been very different and special.*
*S. A. R.*

# Instructor's Preface

*The World of Children* is and is not our own. Children are people, but they are not miniature adults, and how they perceive the world is a never-ending source of fascination and intrigue. The *worlds* of children also differ very much one from another. The worlds of urban, suburban, and rural children may not have that much in common, and the things that are taken for granted in one can be a source of surprise and wonderment to the other. Then, again, the worlds of children in the United States can look very little like the worlds of children in other nations. When children of other nations emigrate to the United States, diverse adjustments and integrations also take place. Capturing, then, the world of children—and the diverse worlds of children—was quite a challenge.

Although it was an arduous task, capturing *The World of Children* was also a source of great fulfillment to the authors. The story of child and adolescent development is at once personal and universal. Not only did this book afford us the satisfactions of parents who, given the slightest opening, show off photos of their children and grandchildren, it also provided us with the fulfillment sought by scientist–authors who commit to pen and paper the methods and principles of a rigorous and fascinating discipline.

Although every page of this book gives us pleasure, we must confess that the idea of it sort of forced itself upon us. As authors, teachers, and researchers, we felt that we needed a new vehicle for teaching the child development course. It therefore became our goal to create a textbook that would present child development with an appropriate balance of scholarly rigor and excitement. This book would motivate students by communicating the engrossing things that children say and do, by allowing our own enthusiasm—and our own family experiences—to shine through, and by inviting students to become involved. In addition, the book would have to integrate the many worlds of children in a natural way, just as children from various backgrounds in the United States navigate naturally through multicultural experiences in their daily lives. As we studied the various experiences of children and adolescents, we learned to appreciate how culture affects development—but we also learned much more. We gained a greater recognition of the possibilities within children in general, because the focus on culture also taught us about the basic physiological and psychological processes that we find in all cultures.

## *Comprehensive and Balanced Coverage*

With *The World of Children,* we want to communicate in content and form the excitement, relevance, and true scientific nature of the discipline of child development. We use a chronological approach, which looks at physical, cognitive, social, and personality development at the different stages of the child's life through adolescence. Chapter 1 presents the history of ways of viewing child development and of contemporary research methods. Chapter 2 is an in-depth discussion of the major theories of child development that influence the field today. Chapters 3 and 4 cover heredity and prenatal and neonatal development. Chapters 5, 6, and 7 explore infancy; Chapters 8, 9, and 10 cover early childhood; Chapters 11, 12, and 13 examine middle childhood; and Chapters 14, 15, and 16 look at adolescence. The book endeavors to show how the different areas of development overlap, and how understanding of one area enhances understanding of the others. In each area, we explore research methodology, up-to-date research findings, and theoretical integration of findings. Although *The World of Children* has a chronological table of contents, each chapter gives full attention to the theoretical questions that attend topical issues in child development. The *Theoretical Interludes,* sections integrated into the discussions, allow us to focus on these questions with depth and academic rigor.

## CRITICAL THINKING ABOUT DEVELOPMENT

Critical thinking helps individuals evaluate claims, arguments, and widely held beliefs in all areas of life. This textbook promotes critical thinking in at least four ways. First, the final section of Chapter 1 is devoted to a discussion of critical thinking about development. Second, the writing style encourages students to think about the issues explored in the book. Third, "Truth or Fiction?" questions appear at the start of each chapter and the answers, known as "Truth or Fiction Revisited", appear in the text when the discussion addresses these questions. Finally, questions called "Thinking About Development" appear in the margins of every chapter. Examples of these questions are

- Agree or disagree with the following statement and support your answer: "Since psychological traits such as shyness and intelligence are influenced by heredity, there is no point in trying to encourage children to be more sociable or to helping poor students do better in school."
- Who is the baby's real mother—the surrogate mother or the wife of the man who fathers the baby?
- Agree or disagree with the following statement and support your answer: "The effects of Head Start programs are illusory. You can't really boost children's IQs."
- Is adolescence a period of "sturm und drang"—storm and stress? If so, why?
- Are there *real* gender differences in cognitive abilities?

## HUMAN DIVERSITY

We have incorporated multicultural research into our discussions in an approach explained in Chapter 1. Throughout the book, the examples, featured material, and "Culture and Development" sections address developmental issues of children from various racial, ethnic, socioeconomic, and religious backgrounds. The emphasis is on diversity within the United States, but cross-cultural comparisons (cultures outside the United States) also are included. To help direct students' critical thinking skills, cultural data charts in the margins summarize key findings. Examples include the following

- Does cultural setting influence parental expectations and behavioral outcomes for children categorized as "difficult"?
- Do different cultural values influence parental child-rearing techniques?
- How do Asian and U.S. attitudes toward achievement differ?
- What percentage of U.S. children live in poverty and are therefore at greater risk for adverse developmental outcomes?
- How does culture influence the development of moral reasoning?

Claire Etaugh specializes in gender research. Related to the diversity theme is the emphasis on studies in gender differences and similarities. The material is incorporated into the text discussion and is obvious in looking at the detailed table of contents. Examples include

- Development of gender roles and gender differences
- Gender differences in play
- Gender and creativity
- Gender and cognitive development
- Gender and moral development
- Women and AIDS

### *Up-to-Date Research and Applications*

The book incorporates the most current information available, while discussing classic studies in the field. It contains over 2,600 references, nearly three-quarters of them from the 1990s. Many in-text applications highlight the relevance of theory and research in child development to daily life. In-text applications include

- Children with AIDS
- Development of reading skills
- What to do about child abuse
- Children in single-parent families
- Mainstreaming of exceptional children

### *Learning Aids and Features*

The central goal of a textbook is to provide students with clear information in a format designed to help them master, think about, and retain the material they read. *The World of Children* contains a number of distinctive learning aids and features designed to meet this goal.

**"Truth or Fiction?" and "Truth or Fiction Revisited" Sections** Truth or Fiction? sections follow the chapter outlines. Truth or Fiction? items stimulate student interest by challenging common knowledge and folklore and by previewing research findings presented in each chapter. Many students consider themselves experts in child development. After all, they observed their own development and that of friends and siblings for many years. Also, some of them are parents. The Truth or Fiction? items prod them to reflect upon the accuracy of their observations.

Truth or Fiction Revisited answers are inserted throughout each chapter following a discussion of the material pertinent to each item. In this way, students are periodically prompted to reflect on their answers to the issues raised in the chapter-opening Truth or Fiction? sections. The Truth or Fiction Revisited items motivate students to compare their preconceptions with scientific knowledge, using their new knowledge to reconsider some of those beliefs.

**THINKING ABOUT DEVELOPMENT AND CULTURAL DATA CHARTS** As we have explained, every chapter has critical thinking features in the margins. "Thinking About Development" questions stimulate students to challenge common beliefs. Cultural data charts summarize important points of key "Culture and Development" sections in visually appealing charts, which also encourage the student to think critically. A three-person (or three-stage) symbol of development draws the reader's attention to these critical thinking exercises. All items marked by this symbol are more fully developed in the workbook that accompanies the textbook.

**GLOSSARIES** *The World of Children* includes two glossaries: a cumulative alphabetical glossary at the end of the book and a running glossary in the margins. The running glossary defines technical terms as they are used in the text. Technical terms are boldfaced in the text the first time they appear. They are defined in the margins of the same pages. Ready access to glossary items permits students to maintain concentration on the chapter. When needed, phonetic spellings are given to help students pronounce technical terms.

**"FOCUS ON RESEARCH" INSERTS** A number of Focus on Research boxes throughout the book elaborate the scientific methods developmentalists use to expand knowledge. These inserts amplify the rigor and depth of the book and include reports of a number of classical and contemporary studies. Examples are

- Selecting the Gender of Your Child: Fantasy or Reality?
- Counting in the Crib
- Children's Eyewitness Testimony
- Is Early Puberty Linked to Childhood Stress?
- The Puzzling Teen-Pregnancy Epidemic

**"DEVELOPING TODAY" INSERTS** Developing Today boxes highlight some of the practical applications and contemporary issues related to scientific advances in child development. They include

- Genetic Engineering
- Prenatal Surgery
- Selecting a Day-Care Center
- Children in War Zones
- Helping Children Use Television Wisely: Suggestions for Parents
- Preventing AIDS: It's More Then Safe(r) Sex
- Warning Signs of Suicide

**CHAPTER SUMMARIES** Each chapter has a summary organized by numbered points. This format helps students review the material in a logical step-by-step manner. Care was taken to include technical terms in the summaries.

## COMPLETE TEACHING PACKAGE

*The World of Children* has a strong, diverse multimedia package, which includes a variety of learning and teaching aids.

***Thinking and Writing About The World of Children* Workbook**
Prepared by Spencer A. Rathus, this workbook comes free with the textbook. *Thinking and Writing About The World of Children* is designed to promote two aspects of studying child development: critical thinking and writing—both in an attempt to understand the world of children as it is and is not our own. The workbook contains a discussion of what critical thinking is, a comprehensive guide to writing about child development, and dozens of writing exercises. By following the critical thinking icons in the textbook, the student revisits the Thinking About Development exercises and the cultural data charts in the textbook. The pages of the workbook are perforated. The exercises may be assigned as a way of encouraging the development of thinking, writing, and data interpretation skills, as a way of providing an opportunity for class participation, and, perhaps, as a way of earning part of the grade for the course.

**Study Guide with Readings** Prepared by Dan Tomasulo of Brookdale Community College, the study guide helps students master, explore, and enjoy the concepts of child development. Each chapter has learning objectives, creative vocabulary exercises, puzzles, practice tests, and readings with critical thinking questions.

**Instructor's Resource Manual** Written by Jo Ann Farver of the University of Southern California, the Instructor's Resource Manual provides extensive information on perforated pages. The manual begins with a course planner, including general teaching suggestions, a sample syllabus, and ways to use the teaching package. Each chapter has an overview and outline, teaching enhancements, ideas for interviews and observational activities, a multicultural reading guide with questions for the students, and a section on audiovisual aids.

**Test Bank** Prepared by Rosemary Price and Gregory Pezzetti of Rancho Santiago College, the test bank provides complete testing information. Each chapter has more than 100 multiple-choice, true-false, and fill-in-the-blank items. The test bank classifies each item as knowledge-recall or applied cognitive type. The test bank is available in both printed and computerized form, which includes Gradebook Software and four versions of EXAMaster software: IBM 3 1/2, IBM 5 1/4, Windows, and Macintosh.

**Overhead Transparencies: Developmental Series** Instructors using *The World of Children* will have access to a set of 50 full-color overhead transparency acetates designed to facilitate understanding of key concepts. These transparencies are meant to supplement (not duplicate) coverage from the textbook.

**Harcourt Brace Video Library** Harcourt Brace offers a large and varied choice of video programs, which complement one another in their various approaches to child development. Use of the videos is based on the Harcourt Brace video policy. See your Harcourt Brace book representative.

**"Childhood" Video Programs** In seven 1-hour programs, Childhood presents an insightful and richly textured examination of the various influences that shape people as individuals and members of families and societies. It offers a strong cross-cultural perspective on child development. Childhood is a production of Thirteen/WNET and the Childhood Project, Inc., part of the Ambrose Video Collection.

**"Time to Grow" Video Programs** The Time to Grow series offers an introductory course in child development consisting of twenty-six 30-minute television programs and coordinated print materials. The series follows a chronological approach, including the most recent theoretical and applied perspectives about effective ways of caring for and working with children.

**"Seasons of Life" Video Programs** A study of lifespan psychology, Seasons of Life includes five 1-hour programs—each covering a chronological phase of the lifespan—that examine the drama of human development. David Hartman is the host with John Kotre, professor of psychology at the University of Michigan-Dearborn.

**"Discovering Psychology" Teaching Modules** The Discovering Psychology video series offers the most salient information from the Discovering Psychology television course. Clips of experiments are interwoven with interviews of such prominent researchers as Jean Piaget, Renée Baillargeon, Judy DeLoache, Michael Meaney, and Eleanor Maccoby. Each module is divided into segments that are less than five minutes each. The two modules that cover development, #10 on Physical and Cognitive Development and #11 on Social and Personality Development, have been made available to instructors using Etaugh/Rathus.

**Harcourt Brace Human Development Videodisk** A new human development videodisk will be available to instructors who use Etaugh/Rathus, *The World of Children.* Quantity of videos and videodisks is based on the Harcourt Brace per-adoption policy.

## Acknowledgments

*The World of Children* owes a great deal of its substance and form to our colleagues, who provided expert suggestions and insights at various stages in its development. Our sincere thanks to the following reviewers and consultants:

Barbara Allgood-Hill, Kent State University; Harry H. Avis, Sierra College; Melita Baumann, Glendale Community College; Margaret Berrio, Cal Poly State University; Bruce Carter, Syracuse University; William Charlesworth, University of Minnesota at Twin Cities; Margaret Cleek, University of Wisconsin at West Bend; Phillip Dale, University of Washington; Carol Lynn Davis, University of Southern Maine; Louise Dean, Los Angeles Valley College; Don Devers, North Virginia Community College; Melanie Diderichs, Mount San Antonio College; Joan Downs, Governors State University; Larry Fenson, San Diego State University; Barbara Foulks, SUNY Geneseo; Kathleen Fox, Salisbury State University; Dennis Goff, Randolph-Macon Woman's College; Jerry Harper, University of Wisconsin at Eau Claire; Yvette Harris, Miami University; Elizabeth Hasson, West Chester University; Wallace Kennedy, Florida State University; Eileen Knight, St. Xavier University; Daniel Lapsley, University of Notre Dame; Karen Lowe, San Diego Mesa College; Laura Massey, Montana State University; Deborah R. McDonald, New Mexico State University; Gregory Pezzetti, Rancho Santiago College; Carolyn Schantz, Wayne State University; Patricia Schmolze, Los Angeles City College; Susan Nakayama Siaw, California State Polytechnical University at Pomona; Beverly Smith, University of New Mexico; Linda Spear, SUNY Binghampton; Ron Taylor, Temple University; Robert Tomlinson, University of Wisconsin at Eau Claire; Robert Wallace, Blinn College; Alida Westman, Eastern Michigan University; Lyn Wickelgren, Metropolitan State College.

We wish to pay special thanks to Algea Harrison. Her sensitive reading of the manuscript helped us in the writing of the Culture and Development sections. She also supplied many of the cultural data charts. We also are grateful to Nancy Wagler, who typed the manuscript and carried out many other tasks essential to the production of the book.

We are indebted to the publishing professionals at Harcourt Brace. It is a privilege to work with them. In particular, we acknowledge the invaluable assistance and support of Tina Oldham, Acquisitions Editor; Meera Dash, Senior Developmental Editor; and Jeff Beckham, Project Editor. Without them, this book could not have been written. Thanks also go to Kathleen Ferguson, Senior Production Manager; Greg Meadors, Picture Editor; Nick Welch, Art Director; and Sheila Shutter, Permissions Editor.

Finally, our heartfelt appreciation goes to our significant others—William Wilsen and Lois Fichner-Rathus—for their patience, moral support, and understanding during the thousands of hours it took to write this book.

*Claire Etaugh*

*Spencer A. Rathus*

## About the Authors

**Claire Etaugh** is Professor of Psychology at Bradley University. She received her Ph.D. in child development from the University of Minnesota. Twenty years ago, she cofounded the Center for the Study of Early Childhood Development at Bradley University and she remains its codirector. A Fellow of the American Psychological Association's Divisions of Developmental Psychology and the Psychology of Women, she has published over ninety scholarly articles in such journals as *Child Development, Developmental Psychology, Merrill-Palmer Quarterly, Psychology of Women, Sex Roles,* and *American Psychologist.*

**Spencer A. Rathus** received his Ph.D. from the State University of New York at Albany. He is on the psychology faculty at St. John's University, where he has taught courses in child development and cognitive-behavior therapy and supervised doctoral trainees in psychotherapy. He has published numerous articles in the areas of developmental psychology, psychological assessment, cognitive-behavior therapy, and deviant behavior. He is the author of the Rathus Assertiveness Schedule and has written many books, including *Psychology* and *Essentials of Psychology.* He has coauthored *Making the Most of College* with Lois Fichner-Rathus; *AIDS—What Every Student Needs to Know* with Susan Boughn; *Adjustment and Growth: The Challenges of Life* and *Behavior Therapy Strategies for Solving Problems in Living* with Jeffrey S. Nevid; *Human Sexuality in a World of Diversity* with Jeffrey S. Nevid and Lois Fichner-Rathus; and *Abnormal Psychology in a Changing World* with Jeffrey S. Nevid and Beverly A. Greene.

[illegible]

## ABOUT THE AUTHORS

[illegible]

# *Student's Preface:* How to Use This Textbook

**The World of Children** was designed to help you understand and think about child development in a way that will benefit you not only in your studies, but also in your experiences. The following pages will show you how to use the learning features of each chapter of the textbook and the free accompanying workbook, **Thinking and Writing About The World of Children.**

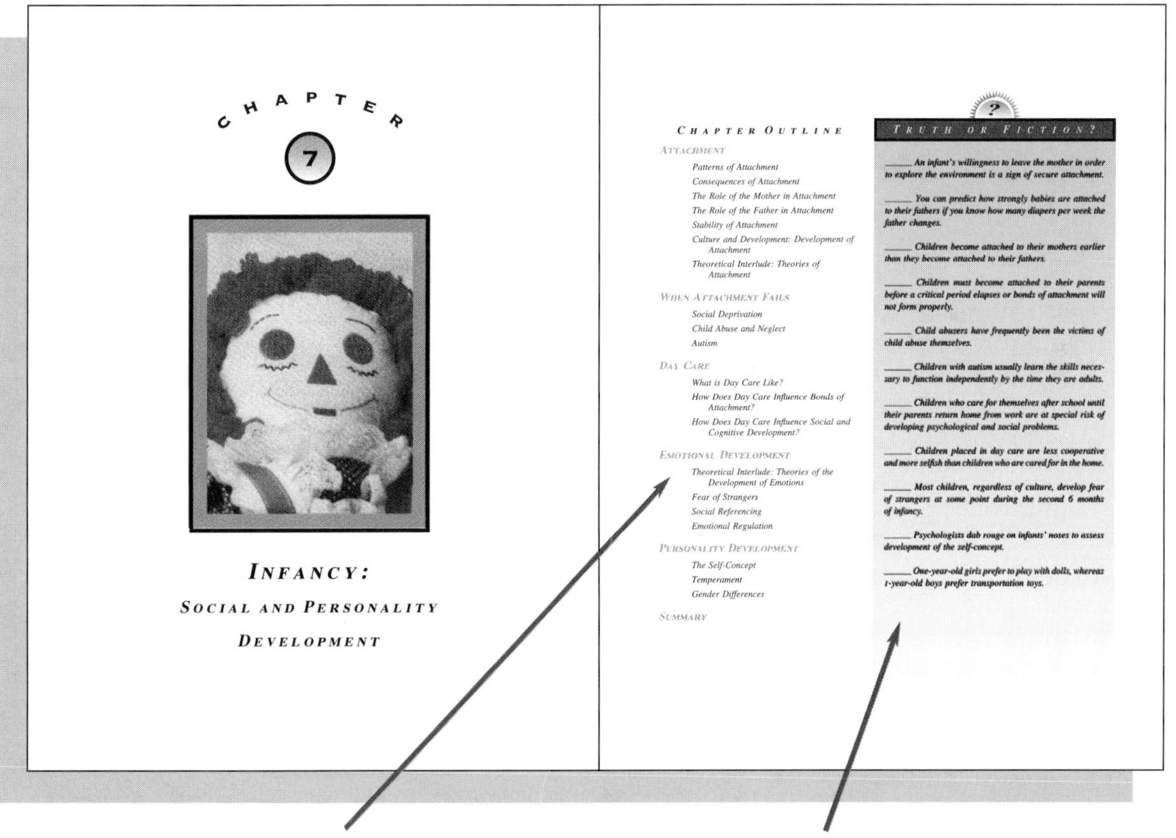

*A Chapter Outline appears at the start of each chapter. Skim this outline to give yourself an overview of the topics and the order in which you will read about them.*

*Truth-or-Fiction? questions open each chapter. Complete this "true-false" test* before *you read the chapter. The interesting issues it raises could lead you to search for the answers in the chapter.*

Characteristics of Newborns 147

is just one of the many ***reflexes*** shown by neonates. Reflexes are simple, unlearned, stereotypical responses that are elicited by certain types of stimulation. They do not require higher brain functions; they occur automatically, without thinking. Reflexes are the most complicated motor activities displayed by newborns. Neonates cannot roll over, sit up, reach for an object that they see, or raise their heads.

***Reflex*** An unlearned, stereotypical response to a stimulus.

***Voluntarily*** Intentionally.

***Neural*** Of the nervous system.

***Rooting reflex*** A reflex in which infants turn their mouths and heads in the direction of a stroking of the cheek or the corner of the mouth.

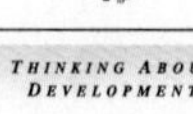

TRUTH OR FICTION REVISITED

*It is true that newborn babies who are placed face down in comfortably warm water will make swimming motions. Swimming movements are reflexive and may reflect our evolutionary history.*

Let us return to our early venture into the water. If you had been placed into the water not a few moments but several months after birth, the results might have been very different and disastrous. After a few months the swimming reflex, like many others, ceases to exist. However, at 6 to 12 months of age infants can learn how to swim ***voluntarily.*** In fact, the transition from reflexive swimming to learned swimming can be reasonably smooth with careful guided practice.

Many reflexes have survival value. Adults and neonates, for example, will reflexively close their eyes when assaulted with a puff of air or sudden bright light. Other reflexes seem to reflect interesting facets of the evolution of the nervous system. The swimming reflex seems to suggest that there was a time when our ancestors profited from being born able to swim.

Pediatricians learn a good deal about the adequacy of newborn babies' ***neural*** functioning by testing their reflexes. The absence or weakness of a reflex may indicate immaturity (as in prematurity); slowed responsiveness, which can result from anesthetics used during childbirth; brain injury; or retardation. Let us examine some of the reflexes shown by neonates.

The rooting and sucking reflexes are basic to survival. In the ***rooting reflex,*** the baby turns the head and mouth toward a stimulus that strokes the cheek, chin, or corner of the mouth. The rooting reflex facilitates finding the mother's nipple in preparation for sucking. Babies will suck almost any object that touches the lips. The sucking reflex grows stronger during the first days after birth and can be lost if not stimulated. As the months go on, reflexive sucking becomes replaced by voluntary sucking.

THINKING ABOUT DEVELOPMENT

In human beings, what kinds of behavior patterns are learned and what kinds are innate (inborn)? Are most differences between people learned or innate?

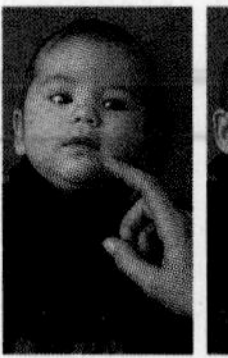

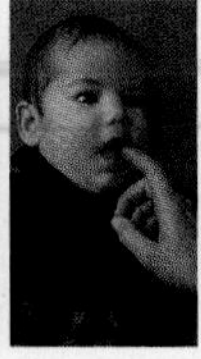

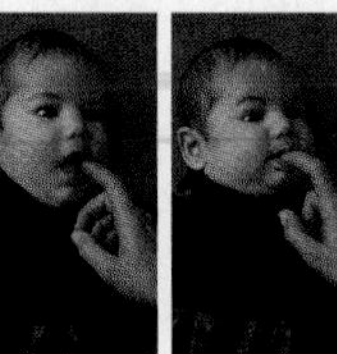

FIGURE 4.10

**THE ROOTING REFLEX.** *Tactile stimulation of the corner of the mouth elicits turning of the head toward the stimulus.*

*TRUTH OR FICTION REVISITED answers one of the Truth or Fiction? questions that you addressed earlier.*

*THINKING ABOUT DEVELOPMENT asks you to agree or disagree with a common bias or belief. Use the three-person symbol to complete the corresponding exercise in your workbook.*

*CULTURE AND DEVELOPMENT SECTIONS discuss children of various ethnic, racial, religious, and socioeconomic backgrounds. See if you can detect any cultural distinctions within the United States, or in contrast to U.S. children.*

*A CULTURAL DATA CHART directs you to a central question about culture and development, summarizing the relevant studies in a chart. The three-person symbol is a reminder that a related exercise appears in your workbook.*

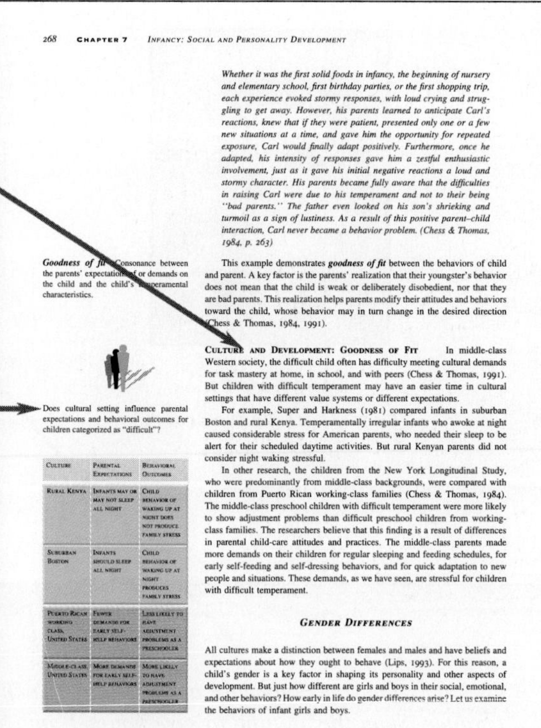

268 CHAPTER 7 INFANCY: SOCIAL AND PERSONALITY DEVELOPMENT

*Whether it was the first solid foods in infancy, the beginning of nursery and elementary school, first birthday parties, or the first shopping trip, each experience evoked stormy responses, with loud crying and struggling to get away. However, his parents learned to anticipate Carl's reactions, knew that if they were patient, presented only one or a few new situations at a time, and gave him the opportunity for repeated exposure, Carl would finally adapt positively. Furthermore, once he adapted, his intensity of responses gave him a zestful enthusiastic involvement, just as it gave his initial negative reactions a loud and stormy character. His parents became fully aware that the difficulties in raising Carl were due to his temperament and not to their being "bad parents." The father even looked on his son's shrieking and turmoil as a sign of lustiness. As a result of this positive parent–child interaction, Carl never became a behavior problem. (Chess & Thomas, 1984, p. 263)*

***Goodness of fit*** Consonance between the parents' expectations of or demands on the child and the child's temperamental characteristics.

This example demonstrates ***goodness of fit*** between the behaviors of child and parent. A key factor is the parents' realization that their youngster's behavior does not mean that the child is weak or deliberately disobedient, nor that they are bad parents. This realization helps parents modify their attitudes and behaviors toward the child, whose behavior may in turn change in the desired direction (Chess & Thomas, 1984, 1991).

**CULTURE AND DEVELOPMENT: GOODNESS OF FIT** In middle-class Western society, the difficult child often has difficulty meeting cultural demands for task mastery at home, in school, and with peers (Chess & Thomas, 1991). But children with difficult temperament may have an easier time in cultural settings that have different value systems or different expectations.

For example, Super and Harkness (1981) compared infants in suburban Boston and rural Kenya. Temperamentally irregular infants who awoke at night caused considerable stress for American parents, who needed their sleep to be alert for their scheduled daytime activities. But rural Kenyan parents did not consider night waking stressful.

In other research, the children from the New York Longitudinal Study, who were predominantly from middle-class backgrounds, were compared with children from Puerto Rican working-class families (Chess & Thomas, 1984). The middle-class preschool children with difficult temperament were more likely to show adjustment problems than difficult preschool children from working-class families. The researchers believe that this finding is a result of differences in parental child-care attitudes and practices. The middle-class parents made more demands on their children for regular sleeping and feeding schedules, for early self-feeding and self-dressing behaviors, and for quick adaptation to new people and situations. These demands, as we have seen, are stressful for children with difficult temperament.

Does cultural setting influence parental expectations and behavioral outcomes for children categorized as "difficult"?

| CULTURE | PARENTAL EXPECTATIONS | BEHAVIORAL OUTCOMES |
|---|---|---|
| RURAL KENYA | INFANTS MAY OR MAY NOT SLEEP ALL NIGHT | CHILD BEHAVIOR OF WAKING UP AT NIGHT DOES NOT PRODUCE FAMILY STRESS |
| SUBURBAN BOSTON | INFANTS SHOULD SLEEP ALL NIGHT | CHILD BEHAVIOR OF WAKING UP AT NIGHT PRODUCES FAMILY STRESS |
| PUERTO RICAN WORKING CLASS, UNITED STATES | FEWER DEMANDS FOR EARLY SELF-HELP BEHAVIORS | LESS LIKELY TO HAVE ADJUSTMENT PROBLEMS AS A PRESCHOOLER |
| MIDDLE-CLASS, UNITED STATES | MORE DEMANDS FOR EARLY SELF-HELP BEHAVIORS | MORE LIKELY TO HAVE ADJUSTMENT PROBLEMS AS A PRESCHOOLER |

GENDER DIFFERENCES

All cultures make a distinction between females and males and have beliefs and expectations about how they ought to behave (Lips, 1993). For this reason, a child's gender is a key factor in shaping its personality and other aspects of development. But just how different are girls and boys in their social, emotional, and other behaviors? How early in life do gender differences arise? Let us examine the behaviors of infant girls and boys.

Information Processing 211

FOCUS ON RESEARCH

### COUNTING IN THE CRIB

Infants as young as 5 months of age have the ability to add and subtract, according to recent research by Karen Wynn (1992a). Wynn's conclusion is based on the fact that infants look longer at unexpected events than expected ones. (You may recall that Baillargeon's studies of object permanence in young infants also made use of this fact.) If babies are able to add and subtract, they should look longer at the "wrong" unexpected answer to an addition or subtraction problem than at the expected "correct" answer. Wynn showed the infants 4-inch Mickey Mouse dolls. One group of babies saw a single doll. Then a screen was put up, blocking the babies' view. While the babies watched, Wynn put another doll behind the screen. The screen was removed, revealing either two dolls (the right answer) or only one doll (the wrong answer). Another group of babies saw two dolls initially. The screen was put up, and the babies watched while one doll was removed. When the screen was removed, the infants saw either one doll (right) or two (wrong). Babies consistently looked longer at the "wrong" answers.

These results show that infants know that adding or subtracting produces some sort of change in the number of objects. But can babies calculate precisely how much change is produced? That is, can they actually count?

To answer this question, Wynn presented a third group of babies with a single doll. She added another doll after the screen went up and then removed the screen, revealing either two Mickeys (correct answer) or three (wrong answer). In both cases, a change was produced. But babies stared longer at the wrong answer of three dolls, indicating that they had calculated exactly how many objects should appear.

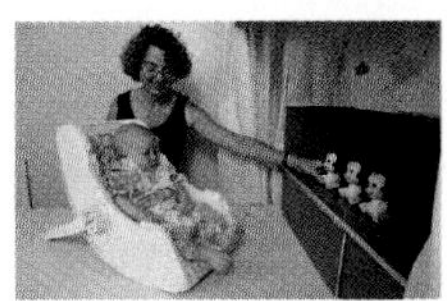

**FIGURE 6.8 COUNTING IN THE CRIB.** *Recent research suggests that 5-month-old infants know when simple calculations are done correctly or incorrectly. The babies stare longer when shown a "wrong answer." Karen Wynn (shown here with a 5-month-old) arrived at these results by showing infants Mickey Mouse dolls. She then added or subtracted a doll behind a screen and presented the baby with the "right" or "wrong" answer.*

Memory improves between 2 and 6 months of age. This improvement may indicate that older infants are more capable than younger ones of encoding (that is, storing) information, retrieving information already stored, or both (Kail, 1990).

A fascinating series of studies by Carolyn Rovee-Collier and her colleagues (Rovee-Collier, 1993) illustrates some of these developmental changes in infant memory (see Figure 6.9). One end of a ribbon was tied to a brightly colored mobile suspended above the infant's crib. The other end was tied to the infant's ankle, so that when the baby kicked, the mobile moved. Babies quickly learned to increase their rate of kicking. To measure memory, the infant's ankle was again fastened to the mobile after a period of one or more days had elapsed. In one study, 2-month-olds remembered how to make the mobile move after delays of up to 3 days, and 3-month-olds remembered for more than a week (Greco et al., 1986).

Infant memory can be improved if babies receive a reminder before they are given the memory test (Rovee-Collier & Shyi, 1992). In one study that used this reminder procedure, babies were shown the moving mobile on the day prior to the memory test, but they were not allowed to activate it. Under these conditions, 3-month-olds remembered how to move the mobile after a 28-day delay (Rovee-Collier, 1993).

*A FOCUS ON RESEARCH FEATURE shows you how some of the most important research about children is carried out. Try to identify the main method and analysis used to explore the researcher's questions.*

Motor Development 185

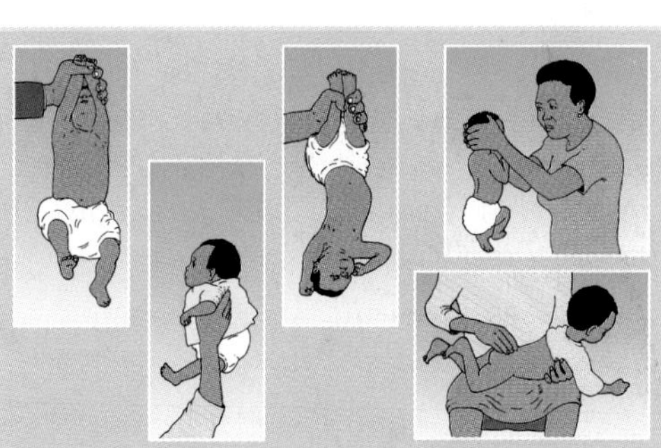

FIGURE 5.15

**ASPECTS OF THE JAMAICAN FORMAL-HANDLING ROUTINE.** *Parents in Africa and in cultures of African origin, such as Jamaica, provide experience from birth onward that stimulates the development of sitting and walking in their babies. These activities, known as* formal handling, *including stretching exercises and massage (as shown here), as well as propping babies in a sitting position, bouncing them on their feet, and exercising the stepping reflex. (Source: Hopkins, 1991).*

### THEORETICAL INTERLUDE: NATURE AND NURTURE IN MOTOR DEVELOPMENT

There seems to be little doubt that both maturation (nature) and experience (nurture) play indispensable roles in various aspects of motor development (Jouen & Lepecq, 1990). Certain types of voluntary motor activities do not seem possible until the brain has matured in terms of myelination and the differentiation of the motor areas of the cortex. While it is true that the neonate shows stepping and swimming reflexes, these behaviors are controlled by more primitive areas of the brain. They disappear when cortical development inhibits some of the functions of the lower areas of the brain, and, when they reappear, their quality is quite different.

Infants also need some opportunity for motor experimentation before they can engage in milestones such as sitting up and walking. But although it may take them several months to sit up and, as described earlier, more months to take their first steps, most of this time can apparently be attributed to maturation. In a classic study, Wayne and Marsena Dennis (1940) reported on the motor development of Native-American Hopi children who spent their first year strapped to a cradleboard (see Figure 5.16). Although denied a full year of experience in locomotion, the Hopi infants gained the capacity to walk early in their second year, at about the same time as children reared in other cultures. A more recent cross-cultural study (Hindley et al., 1966) reported that infants in five European cities began to walk at about the same time (generally between 12 and 15 months), despite cultural differences in encouragement to walk.

*A THEORETICAL INTERLUDE introduces in depth the questions that developmental researchers debate. Make note of the key argument of each side of the debate.*

Day Care 257

*Developing Today*

### SELECTING A DAY-CARE CENTER OR HOME

Selecting a day-care center or home can be an overwhelming task. Standards for day-care centers and homes vary from locale to locale, so licensing is no guarantee of adequate care. To become sophisticated consumers of day care, parents can weigh factors such as the following when making a choice:

1. Is the center or home licensed? By what agency? What standards must be met to acquire a license?
2. What is the ratio of children to care givers? Everything else being equal, care givers appear to do a better job when there are fewer children in their charge. Experts recommend there be at least one care giver for every 4 children under age 2, for every 6 2-year-olds, and for every 10 children ranging from 3 to 5 years of age (Hayes et al., 1990). But it may also be of use to look beyond numbers. Quality is frequently more important than quantity.
3. What are the qualifications of the care givers? How well aware are they of children's needs and patterns of development? Research shows that children fare better when their care givers have specific training in child development (Howes, 1990; Zaslow, 1991). Years of day-care experience and formal degrees are less important. Day-care workers typically are paid poorly. Financial frustrations lead many well-qualified workers to seek work in other fields (Noble, 1993).
4. How safe is the environment? Do toys and swings seem to be in good condition? Are dangerous objects out of reach? Would strangers have a difficult time breaking in? Have children been injured in this center or home?
5. What is served at mealtime? Is it nutritious, appetizing? Will your child eat it? Some babies are placed in day care at 6 months or younger, and parents will need to know what formulas are used.
6. Which care givers will be responsible for your child? What are their backgrounds? How do they seem to relate to children?
7. With what children will your child interact and play?
8. What toys, games, books, and other educational objects are provided?
9. What facilities are present for promoting the motor development of your child? How well-supervised are children when they use new objects such as swings and tricycles?
10. Are the hours offered by the center or home convenient for your schedule?
11. Is the location of the center or home convenient?
12. Are parents permitted to visit unannounced?
13. Do you like the overall environment and feel of the center or home?

interpreted quite differently (Clark-Stewart 1989; Lamb et al., 1992a; Thompson, 1991b).

One key factor is that the Strange Situation may be less stressful for children of employed mothers than for those with nonemployed mothers and, therefore, may be a less valid indicator of attachment for them. Infants whose mothers work encounter daily separation from and reunions with their mother. Young children adapt to repeated separations from their mothers (Field, 1991c). Therefore, infants whose mothers work may be less distressed by her departure in the Strange Situation and less likely to seek her out when she returns. A second point to keep in mind is that the likelihood of insecure attachment is not much greater in day-care babies than in home-reared babies; in fact, most infants in both groups are securely attached (Clarke-Stewart, 1989; Lamb et al., 1992b).

### HOW DOES DAY CARE INFLUENCE SOCIAL AND COGNITIVE DEVELOPMENT?

Day care generally seems to have positive influences on children's social and cognitive development. Infants with day-care experience are more peer oriented and play at higher developmental levels than do home-reared babies. Day-care

*A DEVELOPING TODAY FEATURE helps you to apply contemporary advances in development research to common situations. Discuss with your friends, classmates, or family these practical guidelines.*

90 **CHAPTER 3** *HEREDITY AND PRENATAL DEVELOPMENT*

**TRUTH OR FICTION REVISITED**

***It is possible to learn the gender of one's child prior to birth. Amniocentesis and ultrasound are two of the methods that can provide this information.***

***Chorionic villus sampling*** **(CORE-ee-ON-ick Vill-iss) A method for the prenatal detection of genetic abnormalities that samples the membrane enveloping the amniotic sac and fetus.**

**CHORIONIC VILLUS SAMPLING** ***Chorionic villus sampling*** **(CVS) is similar to amniocentesis but offers the advantage of diagnosing fetal abnormalities much earlier in pregnancy. CVS is carried out during the 9th or 10th week of pregnancy. A small syringe is inserted through the vagina into the uterus. The syringe gently sucks out a few of the threadlike projections (villi) from the outer membrane that envelops the amniotic sac and fetus. Results are available within days of the procedure. However, CVS carries a slightly greater risk of spontaneous abortion than does amniocentesis (Gilbert, 1993; Rosenthal, 1991). Recent studies also suggest that somewhere between 1 in 200 to 1 in 1,000 babies born to women who have CVS may have birth defects involving missing or stubby fingers and toes (Kolata, 1992d; "Study Finds," 1994), so the technique remains controversial.**

*THE RUNNING GLOSSARY lets you learn and review terms at your own pace. It includes pronunciation guidelines for difficult terms.*

FIGURE 3.7

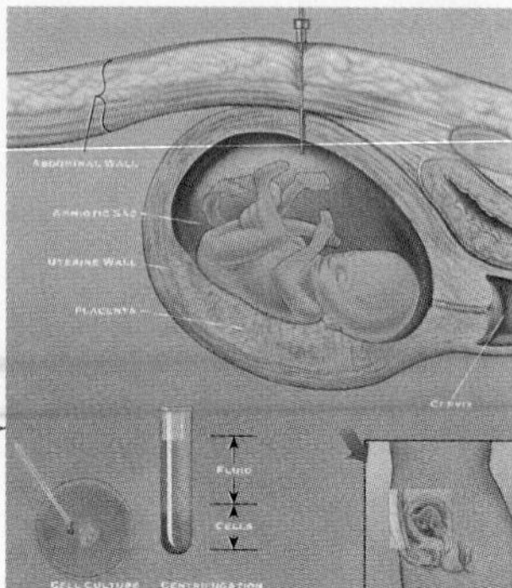


**AMNIOCENTESIS.** *Amniocentesis allows prenatal identification of certain genetic and chromosomal disorders by examining genetic material sloughed off by the fetus into amniotic fluid. Amniocentesis also allows parents to learn the gender of their unborn child. Would you want to know?*

*VISUAL AIDS AND EXPLANATORY CAPTIONS bring clarity, detail, and emphasis to key concepts. They also provide you with a focus for discussing the material with others.*

270 **CHAPTER 7** *INFANCY: SOCIAL AND PERSONALITY DEVELOPMENT*

FIGURE 7.19

**ADULTS TREAT INFANT GIRLS AND BOYS DIFFERENTLY.** *Perhaps the most obvious way in which parents treat their baby girls and boys differently is in their choice of clothing, toys, and room furnishings. If you were to meet these two unfamiliar children, would you have any doubt about their gender?*

Other studies find that parents react favorably when their preschool daughters play with "girls'" toys and their sons play with "boys'" toys. Parents and other adults show more negative reactions when girls play with "boys'" toys and boys play with "girls'" toys (Caldera et al., 1989; Etaugh, 1983; Martin, 1990). Fathers are more concerned than mothers that their children engage in activities viewed as "appropriate" for their gender (Bradley & Gobbart, 1989; Lytton & Romney, 1991).

And so, parents begin to shape the behaviors of their children during the infant years and help lay the foundation for development in early childhood. It is to that period of life that we turn next.

## Summary

1. Attachment is the affectional tie that persons form between themselves and specific others. Attachment in young children is measured by their efforts to maintain contact with care givers and by their display of separation anxiety. Using the Strange Situation method, Ainsworth has identified patterns of secure and insecure (avoidant and ambivalent-resistant) attachment. Different child-rearing attitudes and practices may account for cross-cultural differences in attachment patterns.

2. Securely attached infants and toddlers are happier and more socially competent. They use their primary care givers as a base for exploration. Individual patterns of attachment can change as family conditions and interpersonal relationships change. Babies become attached to both parents at about the same time, although they generally spend less time with their fathers and their mothers are more likely to be the ones who meet their routine needs.

3. Three phases of attachment have been identified: From birth to 3 months, infants show indiscriminate attachment. At about 3 or 4 months, they select familiar figures over strangers. At 6 or 7 months, attachment becomes more clear-cut.

4. There are many theoretical views of attachment, including the cognitive, behavioral, psychoanalytic, "contact comfort," and ethological perspectives.

*A CHAPTER SUMMARY gives you a quick review of the basic principles of the chapter. Focus on one numbered point at a time. If you do not understand anything under that item, go back to the appropriate section of the chapter and review the material until you know it better.*

## Brief Table of Contents

# CONTENTS

O L C
T W
D G K

# Culture and Domains of Development

## *Physical Domain*

### Multicultural Issues



### Cross-cultural Issues



## *Cognitive Domain*

### Multicultural Issues



### Cross-cultural Issues

## Social Domain

### Multicultural Issues



### Cross-cultural Issues

## Gender and Domains of Development

### *Physical Domain*



### *Cognitive Domain*



### *Social Domain*

# The World of Children

# WHAT IS CHILD DEVELOPMENT?

HOW CHILDREN CHANGE AS THEY GROW OLDER AND GROW UP is the subject of this book.

You will see in Chapter 1 that we study child development for many reasons. Among these are the desire to learn about the origins of adult behavior; to investigate the causes, prevention, and treatment of developmental problems; and to optimize conditions of development for all children. In Chapter 1, we also examine the history of child development and some of the current controversies in the field. We introduce you to the research methods used to increase our knowledge of child development. In Chapter 2, we discuss the major theories of development that have guided efforts to better understand children. After these two introductory chapters, the remainder of the book is devoted to charting the course of development from the time of conception through the adolescent years.

# HISTORY, CONTROVERSIES, AND METHODS

## CHAPTER OUTLINE



## TRUTH OR FICTION?

______ *Development and growth are synonymous terms.*

______ *Hispanic Americans are the fastest growing ethnic group in the United States.*

______ *Women were not permitted to attend college in the United States until 1833.*

______ *During the Middle Ages, children were often treated and depicted as miniature adults.*

______ *Children come into the world as "blank tablets"—without preferences or inborn differences in intelligence and specific talents.*

______ *Children were once treated as the property of their parents.*

______ *Some theorists contend that children actively strive to understand and take charge of their worlds, whereas other theorists argue that children respond passively to environmental stimulation.*

______ *Research with rhesus monkeys has helped psychologists understand the formation of attachment in humans.*

______ *Researchers have followed some participants in developmental research for more than 50 years.*

______ *Psychologists would not be able to carry out certain research studies with children if they fully informed the participants as to the purposes and methods of the studies.*

*Your children are not your children.*
*They are the sons and daughters of Life's longing for itself.*
*They come through you but not from you,*
*And though they are with you yet they belong not to you.*
*You may give them your love but not your thoughts,*
*For they have their own thoughts.*
*You may house their bodies but not their souls,*
*For their souls dwell in the house of tomorrow,*
*which you cannot visit, not even in your dreams.*
*You may strive to be like them, but seek not to make them like you.*
*For life goes not backward nor tarries with yesterday . . .*

(KAHLIL GIBRAN, *THE PROPHET*, 1970, P. 17)

What is Gibran suggesting in this poem? Watching a child develop is a wondrous experience. Parents certainly play their part, but they alone do not determine the ultimate outcome.

The development of children is what this book is about, but in our children we see mirrors of ourselves. In a very real sense, we cannot hope to understand ourselves as adults—we cannot catch a glimpse of the remarkable journeys we have taken—without understanding children.

Let us embark on our search for ourselves by answering a basic question: What is child development? Then we shall explore some of the reasons for studying child development. One of them, as suggested, is to gain insight into our own behavior as adults. But there are others, such as looking into the causes of developmental abnormalities and finding ways to prevent or treat them. Next, we examine the importance of studying the diversity of children, focusing on issues of ethnic and gender diversity. Then we go on a brief tour of the history of child development. It may surprise you to learn that until relatively recent times, people were not particularly sensitive to the many ways in which children differ from adults. Next we examine some controversies in child development, such as whether there are distinct stages of development. Then we consider scientific methods for the study of child development. We also examine some of the issues concerning ethics in developmental research. We shall see that many sophisticated methods for studying children have been devised and that ethics helps determine the types of research that are deemed proper and improper. Finally, we explore the role of critical thinking in the study of child development.

## WHAT IS CHILD DEVELOPMENT?

In order to define child development, let us look at two words whose meanings may seem self-evident but may not be: *child* and *development.*

### CHILD

**Child** A person undergoing the period of development from infancy through puberty.

**Infancy** Babyhood. The period of very early childhood, characterized by lack of complex speech; the first 2 years after birth.

You have heard the word *child* all your life, so why bother to define it? We define it, because words in common usage are frequently used in inexact ways.

A ***child*** is a person undergoing the period of development from infancy to puberty—two more familiar words that are frequently used inexactly. The term ***infancy*** derives from Latin roots meaning "not speaking," and infancy is usually defined as the first 2 years of life, or the period of life prior to the development of complex speech. We stress the word *complex,* because many children have large numbers of words and use simple sentences well before their second birthday. ***Puberty*** refers to the period of development during which people gain reproductive capacity. Puberty signals the beginning of ***adolescence,*** a transitional period between childhood and adulthood in most industrial societies. Postpubertal children often continue to acquire academic and vocational skills and gradually attain independence from parents. In some preindustrial societies, however, children may assume adult roles at the time of puberty.

Between infancy and adolescence are two other periods of development. The first is usually called ***early childhood,*** and the second is called ***middle childhood.*** Early childhood encompasses the ages of 2 to 5 years. These are the years before the child starts school, and so early childhood is sometimes referred to as the preschool period. Middle childhood generally is defined as the years from ages 6 to 12. The beginning of this period usually is marked by the child's entry into first grade. Most child development textbooks include discussions of infancy, early childhood, middle childhood, and adolescence, and so does this one. In fact, we shall begin even before infancy. We shall describe the origin of ***germ cells,*** the process of ***conception,*** and the ***prenatal period.***

***Puberty*** (PEW-burr-tee) The stage of development characterized by changes that lead to reproductive capacity.

***Adolescence*** The stage bounded by the advent of puberty at the lower end and the capacity to take on adult responsibilities at the upper end. Puberty is a biological concept, while adolescence is a psychological concept.

***Early childhood*** The period of development from ages 2 to 5; the preschool years.

***Middle childhood*** The period of development from ages 6 to 12; the elementary school years.

***Germ cells*** The cells from which new organisms are developed.

***Conception*** The process of becoming pregnant; the process by which a sperm cell joins with an ovum to begin a new life.

***Prenatal period*** The period of development from conception to birth.

## *Development*

***Development*** is the orderly appearance, over time, of physical structures, psychological traits, behaviors, and ways of adapting to the demands of life. The changes brought on by development are both ***qualitative*** and ***quantitative.*** Qualitative changes are changes in type or kind. Consider ***motor development.*** As we develop, we gain the capacities to lift our heads, sit up, creep, stand, and walk. These changes are qualitative. However, within each of these qualitative changes, there are also developments that are quantitative. Quantitative changes are changes in amount. After babies begin to lift their heads, they lift them higher and higher. Soon after children walk, they also begin to run. And, as their running advances, they gain the capacity to go faster and faster.

***Development*** The processes by which organisms unfold features and traits, grow, and become more complex and specialized in structure and function.

***Qualitative changes*** Changes in type or kind.

***Quantitative changes*** Changes in amount.

***Motor development*** The development of the capacity for movement, particularly that made possible by changes in the nervous system and the muscles.

**FIGURE 1.1**

**MOTOR DEVELOPMENT.** *Development refers to orderly changes, over time, in physical and psychological traits and abilities. The baby in this photo has just mastered the ability to pull herself to a standing position. Soon she will be able to stand alone, and then begin to walk.*

***Growth*** The processes by which organisms increase in size, weight, strength, and other traits as they develop.

***Zygote*** A fertilized egg cell or ovum.

Development also occurs across many dimensions simultaneously—physiological, cognitive, personality, social, emotional, and behavioral. Development is spurred on by internal factors, such as the genetic code, and external factors, such as learning and nutrition.

Are ***growth*** and development synonymous? Not quite, although many people do use them interchangeably. Growth is usually used to refer to changes in size or quantity, whereas development also refers to changes in quality.

During the early days following fertilization, the ***zygote*** *develops* rapidly as cells divide and begin to take on specialized forms. However, there is no gain, or *growth,* in mass, because the zygote does not yet have external sources of nourishment. Language *development* refers to the process by which the child's use of language becomes progressively more sophisticated and complex during the first few years of life. Vocabulary *growth,* by contrast, refers to the simple accumulation of knowledge of the meanings of new words.

## TRUTH OR FICTION REVISITED

*It is not true that* development *and* growth *are synonymous terms. Growth refers to changes in size or quantity. Development is a more comprehensive term. Development refers both to changes in quality, as in the qualitative distinctions between thought processes in the 2-year-old and in the 5-year-old, and to growth.*

### THINKING ABOUT DEVELOPMENT

Do students really need to take course work in child development to understand children? After all, as one student put it, "I've lived through it."

### CHILD DEVELOPMENT: A DEFINITION

Child development, then, is a field of inquiry that attempts to gain knowledge of the processes that govern the appearance and growth of children's physical structures, psychological traits, behavior patterns, and ways of adapting to the demands of life. To test your knowledge of child development, see Developing Today.

Professionals from many fields are interested in child development. They include psychologists, educators, anthropologists, sociologists, nurses, medical researchers, and many others. Each brings his or her own brand of expertise to the quest for knowledge. Intellectual cross-fertilization enhances the skills of developmentalists and enriches the lives of children.

Let us now consider the many reasons why these professionals study child development.

## WHY DO WE STUDY CHILD DEVELOPMENT?

One motive for studying child development also applies to other areas of investigation: curiosity—the desire to learn about things that are little understood. Scientists still find curiosity a valid reason for studying child development. Despite the wealth of research that has been conducted, many important questions about development remain unresolved or only partly resolved.

Other motives have theoretical and practical aspects. Here are some additional reasons for studying child development.

## Developing Today

### How Much Do You Know About Child Development?

So, you think, what is there to learn about child development? After all, you were once a child. Having been one, you should be something of an expert, right?

Perhaps you are. Perhaps you aren't. If you are, we must admit that you are far ahead of where we were as students.

To test your knowledge of child development, indicate whether you think each of the following items is true or false by circling the T or F. Then compare your answers with the key at the end of the chapter.

1. T–F Conception takes place in the uterus.
2. T–F Pregnant women can have just one or two drinks a day without being concerned about their effects on the fetus.
3. T–F Parents must spend the first few hours after birth with their newborn babies if adequate bonding is to take place.
4. T–F Newborn babies sleep about 16 hours a day.
5. T–F Newborn babies usually cannot see for several hours.
6. T–F Nine-month-old babies will usually crawl off the edges of beds, couches, and tables if not prevented from doing so.
7. T–F Although it may be difficult to measure intelligence in newborn babies, a child's IQ remains fixed from birth.
8. T–F Nine-month-old babies who fear strangers are likely to become anxious adults.
9. T–F Babies placed in day care grow less attached to their mothers than babies reared by their mothers in the home.
10. T–F It is better for parents in conflict to stay together for the sake of the children than to get a divorce.
11. T–F More attractive children are usually more popular with peers.
12. T–F Boys are usually more aggressive than girls.
13. T–F Boys usually have greater verbal skills than girls.
14. T–F Television violence contributes to aggressive behavior in child viewers.
15. T–F Most children who wet their beds simply outgrow the problem.
16. T–F Marijuana is the drug most frequently abused by adolescents.

### *To Gain Insight into Our Basic Nature*

For centuries, philosophers, theologians, natural scientists, psychologists, and educators have held different perspectives on development and argued about the basic nature of children. They have argued over whether children are basically antisocial and aggressive or prosocial and loving. They have argued over whether children are conscious and self-aware. They have disputed whether children have a natural curiosity that demands to unravel the mysteries of the universe, or whether children are merely mechanical reactors to environmental stimulation.

If their arguments had remained theoretical—limited only to discussion in the seminar—they might have gained little notice. But their perspectives on child development have led to very different suggestions for child rearing and education. They have an important impact on the daily lives of children, parents, educators, and others who interact with children.

One motive for studying child development, then, is to determine which theoretical perspectives are supported by the evidence. The major theoretical perspectives on child development today are the maturational, psychoanalytic, learning-theory, cognitive-developmental, and ecological perspectives. We refer to each of them later on.

### To Gain Insight into the Origins of Adult Behavior

How do we explain the origins of ***empathy*** in adults? Of antisocial behavior? How do we explain the assumption of "feminine" and "masculine" behavior patterns? The origins of special abilities in language (reading, writing, spelling, articulation) and in mathematics?

There are various ways to explain the origins of adult behavior. Some investigators look to situational influences—that is, the stimuli that impinge on the adult of today. Others look to adult decision making—to a mature weighing of the pluses and minuses in a situation. Still others tend to search for answers in the processes of development.

Consider the example of ***gender roles,*** which are cultural expectations of how females and males should behave. There is no question that society remains biased toward rewarding men for "masculine" behavior and rewarding women for "feminine" behavior. It also seems reasonable that women and men take society's system of rewards and punishments into account, if and when they weigh their satisfaction with their gender-role behavior. But the literature on child development shows that most girls and boys take on what is considered "appropriate" gender-role behaviors during early childhood, largely through processes of ***identification*** and ***socialization,*** as we shall see in Chapter 10. There remains a good deal of controversy about the relative roles of biology and experience in the assumption of gender roles, but no discussion of the origins of gender-role behavior could be meaningful without reference to child development.

### To Gain Insight into the Causes, Prevention, and Treatment of Developmental Abnormalities and Problems

Fetal alcohol syndrome, PKU, SIDS, Down syndrome, autism, hyperactivity, dyslexia, child abuse—these are just a handful of the buzzwords that stir fear in parents and parents-to-be. A major focus in child development research is the search for the causes of such problems, so that they can be prevented and, when possible, treated.

Let us mention just a few examples that are discussed more thoroughly in later chapters. Research has made it possible to identify children with ***PKU*** (phenylketonuria) at birth through analysis of samples of blood or urine. PKU may then be treated through reasonably effective dietary restrictions. In the future it may be possible for parents to preselect boys or girls with certainty. In that case, parents whose male children would be susceptible to sex-linked diseases such as Duchenne muscular dystrophy and hemophilia could avert these tragedies by conceiving girls.

***Empathy*** The ability to share another person's feelings or emotions (from the Greek *en,* meaning "in," and *pathos,* meaning "feeling").

***Gender roles*** Complex clusters of behavior that are considered stereotypical of females and males.

***Identification*** A process in which one person becomes like another through broad imitation and incorporation of the other person's personality traits.

***Socialization*** The systematic exposure of children to rewards and punishments and to role models who guide them into socially acceptable behavior patterns.

***PKU*** Phenylketonuria. A genetic abnormality in which a child cannot metabolize phenylalanine, an amino acid, which consequently builds up in the body and causes mental retardation. If treated with a special diet, retardation is prevented.

### To Optimize the Conditions of Development for All Children

Most children, fortunately, do not encounter developmental abnormalities. However, we remain concerned about optimizing the conditions of their development in order to foster positive traits. At the most basic level, for example, most parents want their infants to survive. They want to provide the best in nutrition and medical care so their children will develop strong and healthy bodies. Parents want their infants to feel secure with them. They want to assure that major transitions, such as the transition from the home to the school, will be as stress-free as possible.

Note just a few of the issues that have been studied in recent years in an effort to optimize the conditions of development:

- The effects of various foods and agents on the development of unborn children
- The effects of intense parent–infant interaction immediately following birth on bonds of attachment
- The effects of bottle-feeding versus breast-feeding on mother–infant attachment and on babies' health
- The effects of day-care programs on parent–child bonds of attachment and on children's social and intellectual development
- The effects of different patterns of child rearing on the fostering of independence, competence, and social adjustment

**Culture and Development: Optimizing Conditions of Development** Evidence is mounting that the United States is not doing as good a job as many other nations in optimizing conditions of development for its children.

Recent statistics compiled by the Children's Defense Fund (1992b) present a bleak picture. Consider the fact that the United States has

- A higher infant mortality rate than 19 other nations.
- A higher infant mortality rate for African-American infants than the overall rates of 31 other nations, including Cuba, Bulgaria, and Kuwait.
- A death rate among preschool children worse than 19 other nations.
- A worse low-birth-weight rate than 30 other nations.

FIGURE 1.2

***Optimizing Conditions of Development.*** *Most parents and day-care facilities try to provide positive and stimulating experiences to optimize the development of their children.*

How do children in the United States compare with children from other nations on measures of optimal conditions of development?

| MEASURE | UNITED STATES COMPARED WITH OTHER NATIONS |
|---|---|
| INFANT MORTALITY RATE | HIGHER THAN 19 OTHER NATIONS<br>HIGHER AMONG AFRICAN AMERICANS THAN 31 OTHER NATIONS |
| DEATH RATE | HIGHER THAN 19 OTHER NATIONS FOR PRESCHOOLERS |
| LOW-BIRTH-WEIGHT RATE | HIGHER THAN 30 OTHER NATIONS<br>HIGHER AMONG AFRICAN AMERICANS THAN 73 OTHER NATIONS |
| POLIO IMMUNIZATION | SMALLER PROPORTION THAN 16 OTHER NATIONS<br>SMALLER PROPORTION OF ETHNIC MINORITY BABIES THAN 69 OTHER NATIONS |
| POVERTY RATES | HIGHER THAN SEVEN OTHER INDUSTRIALIZED WESTERN NATIONS; ONE IN FIVE U.S. CHILDREN IS POOR |

- A low-birth-weight rate among African Americans worse than the overall rates of 73 other countries, including many Third World and former Communist Eastern bloc countries.
- A smaller proportion of babies immunized against polio than 16 other nations.
- A smaller proportion of ethnic minority babies immunized against polio than the overall rates of 69 other nations.
- A higher child poverty rate than seven other industrialized Western countries. One in five U.S. children—14.3 million—is poor, making children the largest category of poor Americans.

Developmentalists increasingly are turning their attention to social problems such as these in an effort to improve the conditions of development of children in the United States as well as in other nations.

To try to optimize conditions of development for all children, we need to understand the diversity of human development. Let us turn now to a consideration of human diversity.

## CULTURE AND DEVELOPMENT: HUMAN DIVERSITY

The field of child development focuses mainly on individuals and is committed to the dignity of the individual child. We cannot understand individual children, however, without an awareness of the richness of human diversity (Bronstein & Quina, 1988; Goodchilds, 1991). Two of the ways in which children diverge or differ from one another are in their ethnicity and their gender.

### *ETHNIC DIVERSITY*

Until recently, much of the research on child development was confined to white, middle-class American children (Greenfield & Cocking, 1994; Lerner, 1991). But we live in a nation and a world of diverse cultures. There is a growing recognition among developmentalists that the cultural context in which the child grows up must be taken into account to better understand children's development and behavior (Greenfield & Cocking, 1994; Nsamenang, 1992; Padilla & Lindholm, 1992; Szapocznik & Kurtines, 1993).

One kind of cultural diversity involves children's ***ethnic groups,*** which tend to unite them according to features such as their cultural heritage, their race, their language, and their common history. One reason for studying ethnic diversity is the changing ethnic makeup of the United States.

Table 1.1 and Figure 1.3 highlight the dramatic changes under way in the United States due to reproductive patterns and immigration. The U.S. Bureau of the Census projects, for example, that the nation's non-Hispanic white population will increase from 191 million in 1992 to 202 million in the year 2050, an increase of 11 million people (see Table 1.1). Because, however, the populations of other ethnic groups in the United States are projected to increase relatively more rapidly, the *percentage* of non-Hispanic white Americans in the total population will *decrease* from 74–75 percent in 1992 to 53 percent in 2050 (Table 1.1). The fastest growing ethnic group consists of Asian Americans (see Figure 1.3).

***Ethnic groups*** Groups of people distinguished by cultural heritage, race, language, and common history.

**TABLE 1.1**

***Ethnic Makeup of the United States: 1992 and 2050***

| Ethnic Group | Millions of People 1992 | Millions of People 2050 | Percent Increase % | Percent of Total U.S. Population 1992 | Percent of Total U.S. Population 2050 |
|---|---|---|---|---|---|
| White Americans (Non-Hispanic) | 191 | 202 | 6 | 74 -75 | 53 |
| Hispanic Americans | 24 | 81 | 238 | 9 | 21 |
| African Americans | 32 | 62 | 94 | 12 | 16 |
| Asian Americans | 9 | 41 | 356 | 3 | 11 |

Source: U.S. Bureau of the Census, 1992. Figures for 2050 are projections.

In 1992 there were 9 million Asian Americans in the United States. They are expected to increase to 41 million by 2050, more than quadrupling their numbers and rising from 3 percent to 11 percent of the U.S. population (Table 1.1). As shown in Table 1.1 and Figure 1.3, the numbers of African Americans and Hispanic Americans (who may be white, black, or Native-American Indian in racial origin) are also growing more rapidly than those of non-Hispanic white Americans. The cultural heritages, languages, and histories of ethnic minority groups are thus likely to have increasing impacts on the cultural life of the United States.

**Truth or Fiction Revisited**

*Asian Americans constitute the fastest growing ethnic group in the United States.*

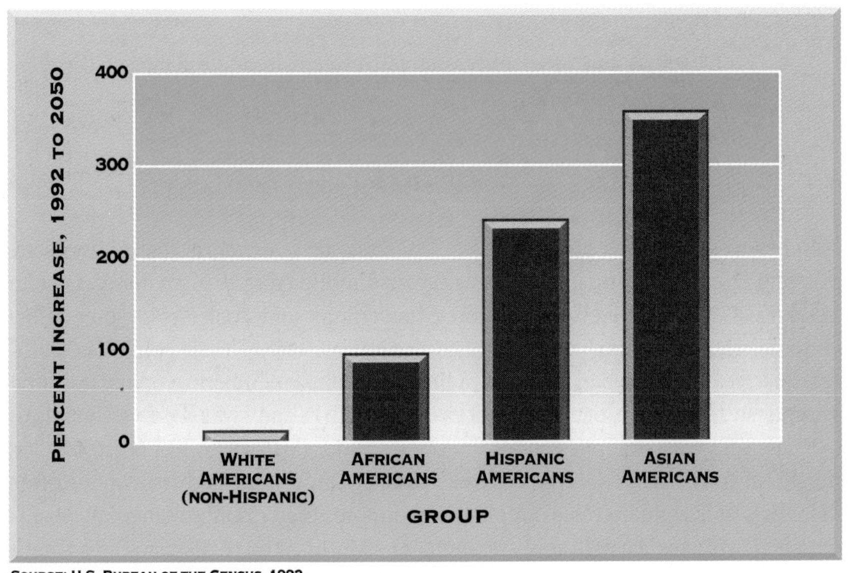


Source: U.S. Bureau of the Census, 1992.

**FIGURE 1.3**

**Percentage Increase of Ethnic Populations in the United States, 1992 to 2050.** *The percentages of Hispanic Americans, African Americans, and Asian Americans are increasing faster than that of white Americans. The fastest growing group consists of Asian Americans. (Source: U.S. Bureau of the Census, 1992).*

Another reason for studying human diversity is to enable us to appreciate the cultural heritages and historical problems of children from various ethnic groups. Too often throughout our history, the traditions, languages, and achievements of ethnic minority groups have been judged by majority standards or disparaged (Betancourt & López, 1993; Jones, 1991; McAdoo, 1993; Sue, 1991). Black English has been considered inferior to standard English, for example, and being reared bilingually has been erroneously considered inferior to being reared to speak English only (see Chapter 12).

It is also important to study diversity in order to provide appropriate educational experiences for children. Educators need to understand children's family values and cultural expectations in order to teach them and guide their learning.

Still another reason for studying diversity concerns psychological intervention and consultation. Psychologists are called upon to help children and families of all ethnic groups solve personal problems, for example. How can psychologists hope to understand the aspirations and problems of children from an ethnic group without understanding the history and cultural heritage of that group (Jones, 1991; Nevid et al., 1994; Sue, 1991)? How can psychologists understand African-American or Hispanic-American children, for example, without sensitivity to the histories of prejudice to which children from these ethnic groups have been exposed? Psychotherapists who work with children and families from ethnic minority groups need to identify and use treatment approaches that are culturally sensitive, relevant, and acceptable (Kazdin, 1993b).

Throughout the text, we consider many issues that address children from various ethnic groups. Just a handful of them are:

- Bilingualism
- Ethnic differences in intelligence test scores—their implications and possible origins
- Alcohol and substance abuse among adolescents from various ethnic minority groups
- The prevalence of suicide among members of different ethnic minority groups
- Patterns of child rearing among parents of various ethnic minority groups
- Development of identity and self-esteem in adolescents of different ethnic backgrounds

## *GENDER*

Another way in which children differ concerns their ***gender***—that is, the state of being female or being male. Gender is not simply a matter of anatomy. Gender involves a complex web of cultural expectations and social roles that affect children's self-concepts and hopes and dreams as well as their behavior.

Just as there have been historic prejudices against members of ethnic minority groups, so have there been prejudices against girls and women. Even much of the scientific research into gender roles and gender differences has been affected by subtle forms of gender bias. Psychologists study boys and men more often than girls and women, for example. Furthermore, they often assume that results obtained with males will apply to females (Matlin, 1993). Psychologists have proposed guidelines for avoiding gender bias in psychological research (Denmark et al., 1988). Some of these guidelines are presented in Table 1.2.

***Gender*** The state of being female or male.

The career aspirations of girls have been traditionally discouraged, and girls have been channeled into the domestic arena. Not until relatively modern times have girls generally been considered suitable for education in the Western world. In fact, girls are still considered unsuited to education in many parts of the world. So many girls and women have been lost to history because of prejudice. Who, for example, is Lucinda Foote? She was a brilliant young woman who is known to us only because of her rejection letter from Yale University in 1792, which confirmed that she was qualified for Yale in every way except for her gender (Lerner, 1993). Women have attended college in the United States only since 1833, when Oberlin opened its doors to women. Today, however, more than half (55 percent) of U.S. college students are female.

**TABLE 1.2**

***Guidelines for Avoiding Gender Bias in Psychological Research***

| PROBLEM | EXAMPLE | CORRECTION |
|---|---|---|
| 1. GENDER STEREOTYPES THAT ARE ASSOCIATED WITH THE TOPIC BEING STUDIED CAN BIAS FORMULATION OF THE RESEARCH QUESTION AND SELECTION OF RESEARCH PARTICIPANTS. | 1. SOME STUDIES HAVE DEFINED NURTURANCE IN TERMS OF THE MOTHER'S TALKING TO AND HOLDING HER BABY AND HAVE STUDIED ONLY WOMEN. | 1. RECOGNIZE THAT NURTURANCE IS NOT A CHARACTERISTIC LIMITED TO FEMALES. STUDY CARETAKERS OF BOTH GENDERS. |
| 2. SELECTION OF GENDER-STEREOTYPED MEASURES DIFFERENTIALLY AFFECTS PERFORMANCE OF GIRLS AND BOYS. | 2. IN STUDIES OF MATHEMATICAL ABILITY,THE CONTENTS OF THE MATH PROBLEM (COMPUTING BASEBALL SCORES, COOKING INGREDIENTS) PRODUCED GENDER DIFFERENCES NOT FOUND WHEN THE CONTENT WAS UNASSOCIATED WITH GENDER-RELATED INTERESTS. | 2. SELECT MEASURES THAT ARE CONTROLLED FOR GENDER-RELATED CONTENT OR INCLUDE THIS AS A DESIGN VARIABLE. |
| 3. RESEARCHERS MAY ASSUME THAT OBTAINED GENDER DIFFERENCES ARE DUE TO INNATE BIOLOGICAL FACTORS, IGNORING THE POSSIBLE ROLE OF ENVIRONMENTAL INFLUENCES. | 3. DIFFERENCES IN FEMALE AND MALE NURTURING BEHAVIOR MAY BE ASSUMED TO BE BIOLOGICALLY BASED BECAUSE WOMEN GIVE BIRTH AND BREAST-FEED, EVEN THOUGH RESEARCH HAS SHOWN NURTURING BEHAVIOR IS STRONGLY INFLUENCED BY CULTURE AND PREVIOUS EXPERIENCE. | 3. USE CAUTION IN ASSUMING INNATE DIFFERENCES EXIST WHEN THE BIOLOGICAL MECHANISMS HAVE NOT BEEN DETERMINED. |
| 4. RESULTS BASED ON ONE GENDER ARE GENERALIZED TO BOTH. | 4. A STUDY CONCLUDING THAT "AGGRESSIVE CHILDREN ARE MORE LIKELY TO BE REJECTED BY PEERS" EXAMINES ONLY AGGRESSIVE BOYS AND THEIR MALE PLAYMATES. | 4. CLEARLY DESCRIBE THE SAMPLE AND DRAW CONCLUSIONS ONLY FOR INDIVIDUALS WITH THOSE CHARACTERISTICS. |

ADAPTED FROM DENMARK ET AL., 1988.

TRUTH OR FICTION REVISITED

*It is true that women were not permitted to attend college in the United States until 1833, when Oberlin began to accept women as students.*

Women today are also making inroads into academic and vocational spheres—such as medicine, law, engineering, and the military—that were traditionally male preserves. Women now earn about one-third of U.S. medical degrees and more than 42 percent of all law degrees. Women currently make up 15 percent of engineering graduates, but only 20 years ago, women accounted for only about 1 percent of engineering graduates ("Earned Degrees," 1992; U.S. Bureau of the Census, 1992). Obvious trends are in place—and overdue.

These opportunities for women are crucial to the development of girls. Children learn early about gender roles and gender-role stereotypes. Cultural opportunities for, and limitations on, adults give children their own senses of what is possible for them and what is not. Just as many children from ethnic minority groups wonder whether they can experience the rewards and opportunities they see in the dominant culture, so do girls wonder whether the career and social roles they admire are available to them. One of the authors (S. R.) learned only recently that his 11- and 9-year-old daughters assumed the presidency of the United States was available only to men. The effects of cultural expectations on girls' self-concepts, motivation, and behavior are clear and compelling.

The focus on human diversity throughout the text will create a better understanding and fuller appreciation of the true extent of children's behavior and mental processes. This broader view of development—and the world—is enriching for its own sake, and it heightens the accuracy and scope of the material. Another way to broaden our view of child development is to take a brief journey through the history of child development.

## HIGHLIGHTS IN THE HISTORY OF CHILD DEVELOPMENT

Child development as a field of scientific inquiry has existed for little more than a century. Before its evolution, attitudes toward children varied greatly.

### *UP THROUGH THE MIDDLE AGES*

In ancient times and in the Middle Ages, children often were viewed as innately evil, and discipline was harsh. Legally, medieval children were treated as property and servants. They enjoyed no civil rights. They could be sent to the monastery,

TRUTH OR FICTION REVISITED

*It is true that during the Middle Ages children were often treated and depicted as miniature adults.*

FIGURE 1.4

***View of Children in the 1600s.*** *Centuries ago, children were viewed as miniature adults. In this 17th-century painting, notice how the body proportions of the young princess (in the middle) are similar to those of her adult attendants.*

married without consultation, or convicted of crimes. Children were nurtured until 7, the "age of reason." Then they were expected to work alongside adults in the home and in the field (Aries, 1962). They ate, drank, and dressed as miniature adults. For much of the Middle Ages, artists depicted children as small adults.

### *The Transition to Modern Times*

The transition to modern times is marked by the thinking of philosophers such as John Locke and Jean-Jacques Rousseau. The Englishman John Locke (1632–1704) believed that the child came into the world as a ***tabula rasa,*** a "blank tablet" or clean slate that was written upon by experience. Locke did not believe that inborn predispositions toward good or evil played an important role in the conduct of the child. Instead, he focused on the role of the environment or of experience. Social approval and disapproval, he believed, are powerful shapers of behavior. Jean-Jacques Rousseau (1712–1778), a Swiss–French philosopher, reversed the stance of the Middle Ages. Rousseau argued that children are inherently good and that, if allowed to express their natural impulses, they will develop into generous and moral individuals.

***Tabula rasa*** (TAB-you-luh RAH-suh) A Latin phrase meaning "blank slate," referring to the view that children are born without ethical, cultural, or vocational preferences and that such preferences are shaped by the environment.

## TRUTH OR FICTION REVISITED

*Throughout this book, we shall see that it is* not *true that children come into the world as "blank tablets"—that is, without preferences or inborn differences in intelligence and specific talents. Although the view of children as blank tablets or clean slates has been advanced by John Locke and others, evidence suggests that there are inherited components of children's psychological traits and basic temperaments. On the other hand, social approval and disapproval are powerful shapers of behavior, as suggested by Locke.*

### UP TO THE PRESENT DAY

During the Industrial Revolution, family life became defined in terms of the nuclear unit of mother, father, and children, rather than the extended family. Children became more visible, fostering awareness of childhood as a special time of life. Still, girls and boys often labored in factories from dawn to dusk up through the early years of the 20th century.

In the 20th century, laws were passed to protect children from severe labor, to require that they attend school until a certain age, and to prevent them from getting married or being sexually exploited. Whereas children were once considered the property of parents to do with as they wished, laws have been passed protecting children from the abuse and neglect of parents and other caretakers. Juvenile courts have been introduced that grant special status to child offenders under the law.

FIGURE 1.5

**A YOUNG CHILD LABORER.** *Children often worked long days in factories up through the early years of this century.*

*It is true that children were once treated as the property of their parents.*

### *Pioneers in the Study of Child Development*

In the 19th and early 20th centuries, many individuals contributed to the advancement of child development as a scientific field of study. They include Charles Darwin, G. Stanley Hall, and Alfred Binet.

The Englishman Charles Darwin (1809–1882) is perhaps best known as the originator of evolutionary theory. But he also was one of the first observers to keep a ***baby biography,*** in which he described his infant son's behaviors in great detail. G. Stanley Hall (1844–1924) is credited with founding child development as an academic discipline. He adapted the new questionnaire method for use with large groups of children so that he could study the "contents of children's minds." After Hall published his major two-volume work, *Adolescence,* in 1904, adolescence became widely perceived as a separate stage of life. The Frenchman Alfred Binet (1857–1911), along with Theodore Simon, developed the first standardized intelligence test at around the turn of the century. Binet's purpose was twofold: to assess individual differences in intellectual functioning and to identify public schoolchildren who might profit from special education.

By the start of the 20th century, child development had emerged as a scientific field of study. Within a short time, major theoretical views of the developing child had begun to emerge, proposed by such developmentalists as Arnold Gesell, Sigmund Freud, John B. Watson, and Jean Piaget. We describe their views in Chapter 2.

As we have seen, philosophers, psychologists, and educators have held very different opinions as to the nature of children. Let us now turn our attention to some of the controversies that continue to color the field of child development.

## Critical Issues in Child Development

We have noted that developmentalists see things in very different ways. Let us consider three of the most important debates in the field.

### *Which Exerts Greater Influence on Children: Nature or Nurture?*

Think about your friends for a moment. Some may be tall and lanky, others, short and stocky. Some are outgoing and sociable; others are more reserved and quiet. One may be a good athlete, another a fine musician. What made them this way? How much does inheritance have to do with it, and how much does the environment play a role?

**Baby biography** A meticulous account of the development of a baby, attending to the sequence and timing of changes.

***Nature*** The processes within an organism that guide that organism to develop according to its genetic code.

***Nurture*** The processes external to an organism that nourish it as it develops according to its genetic code or cause it to swerve from its genetically programmed course. Environmental factors that influence development.

***Genes*** The basic building blocks of heredity.

***Maturation*** The unfolding of genetically determined traits, structures, and functions.

***Primates*** An order of mammals that includes humans, apes, and monkeys.

***Stage*** A distinct period of development that differs qualitatively from other periods. Stages follow one another in an orderly sequence.

Researchers are continually trying to sort out the extent to which human behavior is the result of ***nature*** (heredity) and of ***nurture*** (environmental influences). What aspects of behavior originate in our ***genes*** and are biologically programmed to unfold in the child as time goes on, so long as minimal nutrition and social experience are provided? What aspects of behavior can be traced largely to such environmental influences as nutrition and learning?

Scientists seek the natural causes of behavior in our genetic heritage, the functioning of the nervous system, and in the process of ***maturation.*** Scientists seek the environmental causes of behavior in our nutrition, our cultural and family backgrounds, and in our opportunities to learn about the world, including our cognitive stimulation during early childhood and our formal education.

Some theorists lean heavily toward natural explanations of development, while others lean more heavily toward environmental explanations. But today nearly all researchers would agree that, broadly speaking, nature and nurture each play important roles in virtually every area of child development. Consider the development of language. Language develops only in advanced ***primates*** and appears to be based in structures found in certain areas of the brain. Thus, biology (nature) plays an indispensable role in language development. But children also come to speak the languages spoken by their caretakers. Parent–child similarities in accent and vocabulary provide additional evidence for an indispensable role for learning (nurture) in language development.

### *Is Development Continuous or Discontinuous?*

Do developmental changes occur gradually (continuously), the way a seedling becomes a tree? Or do changes occur in major qualitative leaps (discontinuously) that dramatically alter our bodies and behavior, the way a caterpillar turns into a butterfly?

Some developmentalists have viewed human development as a continuous process in which the effects of learning mount gradually, with no major sudden qualitative changes. Other theorists, in contrast, believe there are a number of rapid qualitative changes that usher in new ***stages*** of development. Maturational theorists point out that the environment, even when enriched, profits us little until we are ready, or mature enough, to develop in a certain direction. For example, newborn babies will not imitate their parents' speech, even when parents speak clearly and deliberately. Nor does aided practice in "walking" during the first few months after birth significantly accelerate the emergence of independent walking.

Stage theorists such as Sigmund Freud and Jean Piaget (see Chapter 2) saw development as being discontinuous. Both theorists saw biological changes as providing the potential for psychological changes. Freud focused on the ways in which physical sexual developments might provide the basis for personality development. Piaget emphasized the ways in which maturation of the nervous system permitted cognitive advances. Stage theorists see the sequences of development as being invariant (occurring in the same order), although they allow for individual differences in timing.

Certain aspects of physical development do appear to occur in stages. For example, from the age of 2 to the onset of puberty, children gradually grow larger. Then the adolescent growth spurt occurs, ushered in by hormones and characterized by rapid biological changes in structure and function (as in the development of the sex organs) as well as in size. So it would appear that a new

**THINKING ABOUT DEVELOPMENT**

Agree or disagree with the following statement and support your answer: "Child development is self-regulated by the unfolding of natural plans and processes."

FIGURE 1.6

***Which Aspects of Development Are Continuous and Which Are Discontinuous?*** *The adolescent growth spurt is an example of discontinuity in development. Psychologists debate whether other aspects of development—such as cognitive development—are most accurately described as continuous or discontinuous.*

stage of life has begun. Psychologists disagree more strongly on whether aspects of development such as cognitive development, attachment, and development of gender roles occur in stages.

### *Are Children Active or Passive?*

In the broad sense, all living organisms are active. However, in the field of child development, the question has a more specific meaning. Are children innately "programmed" to try to act upon and take charge of the world (are they ***active***)? Or are children basically shaped by experience, so that they will fit within almost any behavioral or social mold (are they ***passive***)?

Historical views of children as willful and unruly suggest that people have generally seen children as active—even if mischievous (at best) or evil (at worst). As you read earlier in this chapter, John Locke introduced a view of children as passive beings (blank tablets) upon whom external experience writes features of personality and moral virtue.

At one extreme, educators who view children as passive may assume that they must be motivated to learn by their instructors. Such educators are likely to provide a traditional curriculum with rigorous exercises in spelling, music, and math to promote absorption of the subject matter. They are also likely to apply a powerful system of rewards and punishments to keep children on the straight and narrow.

At the other extreme, educators who view children as active may assume that they have a natural love of learning. Such educators are likely to espouse open education and encourage children to explore an environment rich with learning materials. Rather than attempting to coerce children into specific academic activities, such educators are likely to listen to the children to learn about their unique likes and talents and then support children as they pursue their inclinations.

***Active*** Influencing or acting upon the environment.

***Passive*** Influenced or acted upon by environmental stimuli instead of acting upon the environment.

### TRUTH OR FICTION REVISITED

*It is true that some theorists contend that children actively strive to understand and take charge of their worlds, whereas other theorists argue that children respond passively to environmental stimulation.*

***Empirical*** Based on observation and experimentation.

These are extremes. Most educators would probably agree that children show major individual differences and that some children require more guidance and external motivation than others. In addition, children can be active in some subjects and passive in others. Whether children who do not actively seek to master certain subjects are coerced tends to depend on how important the subject is to functioning in today's society, the age of the child, the attitudes of the parents, and many other factors.

Urie Bronfenbrenner (1977) argues that we miss the point when we assume that children are either entirely active or passive. Children are influenced by the environment, but children also influence the environment. The challenge is to observe the many ways in which children interact with their settings.

These debates are theoretical. Scientists value theory for its ability to tie together observations and suggest new areas of investigation, but they also follow an ***empirical*** approach. That is, they engage in research methods, such as those described in the following section, to find evidence for or against various theoretical positions.

## HOW DO WE STUDY CHILD DEVELOPMENT?

What is the relationship between intelligence and achievement? What are the effects of aspirin and alcohol on the fetus? How can you rear children to become competent and independent? What are the effects of divorce on children?

Many of us have expressed opinions on questions such as these at one time or another. But scientists insist that such questions be answered by research. Strong arguments, reference to authority figures, even tightly knit theories are not considered adequate as scientific evidence. Scientific evidence is obtained by the *scientific method.*

> **THINKING ABOUT DEVELOPMENT**
>
> Agree or disagree with the following statement and support your answer: "The only way to understand children's behavior is from a scientific perspective."

### *THE SCIENTIFIC METHOD*

There are four basic steps to the scientific method:

**STEP I: FORMULATING A RESEARCH QUESTION** The first step is formulation of a research question. Our daily experiences, developmental theory, even folklore help generate questions for research. Daily experience in using day-care centers may motivate us to conduct research to find out whether day care influences children's intellectual or social development or the bonds of attachment between children and their parents. Social-learning principles of observational learning may prompt research into the effects of televised violence.

**Step 2: Developing a Hypothesis** The second step is the development of a hypothesis. A ***hypothesis*** is a specific statement about behavior that is tested through research.

One hypothesis about day care might be that preschool children placed in day care will acquire greater social skills in relating to peers than will preschool children who are cared for in the home. A hypothesis about TV violence might be that elementary school children who watch more violent TV shows tend to behave more aggressively toward their peers.

**Step 3: Testing the Hypothesis** The third step is testing the hypothesis. Psychologists test the hypothesis through carefully controlled information-gathering techniques and research methods, such as naturalistic observation, the case study, the correlational method, and the experiment.

For example, we could introduce day-care and non-day-care children to a new child in a college child-research center and observe how each group acts toward the new acquaintance. Concerning the effects of TV violence, we could have parents help us tally which television shows their children watch and rate the shows for violent content. Each child could receive a total score for exposure to TV violence. We could also gather teacher reports as to how aggressively the children act toward their peers. Then we could determine whether more aggressive children also watch more violence on television. We describe research methods such as these later in the chapter.

**Step 4: Drawing Conclusions about the Hypothesis** The fourth step is drawing conclusions. Psychologists draw conclusions about the accuracy of their hypothesis on the basis of the results of their research findings. When research does not bear out their hypotheses, the researchers may modify the theories from which the hypotheses were derived. Research findings often suggest new hypotheses and new studies.

In our research on the effects of day care, we would probably find that day-care children show somewhat greater social skills than children cared for in the home (see Chapter 7). We would probably also find that more aggressive children spend more time watching televised violence (see Chapter 10). But we shall also see in the following pages that it might be wrong to conclude from the evidence described that TV violence *causes* aggressive behavior.

Now let us consider the information-gathering techniques and the research methods used by developmentalists. Then we shall discuss ethical issues concerning research in child development.

## *Gathering Information*

Two techniques used by developmentalists for gathering information are naturalistic observation and the case-study method.

**Naturalistic Observation** ***Naturalistic observation*** studies of children are conducted in natural, or real-life, settings such as homes, playgrounds, and classrooms. In naturalistic observation, investigators observe the natural behavior of children, trying their best not to interfere with it. Interference could influence the results, so that investigators would be observing child–investigator interactions and not genuine behavior. Thus, researchers may try to blend in with the woodwork by sitting quietly in the back of a classroom or by observing the class through a one-way mirror (see Focus on Research).

***Hypothesis*** (high-POTH-uh-sis) A Greek word meaning ''groundwork'' or ''foundation'' which has come to mean a specific statement about behavior that is tested by research.

***Naturalistic observation*** A method of scientific observation in which children (and others) are observed in their natural environments.

FOCUS ON RESEARCH

### *How Do You Ease Your Child into Nursery School or Day Care?—A Naturalistic Observation Study*

The big moment has arrived—Allison's first day at the day-care center. Although you've done everything to prepare her—lengthy explanations and gradually longer stays in the care of babysitters—she's clutching and crying and begging you not to go. How do parents take leave of their children in such situations? How do the children adjust? A naturalistic observation study by Tiffany Field and her colleagues (1984) provides some clues. They observed leave-takings for infants (ages 3–17 months), toddlers (ages 18–29 months), and preschoolers (ages 30–69 months) at the beginning of the fall semester and again 6 months later.

Various relationships (correlations) were observed between children's gender, age, and behavior. For example, girls were more likely than boys to approach their teachers, and boys were more likely to immediately get involved in play activities. Preschoolers were most likely to kiss and hug their parents, and toddlers were most likely to cry, complain, and cling to their parents. The parents of the toddlers—the group of children for whom adjustment was most difficult—were most likely to try to distract their children by getting them involved in activities in the schoolroom and then quietly slipping out.

Observations made 6 months later showed that children of all age groups spent less time relating to their departing parents. There was less crying, less protesting. The children had generally adjusted to spending their days at nursery school. Interestingly, children whose parents left abruptly showed less distress than children whose parents stayed for several minutes, attempting to distract them.

But a note of caution: This naturalistic observation study uses the correlational method (discussed in this chapter), and it can be misleading to try to ferret out cause and effect from correlational studies. You cannot conclude that parental lingering and distraction caused child distress. It could be that child distress caused the parents to linger and try to sneak out. Or it could be that causal effects were *bidirectional*—that is, that the children and parents influenced each other's behavior in a fluid, continuous fashion.

In any event, a comforting thought may be drawn from this study. Most children do adjust reasonably quickly to nursery school and day care, regardless of the amount of distress they show during the early days.

Naturalistic observation is frequently the first type of study carried out in new areas of investigation. Through careful observation, scientists gather an initial impression of what happens in certain situations. In their interpretation of the data, they may use the mathematical *correlational method,* described later in this chapter, to refine their observations of how strongly different ***variables*** are related. For example, they may explore whether the rate of vocabulary growth is related to gender or to cultural background. Afterwards, they may attempt to investigate cause and effect through experimental research.

***Variables*** Quantities that can vary from child to child, or from occasion to occasion, such as height, weight, intelligence, and attention span.

***Case study*** A carefully drawn biography of the life of an individual.

***Questionnaire*** A method for gathering information in which the subject responds in writing to a set of written questions.

***Standardized test*** A test of some ability or characteristic in which an individual's score is compared to the scores of a group of similar individuals.

**Culture and Development: A Sampling of Naturalistic Observation Studies** A number of important naturalistic observation studies have been done with children of different cultures. We will look at these in greater detail as we touch on the appropriate topics throughout the book. For example, researchers have observed the motor behavior of Native-American Hopi children who are strapped to cradleboards during the first year. They have observed language development in the United States, Mexico, Turkey, Kenya, and China—seeking universals that might suggest a major role for maturation in the acquisition of language skills. They have also observed the ways in which children are socialized in Russia, Israel, Japan and other nations in an effort to determine what patterns of child rearing are associated with development of behaviors such as attachment and independence.

**The Case-Study Method** Another way of gathering information about children is through the ***case-study method.*** The case study is a carefully drawn account or biography of the behavior of an individual child. Parents who keep diaries of their children's activities are involved in informal case studies. Case studies themselves often use a number of different kinds of information about children. In addition to direct observation, case studies may include ***questionnaires, standardized tests,*** and ***interviews*** with the child and his or her parents, teachers, and friends. Information gleaned from school and other records may be included. Scientists who use the case-study method take great pains to record all the relevant factors in a child's behavior, and they are very cautious in drawing conclusions about what leads to what.

Jean Piaget used the case-study method in carefully observing and recording the behavior of children, including his own (see Chapter 6). Sigmund Freud (see Chapter 2) developed psychoanalytic theory largely on the basis of case studies. Freud studied his patients in great depth and followed some of them for many years.

Some of the most fascinating case studies of children are found in baby biographies. Baby biographies are careful observations of children that frequently begin just after birth. As was the case with Piaget's and Charles Darwin's accounts of their own children, baby biographies often include accounts of a parent or observer touching the child or serving as a model for the child and then recording the child's responses.

In many instances, case studies, like naturalistic observation, form the basis for sophisticated correlational and experimental studies that follow. The early case studies of Freud and Piaget have led to countless experiments that have attempted to find evidence to support or disconfirm their theories.

FIGURE 1.7

**Cultural Contexts of Research.** *Researchers have observed language development in many different cultures. They have sought universals that might suggest a major role for maturation in language acquisition.*

## *Research Methods*

The two major research strategies used to study child development are the correlational method and the experimental method.

**The Correlational Method** In the ***correlational method,*** researchers determine whether one behavior or trait being studied is related to, or correlated with, another. Consider, for example, the variables of intelligence and achievement. These variables are assigned numbers such as intelligence test scores and academic grade averages. Then the numbers or scores are mathematically related and expressed as a ***correlation coefficient.*** A correlation coefficient is a number that varies between 1.00 and −1.00.

Numerous studies report ***positive correlations*** between intelligence and achievement. Generally speaking, the higher children score on intelligence tests, the better their academic performance is likely to be. The scores attained on intelligence tests are positively correlated (about 0.60 to 0.70) with overall academic achievement.

There is a ***negative correlation*** between teenagers' working after school and their academic performance. As we shall see in Chapter 15, the more hours teenagers are employed, the lower are their school grades.

Naturalistic observation studies may also use the correlational method. Consider the study by Tiffany Field and her colleagues (1984) described earlier. In this study there were numerous correlations—for example, correlations between children's ages and their behavior at leave-taking, correlations between the gender

***Interview*** A method for gathering information in which the subject responds verbally to the researcher's questions.

***Correlational method*** A method in which researchers determine whether one behavior or trait being studied is related to, or correlated with, another.

***Correlation coefficient*** A number ranging from +1.00 to −1.00 that expresses the direction (positive or negative) and strength of the relationship between two variables.

***Positive correlation*** A relationship between two variables in which one variable increases as the other variable increases.

***Negative correlation*** A relationship between two variables in which one variable increases as the other variable decreases.

FIGURE 1.8

***INTELLIGENCE AND ACHIEVEMENT.*** *Correlations between intelligence test scores and academic achievement—as measured by school grades and achievement tests—tend to be positive and strong. Does the correlation method allow us to say that intelligence* causes *or* is responsible for *academic achievement? Why or why not?*

of children and leave-taking behavior, and correlations between parental behavior at leave-taking and level of child distress, to name but a few.

Much correlational research has also been conducted to learn what patterns of child rearing are associated with positive traits, such as independence and competence with friends and in school. Other correlational studies have explored factors associated with development of gender roles. See Focus on Research for an example of one such study.

**LIMITATIONS OF CORRELATIONAL RESEARCH** Correlational studies can reveal relationships between variables, but they do not show cause and effect. For example, studies have found that children who watch TV containing a lot of violence are more likely to show aggressive behavior at home and in school. It may seem logical to assume that exposure to televised violence makes children more aggressive. But it may be that children who are more aggressive to begin with prefer TV shows that contain a good deal of violence. The relationship between watching televised violence and engaging in aggressive behavior may not be as simple as you might think.

Similarly, studies that relate divorce to behavior and adjustment report that children (especially boys) in divorced families sometimes show more problems than do children in nondivorced families (Hetherington et al., 1992). However, these studies do not show that divorce *causes* these adjustment problems. It could be that the factors that led to divorce (such as parental change, lack of commitment, or conflict) also led to adjustment problems among the children. Or, having a child with problems may put a strain on the parents' marriage and ultimately be a contributing factor to divorce.

In the studies on patterns of child rearing, we must also ask why parents choose to raise their children in certain ways. It is possible the same factors that lead them to make these choices also influence the behavior of their children.

Thus, correlational research does not allow us to place clear "cause" and "effect" labels on variables. To investigate cause and effect, researchers turn to the experimental method.

**The Experiment** Most psychologists would agree that the preferred method for investigating questions of cause and effect is the ***experiment.*** In an experiment, a group of participants (also called ***subjects***) receives a ***treatment*** while another group does not receive the treatment. The subjects are then observed to determine whether the treatment makes a difference in their behavior.

Experiments are used whenever possible, because they allow researchers to directly control the experiences of children and other subjects in order to determine the outcomes of a treatment. Experiments, like other research methods, are usually undertaken to test a hypothesis. For example, a social-learning theorist might hypothesize that television violence will cause aggressive behavior in children because of principles of observational learning. To test this hypothesis, she might devise an experiment in which some children are purposely exposed to televised violence while others are not. Remember that it is not enough to demonstrate that children who *choose* to watch more violence on television behave more aggressively; such evidence is only correlational. We review this research—correlational and experimental—in Chapter 10.

***Independent and Dependent Variables*** In an experiment to determine whether televised violence causes aggressive behavior, experimental subjects would be shown a television program containing violence and its effects on behavior would be measured. Televised violence would be considered an ***independent variable,*** a variable whose presence is manipulated by the experimenters so that its effects may be determined. The measured result, in this case the child's

***Experiment*** A method of scientific investigation that seeks to discover cause-and-effect relationships by introducing independent variables and observing their effects on dependent variables.

***Subjects*** Participants in a scientific study. Many psychologists consider this term dehumanizing and no longer use it in reference to human participants.

***Treatment*** In an experiment, a condition received by participants so that its effects may be observed.

***Independent variable*** A condition in a scientific study that is manipulated (changed) so that its effects may be observed.

FOCUS ON RESEARCH

### *Toys, Chores and Gender Roles: A Correlational Study*

On her eighth birthday, one of the authors (C. E.) eagerly ripped open the wrappings of her birthday presents, hoping to find the one thing she wanted more than anything else. Yes, there it was: a baseball glove! She raced to complete her Saturday chores and then went out to play ball. Do the toys parents give their children and the chores they assign them have any bearing on the child's development of gender roles? A study done many years later by C. E. and Marsha Liss used the correlational method to explore this question. They gave questionnaires before and after a Christmas holiday to children who ranged in age from 5 to 13 years old. The children were asked what gifts they had asked for and had received. They also were asked to list their chores at home and their occupational aspirations.

Many correlations were observed between the behaviors of the children and their parents. For example, there was a positive correlation between children wanting toys that are traditional for their gender and getting them. In other words, girls who asked for "girls'" toys such as dolls received them, and boys who requested "boys'" toys such as toy cars and sports equipment also had their wishes granted. But boys who asked for dolls or girls who asked for baseball gloves generally did not receive them (unlike C. E.'s experience). That is, there was a negative correlation between requesting nontraditional toys and getting them.

Parents who gave "boys'" toys to children of both genders also were more likely to assign children traditionally male chores such as yardwork and taking out the garbage. Both girls and boys who received "boys'" toys and who were assigned traditionally male chores were more likely to aspire to traditionally male-dominated careers.

It may be tempting to conclude from these results that parents' behaviors cause children to develop certain gender-role preferences. But as the section on limitations of correlational research indicates, correlational studies do not allow us to place clear "cause" and "effect" labels on variables. For example, a parent may be more likely to assign traditional "masculine" chores to girls or boys who already display interest in traditional "masculine" activities. In Chapter 10, we shall see that the development of gender roles is a complex process in which children are both influenced by and in turn influence parents, teachers, and other children.

***Dependent variable*** A measure of an assumed effect of an independent variable.

***Experimental subjects*** Participants receiving a treatment in an experiment.

***Control subjects*** Participants in an experiment who do not receive the treatment but for whom all other conditions are held comparable to those of experimental subjects.

behavior, is called a ***dependent variable.*** Its presence or level presumably depends on the independent variables.

***Experimental and Control Groups*** Experiments use experimental and control subjects or groups. ***Experimental subjects*** receive the treatment, while ***control subjects*** do not. Every effort is made to ensure that all other conditions are held constant for both groups of subjects. By doing so, we can have confidence that experimental outcomes reflect the treatments and not chance factors. In a study on the effects of televised violence on children's behavior, children in the experimental group would be shown television programs containing violence, and children in the control group would be shown programs that did not contain violence.

***Random Assignment*** It is also essential that subjects be assigned to experimental or control groups on a chance or random basis. As we saw earlier, we could not conclude much from an experiment on the effects of televised violence on children's aggressive behavior if the children were allowed to choose whether they would be in a group that watched a lot of televised violence or in a group that watched only nonviolent television. This is because, as a group, children who choose to watch televised violence might have aggressive tendencies to begin with. And so, if children who watched violent TV programs wound up showing more aggression, we cannot attribute this difference to the TV viewing itself. It may, instead, reflect the children's greater initial aggressiveness.

In an experiment on the effects of televised violence, we would therefore have to assign children randomly either to view TV violence or nonviolence, regardless of their personal preferences. As you can imagine, this would be difficult, if not impossible, to do in the child's own home. But such studies can be performed in laboratory settings, as we will see in Chapter 10.

Ethical and practical considerations also prevent researchers from doing experiments on the effects of many significant life circumstances such as divorce or different patterns of child rearing. We cannot randomly assign some families to divorce, or to conflict, and other families to perpetual harmony. Nor can we

**FIGURE 1.9**

**WHAT ARE THE EFFECTS OF REWARDS ON LEARNING?** *In this experiment, some children (the experimental group) received a treat when they picked a certain block. Other children (the control group) received nothing. Which group do you think learned this task more quickly? Why?*

randomly assign parents with an authoritarian bent to raising their children in a permissive manner, or vice versa. In some areas of investigation, we must be relatively satisfied with correlational evidence.

When experiments cannot ethically be performed on humans, researchers sometimes have carried out experiments with animals and then generalized the findings to humans. For example, no researcher would wish to separate human infants from their parents to study the effects of isolation on development. But experimenters have deprived rhesus monkeys of early social experience. Such research has helped psychologists investigate the formation of parent–child bonds of attachment (see Chapter 7).

**THINKING ABOUT DEVELOPMENT**

Agree or disagree with the following statement and support your answer: "Research with lower animals cannot really tell us anything about children."

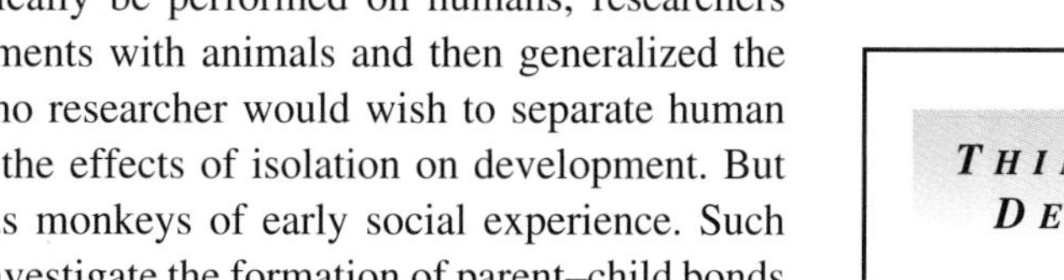

**TRUTH OR FICTION REVISITED**

*It is true that studies of early social deprivation in rhesus monkeys have helped psychologists understand how attachment develops in humans.*

Sometimes researchers are able to conduct a ***natural experiment,*** in which they examine the effect of a naturally occurring independent variable in two settings that are similar in many ways. For example, one of the authors (C. E.) was asked by a local elementary school district to evaluate the effect of resource rooms, called "learning centers," on students' school performance and attitudes. Learning centers were about to open up in some of the schools in the district. C. E. was not able to randomly assign students to participate or not participate in the centers, so she could not perform a true experiment. However, she was able to compare students in a school that had a learning center with students of similar backgrounds who were attending a nearby school that did not have a learning center. Natural experiments like this do not, however, have the same degree of control as do true experiments. Although subjects in the "treatment" and "control" groups are similar, they may differ in some subtle but important ways that affect their response to the variable being studied.

## *STUDYING DEVELOPMENT OVER TIME*

The processes of development occur over time, and researchers have evolved different strategies for comparing children of one age to children (or adults) of other ages. In ***longitudinal research,*** the same children are observed repeatedly over time, and changes in development, such as gains in height or changes in approach to problem solving, are recorded. In ***cross-sectional research,*** children of different ages are observed and compared. It is assumed that when large numbers of children are chosen at random, the differences found in the older age groups are a reflection of how the younger children will develop, given time. Table 1.3 summarizes the major features of cross-sectional and longitudinal research.

***Natural experiment*** Comparison of naturally occurring groups that differ along some dimension of interest, such as children who were exposed prenatally to drugs versus those who were not.

***Longitudinal research*** The study of developmental processes by taking repeated measures of the same group of children at various stages of development.

***Cross-sectional research*** The study of developmental processes by taking measures of children of different age groups at the same time.

**LONGITUDINAL STUDIES** Some ambitious longitudinal studies have followed the development of children and adults for more than half a century. One, the Fels Longitudinal Study, began in 1929. Children were observed twice a year in their homes and twice a year in the Fels Institute nursery school. From time

**TABLE 1.3**

***COMPARISON OF CROSS-SECTIONAL AND LONGITUDINAL RESEARCH***

| | CROSS-SECTIONAL | LONGITUDINAL |
|---|---|---|
| DESCRIPTION | STUDY CHILDREN OF DIFFERENT AGES AT THE SAME POINT IN TIME | STUDY THE SAME CHILDREN REPEATEDLY OVER TIME |
| ADVANTAGES | INEXPENSIVE<br>COMPLETED IN SHORT PERIOD OF TIME<br>NO DROP-OUT OR PRACTICE EFFECTS | FOLLOW DEVELOPMENT OVER TIME<br>STUDY RELATIONSHIP BETWEEN EARLY AND LATER BEHAVIOR |
| DISADVANTAGES | CANNOT STUDY DEVELOPMENT OVER TIME<br>CANNOT STUDY RELATIONSHIP BETWEEN EARLY AND LATER BEHAVIOR<br>DIFFERENT AGE GROUPS MAY NOT BE COMPARABLE (COHORT EFFECT) | EXPENSIVE<br>TAKES A LONG TIME<br>SUBJECTS DROP OUT<br>THOSE WHO DROP OUT MAY DIFFER FROM THOSE WHO DO NOT<br>PRACTICE EFFECTS MAY OCCUR |

**TRUTH OR FICTION REVISITED**

*Researchers have, in fact, followed some participants in developmental research for more than 50 years. Participants have been followed for this length of time in a number of longitudinal research projects.*

to time, various investigators have dipped into the Fels pool of subjects, further testing, interviewing, and observing these individuals as they have grown into adults. In this way, researchers have been able to observe, for example, the development of intelligence and of patterns of independence and dependence.

The Terman Studies of Genius, also begun in the 1920s, tracked children with high IQ scores. As we shall see in Chapter 12, the men in this study, but not the women, went on to high achievements in the professional world. Why is this? Contemporary studies of women show that those with high intelligence generally match the achievements of men and suggest that women of the earlier era were held back by traditional gender-role expectations.

Most longitudinal studies span months or a few years, not decades. In Chapter 13, for example, we shall see that briefer longitudinal studies have found that the children of divorced parents undergo the most severe adjustment problems within a few months of the divorce. By 2 or 3 years afterward, many children have regained their equilibrium, as indicated by improved academic performance, socially appropriate behavior, and other measures (Hetherington et al., 1992).

Longitudinal studies have a number of drawbacks. On a practical level, it can be difficult to enlist volunteers to participate in a study that will last a lifetime, and it can be difficult to have the subjects provide updated addresses. Many participants fall out of touch as the years pass; others die. Furthermore, those who remain in the study tend to be brighter and more motivated than those who drop out. The researchers, of course, must be very patient. To compare 3-year-olds with 6-year-olds, they must wait at least 3 years. And in the early stages of such a study, the idea of comparing 3-year-olds with 21-year-olds remains a distant dream. When the researchers themselves are middle-aged or elderly, they must hope that the candle of yearning for knowledge will be kept lit by a new generation of researchers.

***Cohort effect*** Similarities in behavior among a group of peers that stem from the fact that group members are approximately of the same age. (A possible source of misleading information in cross-sectional research.)

**Cross-Sectional Studies** Because of the drawbacks of longitudinal studies, most research that compares children of different ages is cross-sectional. Most investigators, in other words, gather data on what the "typical" 6-month-old is doing by finding children who are 6 months old today. When they expand their research to the behavior of typical 12-month-olds, they seek another group of children, and so on.

A major drawback to cross-sectional research is the ***cohort effect.*** A cohort is a group of people born at about the same time. As a result, they experience cultural and other events unique to their age group. In other words, children and adults of different ages are not likely to have shared similar cultural backgrounds. People who are 60 years old today, for example, grew up without television. People who are 40 years old today grew up before the era of space travel. When they were children, no explorers had yet left Earth. Today's 30-year-olds did not spend their earliest years with "Sesame Street," a television program that has greatly influenced millions of a somewhat younger cohort of children and young adults. And today's children are growing up taking microcomputers and video games for granted.

Children of past generations also grew up with very different expectations about gender roles and appropriate social behavior. Remember that women in the Terman study generally chose motherhood over careers. Today's girls are growing up with female role models who are astronauts, high government officials, and powerful athletes. Moreover, today more than 60 percent of mothers are in the work force, and their attitudes about women's roles have changed.

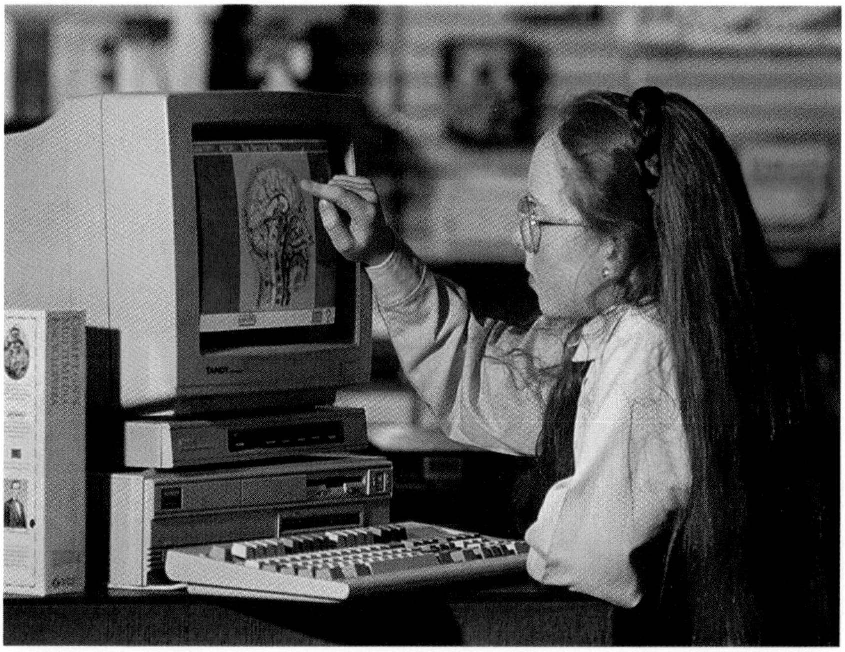

FIGURE 1.10

**An Example of the Cohort Effect?** *Children and adults of different ages experience cultural and other events unique to their age group. This is known as the* cohort effect. *For example, today's children—unlike their parents—are growing up taking microcomputers and video games for granted.*

***Cross-sequential research*** An approach that combines the longitudinal and cross-sectional methods by following individuals of different ages for abbreviated periods of time.

***Time-lag*** The study of developmental processes by taking measures of children of the same age group at different times.

In sum, today's 25-year-olds are not today's 5-year-olds as seen 20 years later. And today's 10-year-olds may not even be today's 5-year-olds as seen 5 years later. The times change, and their influence on children changes also. In longitudinal studies, we know that we have the same individuals as they have developed over 5, 10, and 20 years. In cross-sectional research, we can only hope they will be comparable.

**CROSS-SEQUENTIAL RESEARCH** ***Cross-sequential research*** combines the longitudinal and cross-sectional methods in such a way that many of their individual drawbacks are overcome. In the cross-sequential study, the full span of the ideal longitudinal study is first broken up into convenient segments (see Figure 1.11). For example, let us assume we wish to follow the gender-role attitudes of children from the age of 4 through the age of 12. The typical longitudinal study would take 8 years. However, we can divide this 8-year span in half by attaining two samples of children (a cross-section) instead of one: 4-year-olds and 8-year-olds. We would then interview, test, and observe each group at the beginning of the study (1991) and 4 years later (1995). By the time of the second observation period, the 4-year-olds would have become 8 years old, and the 8-year-olds would have become 12.

An obvious advantage to this collapsed method is that the study is completed in 4 rather than 8 years. Still, the testing and retesting of samples provides some of the continuity of the longitudinal study. By observing both samples at the age of 8 (this is called a ***time-lag*** comparison) we can also determine whether they are, in fact, comparable or whether the 4 years' difference in their birthdates is associated with cultural and other environmental changes that lead to different attitudes. The fact that both groups of children overlap in age at one point (8 years old), when the younger group is tested for the second time and the older group for the first time, may also provide insight as to whether the process of testing itself makes a difference in future performance. That is, differences between samples tested at the same age may reflect the experience of having been tested before, as well as other environmental differences.

This combined method may include more than two samples and briefer time spans. For example, it is possible to recruit five groups of children, not two. If these children are 2, 4, 6, 8, and 10 years old at the outset of the study, they can be followed for 2 years, until their ages overlap, and then be retested. In this way, 10 years of "longitudinal" data can be acquired in 2. Eight years are saved, and some of the objections to longitudinal research are overcome. Quite a bargain.

FIGURE 1.11

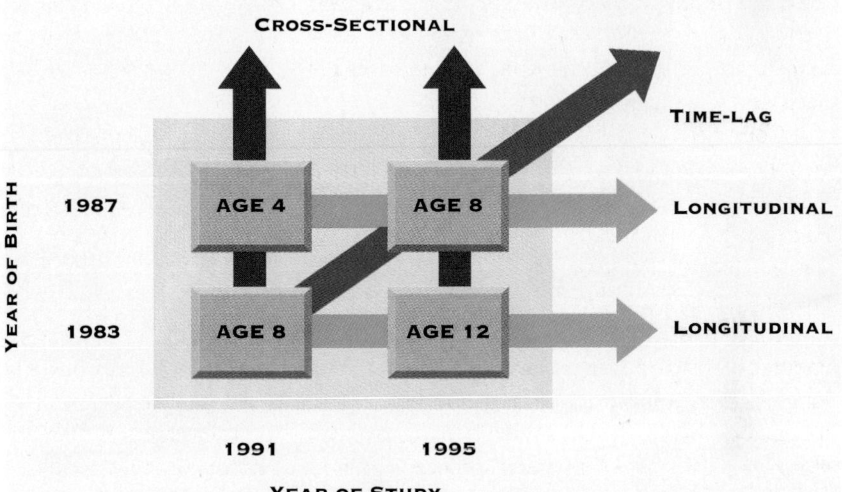


**AN EXAMPLE OF CROSS-SEQUENTIAL RESEARCH.** *Cross-sequential research combines three methods: cross-sectional, longitudinal, and time lag. The child's age at time of testing appears in the boxes. Vertical columns represent cross-sectional comparisons. Horizontal rows represent longitudinal comparisons. Diagonals represent time-lag comparisons.*

### *Ethical Considerations in Child Development*

Psychologists adhere to a number of ethical standards that are intended to promote the dignity of the individual, foster human welfare, and maintain scientific integrity (McGovern et al., 1991). These standards also ensure that psychologists do not undertake research methods or treatments that are harmful to research participants (American Psychological Association, 1992). What are some of the ethical issues involved in child development research?

Various professional groups—such as the American Psychological Association and the Society for Research in Child Development—and government review boards have proposed guidelines for research with children. The overriding purpose of these guidelines is to protect children from harm. These guidelines include the following:

- Researchers are not to use treatments or methods of measurement that may do physical or psychological harm to children.
- Children and their parents must be fully informed of the purposes of the research and about the research methods.
- Children and their parents must provide voluntary consent to participate in the study.
- Children and their parents may withdraw from the study at any time, for any reason.
- Children and their parents should be offered information about the results of the study.
- The identities of the children participating in a study are to remain confidential.
- Researchers should present their research plans to a committee of their colleagues and gain the committee's approval before proceeding.

These guidelines present researchers with a number of hurdles to overcome before proceeding with and while conducting research. But since they protect the welfare of children, the guidelines are valuable.

However, one major dilemma is posed by one of these guidelines, and exceptions are sometimes sought. This is the guideline that suggests children be informed of the purposes of the research. The problem is not that many children are too young to comprehend the research; in such cases, disclosure can be made to their parents instead. But what of those cases in which disclosure of the study's purposes would render the study useless?

Consider a study in which children are exposed to films of adults acting aggressively and are then given the opportunity to act aggressively themselves. What would be the effect of informing children of the purposes of the study? And what if—in order to be perfectly aboveboard—the children were also informed they would be observed through one-way mirrors? Such research could not be accomplished if full disclosure were insisted upon.

Because of this dilemma, researchers are sometimes given the go-ahead by committees of peers to make exceptions to the principle of full disclosure, so long as other safeguards are taken. Such safeguards might include disclosure of the study's purposes and methods to parents, if not the children themselves; reasonable assurance that the procedures will not be harmful; and ***debriefing*** of participants after the study has been carried out.

***Debriefing*** Receiving information about a just-completed research procedure.

TRUTH OR FICTION REVISITED

*It is true that psychologists cannot carry out certain research studies with children if they fully inform the participants as to their purposes and methods. However, participants are debriefed after such studies are completed.*

## CRITICAL THINKING AND DEVELOPMENT

Is breast-feeding superior to bottle-feeding? Is it harmful to spoil children? Are people who were abused as children likely to abuse their own children? Many students (and many parents) will have opinions on some of these issues. The knowledge of research methods that you have gained from this first chapter can help you think more critically. Critical thinking helps us sort out evidence from opinion and truth from fiction.

By thinking critically, we come to challenge widely accepted but erroneous beliefs, including some of those we most cherish. ***Critical thinking*** helps make us into active, astute judges of other people's opinions—including their opinions on development—rather than passive recipients of the latest intellectual fads and tyrannies.

The core of critical thinking is skepticism. An attitude of skepticism encourages students to no longer take certain ''truths'' for granted. Consider the widespread assumption that authority figures such as child development experts usually provide us with factual information and are generally best equipped to make the decisions that affect our lives. But when developmentalists disagree about whether certain child-rearing practices are necessary for normal development, how can they all be correct? We need to learn to seek pertinent information to make our own decisions and to rely on our analytical abilities to judge the accuracy of information. This textbook will help you learn to seek and analyze information that lies within the province of child development, but the critical thinking skills you acquire will be broadly applicable in all of your courses and all of your adult undertakings.

### *PRINCIPLES OF CRITICAL THINKING*

Many of the ''Truth-or-Fiction?'' items presented in this textbook are intended to encourage you to apply principles of critical thinking to the subject matter of development. Some of them reflect truisms, beliefs that are commonly accepted in our culture. Consider a sampling of ''Truth-or-Fiction?'' items from several chapters:

- Breast-feeding and bottle-feeding are equally healthful for infants.
- Crying is the child's earliest use of language.
- Child abusers have frequently been the victims of child abuse themselves.
- Hyperactivity is caused by chemical food additives.
- Bilingual children encounter more academic problems than children who know only one language.

***Critical thinking*** A type of thinking that helps individuals sort out evidence from opinion and truth from fiction.

- ✦ Children with school phobia should not return to school until the origins of the problem are uncovered and resolved.
- ✦ U.S. adolescents are growing taller than their parents.
- ✦ Adolescent boys outperform adolescent girls in mathematics.
- ✦ Parents and peers tend to exert conflicting influences on adolescents.

You will have the opportunity to agree or disagree with these statements in the following chapters. We will refer to a number of them as we elaborate on the principles of critical thinking, however. We may not give you the answers to the items—not yet—but we will provide hints, and we will illustrate some principles of critical thinking as we whet your appetite for studying development. Consider the following principles of critical thinking:

1. *Be skeptical.* Politicians and advertisers strive to convince you of their points of view. Even research reported in the media or in textbooks may take a certain slant. Have the attitude that you will accept nothing as true until you have personally examined the evidence.

   Consider some truisms in the area of child development: "Hyperactivity is caused by chemical food additives"; "U.S. adolescents are growing taller than their parents"; and "Parents and peers tend to exert conflicting influences on adolescents." What does the evidence say?

2. *Examine definitions of terms.* One of the strengths of a scientific approach to development is the use of *operational definitions* of concepts. Operational definitions are framed in terms of the ways in which we measure concepts. In interpreting research, pay attention to how the concepts are defined. Some statements are true when a term is defined in one way but not another. Consider the statement "Crying is the child's earliest use of language." Although we won't drop the answer in your lap, we'll tell you that the correctness of the statement depends on the definition of *language.*

3. *Examine the assumptions or premises of arguments.* What are the assumptions that underlie the view that "Children with school phobia should not return to school until the origins of the problem are uncovered and resolved"? Is there a notion that meaningful behavior change cannot take place unless the underlying causes of problems are discovered and rooted out? Does the evidence support that view?

4. *Be cautious in drawing conclusions from evidence.* Studies for many years had shown that children reared in homes where English was not spoken fared more poorly in school than children reared in English-speaking homes. Therefore, it appeared to some investigators that bilingualism contributed to academic problems. However, more careful analysis of the data showed that children reared in homes where English was not spoken were also frequently subjected to the problems of poverty and social discrimination. Did bilingualism or these social ills contribute to their academic problems?

5. *Consider alternative interpretations of research evidence.* Because there is a connection, or correlation, between experiencing child abuse and abusing one's own children, it may be assumed that being abused as a child causes one to abuse one's own children. If this were so, victims of child abuse would inevitably abuse their own children. This, however, is not the case. Perhaps early victimization by abusive parents shows children one way adults respond to stress, but there is no clear causal connection between being abused and committing abuse.

6. *Do not oversimplify.* Consider the issue of whether breast-feeding and bottle-feeding are equally healthful for infants. Are all instances of breast-feeding comparable, or would that view be oversimplifying? Similarly, are all instances of bottle-feeding alike? The issue is actually quite complex.

7. *Do not overgeneralize.* Consider the statement "Adolescent boys outperform adolescent girls in mathematics." Later in the text, we shall see that mathematics involves many different kinds of skills and that the belief of male superiority is at best an overgeneralization.

8. *Apply critical thinking to all areas of life.* A skeptical attitude and a demand for evidence are not simply academic exercises of value in college courses. They are of value in all areas of life. Be skeptical when you are bombarded by TV commercials, when political causes try to sweep you up, when you see tabloid cover stories about Elvis and UFOs. How many times have you heard the claim "Studies have shown that . . ."? Perhaps such claims sound convincing, but ask yourself, Who ran the studies? Were the researchers neutral scientists or biased toward obtaining certain results? Did the studies possess all of the controls described in your textbook's discussion of research methods?

As noted by the educator Robert M. Hutchins, "The object of education is to prepare the young to educate themselves throughout their lives." One of the primary ways of educating yourself is through critical thinking.

## Summary

1. Childhood spans the years from infancy to puberty. It includes the periods of infancy (birth to 2 years), early childhood (2 to 6 years) and middle childhood (6 to 12 years). Puberty signals the beginning of adolescence, a period between childhood and adulthood. Child development refers to the unfolding and growth of structures, traits, and behavior patterns throughout childhood and adolescence.

2. Researchers study child development for many reasons: to gain insight into human nature; to learn about the origins of adult behavior; to investigate the causes, prevention, and treatment of developmental abnormalities; and to optimize conditions of development for all children.

3. To understand children's development, we must be aware of their diversity. Children differ in their ethnicity and their gender. Ethnicity refers to cultural heritage, race, language, and common history. Gender involves social and cultural definitions of femaleness and maleness.

4. During the Middle Ages children frequently worked alongside their parents. They were treated and depicted as miniature adults.

5. The 17th-century philosopher John Locke argued that children enter the world as blank tablets, and that rewards and punishments foster proper behavior. The 18th-century philosopher Jean-Jacques Rousseau argued that children are innately good.

6. The Industrial Revolution contributed to the awareness of childhood as a special time of life. During the 20th century, compulsory education laws were passed, along with laws that protect children from parental abuse and neglect and from adverse labor conditions.

7. Nineteenth-century scientist Charles Darwin was one of the first to keep a baby biography. Psychologist G. Stanley Hall, who founded the field of child development a century ago, adapted the questionnaire method for use with children and heightened awareness of adolescence as a stage. The mental-testing movement was pioneered by Alfred Binet.

8. There are three major contemporary controversies in child development: Does nature (heredity) or nurture (environmental influences) exert greater impact upon children? Is development continuous (does it occur gradually) or discontinuous (does it occur in stages)? Are children basically active or passive?

9. Developmental psychologists use the scientific method to gather evidence. The four steps of this method are: formulating a research question, developing a hypothesis, testing the hypothesis, and drawing conclusions about the hypothesis.

10. Developmental psychologists use various methods to gather information about children. The naturalistic observation study observes children's behavior where it occurs—the natural setting.

11. The case study is a carefully drawn description of the behavior of an individual. Both Freud and Piaget relied heavily on the case-study method.

12. The correlational method reveals relationships between variables but it does not determine cause and effect.

13. Experiments seek to determine cause and effect by giving experimental subjects a treatment that is not given to control subjects.

14. Natural experiments examine the effects of a naturally occurring variable. However, they do not permit the same degree of control as true experiments.

15. In longitudinal research, the same group of individuals is observed repeatedly at several points in time. In cross-sectional research, individuals of different ages are compared. Both types of research suggest developmental conclusions. Longitudinal research has the drawbacks of taking a long time and of loss of participants over time. A problem with cross-sectional research is that older participants may not be representative of younger participants at advanced ages.

16. The cross-sequential method combines longitudinal and cross-sectional approaches. It saves researchers time and also remedies some of the drawbacks of both types of research.

17. Ethics in child development research are intended to prevent mistreatment of children. Children and/or their parents are informed of research methods and purposes, they are given the opportunity to withdraw from research at any time, and their records are kept confidential.

18. Critical thinking helps individuals evaluate claims, arguments, and widely held beliefs in all areas of life.

**ANSWER KEY TO QUESTIONNAIRE ON KNOWLEDGE OF CHILD DEVELOPMENT, PAGE 7.**

| | | | |
|---|---|---|---|
| 1. F | 5. F | 9. F | 13. F |
| 2. F | 6. F | 10. F | 14. T |
| 3. F | 7. F | 11. T | 15. T |
| 4. T | 8. F | 12. T | 16. F |

CHAPTER

2

# *Theories of Development*

## Chapter Outline

**Theoretical Interlude: Why Do We Have Theories of Child Development?**
- *Theories*
- *Stage Theories versus Continuous Development*

**Maturational Theory**
- *Practical Applications of Maturational Theory*
- *Evaluation of Maturational Theory*

**Psychoanalytic Theories**
- *Sigmund Freud's Theory of Psychosexual Development*
- *Erik Erikson's Theory of Psychosocial Development*

**Learning Theories**
- *Behaviorism*
- *Social-Learning Theory*

**Cognitive Theories**
- *Jean Piaget's Cognitive-Developmental Theory*
- *Information-Processing Theory*

**Ecological Theory**
- *Focus on Reciprocal Processes*
- *Focus on the Larger Context: Systems within Systems*
- *Practical Applications of Ecological Theory*
- *Evaluation of Ecological Theory*

**Theoretical Interlude: Some Integrating Thoughts on Theories of Development**

**Summary**

## Truth or Fiction?

_____ *Early training in sitting up and walking accelerates the development of these skills in infants.*

_____ *Conflict between children and their parents is inescapable.*

_____ *Children can be taught to wake up in the middle of the night if they are about to wet their beds.*

_____ *Punishment doesn't work.*

_____ *Psychologists successfully used painful electric shock to teach a 9-month-old infant not to vomit.*

_____ *Classroom behavior-modification procedures rely largely on old standbys such as ignoring children when they misbehave and praising them for desired behavior.*

_____ *Children are budding scientists who actively intend to learn about and take intellectual charge of their worlds.*

_____ *Some developmentalists see children's strategies for solving problems as "mental programs" that are operated by their "personal computers," or brains.*

_____ *Infants do not simply accept their parents' child-rearing approaches; even newborns influence their parents to treat them in certain ways.*

_____ *Children are influenced not only by their parents, schools, and other local agencies, but also by the ideals and values of the cultures in which they are reared.*

"Give me a dozen healthy infants, well-formed," John B. Watson challenged in 1924, "and my own specified world to bring them up in, and I'll guarantee to train them to become any type of specialist I might suggest—doctor, lawyer, merchant, chief, and, yes, even beggar and thief, regardless of their talents, penchants, tendencies, abilities, vocations, and the race of their ancestors" (adapted from Watson, 1924, p. 82).

Watson, often referred to as the founder of American ***behaviorism,*** was expressing a learning-theory view of children, in keeping with the ideas of British philosopher John Locke, that children come into the world as a *tabula rasa,* or "blank slate," and that their ideas, preferences, tendencies, and skills are shaped by their experiences. In Chapter 1, it was noted that there has long been a nature–nurture controversy in the study of children. In his theoretical approach to understanding children, Watson emphasized the role of *nurture,* or of the physical and social environments, for example, of parental training and approval.

Watson's view was a minority in the long history of approaches to understanding children. *Nature,* or the inherited, genetic characteristics of the child, had long been the more popular explanation of how children get to be what they are. Just 4 years after Watson sounded his clarion call for the behavioral view, Arnold Gesell expressed the idea that biological ***maturation*** was the main principle of development: "All things considered, the inevitableness and surety of maturation are the most impressive characteristics of early development. It is the hereditary ballast which conserves and stabilizes growth of each individual infant" (Gesell, 1928, p. 378).

Watson was talking largely about the behavior patterns children develop, while Gesell was perhaps focusing mainly on physical aspects of growth and development. Still, the behavioral and maturational perspectives remain at opposite ends of the continuum of theories of development. As noted by Sandra Scarr (1985), many scientists fall into the trap of overemphasizing the importance of either nature or nurture at the risk of overlooking the ways in which nature and nurture interact. Just as a child's environments and experiences influence the development of his or her biological endowment, children often place themselves in environments that are harmonious with their personal characteristics. Children, for example, are influenced by teachers and by other students; however, because of the psychological traits they bring to school with them, some children may choose to socialize as much as possible with other children, while other children may prefer the company of teachers, and still other children may prefer to remain by themselves as much as they can.

In this chapter, we first define what is meant by theories of development. We show why it is important to try to construct theories and to show which theories are most helpful in understanding children. Then we examine five contemporary theoretical approaches to understanding children: the maturational, psychoanalytic, learning, cognitive, and ecological approaches. As you may already have realized, each theoretical approach has contributed to our overall understanding of children.

***Behaviorism*** John B. Watson's view that a science or theory of development must study observable behavior only and investigate relationships between stimuli and responses.

***Maturation*** The unfolding of genetically determined traits, structures, and functions.

## THEORETICAL INTERLUDE: WHY DO WE HAVE THEORIES OF CHILD DEVELOPMENT?

Child development is a scientific enterprise. As in other scientific enterprises, developmentalists seek to *describe, explain, predict,* and *control* the events they study.

Developmentalists attempt to describe and explain behavior in terms of concepts such as heredity, perception, language, learning, cognition, emotion, socialization, and gender roles. For example, we may describe learning as a process in which behavior changes as a result of experience. We can be more specific and describe instances of learning in which children memorize the alphabet through repetition, or acquire gymnastic skills through practice in which their performance gradually approximates desired behavior. We may explain how learning occurs in terms of rules or principles that govern learning. Thus we might explain the trainer's use of words such as "fine" and "good" as "reinforcers" that provide the gymnast with "feedback."

### *Theories*

When possible, descriptive terms and concepts are interwoven into ***theories.*** Theories are related sets of statements about events. Theories are based on certain assumptions about behavior, such as Watson's assumption that training outweighs talents and abilities or Gesell's assumption that the unfolding of maturational tendencies is inevitable. Theories also allow us to derive explanations and predictions. Many developmental theories combine statements about psychological concepts (such as learning and motivation), behavior (such as reading or problem solving), and anatomical structures or biological processes (such as maturation of the nervous system). For instance, a child's ability to learn to read is influenced by her or his motivation, attention span, and level of perceptual development.

A satisfactory theory of development must allow us to predict behavior. For instance, a satisfactory theory concerning the development of gender roles will allow us to predict the circumstances under which children will acquire stereotypical feminine or masculine gender-typed behavior patterns or a combination of these patterns. A broadly satisfying, comprehensive theory should have a wide range of applicability. A broad theory of the development of gender roles might apply to children from different cultural and racial backgrounds and, perhaps, to homosexuals as well as heterosexuals. If our observations cannot be adequately explained by or predicted from a given theory, we should consider revising or replacing that theory.

Many theories have been found incapable of explaining or predicting new observations. As a result, they have been revised extensively. For example, Sigmund Freud's psychoanalytic view that assertive career women are suffering from unconscious ***penis envy*** has met with criticism from his followers (such as Karen Horney) and his antagonists alike. Most modern-day, or "neo-," Freudians have developed different views concerning assertive behavior in girls and women.

The notion of controlling behavior is controversial. However, the goal of control does not mean that developmentalists seek to make children do their bidding—as if they were puppets dangling on strings. Instead, it means that professionals consult with parents, teachers, nurses, and children themselves in order to promote the welfare of children. Psychologists, for example, may summarize and interpret theory and research on the effects of day care to help day-care workers provide an optimal child-care environment. Teachers may use learning theory to help children learn to read and write. In each case, the professional is controlling the experiences that children will encounter, but it is clearly with the benefits to the children in mind and also, ultimately, with the understanding and approval of parents.

***Theory*** A formulation of relationships underlying observed events. A theory involves assumptions and logically derived explanations and predictions.

***Penis envy*** In psychoanalytic theory, jealousy of the male sex organ attributed to girls in the phallic stage.

***Stage theory*** A theory of development characterized by hypothesizing the existence of stages.

***Stage*** A distinct period of life that is qualitatively different from other stages. Stages follow one another in an orderly sequence.

***Discrete*** Separate and distinct; made up of distinct parts.

***Maturational theory*** Arnold Gesell's view that development is self-regulated by the unfolding of natural plans (that is, heredity) and processes.

## *Stage Theories versus Continuous Development*

The psychoanalytic theories of Sigmund Freud and Erik Erikson and the cognitive-developmental theory of Jean Piaget are ***stage theories.*** You will recall from Chapter 1 that ***stages*** are relatively ***discrete*** periods of development that differ in quality from other periods. Stages follow one another in a certain sequence. According to Freud, each stage of development is ushered in by biological changes. Each stage is characterized by particular behaviors and holds a distinct potential for the development of various traits and conflicts.

Not all developmental theories are stage theories. Social-learning theorists, for example, view development as a continuous process in which the effects of learning mount gradually, with no major, sudden qualitative leaps.

Let us now consider what each of the major theoretical approaches has to say about the nature and development of the child.

# Maturational Theory

***Maturational theory*** focuses largely on the unfolding of genetically determined developmental sequences. Whereas the theory of Sigmund Freud assumes that biological maturation provides the foundation for changes in personality and emotional development, maturational theory, as propounded by Arnold Gesell (1880–1961), argues that all areas of development are self-regulated by the unfolding of natural plans and processes. Few contemporary students of child development would agree that maturation is the central factor in *all* areas of development. However, very few would dispute that maturation plays the major role in areas such as motor development.

Maturational processes tend to follow invariant sequences. In the case of motor development, children sit up before they stand, and they stand before they walk. It appears that these motor skills are made possible by the progressive maturation of certain parts of the nervous system. Numerous investigators have also wondered whether learning experiences have an important influence on motor development—whether, for example, training can accelerate children's progress through this sequence. In Chapter 5, we shall see that early training only slightly accelerates motor development. No amount of training, moreover, can teach these skills to children whose levels of maturation are not sufficiently advanced. In maturational terms, children must be "ready" to acquire new behavior patterns. The unfolding of natural processes creates the foundation on which experiences can build.

### *Truth or Fiction Revisited*

*Actually, early training in sitting up and walking does not significantly accelerate the development of these skills in infants. Training may slightly speed up the processes of motor development, but motor skills, by and large, are not acquired until children have matured to the point where they are ready to acquire them.*

A few studies have focused on the effects of purposefully preventing infants from practicing certain motor skills during the early months. When children who are deprived of experience in this way are again permitted to move about freely at more advanced ages, they tend to acquire these motor skills almost literally overnight. When we are ready to learn, we tend to learn quickly. When we are not ready, learning proceeds tediously, if it occurs at all. Educators are understandably concerned with knowing when children are ready to acquire academic skills.

### *Practical Applications of Maturational Theory*

The work of Gesell and other maturational theorists has provided standards in many areas of development against which children may be compared to see if they are developing normally (Thelen & Adolph, 1992; Thomas, 1992). Parents (especially first-time parents) frequently consult child-rearing books to check whether the age when their child first sits up, walks, talks, and so forth is typical (or slow or advanced) for its age.

### *Evaluation of Maturational Theory*

Most psychologists acknowledge that maturation—that is, the unfolding of the genetic code—plays a role in the child's development. But they also note how children's environments interact with inherited and maturational tendencies in directing their development. For example, although children cannot throw a ball

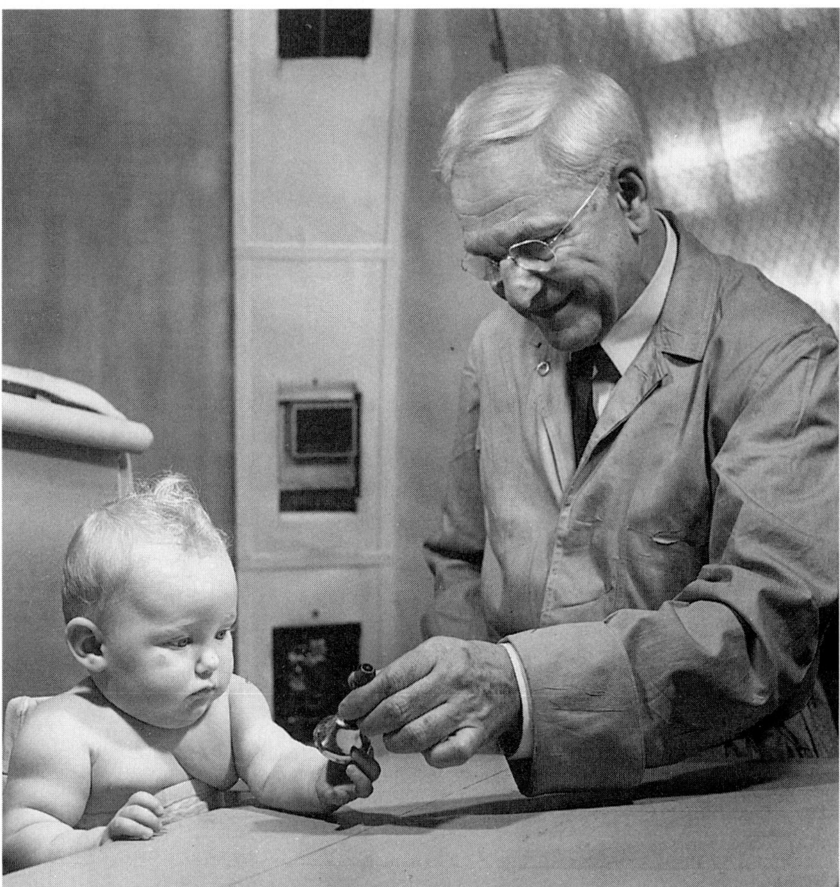

FIGURE 2.1

***Arnold Gesell.*** *Gesell was a major proponent of the maturational theory of child development. This theory focuses largely on the unfolding of genetically determined developmental sequences.*

or play the piano before reaching a certain level of neurological and physical maturation, they also acquire these behaviors through the learning process (Crain, 1992).

Gesell has been criticized for reporting only the "typical" characteristics of children of a given age. He gave no indication of the amount of individual variation that occurs at each age, and so the child's individuality often was overlooked. Moreover, Gesell's standards of "normal" development were based on middle-class children in a university setting and may not apply exactly in other cultural contexts (Crain, 1992).

Now let us consider another theory of development that relies upon the relationship between the biological maturation of the child and stages of development: psychoanalytic theory. Unlike Gesell's approach, the psychoanalytic approach focuses on what is presumed to be children's conflicts with their parents and society at large.

FIGURE 2.2

***SIGMUND FREUD.*** *Freud is the originator of psychoanalytic theory. He proposed five stages of psychosexual development and emphasized the importance of biological factors in the development of personality.*

## PSYCHOANALYTIC THEORIES

He was born with a shock of dark hair—in Jewish tradition, the sign of a prophet. In 1856, in a Czechoslovakian village, a fortune-teller told his mother that she had given birth to an important man, and the child was raised with great expectations. In adulthood, Sigmund Freud himself would be cynical about this notion. Fortune-tellers, after all, earn more favors through good tidings than through forecasts of doom. But, in a sense, the prophecy about Freud may have been realized. Few have shaped our thinking about human nature as deeply as the compassionate physician from Vienna.

Freud (1856–1939) formulated the ***psychoanalytic theory*** of development and the form of psychotherapy called *psychoanalysis.* He focused on the emotional and social development of children and on the origins of ***psychological traits*** such as dependence, obsessive neatness, and vanity.

A basic concept of psychoanalytic theories is that conflict between the child and society is inevitable. Children are viewed as possessing biological instincts that demand gratification. The social processes that limit the child's avenues for seeking this gratification—that guide the child into following parental wishes and social codes—also shape the child's personality.

In this section, we explore Freud's theory of psychosexual development and Erik Erikson's theory of psychosocial development. Each is a stage theory. Each suggests that the child's experiences during early stages have implications for the child's eventual emotional balance and social adjustment.

***Psychoanalytic theory*** The school of psychology, founded by Sigmund Freud, that emphasizes the importance of unconscious, primitive motives and conflicts as determinants of behavior and personality development.

***Psychological trait*** An aspect of personality that is inferred from behavior and assumed to give rise to behavioral consistency.

***Psychodynamic*** Descriptive of Sigmund Freud's view that various forces move through the personality and determine behavior.

### *SIGMUND FREUD'S THEORY OF PSYCHOSEXUAL DEVELOPMENT*

Freud's view of personality is ***psychodynamic.*** Freud taught that even in young children, personality is characterized by a dynamic struggle. Basic drives such as hunger, sex, and aggression inevitably come into conflict with social pressures to behave according to laws, rules, and moral codes. The laws and social rules become internalized; children make them parts of themselves. After doing so, the dynamic struggle becomes a clashing of opposing *inner* forces. The major struggles lie *within.*

## TRUTH OR FICTION REVISITED

*Conflict between children and their parents may be inescapable* according to Freud's psychoanalytic theory, in which children's basic instincts are viewed as selfish and antisocial. *Other theorists, however, do not necessarily agree.*

**THE GEOGRAPHY OF THE MIND: WARMING UP TO THE HUMAN ICEBERG** Freud believed that the human mind was like an iceberg. Only the tip of an iceberg rises above the surface of the water, while the great mass of it resides in the deep. Freud came to believe that people, because of their childhood experiences, are aware of only a small number of the ideas and the impulses that dwell within their minds. Our deepest images, thoughts, fears, and urges remain beneath the surface of conscious awareness, where little light illuminates them. He labeled the region that surfaces into the light of awareness the ***conscious*** part of the mind. He called the regions that lie below the surface the preconscious and the unconscious.

The ***preconscious*** mind contains elements of experience that are presently out of awareness but can be made conscious simply by focusing on them, such as your phone number or what you ate for dinner yesterday. The ***unconscious*** mind contains genetic instincts and urges that we only partially perceive, such as hunger, thirst, sexuality, and aggression. Some unconscious urges cannot be experienced consciously, because mental images and words cannot portray them in all their color and fury.

**THE STRUCTURE OF PERSONALITY: ID, EGO, AND SUPEREGO** Sigmund Freud labeled the clashing forces of personality the *id, ego,* and *superego.* These three ***psychic structures*** cannot be observed directly, but their influence can be inferred from our behavior.

The ***id*** is present at birth. The id represents biological drives and is unconscious. It demands instant gratification of instincts without consideration of law, social custom, or the needs of others.

The ***ego*** begins to develop during the first year of life, when an infant experiences delays prior to receiving gratification. It blossoms as children learn to obtain gratification for themselves, without screaming or crying. The ego provides rational ways of coping with frustration. The ego curbs the appetites of the id and makes plans that are in keeping with social convention so that a person can find gratification yet avoid the disapproval of others. The id lets children know that they are hungry. The ego creates the idea of walking to the refrigerator, warming up some enchiladas, and pouring a glass of milk.

The ego also acts as a watchdog, or censor, that screens the impulses of the id. When the ego senses that socially unacceptable impulses are rising into awareness, it may use psychological defenses, or ***defense mechanisms,*** to prevent them from surfacing. *Repression* is one such psychological defense. ***Repression,*** or motivated forgetting, is the ejecting of unacceptable ideas from awareness. Repression protects children and adults from recognizing impulses they would consider inappropriate in light of their moral values. Other important defense mechanisms include *regression, rationalization,* and *displacement.* In ***regression,*** the individual under stress returns to a form of behavior characteristic of an

***Conscious*** Self-aware.

***Preconscious*** In psychoanalytic theory, not in awareness but capable of being brought into awareness by focusing of attention.

***Unconscious*** In psychoanalytic theory, not available to awareness by simple focusing of attention.

***Psychic structure*** (SIGH-kick) In psychoanalytic theory, a hypothesized mental structure that helps explain different aspects of behavior.

***Id*** The psychic structure, present at birth, that represents physiological drives and is fully unconscious (a Latin word meaning "it").

***Ego*** (EE-go) The second psychic structure to develop, characterized by self-awareness, planning, and the delay of gratification (a Latin word meaning "I").

***Defense mechanism*** In psychoanalytic theory, an unconscious function of the ego that protects it from anxiety-evoking material by preventing accurate recognition of this material.

***Repression*** A defense mechanism in which the individual ejects anxiety-evoking ideas and impulses from awareness.

***Regression*** A defense mechanism in which the individual, under stress, returns to behavior patterns that are characteristic of earlier stages of development (from the Latin *re-*, meaning "back," and *gradi,* meaning "to go").

***Rationalization*** A defense mechanism in which the individual engages in self-deception by finding justifications for unacceptable ideas or behavior.

***Displacement*** A defense mechanism in which ideas or impulses are transferred from threatening or unsuitable objects onto less threatening objects.

***Superego*** The third psychic structure, which functions as a moral guardian and sets forth high standards for behavior.

***Identification*** In psychoanalytic theory, the unconscious assumption of the behavior of another person.

***Eros*** In psychoanalytic theory, the basic instinct to preserve and perpetuate life.

***Libido*** (lib-BEE-doe) In psychoanalytic theory, the energy of eros; the sexual instinct.

***Erogenous zone*** An area of the body that is sensitive to sexual sensations.

***Psychosexual development*** In psychoanalytic theory, the process by which libidinal energy is expressed through different erogenous zones during different stages of development.

***Oral stage*** The first stage of psychosexual development, during which gratification is attained primarily through oral activities such as sucking and biting.

***Fixation*** In psychoanalytic theory, arrested development. Attachment to objects of an earlier stage.

***Anal stage*** The second stage of psychosexual development, when gratification is attained through anal activities such as eliminating wastes.

***Anal-retentive*** Descriptive of behaviors and traits that have to do with "holding in," or the expression of self-control.

***Anal-expulsive*** Descriptive of behaviors and traits that have to do with unregulated self-expression, such as messiness.

earlier stage of development. For example, an adolescent may cry when he is not allowed to use the family car. ***Rationalization*** is the use of self-deceiving justifications for unacceptable behavior. For example, a fifth-grader may blame her cheating on the teacher for leaving the room. ***Displacement*** is the transfer of ideas and impulses from threatening or unsuitable objects to less threatening objects. We shall see that Freud believed that children displace their sexual urges toward their own parents onto people outside the family, in part because of the incest taboo.

The ***superego*** develops throughout early childhood, incorporating the moral standards and values of parents and important members of the community through ***identification.*** Throughout life the superego monitors the intentions of the ego and hands out judgments of right and wrong.

**THE STAGES OF PSYCHOSEXUAL DEVELOPMENT** Freud stirred controversy within the medical establishment of his day by arguing that sexual impulses and their gratification are central factors in children's development. He believed that children's most basic ways of relating to the world, such as sucking and moving their bowels, involve intense sexual feelings.

He also believed that one of the major instincts of the id is ***eros,*** the instinct to preserve and perpetuate life. Eros contains a certain amount of energy, which Freud labeled ***libido.*** This energy is psychological in nature and involves sexual impulses, so Freud considered it *psychosexual.* Libidinal energy is expressed through sexual feelings in different parts of the body, or ***erogenous zones,*** as the child develops. Freud hypothesized five stages of ***psychosexual development:*** oral, anal, phallic, latency, and genital. These are briefly summarized in Figure 2.3.

***The Oral Stage*** During the first year of life, a child experiences much of its world through the mouth. If it fits, into the mouth it goes. This is the ***oral stage.*** Freud argued that oral activities like sucking and biting bring the child sexual gratification as well as nourishment.

Freud believed that children encounter conflicts during each stage of psychosexual development. During the oral stage, conflict centers around the nature and extent of oral gratification. Early weaning can lead to frustration. Excessive gratification, on the other hand, can lead an infant to expect it routinely will be handed everything in life. Insufficient or excessive gratification in any stage can lead to ***fixation*** in that stage and to the development of traits characteristic of that stage. Oral traits include dependency, gullibility, and optimism or pessimism.

Freud theorized that adults with an oral fixation can experience exaggerated desires for oral activities such as smoking, overeating, alcohol abuse, and nail biting. Like the infant whose very survival depends on the mercy of an adult, adults with oral fixations may be disposed toward clinging, dependent interpersonal relationships.

***The Anal Stage*** During the ***anal stage,*** sexual gratification is attained through contraction and relaxation of the muscles that control elimination of waste products. Elimination, which was controlled reflexively during most of the first year of life, comes under voluntary muscular control, even if such control is not reliable at first. The anal stage is said to begin in the second year of life.

During the anal stage, children learn to delay the gratification of eliminating as soon as they feel the urge. The general issue of self-control may become a source of conflict between parent and child, and the issue of self-control frequently finds expression in toilet training. Anal fixations may stem from this conflict and lead to two sets of anal traits. ***Anal-retentive*** traits involve excessive use of self-control. They include perfectionism, a strong need for order, and exaggerated neatness and cleanliness. ***Anal-expulsive*** traits, on the other hand, "let it all hang out." They include carelessness and messiness.

*Freud hypothesized five stages of psychosexual development during childhood and adolescence. Erikson focused more on social relationships and so he speaks of psycho*social *development. Erikson added three more stages to include development in adulthood.*

FIGURE 2.3

***Freud's Psychosexual and Erikson's Psychosocial Stages Compared.***

| AGE | FREUD'S PSYCHOSEXUAL STAGES | ERIKSON'S PSYCHOSOCIAL STAGES |
|---|---|---|
| BIRTH TO 1 YEAR | *Oral Stage*<br>SATISFACTION CENTERS ON ORAL ACTIVITIES SUCH AS SUCKING. | *Basic Trust vs. Mistrust*<br>COME TO TRUST CAREGIVERS, OR FAIL TO DO SO IF CAREGIVERS ARE NEGLECTFUL OR REJECTING. |
| 1 TO 3 YEARS | *Anal Stage*<br>SATISFACTION CENTERS ON ELIMINATION ACTIVITIES. | *Autonomy vs. Shame and Doubt*<br>DEVELOP CONTROL OVER BODY FUNCTIONS AND MOTOR ACTIVITIES, OR DOUBT ONE'S ABILITY TO DEVELOP CONTROL IF SHAMED OR HUMILIATED. |
| 3 TO 6 YEARS | *Phallic Stage*<br>SATISFACTION CENTERS ON GENITAL AREA. OEDIPAL AND ELECTRA COMPLEXES EMERGE AND ARE RESOLVED. | *Initiative vs. Guilt*<br>BEGIN TO DEVELOP INDEPENDENCE FROM PARENTS AND INITIATE BEHAVIORS, OR EXPERIENCE GUILT IF PUNISHED FOR OVERSTEPPING BOUNDARIES. |
| 6 TO 12 YEARS | *Latency Stage*<br>SUPPRESSION OF SEXUAL URGES AND DEVELOPMENT OF SOCIAL SKILLS. | *Industry vs. Inferiority*<br>MASTER TASKS AND FEEL COMPETENT, OR FAIL TO DO SO AND FEEL INFERIOR. |
| ADOLESCENCE | *Genital Stage*<br>REAPPEARANCE OF SEXUALITY IN MORE MATURE FORM. | *Identity vs. Identity Diffusion*<br>FORM A SENSE OF SELF, INCLUDING OCCUPATIONAL AND GENDER ROLES, OR FEEL CONFUSED ABOUT WHO ONE IS. |
| YOUNG ADULTHOOD | | *Intimacy vs. Isolation*<br>FORM INTIMATE TIES TO OTHERS, INCLUDING A SEXUAL PARTNER, OR FAIL TO DO SO AND FEEL ISOLATED. |
| MIDDLE ADULTHOOD | | *Generativity vs. Stagnation*<br>GUIDE AND ENCOURAGE THE YOUNGER GENERATION, OR BECOME SELF-ABSORBED AND STAGNANT. |
| LATE ADULTHOOD | | *Integrity vs. Despair*<br>ACCEPT ONE'S LIFE WITH SATISFACTION AND DIGNITY, OR DESPAIR OVER LIFE'S DISAPPOINTMENTS. |

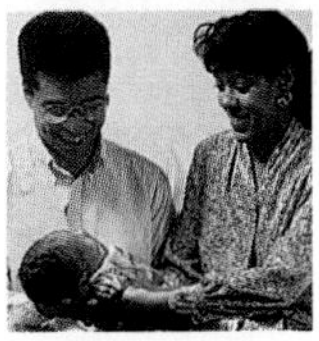

FIGURE 2.4

***THE PHALLIC STAGE.*** *According to Freud, children in the phallic stage develop strong attachments to the parent of the other gender and view the parent of the same gender as a rival.*

***The Phallic Stage*** Children enter the ***phallic stage*** during the third year of life. During this stage, the major erogenous zone becomes the phallic region, including the penis in boys and the clitoris in girls. Parent–child conflict is likely to develop over masturbation, which many parents treat with punishment and threats. During the phallic stage, children may develop strong sexual attachments to the parent of the other gender and begin to view the same-gender parent as a rival for the other parent's affections. Girls may want to marry Daddy, and boys may want to marry Mommy. At the same time, children notice that girls do not have a penis. The girl becomes envious of the boy's penis ("penis envy") and blames mother for not giving her one. The boy fears that father will castrate him ("castration anxiety") and that he, too, will lose his penis.

Feelings of lust, jealousy, envy, and fear are difficult for little children to handle. Home life would be tense indeed if they were aware of them. So these feelings are largely repressed, although their influence is felt through fantasies about marriage and through vague hostilities toward the parent of the same gender. Freud labeled this conflict in boys the ***Oedipus complex,*** after the legendary Greek king who unwittingly killed his father and married his mother. Freud labeled similar feelings in girls the ***Electra complex.*** According to Greek legend, Electra was the daughter of the king Agamemnon. She longed for him after his death and sought revenge against his slayers—her mother and her mother's lover.

The Electra and Oedipus complexes normally become resolved by about the ages of 5 or 6. Children repress their hostilities toward the parent of the same gender and identify with that parent. Identification leads to playing the social and gender roles of the same-gender parent and internalizing that parent's values. Sexual feelings toward the parent of the other gender are repressed for a number of years. When the feelings reemerge during adolescence, they are displaced onto individuals outside the family.

***The Latency Stage*** By the age of 5 or 6, Freud believed, the pressures of the Oedipus and Electra complexes motivate children to repress all sexual urges. In so doing, they enter the ***latency stage,*** a period of life during which sexual feelings remain unconscious. Children use this period to focus on schoolwork and to consolidate earlier learning of, most notably, appropriate gender-role behaviors. During the latency stage, children typically prefer playmates of their own gender.

***The Genital Stage*** Freud wrote that we enter the final stage of psychosexual development, or ***genital stage,*** at puberty. Adolescent females again experience sexual urges toward their fathers and adolescent males toward their mothers. But the ***incest taboo*** provides ample motivation for keeping knowledge of the

***Phallic stage*** The third stage of psychosexual development, characterized by a shift of libido to the phallic region (from the Greek *phallos,* meaning "image of the penis").

***Oedipus complex*** (ED-uh-puss) A conflict of the phallic stage in which the boy wishes to possess his mother sexually and perceives his father as a rival in love.

***Electra complex*** A conflict of the phallic stage in which the girl longs for her father and resents her mother.

***Latency stage*** The fourth stage of psychosexual development, characterized by repression of sexual impulses.

***Genital stage*** The mature stage of psychosexual development, in which gratification is attained through intercourse with an adult of the other gender.

***Incest taboo*** The cultural prohibition against marrying or having sexual relations with a close blood relative.

true objects of these feelings repressed and displacing the feelings onto other adults or adolescents of the other gender. Even so, girls might still be attracted to men who resemble their fathers, and boys might still seek girls "just like the girl that married dear old Dad."

Freud believed that the thrust of *eros,* the life instinct, is aimed at the perpetuation of the species. Therefore, people in the genital stage prefer to find sexual gratification through intercourse with a member of the other gender. In Freud's view, oral or anal stimulation, masturbation, and homosexual activity represent pregenital fixations and immature forms of sexual conduct.

**Practical Applications of Freud's Theory** Freud's ideas have had an impact on at least three areas affecting children: child-rearing practices, education, and therapy. For example, Freud's views about the anal stage have influenced pediatricians and other child-care experts to recommend that toilet training not be started too early nor handled in a punitive manner. Freud's emphasis on the emotional needs of children has influenced educators to be more sensitive to the possible emotional reasons behind a child's misbehavior. He also was an early advocate of sex education in the schools. Freudian theory has had an impact on techniques of child psychotherapy as well (Thomas, 1992).

**Evaluation of Freud's Theory** Freud's theory has had tremendous appeal and has been a major contribution to 20th-century thought. It is one of the richest theories of development, explaining the childhood origins of many varieties of behavior and traits. Freud's theory has also stimulated research on attachment, development of gender roles, moral development, and identification. But despite its richness, Freud's work has been criticized on many grounds (Emde, 1992).

For one thing, Freud developed his theory on the basis of contacts with patients (mostly women) who were experiencing emotional problems. He also concluded that most of his patients' problems originated in childhood conflicts. It is possible that he might have found less evidence of childhood conflict if his sample had consisted of less troubled individuals. He was also dealing with recollections of his patients' pasts, rather than observing children directly. Such recollections are subject to errors in memory, and it may also be that Freud subtly guided his patients into expressing ideas consistent with his own theoretical views.

A number of followers of Freud, such as Erik Erikson and Karen Horney, have argued that Freud placed too much emphasis on human sexuality and biological determinants of behavior, while neglecting the relative importance of social relationships and learning. Others have contended that Freud placed too much emphasis on unconscious motives. They argue that people are motivated by conscious desires to achieve, to have esthetic experiences, and to help others, as well as by the primitive urgings of the id.

A number of critics note that "psychic structures" like the id, ego, and superego have no substance. They are little more than useful fictions, poetic ways to express inner conflict. It is debatable whether Freud himself ever attributed substance to the psychic structures.

Nor has Freud's theory of psychosexual development escaped criticism. Children may begin to masturbate as early as the first year of life, rather than in the phallic stage. As parents can testify from observing their children play doctor, sexuality in the latency stage is not as latent as Freud believed. Much of Freud's thinking concerning the Oedipus and Electra complexes remains simple speculation and lacks empirical support (Watson & Getz, 1990).

Finally, Freud's view of female development and gender-role behavior reflects the ignorance and male-centered prejudice of his times. For example, Freud

FIGURE 2.5

***Karen Horney.*** *Horney, a follower of Freud, argued that he placed too much emphasis on sexual and biological determinants of behavior while neglecting the importance of social factors.*

assumed that girls and women had immature superegos and that their moral development, therefore, was inferior to that of males. This assumption has not been supported by research, however, as we shall see in Chapter 15 (Lips, 1993).

The assumption that girls suffer from penis envy also has been attacked strongly by modern-day psychoanalysts and others. Karen Horney (1967), for example, contended that little girls do not feel inferior to little boys, and that the penis-envy hypothesis is not supported by observations of children. Horney argued that Freud's views reflected a Western cultural prejudice, not good psychological theory.

Psychologist Judith Worell (1990) argues that there has been a historic prejudice against self-assertive, competent women. Many people believe that women should remain passive and submissive, emotional, and dependent on men. In Freud's day these prejudices were even more extreme. Psychoanalytic theory, in its original form, reflected the belief that motherhood and family life were the only proper avenues of fulfillment for women.

Once we have catalogued our criticisms of Freud's views, what of merit is left? A number of things. Freud pointed out that behavior is determined and not arbitrary. He pointed out that childhood experiences can have far-reaching effects on personality. He noted that we have defensive ways of looking at the world, that our cognitive processes can be distorted by our efforts to defend ourselves against anxiety and guilt. If these ideas no longer impress us as unique or innovative, it is largely because they have been so widely accepted since Freud first enunciated them.

## *Erik Erikson's Theory of Psychosocial Development*

Erik Erikson modified and expanded upon Freud's theory. Throughout his early childhood in Germany, Erikson did not know that his natural father had deserted his mother just before his birth in 1902 (Erikson, 1975). Young Erikson was raised by his mother and his stepfather, Theodor Homburger, a pediatrician. Though his mother and stepfather were Jewish, Erikson's blond hair and blue eyes resembled those of his natural father, a Dane. In his stepfather's synagogue he resembled a Gentile. To his classmates he was Jewish. He felt different from other children and alienated from his family. Like many children, he fantasized that he was adopted, the offspring of special parents who had abandoned him. "Who am I?" was a question that permeated his early years.

As he developed, Erikson faced another issue of self-identity: "What am I to do in life?" His stepfather encouraged him to follow in his footsteps and pursue medicine, but Erikson sought his own path. As a youth he studied art and traveled through Europe, leading the bohemian life of an artist. This was a period of serious questioning and soul-searching that Erikson would later label an ***identity crisis.***

The turmoil of his personal quest for identity oriented Erikson toward his life's work: psychotherapy. He met Sigmund Freud and other psychoanalysts in Vienna and plunged into psychoanalytic training under the tutelage of Anna Freud, a distinguished psychoanalyst and the daughter of Sigmund Freud (Hall, 1983). After his graduation from the Vienna Psychoanalytic Institute in 1933, he came to the United States.

***Identity crisis*** According to Erikson, a period of inner conflict during which one examines one's values and makes decisions about life roles.

Erikson's psychoanalytic theory, like that of Freud's, focuses on the development of the emotional life and psychological traits—on social adjustment. But Erikson also focuses on the development of self-identity. Out of the chaos of his own identity problems, Erikson forged a personally meaningful life pattern, and his theory of development differs dramatically from that of his intellectual forebear, Sigmund Freud. To Erikson, development is not the outcome of environmental forces and intrapsychic conflict. Erikson's social relationships had been more crucial than sexual or aggressive instinct as determinants of his development. Therefore, Erikson speaks of psycho*social* rather than psycho*sexual* development. Furthermore, it seemed to Erikson that he had developed his own personality through a series of conscious and purposeful acts. Consequently, he places greater emphasis on the ego and on one's ability to actively deal with life's conflicts than did Freud.

Erikson (1963) extended Freud's five developmental stages to eight in order to include the developing concerns of the various seasons of adulthood. Rather than label his stages after erogenous zones, Erikson labeled stages after the ***life crises*** that the child (and later, the adult) might develop and experience during that stage. Erikson's eight stages are outlined in Figure 2.3.

Erikson proposed that our relationships with others, as well as our levels of physical maturation, give each stage its character. For example, the parent–child relationship and the infant's utter dependence and helplessness are responsible for the nature of the earliest stages of development. The 6-year-old's capacity to profit from the school setting reflects the cognitive capacities to learn to read and to understand the rudiments of mathematics, and the physical/perceptual capacities to sit relatively still and focus on schoolwork.

According to Erikson, early experiences exert a continued influence on future development. With proper parental support during the early years, most children resolve early life crises productively. Successful resolution of each crisis bolsters their senses of identity—of who they are and what they stand for—and their expectations of future success.

FIGURE 2.6

**ERIK ERIKSON.** *Erikson proposed eight stages of psychosocial development extending through the life span. He focused on social relationships and argued that personality development is largely conscious.*

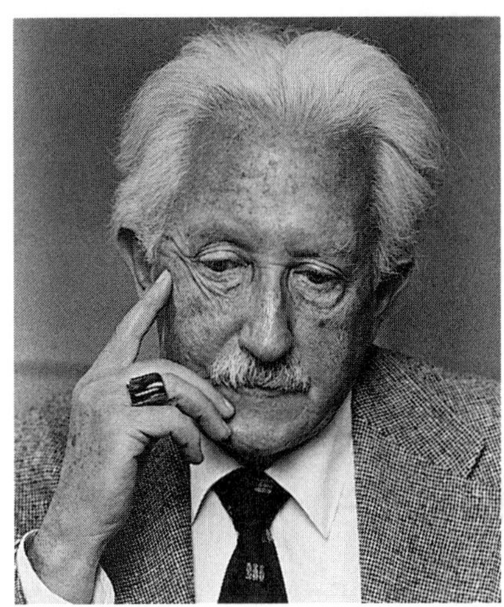

**STAGES OF PSYCHOSOCIAL DEVELOPMENT** Let us now consider each of Erikson's stages of ***psychosocial development.*** Each stage carries a specific developmental task. Successful completion of this task depends heavily on the nature of the child's social relationships at each stage.

The first stage of psychosocial development is labeled ***trust versus mistrust.*** The developmental task of this stage is to develop a sense of trust in one's caregivers that will foster feelings of attachment and pave the way for the development of future intimate relationships. A warm, loving relationship with caregivers during infancy leads to a basic sense of trust in people and the world. A cold, nongratifying relationship with caregivers, however, may lead to a pervasive sense of mistrust.

The second stage, ***autonomy versus shame and doubt,*** occurs during the second and third years. The central tasks are to develop and exercise self-control and independence. Toilet training is one of the challenges faced during the second year. During this year, children also become mobile and inquisitive. Warmly encouraging parents can provide guidance yet teach their children to be proud of their newly developing autonomy. But parents who demand too much too soon at this stage or who are arbitrarily restrictive can lead a child to perceive self-control as an unattainable goal. A lifelong pattern of self-doubt can follow.

The third stage, ***initiative versus guilt,*** takes place during the fourth and fifth years. The central tasks are to test new language, motor and social skills, initiate behavior, and become more independent from one's parents. If the child is supported and encouraged in these efforts, a sense of initiative develops. If, however, the child's initiatives are punished, feelings of guilt may develop.

***Life crisis*** An internal conflict that attends each stage of psychosocial development. Positive resolution of life crises sets the stage for positive resolution of subsequent life crises.

***Psychosocial development*** Erikson's theory, which emphasizes the importance of social relationships and conscious choice throughout the eight stages of development.

***Trust versus mistrust*** The first of Erikson's stages of psychosocial development, during which the child comes to (or not to) develop a basic sense of trust in others.

***Autonomy versus shame and doubt*** Erikson's second stage of psychosocial development, during which the child develops (or does not develop) the capacity to exercise self-control and independence.

***Initiative versus guilt*** Erikson's third stage of psychosocial development, during which the child initiates new activities. Punishment of the child's activities may produce feelings of guilt.

The fourth stage, ***industry versus inferiority,*** occurs during the elementary school years of about 6 to 12. The major developmental task is to acquire the basic academic and cultural skills that will enable one to achieve. A sense of industry will contribute to achievement motivation. A sense of inferiority may turn the child away from attempts to acquire skills and compete with peers.

During the elementary school years, children learn to evaluate their competence by comparing their performance to that of peers. If schoolchildren do well in their studies, in sports, and in their social activities, they are likely to develop a sense of industry and become productive. Fine performance in, say, math may compensate for poor or average athletic performance and vice versa. But if children fail consistently in most areas, they are likely to develop feelings of inferiority and withdraw from the arenas of competition.

The fifth stage, ***identity versus identity diffusion,*** takes place during the teenage years. The central developmental task is for adolescents to develop identity—that is, a sense of who they are and what they stand for. Adolescents may simply adopt the expectations others have for them, or they may examine expectations in the light of their own understanding of the world around them. One aspect of attaining identity is learning "how to connect the roles and skills cultivated earlier with the occupational prototypes of the day" (Erikson, 1963, p. 261)—that is, with jobs. But identity also extends to sexual, political, and religious beliefs and commitments.

If the life crisis of identity versus diffusion is resolved properly, adolescents develop a firm sense of who they are and what they stand for. Identity can then carry them through difficult times and color their achievements with meaning. But if they do not resolve this life crisis properly, they may experience identity diffusion. In this case, they spread themselves thin, running down one blind alley after another and placing themselves at the mercy of leaders who promise to give them the sense of identity they cannot mold for themselves.

We shall briefly discuss Erikson's final three stages of development in order to provide a sense of continuity, although they concern adult development rather than child development.

The life crisis of young adulthood is labeled ***intimacy versus isolation.*** The establishment of intimate relationships is the central task. Young adults who have evolved a firm sense of identity during adolescence are now ready, Erikson believes, to establish relationships such as marriage and abiding friendships with significant others. Failure to establish intimate relationships leads to a sense of social and emotional isolation.

Erikson labels the life crisis of middle adulthood ***generativity versus stagnation.*** He describes generativity as including procreativity (having children), productivity (as in work), and creativity (Erikson, 1983). Generativity assumes that in middle life, people are concerned about the welfare of the next generation and work to make the world a better place in which to live. Failure to do so results in feelings of stagnation and self-absorption.

Erikson's eighth stage, ***integrity versus despair,*** occurs in later adulthood. As we look back and reflect upon our lives, the central task is to maintain our sense of who we are and what we stand for (integrity) in the face of deterioration of physical function and the specter of death. But those who look back on their lives with regret and who fear old age and death experience a feeling of despair.

***Industry versus inferiority*** Erikson's fourth stage of psychosocial development, in which the child masters (or fails to master) many skills during the elementary school years.

***Identity versus identity diffusion*** Erikson's fifth stage of psychosocial development, during which adolescents develop (or fail to develop) a sense of who they are and what they stand for.

***Intimacy versus isolation*** Erikson's sixth stage of psychosocial development; the young-adult years during which persons commit themselves to intimate relationships with others, or else develop feelings of isolation.

***Generativity versus stagnation*** Erikson's seventh stage of psychosocial development; the middle years during which persons find (or fail to find) fulfillment in expressing creativity and in guiding and encouraging the younger generation.

***Integrity versus despair*** Erikson's eighth stage of psychosocial development; the later years during which adults look back on their lives and experience either a sense of satisfaction (integrity) or regret (despair).

**PRACTICAL APPLICATIONS OF ERIKSON'S THEORY** Erikson's views, like Freud's, have influenced child rearing, early childhood education, and therapy with children. In particular, Erikson's views about the existence of an adolescent identity crisis have widely entered the popular culture and affect the way parents and teachers deal with teenagers. For example, some schools help students master the crisis by means of life-adjustment courses and study units on self-understanding in social studies and literature classes (Thomas, 1992).

**Evaluation of Erikson's Theory** Erikson's views have received much admiration and much criticism. They are appealing in that they emphasize the importance of human consciousness and choice and minimize the role—and the threat—of dark, poorly perceived urges. They are also appealing in that they paint us as prosocial and giving, whereas Freud portrayed us as selfish and needing to be forced into adherence to social norms. Erikson has been praised as well for presenting a unified view of development throughout the life span.

There is also some empirical support for the Eriksonian view that positive resolutions of early life crises lead to more positive behavior later on. For example, infants and toddlers who are securely attached to their mothers—children who appear to have a sense of basic trust in their mothers—are more sociable with their peers than are insecure children (Thompson, 1991a). Trust in the mother seems to develop into willingness to relate to others.

On the other hand, some argue that Erikson's concepts are difficult to measure and that it is therefore difficult to test the validity of his theory. Erikson also has been criticized because his views of psychosocial development, especially in adolescence and young adulthood, appear to be based primarily on patterns of male development (see Chapter 16).

**Figure 2.7**

***John B. Watson.*** *Watson is shown here testing the grasping reflex of an infant. As a behaviorist, he believed that the environment is all-important in shaping development.*

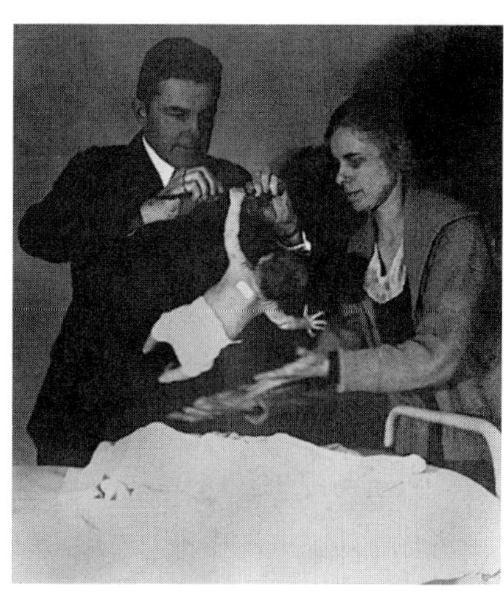

## Learning Theories

During the 1930s, psychologists derived from learning theory an ingenious method for helping 5- and 6-year-old children overcome bed-wetting. Most children at this age wake up and go to the bathroom when their bladders are full. But bed-wetters sleep through bladder tension and reflexively urinate in bed. The psychologists' objective was to teach sleeping children with full bladders to wake up rather than wet their beds.

They placed a special pad beneath the sleeping child. When the pad was wet, an electrical circuit was closed, causing a bell to ring and the sleeping child to waken. After several repetitions, most children learned to wake up before they wet the pad. How? Through a technique called classical conditioning, which we explain in this section.

The so-called bell-and-pad method for bed-wetting is an exotic example of the application of learning theory in child development. However, the great majority of applications of learning theory to development are found in everyday events. For example, children are not born knowing what the letters *A* and *B* sound like or how to tie their shoes. They learn these things. They are not born knowing how to do gymnastics. Nor are they born understanding the meanings of abstract concepts such as big, blue, decency, and justice. All these skills and knowledge are learned.

In this section, we discuss the theories of behaviorism and social learning and see how they are involved in child development. We shall see that children are capable of mechanical learning by association (as in the bell-and-pad method), but we shall also see that children are capable of intentional learning. Children purposefully engage in rote learning and trial-and-error learning. Children purposefully observe and imitate the behavior of other people. We shall also see how the principles of learning have been used in ***behavior modification*** to help children overcome behavior disorders or cope with adjustment problems.

***Behavior modification*** The systematic application of principles of learning to eliminate behavior problems or encourage desired behaviors.

## BEHAVIORISM

***Classical conditioning*** A simple form of learning in which one stimulus comes to bring forth the response usually brought forth by a second stimulus by being paired repeatedly with the second stimulus.

***Stimulus*** A change in the environment that leads to a change in behavior.

***Elicit*** (ee-LISS-it) To bring forth; evoke.

***Unconditioned stimulus*** (UCS) A stimulus that elicits a response from an organism without learning.

***Unconditioned response*** (UCR) An unlearned response. A response to an unconditioned stimulus.

***Conditioned stimulus*** (CS) A previously neutral stimulus that elicits a response, because it has been paired repeatedly with a stimulus that already elicited that response.

***Conditioned response*** (CR) A learned response to a previously neutral stimulus.

Behaviorism in the United States, as noted at the outset of the chapter, was founded by John B. Watson. Watson argued that scientists must address observable behavior only. Therefore, a scientific approach to development must focus on the observable behavior of humans and not on thoughts, plans, fantasies, and other mental images.

Let us see how two types of learning—classical and operant conditioning—have contributed to behaviorism and the understanding of development. Then we shall consider a more recently developed theory of learning that deals with children's cognitive processes as well as their overt behavior—social-learning theory.

**CLASSICAL CONDITIONING** ***Classical conditioning*** is a simple form of learning in which an originally neutral ***stimulus*** comes to bring forth, or ***elicit,*** the response usually brought forth by a second stimulus as a result of being paired repeatedly with the second stimulus.

Like many other important scientific discoveries, classical conditioning was discovered by accident. Russian physiologist Ivan Pavlov (1849–1936) was doing research on the salivary reflex in dogs. He discovered that reflexes can be learned, or conditioned, through association. Pavlov's dogs began salivating in response to clinking food trays, because clinking had been paired repeatedly with the arrival of food. Pavlov then carried out experiments in which he conditioned his dogs to salivate to the sound of a bell, which had been paired with food.

In the bell-and-pad method for bed-wetting, psychologists repeatedly pair tension in the children's bladders with a stimulus that wakes them up (the bell). The children learn to respond to the bladder tension as if it were a bell—that is, they wake up.

The bell is an unlearned or ***unconditioned stimulus*** (UCS). Waking up in response to the bell is an unlearned or ***unconditioned response*** (UCR). Bladder tension is at first a meaningless, or neutral stimulus (see Figure 2.8). Then, through repeated association with the bell, bladder tension becomes a learned or ***conditioned stimulus*** (CS) for waking up. Waking up in response to bladder tension (the CS) is a learned or ***conditioned response*** (CR).

Behaviorists argue that a good deal of emotional learning is acquired through classical conditioning. For example, touching a hot stove is painful, and one or two incidents may elicit a fear response when a child looks at a stove or considers touching it again.

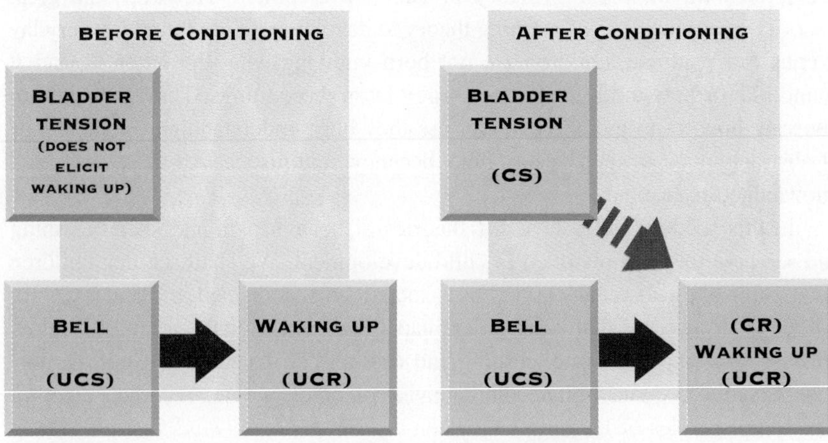


**FIGURE 2.8**

**A SCHEMATIC REPRESENTATION OF CLASSICAL CONDITIONING.** *Prior to conditioning, the bell elicits waking up. Bladder tension, a neutral stimulus, does not elicit waking up. During conditioning, bladder tension always precedes urination, which in turn causes the bell to ring. After conditioning, bladder tension has become a conditional stimulus (CS) that elicits waking up—the conditioned response (CR).*

## Truth or Fiction Revisited

*It is true that children can be taught to wake up in the middle of the night if they are about to wet their beds. In the bell-and-pad method, bladder tension becomes a conditioned stimulus (CS) that elicits the response of waking up.*

**Operant Conditioning** In classical conditioning, children learn to associate stimuli so that a response made to one is then made in response to the other. But in ***operant conditioning,*** children learn to operate on the environment, or to engage in certain behavior, because of the effects of that behavior.

B. F. Skinner introduced one of the central concepts of operant conditioning—the concept of ***reinforcement.*** Reinforcers are stimuli that increase the frequency of the behavior they follow. Most children will increase the frequency of behavior patterns that earn them consequences such as a hug, an A on a test, attention, or social approval. And so, these consequences serve as reinforcers. Some children learn to conform their behavior to social codes and rules to earn the attention and approval of their parents and teachers. Other children, ironically, may learn to misbehave, since misbehavior also draws attention. Children may especially learn to be "bad" when their "good" behavior is routinely ignored or is not "good enough" to earn approval. The poor student is more likely to be drawn into a delinquent subculture than the excellent student, since reinforcement is not likely to be provided by the mainstream culture—for example, by teachers.

In operant conditioning, it matters little how the first desired response is made. The child can happen upon it by chance, as in random trial-and-error learning, or the child can be physically or verbally guided. A 2-year-old child may be shown how to turn the crank on a music box to play a tune by an adult placing his or her hand over the child's and doing the turning. The child is reinforced by the sound of music, and after training she or he will be able to turn the crank alone.

Various behaviors—such as vocalizing, smiling, and looking at specific objects—have been conditioned in very young infants (Gewirtz & Peláez-Nogueras, 1992). For one example, see Focus on Research.

***Types of Reinforcers*** How do we know whether a stimulus is a reinforcer? Any stimulus that increases the frequency of the responses preceding it serves as a reinforcer. Most of the time, food, social approval, and attention serve as reinforcers.

Skinner distinguished between positive and negative reinforcers. ***Positive reinforcers*** increase the frequency of behaviors when they are *applied.* Food and approval usually serve as positive reinforcers. ***Negative reinforcers*** increase the frequency of behaviors when they are *removed.* Children often learn to plan ahead so that they need not fear that things will go wrong. Fear acts as a negative reinforcer in that its removal increases the frequency of the behaviors preceding it (such as studying for a quiz).

Knowledge of results is often an effective reinforcer with children. Many children will work hard to improve skills in spelling, math, and myriad other areas simply for the sake of improvement. White (1959) has advanced the view that we have an ***intrinsic*** motive to master skills and will frequently learn how

**Figure 2.9**

**B. F. Skinner.** *Skinner, a behaviorist, developed the principles of operant conditioning. He focused on the role of reward and punishment in shaping behavior.*

***Operant conditioning*** A simple form of learning in which an organism learns to engage in behavior that is reinforced.

***Reinforcement*** The process of providing stimuli following a response, which has the effect of increasing the frequency of the response.

***Positive reinforcer*** A reinforcer that, when applied, increases the frequency of a response.

***Negative reinforcer*** A reinforcer that, when removed, increases the frequency of a response.

***Intrinsic*** Internal.

FOCUS ON RESEARCH

### OPERANT CONDITIONING OF VOCALIZATIONS IN INFANTS

A classic study by psychologist Harriet Rheingold and her colleagues (1959) demonstrates how reinforcement and extinction can influence the behavior of infants—in this case, vocalization. A female researcher first observed the subjects, 3-month-old infants, for about half an hour to record baseline (preexperimental) measures of the frequency of their vocalizing. Infants averaged about 13–15 vocalizations each. During the conditioning phase of the study, the researcher reinforced the vocalizations with social stimuli, such as encouraging sounds, smiles, and gentle touches. There was a significant increase in the frequency of vocalizing throughout this phase. By the end of an hour of conditioning spread over a two-day period, the average incidence of vocalizations had nearly doubled to about 24–25 within a half hour. During the extinction phase, as during the baseline period, the researcher passively observed each infant, no longer reinforcing vocalization. After two, half-hour extinction periods, average vocalizing had returned to near baseline, about 13–16 per half hour.

to solve problems and manipulate objects for the pleasure of doing so. Children, in other words, frequently find reinforcers for behaviors within rather than outside of themselves. The latter are called ***extrinsic*** reinforcers. Later in the chapter, we shall see that developmentalist Jean Piaget believed that children are intrinsically motivated to understand their worlds.

There is a message in this. We need not always be concerned that children get payoffs for learning. Once children become involved in an area of subject matter and acquire the capacity to manipulate concepts in that area, they may enjoy working for hours simply for its own sake. Other children, however, may not find the development of even basic academic skills reinforcing. They may require regular external reinforcement for manipulating concepts and objects if we are to involve them successfully.

***Extinction*** ***Extinction*** results from repeated performance of operant behavior without reinforcement. After a number of trials, the operant behavior is no longer shown. There are many cases in which children's temper tantrums and crying at bedtime have been extinguished within a few days by simply having parents remain out of the bedroom after the children have been put to bed. Previously, the tantrums and crying had been reinforced by parental attention and company. By changing the reinforcement contingencies of the problem behavior, the behavior was eliminated.

***Punishment*** ***Punishments*** are aversive events that suppress or decrease the frequency of the behavior they follow. Punishing events may be physical (such as spanking), verbal (for example, scolding or criticizing), or involve removal of privileges. Punishments, like rewards, can influence the probability that behavior will be shown. Punishments can rapidly suppress undesirable behavior and may be warranted in emergencies, such as when a child tries to run out into the street. But many learning theorists agree that punishment is usually undesirable, especially in rearing children, for reasons such as the following:

1. Punishment does not in itself suggest an alternative, acceptable form of behavior.

2. Punishment tends to suppress undesirable behavior only under circumstances in which its delivery is guaranteed. It does not take children long to learn that they can "get away with murder" with one parent or one teacher, but not with another.

***Extrinsic*** External.

***Extinction*** A decrease and eventual disappearance of a response in the absence of reinforcement.

***Punishment*** An unpleasant stimulus that suppresses the behavior it follows.

3. Punished children may withdraw from the situation. Severely punished children may run away, cut class, or drop out of school.

4. Punishment can create anger and hostility. After being spanked by their parents, children may hit smaller siblings or destroy objects in the home.

5. Punishment may generalize too far. The child who is punished severely for bad table manners may stop eating altogether. Overgeneralization is more likely to occur when children do not know exactly why they are being punished and when they have not been shown acceptable alternative behaviors.

6. Punishment may be modeled as a way of solving problems or coping with stress. One way that children learn is by observing others. Even though children may not immediately perform the behavior they observe, they may perform it later on, even as adults, when their circumstances are similar to those of the ***model.*** For example, many child abusers were beaten by their own parents (Simons et al., 1991).

It is usually preferable to reward children for desirable behavior than to punish them for unwanted behavior. By ignoring their misbehavior, or by using ***time out*** from positive reinforcement, we can consistently avoid reinforcing children for misbehavior.

**TRUTH OR FICTION REVISITED**

*Punishment* does *work. Punishment can suppress undesired behavior. However, most developmentalists prefer not to use punishment, because punishment can have undesirable side effects, such as creating hostility or causing the child to withdraw.*

To reward or positively reinforce children for desired behavior takes time and care. First, we must pay attention to children when they are behaving well. If we take their desirable behavior for granted and act as if we are aware of them only when they misbehave, we may be encouraging misbehavior.

Second, we must be certain that children are aware of and capable of performing desired behavior. It is harmful and fruitless merely to punish children for unwanted behavior. We must also physically or verbally guide them into making the desired responses and then reward them.

***Making Punishment Effective*** If punishment is to be used with children, it is useful to keep the following in mind (Parke, 1977):

1. Immediate punishment is more effective than delayed punishment. If the child cannot be punished immediately, it is useful to remind the child of the misbehavior before administering the punishment.

2. It is helpful to explain why the misbehavior is worthy of punishment. Punishment then is less likely to seem arbitrary and to elicit hostility.

3. Consistent punishment is more effective than irregular punishment.

4. Although intense punishment suppresses behavior more rapidly than mild punishment, parents and teachers must be careful not to abuse children.

***Model*** A person who engages in behavior that is imitated by another.

***Time out*** A behavior-modification technique in which a child who misbehaves is temporarily placed in a drab, restrictive environment in which reinforcement is unavailable.

***Continuous versus Intermittent Reinforcement*** Some responses are maintained by ***continuous reinforcement.*** You become warmer every time you put on heavy clothing. You become less thirsty every time you drink water. But if you have ever watched people throwing money down the maws of slot machines, you know that behavior can also be maintained by ***intermittent reinforcement.***

During the early stages of learning, it is useful to reinforce every correct response. In this way, the child quickly learns what is expected. In the classroom, the teacher may at first praise children each time they write numbers and letters correctly. But once children have acquired basic skills in writing letters, teachers can turn to intermittent praise or reinforcement.

Learning theorists note that many parents unintentionally teach their children to cry or whine persistently by intermittently reinforcing these behavior patterns. Consider a child who cries when a parent refuses a request for cookies before dinner. If the parent were consistent in ignoring the child's crying, learning theorists predict that it would eventually stop. Why? Because it is not being reinforced. But what happens when a parent ignores the crying on, say, nine occasions, but simply hasn't the heart to ignore the child on the tenth? The child's crying when denied cookies might then become increasingly persistent because of the intermittent reinforcement.

***Shaping*** We can teach children complex behaviors by ***shaping,*** or at first reinforcing small steps toward the behavioral goals. If a child is being taught to use the potty, the parent may first generously reinforce the learner simply for sitting on the potty for a while, even if the child insists on wearing a diaper at the time.

As training proceeds, the parent can demand more before dispensing reinforcement. We can reinforce ***successive approximations*** to the goal. In teaching a 2-year-old child to put on her own coat, it helps first to praise her for trying to stick her arm into a sleeve on a couple of occasions. Then praise her for actually getting her arm into the sleeve, and so on.

**PRACTICAL APPLICATIONS OF OPERANT CONDITIONING** Operant conditioning has numerous applications for child development. Here we focus on just a few.

***Socialization*** Operant conditioning is used every day in the ***socialization*** of young children. For example, as we shall see in Chapter 10, parents and peers influence children to acquire gender-appropriate behaviors through the elaborate use of rewards and punishments. Thus, boys may ignore other boys when they play with dolls and housekeeping toys but play with boys when they use transportation toys.

***Avoidance Learning*** Techniques of ***avoidance learning*** can be used with children who are too young or distressed to respond to verbal forms of therapy. In one example, reported by Lang and Melamed (1969), a 9-month-old infant vomited regularly within 10–15 minutes after eating. Diagnostic workups had found no medical basis for the problem, and medical treatments were to no avail. When the case was brought to the attention of Lang and Melamed, the infant weighed only nine pounds and was in critical condition, being fed by a pump.

The psychologists monitored the infant for the first physical indications (local muscle tension) that vomiting was to occur. When the child tensed prior to vomiting, a tone was sounded, followed by painful but (presumably) harmless electric shock. After two 1-hour treatment sessions, the infant's muscle tensions ceased in response to the tone alone, and vomiting soon ceased altogether. At a 1-year follow-up, the infant was still not vomiting and had caught up in weight.

***Continuous reinforcement*** Reinforcement of all correct responses.

***Intermittent reinforcement*** Reinforcement of some, but not all, correct responses.

***Shaping*** A procedure for teaching complex behavior patterns by means of reinforcing small steps toward the target behavior.

***Successive approximations*** A series of behaviors that become progressively more like the target behavior.

***Socialization*** A process in which children are encouraged to adopt socially desirable behavior patterns through a system of guidance, rewards, and punishments.

***Avoidance learning*** A form of learning in which organisms learn to engage in responses that prevent aversive (painful) stimulation.

**TRUTH OR FICTION REVISITED**

*Psychologists did successfully use painful electric shock to teach a 9-month-old infant not to vomit. The dangerously malnourished infant in the case learned not to vomit and made dramatic gains in weight.*

This remarkable procedure included both classical and operant conditioning. Through repeated pairings, the tone (CS) came to elicit expectation of electric shock (UCS), so that the psychologists could use the painful shock only sparingly. The electric shock and, after classical conditioning, the tone served as punishments. The infant soon learned to suppress the behaviors (muscle tensions) that were followed by punishments. By so doing, punishment was avoided. This learning occurred at an age long before any verbal intervention could have been understood, and it apparently saved the infant's life.

***Behavior Modification in the Classroom*** Many studies have found that when teachers praise and attend to appropriate behaviors and ignore misbehaviors, study behavior and classroom performance improve while disruptive and aggressive behaviors decrease (Greenwood et al., 1992).

Teachers also frequently use time out from positive reinforcement to discourage misbehavior. In this method, children are placed in drab, restrictive environments for a specified time period, usually about 10 minutes, when they behave disruptively. When isolated, they cannot earn the attention of peers or teachers, and no reinforcing activities are present.

It may strike you that these techniques are not new. Perhaps we all know parents who have ignored their children's misbehavior and have heard of teachers making children sit facing the corner. What is novel is the focus on (a) avoiding punishment and (b) being consistent so that undesirable behavior is not intermittently reinforced.

**TRUTH OR FICTION REVISITED**

*Classroom behavior-modification procedures do rely largely on old standbys such as ignoring children when they misbehave and praising them for desired behavior. Behavior-modification procedures apply these methods and others as consistently as possible.*

**THINKING ABOUT DEVELOPMENT**

Agree or disagree with the following statement and support your answer: "Apparently complex child behavior can be explained as the summation of many instances of conditioning."

## SOCIAL-LEARNING THEORY

Behaviorists tend to limit their discussions of human learning to the classical and operant conditioning of observable behaviors. They theorize that learning in children can be fully explained as the summation of numerous instances of the association of stimuli (classical conditioning) or the reinforcement of operant behavior (operant conditioning).

***Social-learning theorists,*** such as Albert Bandura (1989, 1991), have done numerous experiments that show that much of children's learning also occurs by observing parents, teachers, other children, and even characters on television. Children may need some practice to refine their skills, but they acquire much of

***Social-learning theory*** A cognitively oriented learning theory that emphasizes observational learning in the determining of behavior.

**FIGURE 2.10**

***BEHAVIOR MODIFICATION.*** *Teacher praise reinforces desirable behavior in most children. Behavior modification in the classroom applies principles of operant conditioning.*

the basic know-how through observation. Children may also let these skills lie ***latent.*** For example, children (and adults) are not likely to imitate aggressive behavior unless they are provoked and believe they are more likely to be rewarded than punished for aggressive behavior.

As viewed by the behaviorists, learning occurs by means of mechanical conditioning. There is no reference to thought processes that may occur as a result of conditioning and prior to the performance of responses. There is no role for *cognition.* In social-learning theory, by contrast, cognition plays a central role. In fact, Bandura (1991) now labels the theory *social cognitive theory.* To social-learning theorists, learning alters children's mental representation of the environment and influences their belief in their ability to act effectively on the environment. Children choose whether or not to show the new behaviors they have learned. In social-learning theory, children acquire behaviors without necessarily being directly reinforced. Children's values and expectations of reinforcement also influence the likelihood that they will attempt to imitate the behavior they observe.

***Latent*** Hidden.

Social-learning theorists see children as active. They intentionally seek out or create environments in which reinforcers are available. As an example of how a child's behavior and characteristics create a reinforcing environment, consider the child who has artistic ability. The child may develop this skill by taking art lessons and by modeling the behaviors of her art teacher. In doing so, she creates an environment of social reinforcement in the form of praise from others. This reinforcement, in turn, influences the child's view of herself as a good artist (Miller, 1983). This mutual interplay of the child's behavior, cognitive characteristics, and environment is known as ***reciprocal determinism*** (Bandura, 1989).

FIGURE 2.11

**ALBERT BANDURA.** *Bandura and other social-learning theorists have shown that one way children learn is by observing others. Cognition plays an important role in social-learning theory.*

**OBSERVATIONAL LEARNING** ***Observational learning,*** the type of learning of most interest to social-learning theorists, may account for most of human learning. It occurs when children observe how parents cook, clean, or repair a broken appliance. It takes place when children watch teachers solve problems on the blackboard or hear them speak in a foreign language. Observational learning does not occur because of direct reinforcement. Children can learn without engaging in overt responses at all. Learning will occur so long as children pay attention to the behavior of others.

In Chapter 10, we shall see that observational learning is one of the mechanisms by which children appear to acquire their concepts of stereotypical masculine and feminine behavior. In addition to specific behavior patterns, children learn rules and principles from observing others. Consider the area of moral development, which is discussed in Chapter 15. Children have been exposed to adult models who made moral judgments that were more advanced than those shown by the children. In this research, the children tended to advance in their moral reasoning in the direction displayed by the model (Walker, 1982).

In later chapters, we shall also see how both helping behavior and aggression in children are fostered by observational learning.

***Reciprocal determinism*** Mutual interplay of the child's behavior, cognitive characteristics, and environment.

***Observational learning*** The acquisition of expectations and skills by means of observing others. In observational learning, skills can be acquired without being emitted and reinforced.

**IMITATION AND IDENTIFICATION** *Identification,* a term derived from Freud's psychoanalytic theory, refers to children's attempts to internalize the traits of other people. However, from a social-learning-theory perspective, identification may be viewed as a broad process of imitation through which children acquire behavior patterns that are similar to those of other people. Once children are a

FIGURE 2.12

**OBSERVATIONAL LEARNING.** *Children acquire a variety of skills by means of observational learning. Here, a young boy imitates his father shaving.*

few years old, observational learning becomes intentional, and children appear to select models for imitation who show certain positive characteristics.

**MODELS** In social-learning theory, the people after whom children pattern their own behavior are *models.* The traits that encourage children to identify with models include warmth, competence, social dominance, and social status. Traits such as these appear to give models access to the tangible rewards and social success to which children themselves aspire. Children are also likely to imitate models they perceive to be similar to themselves (Thomas, 1992).

**PRACTICAL APPLICATIONS OF SOCIAL-LEARNING THEORY** Social-learning theory has increased our awareness of the importance of models in child rearing and education. Bandura and others have shown the powerful impact not only of live models, but those presented in the media, particularly television (Crain, 1992; Grusec, 1992). In the therapeutic setting, modeling has been used to help reduce fears (see Chapter 10).

**EVALUATION OF LEARNING THEORIES** There is no question that learning theories have done an excellent job of allowing us to describe, explain, predict, and control many aspects of children's behavior. There have been thousands of innovative applications of conditioning and social-learning theory. For example, the use of the bell-and-pad method for bed-wetting is an example of behavior modification that probably would not have been derived from any other theoretical approach. Behavior modification has also been used in innovative ways to deal with autistic children, self-injurious children, and children showing temper tantrums and conduct disorders. Many of the teaching approaches used in educational television shows are based on learning theory.

Despite the demonstrated effectiveness of behavior-modification procedures, learning-theory approaches to child development have been criticized in several ways. First, there is the theoretical question as to whether the conditioning process in children is merely mechanical. Recent research has shown that even infants are able to learn strategies and rules for solving complex problems (Flavell et al., 1993a). Traditional learning theory cannot account for these findings.

Second, it may be that learning theorists have exaggerated the role of learning in development. There is no question that learning is of major importance in the acquisition of motor skills, language, and academic skills. However, behaviorists such as Watson may have erroneously underestimated the prominence of biological-maturational factors in the appearance of basic psychological traits. That is, many learning theorists have not paid sufficient attention to the genetically based individual differences that may place limits on learning (Horowitz, 1992).

Social-learning theorists seem to be working on these theoretical flaws. Today's social-learning theorists view children as being active, not as reacting mechanically to environmental pressures (as Watson saw them). Many social-learning theorists allow for genetically determined individual differences. They also grant cognition an important role.

Now let us consider theories of development that place cognitive processes at the heart of development.

## COGNITIVE THEORIES

Psychologists with a cognitive perspective focus on children's mental processes. They investigate the ways in which children perceive and mentally represent the world, how they develop thought and logic, how they develop the ability to solve problems. Cognitive psychologists, in short, attempt to study all those things we refer to as the *mind.*

Today, the cognitive perspective has many faces. One is the ***cognitive-developmental theory*** advanced by the Swiss biologist Jean Piaget (1896–1980). Another is *information-processing theory.*

***Cognitive-developmental theory*** The stage theory that holds that the child's abilities to mentally represent the world and solve problems unfold as a result of the interaction of experience and the maturation of neurological structures.

### *Jean Piaget's Cognitive-Developmental Theory*

Jean Piaget was born and spent his childhood in Neuchatel, Switzerland. His first intellectual love was biology, and he published his first scientific article at the age of 10. He then became a laboratory assistant to the director of a museum of natural history and engaged in research on mollusks (oysters, clams, snails, and such). The director soon died, and Piaget published their findings himself. On the basis of these papers, he was offered the curatorship of a museum in Geneva, but had to turn it down. After all, he was only 11.

During adolescence Piaget studied philosophy, logic, and mathematics, but took his Ph.D. in biology. In 1920, Piaget obtained a job at the Binet Institute in Paris, where work on intelligence tests was being conducted. His initial task was to adapt a number of verbal reasoning items that had originated in England for use with French children. To do so, Piaget had to try out the items on children of various age groups and see whether they could arrive at correct answers. The task was becoming boring until Piaget became intrigued by the children's *incorrect* answers. Another investigator might have shrugged them off and forgotten them, but young Piaget realized that there were methods to his children's madness. The wrong answers seemed to reflect consistent, if illogical, cognitive processes. Piaget investigated these "wrong" answers by probing the children's responses to seek out the underlying patterns of thought that had led to them. He began to publish a series of articles on children's thought processes.

Piaget wrote and published dozens of books and scores of articles, but his work was almost unknown in English-speaking countries until the mid-1950s. For one thing, Piaget's writing is difficult to understand, even to native speakers of French. For another, it took him a number of years to formulate his full set of theoretical ideas. Additionally, Piaget's views were very different from those

FIGURE 2.13

**JEAN PIAGET.** *Piaget's cognitive-developmental theory is a stage theory that focuses on the ways children adapt to the environment by mentally representing the world and solving problems.*

of other developmentalists. Psychology in England and the United States was dominated by behaviorism and psychoanalysis, and Piaget's writings had a biological-cognitive flavor. They did not fit in. Today the world of child development has been turned topsy-turvy; many English-speaking developmentalists are trying to fit their views to those of Piaget.

> ***THINKING ABOUT DEVELOPMENT***
>
> Agree or disagree with the following statement and support your answer: "Children are natural scientists who actively intend to learn about and manipulate their worlds."

**PIAGET'S VIEW OF THE NATURE OF CHILDREN** Different child development theorists have attempted to explain different types of events and have had very different views of the basic nature of children. Behaviorists such as John B. Watson have focused on the acquisition of overt behavior. They see children as blank slates that are written upon by experience—as reactors to environmental stimulation, not actors. Freud's psychoanalytic theory focuses on personality and emotional development. It portrays children as largely irrational and at the mercy of instinctive impulses—as driven creatures caught between powerful sexual and aggressive urges and the stifling codes of parents and society.

Piaget was concerned with how children form concepts or mental representations of the world and how they manipulate their concepts in order to plan changes in the external world. Freud believed that conscious thought represents only a small portion of what occurs in the mind, and an illusory portion at that. Piaget, by contrast, believed that thought processes are at the heart of what it is to be human. But Piaget, like the behaviorists, recognized that thoughts cannot be measured directly, and so he always tried to link his views on children's mental processes to observable behavior.

Piaget regarded maturing children as natural physicists who actively intend to learn about and take intellectual charge of their worlds. In the Piagetian view, children who squish their food and laugh enthusiastically are often acting as budding scientists. In addition to enjoying a response from parents, they are studying the texture and consistency of their food. (Parents, of course, often prefer that their children practice these experiments in the laboratory, not the dining room.)

> ***TRUTH OR FICTION REVISITED***
>
> *It is true that children are budding scientists who actively intend to learn about and take intellectual charge of their worlds,* according to cognitive-developmental theory. *Behaviorists, however, might not agree.*

**PIAGET'S BASIC CONCEPTS** Researchers from different perspectives tie together different concepts in theoretical packages. Psychoanalysts integrate concepts such as repression and anal traits into principles that govern personality development. Behaviorists tie together concepts such as stimulus and reinforcement into principles that govern processes of learning. Piaget used concepts such as *schemes, adaptation, assimilation, accommodation,* and *equilibration* and tied them together to describe and explain cognitive development.

***Schemes*** Piaget defines the ***scheme*** as a pattern of action or a mental structure that is involved in acquiring or organizing knowledge. According to Piaget, acting on the environment and acquiring knowledge occur simultaneously or are equivalent forms of behavior. As action patterns, schemes tend to be repeated and to occur in certain types of situations.

***Scheme*** According to Piaget, an action pattern or mental structure that is involved in the acquisition and organization of knowledge.

Among older children and adults, a scheme may be the inclusion of an object in a class. For example, the mammal class, or concept, includes a group of animals that are warm-blooded and nurse their young. The inclusion of cats, apes, buffalo, whales, and people in the mammal class involves a series of schemes that expand the child's knowledge of the natural world.

But schemes need not involve words. Babies, for example, are said to have sucking schemes, grasping schemes, and looking schemes. As we shall see in Chapter 4, newborn babies tend to suck things that are placed in their mouths, to grasp objects placed in their hands, and to visually track moving objects. Piaget would say that infants' schemes give meaning to the objects around them. For instance, even in the first months of life infants are responding to objects around them as things I can suck or things I can't suck, things I can grasp or things I can't grasp.

Sucking and grasping are reflexes, but Piaget referred to them as schemes, because the concept of the reflex implies that children behave mechanically—that they do not act until they are stimulated. While neonates do respond mechanically to certain stimuli, they also show some flexibility in their behavior, and Piaget described their behavior as becoming active, intentional, and purposeful even within the first few weeks. Piaget drew a connection between the wordless schemes of infants and the complex mental structures of older children and adults, because both involve the transformation of experience into knowing. Both reflect an active and organized quest for knowledge.

***Adaptation*** ***Adaptation*** refers to the interaction between the organism and the environment. This term reflects Piaget's early interest in biology. According to Piaget, adapting to the environment is a biological tendency found in all organisms. Adaptation consists of two complementary processes, assimilation and accommodation, that occur throughout life.

***Assimilation*** The concept of ***assimilation*** also has its roots in biology. In biology, assimilation is the process by which food is digested and converted into the tissues that compose an animal. The *cognitive* process of assimilation is akin to biological assimilation. Cognitive assimilation is the process by which new objects or events are responded to according to existing schemes or ways of organizing knowledge. Infants, for example, usually try to place new objects in their mouths to suck, feel, or explore them. Piaget would say that the child is assimilating (fitting) a new toy or object into the sucking-an-object activity or scheme.

Similarly, 2-year-olds who refer to sheep and cows as "doggies" or "bow-wows" can be said to be assimilating these new animals into the *doggy* scheme. As they develop, these children will adapt by acquiring proper schemes for interpreting these animals. Their cognitive organization will blossom into a hierarchical structure in which dogs and sheep are assimilated as mammals and mammals are further assimilated as animals.

***Accommodation*** Sometimes, a novel object or event cannot be made to fit (that is, cannot be assimilated into an existing scheme). In that case, the scheme may be changed or a new scheme created in order to incorporate the new event. This process is known as ***accommodation.*** Accommodation is also a biological term, meaning a change in structure that permits an organism to adjust or adapt to a novel object or event, to a new source of stimulation.

Consider the sucking reflex. Within the first month of life, infants begin to modify their sucking behavior as a result of their experiences sucking different objects. The nipple on the bottle is sucked one way; the thumb, a different way. Infants accommodate further by rejecting objects that are too large, that taste bad, or that are of the wrong texture or temperature. They learn that certain things are not to be sucked and may experiment with new ways to relate to them.

Two-year-olds may at first try to assimilate cats and other animals into the "doggy" scheme. However, children accommodate to parental correction and the

***Adaptation*** According to Piaget, the interaction between the organism and the environment. It consists of two processes: assimilation and accommodation.

***Assimilation*** According to Piaget, the incorporation of new events or knowledge into existing schemes.

***Accommodation*** According to Piaget, the modification of existing schemes to permit the incorporation of new events or knowledge.

***Equilibration*** The creation of an equilibrium, or balance, between assimilation and accommodation as a way of incorporating new events or knowledge.

desire to be understood by creating new mental structures, such as classes or categories for cats, cows, sheep, and other animals.

***Equilibration*** Piaget theorized that when children can assimilate new events to existing schemes, they are in a state of cognitive harmony, or equilibrium. When something that does not fit happens along, their state of equilibrium is disturbed and they may try to accommodate to it. The process of restoring equilibrium is termed ***equilibration.*** Piaget believed that the attempt to restore equilibrium is the source of intellectual motivation and lies at the heart of the natural curiosity of the child.

**PIAGET'S STAGES OF COGNITIVE DEVELOPMENT** Piaget (1963) hypothesized that children's cognitive processes develop in an orderly sequence or series of stages. As is the case with motor development, some children may be more advanced than others at particular ages, but the development sequence does not normally vary. Piaget identified four major stages of cognitive development: *sensorimotor, preoperational, concrete operational,* and *formal operational.* These stages are described in Table 2.1 and will be discussed in detail in Chapters 6, 9, 12, and 15.

**TABLE 2.1**

***PIAGET'S STAGES OF COGNITIVE DEVELOPMENT***

| STAGE | APPROXIMATE AGE | DESCRIPTION |
|---|---|---|
| SENSORIMOTOR | BIRTH TO 2 YEARS | THE CHILD LACKS LANGUAGE AND DOES NOT USE SYMBOLS OR MENTAL REPRESENTATIONS OF OBJECTS IN THE ENVIRONMENT. SIMPLE RESPONDING TO THE ENVIRONMENT (THROUGH REFLEXES) DRAWS TO AN END, AND INTENTIONAL BEHAVIOR — SUCH AS MAKING INTERESTING SIGHTS LAST — BEGINS. |
| PREOPERATIONAL | 2 TO 7 YEARS | THE CHILD BEGINS TO REPRESENT THE WORLD MENTALLY, THROUGH THE USE OF SYMBOLS SUCH AS WORDS AND DRAWINGS. BUT LOGICAL MENTAL ACTIONS — CALLED OPERATIONS — ARE ABSENT. |
| CONCRETE OPERATIONAL | 7 TO 12 YEARS | THE CHILD SHOWS LOGICAL MENTAL ACTIONS WHEN DEALING WITH CONCRETE OBJECTS. |
| FORMAL OPERATIONAL | 12 YEARS AND OLDER | MATURE, ADULT THOUGHT EMERGES. THINKING IS CHARACTERIZED BY DEDUCTIVE LOGIC, CONSIDERATION OF VARIOUS POSSIBILITIES BEFORE ACTING TO SOLVE A PROBLEM (MENTAL TRIAL AND ERROR), ABSTRACT THOUGHT (E.G., PHILOSOPHICAL WEIGHING OF MORAL PRINCIPLES), AND THE FORMATION AND TESTING OF HYPOTHESES. |

Piaget believed that the cognitive developments of each stage, and of the substages within them, tend to be universal. One reason for this is that cognitive development largely depends on the maturation of the brain, and, assuming minimal nourishment, the course of maturation will be reasonably similar from child to child. Second, cognitive developments are based on children's interactions with their environments. While it is true that no two children share precisely the same environment, the broad realities are compelling enough that practically all children must learn to cope with them. For example, gravity affects us all, so all children have the opportunity to learn that dropped objects move downward. Children from different cultures may reach for very different objects, but all normally learn that reaching for things enables us to touch or grasp them.

Piaget also believed that the cognitive developments of one stage, or one substage, are made possible by the cognitive achievements of the preceding stage. In Chapter 6, we shall see how stage develops from stage and how substage grows out of substage.

**Practical Applications of Piaget's Theory** Because Piaget's theory focuses on cognitive development, its applications are primarily in educational settings. Teachers following Piaget's views would engage the child actively in solving problems. They would pay particular attention to gearing instruction to the child's developmental level and offering learning activities that challenge the child to advance to the next highest level (Thomas, 1992). For example, 5-year-olds learn primarily through play and direct sensory contact with the environment. Early formal instruction using workbooks and paper may be far less effective with this age group (Crain, 1992).

**Evaluation of Piaget's Theory** Many researchers, using a variety of methods, have found that Piaget may have underestimated the ages when children are capable of doing certain things. It also appears that cognitive skills develop more gradually than Piaget thought, and not in discrete stages. Moreover, Piaget did not pay much attention to individual differences in cognitive development. Here let it suffice to note that Piaget presented us with a view of children very different from the psychoanalytic and behaviorist views and that Piaget provided a strong theoretical foundation for researchers concerned with the sequences in children's cognitive development.

## *Information-Processing Theory*

Another face of the cognitive perspective is *information processing* (Klahr, 1992; Flavell et al., 1993b). Psychological thought has long been influenced by the status of the physical sciences of the day. For example, Freud's psychodynamic theory was related to the development of thermodynamics in the last century. Many of today's cognitive psychologists have been influenced by concepts of computer science. Computers process information to solve problems. Information—encoded so it can be accepted as input—is first fed into the computer. Then it is placed in *memory* while it is manipulated. The information can be stored more permanently on a floppy disk, a hard disk, or another device. In Chapter 12, we shall see that many psychologists speak of people as having short-term memory and a more permanent long-term memory. If information has been placed in long-term memory, it must be retrieved before we can work on it again. To retrieve information from computer storage, we must know the code or name for the data file and the rules for retrieving data files. Similarly, note psychologists, we must have appropriate cues to retrieve information from our own long-term memories, or the information is lost to us.

Thus, many cognitive psychologists focus on information processing in people—the processes by which information is encoded (input), stored (in long-term memory), retrieved (placed in short-term memory), and manipulated to solve problems (output). Our strategies for solving problems are sometimes referred to as our "mental programs" or "software." In this computer metaphor, our brains are the "hardware" that runs our mental programs. Our brains, that is, become genuinely *personal* computers.

**TRUTH OR FICTION REVISITED**

*Some developmentalists do see children's strategies for solving problems as "mental programs" that are operated by their "personal computers," or brains. These are information-processing theorists.*

When psychologists who study information processing contemplate the cognitive development of children, they are likely to talk in terms of the size of the child's short-term memory at a given age and of the number of programs a child can run simultaneously. Research suggests that these are indeed useful ways of talking about children (see Chapter 12).

**PRACTICAL APPLICATIONS OF INFORMATION-PROCESSING THEORY** The most obvious applications of information processing occur in teaching (Thomas, 1992). For example, information-processing models alert teachers to the sequence of steps by which children acquire information, commit it to memory, and retrieve it to solve problems. By understanding this sequence, teachers can provide experiences that give students practice with each stage. The information-processing model is also a useful guide in diagnosing and treating children's learning difficulties. Each "component" in the information-processing "system" can be assessed when the trouble spot has been identified, and methods for correcting the problem can be applied.

**EVALUATION OF INFORMATION-PROCESSING THEORY** Psychologists in the behaviorist tradition argue that cognitions are not directly observable and that cognitive psychologists do not place adequate emphasis on the situational determinants of behavior. Cognitive psychologists counter that human behavior cannot be understood without reference to cognition.

## ECOLOGICAL THEORY

***Ecology*** The branch of biology that deals with the relationships between living organisms and their environment.

***Ecological theory*** The view that explains child development in terms of the reciprocal influences between children and the settings that make up their environment.

***Ecology*** is the branch of biology that deals with the relationships between living organisms and their environment. The ***ecological theory*** of child development addresses aspects of psychological, social, and emotional development, as well as biological development. Ecological theorists explain child development in terms of the interaction between children and the settings in which they live (Bronfenbrenner, 1989).

### *Focus on Reciprocal Processes*

According to Urie Bronfenbrenner, the first proposition of ecological theory is that the traditional, unidirectional approach to understanding child–environment relationships is insufficient. The ecological approach argues that the developmental process cannot be completely understood unless we focus on the ***reciprocal*** interactions between the child and the parents, not just maturational forces (nature) or parental child-rearing approaches (nurture).

***Reciprocal*** Done, felt, or given in return. Referring to a mutual exchange in which each side influences the other.

**TRUTH OR FICTION REVISITED**

*It is true that infants do not simply accept their parents' child-rearing approaches. Newborns* do *influence their parents to treat them in certain ways. Children differ in their basic temperaments. As pointed out by ecological theorists, influences between children and their environments are reciprocal.*

Consider the example of the ways in which parents interact with infants. Some parents may choose to feed newborns on demand, while others may decide to adhere to a schedule in which feedings occur 4 hours apart. Certainly, parental feeding plans will affect the child. But the basic (apparently inborn) temperaments of children differ (see Chapter 7), and some children are more likely than others to accept their parents' feeding patterns. Some children, that is, are basically "easy." Easy children readily develop regular cycles of eating and sleeping and are likely to conform to a rigid feeding schedule. Other children are basically "difficult." Difficult children are slow to develop regular cycles of eating and sleeping. They may not readily adapt to a rigid feeding schedule, and the parents' wishes may have to be modified if the peace is to be kept.

The point is this: Parents are part of the child's environment, and parents do have a major influence on the child, but the influence is not a one-way street.

**FIGURE 2.14**

**URIE BRONFENBRENNER.** *Bronfenbrenner's ecological theory focuses on children's interactions with environmental systems.*

### *Focus on the Larger Context: Systems within Systems*

The development of the child is also influenced "by the relations between these settings [in which the developing person lives] and by larger contexts in which the settings are embedded" (Bronfenbrenner, 1979, p. 21). According to psychologist Sandra Scarr, we must expand our view "of the context in which development occurs. Children have not only an immediate family but contexts of neighborhood, community, and society in which they do or do not get medical care, day care, and school lunches. Parents have work lives and friendship groups that affect how much time of what quality they spend with the children" (1985, p. 510). Scarr adds that we cannot understand children unless we examine the social and cultural aspects of behavior, as well as the biological and psychological aspects.

Bronfenbrenner (1979, 1989) suggests that we can view the setting or contexts of human development as consisting of four systems. Each of these systems is embedded within the next larger context. From narrowest to widest, these systems consist of the *microsystem,* the *mesosystem,* the *exosystem,* and the *macrosystem.*

FIGURE 2.15

***THE CONTEXTS OF HUMAN DEVELOPMENT.*** *According to ecological theory, the systems within which children develop are embedded within larger systems. Children and these systems reciprocally influence each other. (Source: Garbarino, 1982).*

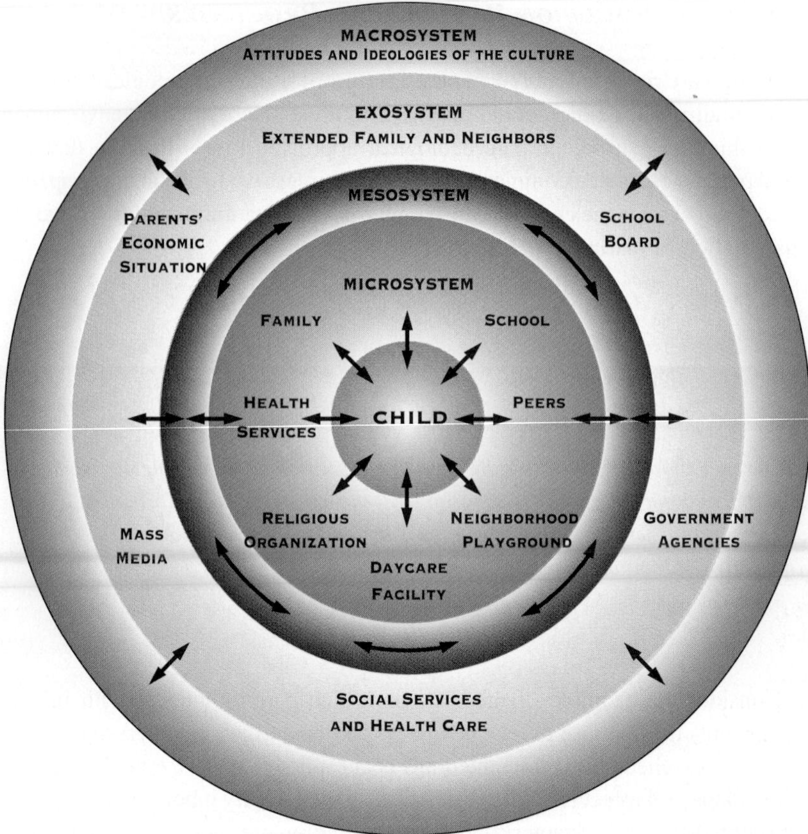


SOURCE: ADAPTED FROM GARBARINO, 1982.

**THE MICROSYSTEM** The ***microsystem*** involves the interactions of the child and other people in the immediate setting, such as the home, the school, or the peer group. Initially, the microsystem is small, involving care-giving interactions with the parents or others, usually at home. As children get older, they do more, with more people, in more places (Garbarino, 1982).

**THE MESOSYSTEM** The ***mesosystem*** involves the interactions of the various settings within the microsystem. For instance, the home and the school interact during parent–teacher conferences. The school and the larger community interact when children are taken on field trips. The ecological approach addresses the joint impact of two or more settings on the child.

**THE EXOSYSTEM** The ***exosystem*** involves the institutions in which the child does not directly participate, but which exert an indirect influence on the child. For example, the school board is part of the child's exosystem in that board members construct curricula for the child's education, determine what books will be in the school library, and so forth. In similar fashion, the parents' workplaces and economic situations determine the hours during which they will be available to the child, help determine what mood they will be in when they interact with the child, and so on. For example, poverty and unemployment cause psychological distress in parents, which in turn decreases their capacity for supportive, consistent, and involved parenting (McLoyd, 1990; Simons et al., 1993). Their children, as a result, may experience adjustment problems both at home and in school (Conger et al., 1993a; Flanagan & Eccles, 1993). Studies

***Microsystem*** The immediate settings with which the child interacts, such as the home, the school, and one's peers (from the Greek *mikros,* meaning "small").

***Mesosystem*** The interlocking settings that influence the child, such as the interaction of the school and the larger community when children are taken on field trips (from the Greek *mesos,* meaning "middle").

***Exosystem*** Community institutions and settings that indirectly influence the child, such as the school board and the parents' workplaces (from the Greek *exo-,* meaning "outside").

that address the effects of housing, health care, television programs, church attendance, government agencies, or even the presence or absence of a telephone on children are all examining the interactions of the exosystem with the child.

***Macrosystem*** The basic institutions and ideologies that influence the child, such as the American ideals of freedom of expression and equality under the law (from the Greek *makros,* meaning ''long'' or ''enlarged'').

***Cross-cultural study*** A comparison of two or more cultures.

**THE MACROSYSTEM** The ***macrosystem*** involves the interaction of children with the beliefs, values, expectations, and life-styles of their cultural settings. ***Cross-cultural studies*** examine children's interactions with their macrosystem in different cultures. There are macrosystems within a particular culture as well. For example, within the United States, the two-wage-earner family, the low-income single-parent household, and the more traditional family with father as sole breadwinner each constitutes a macrosystem. Each exhibits its own characteristic life-style, set of values, and expectations (Bronfenbrenner, 1989).

**CULTURE AND DEVELOPMENT: INFLUENCE OF THE MACROSYSTEM ON THE DEVELOPMENT OF INDEPENDENCE** Cross-cultural studies provide interesting insights into the way children interact with their macrosystems. Consider the development of independence. Among the !Kung people of Namibia, babies are kept in close contact with their mothers during the first year (Konner, 1977). !Kung infants are frequently carried in slings across their mothers' hips that allow them to nurse at will—literally, all day long. The !Kung seem to follow the commandment *The infant shall not go hungry*—not even for 5 seconds. In every way, !Kung mothers try to respond at once to their babies' cries and whims. By Western standards, !Kung babies are incredibly indulged or spoiled. However, overindulgence does not appear to make !Kung babies overly dependent on their mothers. By the time they are capable of walking, they do. They do not cling to their mothers. In comparison to Western children of the same age, !Kung children spend less time with their mothers and more time with their peers.

Also compare Urie Bronfenbrenner's (1973) observations of child rearing in the United States and Russia. Russian babies, as a group, are more likely than U.S. babies to be cuddled, kissed, and hugged. Russian mothers are not quite so solicitous as their !Kung counterparts, but they are highly protective as compared with U.S. mothers. Russian children are taught to take care of themselves at younger ages than U.S. children. By 18 months of age, Russian children are usually learning to dress themselves and are largely toilet trained.

What are some parental practices used by different cultures to foster independent behavior?

| CULTURE | PARENTAL TECHNIQUE |
|---|---|
| !KUNG, AFRICA | CLOSE PHYSICAL CONTACT<br>QUICK RESPONSE TO EXPRESSED NEED |
| UNITED STATES | MODERATE PHYSICAL CONTACT<br>ENCOURAGEMENT OF SELF-EFFORT AND SELF-EXPRESSION |
| RUSSIAN | CLOSE PHYSICAL CONTACT<br>EARLY TRAINING IN SELF-CARE |

**TRUTH OR FICTION REVISITED**

*It is true that children are influenced not only by their parents, schools, and other local agencies but also by the ideals and values of the cultures in which they are reared. Ecological theorists encourage us to focus on the various systems—immediate and extended—that interact with children as they develop.*

## PRACTICAL APPLICATIONS OF ECOLOGICAL THEORY

The ecological (''multisystemic'') approach broadens the strategies for intervention in problems such as juvenile offending and child abuse (Brunk et al.,

1987; Henggeler et al., 1986; Rosenberg, 1987). Bronfenbrenner (1977) suggests projects such as

- ✦ Introducing a ''curriculum for caring'' in which students help care for children of working mothers, help families during crises, and visit the sick and the elderly.
- ✦ Facilitating the entry of children into the educational system by acquainting families with school personnel and encouraging joint activities when children are still preschoolers.
- ✦ Inducing businesses to create more flexible work schedules for parents.

### *Evaluation of Ecological Theory*

Perhaps the most valuable aspect of ecological theory is that it has helped make researchers aware of the systems with which children interact. This awareness has fostered research down relatively new avenues. For example, focus on interactions within the microsystem has led to research on the important, but previously ignored, role of the father in child development (see Chapter 7).

Much research at the level of the mesosystem focuses on the shifts in setting that children encounter as they develop. For example, the health of the child requires interlocking relationships between parents and the health system, just as the education of the child requires the interaction of parents and school personnel. At the level of the exosystem, researchers look into the effects of parents' work lives, welfare agencies, transportation systems, shopping facilities, and so on. At the level of the macrosystem, we may compare child-rearing practices in the United States with those of other countries.

In short, the powerful legacies of the ecological approach are that our perspectives on development are broadened and our research endeavors may be better organized. The ecological approach compels us to pay attention to the power of nature and also to regard the several systems of nurture with greater sophistication.

Our overview of the major theories of development does not begin to cover all of the many contributions made to the field by countless other developmental psychologists. The contributions of two often overlooked groups—women and people of color—are discussed in Developing Today.

## Theoretical Interlude: Some Integrating Thoughts on Theories of Development

Now that we have explored the major theories of development, what can we conclude? After all, the theories do not all address the same aspects of development. One may focus on motor development, another on learning, another on emotional development, and still another on cognitive development. One theory may view development as involving a discrete sequence of stages, while another may view development as continuous. Table 2.2 summarizes some of the important similarities and differences among the theories.

We must also deal with the fact that many theoretical notions have been discarded, or at least revised and updated. For example, Erikson's views revise those of Freud, and social-learning theorists have updated the propositions of the behaviorists.

**TABLE 2.2**

***COMPARISON OF DEVELOPMENTAL THEORIES***

| THEORY AND THEORIST | BASIC IDEA | NATURE OR NURTURE MORE IMPORTANT? | DEVELOPMENT CONTINUOUS OR DISCONTINUOUS? | CHILD ACTIVE OR PASSIVE? |
|---|---|---|---|---|
| MATURATIONAL (GESELL) | DEVELOPMENT PROGRESSES THROUGH AN ORDERLY SEQUENCE DETERMINED BY BIOLOGICAL MATURATION. | NATURE | DISCONTINUOUS | PASSIVE |
| PSYCHOANALYTIC (FREUD) | PERSONALITY DEVELOPS IN FIVE PSYCHOSEXUAL STAGES, POWERED BY UNCONSCIOUS CONFLICTS AMONG THE ID, EGO, AND SUPEREGO. | NATURE, BUT NURTURE ALSO IMPORTANT | DISCONTINUOUS | PASSIVE |
| PSYCHOANALYTIC (ERIKSON) | PERSONALITY DEVELOPS IN EIGHT PSYCHOSOCIAL STAGES THROUGH THE LIFE SPAN. SOCIAL RELATIONSHIPS AND CONSCIOUS THOUGHT ARE IMPORTANT. | NURTURE, BUT NATURE ALSO IMPORTANT | DISCONTINUOUS | ACTIVE |
| LEARNING: BEHAVIORISM (PAVLOV, SKINNER) | CHANGES IN BEHAVIOR RESULT FROM EXPERIENCE. PUNISHMENT AND SHAPING ARE IMPORTANT. | NURTURE | CONTINUOUS | PASSIVE |
| LEARNING: SOCIAL (BANDURA) | CHILDREN LEARN BY OBSERVING AND IMITATING OTHERS. RECIPROCAL DETERMINISM IS IMPORTANT. | NURTURE | CONTINUOUS | ACTIVE |
| COGNITIVE: COGNITIVE-DEVELOPMENTAL (PIAGET) | THINKING AND PROBLEM SOLVING DEVELOP IN FOUR QUALITATIVELY DIFFERENT STAGES. ASSIMILATION, ACCOMMODATION, EQUILIBRATION ARE IMPORTANT. | NATURE AND NURTURE BOTH IMPORTANT | DISCONTINUOUS | ACTIVE |
| COGNITIVE: INFORMATION-PROCESSING | CHILD'S MIND IS COMPARED TO A COMPUTER. FOCUS IS ON STORING AND RETRIEVING INFORMATION AND USING "MENTAL PROGRAMS" TO SOLVE PROBLEMS. | NATURE ("HARDWARE") AND NURTURE ("SOFTWARE") BOTH IMPORTANT | CONTINUOUS | ACTIVE |
| ECOLOGICAL (BRON-FENBRENNER) | CHILDREN AND THEIR SOCIAL ENVIRONMENTS RECIPROCALLY INFLUENCE EACH OTHER. FOUR ENVIRONMENTAL SYSTEMS ARE THE MICROSYSTEM, MESOSYSTEM, EXOSYSTEM, AND MACROSYSTEM. | NURTURE | CONTINUOUS | ACTIVE |

## Developing Today

### CONTRIBUTIONS OF WOMEN AND PEOPLE OF COLOR TO THE STUDY OF CHILD DEVELOPMENT

When historians of psychology are asked to rank the most important historic figures in psychology, many of the names we have just discussed are mentioned: Skinner, Freud, Piaget, Watson, and Pavlov (Hilgard, 1993; Korn et al., 1991). Besides being significant figures in the field of child development, what else do these individuals have in common? They are all white males. Critics assert that such lists create the erroneous impression that women and people of color have not made major contributions to the history of psychology (Korn et al., 1991).

In the early years of psychology, women and ethnic minority psychologists often faced discrimination and their contributions were not always recognized (Paludi, 1992). Fortunately, that situation has begun to change.

Consider just a few of the women who have made important contributions to the field of child development. Nancy Bayley developed the most widely used scale of infant intelligence (see Chapter 6). Eleanor Gibson introduced the visual cliff, one of the best-known techniques for studying depth perception in infants (see Chapter 5). Margaret Kuenne Harlow advanced our understanding of the importance of tactile stimulation in attachment formation (see Chapter 7).

Psychologists of different ethnic backgrounds have made their mark in child development as well. For example, African-American psychologists Kenneth Clark and Mamie Phipps Clark studied the self-concepts of African-American children and influenced a key Supreme Court decision on desegregation (Korn et al., 1991). Hispanic psychologist Jorge Sanchez was among the first to show how intelligence tests are culturally biased to the detriment of Mexican-American children. Asian-American psychologist Stanley Sue (see Chapter 12) has engaged in prominent research on racial differences in academic achievement and has discussed these differences in terms of adaptation to discrimination, among other factors.

True—child development was once the province of white males. Today, however, more than half (56 percent) of the Ph.D's in psychology and more than three-fourths (78 percent) of the Ph.D's in developmental psychology are awarded to women (Ostertag & McNamara, 1991). African Americans, Asian Americans, Hispanics, and Native Americans receive about 9 percent of all Ph.D's awarded in psychology (National Science Foundation, 1991)—far below their representation in the general population, unfortunately. Even so, fewer than two psychology Ph.D's in five are now received by white males. Child development and the other fields of psychology, like the world in which they exist, are showing diversification.

**FIGURE 2.16 KENNETH AND MAMIE PHIPPS CLARK.** *Women and people of color have made important contributions to psychology that were not always recognized. Kenneth Clark and Mamie Phipps Clark studied the self-concepts of African-American children and influenced a key Supreme Court decision on desegregation.*

Nonetheless, despite the differences in the theories, and despite the need for revision, there may be emerging a central core of knowledge about children. For example, it would be erroneous to ignore the powerful role of maturation in the child's biological development and the appearance of the child's basic temperament, although the extent of the role of maturation is somewhat more open to dispute in the development of intelligence and academic skills.

Let us try to develop an integrating list of propositions on development—a theory-derived list that appears to have been generally supported by research. Such a list might look like this:

1. The heredity of the child provides for a measure of stability in development. For example, as we shall see in Chapter 5, children whose physical development is delayed by malnourishment tend to catch up when nourishment becomes more adequate. (maturational theory)
2. Children may not only inherit physical traits such as hair and eye color but also predispositions toward basic temperament and factors such as basic approaches to cognitive tasks. (maturational theory)
3. Early childhood experiences can have far-reaching effects on adult personality and emotional life. (Freud's psychoanalytic theory)
4. Our early social relationships influence our tendencies to view the world as generally benevolent or malevolent and color our future relationships. (Freud's and Erikson's psychoanalytic theories)
5. To some degree, we are the conscious architects of our own personalities. (Erikson's psychoanalytic theory; social-learning theory; cognitive-developmental theory)
6. Children are capable of learning to associate stimuli very early in life, long before they can verbalize the associations. (learning theory)
7. Rewards and, in many cases, punishments work. Pleasant stimuli tend to encourage children to repeat the rewarded behavior, while aversive stimuli tend to suppress the punished behavior. (learning theory)
8. Children also learn from observing the behavior of others—parents, siblings, peers, teachers, television characters, even characters in books. (social-learning theory)
9. Children do not only react mechanically to external stimulation. They also try to understand the world about them—to form accurate mental representations of external objects and to discover what leads to what. (cognitive-developmental theory; information-processing theory)
10. Children (and adults) tend to interpret new events according to existing ways of perceiving the world, but we can also accommodate by changing the ways we perceive the world when new events do not fit existing schemes. (cognitive-developmental theory)
11. Children are not only influenced by their environments; children also influence their environments, so that the influences are reciprocal. (ecological theory)
12. To develop a comprehensive understanding of the forces that act upon children, we must consider many interacting systems, ranging from systems as concrete as the immediate family to systems as abstract as the ideals of the cultures in which children are reared. (ecological theory)

If it strikes you that there is some truth to each of these statements, then perhaps each theory of development has something of value to tell us. Each theory sheds light on meaningful aspects of development. In later chapters, we shall return to these theories to see how they further enhance our understanding of child development.

## Summary

1. Scientists who study child development seek to describe, explain, predict, and control various aspects of development. Theories are based on assumptions about behavior, and theories allow us to derive explanations and predictions about child development.

2. Stage theorists view development as consisting of discrete periods that differ qualitatively from other periods. Stages follow one another in invariant sequences.

3. Maturational theory focuses on the unfolding of genetically determined developmental sequences. Maturational theorist Arnold Gesell argued that all areas of development are self-regulated by the unfolding of natural plans and processes.

4. Sigmund Freud's psychoanalytic theory focuses on personality and emotional development and assumes that children are driven by instincts and inevitably encounter conflict with parents. Freud hypothesized the existence of three psychic structures: the id, which provides instinctive motives; the ego, which represents reason and makes plans; and the superego, which functions as the conscience. Defense mechanisms protect the ego from anxiety by repressing unacceptable ideas or distorting reality.

5. According to Freud, children undergo five stages of psychosexual development as psychosexual energy is transferred from one erogenous zone to another: the oral, anal, phallic, latency, and genital stages.

6. Erik Erikson's psychoanalytic theory in contrast to Freud's, has eight stages of development, three of which occur during adulthood. Erikson's theory concerns stages of psychosocial development rather than psychosexual development. Erikson's theory also argues that personality development is largely conscious.

7. Learning theorists view development in terms of changes in behavior that result from experience. In classical conditioning, an originally neutral stimulus (the conditioned stimulus) comes to elicit the response usually brought forth by a second stimulus (the unconditioned stimulus) by being paired repeatedly with the second stimulus.

8. In operant conditioning, children increase the frequency of behaviors that are reinforced and decrease the frequency of behaviors that are punished. Children may acquire complex motor skills through shaping, in which successive approximations to the target behavior pattern are reinforced.

9. Positive reinforcers (such as food and approval) increase the frequency of behaviors when they are applied. Negative reinforcers (such as pain and fear) increase the frequency of the behaviors that result in their removal.

10. Social-learning theorists such as Albert Bandura have shown that children also learn by observing others. Learning occurs through reciprocal determinism, the interplay of the child's behavior, his or her cognitive characteristics, and the environment.

11. Jean Piaget's cognitive-developmental theory is a stage theory that focuses on the ways in which children adapt to the environment by mentally representing the world and solving problems.

12. Piaget theorized that children respond to stimulation with organized actions or mental operations termed schemes. Children assimilate new events into existing schemes when possible, and, when they cannot, they accommodate by modifying their schemes. Restoration of balance between assimilation and accommodation is termed equilibration.

13. Information-processing theorists view cognitive development in terms of children's advances in the input, storage, retrieval, manipulation, and output of information.

14. Ecological theorists such as Urie Bronfenbrenner focus on children's interactions with environmental systems. They propose that children and their environments exert reciprocal influences upon one another.

15. Ecological theory hypothesizes the existence of four systems that influence children: the microsystem, or immediate setting, such as the home or school; the mesosystem, which involves the interactions of various settings; the exosystem, or influential institutions in which the child does not directly participate (for example, the parents' workplaces); and the macrosystem, or cultural values, beliefs, and life-styles.

# BEGINNINGS

THE WONDER OF HUMAN DEVELOPMENT BEGINS LONG BEFORE the baby is born. In one sense, it begins even before the moment of conception, with the formation of egg and sperm cells in the bodies of the parents-to-be. Once an egg and sperm cell unite, our genetic makeup is determined. But the newborn baby is not the result of heredity alone. Development also is influenced by environmental events that occur during the prenatal period, such as the mother's health, her diet, and drugs she may take.

In Chapter 3, we discuss the roles of heredity and environment in development. We describe the process of conception and the stages of prenatal development. In Chapter 4, we examine the stages and methods of childbirth. We conclude with a look at the characteristics and capabilities of that remarkable organism: the newborn baby.

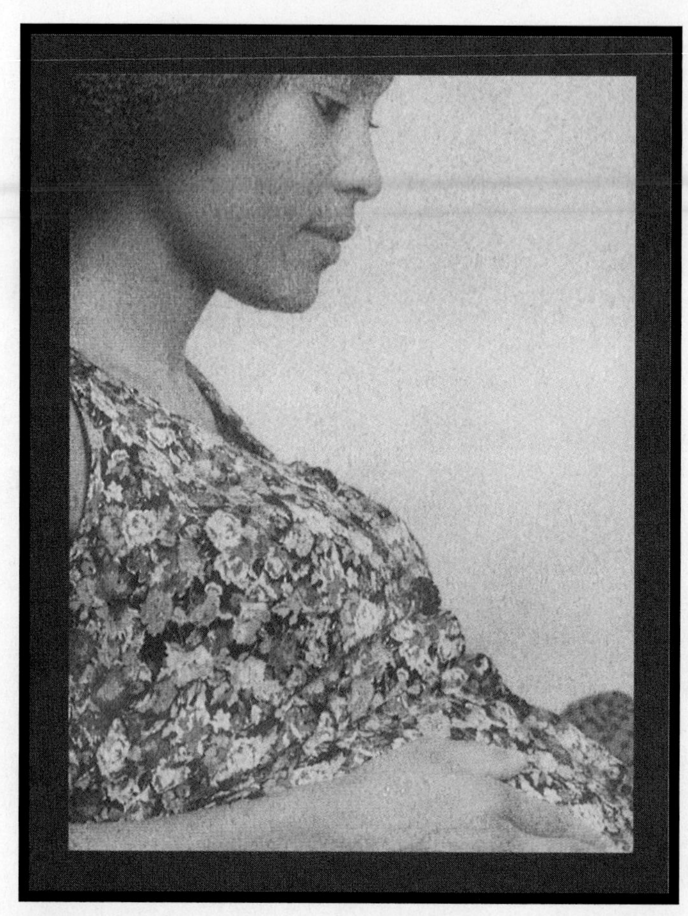

# *HEREDITY AND PRENATAL DEVELOPMENT*

## Chapter Outline

**Influence of Heredity on Development**

- *Genes and Chromosomes*
- *Mitosis and Meiosis*
- *Identical and Fraternal Twins*
- *Dominant and Recessive Traits*
- *Chromosomal and Genetic Abnormalities*
- *Genetic Counseling and Prenatal Testing*

**Heredity and Environment**

- *Consanguinity Studies*
- *Twin Studies*
- *Adoption Studies*

**Conception: Against All Odds**

- *Ova*
- *Sperm Cells*

**Other Ways to Conceive**

- *Infertility Problems*
- *Artificial Insemination*
- *In Vitro Fertilization*
- *Embryonic Transplant*
- *Surrogate Mothers*

**Stages of Prenatal Development**

- *The Germinal Stage*
- *The Embryonic Stage*
- *The Fetal Stage*

**Environmental Influences on Prenatal Development**

- *Nutrition*
- *Diseases and Disorders of the Mother*
- *Drugs Taken by the Parents*
- *Environmental Hazards*
- *Maternal Stress*
- *The Mother's Age*

**Summary**

## Truth or Fiction?

______ *Brown eyes are dominant over blue eyes.*

______ *Sickle-cell anemia is most prevalent among African Americans.*

______ *It is not possible to learn the gender of one's child prior to birth.*

______ *Identical twins are more likely than fraternal twins to share disorders such as schizophrenia and vulnerability to alcoholism.*

______ *Developing embryos have been successfully transferred from the uterus of one woman to the uterus of another.*

______ *Newly fertilized egg cells survive without any nourishment from the mother for more than a week.*

______ *Your heart started beating when you were only one-fourth of an inch long and weighed a fraction of an ounce.*

______ *If it were not for the secretion of male sex hormones a few weeks after conception, we would all develop as females.*

______ *Fetuses suck their thumbs and hiccough, sometimes for hours on end.*

______ *Embryos and fetuses take what they need from their mothers. Therefore, pregnant women need not be too concerned about their diets.*

______ *Babies can be born addicted to narcotics and other drugs.*

On a summerlike day in October, Michele and her husband, Matt, rush out to their jobs as usual. While Michele, an attorney, is preparing a case for court a very different drama is unfolding in her body. Hormones are causing a follicle (egg container) in one of her ***ovaries*** to rupture and release an egg cell, or ***ovum.*** When it is released, the ovum begins a slow journey down a 4-inch-long ***Fallopian tube*** to the ***uterus.*** It is within this tube that one of Matt's sperm cells will unite with it. Like all women, Michele possessed at birth all the egg cells she will ever have. How this particular ovum was selected to mature and be released this month is unknown. For a day or so following ***ovulation,*** however, Michele will be capable of becoming pregnant.

Michele had used a kit bought in a drugstore to predict when she would ovulate. When the results indicated she was about to ovulate, she and Matt had sexual intercourse that night. Matt ejaculated hundreds of millions of sperm. Only a few thousand had survived the journey through the cervix and uterus to the Fallopian tubes. Several bombarded the ovum, attempting to penetrate. Only one succeeded. The single-cell fertilized ovum, or ***zygote,*** is 1/175th of an inch long—a tiny beginning.

In this chapter, we explore heredity and ***prenatal*** development. In a sense, development begins before the moment of conception. Development also involves the origins of the genetic structures that determine that the being conceived by Matt and Michele will grow arms rather than wings, a mouth rather than gills, and hair rather than scales. And so, our discussion begins with an examination of the building blocks of heredity: genes and chromosomes. We describe the process of conception itself and find that the odds against any one sperm uniting with an ovum are astronomical. We then trace human growth and development through the 9 months of ***gestation.*** Although many parents feel that their pregnancies tend to drag on, especially toward the end, we see that the major organ systems and all the structures that make us human actually take form with great rapidity.

***Ovary*** A female reproductive organ, located in the abdomen, that produces female reproductive cells (ova).

***Ovum*** A female reproductive cell.

***Fallopian tube*** A tube through which ova travel from an ovary to the uterus.

***Uterus*** The hollow organ within females in which the embryo and fetus develop.

***Ovulation*** The releasing of an ovum from an ovary.

***Zygote*** A fertilized ovum.

***Prenatal*** Before birth.

***Gestation*** The period of carrying young from conception until birth.

***Heredity*** The transmission of traits and characteristics from parent to child by means of genes.

***Genetics*** The branch of biology that studies heredity.

***Behavior genetics*** The study of the genetic transmission of structures and traits that give rise to behavior.

## INFLUENCE OF HEREDITY ON DEVELOPMENT

Consider some of the facts of life:

- People cannot breathe underwater (without special equipment).
- People cannot fly (without special equipment).
- Fish cannot learn to speak French or dance an Irish jig, even if you raise them in enriched environments and send them to finishing school (which is why we look for tuna that taste good, not for tuna with good taste).

We cannot breathe underwater or fly, because we have not inherited gills or wings. Fish are similarly limited by their ***heredity,*** or the biological transmission of traits and characteristics from one generation to another. Because of their heredity, fish cannot speak French or do a jig.

Heredity plays a momentous role in the determination of human traits. The structures we inherit both make our behaviors possible and place limits on them (Loehlin, 1992). The field within the science of biology that studies heredity is called ***genetics. Behavior genetics*** is a specialty that bridges the sciences of psychology and biology. It is concerned with the transmission of structures and traits that give rise to patterns of behavior.

Genetic (inherited) influences are fundamental in the transmission of physical traits, such as height, hair texture, and eye color. Genetics also appear to be a factor in intelligence and in the origins of personality traits such as activity level, sociability, shyness, fearfulness, ***neuroticism,*** and ***empathy*** (Heath et al., 1992; Loehlin, 1992; Saudino & Eaton, 1993; Stevenson, 1992). Genetic influences are also implicated in psychological disorders such as schizophrenia, depression, and alcoholism (Plomin & McClearn, 1993).

> **THINKING ABOUT DEVELOPMENT**
>
> Agree or disagree with the following statement and support your answer: "Since psychological traits such as shyness and intelligence are influenced by heredity, there is no point in trying to encourage children to be more sociable or helping poor students do better in school."

***Neuroticism*** A personality trait characterized by anxiety and emotional instability.

***Empathy*** The ability to share another person's feelings or emotions.

## GENES AND CHROMOSOMES

***Chromosomes*** are the rod-shaped structures found in the nuclei of the body's cells. A normal human cell contains 46 chromosomes organized into 23 pairs. Each chromosome contains thousands of segments called ***genes.*** Genes are the biochemical materials that regulate the development of traits. Some traits, such as blood type, appear to be transmitted by a single pair of genes—one of which is derived from each parent. Other traits, referred to as ***polygenic,*** are determined by combinations of pairs of genes.

We have about 100,000 genes in every cell in our bodies. Genes consist of large, complex molecules of the substance ***deoxyribonucleic acid* (DNA)**. The form of DNA was first demonstrated in the 1950s by James Watson and Francis Crick (1958). As you can see in Figure 3.1, DNA takes the form of a double spiral, or helix, similar in appearance to a twisting ladder. In all living things, from one-celled animals to fish to people, the sides of the "ladder" consist of alternating segments of phosphate (P) and simple sugar (S). The "rungs" of the ladder are attached to the sugars and consist of one of two pairs of bases, either *adenine* with *thymine* (A with T) or *cytosine* with *guanine* (C with G). The sequence of the "rungs" is the genetic code that will cause the developing organism to grow arms or wings, skin or scales.

***Chromosomes*** Rod-shaped structures composed of genes that are found within the nuclei of cells.

***Gene*** The basic unit of heredity. Genes are composed of deoxyribonucleic acid (DNA).

***Polygenic*** Resulting from many genes.

***Deoxyribonucleic acid (DNA)*** Genetic material that takes the form of a double helix composed of phosphates, sugars, and bases.

## MITOSIS AND MEIOSIS

We all begin life as a single cell, or zygote, that divides again and again. There are two types of cell division: *mitosis* and *meiosis.* ***Mitosis*** is the cell-division process by which growth occurs and tissues are replaced. Through mitosis, the identical genetic code is carried into each new cell in the body. To accomplish this, the strands of DNA break apart, or "unzip" (see Figure 3.2). The double helix is then rebuilt in the cell. Each incomplete rung combines with the appropriate "partner" element (that is, G combines with C, A with T, and so on) to form a complete ladder. The two resulting identical copies of the DNA strand move apart when the cell divides, each becoming a member of one of the newly formed cells. As a consequence, the genetic code is identical in every cell of the body unless ***mutations*** occur through radiation or other environmental influences. Mutations are also believed, on rare occasions, to occur by chance.

Sperm and ova are produced through ***meiosis,*** or reduction division. In meiosis, the 46 chromosomes within the cell nucleus first line up into 23 pairs. When the cell divides, one member of each pair goes to each newly formed cell. As a consequence, each new cell nucleus contains only 23 chromosomes, not 46. And so, a cell that results from meiosis has half the genetic material of one that results from mitosis.

Through reduction division, or meiosis, we receive 23 chromosomes from our father's sperm cell and 23 from our mother's ovum. When a sperm cell fertilizes an ovum, the chromosomes form 23 pairs (Figure 3.3). Twenty-two of the pairs are ***autosomes,*** chromosomes that are matched pairs and possess genetic information concerning the same set of traits. The 23rd pair consists of

***Mitosis*** The form of cell division in which each chromosome splits lengthwise to double in number. Half of each chromosome combines with chemicals to retake its original form and then moves to the new cell.

***Mutation*** A sudden variation in an inheritable characteristic, as by an accident that affects the composition of genes.

***Meiosis*** The form of cell division in which each pair of chromosomes splits, so that one member of each pair moves to the new cell. As a result, each new cell has 23 chromosomes.

***Autosome*** Either member of a pair of chromosomes (with the exception of sex chromosomes).

***Sex chromosome*** A chromosome in the shape of a Y (male) or X (female) that determines the sex of the child.

FIGURE 3.1

***The Double Helix of DNA.*** *DNA consists of phosphate, sugar, and a number of bases. It takes the form of a double spiral, or helix.*

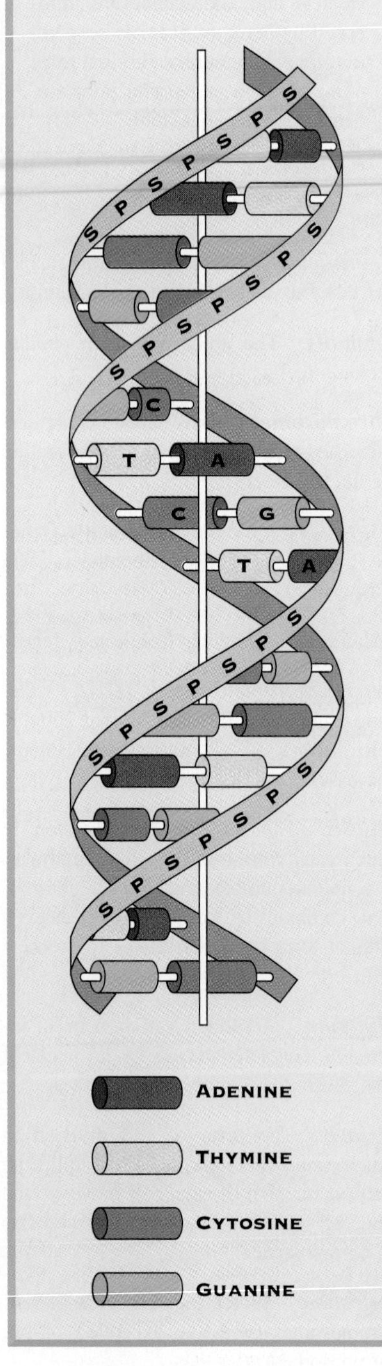


***sex chromosomes*** that look different and determine our gender. We all receive an X sex chromosome (so called because of its X shape) from our mothers. If we receive an X sex chromosome from our fathers, we develop into females. If we receive a Y sex chromosome (named after its Y shape) from our fathers, we develop into males.

### *Identical and Fraternal Twins*

Now and then, a zygote divides into two cells that separate so that each subsequently develops into an individual with the same genetic makeup. These individuals are known as identical or ***monozygotic (MZ) twins.*** If the woman produces two ova in the same month, and they are each fertilized by a different sperm cell, they develop into fraternal or ***dizygotic (DZ) twins.***

MZ twins are rarer than DZ twins, occurring once in about every 270 pregnancies (Cassill, 1982; Scheinfeld, 1973). MZ twins occur with equal frequency in all ethnic groups, but the incidence of DZ twins varies in different ethnic groups. Whites in the United States have about 1 chance in 90 of having DZ twins. African Americans have 1 chance in 70, whereas Asian Americans have only about 1 chance in 150.

DZ twins run in families. If a woman's mother was a twin, chances are one in eight that she will bear twins. If a woman has previously borne twins, the chances similarly rise to one in eight that she will bear twins in subsequent pregnancies. Similarly, women who have borne several children have an increased likelihood of twins in subsequent pregnancies.

As women reach their 40s, ovulation becomes less regular, resulting in a number of months when more than one ovum is released. Thus the chances of twins increase with the woman's age. Fertility drugs also enhance the chances of multiple births (Rosenthal, 1992b).

### *Dominant and Recessive Traits*

Traits are determined by pairs of genes. Each member of a pair of genes is referred to as an ***allele.*** When both of the alleles for a trait, such as hair color, are the same, the person is said to be ***homozygous*** for that trait. When the alleles for a trait differ, the person is ***heterozygous*** for that trait.

Gregor Mendel (1822–1884), an Austrian monk, established a number of laws of heredity through his work with plants. Mendel realized that some traits may result from an ''averaging'' of the genetic instructions carried by the parents. When the effects of both alleles are shown, there is said to be incomplete dominance or codominance.

Mendel also discovered the ''law of dominance.'' For example, the offspring from the crossing of purebred tall peas and purebred dwarf peas were tall, suggesting that tallness is dominant over dwarfism. We now know that many genes determine ***dominant traits*** or ***recessive traits.*** When a dominant allele is paired with a recessive allele, the trait determined by the dominant allele appears in the individual.

Brown eyes, for instance, are dominant over blue eyes. If one parent carried genes for only brown eyes, and the other for only blue eyes, the children would invariably have brown eyes. But brown-eyed parents may also carry recessive genes for blue eyes, as shown in Figure 3.4. Similarly, the offspring of Mendel's crossing of purebred tall and purebred dwarf peas were not pure. They carried recessive genes for dwarfism.

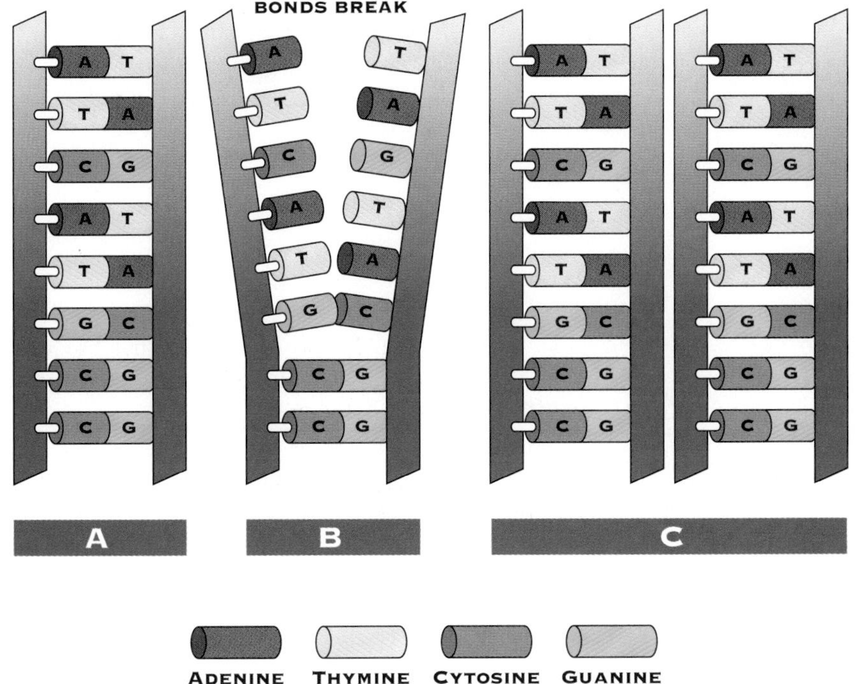

***Mitosis.*** *Part A shows a segment of a strand of DNA before mitosis. During mitosis, chromosomal strands of DNA "unzip" as shown in part B. As shown in part C, the double helix is rebuilt in the cell as each incomplete "rung" combines with appropriate molecules. The resulting identical copies of the DNA strand move apart when the cell divides, each joining one of the new cells.*

***Monozygotic (MZ) twins*** Twins that derive from a single zygote that has split into two; identical twins. Each MZ twin carries the same genetic code.

***Dizygotic (DZ) twins*** Twins that derive from two zygotes; fraternal twins.

***Allele*** A member of a pair of genes.

***Homozygous*** Having two identical alleles.

***Heterozygous*** Having two different alleles.

***Dominant trait*** A trait that is expressed.

***Recessive trait*** A trait that is not expressed when the gene or genes involved have been paired with dominant genes. Recessive traits are transmitted to future generations and expressed if they are paired with other recessive genes.

***Carrier*** A person who carries and transmits characteristics but does not exhibit them.

If the recessive gene from one parent should combine with the recessive gene from the other, the recessive trait will be shown. As suggested by Figure 3.4, approximately 25 percent of the offspring of brown-eyed parents who carry recessive blue eye color will have blue eyes. Mendel found that 25 percent of the offspring of parent peas that carried recessive dwarfism would be dwarfs.

Our discussion of eye color has been simplified. The percentages are not always perfect, because other genes may alter the expression of the genes for brown and blue eyes, producing hazel, or greenish, eyes. Some genes also switch other genes "on" or "off" at various times during development. For example, we normally reach reproductive capacity in the teens and not earlier, and men who go bald usually do so during adulthood. Similarly, the heart and the limbs develop at different times in the embryo, again because of the switching on of certain genes by other genes.

People who bear one dominant gene and one recessive gene for a trait are said to be ***carriers*** of the recessive gene. In the cases of recessive genes that

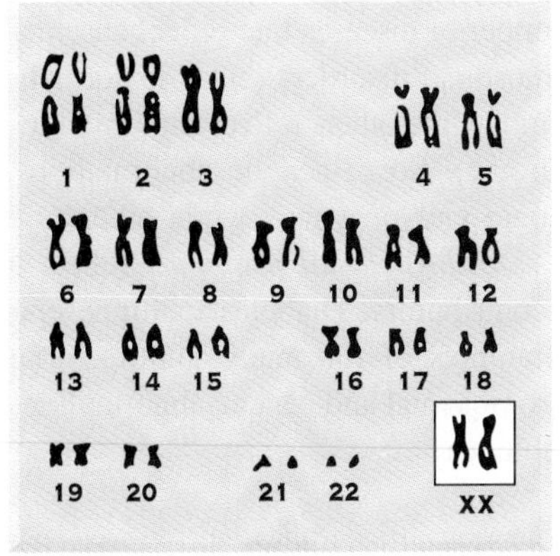


FEMALE

1 2 3 4 5
6 7 8 9 10 11 12
13 14 15 16 17 18
19 20 21 22 XY

MALE

FIGURE 3.3

***The 23 Pairs of Human Chromosomes.*** *People normally have 23 pairs of chromosomes. Females have two X chromosomes, whereas males have an X and a Y sex chromosome.*

FIGURE 3.4

***THE TRANSMISSION OF DOMINANT AND RECESSIVE TRAITS.*** *Two brown-eyed parents each carry a gene for blue eyes. Their children have an equal opportunity of receiving genes for brown eyes and blue eyes. In such cases, 25 percent of the children show the recessive trait—blue eyes. The other 75 percent show the dominant trait—brown eyes. But two of three who have brown eyes carry the recessive trait for transmittal to future generations.*

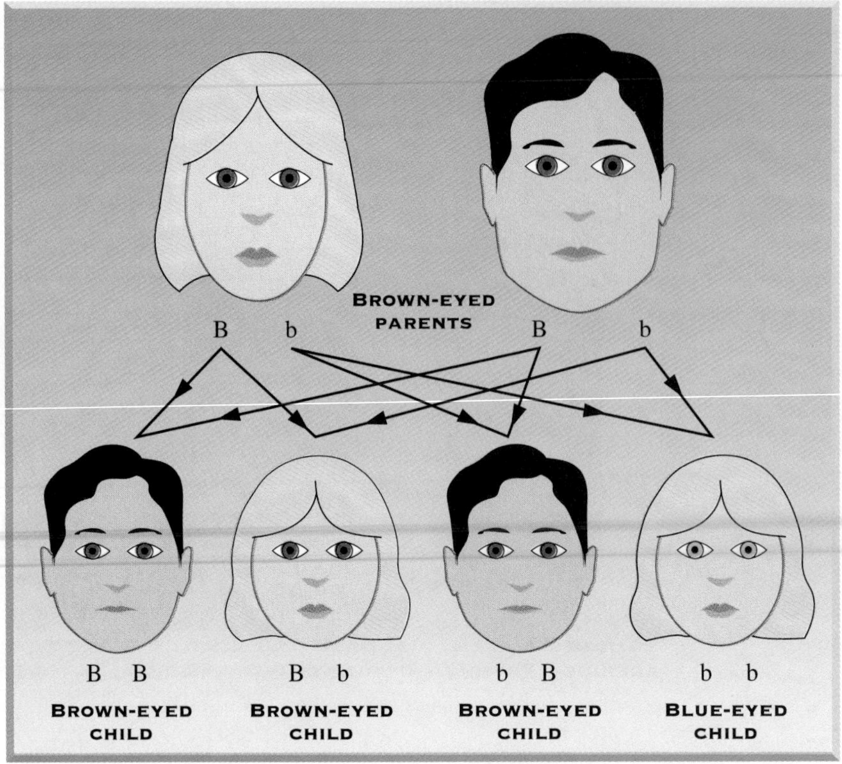


give rise to serious illnesses, carriers of those genes are fortunate to have dominant genes that cancel their effects. Unfortunately, carriers can still transmit their recessive genes to their children.

*It is true that brown eyes are dominant over blue eyes. Blue eye color is carried by a recessive gene.*

### CHROMOSOMAL AND GENETIC ABNORMALITIES

What happens when we do not have the normal complement of 46 chromosomes or when genes are defective? There are a number of diseases that reflect chromosomal or genetic abnormalities. Some chromosomal disorders reflect abnormalities in the autosomes (such as Down syndrome), while others reflect abnormalities in the sex chromosomes (as in XYY syndrome). Some genetic abnormalities, such as cystic fibrosis, are caused by a single pair of genes, while others are caused by complex combinations of genes. ***Multifactorial problems*** reflect a genetic predisposition and environmental contributors. Diabetes mellitus, epilepsy, and peptic ulcers are but a few examples of the many multifactorial problems people encounter. A number of chromosomal and genetic abnormalities are discussed below and summarized in Table 3.1.

***Multifactorial problems*** Problems that stem from the interaction of heredity and environmental factors.

**CHROMOSOMAL ABNORMALITIES** Occasionally, children do not have the normal complement of 46 chromosomes. Behavioral as well as physical abnormalities may then result. The risk of chromosomal abnormalities rises with the age of the parents (Hamamy et al., 1990).

***Down Syndrome*** In ***Down syndrome***, the 21st pair of chromosomes has an extra, or third, chromosome. Down syndrome is thought to be caused by faulty division of the 21st pair of chromosomes during meiosis. The extra chromosome is contributed by the mother in about 95 percent of cases (Antonarakis et al., 1991) and becomes increasingly likely as women age. Among mothers in their early 20s, Down syndrome occurs in about 1 birth in 1,500. By age 35, the figure rises to 1 birth in 350, and by age 45, to 1 birth in every 38 (Evans et al., 1989). The risk of Down syndrome also increases when the father is 50 years or older (Erickson & Bjerkedal, 1981).

***Down syndrome*** A chromosomal abnormality characterized by mental retardation and caused by an extra chromosome in the 21st pair.

The eyes of children with Down syndrome show a downward-sloping fold of skin at the inner corners. Children with Down syndrome also have characteristic round faces, protruding tongues, and broad, flat noses. Their motor development lags behind that of normal children, and they are moderately to severely mentally retarded. They often suffer from respiratory problems and heart malformations, problems that tend to claim their lives by middle age (Cicchetti & Beeghly, 1990).

The development and adjustment of children with Down syndrome are related to their acceptance by their families. Down-syndrome children reared in the home develop more rapidly and achieve higher levels of functioning than those reared in institutions (Spiker, 1990). Although the birth of a child with Down syndrome is usually traumatic for a family, in most cases the child gains acceptance and comes to provide the family with a source of pleasure (Gath, 1992; Shonkoff et al., 1992).

***Sex-Linked Chromosomal Abnormalities*** A number of disorders stem from abnormal numbers of sex chromosomes and are therefore said to be sex-linked. Most individuals with an abnormal number of sex chromosomes show reduced fertility and cannot reproduce.

Approximately 1 male in 700 has an extra Y chromosome, which is associated with the heightening of male secondary sex characteristics. XYY males are somewhat taller than average and develop heavier beards. They are often mildly retarded, particularly in language development. Despite previous speculations

FIGURE 3.5

**DOWN SYNDROME.** *The development and adjustment of children with Down syndrome are related to their acceptance by their families. Down-syndrome children reared at home develop more rapidly and achieve higher levels of functioning than those reared in institutions.*

**TABLE 3.1**

***CHROMOSOMAL AND GENETIC ABNORMALITIES***

| DISORDER | DESCRIPTION | INCIDENCE |
|---|---|---|
| CYSTIC FIBROSIS | A FATAL GENETIC DISEASE IN WHICH THE PANCREAS AND LUNGS BECOME CLOGGED WITH MUCUS, IMPAIRING THE PROCESSES OF RESPIRATION AND DIGESTION. | 1 IN 2,000 WHITES; 1 IN 20 WHITES IS A CARRIER. |
| DOWN SYNDROME | A CONDITION, CHARACTERIZED BY A THIRD CHROMOSOME ON THE 21ST PAIR, IN WHICH THE CHILD SHOWS A CHARACTERISTIC FOLD OF SKIN OVER THE EYE AND MENTAL RETARDATION. RISK INCREASES AS PARENTS INCREASE IN AGE. | 1 IN 800; 1 IN 350 FOR WOMEN OVER 35. |
| HEMOPHILIA | A SEX-LINKED DISORDER IN WHICH THE BLOOD FAILS TO CLOT PROPERLY. | 1 IN 10,000 MALES. |
| HUNTINGTON'S DISEASE | A FATAL NEUROLOGICAL DISORDER WITH ONSET IN MIDDLE ADULTHOOD. | 1 IN 18,000. |
| KLINEFELTER'S SYNDROME (XXY) | A SEX-CHROMOSOME DISORDER CAUSING MILD RETARDATION, INFERTILITY, AND LESSENING OF MALE SECONDARY SEX CHARACTERISTICS. | 1 IN 500 MALES. |
| NEURAL-TUBE DEFECTS | DISORDERS OF THE BRAIN OR SPINE, SUCH AS ANENCEPHALY, IN WHICH PART OF THE BRAIN IS MISSING, AND SPINA BIFIDA, IN WHICH PART OF THE SPINE IS EXPOSED OR MISSING. ANENCEPHALY IS FATAL SHORTLY AFTER BIRTH, BUT SOME SPINA BIFIDA VICTIMS SURVIVE FOR A NUMBER OF YEARS, ALBEIT WITH SEVERE HANDICAPS. | 1 IN 1,000. |

CONTINUED

about the behavior related to XYY syndrome, most individuals with XYY syndrome do not show records of aggressive criminal behavior (Graham, 1991).

About 1 male in 500 has ***Klinefelter's syndrome,*** which is caused by an extra X sex chromosome (XXY). XXY males produce less testosterone than normal males, and the secondary sex characteristics, such as deepening of the voice and a male pattern of bodily hair, do not develop. XXY males are infertile and usually have enlarged breasts and poor muscle development. They are usually mildly mentally retarded, particularly in language skills (Graham, 1991).

About 1 girl in 2,000 has a single X sex chromosome and as a result develops ***Turner's syndrome.*** The external genitals of girls with this disorder are normal, but their ovaries are poorly developed, and they produce reduced amounts of estrogen. Because of low estrogen production, they do not develop breasts or menstruate. Girls with this problem are shorter than average and infertile. They generally have normal intelligence except for deficits in spatial perception. In fact, their school performance often is above average (Hall et al., 1982; McCauley et al., 1987).

About 1 girl in 1,000 has XXX sex chromosomal structure. These girls are normal in appearance. However, they tend to show lower-than-average language skills and poorer memory for recent events, suggestive of mild mental retardation (Rovet, 1993).

***Klinefelter's syndrome*** A chromosomal disorder found among males that is caused by an extra X sex chromosome and characterized by infertility and mild mental retardation.

***Turner's syndrome*** A chromosomal disorder found among females that is caused by having a single X sex chromosome and characterized by infertility.

| DISORDER | DESCRIPTION | INCIDENCE |
|---|---|---|
| PHENYLKETO-NURIA (PKU) | A DISORDER IN WHICH CHILDREN CANNOT METABOLIZE PHENYLALANINE, WHICH BUILDS UP AND CAUSES MENTAL RETARDATION. DIAGNOSED AT BIRTH AND CONTROLLED BY DIET. | 1 IN 10,000; 1 IN 80 WHITES IS A CARRIER. |
| SICKLE-CELL ANEMIA | A BLOOD DISORDER THAT MOSTLY AFFLICTS AFRICAN AMERICANS. DEFORMED BLOOD CELLS OBSTRUCT SMALL BLOOD VESSELS, DECREASING THEIR CAPACITY TO CARRY OXYGEN AND HEIGHTENING THE RISK OF OCCASIONALLY FATAL INFECTIONS. | 1 IN 375 AFRICAN AMERICANS; 1 IN 10 AFRICAN AMERICANS AND 1 IN 20 HISPANICS IS A CARRIER. |
| TAY-SACHS DISEASE | A FATAL NEUROLOGICAL DISORDER THAT AFFLICTS JEWS OF EASTERN EUROPEAN ORIGIN. | 1 IN 3,000 JEWS OF EASTERN EUROPEAN ORIGIN; 1 IN 30 IN THIS GROUP IS A CARRIER. |
| THALASSEMIA (COOLEY'S ANEMIA) | A DISORDER PRIMARILY AFFLICTING THOSE OF MEDITERRANEAN ORIGIN THAT CAUSES WEAKNESS AND SUSCEPTIBILITY TO SOMETIMES FATAL INFECTIONS. | 1 IN 400 IN GREEK AMERICANS AND ITALIAN AMERICANS; 1 IN 10 IN THESE GROUPS IS A CARRIER. |
| TURNER'S SYNDROME | A SEX-CHROMOSOME DISORDER CAUSING SHORTNESS, INFERTILITY, AND DEFECTS IN SPATIAL PERCEPTION. | 1 IN 2,000 FEMALES. |
| XXX | A SEX-CHROMOSOME DISORDER CAUSING MILD RETARDATION. | 1 IN 1,000 FEMALES. |
| XYY | A SEX-CHROMOSOME DISORDER CAUSING MILD RETARDATION AND HEIGHTENING OF MALE SECONDARY SEX CHARACTERISTICS. | 1 IN 700 MALES. |

SOURCES: CUMMINGS, 1991; MCKUSICK, 1992.

**GENETIC ABNORMALITIES** A number of disorders have been attributed to defective genes.

***PKU*** The enzyme disorder ***phenylketonuria (PKU)*** is transmitted by a recessive gene and affects about 1 child in 10,000 (DeAngelis, 1993). Therefore, if both parents are carriers, PKU will be transmitted to one child in four (as in Figure 3.4). One child in four will *not* carry the recessive gene. The other two children in four will, like their parents, be carriers.

Children with PKU cannot metabolize the amino acid *phenylalanine.* As a consequence, it builds up in their bodies and damages the central nervous system. The results are mental retardation and emotional disturbance. We have no cure for PKU, but PKU can be detected in newborn children through blood or urine analysis. Children with PKU who are placed on diets low in phenylalanine within 3 to 6 weeks after birth develop normally. The diet prohibits all meat, poultry, fish, dairy products, beans, and nuts. Fruits, vegetables, and some starchy foods are allowed. Pediatricians recommend staying on the diet at least until adolescence, and some encourage staying on it for life (Hunt & Berry, 1993).

***Huntington's Disease*** ***Huntington's disease,*** the disease that afflicted folksinger Woody Guthrie, is a fatal progressive degenerative disorder and is a dominant trait. Physical symptoms include uncontrollable muscle movements. Psychological symptoms include loss of intellectual functioning and personality change. Because its onset is delayed until middle adulthood, many individuals

***Phenylketonuria (PKU)*** (fee-nill-key-tone-NEW-ree-uh) A genetic abnormality in which phenylalanine builds up and causes mental retardation.

***Huntington's disease*** A fatal genetic neurologic disorder whose onset is in middle age.

What hereditary diseases are associated with different ethnic backgrounds?

| Ethnic Background | Disease | Incidence |
|---|---|---|
| African American | Sickle-Cell Anemia | 1 in 375; 1 in 10 is a carrier |
| Hispanic | Sickle-Cell Anemia | 1 in 20 is a carrier |
| Jewish families of Eastern European Origin | Tay-Sachs | 1 in 3,000; 1 in 30 is a carrier |
| White American | Cystic Fibrosis | 1 in 2,000; 1 in 20 is a carrier |
| Greek American; Italian American | Thalassemia | 1 in 400; 1 in 10 is a carrier |

with the defect have borne children only to discover years later that they, and possibly half of their offspring, will inevitably develop it (Angier, 1993).

***Sickle-Cell Anemia*** ***Sickle-cell anemia*** is caused by a recessive gene. Sickle-cell anemia is most common among African Americans but also occurs in people from Central and South America, the Caribbean, the Mediterranean countries, and the Middle East (Leary, 1993b). Nearly 1 African American in 10 and 1 Hispanic American in 20 is a carrier. In sickle-cell anemia, red blood cells take on a sickle shape and clump together, obstructing small blood vessels and decreasing the oxygen supply. Results can include painful and swollen joints, jaundice, and potentially fatal conditions such as pneumonia and heart and kidney failure (Platt et al., 1991).

**TRUTH OR FICTION REVISITED**

*Sickle-cell anemia is, in fact, most prevalent among African Americans. There is also a relatively high incidence among Hispanic Americans.*

***Tay–Sachs Disease*** ***Tay–Sachs disease*** is a fatal degenerative disease of the central nervous system caused by a recessive gene. It is most prevalent among children in Jewish families of East European origin. About 1 in 30 U.S. Jews of East European background carries the recessive gene for the defect, and so the chance that a Jewish couple will both carry the gene is about 1 in 900. Victims of Tay–Sachs disease gradually lose muscle control. They become blind and deaf, retarded and paralyzed, and die by the age of 5.

***Cystic Fibrosis*** ***Cystic fibrosis,*** also caused by a recessive gene, is the most common fatal hereditary disease among whites. About 30,000 Americans have the disorder, but another 12 million (1 in every 20 people) are carriers. Children with the disease suffer from excessive production of thick mucus that clogs the pancreas and lungs. Most victims die of respiratory infections in their 20s (Angier, 1993; Graham, 1991).

***Sex-Linked Genetic Abnormalities*** Some genetic defects, such as ***hemophilia,*** are carried on only the X sex chromosome. For this reason, they are referred to as ***sex-linked.*** Those defects also involve recessive genes. Females, who have two X sex chromosomes, are less likely than males to show sex-linked disorders, since the genes that cause the disorder would have to be present on both of a female's sex chromosomes for the disorder to be expressed. Sex-linked diseases are more likely to afflict sons of female carriers, since they have only one X sex chromosome, which they inherit from their mothers. Queen Victoria was a carrier of hemophilia and transmitted the blood disorder to many of her children, who, in turn, carried it into a number of the ruling houses of Europe. For this reason, hemophilia has been referred to as the "royal disease."

One form of ***muscular dystrophy,*** Duchenne muscular dystrophy, is sex-linked. Muscular dystrophy is characterized by a weakening of the muscles that can lead to wasting away, inability to walk, and sometimes death. Other sex-linked abnormalities include diabetes, color blindness, and some types of night blindness.

***Sickle-cell anemia*** A genetic disorder that decreases the blood's capacity to carry oxygen.

***Tay–Sachs disease*** A fatal genetic neurological disorder.

***Cystic fibrosis*** A fatal genetic disorder in which mucus obstructs the lungs and pancreas.

***Hemophilia*** A genetic disorder in which blood does not clot properly.

***Sex-linked genetic abnormalities*** Abnormalities due to genes that are found on the X sex chromosome. They are more likely to be shown by male offspring (who do not have an opposing gene from a second X chromosome) than by female offspring.

***Muscular dystrophy*** (DISS-tro-fee) A chronic disease characterized by a progressive wasting away of the muscles.

## GENETIC COUNSELING AND PRENATAL TESTING

It is now possible to detect the genetic abnormalities responsible for hundreds of diseases (Schmeck, 1990). In an effort to help parents avert these predictable tragedies, ***genetic counseling*** is becoming widely used. In this procedure, information about a couple's genetic background is compiled to determine the possibility that their union may result in genetically defective children. Some couples facing a high risk of passing along genetic defects to their children elect to adopt children rather than have their own.

***Genetic counseling*** Advice concerning the probabilities that a couple's children will show genetic abnormalities.

***Amniocentesis*** (AM-nee-oh-sen-TEE-sis) A procedure for drawing and examining fetal cells sloughed off into amniotic fluid to determine the presence of various disorders.

***Spina bifida*** A neural tube defect that causes abnormalities of the brain and spine.

**AMNIOCENTESIS** Pregnant women may also confirm the presence of certain genetic and chromosomal abnormalities in their unborn children through ***amniocentesis,*** a procedure carried out about 14 to 16 weeks after conception. Fluid is withdrawn by a syringe from the amniotic sac (or "bag of waters") containing the fetus. Sloughed-off fetal cells are then separated from amniotic fluid, grown in a culture, and examined microscopically for genetic abnormalities.

Amniocentesis is commonly carried out with women who become pregnant after the age of 35, since the chances of Down syndrome increase dramatically as women approach or pass the age of 40 (Gilbert, 1993). But women carrying the children of aging fathers may also wish to have amniocentesis. Amniocentesis can detect the presence of well over 100 chromosomal and genetic abnormalities, including sickle-cell anemia, Tay–Sachs disease, ***spina bifida,*** muscular dystrophy, and Rh incompatibility in the fetus (Gilbert, 1993). Women who (or whose partners) carry or have a family history of any of these disorders are advised to have amniocentesis performed. If the test reveals the presence of a serious disorder, the parents may decide to abort the fetus. Or, they may decide to continue the pregnancy and prepare themselves to raise a child who has special needs.

Amniocentesis also permits parents to learn the gender of their unborn child through examination of the sex chromosomes. But because the test carries some risk of miscarriage (in about 1 in 100 who undergo the procedure), it is considered unwise to have amniocentesis done solely for this purpose. If you were having amniocentesis, would you want to know the gender of your child, or would you prefer to wait?

FIGURE 3.6

***RECEIVING GENETIC COUNSELING.*** *Genetic counseling helps potential parents weigh the probabilities that their children will bear genetic defects. These defects can frequently be detected by amniocentesis or chorionic villus sampling, ultrasound, blood test, or fetoscopy.*

*It is possible to learn the gender of one's child prior to birth. Amniocentesis and ultrasound are two of the methods that can provide this information.*

***Chorionic villus sampling*** (CORE-ee-ON-ick Vill-iss) A method for the prenatal detection of genetic abnormalities that samples the membrane enveloping the amniotic sac and fetus.

**CHORIONIC VILLUS SAMPLING** ***Chorionic villus sampling*** (CVS) is similar to amniocentesis but offers the advantage of diagnosing fetal abnormalities much earlier in pregnancy. CVS is carried out during the 9th or 10th week of pregnancy. A small syringe is inserted through the vagina into the uterus. The syringe gently sucks out a few of the threadlike projections (villi) from the outer membrane that envelops the amniotic sac and fetus. Results are available within days of the procedure. However, CVS carries a slightly greater risk of spontaneous abortion than does amniocentesis (Gilbert, 1993; Rosenthal, 1991). Recent studies also suggest that somewhere between 1 in 200 to 1 in 1,000 babies born to women who have CVS may have birth defects involving missing or stubby fingers and toes (Kolata, 1992d; "Study Finds," 1994), so the technique remains controversial.

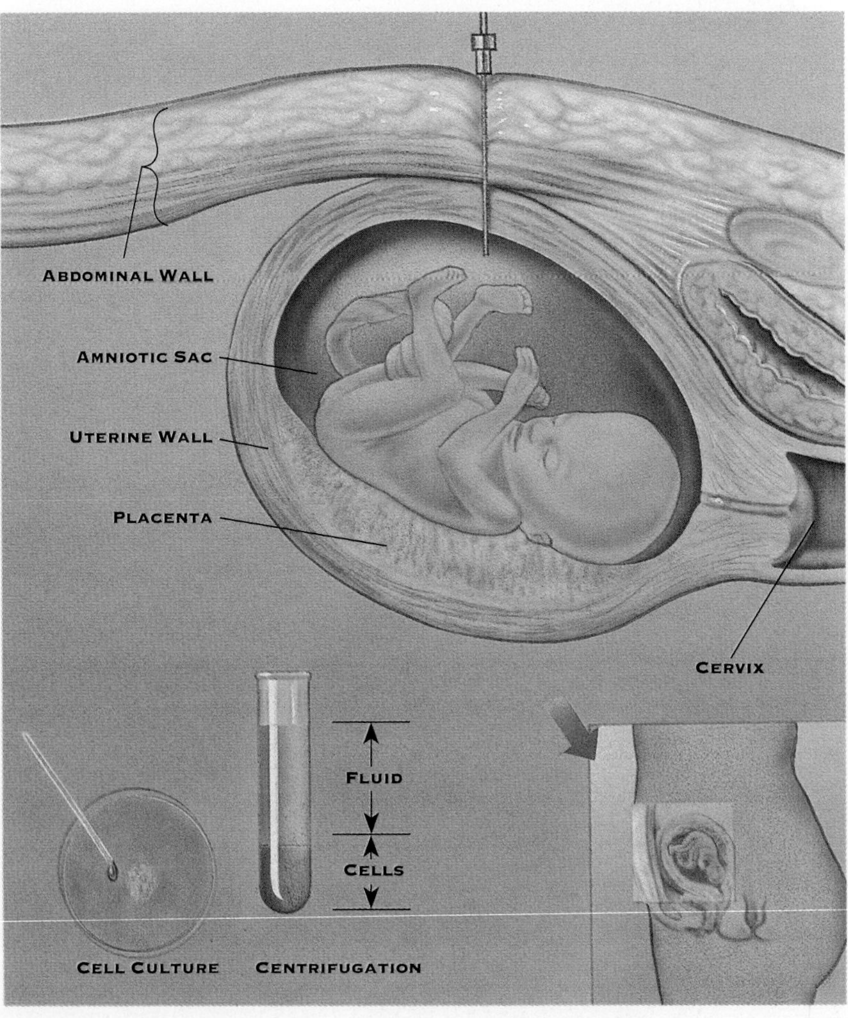


FIGURE 3.7

**AMNIOCENTESIS.** *Amniocentesis allows prenatal identification of certain genetic and chromosomal disorders by examining genetic material sloughed off by the fetus into amniotic fluid. Amniocentesis also allows parents to learn the gender of their unborn child. Would you want to know?*

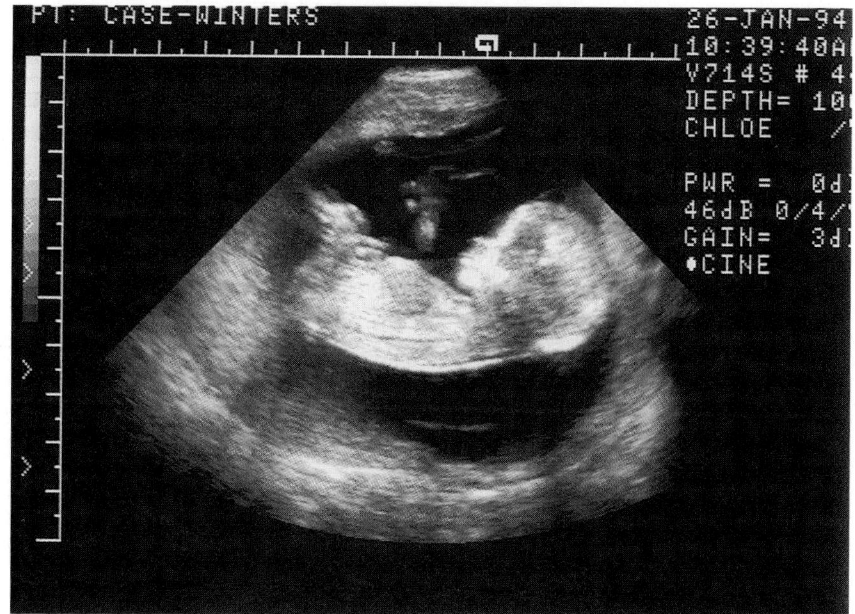


**FIGURE 3.8**

***SONOGRAM OF A 5-MONTH-OLD FETUS.*** *In the ultrasound technique, soundwaves are bounced off the fetus and provide a picture called a* sonogram *that enables professionals to detect various abnormalities.*

**ULTRASOUND** Another common method of prenatal testing is the use of ***ultrasound*** to form a picture of the fetus. The picture is referred to as a ***sonogram.*** Ultrasound is so high in pitch that it cannot be detected by the human ear. However, it can be bounced off the fetus in the same way that radar is bounced off objects to form a picture of the object (see Figure 3.8).

Ultrasound is used as an adjunct to amniocentesis or CVS in order to better determine the position of the fetus. In this way the physician performing the procedure can make sure the needle enters the sac surrounding the fetus, and not the fetus itself. Ultrasound is also employed to locate fetal structures when intrauterine transfusions are necessary for the survival of a fetus with Rh disease.

Ultrasound also is used to track the growth of the fetus, to determine fetal age and gender, and to detect multiple pregnancies and structural abnormalities. While ultrasound is beneficial for pregnant women at risk of serious medical problems, it does not improve birth outcomes for women with low-risk pregnancies (Ewigman et al., 1993). The American College of Obstetricians and Gynecologists therefore recommends that ultrasound should not be administered routinely (Leary, 1993c). No ill effects have yet been detected from normal levels of ultrasound, however (Brody, 1990d).

**BLOOD TESTS** Parental blood tests can reveal the presence of recessive genes for a variety of disorders, such as sickle-cell anemia, Tay–Sachs disease, and cystic fibrosis (Schmeck, 1990). When both parents carry genes for these disorders, the disorders can be detected in the fetus by means of amniocentesis or CVS.

Another kind of blood test, the ***alpha-fetoprotein assay,*** is used to detect neural tube defects such as spina bifida and certain chromosome abnormalities (Cunningham & Gilstrap, 1991; Hobbins, 1991). Neural tube defects cause an elevation in the alpha-fetoprotein (AFP) level in the mother's blood. Elevated AFP levels also are associated with increased risk of fetal death (Waller et al., 1991). However, the mother's AFP level also varies with other factors. For this reason, the diagnosis of neural tube defect is confirmed by other methods of observation, such as amniocentesis, ultrasound or ***fetoscopy.***

***Ultrasound*** Sound waves too high in pitch to be sensed by the human ear.

***Sonogram*** A procedure for using ultrasonic sound waves to create a picture of an embryo or fetus.

***Alpha-fetoprotein assay*** A blood test that assesses the mother's blood level of alpha-fetoprotein, a substance that is linked with fetal neural-tube defects.

***Fetoscopy*** (fee-TOSS-co-pea) Surgical insertion of a narrow tube into the uterus in order to examine the fetus.

***In vitro fertilization*** (VEE-tro) Fertilization of an ovum in a laboratory dish.

**FETOSCOPY** In fetoscopy, a narrow tube is surgically inserted through the abdomen into the uterus to allow examination of the fetus during the second and third trimesters of pregnancy. A small lens and a light can be attached to the fetoscope, permitting visual examination. A small needle may also be attached, which enables the direct withdrawal of a blood sample from the fetus. Fetoscopy, like CVS, is riskier than amniocentesis and its use is more limited. A new experimental technique called *embryoscopy* appears to be safer and allows visual examination of the fetus and embryo as early as the first trimester (Kolata, 1993).

In the future, we may be able to modify problem genes while babies are developing within the uterus (see Developing Today: Genetic Engineering). Researchers now are able to identify genetic defects such as cystic fibrosis in embryos only a few days old. In one landmark study, embryos obtained by ***in vitro fertilization*** were examined for cystic fibrosis. Both parents were carriers of the disease. Only healthy embryos were implanted in the mother's uterus, and a healthy child was born (Handyside et al., 1992). But this technique is still in the experimental stage. For the time being, families whose unborn children face serious genetic disorders can only choose whether or not to have an abortion, which raises painful personal dilemmas for some couples.

## *Developing Today*

### GENETIC ENGINEERING

Someday, genetic engineering may provide couples with genetically abnormal embryos the possibility of correcting the problem in the uterus. In genetic engineering, the genetic structures of organisms are changed by direct manipulation of their cells. Even as you read these words, patents are pending on new life forms—mostly microscopic—that biologists and corporations hope will be marketable.

Innovations in genetic engineering have already given us screening for fatal hereditary diseases such as Huntington's disease and cystic fibrosis (Rossiter & Caskey, 1993; Wexler, 1993). The following are in various stages of development:

- Vaccines for diseases such as hepatitis and herpes.
- Ways of detecting predispositions for disorders such as cancer or manic-depression by studying a newborn's (or fetus's) genetic code (Annas, 1993).
- Modification of the genetic codes of fetuses or children to prevent or cure disease. For example, a 4-year-old girl recently was the first to get new genes in an effort to cure a severe inherited immune deficiency disorder. Prior to treatment, the girl and her family rarely left home for fear of bringing back even a minor infection, which could have been life-threatening. Within a year after receiving gene therapy, the child's immune system responded so well that she could swim, take dancing lessons, and even go to school (Greenough, 1993).
- Insertion of foreign genes into human lymphocytes (white blood cells) to enhance the cells' ability to combat cancer and other diseases (Angier, 1992b; Rossiter & Caskey, 1993).
- Creation of wonder drugs from DNA.

Many of the ways in which science has permitted us to intervene in the reproductive process have engendered heated controversy. Some people, including a number of religious leaders, fear that we are converting natural biological processes into a calamity that will have profound moral consequences and change the face of our species (and others) in ways that we cannot foresee. Other people fear the invention of various kinds of biological monsters or disease agents—most of them microscopic—that we may not be able to control.

What is there to conclude? Ugly scenarios are indeed possible, but so are splendid, health-enhancing outcomes. As scientists, we believe there is no such thing as bad knowledge—only bad use of knowledge. As citizens, it is our duty to keep abreast of technical innovations and to ensure that their applications are beneficial.

## Heredity and Environment

The sets of traits that we inherit from our parents are referred to as our ***genotypes.*** But none of us is the result of heredity, or genotype, alone. Heredity provides the biological basis for a ***reaction range*** in the expression of traits. Our inherited traits can vary in expression, depending on environmental conditions. In addition to inheritance, the expression of our traits is also influenced by nutrition, learning, exercise, and—unfortunately—accident and illness. A potential Shakespeare who is reared in an impoverished neighborhood and never taught to read or write is unlikely to create a *Hamlet.* Thus, behavior appears to represent the interaction between heredity and environment. Our actual sets of characteristics or behaviors at any point in time are referred to as our ***phenotypes,*** the product of genetic and environmental influences.

Researchers have developed a number of strategies to help determine the relative effects of heredity and environment on development. Let us briefly examine some of these methods:

### *Consanguinity Studies*

Researchers study the distribution of a particular behavior pattern among relatives who differ in degree of genetic closeness. The more closely people are related, the more genes they have in common. Parents and children have a 50 percent overlap in their genetic endowments, and so do siblings (brothers and sisters), on average. Aunts and uncles have a 25 percent overlap with nieces and nephews, and so do grandparents with their grandchildren. First cousins share 12.5 percent of their genetic endowment. So if genes are implicated in a behavior pattern, people who are more closely related should be more likely to share the pattern.

### *Twin Studies*

Remember that monozygotic (MZ) twins share 100 percent of their genes, while dizygotic (DZ) twins have only a 50 percent overlap, just as other siblings do. If MZ twins show greater similarity on some behavior than DZ twins, a genetic basis for the behavior is indicated.

MZ twins resemble each other more closely than DZ twins on a number of physical and psychological traits. MZ twins look alike and are closer in height and weight than DZ twins. This finding holds even when the identical twins are reared apart and the fraternal twins are reared together (Stunkard et al., 1990). Other physical similarities between pairs of MZ twins may be more subtle, but they are also strong. For example, research shows that MZ twin sisters begin to menstruate about one to two months apart, whereas DZ twins begin to menstruate about a year apart. MZ twins are more alike than DZ twins in their blood pressure, brain wave patterns and even in their speech patterns, gestures, and mannerisms (Lykken et al., 1992). MZ twins resemble one another more strongly than DZ twins in intelligence and in personality traits such as sociability, anxiety, friendliness, and conformity (Loehlin, 1992). Also, MZ twins are more likely than DZ twins to share psychological disorders such as ***autism,*** depression, schizophrenia, and even vulnerability to alcoholism (Plomin & McClearn, 1993; McGue et al., 1992). In one study on autism, the ***concordance*** rate for MZ twins was 96 percent. The concordance rate for DZ twins was only 24 percent (Ritvo et al., 1985).

***Genotype*** The genetic form or constitution of a person as determined by heredity.

***Reaction range*** The variability in the expression of inherited traits as they are influenced by environmental factors.

***Phenotype*** The actual form or constitution of a person as determined by heredity and environmental factors.

***Autism*** A developmental disorder characterized by failure to relate to others, communication problems, intolerance of change, and ritualistic behavior (see Chapter 7).

***Concordance*** Agreement.

## TRUTH OR FICTION REVISITED

*Identical twins are, in fact, more likely than fraternal twins to share disorders such as schizophrenia and vulnerability to alcoholism. Identical twins are very much alike in certain behavior patterns as well as in their physical traits.*

Of course, twin studies are not perfect. MZ twins may resemble each other more closely than DZ twins partly because they are treated more similarly. MZ twins frequently are dressed identically, and parents sometimes have difficulty telling them apart (Vandell, 1990).

One way to get around this difficulty is to find and compare MZ twins who were reared in different homes. Any similarities between MZ twins reared apart cannot be explained by a shared home environment and would appear to be largely a result of heredity. In the fascinating Minnesota Study of Twins Reared Apart (T. J. Bouchard et al., 1990; Lykken et al., 1992), researchers have been measuring the physiological and psychological characteristics of 56 sets of MZ adult twins who were separated in infancy and reared in different homes. The MZ twins reared apart are about as similar as MZ twins reared together on a variety of measures of intelligence, personality, temperament, occupational and leisure-time interests, and social attitudes. These traits thus would appear to have a genetic underpinning.

### ADOPTION STUDIES

Adoption studies in which children are separated from their natural parents at an early age and reared by adoptive parents provide special opportunities for sorting out nature and nurture. As we shall see in discussions of the origins of intelligence (Chapter 12) and of various problem behaviors (Chapters 11 and 14), psychologists look for the relative similarities between children and their

FIGURE 3.9

**IDENTICAL TRIPLETS REARED APART.** *Reunited at the age of 19, Robert Shafran, David Kellman, and Eddie Galland not only are physically alike but have many similar mannerisms and interests.*

adoptive and natural parents. When children who are reared by adoptive parents are nonetheless more similar to their natural parents in a trait, a powerful argument is made for a genetic role in the appearance of that trait.

***Endometrium*** The inner lining of the uterus.

## Conception: Against All Odds

Conception is the union of an ovum and a sperm cell. Conception, from one perspective, is the beginning of a new human life. But conception is also the end of a fantastic voyage in which one of several hundred thousand ova produced by the woman unites with one of several hundred million sperm produced by the man in the average ejaculate.

### *Ova*

Although women at birth already contain their 400,000 ova, the ova are immature in form. The ovaries also produce the female hormones estrogen and progesterone. At puberty, in response to hormonal command, some ova begin to mature. Each month, one egg (occasionally more than one) is released from its ovarian follicle about midway during the menstrual cycle and enters a nearby Fallopian tube. It might take 3 to 4 days for an egg to be propelled by small, hairlike stuctures called *cilia* and, perhaps, by contractions in the wall of the tube, the few inches to the uterus. Unlike sperm, eggs do not propel themselves.

If the egg is not fertilized, it is discharged through the uterus and the vagina—sloughed off, along with the ***endometrium*** that had formed to support an embryo, in the menstrual flow. During a woman's reproductive years, only about 400 ova (that is, 1 in 1,000) will ripen and be released. How these ova are selected is a mystery.

In an early stage of development, egg cells contain 46 chromosomes. Each developing egg cell contains two X sex chromosomes. After meiosis, each ovum contains 23 chromosomes, one of which is an X sex chromosome.

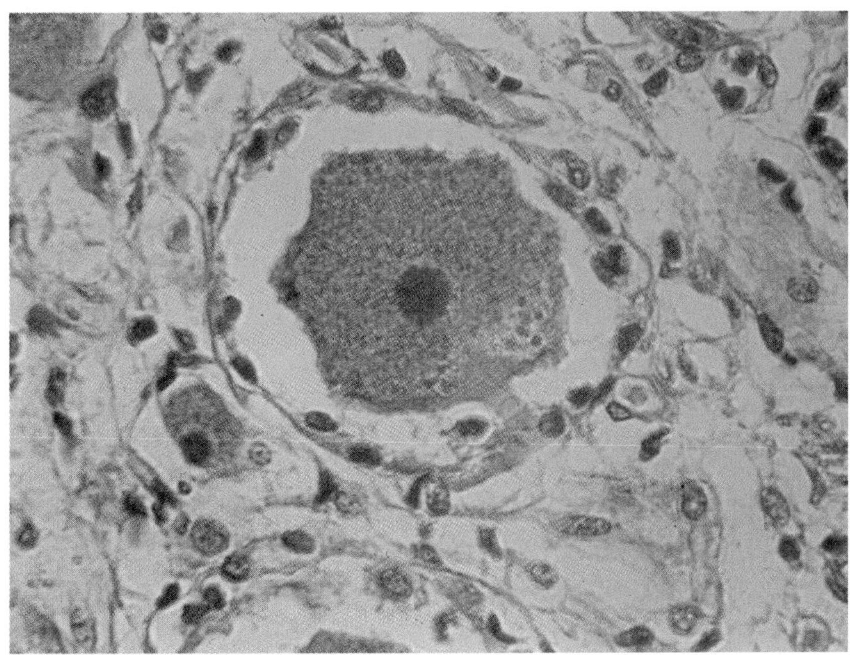

FIGURE 3.10

***A Ripening Ovum in an Ovarian Follicle.*** *At puberty, some ova begin to mature. Each month one egg (occasionally more than one) is released from its ovarian follicle and enters a Fallopian tube.*

***Spontaneous abortion*** Unpremeditated, accidental abortion.

Ova are much larger than sperm. (The chicken egg and the 6-inch ostrich egg are each just *one cell.*) Human ova are barely visible to the eye, but their bulk is still thousands of times larger than that of sperm cells.

### *SPERM CELLS*

Sperm cells develop through several stages. In one early stage, like ova, they each contain 46 chromosomes, including one X and one Y sex chromosome. After meiosis, each sperm has 23 chromosomes. Half have X sex chromosomes, and the other half have Y sex chromosomes. Each sperm cell is about 1/500th of an inch long, one of the smallest types of cells in the body. Sperm with Y sex chromosomes appear to swim faster than sperm with X sex chromosomes. This is one of the reasons why between 120 and 150 boys are conceived for every 100 girls. Male fetuses suffer a higher rate of ***spontaneous abortion*** than females, however, often during the first month of pregnancy. At birth, boys outnumber girls by a ratio of only 105 to 100 (Gualtieri & Hicks, 1985). Boys also have a higher incidence of infant mortality, which further equalizes the numbers of girls and boys in a population by the time they show an interest in pairing off.

The 200 to 400 million sperm in an average ejaculate may seem a wasteful investment since only one can fertilize an ovum. But only 1 in 1,000 will ever arrive in the vicinity of an ovum. Millions deposited in the vagina simply flow out of the woman's body because of gravity, unless she remains prone for quite some time. Normal vaginal acidity kills many more. Many surviving sperm swim against the current of fluid coming from the cervix (see Figure 3.11).

Surviving sperm may reach the Fallopian tubes 60–90 minutes after ejaculation. About half the sperm enter the wrong tube—that is, the one without the egg. Perhaps 2,000 enter the right tube. Fewer still manage to swim the final two inches against the currents generated by the cilia that line the tube. Recent research suggests that the sperm cells are attracted by a compound secreted by the ovum (Angier, 1992a).

Of all the sperm swarming around the egg, only one enters (see Figure 3.12). Its "selection" is another biological mystery. Other sperm are unable to enter. The chromosomes from the sperm cell line up across from the corresponding chromosomes in the egg cell. Conception finally occurs as the chromosomes combine to form 23 new pairs with a unique set of genetic instructions.

FIGURE 3.11

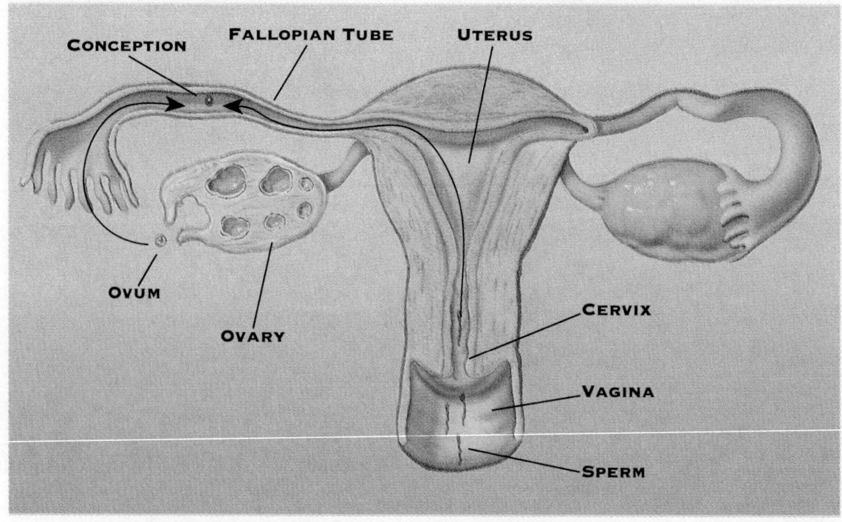


***FEMALE REPRODUCTIVE ORGANS.*** *Conception is something of an obstacle course. Sperm must survive the pull of gravity, vaginal acidity, risk winding up in the wrong Fallopian tube, and surmount other hurdles before they reach the ovum. (Source: Moore, 1989).*

## Other Ways to Conceive

For couples who want children, few problems are more frustrating than inability to conceive. Physicians often recommend that couples try to conceive on their own for 6 months before seeking medical assistance. The term *infertility* usually is not applied until the couple has failed to conceive for a year.

### *Infertility Problems*

At least 10 percent of U.S. couples has fertility problems (Hopkins, 1992). In about 4 of 10 cases, the problem lies with the man. Fertility problems in the male include (a) low sperm count, (b) irregularly shaped sperm, (c) low sperm ***motility,*** (d) infectious diseases, and (e) direct trauma to the testes (Rathus et al., 1993). Low (or zero) sperm count is the most common infertility problem among men.

Women may be infertile because of (a) failure to ovulate, (b) infections, (c) ***endometriosis,*** and (d) obstructions or malfunctions in the reproductive tract (Rathus et al., 1993). The most frequent infertility problem in women, failure to ovulate, may stem from causes such as hormonal irregularities, malnutrition, and stress.

Local infections may scar the Fallopian tubes and other organs, impeding the passage of sperm or ova. Such infections include ***pelvic inflammatory disease (PID)***—a term that refers to several diseases caused by bacteria and viruses, such as the sexually transmitted disease gonorrhea.

In endometriosis, cells break away from the uterine lining and grow elsewhere. They can block the Fallopian tubes or interfere with conception for reasons that are not well understood. Hormone treatments and surgery are sometimes successful in reducing endometriosis to the point where women can conceive.

Let us now consider some of the methods that have been developed in recent years to help infertile couples bear children.

***Motility*** Self-propulsion.

***Endometriosis*** Inflammation of endometrial tissue sloughed off into the abdominal cavity rather than out of the body during menstruation and characterized by abdominal pain and, sometimes, infertility.

***Pelvic inflammatory disease (PID)*** Any of a number of diseases that infect the abdominal region, impairing fertility.

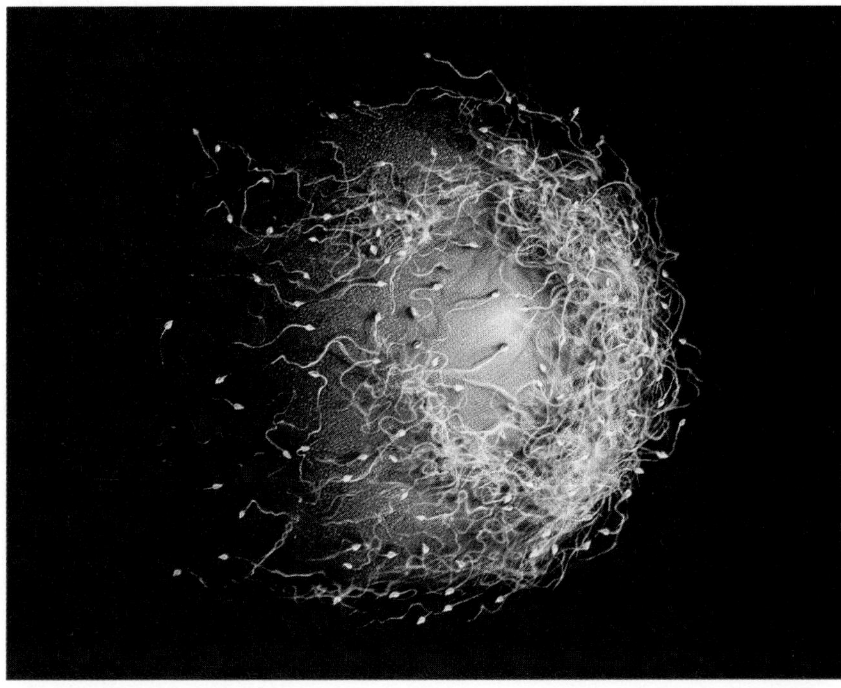

**Figure 3.12**

***Human Sperm Swarming Around an Ovum in a Fallopian Tube.*** *Fertilization normally occurs in a Fallopian tube, not in the uterus. Thousands of sperm may wind up in the vicinity of an ovum, but only one fertilizes it. How this sperm cell is "selected" remains one of the mysteries of nature.*

### ARTIFICIAL INSEMINATION

Multiple ejaculations of men with low sperm counts can be collected and quick-frozen. The sperm can then be injected into the woman's uterus at the time of ovulation. This is one ***artificial insemination*** procedure. Sperm from men with low sperm motility can also be injected into their partners' uteruses, so that the sperm can begin their journey closer to the Fallopian tubes. When a man is completely infertile or has an extremely low sperm count, his partner can be artificially inseminated with the sperm of a donor who resembles the man in physical traits. The child then bears the genes of one of the parents, the mother.

### IN VITRO FERTILIZATION

Louise Brown, the world's first "test-tube baby," was born in England in 1978 after having been conceived by means of *in vitro fertilization* (IVF). In this method, which may be used when the Fallopian tubes are blocked, mature ova are surgically removed from the mother's ovary and placed in a laboratory dish along with the father's sperm. Fertilized ova are then injected into the mother's uterus to become implanted in the uterine wall. A variation known as ***donor IVF*** can be used when the intended mother does not produce ova. An ovum from another women is fertilized and injected into the uterus of the mother-to-be (Schulman & Bustillo, 1989).

At this time, in vitro fertilization remains costly—between $7,000 and $11,000 per try. It can take several tries to achieve a pregnancy, since only about 15 to 20 percent of attempts lead to births (Miller, 1992).

### EMBRYONIC TRANSPLANT

A related method, ***embryonic transplant,*** involves moving the embryo into a host uterus (Schwartz, 1991). This procedure is used when a woman cannot produce ova. Another woman is artificially inseminated with sperm from the infertile woman's husband. After a few days, the embryo is removed and transferred to the wife's uterus.

Sometimes, a woman can produce ova but cannot carry a pregnancy to term. In this case, her ova are fertilized by her husband's sperm by means of the IVF procedure. The fertilized egg is then implanted in the uterus of another woman, who carries the baby to term. This was the procedure followed in the publicized case of 53-year-old Geraldine Wesolowski, who gave birth in December 1992 to her own grandson. She agreed to carry the child for her daughter-in-law, whose uterus had been surgically removed (Gruson, 1993).

***Artificial insemination*** Injection of sperm into the uterus to fertilize an ovum.

***Donor IVF*** The transfer of a donor's ovum, fertilized in a laboratory dish, to the uterus of another woman.

***Embryonic transplant*** The transfer of an embryo from the uterus of one woman to that of another.

**TRUTH OR FICTION REVISITED**

*It is true that developing embryos have been successfully transferred from the uterus of one woman to the uterus of another. Embryonic transplant is just one of several recent advances in reproductive technology.*

### *Surrogate Mothers*

In recent years, stories about ***surrogate mothers*** have filled the headlines. Surrogate mothers bring newly conceived babies to term for other women who are infertile. (The word *surrogate* means "substitute".) Surrogate mothers are artificially inseminated by the husbands of infertile women. The baby thus carries the genes of the father. Surrogate mothers are usually paid fees ranging from

***Surrogate mother*** A woman who is artificially inseminated and carries to term a child who is then given to another woman, typically the spouse of the sperm donor.

## *Developing Today*

### *Surrogate Motherhood: Who is the Real Mother?*

The "Baby M" case caused a great deal of controversy in the late 1980s. Although there had been several hundred earlier cases of surrogate motherhood, this was the first to attract widespread public attention, largely because the surrogate mother changed her mind. The individuals in this drama were a married couple, Elizabeth and William Stern; the surrogate mother, Mary Beth Whitehead; and Baby M (Melissa Stern). Elizabeth Stern had multiple sclerosis, which could have been worsened by pregnancy. An infertility clinic arranged a contact with the prospective surrogate mother, Mary Beth Whitehead. A contract was signed, specifying payment after the birth and relinquishment of the baby. Whitehead first gave up Baby M, then requested the baby back for a few days. She fled to another state with Baby M, who was recovered after 3 months. The Sterns received legal custody, but Whitehead was given visitation rights (Schwartz, 1991).

This case makes us ponder the question of who a baby's real mother is—the surrogate mother or the wife of the man who fathers the baby? What does it mean to be a mother? In the biological sense, does not being a mother begin with the contribution of an ovum and proceed with carrying a child to term? But in a psychological sense, does not wanting a child and doing everything one can to obtain and nurture a child constitute motherly behavior? Does motherly behavior make one a mother? Millions of adoptive parents would argue that it most certainly does.

Some social critics also argue that surrogate motherhood is one more instance of exploitation of women, especially poor women. Affluent infertile couples are viewed as hiring the body of a woman, a practice that some find uncomfortably reminiscent of prostitution (Schwartz, 1991). Yet, some surrogate mothers derive an immense satisfaction from the altruistic act of giving a child to a couple who cannot have one.

**Figure 3.13 Who Is the Real Mother?** *In cases that might have tried the wisdom of Solomon, courts have recently dealt with suits by surrogate mothers for custody of their children. Here, Mary Beth Whitehead, a principal in the "Baby M" case, is surrounded by supporters.*

Under those circumstances, can we say that the surrogate is being exploited?

And what about the young college women who offer to sell their eggs to infertile couples for use in donor IVF procedures (Kolata, 1991)? Even though they will not bear the baby during pregnancy, can they later claim legal rights to the child on the basis of their genetic contribution?

Many ethical, emotional, and legal issues remain unresolved. In your opinion, how far should medical science be allowed to go in making reproductive alternatives available to infertile couples?

## Focus on Research

### *Selecting the Gender of Your Child: Fantasy or Reality?*

What would happen if we could select the gender of our children? Would we predominantly select boys or girls? Would it all balance out in the end? Let us look at the technology that makes gender selection possible and then consider some of the implications.

**Shettles' Approach** Landrum Shettles (1982) notes that sperm bearing the Y sex chromosome are smaller than those bearing the X sex chromosome and are faster swimmers. But sperm with the X sex chromosome are more durable. From these assumptions, Shettles and other researchers derive a number of strategies for selecting the gender of one's children.

To increase the chances of having a girl, (a) the couple should engage in sexual intercourse two days (or slightly more) before ovulation; (b) the woman should make the vagina less hospitable to Y-bearing sperm by douching with 2 tablespoons of vinegar per quart of warm water to raise vaginal acidity before intercourse; (c) the woman should avoid orgasm on the (debatable) assumption that orgasm facilitates the journey of sperm; and (d) the man should ejaculate with shallow penetration.

To increase the chances of having a boy, (a) the man should not ejaculate for several days preceding his partner's expected time of ovulation; (b) the couple should engage in sexual intercourse on the day of ovulation; (c) the man should penetrate deeply at the moment of ejaculation; and (d) the woman should make the vagina more hospitable to Y-bearing sperm by douching with 2 tablespoons of baking soda per quart of warm water before intercourse. This will lower vaginal acidity.

A combination of these methods has been asserted to result in the conception of a child of the desired sex in about 80 percent of cases, but many observers regard these figures as exaggerated (Carson, 1988).

**Sperm-Separation Procedures** Several sperm-separation procedures are now in use (Jancin, 1988). One is based on the swimming rates of X- and Y-bearing sperm. In this method, designed to maximize the chances of conceiving a boy, semen is placed at the top of a test tube containing albumin. Albumin, a thick liquid protein similar to egg white, impedes the progress of X-bearing sperm more than that of the faster swimming Y-bearing sperm. The Y-bearing sperm move to the bottom more rapidly than the X-bearing sperm. The sperm at the bottom of the tube are collected and used in artificial insemination. This method reportedly has led to conception of boys 75 percent of the time, as compared with the usual 53 percent (Glass & Ericsson, 1982). Another method, pioneered in Japan, separates Y- from X-bearing sperm on the basis of the differences in electrical charges

---

$10,000 to $20,000 and sign agreements to surrender the baby. (These contracts have been annulled in some states, however, so that surrogate mothers cannot be forced to hand over their babies.)

Biologically, surrogate motherhood might seem the mirror image of the more common artificial insemination technique in which a fertile woman is artificially inseminated with sperm from a donor. But the methods are psychologically very different. For example, sperm donors usually do not know the identity of the women who have received their sperm or follow the child's prenatal development. Surrogate mothers, however, are involved throughout the course of prenatal development.

**Thinking About Development**

Who is the baby's real mother—the surrogate mother or the wife of the man who fathers the baby?

Ethical and legal dilemmas revolve around the fact that surrogate mothers have a genetic link to the babies they conceive. If they change their minds and do not want to hand the babies over to the contractual parents, there can be legal struggles, as in the publicized "Baby M" case (Schwartz, 1991). This case, and some of the legal and ethical dilemmas it raises, are discussed further in the Developing Today on surrogate motherhood.

Just as new technologies are enhancing the chances for infertile couples to become parents, new methods seem to be leading to the day when we can preselect the gender of our children. For a discussion of these methods and the issues involved, see Focus on Research.

*continued*

on the two types. Sperm-separation approaches reportedly result in success rates of about 80 percent (Carson, 1988).

**Culture and Development: Selecting the Gender of One's Child** Gender preference research done in the United States over the last 60 years shows that men have a moderate preference for a male. Women have a weaker male preference (Pooler, 1991). A preference for male children is found in most other countries as well

Consider the example of China. Chinese scientists note that the preference for boys is jeopardizing China's family-planning goal of one child per family. The preference stems from the belief that sons can do more in the fields and the tradition that sons provide for aging parents. Thus, it is considered a misfortune for a family to be without a male child (Hu, 1988; Kristof, 1993b). Given the prejudice against girls, what might happen if Chinese couples could choose the gender of their children but remained pressured to have only one child? Would China's population problems be eliminated in a generation? Would sufficient numbers of girls be born to stabilize the population?

A form of "family planning" *after birth* may already be taking place in China and other nations (Kristof, 1993a,b; WuDunn, 1991). A 1990 census in China raises suspicions that 8 percent of infant girls who were born in China are "missing." This amounts to 900,000 missing girls per year (Kristof, 1993a). Some of these infant girls may have been killed at birth by midwives on the orders of parents who desire to have sons. Some have been abandoned or given up for adoption (Porter, 1993; WuDunn, 1991). Others are being reared secretly by parents who seek to evade the one-child-per-family rule. Most Chinese deny that female infanticide is a common practice, but Kristof (1993a) reports that in rural areas, some newborn girls are drowned by midwives who keep a bucket by the mother's side for this purpose.

Many nations other than China have traditionally valued sons more than daughters. Based on the usual male-to-female birth ratio, Kristof (1991) estimates that nearly 23 million women are "missing" in India, 3 million in Pakistan, 1.6 million in Bangladesh, 600,000 in Egypt, and 200,000 in Nepal. The prevalence of infanticide is unknown, but in many cases baby girls may die at a young age from various kinds of neglect. For example, an infant daughter with diarrhea may be ignored, whereas the same problem in a boy is viewed as a crisis that requires medical help. When food is scarce in a poor family, boys may receive more than their fair share.

In recent years, technology has provided parents with yet another gender selection option: the use of amniocentesis or ultrasound. In many parts of India and China, these tests are widely used to determine the gender of the child. If it is a female, it is almost always aborted (Gargan, 1991; Kristof, 1993a,b).

Given the preference for boys in many cultures, the proportion of male births might increase dramatically if gender selection techniques were even more widely available. For this reason, social critics brand gender selection technology as "stupendously sexist" (Powledge, 1981).

## Stages of Prenatal Development

The months following conception are eventful, indeed. We can date pregnancy from the onset of the last menstrual period before conception, which makes the normal gestation period 280 days. We can also date pregnancy from the assumed date of fertilization, which normally occurs 2 weeks after the beginning of the woman's last menstrual cycle. With this accounting method, the gestation period is 266 days.

Soon after conception, the single cell formed by the union of sperm and egg begins to multiply—becoming two cells, then four, then eight, and so on. During the weeks and months that follow, tissues, organs, and structures begin to form, and the fetus gradually takes on the unmistakable shape of a human being. By the time a fetus is born, it consists of hundreds of billions of cells—more cells than there are stars in the Milky Way galaxy. Prenatal development is divided into three periods: the germinal stage (approximately the first 2 weeks), the embryonic stage (the 3rd through the 8th weeks), and the fetal stage (the 3rd month through birth). We also commonly speak of prenatal development in terms of three trimesters of 3 months each. For some of the highlights of prenatal development, see Table 3.2.

**TABLE 3.2**

***HIGHLIGHTS OF PRENATAL DEVELOPMENT***

| FIRST TRIMESTER | |
|---|---|
| EMBRYO | |
| 3 WEEKS | HEAD AND BLOOD VESSELS FORM<br>BRAIN BEGINS TO DEVELOP |
| 4 WEEKS | HEART BEGINS TO BEAT AND PUMP BLOOD<br>ARM BUDS AND LEG BUDS APPEAR<br>EYES, EARS, NOSE, AND MOUTH FORM<br>NERVES BEGIN TO DEVELOP<br>WEIGHS A FRACTION OF AN OUNCE AND IS 1/2 INCH LONG |
| 5-8 WEEKS | HANDS AND FEET DEVELOP, WEBBED FINGERS AND TOES FORM<br>UNDIFFERENTIATED SEX ORGANS APPEAR<br>TEETH BUDS DEVELOP<br>KIDNEYS AND LIVER START FUNCTIONING<br>WEIGHS 1/30 OF AN OUNCE AND IS 1 INCH LONG |
| FETUS | |
| 9-12 WEEKS | ALL MAJOR ORGAN SYSTEMS ARE FORMED<br>FINGERS AND TOES ARE FULLY FORMED<br>EYES CAN BE CLEARLY DISTINGUISHED<br>SEX OF THE FETUS CAN BE DETERMINED VISUALLY<br>FETUS RESPONDS TO EXTERNAL STIMULATION<br>WEIGHS 1 OUNCE AND IS 3 INCHES LONG |
| SECOND TRIMESTER | |
| 13-16 WEEKS | MOTHER DETECTS FETAL MOVEMENT<br>MANY REFLEXES ARE PRESENT<br>FINGERNAILS AND TOENAILS FORM |
| 17-20 WEEKS | HAIR DEVELOPS ON HEAD<br>FINE, DOWNY HAIR (LANUGO) COVERS BODY<br>FETUS SUCKS THUMB AND HICCOUGHS |
| 21-24 WEEKS | EYES OPEN AND SHUT<br>LIGHT AND SOUNDS ARE PERCEIVED<br>FETUS ALTERNATES BETWEEN PERIODS OF SLEEP AND WAKEFULNESS<br>SKIN LOOKS RUDDY BECAUSE BLOOD VESSELS SHOW THROUGH THE SURFACE<br>SURVIVAL RATE IS LOW IF FETUS IS BORN<br>WEIGHS ABOUT 2 POUNDS AND IS 14 INCHES LONG |
| THIRD TRIMESTER | |
| 25-28 WEEKS | ORGAN SYSTEMS MATURE FURTHER<br>FATTY LAYER BEGINS TO DEVELOP UNDER THE SKIN<br>FETUS TURNS HEAD DOWN IN THE UTERUS<br>CHANCES OF SURVIVAL ARE GOOD IF BORN<br>WEIGHS 3-4 POUNDS AND IS 16 INCHES LONG |
| 29-36/38 WEEKS | ORGAN SYSTEMS FUNCTION WELL<br>FATTY LAYER DEVELOPS FURTHER<br>ACTIVITY LEVEL DECREASES IN WEEKS BEFORE BIRTH<br>WEIGHT INCREASES TO ABOUT 7-7 1/2 POUNDS AND LENGTH TO 20 INCHES |

## *THE GERMINAL STAGE*

Within 36 hours after conception, the zygote divides into two cells. It then divides repeatedly as it proceeds on its journey to the uterus. Within another 36 hours, it has become 32 cells. It takes the zygote 3 to 4 days to reach the uterus. The

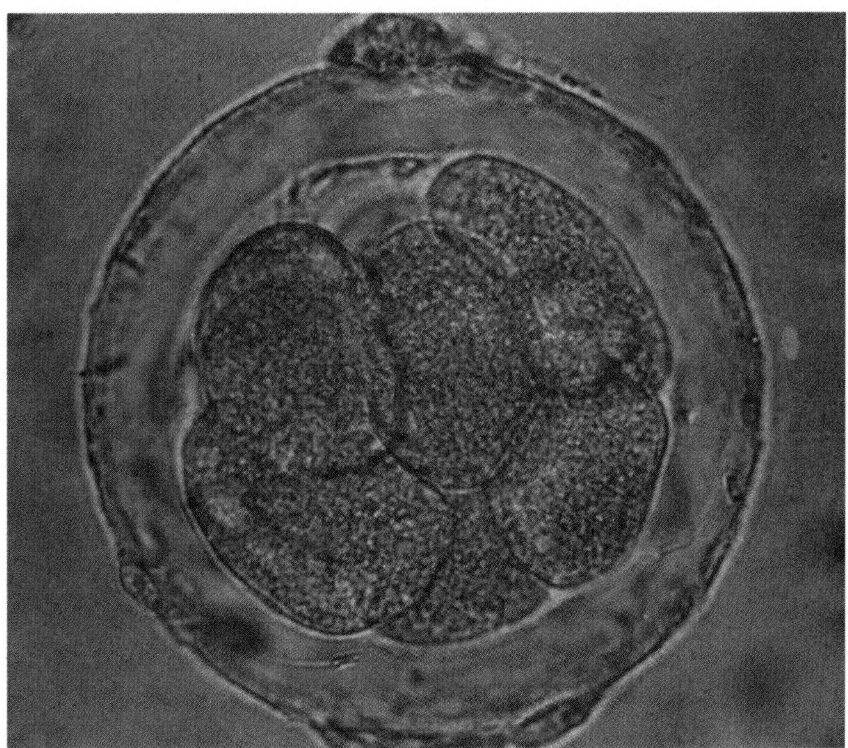

FIGURE 3.14

***The Eight-Cell Stage.*** *Early in the germinal stage of development, the dividing ball of cells consists of eight cells.*

mass of dividing cells wanders about the uterus for another 3 to 4 days before it begins to become implanted in the uterine wall. Implantation takes another week or so. The period from conception to implantation is called the ***germinal stage*** (see Figure 3.15).

A few days into the germinal stage, the dividing cell mass takes the form of a fluid-filled ball of cells called a ***blastocyst.*** A blastocyst already shows cell differentiation. Cells begin to separate into groups that will eventually become different structures. Two distinct inner layers of cells are forming within a thickened mass of cells called the ***embryonic disk.*** These cells will become the embryo and eventually the fetus.

The outer part of the blastocyst, or ***trophoblast,*** at first consists of a single layer of cells. But it rapidly differentiates into four membranes that will protect and nourish the embryo. One membrane produces blood cells until the embryo's liver develops and takes over this function. Then the membrane disappears. Another membrane develops into the umbilical cord and the blood vessels of the placenta. A third develops into the amniotic sac, and the fourth becomes the chorion, which will line the placenta.

Prior to implantation, the dividing cluster of cells is nourished solely by the yolk of the original egg cell and it does not gain in mass. The blastocyst can gain in mass only from outside nourishment, which it will gain once implanted in the uterine wall.

***Germinal stage*** The period of development between conception and the implantation of the embryo in the uterine wall.

***Blastocyst*** A stage within the germinal period of prenatal development in which the zygote has the form of a sphere of cells surrounding a cavity of fluid.

***Embryonic disk*** The platelike inner part of the blastocyst that differentiates into the ectoderm, mesoderm, and endoderm of the embryo.

***Trophoblast*** The outer part of the blastocyst, from which the amniotic sac, placenta, and umbilical cord develop.

TRUTH OR FICTION REVISITED

*It is true that newly fertilized egg cells survive without any nourishment from the mother for more than a week. They do so before they become implanted in the uterus.*

**FIGURE 3.15**

***THE OVARIAN CYCLE, CONCEPTION, AND THE EARLY DAYS OF THE GERMINAL STAGE.*** *The zygote first divides about 36 hours after conception. Continuing division creates the hollow sphere of cells termed the* blastocyst. *The blastocyst normally becomes implanted in the wall of the uterus. (Source: Moore, 1989).*

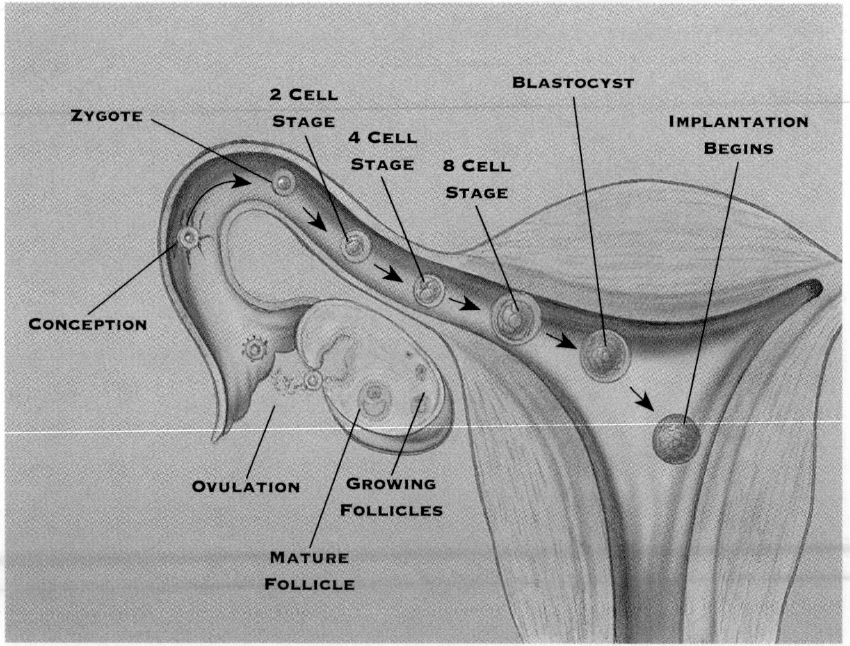


Implantation may be accompanied by some bleeding, which results from the normal rupturing of some small blood vessels that line the uterus. Bleeding can also be a sign of miscarriage (which is also called *spontaneous abortion*). Miscarriage usually stems from abnormalities in the developmental process. Many women miscarry early in pregnancy, but their menstrual flows appear about on schedule, so that they may not even realize they had conceived. Nearly a third of all pregnancies result in miscarriage, the majority of them occurring in the first 3 months (Wilcox et al., 1988). However, most women who experience implantation bleeding do not miscarry but go on to have normal pregnancies and normal babies.

## THE EMBRYONIC STAGE

***Embryonic stage*** The stage of prenatal development that lasts from implantation through the eighth week and is characterized by the development of the major organ systems.

***Cephalocaudal*** From head to tail.

***Proximodistal*** From the inner part (or axis) of the body outward.

***Ectoderm*** The outermost cell layer of the newly formed embryo, from which the skin and nervous system develop.

***Neural tube*** A hollowed-out area in the blastocyst from which the nervous system develops.

***Endoderm*** The inner layer of the embryo, from which the lungs and digestive system develop.

The ***embryonic stage*** lasts from implantation until about the eighth week of development. During this stage, the major body organ systems differentiate. Development follows two general trends—***cephalocaudal*** (Latin for "head to tail") and ***proximodistal*** (Latin for "near to far"). The apparently oversized heads of embryos and fetuses at various stages of prenatal development show that growth of the head takes precedence over the growth of the lower parts of the body (see Figure 3.16). You can also think of the body as containing a central axis that coincides with the spinal cord. The growth of the organ systems close to this axis (that is, *proximal* to the axis) takes precedence over the growth of the extremities, which are farther away (that is, *distal* to the axis). Relatively early maturation of the brain and organ systems that lie near the central axis allows these organs to play important roles in the further development of the embryo and fetus.

During the embryonic stage, the outer layer of cells of the embryonic disk, or ***ectoderm,*** develops into the nervous system, sensory organs, nails, hair, teeth, and the outer layer of skin. At about 21 days, two ridges appear in the embryo and fold to compose the ***neural tube,*** from which the nervous system will develop. The inner layer, or ***endoderm,*** forms the digestive and respiratory systems, the liver, and the pancreas. A bit later during the embryonic stage, the ***mesoderm,*** a middle layer of cells, becomes differentiated. The mesoderm develops into the excretory, reproductive, and circulatory systems; the muscles; the skeleton; and the inner layer of the skin.

**Mesoderm** The central layer of the embryo, from which the bones and muscles develop.

During the third week after conception, the head and blood vessels begin to form. During the fourth week, a primitive heart begins to beat and pump blood—in an organism that is only one-fourth of an inch in length and weighs a fraction of an ounce. The heart will continue to beat without rest every minute of every day for perhaps 80 or 90 years. Arm buds and leg buds begin to appear toward the end of the first month. Eyes, ears, nose, and mouth begin to take shape. By this time, the nervous system, including the brain, has also begun to develop.

## TRUTH OR FICTION REVISITED

*Your heart did, in fact, start beating when you were only one-fourth of an inch long and weighed a fraction of an ounce. You reached this size about one month after conception.*

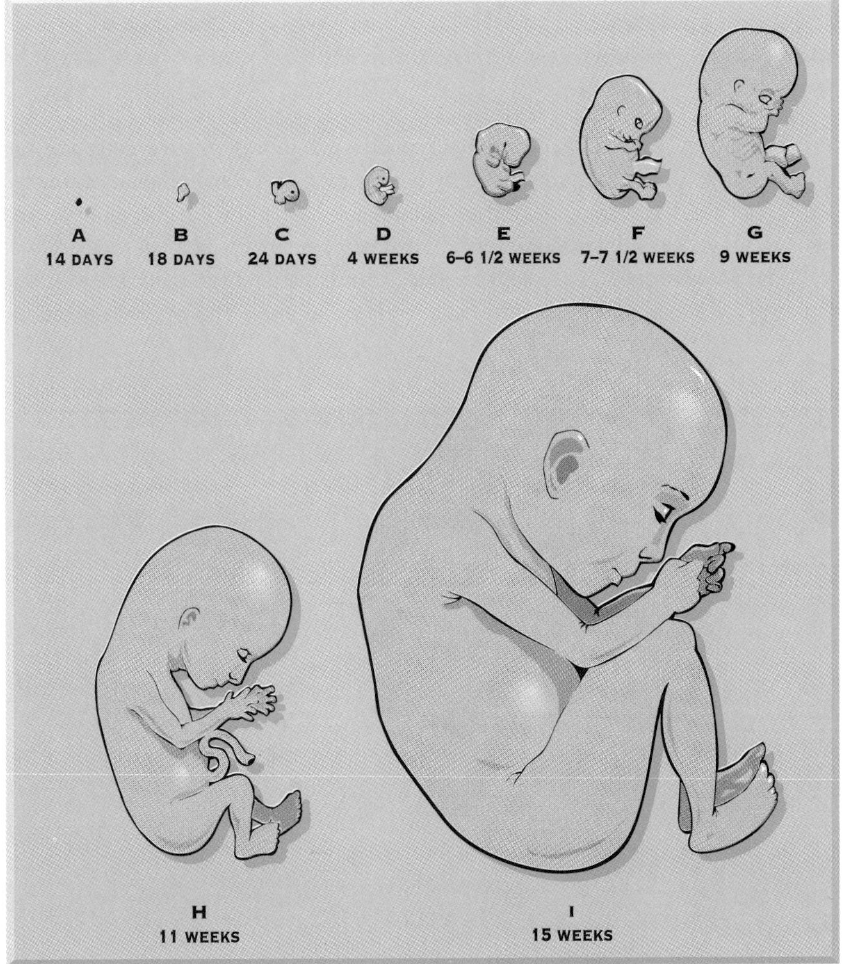


FIGURE 3.16

**HUMAN EMBRYOS AND FETUSES AT VARIOUS STAGES OF DEVELOPMENT.** *Development is cephalocaudal and proximodistal. Growth of the head takes precedence over the growth of the lower parts of the body. Growth of the organs near the center of the body takes precedence over those near the extremities. (Source: Rathus et al., 1993).*

***Androgens*** Male sex hormones.

***Amniotic sac*** The sac containing the fetus.

***Amniotic fluid*** Fluid within the amniotic sac that suspends and protects the fetus.

***Placenta*** (pluh-SENT-uh) An organ connected to the uterine wall and to the fetus by the umbilical cord. The placenta serves as a relay station between mother and fetus for exchange of nutrients and wastes.

In accord with the principle of proximodistal development, the upper arms and legs develop before the forearms and lower legs. Next come hands and feet, followed at 6 to 8 weeks by webbed fingers and toes. By the end of the second month, the limbs are elongating and separated. The webbing is gone. The head has become rounded and the facial features distinct—all in an embryo about 1 inch long and weighing 1/30th of an ounce. During the second month the nervous system begins to transmit messages. By the end of the embryonic period, teeth buds have formed. The embryo's kidneys are filtering acid from the blood, and its liver is producing red blood cells.

By 5 to 6 weeks, when the embryo is only a quarter to a half an inch long, nondescript sex organs have formed. By about the seventh week, the genetic code (XY or XX) begins to assert itself, causing sex organs to differentiate. If a Y sex chromosome is present, testes form and begin to produce ***androgens,*** which further masculinize the sex organs. In the absence of male sex hormones, the embryo will develop female sex organs. Female sex hormones are not needed to induce these changes. By about 4 months after conception, males and females show distinct external genital structures.

*TRUTH OR FICTION REVISITED*

*If it were not for the secretion of male sex hormones a few weeks after conception, we would, in fact, all develop as females—at least in terms of visible sex characteristics. Male sex hormones spur the development of male sex organs.*

The embryo and fetus develop suspended within a protective ***amniotic sac*** in the uterus. The sac is surrounded by a clear membrane and contains ***amniotic fluid.*** The fluid serves as a kind of natural air bag, allowing the embryo and fetus to move around without injury. It also helps maintain an even temperature.

The ***placenta*** is a mass of tissue that permits the embryo (and, later on, the fetus) to exchange nutrients and wastes with the mother. The placenta is unique

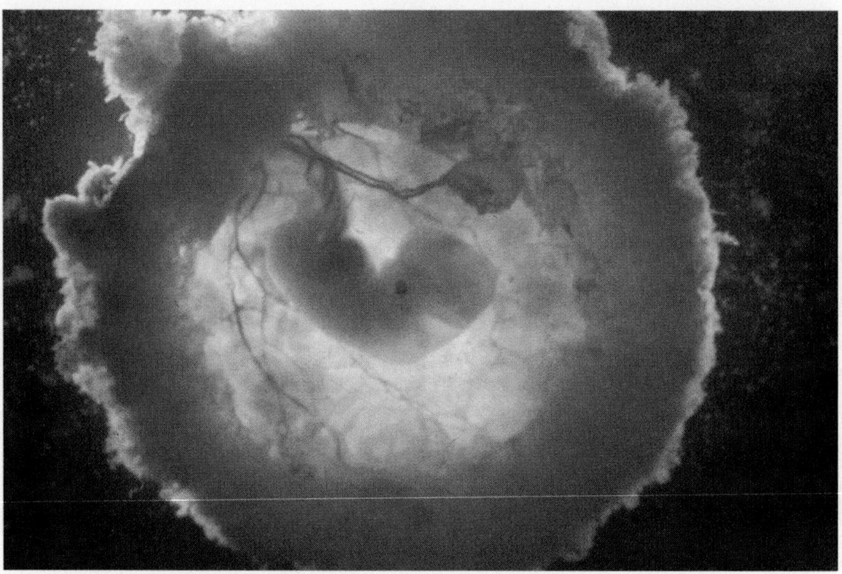

FIGURE 3.17

**A HUMAN EMBRYO AT 7 WEEKS.** *At this late part of the embryonic stage, the major organ systems have already become differentiated, except for the sex organs.*

in origin; it grows from material supplied by both mother and embryo. The fetus is connected to the placenta by the ***umbilical cord.*** The mother is connected to the placenta by the system of blood vessels in the uterine wall.

The circulatory systems of mother and baby do not mix. A membrane in the placenta permits only certain substances to pass through. Oxygen and nutrients pass from the mother to the embryo. Carbon dioxide and other wastes pass from the child to the mother, where they are removed by the mother's lungs and kidneys. Unfortunately, a number of other substances can pass through the placenta. They include some microscopic disease organisms—such as those that cause syphilis, German measles, and AIDS—and some drugs, including aspirin, narcotics, alcohol, and tranquilizers.

The placenta also secretes hormones that preserve the pregnancy, prepare the breasts for nursing, and stimulate the uterine contractions that prompt childbirth. Ultimately, the placenta passes from the woman's body after the child is delivered. For this reason, it is also called the *afterbirth.*

***Umbilical cord*** A tube that connects the fetus to the placenta.

***Fetal stage*** The stage of development that lasts from the beginning of the ninth week of pregnancy through birth and is characterized by gains in size and weight and maturation of the organ systems.

### *The Fetal Stage*

The ***fetal stage*** lasts from the beginning of the third month until birth. The fetus begins to turn and respond to external stimulation at about the ninth or tenth week. By the end of the first trimester, all the major organ systems have been formed. The fingers and toes are fully formed. The eyes can be clearly distinguished, and the sex of the fetus can be determined visually.

The second trimester is characterized by further maturation of fetal organ systems and dramatic gains in size. The brain continues to mature, contributing to the fetus's ability to regulate its own basic body functions. During the second trimester, the fetus advances from 1 ounce to 2 pounds in weight and grows four to five times in length, from about 3 inches to 14 inches. Soft, downy hair grows above the eyes and on the scalp. The skin turns ruddy because of blood vessels that show through the surface. (During the third trimester, fatty layers will give the skin a pinkish hue.)

By the end of the second trimester, the fetus opens and shuts its eyes, sucks its thumb, alternates between periods of wakefulness and sleep, and perceives

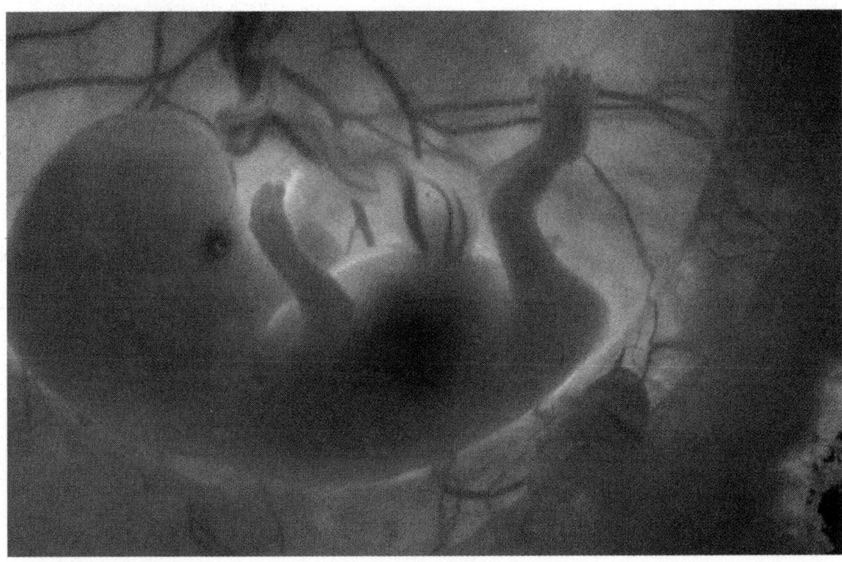

FIGURE 3.18

***A Human Fetus at 12 Weeks.*** *By the end of the first trimester, formation of all the major organ systems is complete. Fingers and toes are fully formed, and the sex of the fetus can be determined visually.*

FIGURE 3.19

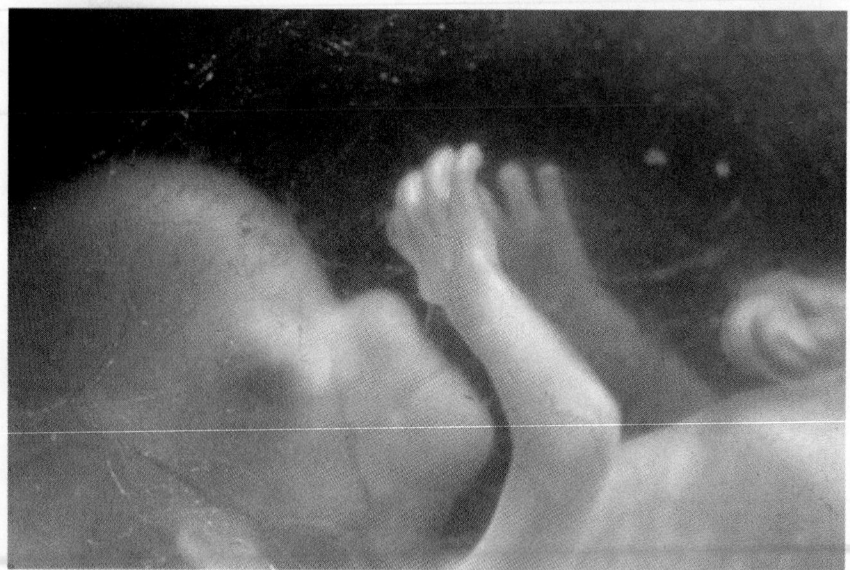

**A HUMAN FETUS AT 4½ MONTHS.** *At this midway point between conception and birth, the fetus is covered with fine, downy hair called* lanugo.

light and sounds. There are also sharp spasms of the diaphragm, or fetal hiccoughs, which may last for hours. Toward the end of the second trimester, the fetus nears the ***age of viability.*** Still, only about one baby in two born at the end of the second trimester who weighs less than 2 pounds will survive, even with expert medical care (Lin, 1989).

TRUTH OR FICTION REVISITED

*Fetuses do suck their thumbs and hiccough, and the hiccoughing does last sometimes for hours on end—as many pregnant women will attest.*

During the third trimester, the organ systems of the fetus continue to mature. The heart and lungs become increasingly capable of sustaining independent life. The fetus gains about 5½ pounds and doubles in length. Newborn boys average about 7½ pounds and newborn girls about 7 pounds.

During the seventh month, the fetus normally turns upside down in the uterus so that delivery will be headfirst. By the end of the seventh month, the fetus will have almost doubled in weight, gaining another 1 pound 12 ounces, and will have increased another 2 inches in length. If born now, chances of survival are nearly 90 percent (Ekvall, 1993b). If born at the end of the eighth month, the odds are overwhelmingly in favor of survival.

**FETAL PERCEPTION: BACH AT BREAKFAST AND BEETHOVEN AT BRUNCH?** When S. R. was a beginning graduate student and thought he knew everything, he was astounded by what he thought was the naiveté of parents-to-be who listened to Bach or Beethoven or who read Shakespeare to promote the cultural development of their fetuses. But in more recent years, he admits that he and his wife have made more of an effort to expose their fetuses to good music as well.

Research shows that by the 13th week of pregnancy, the fetus does respond to sound waves. In a classic experiment, Sontag and Richards (1938) rang a bell

***Age of viability*** The age at which a fetus can sustain independent life.

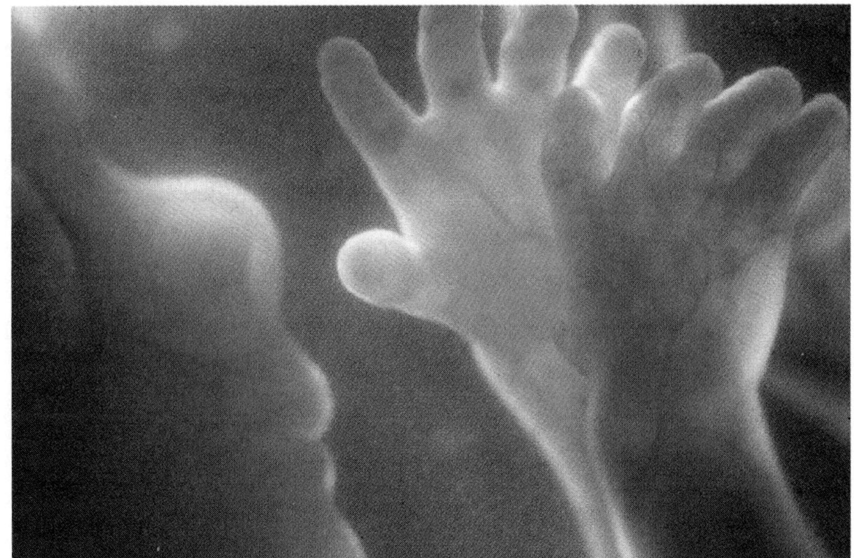

FIGURE 3.20

***The Hands of a Human Fetus at 5 Months.*** *By 5 months of age, the hands have been fully formed for a month or so. At this age, the fetus may occasionally suck its thumb.*

near the mother and the fetus responded with muscle movements similar to those of the startle reflex shown after birth. During the third trimester, fetuses respond to sounds of different frequencies through a variety of movements and changes in heart rate, suggesting that by this time they can discriminate pitch (Bernard & Sontag, 1947).

An experiment by DeCasper and Fifer (1980) is even more intriguing. In this study, women read the Dr. Seuss book *The Cat in the Hat* out loud twice daily during the final month and a half of pregnancy. After birth, their babies were given special pacifiers: sucking on them in one way would activate recordings of their mothers reading *The Cat in the Hat.* Sucking on them in another way would activate their mothers' readings of another book—*The King, the Mice, and the Cheese*—which was written in very different cadences. The newborns chose to hear *The Cat in the Hat.* Using similar research methods, DeCasper and his colleagues also found that newborns prefer the mother's voice to that of their father or an unfamiliar woman (DeCasper & Prescott, 1984; DeCasper & Spence, 1986, 1991). Presumably, preference for the mother's voice is established through prenatal exposure.

So, during the latter days of pregnancy, Bach at breakfast and Beethoven at brunch may not be a bad idea. It just may do more than help the food go down.

**Fetal Movements** In the middle of the fourth month, the mother usually detects the first fetal movements (Eaton & Saudino, 1992). By the end of the second trimester, the fetus moves its limbs so vigorously that the mother may complain of being kicked—often at 4 a.m. The fetus also turns somersaults, which are clearly felt by the mother. Fortunately, the umbilical cord will not break or become dangerously wrapped around the fetus, no matter how many acrobatic feats the fetus performs.

Fetuses show different patterns of prenatal activity (Sontag, 1966). Slow squirming movements begin at about 5 or 6 months. Sharp jabbing or kicking movements begin at about the same time and increase in intensity until shortly prior to birth. As the fetus grows it becomes cramped in the uterus, and movement is constricted. Many women become concerned that their fetuses are markedly less active during the ninth month than previously, but most of the time this change is normal.

Different fetuses show different levels of activity. Moreover, prenatal activity predicts activity levels after birth. For instance, highly active fetuses show more advanced motor development 6 months after birth than do their more lethargic counterparts (Richards & Nelson, 1938).

## ENVIRONMENTAL INFLUENCES ON PRENATAL DEVELOPMENT

Scientific advances have not only helped us chronicle the details of prenatal development. They have also made us keenly aware of the types of things that can go wrong and what we can do to prevent these problems, even including prenatal surgery (see Developing Today: Prenatal Surgery). In this section, we consider some of the environmental factors that have an impact on prenatal development. These include nutrition, diseases and disorders of the mother, drugs, environmental hazards, maternal stress, and the mother's age.

### *NUTRITION*

It is a common misconception that fetuses take what they need from their mothers, even at the expense of their mothers' own nutritional needs. If this were true, pregnant women would not have to be highly concerned about their diets. But malnutrition in the mother, especially during the last trimester when the fetus should be making rapid gains in weight, has been linked to low birth weight, prematurity, stunted growth, retardation of brain development, cognitive deficiencies, and behavioral problems (Bauerfeld & Lachenmeyer, 1992; Ekvall, 1993c).

**TRUTH OR FICTION REVISITED**

*It is only a myth that embryos and fetuses take what they need from their mothers. Therefore, pregnant women do need to be concerned about their diets.*

Maternal malnutrition can lead to long-term behavioral effects. Studies done in Mexico, Guatemala, and South America indicate that children whose mothers were malnourished during their pregnancies show deficits in motor and cognitive skills and general intelligence (Schultz, 1990). Fortunately, the effects of fetal malnutrition may be overcome by a supportive, care-giving environment. In one study, for example, children who had suffered fetal malnutrition but participated from early infancy in an enriched day-care program showed better intellectual and social skills at 3 years of age than similarly malnourished children who had not participated in the program (Zeskind & Ramey, 1981).

Evidence on supplementing the diets of pregnant women who might otherwise be deficient in their intake of calories and protein also shows modest positive effects on the motor development of their infants. In one study, 8-month-old children of Taiwanese women who had received prenatal calorie and protein supplements showed more advanced motor development than controls, as measured by crawling and sitting, pulling themselves to a standing position, and making stepping movements (Joos et al., 1983).

## *Developing Today*

### *Prenatal Surgery*

Six months into her pregnancy, a 27-year-old Michigan woman learned that her unborn child was suffering from a potentially fatal problem. A hernia (or hole) in the diaphragm had caused the baby's abdominal organs to move into its chest cavity, threatening to crush its lungs. This defect is fatal in 75 percent of cases. Until recently, nothing could have been done but await the birth of a child doomed to likely death. But in June 1989, surgeon Michael Harrison made an incision into the mother's uterus and then into the rib cage of the fetus. The abdominal organs were repositioned and the diaphragm repaired. Seven weeks later, Blake Schultz was born in good health (M. R. Harrison et al., 1990). This was the first case of successful major surgery performed on a fetus.

In the 1980s and 1990s, advances in fetal diagnosis and treatment have made it possible to treat a number of fetal conditions (Longaker et al., 1992). *Rh incompatibility,* a potentially fatal blood incompatibility between the fetus and the mother, can be treated by fetal transfusions as early as the 18th week of pregnancy. Several fetuses also have had operations to drain abnormal accumulations of cerebrospinal fluid around the brain in a condition called *hydrocephalus.*

Still others have been treated for urinary-tract blockage that threatens to destroy their kidneys and lungs (Ohlendorf–Moffat, 1991). In this procedure, ultrasound guides physicians as they insert a hollow tube into the swollen bladder of the fetus. The other end of the tube drains into the amniotic sac. Amniotic fluid is largely formed from fetal urine, and the shunt permits this process to continue despite blockage in the urinary tract. Additional surgery is undertaken after delivery to remove the shunt and permanently unblock the urinary tract itself.

A review of the first 17 human cases of fetal surgery reported no serious maternal complications or effects on later fertility (Longaker et al., 1992).

Some prenatal surgery techniques remain highly experimental. For example, the first fetus-to-fetus transplant was performed in 1992 (Begley, 1993). Liver cells from a 13-week-old spontaneously aborted fetus were injected into a 15-week-old fetus with a rare inherited enzyme deficiency. Six months after birth, the child who received the transplant was producing the missing enzyme. Many other genetic disorders, including sickle-cell anemia, thalassemia, and certain immune system deficiencies also might be correctable before birth with transplants of fetal tissue.

The use of fetal tissue for transplants and medical research has raised a number of ethical questions (Woodward, 1993). What limits should be observed when experimenting with human fetuses? Does a mother have the right to donate an aborted fetus to science? May she decide who receives the fetal organs or tissue? Does a woman have a right to conceive a child for the purpose of aborting it so that its cells can be used to treat an ill relative? How do you feel about these issues?

A related question concerns a couple's right to bear a child to save the life of another child. Consider Mary and Abe Ayala, whose 17-year-old daughter suffered from fatal leukemia. The only hope for a cure was a bone marrow transplant from someone whose tissues were a close match. The Ayalas decided to have a second child, hoping that its bone marrow would match that of their ill daughter. Luckily, it did. When the baby was 14 months old, a small amount of bone marrow was withdrawn from her hip bone and injected into her older sister. Today, both sisters are healthy and leading normal lives (Bishop, 1993).

From a moral standpoint, were the Ayalas justified in their decision?

Pregnant women require the following food elements to maintain themselves and to give birth to healthy babies: protein, most heavily concentrated in meat, fish, poultry, eggs, beans, milk, and cheese; vitamin A, found in milk and vegetables; vitamin B, found in wheat germ, whole grain breads, and liver; vitamin C, found in citrus fruits; vitamin D, derived from sunshine, fish-liver oil, and vitamin-D-fortified milk; vitamin E, found in whole grains, some vegetables, eggs, and peanuts; iron, concentrated heavily in meat—especially liver—egg yolks, fish, and raisins; the trace minerals zinc and cobalt, found in seafood; calcium, found in dairy products; and, yes, calories (Ekvall, 1993b; Schultz, 1990). Recent research also demonstrates the importance of consuming folic acid, which is found in leafy green vegetables. Pregnant women who take extra folic acid greatly reduce the risk of giving birth to babies with devastating neural tube defects, which can cause paralysis and death (Brody, 1994). While women who eat a well-rounded diet do not require food supplements, most doctors recommend vitamin and mineral supplements to be on the safe side.

Women can expect to gain quite a bit of weight during pregnancy because of the growth of the placenta, amniotic fluid, and the fetus itself. Women who do not restrict their diet during pregnancy normally will gain 25 to 35 pounds. Overweight women may gain less, and slender women may gain more (Ekvall, 1993b; "Women Can Gain," 1990). Regular weight gains are most desirable, about one-half pound per week during the first half of pregnancy, and one pound per week during the second half. Sudden large gains or losses in weight should be discussed with the doctor.

Over the years, the pendulum has swung back and forth between views of ideal weight gains during pregnancy. Early in this century, it was believed that greater weight gains would assure proper nutrition for mother and fetus. During the 1960s and part of the 1970s, pregnant women were advised to watch their weight. It was felt that excess weight posed risks for the mother and might be hard to take off following pregnancy—concerns with some basis in fact. But now the pendulum has swung again. It is now known that low weight gain during pregnancy increases the chances of having a premature or low-birth-weight baby (Scholl et al., 1991). Recent research indicates that women who gain 25 to 35 pounds during pregnancy are more likely to have healthy babies than those who gain less (Ekvall, 1993b; "Women Can Gain," 1990). But a woman in the seventh or eighth month who finds herself overshooting a weight-gain target of, say, 25–30 pounds, should avoid a crash diet—especially during the period when the fetus is making its most dramatic gains in weight.

## *DISEASES AND DISORDERS OF THE MOTHER*

Environmental influences or agents that can harm the developing embryo or fetus are called ***teratogens.*** These include drugs taken by the mother such as thalidomide and alcohol, as well as substances produced by the mother's body, such as Rh-positive antibodies. Other teratogens include metals such as lead and mercury, radiation, excessive hormones, and disease-causing organisms such as bacteria and viruses. Many disease organisms cannot pass through the placenta and infect the embryo or fetus, but extremely small organisms, such as those responsible for AIDS, syphilis, mumps, chicken pox, and measles, can. Some disorders such as toxemia are not transmitted to the embryo or fetus but adversely affect the environment within which it develops.

**CRITICAL PERIODS OF VULNERABILITY** Exposure to particular teratogens is most harmful during certain ***critical periods.*** These critical periods correspond to the times during which certain organs are developing. For example, the heart develops rapidly during the third to fifth weeks after conception. As you can see in Figure 3.21, the heart is most vulnerable to certain teratogens at this time. The arms and legs, which develop later, are most vulnerable during the fourth through eighth weeks. Since the major organ systems differentiate during the embryonic stage, the embryo is generally more vulnerable to teratogens than the fetus. But many teratogens are harmful throughout the entire course of prenatal development.

Let us now consider the effects of specific teratogens. Many of these effects are summarized in Table 3.3.

***Teratogens*** Environmental influences or agents that can damage the embryo or fetus (from the Greek *teras,* meaning "monster").

***Critical period*** A period during which an embryo is particularly vulnerable to a certain teratogen.

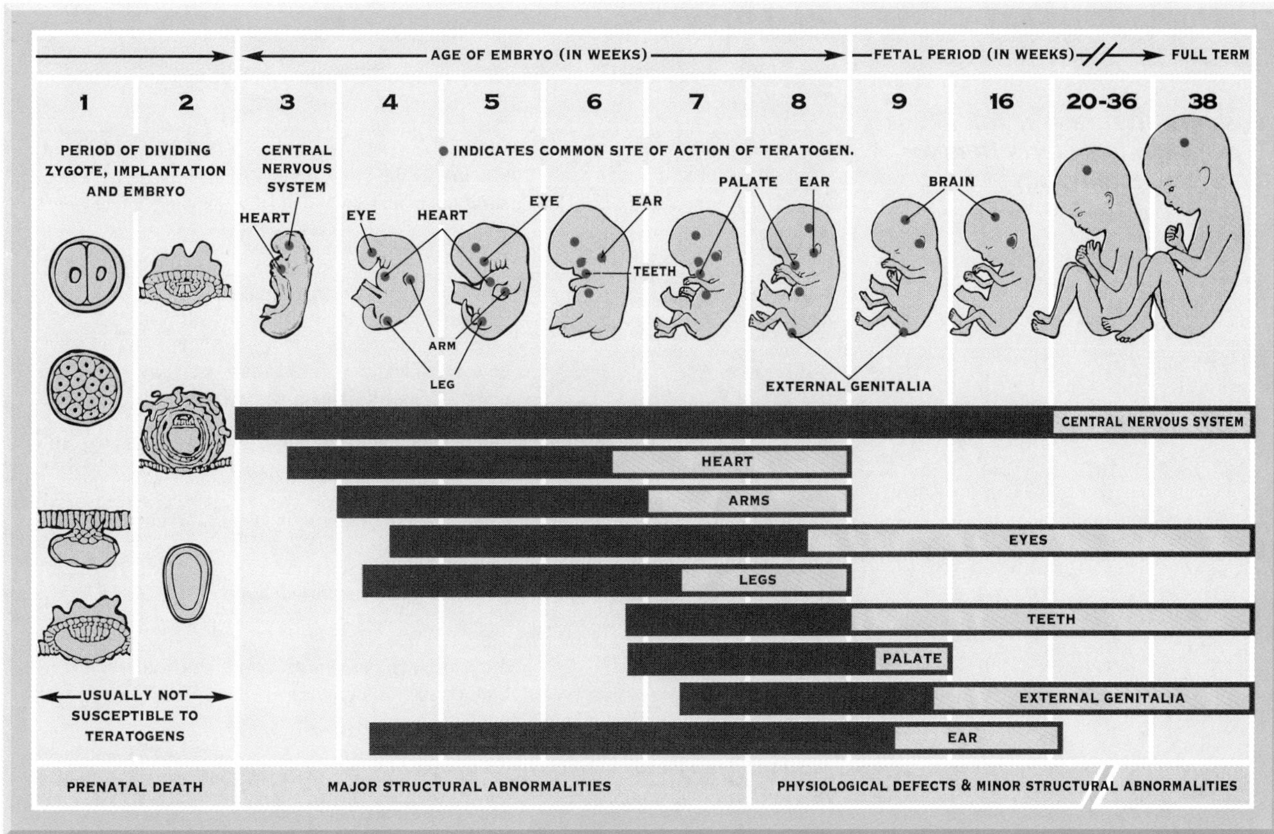


FIGURE 3.21

***Critical Periods in Prenatal Development.*** *The developing human is most vulnerable to teratogens during the embryonic period, when the organ systems are forming. The periods of greatest vulnerability for organ systems are shown in red. Periods of lesser vulnerability are shown in yellow. (Source: Moore, 1989).*

**Rubella** *Rubella* (German measles) is a viral infection. Women who contract rubella during the first month or two of pregnancy, when the major organ systems are undergoing rapid differentiation, may bear children who suffer from deafness, mental retardation, heart disease, or cataracts (Moore, 1989). Risk of these disorders declines as the pregnancy progresses.

Many adult women had rubella as children and acquired immunity in this way. Women who are uncertain as to whether they have had rubella may be tested. If they are not immune, they can be vaccinated prior to pregnancy. Inoculation during pregnancy is risky because the vaccine gives the mother a mild case of the disease, which can affect the unborn child (Anderson & Golbus, 1989).

Increased awareness of the dangers of rubella during pregnancy and of the protective effects of inoculation has led to a dramatic decline in the number of children born in the United States with defects caused by rubella, from about 20,000 cases in 1964–1965 to fewer than 10 in 1985 (Cochi et al., 1989).

**Syphilis** *Syphilis* is a sexually transmitted disease that can cause miscarriage, ***stillbirth,*** or ***congenital*** syphilis (Rathus et al., 1993). Congenital syphilis can impair vision and hearing, damage the liver, or deform the bones and teeth. Routine blood tests early in pregnancy can diagnose syphilis and other problems. Because the bacteria that cause syphilis do not readily cross the placental membrane during the first months of pregnancy, the fetus will probably not contract syphilis if an infected mother is treated successfully with antibiotics before the fourth month of pregnancy.

***Rubella*** A viral infection that can cause retardation and heart disease in the embryo. Also called German measles.

***Syphilis*** A sexually transmitted disease that, in advanced stages, can attack major organ systems.

***Stillbirth*** The birth of a dead fetus.

***Congenital*** Present at birth; resulting from the prenatal environment.

**TABLE 3.3**

***POSSIBLE EFFECTS ON THE FETUS OF CERTAIN AGENTS DURING PREGNANCY***

| AGENT | POSSIBLE EFFECT |
|---|---|
| ACCUTANE (AN ACNE TREATMENT) | MALFORMATION OF ORGANS, MISCARRIAGE |
| ALCOHOL | MENTAL RETARDATION, GROWTH RETARDATION, FACIAL AND HEART DEFECTS, BEHAVIORAL PROBLEMS (FETAL ALCOHOL SYNDROME) |
| ASPIRIN (LARGE DOSES) | RESPIRATORY PROBLEMS, BLEEDING |
| CAFFEINE (COFFEE, MANY SOFT DRINKS, CHOCOLATE, ETC.) | LOW BIRTH WEIGHT, MISCARRIAGE |
| CIGARETTES | LOW BIRTH WEIGHT, PREMATURE DELIVERY, FETAL DEATH, LEARNING DISORDERS, BEHAVIORAL PROBLEMS |
| COCAINE | STILLBIRTH, LOW BIRTH WEIGHT, BIRTH DEFECTS, NEUROLOGICAL AND BEHAVIORAL PROBLEMS |
| DIETHYLSTILBESTROL (DES) | CANCER OF THE CERVIX OR TESTES, INFERTILITY, IMMUNE SYSTEM DISORDERS |
| HEAVY SEDATION DURING LABOR | BRAIN DAMAGE, ASPHYXIATION |
| HEROIN, MORPHINE, METHADONE, AND OTHER NARCOTICS | ADDICTION, PREMATURITY, LOW BIRTH WEIGHT, MOTOR AND ATTENTION DEFICITS |
| HOT TUBS, SAUNAS | BIRTH DEFECTS |
| LEAD | SLOWED MENTAL DEVELOPMENT |
| MARIJUANA | PREMATURE DELIVERY, FAILURE TO HABITUATE |
| MERCURY | MENTAL RETARDATION, NEUROLOGICAL PROBLEMS |
| PAINT FUMES (SUBSTANTIAL EXPOSURE) | MENTAL RETARDATION |
| PCBs | LOW BIRTH WEIGHT, MOTOR AND MEMORY DEFICITS, DECREASED RESPONSIVENESS |
| PROGESTIN | MASCULINIZATION OF FEMALE EMBRYOS, POSSIBLE HEIGHTENED AGGRESSIVENESS |
| RADIATION | MALFORMATION OF ORGANS |
| RUBELLA (GERMAN MEASLES) | MENTAL RETARDATION, NERVE DAMAGE IMPAIRING VISION AND HEARING |
| STREPTOMYCIN | HEARING LOSS |
| TETRACYCLINE | YELLOW TEETH, BONE ABNORMALITIES |
| THALIDOMIDE | DEFORMED OR MISSING LIMBS |
| VITAMIN A (LARGE DOSES) | CENTRAL NERVOUS SYSTEM DAMAGE, SMALL HEAD SIZE |
| VITAMIN D (LARGE DOSES) | HEART DEFECTS |

A VARIETY OF CHEMICAL AND OTHER AGENTS HAVE BEEN FOUND HARMFUL TO THE FETUS OR ARE STRONGLY IMPLICATED IN FETAL DAMAGE. PREGNANT WOMEN SHOULD CONSULT THEIR PHYSICIANS ABOUT THEIR DIETS, VITAMIN SUPPLEMENTS, AND USE OF ANY DRUGS–INCLUDING DRUGS AVAILABLE WITHOUT A PRESCRIPTION.

Sad to say, the incidence of congenital syphilis has grown since the late 1980s and the disease now afflicts thousands of newborns nationwide. Health experts believe that the increase is related to a growing use of crack cocaine among women who contract syphilis while trading sex for drugs (Lewin, 1992a).

Other sexually transmitted diseases in the mother that also affect the unborn child are chlamydia, genital herpes, and AIDS.

**AIDS** ***AIDS*** (acquired immune deficiency syndrome) disables the body's immune system, leaving victims prey to a wide variety of fatal illnesses, including respiratory disorders and certain types of cancer. Current data indicate that nearly all individuals who are infected by the human immunodeficiency virus (HIV), which causes AIDS, will develop the disease, which almost always results in death within a few years (Rathus & Boughn, 1993). AIDS is now the eighth leading cause of death among children 1–4 years of age (Children's Defense Fund, 1992a).

The HIV virus can be transmitted by means of either heterosexual or homosexual contact, blood transfusions, and by sharing hypodermic needles while shooting up drugs. Studies show that 14–32 percent of babies born to mothers who have the HIV virus end up infected ("Caesarean Delivery," 1993; Lee, 1993; Navarro, 1993a). Recent research suggests that about half of these infected infants get the virus while still in the uterus, and half get it during the birth process (Miles et al., 1993). During childbirth, the rupturing of blood vessels in the mother and baby provide an opportunity for an exchange of blood and transmission of the virus (Goedert et al., 1991). The virus also can be transmitted in breast milk (Blackman, 1991; Lederman, 1992). Children have also received AIDS through blood transfusions, but the proportion of children who contract AIDS in this manner has decreased dramatically due to better blood testing (Children's Defense Fund, 1992a; Jones et al., 1992).

Minority children are disproportionately infected with the HIV virus, with African Americans accounting for over half and Hispanics for almost one quarter of the pediatric cases of AIDS (Perkin, 1993). Inner city neighborhoods, where there is widespread intravenous drug use, have been especially hard hit (Leary, 1993a).

Pregnant women who have or who fear they have AIDS or other sexually transmitted disorders should discuss them frankly with their physicians. In some cases, measures can be taken that will help protect their children.

**TOXEMIA** ***Toxemia*** is a life-threatening disease, characterized by high blood pressure, that may afflict women late in the second or early in the third trimester. The first stage of toxemia, *preeclampsia,* is evidenced by protein in the urine, swelling from fluid retention, and high blood pressure and may be relatively mild. As preeclampsia worsens, the mother may have headaches and visual problems from the heightened blood pressure, along with abdominal pain. *Eclampsia,* the final stage, may bring convulsions, coma, and death of the mother or fetus. Women with toxemia often have ***premature*** or undersized babies.

Toxemia appears to be linked to malnutrition, but the causes are unclear. Ironically, undernourished women may gain weight rapidly through fluid retention, but their swollen appearance may then discourage eating. Pregnant women who gain weight rapidly but have not increased their food intake should consult their obstetricians.

***AIDS*** Acronym for acquired immune deficiency syndrome. A fatal, usually sexually transmitted disease that is caused by a virus and cripples the body's immune system, making the person vulnerable to opportunistic diseases.

***Toxemia*** A life-threatening disease that can afflict pregnant women and is characterized by high blood pressure.

***Premature*** Born before the full term of gestation.

**RH INCOMPATIBILITY** In ***Rh incompatibility,*** antibodies produced by the mother are transmitted to a fetus or newborn infant and cause brain damage or death. *Rh* is a blood protein that is found in the red blood cells of some individuals. Rh incompatibility occurs when a woman who does not have this factor, and is thus *Rh negative,* is carrying an *Rh-positive* fetus, which may happen if the father is Rh positive. This negative–positive combination occurs in about 10 percent of marriages in the United States but becomes a problem only in a minority of the resulting pregnancies. Rh incompatibility does not usually adversely affect a first child because women will typically not have formed antibodies to the Rh factor.

Since mother and fetus have separate circulatory systems, it is unlikely that Rh-positive fetal red blood cells will enter the mother's body. But the chances of an exchange of blood increase during childbirth, especially when the placenta detaches from the uterine wall. If an exchange of blood occurs, the mother produces Rh-positive antibodies to the baby's Rh-positive blood. These antibodies may enter the fetal bloodstream during subsequent pregnancies or deliveries and attack the red blood cells, causing anemia, mental deficiency, or death to the fetus.

If an Rh-negative mother is injected with a substance called *Rh immune globulin* within 72 hours after delivery of an Rh-positive baby, she will not develop the dangerous antibodies (Beeson, 1989). A fetus or newborn child at risk of Rh disease may also receive a preventive blood transfusion, which removes the mother's antibodies from its blood.

## *DRUGS TAKEN BY THE PARENTS*

In this section, we discuss the effects of various drugs on the unborn child—prescription drugs, over-the-counter drugs, and illegal drugs. Even commonly used medications, such as aspirin, may be harmful to the fetus (Anderson & Golbus, 1989). If a woman is pregnant or thinks she may be, it is advisable for her to consult her obstetrician before taking any drugs, not just prescription medications. A physician usually can recommend a safe and effective substitute for a drug that could potentially harm a developing fetus.

**THALIDOMIDE** ***Thalidomide*** was marketed in the early 1960s as a safe treatment for insomnia and nausea. It was available in Germany and England without prescription. Within a few years, over 10,000 babies with missing or stunted limbs had been born in these countries and elsewhere as a result of their mothers having taken thalidomide during pregnancy (Fleisher, 1987).

Thalidomide provides a dramatic and tragic example of the critical periods of vulnerability to various teratogens. The extremities undergo rapid development during the last 4 weeks of the embryonic stage (see Figure 3.21). Thalidomide taken during this period of development almost invariably causes limb deformities (Anderson & Golbus, 1989).

**ANTIBIOTICS** Several antibiotics may be harmful to the fetus. Tetracycline, which is frequently prescribed for flu symptoms and colds, may lead to yellowed teeth and bone abnormalities. Other antibiotics have been implicated in hearing loss (Anderson & Golbus, 1989; Hamod & Khouzami, 1988).

**HORMONES** Women at risk for miscarriages have been prescribed hormones such as progestin and DES to help maintain their pregnancies.

***Rh incompatibility*** A condition in which antibodies produced by the mother are transmitted to the child and may cause brain damage or death.

***Thalidomide*** A sedative used in the 1960s that has been linked to birth defects, especially deformed or absent limbs.

***Progestin*** is similar in chemical composition to male sex hormones. When taken at about the time that male sex organs begin to differentiate in the embryo, progestin can masculinize the external sex organs of embryos with a female (XX sex chromosome) genotype. Progestin taken during pregnancy also has been linked to increased levels of aggressive behavior during childhood (Reinisch, 1981) and to masculinelike play patterns in girls (Hines, 1982).

***Progestin*** A hormone used to maintain pregnancy that can cause masculinization of the fetus.

***DES*** (short for *diethylstilbestrol*), a powerful estrogen, was given to many women during the 1940s and 1950s to help prevent miscarriage. DES appears to have caused cervical and testicular cancer in some of the children of women who used it to maintain their pregnancies (Melnick et al., 1987). Among daughters of DES users, about 1 in 1,000 will develop cancer in the reproductive tract (Melnick et al., 1987). Daughters of DES users also are more likely to have babies who are premature or of low birth weight (Linn et al., 1988). Both daughters and sons whose mothers took DES have higher than average rates of infertility and immune system disorders (Brody, 1993c).

***DES*** Abbreviation for diethylstilbestrol, a powerful estrogen that has been linked to cancer in the reproductive organs of children of women who used the hormone when pregnant.

**Vitamins** While pregnant women are often prescribed daily multivitamins to maintain their own health and to promote the development of their fetuses, too much of a good thing can be dangerous. High doses of vitamins A and D have been associated with central nervous system damage, small head size, and heart defects (Anderson & Golbus, 1989).

**Heroin and Methadone** Maternal addiction to heroin or methadone is linked to low birth weight, prematurity, and toxemia (Anderson & Golbus, 1989). Narcotics such as heroin and methadone readily cross the placental membrane. These drugs are highly addictive, and the fetuses of women who use them regularly during pregnancy can become addicted to them.

The addicted newborns may be given the narcotic shortly after birth so they will not suffer withdrawal symptoms such as muscle tremors, fever, intestinal problems, difficulty in breathing, and, in severe cases, convulsions and death.

**TRUTH OR FICTION REVISITED**

*It is true that babies can be born addicted to narcotics and other drugs. A variety of drugs cross the placental membrane and influence the fetus.*

The neonates are then usually withdrawn gradually from the drug. Still, infant mortality, usually from respiratory problems, is more likely to occur among the children of mothers addicted to heroin or methadone. Behavioral effects still are apparent years later. For example, infants whose mothers were on methadone maintenance programs throughout pregnancy are slower in motor and language development at the age of 2 years (Hans et al., 1992). During the elementary school years, methadone-exposed children exhibit more anxiety and aggression than non-exposed children (deCubas & Field, 1993).

**Marijuana** Using marijuana during pregnancy may pose certain risks for the fetus, as shown in Table 3.3 (Abel & Sokol, 1988; Lester & Dreher, 1989). For example, babies of women who regularly used marijuana have been

FIGURE 3.22

***Fetal Alcohol Syndrome (FAS).*** *The children of many mothers who drank alcohol during pregnancy exhibit FAS. This syndrome is characterized by developmental lags and such facial features as an underdeveloped upper jaw, a flattened nose, and widely spaced eyes.*

found to show increased tremors and startling and failure to ***habituate*** to a stimulus, possibly indicating immature nervous system development.

**Cocaine** Recent studies clearly show the harmful effects on the fetus of using cocaine (including its highly addictive form, crack). Abuse of cocaine by women during pregnancy increases the risk of stillbirth, low birth weight and birth defects (Coles et al., 1992; Woods et al., 1993). The infants are often excitable, irritable, easily overstimulated, or lethargic (Lester et al., 1991; Treaster, 1993). As they get older, they are more likely to show learning and behavioral disabilities such as hyperactivity, disorganization, slowed language and cognitive development, and problems relating to others (Arendt et al., 1993; Chasnoff et al., 1992; Hawley et al., 1993; Singer et al., 1992).

Cocaine-using fathers also may produce birth defects in their offspring. A recent experiment found that cocaine appears to attach itself to the sperm of men who use the drug. When the cocaine-carrying sperm enters the egg during conception, birth defects may result ("Cocaine-using Fathers," 1991).

Some of the developmental problems of children exposed to cocaine during fetal life may not be due directly to the drug itself. Cocaine-abusing parents often do not nurture or supervise their children adequately (Hawley, 1993). This pattern of parental neglect and rejection may help explain why many children of cocaine abusers are insecurely attached to their parents (Rodning et al., 1991). One study found that children exposed to cocaine-abusing parents at home had more serious behavior problems than those exposed to cocaine during prenatal life (Youngstrom, 1991). So it appears that inadequate parenting can compound the effects of early drug exposure. By the same token, good parenting can help counteract the effects of early exposure to drugs. Research shows that if babies who have been exposed to drugs in the uterus are raised in a relatively warm, stable, and caring home environment, the long-term developmental outcome may be positive (Youngstrom, 1991; Zuckerman & Frank, 1992).

**Alcohol** Nearly 40 percent of children of mothers who drank heavily during pregnancy develop ***fetal alcohol syndrome (FAS)*** (Rosenthal, 1990b). Infants with FAS are frequently undersized and have smaller than average brains. They may have limb deformities and heart problems. They have distinct facial features, including widely spaced eyes, a flattened nose, and an underdeveloped upper jaw (Astley et al., 1992; Huber & Ekvall, 1993), as shown in Figure 3.22. Behavioral problems may include mental retardation, hyperactivity, distractibility, learning disabilities, and poor motor coordination (Autti–Rämö et al., 1992; Streissguth et al., 1992; Youngstrom, 1992a).

The characteristic facial deformities of FAS diminish as the child moves into adolescence and most such children catch up in height and weight (Spohr et al., 1993). But the intellectual, academic, and behavioral deficits of individuals with FAS persist into adolescence and adulthood. Recent studies by Ann Streissguth and her colleagues (1991; Olson et al., 1992), for example, found that the average academic functioning of adolescents and young adults with FAS was at the second- to fourth-grade level. Maladaptive behaviors such as poor judgment, distractability, and difficulty perceiving social cues were common.

Certain racial and ethnic groups appear to be more vulnerable to the effects of alcohol than others, perhaps because of genetic factors. African-American women are seven times more likely to have fetal-alcohol affected children than are white women with similar drinking habits. And FAS is 30 times more common among Native Americans than whites (Rosenthal, 1990b).

***Habituate*** Pay less attention to a repeated stimulus.

***Fetal alcohol syndrome (FAS)*** A cluster of symptoms shown by children of women who drink heavily during pregnancy, including characteristic facial features and mental retardation.

What about the effects of what is commonly called "social drinking"? Many physicians allow their pregnant patients a glass of wine with dinner. However, research has found that even moderate drinkers place their offspring at increased risk for a somewhat less severe set of effects known as ***fetal alcohol effect (FAE).*** For example, one study of nearly 32,000 women reported that pregnant women who had as few as one or two drinks a day were more likely to miscarry and to have growth-retarded babies than women who did not drink at all (Mills et al., 1984). By the age of 4, children whose mothers had only three to five drinks a week during midpregnancy show deficits that may predict academic difficulties. They show longer reaction time and attention deficits, lower intelligence, and poorer motor functioning than 4-year-olds whose mothers did not drink during pregnancy (Barr et al., 1990; Streissguth et al., 1992).

***Fetal alcohol effect (FAE)*** A cluster of symptoms less severe than those of FAS shown by children of women who drink moderately during pregnancy.

The safest course for a pregnant woman is to abstain from alcohol. If she does drink, drinking small amounts of alcohol may be less risky than drinking larger amounts, *but there is no guaranteed safe minimum.* It also makes sense for women who are trying to become pregnant—or who are not taking precautions against becoming pregnant—to assume that they may conceive a child any month and to modify their drinking habits accordingly.

And what of the father's drinking habits? Recent research indicates that the father's alcohol consumption just before conception may create risks. In one study, for example, newborns whose fathers regularly drank at least two glasses of wine or two bottles of beer per day prior to conception weighed less than babies whose fathers drank only occasionally (Merewood, 1991).

**CAFFEINE** Many pregnant women consume caffeine in the form of coffee, tea, soft drinks, chocolate, and nonprescription drugs. The findings of research on caffeine's effects on the developing fetus have been inconsistent. Some studies report no adverse findings (Mills et al., 1993; McDonald et al., 1992a). But others find that the more coffee a pregnant woman drinks, the more likely she is to have a miscarriage or a low-birth-weight baby (Armstrong et al., 1992; McDonald et al., 1992b). The most prudent course of action for pregnant women is to follow the recommendation of the Food and Drug Administration: Either avoid caffeine, or use it only in moderation.

**CIGARETTES** Smoking during pregnancy increases the likelihood of having a low-birth-weight or preterm baby (McDonald et al., 1992b; Wen et al., 1990). Women who smoke during pregnancy also are more likely to have miscarriages, stillbirths, and babies who die soon after birth (Armstrong et al., 1992; Berkowitz, 1988).

Maternal smoking may also have long-term negative effects on the child's development. Children whose mothers smoked during pregnancy are more likely to show short attention spans, hyperactivity, lower cognitive and language scores, and relatively poor school performance (Berkowitz, 1988; Fried et al., 1992).

A father's smoking may also hold dangers. Men who smoke are more likely than nonsmokers to produce abnormal sperm. Babies of fathers who smoke have higher rates of birth defects and infant mortality (Evans, 1981) and lower birth weights (Schwartz–Bickenbach et al., 1987). Fathers who smoke around the time of conception increase their child's risk of later developing cancer (Merewood, 1991).

Smoking after the baby is born also is harmful. Children of smokers are more likely to develop respiratory infections, asthma, and certain kinds of cancer. They also score lower on tests of reasoning ability and vocabulary and show

FIGURE 3.23

**WHY START A NEW LIFE UNDER A CLOUD?** *This American Cancer Society poster dramatizes the risks posed by maternal smoking during pregnancy.*

more behavior problems than children of nonsmokers (Chilmonczyk et al., 1993; Martinez et al., 1992; U.S. Environmental Protection Agency, 1993; Weitzman et al., 1992).

### *Environmental Hazards*

**Lead** The harmful effects of lead exposure on children have been known for some time (Yule, 1992). Only recently have we learned that lead affects the fetus as well. In one longitudinal study, newborns who had even mildly elevated levels of lead in their umbilical cord blood showed slower mental development at 1 and 2 years of age (Bellinger et al., 1987). By age 6, the cognitive functioning of these children had improved if they no longer were exposed to elevated lead levels in the home. But those children who continued to be exposed to higher lead levels still showed cognitive deficits (Bellinger et al., 1991).

**Mercury** The devastating effects of mercury on the developing fetus were first recognized among the Japanese who lived around Minimata Bay. Industrial waste containing mercury was dumped into the bay and accumulated in the fish that were a major food source for local residents. Children born to women who had eaten the fish during pregnancy often were profoundly retarded and neurologically damaged (Vorhees & Mollnow, 1987). Prenatal exposure to even small amounts of mercury and other heavy metals such as cadmium and chromium can produce subtle deficits in cognitive functioning and physical health (Lewis et al., 1992).

**PCBs** Polychlorinated biphenyls (PCBs) are chemicals used in many industrial products. Like mercury, they accumulate in fish that feed in polluted waters. Newborns whose mothers had consumed PCB-contaminated fish from Lake Michigan were smaller and showed poorer motor functioning and less responsiveness than newborns whose mothers had not eaten these fish. Furthermore, even those PCB-exposed infants who appeared normal at birth showed deficits in memory at 7 months and at 4 years of age (Jacobson & Jacobson, 1990; Jacobson et al., 1992).

**Radiation** Fetal exposure to radiation in high doses can cause defects in a number of organs, including the eyes, central nervous system, and skeleton (Michel, 1989). Pregnant women who were exposed to atomic radiation during the bombing of Hiroshima and Nagasaki in World War II gave birth to babies who were more likely to be mentally retarded in addition to being physically deformed (Yamazaki & Schull, 1990). The effects of low exposure levels of radiation remain unclear. The best advice for a pregnant woman is to avoid any unnecessary exposure to x-rays.

**Exposure of Fathers** Until recently, studies of the effects of environmental hazards on the fetus focused on the pregnant woman's exposure to these dangers. Recent research suggests that men exposed to such substances as lead and nuclear radiation also may produce children with serious abnormalities (Merewood, 1991; Purvis, 1990). For example, children of fathers employed in jobs with high exposure to lead had three times more kidney tumors than children whose fathers were not exposed (Davis, 1991). Another recent study found a higher incidence of leukemia among children whose fathers worked in nuclear plants where they were exposed to high levels of radiation prior to the children's conception ("British Study Finds," 1990).

## *Maternal Stress*

While pregnancy can be a time of immense gratification for women, it can also be a time of stress. The baby might be unplanned and unwanted. Parents might not have the financial resources or the room for the child. The mother might be experiencing physical discomforts because of the pregnancy. She might also fear the birth process itself or be concerned as to whether the baby will be normal.

But how does a mother's emotional state influence her unborn child? Although emotions are psychological feeling states, they also have physiological components. For example, they are linked to the secretion of hormones such as ***adrenalin.*** Adrenalin stimulates the mother's heart rate, respiratory rate, and many other bodily functions. Hormones pass through the placenta and also have a physiological influence on the unborn child.

The effects of maternal stress on the fetus are open to question. There are some reports that anxious, stressed mothers are more likely to have pregnancy and labor complications and premature or low-birth-weight babies (Lobel et al., 1992; Omer & Everly, 1988; Ward, 1991). Other studies show that the infants of emotionally anxious or distressed women have high activity levels both before and after birth. These babies have also been described as irritable, poor sleepers, and prone to gastrointestinal problems (Van den Bergh, 1990). On a more positive note, psychological and emotional support from others during pregnancy can reduce the complications associated with maternal stress (Norbeck & Tilden, 1983).

There are also confounding factors in the research on the effects of maternal stress. For example, pregnant women who are under stress may be more likely to consume alcohol or smoke cigarettes. The apparent effects of prenatal stress thus might actually be due to exposure to these harmful substances.

In sum, while some reports on the effects of maternal stress have been alarming, other evidence on the issue is less convincing. It makes sense for pregnant women to regulate the stresses affecting them, just as it makes sense for all of us to be aware of and regulate the stresses to which we are exposed. But it may be that the effects of maternal stress upon the fetus are mostly temporary.

## *The Mother's Age*

From a biological vantage point, the 20s may be the ideal age for women to bear children. Teenage mothers have a higher incidence of infant mortality and children with low birth weight (Wegman, 1992). Teenagers who become pregnant place a burden on bodies that may not have adequately matured to facilitate pregnancy and childbirth. Teenage mothers also are less educated and are less likely to seek prenatal care. All of these factors are associated with a greater likelihood of high-risk pregnancy (Rossetti, 1990).

What about women over the age of 30? There is evidence that women's fertility declines gradually until the mid-30s, after which it declines more rapidly (McFalls, 1990). Women beyond their middle 30s may have passed the point at which their reproductive systems function most efficiently. As noted, women possess all their ova in immature form at birth. Over 30 years, these cells are exposed to the slings and arrows of an outrageous environment of toxic wastes, chemical pollutants, and radiation, thus increasing the risk of chromosomal abnormalities such as Down syndrome (Evans et al., 1989). Women who wait until their 30s or 40s to have children also increase the likelihood of having stillborn or preterm babies (Cnattingius et al., 1992). But the risk of bearing a premature

***Adrenalin*** A hormone that generally arouses the body, increasing the heart and respiration rates.

or unhealthy baby still is relatively small even for older first-time mothers (Berkowitz et al., 1990). This news should be encouraging for women who want or need to delay marriage and bearing children until their 30s or 40s.

Whatever the age of the mother, the events of childbirth provide some of the most memorable moments in the lives of parents. In Chapter 4, we examine the process of birth and the characteristics of the newborn child.

## Summary

1. With the exception of ova (egg cells) and sperm, human cells carry 46 chromosomes (23 pairs of chromosomes) in their nuclei. Chromosomes contain genes, the units of heredity. Some traits are transmitted by single pairs of genes, whereas others are polygenic—transmitted by more than one pair of genes.

2. There are two types of cell division: mitosis and meiosis. In mitosis, the original 46 chromosomes duplicate themselves. One copy of each chromosome moves to each of the two new cells. Ova and sperm cells are formed by meiosis. Each pair of chromosomes splits, and 23 migrate into each ovum and sperm. At conception, the 23 chromosomes in the ovum and the 23 in the sperm cell unite, forming a zygote with 46 chromosomes.

3. Girls carry two X sex chromosomes. Boys carry one X and one Y sex chromosome. Identical (monozygotic) twins are formed when one zygote divides into two organisms. Fraternal (dizygotic) twins are conceived when two sperm fertilize two ova.

4. Dominant genetic traits are expressed when they pair up with recessive genes. Recessive traits are not expressed unless they pair up with other recessive genes or are unopposed by another gene.

5. There are a number of chromosomal abnormalities, including Down syndrome. Other chromosomal abnormalities, such as Klinefelter's syndrome and Turner's syndrome, stem from abnormal numbers of sex chromosomes. Genetic abnormalities include phenylketonuria (PKU), sickle-cell anemia, Tay–Sachs disease, and cystic fibrosis.

6. Genetic counseling helps potential parents weigh the probabilities that their children will be afflicted by such disorders. These abnormalities can frequently be detected by amniocentesis or chorionic villus sampling, ultrasound, blood tests, or fetoscopy.

7. Development reflects the interaction of genetic and environmental influences. Our genotype is our genetic makeup. Genes provide a reaction range for the expression of inherited traits. Our phenotype, or actual, exhibited traits, is influenced both by genetics (nature) and environmental factors (nurture).

8. Research strategies used to study the relative effects of heredity and environment on behavior include consanguinity studies, twin studies, and adoption studies.

9. New reproductive technologies may be used when fertility problems cannot be corrected: artificial insemination, in vitro fertilization (IVF), donor IVF, embryonic transplant, and surrogate motherhood.

10. During the germinal stage of prenatal development, the zygote divides repeatedly and becomes implanted in the uterine wall about 10 to 14 days after conception.

11. The major organ systems, amniotic sac, placenta, and umbilical cord are formed during the embryonic stage, which lasts from the second through the eighth weeks following conception.

12. The fetal stage lasts from the ninth week through birth, which takes place about 266 days (9 months) after conception. The fetal stage is marked by further gains in length and weight and maturation of organ systems.

13. Inadequate maternal diet has been linked to low birth weight and infant mortality. There are critical periods during prenatal development when the embryo and fetus are most vulnerable to certain substances (called *teratogens*) because of the structures that are differentiating at the time.

14. Various maternal diseases and disorders lead to birth defects or other problems in the child. These include rubella (German measles), congenital syphilis, AIDS, toxemia, and Rh incompatibility.

15. Drugs taken by the mother pass through the placenta and can harm the child. These include hormones such as DES and progestin and narcotics such as heroin, methadone, marijuana, cocaine, alcohol, caffeine, and tobacco.

16. Exposure of mothers and fathers to various environmental hazards such as lead, mercury, PCBs, and radiation can cause various physical and behavioral abnormalities in the child.

17. Periodic maternal stress probably has only temporary effects.

18. Women in their teens are more likely to have complications during pregnancy and to bear children with birth defects than women in their 20s. Women over 30 have increased risk of bearing children with chromosome abnormalities but otherwise have little extra risk of having unhealthy babies.

CHAPTER

4

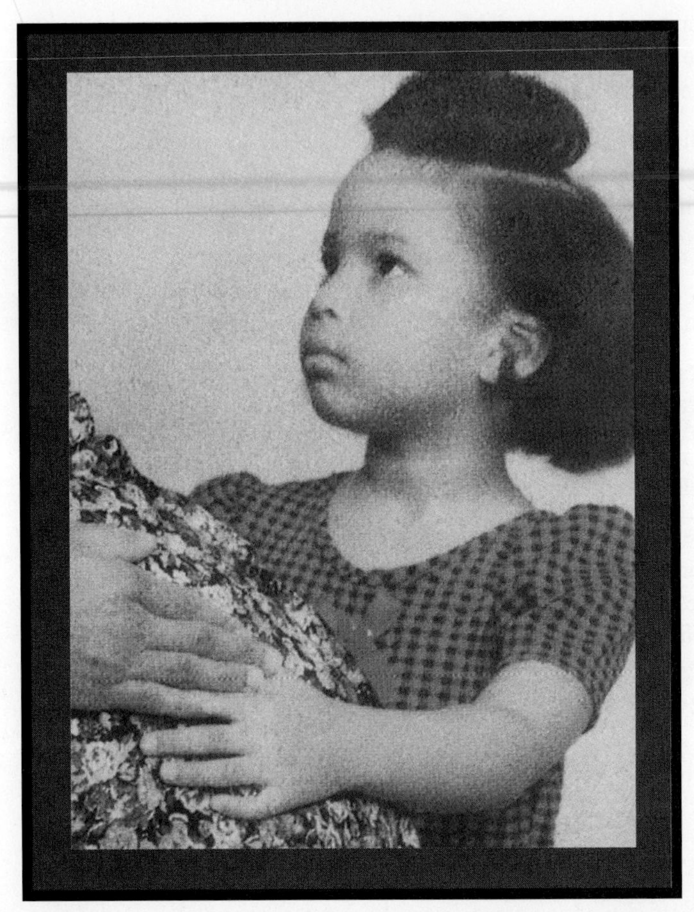

# *Birth and the Neonate: In the New World*

## CHAPTER OUTLINE

## TRUTH OR FICTION?

______ *The fetus signals the mother when it is ready to be born.*

______ *Soon after birth, babies are slapped on the buttocks to clear passageways for air and stimulate independent breathing.*

______ *Local or regional anesthetics used by mothers during childbirth have no effect on the child.*

______ *Women who give birth according to the Lamaze method experience no pain during labor.*

______ *Home births are as safe as hospital births for women with low-risk pregnancies.*

______ *Once their physical needs have been taken care of, preterm infants should be left undisturbed as much as possible until they achieve normal birth weights.*

______ *It is essential for parents to have extended early contact with their newborn children if adequate bonding is to take place.*

______ *Newborn babies who are placed face down in comfortably warm water will attempt to swim.*

______ *Newborn babies are capable of learning.*

______ *Newborn babies require about twice the amount of sleep that adults do.*

______ *Babies who are picked up as soon as they start to cry become spoiled and cry more often than babies whose mothers wait a while to pick them up.*

During the last few weeks, before she gave birth, said Michele, "I couldn't get my mind off the pregnancy—what it was going to be like when I finally delivered Lisa. I'd had the amniocentesis, but I was still hoping and praying everything would be normal with her. And it was just so darned hard to get around."

During the last weeks of pregnancy it is normal, especially for first-time mothers, to worry about the mechanics of delivery and whether the child will be normal. As they near full ***term,*** women become increasingly heavy and literally "bent out of shape." It may require a feat of balance and ingenuity to get up from a chair or out of bed. Muscle tension from supporting the fetus may cause backaches. Some women have the feeling that their pregnancies will never end.

They do, of course, or else this book would not have been written.

Early in the last month of pregnancy, as noted in Chapter 3, the head of the fetus settles in the pelvis. This is called *dropping* or *lightening*. Since lightening decreases pressure in the diaphragm, the mother may, in fact, feel lighter.

The first uterine contractions are called ***Braxton-Hicks contractions,*** or false labor contractions. They are relatively painless and may be experienced as early as the sixth month of pregnancy. They tend to increase in frequency as the pregnancy progresses and may serve to tone the muscles that will be used in delivery. Although they may be confused with actual labor contractions, real labor contractions are more painful and regular and are also usually intensified by walking.

A day or so before labor begins, increased pelvic pressure from the fetus may rupture superficial blood vessels in the birth canal so that blood appears in vaginal secretions. The mucus tissue that had plugged the cervix and protected the uterus from infection becomes dislodged. At about this time, 1 woman in 10 also has a rush of warm liquid from the vagina. This liquid is amniotic fluid, and its discharge means that the amniotic sac has burst. The amniotic sac usually does not burst until the end of the first stage of childbirth, as described below. Indigestion, diarrhea, an ache in the small of the back, and abdominal cramps are also common signs that labor is beginning.

The initiation of labor may be triggered by secretion of hormones by the adrenal and pituitary glands of the fetus. This suggests that the fetus has a way of signaling the mother when it is mature enough to sustain life outside the uterus. The fetal hormones stimulate the placenta and the uterus to secrete ***prostaglandins,*** which cause labor contractions by exciting the muscles of the uterus. Later during labor, the pituitary gland releases ***oxytocin,*** a hormone that stimulates contractions strong enough to expel the baby.

***Term*** A set period of time.

***Braxton–Hicks contractions*** The first, usually painless, contractions of childbirth.

***Prostaglandins*** (pross-tuh-GLAND-ins) Hormones that stimulate uterine contractions.

***Oxytocin*** (ox-see-TOE-sin) A pituitary hormone that stimulates labor contractions (from the Greek *oxys,* meaning "quick," and *tokos,* meaning "birth").

***Neonate*** A newborn child (from the Greek *neos,* meaning "new," and the Latin *natus,* meaning "born").

**TRUTH OR FICTION REVISITED**

*It is probably true that the fetus signals the mother when it is ready to be born. There is evidence that hormones secreted by the fetus normally stimulate the mother to begin childbirth.*

In this chapter we discuss the events of childbirth and the characteristics of the ***neonate.*** Arriving in the new world may be a bit more complex than you had thought, and it may also be that newborn babies can do a bit more than you had imagined.

## THE STAGES OF CHILDBIRTH

Childbirth begins with the onset of regular uterine contractions and occurs in three stages.

### *THE FIRST STAGE*

In the first stage, uterine contractions cause the cervix to become ***effaced*** and ***dilated*** to about 4 inches (10 cm) in diameter, so that the baby may pass through it. Most of the pain of childbirth is caused by the stretching of the cervix. When the cervix dilates easily and quickly, there may be little or no pain at all.

The first stage may last from a few hours to more than a day. Twelve to 24 hours is about average for a first pregnancy. Later pregnancies take about half this time. The initial contractions are usually not very painful and are spaced 10 to 20 minutes apart. They may last from 20 to 40 seconds each.

As time elapses, contractions become more frequent, regular, and strong. A woman is usually advised to go to the hospital when they are 4 to 5 minutes apart. Until the end of the first stage of labor, she will normally be in a labor room with the father-to-be.

If the woman is to be "prepped"—that is, if her pubic hair is to be shaved—it takes place now. The prep is intended to lower the chances of infection during delivery and to facilitate the performance of an ***episiotomy*** (described below). A woman may now also be given an enema to prevent an involuntary bowel movement during contractions of labor. However, many women find prepping and enemas degrading and seek obstetricians who do not perform them routinely. The medical necessity of these procedures has been questioned (Scott et al., 1990).

During the first stage of childbirth, ***fetal monitoring*** may be used. One kind of monitoring is an electronic sensing device strapped around the woman's abdomen. It can measure the fetal heart rate as well as the frequency, strength, and duration of the mother's contractions. Another type of fetal monitor has electrodes that are attached directly to the scalp of the baby. Abnormal heart rate alerts the medical staff to possible fetal distress so that appropriate steps can be taken, such as speeding up the delivery by means such as ***forceps*** or the ***vacuum extraction tube.*** The forceps is a curved instrument that fits around the baby's head and allows the baby to be pulled out of the mother's body. The vacuum extraction tube relies on suction to pull the baby through the birth canal.

When the cervix is nearly fully dilated, the head of the fetus begins to move into the vagina, or birth canal. This process is called ***transition.*** During transition, which lasts about 30 minutes or less, contractions usually are frequent and strong.

### *THE SECOND STAGE*

The second stage of childbirth follows transition. It begins when the baby first appears at the opening of the birth canal (Figure 4.1). The second stage is shorter than the first stage. It lasts from a few minutes to a few hours, and ends with the birth of the baby. The woman may be taken to a delivery room for the second stage of childbirth.

With each contraction in the second stage, the skin surrounding the birth canal stretches farther and the baby is propelled farther along. When the baby's head starts to emerge from the birth canal, it is said to have *crowned.* Typically, the baby emerges fully within a few minutes.

***Efface*** To rub out or wipe out; to become thin.

***Dilate*** To make wider or larger.

***Episiotomy*** (ep-pee-zee-OTT-to-me) A surgical incision in the perineum that widens the vaginal opening, preventing random tearing during childbirth.

***Fetal monitoring*** The use of instruments to track the heart rate and oxygen levels of the fetus during childbirth.

***Forceps*** A curved instrument that fits around the head of the baby and permits it to be pulled through the birth canal.

***Vacuum extraction tube*** An instrument that uses suction to pull the baby through the birth canal.

***Transition*** The initial movement of the head of the fetus into the birth canal.

FIGURE 4.1

***THE STAGES OF CHILDBIRTH.*** *In the first stage, uterine contractions efface and dilate the cervix to about 4 inches so that the baby may pass. The second stage begins with movement of the baby into the birth canal and ends with birth of the baby. During the third stage, the placenta separates from the uterine wall and is expelled through the birth canal. (Source: Rathus et al., 1993).*

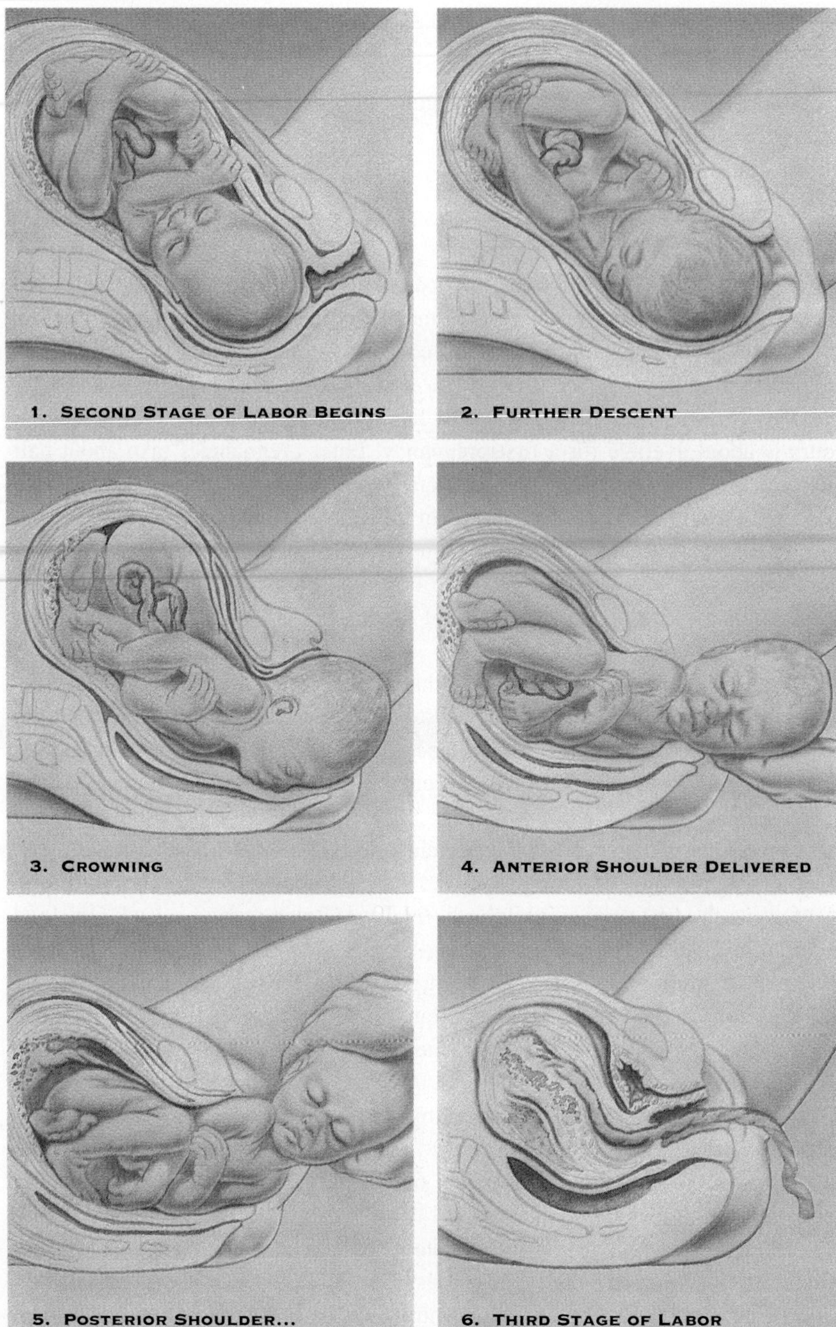


When the baby's head is crowned, an *episiotomy* may be performed. Most women do not feel the incision because pressure from the baby's emerging head tends to numb the area. The episiotomy, like prepping and the enema, is controversial and is not practiced in Europe. The incision may cause itching and discomfort as it heals. Discomfort may interfere with sexual relations for several months following delivery. Today, many U.S. obstetricians no longer perform the episiotomy routinely, although most agree that an episiotomy is preferable to random tearing that can occur if the tissue of the ***perineum*** becomes severely effaced.

***Perineum*** The area between the female's genital region and the anus.

Whether or not an episiotomy is performed, the baby's passageway to the outside world is, at best, a tight fit. For this reason, the shape of the baby's head and facial features may be distended. The head may be elongated, the nose flattened, and the ears bent—as though the new arrival had been involved in a vicious prizefight. Parents are frequently concerned about whether the baby's features will return to their proper shape, but they almost always do.

Once the baby's head emerges from the mother's body, mucus is removed from its mouth by suction so that the passageway for breathing will not be obstructed. This procedure is repeated when the baby is fully delivered. Because of the use of suction, the baby is no longer routinely held upside down to help expel mucus. Nor is the baby slapped on the buttocks to stimulate breathing, as in so many old films.

**TRUTH OR FICTION REVISITED**

*It is no longer true that newborn babies are slapped on the buttocks to clear passageways for air and stimulate independent breathing. Today, the babies' air passages are cleared by suction.*

When the baby is breathing adequately on its own, the umbilical cord is clamped and severed about 3 inches from the baby's body. At about 266 days after conception, mother and infant have finally become separate beings. The stump of the umbilical cord will dry and fall off in about 7 to 10 days.

The baby may then be taken by a nurse, so that various procedures can be performed while the mother is in the third stage of labor. The baby is usually given a plastic identification bracelet and footprinted. Most states require that drops of silver nitrogen or an antibiotic ointment (erythromycin) be put into the baby's eyes to prevent bacterial infections. The newborn may also receive an injection of vitamin K, since neonates do not manufacture this vitamin. Vitamin K helps ensure that the baby's blood will clot normally in the event of bleeding.

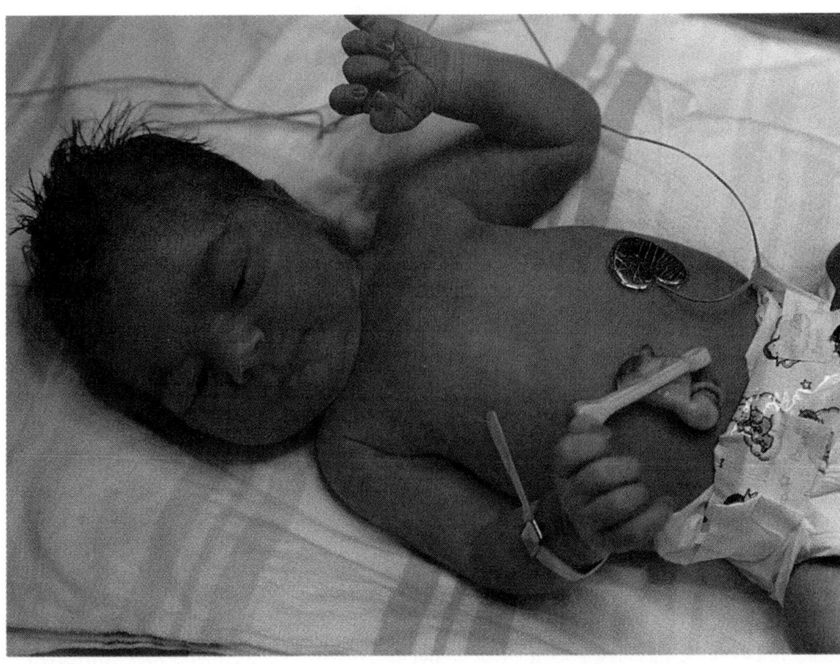

**FIGURE 4.2**

***A Clamped and Severed Umbilical Cord.*** *The stump of the cord dries and falls off in about 10 days.*

### *The Third Stage*

During the third stage or *placental* stage of childbirth, which may last from a few minutes to an hour or more, the placenta separates from the uterine wall and is expelled along with fetal membranes. There may be some bleeding. The uterus begins the process of contracting to a smaller size. The attending physician sews the episiotomy and any tears in the perineum.

## METHODS OF CHILDBIRTH

Until this century, childbirth typically was an intimate procedure that took place at home and involved the mother, a ***midwife,*** family, and friends. In the United States today, it is most often a hospital procedure performed by an obstetrician who uses surgical instruments and anesthetics to help protect mother and child from infection, complications, and pain. While the use of modern medicine has saved lives, it has also made childbearing more impersonal. Social critics argue that it has, to a large degree, wrested from women control over their own bodies and, through drugs, denied many women the experience of giving birth.

In this section, we consider a number of contemporary methods for facilitating childbirth.

### *Medicated Childbirth*

*In sorrow thou shalt bring forth children. (Genesis 3:16)*

The Bible suggests that in ancient times, people viewed suffering during childbirth as a woman's lot. But during the past two centuries, the development of modern medicine and effective ***anesthetics*** has led many people to believe that women need not experience discomfort during childbirth. Today, some anesthesia is used in most U.S. deliveries.

***General anesthesia*** was popularized in England when Queen Victoria delivered her eighth child under chloroform anesthesia in 1853. General anesthesia, like the chloroform of old, achieves its anesthetic effect by putting the woman to sleep. Sodium pentothal, a barbiturate, is injected into the vein of the arm, producing general anesthesia. ***Tranquilizers*** such as Valium, oral barbiturates such as sodium seconal, and narcotics such as Demerol, are not anesthetics, but they may be used to reduce anxiety and pain without inducing sleep.

General anesthetics, tranquilizers, and narcotics decrease the strength of uterine contractions during delivery and, by crossing the placental membrane, lower the overall physiological and behavioral responsiveness of the neonate (Brazelton et al., 1987). Negative effects include abnormal patterns of sleep and wakefulness and decreased attention and social responsiveness for at least the first 6 weeks of life (Broman, 1983; Sepkoski, 1985). The higher the dosage, the greater the impact.

A major question is whether these anesthetics have long-term effects on the child. The evidence is mixed (Brazelton, 1990a). Some studies show no long-term effects. Others, however, suggest that children whose mothers received heavy doses of anesthetics during delivery lag in their motor development and cognitive functioning at least through 7 years of age (Brackbill et al., 1985).

Regional or ***local anesthetics*** deaden the pain in certain areas of the body without generally decreasing the mother's alertness or putting her to sleep. For these reasons, it has also been hoped that they would also have less impact on

***Midwife*** An individual who helps women in childbirth (from Old English roots meaning "with woman").

***Anesthetics*** Agents that produce partial or total loss of the sense of pain (from Greek roots meaning "without feeling").

***General anesthesia*** The process of eliminating pain by putting the person to sleep.

***Tranquilizer*** A drug that reduces feelings of anxiety and tension.

***Local anesthetic*** A method that reduces pain in an area of the body.

the neonate. In the *pudendal block,* the mother's external genitals are numbed by local injection. In an *epidural block,* anesthesia is injected into the spinal canal, temporarily numbing the body below the waist. Anesthesia is injected directly into the spinal cord in the *spinal block,* which also numbs the body from the waist down.

It appears that local anesthesia does decrease the strength and lower the activity levels of neonates, at least during the first 8 hours following birth (Brackbill et al., 1985; Brazelton et al., 1987). Even low doses of local anesthesia make the baby less alert (Lester et al., 1982).

**TRUTH OR FICTION REVISITED**

*Actually, local or regional anesthetics used by mothers during childbirth do have an effect on the child, although less of an effect than general anesthesia.*

Some researchers have also found that medicated childbirth negatively influences parent–baby interactions during the month after birth (Hollenbeck et al., 1984). Why should this be so?

Medicated babies are less responsive after birth, and it is possible that their relationships with their mothers get off on the wrong foot. Perhaps the mothers' first impressions of lower responsiveness persist even after their babies' responsiveness levels have risen to normal. Note also that most studies in this area are "natural experiments." Mothers are not randomly assigned to medication or no-medication groups. Some mothers ask for medication, others do not. Thus, it might be that the same factors that influence some mothers to refuse medication also influence them to appreciate their children more. Given that questions remain about the effects of medicated delivery on the child, one such factor could be greater concern about the welfare of their babies. It could also be that the mothers who do not ask for medication are better prepared for childbirth—and child rearing.

Women who have general anesthesia and are unconscious throughout childbirth have more negative feelings about childbirth and the baby than women using any other method. Women who receive spinal or other blocks have relatively more positive feelings about childbirth and their babies, but they feel detached somewhat from the childbirth process (Leifer, 1980).

### NATURAL CHILDBIRTH

Partly as a reaction against the use of anesthetics, English obstetrician Grantly Dick-Read endorsed ***natural childbirth*** in his 1944 book, *Childbirth Without Fear.* Dick-Read argued that women's labor pains are heightened by their fear of the unknown and resultant muscle tensions. Dick-Read helped shape modern childbirth practices by educating women about the biological aspects of reproduction and delivery, encouraging physical fitness, and teaching relaxation and breathing exercises.

### PREPARED CHILDBIRTH

Most women who are pregnant for the first time expect pain and discomfort during childbirth (Leifer, 1980). Certainly the popular media image of childbirth

***Natural childbirth*** A method of childbirth in which women use no anesthesia and are educated about childbirth and strategies for coping with discomfort.

***Lamaze method*** A childbirth method in which women are educated about childbirth, learn to relax and breathe in patterns that conserve energy and lessen pain, and have a coach (usually the father) present during childbirth. Also termed *prepared childbirth.*

is one in which the woman sweats profusely and screams and thrashes in pain. The French obstetrician Fernand Lamaze shared this impression until he visited the Soviet Union in 1951. He found that many Russian women bore babies without anesthetics or pain. Lamaze took back to Western Europe with him the techniques of the Russian women, which were brought to the United States in the 1950s as the ***Lamaze method,*** or *prepared childbirth.* Acknowledging his debt to the conditioning concepts of Ivan Pavlov (see Chapter 2), Lamaze (1981) contends that women can learn to *dissociate* uterine contractions from pain and fear by associating *other* responses with contractions. Women can be taught to think of pleasant images, such as beach scenes, while they are in delivery, and they can engage in breathing and relaxation exercises.

A pregnant woman attends Lamaze classes accompanied by a "coach"—usually the father-to-be—who will aid her in the delivery room by timing contrac-

FIGURE 4.3

**AN EXERCISE CLASS FOR PREGNANT WOMEN.** *Years ago, the rule of thumb was that pregnant women were not to exert themselves. Today, it is recognized that exercise is healthful for pregnant women, because it promotes cardiovascular fitness and increases muscle strength. Fitness and strength are assets during childbirth—and at other times.*

tions, offering moral support, and coaching her in patterns of breathing and relaxation. During each contraction, the woman breathes in a specific, rehearsed manner. She is taught how to relax muscle groups throughout her body, then how to contract a single muscle while others remain at ease. The rationale is that during labor she will be able, upon cue, to keep other muscles relaxed while the uterus contracts. In this way she will conserve energy, minimize bodily tension and pain, and experience less anxiety.

The woman is also educated about the process of childbirth. The father-to-be is integrated into the process, and it has been reported that their relationship is strengthened and that the woman feels less alone during delivery as a result (Dooker, 1980; Wideman & Singer, 1984). The father, as well as the mother, takes pride in "their" accomplishment of childbirth (Bing, 1983). Women using the Lamaze method have generally positive feelings about childbirth and about their babies (Leifer, 1980). They usually report some pain during delivery and frequently use anesthetics (Wuitchik et al., 1990), but the method appears to enhance women's self-esteem by giving them a sense of control over the delivery (Dooker, 1980; May & Perrin, 1985).

**TRUTH OR FICTION REVISITED**

*It is not true that women who give birth according to the Lamaze method experience no pain. Women bearing children according to this method are better prepared for childbirth. However, they often request anesthesia as childbirth proceeds.*

Continuous support during labor may be provided by individuals other than the father, of course. A woman's mother, sister, or friend also may serve as a

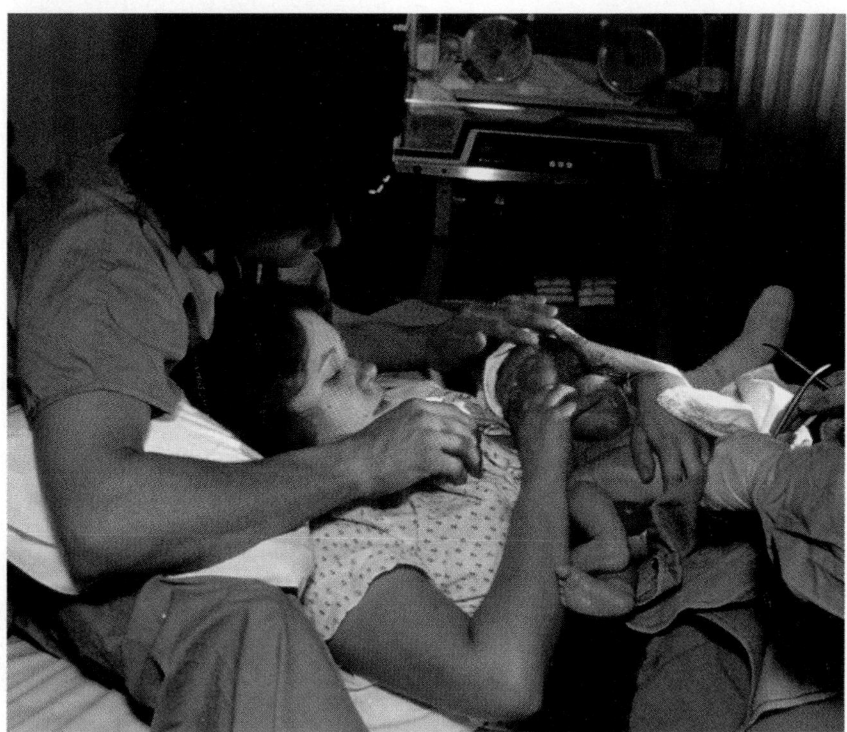

FIGURE 4.4

**FATHER IN THE DELIVERY ROOM.** *Today, the father is usually integrated into the process of childbirth. The father and mother take pride in "their" accomplishment of childbirth.*

***Leboyer method*** A childbirth method that focuses on gently easing the neonate into the world. Also termed *gentle childbirth.*

labor coach. Four recent studies in three countries have demonstrated the positive impact of continuous emotional support during labor by an experienced female companion known as a *doula* (Kennell & McGrath, 1993; Kennell et al., 1991). Women in a U.S. hospital who had a doula randomly assigned to them during labor had fewer Caesarean deliveries, less anesthesia, and shorter labors than women without a doula. In a similar South African study, doula-supported women reported less pain and anxiety during labor. Six weeks after childbirth, they were less likely to experience post-partum depression. Two studies in Guatemala found that women who were randomly assigned the support of a doula showed more affectionate interactions with their babies after delivery. Emotional support during labor clearly has beneficial effects for both mothers and infants.

### *"Birth without Violence": The Leboyer Method*

Natural and prepared methods of childbirth address the comfort of the mother. In the book *Birth without Violence,* French physician Frederick Leboyer (1975) advocates another form of reaction against the institutionalization of childbearing by focusing on gently easing the infant into the world. In the ***Leboyer method,*** or *gentle birth,* the physician or midwife eases the baby along the birth canal, with fingers under its armpits. Hospital delivery rooms tend to be noisy, harshly lit places where babies are separated from their mothers after birth so that the various procedures described earlier can be carried out and the mother can rest. Leboyer tames the hospital setting by lowering the lighting and instructing attendants to keep their voices hushed. After birth, the baby is placed on its

FIGURE 4.5

**LEBOYER METHOD.** *One of the practices of the Leboyer method is placing the newborn baby on the mother's abdomen after birth. This practice is widely adopted today, even by mothers who do not use other aspects of the Leboyer method. Some parents and professionals believe that it is one element in the bonding process.*

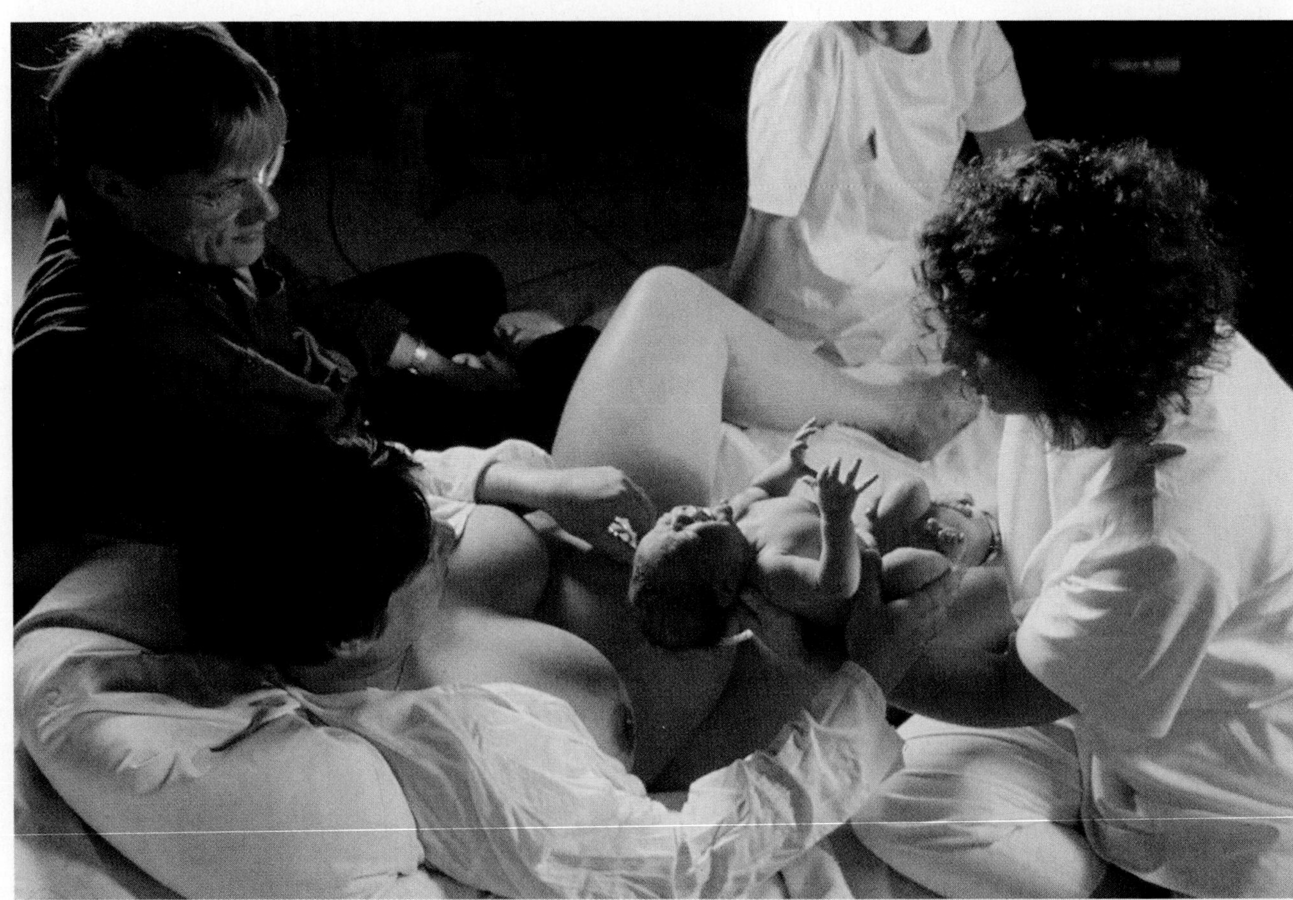

mother's abdomen and is held by her until it begins breathing strongly on its own. Only then is the umbilical cord cut. In other methods of childbirth, the umbilical cord is cut upon delivery. Leboyer has noted that his method permits the baby to escape the violence of being slapped on the buttocks, but as noted earlier, today babies are (gently) suctioned rather than slapped. Next, the baby is given a warm bath—frequently by the father (Berezin, 1980). When the newborn opens its eyes and flexes its limbs, it is returned to the mother for cuddling and feeding.

There is little research on the Leboyer method. The few studies that have been done suggest that gentle birth techniques have little or no influence on later development (Maziade et al., 1986). One study compared babies delivered by the Leboyer method to babies delivered by other means an hour after birth, and at follow-ups of 24 hours, 72 hours, and 8 months (Nelson et al., 1980). No differences were found in the responsiveness of the babies or in the health of the babies or their mothers. At 8 months, the mothers reported that they *thought* that the Leboyer method had helped their children, even though their views were not supported by objective evidence. It seems that we generally expect more from "special" treatments and are disposed toward rating them positively.

***Caesarean section*** A method of childbirth in which the neonate is delivered through a surgical incision in the abdomen.

***Breech position*** A position in which the fetus enters the birth canal buttocks-first.

***Transverse position*** A position in which the fetus lies crosswise across the opening to the birth canal.

## *Caesarean Section*

In a ***Caesarean section*** (or C-section), the baby is delivered by surgery rather than through the vagina. In this procedure, by which Julius Caesar is said to have been delivered (hence the name), incisions are made in the abdomen and the uterus, and the baby is removed. The incisions are then sewn up, and the mother is capable of walking about on the same day, although there is discomfort. Today, C-sections typically are performed near the top line of the mother's pubic hair. This so-called "bikini cut" is all but invisible.

The C-section has become increasingly common in the United States. It is used in nearly 24 percent of childbirths today, as compared with 10 percent in 1975 ("349,000 Caesareans," 1993). The C-section typically is recommended when normal delivery is expected to be difficult or threatening to the health of the mother or child. Difficult vaginal deliveries can occur when the mother is weak or fatigued, the baby is very large, or the mother's pelvis is small or misshapen. C-sections may also be performed when the baby is in the ***breech position*** (buttocks downward), in the ***transverse position*** (lying crosswise), or in distress. Babies' contact with herpes infections in the birth canal can also be avoided by use of the C-section (Rathus & Boughn, 1993).

The C-section has its disadvantages. Women receiving C-sections have a higher risk of infection than women who deliver vaginally, and their physical recoveries from childbirth are prolonged. Some health professionals assert that many C-sections are unnecessary. They note that the rate of C-sections is substantially higher in the United States than in other industralized countries that also have advanced medical care (Notzon, 1990). Because of these criticisms, the rate of increase in C-sections in the United States has been leveling off in recent years ("349,000 Caesareans," 1993)

## *Alternatives to the Hospital: Where Should a Child Be Born?*

Most babies in the United States are born in hospitals. The advantage of hospital delivery is the availability of medical equipment and personnel in case of complications. But hospitals can be expensive and impersonal and their use may reinforce the perception that pregnancy is an illness that requires medical treatment, rather than a natural process. The hospital environment encourages patients to surrender responsibility to the physician and to take a passive role in their own well-being. For these reasons, in recent years many pregnant women have sought alternative birthplaces.

**BIRTHING CENTERS** Birthing centers attempt to provide the backup facilities found in hospitals, combined with the atmosphere of a home delivery. Unheard of 20 years ago, there are now nearly 150 in the United States. Birthing centers are sometimes located within or adjacent to medical centers so that medical equipment is nearby in case of emergency (Belkin, 1992).

The birthing room itself is usually decorated and furnished cheerfully, like a bedroom. Family, friends, and siblings of the baby may be present. Women in labor move about, eat, drink, rest, or talk with family and friends as they wish. After the birth, the family usually remains together to share in the happy event. As in the Leboyer method, the neonate is placed on the mother's abdomen, where it has the opportunity to be cuddled and to experience eye contact. Many U.S. hospitals today also have birthing rooms and take a more family-centered approach to childbirth (see Developing Today).

**HOME BIRTHS** Home birth has also increased in popularity in recent years. Home delivery provides familiar surroundings and also enhances the perception that the woman and her family are in control.

Some advocates of home delivery argue that when a pregnant woman is screened carefully for potential complications, and when she has a history of normal births, home delivery may be quite safe. Opponents assert that women cannot be screened for every possible complication and that home delivery poses unnecessary risks to mother and child. Many physicians, in fact, refuse to deliver babies in the home. But recent research suggests that for low-risk pregnancies, home birth assisted by a midwife is as safe as physician-assisted hospital delivery (A.M. Durand, 1992).

## *Developing Today*

### *A FAMILY-CENTERED APPROACH TO CHILDBIRTH*

In recent years, childbirth has been becoming more family-centered, as opposed to hospital- or doctor-centered. Margaret Matlin (1993, p. 381) summarizes some of the trends toward family-centered childbirth:

1. Labor is not artificially induced simply because it is more convenient for the physician.
2. Women are allowed to take an upright (sitting) position during delivery, rather than the flat-on-the-table, feet-in-the-stirrups approach.
3. Birth practices that have little or no health benefits—such as routine enema, shaving of the genital area, a ban on the consumption of food, and episiotomy—are modified.
4. Routine use of anesthetics is discouraged.
5. A supportive family member or friend is present.
6. Alternative physical locations for childbirth are explored.
7. Siblings are permitted to share in the birth of the new baby, and they are carefully prepared for the event.

*Home births appear to be as safe as hospital births for women who are in good health and who have low-risk pregnancies.*

### ALTERNATIVE TO THE OBSTETRICIAN: THE MIDWIFE

Many countries around the world, including those in Europe, have long used midwives to deliver babies. In the last 20 years, the choice of a midwife for prenatal care and delivery has become increasingly popular in the United States as well (Brody, 1993d). Midwives today are nearly all registered nurses with advanced training in gynecology and obstetrics. Currently, they attend between 3 and 4 percent of hospital-based births and about a third of deliveries in birthing centers (Brody, 1993d).

According to one study (Declercq, 1992), midwives who work in hospitals serve mothers with higher than average risk of birth complications. These women are younger than the average mother and are more likely to be unmarried, foreign-born, and members of minority groups. They receive less prenatal care. Despite these risks, the study found that babies had better than average outcomes when their births were attended by midwives either in or out of hospitals. The babies were less likely to have low birth weight. They also scored better on the Apgar scale, a measure of the newborn's general state of health that we describe more fully later in the chapter. Another review examined 15 studies that compared the outcomes of births attended by physicians or by certified nurse-midwives (Brown & Grimes, 1993). Again, the babies delivered by the midwives did as well or better than the physician-assisted babies in terms of birth weight and Apgar scores. In addition, women who had been attended by midwives left the hospital sooner and were more likely to breast-feed. These positive outcomes indicate that midwives are providing a reasonable alternative to physician-assisted birth.

## BIRTH PROBLEMS

Although the great majority of deliveries are unremarkable from a medical standpoint, perhaps every delivery is most remarkable from the parents' point of view. Still, there are a number of problems that can and do occur. In this section, we discuss anoxia and preterm and low-birth-weight neonates.

### ANOXIA

Prenatal ***anoxia*** can cause brain damage and associated problems such as mental retardation and neurological impairment. Prolonged cutoff of the baby's oxygen supply during delivery can also cause cerebral palsy and, in extreme cases, death.

The fetus and emerging baby receive oxygen through the umbilical cord. Passage through the birth canal is tight, and the umbilical cord is usually squeezed during the process. If the squeezing is temporary, the effect is like holding one's breath for a moment, and no problems are likely to ensue. (In fact, slight oxygen deprivation at birth is not unusual because the transition from receiving oxygen through the umbilical cord to breathing on its own may not take place immediately

***Anoxia*** A condition characterized by lack of oxygen.

after the baby is born.) But if constriction of the umbilical cord is prolonged, anoxia can result. Prolonged constriction is more likely during a breech presentation, when the baby's body may press the umbilical cord against the birth canal.

Fetal monitoring can help detect anoxia before it causes damage. A C-section can be performed if the fetus seems to be in distress. Fortunately, even infants who initially show impaired development as a result of anoxia often improve and show little damage by the time they are in the early school years (Stechler & Halton, 1982). One longitudinal study found that the effects of a difficult birth were largely overcome when children experienced a stable and stimulating rearing environment. Unless there was serious damage to the nervous system, later physical and psychological impairment resulted only when children grew up under persistently poor rearing conditions (Werner & Smith, 1992).

## *PRETERM AND LOW-BIRTH-WEIGHT INFANTS*

Since the fetus makes dramatic gains in weight during the last weeks of pregnancy, prematurity and low birth weight usually go hand in hand. A baby is considered premature or ***preterm*** when birth occurs at or before 37 weeks of gestation, as compared with the normal 40 weeks. A baby is considered to have a low birth weight when it weighs less than 5½ pounds (about 2,500 grams). When a baby is low in birth weight, even though it is born at full term, it is referred to as ***small for dates.*** Small-for-dates babies, as a group, tend to remain shorter and lighter than their age-mates (Barros et al., 1992; Niedbala & Tsang, 1993), while preterm babies who survive are more likely to achieve normal heights and weights.

About 7 percent of children are born preterm or low in birth weight, although the incidence varies in different racial and ethnic groups (see Developing Today). Newborns weighing between 3¼ and 5½ pounds are 7 times more likely to die than infants of normal birth weight, while those weighing less than 3¼ pounds (1,500 grams) are nearly 100 times more likely to die (Overpeck et al., 1992).

**SIGNS OF PREMATURITY** Preterm babies show characteristic signs of immaturity. They are relatively thin, because they have not yet formed the layer of fat that gives so many full-term children their round, robust appearance. They often have fine, downy hair referred to as ***lanugo,*** and an oily, white substance on the skin known as ***vernix.*** Lanugo and vernix disappear within a few days or weeks. If they are born 6 weeks or more prior to full term, their nipples will not yet have emerged. The testicles of boys born this early will not yet have descended into the scrotum. However, the nipples develop further and the testes descend after birth.

The muscles of preterm babies are immature. As a result, the babies' vital sucking and breathing reflexes are weak. The muscles of preterm babies may not be mature enough to sustain independent breathing. Also, the walls of the tiny air sacs within their lungs may tend to stick together because they do not yet secrete ***surfactants,*** substances that lubricate the walls of the sacs (Avery & Merritt, 1991). As a result, babies born more than a month prior to full term may breathe irregularly or suddenly stop breathing, evidence of a cluster of problems known as ***respiratory distress syndrome.*** About 14 percent of babies born one month early show the syndrome, and it is found more frequently among infants born still earlier (Lin, 1989). Respiratory distress syndrome causes a large percentage of U.S. neonatal deaths. The immune systems of preterm babies may also be underdeveloped, making them vulnerable to infections.

Major strides have been made in helping low-birth-weight children survive. Still, low-birth-weight children who do survive often have problems, including

***Preterm*** Born at or prior to completion of 37 weeks of gestation.

***Small for dates*** Descriptive of neonates who are unusually small for their age.

***Lanugo*** (lan-OO-go) Fine, downy hair that covers much of the body of the neonate, especially preterm babies.

***Vernix*** An oily, white substance that coats the skin of the neonate, especially preterm babies.

***Surfactants*** Substances that lubricate the walls of the air sacs in the lungs.

***Respiratory distress syndrome*** A cluster of breathing problems, including weak and irregular breathing, to which preterm babies are particularly prone.

below-average verbal ability and academic achievement and various physical, motor, perceptual, neurological, and behavioral impairments (Byrne et al., 1993; Goldson, 1992; Gross et al., 1992; Hoy et al., 1992).

Preterm infants with very low birth weights (under 1,500 grams) are likely to show the greatest cognitive deficits and developmental delays (Hack et al., 1992; Rose et al., 1992a; Roussounis et al., 1993; Simensen & Marshall, 1992). Still, medical advances in recent years have greatly reduced the severity and incidence of handicaps among babies with very low birth weights (Kitchen et al., 1991; Robertson et al., 1992). A recent review of 111 studies that followed the development of very low birth weight babies into the preschool years and beyond reported that 75 percent had no disabilities (Escobar et al., 1991).

**Incubator** A heated, protective container in which premature infants are kept.

**Retrolental fibroplasia** A form of blindness that stems from excessive oxygen, as may be found in an incubator.

**Womb simulator** An artificial environment that mimics some of the features of the womb, particularly temperature, sounds, and rocking movements.

**Treatment of Preterm Babies** Because of their physical frailty, preterm infants usually remain in the hospital and are placed in ***incubators*** that maintain a temperature-controlled environment and afford some protection from disease. They may be given oxygen, although excessive oxygen can cause permanent eye injury or a form of blindness referred to as ***retrolental fibroplasia.***

A generation ago, preterm babies were left as undisturbed as possible. For one thing, concern was aroused by the prospect of handling such a tiny, frail creature. For another, preterm babies would not normally experience interpersonal contact or other sources of external stimulation until full term.

However, experiments carried out over the past two decades have suggested that preterm infants profit from early stimulation just as do full-term babies. One type of approach attempts to compensate somewhat for early removal from the uterus by exposing preterm infants to treatments that provide features of the intrauterine environment. These treatments include recordings of maternal heartbeats as they might be heard from within the uterus and placement in incubator waterbeds and ***womb simulators*** whose movements presumably capture some of the sensations of floating within the amniotic sac (Thoman, 1993).

Another approach is to provide preterm infants with the types of experiences that full-term babies receive. The babies may be cuddled, rocked, talked and sung to, exposed to recordings of their mothers' voices, and have mobiles placed within view. One study combined mechanical rocking with a recorded heartbeat for several 15-minute periods on a daily basis (Barnard & Bee, 1983). Immediately following the treatment, the infants showed increased activity levels. At a 2 year follow-up, their intellectual functioning was significantly ahead of preterm babies not given this treatment. Other recent innovations in stimulating premature babies include massage (Field, 1992b), and "kangaroo care," in which the baby spends several hours a day lying skin to skin, chest to chest, with one of its parents (Anderson, 1993; Rosenthal, 1992a). By and large, preterm infants exposed to stimulation tend to gain weight more rapidly, show fewer respiratory problems, and make greater advances in motor, intellectual, and neurological development than controls (Rosenthal, 1992a; Scafidi et al., 1990; Sparling et al., 1991).

## Truth or Fiction Revisited

*It is not true that preterm infants should be left undisturbed as much as possible until they achieve normal birth weights. It seems that stimulation fosters their development.*

## Developing Today

### Culture and Development: Low Birth Weight, Infant Mortality and Prenatal Care

The incidence of low birth weight and infant death varies in different racial and ethnic groups, as illustrated in the figures here. You can see in Figure 4.6 that African-American mothers are most likely to have low-birth-weight babies. Since babies of low birth weight are more likely to die, it is not surprising that the infant mortality rate also is highest among African-American babies (see Figure 4.7).

African-American mothers, compared with white mothers, are more likely to be teenaged, have lower educational levels, and get less prenatal care. These are all risk factors for low birth weight. However, even when comparing African-American and white mothers who are similar in age, educational level, amount of prenatal care, and other factors, African-American women still are more likely to have low-birth-weight infants. To add to this puzzle, the risk of low birth weight in other disadvantaged ethnic minority groups—such as Mexican Americans and Native Americans—is much less than the risk for African Americans and only slightly higher than that for whites (Garcia-Coll, 1990; Healthy People 2000, 1990).

No single cause is responsible for the high incidence of low-birth-weight infants among African Americans. Four common pregnancy problems account for most cases of low birth weight: infection or rupture of the amniotic membranes, premature labor, high blood pressure and hemorrhaging (Kempe et al., 1992). African-American women are three times as likely as white women to experience these problems.

Why do African-American women have more difficult pregnancies than white women? One logical reason might be differences in prenatal care. Comprehensive prenatal care generally is connected with higher birth weights (McLaughlin et al., 1992). As you can see in Figure 4.8, only 61 percent of African-American mothers received prenatal care in 1988, compared with 79 percent of whites. (Asian and Cuban mothers had even higher rates of prenatal care.) But before we conclude that lower rates of prenatal care are responsible for the higher incidence of African-American low-birth-weight babies, look at the figures for other ethnic groups. Premature babies are relatively rare among Mexican-American and Native-American women. And yet these women are just as poor as African-American women and are no more likely to receive prenatal care (Davidson & Fukushima, 1992). So the puzzle remains unsolved for now.

**FIGURE 4.6**

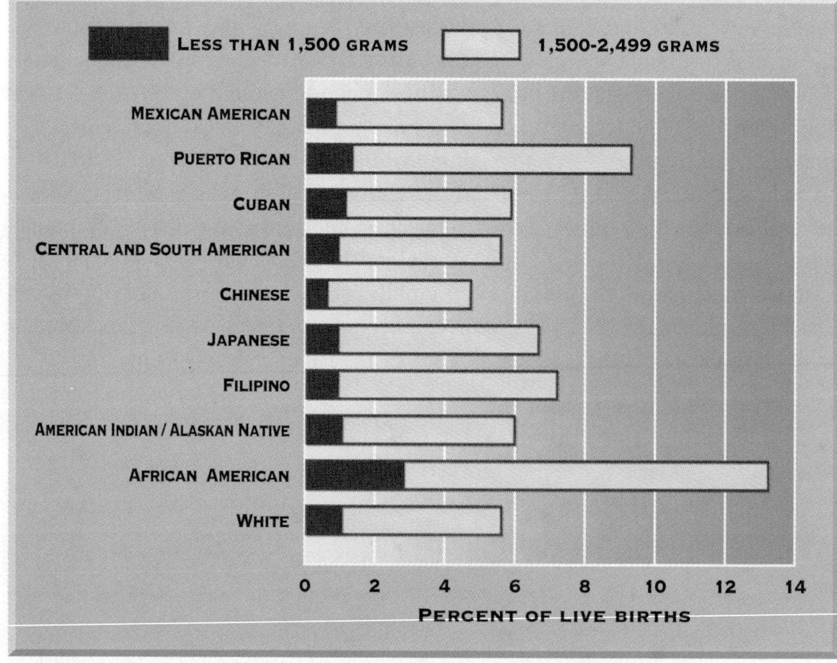


NOTE: DATA ON HISPANIC ORIGIN OF MOTHER ARE FROM 30 STATES AND THE DISTRICT OF COLUMBIA.
SOURCE: NATIONAL CENTER FOR HEALTH STATISTICS, NATIONAL VITAL STATISTICS SYSTEM.

**Low Birth Weight, According to Race/Ethnicity of Mother: United States 1988.** *African-American women are more likely than white women to have low-birth-weight babies, even when controlling for risk factors such as age, educational level, and amount of prenatal care. The risk of low birth weight in other disadvantaged ethnic minority groups also is less than the risk for African Americans. Are differences in prenatal care responsible? See Figure 4.8. (Source: Healthy People 2000, 1990).*

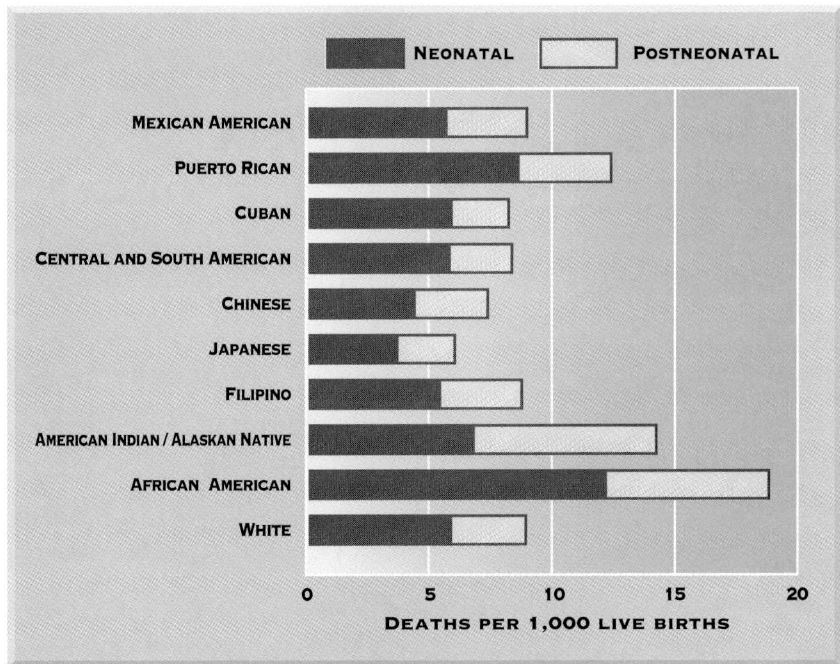


NOTE: DATA ON HISPANIC ORIGIN OF MOTHER ARE FROM 23 STATES AND THE DISTRICT OF COLUMBIA.
SOURCE: NATIONAL CENTER FOR HEALTH STATISTICS, NATIONAL VITAL STATISTICS SYSTEM.

FIGURE 4.7

***INFANT MORTALITY RATES, ACCORDING TO RACE/ETHNICITY OF MOTHER: UNITED STATES, 1983–1985.*** *Infant mortality rates are highest for African Americans, followed by Native Americans and Puerto Ricans. Asian-American groups have the lowest infant mortality rate. These trends appear to be related to differences in the incidence of low-birth-weight babies in various ethnic groups. (See Figure 4.6). (Source: Healthy People 2000, 1990)*

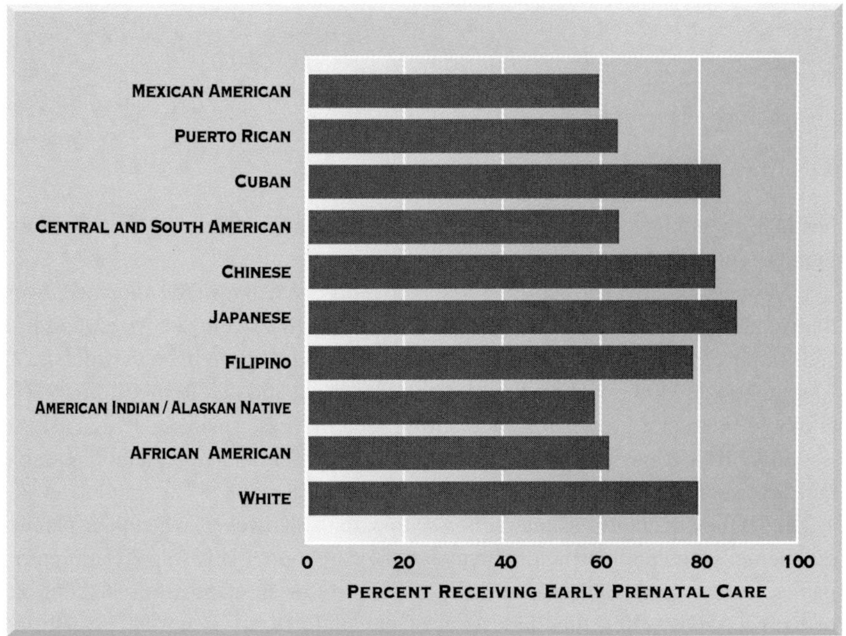


NOTE: EARLY PRENATAL CARE IS DEFINED AS CARE BEGINNING IN THE FIRST TRIMESTER OF PREGNANCY. DATA ON HISPANIC ORIGIN OF MOTHER ARE FROM 30 STATES AND THE DISTRICT OF COLUMBIA.
SOURCE: NATIONAL CENTER FOR HEALTH STATISTICS, NATIONAL VITAL STATISTICS SYSTEM.

FIGURE 4.8

***EARLY PRENATAL CARE, ACCORDING TO RACE/ETHNICITY OF MOTHER: UNITED STATES, 1988.*** *African-American mothers are less likely to receive prenatal care than white American, Asian-American, or Cuban mothers. Does this account for the higher incidence of African-American babies of low birth weight? One puzzling fact is that Mexican-American and Native-American women have fewer premature babies than African-American women, yet they are just as poor and are no more likely to receive prenatal care. (Source: Healthy People 2000, 1990).*

**PARENTS AND PRETERM NEONATES** Parents, unfortunately, often do not treat preterm newborns as well as they treat full-term newborns. For one thing, preterm neonates are less attractive than full-term babies. Preterm infants usually do not have the robust, appealing appearance of many full-term babies. Their cries are more high-pitched and grating (Frodi & Senchak, 1990). Fear of hurting these babies can further discourage parents from handling them, even when the

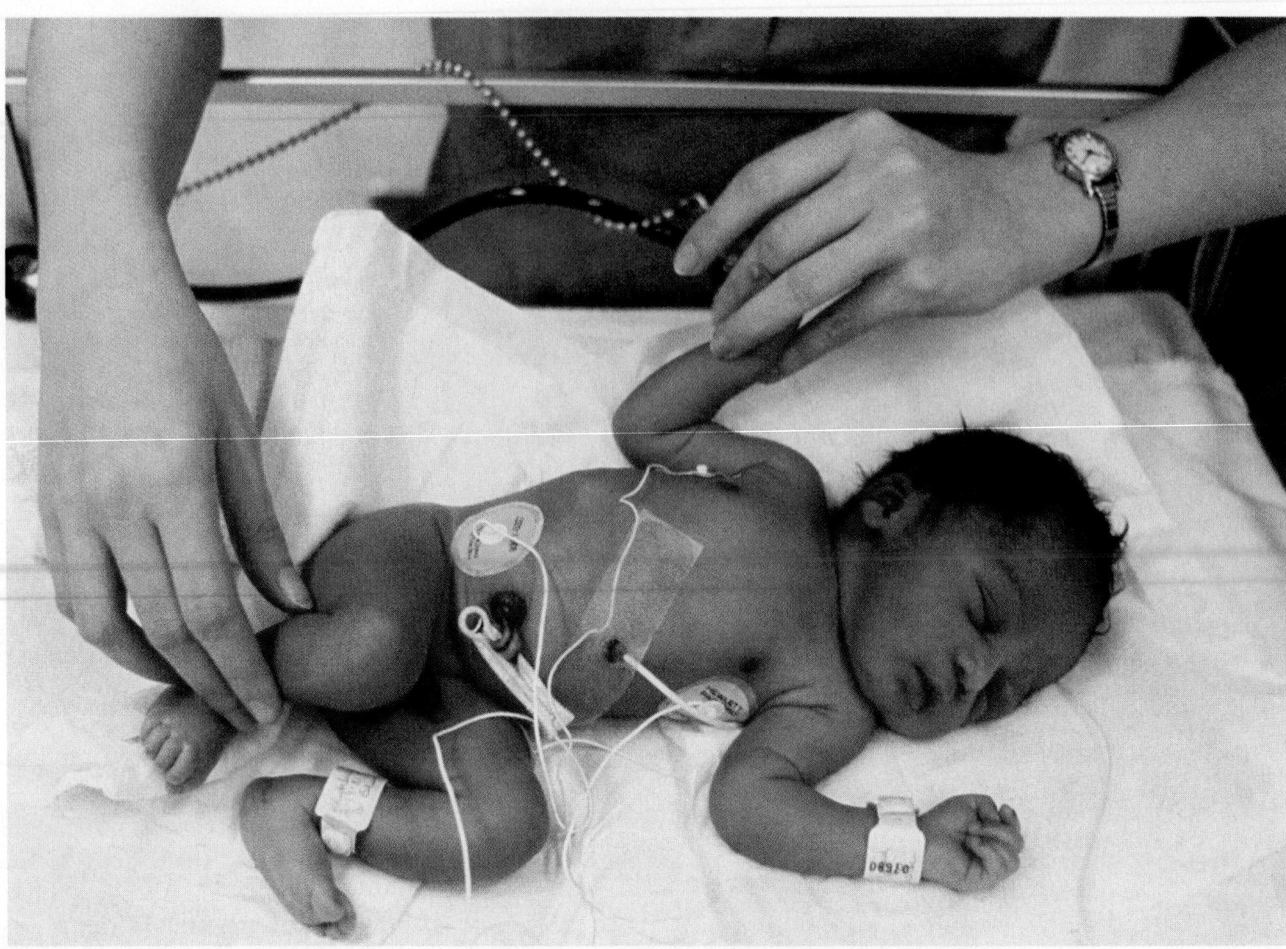

FIGURE 4.9

***STIMULATING A PRETERM INFANT.*** *It was once believed that preterm infants should be left as undisturbed as possible. Today, however, it is recognized that preterm infants usually profit from various kinds of stimulation.*

hospital encourages it. Preterm children are also more likely to be abused by their parents in later years (Korner, 1987).

Mothers of preterm babies frequently report that they feel alienated from them and harbor feelings of failure, guilt, and low self-esteem. They respond less sensitively to their infants' behavior than mothers of full-term babies (Pederson & Moran, 1993). Mothers of preterm infants also touch and talk to their infants less and hold them at a greater distance during feeding (Eckerman & Oehler, 1992).

Once they come home from the hospital, preterm infants remain more passive and less sociable than full-term infants (Crnic et al., 1983; Garcia-Coll et al., 1992), so they demand less interaction with parents. However, when their parents do interact with them during the first year, they are more likely to poke at preterm babies, caress them, and talk to them, apparently in an effort to prod them out of their passivity. Yet, this high level of parental activity is not necessarily all positive in nature. Parents and preterm babies smile at one another less frequently during the first year than do parents and full-term babies (Field, 1980; Garner & Landry, 1992). Preterm babies also show less positive emotional tone in their vocalizations (Crnic et al., 1983). Mothers of preterm babies report feeling overprotective toward them. This may explain why 1-year-old preterm infants explore less and stay closer to their mothers than do full-term babies of the same age (Macey et al., 1987).

Preterm infants fare better when they have responsive and caring parents. Longitudinal research shows that preterm children who are reared in attentive and responsive environments attain higher intelligence test scores, have higher self-esteem, show more positive social skills, and have fewer behavioral and emotional problems in childhood than do preterm children reared in less responsive homes (Beckwith et al., 1992; Goldberg et al., 1989; Pfeiffer & Aylward, 1990).

**Intervention Programs** Intervention programs aimed at helping parents adjust to the birth and care of a low-birth-weight infant can be beneficial to both the parents and the baby (Parker et al., 1992; Zahr et al., 1992). In one such program, a specially trained nurse provided mothers with information, practical experience handling the infant, and emotional support. At the completion of the program, the mothers reported greater self-confidence and satisfaction with mothering and more favorable perceptions of their infants' temperament than did mothers who were not in the program (Rauh et al., 1988). At 3, 7, and 9 years of age, children of participating mothers showed more advanced intellectual development than control children (Achenbach et al., 1990, 1993).

In another intervention program, the Infant Health and Development Program, parents of preterm babies in eight different locations were visited by child development specialists during their children's first 3 years. Parents were taught what to expect from their baby and how to respond to foster the child's development. Between the ages of 1 and 3, the children attended a day-care program that focused on language, social, and motor skills. At age 3, the children showed more advanced intellectual functioning and fewer behavior problems than preterm babies who were not in the program (Brooks-Gunn et al., 1993; Ramey et al., 1992).

## The Postpartum Period

The weeks following delivery are called the ***postpartum period.*** The first few days postpartum are frequently happy ones. The long wait is over. The discomforts (and fear) of labor are gone. In the great majority of cases the baby is normal, and the mother may be pleased that she is getting her figure back. However, a number of women experience feelings of depression in the days and sometimes weeks and months following childbirth. In this section, we discuss two issues of the postpartum period: maternal depression and bonding.

### *Maternal Depression*

Women frequently encounter one of two types of depression during the postpartum period.

**Maternity Blues** The first type of depression is less severe. It is called ***maternity blues,*** and it is experienced by 50 to 80 percent of new mothers (Harding, 1989). The maternity blues are characterized by sadness, crying, and irritability. This mood state typically occurs around the third day after delivery and lasts about 2 days. Hormonal changes that occur after delivery may play a role in triggering the maternity blues. Maternity blues are also more common following a first pregnancy, and they may reflect the mother's adjustment to the changes that are about to take place in her daily life. New fathers too may feel

***Postpartum period*** The period that immediately follows childbirth.

***Maternity blues*** Crying and feelings of sadness, anxiety and tension, irritability, and anger that half or more women experience within a few days after childbirth.

***Postpartum depression*** More severe, prolonged depression that afflicts 10 percent of women after childbirth, and is characterized by sadness, apathy, feelings of worthlessness, difficulty concentrating, and physical symptoms.

***Bonding*** The process of forming bonds of attachment between parent and child.

overwhelmed or unable to cope. Perhaps more fathers might experience "paternity blues" but for the fact that mothers generally perform most of the child-rearing chores.

**POSTPARTUM DEPRESSION** About 10 percent of women have severe feelings of depression that last for several weeks or months following delivery (Campbell & Cohn, 1991; O'Hara et al., 1991). These feelings are termed ***postpartum depression,*** and they are characterized by extreme sadness, apathy, despair, feelings of worthlessness, difficulty concentrating, and changes in sleep and appetite patterns. Mothers with postpartum depression interact more negatively with their infants than do nondepressed mothers (Campbell et al., 1992, 1993; Field, 1992a).

Like the maternity blues, postpartum depression may reflect both physiological and psychological factors. Hormonal changes may be linked to postpartum depression, but women with postpartum depression are more likely than those with maternity blues to have had depressive episodes prior to and during pregnancy (O'Hara et al., 1991). Postpartum depression, also like the maternity blues, may be heightened by concerns about maternal adequacy and the changes that will occur in personal and family life (Belsky & Pensky, 1988; Ruble et al., 1990). Psychological stresses such as marital problems or the challenges of adjusting to a sick or unwanted baby may increase a woman's susceptibility to postpartum depression (Gitlin & Pasnay, 1989).

Infants with so-called "difficult" temperaments (see Chapter 7) may also contribute to postpartum depression. Their intense emotional reactions, prolonged and vigorous crying episodes, and irregular sleeping and eating patterns are stressful in and of themselves. They also place a severe strain on the mother's sense of competence (Cutrona & Troutman, 1986; Whiffen & Gotlib, 1989). A network of social support is helpful to the mother at this time (Campbell et al., 1992; Leadbeatter & Linares, 1992). But even without such support, mood improves spontaneously for most depressed mothers between 2 weeks and 5 months after childbirth (Fleming et al., 1992).

## *BONDING*

In Chapter 7, we fully explore the nature of parent–child attachment. Here let us consider the view that the first hours postpartum provide a special opportunity for ***bonding*** between parents and newborns.

One study that has stirred controversy on this issue was carried out by Marshall Klaus and John Kennell (1976). They assert that the first few hours after birth present a "maternal-sensitive" period during which the mother is particularly disposed, largely because of hormone levels, to form a bond with the neonate.

In their study, one group of mothers was randomly assigned to standard hospital procedure in which their babies were whisked away to the nursery shortly after birth. Throughout the remainder of the hospital stay, the babies visited with their mothers for half-hour periods at feeding time. The other group of mothers spent a half-hour with their neonates within 3 hours after birth, and they spent 5 hours a day with their infants for the remainder of the stay. The hospital staff encouraged and reassured the group of mothers who had extended contact.

Follow-ups over a 2-year period suggested that extended contact benefitted both the mothers and children (Klaus & Kennell, 1978). For example, extended-contact mothers were more likely than controls to cuddle their babies, pick them up and soothe them when they cried, and interact with them. Some later studies also suggested that extended early contact may lead to better parent–child relationships, at least on a short-term basis (Fleming, 1989; Goldberg, 1983; Thomson & Kramer, 1984).

Critics note that these studies of bonding are fraught with methodological problems, however (Goldberg, 1983; Thomson & Kramer, 1984). Perhaps the most telling criticism is that it is impossible to determine if the benefits resulted from the extended contact or from parents' knowledge that they were in a special group. For example, not only did mothers in the Klaus and Kennell study receive extra time with their babies, but the hospital staff gave them encouragement and support. Did their infants fare better because of superior bonding, or because the hospital staff taught them that their relationships with their children were special and instructed them how to play with their babies and care for them? In short, research is not compelling that the hours after birth are critical, or that failure to "form bonds" during this time will result in a second-rate parent–child relationship (Eyer, 1993). There are countless millions of fine parent–child relationships in which the parents were denied these early hours with their children (Rutter, 1981). Even Kennell and Klaus (1984) have toned down their views in their more recent writings. They now view the hours after birth as just one element in a complex and prolonged bonding process.

**TRUTH OR FICTION REVISITED**

*It has not been shown that it is essential for parents to have extended early contact with their newborn children if adequate bonding is to take place. Most scholars agree that early extended contact is just one possible element of a complex and prolonged bonding process.*

## CHARACTERISTICS OF NEWBORNS

Many neonates come into the world looking a bit fuzzy, because the lanugo has not yet disappeared, although full-term babies show less of this downy substance than preterm babies do. Full-term babies also show something of the protective oily coating or vernix shown by preterm babies. It dries up within a few days. Newborns tend to be pale, regardless of race. Their skin is thin, and the blood flowing through surface capillaries creates a pinkish cast.

In this section, we discuss several aspects of the behavior of newborn children. Newborns may be utterly dependent on others, but they are probably more aware of their surroundings than you had imagined, and they make rapid adaptations to the world around them.

### *ASSESSING THE HEALTH OF NEWBORNS*

The newborn's overall level of health is usually evaluated at birth according to the ***Apgar scale,*** developed by Virginia Apgar in 1953. Apgar scores are based on five signs of health, as shown in Table 4.1. The neonate can receive a score of 0, 1, or 2 on each sign. The total Apgar score can, therefore, vary from 0 to 10. A score of 7 or above usually indicates that the baby is not in danger. A

***Apgar scale*** A measure of a newborn's health that assesses appearance, pulse, grimace, activity level, and respiratory effort.

**TABLE 4.1**

*THE APGAR SCALE*

| SIGN | POINTS 0 | 1 | 2 |
|---|---|---|---|
| APPEARANCE COLOR | BLUE, PALE | BODY PINK, EXTREMITIES BLUE | ENTIRELY PINK |
| PULSE HEART RATE | ABSENT (NOT DETECTABLE) | SLOW–BELOW 100 BEATS/MINUTE | RAPID–100-140 BEATS/MINUTE |
| GRIMACE REFLEX IRRITABILITY | NO RESPONSE | GRIMACE | CRYING, COUGHING, SNEEZING |
| ACTIVITY LEVEL MUSCLE TONE | COMPLETELY FLACCID, LIMP | WEAK, INACTIVE | FLEXED ARMS AND LEGS; RESISTS EXTENSION |
| RESPIRATORY EFFORT BREATHING | ABSENT (INFANT IS APNEIC) | SHALLOW, IRREGULAR, SLOW | REGULAR BREATHING; LUSTY CRYING |

score below 4 suggests that the baby is in critical condition and requires medical attention. By 1 minute after birth, most normal babies attain scores of 8 to 10 (Bornstein & Lamb, 1992).

An acronym using the name APGAR is commonly used to aid in remembering the five criteria:

A: the general *appearance* or color of the newborn infant

P: the *pulse* or heart rate

G: *grimace* (the 1-point indicator of reflex irritability)

A: general *activity* level or muscle tone

R: *respiratory* effort, or rate of breathing

The ***Brazelton Neonatal Behavioral Assessment Scale,*** developed by pediatrician T. Berry Brazelton, measures neonates' reflexes and other behavior patterns (Brazelton et al., 1987; Brazelton, 1990b). The test screens neonates for behavioral and neurological problems by assessing four areas of behavior—motor behavior, including muscle tone and most reflexes; response to stress, as shown, for example, by the startle reflex; adaptive behavior, such as orientation to the examiner and responsiveness to cuddling; and control over physiological state, as shown by quieting oneself after being disturbed.

## *REFLEXES*

***Brazelton Neonatal Behavioral Assessment Scale*** A measure of a newborn's motor behavior, response to stress, adaptive behavior, and control over physiological state.

If soon after birth you had been held gently for a few moments with your face down in comfortably warm water, you would not have drowned. Instead of breathing the water in, you would have exhaled slowly through the mouth and engaged in swimming motions. (We urge readers not to test babies for this reflex. The hazards are obvious.) This swimming response is innate, or inborn, and it is just one of the many ***reflexes*** shown by neonates. Reflexes are simple, unlearned, stereotypical responses that are elicited by certain types of stimulation. They do not require higher brain functions; they occur automatically, without thinking. Reflexes are the most complicated motor activities displayed by newborns. Neonates cannot roll over, sit up, reach for an object that they see, or raise their heads.

***Reflex*** An unlearned, stereotypical response to a stimulus.

***Voluntarily*** Intentionally.

***Neural*** Of the nervous system.

***Rooting reflex*** A reflex in which infants turn their mouths and heads in the direction of a stroking of the cheek or the corner of the mouth.

## TRUTH OR FICTION REVISITED

*It is true that newborn babies who are placed face down in comfortably warm water will make swimming motions. Swimming movements are reflexive and may reflect our evolutionary history.*

Let us return to our early venture into the water. If you had been placed into the water not a few moments but several months after birth, the results might have been very different and disastrous. After a few months the swimming reflex, like many others, ceases to exist. However, at 6 to 12 months of age infants can learn how to swim ***voluntarily.*** In fact, the transition from reflexive swimming to learned swimming can be reasonably smooth with careful guided practice.

Many reflexes have survival value. Adults and neonates, for example, will reflexively close their eyes when assaulted with a puff of air or sudden bright light. Other reflexes seem to reflect interesting facets of the evolution of the nervous system. The swimming reflex seems to suggest that there was a time when our ancestors profited from being born able to swim.

Pediatricians learn a good deal about the adequacy of newborn babies' ***neural*** functioning by testing their reflexes. The absence or weakness of a reflex may indicate immaturity (as in prematurity); slowed responsiveness, which can result from anesthetics used during childbirth; brain injury; or retardation. Let us examine some of the reflexes shown by neonates.

The rooting and sucking reflexes are basic to survival. In the ***rooting reflex,*** the baby turns the head and mouth toward a stimulus that strokes the cheek, chin, or corner of the mouth. The rooting reflex facilitates finding the mother's nipple in preparation for sucking. Babies will suck almost any object that touches the lips. The sucking reflex grows stronger during the first days after birth and can be lost if not stimulated. As the months go on, reflexive sucking becomes replaced by voluntary sucking.

### THINKING ABOUT DEVELOPMENT

In human beings, what kinds of behavior patterns are learned and what kinds are inate (inborn)? Are most differences between people learned or inate?

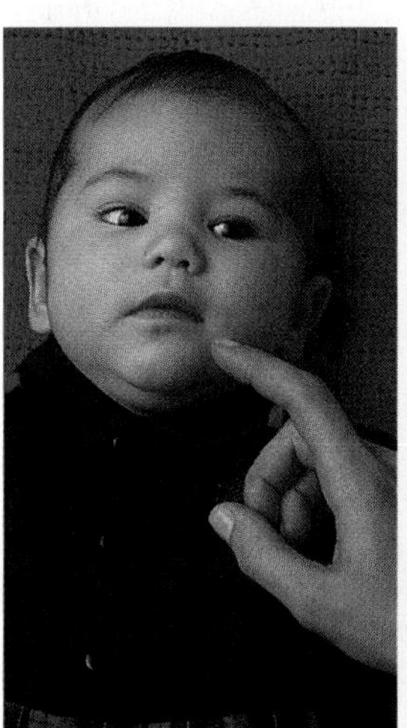
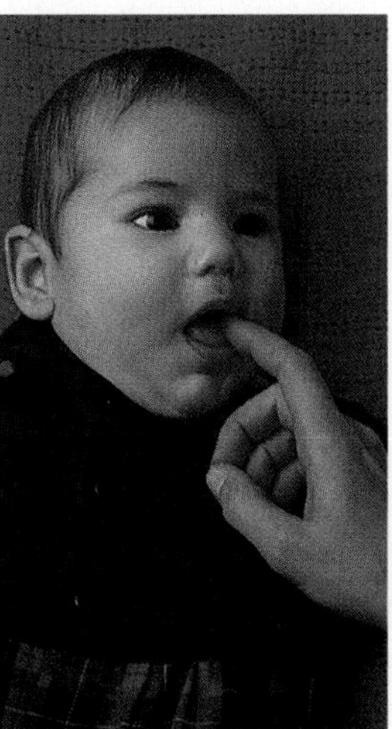
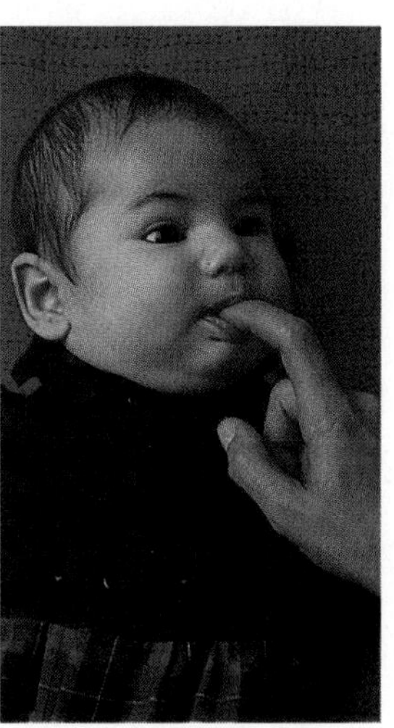

FIGURE 4.10

**THE ROOTING REFLEX.** *Tactile stimulation of the corner of the mouth elicits turning of the head toward the stimulus.*

FIGURE 4.11

***Testing the Sucking Reflex.*** *The sucking reflex grows stronger during the days after birth. After several months, reflexive sucking is replaced by voluntary sucking.*

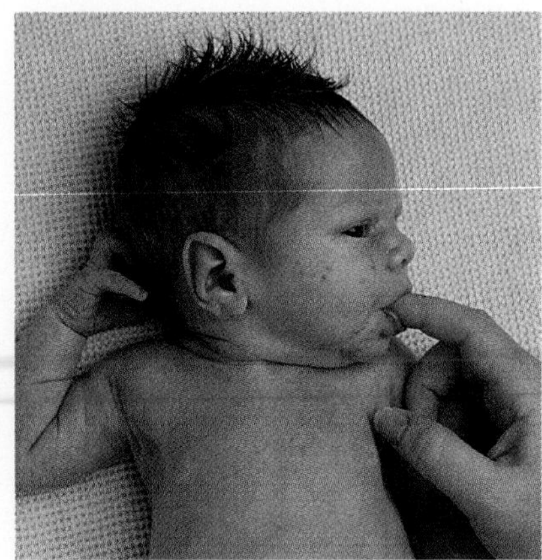

In the startle or ***Moro reflex,*** the back arches and the legs and arms are flung out and then brought back toward the chest, with the arms in a hugging motion. The Moro reflex occurs when a baby's position is suddenly changed or support for the head and neck is suddenly lost. It can also be elicited by loud noises, by bumping the baby's crib, or by jerking the baby's blanket. The Moro reflex is usually lost by 6 to 7 months after birth, although similar movements can be found in adults who suddenly lose support. Absence of the Moro reflex can indicate immaturity or brain damage.

During the first few weeks following birth, babies show an increasing tendency to reflexively grasp fingers or other objects pressed against the palms of their hands. In this ***grasping reflex,*** or *palmar reflex,* they use four fingers only (the thumbs are not included). The grasping reflex is stronger when babies are simultaneously startled. Most babies can support their own weight in this way. They can be literally lifted into the air as they reflexively cling with two hands. Some babies can actually support their weight with just one hand. (Please do not try this, however!) Absence of the grasping reflex may indicate depressed activity of the nervous system, which can stem from use of anesthetics during childbirth. The grasping reflex is usually lost by 3 to 4 months of age, and babies generally show voluntary grasping by 5 to 6 months. The Moro and grasping reflexes, like the swimming reflex, may suggest something about our evolutionary history. For example, the startle and grasping reflexes could work together to allow baby monkeys to cling to their mothers (Field, 1990).

One or 2 days after birth, babies show a reflex that mimics walking. When held under the arms and tilted forward so that the feet press against a solid surface, a baby will show a ***stepping reflex*** in which the feet are advanced alternately. A full-term baby "walks" heel to toe, whereas a preterm infant is more likely to remain on tiptoe. The stepping reflex usually disappears by about 3 or 4 months of age.

**Moro reflex** A reflex in which infants arch their back, fling out their arms and legs, and draw them back toward the chest in response to a sudden change in position.

**Grasping reflex** A reflex in which infants grasp objects that cause pressure against the palms.

In the ***Babinski reflex,*** the neonate fans or spreads the toes in response to stroking of the foot from heel to toes. The Babinski reflex normally disappears toward the end of the first year, to be replaced by curling downward of the toes. Persistence of the Babinski reflex may suggest defects of the lower spinal cord, lagging development of nerve cells, or other disorders.

The ***tonic-neck reflex*** is observed when the baby is lying on its back and turns its head to one side. The arm and leg on that side extend, while the limbs

FIGURE 4.12

***The Moro Reflex.*** *The startle, or Moro, reflex is elicited by sudden changes as loud noises or loss of support of the head and neck.*

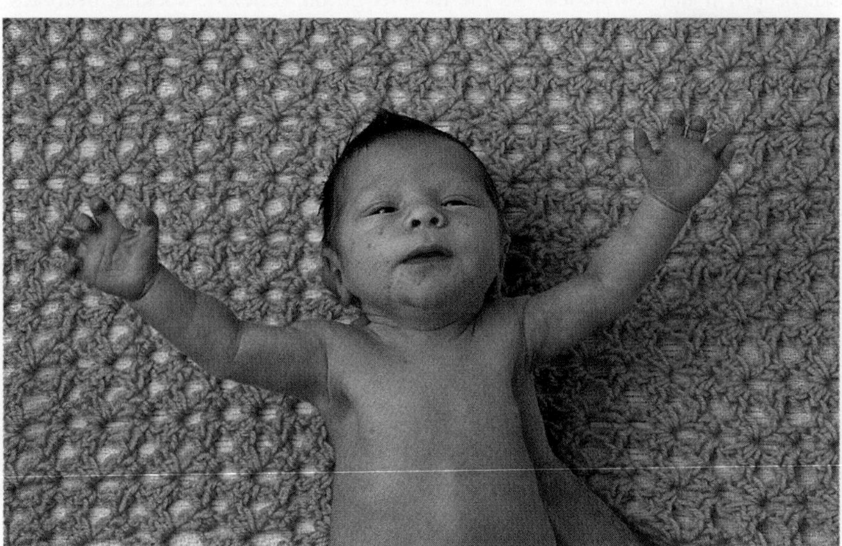

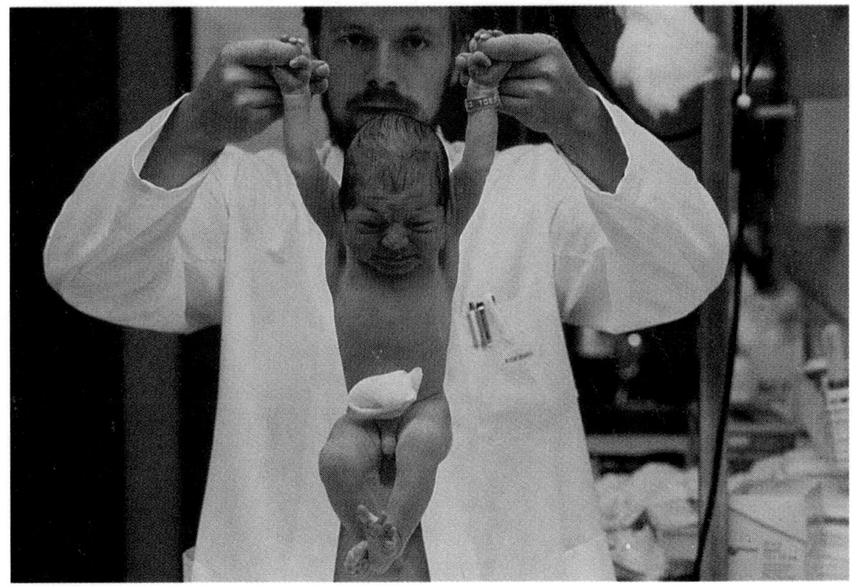

FIGURE 4.13

***The Grasping Reflex.*** *Newborns reflexively grasp objects pressed against the palms of their hands. By 3 to 4 months, the grasping reflex is lost and is gradually replaced by voluntary grasping.*

***Stepping reflex*** A reflex in which infants take steps when held under the arms and leaned forward so that the feet press against the ground.

***Babinski reflex*** A reflex in which infants fan their toes when the undersides of their feet are stroked.

***Tonic-neck reflex*** A reflex in which infants turn their head to one side, extend the arm and leg on that side, and flex the limbs on the opposite side. Also known as the "fencing position."

***Habituate*** Show a decline in interest as a repeated stimulus becomes familiar.

on the opposite side flex. You can see why this reflex sometimes is known as the "fencing position."

Some reflexes, such as breathing and blinking the eye in response to a puff of air, remain with us for life. Others, such as the sucking and grasping reflexes, are gradually replaced by voluntary sucking and grasping after a number of months. Still others, such as the Moro and Babinski reflexes, disappear, indicating that the nervous system is maturing on schedule.

### *Culture and Development: Neonatal Behavior*

Newborns from different ethnic groups show some differences in their behavior. For example, compared with white newborns, Chinese-American, Japanese-American, and Navajo infants are less likely to fret or cry, are calmed more readily when upset, are less excitable, and ***habituate*** faster to repeated presentation of stimuli (Chisholm, 1983; Kagan, 1992). These differences are thought to reflect a variety of factors including genetic endowment, the prenatal environment, and the mother's reproductive history (Garcia-Coll, 1990). Cultural differences in the way parents respond to their babies may strengthen early biologically based differences in emotional reactivity. For example, Japanese mothers are much more likely than American mothers to carry their infants and to sleep with them. Japanese mothers also are more apt to try to minimize their infant's crying and to emotionally indulge them (Camras et al., 1992). These maternal behaviors may contribute to the lower emotional reactivity of Japanese infants.

We have seen how neonates respond to their new environment. But in order to respond, they must first *sense.* Let us now consider some of the sensory capabilities of the neonate.

FIGURE 4.14

***The Stepping Reflex.*** *The stepping reflex mimics walking. It is elicited by tilting the baby forward so that its feet press against a solid surface. True walking does not appear until the beginning of the second year.*

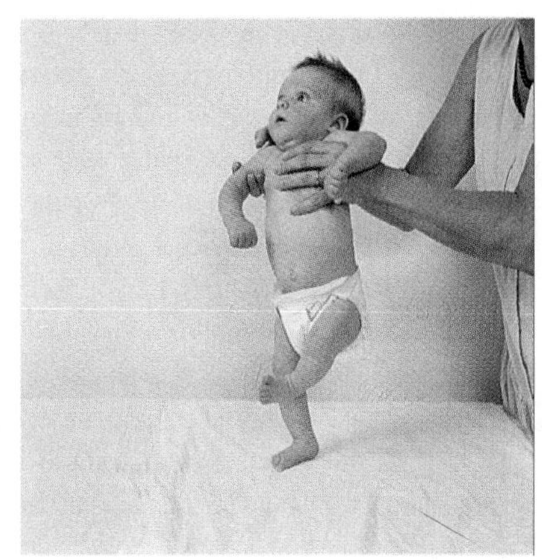

### *Sensory Capabilities*

In 1890, William James, one of the founders of modern psychology, wrote that the newborn baby must sense the world "as one great blooming, buzzing confusion." The neonate emerges from being literally suspended in a temperature-controlled environment to being—again, in James's words—"assailed by eyes,

FIGURE 4.15

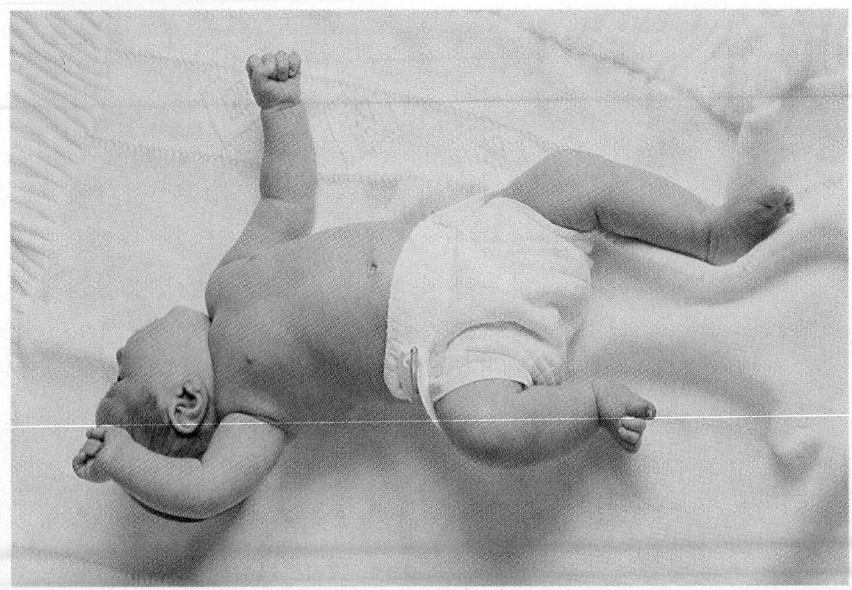

**THE TONIC-NECK REFLEX.** *The tonic-neck reflex, or "fencing position," is observed when the baby is on its back and turns its head to one side. The arm and leg on that side extend, while the limbs on the other side flex.*

What are some different neonatal behaviors exhibited by ethnic groups reflective of genetic endowment, prenatal environment, and mothers' reproductive history and postnatal behavior?

| CULTURE | BEHAVIOR |
|---|---|
| CHINESE AMERICAN<br>JAPANESE AMERICAN<br>NAVAJO | LESS LIKELY TO FRET OR CRY<br>MORE SOOTHABLE<br>LESS EXCITABLE<br>QUICK TO HABITUATE |
| WHITE AMERICAN | MORE LIKELY TO FRET OR CRY<br>LESS SOOTHABLE<br>MORE EXCITABLE<br>SLOW TO HABITUATE |

ears, nose, skin, and entrails at once." In this section, we describe the sensory capabilities of newborn children, and we see that James, for all his eloquence, probably exaggerated the disorganization of the neonate.

**VISION** Neonates can see, but they do not possess great sharpness of vision, or ***visual acuity.*** Visual acuity is expressed in numbers such as 20/20 or 20/200. Think for a moment of the big *E* on the Snellen chart (Figure 4.16), which you have probably seen during many eye examinations. If you were to stand 20 feet from the Snellen chart and could see only the E, we would say

## FOCUS ON RESEARCH

### STUDYING VISUAL ACUITY IN NEWBORN INFANTS: HOW DO YOU GET BABIES TO TELL YOU HOW WELL THEY CAN SEE?

How do psychologists determine the visual acuity of neonates? Naturally, they can't ask babies to report how well they see, but psychologists can determine what babies are looking at and draw conclusions from this information.

One method of observing what a baby is looking at is by using a "looking chamber" of the sort used in research by Robert Fantz and his colleagues (1975) (see Figure 4.17). In this chamber, the baby lies on its back, with two panels above. Each panel contains a visual stimulus. The researcher observes the baby's eye movements and records how much time is spent looking at each panel. A similar strategy can be carried out in the baby's natural environment. Filtered lights and a movie or TV camera can be trained on the baby's eyes. Reflections from objects in the environment can then be recorded to show what the baby is looking at.

Newborn babies will stare at almost any nearby object for minutes—golf balls, wheels, checkerboards, bull's-eyes, circles, triangles, even lines (Maurer & Maurer, 1976). But babies have their preferences, as measured by the amount of time they spend fixating on (looking at) certain objects. For example, they will spend more time looking at black and white stripes than at gray blobs. This fact suggests one strategy for measuring visual acuity in the neonate. As black and white stripes become narrower, they eventually take on the appearance of that dull gray blob. And, as they are progessively narrowed, we can assume that babies continue to discriminate them as stripes only so long as they spend more time looking at them than at blobs.

Studies such as these suggest that newborns are very nearsighted. But we should remember that they, unlike adults or older children, are not motivated to "perform" in such experiments. If they were, they might show somewhat greater acuity.

that your vision is 20/200. This would mean that you can see from a distance of 20 feet what a person with normal vision can discriminate from a distance of 200 feet. In such a case, you would be quite nearsighted. You would have to be unusually close to an object to discriminate its details.

Expressed in these terms, investigators have arrived at various approximations of the visual acuity of newborn babies, with the best estimates in the neighborhood of 20/600 (Banks & Salapatek, 1983). Neonates can best see objects that are about 7 to 9 inches away from their eyes. Newborn babies also see best through the centers of their eyes. They do not have the peripheral vision of older children. To learn how psychologists measure the visual acuity of infants, turn to the Focus on Research.

Neonates can visually detect movement, and many neonates can ***track*** movement the first day after birth. In fact, they appear to prefer (that is, they spend more time looking at) moving objects to stationary objects (Kellman & von Hofsten, 1992). In one study (Haith, 1966), for example, 1- to 4-day-old neonates were exposed to moving or nonmoving lights while sucking on a pacifier. The frequency of their sucking decreased significantly when moving lights were presented, suggesting that they preferred this visual stimulus.

***Visual accommodation*** refers to the self-adjustments made by the lens of the eye to bring objects into focus. If you hold your finger at arm's length and bring it gradually nearer, you will feel tension in your eyes as your lenses automatically foreshorten and thicken in an effort to maintain the image in focus. When you move the finger away, the lens accommodates by lengthening and flattening, thereby keeping the finger in focus. Neonates show little or no visual accommodation; they see as through a fixed-focus camera. Objects placed somewhere between 7 and 9 inches away are in clearest focus for most neonates, although this range can be somewhat expanded when lighting conditions are very bright. Interestingly, this is about the distance of the face of an adult who is cradling a newborn in the arms. It has been speculated that this sensory capacity for gazing into others' eyes may promote attachment between neonates and caregivers. Visual accommodation improves dramatically within the first 2 months (Hainline & Abramov, 1992).

FIGURE 4.16

**THE SNELLEN CHART.** *The Snellen chart is used in eye examinations to provide an approximate measure of visual acuity.*

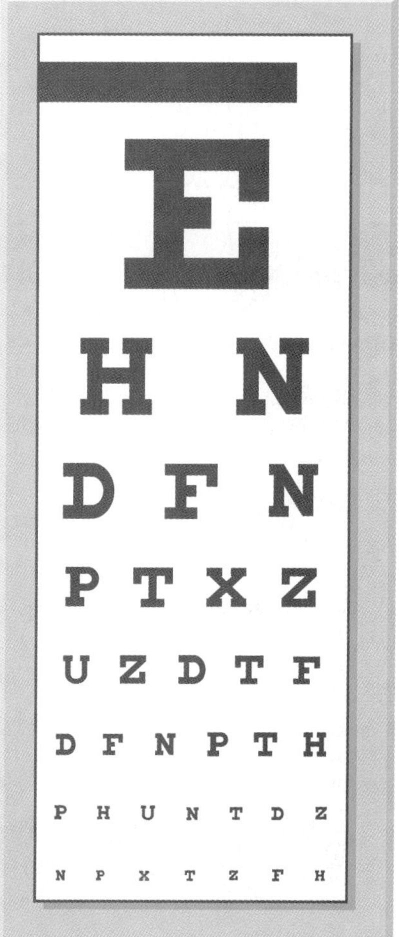


***Visual acuity*** Keenness or sharpness of vision.

***Track*** Visually follow.

***Visual accommodation*** The automatic adjustments made by the lenses of the eyes to bring objects into focus.

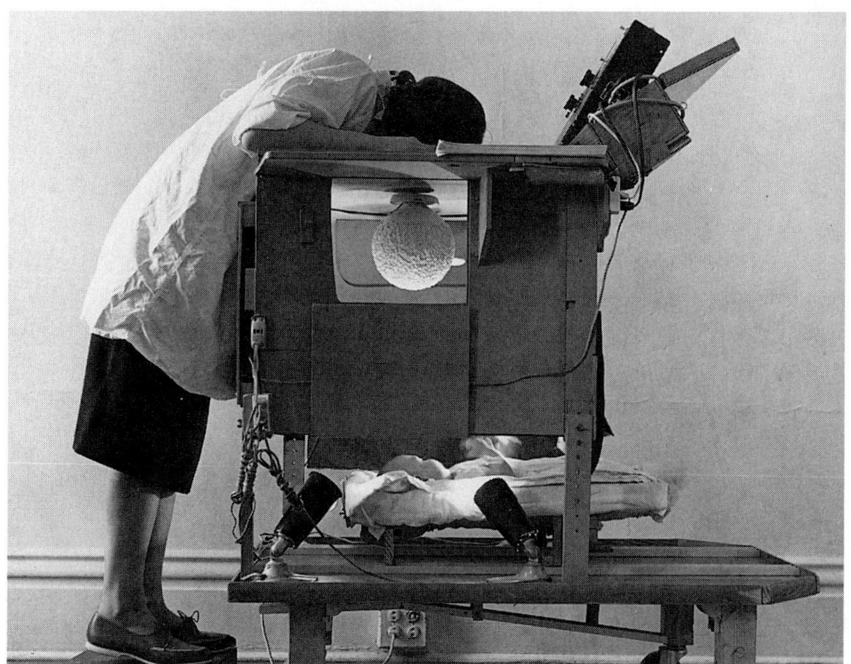

FIGURE 4.17

**THE LOOKING CHAMBER.** *With this chamber, the researcher can observe the baby's eye movements and record how much time is spent looking at a visual stimulus.*

***Convergence*** The inward movement of the eyes as they focus on an object that is drawing nearer.

***Intensity*** Brightness.

***Saturation*** Richness or purity of a color.

***Hue*** Color.

Now bring your finger toward your eyes trying to maintain a single image of the approaching finger. If you do so, it is because your eyes turn inward, or *converge* on the finger, resulting in a crossed-eyes look and feelings of tension in the eye muscles (see Figure 4.18). ***Convergence*** is made possible by the coordination of the eye muscles. Neonates do not have the muscular control to converge their eyes on an object that is very close to them. For this reason, one eye may be staring off to the side, while the other fixates on an object straight ahead. Convergence does not occur until 7 or 8 weeks of age for near objects. Newborns do show some convergence for objects that are at intermediate viewing distances (Aslin, 1987).

The degree to which neonates perceive color remains an open question. The research problem is that colors vary in ***intensity*** (that is, brightness) and ***saturation*** (richness), as well as in ***hue.*** For this reason, when babies appear to show preference for one color over another, we cannot be certain that they are responding to the hue. They may also be responding to the difference in brightness or saturation. So, you say, simply change hues and keep intensity and saturation constant. A marvelous idea—but easier said than done, unfortunately.

Physiological observations also cast doubt on the capacity of neonates to have highly developed color vision. There are two types of cells in the retina of the eye that are sensitive to light: ***rods*** and ***cones.*** Rods transmit sensations of light and dark, and cones transmit sensations of color. At birth, the cones are less well-developed than rods in structure.

FIGURE 4.18

***CONVERGENCE OF THE EYES.*** *Newborns do not have the muscular control to converge their eyes on an object that is very close to them. However, they do show some convergence for objects at intermediate viewing distances.*

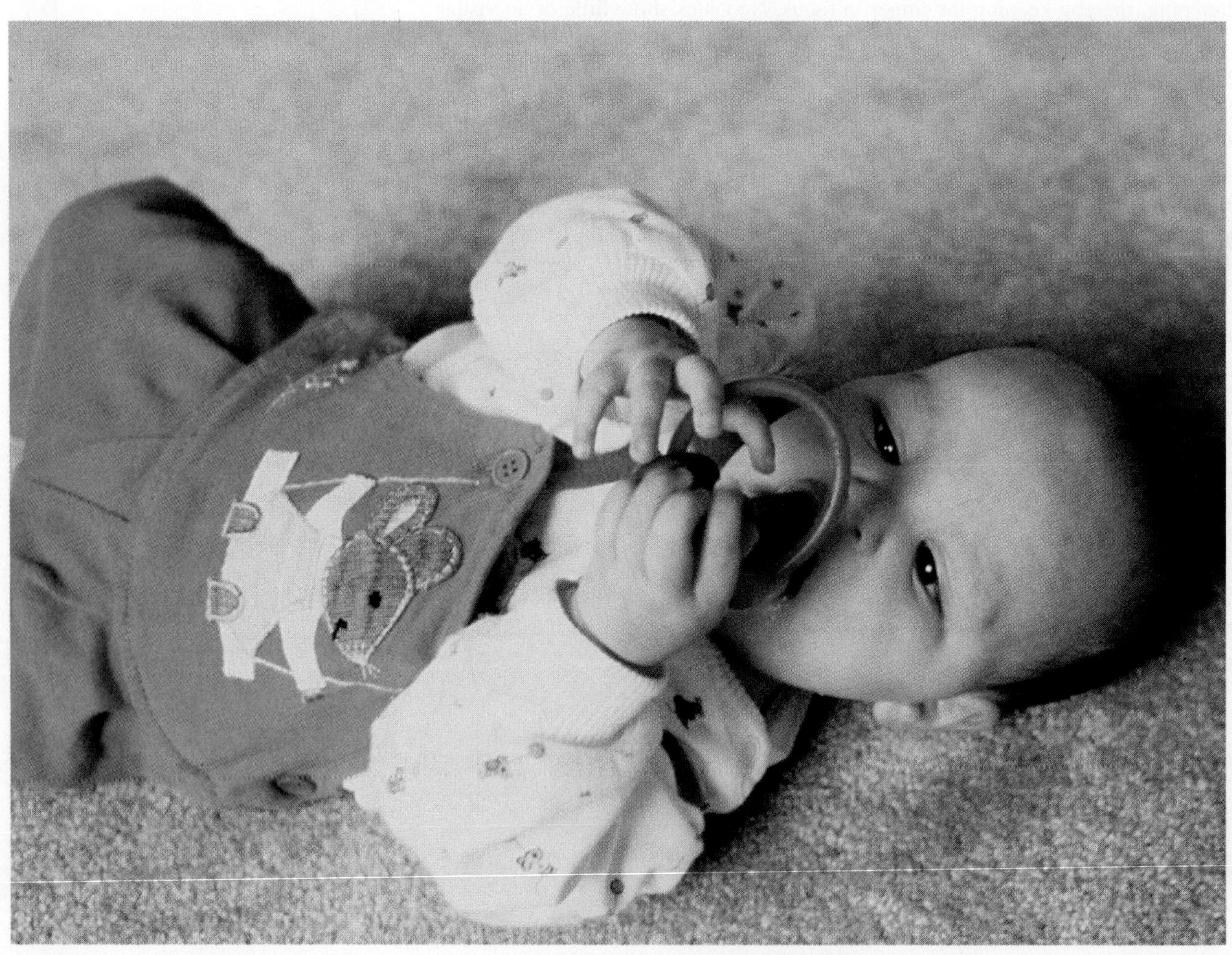

Recent studies indicate that infants under 1 month of age do not show the ability to discriminate stimuli that differ in color. Two-month-olds can do so, but require large color differences. By 3 months, infants can see most, if not all, the colors of the visible spectrum (Banks & Shannon, 1993; Brown; 1990; Teller & Lindsey, 1993).

Even at birth, babies do not just passively respond to visual stimuli. For example, babies placed in absolute darkness open their eyes wide and actively search the visual field, moving their eyes two to three times a second (Haith, 1986).

**Hearing** Fetuses respond to sound months before they are born, as noted in Chapter 3. Although myelination of the auditory pathways is not complete prior to birth, fetuses' middle and inner ears normally reach their mature shapes and sizes before they are born (Aslin et al., 1983). Normal neonates can also hear remarkably well, unless their middle ears are clogged with amniotic fluid. In fact, most neonates will turn their heads toward unusual sounds, such as that of a shaking rattle (Clarkson et al., 1985).

Newborn infants have the capacity to respond to sounds of different ***amplitude*** and to ***pitch.*** They are more likely to respond to high-pitched sounds than to low-pitched sounds (Morrongiello & Clifton, 1984; Werner & Gillenwater, 1990). By contrast, speaking or singing to infants softly, in a relatively low-pitched voice, can have a soothing effect (Papousek et al., 1991). This may explain the widespread practice in many cultures of singing lullabies to infants to promote sleep (Trehub et al., 1993).

It may well be that the sense of hearing plays a role in the formation of affectional bonds between neonates and their mothers that goes well beyond the soothing potential of the mothers' voices. Research indicates that newborn babies prefer their mothers' voices to those of other women, but do not show similar preferences for the voices of their fathers (DeCasper & Prescott, 1984; Freeman et al., 1993). It may seem tempting to conclude that the human nervous system is "prewired" to respond positively to the voice of one's biological mother. However, you will recall from Chapter 3 that neonates have already had several months of experience in the uterus, and, for a good part of this time, they have been capable of sensing sounds. Since they are predominantly exposed to prenatal sounds produced by their mothers, learning appears to play a role in neonatal preferences.

There is fascinating evidence that newborns are particularly responsive to the sounds and rhythms of speech, although they do not show preferences for specific languages. Condon and Sander (1974) filmed the bodily responses of 12-hour- to 2-week-old infants to human speech (English or Chinese), disconnected vowel sounds, and tapping. The babies—most of whom were under 2 days old—tended to synchronize the movements of their heads, arms, and legs to the pattern of speech. They were equally adept at "dancing" to the sounds of English and Chinese, but showed little synchronization with the disconnected vowels or the tapping. It has also been shown that newborns can discriminate between different speech sounds (Molfese et al., 1991). And they can discriminate between new sounds of speech and those that they have heard before (Brody et al., 1984).

**Smell: The Nose Knows Rather Early** Neonates can definitely discriminate distinct odors, such as those of onions and anise (licorice). They show more rapid breathing patterns and increased bodily movement in response to powerful odors. They also turn away from unpleasant odors, such as ammonia and vinegar, as early as the first day after birth (Engen & Lipsitt, 1965; Rieser et al., 1976).

***Rods*** Rod-shaped receptors of light that are sensitive to intensity only. Rods permit black-and-white vision.

***Cones*** Cone-shaped receptors of light that transmit sensations of color.

***Amplitude*** Height. The higher the amplitude of sound waves, the louder they are.

***Pitch*** The highness or lowness of a sound, as determined by the frequency of sound waves.

The nasal preferences of newborns are quite similar to those of older children and adults (Steiner, 1979; Ganchrow et al., 1983). When a cotton swab saturated with the odor of rotten eggs was passed beneath their noses, newborn infants spat, stuck out their tongues, wrinkled their noses, and blinked their eyes. However, they showed smiles and licking motions when presented with the odors of chocolate, strawberry, vanilla, butter, bananas, and honey. (It would be interesting to run a longitudinal study to determine whether newborns who show relatively less response to the aromas of chocolate, butter, and honey are more slender during later childhood and adulthood).

Research by Aidan Macfarlane (1975, 1977) and others suggests that the sense of smell, like hearing, may provide a vehicle for mother–infant recognition and attachment. Macfarlane suspected that neonates may be sensitive to the smell of milk, because, when held by the mother, they tend to turn toward her nipple before they have had a chance to see or touch it. In one experiment, Macfarlane placed nursing pads above and to the sides of neonates' heads. One pad had absorbed milk from the mother, and the other was clean. Neonates less than a week old spent more time turning to look at their mothers' pads than at the new pads.

In the second phase of this research, Macfarlane suspended pads with milk from the neonates' mothers and strangers to the sides of the babies' heads. For the first few days following birth, the infants showed no preference for the pads. However, by the time they were 1 week old, they spent more time looking at their mothers' pads than at the strangers'. It appears that they learned to respond positively to the odor of their mothers' milk during the first few days. Afterward, a source of this odor received preferential treatment even when the infants were not nursing.

Breast-fed 15-day-old infants also prefer their mother's axillary (underarm) odor to odors produced by other lactating women and by non-lactating women. Bottle-fed infants do not show this preference (Cernoch & Porter, 1985; Porter et al., 1992). The authors explain this difference by suggesting that breast-fed infants may be more likely than bottle-fed infants to be exposed to their mother's axillary odor. That is, mothers of bottle-fed infants usually remain clothed. Axillary odor, along with odors from breast secretions, might contribute to the early development of recognition and attachment.

**FIGURE 4.19**

***FACIAL EXPRESSIONS ELICITED BY SWEET, SOUR, AND BITTER SOLUTIONS.*** *Newborns are sensitive to different tastes, as shown by their facial expressions when tasting (a) sweet, (b) sour, and (c) bitter solutions.*

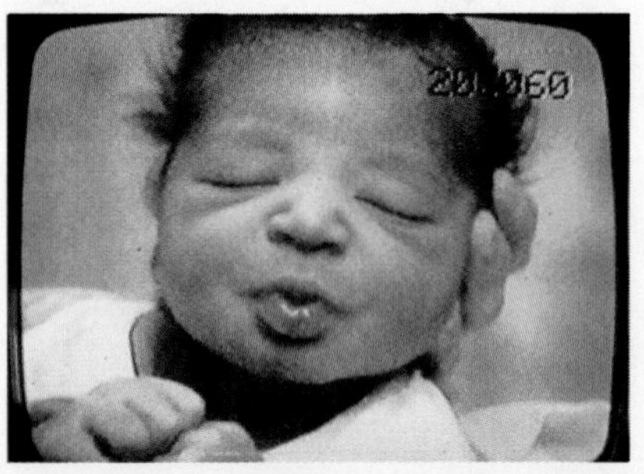

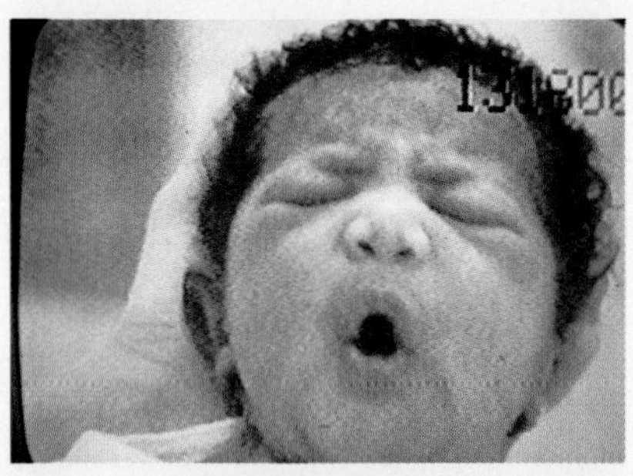

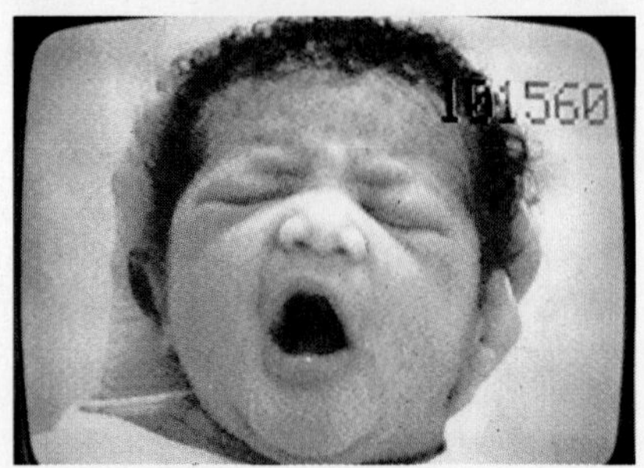

**TASTE** Newborns are sensitive to different tastes. Research shows that newborn infants form facial expressions similar to those of adults in response to various kinds of fluids. In one study, neonates swallowed without showing any facial expression suggestive of a positive or negative response when distilled water was placed on their tongues (Steiner, 1979). Sweet solutions were met with smiles, licking, and eager sucking. Sour fluids frequently elicited pursing of the lips, nose wrinkling, and eye blinking, while bitter solutions stimulated spitting, gagging, and sticking out of the tongue. The absence of a distinctive facial response to salty liquids suggests that newborns are not very sensitive to the taste of salt (Rosenstein & Oster, 1988).

Sweet solutions have a calming effect on newborns (Blass & Smith, 1992; Smith et al., 1990). Furthermore, sweeter solutions increase the heart rates of newborn infants, suggesting heightened arousal, but slow down their rates of sucking (Crook & Lipsitt, 1976). Some have interpreted this finding as an infant effort to savor the sweeter solution—to make the flavor last. Although we do not know why infants ingest sweet foods more slowly, this difference is useful in preventing overeating. Sweet foods tend to be high in calories, and by eating them slowly infants give their brains more time (a) to respond to bodily signals that they have eaten enough and (b) to consequently stimulate them to stop eating. Ah, to have the wisdom of a newborn baby!

**Touch and Pain** The sense of touch is an extremely important avenue of learning and communication for babies. Not only do the skin senses provide information about the external world, but the sensations of skin against skin also appear to provide feelings of comfort and security that may be major factors in the formation of bonds of attachment between infants and their care givers, as we shall see in Chapter 7.

Newborn babies are sensitive to touch. As noted earlier in the chapter, many reflexes—including the rooting, sucking, Babinski, and grasping reflexes, to name a few—are activated by pressure against the skin. However, newborns do not seem as sensitive to pain as slightly older babies are (Reisman, 1987). Considering the squeezing that takes place during childbirth, relative insensitivity to pain may be quite adaptive. Although they are less sensitive to pain, newborns do perceive pain. For example, babies who are circumcised display the short, high-pitched cries that are characteristic of infants who are under stress or seriously ill (Porter et al., 1988).

***Thinking About Development***

Agree or disagree with the following statement and support your answer: "A baby's behavior is under the governance of pleasure and pain."

## *Learning*

The somewhat limited sensory capabilities of neonates suggest that they may not learn as rapidly as older children do. After all, we must sense clearly those things we are to learn about. However, neonates seem capable of at least two basic forms of learning: classical and operant conditioning.

**Classical Conditioning of Neonates** In classical conditioning of neonates, involuntary responses are conditioned to new stimuli. In a typical study (Lipsitt, 1990b), newborns were taught to blink in response to a tone. Blinking (UCR) was elicited by a puff of air directed toward the infant's eye (UCS). A tone was sounded (CS) as the puff of air was delivered. After repeated pairings, sounding the tone (CS) gained the capacity to elicit blinking (CR).

Classical conditioning takes longer in newborns than in older infants. By the end of the first month, babies already have improved their ability to show classical conditioning and to retain what they have learned (Little et al., 1984). But even newborns are equipped to learn that events peculiar to their own environments (touches or other conditioned stimuli) may mean that a meal is at hand—or, more accurately, at mouth. One neonate may learn that a light switched on overhead precedes a meal. Another may learn that feeding is preceded by the rustling of a carpet of thatched leaves. The conditioned stimuli are culture-specific; the capacity to learn is universal.

**Operant Conditioning of Neonates** Operant conditioning, like classical conditioning, can take place in neonates. We already have seen a good example of such conditioning in Chapter 3. You will recall that newborns learned to suck on a pacifier in a certain way that activated a recording of their mothers reading *The Cat in the Hat* (DeCasper & Fifer, 1980; DeCasper & Spence, 1991). The mothers had read this story aloud during the final weeks of pregnancy. In this example, the infants' sucking reflexes were modified through the reinforcement of hearing their mothers read a familiar story.

The younger the child, the more important it is that reinforcers be administered rapidly. Among newborns, it seems that reinforcers must be administered

FIGURE 4.20

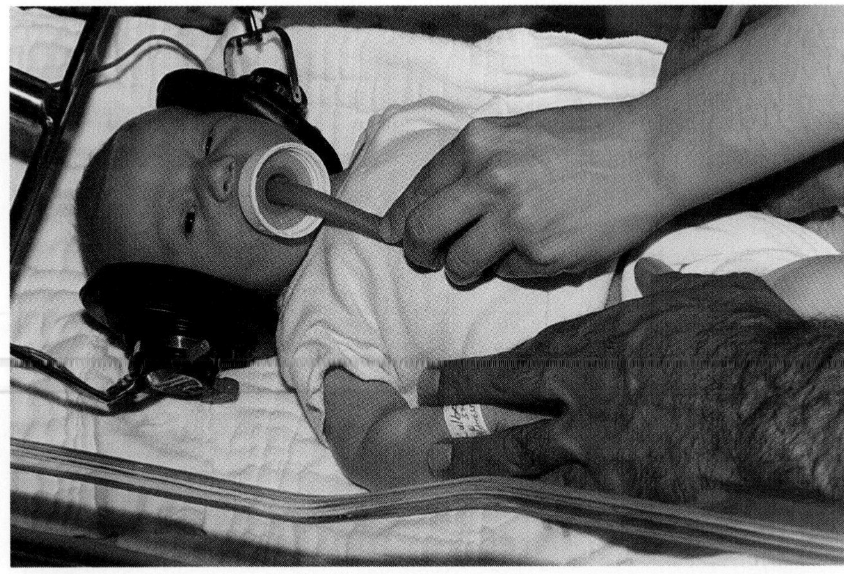

***Newborn Sucking to Hear Its Mother's Voice.*** *Newborns learned to suck on a pacifier in a certain way to activate a recording of their mothers reading* The Cat in the Hat. *Their mothers had read the story aloud during the final weeks of pregnancy.*

within a second after the desired behavior is performed if learning is to occur (Millar, 1972). Infants ages 6–8 months can learn if the reinforcer is delayed by two seconds, but if the delay is three seconds or more, learning does not take place (Millar, 1990).

TRUTH OR FICTION REVISITED

*Newborn babies are definitely capable of learning. They may be conditioned, but immediate reinforcements are required.*

There are large individual differences in conditionability among newborn children. Some can be conditioned with relatively few trials, while others apparently cannot be conditioned at all (Fitzgerald & Brackbill, 1976). However, it would be premature to attribute differences in conditionability to differences in intelligence. Although intelligence is often loosely thought of as learning ability, conditionability is not comparable with the complex cognitive tasks that define intellectual performance in older children. And, as we shall see in Chapter 6, measures of intelligence in infants do not correlate very well with measures of intelligence that are taken at later ages.

### *Sleeping and Waking States*

A number of different ***states*** of sleep and wakefulness have been identified in newborns and infants, as shown in Table 4.2 (Berg & Berg, 1987; Colombo et al., 1989). Although individual babies differ in the amount of time they spend in each of these states, sleep clearly predominates over wakefulness in the early days and weeks of life.

As adults, we spend about one-third of our time sleeping. Newborn infants greatly outdo us, spending two-thirds of their time, or about 16 hours per day, in sleep. And in one of life's basic challenges to parents, neonates do not sleep their 16 hours consecutively.

***States*** Levels of sleep and wakefulness in infants.

## TRUTH OR FICTION REVISITED

*It is true that newborn babies require about twice the amount of sleep that adults do. They sleep 16 hours per day on the average.*

Individual infants require different amounts of sleep and follow different patterns of sleep, but virtually all infants distribute their sleeping throughout the day and night through a series of naps. The typical infant has about six cycles of waking and sleeping in a 24-hour period (Bamford et al., 1990). The longest nap typically approaches 4½ hours, and the neonate is usually awake for a little more than 1 hour during each cycle.

This pattern of waking and sleeping changes rapidly and dramatically over the course of the years (Berg & Berg, 1987; Lowrey, 1986). Even after a month or so, the infant has fewer but longer sleep periods and will usually take longer naps during the night. Parents whose babies do not know the difference between night and day usually teach them the difference by playing with them during daytime hours, once feeding and caretaking chores have been carried out, and by putting them back to sleep as soon as possible when they awaken hungry during the night. Most parents do not require professional instruction in this method. At 3:00 A.M., parents are not likely to feel playful.

By the ages of about 6 months to a year, many infants begin to sleep through the night. Some infants start sleeping through the night even earlier (Anders et al., 1992). A number of infants begin to sleep through the night for a week or so and then revert to their wakeful ways again for a while.

**REM AND NREM SLEEP** Sleep itself is not a consistent state. Figure 4.21 shows that sleep can be divided into ***rapid-eye-movement (REM) sleep*** and ***non-rapid-eye-movement (NREM) sleep.*** Studies with the ***electroencephalograph (EEG)*** show that we can subdivide NREM sleep into four additional stages of sleep, each with its characteristic brain waves, but our discussion will be limited to REM and NREM sleep. REM sleep is characterized by rapid eye

***Rapid-eye-movement (REM) sleep*** A period of sleep during which we are likely to dream, as indicated by rapid eye movements.

***Non-rapid-eye-movement (NREM) sleep*** Periods of sleep during which we are unlikely to dream.

***Electroencephalograph (EEG)*** An instrument that measures electrical activity of the brain.

**TABLE 4.2**

***STATES OF SLEEP AND WAKEFULNESS IN INFANCY***

| STATE | DESCRIPTION |
|---|---|
| QUIET SLEEP (NREM) | REGULAR BREATHING, EYES CLOSED, NO MOVEMENT |
| ACTIVE SLEEP (REM) | IRREGULAR BREATHING, EYES CLOSED, RAPID EYE MOVEMENT, MUSCLE TWITCHES |
| DROWSINESS | REGULAR OR IRREGULAR BREATHING, EYES OPEN OR CLOSED, LITTLE MOVEMENT |
| ALERT INACTIVITY | REGULAR BREATHING, EYES OPEN, LOOKING AROUND, LITTLE BODY MOVEMENT |
| ALERT ACTIVITY | IRREGULAR BREATHING, EYES OPEN, ACTIVE BODY MOVEMENT |
| CRYING | IRREGULAR BREATHING, EYES OPEN OR CLOSED, THRASHING OF ARMS AND LEGS, CRYING |

SOURCES: BASED ON BERG & BERG, 1987; COLOMBO ET AL., 1989.

***Autostimulation theory*** The view that REM sleep in infants fosters the development of the brain by stimulating neural activity.

movements that can be observed beneath closed lids. The EEG patterns produced during REM sleep resemble those of the waking state. For this reason, REM sleep is also called *paradoxical sleep.* However, we are difficult to awaken during REM sleep. Adults who are roused during REM sleep report that they have been dreaming about 80 percent of the time. Adults report dreaming only about 20 percent of the time when they are awakened during NREM sleep. The reasons for dreaming remain a mystery, although the content of dreams most often parallels the experiences of the waking day.

Note from Figure 4.21 that neonates spend about half their time sleeping in REM sleep. By 6 months or so, REM sleep accounts for only about 30 percent of the baby's sleep, and by 2 to 3 years, REM sleep drops off to about 20–25 percent (Coons & Guilleminault, 1982). There is a dramatic falling off in the total number of hours spent in sleep as we develop. Figure 4.21 shows that the major portion of the drop-off can be attributed to lessened REM sleep.

Why does the amount of REM sleep decline? According to ***autostimulation theory,*** the brain requires a certain amount of neural activity to develop properly (Roffwarg et al., 1966). This activity can be stimulated from internal or external sources. In older children and adults, external sources of stimulation are provided by activity, a vast and shifting array of sensory impressions, and, perhaps, thought processes during the waking state. The newborn, however, spends its brief waking periods largely isolated from the kaleidoscope of events of the world outside and is not likely to be lost in deep thought. Thus, in the waking state, the brain may not be provided with the needed stimulation. As a compensatory measure, the neonate spends relatively more time in REM sleep, which most closely parallels the waking state in terms of brain waves. While infants are in REM sleep, internal physiological stimulation spurs the brain on to appropriate development. Preterm babies spend even greater proportions of their time in REM sleep than full-term babies, perhaps—goes the argument—because they might require relatively greater stimulation of the brain.

In support of autostimulation theory, one study found that circumcised neonates spent less time in REM sleep than did noncircumcised neonates (Emde et al., 1971). The process of circumcision is highly stimulating to neonates, and perhaps this external experience decreases the amount of internal stimulation or

FIGURE 4.21

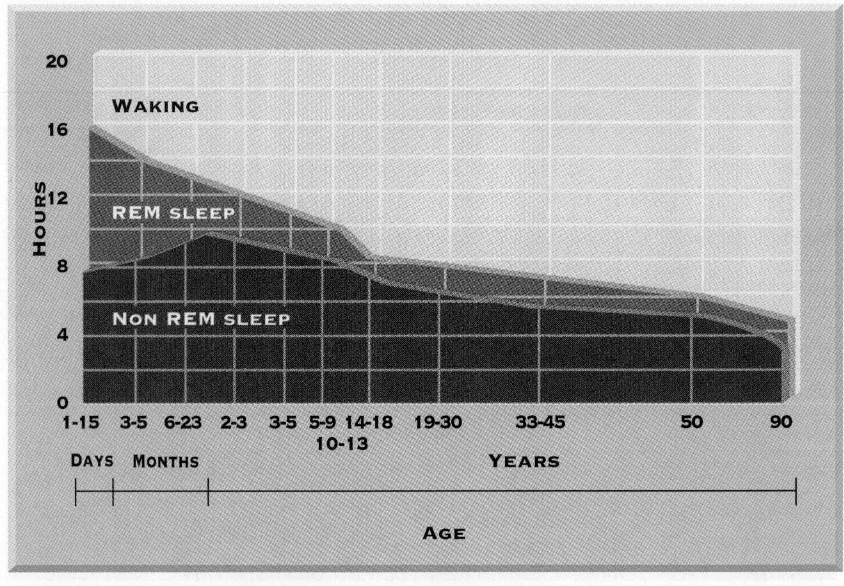


**REM SLEEP AND NREM SLEEP.** *Newborns spend nearly 50 percent of their time sleeping in rapid-eye movement (REM) sleep. The percentage of time spent in REM sleep drops off to 20–25 percent for 2- to 3-year-olds. As we mature, we sleep fewer hours, and most of the dropoff can be attributed to decline in REM sleep. (Source: Roffwarg et al., 1966)*

autostimulation they require. Another study found that infants who spent a good deal of time fixating on visual stimuli while awake showed temporary decreases in REM sleep (Boismier, 1977). Again, external stimulation might have reduced the need for internal stimulation.

A different view is that protein synthesis plays an important role in REM sleep. Protein concentrations in the brain increase during REM and decrease during REM deprivation (McGinty & Drucker-Colin, 1982). The large amount of time infants spend in REM sleep may indicate increased levels of protein synthesis during this period of rapid development (Berg & Berg, 1987).

**Sudden Infant Death Syndrome** One tragic disorder of infancy that strikes during sleep is ***Sudden Infant Death Syndrome (SIDS),*** sometimes called *crib death.* In the typical case, a baby goes to sleep, apparently in perfect health, and is found dead the next morning. There is no sign that the baby struggled or was in pain. About 5,400 infants in the United States die annually of SIDS during their first year. This represents about 1 child in 770 (Centers for Disease Control, 1993). SIDS is the most common cause of death in infants between the ages of 1 month and 1 year (Oberfield & Gabriel, 1991). New parents frequently live in dread of SIDS and check their babies regularly through the night to see if they are breathing. It is not abnormal, by the way, for babies occasionally to suspend breathing for a moment. The intermittent suspension of respiration is called ***apnea,*** and the buildup of carbon dioxide usually spurs a return to breathing. Babies who succumb to SIDS may have more episodes of apnea than normal (Hunt, 1990).

Although it is known that SIDS does not result from suffocation or from choking on regurgitated food, its causes remain largely obscure. Currently one of the most compelling hypotheses is that SIDS results from abnormal control of cardiac and respiratory functioning by the brain stem (Hunt, 1992; Oberfield & Gabriel, 1991). Still, there are a number of ***risk factors*** associated with the disorder, and parents whose situations seem to fit the stereotypical picture may wish to take special heed. SIDS is more common among

- babies ages 2–4 months
- premature and low-birth-weight infants
- male infants
- families of lower socioeconomic status
- African-American families
- babies of teenage mothers
- babies whose mothers smoked during or after pregnancy or used narcotics during pregnancy (Children's Defense Fund, 1992b; Gilbert-Barness & Barness, 1992; Hunt, 1992; Schoendorf & Kiely, 1992).

Recent studies also have found a slightly higher risk of SIDS among babies who sleep on their stomachs (Ponsonby et al., 1993; Poets & Southall, 1993). These findings have led the American Academy of Pediatrics to recommend putting babies down to sleep on their sides or back (AAP Task Force, 1992).

No remedy for SIDS is in the offing. Home monitoring systems have been developed to alert parents to episodes of apnea and to give them time to

***Sudden Infant Death Syndrome (SIDS)*** The death, while sleeping, of apparently healthy babies who stop breathing for unknown medical reasons. Also called crib death.

***Apnea*** (AP-knee-uh) Temporary suspension of breathing (from the Greek *a-,* meaning "without," and *pnoie,* meaning "wind").

***Risk factors*** Variables such as ethnicity and social class that are associated with the likelihood of problems but do not directly cause problems.

intervene—as by artificial respiration. However, use of home monitors can be stressful for the families (Wasserman, 1984). Moreover, there is no evidence that SIDS rates have been reduced as a result of using monitors (Blakeslee, 1989).

**CRYING** No discussion of the sleeping and waking states of the neonate would be complete without mentioning crying—a comment that parents will view as an understatement. We have known a number of first-time parents who have attempted to follow an imaginary 11th commandment: "The baby shall not cry." Some parents have entered into conflict with hospital nurses who tell them not to worry when their babies are crying on the other side of the nursery's glass partition. Nurses frequently tell parents that their babies *must* cry, that crying helps clear their respiratory systems of any fluids that linger from the amniotic sac and that it stimulates the circulatory system.

Whether crying is healthful and necessary remains an open question, but at least some crying among babies seems universal. Some scholars have thought of crying as a sort of primitive language, but it is not. Languages contain units and groupings of sounds that symbolize objects and events. Crying does not. Still, crying appears to be both expressive and functional. Crying, that is, serves as an infant's expressive response to aversive stimulation and also stimulates caretakers to do something to help. Crying thus communicates something, even though it is not a form of language.

There are a number of different types of cries. Schaffer (1971) suggests the existence of three distinct patterns: crying that stems from (a) hunger, (b) anger, and (c) pain. A sudden, loud, insistent cry associated with flexing and kicking of the legs may indicate colic (pain due to gas or other sources of distress in the digestive tract). The baby may seem to hold its breath for a few moments, then gasp and begin to cry again. Crying from colic can be severe and persistent—sometimes lasting for hours (Barr et al., 1992; Lester et al., 1992). Much to the relief of parents, colic tends to disappear by the third to sixth month, as a baby's digestive system matures.

Prior to parenthood, many people wonder whether they will be able to recognize the meaning of their babies' cries, but it usually does not take them long. Parents are also somewhat better than nonparents at interpreting the cries of unfamiliar babies, probably because of their greater experience with infant cries and care giving (Green et al., 1987; Gustafson & Harris, 1990).

Parents and other people, including children, have similar physiological responses to infant crying—increases in heart rate, blood pressure, and sweating (Frodi, 1985). Infant crying makes them feel irritated and anxious and motivates them to run to the baby to try to relieve the distress. Adults perceive high-pitched crying to be more urgent, distressing, and sick sounding than low-pitched crying (Crowe & Zeskind, 1992; Lester et al., 1992).

In fact, certain kinds of high-pitched cries, if prolonged, can serve as a sign of abnormal development. For example, the cries of chronically distressed infants differ from those of normal infants in both rhythm and pitch. Patterns of crying may be indicative of such problems as chromosomal abnormalities, infections, fetal malnutrition, and exposure to narcotics (Huntington et al., 1990; Sepkoski et al., 1993). A striking example of the link between crying and a physical disorder is the syndrome called *cri du chat,* French for "cry of the cat." This is a genetic disorder that produces abnormalities in the brain, atypical facial features, and a high-pitched, squeaky cry.

***Pacifier*** An artificial nipple or teething ring that soothes babies.

**SOOTHING** How can a crying baby be soothed? For one thing, sucking seems to function as a built-in tranquilizer. Sucking on a ***pacifier*** decreases crying and agitated movement in neonates who have not yet had the opportunity to feed (Kessen et al., 1967). Therefore, the soothing function of sucking need not be learned through experience.

Parents find many other ways to soothe infants, including picking them up, patting, caressing and rocking them, and speaking to them in a low voice (Acebo & Thomas, 1992; Gustafson & Harris, 1990). Parents then usually try to find the specific cause of the distress by offering a bottle or pacifier or checking the diaper. These responses to a crying infant are shown by parents in cultures as diverse as those of the United States, France, and Japan (Bornstein et al., 1992b).

Learning occurs quickly during the soothing process. Parents learn by trial and error what types of embraces and movements are likely to soothe their infants. And infants learn quickly that crying is followed by being picked up or other forms of intervention. Parents sometimes worry that if they pick up the crying baby quickly, they are reinforcing the baby for crying. In this way, they believe, the child may become spoiled and find it progressively more difficult to engage in self-soothing to get to sleep.

Do babies who are picked up quickly cry more often or less often? Does picking them up reassure and soothe them, or does it simply reinforce crying? A classic study by Mary Ainsworth and her colleagues (1974) suggests that parents may not have to worry about whether they are attempting to soothe their babies too quickly. The Ainsworth group visited the homes of newborn babies every 3 weeks for the first year. Babies who were picked up and soothed quickly cried less, not more, frequently than those who were picked up after more time had elapsed. This study suggests that the main effect of picking up babies may be to soothe and reassure them, rather than to encourage further crying (Crockenberg & Smith, 1982).

FIGURE 4.22

**SOOTHING.** *How can a crying baby be soothed? Picking the baby up, talking to it quietly, patting, stroking, and rocking all seem to have calming effects.*

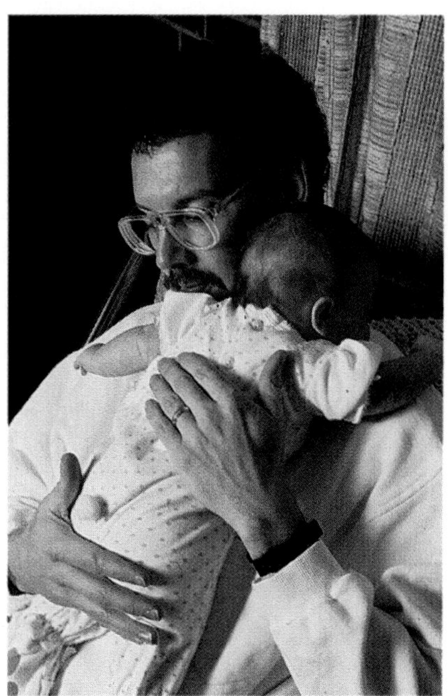

## TRUTH OR FICTION REVISITED

*Actually, it is not true that babies who are picked up as soon as they start to cry become spoiled and cry more often than babies whose mothers wait a while to pick them up. Babies who are picked up quickly may cry less, not more, frequently than babies who are picked up after a delay.*

Before leaving the Ainsworth study, we must issue the caveat that we issue with all correlational studies. The researchers did not randomly assign one group of mothers to quick soothing and another group of mothers to delayed soothing. Instead, they compared the behavior of babies whose mothers chose to soothe quickly or to delay. It could be, for example, that the mothers who chose to soothe quickly were generally more affectionate and concerned about their babies' moods and that this in itself might account for the behavioral differences in the babies.

Fortunately, as infants mature and learn, crying tends to become replaced by less upsetting verbal requests for intervention. And among adults, soothing techniques take very different forms—a bouquet of flowers or admission that one started the argument.

## Summary

1. Childbirth begins with the onset of regular contractions of the uterus. The fetus may signal the mother through hormones that it is mature enough to be born. There are three stages of childbirth. In the first, the cervix becomes effaced and dilated. In the second, the baby is born. During the third stage, the placenta passes from the mother's body.

2. Many women receive general or local anesthetics during childbirth. Evidence is mixed as to whether medicated childbirth has any negative long-term effects.

3. In natural childbirth and the Lamaze method of prepared childbirth, women are educated about childbirth and taught breathing and muscle relaxation exercises. The Leboyer method eases the baby gently into the world.

4. Caesarean sections are frequently carried out when the baby is in the breech (buttocks downward) position or when difficult labor is expected for another reason.

5. So-called alternate birth centers and home births have grown in popularity. They appear to be as safe as hospital births for women who have low-risk pregnancies. Midwives are increasingly used for prenatal care and delivery.

6. Anoxia, or oxygen deprivation, at birth can result in neurological or intellectual impairment.

7. Preterm and low-birth-weight babies are at higher risk for infant mortality and developmental delays, but stimulation can foster their development.

8. Following birth, many mothers experience temporary feelings of depression termed *maternity blues.* Prolonged depression, called *postpartum depression,* may reflect a combination of fluctuating hormone levels, a history of problems, stress, a difficult temperament in the neonate, and lack of social support.

9. Some developmentalists have argued that extended parent–infant contact during the postpartum period is essential to the bonding process, but research supporting this view has been criticized.

10. The Apgar scale assesses the neonate's color, heart rate, reflex irritability, muscle tone, and respiratory effort. The Brazelton Neonatal Behavioral Assessment Scale measures neonatal motor and adaptive behavior, response to stress, and physiological state.

11. Neonates possess a number of reflexes, including the rooting, sucking, Moro, grasping, stepping, Babinski, and tonic-neck reflexes. Some reflexes disappear as infants mature, and reflexes are taken as indexes of neurological development.

12. Neonates have somewhat limited visual capabilities which improve sharply within the first two months. Hearing acuity is excellent at birth. Neonates can discriminate odors and tastes. They are sensitive to touch but are less sensitive to pain than slightly older babies are.

13. Neonates appear capable of learning by means of classical and operant conditioning. However, they may require higher numbers of repetitions than older children.

14. Neonates sleep about 16 hours per day, and nearly half of this sleep is rapid-eye-movement (REM) sleep. Neonates distribute sleep into about six cycles of waking and sleeping per day.

15. Sudden infant death syndrome (SIDS) is the death, while asleep, of apparently healthy babies who stop breathing for unknown medical reasons. It is the leading cause of death of infants between the ages of 1 month and 1 year.

16. Infants cry for reasons such as hunger, anger, pain, and fatigue. Parents quickly learn to interpret their infants' cries. Infants can be soothed in many ways. Those who are soothed rapidly do not cry more frequently than infants whose parents delay picking them up.

# INFANCY

WHAT A FASCINATING CREATURE THE NEWBORN IS: TINY, SEEMingly helpless, apparently oblivious to its surroundings, yet perfectly formed and fully capable of letting its caretakers know when it is hungry, thirsty, or uncomfortable. And what a fascinating creature is the same child 2 years later: running, climbing, playing, talking, hugging, and kissing.

It is hard to believe that only 2 short years can bring about such remarkable changes. Certainly no 2-year period in the life of an adult produces anything like it. During the years from birth to age 2, children experience the most rapid physical, cognitive, social, and personality growth of their lives. Nearly every day, it seems, brings with it a new accomplishment, much to the delight of the child's family.

In Chapters 5, 6, and 7, we explore the different areas of growth and development in infancy.

O L C
W
D G K

# INFANCY:
## PHYSICAL DEVELOPMENT

## Chapter Outline

### Physical Growth and Development

*Sequences of Physical Development*

*Growth Patterns in Height and Weight*

*Nutrition*

### Development of the Brain and Nervous System

*Development of Neurons*

*Development of the Brain*

### Motor Development

*Lifting and Holding the Torso and Head*

*Control of the Hands*

*Locomotion*

*Culture and Development: Motor Development*

*Theoretical Interlude: Nature and Nurture in Motor Development*

### Sensory and Perceptual Development

*Development of Vision*

*Development of Hearing*

*Development of Coordination of the Senses*

*Theoretical Interlude: Do Children Play an Active or Passive Role in Perceptual Development?*

*Theoretical Interlude: Nativism and Empiricism in Perceptual Development*

### Summary

## Truth or Fiction?

______ *The head of the newborn child only doubles in length by adulthood, but the legs increase in length by about five times.*

______ *Infants triple their birth weight by age 1.*

______ *Infants should be fed skim milk to prevent later obesity.*

______ *We are born with all the nerve cells we'll ever have.*

______ *A child's brain reaches nearly 70 percent of its adult weight by age 1.*

______ *White U.S. infants sit, walk, and run at earlier ages than African and African-American infants do.*

______ *Hopi babies spend the first year of life strapped to a board, yet they begin to walk at about the same time as children who are reared in other cultures.*

______ *Newborn babies are nearsighted.*

______ *Two-month-old babies prefer to look at human faces rather than at brightly colored objects.*

______ *Infants need to have some experience crawling before they develop fear of heights.*

______ *Newborn kittens raised with a patch over one eye will lose vision in that eye.*

he authors are keen observers of children—that is, our own—and, from our experiences, we have derived the following basic principles of physical growth and development:

- Just when you think your child has finally begun to make regular gains in weight, she will begin to lose weight or go for several months without gaining an ounce.
- No matter how early your child sits up or starts to walk, your neighbor's child will do it earlier.
- Children first roll over when one parent is watching but will steadfastly refuse to repeat it when the other parent is called in.
- Children will begin to get into everything *before* you get childproof latches on the cabinets.
- Every advance in locomotor ability will provide your child with new ways in which to get hurt.
- Children will display their most exciting developmental milestones when there is no film in the camera.

More seriously, in this chapter we discuss various aspects of physical development during infancy. We examine changes in physical growth, the development of the brain and the nervous system, motor development, and the development and coordination of sensory and perceptual capabilities such as vision and hearing.

## PHYSICAL GROWTH AND DEVELOPMENT

During the first 2 years of life, children make enormous strides in their physical growth and development. In this section, we explore sequences of physical development, changes in height and weight, and nutrition.

### *SEQUENCES OF PHYSICAL DEVELOPMENT*

Three important sequences of physical development are known as *cephalocaudal development, proximodistal development,* and *differentiation.*

**CEPHALOCAUDAL DEVELOPMENT** The word ***cephalocaudal*** derives from the Greek *kephale,* meaning "head" or "skull," and from the Latin *cauda,* meaning "tail." It refers to the fact that development proceeds from the upper part of the head to the lower parts of the body.

When we consider the central role of the brain, which is contained within the skull, the cephalocaudal sequence appears quite logical. The brain regulates essential functions, such as heartbeat. Through the secretion of hormones, the brain also regulates the growth and development of the body and influences basic drives, such as hunger and thirst.

As you may recall from Chapter 3, the head develops more rapidly than the rest of the body during the embryonic stage. By 8 weeks after conception, the head constitutes half of the entire length of the embryo. The brain develops more rapidly than the spinal cord. Arm buds form before leg buds. Most neonates have a strong, well-defined sucking reflex, although their legs are spindly and their

***Cephalocaudal*** (SEFF-uh-low-CAW-d'l) From top to bottom; from head to tail.

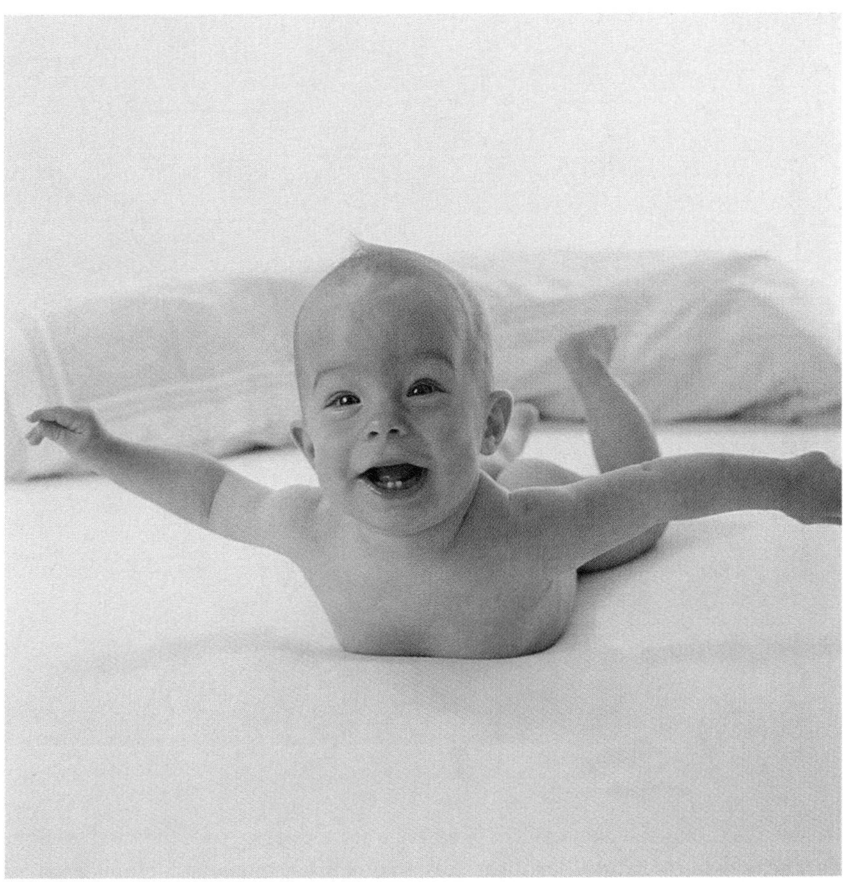

FIGURE 5.1

**CEPHALOCAUDAL DEVELOPMENT.** *Babies gain control over their head and upper body before they gain control over their lower body.*

limbs move back and forth only in diffuse excitement or agitation. Infants can hold up their heads before they gain control over their arms, their torsos, and, finally, their legs (see Figure 5.1). They can sit up before they can crawl and walk. When they first walk, they use their hands to hold on to a person or object for support.

The lower parts of the body, because they get off to a later start, must do more growing to reach adult size. For example, the head doubles in length between birth and maturity, but the torso triples in length. The arms increase their length about four times, but the legs and feet do so by about five times.

## TRUTH OR FICTION REVISITED

*It is true that the head of the newborn child only doubles in length by adulthood, whereas the legs increase in length by about five times. Consistent with the principle of cephalocaudal development, the head at birth is already well-developed relative to the limbs.*

**PROXIMODISTAL DEVELOPMENT** Recall from Chapter 3 that the ***proximodistal*** principle refers to the fact that growth and development proceed from the trunk outward—from the body's central axis toward the periphery. This principle, too, makes a good deal of sense. The brain and spinal cord follow a central axis down through the body, and it is essential that the nerves be in place

***Proximodistal*** From near to far; from the central axis of the body outward to the periphery.

FIGURE 5.2

***PROXIMODISTAL DEVELOPMENT.*** *Babies can grab large objects before picking up tiny things with their fingers.*

before the infant can gain control over the arms and legs. Also, the life functions of the newborn baby—heartbeat, respiration, digestion, and elimination of wastes—are all carried out by organ systems close to the central axis. These must be in operation or ready to operate when the child is born.

In terms of motor development, babies gain control over their trunks and their shoulders before they can control their arms, hands, and fingers. They make clumsy swipes at objects with their arms before they can voluntarily grasp them with their hands. Babies can grab large objects before picking up tiny things with their fingers (see Figure 5.2). Similarly, infants gain control over their hips and upper legs before they can direct their lower legs, feet, and toes.

**DIFFERENTIATION** As children mature, their physical reactions become less global and more specific. The tendency of responses to become more specific and distinct is called ***differentiation.*** If a neonate's finger is pricked or burned, the baby may withdraw the finger, but will also thrash about, cry, and show general signs of distress. Toddlers are also likely to cry and show distress, but are more likely to withdraw the finger and less likely to thrash about. An older child or adult is also likely to withdraw the finger, but less likely to wail and show general distress.

## *GROWTH PATTERNS IN HEIGHT AND WEIGHT*

The most dramatic gains in height and weight occur during prenatal development. Within a span of 9 months, children develop from a zygote about 1/175 of an inch long to a neonate about 20 inches in length. Weight increases by a factor of billions.

***Differentiation*** The processes by which behaviors and physical structures become more specialized.

During the first year after birth, gains in height and weight are also dramatic, although not by the standards of prenatal gains. Babies usually double their birth weight in about 5 months and triple it by the first birthday (Wardlaw & Insel, 1993). Their height increases by about 50 percent in the first year, so that a child whose length at birth was 20 inches is likely to be about 30 inches tall at 12 months.

## TRUTH OR FICTION REVISITED

*It is true that infants triple their birth weight by age 1. They also add about 10 inches to their height.*

Growth in infancy has long been viewed as a slow and steady process. Growth charts in pediatricians' offices resemble the smooth, continuous curves shown in Figure 5.3. But a recent study indicates that babies grow in spurts and that 90–95 percent of the time they are not growing at all (Lampl et al., 1992). The study measured the height of babies throughout their first 21 months. The researchers found that the babies would remain the same size for 2 to 63 days and then would shoot up in length from a fifth of an inch (.5 centimeters) to a full inch (2.5 centimeters) in less than 24 hours. Parents who swear that their babies sometimes consume enormous amounts of food and then grow overnight no longer can be dismissed as simply exaggerating (Kolata, 1992e).

Infants grow another 4 to 6 inches during the second year, and gain about 4 to 7 pounds. Boys generally reach half of their adult height by the second birthday. Girls, however, mature more quickly than boys and are likely to reach

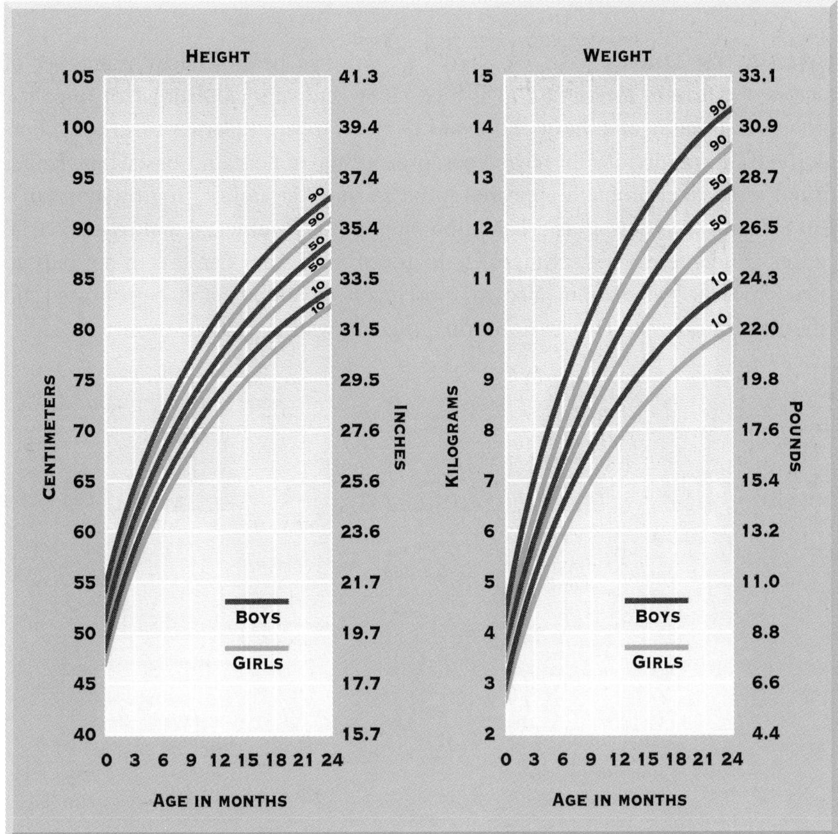


SOURCE: NATIONAL CENTER FOR HEALTH STATISTICS.

FIGURE 5.3

***GROWTH CURVES FOR HEIGHT AND WEIGHT FROM BIRTH TO AGE 2 YEARS.*** *The numbers on the curves indicate the percentiles for height and weight at different ages. Lines labeled 90 show the height and weight of children who are taller and heavier than 90 percent of children of a particular age. Lines marked 50 indicate the height and weight of the average child of a given age. Half of their age-mates are shorter and lighter and half are heavier and taller. Lines labeled 10 designate children who are taller and heavier than only 10 percent of children their age. (Source: National Center for Health Statistics, 1979.)*

***Failure to thrive (FTT)*** A disorder of impaired growth in infancy and early childhood.

half of their adult height at the age of 18 months (Tanner, 1989). Taller than average infants, as a group, tend to slow down in their growth rates. Shorter than average infants, as a group, tend to speed up. This is not to suggest that there is no relationship between infant and adult heights, or that we all wind up in an average range. Tall infants, as a group, wind up taller than short infants, but in most cases not by as much as seemed likely during infancy.

**CHANGES IN BODY PROPORTIONS** In rendering the human form, Greek classical sculptors followed the rule of the "Golden Section": The length of the head must equal one-eighth of the height of the body (including the head). The ideal of human beauty may be so, but the reality is that, among adults, the length of the head actually varies from about one-eighth to one-tenth of the entire body. Among children, the head is proportionately larger (see Figure 5.4).

As noted earlier, development proceeds in a cephalocaudal manner. A few weeks after conception, an embryo is almost all head. When entering the fetal stage, the head is about half the length of the unborn child. In the neonate, it is about one-quarter of the length of the body. The head gradually diminishes in proportion to the rest of the body, even though it doubles in size by adulthood (Rosenblith & Sims-Knights, 1989).

Among adults, the arms are nearly three times the length of the head. The legs are about four times as long—nearly half the length of the body. Among newborns, the arms and legs are about equal in length. Each is only about 1½ times the length of the head. By the first birthday, the neck has begun to lengthen visibly, as have the arms and legs. The arms grow more rapidly than the legs do at first (an example of the cephalocaudal trend), and by the second birthday, the arms are actually longer than the legs. The legs then grow more rapidly, soon catching up with and surpassing the arms in length.

**FAILURE TO THRIVE** A child's growth can be slowed by a number of factors. ***Failure to thrive (FTT)*** is a common and serious disorder of impaired growth in infancy and early childhood (Kelsey, 1993; Polan et al., 1991). Formerly, FTT was divided into two types, organic and nonorganic, based on whether or not a physical problem appeared to be causing the failure to grow normally. But FTT now is viewed as a condition having both biological and psychosocial causes (Budd et al., 1992; Singer et al., 1990). FTT has been linked not only to slow physical growth, but also to subsequent developmental, behavioral, and emotional problems (Drotar & Sturm, 1992; Powell & Bettes, 1992).

FIGURE 5.4

***CHANGES IN THE PROPORTIONS OF THE BODY.*** *Development proceeds in a cephalocaudal direction. The head is proportionately larger among younger children.*

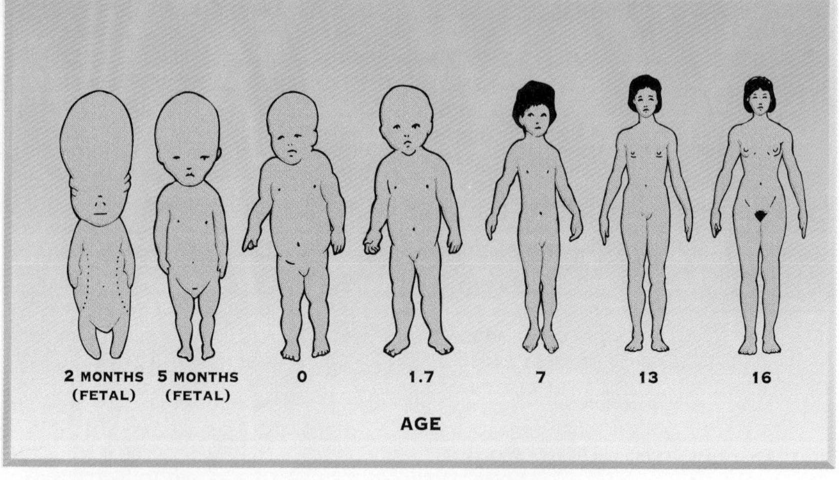

Deficiencies in mother–child interaction are thought to play a major role in the development of FTT. For example, mothers of FTT infants, compared with mothers of healthy infants, show fewer adaptive social interactions and fewer positive emotions toward their infants and terminate feedings in a more arbitrary manner (Drotar, 1991; Hutcheson et al., 1993). Mothers of children with FTT also are more likely to have various psychological and personality disorders than mothers of healthy children (Polan et al., 1991).

Since FTT often results from many different factors, treatment may not be easy. These children need both nutritional support and attention to the psychosocial problems that may be present (Bithoney et al., 1991; Kelsey, 1993).

**Catch-up Growth** A child's growth can be slowed from its genetically predetermined course by many organic factors, including illness and dietary deficiency. However, once the problem is alleviated, the child's rate of growth frequently accelerates and returns to approximate its normal, deflected course. The tendency to return to one's genetically determined pattern of growth is referred to as ***canalization*** (Tanner, 1989).

## *Nutrition*

The overall nutritional status of infants and children in the United States is fairly good compared with that of children in many other countries. The nutritional status of poor children has improved considerably in recent years, helped by various federal programs such as Food Stamps, the Supplemental Food Program for Women, Infants and Children (WIC), the Child Care Food Program and the National School Breakfast and Lunch programs. Even so, babies and young children from low-income families are more likely than other children to display signs of poor nutrition such as retarded growth and anemia (National Center for Children in Poverty, 1990; Wardlaw & Insel, 1993). Just what are the nutritional needs of infants?

**Nutritional Needs of Infants** From the time of birth, infants should be fed either breast milk or iron-fortified infant formula. The introduction of solid foods is recommended when the infant is able to indicate hunger by leaning forward and indicate fullness by turning away from food. This stage normally occurs at 4 to 6 months of age. The first solid food usually is iron-enriched cereal, followed by strained fruits, then vegetables, and finally meats, poultry, and fish. Whole cow's milk is normally delayed until the baby is 9 to 12 months old. Finger foods such as teething biscuits are introduced in the latter part of the first year.

Here are some useful guidelines for infant nutrition (Ekvall, 1993a; Niedbala & Ekvall, 1993):

- Build up to a variety of foods.
- Heed your baby's appetite to avoid overfeeding or underfeeding.
- Don't restrict fat and cholesterol too much. (For example, don't substitute skim milk for whole milk.) Babies *need* fat and calories.
- Don't overdo high-fiber foods.
- Avoid items with added sugar and salt.
- Encourage high-iron foods; babies need more iron, pound for pound, than adults.

***Canalization*** The tendency of growth rates to return to genetically determined patterns after undergoing environmentally induced change.

## TRUTH OR FICTION REVISITED

*It is not true that infants should be fed skim milk to avoid later obesity. Infants need fat and calories in their diets. When they start drinking cow's milk, whole milk should be used, not skim milk.*

### THINKING ABOUT DEVELOPMENT

Agree or disagree with the following statement and support your answer: "Breast-feeding is better for babies than bottle-feeding."

**BREAST-FEEDING VERSUS BOTTLE-FEEDING: DOES IT MAKE A DIFFERENCE?** Today, slightly over half of U.S. women breast-feed their children. White women are more likely than African-American or Hispanic women to breast-feed (Ekvall, 1993c; Ryan et al., 1991). Breast-feeding was the standard way of feeding infants until the early 1930s, when infant formulas were developed. Over the next three decades, breast-feeding declined dramatically, but then increased in popularity until the mid 1980s. Now, breast-feeding is again on the decline (Hilts, 1991).

Why do women bottle-feed their children? Many women return to the work force soon after childbirth and are unavailable for regular breast-feeding. Some parents prefer to share child feeding responsibilities, and the father, of course, is well equipped to hold a bottle. Other women find bottle-feeding more convenient and trouble-free. The decision about whether to breast-feed is taken very seriously by most parents. A number of issues have been raised about the relative physical and psychological merits of breast- and bottle-feeding for infants. For a discussion of these issues, see Developing Today.

**CULTURE AND DEVELOPMENT: BREAST-FEEDING AND BOTTLE-FEEDING** Some people have viewed bottle-feeding as more modern than breast-feeding, since it helps free women from a traditional task that hampers their availability to the work force. For this reason, bottle-feeding has been increasing in many developing nations as they move toward industrialization (see Figure 5.5). Unfortunately, in many cases the practice has backfired. Many poverty-stricken mothers

## Developing Today

### MOTHER'S MILK: THE ULTIMATE FAST FOOD?

Mother's milk has been referred to as the ultimate fast food or the perfect health food (Eiger & Olds, 1986). Mother's milk is superior to cow's milk or formula in its balance of nutrients. It contains antibodies that help infants fend off diseases the mother has had, or against which the mother has been inoculated, such as tetanus, chicken pox, typhoid, and smallpox. Breast milk also helps prevent respiratory infections and allergies (Ekvall, 1993c; Jason, 1991). So is breast-feeding ultimately better for babies than bottle-feeding?

In the United States, nutritious alternatives to breast milk are readily available and sanitation is generally good. Mortality rates of breast-fed and bottle-fed babies are about the same (Jason, 1991). Breast-fed babies may contract fewer illnesses (DeBruyne & Rolfes, 1989). On the other hand, alcohol, many drugs taken by the mother, environmental hazards such as PCBs, and the HIV virus, which causes AIDS, are passed along to babies through breast milk (Lederman, 1992; Mennella & Beauchamp, 1991). So breast milk may not always be as pure as it would seem. Long-term comparisons of breast-fed and bottle-fed U.S. children show few, if any, significant differences (Wardlaw & Insel, 1993). Most U.S. women are probably well-advised to choose whether to breast- or bottle-feed on the basis of financial considerations or personal preferences and not to be overly concerned about the long-term effects of their decisions on the physical or psychological development of their infants.

**FIGURE 5.5**

***BOTTLE-FEEDING VERSUS BREAST-FEEDING.*** *Bottle-feeding has been viewed as a way of freeing women in developing nations to join the work force. Unfortunately, formulas have been watered down by many poor women in developing countries, so that bottle-fed children often have been malnourished.*

water down the formula, thus providing their babies with inadequate nutrition. Some prepare the formula under unsanitary conditions or place it in unsanitized bottles, causing infant deaths. For these reasons, the United Nations Children's Fund urges that mothers in developing countries breast-feed their children for the first 4 to 6 months of life (Grant, 1993).

**CULTURE AND DEVELOPMENT: MALNUTRITION** An estimated 40 to 60 percent of children around the world suffer from mild to moderate malnutrition and another 3 to 7 percent are severely malnourished (Lozoff, 1989; Sigman et al., 1991). There are many reasons for malnutrition in developing countries, including famine, war, and poverty. Another contributing factor, as we have seen, is the decline of breast-feeding. Surprisingly, much of today's malnutrition may occur in areas where food is adequate. The major problem often is poor health care, which leads to frequent illness, which, in turn, reduces the child's appetite and lowers food intake, causing malnutrition (Grant, 1994). The combination of frequent illness and malnutrition leads to stunted physical and mental growth, impaired attention span, low activity level, and reduced social responsiveness (Ricciuti, 1993).

The long-term effects of severe malnutrition are illustrated by a longitudinal study conducted in Barbados by Janina Galler and her colleagues (1989, 1990). They compared children who had experienced severe protein malnutrition during the first year of life with children who had received adequate nutrition. By age 11, the undernourished children had caught up in physical growth, but they continued to show cognitive and behavioral deficits such as impaired attention, poor school performance, and distractibility. These problems continued through age 18.

Even mild to moderate malnutrition adversely affects the physical, cognitive, and motor development of children. A series of studies in Kenya and Egypt compared infants and children who suffered mild to moderate malnutrition with children who were well-nourished (Espinosa et al., 1992; Sigman & Sena, 1993; Wachs, 1993). The children with less adequate diets were shorter and weighed less. They were less active, showed less advanced forms of play, and appeared more anxious. They also had lower scores on tests of verbal skills and other

What cultural factors have contributed to the decline in breast-feeding?

| CULTURE | FACTORS |
|---|---|
| UNITED STATES | INCREASE IN NUMBER OF WOMEN IN WORK PLACE<br><br>AVAILABILITY OF SAFE, CONVENIENT ALTERNATIVES<br><br>VIEWED AS CONSTRAINING WOMEN TO TRADITIONAL TASKS |
| DEVELOPING COUNTRIES | BOTTLE-FEEDING VIEWED AS MORE MODERN THAN BREAST-FEEDING<br><br>INCREASE IN INDUSTRIALIZATION<br><br>VIEWED AS CONSTRAINING WOMEN TO TRADITIONAL TASKS |

FIGURE 5.6

***MALNOURISHED CHILD.*** *An estimated 40–60 percent of children around the world suffer from mild to moderate malnutrition and another 3–7 percent are severely malnourished.*

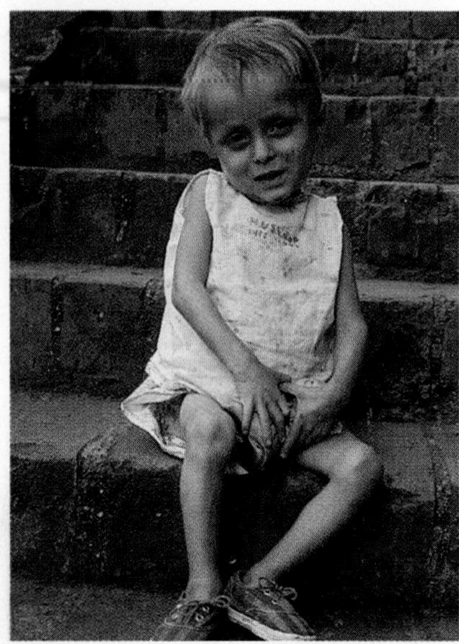

cognitive abilities. As adolescents and young adults, they remained behind their peers in reading, vocabulary, and general knowledge (Pollitt et al., 1993).

The good news is that the effects of malnutrition early in life can be reversed to some extent. Malnourished Guatemalan children who received food supplements during the first years of life became more socially involved, more interested in the environment, and more active (Barrett et al., 1982). In another study (Super et al., 1990), Colombian infants at risk of malnutrition were assigned randomly to one of four groups. One group received food supplements for the entire family from the middle of the mother's pregnancy until the child was 3 years old. In another group, home visitors tutored mothers in how to stimulate their children's cognitive and social development. A third group received both food supplements and visits, and the fourth group received neither. At 3 years of age, children who had received food supplements were taller and heavier than those who had not. This effect remained when the children reached age 6. The combination of food supplements plus home visits had an even stronger effect on children's growth.

## DEVELOPMENT OF THE BRAIN AND NERVOUS SYSTEM

The nervous system is a system of ***nerves*** involved in heartbeat, visual-motor coordination, thought and language, and so on. The human nervous system is more complex than that of lower animals. Although elephants and whales have heavier brains, our brains constitute a larger proportion of our body weight.

### *DEVELOPMENT OF NEURONS*

The basic units of the nervous system are ***neurons.*** Neurons are cells that are specialized to receive and transmit messages from one part of the body to another. The messages transmitted by neurons account for phenomena as varied as reflexes, the perception of an itch from a mosquito bite, the visual-motor coordination of a skier, the composition of a concerto, and the solution of a math problem.

A person is born with about 20 billion neurons in the brain, which is all that he or she will ever have (Wilson, 1990a). Neurons vary according to their functions and locations in the body. Some neurons in the brain are only a fraction of an inch in length, while neurons in the leg grow to be several feet long. Each neuron possesses a cell body, dendrites, and an axon (see Figure 5.7). The ***dendrites*** are short fibers that extend from the cell body and receive incoming messages from up to 1,000 adjoining neurons. The ***axon*** extends trunklike from the cell body and accounts for much of the difference in length in neurons, ranging up to several feet in length if it is carrying messages from the toes upward. Messages are released from axon terminals in the form of chemicals

***Nerves*** Bundles of axons from many neurons.

***Neurons*** Nerve cells.

***Dendrite*** A rootlike part of a neuron that receives impulses from other neurons (from the Greek *dendron,* meaning "tree").

***Axon*** A long, thin part of a neuron that transmits impulses to other neurons through small branching structures called *axon terminals.*

TRUTH OR FICTION REVISITED

*It is true that we are born with all the nerve cells we'll ever have. However, the nervous system grows through the proliferation of connections between cells and through the lengthening of axons.*

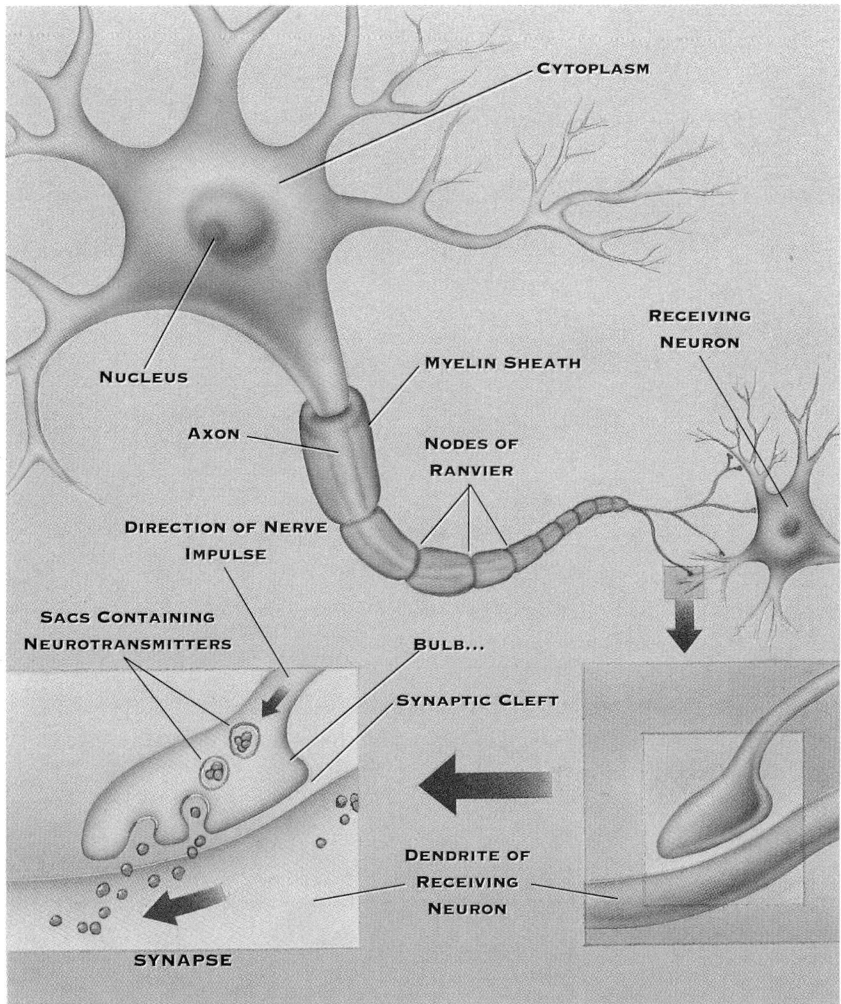


FIGURE 5.7

***The Anatomy of a Neuron.*** *"Messages" enter neurons through dendrites, are transmitted along the axon, and then are sent through axon terminals to muscles, glands, and other neurons.*

called ***neurotransmitters.*** These messages are then received by the dendrites of adjoining neurons, muscles, or glands. As the child matures, the axons of neurons grow in length, and the dendrites and axon terminals proliferate, creating vast interconnected networks for the transmission of complex messages.

Many neurons are tightly wrapped with white, fatty ***myelin sheaths.*** The high fat content of the myelin sheath insulates the neuron from electrically charged atoms in the fluids that encase the nervous system. In this way, leakage of the electric current being carried along the axon is minimized, and messages are conducted more efficiently.

The term ***myelination*** refers to the process by which axons are coated with myelin. Myelination is not complete at birth. Myelination is part of the maturation process that leads to the abilities to crawl and walk during the first year after birth. Incomplete myelination accounts for some of the helplessness of newborns (Rosenblith & Sims-Knight, 1989). In the disease ***multiple sclerosis,*** myelin is replaced by a hard, fibrous tissue that disrupts the timing of neural transmission and in this way interferes with muscle control.

***Neurotransmitter*** A chemical substance involved in the transmission of neural impulses from one neuron to another.

***Myelin sheath*** (MY-uh-lin) A fatty, whitish substance that encases and insulates neurons, permitting more rapid transmission of neural impulses.

***Myelination*** The process by which axons are coated with myelin.

***Multiple sclerosis*** A disorder in which myelin is replaced by hard fibrous tissue that impedes neural transmission.

### *Development of the Brain*

The brain of the newborn baby weighs a little less than a pound—nearly one-fourth of its adult weight. In keeping with the principles of cephalocaudal growth,

FIGURE 5.8

***GROWTH OF BODY SYSTEMS AS A PERCENTAGE OF TOTAL POSTNATAL GROWTH.*** *The brain of the neonate weighs about one-fourth its adult weight. In keeping with the principle of cephalocaudal growth, it will triple in weight by the first birthday, reaching nearly 70 percent of its adult weight.*

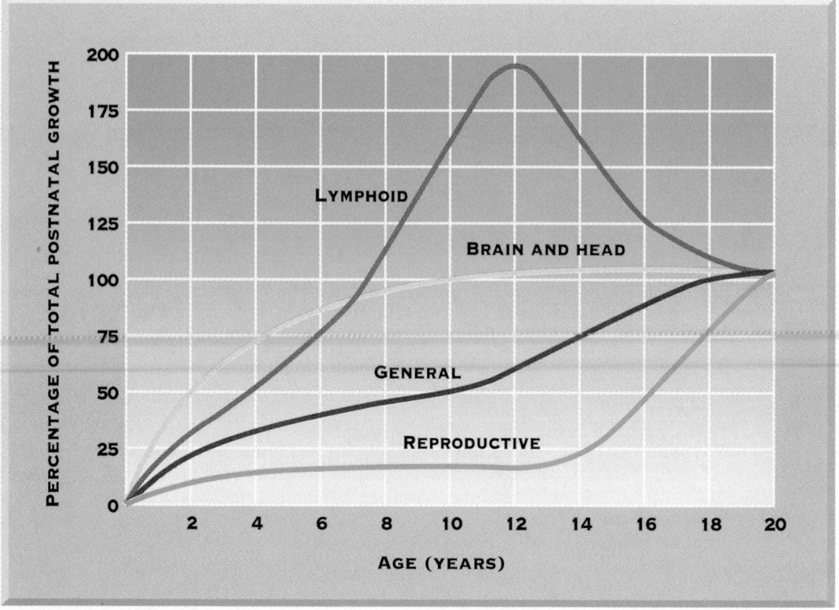


the brain triples in weight by the first birthday, reaching nearly 70 percent of its adult weight (see Figure 5.8). Let us look at the brain, as shown in Figure 5.9, and discuss the development of the structures within.

?

TRUTH OR FICTION REVISITED

*It is true that a child's brain reaches nearly 70 percent of its adult weight by the age of 1 year. This is another example of the principle of cephalocaudal growth. The brain develops relatively early.*

**STRUCTURES OF THE BRAIN** Many nerves that connect the spinal cord to higher levels of the brain pass through the ***medulla.*** The medulla is vital in the control of basic functions such as heartbeat and respiration. The medulla is part of an area called the *brain stem,* which may be implicated in Sudden Infant Death Syndrome (see Chapter 4).

Above the medulla lies the ***cerebellum,*** which is Latin for ''little brain.'' The cerebellum helps the child maintain balance, control motor behavior, and coordinate eye movements with bodily sensations.

The ***cerebrum*** is the crowning glory of the brain. It makes possible the breadth and depth of human learning, thought, memory, and language. Only in human beings does the cerebrum constitute such a large proportion of the brain. The surface of the cerebrum consists of two hemispheres—left and right—that become increasingly wrinkled, or convoluted, as the child develops, coming to show ridges and valleys called *fissures.* This surface is the *cerebral cortex.* The convolutions allow a great deal of surface area to be packed into the brain.

***Medulla*** (meh-DULL-ah) An oblong-shaped area of the hindbrain involved in heartbeat and respiration.

***Cerebellum*** (sara-BELL-um) The part of the hindbrain involved in muscle coordination and balance.

***Cerebrum*** (sir-REE-brum) The large mass of the forebrain, which consists of two hemispheres.

**GROWTH SPURTS OF THE BRAIN** The brain makes gains in size and weight in different ways. One is in the formation of neurons, a process complete

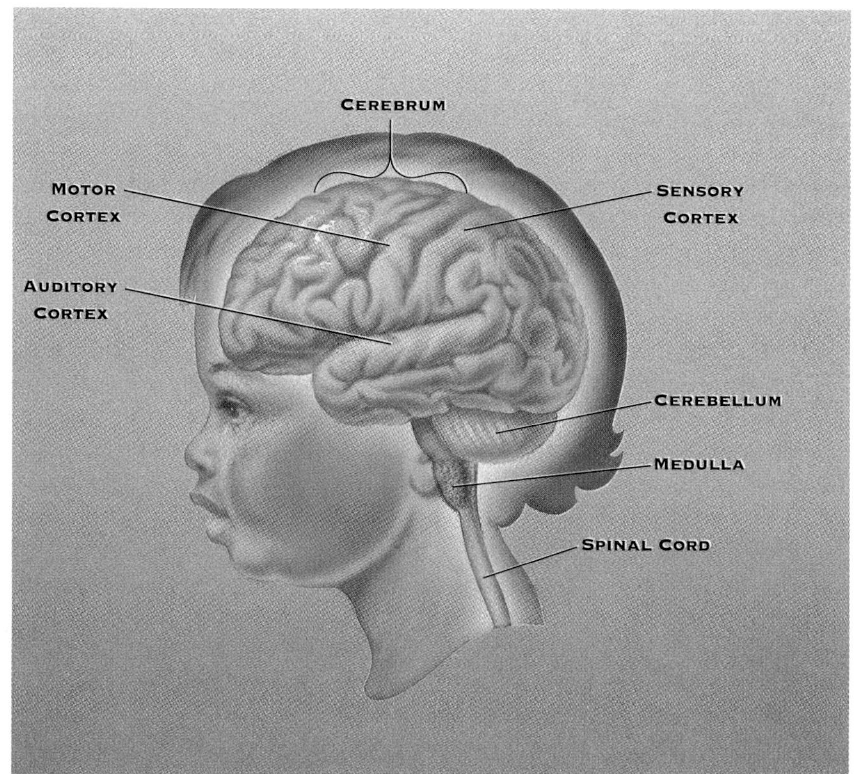


FIGURE 5.9

***STRUCTURES OF THE BRAIN.*** *This vertical cross-section model of the brain shows some of the most important structures.*

by birth. The first major growth spurt of the brain occurs during the fourth and fifth months of prenatal development, when neurons proliferate. A second growth spurt in the brain occurs between the 25th week of prenatal development and the end of the second year after birth. Whereas the first growth spurt of the brain was due to the formation of neurons, the second growth spurt is due primarily to the proliferation of dendrites and axon terminals (see Figure 5.10).

**BRAIN DEVELOPMENT IN INFANCY** There is a clear link between what infants can do and the myelination of areas within the brain. At birth, the parts of the brain involved in heartbeat and respiration, sleeping and arousal, and reflex activity are fairly well myelinated and functional.

Myelination of motor pathways allows newborn infants to show stereotyped reflexes, but otherwise their motor activity tends to be random and diffuse. Myelination of the motor area of the cerebral cortex begins at about the fourth month of prenatal development. Myelin develops rapidly along the major motor

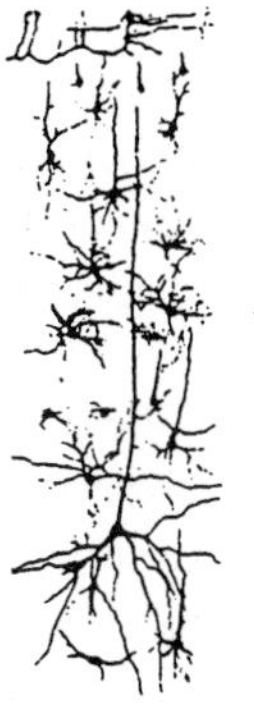

FIGURE 5.10

***INCREASE IN NEURAL CONNECTIONS IN THE BRAIN.*** *A major growth spurt in the brain occurs between the 25th week of prenatal development and the end of the second year after birth. This growth spurt is due primarily to the proliferation of dendrites and axon terminals. (Source: Conel, 1959).*

pathways from the cerebral cortex during the last month of pregnancy and continues after birth. The development of voluntary motor activity coincides with myelination as the diffuse movements of the neonate come under increasing control. The process of myelinating the motor pathways is largely complete by the age of 2 (O'Leary, 1990).

Although newborn babies respond to touch and can see and hear quite well, the areas of the cortex that are involved in vision, hearing, and the skin senses are less well myelinated at birth. As myelination progresses and the interconnections between the various areas of the cortex thicken, children become increasingly capable of complex and integrated sensorimotor activities (Tanner, 1989).

In Chapter 3, it was noted that newborns whose mothers read *The Cat in the Hat* aloud during the last few weeks of pregnancy showed a preference for this story. It turns out that myelination of the neurons involved in the sense of hearing begins at about the sixth month of pregnancy—coinciding with the period in which fetuses begin to respond to sound. Myelination of these pathways is developing rapidly at term and continues until about the age of 4 (Rosenblith & Sims-Knight, 1989).

Although the fetus shows some response to light during the third trimester, it is hard to imagine what use the fetus could have for vision. It turns out that the neurons involved in vision begin to myelinate only shortly before full term, but then they complete the process of myelination rapidly. Within a short 5 to 6 months after birth, vision has become the dominant sense.

**NATURE AND NURTURE IN THE DEVELOPMENT OF THE BRAIN** Development of the sensory and motor areas of the brain starts on course as a result of maturation, but sensory stimulation and motor activity during early infancy may also contribute to the development (Werry, 1991). Experience seems to fine tune the unfolding of the genetic code (Gottlieb, 1991).

Research with animals shows how the flood of sensory stimulation that newborns experience apparently spurs growth of the cortex. Researchers have created rat ''amusement parks'' to demonstrate the effects of enriched environments on neural development. Rats have been given toys such as ladders, platforms, and boxes. They have been provided with exploratory sessions in mazes and in fields with barriers. In these studies, the ''enriched'' rats invariably develop heavier brains than control animals. The weight differences in part reflect greater numbers of dendrites and axon terminals (Werry, 1991). On the other hand, animals raised in darkness show shrinkage of the visual cortex and impaired visual behavior (Greenough et al., 1987).

Human brains also are affected by experience. Infants actually have more connections among their neurons than adults do (Rakic, 1991). Those connections that are activated by experience survive; the others do not (Casaer, 1993; Greenough, 1991).

The great adaptability of the brain appears to be a double-edged sword. Adaptability allows us to develop different patterns of neural connections to meet the demands of our different environments. However, lack of stimulation—especially during critical early periods of development (as we shall see later)—can apparently impair our adaptability.

The nourishment the brain receives, like early experience, plays a role in its achieving the upper limits of the reaction range permitted by the child's genes. As noted in Chapter 3, inadequate nutrition in the fetus, especially during the prenatal growth spurt of the brain, has several negative effects. These include smallness in the overall size of the brain, the formation of fewer neurons, and less myelination (Bauerfeld & Lachenmeyer, 1992; Ekvall, 1993a).

## Motor Development

"When did your baby first sit up?" "When did he walk?" "Allyn couldn't walk yet at 10 months, but she zoomed after me in her walker, giggling her head off." "Anthony was walking forward *and* backward by the age of 13 months".

These are some of the types of comments parents make about their children's motor development. Motor development provides some of the most fascinating changes in infants, in part because so much seems to happen so quickly—and so much of it during the first year.

Motor development, like physical development, follows patterns of cephalocaudal and proximodistal development, and differentiation. As noted earlier in this chapter, for example, infants gain control of their heads and upper torsos before they can effectively use their arms. This trend illustrates cephalocaudal development. Babies also can control their trunks and shoulders before they can use their hands and fingers, demonstrating the proximodistal trend in development.

### *Lifting and Holding the Torso and Head*

Newborn babies can move their heads slightly to the side. This permits them to avoid suffocation if they are lying face down and their noses or mouths are obstructed by the bedding. At about 1 month, babies raise their heads. By about 2 months, they can also lift their chests while lying in a prone position.

When neonates are held, their heads must be supported. But by 3 to 6 months of age, babies generally manage to hold their heads quite well, so that supporting the head is no longer necessary. Unfortunately, babies who can normally support their heads cannot do so when they are lifted or moved about in a jerky manner, and babies who are not handled carefully can develop neck injuries.

### *Control of the Hands*

The development of hand skills is a clear example of the process of proximodistal development. Babies will track (follow) slowly moving objects with their eyes from shortly after birth, but generally will not reach for them. They show a grasp reflex, as described in Chapter 4, but they do not reliably reach for the objects that appear to interest them. Voluntary reaching and grasping require visual–motor coordination. By about 3 months of age, infants will make clumsy swipes at objects, failing in efforts to grasp them, because their aim is poor or they close their hands too soon or too late.

Between 4 and 6 months, infants become increasingly successful at grasping objects (Mathew & Cook, 1990; Tallandini et al., 1990). However, they may not know how to let go of an object and may hold on to it indefinitely, until their attention is diverted and the hand opens accidentally. Four to 6 months is a good age for giving children rattles, large plastic spoons, mobiles, and other brightly colored hanging toys that are harmless when they wind up in the mouth.

Babies first hold objects between their fingers and their palm. The oppositional thumb does not come into play until 9 to 12 months or so. Use of the thumb gives infants the ability to pick up tiny objects in what is called a ***pincer grasp,*** as seen in Figure 5.11 (Thomas, 1990). By about 11 months, infants can hold objects in each hand and inspect them in turn.

Another measure of visual–motor coordination is the ability to stack blocks. On the average, children can stack two small blocks at the age of 15 months,

***Pincer grasp*** The use of the opposing thumb to grasp objects.

FIGURE 5.11

***Pincer Grasp.*** *Babies first hold objects between their fingers and palm. Once the oppositional thumb comes into play at about 9 to 12 months of age, babies are able to pick up tiny objects using what is called a* pincer grasp.

three blocks at 18 months, and five blocks at 24 months. At about 24 months, children also can copy horizontal and vertical lines.

## *Locomotion*

***Locomotion*** is movement from one place to another. Children gain the capacity to move their bodies about through a sequence of activities that includes rolling over, sitting up, crawling, creeping, walking, and running (see Figure 5.12). There is a great deal of variation in the ages at which infants first engage in these activities, but the sequence remains generally invariant. A number of children will skip a step, however. For example, an infant may creep without ever having crawled.

Most infants can roll over, from back to stomach and stomach to back, by about 6 months. They are also capable of sitting (and holding their upper bodies, necks, and heads) for extended periods if they are supported by a person or placed in a seat with a strap, such as a high chair. By about 7 months, infants usually begin to sit up by themselves.

At about 8 to 9 months, most infants begin to crawl, a motor activity in which they lie prone and use their arms to pull themselves along, dragging their bellies and feet behind. Creeping, a more sophisticated form of locomotion in which infants move themselves along up on their hands and knees, requires a good deal more coordination and usually appears a month or so after crawling (see Figure 5.13).

There are fascinating alternatives to creeping. Some infants travel from one place to another by rolling over and over. Some lift themselves and swing their arms while in a sitting position, in effect dragging along on their buttocks. Still others do a ''bear walk'' in which they move on their hands and feet, without allowing their elbows and knees to touch the floor. And some, as noted, just crawl until they are ready to stand and walk from place to place while holding on to chairs, other objects, and people.

Standing overlaps with crawling and creeping. Most infants can remain in a standing position if holding on to something by about 8 or 9 months. At this age they may also be able to walk a bit when supported by adults. This walking

***Locomotion*** Movement from one place to another.

FIGURE 5.12

***Motor Development in Infancy.*** *Motor development proceeds in an orderly sequence, but there is considerable variation in the timing of the marker events shown in this figure. An infant who is a bit behind most likely will develop with no problems at all, and a precocious infant will not necessarily become a rocket scientist (or gymnast).*

is voluntary and does not have the stereotyped appearance of the walking reflex described in Chapter 4. About 2 months later, they can pull themselves to a standing position by holding on to the sides of their cribs or other objects and can also stand briefly without holding on. Shortly afterward, they walk about unsteadily while holding on. By 12 to 15 months or so they walk by themselves, earning them the name ***toddler.*** Attempts at mastering each of these new motor skills often are accompanied by signs of pleasure such as smiling, laughing, and babbling (Mayes & Zigler, 1992).

***Toddler*** A child who walks with short, uncertain steps. Toddlerhood lasts from about 18 to 30 months of age.

FIGURE 5.13

***CREEPING.*** *Creeping requires considerable coordination of arm and leg movements. Creeping usually appears a month or so after crawling.*

Toddlers soon run about in a bowlegged fashion, supporting their relatively heavy heads and torsos by spreading their legs. Because they are top-heavy and inexperienced, they fall frequently. Some toddlers require a good deal of consoling when they fall. Others spring right up and run on again with barely an interruption. Toddlers are surprisingly skillful at navigating safely down both steep and shallow slopes (Weiner & Adolph, 1993). They walk down shallow slopes but prudently elect to slide or crawl down steep ones.

The ability to move about on the legs provides children with new freedom. It allows them to get about rapidly and grasp objects that were formerly out of reach. A large ball to toss and run after is about the least expensive and most enjoyable toy toddlers can be given.

As children mature, their muscle strength, the density of their bones, and their balance and coordination all improve. By 2 years of age, they can climb steps one at a time, placing both feet on each step. They can run well, walk backward, kick a large ball, and jump several inches.

### CULTURE AND DEVELOPMENT: MOTOR DEVELOPMENT

***Formal handling*** A series of activities used by parents in Africa and in cultures of African origin to stimulate sitting and walking in their infants.

African and African-American infants generally reach such motor milestones as sitting, walking, and running before white infants. This finding has been obtained for both premature and full-term infants (Allen & Alexander, 1990; Capute et al., 1985) and in Third World countries as well as in the United States (Garcia-Coll, 1990).

### TRUTH OR FICTION REVISITED

*It is not true that white U.S. infants sit, walk, and run at earlier ages than African and African-American infants do. The reverse is true. Parents in Africa and in some cultures of African origin provide considerable early stimulation and practice in these aspects of motor development.*

While genetic factors may be involved in the earlier motor development of African and African-American infants, environmental factors also appear to play a role (see Figure 5.15). The areas of motor development in which African infants excel are those in which they have received considerable stimulation and practice. For example, African babies sit and walk earlier than American babies, but they do not crawl any sooner (Rogoff & Morelli, 1989). Parents in Africa and in cultures of African origin, such as Jamaica, place considerable importance on the development of sitting and walking. Crawling is not a culturally valued behavior because it is seen as being hazardous and apelike (Hopkins, 1991; Hopkins & Westra, 1990). African and Jamaican parents provide experiences from birth onward that stimulate the development of sitting and walking in their babies. These activities, known as ***formal handling,*** consist of stretching exercises and massages that start shortly after birth. From the second or third months, other activities are added, such as propping babies in a sitting position, bouncing them on their feet, and exercising the stepping reflex. But African and Jamaican babies typically are not placed on the ground on their stomachs and so do not receive much practice in crawling.

FIGURE 5.14

***WALKING.*** *By 12 to 15 months or so, babies walk by themselves, earning them the name* toddler.

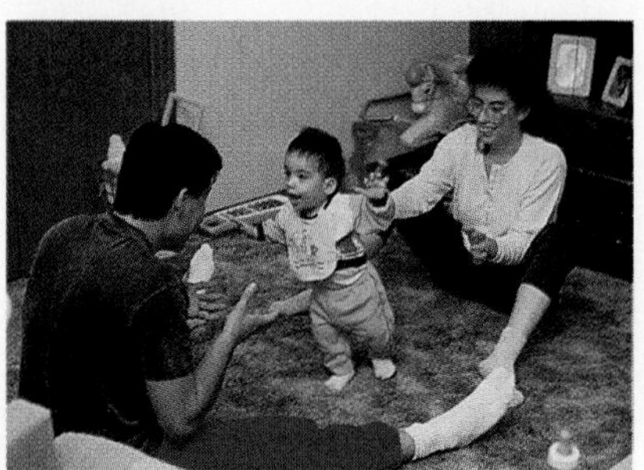

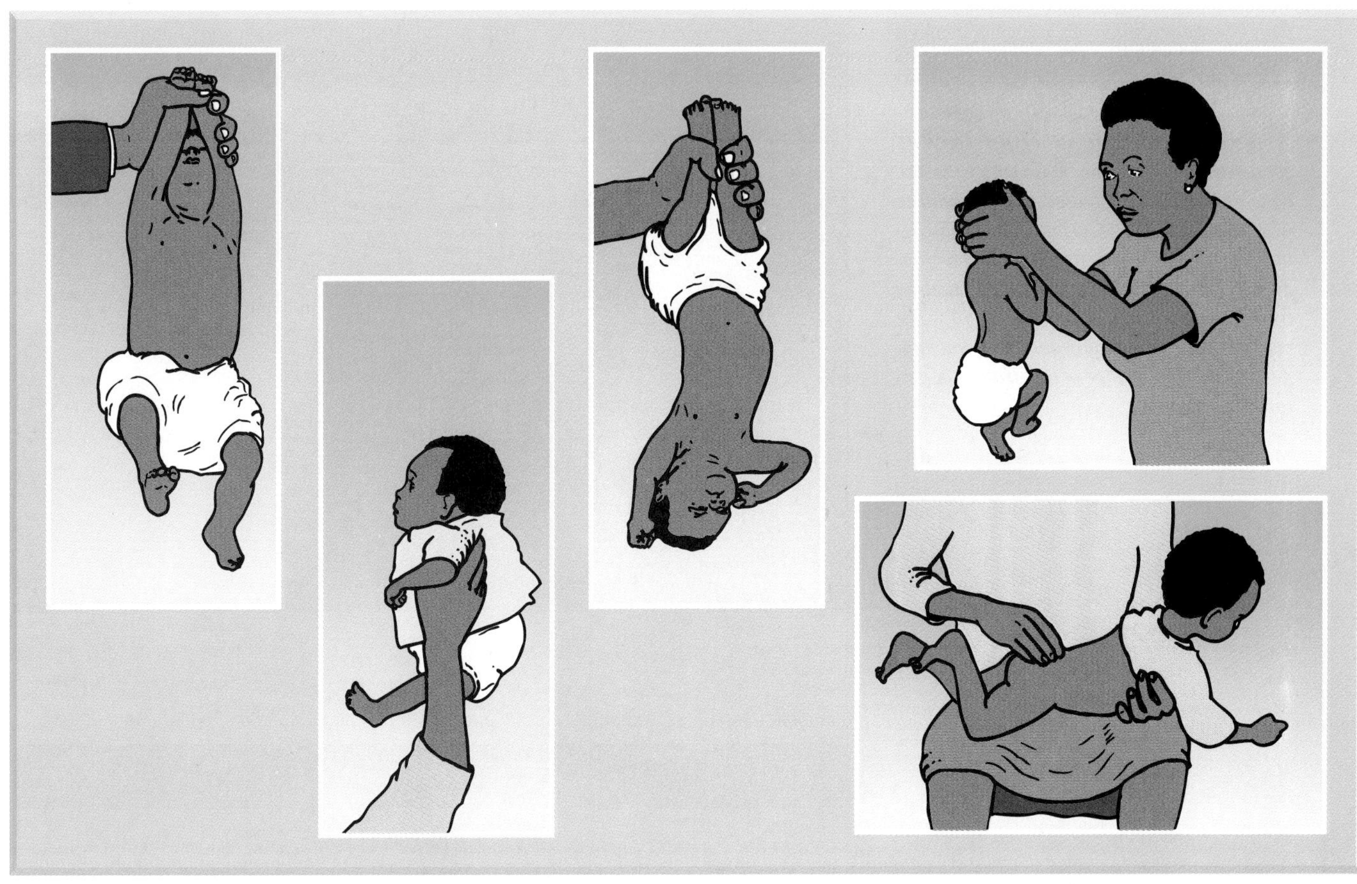

FIGURE 5.15

***Aspects of the Jamaican Formal-Handling Routine.*** *Parents in Africa and in cultures of African origin, such as Jamaica, provide experience from birth onward that stimulates the development of sitting and walking in their babies. These activities, known as* formal handling, *including stretching exercises and massage (as shown here), as well as propping babies in a sitting position, bouncing them on their feet, and exercising the stepping reflex. (Source: Hopkins, 1991).*

## *Theoretical Interlude: Nature and Nurture in Motor Development*

There seems to be little doubt that both maturation (nature) and experience (nurture) play indispensable roles in various aspects of motor development (Jouen & Lepecq, 1990). Certain types of voluntary motor activities do not seem possible until the brain has matured in terms of myelination and the differentiation of the motor areas of the cortex. While it is true that the neonate shows stepping and swimming reflexes, these behaviors are controlled by more primitive areas of the brain. They disappear when cortical development inhibits some of the functions of the lower areas of the brain, and, when they reappear, their quality is quite different.

Infants also need some opportunity for motor experimentation before they can engage in milestones such as sitting up and walking. But although it may take them several months to sit up and, as described earlier, more months to take their first steps, most of this time can apparently be attributed to maturation. In a classic study, Wayne and Marsena Dennis (1940) reported on the motor development of Native-American Hopi children who spent their first year strapped to a cradleboard (see Figure 5.16). Although denied a full year of experience in locomotion, the Hopi infants gained the capacity to walk early in their second year, at about the same time as children reared in other cultures. A more recent cross-cultural study (Hindley et al., 1966) reported that infants in five European cities began to walk at about the same time (generally, between 12 and 15 months), despite cultural differences in encouragement to walk.

FIGURE 5.16

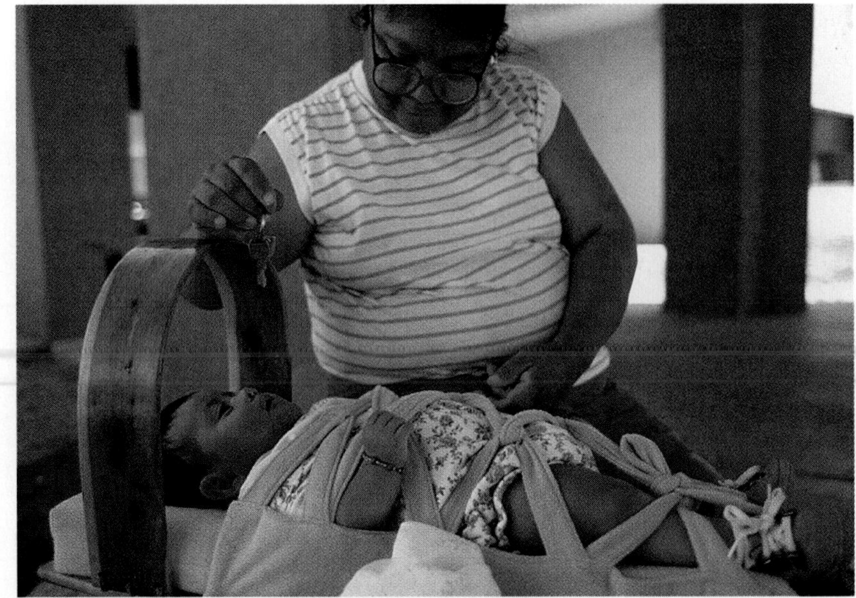

***A Native-American Hopi Infant Strapped to a Cradleboard.*** *Researchers have studied Hopi children who are strapped to cradleboards during the first year to see if their motor development is delayed significantly. Once released from their boards, Hopi children make rapid advances in motor development, suggesting the importance of maturation in motor development.*

## TRUTH OR FICTION REVISITED

*Hopi babies who are strapped to a board for the first year of life do begin to walk at about the same time as children who are reared in other cultures. Maturation seems to be the central factor in the development of basic motor skills. Any negative effects from sensorimotor deprivation do not appear to last in Hopi children.*

Does the Hopis' cultural custom of strapping infants to cradleboards interfere with motor development?

| Culture | Early Social Environment | Behavioral Outcome |
|---|---|---|
| Hopi | Strapped to a cradleboard | Both groups begin to walk early in the second year |
| Other U.S. children | Allowed to move about freely | |

On the other hand, evidence is mixed as to whether specific training can accelerate the appearance of motor skills. For example, in a classic study with identical twins, Arnold Gesell (1929) gave one twin extensive training in hand coordination, block building, and stair climbing from early infancy. The other was allowed to develop on his own. But as time passed, the untrained twin became as skilled in these activities as the other.

Later research indicates that the appearance and development of motor skills can be accelerated by training (Zelazo et al., 1993). Yet this effect is slight, at best; guided practice in the absence of neural maturation can have only limited results. There is also no evidence that this sort of training leads to eventual superior motor skills or other advantages.

Although being strapped to a cradleboard did not permanently prevent the motor development of Hopi infants, Wayne Dennis (1960) reported that infants in an Iranian orphanage were significantly retarded in their motor development. In contrast to the Hopi infants, the institutionalized infants were exposed to extreme social and physical deprivation. Under these conditions, they grew apathetic, and all aspects of development suffered. But there is also a bright side to this tale of deprivation. The motor development of infants in a Lebanese orphanage accelerated dramatically in response to such minimal intervention as being propped up in their cribs and being given a few colorful toys (Dennis & Sayegh, 1965).

Nature, as noted, provides the reaction range for the expression of inherited traits. Nurture determines whether the child will develop skills in accord with the upper limits of the inherited range. Recent research by Esther Thelen and her colleagues indicates that even a fundamental skill such as locomotion is determined by a complex interplay of both maturational and environmental factors (Thelen, 1990; Thelen & Ulrich, 1991). There may be little purpose in trying to train children to enhance their motor skills before they are ready. Once they are ready, however, teaching and practice do make a difference. One does not become an Olympic athlete without "good genes." But one also usually does not become an Olympic athlete without high-quality training. And since motor skills are important to the self-concepts of children, good teaching is all the more important.

***Thinking About Development***

Agree or disagree with the following statement and support your answer: "Outstanding athletes are born, not made."

## Sensory and Perceptual Development

What a world we live in—green hills and reddish skies; rumbling trucks, murmuring brooks, and voices; the sweet and the sour; the acrid and the perfumed; the metallic and the fuzzy. What an ever-changing display of sights, sounds, tastes, smells, and touches.

The pleasures of the world, and its miseries, are known to us through sensory impressions and the organization of these impressions into personal inner maps of reality. Our eyes; our ears; the sensory receptors in our noses and our mouths; our skin senses—these are our tickets of admission to the world.

In Chapter 4, we examined the sensory capabilities of the neonate. In this section, we follow infants to learn how they develop their abilities to integrate disjointed sensory impressions into meaningful patterns of events known as *perceptions.* We see what sorts of things capture the attention of young babies, and we see how young children become purposeful seekers of information—selecting the sensory impressions they will choose to capture and weeding out the sensory chaff. We will focus on the development of vision and hearing, since most of the research on sensory and perceptual development after the newborn period has been done in these areas.

We shall see that many things that are obvious to us are not obvious to young infants. You may know that a coffee cup is the same whether you see it from above or from the side, but make no such assumptions about the baby. You may know that a baby's mother is the same size whether she is standing next to the baby or approaching from two blocks away, but do not assume that the baby agrees with you.

We cannot ask infants to explain why they look at some things and not at others. Nor can we ask them if their mother appears to be the same size whether she is standing close to them or far away. But the clever methods that have been devised by investigators of childhood sensation and perception to answer these questions provide us with fascinating insights into the perceptual processes of even the neonate. These methods reveal that many basic perceptual competencies are present early in life (Pick, 1991).

### *Development of Vision*

We explored some of the visual capabilities of newborn babies in Chapter 4. In this section, let us examine the developing visual capacities of the infant.

**Development of Visual Acuity and Peripheral Vision** As we saw in Chapter 4, newborns are very nearsighted. The most dramatic gains in visual acuity are made between birth and 6 months of age, with acuity reaching about 20/50 (Haith, 1990). Gains in visual acuity then become more gradual, approximating adult levels (20/20) by about 3 to 5 years of age (Fielder et al., 1992).

*Newborn babies are, in fact, nearsighted. By 6 months their visual acuity approaches adult levels, however.*

Newborns also have poor peripheral vision (Courage & Adams, 1993). Adults can perceive objects that are nearly 90 degrees off to the side (that is, directly to the left or right), although objects at these extremes are unclear. Newborn babies cannot perceive visual stimuli that are off to the side by an angle of more than 30 degrees, but their peripheral vision expands to an angle of about 45 degrees by the age of 7 weeks (Macfarlane et al., 1976). By 6 months of age, their peripheral vision is about equal to that of an adult (Cohen et al., 1979).

Let us now consider the development of visual perception. In so doing we shall see that infants frequently prefer the strange to the familiar and will avoid going off the deep end—sometimes.

**VISUAL PREFERENCES: HOW DO YOU CAPTURE A CHILD'S ATTENTION?** What are the things that capture the attention of babies? How do visual preferences develop? You will remember from Chapter 4 that young babies attend longer to stripes than blobs, a finding that has been used in much of the research on visual acuity. By 8 to 12 weeks, most babies also show distinct preferences for curved lines over straight ones (Fantz et al., 1975).

Fantz (1961) also wondered whether there was something intrinsically interesting about the human face that drew the attention of babies. To investigate this question, he showed 2-month-old infants the six disks illustrated in Figure 5.17.

FIGURE 5.17

***PREFERENCES FOR VISUAL STIMULI IN 2-MONTH-OLDS.*** *Infants appear to prefer complex to simple visual stimuli. By the time they are 2 months old, they also tend to show preference for the human face.*

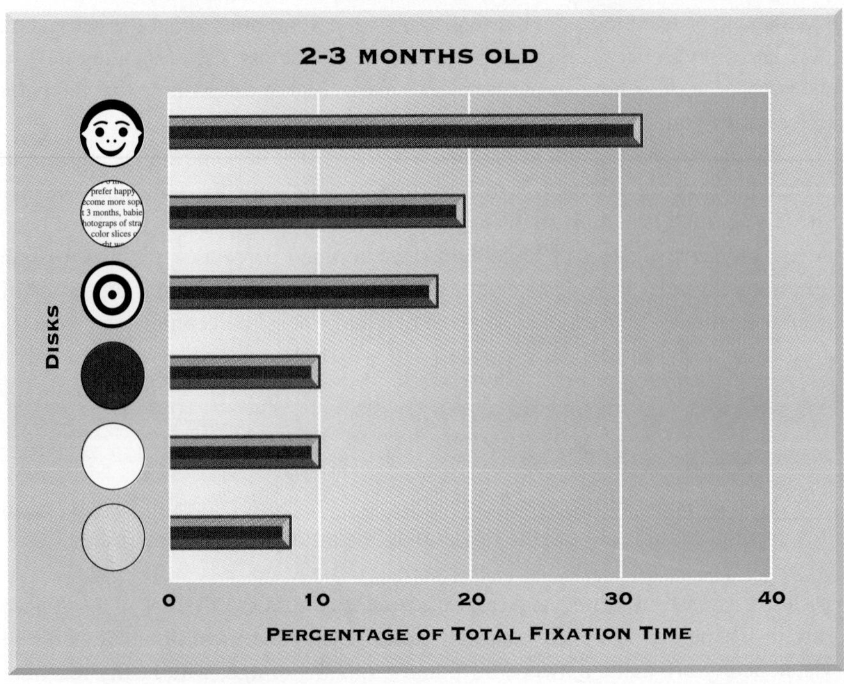

One contained a caricature of human features, another newsprint, and still another a bull's-eye. The remaining three were featureless but colored red, white, and yellow. In this study, the babies fixated significantly longer on the human face.

Subsequent studies have suggested that the babies in the Fantz (1961) study may not have preferred the human face so much because it was a face as because it had a complex, intriguing pattern of dots (eyes) within an outline. In some of these studies, babies have been shown drawings that resemble a face and other drawings that contain the same elements of a face (such as eyes, nose, and mouth) but in scrambled order. Under 2 months of age, babies pay about an equal amount of attention to both types of drawings. But by 2 months of age, they begin to prefer the "real" face to the scrambled one (Johnson et al., 1992; Morton & Johnson, 1991).

**TRUTH OR FICTION REVISITED**

*It is true that 2-month-old babies prefer to look at human faces rather than at brightly colored objects. The question is whether they prefer faces because they are faces or because faces are complex stimuli.*

Even newborns can discriminate their mother's face from a stranger's (Bushnell et al., 1989; Walton et al., 1992). By 3 to 5 months of age, they respond differently to happy, surprised, and sad faces (Muir & Hains, 1993; Nelson & Ludemann, 1989). Moreover, infants as young as 2 months of age prefer attractive faces to unattractive faces (Langlois et al., 1990, 1991). These results suggest the intriguing hypothesis that standards of attractiveness may have an inborn component.

Newborn babies appear to direct their attention to the edges of objects. This pattern persists for the first several weeks (Bronson, 1991). When they are given the opportunity to look at human faces, 1-month-old babies tend to pay most attention to the "edges"—that is, the chin, an ear, or the hairline. Two-month-old babies move in from the edge, as shown in Figure 5.18. They focus particularly

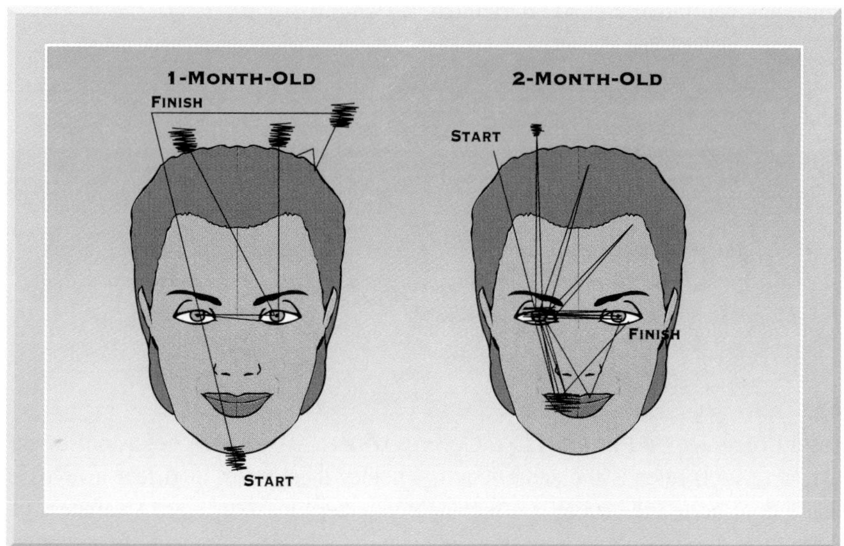


**FIGURE 5.18**

***EYE MOVEMENTS OF 1- AND 2-MONTH-OLDS.*** *One-month-olds direct their attention to the edges of objects. Two-month-olds "move in from the edge." When looking at a face, for example, they focus on the eyes and other inner features. (Source: Salapatek, 1975).*

FIGURE 5.19

***The Visual Cliff Experiment.*** *This young explorer has the good sense not to crawl out onto an apparently unsupported surface, even when mother beckons from the other side.*

on the eyes, though they also inspect other inner features, such as the mouth and nose (Nelson & Ludemann, 1989).

Some researchers (Haith, 1979) explain babies' tendencies to scan from the edges of objects inward by noting that for the first several weeks of life, babies seem to be essentially concerned with *where* things are. Their attention is captured by movement and sharp contrasts in brightness and shape, such as those that are found where the edges of objects stand out against their backgrounds. But by about 2 months, babies tend to focus on the *what* of things. They may locate objects by looking at their edges, but now they scan systematically within the boundaries of objects (Bronson, 1990).

**Development of Depth Perception: On *Not* Going Off the Deep End** Infants generally respond to cues for depth by the time they are able to crawl about (6 to 8 months of age or so), and most have the good sense to avoid "going off the deep end"—that is crawling off ledges and tabletops into open space (Campos et al., 1978). In a classic study on depth perception, Eleanor Gibson and Richard Walk (1960) placed infants of various ages on a fabric-covered runway that ran across the center of a clever device called a *visual cliff* (see Figure 5.19). The visual cliff consists of a sheet of plexiglass that covers a cloth with a high-contrast checkerboard pattern. On one side the cloth is placed immediately beneath the plexiglas, and on the other, it is dropped about 4 feet below. Since the plexiglas alone would easily support the infant, this is a visual cliff rather than an actual cliff. In the Gibson and Walk study, 8 out of 10 infants who had begun to crawl refused to venture onto the seemingly unsupported surface, even when their mothers beckoned encouragingly from the other side.

Psychologists can assess babies' emotional responses to the visual cliff long before they can crawl. For example, Joseph Campos and his colleagues (1970) found that 1-month-old infants showed no change in heart rate when placed face down on the visual cliff. Apparently, they did not perceive the depth of the cliff. At 2 months of age, the infants showed decreases in heart rate when so placed, which psychologists interpret as a sign of interest. The heart rates of 9-month-olds accelerated when the infants were placed on the cliff, which is interpreted as a fear response. It may be that infants need to have some experience crawling about (and, perhaps, accumulating some bumps) before they develop fear of heights. The 9-month-olds but not the 2-month-olds had had such experience. Other studies support the view that babies usually do not develop fear of heights until they can move around (Bertenthal & Campos, 1990).

*TRUTH OR FICTION* ***REVISITED***

*It is apparently true that infants need to have some experience crawling about before they develop fear of heights. Infants typically do not show fear of the visual cliff unless they have had such experience.*

**Development of Perceptual Constancies** It may not astonish you that a 12-inch ruler is the same length whether it is 2 feet or 6 feet away. Or that a door across the room is a rectangle whether closed or ajar. Awareness of these facts depends not on sensation alone, but on the development of perceptual constancies. ***Perceptual constancy*** is the tendency to perceive an object to be the same, even though the sensations produced by the object may differ under various conditions.

Consider again the example of the ruler. When it is 2 feet away, its image, as focused on the retina, is a certain length. This length is the image's "retinal size." From 6 feet away, the 12-inch ruler is only one-third as long in terms of retinal size, but we perceive it as being the same size because of ***size constancy.*** Size constancy is the tendency to perceive the same objects as being of the same size even though their retinal sizes vary as a function of their distance. From 6 feet away, a 36-inch yardstick casts an image equal in retinal size to the 12-inch ruler at 2 feet, but—if recognized as a yardstick—it is perceived as longer, again because of size constancy.

In a classic study of the development of size constancy, Thomas Bower (1974) conditioned 2½- to 3-month-old babies to turn their heads to the left when shown a 12-inch cube from a distance of 3 feet. He then presented them with three experimental stimuli: (a) a 12-inch cube 9 feet away, whose retinal size was smaller than that of the original cube; (b) a 36-inch cube 3 feet away, whose retinal size was larger than that of the original cube; and (c) a 36-inch cube 9 feet away, whose retinal size was the same as that of the original cube. The infants turned their heads most frequently in response to the first experimental cube, although its retinal image was only one-third the length of that to which they had been conditioned, suggesting that they had achieved size constancy. Later studies have confirmed Bower's finding that size constancy is present in early infancy. Some research suggests that even newborns possess rudimentary size constancy (Granrud, 1987; Slater et al., 1990).

***Shape constancy*** is the tendency to perceive an object as having the same shape even though, when perceived from another angle, the shape projected onto the retina may change dramatically. When the top of a cup or a glass is seen from above, the visual sensations are in the shape of a circle. When seen from a slight angle, the sensations are elliptical, and when seen from the side, the retinal image is the same as that of a straight line. However, we still perceive the rim of the cup or glass as being a circle, because of our familiarity with the object. In the first few months after birth, young babies see the features of their mothers, of bottles, of cribs, and of toys from all different angles, so that by the time they are 4 or 5 months old, a broad grasp of shape constancy seems to be established, at least under certain conditions (Aslin, 1987; Dodwell et al., 1987). Strategies for studying the development of shape constancy are described in Focus on Research.

***Perceptual constancy*** The tendency to perceive objects as the same although sensations produced by them may differ when, for example, they differ in position or distance.

***Size constancy*** The tendency to perceive objects as being the same size although the sizes of their retinal images may differ as a result of distance.

***Shape constancy*** The tendency to perceive objects as being the same shape although the shapes of their retinal images may differ when the objects are viewed from different positions.

## *Development of Hearing*

Newborns can crudely orient their heads in the direction of a sound (Aslin, 1987). By 18 months, the accuracy of sound-localizing ability approaches that of adults (Morrongiello et al., 1990). Sensitivity to sounds increases in the first few months of life (Trehub et al., 1991; Werner & Bargones, 1992). As infants mature, the range of the pitch of the sounds they can sense gradually expands to include the adult 20–20,000 cycles per second. The ability to detect differences in the pitch and loudness of sounds improves considerably throughout the preschool years (Jensen & Neff, 1993). Auditory acuity also improves gradually over the first several years (Aslin, 1987), although the hearing of babies can be so fine that many parents complain their napping infants will awaken at the slightest sound. Some do, especially if parents have been overprotective in attempting to keep

FOCUS ON RESEARCH

### *Strategies for Studying the Development of Shape Constancy*

People are said to show shape constancy when they perceive an object as having the same shape even though, when viewed from another angle, the shape projected onto the retina may be very different. We can determine whether babies have developed shape constancy through the process of habituation, which, as you may recall from Chapter 3, involves paying less attention to a repeated stimulus.

**Habituation** Once they are a few months old, infants show a preference for novel objects. They have become habituated to familiar objects, and—if we can take the liberty of describing their responses in adult terms—they are apparently bored by them. Certain bodily responses indicate interest in an object—for example, a slower heart rate (as with 2-month-old babies placed face-down on a visual cliff) and concentrated gazing. Therefore, when infants have become habituated to an object, their heart rates speed up moderately, and they no longer show concentrated gazing.

Here, then, is the research strategy. Show an infant stimulus A for a prolonged period of time. At first the heart rate will slow, and the infant will focus on the object. But as time goes on, the heart rate will again rise to prestimulated levels, and the baby's gaze will wander. Now show the infant stimulus B. If the heart rate again slows, and the gaze again becomes concentrated, we can infer that stimulus B is perceived as a novel (different) object. But if the heart rate and pattern of gazing does not change, we can infer that the baby does not perceive a difference between stimuli A and B.

Here is the 64-day-old question: If stimuli A and B are actually the same object, but are seen from different angles, what does it mean when the baby's heart rate and pattern of gazing do not change? We can assume that lack of change means that the baby perceives stimuli A and B to be the same—in this case, the same object. Therefore, we can conclude that the baby has developed shape constancy.

Using a strategy similar to that above, Caron and his colleagues (1979) first habituated 3-month-old babies to a square shown at different angles. The babies then were presented with one of two test stimuli: (a) the identical square, shown at an entirely new angle or (b) a novel figure (a trapezoid) shown at the new angle. The two test stimuli projected identical trapezoidal images on the retina, even though their real shapes were different. Infants who were shown the square at the new angle showed little change in response. However, babies shown the trapezoid did show different responses. Therefore, it seems that babies perceived the trapezoid as novel, even though it cast the same retinal image as the square. But the infants were able to recognize the ''real'' shape of the square despite the fact that it cast a trapezoidal image on the retina. In other words, they showed shape constancy.

their rooms as silent as possible. Babies who are normally exposed to a backdrop of moderate noise levels become habituated to them and are not likely to awaken unless there is a sudden, sharp noise.

By the age of 1 month, infants perceive differences between speech sounds that are highly similar. In a classic study relying on the ***habituation*** method, babies of this age could activate a recording of "bah" by sucking on a nipple (Eimas et al., 1971). As time went on, habituation occurred, as shown by decreased sucking in order to hear the "bah" sound. Then the researchers switched from "bah" to "pah." If the sounds had seemed the same to the infants, their lethargic sucking patterns would have continued. But they immediately sucked harder, suggesting that they perceived the difference. Other researchers have found that within another month or two, babies reliably discriminate three-syllable words such as *marana* and *malana* (Kuhl, 1987).

Babies can discriminate the sounds of their parent's voices by 3½ months of age. In one study, infants of this age were oriented toward their parents as they reclined in baby seats. The researchers (Spelke & Owsley, 1979) played recordings of the mother's or father's voice, while the parents themselves remained inactive. The babies reliably looked at the parent whose voice was being played.

***Habituation*** Paying less attention to a repeated stimulus.

Young infants are capable of perceiving most of the speech sounds present in the world's languages. But after exposure to one's native language, infants gradually lose the capacity to discriminate those sounds that are not found in the native language. Prior to 6 months of age, for example, infants reared in an English-speaking environment could discriminate sounds found in Hindi (a language of India) and Salish (a Native American language). But by 10 to 12 months of age, they had lost the ability to do so, as shown in Figure 5.20 (Werker, 1989).

Infants also learn at an early age to ignore small, meaningless variations in the sounds of their native language. Adults do this routinely. For example, if someone speaking your language has a head cold or a slight accent, you ignore the minor variations in the person's pronunciation and hear these variations as the same sound. But when you hear slight variations in the sounds of a foreign language, you might assume that each variation carries a different meaning and so you hear the sounds as different.

Infants show this ability to screen out meaningless sounds as early as 6 months of age. Patricia Kuhl and her colleagues (1992) presented American and Swedish babies with pairs of sounds in either their own language or the other language. The babies were trained to look over their shoulder when they heard a difference in the sounds and to ignore sound pairs that seemed to be the same. The babies routinely ignored variations in sounds that were part of their language, because they apparently perceived them as being the same sound. But they noticed slight variations in the sounds of the other language. A later study demonstrated this same ability in babies as young as 2 months of age (Marean et al., 1992).

By the first birthday, many infants understand many words, and some may even say a word or two of their own. During infancy the auditory apparatus for language learning is well in place.

## *Development of Coordination of the Senses*

We have seen that newborn babies crudely orient their heads toward sounds and pleasant odors. In this way, they increase the probability that the sources of the sounds and odors will also be sensed through visual scanning. Young infants also have the ability to recognize that an object experienced in one sensory modality is the same as an identical object experienced in a different modality.

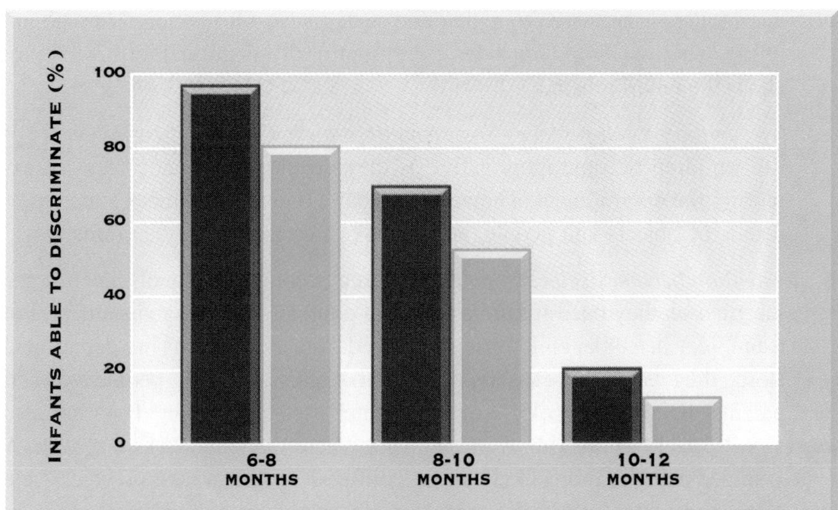


FIGURE 5.20

**Declining Ability to Discriminate Sounds of Other Languages.** *Infants show a decline in the ability to discriminate sounds not found in their native language. Before 6 months of age, babies from English-speaking families could discriminate sounds found in Hindi (red bars) and Salish, a Native-American language (green bars). By 10 to 12 months of age, they could no longer do so. (Source: Werker, 1989).*

***Cross-modal transfer*** The ability to recognize that an object experienced in one sensory modality is the same as an identical object experienced in a different modality.

This ability, known as ***cross-modal transfer,*** has been demonstrated in infants as young as 1 month of age (Bushnell, 1993; Rose & Ruff, 1987). One experiment demonstrating cross-modal transfer in 12-month-olds takes advantage of the fact that children of this age prefer novel to familiar sources of stimulation. Susan Rose and Esther Orlian (1991) allowed the infants to handle, but not see, an object (for example, a plastic triangle). This object and a novel object (for example, a plastic cross) then were shown to the infants, but they were not allowed to touch them. The children spent more time looking at the novel object. This indicates that they recognized the handled object, even though they were now experiencing it visually.

## *Theoretical Interlude: Do Children Play an Active or Passive Role in Perceptual Development?*

Newborn infants may have more sophisticated sensory capabilities than you expected. Still, their ways of perceiving the world are largely mechanical, or passive. The description of a stimulus *capturing* a baby's attention seems quite appropriate. Neonates seem to be generally at the mercy of external stimuli. When a bright light strikes, they attend to it. If the light moves slowly across the plane of their vision, they track it.

As time passes, broad changes occur in the perceptual processes of children, and the child's role in perception appears to become decidedly more active. Developmental psychologist Eleanor Gibson (1969, 1991) notes a number of these changes:

1. *Intentional action replaces "capture."* As infants mature and gain experience, purposeful scanning and exploration of the environment take the place of mechanical movements and passive responses to potent stimulation.

   Consider the scanning "strategies" of newborn infants. In a lighted room, newborn babies move their eyes mostly from left to right and back again. Mechanically, they sweep a horizontal plane. If they encounter an object that contrasts sharply with the background, their eye movements bounce back and forth against the edges. However, even when newborns awaken in a dark room, they show the stereotypical horizontal scanning pattern, with about two eye movements per second (Haith, 1990).

   The stereotypical quality of these initial scanning movements suggests that they are inborn. They provide strong evidence that the neonate is neurologically prewired to gather and seek visual information. They do not reflect what we would consider a purposeful, or intentional, effort to learn about the environment.

2. *Systematic search replaces unsystematic search.* Over the first few years of life, children become more active as they develop systematic ways of exploring the environment. They come to pay progressively more attention to details of objects and people, and to make finer and finer discriminations.

3. *Attention becomes selective.* Older children become capable of selecting the information they need from the welter of confusion in the environment. For example, when older children are separated from their parents in a department store, they have the capacity to systematically scan for people of their parents' height, hair color, vocal characteristics, and so on. They are also more capable of discriminating the spot where the parent was last seen. A younger child is more likely to be confused by the welter of voices and faces and aisles and to be unable to extract essential information from this backdrop.

4. *Irrelevant information becomes ignored.* Older children gain the capacity to screen out, or deploy their attention away from, stimuli that are irrelevant to the task at hand. This might mean shutting out the noise of cars in the street or radios in the neighborhood in order to focus on a book.

**_Nativism_** The view that children are born with predispositions to perceive the world in certain ways.

**_Empiricism_** The view that experience determines the ways in which children perceive the world.

Children, in short, develop from passive, mechanical reactors to the world about them into active, purposeful seekers and organizers of sensory information. They develop from beings whose attention is diffuse and "captured" into people who make decisions as to what they will attend to. This is a process that, like so many others, appears to depend on both maturation and experience.

Let us now screen out distractions and turn our attention to consideration of the importance of maturation and experience in perceptual development.

## *Theoretical Interlude: Nativism and Empiricism in Perceptual Development*

The nature–nurture issue is found in perceptual development, just as it is in other dimensions of development. In the area of perception, the issue can be traced to the philosophers of the 17th and 18th centuries. René Descartes and Immanuel Kant took the ***nativist*** view that children are born with predispositions to perceive the world in certain ways. Kant, for example, believed that our innate makeup causes us to sense and organize the objects of the world according to certain "categories." We perceive some things and are oblivious to others because of our inborn ways of organizing the world outside.

George Berkeley and John Locke took the ***empiricist*** view that experience determines our ways of perceiving the world. Locke, for example, argued that mental representations reflect the impact of the world on the sense organs. There is no particular inborn way of organizing sensations of the world. The world, instead, impresses the mind with its own stamp.

Today, few developmentalists subscribe to either extreme. Most would agree that nature (the nativist view) and nurture (the empiricist view) interact to give shape to perceptual development.

**Evidence for the Nativist View** There is compelling evidence that our inborn sensory capacities play a crucial role in our perceptual development. For one thing, newborn babies have already come into the world with a good number of perceptual skills. They can see nearby objects quite well, and their hearing is usually fine. They are also born with tendencies to track moving objects, to systematically scan the horizon, and to prefer certain kinds of stimuli to others. Preferences for different kinds of visual stimuli appear to unfold on schedule as the first months wear on. Sensory changes, like the motor changes discussed earlier in this chapter, appear to be linked to maturation of the nervous system.

For these reasons, it seems clear that we do have certain inborn ways of responding to sensory input—certain "categories" and built-in limits—that allow us to perceive certain aspects of the world of physical reality.

**Evidence for the Empiricist View** Evidence that experience plays a crucial role in perceptual development is also compelling. We could use any of hundreds of studies with children and other species to make the point, but, for the sake of convenience, let us limit our discussion to some experiments with kittens that appear to confirm observations of children.

Numerous studies have shown, for example, that there are critical periods in the perceptual development of children and lower animals. Failure to receive adequate sensory stimulation during these critical periods can result in permanent sensory deficits (Greenough et al., 1987). For example, newborn kittens raised with a patch over one eye wind up with few or no cells in the visual area of the cerebral cortex that would normally be activated by sensations of light that enter that eye. In effect, that eye becomes blind, even though sensory receptors in the eye itself may fire in response to light. On the other hand, if the eye of an adult cat is patched for the same amount of time, the animal will not lose vision in that eye. The critical period apparently will have passed. Similarly, if medical problems require that a child's eye must be patched for an extensive period of time during the first year, the child's visual acuity in that eye may be impaired.

**TRUTH OR FICTION REVISITED**

*It is true that newborn kittens raised with a patch over one eye will lose vision in that eye. Such evidence with kittens supports the view that there are critical periods for the development of visual abilities.*

And so, with perceptual development, as with other dimensions of development, nature and nurture play indispensable roles. Nature continues to guide the unfolding of the child's physical systems. Nurture continues to interact with nature in the development of these systems. Earlier in this chapter, we saw how sensorimotor experiences thicken the cortex of the brain. We also have seen how sensory experiences are linked to the development of neurons in the cortex. Inborn physical structures place limits on our abilities to respond to the world, but experience continues to help shape our most basic physical structures.

In the next chapter, we will see how nature and nurture influence the development of thought and language in infants.

## Summary

1. Physical growth and development are characterized by cephalocaudal and proximodistal sequences and differentiation. Development proceeds from head to tail (cephalocaudal) and from the trunk, or central axis, to the extremities (proximodistal). Motor responses become more distinct and specific (differentiation).

2. Changes in height and weight are most dramatic during the first year, with infants adding about 10 inches (50 percent) to their height and tripling their birth weight. Growth occurs in spurts.

3. Failure to thrive (FTT) is a growth disorder linked to later developmental, behavioral, and emotional problems.

4. Illness and dietary deficiency can slow children from growing at their genetically predetermined rates. However, they tend to catch up once the problem is resolved.

5. Breast milk is better balanced nutritionally than cow's milk and carries antibodies that help protect babies from certain infections and allergies. But

harmful substances can also pass from mothers to babies through breast milk. U.S. bottle-fed babies thrive and do as well as breast-fed babies.

6. Malnutrition both before and after birth adversely affects physical, cognitive, and behavioral development, although these effects can be reversed to some extent.

7. Children have all the neurons they will ever have at birth. The brain undergoes a prenatal growth spurt during which neurons are formed. A second growth spurt that begins during the last months of pregnancy and continues through infancy is due to proliferation of dendrites and axon terminals. The brain has 25 percent of its adult weight at birth and 70 percent of its adult weight by the first birthday.

8. The progress of myelination and the development of voluntary, complex behavior patterns are linked. Experience appears to fine-tune development of the brain.

9. Motor development follows generally invariant sequences, although the ages at which developmental milestones occur vary widely. African and African-American infants show earlier motor development than white infants. Both genetic and environmental factors may be involved.

10. Infants who are prevented from practicing motor skills nevertheless reach milestones such as sitting up and walking at normal ages, suggesting the powerful role of maturation. Early training in motor skills has limited effects. Extreme social and physical deprivation can retard motor development, but deprived children who later receive stimulation show some capacity to catch up.

11. Dramatic gains in visual acuity are made between birth and 6 months, with acuity approaching adult levels by 3 to 5 years of age. Two-month-old babies prefer to view faces rather than brightly colored disks. One-month-olds are visually captured by the edges of objects, while 2-month-olds prefer to scan within the edges.

12. Babies develop some form of depth perception by about 2 months of age. By 7 to 9 months of age, when they have developed the capacity to crawl, most infants show fear when placed on the visual cliff.

13. Size constancy is present by 3 months and perhaps at birth. Shape constancy develops by 4 to 5 months.

14. Auditory acuity improves over the first months, and the range of detectable pitches expands. Infants can perceive most of the sounds present in all languages, but gradually lose the capacity to discriminate those not found in the language to which they are exposed.

15. Cross-modal transfer, the ability to recognize the same object in two different sensory modalities, appears by the age of 1 month.

16. One theoretical issue is whether children's perceptual processes are basically active or passive. Gibson describes four shifts in perception and attention that show perceptual processes become increasingly active: (a) Intentional action replaces capture of the senses; (b) systematic search replaces unsystematic search; (c) attention becomes selective; and (d) irrelevant information becomes ignored.

17. Another issue concerns nature and nurture: the extent to which perceptual development is guided by inborn tendencies to perceive the world in certain ways (the nativist view) or by experience (the empiricist view). Both nature and nurture appear to be important.

# *INFANCY:*
## *COGNITIVE DEVELOPMENT*

## Chapter Outline

## Truth or Fiction?

______ *Cognitive development does not occur prior to development of the ability to use language.*

______ *When favorite toys are placed behind a screen, they no longer exist so far as 2-month-old babies are concerned.*

______ *Infants are able to add and subtract by the age of 5 months.*

______ *Tests have been developed for measuring intelligence in infants.*

______ *We can predict how intelligent a person will be as an adult as early as the age of 1 year.*

______ *Crying is the child's earliest use of language.*

______ *Deaf children do not babble.*

______ *Most of children's earliest words are names for things.*

______ *To a 2-year-old, the word combinations "Go Mommy" and "Mommy go" have the same meaning.*

______ *Children learn language faster when their parents correct their errors.*

______ *Children are "preprogrammed" to listen to language in such a way that they deduce rules of grammar.*

*"Laurent . . . resumes his experiments of the day before. He grabs in succession a celluloid swan, a box, etc., stretches out his arm and lets them fall. He distinctly varies the position of the fall. Sometimes he stretches out his arm vertically, sometimes he holds it obliquely, in front of or behind his eyes, etc. When the object falls in a new position, he lets it fall two or three times more on the same place, as though to study the spatial relation; then he modifies the situation."*

Is this the description of a scientist at work? In a way, it is. For although Swiss psychologist Jean Piaget (1963) was describing his 11-month-old son, Laurent, children of this age frequently act like scientists, performing what Piaget called "experiments in order to see."

This chapter chronicles the developing thought processes of infants and toddlers—that is, their cognitive development. We focus on the sensorimotor stage of cognitive development hypothesized by Piaget. Then we examine infant memory and imitation. We next explore individual differences in infant intelligence. Finally, we turn our attention to a remarkable aspect of cognitive development: language.

## COGNITIVE DEVELOPMENT: JEAN PIAGET

Cognitive development focuses on the development of children's ways of perceiving and mentally representing the world. As noted in Chapter 2, Piaget labeled children's concepts of the world ***schemes.*** He hypothesized that children attempt to ***assimilate*** new events into existing schemes and, when assimilation does not allow the child to make sense of novel events, children try to ***accommodate*** by modifying existing schemes.

Piaget (1963) hypothesized that children's cognitive processes develop in an orderly sequence, or series of stages. As is the case with motor and perceptual development, some children may be more advanced than others at particular ages, but the developmental sequence does not normally vary (Thomas, 1992). Piaget identified four major stages of cognitive development: *sensorimotor, preoperational* (see Chapter 9), *concrete operational* (see Chapter 12), and *formal operational* (see Chapter 15). In this chapter, we discuss the sensorimotor stage.

***Scheme*** According to Piaget, an action pattern or mental structure that is involved in the acquisition or organization of knowledge.

***Assimilation*** According to Piaget, the incorporation of new events or knowledge into existing schemes.

***Accommodation*** According to Piaget, the modification of existing schemes in order to incorporate new events or knowledge.

### *THE SENSORIMOTOR STAGE*

Piaget's descriptions of the cognitive development of infants during the first 2 years generally rely on observations of their sensory and motor activity. Although it may be difficult for us to imagine how we can develop and use cognitive processes in the absence of language, children do so in many ways.

**TRUTH OR FICTION REVISITED**

*Cognitive development actually does occur prior to development of the ability to use language. Many cognitive developments—for example, the attainment of mental representation and mental trial and error—take place during what Piaget referred to as the* sensorimotor *stage of cognitive development.*

**TABLE 6.1**

***THE SIX SUBSTAGES OF THE SENSORIMOTOR STAGE, ACCORDING TO PIAGET***

| SUBSTAGE | SOME MAJOR EVENTS |
|---|---|
| 1. SIMPLE REFLEXES (0 TO 1 MONTH) | ASSIMILATION OF NEW OBJECTS INTO REFLEXIVE RESPONSES; BABIES "LOOK AND SEE". INBORN REFLEXES CAN BE MODIFIED BY EXPERIENCE. |
| 2. PRIMARY CIRCULAR REACTIONS (1 TO 4 MONTHS) | REPETITION OF ACTIONS THAT MAY HAVE INITIALLY OCCURRED BY CHANCE BUT THAT HAVE SATISFYING OR INTERESTING RESULTS; BABIES "LOOK IN ORDER TO SEE". THE FOCUS IS ON THE INFANT'S BODY. BABIES DO NOT YET DISTINGUISH BETWEEN THEMSELVES AND EXTERNAL WORLD. |
| 3. SECONDARY CIRCULAR REACTIONS (4 TO 8 MONTHS) | REPETITION OF SCHEMES THAT HAVE INTERESTING EFFECTS ON THE ENVIRONMENT. THE FOCUS SHIFTS TO EXTERNAL OBJECTS AND EVENTS. THERE IS INITIAL AWARENESS THAT SCHEMES CAN INFLUENCE THE EXTERNAL WORLD. |
| 4. COORDINATION OF SECONDARY SCHEMES (8 TO 12 MONTHS) | COORDINATION OF SECONDARY SCHEMES, SUCH AS LOOKING AND GRASPING TO ATTAIN SPECIFIC GOALS; BEGINNING OF INTENTIONALITY AND MEANS-END DIFFERENTIATION; IMITATION OF ACTIONS NOT ALREADY IN INFANTS' REPERTOIRES. |
| 5. TERTIARY CIRCULAR REACTIONS (12 TO 18 MONTHS) | PURPOSEFUL ADAPTATION OF ESTABLISHED SCHEMES TO SPECIFIC SITUATIONS; BEHAVIOR TAKES ON EXPERIMENTAL QUALITY; OVERT TRIAL AND ERROR IN PROBLEM SOLVING. |
| 6. INVENTION OF NEW MEANS THROUGH MENTAL COMBINATIONS (18 TO 24 MONTHS) | MENTAL TRIAL AND ERROR IN PROBLEM SOLVING; MENTAL DETOURS BASED ON COGNITIVE MAPS; DEFERRED IMITATION; SYMBOLIC PLAY. INFANTS' COGNITIVE ADVANCES ARE MADE POSSIBLE BY THEIR MENTAL REPRESENTATIONS AND THE BEGINNINGS OF SYMBOLIC THOUGHT. |

During the sensorimotor stage, infants progress from responding to events with reflexes, or ready-made schemes, to goal-oriented behavior that involves awareness of past events. During this stage, they come to form mental representations of objects and events, to hold complex pictures of past events in mind, and to solve problems by mental trial and error (Yates, 1991).

Piaget divided the sensorimotor stage into six substages, each of which is characterized by more complex behavior than the preceding substage. But there is also continuity from substage to substage. Each could be characterized as a variation on a theme in which earlier forms of behavior are repeated, varied, and coordinated. The approximate time periods of the substages and some characteristics of each are summarized in Table 6.1.

**SIMPLE REFLEXES** The first substage covers the first month after birth. It is dominated by the assimilation of sources of stimulation into inborn reflexes such as grasping, visual tracking, crying, sucking, and crudely turning the head toward a sound (see Figure 6.1).

At birth, reflexes may have a stereotypical, inflexible quality. But even within the first few hours, newborns begin to modify reflexes as a result of experience. For example, infants will adapt (accommodate) patterns of sucking to the shape of the nipple and the rate of flow of fluid.

During the first month or so, infants apparently make no connection between stimulation perceived through different sensory modalities. They make no effort

**FIGURE 6.1**

***SIMPLE REFLEXES.*** *Even within hours after birth, newborns begin to modify reflexes as a result of experience. For example, they adapt sucking patterns to the shape of the nipple.*

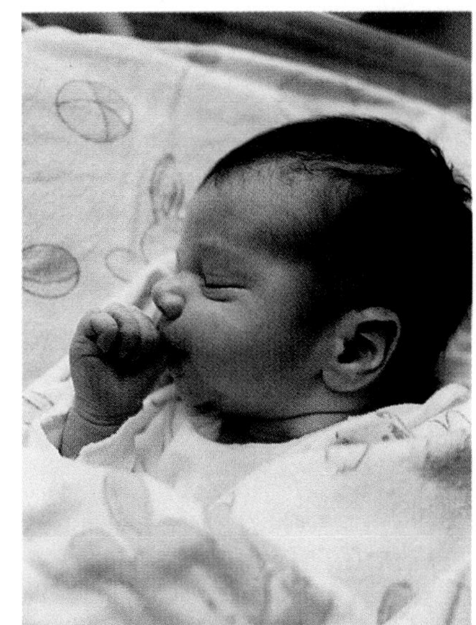

FIGURE 6.2

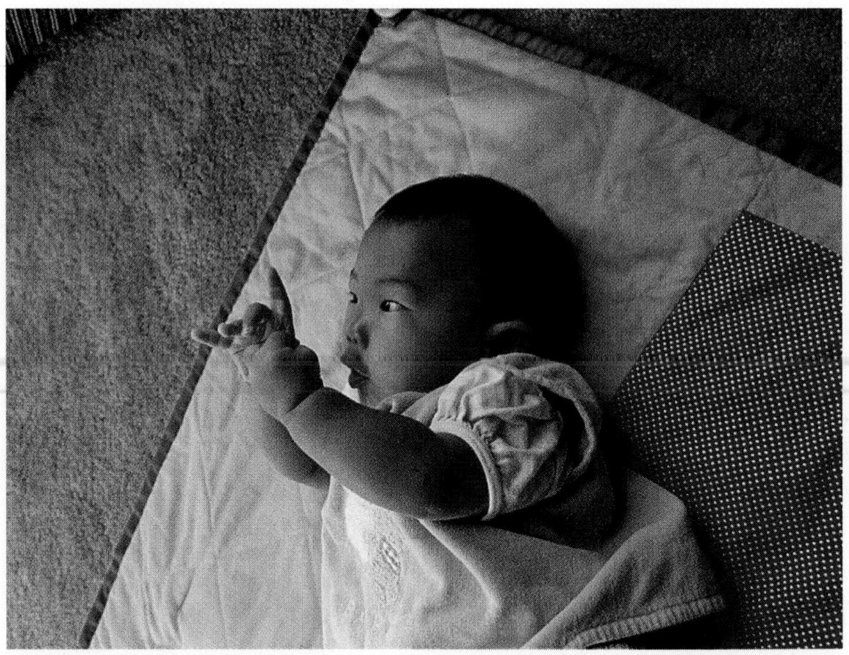

***PRIMARY CIRCULAR REACTIONS.*** *In the substage of primary circular reactions, infants repeat actions that involve their bodies. The 3-month-old in this picture is also beginning to coordinate visual and sensorimotor schemes—that is, looking at the hand is becoming coordinated with holding it in the field of vision.*

to grasp objects that they visually track. Crude turning toward sources of auditory and olfactory stimulation has a ready-made look about it that cannot be considered purposeful searching.

**PRIMARY CIRCULAR REACTIONS** The second substage, primary circular reactions, lasts from about 1 to 4 months of age and is characterized by the beginnings of the coordination of various sensorimotor schemes. In this substage, babies tend to repeat stimulating actions that first occurred by chance. A circular reaction is a behavior that is repeated. ***Primary circular reactions*** are those that focus on the infant's own body rather than on the external environment (see Figure 6.2). Piaget noticed the following primary circular reaction in his son Laurent:

> *At 2 months 4 days, Laurent by chance discovers his right index finger and looks at it briefly. At 2 months 11 days, he inspects for a moment his open right hand, perceived by chance. At 2 months 17 days, he follows its spontaneous movement for a moment, then examines it several times while it searches for his nose or rubs his eye.*
>
> *At 2 months 21 days, he holds his two fists in the air and looks at the left one, after which he slowly brings it toward his face and rubs his nose with it, then his eye. A moment later the left hand again approaches his face; he looks at it and touches his nose. He recommences and laughs five or six times in succession while moving the left hand to his face. He seems to laugh before the hand moves, but looking has no influence on its movement. He laughs beforehand but begins to smile again on seeing the hand. Then he rubs his nose. At a given moment he turns his head to the left, but looking has no effect on the direction. The next day, same reaction. At 2 months 23 days, he looks at his right hand, then at his clasped hands (at length). At 2 months 24 days, at last it may be stated that looking acts on the orientation of the hands which tend to remain in the visual field (Piaget, 1963, pp. 96–97).*

***Primary circular reactions*** The repetition of actions that first occurred by chance and that focus on the infant's own body.

And so Laurent, early in the third month, visually tracks the behavior of his hand, but his visual observations do not seem to influence their movement. At about 2 months 21 days, Laurent can apparently exert some control over his hands, because he seems to know when a hand is about to move (and entertain him). But the link between looking at and moving the hands remains weak. A few days later, however, his looking "acts" on the hands, causing them to remain in his field of vision. Sensorimotor coordination has been achieved. An action is repeated because it stimulates the infant.

In terms of assimilation and accommodation, the child is attempting to assimilate the motor scheme (moving the hand) into the sensory scheme (looking at it). But the schemes do not automatically fit. Several days of apparent trial and error pass during which the infant seems to be trying to make accommodations so that they will fit.

Goal-directed behavior makes significant advances during the second substage. During the month after birth, infants visually track objects that contrast with their backgrounds, especially moving objects. But this ready-made behavior is largely automatic, so that the infant is "looking and seeing." But by the third month, as with Laurent, objects may be examined repeatedly and intensely. It seems clear that the infant is no longer simply looking and seeing, but is now "looking *in order* to see." And by the end of the third month, Laurent seems to be moving his hands *in order to look* at them.

Since Laurent (and other infants) will repeat actions that allow them to see, cognitive-developmental psychologists consider sensorimotor coordination self-reinforcing. Laurent does not seem to be looking or moving his hands because these acts allow him to satisfy a more basic drive such as hunger or thirst. The desire to prolong stimulation may be just as basic.

***Secondary circular reactions*** The repetition of actions that produce an effect on the environment.

**Secondary Circular Reactions** The third substage lasts from about 4 to 8 months and is characterized by ***secondary circular reactions,*** in which patterns of activity are repeated because of their effect on the environment. In the second substage of primary circular reactions, infants are focused on their own bodies. In the third substage of secondary circular reactions, the focus shifts to objects and environmental events. Infants may now learn to pull strings in order to make a plastic face appear or to shake an object in order to hear it rattle (see Figure 6.3).

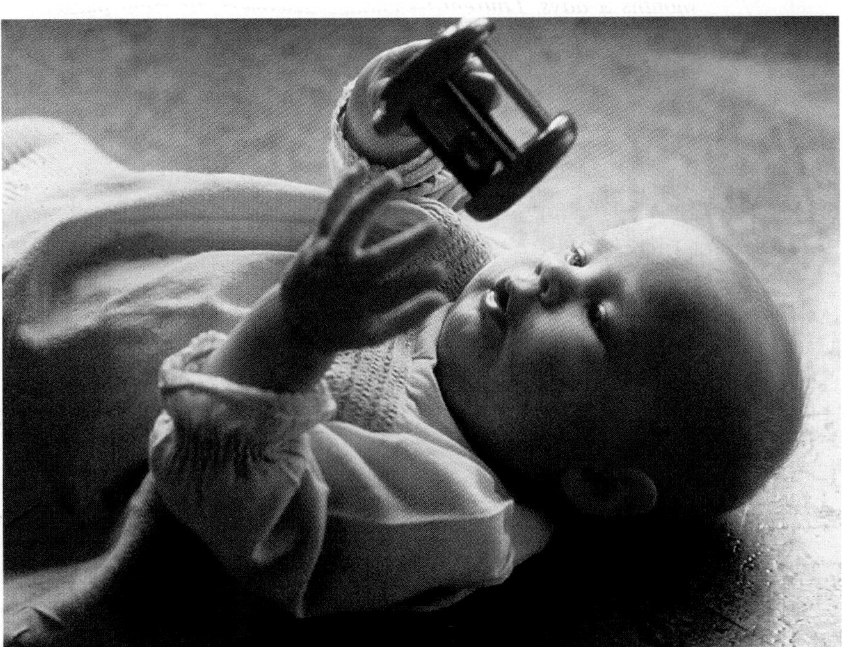

FIGURE 6.3

**Secondary Circular Reactions.** *In the substage of secondary circular reactions, patterns of activity are repeated because of their effect on the environment. This baby shakes a rattle to produce an interesting sound.*

Although infants in this substage track the trajectory of moving objects, they abandon their searches when the objects disappear from view. As we shall see later in this chapter, the object concepts of infants are quite limited at these ages, especially the age at which the third substage begins.

**COORDINATION OF SECONDARY SCHEMES** In the fourth substage, infants no longer act simply to prolong interesting occurrences. Now they can coordinate schemes to attain specific goals. Infants begin to show intentional, goal-directed behavior in which they differentiate between the means of achieving a goal and the goal or end itself. For example, as seen in Figure 6.4, they may lift a piece of cloth in order to reach a toy that they had seen a parent place under the cloth earlier. In this example, the scheme of picking up the cloth (the means) is coordinated with the scheme of reaching for the toy (the goal or end).

The above example indicates that the infant has mentally represented the toy placed under the cloth. Consider another example. At the age of 5 months, one of Piaget's daughters, Lucienne, was reaching across her crib for a toy. As she did so, Piaget obscured the toy with his hand. Lucienne pushed her father's hand aside, but in doing so, she became distracted and began to play with the hand. A few months later, Lucienne did not allow her father's hand to distract her from the goal of reaching the toy. She moved the hand firmly to the side and then grabbed the toy. The mental representation of the object appears to have become more persistent. The intention of reaching the object was also maintained, and so the hand was perceived as a barrier and not as another interesting stimulus.

During the fourth substage, infants also gain the capacity to copy actions that are not in their own repertoires. Infants can now imitate many gestures and sounds they had previously ignored. The imitation of a new facial gesture implies

FIGURE 6.4

***COORDINATION OF SECONDARY SCHEMES.*** *During this substage, infants coordinate their behaviors to attain specific goals. This infant lifts a piece of cloth to retrieve a toy that has been placed under the cloth.*

**FIGURE 6.5**

***TERTIARY CIRCULAR REACTIONS.*** *In this substage, infants vary their actions in a trial-and-error fashion to learn how things work. This baby is fascinated by what happens when you pull tissues out of a box.*

that infants have mentally represented their own faces and can tell what parts of their faces they are moving through feedback from facial muscles. For example, when a girl imitates her mother sticking out her tongue, it would appear that she has coordinated moving her own tongue with feedback from muscles in the tongue and mouth. In this way, imitation suggests a great deal about the child's emerging self-concept.

**TERTIARY CIRCULAR REACTIONS** In the fifth substage, which lasts from about the ages of 12 to 18 months, Piaget looked upon the behavior of infants as characteristic of budding scientists. Infants now engage in ***tertiary circular reactions,*** or purposeful adaptations of established schemes to specific situations. Behavior takes on a new experimental quality, and infants may vary their actions dozens of times in a deliberate trial-and-error fashion in order to learn how things work (see Figure 6.5). Piaget's description of Laurent's behavior at the beginning of this chapter is a good example of tertiary circular reactions.

Piaget reported another example of tertiary circular reactions by his daughter Jacqueline. The episode was an experiment in which Piaget placed a stick outside of Jacqueline's playpen, which had wooden bars (Piaget, 1963). At first, Jacqueline grasped the stick and tried to pull it sideways into the playpen. The stick was too long and could not fit through the bars. Over a number of days of trial and error, however, Jacqueline discovered that she could bring the stick between the bars by turning it upright. In future presentations, she would immediately turn the stick upright and bring it in.

Jacqueline's eventual success with the stick was the result of overt trial and error. In the sixth substage, described below, the solution to problems is often more sudden, suggesting that children have manipulated the elements of the problems in their minds and engaged in mental trial and error before displaying the correct overt response.

**INVENTION OF NEW MEANS THROUGH MENTAL COMBINATIONS** The sixth substage lasts from about 18 to 24 months of age. It serves as a transition between sensorimotor development and the symbolic thought that characterizes the preoperational stage. External exploration is replaced by mental exploration.

***Tertiary circular reactions*** The purposeful adaptation of established schemes to new situations.

Recall Jacqueline's trials (in more ways than one) with the stick. Piaget cleverly waited until his other children, Lucienne and Laurent, were 18 months old, and then he presented them with the playpen and stick problem. By waiting until 18 months, he could attribute differences in their performance to advanced age instead of a possible warm-up effect from earlier tests. Rather than engage in overt trial and error, the 18-month-old children sat and studied the situation for a few moments. Then they grasped the stick, turned it upright, and brought it into the playpen with little overt effort.

Jacqueline had at first failed with the stick. She then turned it every which way, happening upon a solution almost by chance. Lucienne and Laurent solved the problem fairly rapidly, suggesting that they mentally represented the stick and the bars of the playpen and perceived that the stick would not fit through as it was. They must then have rotated the mental image of the stick until they perceived a position that would allow the stick to pass between the bars.

At around 18 months old, children may also use imitation to symbolize or stand for a plan of action. Consider how Lucienne goes about retrieving a watch chain her father placed in a match box. It seems that symbolic imitation serves her as a way of thinking out loud.

> *I put the chain back into the box and reduce the opening. [Lucienne] is not aware of [how to open and close] the match box. [She] possesses two preceding schemes: turning the box over in order to empty it of its contents, and sliding her fingers into the slit to make the chain come out. [She] puts her finger inside and gropes to reach the chain, but fails. A pause follows during which Lucienne manifests a very curious reaction. . . .*
>
> *She looks at the slit with great attention. Then, several times in succession, she opens and shuts her mouth, at first slightly, then wider and wider! Apparently Lucienne understands the existence of a cavity . . . and wishes to enlarge that cavity. The attempt at representation which she thus furnishes is expressed plastically. That is to say, due to inability to think out the situation in words or clear visual images, she uses a simple motor indication as "signifier" or symbol. [Lucienne then] puts her finger in the slit, and, instead of trying as before to reach the chain, she pulls so as to enlarge the opening. She succeeds and grasps the chain (Piaget, 1963, pp. 337–338).*

In Chapter 9, it will be seen that children at this age also begin to use symbolic (or "pretend") play. For example, an 18–24-month-old child who is scolded by parents for throwing food may later return the scolding through play with dolls, or even imaginary figures.

## DEVELOPMENT OF OBJECT PERMANENCE

One important sign of the development of cognitive processes is the appearance of ***object permanence,*** the recognition that an object or person continues to exist when out of sight. Your child development textbook continues to exist when you accidentally leave it in the library after studying for the big test, and a baby's mother continues to exist even when she is in another room. Your realization that your book exists, although out of view, is an example of object permanence. If a baby acts as if its mother no longer exists when she is out of sight, the baby does not have the concept of object permanence.

**_Object permanence_** Recognition that objects continue to exist even when they are not seen.

According to Jean Piaget, various facets of object permanence develop during infancy and correspond to the stages and substages of the child's general cognitive development (Flavell et al., 1993b). The development of object permanence is tied into children's general tendency to form mental representations of sensory impressions.

Neonates show no tendency to respond to objects that are not within their immediate sensory grasp. By 2 months, infants may show some surprise if an object (such as a toy duck) is placed behind a screen and then taken away so that when the screen is lifted, it is absent. However, they make no effort to search for the missing object. Through the first 6 months or so, when the screen is placed between the object and the baby, the baby behaves as though it is no longer there (see Figure 6.6).

**TRUTH OR FICTION REVISITED**

*When favorite toys are placed behind a screen, they do cease to exist so far as 2-month-old babies are concerned. At this age, out of sight apparently means out of existence.*

There are some interesting advances in the development of the object concept by about the sixth month (Piaget's substage 3). For example, a baby at this age will tend to look for an object that has been dropped, behavior that suggests some form of object permanence. By this age, there is also reason to believe that the baby perceives a mental representation (image) of an object, such as a favorite toy, in response to sensory impressions of part of the object. This is shown by the baby's reaching for a preferred object when it has been partially hidden by a cloth.

By the ages of 8 to 12 months (Piaget's substage 4), infants will seek to retrieve objects that have been completely hidden behind screens. But in observing his own children, Piaget (1963) noted an interesting error known as the *A not B error.* Piaget repeatedly hid a toy behind a screen (A), and each time his infant removed the screen and retrieved it. Then, as the infant watched, Piaget hid the toy behind another screen (B) in a different place. Still, the infant tried to recover the toy by pushing aside the first screen (A). It is as though the child had learned that a certain motor activity would reinstate the missing toy. The child's concept of the object did not, at this age, extend to recognition that objects usually remain in the place where they have been most recently mentally represented.

Recent research, however, indicates that under certain conditions, 8–12-month-olds do not show the A not B error (Harris, 1987; Small, 1990). For example, if infants are allowed to search for the object immediately after seeing it hidden, the error often does not occur. But if they are forced to wait 5 or more seconds before looking, they are likely to commit the A not B error (Wellman et al., 1986).

In Chapter 7, we shall see that most children have developed some notion of object permanence before they develop emotional bonds to specific caregivers. It seems logical that infants must have permanent representations of their mothers before they will show distress at being separated from their mothers. But wait, you say? Won't even 3- or 4-month-old babies cry when mother leaves and then stop crying when she comes and picks them up? Doesn't this behavior pattern show object permanence in very young infants? Don't these babies "miss" their mothers when they are gone (that is, perceive their continued existence in their absence) and try to get them back? Excellent questions, but the answer is "Not necessarily." Babies appear to appreciate the comforts provided by their mothers' presence and to express displeasure when they come to an end (as when their

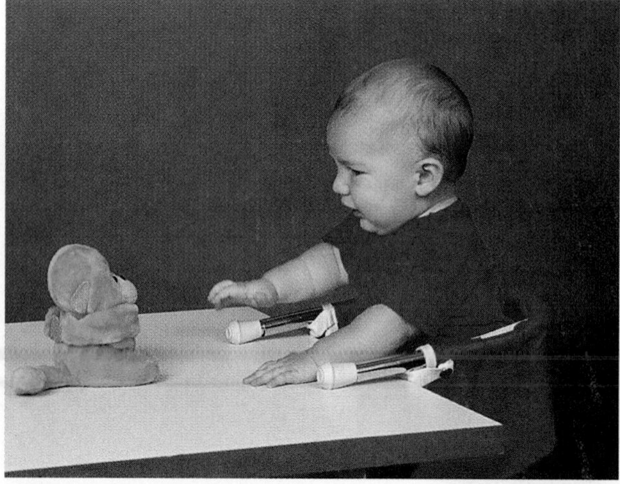

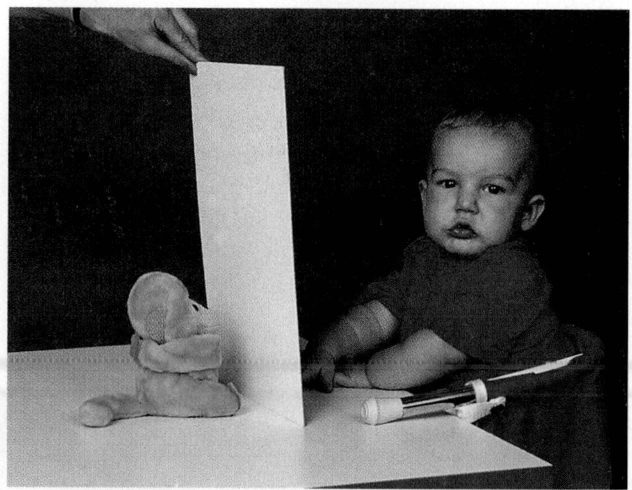

FIGURE 6.6

***DEVELOPMENT OF OBJECT PERMANENCE.*** *To the infant at the top, who is in the early part of the sensorimotor stage, out of sight is truly out of mind. Once a sheet of paper is placed between the infant and the toy monkey, the infant loses all interest in the toy. From evidence of this sort, Piaget concluded that the toy is not mentally represented. The bottom series of photos shows a child in a later part of the sensorimotor stage. This child does mentally represent objects and pushes through a towel to reach an object that has been screened from sight.*

mothers leave the room). The expression of displeasure frequently results in the reinstatement of pleasure (being held, fed, and spoken to). Therefore, babies may learn to engage in these protests when their mothers leave because of the positive consequences of protesting—and not because they have developed object permanence.

Nevertheless, recent studies by Renee Baillargeon and her colleagues (Baillargeon, 1993; Baillargeon et al., 1990) show that some rudimentary knowledge of object permanence may actually be present as early as 3½ months of age. In one clever study, Baillargeon (1987) first showed 3½- and 4½-month-olds the event illustrated in the top part of Figure 6.7. A screen rotated back and forth through a 180-degree arc like a drawbridge. After several trials, the infants showed habituation; that is, they spent less and less time looking at the screen. Next, a box was placed in the path of the screen, as shown in the middle drawing of Figure 6.7. The infant could see the box at the beginning of each trial, but could no longer see it when the screen reached the box. In one condition, labeled the "possible event," the screen stopped when it reached the box. In another condition, labeled the "impossible event," the screen rotated through a full 180-degree arc, as though the box were no longer behind it. (How could this happen? Unknown to the infant, a trapdoor was released, causing the box to drop out of the way). The infants looked longer at the "impossible event" than at the "possible" one. Babies tend to look longer at unexpected events. So their behavior indicates they were surprised that the screen did not stop when it reached the box. This reaction indicates that children as young as 3½ months of age realized that the box continued to exist even when it was hidden behind the screen (Baillargeon,

1991). But why then do infants not actively look for hidden objects until about 8 months of age? It may be that Piaget was correct in stating that coordination of acts (such as removing a barrier in order to reach a toy) does not occur until this later age (Baillargeon et al., 1990).

## *Evaluation of Piaget's Theory*

Piaget's theory remains the most comprehensive model of infant cognition. Many of his observations of his own three infants have been confirmed by others. The pattern and sequence of events he described have been observed among American, European, African, and Asian babies (Werner, 1988). Still, recent research has raised questions about the validity of many of Piaget's claims (Flavell et al., 1993b).

For one thing, most cognitive researchers now agree that cognitive development is not as tied to discrete stages as Piaget believed (Flavell et al., 1993b). The heart of the stage-theory approach is that changes are discontinuous. In the case of Piaget's theory, children's responses to the world, as governed by their cognitive processes, would have to change relatively suddenly. While later cognitive acquisitions do appear to build on earlier ones, the process appears to be more gradual than discontinuous.

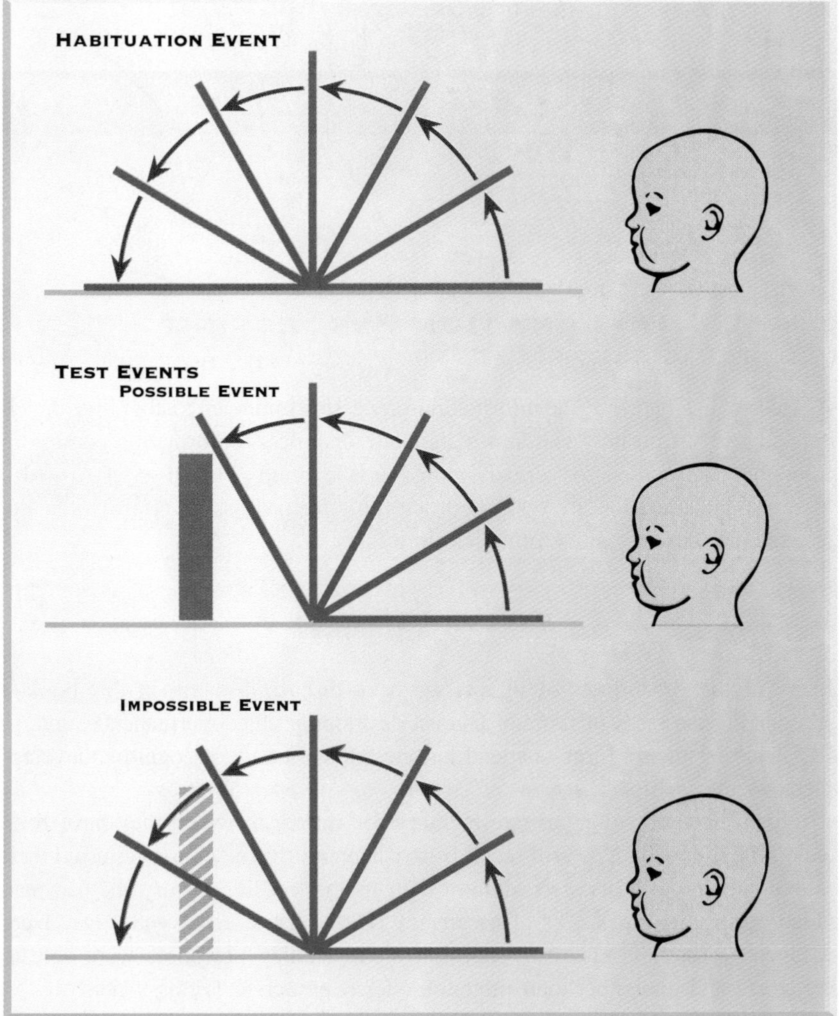


FIGURE 6.7

***Object Permanence Before 4 Months of Age?*** *Renee Baillargeon (1987) used the technique shown here to demonstrate that knowledge of object permanence may exist prior to 4 months of age. She first showed infants a screen rotated back and forth like a drawbridge (top drawing). After infants showed habituation, a box was placed in the path of the screen. The middle drawing shows a possible event—the screen stops when it reaches the box. The bottom drawing shows an impossible event—the screen rotates through a full 180-degree arc as though the box were no longer behind it. (The experimenter had removed it, unknown to the infant.) Babies looked longer at the impossible event, indicating they realized the box still existed even when hidden behind the screen. (Source: Baillargeon, 1987).*

***Deferred imitation*** The imitation of people and events that occurred hours, days, or weeks ago.

A second criticism of Piaget's theory is that he appears to have underestimated the young infant's competence (Flavell et al., 1993b). For example, as we saw earlier in this chapter, babies display object permanence at a much earlier age than Piaget believed.

Another example of early infant competence is provided by studies on ***deferred imitation,*** which is imitation of an action that may have occurred hours, days, or even weeks earlier. A young child may do an excellent imitation of Mommy mowing the lawn or Daddy changing the baby (by using a doll). The presence of deferred imitation suggests that children have mentally represented complex behavior patterns and actions. Piaget believed that deferred imitation appears at about 18 months, but more recent findings indicate that infants can show deferred imitation as early as 9 months of age (Meltzoff, 1988). In Meltzoff's study, 9-month-old infants watched an adult perform a series of novel actions, such as pushing a button on a box to produce a beeping sound. When given a chance to play with the same objects 24 hours later, many of the babies reproduced the actions they had seen the adult perform.

A final example of infant competence that occurs much earlier than Piaget predicted comes from recent research that suggests that 5-month-old infants are able to grasp simple arithmetic concepts such as addition and subtraction (see Focus on Research). In Piaget's view, numerical abilities did not emerge until the preoperational stage, which begins at approximately 2 years of age.

*It is true that infants as young as 5 months of age have the ability to add and subtract.*

## INFORMATION PROCESSING

As we saw in Chapter 2, the information-processing approach to cognitive development focuses on how children manipulate or process information coming in from the environment or already stored in the mind (Flavell et al., 1993b). Memory and imitation are two important tools for processing information. Let us examine these cognitive processes in infants.

### *INFANTS' MEMORY*

Many of the capabilities of infants we have discussed so far in this book—recognizing the faces of familiar people, developing object permanence, and, in fact, learning in any form—depend on one critical aspect of cognitive development: memory (Lipsitt, 1990a).

Even newborns demonstrate memory for stimuli to which they have been exposed previously. You will recall from Chapter 4 that newborns adjusted their rate of sucking to hear a recording of their mother reading a story she had read aloud during the last weeks of pregnancy (DeCasper & Fifer, 1980; DeCasper & Spence, 1991). Remember, too, that breast-feeding newborns were able to recognize and remember their mother's odor (Cernoch & Porter, 1985).

**FOCUS ON RESEARCH**

### *COUNTING IN THE CRIB*

Infants as young as 5 months of age have the ability to add and subtract, according to recent research by Karen Wynn (1992a). Wynn's conclusion is based on the fact that infants look longer at unexpected events than expected ones. (You may recall that Baillargeon's studies of object permanence in young infants also made use of this fact.) If babies are able to add and subtract, they should look longer at the "wrong" unexpected answer to an addition or subtraction problem than at the expected "correct" answer. Wynn showed the infants 4-inch Mickey Mouse dolls. One group of babies saw a single doll. Then a screen was put up, blocking the babies' view. While the babies watched, Wynn put another doll behind the screen. The screen was removed, revealing either two dolls (the right answer) or only one doll (the wrong answer). Another group of babies saw two dolls initially. The screen was put up, and the babies watched while one doll was removed. When the screen was removed, the infants saw either one doll (right) or two (wrong). Babies consistently looked longer at the "wrong" answers.

These results show that infants know that adding or subtracting produces some sort of change in the number of objects. But can babies calculate precisely how much change is produced? That is, can they actually count?

To answer this question, Wynn presented a third group of babies with a single doll. She added another doll after the screen went up and then removed the screen, revealing either two Mickeys (correct answer) or three (wrong answer). In both cases, a change was produced. But babies stared longer at the wrong answer of three dolls, indicating that they had calculated exactly how many objects should appear.

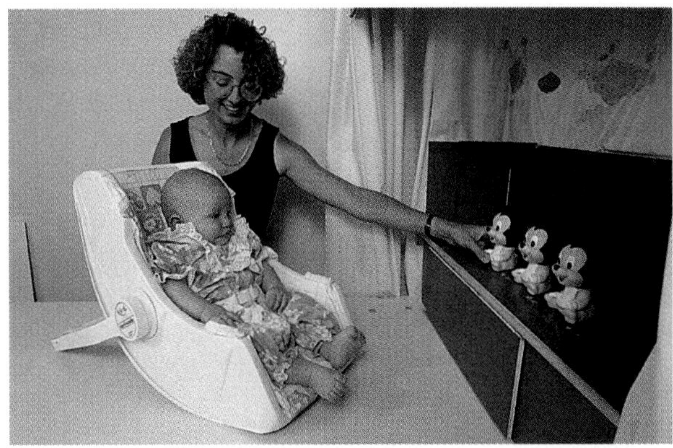

**FIGURE 6.8 COUNTING IN THE CRIB.** *Recent research suggests that 5-month-old infants know when simple calculations are done correctly or incorrectly. The babies stare longer when shown a "wrong answer." Karen Wynn (shown here with a 5-month-old) arrived at these results by showing infants Mickey Mouse dolls. She then added or subtracted a doll behind a screen and presented the baby with the "right" or "wrong" answer.*

Memory improves between 2 and 6 months of age. This improvement may indicate that older infants are more capable than younger ones of encoding (that is, storing) information, retrieving information already stored, or both (Kail, 1990).

A fascinating series of studies by Carolyn Rovee-Collier and her colleagues (Rovee-Collier, 1993) illustrates some of these developmental changes in infant memory (see Figure 6.9). One end of a ribbon was tied to a brightly colored mobile suspended above the infant's crib. The other end was tied to the infant's ankle, so that when the baby kicked, the mobile moved. Babies quickly learned to increase their rate of kicking. To measure memory, the infant's ankle was again fastened to the mobile after a period of one or more days had elapsed. In one study, 2-month-olds remembered how to make the mobile move after delays of up to 3 days, and 3-month-olds remembered for more than a week (Greco et al., 1986).

Infant memory can be improved if babies receive a reminder before they are given the memory test (Rovee-Collier & Shyi, 1992). In one study that used this reminder procedure, babies were shown the moving mobile on the day prior to the memory test, but they were not allowed to activate it. Under these conditions, 3-month-olds remembered how to move the mobile after a 28-day delay (Rovee-Collier, 1993).

FIGURE 6.9

***Investigating Infant Memory.*** *In this technique, developed by Renee Rovee-Collier, the baby's ankle is connected to a mobile by a ribbon. Babies quickly learn to kick to make the mobile move. Two- and 3-month-olds remember how to perform this feat after a delay of a few days. If given a reminder of simply viewing the mobile, their memory lasts for 2 to 4 weeks.*

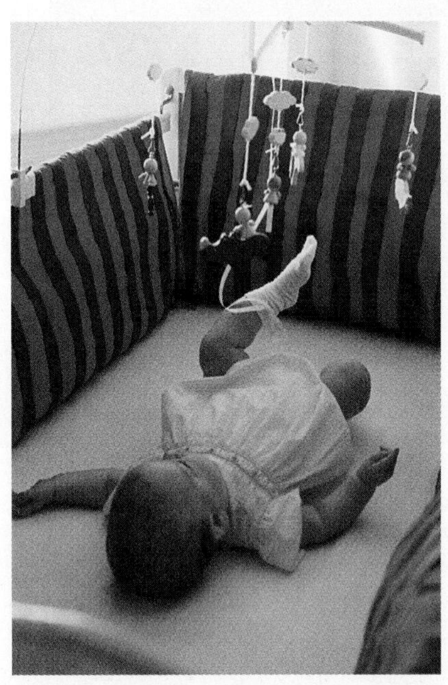

### *Imitation*

Imitation is the basis for much of human learning. Earlier in the chapter, we saw that deferred imitation—the imitation of actions after a time delay—occurs as early as 9 months of age. But infants apparently have the capacity to imitate certain actions at a much earlier age. In recent experiments, neonates only 0.7 to 71 hours old were found to imitate adults who opened their mouths or stuck out their tongues (Anisfeld, 1991; Meltzoff, 1990; Meltzoff & Moore, 1992) (see Figure 6.10).

Before you become too impressed with this early imitative ability of newborns, you should know that some studies have not found imitation in early infancy (Abravanel & DeYong, 1991). Furthermore, 6-week-old babies stick out their tongues when nonhuman stimuli, such as small balls or felt-tipped pens, are moved toward their mouths (Jacobson, 1979). This cannot be considered imitative behavior because it did not occur in response to another person's engaging in the same (or highly similar) behavior.

One key factor may be the infants' age. The studies that find imitation generally have been done with very young babies—up to 2 weeks old—while the studies that do not find imitation have tended to use older infants (Reissland, 1988). So perhaps the imitation of newborns is reflexive, disappearing for a while and reemerging later (Anisfeld, 1991; Reissland, 1988).

## Individual Differences in Infant Intelligence

Up to now, we have discussed cognitive development as though it proceeded in the same way or pace for all infants. But there are individual differences in the development of cognition. Efforts to understand the development of infant differences in cognitive development have relied on so-called scales of infant development or infant intelligence.

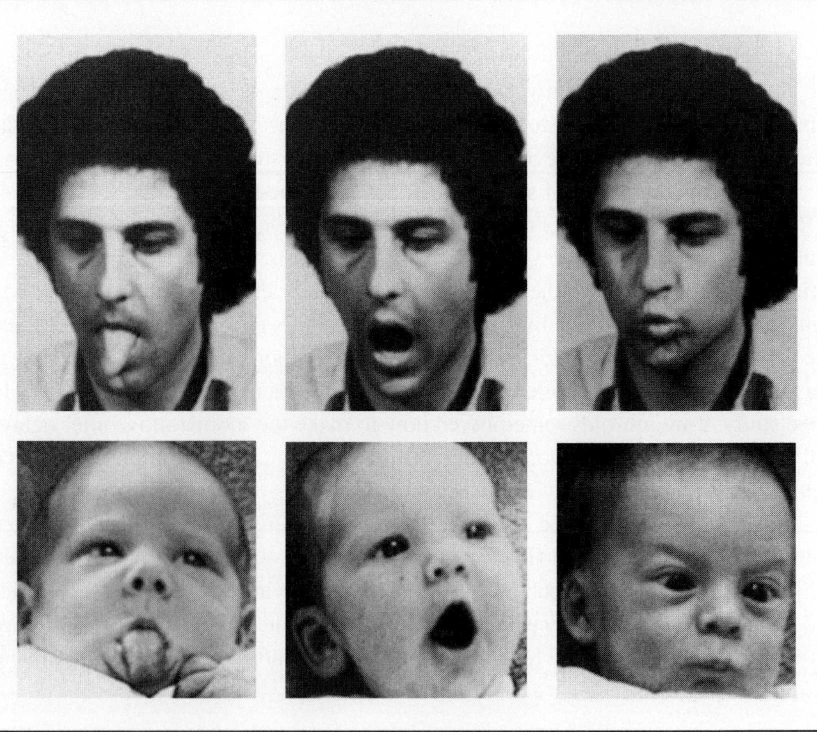

FIGURE 6.10

***Imitation in Infants.*** *These 2- to 3-week-old infants are imitating the facial gestures of an adult experimenter.*

## TRUTH OR FICTION REVISITED

*It is true that tests have been developed for measuring intellectual functioning in infants, but they assess sensorimotor functions to screen infants for neurological and cognitive problems. Different kinds of behaviors are considered indicative of intellectual functioning in older children.*

Measuring cognition or intelligence in infants is very different from measuring it in adults. Infants cannot, of course, be assessed by asking them to explain the meanings of words, the similarity between concepts, or the rationales for social rules. One of the most important tests of intellectual development among infants contains very different kinds of items. It is the Bayley Scales of Infant Development, constructed in 1933 by psychologist Nancy Bayley and revised most recently in 1993.

The Bayley test currently consists of 178 mental-scale items and 111 motor-scale items. The mental scale assesses verbal communication, perceptual skills, learning and memory, and problem-solving skills. The motor scale assesses gross motor skills, as in standing, walking, and climbing, and fine motor skills, as shown by ability to manipulate the hands and fingers. A behavior rating scale based on examiner observation of the child during the test is also used. The behavior rating scale assesses attention span, goal directedness, persistence, and aspects of social and emotional development. Table 6.2 contains sample items

**TABLE 6.2**

***Items From the Bayley Scales of Infant Development***

| Age | Mental-Scale Items | Motor-Scale Items |
|---|---|---|
| 1 month | Baby quiets when picked up. | Baby makes a postural adjustment when put to examiner's shoulder. |
| 2 months | When examiner presents two objects (bell and rattle) above infant in crib, she glances back and forth from one to the other. | Baby holds her head steady when being carried about in vertical position. |
| 5 months | Baby is observed to transfer object from one hand to the other during play. | When seated at a feeding-type table and presented with a sugar pill out of reach, baby attempts to pick it up. |
| 8 months | When object in plain view of baby (on table) is covered by a cup, baby removes cup to recover toy. | Baby raises herself to a sitting position. |
| 12 months | Baby imitates words when examiner says them. | When asked by examiner, baby stands up from a position lying on her back on the floor. |
| 14-16 months | Baby builds a tower with two cubes after demonstration by examiner. | Baby walks alone with good coordination. |

Ages given correspond to level at which 50 percent of infants pass item.
Source: Bayley, 1993.

FIGURE 6.11

***The Bayley Scales of Infant Development.*** *The Bayley Scales, shown here, measure the infant's mental and motor development. (Source: Bayley, 1993).*

from the mental and motor scales and shows the ages at which 50 percent of the infants taking the test passed the items.

### *Purposes and Problems in Testing Infants*

As you can imagine, it is no easy matter to test an infant. The items must be administered on a one-to-one basis by a patient tester, and it can be difficult to judge whether the infant is showing the targeted response. Why, then, do we test infants?

One reason is to screen babies for handicaps. A highly trained tester may be able to detect early signs of sensory or neurological problems. In addition to the Bayley Scales, a number of tests have been developed to screen infants for such difficulties, including the Brazelton Neonatal Behavioral Assessment Scale (see Chapter 4) and the Denver Developmental Screening Test (Frankenburg et al., 1992; Mayes, 1991).

A second use of infant scales is to make developmental predictions. Here the scales do not fare so well.

### *The Instability of Intelligence Scores Attained at Early Ages*

How well do infant scales predict later intellectual performance? The answer is somewhat unclear. Certain items on the Bayley Scales have been found to predict specific intellectual skills later in childhood. For example, Linda Siegel found that Bayley items measuring infant motor skills predicted subsequent fine-motor and visual-spatial skills at 6 to 8 years of age. Bayley language items also predicted language skills at the same age (Siegel, 1992).

But overall or global scores on the Bayley and other infant scales do not predict school grades or later IQ scores very well (Colombo, 1993; Storfer, 1990). Why do infant tests fail to do a good job of predicting IQ scores among preschoolers and school-aged children? First of all, cognitive functioning seems to change so quickly during infancy that reliable measurement may be impossible.

Second, the sensorimotor test items used during infancy may not be strongly related to the verbal and symbolic items used at later ages (Colombo, 1993; Seefeldt, 1990; Thompson et al., 1991b).

***Visual recognition memory*** An infant's ability to discriminate previously seen objects from novel objects.

*TRUTH OR FICTION REVISITED*

*Actually, we cannot predict how intelligent a person will be as an adult as early as the age of 1 year. Correlations between measures of intellectual functioning at infancy and later on are weak to moderate at best.*

### *USE OF VISUAL RECOGNITION MEMORY: AN EFFORT TO ENHANCE PREDICTABILITY*

In a continuing effort to find aspects of intelligence and cognition that might remain consistent from infancy through later childhood, a number of researchers have recently focused on ***visual recognition memory.*** This procedure is based on habituation, as are many of the methods for assessing perceptual development (see Chapter 5).

Let us consider a longitudinal study of this type. Susan Rose and her colleagues (Rose et al., 1992b) showed 7-month-old babies pictures of two identical faces. After 20 seconds, the pictures were replaced with one picture of a new face and a second picture of the familiar face. The amount of time the infants spent looking at each of the faces in the second set of pictures was recorded. Some infants spent more time looking at the new face than the older face, suggesting that they had better memory for visual stimulation. The children were given standard IQ tests yearly from ages 1 through 6. It was found that the children with greater visual recognition memory later attained higher IQ scores.

A number of other studies have examined the relationship between either infant visual recognition memory or preference for novel stimulation (which is a related measure) and later IQ scores (Colombo, 1993; Fagan & Detterman, 1992; McCall & Carriger, 1993). The average correlation between the earlier and later measures is about +.45. These moderate correlations are stronger than the correlations attained using more traditional assessment techniques. Perhaps infants' tendencies to scan stimuli and retain images will yield even more precise measures in future years.

In sum, scales of infant development may provide useful data as screening devices, as research instruments, or simply for describing the things that infants do and do not do. However, their predictive power as intelligence tests has so far been disappointing. Tests of visual recognition hold better promise as predictors of later intelligence.

Now let us turn our attention to a fascinating aspect of cognitive development, the development of language.

*THINKING ABOUT DEVELOPMENT*

Agree or disagree with the following statement and support your answer: "A child who scored well on an infant development test will get good grades in school."

## LANGUAGE DEVELOPMENT

By the end of the toddler years, children possess an impressive array of language skills. In this section, we trace language development from early crying and cooing through the production of two-word sentences. We then consider theoretical views of language development.

FIGURE 6.12

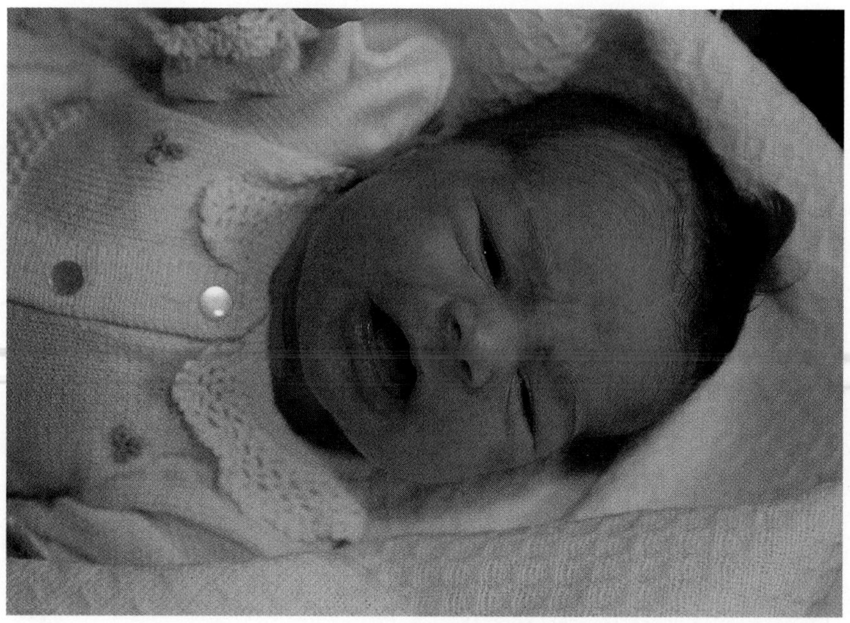

***Crying.*** *Crying is a prelinguistic vocalization that most adults find aversive and strive to bring to an end.*

## *Early Vocalizations*

Children develop language according to an invariant sequence of steps, or stages, as outlined in Table 6.3. We begin with the early ***prelinguistic*** vocalizations of crying, cooing, and babbling.

**Crying, Cooing, and Babbling** Newborn children, as parents are well aware, have an unlearned but highly effective form of verbal expression: crying and more crying (see Figure 6.12). Crying is accomplished by blowing air through the vocal tract. There are no distinct, well-formed sounds. Crying is about the only sound that infants make during the first month.

During the second month, infants begin ***cooing.*** Babies use their tongues when they coo. For this reason, coos are more articulated than cries. Coos are often vowel-like, and may resemble extended "oohs" and "ahs." Cooing appears linked to feelings of pleasure or positive excitement. Babies tend not to coo when they are hungry, tired, or in pain.

Cries and coos are innate but can be modified by experience. When parents respond positively to cooing by talking to their babies, smiling at them, and imitating them, cooing increases. Early parent–child "conversations," in which parents respond to coos and then pause as the baby coos, may foster early infant awareness of turn-taking as a way of verbally relating to other people.

Cries and coos do not represent objects or events as true words do. So they are prelinguistic.

**?**

**Truth or Fiction Revisited**

*Crying is* not *the child's earliest use of language. Crying, along with cooing and babbling, are* prelinguistic *vocalizations.*

***Prelinguistic*** Prior to the development of language.

***Cooing*** Prelinguistic, articulated vowel-like sounds that appear to reflect feelings of positive excitement.

***Babbling*** The child's first vocalizations that have the sounds of speech.

By about 8 months of age, cooing decreases markedly. Somewhere between 6 and 9 months, children begin to babble. ***Babbling*** is the first vocalizing that sounds like human speech. In babbling, babies frequently combine consonants and vowels, as in *ba, ga,* and, sometimes, the much valued *dada* (Mitchell & Kent, 1990). At first, "dada" is purely coincidental (sorry, you dads), despite the family's jubilation over its appearance.

In verbal interactions between infants and adults, the adults frequently repeat the syllables produced by their babies. They are likely to say "dadada" or "bababa" instead of simply "da" or "ba." Such redundancy apparently helps

**TABLE 6.3**

***Milestones in Language Development in Infancy***

| Approximate Age | Vocalization and Language |
|---|---|
| Birth | Cries |
| 12 weeks | Markedly less crying than at 8 weeks; when talked to and nodded at, smiles, followed by squealing-gurgling sounds (usually called *cooing*) that are vowel-like in character and pitch-modulated; sustains cooing for 15-20 seconds. |
| 16 weeks | Responds to human sounds more definitely; turns head; eyes seem to search for speaker; occasionally some chuckling sounds. |
| 20 weeks | Vowel-like cooing sounds begin to be interspersed with more consonantal sounds; acoustically, all vocalizations are very different from the sounds of the mature language of the environment. |
| 6 months | Cooing changing into babbling resembling one-syllable utterances; neither vowels nor consonants have very fixed recurrences; most common utterances sound somewhat like *ma, mu, da,* or *di.* |
| 8 months | Reduplication (or more continuous repetitions) becomes frequent; intonation patterns become distinct; utterances can signal emphasis and emotions. |
| 10 months | Vocalizations are mixed with sound-play such as gurgling or bubble blowing; appears to wish to imitate sounds, but the imitations are never quite successful. |
| 12 months | Identical sound sequences are replicated with higher relative frequency of occurrence, and words (*mamma* or *dadda*) are emerging; definite signs of understanding some words and simple commands ("Show me your eyes"). |
| 18 months | Has a definite repertoire of 3-50 words; vocabulary explosion begins; still much babbling but now of several syllables with intricate intonation pattern; no attempt at communicating information and no frustration when not understood; vocabulary may include such words as *thank you* or *come here,* but there is little ability to join any of the words into spontaneous two-word phrases; understanding is progressing rapidly. |
| 24 months | Vocabulary of more than 50 words (some children seem to be able to name everything in environment); begins spontaneously to join vocabulary items into two-word phrases; all phrases seem to be own creations; definite increase in communicative behavior and interest in language. |

The ages in this table are approximations. Parents need not assume that their children will have language problems if they are somewhat behind.
Source: Adapted from Lenneberg, 1967, pp. 128-130.

infants discriminate these sounds from others and further encourages them to imitate their parents (Goodsitt et al., 1984).

After infants have been babbling for a few months, parents often believe that their children are having conversations with themselves. At 10 to 12 months, infants tend to repeat syllables, showing what linguists refer to as ***echolalia.*** Parents overhear them going on and on, repeating consonant–vowel combinations (''ah-bah-bah-bah-bah''), pausing, then switching to other combinations.

Toward the end of the first year, infants are also using patterns of rising and falling ***intonation*** that resemble the sounds of adult speech. It may sound as if the infant is trying to speak the parents' language. In fact, parents may think that their children are babbling in English, or in whatever tongue is spoken in the home (Bates et al., 1987).

**CULTURE AND DEVELOPMENT: BABBLING** Babbling, like crying and cooing, appears inborn. Children from different cultures, where languages sound very different, all seem to babble the same sounds, including many they could not have heard (Oller, 1981). Babbling also occurs in deaf babies, although its onset is delayed (Oller & Eilers, 1988). Deaf babies of deaf parents babble with their hands as well, using repetitive gestures that resemble the vocal babbling of hearing infants (Petittio & Marentette, 1991).

**TRUTH OR FICTION REVISITED**

*Deaf children do, in fact, babble. Babbling appears in children who cannot hear, providing evidence that babbling emerges innately and does not represent imitation.*

Despite the fact that it is innate, babbling is readily modified by the child's language environment. One study followed babies growing up in French-, Chinese-, and Arabic-speaking households (de Boysson-Bardies et al., 1989). At 4 to 7 months of age, the infants began to use more of the sounds in their language environment; foreign phonemes began to drop out. The role that experience plays in language development is further indicated by the fact that the babbling of deaf infants never begins to approximate the sounds of the parents' language. Deaf children tend to lapse into silence by the end of the first year.

## DEVELOPMENT OF VOCABULARY

Vocabulary development refers to the child's learning of the meanings of words. Generally speaking, children's ***receptive vocabulary*** development outpaces their ***expressive vocabulary*** development (Baker & Cantwell, 1991). This means that at any given time, they can understand more words than they can use. One study, for example, found that 12-month-olds could speak an average of 13 words but could comprehend the meaning of 84 words (Thal & Bates, 1990). In fact, infants usually understand much of what others are saying well before they themselves utter any words at all.

**THE CHILD'S FIRST WORDS** Ah, that long-awaited first word! What a milestone! Sad to say, many parents miss it. They are not quite sure when their infants utter their first word, often because the first word is not pronounced clearly or because pronunciation varies from usage to usage.

***Echolalia*** (Eck-oh-LAY-lee-uh) Automatic repetition of sounds or words.

***Intonation*** The use of pitches of varying levels to help communicate meaning.

***Receptive vocabulary*** The extent of one's knowledge of the meanings of words that are communicated to one by others.

***Expressive vocabulary*** The sum total of the words that one can use in the production of language.

The first word typically is spoken between 11 and 13 months, but a range of 8 to 18 months is considered normal (Baker & Cantwell, 1991; Bates et al., 1992). First words tend to be brief, consisting of one or two syllables. Each syllable is likely to consist of a consonant followed by a vowel. Vocabulary acquisition is slow at first. It may take children 3 or 4 months to achieve a vocabulary of 10 to 30 words after the first word is spoken (deVilliers & deVilliers, 1992).

By about 18 months, children may be producing up to about 50 words. Many of them are quite familiar, such as *no, cookie, mama, hi,* and *eat.* Others, such as *allgone* and *bye-bye,* may not be found in the dictionary, but they function as words. That is, they are used consistently to symbolize the same meaning.

More than half (65 percent) of children's first words comprise what Katherine Nelson (1973) refers to as "general nominals" and "specific nominals." General nominals are like nouns in that they include the names of classes of objects (*car, ball, doggy*), animals (*doggy, poo-cat*), and people (*boy*). But they also include both personal and relative pronouns (*she* and *that*). Specific nominals are proper nouns, such as *Daddy* (used as the father's name, not the category of men to which he belongs) and *Rover.* As noted in Chapter 5, the attention of infants seems to be captured by movement. Words expressing movement are frequently found in early speech (Stockman & Vaughn-Cooke, 1992). Nelson (1973, 1981) found that of children's first 50 words, the most common words were names for people, animals, and objects that move (*Mommy, car, doggy*) or that can be moved (*dolly, milky*); action words (*bye-bye*); a number of modifiers (*big, hot*); and expressive words (*no, hi, oh*).

**TRUTH OR FICTION REVISITED**

*Most of children's earliest words are names for things. These are referred to as* nominals.

Nelson found a surprising diversity in the nominals used by these children, reflecting the objects that surrounded them and what was important to their parents. Some children, for example, may number words as exotic as "ohgi" (yogurt) and "bay" (bagel) among their first 50 or so, whereas others accumulate more traditional nominals such as *baby, ball,* and *juice* (Bloom, 1993). These first words that children produce tend to be words their parents frequently use when talking to them (Barrett et al., 1991; Hart, 1991).

At about 18 to 22 months of age, there is a rapid burst in the number of new words learned (Reznick & Goldfield, 1992). The child's vocabulary may increase from 50 to more than 300 words in just a few months (Bates et al., 1992). This vocabulary spurt could also be called a "naming explosion," since almost 75 percent of the words added during this time are nouns (Goldfield & Reznick, 1990). The rapid pace of vocabulary growth continues through the preschool years, with children acquiring an average of nine new words per day (Rice, 1989).

**REFERENTIAL AND EXPRESSIVE STYLES IN LANGUAGE DEVELOPMENT** Nelson (1981) also found that some children prefer a *referential* approach in their language development, whereas others take a more *expressive* approach.

Children who show the ***referential language style*** use language primarily to label objects in their environments. Their early vocabularies consist mainly of nominals. Children who use an ***expressive language style*** use language primarily as a means for engaging in social interactions. Children with an expressive style use more pronouns and many words involved in social routines, such as *stop, more,* and *all gone.* More children use an expressive style than a referential style (Hampson, 1989), but most use a combination of the styles.

Why do some children prefer a referential style and others an expressive style? It may be that some children are naturally oriented toward objects, whereas others are primarily interested in social relationships. Nelson also found that the mother's ways of teaching her children play a role. Some mothers focus on labeling objects for their children as soon as they notice their vocabularies expanding in the second year. Other mothers are more oriented toward social interactions themselves, teaching their children to say "hi," "please," and "thank you."

**OVEREXTENSION** Young children try to talk about more objects than they have words for, and so they often extend the meaning of one word to refer to things and actions for which they do not have words. This process is called ***overextension.*** Eve Clark (1973, 1975) studied diaries of infants' language development and found that overextensions generally are based on perceived similarities in function or form between the original object or action and the new one to which the first word is being extended. She provides the example of the word "mooi," which one child originally used to designate the moon. Then "mooi" became overextended to designate all round objects, including the letter *o* and cookies and cakes.

Clark (1973) also found that overextensions gradually pull back to their proper references as the child's vocabulary and ability to classify objects develops. Consider the example of a child who first refers to a dog as a "bow-wow." The word *bow-wow* then becomes overextended to also refer to horses, cats, and cows. In effect, *bow-wow* comes to mean something akin to "familiar animal." Next the child learns to use the word *moo* to refer to cows. But *bow-wow* still remains extended to horses and cats. As the child's vocabulary develops, she acquires the word *doggy.* So dogs and cats may now be referred to either with *bow-wow* or *doggy.* Eventually, each animal has one or more correct names.

## DEVELOPMENT OF SENTENCES: TELEGRAPHIC SPEECH

Although children first use one-word utterances, these utterances appear to express the meanings of sentences. Roger Brown (1973) calls brief expressions that have the meanings of sentences ***telegraphic*** speech. When we as adults write telegrams, we use principles of syntax to cut out all the unnecessary words. "Home Tuesday" might stand for "I expect to be home on Tuesday." Similarly, only the essential words are used in children's telegraphic speech—in particular, nouns, verbs, and some modifiers.

**MEAN LENGTH OF UTTERANCE** Brown (1973, 1977) has extensively studied telegraphic speech in children. He describes telegraphic speech in terms of children's ***mean length of utterance,*** or MLU. The MLU is defined as the average number of ***morphemes*** children use in their sentences. Morphemes are the smallest units of meaning in a language. A morpheme may be a whole word or part of a word, such as a prefix or suffix. For example, the word *walked*

***Referential language style*** Using language primarily as a means for labeling objects.

***Expressive language style*** Using language primarily as a means for engaging in social interaction.

***Overextension*** Using words in situations in which their meanings become extended, or inappropriate.

***Telegraphic*** Referring to speech in which only the essential words are used, as in a telegram.

***Mean length of utterance*** The average number of morphemes used in an utterance.

***Morpheme*** The smallest unit of meaning in a language.

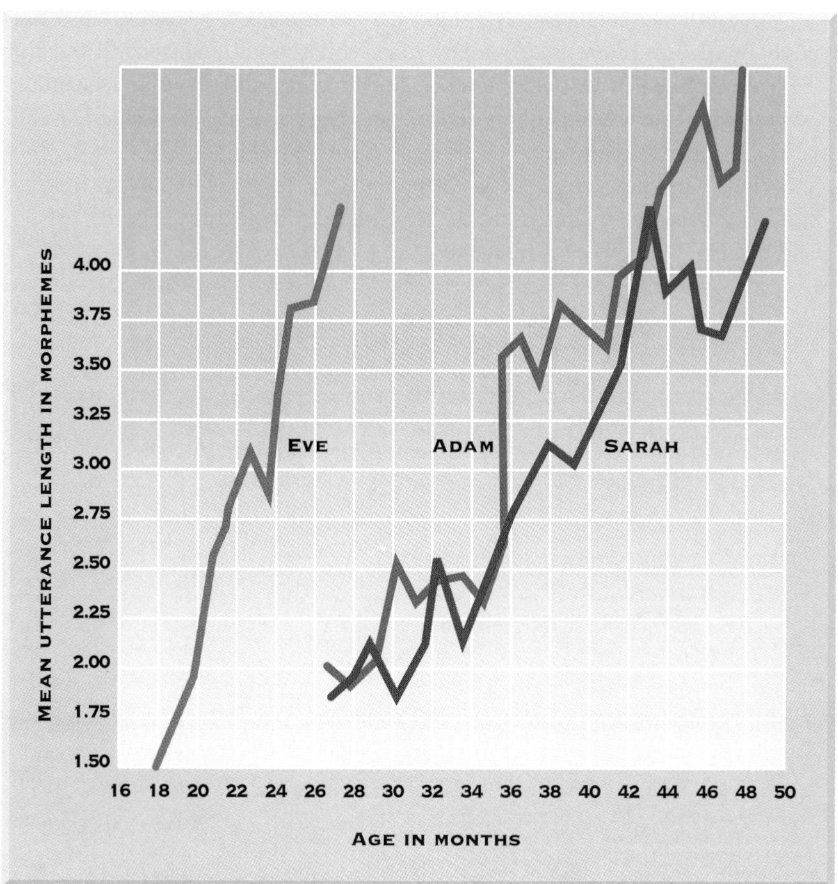


FIGURE 6.13

***MEAN LENGTH OF UTTERANCE FOR THREE CHILDREN.*** *Some children begin speaking earlier than others. However, the mean length of utterance increases rapidly once speech begins.*

consists of two morphemes: the verb *walk* and the suffix *ed,* which changes the verb to the past tense. In Figure 6.13, we see the relationship between chronological age and MLU for three children tracked by Brown: Eve, Adam, and Sarah.

The patterns of growth in MLU are similar for each child, showing swift upward movement, broken by intermittent and brief regressions. Figure 6.13 also shows us something about individual differences. Eve was precocious compared to Adam and Sarah, extending her MLU at much earlier ages. However, as suggested earlier, the receptive language of all three children would have exceeded their expressive language at any given time. Also, Eve's earlier extension of MLU does not guarantee that she will show more complex expressive language than Adam and Sarah at maturity.

Let us now consider the features of two types of telegraphic speech: the *holophrase* and *two-word utterances.*

**HOLOPHRASES** Single words that are used to express complex meanings are called ***holophrases.*** For example, *Mama* may be used by the child to signify meanings as varied as "There goes Mama," "Come here, Mama," and "You are Mama." Most children readily teach their parents what they intend by augmenting their holophrases with gestures, intonations, and reinforcers. That is, they act delighted when parents do as requested and howl when they do not.

**TWO-WORD SENTENCES** At about the time the child's vocabulary consists of 50 to 100 words (usually somewhere between 18 and 24 months of age), telegraphic two-word sentences begin to appear (Baker & Cantwell, 1991; Bates

***Holophrase*** A single word used to express complex meanings.

***Syntax*** The rules in a language for placing words in proper order to form meaningful sentences (from the Latin *syntaxis*, meaning "joining together").

et al., 1992). In the sentence "That ball," the words *is* and *a* are implied. Several types of two-word sentences are used by young children and are listed in Table 6.4.

Two-word sentences, while brief and telegraphic, still show understanding of ***syntax*** (deVilliers & deVilliers, 1992). The child will say "Sit chair" to tell a parent to sit in a chair, not "Chair sit." The child will say "My shoe," not "Shoe my," to show possession. "Mommy go" means Mommy is leaving, while "Go Mommy" expresses the wish for Mommy to go away. For this reason, "Go Mommy" is not heard frequently.

## TRUTH OR FICTION REVISITED

*To a 2-year-old, the word combinations "Go Mommy" and "Mommy go" actually have very different meanings. Word order is essential to meaning even in these apparently simple two-word utterances.*

**TABLE 6.4**

***SOME USES OF CHILDREN'S TWO-WORD SENTENCES***

| TYPE OF UTTERANCE | EXAMPLE | TYPE OF KNOWLEDGE SUGGESTED BY SENTENCE |
|---|---|---|
| NAMING, LOCATING | THAT BALL.<br>CAR THERE. | OBJECTS EXIST AND THEY HAVE NAMES. |
| NEGATING | MILK ALLGONE.<br>NO EAT. | OBJECTS MAY BECOME USED UP OR LEAVE.<br>PEOPLE MAY CHOOSE NOT TO DO THINGS. |
| DEMANDING, EXPRESSING DESIRE | WANT MOMMY.<br>MORE MILK. | OBJECTS CAN BE REINSTATED; QUANTITIES CAN BE INCREASED. |
| AGENT-ACTION | MOMMY GO.<br>DOGGY BARK. | PEOPLE, ANIMALS, AND OBJECTS ACT OR MOVE. |
| ACTION-OBJECT | HIT YOU. | ACTIONS CAN HAVE OBJECTS. |
| AGENT-OBJECT | DADDY CAR. | PEOPLE DO THINGS TO OBJECTS (ALTHOUGH, IN THIS UTTERANCE, THE ACTION IS NOT STATED.) |
| ACTION-LOCATION | SIT CHAIR. | A PERSON (UNSTATED) IS ENGAGING IN AN ACT IN A PLACE. |
| ACTION-RECIPIENT | GIVE MAMA. | AN OBJECT (UNSTATED) IS BEING MOVED IN RELATION TO A PERSON. |
| ACTION-INSTRUMENT | CUT KNIFE. | AN INSTRUMENT IS BEING USED FOR AN ACT. |
| ATTRIBUTION | PRETTY MOMMY.<br>BIG GLASS. | PEOPLE OR OBJECTS HAVE TRAITS OR QUALITIES. |
| POSSESSION | MOMMY CUP.<br>MY SHOE. | PEOPLE POSSESS OBJECTS. |
| QUESTION | WHERE MOMMY?<br>WHERE MILK? | PEOPLE CAN PROVIDE INFORMATION WHEN THEY ARE PROMPTED. |

SOURCE: ADAPTED FROM SLOBIN, 1972.

Martin Braine (1976) described the grammar of two-word sentences as consisting of a *pivot word* and an *open word.* According to Braine, a pivot word is a frequently occurring word that is attached to a variety of other words, known as open words. For example, a child might say "Mommy go," "Daddy go," and "Car go." In these utterances, *go* is the pivot word and *Mommy, Daddy,* and *car* are open words. In this example, the pivot word occurred in the second position but it can also occur in the first position ("More milk," "More read," "More swing").

**Models** In social-learning theory, persons who engage in behaviors that are imitated by others.

**CULTURE AND DEVELOPMENT: TWO-WORD SENTENCES** Two-word sentences appear at about the same time in the development of all languages (Slobin, 1973). Also, the sequence of emergence of the types of two-word utterances (for example, first, agent-action, then action-object, location, and possession) is the same in languages as diverse as English, Luo (an African tongue), German, Russian, and Turkish (Slobin, 1983). This is an example of the point that language develops in a series of steps that appear to be invariant. The lack of wide cultural differences in the developmental sequence can be seen as supporting the view that the human tendency to develop language according to universal processes is innate (Slobin, 1988).

## *THEORETICAL INTERLUDE: THEORIES OF LANGUAGE DEVELOPMENT*

Countless billions of children have learned the languages spoken by their parents and have passed them down, with minor changes, from generation to generation. But how do they do so? In this section, we discuss the learning-theory and nativist views of language development.

**LEARNING-THEORY VIEWS** In Chapter 5, we saw that learning plays a role in motor development and perceptual development. The role of learning in language development is even more obvious. Children who are reared in English-speaking homes learn English, not Japanese or Russian. Learning theorists usually explain language development in terms of imitation and reinforcement.

***The Role of Imitation*** From a social-learning perspective, parents serve as ***models.*** Children learn language, at least in part, by observation and imitation. It seems likely that many vocabulary words, especially nouns and verbs (including irregular verbs), are learned by imitation.

But imitative learning does not explain why children spontaneously utter phrases and sentences that they have *not* observed (J. Harris, 1990). Parents, for example, are unlikely to model utterances such as "bye-bye sock" and "allgone Daddy," but children do say them.

And children sometimes steadfastly *avoid* imitating certain language forms suggested by adults, even when the adults are insistent. Note the following exchange between 2-year-old Ben and a (very frustrated) adult:

*Ben: I like these candy. I like they.*
*Adult: You like them?*
*Ben: Yes, I like they.*
*Adult: Say* them.
*Ben: Them.*
*Adult: Say "I like* them."
*Ben: I like them.*
*Adult: Good.*

*Ben: I'm good. These candy good too.*
*Adult: Are they good?*
*Ben: Yes. I like they. You like they? (Kuczaj, 1982, p. 48).*

Ben is not resisting the model because of obstinancy. He does repeat "I like them" when asked to do so. But when given the opportunity, afterward, to construct the object "them," he reverts to using the subjective form, "they." Ben is more likely at this period in his development to use his (erroneous) understanding of syntax spontaneously to actively produce his own language, instead of just imitating a model.

***The Role of Reinforcement*** In his landmark book, *Verbal Behavior,* B. F. Skinner outlined his view of the role of reinforcement in language development: "A child acquires verbal behavior when relatively unpatterned vocalizations, selectively reinforced, assume forms which produce appropriate consequences in a given verbal community" (Skinner, 1957, p. 31).

Skinner allows that prelinguistic vocalizations such as cooing and babbling may be inborn. But parents reinforce children for babbling that approximates the form of real words, such as "da," which, in English, resembles "dog" or "daddy." Children, in fact, do increase their babbling when it results in adults smiling at them, stroking them, and talking back to them. We have seen that as the first year progresses, children babble the sounds of their native tongues with increasing frequency; foreign sounds tend to drop out. The behaviorist explains this pattern of changing frequencies in terms of reinforcement (of the sounds of the adults' language) and ***extinction*** (of foreign sounds). An alternate (nonbehavioral) explanation is that children actively attend to the sounds in their linguistic environments and are intrinsically motivated to utter them.

From Skinner's (1957, 1983) perspective, children acquire their early vocabularies through ***shaping.*** That is, parents require that children's utterances be progressively closer to actual words before they are reinforced. In support of Skinner's position, more recent research shows that reinforcement accelerates the growth of vocabulary in young children (Whitehurst & Valdez-Menchaca, 1988). Skinner viewed multiword utterances as complex stimulus–response chains that are also taught by shaping. As children's utterances increase in length, parents foster correct word order by uttering sentences to their children and reinforcing imitation. As with Ben, when children make grammatical errors, parents recast their utterances correctly. They reinforce the children for repeating them.

But recall Ben's refusal to be shaped into correct syntax. If the reinforcement explanation of language development were sufficient, parents' reinforcement would facilitate children's learning of syntax and pronunciation. We do not have such evidence. For one thing, parents are more likely to reinforce their children for the accuracy, or "truth value," of their utterances than for their grammatical correctness (Brown, 1973). Parents, in other words, generally accept the syntax of their children's vocal efforts. The child who points down and says "The grass is purple" is not likely to be reinforced, despite correct syntax. But the enthusiastic child who shows her empty plate and blurts out "I eated it all up" is likely to be reinforced, despite the grammatical incorrectness of "eated." Research confirms that while parents do expand and rephrase their children's ungrammatical utterances more than their grammatically correct ones, they do not overtly correct their children's language mistakes (Bohannon & Stanowicz, 1988; Coley, 1993; Penner, 1987).

Also, selective reinforcement of children's pronunciation, in fact, may backfire. Children whose parents reward proper pronunciation but correct poor pronunciation develop vocabulary more slowly than children whose parents are more tolerant about pronunciation (Nelson, 1973).

***Extinction*** A decrease and eventual disappearance of a response in the absence of reinforcement.

***Shaping*** In learning theory, the gradual building of complex behavior patterns by means of reinforcing successive approximations of the target behavior.

## TRUTH OR FICTION REVISITED

*Children do* not *learn language faster when their parents correct their errors. Correcting children's pronunciation, for example, may actually slow down language development.*

Learning-theory approaches also cannot account for the invariant sequences of language development and for children's spurts in acquisition. Even the types of two-word utterances emerge in a consistent pattern in diverse cultures. Although timing differs from child to child, the types of questions used, passive versus active sentences, and so on all emerge in the same order. It is unlikely that parents around the world teach language skills in the same sequence.

On the other hand, there is ample evidence that aspects of the child's language environment influence the development of language. Much of the research in this area has focused on the ways in which adults—especially mothers—interact with their children (see Figure 6.14).

Studies show that language growth in young children is enhanced when mothers and other adults do the following things:

- Use a simplified form of speech known as "motherese" (See Developing Today)
- Use questions that engage the child in conversation (Hoff-Ginsberg, 1986, 1990)
- Relate their speech to the child's utterance; for example, saying "Yes, your doll is pretty" in response to the child's statement "My doll" (Hoff-Ginsberg, 1991)
- Join the child in paying attention to a particular activity or toy (Akhtar et al., 1991; Tamis-LeMonda & Bornstein, 1991; Oram & Oshima-Takane, 1993)

FIGURE 6.14

***FOSTERING LANGUAGE DEVELOPMENT.*** *Language growth in young children is enhanced when parents and caregivers engage the child in conversation about activities and objects in the environment.*

- Describe aspects of the environment occupying the infant's current focus of attention (Dunham & Dunham, 1992)
- Read to the child (Hale & Windecker, 1993; Scarborough, 1993; Whitehurst et al., 1993)
- Talk a lot to the child (Huttenlocher et al., 1991)

***Culture and Development: Talking to Infants*** Mothers in different cultures show certain similarities in the way they talk to their infants, but cultural variations in their speech patterns exist as well. For example, a recent study analyzed how Argentinian, French, Japanese and American mothers spoke to their 5- and 13-month-old infants (Bornstein et al., 1992a). Mothers in all four cultures spoke more to older infants. When the infants were 5 months old, mothers' speech was more heavily laced with expressive statements such as greetings, songs, nonsense sounds, and endearing terms. As children got older, mothers in all groups provided more information in their speech. They made statements, gave reports about the baby, mother, or environment, and asked the child questions.

What cultural values are associated with different informational speech patterns among mothers?

| CULTURE | TYPE OF INFORMATION | CULTURAL VALUE |
|---|---|---|
| ARGENTINIAN | DIRECT STATEMENTS | EMPHASIS ON DIRECTIVE VIEW OF CHILD REARING |
| FRENCH | CONVEY LIMITED INFORMATION | EMPHASIS ON EMOTIONAL SUPPORT<br>LESS EMPHASIS ON STIMULATING ACHIEVEMENT |
| AMERICAN | ASK QUESTIONS | EMPHASIS ON CHILD AS AN ACTIVE LEARNER |
| JAPANESE | EXPRESSIVE SPEECH | EMPHASIS ON EMOTIONAL CLOSENESS AND INTERDEPENDENCE |

But there were also variations in the speech of mothers in the four cultures that appeared to reflect cultural values and beliefs. Japanese mothers used expressive speech more often than Western mothers did, consistent with the Japanese mothers' child-rearing emphasis on social and emotional closeness and interdependence. Mothers from the three Western cultures favored speech containing information. This may reflect American and European traditions of encouraging interpersonal independence and interest in the environment (Barratt et al., 1993; Tamis-LeMonda et al., 1992).

Even within the three Western cultures, there were differences in the types of information mothers provided to their babies. Argentinian mothers used more direct statements, perhaps reflecting their more directive view of child rearing. U.S. mothers asked the most questions, possibly indicating an emphasis on the child as an active learner. French mothers conveyed less information in their speech than other Western mothers. French mothers are thought to place less emphasis on stimulating achievement and more emphasis on emotional support (Bornstein et al., 1992a).

Do these variations in maternal speech affect the baby's behavior? The answer seems to be yes. For example, at 13 months of age, American babies are more advanced than Japanese babies in vocabulary development, possibly reflecting the more information-oriented speech of American mothers (Tamis-LeMonda et al., 1992).

While the environment certainly plays a role in language development, it does not account for some of its features, as we have seen. We must look to other theoretical approaches to explain the regularity of the sequences of language development. Perhaps the sequences are governed in some way by the development of biological structures, according to the unfolding of the genetic code. Perhaps children have a native capacity to speak.

**NATIVIST VIEWS** The nativist view of language development holds that innate or inborn factors cause children to attend to and acquire language in certain ways (Maratsos, 1983). From this perspective, children bring an inborn tendency in the form of neurological "prewiring" to language learning.

***Psycholinguistic theory*** The view that language learning involves an interaction between environmental influences and an inborn tendency to acquire language. The emphasis is on the inborn tendency.

***Psycholinguistic Theory*** According to ***psycholinguistic theory,*** language acquisition involves an interaction between environmental influences—such as exposure to parental speech and reinforcement—and an inborn tendency

## *Developing Today*

### "MOTHERESE"

One fascinating way adults influence the language development of young children is through the use of baby talk or "motherese." But "motherese" is a limiting term, because fathers, siblings, and people who are not related at all, including older children, also use motherese when talking to babies (Fernald, 1991; Trehub et al., 1993). Motherese occurs in languages as different as Arabic, English, Comanche, Italian, French, German, Xhosa (an African language), Japanese, and Mandarin Chinese (Fernald, 1991; Fernald & Morikawa, 1993; Papousek et al., 1991).

Developmentalists who have studied motherese find that it has a number of characteristics (Fernald & Mazzie, 1991; Gleitman & Wanner, 1988; Trehub et al., 1993):

1. Motherese is spoken more slowly than speech addressed to adults. Motherese is spoken at a higher pitch, and there are distinct pauses between ideas.
2. Sentences are brief, and adults make the effort to speak in a grammatically correct manner.
3. Sentences are simple in syntax. The focus is on nouns, verbs, and just a few modifiers.
4. Key words are put at the ends of sentences and are spoken in a higher and louder voice.
5. The diminutive morpheme "y" is frequently added to nouns. "Dad" becomes "Daddy" and "horse" becomes "horsey."
6. Motherese is repetitive. Adults repeat sentences several times, sometimes using minor variations, as in "Show me your nose." "Where is your nose?" "Can you touch your nose?" Adults also repeat children's utterances, often rephrasing them in an effort to expand children's awareness of their expressive opportunities. If the child says, "Baby shoe," the mother may reply, "Yes, that's your shoe. Shall Mommy put the shoe on baby's foot?"
7. Motherese includes a type of repetition called *reduplication*. "Yummy" becomes "yummy-yummy." "Daddy" may alternate with "Da-da."
8. Vocabulary is concrete, referring, when possible, to objects that are in the immediate environment. For example, stuffed lions may be referred to as "kitties". This purposeful overextension is intended to avoid confusing the child by adding too many new labels.
9. Objects may be overdescribed by being given compound labels. Rabbits may become "bunny rabbits," and cats may become "kitty cats." In this way parents may try to be sure that they are connecting with the child by using at least one label that the child will recognize.
10. Parents speak for the children, as in "Is baby tired?" "Oh, we're so tired." "We want to take our nap now, don't we?" This parent is pretending to have a two-way conversation with the child. In this way, parents seem to be trying to help their children express themselves by offering children models of sentences they can use later on.
11. Users of motherese stay a step ahead of the child. As children's vocabularies grow and their syntax develops, adults step up their own language levels—remaining just ahead of the child. In this way, adults seem to be encouraging the child to continue to play catch-up.

And so, adults and older children use a variety of strategies to communicate with young children and to draw them out. Does it work? Does motherese foster language development?

Research on the effects of motherese is supportive of its use. Infants as young as 2 days old prefer baby talk over adult talk (Cooper & Aslin, 1990). The short, simple sentences and high pitch used in motherese are more likely to produce a response from the child and to enhance vocabulary development than are complex sentences and those spoken in a lower pitch (Fernald, 1992; Murray et al., 1990). Children who hear their utterances repeated and recast do seem to learn from the adults who are modeling the new expressions (Farrar, 1992; Nelson, 1989b). Repetition of children's vocalizations also appears to be one method of reinforcing vocalizing. In sum, motherese may be of significant help in fostering children's language development.

**FIGURE 6.15 "MOTHERESE."** *Adults and older children use a simplified form of language known as "motherese" when they talk to babies.*

to acquire language, which Chomsky (1988, 1990) and some others refer to as a ***language acquisition device (LAD).*** Evidence for an inborn tendency is found in the universality of human language abilities; in the regularity of the early production of sounds, even among deaf children; and in the invariant sequences of language development, regardless of which language the child is learning.

The inborn tendency primes the nervous system to learn grammar. On the surface, languages differ a great deal in their vocabulary and grammar. Chomsky refers to these elements as the ***surface structure*** of language. However, the LAD serves children all over the world because languages share what Chomsky refers to as a "universal grammar"—an underlying ***deep structure*** or set of rules for transforming ideas into sentences. From Chomsky's perspective, children are predisposed to attend to language and to deduce the transformational rules. Consider an analogy with computers: According to psycholinguistic theory, the universal grammar that resides in the LAD is the basic operating system of the computer, whereas the particular language that a child learns to use is the word-processing program.

## TRUTH OR FICTION REVISITED

*Evidence suggests that it is true that children are "pre-programmed" to listen to language in such a way that they deduce rules of grammar. The preprogramming has also been referred to as* neural prewiring *or as a* language acquisition device *(LAD).*

***Brain Structures Involved in Language*** The biological structures that may provide the basis for the functions of the LAD appear to be based in the left hemisphere of the cerebral cortex for about 95 percent of right-handed people and about 70 percent of left-handed people (Springer & Deutsch, 1989).

Even at birth, the sounds of speech elicit greater electrical activity in the left hemisphere than in the right, as indicated by the activity of brain waves. This pattern does not hold for non-speech-related sounds. Music tends to elicit greater electrical activity in the right hemispheres of infants (Young & Gagnon, 1990).

Within the left hemisphere of the cortex, the two areas most involved in speech are *Broca's area* and *Wernicke's area* (see Figure 6.16). Even in the human fetus, Wernicke's area is usually larger in the left hemisphere than the right (Wilson, 1990b). Damage to either area is likely to cause an ***aphasia,*** or disruption in the ability to understand or produce language.

Broca's area is located near the section of the motor cortex that controls the muscles of the tongue and throat and of other areas of the face that are used when speaking. When Broca's area is damaged, people speak slowly and laboriously, with simple sentences—a pattern known as ***Broca's aphasia.*** Their ability to understand the speech of others is relatively unaffected, however. Wernicke's area lies near the auditory cortex and is connected to Broca's area by nerve fibers. People with damage to Wernicke's area may show ***Wernicke's aphasia.*** Although they usually speak freely and with proper syntax, their abilities to comprehend other people's speech and to think of the words to express their own thoughts are impaired (Wilson, 1990a). Thus, Wernicke's area seems to be essential to understanding the relationships between words and their meanings. More recent research shows that language areas in addition to Broca's and Wernicke's are found elsewhere in the brain and that each person may have a

***Language Acquisition Device (LAD)*** In psycholinguistic theory, neural "prewiring" that facilitates the child's learning of grammar.

***Surface structure*** The superficial grammatical construction of a sentence.

***Deep structure*** The underlying meaning of a sentence.

***Aphasia*** A disruption in the ability to understand or produce language.

***Broca's aphasia*** A form of aphasia caused by damage to Broca's area and characterized by slow, laborious speech.

***Wernicke's aphasia*** A form of aphasia caused by damage to Wernicke's area and characterized by impaired comprehension of speech and difficulty in attempting to produce the right word.

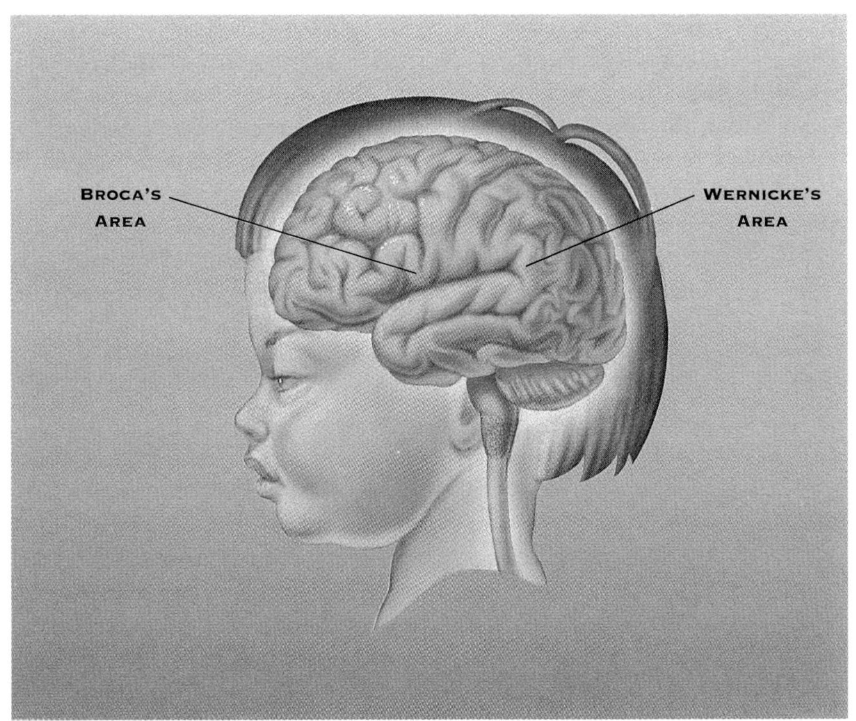


FIGURE 6.16

***Broca's and Wernicke's Areas of the Cerebral Cortex.*** *Areas of the (usually left) hemisphere most involved in speech are Broca's area and Wernicke's area. Damage to either area can produce an aphasia—that is, a disruption of the ability to understand or produce language.*

unique pattern of organization for language ability (Blakeslee, 1991a; Ojemann, 1991).

***The Sensitive Period*** Lenneberg (1967) proposes that there is a ***sensitive period*** for learning language that begins at about 18 to 24 months and lasts until puberty. During the sensitive period, neural development (as in the differentiating of brain structures) provides a degree of plasticity that facilitates language learning.

Evidence for a sensitive period is found in recovery from brain injuries in some people. Injuries to the hemisphere that controls language (usually the left) can impair or destroy the ability to speak. But prior to puberty, children suffering left-hemisphere injuries frequently recover a good deal of speaking ability. Lenneberg (1967) suggests that in very young children, left-hemisphere damage may encourage the development of language functions in the right hemisphere. But adaptation ability wanes in adolescence, when brain tissue has reached adult levels of differentiation.

The best way to determine whether people are capable of acquiring language once they have passed puberty would be to run an experiment in which one or more children were reared in such severe isolation that they were not exposed to language until puberty. Of course, such an experiment could not be run because of ethical and legal barriers.

However, the disturbing case history of Genie offers insights into the issue of whether there is a sensitive period for language development (Curtiss, 1977; Rymer, 1993). Genie's father locked her in a small room at the age of 20 months and kept her there until she was 13. Her social contacts during this period were limited to her mother, who entered the room only to feed Genie, and to beatings by her father. When Genie was rescued, she weighed only about 60 pounds, did not speak, was not toilet trained, and could barely stand. Genie was placed in a foster home, where she was exposed to English for the first time in nearly 12 years. Her language development followed the normal sequence of much younger children in a number of ways, but she never acquired the proficiency of children reared under normal circumstances. Five years after her liberation, Genie's

***Sensitive period*** In linguistic theory, the period from about 18 months to puberty when the brain is thought to be especially capable of learning language because of plasticity of the brain.

### THINKING ABOUT DEVELOPMENT

Agree or disagree with the following statement and support your answer: "Children acquire language on the basis of experience."

language remained largely telegraphic. She still showed significant problems with syntax—failing, for example, to reverse subjects and verbs to phrase spontaneous questions. She showed confusion concerning the use of the past tense (adding *ed* to words) and had difficulty using negative helping verbs such as *isn't* and *haven't.*

Genie's language development provides some support for the sensitive-period hypothesis, although it is possible that her language problems can also be attributed to her long years of malnutrition and abuse. It is also possible that she was retarded to begin with. Her efforts to acquire English after puberty were clearly laborious, and the results were substandard when compared even to the language of many 2- and 3-year-olds.

Further evidence for the sensitive-period hypothesis is provided by a recent study of a 9-year-old deaf boy named Simon (Newport, 1992). Researchers who studied Simon from the time he was 2½ years old reported that he signed in ***American Sign Language (ASL)*** using correct grammar, even though he had been exposed only to grammatically incorrect ASL by his parents and their friends, who also were deaf. Simon's parents and their friends had not learned to sign until they were teenagers. At that age, people often learn languages imperfectly. But Simon showed early mastery of grammatical rules that his parents used incorrectly or not at all. Simon's deduction of these rules on his own supports the view that the tendency to acquire language is inborn and also provides evidence that such learning occurs most readily during a sensitive period early in life.

***American Sign Language (ASL)*** The communication of meaning through the use of symbols that are formed by moving the hands and arms. The language used by some deaf people.

To sum up, the development of language in infancy is a product of both environmental and biological factors. It is becoming clear that the child brings a built-in readiness to the task of language acquisition. At the same time, the opportunity to hear spoken language and to interact verbally with others is of utmost importance (deVilliers & deVilliers, 1992). In the next chapter, we shall examine how interaction with others affects the social development of the infant.

## Summary

1. Cognitive development concerns the ways in which children mentally represent the world and manipulate symbols at various ages and stages of development.

2. Piaget hypothesized the existence of four stages of cognitive development. The sensorimotor stage lasts from the ages of 0 to 2 and consists of six substages. The first substage is dominated by inborn reflexes that are modified by experience. The second substage is characterized by primary circular reactions, in which infants repeat interesting responses that focus on their own body. In the third substage, secondary circular reactions, infants repeat schemes that have an effect on the environment. The fourth substage is characterized by the coordination of secondary schemes. In the fifth substage, infants use tertiary circular reactions, which are purposeful adaptations of established schemes to specific situations. In the sixth substage, invention of new means through mental combinations, infants use mental trial and error to solve simple problems.

3. Object permanence is the recognition that objects continue to exist whether or not they are in sight. Infants gradually develop more sophisticated forms of object permanence during the first 2 years.

4. Recent research indicates that Piaget underestimated the competence of young infants.

5. Memory improves between 2 and 6 months of age and is enhanced if babies receive a reminder before a memory test.

6. Infants are able to imitate certain facial expressions within the first 2 weeks after birth.

7. Individual differences in infant intelligence are measured by sensorimotor types of items that do not predict later IQ scores very well. Tests of visual recognition hold better promise as predictors of later IQ.

8. Prelinguistic vocalizations include crying, cooing, and babbling. Children at first babble sounds found in many languages, but soon utter more of the sounds spoken in the home.

9. First words are frequently spoken toward the end of the first year. Children use single words (holophrases) at about 18 months and two-word utterances a few months later. These brief utterances are referred to as *telegraphic speech.*

10. Vocabulary growth shows a rapid burst at about 18 to 22 months. The rate of acquisition of receptive vocabulary outpaces that of expressive vocabulary.

11. Some children show a referential language style, using language primarily to label objects. Others show an expressive language style, using language primarily to engage in social interaction.

12. Young children overextend the meanings of words, using them in situations for which they do not have words.

13. Brown describes children's telegraphic utterances in terms of the mean length of utterance (MLU), or the number of morphemes that are used per utterance.

14. Learning-theory explanations of language development emphasize the roles of imitation and reinforcement in learning. Language development is enhanced when adults engage the child in conversation, respond to the child's speech in a contingent manner, focus on the same activity or object as the child, and use a simplified form of speech called "motherese."

15. Nativist views emphasize innate factors in language development. Psycholinguistic theory hypothesizes the existence of a language acquisition device (LAD)—neural "prewiring" that spurs children to attend to and deduce rules of grammar.

16. For most people, language functions appear to be based on structures in the left hemisphere of the cerebral cortex: Broca's area and Wernicke's area.

17. Lenneberg suggests that there is a sensitive period for language acquisition that begins at about 18 to 24 months and lasts until puberty.

CHAPTER

7

# INFANCY: SOCIAL AND PERSONALITY DEVELOPMENT

## CHAPTER OUTLINE

## TRUTH OR FICTION?

______ *An infant's willingness to leave the mother in order to explore the environment is a sign of secure attachment.*

______ *You can predict how strongly babies are attached to their fathers if you know how many diapers per week the father changes.*

______ *Children become attached to their mothers earlier than they become attached to their fathers.*

______ *Children must become attached to their parents before a critical period elapses or bonds of attachment will not form properly.*

______ *Child abusers have frequently been the victims of child abuse themselves.*

______ *Children with autism usually learn the skills necessary to function independently by the time they are adults.*

______ *Children who care for themselves after school until their parents return home from work are at special risk of developing psychological and social problems.*

______ *Children placed in day care are less cooperative and more selfish than children who are cared for in the home.*

______ *Most children, regardless of culture, develop fear of strangers at some point during the second 6 months of infancy.*

______ *Psychologists dab rouge on infants' noses to assess development of the self-concept.*

______ *One-year-old girls prefer to play with dolls, whereas 1-year-old boys prefer transportation toys.*

If this chapter had been written by the poet John Donne, it might have begun, "No children are islands unto themselves." Children come into this world fully dependent on others for their survival and well-being. This chapter is about some of the consequences of that absolute dependency. It is about the social relationships between infants and care givers and the development of the bonds of affection or attachment that usually—but not always—bind them. It is about the behaviors of infants that prompt social and emotional responses from adults and the behaviors of adults that prompt social and emotional responses from infants. It is also about infants' unique and different ways of reacting socially and emotionally.

Let us first consider the issue of attachment and the factors that contribute to its development. Then we shall examine some circumstances that interfere with the development of attachment: social deprivation, child abuse, and autism. We turn next to a discussion of day care. Finally, we look at the development of emotions and personality in infancy, including the self-concept, temperament, and gender differences.

## ATTACHMENT

At the age of 2, the daughter of one of the authors (S. R.) almost succeeded at preventing publication of this book. When he locked himself into his study, she positioned herself outside the door and called, "Daddy, oh Daddy." At other times she would bang on the door or cry. When Daddy would give in (several times a day) and open the door, she would run in and say, "I want you to pick up me," and hold out her arms or climb into his lap. How would he ever finish the book?

Being a psychologist, solutions came easily. For example, he could write outside his home. But this solution had the drawback of distancing him from his family. Another solution was to let his daughter cry and ignore her. If he refused to reinforce crying, crying would become extinguished. There was only one problem with this solution. He didn't *want* to extinguish her efforts to get to him. ***Attachment,*** you see, is a two-way street.

Attachment is what most people refer to as affection or love. Mary Ainsworth (1989), one of the preeminent researchers in attachment, defines attachment as an emotional tie that is formed between one animal or person and another specific individual. Attachment keeps organisms together and tends to endure. John Bowlby (1988; Ainsworth & Bowlby, 1991) believes that attachment is essential to the very survival of the infant. He argues that babies are born with behaviors—crying, smiling, clinging—that elicit protective care-giving responses from parents.

Babies and children try to maintain contact with care givers to whom they are attached. They engage in eye contact, pull and tug at them, and ask to be picked up. When they cannot maintain contact, infants show behaviors suggestive of ***separation anxiety.*** They may thrash about, fuss, cry or screech, or whine. Parents who are seeking a few minutes to attend to their own legitimate needs sometimes see these behaviors as manipulative and, in a sense, they are. That is, children learn that the behaviors achieve desired ends. But what is wrong with "manipulating" a loved one to end one's distress?

***Attachment*** An affectional bond between individuals characterized by a seeking of closeness or contact and a show of distress upon separation.

***Separation anxiety*** Fear of being separated from a target of attachment—usually a primary care giver.

### *PATTERNS OF ATTACHMENT*

One procedure used widely in research on the development of attachment is the Strange Situation method developed by Mary Ainsworth and described in Focus

FOCUS ON RESEARCH

## THE STRANGE SITUATION METHOD

In the Strange Situation method of measuring attachment, an infant is exposed to a series of separations and reunions with a care giver (usually the mother) and a stranger who is a confederate of the researchers. Children are led through eight episodes (Ainsworth et al., 1978).

1. The mother carries the infant into the laboratory room.
2. The mother puts the infant down and then sits quietly in a chair. She does not interact with the infant unless the infant seeks her attention.
3. A stranger enters the room and converses with the mother. The stranger then gradually approaches the infant with a toy. The mother leaves the room.
4. If the infant is involved in active play, the stranger observes unobtrusively. If the infant is passive, the stranger tries to interest him or her in a toy. If the infant shows distress (as by crying), the stranger tries to comfort him or her.
5. The mother returns and the stranger leaves. After the infant has again begun to play, the mother also departs.
6. The infant is left alone briefly.
7. The stranger reenters the room and behaves as described in number 4.
8. The mother returns and the stranger leaves.

Based on studies using the Strange Situation method, Ainsworth and her colleagues (1978) have identified three patterns of attachment, which are described in the text of this chapter.

**FIGURE 7.1 THE STRANGE SITUATION.** *These photos show a 12-month-old child in the Strange Situation. In (a), the child plays with toys, glancing occasionally at mother. In (b), the stranger approaches with a toy. While the child is distracted, mother leaves the room. In (c), mother returns after a brief absence. The child crawls to her quickly and clings to her when picked up. In (d), the child cries when mother again leaves the room. What pattern of attachment is this child showing?*

A

B

C

D

***Secure attachment*** A type of attachment characterized by mild distress at leave-takings, seeking nearness to an attachment figure, and being readily soothed by the figure.

***Avoidant attachment*** A type of insecure attachment characterized by apparent indifference to the leave-takings of, and reunions with, an attachment figure.

***Ambivalent/resistant attachment*** A type of insecure attachment characterized by severe distress at the leave-takings of, and ambivalent behavior at reunions with, an attachment figure.

***Disorganized–disoriented attachment*** A type of insecure attachment characterized by dazed and contradictory behaviors toward an attachment figure.

***Kibbutz*** (key-BOOTS) An Israeli farming community in which children are reared in group settings.

***Metapelet*** A child-rearing professional in a kibbutz.

on Research. By using the Strange Situation method, Ainsworth and her colleagues (1978) have identified various patterns of attachment. Broadly speaking, babies have either ***secure attachment*** or insecure attachment. Ainsworth and other investigators have found that about 65 to 70 percent of middle-class U.S. babies are securely attached. In the Strange Situation test, babies who are securely attached mildly protest mother's departure, seek interaction upon reunion, and are readily comforted by her.

The two major types of insecure attachment identified by Ainsworth and her colleagues are ***avoidant attachment*** and ***ambivalent/resistant attachment.*** Approximately 20 to 25 percent of U.S. babies show avoidant attachment. These babies are least distressed by their mothers' departure. They play without fuss when alone and ignore their mothers upon reunion. Ambivalent/resistant babies comprise another 10 to 15 percent of the samples. These babies are the most emotional. They show severe signs of distress when their mothers leave and show ambivalence upon reunion by alternately clinging to and pushing away their mothers. More recently, a third category of insecure attachment, ***disorganized–disoriented,*** has been proposed (Main & Hesse, 1990). Babies showing this pattern appear dazed, confused, or disoriented. They may show contradictory behaviors, such as moving toward the mother while looking away from her.

**CULTURE AND DEVELOPMENT: PATTERNS OF ATTACHMENT** How widespread are these attachment patterns worldwide? Studies using the Strange Situation in seven European and Asian countries have found that secure attachments predominate, just as in the United States. Avoidant attachments are more common in some European countries, especially Germany, than in the United States. While avoidant attachment is more common than ambivalent/resistant attachment in most countries, the opposite pattern has been found for Japan and Israel (van IJzendoorn & Kroonenberg, 1988; van IJzendoorn et al., 1992; Sagi et al., 1991).

Different child-rearing practices and attitudes may account for these differences in attachment patterns. For example, German parents encourage independence in the child at an early age. Compared with American parents, they are less likely to pick up a crying baby and more likely to leave the baby alone in bed (Grossmann & Grossmann, 1991). This pattern may be more likely to foster avoidant attachment in the child. Japanese mothers, on the other hand, emphasize close and continuous contact with their babies and rarely leave them with other caretakers (Barratt et al., 1993; Takahashi, 1990). These infants are not used to being alone or with strangers, which may account for their distressed behavior in the Strange Situation.

The Israeli studies have involved children raised in a collective farm community known as a ***kibbutz.*** Parents visit and play with their children frequently during the day and evening. The children's primary care and training, however, is entrusted to a child-rearing specialist called a ***metapelet,*** who also spends the night with the children. Despite the reduced parent–child contact, kibbutz life does not seem to impair parent–child bonds of attachment (Maccoby & Feldman, 1972). Babies, however, appear to become equally attached to their metapelet (Van IJzendoorn et al., 1992).

How can we explain the finding that kibbutz-reared children show a higher incidence of ambivalent/resistant attachment than avoidant attachment? Like the Japanese child, the kibbutz-reared child has close, continuous contact with its primary caretakers but little contact with strangers. For both these groups of children, then, the Strange Situation may produce intense distress.

FIGURE 7.2

***Child-Rearing Practices and Attachment Behavior.*** *Japanese mothers emphasize close, continuous contact with their babies and rarely leave them with other caretakers. Might this account for the distress shown by Japanese babies in the Strange Situation?*

### *Consequences of Attachment*

Securely attached infants and toddlers are happier, more sociable with unfamiliar adults, more cooperative with parents, and get along better with peers than do insecurely attached children (Belsky et al., 1991a; Thompson, 1991a). They use the mother as a secure base from which to venture out and explore the environment (Ainsworth & Bowlby, 1991). Securely attached toddlers also have longer attention spans, are less impulsive, and are better at solving problems (Frankel & Bates, 1990; Lederberg & Mobley, 1990; Olson et al., 1990). At ages 5 and 6, securely attached children are better liked by peers and teachers, are more competent, are less aggressive, and have fewer behavior problems than insecurely attached children (Lyons-Ruth et al., 1993; Suess et al., 1992; Youngblade & Belsky, 1992). We must keep in mind that these positive developmental outcomes may be caused not only by secure infant attachments but also by the continuation of good parent–child relationships into childhood (Lamb, 1987).

**TRUTH OR FICTION REVISITED**

*It is true that an infant's willingness to leave the mother in order to explore the environment is considered a sign of secure attachment.*

### *The Role of the Mother in Attachment*

Attachment is one measure of the quality of care that infants receive (Rosen & Rothbaum, 1993). The mothers of securely attached babies are more likely to be affectionate, cooperative, reliable, and predictable in their care giving. They respond more sensitively to their babies' smiles, cries, and other social behaviors (Cox et al., 1992; Isabella, 1993; Rosen & Rothbaum, 1993).

Providing economically stressed mothers with support services can enhance their involvement with their infants and increase secure attachment. In one study, low-income women received child-care information and social support from

What are the cultural child-rearing practices and attitudes that account for attachment patterns other than the predominant pattern of secure attachment?

| Culture | Insecure Attachment Patterns | Child-Rearing Practices and Attitudes (compared with other European and Asian countries) |
|---|---|---|
| Germany | Avoidant | Less likely to pick up crying baby<br>More likely to leave alone in bed |
| Japan | Ambivalent/ resistant | Less likely to leave infant with strangers<br>More likely to emphasize close, continuous contact with mother |
| Israel | Ambivalent/ resistant | Less likely to leave infant with strangers<br>More likely to emphasize close, continuous contact with primary caretakers |

**THINKING ABOUT DEVELOPMENT**

Agree or disagree with the following statement and support your answer: "Women have 'natural instincts' that induce them to love and become attached to their children."

home visitors during pregnancy and for a year following childbirth (Jacobson & Frye, 1991). In another study, low-income women suffering from depression received similar support services until their child was 18 months old (Lyons-Ruth et al., 1990). In both instances, children whose mothers received support services showed more secure attachment than control children whose mothers had not. Even something as simple as increasing the amount of physical contact between mothers and their infants appears to promote greater maternal responsiveness and more secure attachment between infant and mother (Anisfeld et al., 1990).

Insecure attachment is found more frequently among babies whose mothers are mentally ill or who abuse them (Teti et al., 1992; van IJzendoorn et al., 1992). It is found more often among babies whose mothers are slow to meet their needs or who meet them in a cold manner (DeMulder & Radke-Yarrow, 1991; Izard et al., 1991).

Although it is tempting to seek the causes of secure and insecure attachment in the mother's behavior, that is not the whole story. Security of attachment seems to depend on the baby's temperament, as well as on the mother's behavior and personality (Fagot & Kavanaugh, 1993; Mangelsdorf et al., 1990). Babies who are more active and irritable and who display more negative emotion are more likely to develop insecure attachment (Fox, 1992; Vaughn et al., 1992). Such babies may elicit parental behaviors that are not conducive to the development of secure attachment. For example, mothers of "difficult" children are less responsive to their children and report that they feel less emotionally close to them (Sheeber & Johnson, 1992; Spangler, 1990). Care givers respond to babies' behavior, just as the babies respond to care givers' behavior. The processes of attachment move in two directions.

### THE ROLE OF THE FATHER IN ATTACHMENT

Did you know that you can predict how well babies are attached to their fathers if you know how many diapers the fathers change each week? Gail Ross and her colleagues (1975) found that the more diapers the father changed, the stronger the attachment. No, there is no magical connection between diapers and love. Rather, the number of diapers the father changes roughly reflects his involvement in child rearing.

**TRUTH OR FICTION REVISITED**

*Yes, you can predict how strongly babies are attached to their fathers if you know how many diapers per week the father changes. This "diaper index" provides a rough measure of a father's involvement with his children.*

Until recently, fathers had been largely left out of the theory and research concerning attachment. A major reason was the traditional division of labor in most societies. The father was the breadwinner and the mother the primary care giver to the children. Mothers have been given the responsible roles of feeder, changer, and comforter of children. Fathers have more or less been expected to play with, enjoy, and, perhaps, discipline them (Draper, 1990).

**INVOLVEMENT OF FATHERS** How involved is the average father with his children? Fathers are just as capable as mothers of acting competently and

FIGURE 7.3

***Fathers and Attachment.*** *The number of diapers a father changes reflects his involvement in child rearing. Children develop strong attachments to fathers as well as mothers, especially if the father interacts positively and affectionately with the child.*

sensitively toward their infants (Lamb & Oppenheim, 1989; Parke & Tinsley, 1987). But studies of U.S. parents show that father–child interactions differ qualitatively and quantitatively from mother–child interactions (Lamb & Oppenheim, 1989). Mothers engage in far more interactions with their infants (Belsky et al., 1989). Most fathers spend much less time on basic child care tasks, such as feeding and diaper changing, than mothers do. Fathers are more likely to play with their children than to feed or clean them (Cowan, 1992; Lamb et al., 1992). Fathers more often than mothers engage in physical, rough-and-tumble play, such as tossing their babies into the air and poking them. Mothers are more likely to play games like pat-a-cake and peekaboo and to play games involving toys (Bretherton et al., 1993; Carson et al., 1993).

**Culture and Development: Mothers' and Fathers' Involvement with their Infants** How does the cultural context affect the involvement of mothers and fathers with their infants? Recent studies have examined variations in parents' interactions with their babies in many different cultures in Africa, Asia, and Western Europe (Nugent et al., 1991), as well as within the United States (Hossain & Roopnarine, in press). One consistent finding in both Western and Eastern societies is that mothers are usually more affectionate and attentive to their children than are fathers (Berndt et al., 1993). Some patterns of parenting, however, vary across cultures.

For example, in one study done in New Delhi, India, mothers were more likely than fathers to pick up, hold, feed, comfort, and show affection to their 1-year-old infants (Roopnarine et al., 1990). Fathers engaged in more rough play than mothers, and mothers were more likely to play peekaboo. So far, this sounds a lot like the behavior of U.S. mothers and fathers. But there were differences as well. When Indian parents held their babies, they were more likely to display affection than to comfort or play with them. This is the reverse of the American pattern. Rough physical play also was much less frequent among the Indian parents. The researchers suggest that Indian cultural values emphasizing tranquility and nonaggressiveness may account for these differences.

**FACTORS INFLUENCING INVOLVEMENT OF FATHERS** Which fathers are most likely to be involved with their infants? Fathers who are more actively involved believe that the father plays an important role in the child's development (Palkovitz, 1984). Fathers also are more involved with their infants when they have positive attitudes toward parenting and their marriage (Belsky et al., 1989; Cox et al., 1992; Noppe et al., 1991). Involved fathers are more likely to believe that infants are socially and cognitively competent (and thus, perhaps more interesting to interact with!) (Ninio & Rinotti, 1988).

**ATTACHMENT TO FATHERS** How strongly, then, do infants become attached to their fathers? The answer seems to depend on the quality of the time the father spends with the baby (Easterbrooks & Goldberg, 1984). The more positive and physically affectionate the interaction between the father and his infant, the stronger the attachment of the child (Cox et al., 1992). Infants under stress still seek out mothers more than fathers (Lamb et al., 1992b). But when observed at their natural activities in the home and other familiar settings, they seek proximity and contact with their fathers about as often as with their mothers (Lamb, 1981).

It appears that babies develop attachments for both parents at about the same time (Lamb et al., 1992b). This is interesting for two reasons. First, it flies in the face of Freudian theory, which argues that babies become more attached to their mothers—providers of "oral gratification"—during the first year. Second, most mothers provide a markedly greater amount of care giving than fathers do during the first few months.

Babies who are securely attached to one parent are likely to be securely attached to the other (Fox et al., 1991; Fox, 1992). But infants who are securely attached to only one parent are as likely to be attached to the father as to the mother (Main & Weston, 1981).

**TRUTH OR FICTION REVISITED**

*It is not true that children become attached to their mothers earlier than they become attached to their fathers. Despite the Freudian view of the special early importance of the mother, children appear to become attached to both parents at about the same time.*

### STABILITY OF ATTACHMENT

Individual patterns of attachment tend to persist when care-giving conditions remain consistent (Main & Cassidy, 1988). Attachment patterns can change, however, when conditions of child care change appreciably (Thompson, 1991a). Egeland and Sroufe (1981) followed a number of infants who were severely neglected and others who received high-quality care from 12 to 18 months of age. Attachment patterns remained stable (secure) for infants receiving fine care. However, many neglected infants changed from insecurely to securely attached over the 6-month period, sometimes because of a relationship with a supportive family member, sometimes because home life grew less tense. Other studies show that children can become less securely attached to care givers when the quality of home life deteriorates (Egeland & Farber, 1984; Thompson et al., 1982).

Even when children are adopted as late as the age of 4, they can become securely attached to their adoptive parents (Hodges & Tizard, 1989). Young children show resilience in their social and emotional development. Early insecurities apparently can be overcome.

## CULTURE AND DEVELOPMENT: DEVELOPMENT OF ATTACHMENT

Several important cross-cultural studies have led to a theory of stages of attachment. In one study, Ainsworth (1967) tracked the attachment behaviors of Ugandan infants. Over a 9-month period, she noted their efforts to maintain contact with the mother, their protests when separated, and their use of the mother as a base for exploring the environment. At first the Ugandan infants showed ***indiscriminate attachment.*** That is, they showed no particular preferences for the mother or another familiar care giver. Specific attachment to the mother, as evidenced by separation anxiety and other behaviors, began to develop at about 4 months and grew intensely by about 7 months. Fear of strangers developed 1 or 2 months later.

In another study, shown in Figure 7.4, Scottish infants showed indiscriminate attachment during the first 6 months or so after birth (Schaffer & Emerson, 1964). Then indiscriminate attachment waned. Specific attachments to the mother and other familiar care givers intensified, as demonstrated by the appearance of separation anxiety, and remained at high levels through the age of 18 months. Fear of strangers occurred a month or so after the intensity of specific attachments began to mushroom. Thus, in both this and the Ugandan study, fear of strangers followed separation anxiety and the development of specific attachments by a number of weeks. Other cross-cultural studies have found that the onset of separation anxiety occurs earliest in cultures in which mothers care for their infants almost exclusively and are in close physical contact with them for extended periods (Crowell & Waters, 1990).

From studies such as these, Ainsworth and her colleagues (1978) identified the following three phases of attachment:

1. The ***initial-preattachment phase,*** which lasts from birth to about 3 months and is characterized by indiscriminate attachment.
2. The ***attachment-in-the-making phase,*** which occurs at about 3 or 4 months and is characterized by preference for familiar figures.
3. The ***clear-cut-attachment phase,*** which occurs at about 6 or 7 months and is characterized by intensified dependence on the primary care giver—usually the mother.

Most infants have more than one adult care giver, however, and are likely to form multiple attachments—to father, day-care providers, grandparents, and other care givers, as well as to mother. In most cultures, single attachments are the exception, not the rule (Howes & Matheson, 1992a).

***Indiscriminate attachment*** The display of attachment behaviors toward any person.

***Initial-preattachment phase*** The first phase in the formation of bonds of attachment, lasting from birth to about 3 months of age and characterized by indiscriminate attachment.

***Attachment-in-the-making phase*** The second phase in the development of attachment, occurring at 3 or 4 months of age and characterized by preference for familiar figures.

***Clear-cut-attachment phase*** The third phase in the development of attachment, occurring at 6 or 7 months of age and characterized by intensified dependence on the primary care giver.

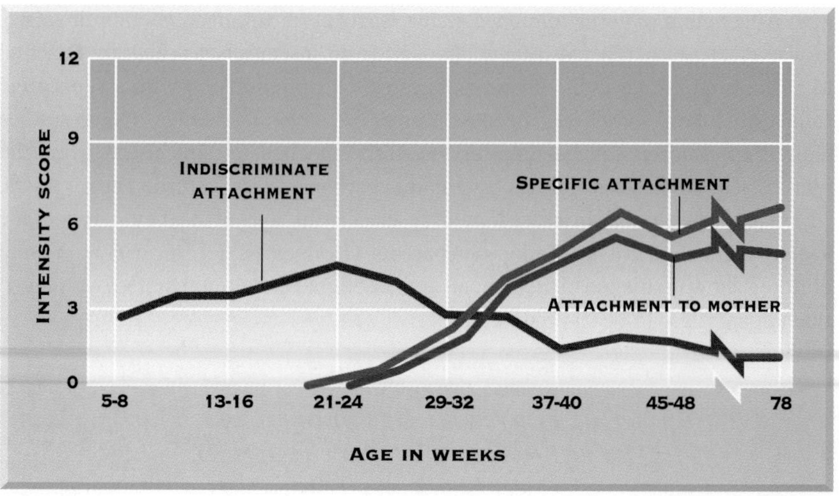


FIGURE 7.4

**THE DEVELOPMENT OF ATTACHMENT.** *During the first 6 months, infants tend to show indiscriminate attachment. Indiscriminate attachment then wanes while specific attachments grow intense and remain at high levels. Fear of strangers develops a month or so after the intensity of specific attachments begins to blossom.*

## *THEORETICAL INTERLUDE: THEORIES OF ATTACHMENT*

Attachment, like so many other behavior patterns, seems to develop as a result of the interaction of nature and nurture. Different theorists emphasize one or the other of these influences.

**A COGNITIVE VIEW OF ATTACHMENT** The cognitive view focuses on the contention that an infant must have developed some concept of object permanence before specific attachment becomes possible. In other words, if care givers are to be missed when absent, the infant must perceive that they continue to exist. We have seen that infants tend to develop specific attachments at about 6 to 7 months. In support of the cognitive view, recall that rudimentary object permanence concerning physical objects develops somewhat earlier (Chapter 6).

**A BEHAVIORAL VIEW OF ATTACHMENT: CARE GIVER AS REINFORCER** Early in the century, behaviorists argued that attachment behaviors are learned through conditioning. Care givers feed their infants and tend to their other physiological needs. Thus, infants associate their care givers with gratification and learn to approach them to meet their needs. From this perspective, a care giver becomes a conditioned reinforcer.

The feelings of gratification that are associated with meeting specific needs generalize into feelings of security when the care giver is present.

**PSYCHOANALYTIC VIEWS OF ATTACHMENT: CARE GIVER AS LOVE OBJECT** Psychoanalytic theorists view the development of attachment somewhat differently from behaviorists. The care giver, usually the mother, becomes not just a "reinforcer" but a love object who forms the basis for all later attachments.

In both the psychoanalytic and behaviorist views, however, the care givers's role in gratifying the child's needs is of paramount importance. You will recall from Chapter 2 that Sigmund Freud emphasized the importance of oral activities such as eating in the first year of life. Freud believed that the infant becomes emotionally attached to the mother during this time, because she is the primary satisfier of the infant's needs for food and sucking.

Remember from the same chapter that Erik Erikson also believed the first year to be critical for developing a sense of trust in the mother. This sense of trust fosters feelings of attachment. Erikson stressed that the mother's sensitivity to all the child's needs, and not just the need for food, is essential for the child to develop trust and attachment.

**The Harlows' View of Attachment: Care Giver as a Source of Contact Comfort** Harry and Margaret Harlow conducted an ingenious series of experiments that demonstrate feeding is not as critical to the attachment process as Freud suggested (Harlow & Harlow, 1966). In one study, the Harlows placed rhesus monkey infants in cages with two surrogate mothers, as shown in Figure 7.5. One "mother" was made from wire mesh, from which a baby bottle was extended. The other surrogate mother was made of soft, cuddly terry cloth. Infant monkeys spent most of their time clinging to the cloth mother, even though she did not offer food. The Harlows concluded that monkeys—and perhaps humans—have a need for ***contact comfort*** that is as basic as the need for food. Gratification of the need for contact comfort, rather than hunger, might be why infant monkeys (and babies) cling to their mothers. Put another way, it might be that the path to a baby's heart is through its skin, not its stomach.

**An Ethological View of Attachment: Smiling and Imprinting** ***Ethologists*** note that for many animals, attachment is an inborn ***fixed action pattern (FAP).*** The FAP of attachment, like other FAPs, is theorized to occur in the presence of a species-specific ***releasing stimulus.*** According to John Bowlby (1988; Ainsworth & Bowlby, 1991), one component of the FAP of attachment in humans, and its releasing stimulus, is a baby's smile in response to a human voice or face (see Figure 7.6). Bowlby proposes that the baby's smile helps ensure survival by eliciting affection in its care givers. By 2 to 3 months of age, the human face begins to elicit a ***social smile*** (Emde et al., 1976). The development of smiling seems to follow the same sequence in many cultures. Smiling responses increase dramatically between 2 to 4 months of age in Native American infants, in infants reared in Israeli middle-class homes and on the kibbutz, in Bedouin Arabs, African hunter-gatherers and agriculturists, and infants in metropolitan Japan (Werner, 1988).

***Contact comfort*** The pleasure derived from physical contact with another; a hypothesized need or drive for physical contact with another.

***Ethologist*** A scientist who studies the behavior patterns that are characteristic of various species.

***Fixed action pattern (FAP)*** An instinct; a stereotyped form of behavior that is characteristic of a species and is triggered by a releasing stimulus.

***Releasing stimulus*** A stimulus that elicits a fixed action pattern (FAP).

***Social smile*** A smile that occurs in response to a human voice or face.

FIGURE 7.5

**Attachment in Infant Monkeys.** *Although this rhesus monkey infant is fed by the "wire mother," it spends most of its time clinging to a soft, cuddly "terry-cloth mother." It knows where to get a meal, but contact comfort is apparently a more central determinant of attachment in infant monkeys (and infant humans?) than is the feeding process.*

FIGURE 7.6

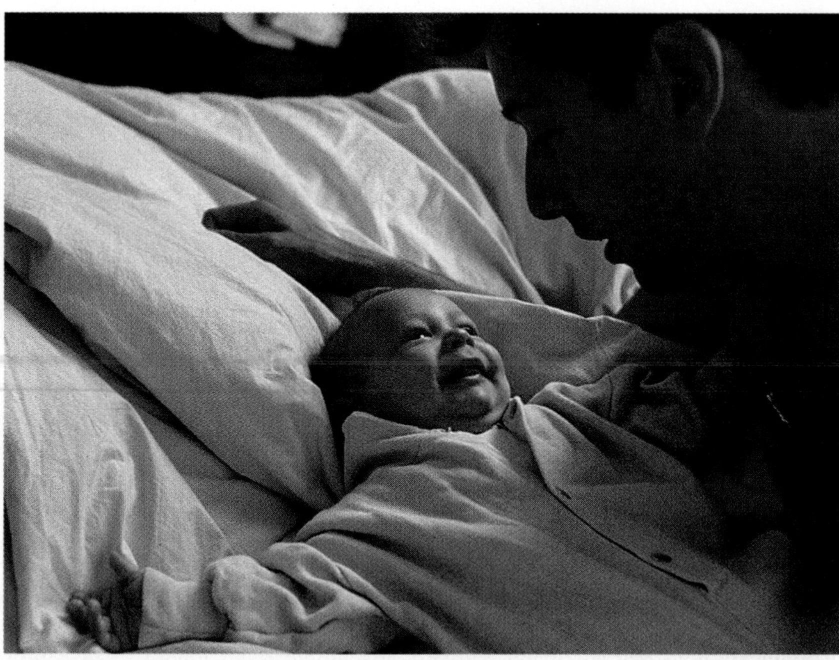

***SMILING.*** *Smiling in babies is elicited by human facial features and seems to be an important ingredient in the formation of parent–infant bonds of attachment.*

The FAP of attachment is also theorized to occur during a ***critical period*** of life. If it does not, it may never occur. During this period, young animals are capable of forming an instinctive attachment to their mothers or parents if the releasing stimuli are present. Waterfowl become attached during the critical period to the first moving object they encounter. It is as if the image of the moving object becomes ''imprinted'' upon the young animal, so the formation of an attachment in this manner is called ***imprinting.***

Ethologist Konrad Lorenz (1962, 1981) became well known when pictures of his ''family'' of goslings were made public (see Figure 7.7). How did Lorenz acquire his ''family''? He was present when the goslings hatched and during their critical periods, and he allowed them to follow him. The critical period for geese and ducks begins when they first engage in locomotion and ends when they develop fear of strangers. The goslings followed Lorenz persistently, ran to him when frightened, honked with distress at his departure, and tried to overcome barriers placed between them and him. If you substitute crying for honking, it all sounds rather human.

***Critical period*** A period of development during which a releasing stimulus can elicit a fixed action pattern (FAP).

***Imprinting*** The process by which some animals exhibit the fixed action pattern (FAP) of attachment in response to a releasing stimulus. The FAP occurs during a critical period and is difficult to modify.

If imprinting occurs with children, it does not follow the mechanics that apply to waterfowl. As shown by the 4-year-old adoptees who formed strong attachments to their adoptive parents (Tizard et al., 1976), there is apparently no critical period for the development of attachment in humans. Klaus and Kennell (1978) suggested that there might be a weaker ''maternal-sensitive'' period, governed by hormones, for becoming attached to a newborn. But the evidence for even this watered-down sensitive period is questionable, as noted in Chapter 4.

TRUTH OR FICTION REVISITED

*It is not true that children must become attached to their parents before a critical period elapses for attachment bonds to form properly.*

**FIGURE 7.7**

***IMPRINTING.*** *Quite a following? Konrad Lorenz may not look like Mommy to you, but these goslings became attached to him because he was the first moving object they perceived and followed. This type of attachment process is referred to as* imprinting.

In sum, attachment in humans appears to be a complex process that continues for months or years. Certainly, it includes learning in the broad sense of the term—as opposed to a limited, mechanistic-behaviorist sense. Attachment involves infant perceptual and cognitive processes, and the type of attachment that develops is related to the quality of the care-giver–infant relationship. The care giving itself, and infant responsiveness, such as infant smiling, appear to spur the development of attachment. Let us now turn our attention to a number of circumstances that may interfere with the development of attachment: social deprivation, child abuse, and autism.

## WHEN ATTACHMENT FAILS

We have looked at the effects on attachment of rearing children in a group setting (the kibbutz) in which children continue to have contact with their parents. What happens when children are reared in group settings such as some orphanages where they have no contact with parents and little contact with other care givers? What happens when parents neglect or abuse their children? In both cases, children's attachments may be impaired. Some children also fail to develop attachments as a result of a disorder called *autism.* In this section, we consider the effect of social deprivation, child abuse, and autism on the development of attachment.

### *SOCIAL DEPRIVATION*

Studies of children reared in institutions where they receive little social stimulation from care givers are limited in that they are correlational. In other words, family factors that led to the children's placement in institutions may also have contributed to their developmental problems. Ethical considerations prevent us from conducting experiments in which we randomly assign children to social deprivation. However, experiments of this kind have been undertaken with rhesus monkeys, and their results are consistent with those of the correlational studies of children. Let us first examine these animal experiments and then turn to the correlational research involving children.

**EXPERIMENTS WITH MONKEYS** As we noted earlier, the Harlows and their colleagues conducted a number of studies of rhesus monkeys who were ''reared by'' wire-mesh and terry-cloth surrogate mothers. In later studies, rhesus monkeys were reared without even this questionable ''social'' support. They were raised without seeing any other animal, whether monkey or human.

The Harlows (Harlow et al., 1971) found that rhesus infants reared in this most solitary confinement later avoided contact with other monkeys. They did not engage in the characteristic playful chasing and romping. Instead, they cowered in the presence of others and failed to respond to them. Nor did they make any effort to fend off attacks by other monkeys. Rather, they sat in the corner, clutching themselves and rocking back and forth. Females who later had children of their own tended to ignore or abuse them (Higley et al., 1989).

Can the damage done by social deprivation be overcome? When monkeys deprived for 6 months or more are placed with younger, 3- to 4-month-old females for a couple of hours a day, the younger monkeys make efforts to initiate social interaction with their deprived elders (see Figure 7.8). Many of the deprived monkeys begin to play with the youngsters after a few weeks and many of them eventually expand their social contacts to other rhesus monkeys of various ages (Suomi et al., 1972). Perhaps of greater interest is the related finding that socially withdrawn 4- and 5-year-old children make gains in their social and emotional development when they are provided with younger playmates (Furman et al., 1979).

**STUDIES WITH CHILDREN** Institutionalized children whose material needs are met but who receive little social stimulation from care givers encounter problems in their physical, intellectual, social, and emotional development (Grusec & Lytton, 1988; Provence & Lipton, 1962; Spitz, 1965). Spitz (1965) noted that many institutionalized children appear to develop a syndrome characterized by withdrawal and depression. They show progressively less interest in their world and become progressively inactive. Some of them die.

Consider a report of life in one institution (Provence & Lipton, 1962). Infants were maintained in separate cubicles for most of their first year to ward off infectious diseases. Adults tended to them only to feed and change their diapers. As a rule, baby bottles were propped up in the infants' cribs. Attendants rarely responded to the babies' cries, and the infants were rarely played with or spoken to. By the age of 4 months, the infants in this institution showed little interest in adults. They rarely tried to gain their attention, even when in distress. A few months later, some of them sat withdrawn in their cribs and rocked back and forth, almost like the Harlows' monkeys. Language deficiencies were striking. As the first year progressed, little babbling was heard within the infants' cubicles. None was speaking even one word at 12 months.

Why do children whose material needs are met show such dramatic deficiencies? Is it because they do not receive the love and affection of a mother or stable surrogate mother? Or is it that they do not receive adequate sensory or social stimulation?

The answer may, in part, depend on the age of the child. Studies by Leon Yarrow and his colleagues (1971; Yarrow & Goodwin, 1973) suggest that deficiencies in sensory stimulation and social interaction may cause more problems than lack of love in infants who are too young to have developed specific attachments. However, once infants have developed specific attachments, separation from their primary care givers can lead to major problems.

In the first study, the development of 53 adopted children was followed over a 10-year period (Yarrow et al., 1971). The researchers compared the development of three subgroups: (a) children who were transferred to their permanent adoptive homes almost immediately after birth; (b) children who were given temporary foster mothers and then transferred to permanent adoptive homes before they were 6 months old; and (c) children who were transferred from temporary foster mothers to their permanent adoptive homes after they were 6 months old. At the age of 10, children in the first two groups showed no differences in social and emotional development. However, children in the third group showed significantly less ability to relate to other people. Perhaps their deficits resulted from being separated from their initial foster mothers, after they had become attached to them.

In the second study, Yarrow and Goodwin (1973) followed the development of 70 adopted children who were separated from temporary foster parents between birth and the age of 16 months. The researchers found strong correlations between the age at which the children were separated and feeding and sleeping problems,

**FIGURE 7.8**

***MONKEY THERAPISTS.*** *In the top photo, a 3- to 4-month-old rhesus monkey "therapist" tries to soothe a monkey who was reared in social isolation. The deprived monkey remains withdrawn. She clutches herself into a ball and rocks back and forth. The bottom photo was taken several weeks later and shows that deprived monkeys given young "therapists" can learn to play and adjust to community life. Socially withdrawn preschoolers have similarly profited from exposure to younger peers.*

FIGURE 7.9

**THE DEVELOPMENT OF ADOPTED CHILDREN SEPARATED FROM TEMPORARY FOSTER PARENTS.** *The older the child at time of separation, the more likely it is that behavioral disturbances will occur. (Source: Yarrow & Goodwin, 1973).*

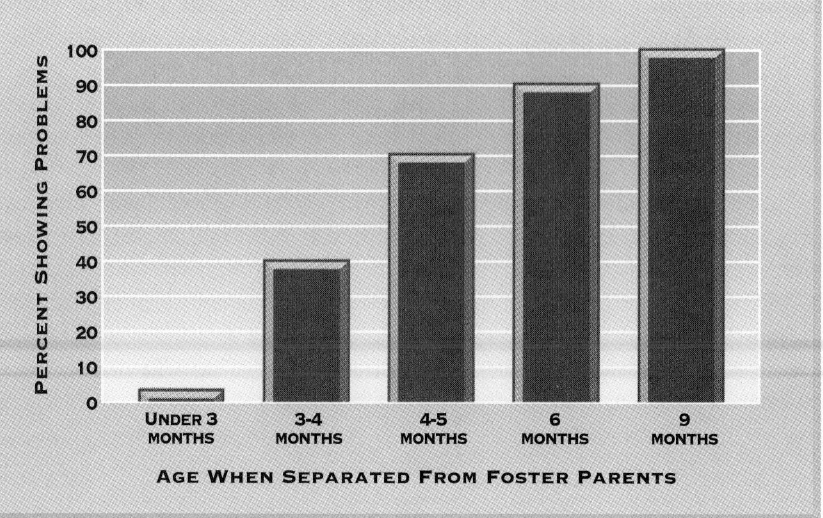


decreased social responsiveness, and extremes in attachment behaviors (see Figure 7.9). Disturbed attachment behaviors included excessive clinging to the new mother and violent rejection of her. None of the children who were separated from the initial foster mothers prior to the age of 3 months showed moderate or severe disturbances. All of the children who were separated at 9 months or older did show such disturbances. From 40 to 90 percent of the children separated between the ages of 3 and 9 months showed moderate to severe disturbances. The incidence of problems increased as the age advanced.

The Yarrow studies suggest that babies in institutions, at least up to the age of 3 months or so, may require general sensory and social stimulation more than a specific relationship with a primary care giver. After the age of 3 months, some disturbance is likely if there is instability in the care-giving staff. By the ages of 6 to 9 months, disturbance seems to be guaranteed if there is instability in the position of primary care giver. Fortunately, there is also evidence that children show some capacity to recover from early social deprivation.

**THE CAPACITY TO RECOVER FROM SOCIAL DEPRIVATION** Studies with animals and children show that early social deprivation is linked to developmental deficits. However, other studies suggest that infants also have powerful capacities to recover from deprivation.

Kagan and Klein (1973) report that many children may be able to recover fully from 13 or 14 months of deprivation. The natives in an isolated Guatemalan village believe that fresh air and sunshine will make children ill. Children are thus kept in windowless huts until they can walk. They are also played with infrequently. During their isolation, the infants behave apathetically, and they are physically and socially retarded when they start to walk. However, by 11 years of age, they are alert, active, and as intellectually competent as U.S. children of the same age.

A longitudinal study of orphanage children also provides dramatic evidence of the ability of children to recover from social deprivation (Skeels, 1966). In this study, a group of 19-month-old apparently retarded children was placed in the care of older institutionalized girls who spent a great deal of time playing with, talking to, and generally nurturing them. This placement occurred many months past the age at which specific attachments develop. However, 4 years after being placed with the girls, the ''retarded'' children made dramatic gains in intelligence-test scores, whereas children remaining in the orphanage showed declines in IQ scores.

The children placed in the care of the older girls also appeared to be generally well-adjusted. By the time Skeels reported on their progress in 1966, most were married and were rearing children of their own who showed no intellectual or social deficits. Unfortunately, many of the children who had been left in the orphanage were still in some type of institutional setting. Few of them showed normal social and emotional development. Few were functioning as independent adults.

The good news from this and other studies is that many children who have been exposed to early social deprivation can catch up in their social and emotional development and lead normal adult lives if they receive individual attention and environmental stimulation (Landesman, 1990). The bad news is that society has not yet allocated the resources to give all children the opportunity to do so.

## *Child Abuse and Neglect*

So far, we have examined what happens when children are reared in settings in which their contact with parents either is reduced or absent. But living with one's parents, unfortunately, does not guarantee that a child will receive tender loving care. Unfortunately, there's no place like home—for violence (see Figure 7.10). Consider the following statistics from a national survey of 1,428 parents (Straus & Gelles, 1990):

- 54.9 percent of parents have slapped or spanked their children.
- 30.7 percent of parents have pushed, grabbed, or shoved their children.
- 9.7 percent have hit their children with an object.
- 2.7 percent have thrown something at their children.
- 1.3 percent have kicked or bitten their children, or hit them with their fists.
- .6 percent have beaten up their children.
- .2 percent have threatened their children with a knife or gun.
- .2 percent have actually used a knife or a gun on their children.

Nearly 3 million children in the United States are reported to be neglected or abused each year by their parents or adult caretakers (McWhirter et al., 1993; Shapiro, 1993). Of these, more than 150,000 are sexually abused (Trickett & Putnam, 1993). Researchers believe that many cases of child abuse go unreported and that the actual incidence is much higher (Emery, 1989; Giovannoni, 1989). The rate of reported child abuse in 1990 was more than four times the rate in 1970. Although some of this increase may be a result of improving reporting procedures, it appears that abuse itself is increasing at an alarming pace (Miringoff, 1992).

Six different types of child maltreatment are recognized (U.S. Department of Health and Human Services, 1988):

- Physical abuse: actions causing pain and physical injury
- Sexual abuse: sexual molestation, exploitation, and intercourse

FIGURE 7.10

**ABUSED CHILD.** *Tragically, nearly 3 million children in the United States are reported to be neglected or abused each year.*

- Emotional abuse: actions impairing the child's emotional, social, or intellectual functioning
- Physical neglect: failure to provide adequate food, shelter, clothing, or medical care
- Emotional neglect: failure to provide adequate nurturance and emotional support
- Educational neglect: permitting or forcing the child to be truant

Neglect is more common that abuse. Although blatant abuse is more horrifying, more injuries, illnesses, and deaths result from neglect (Finkelhor & Dziuba-Leatherman, 1994; Wolock & Horowitz, 1984).

**EFFECTS OF CHILD ABUSE** Sad to say, abused children show an alarming incidence of personal and social problems and abnormal behavior patterns. Maltreated children are more aggressive, angry, and noncompliant than other children. At the same time, they also are more withdrawn and avoid interacting with peers. Maltreated children are more likely to be insecurely attached to their parents. They rarely express positive emotions, have lower self-esteem, and show impaired cognitive functioning (Cicchetti & Barnett, 1991; Salzinger et al., 1993; Sternberg et al., 1993; Toth et al., 1992). As they get older, maltreated children are at greater risk for developing such problems as delinquency, academic failure, substance abuse, and emotional and behavioral problems (Eckenrode et al., 1993; Kendall-Tackett et al., 1993; Trickett & Putnam, 1993; Watkins & Bentovim, 1992).

**CAUSES OF CHILD ABUSE** A number of factors contribute to the probability that parents will abuse their children. They include situational stress, a history of child abuse in at least one of the parents' families of origin, lack of adequate coping and problem-solving skills, deficiency of basic child-rearing skills, unrealistic expectations of a child at a given developmental level, and substance abuse (Famularo et al., 1992; Kaplan, 1991; Vasta, 1990).

There are many sources of stress, including such life changes as parental conflict, divorce or separation, the loss of a job, moving, and the birth of a new family member. Unemployment seems to be a particularly predisposing life change. Child abuse increases among the unemployed (Price, 1992; Straus & Smith, 1990; Wolfner & Gelles, 1993).

Stress is created by crying infants themselves (Green et al., 1987). Ironically, infants who are already in pain of some kind and relatively difficult to soothe may be more likely to be abused (Frodi, 1985). Abusive parents may find the cries of their infants to be particularly aversive, and so the infants' crying may precipitate abusive behavior (Crowe & Zeskind, 1992; Zeskind & Shingler, 1991). Children who act disobediently, inappropriately, or unresponsively also are at greater risk of abuse (Bugental et al., 1990; Trickett & Kuczynski, 1986). Why? Parents tend to become frustrated and irritated when their children show prolonged signs of distress or misbehavior. Abusive mothers are more likely than nonabusive mothers to assume that their children's misbehavior is intentional, even when it is not (Bauer & Twentyman, 1985). Within our culture, intentional misconduct is seen as more deserving of punishment than incidental misconduct. Abusive mothers also tend to believe that they have little control over their child's misbehaviors (Bugental et al., 1989). Parents who abuse often have high standards of achievement for the child, but at the same time, they are dissatisfied with the child and don't enjoy parenting very much (Trickett et al., 1991).

What of the role of failure of attachment in abuse? In Chapter 4, we noted that parents of preterm children have more difficulty becoming attached to them. One reason may be that the early parent–infant relationship is interrupted by hospital procedures. Preterm children are more likely than their full-term counterparts to be abused (Crittenden & Ainsworth, 1989). With prematurity, of course, we are not only dealing with possible failures in attachment. Preterm children are also more likely to develop illnesses and other problems. As a consequence, they may cry more frequently and generally make more demands on their parents.

Abusive parenting tends to run in families (Simons et al., 1991), but it must be emphasized that *the majority of children who are abused do not abuse their own children* (Kaufman & Zigler, 1989). This fact is extremely important because many adults who were victims of child abuse are (unjustifiably) concerned that they are destined to abuse their own children. One study found that abused mothers who were able to break the cycle of abuse were more likely to have received emotional support from a nonabusive adult during childhood, to have participated in therapy in some point in their lives, and to have had a nonabusive and supportive mate (Egeland et al., 1988).

**TRUTH OR FICTION REVISITED**

*Child abusers have, in fact, frequently been the victims of child abuse themselves. Many child abusers have been exposed to violent role models. Let us note, however, that the majority of people who were abused as children do not abuse their own children.*

Why do *some* victims of child abuse become abusive themselves? One possibility is that their parents serve as role models. If children grow up observing their parents using violence as a means of coping with stress and feelings of anger, they are less likely to learn to diffuse anger through techniques such as humor, verbal expression of feelings, reasoning, or even counting to 10 to let the anger pass.

Exposure to violence in their own homes may also lead some children to accept family violence as a norm. They may see little or nothing wrong in it.

Certainly, there are any number of ''justifications'' they can find for violence—if they are seeking them. One is the age-old adage, ''Spare the rod, spoil the child.'' Another is the belief that they are hurting their children ''for their own good''—to discourage behavior that is likely to get them into trouble.

Still another ''justification'' of child abuse is the sometimes cloudy distinction between the occasional swat on the rear end and spanking or other types of repeated hitting. Child abusers may argue that all parents hit their children (which is not true), and they may claim not to understand why outsiders are making such a fuss about their private family behavior. Child abusers who come from families in which they were subjected to abuse also may be more likely to have the (incorrect) perspective that ''everyone does it.''

Nevertheless, child abuse must be conceptualized and dealt with as a crime of violence. Whether or not child abusers happen to be victims of abuse themselves, child abusers are criminals and their children must be protected from them.

**WHAT TO DO** Dealing with child abuse is a frustrating task. Social agencies and the courts can find it as difficult to distinguish between spanking and abuse as many abusers do. Because of the belief in this country that parents have the right to rear their children as they wish, police and the courts have also historically tried to avoid involvement in domestic quarrels and family disputes (Hart & Brassard, 1987).

However, the alarming incidence of child abuse has spawned new efforts at detection and prevention (Emery, 1989; Gelles & Conte, 1990; Willis et al., 1992). Many states require helping professionals such as psychologists and physicians to report any suspicion of child abuse. Many states legally require *anyone* who suspects child abuse to report it to authorities.

A number of techniques have been developed to help prevent child abuse (Olds & Henderson, 1989; Willis et al., 1992). One approach focuses on strengthening parenting skills among the general population (Altepeter & Walker, 1992). Parent-education classes in high school are an example of this approach.

A second approach targets groups at high risk for abuse, such as poor, single teen mothers (Kaufman & Zigler, 1992; Roberts et al., 1991). In some programs, for example, home visitors help the new mother develop skills in parenting and home management.

A third technique focuses on presenting information about abuse and providing support to families. For instance, many locales have child abuse hotlines. Private citizens who suspect child abuse may call for advice. Parents who are having difficulty controlling aggressive impulses toward their children are encouraged to call. Some hotlines are serviced by groups such as Parents Anonymous, whose members have had similar difficulties and may help callers diffuse feelings of anger in less harmful ways.

Other potentially helpful measures include increased publicity on the dimensions of the child-abuse problem. The public may also need more education about where an occasional swat on the behind ends and child abuse begins. Perhaps the format for such education could be something like, ''If you are doing such and such, make no mistake about it—you are abusing your child.''

## AUTISM

***Autism*** A developmental disorder characterized by extreme aloneness, communication problems, intolerance of change, and ritualistic behavior.

In this chapter, we have been examining the development of attachment. Sadly, there are some children who fail to develop attachments to others. These children suffer from a severe disorder known as ***autism.*** Autism strikes 4 to 5 children in 10,000, usually before the age of 36 months (Hertzig & Shapiro, 1990). It is four to five times more common among boys than girls, but when girls are

FIGURE 7.11

**AUTISM.** *The most poignant feature of autism is the child's utter aloneness.*

affected, they are more severely affected (Olley, 1992; Volkmar, 1991). Perhaps the most poignant feature of infantile autism is the child's utter aloneness (see Figure 7.11). Autistic children are uninterested in social interaction, and their attachment to others is weak or absent. Other symptoms of autism include communication problems, intolerance of change, and ritualistic or stereotypical behavior (Baron-Cohen & Bolton, 1993; Rutter, 1991).

Parents of autistic children frequently report that they were "good babies." This usually means that they made few demands. However, as autistic children develop, they tend to shun affectionate contacts such as hugging, cuddling, and kissing (Borden & Ollendick, 1992; Olley, 1992).

Their speech development lags. There is a dearth of babbling and communicative gesturing during the first year. They may show ***mutism, echolalia,*** and pronoun reversal, referring to themselves as "you" or "he." About half of autistic children develop some functional language by middle childhood (Wetherby & Prizant, 1992). But even those who speak exhibit unusual language characteristics and problems in using speech in social interactions (Stone & Caro-Martinez, 1990; Volden & Lord, 1991).

Autistic children become bound by ritual in their demands of others and in their own behavior. Even slight changes in routines or in physical aspects of the environment may cause extreme distress (Howlin & Yule, 1990). Autistic children also show deficits in peer play, imaginative play, imitation skills, and emotional expression (Stone & Lemanek, 1990; Yirmiya et al., 1992).

**CAUSES OF AUTISM** Psychoanalytic and learning-theory approaches have argued that children become autistic in response to rejection by, or lack of adequate reinforcement from, their parents. From this perspective, autistic behavior patterns shut out the cold outside world. But recent evidence makes it clear that deviant child-rearing practices do not account for autism. Parents of autistic children do not exhibit specific deficits in child-rearing practices, nor do they show unusual personality traits (Volkmar, 1991; Borden & Ollendick, 1992).

Various lines of evidence suggest the importance of neurobiological factors in autism. The role of genetic mechanisms has been examined in twin studies.

***Mutism*** The inability or refusal to speak.

***Echolalia*** The automatic repetition of sounds or words.

In one twin study, 10 of 11 identical twins of autistic children showed the disorder, as compared with none of 10 fraternal twins of autistic children (Steffenburg et al., 1989). This striking difference in concordance rates for identical and fraternal twins suggests the importance of hereditary factors in the development of autism. Moreover, autism is sometimes associated with a variety of genetic abnormalities, such as phenylketonuria (PKU) and Down syndrome (Hynd & Hooper, 1992).

Many autistic children also have abnormal brain wave patterns or seizures. In addition, autistic individuals exhibit elevated levels of serotonin, a neurotransmitter (Anderson & Cohen, 1991; Tsai & Ghaziuddin, 1992). These findings indicate some degree of central nervous system involvement.

**TREATMENT AND OUTCOME** The effectiveness of treatment for autism is far from encouraging. Behavioral methods for attacking autistic behavior patterns have met with some success. For example, operant conditioning methods have encouraged autistic children to develop social skills, to pay attention to a therapist, and to stop self-mutilative behavior (Cox & Schopler, 1991; Vitulano & Tebes, 1991). O. Ivar Lovaas and his colleagues (Lovaas et al., 1989; McEachin et al., 1993) have reported the results of a long-term experiment with 19 autistic children, who at age 2 or 3 received 40 hours of one-to-one behavior modification per week for at least 2 years. By the age of 11, most of the children in the program were functioning much better than those in a control group. Nine of the children were attending regular classes and scored within the normal range on tests of intelligence and social adjustment. The results are somewhat confounded by the fact that a number of autistic children were not accepted into the program because of extremely low levels of functioning. Still, the study offers some encouragement.

There are also reports now and then that drugs such as tranquilizers and serotonin-reducing medications are showing some promise with autistic children (Tsai, 1992). A recent study found that clomipramine, a drug often used to treat obsessive–compulsive disorders, decreased or eliminated a variety of symptoms in 75 percent of a group of autistic children (Gordon et al., 1993). Other approaches have included educational mainstreaming, involvement of families in treatment, and residential programs (Berkell, 1992; V. M. Durand, 1992; Handleman, 1992; Powers, 1992).

Over the years, only a small minority of autistic children have developed into adults who live independently and hold jobs (Baron-Cohen & Bolton, 1993; Goleman, 1993; Szatmari et al., 1989). Those children who develop useful verbal skills and who have an IQ in the normal range are the most likely to achieve satisfactory social adjustment in adulthood (Howlin & Yule, 1990).

*Unfortunately, it is not true that children outgrow autism. Most are not able to live independent lives as adults.*

We have been examining the development of attachment and some of the circumstances that may interfere with its development. In recent years, a lively debate has sprung up concerning the effects of day care on children's attachment, as well as on their social and cognitive development. Let us turn now to a consideration of these issues.

## DAY CARE

Fewer than 7 percent of U.S. families now fit the model of a breadwinner husband and a full-time-homemaker wife (Silverstein, 1991). More than two-thirds of today's mothers are employed outside the home. This figure includes more than 55 percent of mothers of children less than 1 year old (U.S. Bureau of the Census, 1992). Financial pressures are likely to increase this number.

When both parents of young children spend the day on the job, the children must be taken care of by others, although many older children take care of themselves after school until their parents come home. Studies of children at least 9 years of age who care for themselves after school have found no significant problems on several measures of psychological, social, and intellectual functioning (Berman et al., 1992; Diamond et al., 1989; Galambos & Maggs, 1991; Vandell & Ramanan, 1991; Woodard & Fine, 1991).

**TRUTH OR FICTION REVISITED**

*Children who care for themselves after school do not appear to be at special risk for developing psychological and social problems.*

But what of younger children whose care is entrusted to others while their parents are at work? Is their attachment to parents affected? What about their social and cognitive development? In this section, we examine different types of day-care arrangements and then consider the effects of day care on the child's development.

### *WHAT IS DAY CARE LIKE?*

Close to 6 million U.S. preschool children now receive some form of day care (U.S. Bureau of the Census, 1992). There are four major types of day care:

**FIGURE 7.12**

**MATERNAL EMPLOYMENT.** *More than two-thirds of mothers in the United States are employed outside the home. This figure includes more than 55 percent of mothers of children less than 1 year old.*

group day care, family day care, in-home care, and care by relatives outside the immediate family (Hofferth et al., 1991). In *group day care,* children receive care in a nursery school or day-care center that may be private but is frequently affiliated with a university, church, housing project, or community agency. *Family day care* is provided by parents who take the children of others into their homes. In a number of states, people who offer family day care must be licensed. *In-home care* (baby-sitting) is care in the child's home by a nonrelative. Finally, relatives may look after the child either in their own home or the child's home.

Even when the mother is employed, the most common arrangement for infants and toddlers is to be cared for by one of their parents. The parents may work alternate shifts in order to share child-care responsibilities (Caruso, 1992). Family day care is the second most common arrangement for infants and toddlers. Group day care is the most popular form of child care for older preschoolers (Hofferth et al., 1991).

Children's experiences in day care vary. Some children are placed in centers or day-care homes for a few hours a week, and others for the entire day, 5 days a week. Some day-care centers or homes have an adult care giver for every three children, and others place as many as 12 children in the care of one adult (Hofferth & Phillips, 1991). Infants require more care than older children. Thus, a care giver in a day-care center typically is assigned no more than 4 or 5 infants under 18 months of age, but might be given responsibility for 10 or 11 3-year-olds (Hayes et al., 1990). The purposes and personnel of day-care settings also vary. Some programs are intended to provide early cognitive stimulation to prepare children for entry into elementary school. Others focus on custodial care and entertainment. Some have college-educated personnel. Others have care givers who function on the basis of life experience or specific training. Standards for the licensing of day-care centers and homes vary from locale to locale. Parents, therefore, need to determine the adequacy of the day-care setting they are considering for their children.

Most parents want day-care centers and homes to provide more than the basics of food, warmth, and security. They want the care givers in these settings to stimulate their children intellectually, to provide a variety of toys and games, and to provide successful peer interactions and experience in relating to adults other than family members.

What should parents look for when they are in the process of selecting a day-care center or family day-care home for their child? Some suggestions are offered in Developing Today.

## *How Does Day Care Influence Bonds of Attachment?*

Many parents wonder whether day care will affect their children's attachment to them. After all, the child will be spending more hours away from them at a tender age. During these periods, their child's needs will be met by outsiders. Parents also have mixed feelings about day care. If they had the time and money, most parents would prefer to care for their children personally. And so parents often feel some guilt about placing their children in day care.

Are such concerns valid? The issue has been hotly debated. Some studies have found that infants who are in day care full-time (more than 20 hours a week) are somewhat more likely than children without day-care experience to show insecure attachment in the Strange Situation (Baydar & Brooks-Gunn, 1991; Belsky & Rovine, 1988). Some psychologists have concluded from these studies that a mother who works full-time puts her infant at risk for developing emotional insecurity (Belsky, 1990a, b). Others feel that these results may be

## Developing Today

### Selecting a Day-Care Center or Home

Selecting a day-care center or home can be an overwhelming task. Standards for day-care centers and homes vary from locale to locale, so licensing is no guarantee of adequate care. To become sophisticated consumers of day care, parents can weigh factors such as the following when making a choice:

1. Is the center or home licensed? By what agency? What standards must be met to acquire a license?
2. What is the ratio of children to care givers? Everything else being equal, care givers appear to do a better job when there are fewer children in their charge. Experts recommend there be at least one care giver for every 4 children under age 2, for every 6 2-year-olds, and for every 10 children ranging from 3 to 5 years of age (Hayes et al., 1990). But it may also be of use to look beyond numbers. Quality is frequently more important than quantity.
3. What are the qualifications of the care givers? How well aware are they of children's needs and patterns of development? Research shows that children fare better when their care givers have specific training in child development (Howes, 1990; Zaslow, 1991). Years of day-care experience and formal degrees are less important. Day-care workers typically are paid poorly. Financial frustrations lead many well-qualified workers to seek work in other fields (Noble, 1993).
4. How safe is the environment? Do toys and swings seem to be in good condition? Are dangerous objects out of reach? Would strangers have a difficult time breaking in? Have children been injured in this center or home?
5. What is served at mealtime? Is it nutritious, appetizing? Will your child eat it? Some babies are placed in day care at 6 months or younger, and parents will need to know what formulas are used.
6. Which care givers will be responsible for your child? What are their backgrounds? How do they seem to relate to children?
7. With what children will your child interact and play?
8. What toys, games, books, and other educational objects are provided?
9. What facilities are present for promoting the motor development of your child? How well-supervised are children when they use new objects such as swings and tricycles?
10. Are the hours offered by the center or home convenient for your schedule?
11. Is the location of the center or home convenient?
12. Are parents permitted to visit unannounced?
13. Do you like the overall environment and feel of the center or home?

interpreted quite differently (Clark-Stewart 1989; Lamb et al., 1992a; Thompson, 1991b).

One key factor is that the Strange Situation may be less stressful for children of employed mothers than for those with nonemployed mothers and, therefore, may be a less valid indicator of attachment for them. Infants whose mothers work encounter daily separation from and reunions with their mother. Young children adapt to repeated separations from their mothers (Field, 1991c). Therefore, infants whose mothers work may be less distressed by her departure in the Strange Situation and less likely to seek her out when she returns. A second point to keep in mind is that the likelihood of insecure attachment is not much greater in day-care babies than in home-reared babies; in fact, most infants in both groups are securely attached (Clarke-Stewart, 1989; Lamb et al., 1992b).

### How Does Day Care Influence Social and Cognitive Development?

Day care generally seems to have positive influences on children's social and cognitive development. Infants with day-care experience are more peer oriented and play at higher developmental levels than do home-reared babies. Day-care children are also more likely to share their toys. They are more independent, self-confident, outgoing, and affectionate as well as more helpful and cooperative with peers and adults (Clarke-Stewart, 1991, Field, 1991b). Participation in day care also is associated with better school performance during the elementary school years, especially for children from low-income families (Andersson, 1992; Caughy et al., in press; Vandell & Ramanan, 1992). And so, day care appears to help in the formation of social skills and enhance cognitive development.

## TRUTH OR FICTION REVISITED

*Children placed in day care are in fact* more *cooperative and* more *likely to share than children who are cared for in the home.*

Some studies, however, have found that children in day care are less compliant and more aggressive toward peers and adults than are children not in day care (Belsky & Eggebeen, 1991; Honig & Park, 1993). Allison Clarke-Stewart (1989, 1990) suggests that greater aggression and noncompliance may be indicative of greater independence, rather than social maladjustment. Put another way, children with day-care experience may be more likely to think for themselves and want their own way.

There is yet another possibility. Studies of children in full-time day care or home care involve children whose parents had already chosen whether or not to use day care. It could be that preexisting personality differences in the children played a role in influencing parents to place them, or not to place them, in day care. Perhaps parents with more aggressive and less cooperative children are more highly motivated to use day care. Remember that the studies on day care have been correlational and not experimental. Infants have not been assigned at random to day care or home care. And so one must consider the possibility that any group differences preexisted and were not the result of day care.

Even if day care sometimes fosters aggressiveness and lower compliance, these outcomes are by no means inevitable (see Figure 7.13). Recent studies have found that children who attend better quality day-care centers and homes are more socially competent (for example, more considerate and friendly) than children who attend lower quality day-care centers and homes (Howes et al., 1992; Kontos, 1993; Zaslow, 1991).

Increasing numbers of parents will require day care for their children in the 1990s. Finding high-quality, affordable, reliable child care is one of the most pressing problems faced by working parents today (Benin & Chong, 1993). It would seem that a major goal for researchers and policymakers must be to ensure that high-quality day care is made available to infants and young children in order to optimize their cognitive, social, and emotional development (Lamb et al., 1992a).

On that note, let us now turn our attention to the development of emotions in infants.

## EMOTIONAL DEVELOPMENT

Emotions color our lives. We are green with envy, red with anger, blue with sorrow. Positive emotions such as love can fill our days with pleasure. Negative emotions such as fear, depression, and anger can fill us with dread and make each day a chore.

**FIGURE 7.13**

***CHILDREN IN DAY CARE.*** *Day care generally has a positive influence on children's social and cognitive development. As shown in this photo, children with day-care experience are more helpful and cooperative with other children and adults and they are more likely to share their toys.*

An ***emotion*** is a state of feeling that has physiological, situational, and cognitive components. Physiologically, when emotions are strong, our hearts may beat more rapidly and our muscles may tense. Situationally, we may feel fear in the presence of a threat and joy or relief in the presence of a loved one. Cognitively, fear is accompanied by the idea that we are in danger.

**Emotion** A state of feeling that has physiological, situational, and cognitive components.

## *THEORETICAL INTERLUDE: THEORIES OF THE DEVELOPMENT OF EMOTIONS*

There are a number of theories concerning the development of emotions. Basically they break down into two camps. The first, proposed originally by Katherine Bridges (1932), holds that we are born with a single emotion and that other emotions become differentiated as time passes. The second, proposed by Carroll Izard (1991, 1992), holds that all emotions are present and adequately differentiated at birth. However, they are not shown all at once. Instead, they emerge in response to the child's developing needs and maturational sequences.

**BRIDGES' AND SROUFE'S THEORY** On the basis of her observations of babies, Bridges proposed that newborns experience one emotion—diffuse excitement. By 3 months, two other emotions have differentiated from this general state of excitement—a negative emotion, distress, and a positive emotion, delight. By 6 months, fear, disgust, and anger will have developed from distress. By 12 months, elation and affection will have differentiated from delight. Jealousy develops from distress, and joy develops from delight—both during the second year.

Alan Sroufe (1979) has advanced Bridges' theory, focusing on the ways in which cognitive development may provide the basis for emotional development. Jealousy, for example, could not become differentiated without some understanding of object permanence (the continuing existence of people and objects) and possession.

Sroufe also links development of fear of strangers to the perceptual cognitive capacity to discriminate the faces of familiar people from those of unfamiliar people. As noted in Chapter 6, infants usually show distress at the mother's departure after they have developed a rudimentary concept of object permanence.

**IZARD'S THEORY** Carroll Izard (1991, 1992) proposes that infants are born with discrete emotional states. However, the timing of their appearance is linked to the child's cognitive development and social experiences. For example, Izard and his colleagues (1987) reported that 2-month-old babies receiving inoculations showed distress, whereas older infants showed anger.

Izard's view may sound very similar to Sroufe's. Both suggest an orderly unfolding of emotions such that they become more specific as time passes. However, in keeping with Izard's view, researchers have found that a number of different emotions appear to be shown by infants at ages earlier than those suggested by Bridges and Sroufe. In one study of emotions shown by babies during the first 3 months, 99 percent of the mothers interviewed reported that their babies showed the emotion of interest. Ninety-five percent of mothers reported joy; 84 percent, anger; 74 percent, surprise; and 58 percent, fear (Johnson et al., 1982). These figures are based on mothers' reports, and it is possible that the infants were actually showing more diffuse emotions (Murphy, 1983). Perhaps the mothers were reading specific emotions into the babies' behavior based on their own knowledge of appropriate (adult) emotional reactions to the infants' situations. This problem extends to Izard's interpretations of infants' facial expressions.

Izard (1983) claims to have found many discrete emotions at the age of 1 month by using his Maximally Discriminative Facial Movement Scoring System. Figure 7.14 shows some infant facial expressions that Izard believes are associated with the basic emotions of anger–rage, enjoyment–joy, fear–terror, and interest–excitement. Izard and his colleagues report that facial expressions indicating interest, disgust, and pain are present at birth. They and others have observed anger and sadness expressions at 2 months of age, surprise expressions at 4 months, and fear expressions at 7 months (Izard & Malatesta, 1987; Lewis et al., 1990). However, some researchers have suggested that this type of research is fraught with problems. First, observers cannot always accurately identify the emotions shown in slides or drawings of infant facial expressions (Oster et al., 1992). Second, we cannot know the exact relationship between a facial expression and an infant's inner feelings, which, of course, are private events (Camras et al., 1993). In other words, even if the drawings accurately represent young infants' facial expressions, we cannot be certain they express the specific emotions they would suggest if they were exhibited by older children and adults.

In sum, researchers agree that a handful of emotions are shown by infants during the first few months. They agree that other emotions develop in an orderly manner. They agree that emotional development is linked to cognitive development and social experience. They do not agree as to exactly when specific emotions are first shown or whether discrete emotions are present at birth.

Enough disagreement. Let us discuss an emotion that we'll all agree is very little fun: fear. We will focus on a common fear of infants, the fear of strangers.

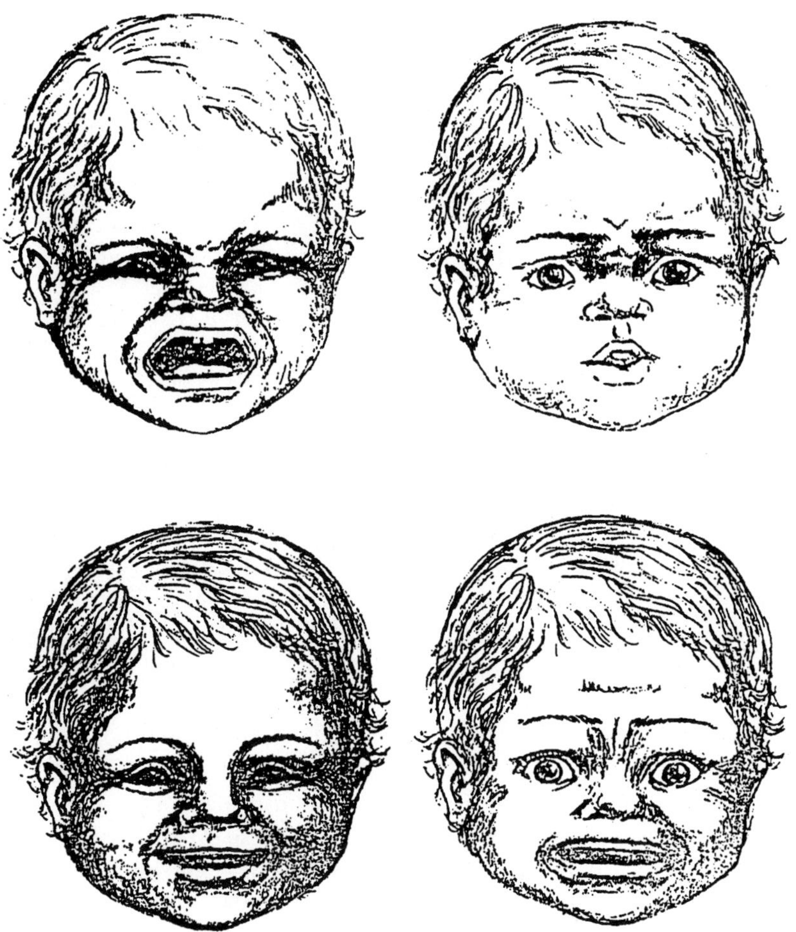

FIGURE 7.14

***Illustrations from Izard's Maximally Discriminative Facial Movement Scoring System.*** *What emotion do you think is being experienced by each of these infants? (Source: Izard, 1983).*

### Fear of Strangers

Most infants develop a fear of strangers, sometimes referred to as ***stranger anxiety.*** Stranger anxiety appears at about 6 to 9 months in many different cultures, including those of the United States, Great Britain, Guatemala, and Zambia (Smith, 1979). By 4 or 5 months, infants smile more in response to their mothers than to strangers. At this age, infants may compare the faces of strangers and their mothers, looking back and forth. Somewhat older infants show marked distress by crying, whimpering, gazing fearfully, and crawling away. Fear of strangers peaks between 9 and 12 months of age and declines in the second year (Marks, 1987). A second peak of fearfulness often occurs between 18 and 24 months, with a decline in the third year (Thompson & Limber, 1990).

***Stranger anxiety*** A fear of unfamiliar people that emerges between 6 and 9 months of age.

*Truth or Fiction Revisited*

*It is true that most children around the world develop fear of strangers at some point during the second 6 months of infancy.*

FIGURE 7.15

***STRANGER ANXIETY.*** *Infants in many cultures develop a fear of strangers, known as* stranger anxiety, *at about 6 to 9 months of age. This baby shows clear signs of distress when held by a stranger, even though mother is close by. How would* you *behave around an unfamiliar child to minimize its stranger anxiety?*

Children who have developed fear of strangers show less distress in response to strangers when their mothers are present. Babies are less likely to show fear of strangers when they are held by their mothers than when they are placed a few feet away (Thompson & Limber, 1990). Children also are less likely to show fear of strangers when they are in familiar surroundings, such as their homes, than when they are in the laboratory (Sroufe et al., 1974).

In terms of proximity, the fear response to strangers is the mirror image of attachment. Children attempt to remain near people to whom they are attached. However, the closer they are to strangers, the greater their signs of distress (Boccia & Campos, 1989). They are most distressed when the strangers touch them. For this reason, if you find yourself in a situation in which you are trying to comfort an infant who does not know you, it may be more effective to talk in a friendly and soothing manner from a distance. Reconsider rushing in and picking up the child (see Figure 7.15). Your behavior with an unfamiliar child also can make a difference. Studies have found that adults who are active and friendly—who gesture, smile, and offer toys—receive more positive response from 6- to 18-month-olds than strangers who are quiet and passive (Bretherton et al., 1981; Mangelsdorf, 1992).

## SOCIAL REFERENCING

As we shall see in Chapter 10, observing unafraid models may help children reduce their fears. Essentially, the models provide information about how to act in a frightening situation. Sometimes we are faced with a situation that is new and ambiguous, and we are not sure how to act. Under these circumstances, we may seek out another person's perception of the situation to help us form our own understanding of it. This process is known as ***social referencing*** (Feinman & Lewis, 1983; Rosen et al., 1992). Babies display social referencing as early as 6 months of age, using their care giver's facial expressions or tone of voice to provide clues on how to respond (Walden & Baxter, 1989). In one study, for example, 8-month-old infants were friendlier to a stranger when their mothers

***Social referencing*** Using another person's reaction to a situation to form one's own assessment of it.

exhibited a friendly facial expression in the stranger's presence than when she displayed a worried expression (Boccia & Campos, 1989).

Infants also use their mother's facial expression to help them interpret ambiguous situations. Do you remember our discussion of the visual cliff in Chapter 6? You will recall that infants are reluctant to cross the deep side of the cliff. James Sorce and his colleagues (Sorce et al., 1985) adjusted the deep side of a visual cliff so that it was neither very deep nor very shallow. In this situation, 1-year-old babies initially hesitated and looked back and forth at the drop-off and at their mother's face. If the mother's facial expression exhibited joy or interest, most infants crossed the deep side. But if the mother looked fearful or angry, few infants crossed.

Infants will use emotional signals from their fathers as often as those from their mothers (Dickstein & Parke, 1988; Hirshberg & Svejda, 1990). They also are influenced by the emotional expressions of a familiar day-care worker (Camras & Sachs, 1991) and even of a friendly adult whom they have just met (Klinnert et al., 1986).

### *Emotional Regulation*

We have just seen how infants use emotional signals from an adult to help them cope with uncertainty. Another important feature of early emotional development is known as ***emotional regulation*** (Kopp, 1992; Thompson, 1990). Emotional regulation refers to the ways in which young children control their own emotions. Even very young infants display certain behaviors to control unpleasant emotional states. They may look away from a disturbing event or suck their thumbs (Rothbart et al., 1992; Tronick, 1989). Care givers play an important role in helping infants learn to regulate their emotions. Early in life, a two-way communication system develops in which the infant signals the care giver that help is needed and the care giver responds. Claire Kopp (1989, p. 347) gives an example of how this system works:

> *A 13-month-old, playing with a large plastic bottle, attempted to unscrew the cover, but could not. Fretting for a short time, she initiated eye contact with her mother and held out the jar. As her mother took it to unscrew the cover, the infant ceased fretting.*

## Personality Development

***Personality*** refers to each individual's distinctive ways of responding to people and events. In this section, we examine important aspects of personality development in the infant years. First, we look at the emergence of the self-concept. We then turn to a discussion of temperament. Finally, we consider gender differences in behavior.

### *The Self-Concept*

We are not born knowing that we exist. At birth, the world may be a confusing blur of sights, sounds, and inner sensations. When our hands first come into view, there is little evidence we realize that that hand "belongs" to us and that we are somehow separate and distinct from the world outside.

The sense of self, or the ***self-concept,*** appears to emerge gradually during infancy. At some point, infants understand the hand they are moving in and out

***Emotional regulation*** Techniques for controlling one's emotional states.

***Personality*** Each individual's distinctive ways of responding to people and events.

***Self-concept*** One's impression of oneself; self-awareness.

FIGURE 7.16

**SELF-AWARENESS.** *In the middle of the second year, infants begin to develop self-awareness, which has a powerful impact on social and emotional development.*

of sight is "their" hand. At some point, they understand that their own bodies extend only so far and that at a certain point, external objects and the bodies of others begin (see Figure 7.16).

**DEVELOPMENT OF THE SELF-CONCEPT** Psychologists have devised ingenious methods to assess the development of the self-concept among infants. One of these is the mirror technique. This technique involves the use of a mirror and a dot of rouge. Before the experiment begins, the researcher observes the infant for baseline data on how frequently the infant touches his or her nose. Then the mother places rouge on the infant's nose, and the infant is placed before a mirror. Not until about the age of 18 months do infants begin to touch their own noses upon looking in the mirror (Butterworth, 1990; Schneider-Rosen & Cicchetti, 1991).

Nose touching suggests that children recognize themselves and that they have a mental picture of themselves that allows them to perceive that the dot of rouge is an abnormality. By 30 months, most infants also can point to pictures of themselves and they begin to use their own name spontaneously (Bullock & Lütkenhaus, 1990; Stipek et al., 1990).

**TRUTH OR FICTION REVISITED**

*Psychologists do, in fact, assess development of the self-concept by dabbling rouge on infants' noses. Infants who touch their colored noses upon looking in a mirror are assumed to have a concept of themselves that deviates from the image they see.*

Self-awareness has a powerful impact on social and emotional development (Asendorpf & Baudonnière, 1993; Lewis, 1991). Knowledge of the self permits the child to develop notions of sharing and cooperation. In one study, for example, 2-year-olds who had a better developed sense of self were more likely to cooperate with other children (Brownell & Carriger, 1990).

Self-awareness also makes possible the development of "self-conscious" emotions such as embarrassment, envy, empathy, pride, guilt, and shame (Lewis, 1990). One illustration of the development of these "self-conscious" emotions comes from a recent study by Deborah Stipek and her colleagues (1992). They found that children over the age of 21 months often seek their mother's attention and approval when they have successfully completed a task, whereas younger toddlers do not.

**Psychoanalytic Views of the Self-Concept** Margaret Mahler (Mahler et al., 1975), a psychoanalyst, has proposed that development of self-concept comes about through a process of ***separation–individuation*** that lasts from about 5 months until 3 years of age. Separation involves the child's growing perception that her mother is separate from herself. Individuation refers to the child's increasing sense of independence and autonomy.

***Separation–individuation*** The child's increasing sense of becoming separate from and independent of the mother.

***Temperament*** Individual differences in styles of reaction that are present very early in life.

The word "autonomy" may remind you of a similar view proposed by Erik Erikson that was discussed in Chapter 2. Erikson states that the major developmental task of the child from ages 2 to 3 is acquiring a sense of autonomy and independence from parents (see Figure 7.17). Remember that Freud, too, believed that children of this age are gaining greater independence and control. His focus, however, was primarily on such bodily functions as toileting behavior.

One of the ways toddlers demonstrate their growing autonomy, much to the dismay of their parents, is by refusing to comply with parental requests or commands. Studies of toddlers and preschoolers between the ages of 1½ and 5 years have found that as children grow older, they adopt more skillful ways of expressing resistance to parental requests (Klimes-Dougan, 1993; Kuczynski & Kochanska, 1990). For example, young toddlers are more likely to ignore a parent's request or defy it ("No, I won't," accompanied by foot stamping). Older toddlers and preschoolers are more likely to make excuses ("I'm not hungry") or engage in negotiations ("Can I just eat *some* of my vegetables?").

### *Temperament*

Each child has a characteristic way of reacting and adapting to the world. The term ***temperament*** refers to stable individual differences in styles of reaction that are present very early in life. Some researchers believe that temperament forms the basic core of personality (Goldsmith et al., 1987; Strelau & Angleitner, 1991).

**Characteristics of Temperament** Temperament includes many aspects of behavior. Alexander Thomas and Stella Chess, in their well-known New York Longitudinal Study, followed the development of temperament in 133 girls and boys from birth to young adulthood (Chess & Thomas, 1991; Thomas & Chess, 1989). They identified the following nine characteristics of temperament:

1. Activity level: How active is the child?
2. Regularity: How regular are the child's biological functions, such as eating and sleeping?
3. Approach or withdrawal: Does the child respond positively or negatively to new situations and people?
4. Adaptability: How easily does the child adapt to new situations?
5. Response threshold: How sensitive is the child to sensory stimulation?

**Figure 7.17**

**Development of Independence.** *This 2-year-old is learning how to be more independent. Two-year-olds may insist on performing certain tasks, such as dressing or feeding themselves, even though the results may leave something to be desired from an adult's point of view.*

6. Response intensity: How intensely does the child respond?
7. Mood quality: Is the child's mood usually cheerful or unpleasant?
8. Distractibility: How easily is the child distracted?
9. Attention span and persistence: How long does the child stay with a particular activity?

**TYPES OF TEMPERAMENT** Thomas and Chess found that from the first days of life, many of the children in their study could be classified into one of three types of temperament: "easy" (40 percent of their sample), "difficult" (10 percent), and "slow to warm up" (15 percent). Some of the differences among these three types of children are shown in Table 7.1. As you can see, the easy child has regular sleep and feeding schedules, approaches new situations (such as a new food, a new school, or a stranger) with enthusiasm and adapts easily to them, and is generally cheerful. It's obvious why such a child would be relatively easy for parents to raise.

The difficult child, on the other hand, has irregular sleep and feeding schedules, is slow to accept new people and situations, takes a long time to adjust to new routines, and responds to frustrations with tantrums and loud crying. Parents find this type of child more difficult to deal with (Chess & Thomas, 1991). The slow-to-warm-up child falls somewhere between the other two. These children have somewhat irregular feeding and sleeping patterns and do not react as strongly as difficult children. They initially respond negatively to new experiences and adapt slowly only after repeated exposure (Chess & Thomas, 1984).

You will notice that only 65 percent of the children studied by Chess and Thomas fit into one of the three types of temperament. Some children are more inconsistent and show a mixture of temperament traits. For example, a toddler may have a pleasant disposition but be frightened of new situations.

**STABILITY OF TEMPERAMENT** How stable is temperament? Evidence indicates at least moderate consistency from infancy into childhood, adolescence,

**TABLE 7.1**

***TYPES OF TEMPERAMENT***

| TEMPERAMENT CATEGORIES | TEMPERAMENT TYPES: EASY | DIFFICULT | SLOW TO WARM UP |
|---|---|---|---|
| REGULARITY OF BIOLOGICAL FUNCTIONING | REGULAR | IRREGULAR | SOMEWHAT IRREGULAR |
| RESPONSE TO NEW STIMULI | POSITIVE APPROACH | NEGATIVE WITHDRAWAL | NEGATIVE WITHDRAWAL |
| ADAPTABILITY TO NEW SITUATIONS | ADAPTS READILY | ADAPTS SLOWLY OR NOT AT ALL | ADAPTS SLOWLY |
| INTENSITY OF REACTION | MILD OR MODERATE | INTENSE | MILD |
| QUALITY OF MOOD | POSITIVE | NEGATIVE | INITIALLY NEGATIVE; GRADUALLY MORE POSITIVE |

SOURCES: CHESS AND THOMAS, 1991; THOMAS AND CHESS, 1989.

FIGURE 7.18

***Differences in Temperament.*** *Differences in temperament emerge in early infancy. The photo on the left shows the positive reactions of a 5-month-old girl being fed a new food for the first time. The photo on the right shows the very different response of another girl of about the same age when introduced to a new food.*

and young adulthood (Asendorpf, 1993; Broberg, 1993; Kochanska & Radke-Yarrow, 1992). The infant who is highly active and cries frequently in unfamiliar situations often becomes a fearful toddler (Kagan & Snidman, 1991). An anxious, unhappy toddler tends to become an anxious, unhappy adolescent (Lerner et al., 1988). The child who refuses to accept new foods during infancy may scream when getting the first haircut, refuse to leave mother's side during the first day of kindergarten, and have difficulty adjusting to college as a young adult. Difficult children in general are at greater risk for developing behavior disorders and adjustment problems later in life (Coon et al., 1992; Mehregany, 1991; Tubman et al., 1992).

Many researchers believe that such consistency indicates that temperament is influenced by genetic factors (Braungart et al., 1992; Goldsmith et al., 1987). Indeed, studies suggest that many aspects of temperament—such as activity level, shyness, fearfulness, sociability, and emotionality—are influenced by heredity (Emde et al., 1992; Kagan et al., 1993; Plomin & McClearn, 1993). Another intriguing bit of evidence that temperament has an innate component is that infants and young children with different temperaments have different patterns of electrical activity in the left and right sides of their brain's cortex. A series of studies by Nathan Fox and his colleagues has found that less cheerful infants, children, and adults show greater right-brain activity, whereas happier individuals demonstrate greater left-brain activity (Adler, 1993a; Fox, 1991).

***Thinking About Development***

Agree or disagree with the following statement and support your answer: "An individual's temperament is inborn and cannot be changed by experience."

**Goodness of Fit: The Role of Environment** Environment also affects the development of temperament. An initial biological predisposition toward a certain temperament may be strengthened or weakened by the parents' reaction to the child. Consider the following: Parents may react to a difficult child by becoming less available and less responsive (Spangler, 1990). They may insist on imposing rigid care-giving schedules, which in turn can cause the child to become even more difficult to handle (Power et al., 1990). This example illustrates a discrepancy, or *poor fit,* between the child's behavior style and the parents' expectations and behaviors.

On the other hand, parents may respond in such a way as to modify a child's initial temperament in a more positive direction. Take the case of Carl, who in early life was one of the most difficult children in the New York Longitudinal Study:

*Whether it was the first solid foods in infancy, the beginning of nursery and elementary school, first birthday parties, or the first shopping trip, each experience evoked stormy responses, with loud crying and struggling to get away. However, his parents learned to anticipate Carl's reactions, knew that if they were patient, presented only one or a few new situations at a time, and gave him the opportunity for repeated exposure, Carl would finally adapt positively. Furthermore, once he adapted, his intensity of responses gave him a zestful enthusiastic involvement, just as it gave his initial negative reactions a loud and stormy character. His parents became fully aware that the difficulties in raising Carl were due to his temperament and not to their being "bad parents." The father even looked on his son's shrieking and turmoil as a sign of lustiness. As a result of this positive parent–child interaction, Carl never became a behavior problem. (Chess & Thomas, 1984, p. 263)*

***Goodness of fit*** Consonance between the parents' expectations of or demands on the child and the child's temperamental characteristics.

This example demonstrates ***goodness of fit*** between the behaviors of child and parent. A key factor is the parents' realization that their youngster's behavior does not mean that the child is weak or deliberately disobedient, nor that they are bad parents. This realization helps parents modify their attitudes and behaviors toward the child, whose behavior may in turn change in the desired direction (Chess & Thomas, 1984, 1991).

Does cultural setting influence parental expectations and behavioral outcomes for children categorized as "difficult"?

| CULTURE | PARENTAL EXPECTATIONS | BEHAVIORAL OUTCOMES |
|---|---|---|
| RURAL KENYA | INFANTS MAY OR MAY NOT SLEEP ALL NIGHT | CHILD BEHAVIOR OF WAKING UP AT NIGHT DOES NOT PRODUCE FAMILY STRESS |
| SUBURBAN BOSTON | INFANTS SHOULD SLEEP ALL NIGHT | CHILD BEHAVIOR OF WAKING UP AT NIGHT PRODUCES FAMILY STRESS |
| PUERTO RICAN WORKING CLASS, UNITED STATES | FEWER DEMANDS FOR EARLY SELF-HELP BEHAVIORS | LESS LIKELY TO HAVE ADJUSTMENT PROBLEMS AS A PRESCHOOLER |
| MIDDLE-CLASS, UNITED STATES | MORE DEMANDS FOR EARLY SELF-HELP BEHAVIORS | MORE LIKELY TO HAVE ADJUSTMENT PROBLEMS AS A PRESCHOOLER |

**CULTURE AND DEVELOPMENT: GOODNESS OF FIT** In middle-class Western society, the difficult child often has difficulty meeting cultural demands for task mastery at home, in school, and with peers (Chess & Thomas, 1991). But children with difficult temperament may have an easier time in cultural settings that have different value systems or different expectations.

For example, Super and Harkness (1981) compared infants in suburban Boston and rural Kenya. Temperamentally irregular infants who awoke at night caused considerable stress for American parents, who needed their sleep to be alert for their scheduled daytime activities. But rural Kenyan parents did not consider night waking stressful.

In other research, the children from the New York Longitudinal Study, who were predominantly from middle-class backgrounds, were compared with children from Puerto Rican working-class families (Chess & Thomas, 1984). The middle-class preschool children with difficult temperament were more likely to show adjustment problems than difficult preschool children from working-class families. The researchers believe that this finding is a result of differences in parental child-care attitudes and practices. The middle-class parents made more demands on their children for regular sleeping and feeding schedules, for early self-feeding and self-dressing behaviors, and for quick adaptation to new people and situations. These demands, as we have seen, are stressful for children with difficult temperament.

## *GENDER DIFFERENCES*

All cultures make a distinction between females and males and have beliefs and expectations about how they ought to behave (Lips, 1993). For this reason, a child's gender is a key factor in shaping its personality and other aspects of development. But just how different are girls and boys in their social, emotional, and other behaviors? How early in life do gender differences arise? Let us examine the behaviors of infant girls and boys.

**Behaviors of Infant Girls and Boys** Girls are more advanced in their motor development: they sit, crawl, and walk earlier than boys do (Hutt, 1978; Matlin, 1993). Girl and boy babies are quite similar in their responses to sights, sounds, tastes, smells, and touch. While a few studies have found that infant boys are more active and irritable than girls, others have not (Cossette et al., 1991; Matlin, 1993). Girls and boys also are similar in their social behaviors. They are equally likely to smile at people's faces, for example, and do not differ in their dependency on adults (Maccoby & Jacklin, 1974; Matlin, 1993). One area in which girls and boys begin to differ early in life is their preference for certain toys and play activities. By 12 to 18 months of age, girls prefer to play with dolls, doll furniture, dishes, and toy animals, while boys prefer vehicles, tools, and sports equipment (Caldera et al., 1989; Etaugh, 1983; Hanna, 1993).

**TRUTH OR FICTION REVISITED**

*It is true that 1-year-old girls prefer to play with dolls, whereas 1-year-old boys prefer transportation toys. The question is whether this gender difference is innate or a consequence of early social learning.*

**Adults' Behaviors Toward Infant Girls and Boys** One reason for these early gender differences in play preferences seems to be that adults respond differently to girls and boys. In some studies, for example, adults are presented with an unfamiliar infant who is dressed in boy's clothes and has a boy's name, while other adults are introduced to a baby with a girl's name and dressed in girl's clothing. (In reality, it is the same baby who simply is given different names and clothing.) When adults believe they are playing with a girl, they are more likely to offer ''her'' a doll; when they think the child is a boy, they are more likely to offer a football or a hammer. ''Boys'' also are encouraged to engage in more physical activity than are ''girls'' (Stern & Karraker, 1989). And perhaps it is no wonder, for infants labeled as ''girls'' are perceived as littler and softer (as well as nicer and more beautiful) than infants labeled as ''boys'' (Vogel et al., 1991).

**Parents' Behaviors Toward Sons and Daughters** How do parents behave toward their own infants? Similar to the adults with the unfamiliar babies, parents are more likely to encourage rough-and-tumble physical activity in their sons than in their daughters. Fathers are especially likely to do this (Siegel, 1987). On the other hand, parents talk more to their infant daughters than to their infant sons (Matlin,1993). They also smile more at their daughters, are more emotionally expressive toward them, and focus more on emotions when talking to them (Fivush, 1993; Malatesta et al., 1989).

Perhaps the most obvious way in which parents treat their baby girls and boys differently is in their choice of clothing, room furnishings, and toys. Even very young infant girls are likely to be decked out in a pink or perhaps yellow dress, embellished with ruffles and lace, whereas infant boys wear blue or red (Pomerleau et al., 1990; Shakin et al., 1985). Parents also provide their baby girls and boys with different bedroom decorations and toys. For example, examination of the contents of rooms of children from 5 months to 6 years of age found that boys' rooms were often decorated with animal themes and with blue bedding and curtains. Girls' rooms featured flowers, lace, ruffles, and pastel colors (Pomerleau et al., 1990; Rheingold & Cook, 1975). Girls owned more dolls, while boys had more vehicles, military toys, and sports equipment.

FIGURE 7.19

***ADULTS TREAT INFANT GIRLS AND BOYS DIFFERENTLY.*** *Perhaps the most obvious way in which parents treat their baby girls and boys differently is in their choice of clothing, toys, and room furnishings. If you were to meet these two unfamiliar children, would you have any doubt about their gender?*

Other studies find that parents react favorably when their preschool daughters play with ''girls''' toys and their sons play with ''boys''' toys. Parents and other adults show more negative reactions when girls play with ''boys''' toys and boys play with ''girls''' toys (Caldera et al., 1989; Etaugh, 1983; Martin, 1990). Fathers are more concerned than mothers that their children engage in activities viewed as ''appropriate'' for their gender (Bradley & Gobbart, 1989; Lytton & Romney, 1991).

And so, parents begin to shape the behaviors of their children during the infant years and help lay the foundation for development in early childhood. It is to that period of life that we turn next.

## Summary

1. Attachment is the affectional tie that persons form between themselves and specific others. Attachment in young children is measured by their efforts to maintain contact with care givers and by their display of separation anxiety. Using the Strange Situation method, Ainsworth has identified patterns of secure and insecure (avoidant and ambivalent-resistant) attachment. Different child-rearing attitudes and practices may account for cross-cultural differences in attachment patterns.

2. Securely attached infants and toddlers are happier and more socially competent. They use their primary care givers as a base for exploration. Individual patterns of attachment can change as family conditions and interpersonal relationships change. Babies become attached to both parents at about the same time, although they generally spend less time with their fathers and their mothers are more likely to be the ones who meet their routine needs.

3. Three phases of attachment have been identified: From birth to 3 months, infants show indiscriminate attachment. At about 3 or 4 months, they select familiar figures over strangers. At 6 or 7 months, attachment becomes more clear-cut.

4. There are many theoretical views of attachment, including the cognitive, behavioral, psychoanalytic, ''contact comfort,'' and ethological perspectives.

5. Severe social and emotional deficits may develop when children's material needs are met but they are socially deprived. Socially deprived rhesus monkeys may overcome social and emotional deficits when exposed to the social stimulation of younger monkeys. Exposure to children younger than themselves has also fostered the social development of socially withdrawn preschoolers.

6. Babies need sensory stimulation and social interaction. After the age of 3 months or so, stability of care givers becomes important. Children can recover from early social deprivation if they receive individual attention and environmental stimulation.

7. Child maltreatment includes physical, sexual, and emotional abuse and physical, emotional, and educational neglect. Abused children show a variety of social and emotional problems. Many factors contribute to child abuse: situational stress, a history of abuse in the abusers' families of origin, acceptance of violence as normal, and failure to develop a strong attachment to one's children.

8. Autism is characterized by a failure to form attachments, communication problems, intolerance of change, and ritualistic behavior.

9. Day care has not been shown to impair mother–child bonds of attachment. Day care generally has a positive effect on children's social and cognitive development.

10. Theories of emotional development fall into two camps: (a) Bridges and Sroufe propose that diffuse excitement is present at birth and differentiates into other emotions; (b) Izard proposes that several discrete emotions are present at birth, even if they are not all shown at once.

11. Fear of strangers appears at 6 to 9 months and peaks at about 1 year of age. The strength of the reaction depends on many factors, such as the proximity of the stranger and of the mother.

12. Babies show social referencing by 6 months of age, using their care giver's facial expressions or tone of voice to provide cues on how to respond in ambiguous situations. Young children learn to control their emotions in a process called *emotional regulation.*

13. Children seem to become self-aware, as assessed by the mirror method, by about 18 months. Self-awareness lays the groundwork for the development of social cooperation and of emotions such as embarrassment and pride.

14. According to Mahler, the self-concept develops from a process of separation (from mother) and individuation (increasing independence and autonomy). Erikson and Freud also stress the development of autonomy and control at ages 2–3 years.

15. Temperament refers to stable individual differences in styles of reaction that appear early in life. Temperamentally easy children have regular schedules, adapt easily to new situations, and are generally cheerful; difficult children have irregular schedules, are slow to adapt, and display negative moods; slow-to-warm-up children fall between these two types.

16. Temperament is moderately consistent from infancy into young adulthood, with both heredity and environment playing a role. The degree of fit between the child's temperament and the parents' expectations and behaviors may be good or poor.

17. Infant girls and boys are similar in their perceptual responses and social behaviors. Gender differences in toy preferences appear early in the second year. Parents, especially fathers, and other adults treat infant girls and boys differently.

# PART IV

# EARLY CHILDHOOD

EARLY CHILDHOOD, THE YEARS FROM 2 TO 6, IS ALSO KNOWN as the preschool period. Children continue to make great strides in their physical, cognitive, social, and personality development.

Physical growth is slower than it was in infancy. Children become taller and leaner, and by the end of early childhood they look more like adults than infants. An explosion of motor skills occurs as children become stronger, faster, and better coordinated.

Language improves enormously, and children can carry on conversations with others. As cognitive skills develop, a new world of make believe or "pretend" play emerges. Curiosity and eagerness to learn are hallmarks of the preschool years.

Increased physical and cognitive capabilities enable the child to emerge from total dependence upon parents and care givers to become part of the broader world outside the family. Peers take on an increasingly important role in the life of the preschooler. Children begin to acquire a sense of their own abilities and shortcomings.

We examine all these developments of early childhood—physical, cognitive, social, and personality—in Chapters 8, 9, and 10.

# *Early Childhood:*

## *Physical Development*

## Chapter Outline



## Truth or Fiction?

______ *The brain develops more quickly than any other organ in early childhood.*

______ *Throughout early childhood, boys outperform girls in motor skills.*

______ *Children's levels of motor activity increase gradually during the preschool years.*

______ *Sedentary parents are more likely to have "couch potatoes" for children.*

______ *Left-handed people are more prone to allergies and learning disabilities than right-handed people are.*

______ *A disproportionately high percentage of 12- and 13-year-old math whizzes are left-handed.*

______ *Accidents are the most common cause of death among children in the United States.*

______ *Sleepwalkers become violently agitated if they are awakened during an episode.*

______ *It is normal for children who have gained bladder control to continue to have bed-wetting accidents at night for a year or more.*

______ *Boys are more likely than girls to wet their beds.*

*Mark is a 2-year-old having lunch in his high chair. He begins eating by taking fistfuls of hamburger and shoving them into his mouth. He picks up his cup with both hands and drinks milk. Mark starts banging his spoon on his tray and his cup. He kicks his feet against the chair. He throws hamburger on the floor.*

*Compare Mark's behavior with that of Larry, age 3½, who is getting ready for bed. Larry carefully pulls his plastic train track apart and places each piece in the box. Then he walks to the bathroom, brings his stool over to the sink, and stands on it. He takes down his toothbrush and toothpaste, opens the cap, squeezes toothpaste on the brush, and begins to brush his teeth.*

(ADAPTED FROM ROWEN, 1973)

During the preschool years, physical and motor development proceeds, literally, by leaps and bounds. While toddlers like Mark are occupied by grasping, banging and throwing things, 3-year-olds like Larry are busy manipulating objects and exercising their newly developing fine motor skills. In this chapter, we explore these and other aspects of physical and motor development in the early years.

## GROWTH PATTERNS

Let us begin looking at the physical development of the child by examining changes in height and weight.

### *HEIGHT AND WEIGHT*

Following the dramatic gains in height of the first 2 years, the rate of growth slows down during the preschool years. Girls and boys tend to gain about 2 to 3 inches in height per year throughout early childhood. Weight gains also remain fairly even at about 4 to 6 pounds per year (see Figure 8.1). Children become increasingly slender during early childhood, as they gain in height and lose some of their "baby fat" (Meredith, 1987). Another interesting feature to note in Figure 8.1 is that boys as a group are only slightly taller and heavier than girls in early childhood. Noticeable variations in growth patterns also occur from child to child.

### *DEVELOPMENT OF THE BRAIN*

One of the important physical developments of early childhood is the increasing maturation of the brain. The brain develops more quickly than any other organ in early childhood. At 2 years of age, for example, the brain already has attained 75 percent of its adult weight. And by the age of 5, the brain has reached 90

**TRUTH OR FICTION REVISITED**

*It is true that the brain develops more quickly than any other organ in early childhood. By the age of 5, it has attained 90 percent of its adult weight. This is another example of the cephalocaudal trend in development.*

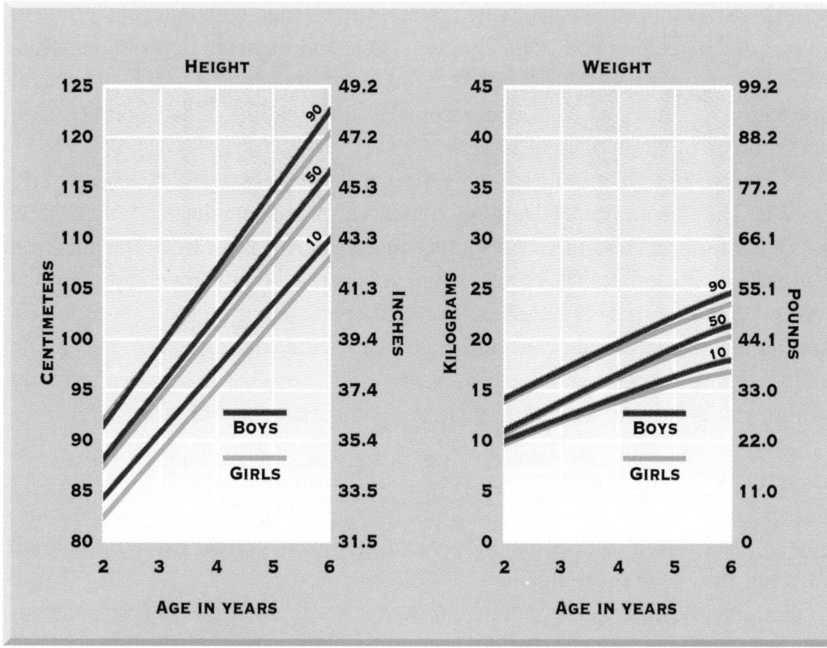


SOURCE: NATIONAL CENTER FOR HEALTH STATISTICS.

**FIGURE 8.1**

***GROWTH CURVES FOR HEIGHT AND WEIGHT, AGES 2 TO 6 YEARS.*** *The numbers on the curves indicate the percentiles for height and weight at different ages. The growth rate slows down during early childhood. As in infancy, boys are only slightly taller and heavier than girls. Variations in growth patterns from child to child are evident. (Source: National Center for Health Statistics).*

percent of its adult weight, even though the total body weight of the 5-year-old is barely one-third of what it will be as an adult (Tanner, 1989).

The increase in brain size is due in part to the continuing process of myelination of nerve fibers (see Chapter 5). Completion of the myelination of the neural pathways that link the cerebellum to the cerebral cortex facilitates the development of fine motor skills. The cerebellum is involved in balance as well as coordination, and the young child's balancing abilities also increase dramatically as myelination of these pathways nears completion.

**BRAIN DEVELOPMENT AND VISUAL SKILLS** The development of the brain also is linked to improvements in children's ability to attend to and process visual information. These skills are critical in learning to read (Bornstein, 1992). The parts of the brain that enable the child to sustain attention and screen out distractions become increasingly myelinated between the ages of about 4 and 7 (Higgins & Turnure, 1984). As a consequence, most children are ready to focus on schoolwork at some time between these ages.

The speed with which children process visual information improves throughout childhood, reaching adult levels at the beginning of adolescence (Wilson et al., 1992). The child's ability to systematically scan visual material also improves in early childhood. For example, one classic study presented children with pairs of pictures of similar looking houses and asked the children whether or not the houses were identical (Vurpillot, 1968). Four-year-olds almost never showed thorough, systematic visual scanning of the features of the houses, whereas 9-year-olds frequently did so.

***THINKING ABOUT DEVELOPMENT***

Agree or disagree with the following statement and support your answer: "Some children are left-brained, and others are right-brained."

**RIGHT BRAIN/LEFT BRAIN?** In recent years, it has become popular to speak of some people as being "right-brained" or "left-brained." We have even heard it said that some instructional methods are aimed at the right brain (presented in an emotionally laden, esthetic way), while others are aimed at the left brain (logical and straightforward).

The notion is that the hemispheres of the brain are involved in different kinds of intellectual and emotional functions and responses. For the great majority

***Corpus callosum*** The thick bundle of nerve fibers that connects the left and right hemispheres of the brain.

***Plasticity*** The tendency of new parts of the brain to take up the functions of injured parts of the brain.

***Gross motor skills*** Skills employing the large muscles used in locomotion.

of us, the left hemisphere is looked on as more concerned with logic and problem solving, understanding and producing language, and mathematical computation. The right hemisphere is considered more involved in decoding visual and spatial information, esthetic and emotional responses, imagination, understanding metaphors, and creative mathematical reasoning (Halpern, 1992).

Actually, these functions are not split up so precisely as has been popularly believed. The functions of the left and right hemispheres overlap to some degree, and the hemispheres also tend to respond simultaneously as we focus our attention on one thing or another. They are aided to "cooperate" by the myelination of the ***corpus callosum***—a thick bundle of nerve fibers that connects the hemispheres. Myelination of the corpus callosum proceeds rapidly during early and middle childhood and is largely complete by the age of 8. By that time, we apparently have greater ability to integrate logical and emotional functioning.

**PLASTICITY OF THE BRAIN** We have just seen that parts of the brain tend to have specialized functions. Specialization allows our behavior to be more complex. But specialization also means that injuries to certain parts of the brain can result in loss of these functions.

Fortunately, the brain also shows ***plasticity.*** The brain frequently can compensate for injuries to particular areas. This compensatory ability is greatest up until the ages of 8 or 9 (Williams, 1983). When we suffer damage to the areas of the brain that control language, we may lose the ability to speak or understand language. However, other areas of the brain may assume these functions in young children who suffer such damage. As a result, they sometimes dramatically regain the ability to speak or comprehend language (Gardner, 1982). In adolescence and adulthood, regaining such functions may be impossible.

There are at least two factors involved in the brain's plasticity. One is "sprouting," or the growth of new dendrites. New dendrites to some degree can allow for the rearrangement of neural circuits. The second is the redundancy of certain neural connections. In some cases, similar functions are found in two or more locations within the brain, although they are developed to different degrees. If one location is damaged, the other one, in time, may be able to develop greater proficiency in performing the function.

## MOTOR DEVELOPMENT

The preschool years witness an explosion of motor skills, as children's nervous systems mature and their movements become more precise and coordinated (Cratty, 1986). Let us examine the development of motor skills in early childhood.

### *GROSS MOTOR SKILLS*

During the preschool years, children make great strides in the development of ***gross motor skills,*** which involve the large muscles used in locomotion (see Table 8.1). At about the age of 3, children can balance on one foot. By 3 or 4, they can walk up stairs as adults do, by placing a foot on each step. By 4 or 5, they can skip and pedal a tricycle (Cratty, 1986). Older preschoolers are better able to coordinate two tasks, such as singing and running at the same time, than are younger preschoolers (Whitall, 1991). Preschool children largely appear to acquire motor skills by teaching themselves and observing the behavior of other children. The opportunity to play with other children seems more important than adult instruction at this age.

**FIGURE 8.2**

***Gross Motor Skills.*** *During the preschool years, children make great strides in the development of gross motor skills. By 4 or 5, they can pedal a tricycle quite skillfully.*

Throughout early childhood, girls and boys are not far apart in their motor skills. Girls are somewhat better in tasks requiring balance and precision of movement. Boys, on the other hand, show some advantage in throwing and kicking (Cratty, 1986).

**TRUTH OR FICTION REVISITED**

*It is not true that boys outperform girls in motor skills throughout early childhood. Girls excel in activities that require balance and precision of movement.*

Individual differences are more impressive than gender differences throughout early and middle childhood. Some children develop motor skills earlier than others. Some are genetically predisposed toward developing better coordination or more strength than others. Motivation and practice also are extremely important in children's acquisition of motor skills. Motor experiences in infancy may affect the development of motor skills in early childhood. For example, children with early crawling experience perform better than noncrawlers on tests of motor skills in the preschool years (McEwan et al., 1991).

**FIGURE 8.3**

***Gender and Motor Skills.*** *Throughout early childhood, girls and boys are not far apart in their motor skills. Girls are somewhat better in tasks requiring balance and precision of movement. Boys show some advantage in throwing and kicking.*

**TABLE 8.1**

***DEVELOPMENT OF GROSS MOTOR SKILLS IN EARLY CHILDHOOD***

| 2 YEARS (24-35 MONTHS) | 3 YEARS (36-47 MONTHS) | 4 YEARS (48-59 MONTHS) | 5 YEARS (60-71 MONTHS) |
|---|---|---|---|
| RUNS WELL STRAIGHT AHEAD | GOES AROUND OBSTACLES WHILE RUNNING | TURNS SHARP CORNERS WHILE RUNNING | RUNS LIGHTLY ON TOES |
| WALKS UPSTAIRS, TWO FEET TO A STEP | WALKS UPSTAIRS, ONE FOOT TO A STEP | WALKS DOWNSTAIRS, ONE FOOT TO A STEP | |
| KICKS A LARGE BALL | KICKS A LARGE BALL EASILY | | |
| JUMPS DISTANCE OF 4 TO 14 INCHES | JUMPS FROM BOTTOM STEP | JUMPS FROM HEIGHT OF 12 INCHES | JUMPS DISTANCE OF 3 FEET |
| THROWS A SMALL BALL WITHOUT FALLING | CATCHES A BOUNCED BALL, USING TORSO AND ARMS TO FORM A BASKET | THROWS A BALL OVERHAND | CATCHES A SMALL BALL USING HANDS ONLY |
| PUSHES AND PULLS LARGE TOYS | GOES AROUND OBSTACLES WHILE PUSHING AND PULLING TOYS | TURNS SHARP CORNERS WHILE PUSHING AND PULLING TOYS | |
| HOPS ON ONE FOOT, 2 OR MORE HOPS | HOPS ON ONE FOOT, UP TO 3 HOPS | HOPS ON ONE FOOT, 4 TO 6 HOPS | HOPS 2 TO 3 YARDS FORWARD ON EACH FOOT |
| TRIES TO STAND ON ONE FOOT | STANDS ON ONE FOOT | STANDS ON ONE FOOT 3 TO 8 SECONDS | STANDS ON ONE FOOT 8 TO 10 SECONDS |
| CLIMBS ON FURNITURE TO LOOK OUT OF WINDOW | CLIMBS NURSERY-SCHOOL APPARATUS | CLIMBS LADDERS | CLIMBS ACTIVELY AND SKILLFULLY |
| | | SKIPS ON ONE FOOT | SKIPS ON ALTERNATE FEET |
| | | RIDES A TRICYCLE WELL | RIDES A BICYCLE WITH TRAINING WHEELS |

THE AGES PRESENTED ARE AVERAGES; THERE ARE WIDE INDIVIDUAL VARIATIONS.

## *PHYSICAL ACTIVITY*

Preschool children spend quite a bit of time engaging in physical activity. One recent study, for example, found that preschoolers spent an average of more than 25 hours a week in large muscle activity (Poest et al., 1989). Younger preschoolers are even more likely than older ones to engage in physically oriented play such as grasping, banging, and mouthing objects (Fromberg, 1990). Consequently, they need more space and less furniture in a preschool or day-care setting. Contrary to what you might expect, children who are the most physically active tend to show less well-developed motor skills (Eaton & Yu, 1989).

Motor activity level begins to decline after 2 or 3 years of age. Children become less restless and are able to sit still for longer periods of time (Eaton & Yu, 1989). Between the ages of 2 and 4, children show an increase in sustained, focused attention during free play (Ruff & Lawson, 1990).

**TRUTH OR FICTION REVISITED**

*Children's levels of motor activity actually decrease during the preschool years so that children become more capable of sustained focused attention.*

**ROUGH-AND-TUMBLE PLAY** One form of physical and social activity often observed in young children is known as ***rough-and-tumble play.*** Rough-and-tumble play consists of running, chasing, fleeing, wrestling, hitting with an open hand, laughing, and making faces (Garvey, 1990). Rough-and-tumble play should not be confused with aggressive behavior (Kagan, 1990). Aggression involves hitting with fists, pushing, taking, grabbing, and angry looks. Unlike aggression, rough-and-tumble play helps develop both physical and social skills in children (Pellegrini & Perlmutter, 1988).

**CULTURE AND DEVELOPMENT: ROUGH-AND-TUMBLE PLAY** Play-fighting and chasing activities are found among young children in societies around the world (Whiting & Edwards, 1988). But the particular form that rough-and-tumble play takes is influenced by culture and environment. For example, rough-and-tumble play among girls is quite common among the Pilaga Indians and the !Kung of Botswana but less common among girls in the United States. In the United States, rough-and-tumble play usually occurs in groups made up of the same gender. However, the !Kung girls and boys engage in rough-and-tumble play together. And among the Pilaga, girls often are matched off against the boys (Garvey, 1990).

***Rough-and-tumble play*** Play fighting and chasing.

**FIGURE 8.4**

**ROUGH-AND-TUMBLE PLAY.** *Play-fighting and chasing activities—known as rough-and-tumble play—are found among young children in societies around the world.*

FIGURE 8.5

***ACTIVITY LEVEL.*** *Children who are physically active are more likely to have physically active parents. Most likely, both genetic and environmental factors are involved.*

**INDIVIDUAL DIFFERENCES IN ACTIVITY LEVEL** Children differ widely in their activity levels. Some children are much more active than others. Children who are physically active are more likely to have physically active parents (Poest et al., 1989). In one recent study of 4- to 7-year-olds (Moore et al., 1991), children of active mothers were twice as likely to be active as children of inactive mothers. Children of active fathers were 3.5 times as likely to be active as children of inactive fathers. A number of possible mechanisms may account for this relationship. First, active parents may serve as role models for activity. Second, sharing of activities by family members may be responsible. Parents who are avid tennis players may involve their children in games of tennis from an early age. By the same token, "couch potato" parents who prefer to view tennis on television rather than play it may be more likely to share this sedentary activity with their children. A third factor is that active parents may encourage and support their child's participation in physical activity. Finally, a tendency to be active or inactive may be transmitted genetically. Results from twin studies (see Chapter 2) show evidence of genetic influences on activity level (Saudino & Eaton, 1993; Stevenson, 1992). Most likely, both genetic and environmental factors are involved in determining a child's activity level.

TRUTH OR FICTION REVISITED

*It is true that sedentary parents are more likely to have "couch potatoes" for children, but we are not certain why this is so. For example, do active parents serve as active role models for children? Is activity level genetically transmitted? Are there interactions among these and other factors?*

**GENDER DIFFERENCES IN MOTOR ACTIVITY** During early childhood, boys tend to be more active than girls, at least in some settings (Danner et al., 1991). Boys spend more time than girls in large muscle activities (Poest et al.,

1989). One study found that preschool boys were more active than girls during indoor play but that girls and boys were equally active outdoors (Maccoby & Jacklin, 1987). Boys tend to be more fidgety and distractible than girls, and to spend less time focusing on tasks (McGuinness, 1990).

Why are boys more active and restless than girls? One interesting theory is that boys of a given age are less mature physically than girls of the same age. We have just seen that children become less active as they develop. Therefore, the apparent gender difference in activity level may really be only a maturational difference (Eaton & Yu, 1989). While maturation does appear to account for some of the gender difference in activity level, it is not the whole story. Other factors such as parental encouragement and reward of motor activity in boys and discouragement of such behavior in girls probably are involved as well.

Boys also are more likely than girls to engage in rough-and-tumble play (Moller et al., 1992; Pellegrini, 1990). What might account for this gender difference? Some psychologists suggest that biologically based reasons may be partly responsible (Maccoby, 1990a, 1991b). Others argue that the socializing influences of the family and culture at large promote play differences among girls and boys (Caplan & Larkin, 1991; Meyer et al., 1991).

FIGURE 8.6

***Fine Motor Skills.*** *Control over the wrists and fingers enables children to hold a pencil, play musical instruments, and, as shown in this photograph, to play with stack toys.*

## *Fine Motor Skills*

***Fine motor skills*** develop gradually and lag behind gross motor skills. This is yet another example of the proximodistal trend in development discussed in Chapter 5. Fine motor skills involve the small muscles used in manipulation and coordination. Control over the wrists and fingers enables children to hold a pencil properly, dress themselves, and stack blocks (see Table 8.2). Preschoolers can labor endlessly in attempting to tie their shoelaces and to get their jackets zipped. There are terribly frustrating (as well as funny) scenes of alternating between steadfast refusal to allow a parent to intervene and requesting the parent's help.

***Fine motor skills*** Skills employing the small muscles used in manipulation, such as those in the fingers.

TABLE 8.2

***Development of Fine Motor Skills in Early Childhood***

| 2 Years (24-35 months) | 3 Years (36-47 months) | 4 Years (48-59 months) | 5 Years (60-71 months) |
|---|---|---|---|
| Builds tower of 6 cubes | Builds tower of 9 cubes | Builds tower of 10 or more cubes | Builds three steps from six blocks with model |
| Copies vertical and horizontal lines | Copies circle and cross | Copies square | Copies triangle and star |
| | Copies letters | Prints simple words | Prints first name and numbers |
| Imitates folding paper | | Imitates folding paper three times | Imitates folding triangle from square paper |
| Paints on easel with brush | Holds crayon with fingers, not fist | Uses pencil with correct hand grip | Traces around diamond drawn on paper |
| Places simple shapes in correct holes | Strings 4 beads with large needle | Strings 10 beads | Laces shoes |

The ages presented are averages; there are wide individual variations.

## CHILDREN'S DRAWINGS

***Placement stage*** An early stage in drawing in which 2-year-olds place their scribbles in various locations on the page (such as in the middle or near a border).

***Shape stage*** A stage in drawing, attained by age 3, in which children draw basic shapes such as circles, squares, triangles, crosses, Xs and odd shapes.

***Design stage*** A stage in drawing immediately following the shape stage in which children begin to combine shapes.

***Pictorial stage*** A stage in drawing attained between ages 4 and 5 in which designs begin to resemble recognizable objects.

The development of drawing in young children is closely linked to the development of both motor and cognitive skills. Children first begin to scribble during the second year of life. Initially, they seem to enjoy making marks for the sheer enjoyment of it (Eisner, 1990). At the age of 18 months, the daughter of one of the authors (C. E.) was especially intrigued with the bright red marks she could produce on the sofa with her mother's lipstick!

Is this scribbling just random motor activity? Rhoda Kellogg (1970) has studied more than a million drawings made by children. Her conclusion is that there is a meaningful pattern to be found among children's scribbles. She identifies 20 basic scribbles that she considers the building blocks of all art: vertical, horizontal, diagonal, circular, curving, waving or zigzagging lines, and dots (see Figure 8.7).

Children go through four stages as they progress from making scribbles to drawing pictures. These are the ***placement, shape, design,*** and ***pictorial stages*** (see Figure 8.8). Two-year-olds place their scribbles in various locations on the page (for instance, in the middle of the page or near one of the borders). By age 3, children are starting to draw basic shapes: circles, squares, triangles, crosses, Xs, and odd shapes. As soon as they can draw shapes, children begin to combine them in the design stage. Between 4 and 5, the child reaches the pictorial stage, in which designs begin to resemble recognizable objects.

Children's early drawings tend to be symbolic of a broad category rather than very specific. For example, a child might draw the same simple building whether she is asked to draw a school or a house (Tallandini & Valentini, 1991). Children between 3 and 5 years old usually do not start out to draw a particular thing. They are more likely to first see what they have drawn and then name it (Winner, 1989). As motor and cognitive skills continue to improve after the ages of 5, children become able to purposely draw something they have in mind (Matthews, 1990). They also become better at copying simple and complex figures (Karapetsas & Kantas, 1991; Pemberton, 1990).

FIGURE 8.7

**THE TWENTY BASIC SCRIBBLES.** *By the age of 2, children can scribble. Rhoda Kellogg has identified these 20 basic scribbles as the building blocks of the young child's drawings. (Source: Kellogg, 1970).*

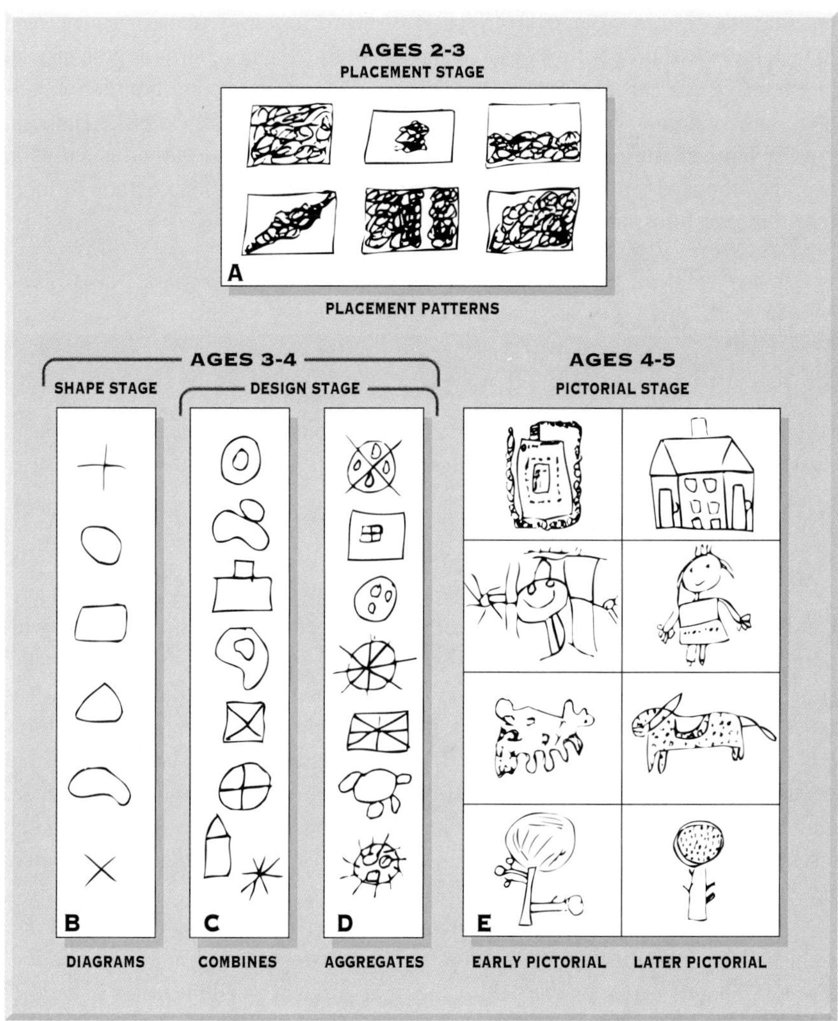


FIGURE 8.8

***The Four Stages in Children's Drawings.*** *Children go through four stages in drawing pictures. (a) They first place their scribbles in various locations on the page. They then (b) draw basic shapes, and (c, d) combine shapes into designs. Finally, (e) they draw recognizable objects. (Source: Kellogg, 1970).*

## *Handedness*

***Handedness*** emerges during infancy. By 2 to 3 months, a rattle placed in the infant's hand is held longer with the right hand than with the left (Fitzgerald et al., 1991). By 6 months, the majority of infants show a clear-cut right-hand preference in reaching and grasping things (Shucard & Shucard, 1990). This preference becomes even more strongly established during the early childhood years (McManus et al., 1988). Overall, about 90 percent of people are right-handed, although left-handedness is found more frequently in boys than girls (Bryden et al., 1991; Coren & Halpern, 1991). Children usually are labeled right-handed or left-handed on the basis of their handwriting preferences (Peters, 1990). However, we should note that some people write with one hand but pitch a baseball or hold a toothbrush with the other.

**Left-Handedness: Myths and Realities** It has been generally believed that children who prefer the left hand for writing are less well-coordinated and more disposed toward reading disabilities and other academic problems than right-handed children (L. J. Harris, 1990; Schwartz, 1990). The word *gawky,* with its connotations of clumsiness, derives from the French word *gauche,* which means both "left" and also "clumsy." The word *sinister,* meaning evil or

***Handedness*** The tendency to prefer using the left or right hand in writing and other activities.

unfortunate, similarly comes from the Latin word for "left" (Coren, 1992). And in fact, increased proportions of left-handers are found among groups with special problems ranging from allergies to learning disabilities, mental retardation, autism, schizophrenia, criminality, and alcoholism (Coren 1990; Coren & Halpern, 1991). Some studies even appear to indicate that left-handed individuals die, on average, about 8 years earlier than right-handers (Coren, 1992), although more recent research disputes this claim (Salive et al., 1993).

### TRUTH OR FICTION REVISITED

*It is true that left-handed people are more prone to problems such as allergies and learning disabilities than right-handed people are, but the reasons for these differences are unclear.*

Because of the negative stereotypes associated with left-handedness, left-handed children for many years were encouraged to switch to writing with their right hands (Hoosain, 1991; Porac & Buller, 1990). This "encouragement" sometimes was quite unpleasant. The father of one of the authors (C. E.) was repeatedly rapped on the knuckles by his first-grade teacher for writing with his left hand. Even today, social pressure against using the left hand for writing persists in many parts of the world, including Italy, Germany, Russia, Japan, China, and many African nations (L. J. Harris, 1991). However, recent research strongly suggests that the negative stereotypes of the left-handed child may be exaggerated.

In one study, Peters (1990) compared the performance of left-handed and right-handed individuals on a number of tests of motor skill and coordination. The left-handers performed as well as the right-handers on all the tasks. In another recent series of studies, Camilla Benbow (O'Boyle & Benbow, 1990) related handedness and other factors to scores on the math part of the Scholastic Aptitude Test (SAT) among 12- and 13-year-olds. (The SAT is designed to assess older adolescents applying for college admission.) Twenty percent of the highest scoring group was left-handed. Only 10 percent of the general population is left-handed, so it appears that left-handed children are more than adequately represented among the most academically gifted.

### TRUTH OR FICTION REVISITED

*It is true that a disproportionately high percentage of 12- and 13-year-old math whizzes are left-handed.*

Left-handedness (or use of both hands) also has been associated with success in athletic activities such as fencing, boxing, basketball, and baseball (Coren, 1992; L. J. Harris, 1990). Higher frequencies of left-handedness also are found among musicians, architects, and artists (Natsopoulos et al., 1992; O'Boyle & Benbow, 1990). Notable examples of left-handed artists include Leonardo da Vinci, Michelangelo, and Pablo Picasso.

How can it be that left-handedness is associated with both talent and giftedness on the one hand (excuse the pun!) and with problems and deficits on the

FIGURE 8.9

***Left-Handedness.*** *Left-handed children are no clumsier than right-handed children, although they may be more likely to develop allergies. Left-handedness is associated with both positive and negative aspects of academic performance.*

other? To answer this question, we need to examine briefly some theories of how handedness develops.

**Theoretical Interlude: Theories of Handedness** According to genetic theories of handedness, most humans have an inborn bias toward right handedness and toward control of handedness and language by the left cerebral hemisphere. A small number have an inborn bias toward left-handedness (Schwartz, 1990). Norman Geschwind has expanded on this view by arguing that certain prenatal influences act to diminish the genetic predisposition toward right-handedness. Specifically, he proposes that exposure to excessive amounts of the hormone testosterone in prenatal life slows development of the left hemisphere, causing an increase both in left-handedness and in problems such as learning disorders and immunological and allergic diseases (Bakan, 1990; Habib et al., 1990; McManus & Bryden, 1991). A related theory is that various pregnancy and birth complications may increase both left-handedness and some of the problems just mentioned (Coren & Searleman, 1990). Both of these views propose that at least some cases of left-handedness are due to damage or delayed development in the left hemisphere. But the same prenatal hormones that slow left-hemisphere development could speed up the development of the right hemisphere (O'Boyle & Benbow, 1990). As we saw earlier in this chapter, the right hemisphere seems to control mathematical reasoning and spatial abilities (Halpern, 1992). So right-hemisphere development could account for a combination of left-handedness and ability in math, as well as in art and architecture.

In sum, there is no convincing evidence that left-handed children are clumsier than right-handed children. They are somewhat more prone toward developing allergies. Academically speaking, left-handedness is associated with positive as well as negative academic performance. Since handedness may reflect the differential development of the hemispheres of the cortex, it is doubtful that struggling to write with the nondominant hand would correct any academic shortcoming that may exist in some left-handed children—any more than training right-handed children to write with their left hands would increase their math ability.

## NUTRITION

Nutrition affects both physical and behavioral development. In this section, we examine children's nutritional needs and their eating behavior.

### NUTRITIONAL NEEDS

As children move from infancy into the preschool years, their nutritional needs change somewhat. True, they still need to consume the basic foodstuffs: proteins, fats, carbohydrates, minerals, and vitamins. But more calories are required as children get older. For example, the average 4- to 6-year-old needs 1,800 calories compared with only 1,300 for the average 1- to 3-year-old (Ekvall, 1993b). However, preschoolers grow at a slower rate than infants. This means that preschoolers need fewer calories per pound of body weight.

### EATING BEHAVIORS

During the second and third years, a child's appetite typically decreases and becomes erratic, often causing parents great worry (see Figure 8.10). But it must be remembered that the child is growing more slowly now and needs fewer calories. Also, young children who eat less at one meal typically compensate by eating more at another (Shea et al., 1992). Strong (and strange) preferences for particular foods may develop (Lucas, 1991). Between the ages of 2 and 3, one of the authors (C. E.) insisted on eating only sour cream and canned fruit cocktail for dinner!

Many children (and adults) consume excessive amounts of sugar and salt, which can be harmful to their health. Infants seem to be born liking the taste of sugar, although they are fairly indifferent to salty tastes. But preference for both sweet and salty foods increases if children are repeatedly exposed to them during childhood (Sullivan & Birch, 1990). The message to parents is clear: Give your child food in the way you want the child to accept it in the future. One of the authors (C. E.) switched her daughter Andi to skim milk during the preschool

**FIGURE 8.10**

***FOOD AVERSIONS.*** *Strong preferences—and aversions—for certain foods may develop in early childhood.*

years. As a young adult, Andi still prefers the taste of skim milk to milk with higher fat content.

Parents also serve as role models in the development of food preferences. If a parent displays an obvious dislike for vegetables, children may develop a similar dislike (Rozin, 1990). Parents need to be careful not to be too rigid in trying to control their children's eating at mealtimes. Research has found that excessive parental demands in this area are associated with later problems of weight control and difficulty in controlling food intake at college age (Birch, 1990).

What, then, is the best way to get children to eat their green peas or spinach or other disliked food? (Notice that it is never *dessert* that the child refuses to eat.) According to Leann Birch, bribing or rewarding a child to eat a new food does not help and may even backfire. She recommends instead that adults encourage the child to taste tiny amounts of the food 8 or 10 times within a period of a few weeks so that it becomes more familiar (Kutner, 1993b).

## HEALTH AND ILLNESS

How healthy are children in the United States and in other countries? What are some of the common illnesses and environmental hazards encountered by young children? Let us examine each of these questions.

### *Minor Illnesses*

The incidence of minor illness in childhood is high. We are referring to respiratory infections such as colds and to gastrointestinal upsets such as nausea, vomiting, and diarrhea. These illnesses typically last only a few days and are not life threatening (Parmelee, 1986). It is important to keep in mind, however, that while diarrheal illness in the United States is mild, it is one of the leading killers of children in developing countries (Grant, 1993).

U.S. children between the ages of 1 and 3 generally average eight to nine minor illnesses a year. Between the ages of 4 and 10, this drops to about four to six illnesses a year. You may be surprised to learn that being ill can actually have beneficial effects on a child's development. Illnesses provide opportunities for children to learn more about themselves and their feelings. Children also gain a better understanding of caring behavior as their parents and other care givers help them cope with their illness (Parmelee, 1986).

### *Major Illnesses*

Advances in immunization, along with the development of antibiotics and other medications, have dramatically reduced the incidence of serious and potentially fatal childhood diseases in the United States. More than 97 percent of schoolchildren have been inoculated against major childhood illnesses such as rubella (German measles), measles, tetanus, mumps, whooping cough, diphtheria, and polio. Consequently, these diseases are no longer the threat they once were (Szilagyi et al., 1993).

But all is not well with the state of children's health in the United States. According to recent reports, the United States is lagging behind other industrialized nations in providing health care for young children ("Preventive Health Care," 1992; Wegman, 1992). The infant mortality rate is higher in the United States than in 20 other industrialized countries, with U.S. rates nearly double

**THINKING ABOUT DEVELOPMENT**

Agree or disagree with the following statement and support your answer: "Good health is basically a matter of heredity or good luck. Parents cannot really do much to enhance the health or stave off illness of their children."

***Oral rehydration therapy*** A treatment involving administration of a salt and sugar solution to a child who is dehydrated from diarrhea.

those of Japan, Finland, and Sweden. Immunization rates for U.S. preschoolers also are lower than they are in 69 other countries (Brody, 1993e). In fact, the proportion of U.S. preschoolers immunized against the major preventable childhood diseases has been dropping. Currently, fewer than half of 2-year-olds are properly immunized. (See Table 8.3 for a listing of ages when children should receive vaccinations.) Immunization rates are particularly low among poor minority children in urban settings (Marks, 1993). As a result, outbreaks of measles, mumps, rubella, and whooping cough in the early 1990s reached epidemic proportions (Brody, 1993e; McConnochie & Roghmann, 1992; Szilagyi et al., 1993). What is the reason for this state of affairs? The United States may have the world's most sophisticated medical technology, but other industrialized nations appear to do a much better job of providing comprehensive preventive health care to people of all socio-economic classes ("Preventive Health Care," 1992). As a first step toward rectifying this situation, the United States government established a program in 1993 that guarantees free immunizations for children who are poor or uninsured (Pear, 1993).

An estimated 31 percent of U.S. children under 18 years of age, or almost 20 million children, also suffer from some type of chronic illness (Newacheck & Taylor, 1992). These include such major disorders as arthritis, diabetes, cerebral palsy, and cystic fibrosis. Other chronic medical problems such as asthma and migraine headaches are less serious but still require extensive health supervision.

### CULTURE AND DEVELOPMENT: CHILDREN'S HEALTH

While many of the major childhood diseases have been largely eradicated in the United States and other industrialized nations, they remain fearsome killers of children in developing countries. Around the world, nearly 13 million children die each year. Two-thirds of these children will die of just six diseases, as shown in Figure 8.11. The most frequent of these is pneumonia, followed by diarrhea, measles, tetanus, whooping cough, and tuberculosis (Grant, 1993).

The tragedy is that low-cost measures such as vaccines, antibiotics, and a technique called ***oral rehydration therapy*** could prevent most of these deaths.

**TABLE 8.3**

***WHEN CHILDREN SHOULD BE IMMUNIZED***

■ RECOMMENDED BY THE AMERICAN ACADEMY OF PEDIATRICS

| VACCINATION OR TEST | COST* | AGE IN MONTHS: 2 | 4 | 6 | 12 | 12 TO 15 | 15 | 15 TO 18 | AGE IN YEARS: 4 TO 6 | 11 TO 12 | 14 TO 16 |
|---|---|---|---|---|---|---|---|---|---|---|---|
| DIPHTHERIA-TETANUS-PERTUSSIS | $9.97 | ■ | ■ | ■ | | | | ■ | ■ | | |
| TETANUS-DIPHTHERIA | | | | | | | | | | | ■ |
| POLIO | 9.91 | ■ | ■ | | | | | ■ | ■ | | |
| MEASLES | 25.29 (measles, mumps, rubella) | | | | † | | ■ | | | ■ | |
| MUMPS | | | | | | | ■ | | | ■ | |
| RUBELLA | | | | | | | ■ | | | ■ | |
| HEMOPHILUS INFLUENZA TYPE B | | ■ | ■ | ■ | | | ■ | | | | |
| TUBERCULOSIS TEST | | | | | | ■ | | | | | |

*AVERAGE COST FROM A PRIVATE DOCTOR IN 1992, WHERE AVAILABLE.

†THE RECOMMENDED AGE FOR THE FIRST MEASLES SHOT IS 12 MONTHS IN NEW YORK CITY AND OTHER PLACES WHERE THE DISEASE IS WIDESPREAD.

SOURCES: DEPARTMENT OF HEALTH AND HUMAN SERVICES; AMERICAN ACADEMY OF PEDIATRICS. CITED IN MARKS, 1993.

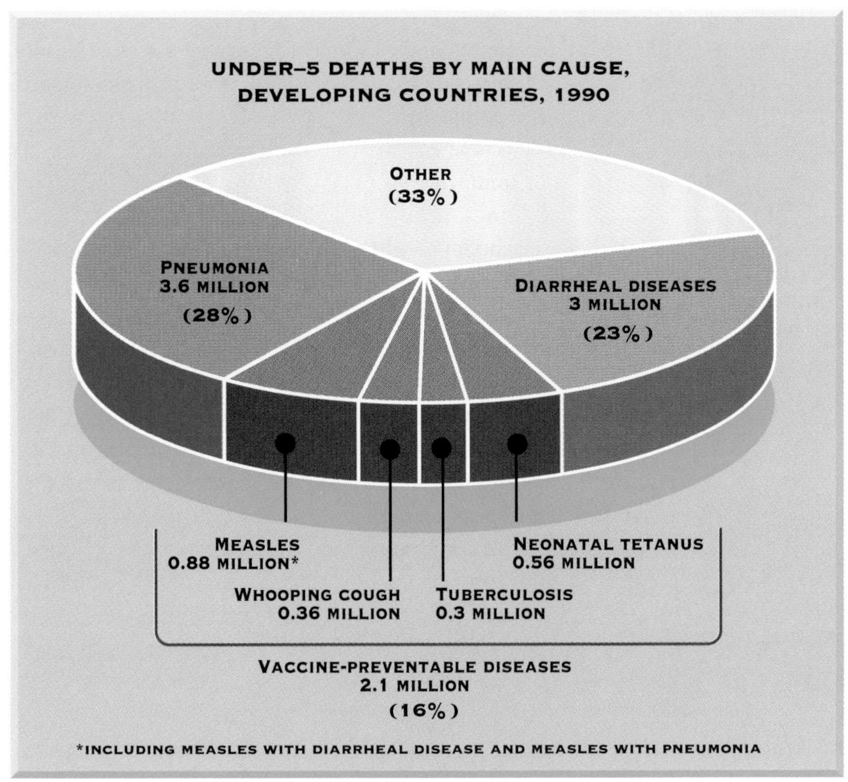


FIGURE 8.11

**CHILD DEATHS.** *Two-thirds of the nearly 13 million child deaths in the world each year are caused by pneumonia, diarrhea, or the vaccine-preventable diseases of measles, tetanus, whooping cough, and tuberculosis. (Source: Grant, 1993).*

Oral rehydration therapy involves giving a simple homemade salt and sugar solution to a child who is dehydrated from diarrhea. One piece of good news is that oral rehydration therapy now is being used by one in three of the developing world's families and is preventing an estimated 1 million child deaths every year. Another promising step is that over 80 percent of children in developing countries now are immunized against tuberculosis, measles, polio, diphtheria, tetanus, and whooping cough (Grant, 1993).

### *Environmental Hazards*

In recent years, there has been increasing concern about the effects of environmental hazards on the health of children. One such hazard is air pollution. Children living in areas with high levels of contaminants in the atmosphere show retarded physical growth as compared with children living in environments with cleaner air (Netriova et al., 1990).

One of the most potent and widespread sources of health problems is lead. As we saw in Chapter 3, prenatal exposure to even mildly elevated lead levels can have harmful effects on the fetus. Unfortunately, many children continue to be exposed to lead in the early years of life, principally by eating chips of lead paint from their homes or by breathing in dust from the paint (Shannon & Graef, 1992; Weitzman et al., 1993). Infants fed formula made with tap water also are at risk of lead poisoning, since the pipes that carry water into most homes often contain lead ("Is There Lead?" 1993). To help you assess the risk of lead poisoning in children under 6 years of age, see the Developing Today on lead poisoning.

Lead causes neurological damage and may result in lowered intelligence and developmental delays (Baghurst et al., 1992; Mahaffey, 1992; Wasserman et al., 1992). Even lead levels that until recently were thought to be harmless have been linked to learning disabilities and other deficits in cognitive functioning (Bellinger et al., 1992; Ruff et al., 1993; Yule, 1992). In recognition of this fact, the U.S. Centers for Disease Control and Prevention in 1991 lowered the amount of lead in the body considered to be safe ("Is There Lead?" 1993).

## Developing Today

### LEAD POISONING: ASSESSING THE RISK

New Medicaid rules say that doctors should ask these questions to assess the risk of lead poisoning in children 6 months to 6 years old:

- Does your child live in or regularly visit a house, a day-care center, or a nursery school that was built before 1960 and has peeling or chipping paint?
- Does your child live in a home built before 1960 that is being remodeled or renovated?
- Does your child live near a heavily traveled major highway where soil and dust may be contaminated with lead?
- Have any of your children or their playmates had lead poisoning?
- Does your child often come in contact with an adult who works with lead—in construction, welding, plumbing, pottery, or other trades?
- Does your child live near a lead smelter, a battery-recycling plant, or other industrial sites likely to release lead?
- Does your home plumbing have lead pipes or copper with lead solder joints?

If the answer to any of these questions is yes, the government says, a child has a substantial risk of exposure to lead and should be given a blood lead test as soon as one can be arranged. If the answers to all questions are negative, the child is said to have a low risk, but should nevertheless be tested for lead poisoning at 12 months of age and again, if possible, at 24 months, federal officials say.

*SOURCE: Pear (1993).*

Currently, about 4 million children, or 17 percent of all American children, are estimated to have harmful levels of lead in their blood (Needleman & Jackson, 1992). Even though children from all social and economic groups are affected, poor children are at greatest risk. They more often live in old dilapidated buildings with flaking lead-based paint and in areas with high lead contamination from industry and vehicles (Brody, 1992d; Suro, 1993).

Children growing up in inner-city neighborhoods are exposed to another very different kind of environmental hazard. They may experience sudden, lethal violence, as described in more detail in Developing Today: Children in War Zones.

### ACCIDENTAL INJURY

Accidents are now the cause of more deaths in U.S. children than the next six most frequent causes combined (Christophersen, 1989). Accidents also are the major killer of children in most countries of the world, except for those developing nations still racked by high rates of malnutrition and disease (Mohan & Romer, 1991). Injuries are responsible for nearly half the deaths of children 1–4 years of age and more than half the deaths of children 5–14 years old. Motor vehicle

**TRUTH OR FICTION REVISITED**

*Accidents are, in fact, the most common cause of death among children in the United States.*

accidents are the most common cause of death in young children in the United States, followed by drowning and fires (Greensher, 1991; Mann et al., 1992). For most types of injuries, boys outnumber girls around the world at all ages and in all socioeconomic groups (Rossetti, 1990; Taket et al., 1991).

**Culture and Development: Accidental Injury** Both fatal and nonfatal accidental injuries occur more often among low-income children than among others. For example, poor children are five times as likely to die from fires and more than twice as likely to die in motor vehicle accidents (National Center for Children in Poverty, 1990). The high accident rate of low-income children probably results partly from living in dangerous housing and neighborhoods. Poor parents also are less likely than higher income parents to take such preventive measures as using infant car seats, fastening children's seat belts, installing smoke detectors, or having the telephone number of a poison control center. The families of children who are injured frequently may be more disorganized and under more stress than other families. The injuries often occur when family members are distracted and children may be under minimal supervision (Rossetti, 1990).

**Prevention of Accidental Injury** Legislation has helped reduce certain child injuries. For example, all 50 states now require child safety seats in automobiles (see Figure 8.12). These laws have contributed to a decrease in

***Post-traumatic stress disorder*** A disorder that follows a psychologically distressing event that is outside the range of normal human experience. It is characterized by symptoms such as intense fear, avoidance of stimuli associated with the event, and reliving of the event.

## *Developing Today*

### *Children in War Zones*

> She is only 6 years old, but her most important family responsibility is to find her 2-year-old sister and hide with her in the bathtub wherever she sees someone with a gun or hears shooting. She has had to do this only twice in the last few months, but it is always on her mind—showing up in nightmares, nervousness and a constant vigilance (Goleman, 1992b, p. E7).

The child described above does not live in Bosnia, Northern Ireland, or Somalia. She lives in a housing project in northern California.

James Garbarino and his colleagues (1991, Garbarino, 1992) have studied children around the world who have experienced war-torn conditions. Most of these children exhibit symptoms of ***post-traumatic stress disorder,*** such as nightmares, insomnia, anxiety, extreme vigilance, and reduced expectations for the future. Symptoms of the disorder often are shown by children who have experienced natural disasters, witnessed extreme violence, or have been victims of sexual and physical abuse (Livingston, 1991; Michaelson, 1993a). The symptoms may last for years (Davidson & Baum, 1990; Terr, 1991).

Garbarino and others (Martinez & Richters, 1993; Richters & Martinez, 1993) have found signs of post-traumatic stress disorder in children growing up in inner cities, where violence occurs frequently but unpredictably. Statistics indicate that 30 percent of inner-city children have seen someone killed before they reach the age of 15, and more than 70 percent have witnessed a beating (Goleman, 1992b). One survey of African-American eighth-graders living in an extremely violent low-income neighborhood in Chicago found that 55 percent of the boys and 45 percent of the girls had seen someone shot (Shakoor & Chalmers, 1991). Another survey of elementary school children in New Orleans reported that 90 percent had witnessed violence, 70 percent had seen a weapon used, and 40 percent had seen a dead body (Groves et al.,1993). A 1993 poll of 6th- to 12th-grade students in 96 schools across the country indicates that exposure to violence is not confined to cities. While 40 percent of inner-city children said they knew someone who had been killed or injured by a gun, the rate was 36 percent among suburban children and 43 percent among those living in rural areas (Chira, 1993c).

Unless solutions are found to such community violence, some children in this country will continue to suffer the effects of living in a war zone.

FIGURE 8.12

***Car Safety.*** *Automobile accidents are the most common cause of death in young children in the United States. All 50 states now require child-restraint seats in automobiles. These laws have contributed to a reduction in child deaths and injuries.*

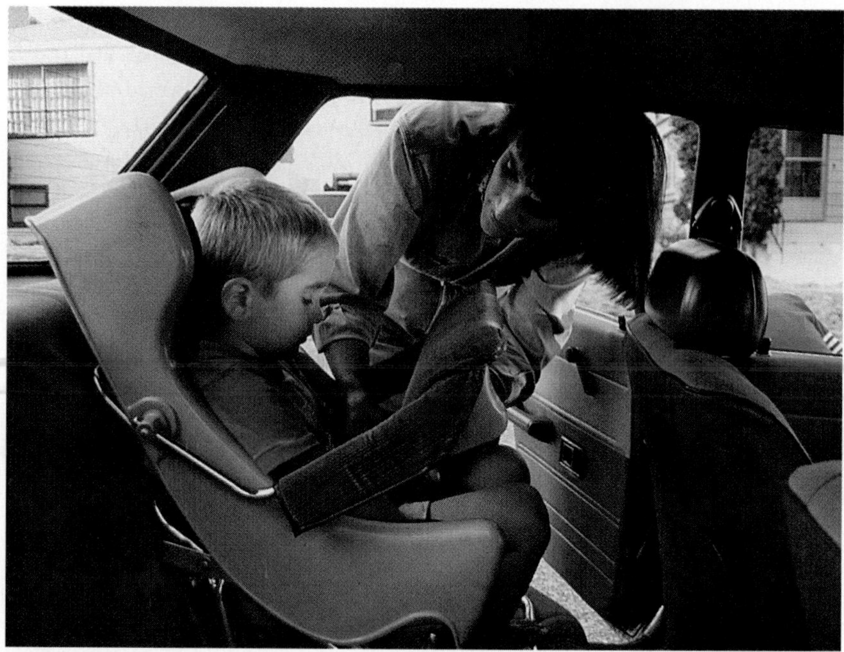

child deaths due to automobile injuries (Osberg & DiScala, 1992). Most large cities in the United States also now have laws mandating the installation of window guards on all high-rise residential buildings. In New York City, this has resulted in a sharp reduction in the number of children killed by falling out of windows (Christophersen, 1989). And in a number of countries, the risks of injury to children have been substantially reduced as a result of legislation requiring manufacturers to meet certain safety standards for such items as toys and flammable clothing (Havard, 1991).

But remember that young children are active and curious creatures. Legislation cannot substitute for the parents' and care givers' responsibility for monitoring the child's behavior and environment (Gärling & Gärling, 1993; Glik et al., 1993). Unfortunately, some parents neglect to engage in good safety practices. A 1992 U.S. Department of Transportation Survey, for example, found that 16 percent of parents didn't use a child safety seat. And of the parents who did use a seat, 36 percent did not use it correctly (''Child Safety Seats,'' 1992).

Other approaches to injury control in addition to legislation include providing health education to parents (Peterson & Roberts, 1992). Expectant parents seem particularly receptive to such messages. Another injury control strategy involves directly rewarding parents and children for engaging in good safety behaviors such as wearing seat belts. These techniques have met with some success (Christophersen, 1989; Frank et al., 1992).

## Sleep Patterns and Sleep Disorders

Children in the early years do not need as much sleep as infants. Most 2- and 3-year-olds sleep about 10 hours at night and also have one nap during the day (Handford et al., 1991). In the United States, the young child's bedtime routine typically includes putting on pajamas, brushing teeth, and being read a story. Many young children also take a favorite object—such as a blanket or stuffed animal—to bed with them (Morelli et al., 1992a). These so-called ***transitional objects*** are seen as helping children make the transition to greater independence and separation from their parents.

***Transitional object*** A soft, cuddly object often carried to bed by a child to ease the separation from parents.

### *Culture and Development: Sleeping Arrangements*

The commonly accepted practice in middle-class U.S. families is for infants and children to sleep in separate beds and in separate rooms from their parents. Child-care experts in the U.S. have endorsed this practice. Sleeping in the same room, they warn, can lead to problems such as the development of overdependence, the difficulty of breaking the habit when the child gets older, and sexual stimulation of the child (Morelli et al., 1992a).

Yet, in many non–U.S. cultures, children sleep with their mothers for the first few years of life, often in the same bed (Barratt et al., 1993; Whiting & Edwards, 1988). This practice, known as *co-sleeping,* occurs in cultures that are technologically advanced as well as in those that are less technologically sophisticated. Children in Japanese cities, for example, often sleep with a parent or other adult family member into the adolescent years (Takahashi, 1990).

In the United States, mothers who are college educated are less likely to sleep with or near their babies than mothers with a high school education (Wolf & Lozoff, 1989). In parts of rural eastern Kentucky, the majority of infants and toddlers sleep in the same bed or same room as their parents (Abbott, 1992).

Resistance to going to bed occurs regularly in 20 to 40 percent of U.S. infants and preschoolers (Johnson, 1991) but seldom occurs in cultures that practice co-sleeping. Some psychologists believe that the resistance shown by some young U.S. children at bedtime is caused by the stress of separating from their parents and going off to bed by themselves. This view is supported by the finding that young children who sleep with or near their parents are less likely to use transitional objects or to suck their thumbs at night than children who sleep alone (Morelli et al., 1992a; Wolf & Lozoff, 1989).

How do sleeping arrangements differ by culture, and what are the behavioral outcomes?

| Culture | Sleeping Arrangement | Behavioral Outcome |
|---|---|---|
| Middle-class United States | Infants and children sleep in separate beds and rooms from their parents. | Shows more resistance to going to bed; more likely to use transitional objects or suck thumb at night. |
| Many non-U.S. cultures; Japan | Infants and children share parents' bed or sleep near parents or other adult family members. | Shows less resistance to going to bed; less likely to use transitional objects or suck thumb at night. |

### *Sleep Disorders*

A number of disorders disturb the sleep of children. In this section we shall discuss night terrors, nightmares, and sleepwalking.

**Night Terrors and Nightmares** ***Night terrors*** are much more severe than the anxiety dreams we refer to as ***nightmares.*** For one thing, night terrors usually occur during deep (stages 3 and 4) sleep. Nightmares take place during rapid-eye-movement (REM) sleep, when about 80 percent of normal dreams occur. Night terrors tend to occur early during the night, nightmares in the morning hours (Barabas, 1990).

Night terrors usually begin in childhood or early adolescence and are outgrown by late adolescence (Handford et al., 1991). Children who encounter night terrors wake up suddenly with a surge in heart and respiration rates, talk incoherently, and thrash about wildly. They sometimes scream piercingly. Children are not completely awake during night terrors and may fall back into more restful sleep as suddenly as they awoke. It can be difficult to awaken them during night terrors. Once awakened, children may be disoriented and difficult to soothe. Memories of night terrors are not very vivid and usually cannot be recalled at all. Fortunately, the incidence of night terrors wanes dramatically as children develop and spend progressively less time in deep sleep. They are all but absent among adults.

Children are easier to awaken during nightmares, and they tend to recall nightmares more vividly than night terrors. The heart and respiration rates of children who are having nightmares show less arousal than those of children who are experiencing night terrors. About one-third of all preschool children

***Night terrors*** Frightening, dreamlike experiences that occur during the deepest stage of NREM sleep, shortly after the child has gone to sleep.

***Nightmares*** Frightening dreams that occur during REM sleep, often in the morning hours.

***Insomnia*** One or more of a number of sleep problems—difficulty falling asleep, difficulty remaining asleep during the night, and waking early.

***Somnambulism*** Sleepwalking (from the Latin *somnus,* meaning ''sleep,'' and *ambulare,* meaning ''to walk'').

have had at least one nightmare (Hawkins & Williams, 1992). Children are more likely to experience nightmares when they are undergoing situational stress, such as moving to a new neighborhood, attending school for the first time, or adjusting to a parental divorce (Barabas, 1990).

Children who have frequent nightmares or night terrors may come to fear going to sleep. They may show distress at bedtime, refuse to get into their pajamas, and insist that the lights be kept on during the night. As a result, they can develop ***insomnia.*** Children with frequent nightmares or night terrors need their parents' understanding and affection. Yelling at them to stop their ''immature'' refusal to have the lights out and return to sleep will not alleviate their anxieties.

**SLEEPWALKING** Sleepwalking, or ***somnambulism,*** is much more common among children than adults. As do night terrors, sleepwalking also tends to occur during deep (stages 3 and 4) sleep (Barabas, 1990; Handford et al., 1991). Onset is usually between the ages of 3 and 8.

During medieval times, it was believed that sleepwalking was a sign of possession by evil spirits. Psychoanalytic theory suggests that sleepwalking allows people the chance to express feelings and impulses they would inhibit while awake. But children who sleepwalk have not been shown to have any more trouble controlling impulses than other children do. Moreover, what children *do* when they sleepwalk is usually too boring to suggest exotic motivation. They may rearrange toys, go to the bathroom, go to the refrigerator and have a glass of milk. Then they return to their rooms and go back to bed. In the morning they seem to have no recall of the episode, which is consistent with night terrors, which also occur during deep sleep. Sleepwalking episodes may be very brief; most tend to last no longer than half an hour.

There are some myths about sleepwalking—namely that sleepwalkers' eyes are closed, that they will avoid harm, and that they will become violently agitated if they are awakened during an episode. All of these are false. Sleepwalkers' eyes are usually open, although they may respond to onlooking parents as furniture to be walked around, and not as people. Children may incur injury when sleepwalking, just as they may when awake. And, finally, children may be difficult to rouse when they are sleepwalking, as during night terrors. But if they are awakened, they are more likely to show confusion and disorientation (again, as during night terrors) than violence.

*It is not true that sleepwalkers become violently agitated if they are awakened during an episode. They may be disoriented and confused, but violence is rare.*

Today, sleepwalking among children is assumed to reflect immaturity of the nervous system and not the acting out of dreams or of psychological conflicts. As in the case of night terrors, the incidence of sleepwalking drops dramatically as children develop. When night terrors or sleepwalking are persistent, it may be wise to discuss them with the pediatrician.

## ELIMINATION DISORDERS

The elimination of waste products occurs reflexively in neonates. As children develop, their task is to learn to inhibit the reflexes that govern urination and bowel movements. The process by which parents teach their children to inhibit these reflexes is referred to as *toilet training*. The inhibition of eliminatory reflexes makes polite conversation possible.

Most U.S. children are reasonably well toilet trained between the ages of 3 and 4 (Liebert & Fischel, 1990). They continue to have accidents at night for about another year.

### TRUTH OR FICTION REVISITED

*It is, in fact, normal for children who have gained bladder control to continue to have "accidents" at night for a year or more. Bed-wetting is not considered a problem unless it is persistent.*

In toilet training, as in so many other areas of physical growth and development, maturation plays a crucial role. During the first year, only an exceptional child can be toilet trained, even when parents devote a great deal of time and energy to the task. If parents wait until the third year to begin toilet training, the process usually runs relatively rapidly and smoothly (see Figure 8.13).

FIGURE 8.13

**TOILET TRAINING.** *If parents wait until the third year to begin toilet training, the process usually goes relatively rapidly and smoothly.*

***Enuresis*** (en-you-REE-sis) Failure to control the bladder (urination) once the normal age for control has been reached.

***Bed-wetting*** Failure to control the bladder during the night.

An end to diaper changing is not the only reason parents are motivated to toilet train their children. Parents often experience pressure from grandparents, other relatives, and friends who point out that so and so's children were all toilet trained before the age of _____ . (You fill it in. Choose a number that will make most of us feel like inadequate parents.) Parents, in turn, may pressure their children to become toilet trained. And so, toilet training can become a major arena for parent–child conflict.

Children who do not become toilet trained within reasonable time frames are said to have either *enuresis, encopresis,* or both.

## *ENURESIS*

***Enuresis*** is the failure to control the bladder (urination) once the "normal" age for achieving control of the bladder has been reached. Conceptions as to the normal age vary. The American Psychiatric Association (1987) is reasonably lenient on the issue and places the cutoff age at 5 years. The frequency of "accidents" is also an issue. The American Psychiatric Association does not consider such accidents enuresis unless the incidents occur at least twice a month for 5- and 6-year-olds or once a month for children who are older.

A nighttime accident is referred to as ***bed-wetting.*** Nighttime control is more difficult to achieve than daytime control. At night, children must first wake up when their bladders are full. Only then can they go to the bathroom.

Bed-wetting is more common among boys than girls. Nearly 12 percent of boys and 8 percent of girls in the early elementary school years still wet their beds at night (Liebert & Fischel, 1990). The incidence drops to about 5 percent for children 10 to 15 years old (Leary, 1992).

### *TRUTH OR FICTION REVISITED*

*It is true that boys are more likely than girls to wet their beds. Boys are also more likely to soil.*

**CAUSES OF ENURESIS** Enuresis can have organic causes, such as infections of the urinary tract or kidney problems. Numerous psychological explanations of enuresis have also been advanced (Mikkelsen, 1991).

Psychoanalytic theory suggests that enuresis is a way of expressing hostility toward parents (because of their harshness in toilet training) or a form of symbolic masturbation. These views are largely unsubstantiated. Learning theorists point out that enuresis is most common among children whose parents attempted to train them early. Early failures might have conditioned anxiety to attempts to control the bladder. Conditioned anxiety, then, prompts, rather than inhibits, urination.

Situational stresses seem to play a role. Children are more likely to wet their beds when they are entering school for the first time, when a sibling is born, or when they are ill. There may also be a genetic component, in that the concordance rate for enuresis is higher among MZ twins than among DZ twins (Barabas, 1990).

It has also been noted that bed-wetting tends to occur during the deepest stage of sleep. This is also the stage when night terrors and sleepwalking take place. For this reason, bed-wetting could be considered a sleep disorder. Like sleepwalking, bed-wetting could reflect immaturity of certain parts of the nervous system. Just as children outgrow night terrors and sleepwalking, they also tend to outgrow bed-wetting. In most cases bed-wetting resolves itself by adolescence, and usually by the age of 8.

**Encopresis** Failure to control the bowels once the normal age for bowel control has been reached. Also called *soiling*.

**Treatment** When parents (and children) feel that they cannot wait for bed-wetting to resolve itself, they may turn to behavioral methods that condition the child to awaken when their bladders are full. One reasonably reliable method for conditioning is the bell-and-pad method (Mikkelsen, 1991), described in Chapter 2.

Often, all that is needed is reassurance that neither parents nor children are necessarily to blame for bed-wetting and that most children will outgrow it.

## *Encopresis*

Soiling, or ***encopresis,*** is lack of control over the bowels. Soiling, like enuresis, is more common among boys. However, the overall incidence of soiling is lower than that of enuresis. About 1 to 2 percent of children at the ages of 7 and 8 have problems controlling their bowels (Liebert & Fischel, 1990).

Soiling, in contrast to enuresis, is more likely to occur during the day. Thus it can be acutely embarrassing to the child. Classmates may avoid or poke fun at the soiler. Since bowel movements have a powerful odor, teachers may find it difficult to function as though nothing of importance has occurred. Parents, too, eventually become aggravated by persistent soiling and may heighten their demands for self-control, using powerful punishments for failure. As a result of all this, children with encopresis may begin to hide soiled underwear (Mikkelsen, 1991). They may perceive themselves as less competent than other children (Johnson & Moely, 1993). They may isolate themselves from schoolmates, pretending to be sick in the morning to stay at home. Their anxiety level increases. And since anxiety prompts bowel movements, control can become increasingly elusive.

**Causes of Encopresis** Encopresis stems from both physical causes, such as chronic constipation, and psychological factors. Soiling may follow harsh punishment of toilet accidents, especially in children who are already anxious or under stress (Brody, 1992a). It is as if the harshness of the punishment focuses the child's attention on soiling. The child then begins to ruminate about soiling, so that it becomes a major concern.

**Treatment: Toilet Training in a Day?** Operant conditioning methods are usually helpful in dealing with soiling. Such methods use reward (by praise and other means) of incidents of self-control, which parents would normally take for granted. They use mild punishments for continued soiling, such as a gentle reminder to pay more attention to bowel sensations and having the child clean the soiled underwear (Stark et al., 1991).

Richard Foxx and Nathan Azrin (1973) trained normal children ranging in age from 20 to 36 months to control their bladders and bowels through only one day of intense operant conditioning. They shaped self-control by reinforcing the children for engaging in each of the steps involved in using the potty—approaching the potty, taking down their pants, sitting, eliminating, wiping themselves, and so on. Reinforcers included praise, embraces, and special treats. Following treatment, the children had an average of one accident a week, as compared with a pretreatment average of six a day. Parents have learned to use this method, with about a 90 percent success rate, although it usually takes them 6 weeks rather than a day (Liebert & Fischel, 1990).

While these principles and treatment methods are simple enough, parents of children who soil frequently may not understand this approach or may resist it. In these cases, it may be necessary for therapists to work on family interactions as well as toilet training (Thapar et al., 1992).

The various treatments of encopresis—some emphasizing learning, others emphasizing family relationships—remind us once again of the close ties that exist among the areas of physical, cognitive, and social development. We now leave our exploration of physical development in early childhood and begin an examination of cognitive development in Chapter 9.

## Summary

1. Throughout early childhood, children tend to gain 2 to 3 inches and 4 to 6 pounds per year.

2. There is a strong link between the progress of myelination and the development of complex motor skills, as well as the ability to attend to and process visual information.

3. The functions of the left and right hemispheres of the brain are somewhat specialized, with the left side more involved in logic and language functions and the right side more involved in esthetic and emotional responses and in spatial and mathematical functions.

4. The brain shows plasticity in early childhood, so that injury-related losses of function can sometimes be taken up by new areas of the brain.

5. In early childhood, children make great strides in the development of the gross motor skills used in locomotion. Girls and boys are not far apart in motor development during these years, but girls tend to be somewhat more flexible and boys tend to be slightly stronger.

6. The activity level of preschool children is high. After age 2 or 3, activity level declines and children are capable of longer periods of sustained attention. Rough-and-tumble play involves play fighting and chasing. It is more frequent among boys than girls.

7. Individual differences in activity level may result from both genetic and environmental factors. Boys are more active than girls in some settings.

8. Fine motor skills develop gradually and lag behind gross motor skills.

9. Children go through four stages as they progress from making scribbles to drawing pictures; placement, shape, design, and pictorial.

10. There are stereotypes that left-handed children are less well-coordinated and more prone to academic problems than right-handed children, but recent research does not support these stereotypes.

11. As preschoolers' growth rate slows, appetite decreases and strong food preferences develop.

12. Minor illnesses are common in childhood, but the incidence of serious childhood diseases has decreased dramatically in the United States as a result of immunization and other medical advances. The United States still is lagging behind other industrialized nations in providing health care for young children, however.

13. Exposure to lead causes neurological damage and cognitive deficits. Poor children are at greater risk of lead poisoning.

14. Accidental injury is the greatest killer of children. Accidents are more common among boys and low-income children.

15. Preschool children need less sleep than infants. Children in middle-class U.S. families typically sleep in separate beds and in separate rooms from their parents, unlike children in many non–U.S. cultures.

16. Most nightmares occur during REM sleep. Night terrors are more severe than nightmares and occur during deep (non-REM) sleep. Sleepwalking also occurs during deep sleep. Despite myths to the contrary, sleepwalkers walk with their eyes open, may hurt themselves, and are not violent when awakened, although they may be disoriented and confused.

17. Enuresis is failure to control the bladder after the normal age of gaining control. Encopresis is lack of bowel control. Both enuresis and encopresis are more common among boys.

# *EARLY CHILDHOOD:*

## *COGNITIVE DEVELOPMENT*

## Chapter Outline

## Truth or Fiction?

______ *Imaginary playmates are signs of loneliness or of psychological problems.*

______ *Two-year-olds tend to assume that their parents are aware of everything that is happening to them, even when their parents are not present.*

______ *Three-year-old children may believe that it gets dark outside so that they can go to sleep.*

______ *Preschool children are unable to separate their beliefs from those of another person.*

______ *Even 1- and 2-year-olds can remember past events.*

______ *Three-year-old children spontaneously use rehearsal to help them remember things.*

______ *Children's levels of intelligence are influenced by early learning experiences.*

______ *A highly academic preschool education provides children with advantages in school later on.*

______ *Preschoolers often cannot differentiate between commercials and television programs themselves.*

______ *Three-year-olds say "Daddy goed away" instead of "Daddy went away" because they* do *understand rules of grammar.*

One of the authors (S. R.) was confused when his daughter Allyn, at the age of 2½, insisted that he continue to play "Billy Joel" on the stereo. Put aside the question of her taste in music. His problem stemmed from the fact that when Allyn asked for Billy Joel, the name of the singer, she could be satisfied only by his playing the first song of the album, "Moving Out." When "Moving Out" had ended and the next song, "The Stranger," had begun to play, she would insist that he play "Billy Joel" again. "That *is* Billy Joel," he would protest. "No, no," she would insist, "I want *Billy Joel!*"

Finally, it dawned on him that "Billy Joel," for her, symbolized the song "Moving Out," not the name of the singer. Of course his insistence that the second song was also "Billy Joel" could not satisfy her! She was conceptualizing *Billy Joel* as a property of a particular song, not as the name of a person who could sing many songs.

From about the ages of 2 to 4, children tend to show a good deal of confusion between symbols and the objects they represent. At their level of cognitive development, they do not recognize that words are arbitrary symbols for objects and events and that people could get together and decide to use different words for things. Instead, children of this age tend to think of words as inherent properties of objects and events.

This chapter discusses cognitive development during early childhood. First we examine the preoperational stage of cognitive development proposed by Swiss psychologist Jean Piaget. Then we consider other aspects of cognitive development, such as how children acquire a "theory of mind" and develop memory. We shall look at the influence of parents, preschool education, and television on cognitive development. Finally, we continue our exploration of language development.

## JEAN PIAGET'S PREOPERATIONAL STAGE

According to Piaget, the ***preoperational stage*** of cognitive development lasts from about the ages of 2 to 7. In this section, we examine the characteristics of children in this stage.

### SYMBOLIC THOUGHT

Preoperational thought is characterized by the use of symbols to represent objects and the relationships among them. Perhaps the most important kind of symbolic activity of young children is language. Language takes on greater importance in this stage of cognitive development, as children become increasingly verbal. But we shall see that children's early usage of language leaves something to be desired in the realm of logic.

You will recall from Chapter 8 that children begin to scribble and draw pictures in the early years. These drawings are symbols of objects, people, and events in children's lives. Another example of symbolism that emerges during these years is ***symbolic play,*** also known as ***pretend play.***

***Preoperational stage*** The second stage in Piaget's scheme, characterized by inflexible and irreversible mental manipulation of symbols.

***Symbolic play; pretend play*** Play in which children make believe that objects and toys are other than what they are.

### SYMBOLIC OR PRETEND PLAY

Children's "let's pretend" type of play may seem immature to busy adults meeting the realistic demands of the business world, but symbolic or pretend play requires cognitive sophistication (Doyle et al., 1991; Lillard, 1993; Lyytinen, 1992).

According to Piaget (1962), pretend play usually begins in the second year, when the child begins to symbolize objects. Piaget argued that the ability to engage in pretend play is based on the use and recollection of symbols—that is, on mental representations of things children have encountered or heard about. At 19 months, Allyn picked up a pine cone and looked it over. Her older sister said, "That's a pine cone." Allyn started pretending to lick it, as if it were an ice cream cone.

Pretend play first appears at about 12 or 13 months when children pretend to engage in familiar activities such as sleeping or feeding themselves. By 15 to 20 months, children are able to shift their focus from themselves to others. A child at this age may pretend to feed her doll instead of herself (see Figure 9.1). By 30 months of age, the child can make believe that the other object takes an active role. For example, the child may pretend that the doll is feeding itself (Campbell, 1990; McCune, 1993).

Pretend play increases during the preschool years and also becomes more complex (Garvey, 1990; Tamis-LeMonda & Bornstein, 1991, 1993). Children begin to integrate pretend play acts into longer, coordinated sequences (Harris & Kavanaugh, 1993; Lyytinen, 1991). For example, a 2-year-old might simply comb a doll's hair. An older preschooler is more likely to comb the doll's hair, put clothes on the doll, make it sit down at a table, pretend to make tea, and offer some to the doll.

Imaginary friends are one example of pretend play. At age 2, Allyn acquired an imaginary playmate named "Loveliness." He told Allyn to do lots of things—move things from here to there, get food for him, and so on. At times, Allyn was overheard talking to Loveliness in her room. As many as 65 percent of preschool children have such friends (Singer & Singer, 1990), and they are more common among firstborn and only children. Having an imaginary playmate does not mean that the child is lonely. Nor, although it involves fantasy, does it mean that the child is having difficulty maintaining contact with reality. In fact, children with imaginary companions are less aggressive, more cooperative, more creative, have more real friends, show a greater ability to concentrate, and are more advanced in their language development (Meador, 1992; Singer, 1991; M. Taylor et al., 1993).

FIGURE 9.1

**PRETEND PLAY.** *Pretend play usually begins in the second year, when the child begins to form mental representations of objects. Pretend play increases and becomes more complex during the preschool years. This 2½-year-old may engage in a sequence of play acts such as making a doll sit down at the table and offering it a pretend cup of tea.*

**TRUTH OR FICTION REVISITED**

*Imaginary playmates are not signs of loneliness or of psychological problems. Research suggests that children with imaginary playmates are better able to focus their attention than other children and are relatively advanced in language development.*

### OPERATIONS

***Operations*** Flexible, reversible mental manipulations of objects, in which objects can be mentally transformed and then returned to their original states.

***Egocentrism*** Inability to perceive the world from another person's point of view.

Any resemblance between the logic of children ages 2 to 7 and your own very often appears to be purely coincidental.

The peculiar nature of young children's logic reflects the fact that they are generally not capable of performing what Piaget refers to as ***operations.*** Or, if they can perform some operations, the circumstances under which they can perform them are limited.

Operations are mental acts (or schemes) in which objects are changed or transformed and can then be returned to their original states. Mental operations are flexible and reversible.

Consider the example of planning a move in checkers or chess. A move in either game requires knowledge of the rules of the game. The child who plays the game well (as opposed to just making moves) is able to picture the results of the move—how, in its new position, the piece will support or be threatened by other pieces and how other pieces might be left undefended by the move. Playing checkers or chess well requires that the child be able to picture, or focus on, different parts of the board and on relationships between pieces at the same time. By considering several moves, the child shows flexibility. By picturing the board as it would be after a move, and then as it is, the child shows reversibility.

Having said all this, let us return to the fact that this section is about preoperational children—children who cannot yet engage in flexible and reversible mental operations. The preoperational stage of cognitive development is characterized by many features, including egocentrism, immature notions about causality in the physical world, confusion between mental and physical events, and ability to focus on only one dimension at a time.

### EGOCENTRISM

One consequence of one-dimensional thinking is ***egocentrism.*** Preoperational children cannot understand that other people do not see things as they do. One of the authors (S. R.) asked his 2½-year-old daughter Allyn to tell him about a trip to the store with her mother. Her response was, "You tell me." It did not occur to her that he could not see the world through her eyes.

**TRUTH OR FICTION REVISITED**

*Two-year-olds do tend to assume that their parents are aware of everything that is happening to them, even when their parents are not present. Two-year-olds tend to be egocentric—to assume that others perceive the world as they do.*

Egocentrism, in Piaget's use of the term, does not mean that preoperational children are selfish (although, of course, they may be). It means that they have not yet developed a complete understanding that other people may have different perspectives on the world. They often view the world as a stage that has been erected to meet their needs and amuse them.

Piaget used the so-called three-mountains test (see Figure 9.2) to show that egocentrism means that young children literally cannot take the viewpoints of others. In this demonstration, the child sits at a table before a model of three mountains. The mountains differ in color. One also has a house on it, and another a cross at the summit.

Piaget then places a doll elsewhere around the table and asks the child what the doll sees. The language abilities of very young children do not permit them to provide verbal descriptions of what can be seen from where the doll is situated, so they can answer in one of two ways. They can either select a photograph taken from the proper vantage point, or they can construct another model of the mountains, as they would be seen by the doll. The results of an experiment with the three-mountains test suggest that 4-year-olds frequently do not understand the problem, and that 5- and 6-year-olds usually select photos or build models that correspond to their own viewpoints (Laurendeau & Pinard, 1970).

**FIGURE 9.2**

***THE THREE-MOUNTAINS TEST.*** *Piaget used the so-called three-mountains test to learn whether children at certain ages are egocentric or can take the viewpoints of others. Other methods for assessing egocentrism show different findings. (Source: Piaget & Inhelder, 1969).*

### *CAUSALITY*

Preoperational children's responses to questions such as "Why does the sun shine?" may show some other facets of egocentrism. At the age of 2 or so, they may simply answer that they do not know, or change the subject. But children a year or two older may report themselves as doing things because they *want* to do them, or, perhaps, "Because Mommy wants me to." In egocentric fashion, this explanation of behavior is extended to inanimate objects. And so, the sun may be thought of as shining because it wants to shine or because someone (or something) else wants it to shine.

A preoperational child might also respond that the sun shines "to keep me warm." In this case, the sun's behavior is thought of as being caused by *will*—perhaps the sun's voluntary wish to bathe the child in its rays, or the child's wish to remain warm. In either case, such an answer places the child at the center of the conceptual universe. The sun itself becomes as much an instrument as a light bulb.

Piaget considers this type of structuring of cause and effect ***precausal.*** Preoperational children believe that things happen for reasons, and not by accident. However, unless preoperational children are quite familiar with the natural causes of an event, their reasons are likely to have an egocentric, psychological flavor and not be based on physical causes or natural law.

Preoperational children are likely to offer mechanical explanations for familiar events (Gelman, 1978), such as how food gets onto a dish ("Mommy put it there") or why a tower of blocks falls ("It's too tall"). But consider the question "Why does it get dark outside?" The preoperational child usually does not have knowledge of the earth's rotation and is likely to answer something like "So I can go to sleep."

Another example of precausal thinking is ***transductive reasoning.*** In transductive reasoning, children reason by going from one specific isolated event to another. For example, a 3-year-old may argue that she should go on her swings in the backyard because it is light outside, or that she should *not* go to sleep because it is light outside. That is, separate specific events, daylight and going on the swings (or being awake) are thought of as having cause-and-effect relationships.

***Precausal*** A type of thought in which natural cause-and-effect relationships are attributed to will and other preoperational concepts.

***Transductive reasoning*** Reasoning from the specific to the specific.

TRUTH OR FICTION REVISITED

*Three-year-old children may, in fact, believe that it gets dark outside so that they can go to sleep. The child lacks scientific knowledge and is egocentric.*

***Animism*** The attribution of life and intentionality to inanimate objects.

***Artificialism*** The belief that environmental features were made by people.

By contrast, older children and adults usually show *inductive reasoning* and *deductive reasoning.* In inductive reasoning, we go from the specific to the general, as in, "I get tired when I jog; therefore, exercise must be fatiguing." (A good reason to avoid jogging.) In deductive reasoning, we go from the general to the specific, as in "Exercise is fatiguing; therefore, if I jog I'll get tired." (Another good reason to avoid jogging.)

Preoperational children also show ***animism*** and ***artificialism*** in their attributions of causality. In animistic thinking, they attribute life and intentions to inanimate objects, such as the sun and the moon. ("Why is the moon gone during the day?" "It is afraid of the sun.") Artificialism is the belief that environmental features such as rain and thunder have been designed and contructed by people. In *Six Psychological Studies,* Piaget (1967) wrote that "Mountains 'grow' because stones have been manufactured and then planted. Lakes have been hollowed out, and for a long time the child believes that cities are built [prior to] the lakes adjacent to them" (p. 28). Other examples of egocentrism, animism, and artificialism are shown in Table 9.1.

TABLE 9.1

*EXAMPLES OF PREOPERATIONAL THOUGHT*

| TYPE OF THOUGHT | SAMPLE QUESTIONS | TYPICAL ANSWERS |
|---|---|---|
| EGOCENTRISM | WHY DOES IT GET DARK OUT?<br>WHY DOES THE SUN SHINE?<br>WHY IS THERE SNOW?<br>WHY IS GRASS GREEN?<br><br>WHAT ARE TV SETS FOR? | SO I CAN GO TO SLEEP.<br>TO KEEP ME WARM.<br>FOR ME TO PLAY IN.<br>BECAUSE THAT'S MY FAVORITE COLOR.<br>TO WATCH MY FAVORITE SHOWS AND CARTOONS. |
| ANIMISM (ATTRIBUTING LIFE TO INANIMATE OBJECTS) | WHY DO TREES HAVE LEAVES?<br>WHY DO STARS TWINKLE?<br><br>WHY DOES THE SUN MOVE IN THE SKY?<br>WHERE DO BOATS GO AT NIGHT? | TO KEEP THEM WARM.<br>BECAUSE THEY'RE HAPPY AND CHEERFUL.<br>TO FOLLOW CHILDREN AND HEAR WHAT THEY SAY.<br>THEY SLEEP LIKE WE DO. |
| ARTIFICIALISM (ASSUMING THAT ENVIRONMENTAL FEATURES HAVE BEEN FASHIONED BY PEOPLE) | WHAT MAKES IT RAIN?<br><br>WHY IS THE SKY BLUE?<br>WHAT IS THE WIND?<br>WHAT CAUSES THUNDER?<br>HOW DOES A BABY GET IN MOMMY'S TUMMY? | SOMEONE EMPTYING A WATERING CAN.<br>SOMEBODY PAINTED IT.<br>A MAN BLOWING.<br>A MAN GRUMBLING.<br>JUST MAKE IT FIRST. (HOW?) YOU PUT SOME EYES ON IT, PUT THE HEAD ON, (ETC.). |

SOURCE: ADAPTED FROM COWAN, 1978; TURNER & HELMS, 1983.

### *Confusion of Mental and Physical Events*

According to Piaget, the preoperational child has difficulty making distinctions between mental and physical phenomena (Beilin & Pearlman, 1991). For example, children from about the ages of 2 to 4 tend to show a good deal of confusion between symbols and the objects or things that they represent. Egocentrism contributes to the assumption that their thoughts are exact reflections of external reality. They do not recognize that words are arbitrary and that people could agree to use different words to refer to things. In *Play, Dreams and Imitation in Childhood,* Piaget (1962) asks a 4-year-old child, "Could you call this table a cup and that cup a table?" "No," the child responds. "Why not?" "Because," explains the child, "you can't drink out of a table!"

Another example of the preoperational child's confusion of the mental and the physical is the tendency to believe that dreams are real. Dreams are cognitive events that originate within the dreamer, and they seem to be perceived through the dreamer's sensory modalities (eyes, ears, and so on), even though the eyes are closed and the night casts no sound upon the ears. These facts are understood by 7-year-olds. However, many 4-year-olds believe that dreams are real. They think their dreams are visible to others and that dreams come from the outside. It is as though they were watching a movie (Crain, 1992).

Do adult beliefs about dreams in a culture influence children's development of understanding of dreams?

| Culture | Adult Beliefs | Development of Children's Understanding |
|---|---|---|
| United States | Dreams are not real. | Dreams first are real, then not real. |
| Swiss | Dreams are not real. | Dreams first are real, then not real. |
| Atayal of Formosa | Dreams are real. | Dreams first are real, then not real, then real. |

**Culture and Development: Origin of Knowledge About Dreams**
Do children gradually discover the properties of dreams on their own, as Piaget believed? Or do they learn about dreams from adults? In the United States, a parent comforts a child who has had a bad dream by saying something like "It was only a dream; it didn't really happen." But in some aboriginal cultures, such as the Atayal of Formosa, adults believe that dreams are real. In spite of these adult beliefs, Lawrence Kohlberg (1966) found that Atayal children initially go through the same stages in their understanding of dreams that American and Swiss children do. In other words, they first believe that dreams are real, then realize that they are not. Ultimately, however, they adopt the adult view that dreams are real.

### *Focus on One Dimension at a Time*

To gain further insight into preoperational thinking, consider these two problems: Imagine that you pour water from a low, wide glass into a tall, thin glass, as in Figure 9.3. Now, does the tall, thin glass contain more, less, or the same amount of water as was in the low wide glass? We won't keep you in suspense. If you said the same (with possible minor exceptions for spillage and evaporation), you were correct.

Now that you're rolling, here's another problem. If you flatten a ball of clay into a pancake, do you wind up with more, less, or the same amount of clay? If you said the same, you are correct once more. To arrive at the correct answers to these questions, you must understand the law of ***conservation.*** This law holds that properties of substances such as volume, mass, and number remain the same—or are *conserved*—even if you change their shape or arrangement.

**Conservation** Conservation requires the ability to focus on two aspects of a situation at once, such as height and width. Conserving the volume, mass or number of a substance requires recognition that a change in one dimension can compensate for a change in another. But the preoperational boy in Figure

***Conservation*** The principle that properties of substances such as weight and mass remain the same (are conserved) when superficial characteristics such as their shapes or arrangement are changed.

FIGURE 9.3

**CONSERVATION.** *The boy in this photograph agreed that the amount of water in two identical containers is equal. He then watched as water from one container was poured into a tall, thin container. When asked whether the amounts of water in the two containers are now the same, he says no. Apparently, he is impressed by the height of the new container, and, prior to the development of conservation, he focuses on only one dimension of the situation at a time—in this case, the height of the new container.*

9.3 focuses on just one dimension at a time, a characteristic of thought that Piaget called ***centration.*** First, the boy is shown two tall, thin glasses of water and agrees that they have the same amount of water. Then, while he watches, water is poured from one tall glass into a squat glass. Asked which glass has more water, he points to the tall glass. Why? When he looks at the glasses, he is "overwhelmed" by the fact that the thinner glass is taller.

The preoperational child focuses on the most apparent dimension of the situation—in this case, the greater height of the thinner glass. He does not realize that the gain in width in the squat glass compensates for the loss in height. If you ask him whether any water has been added or taken away in the pouring process, he will readily reply no. But if you then repeat the question about which glass has more water, he will again point to the taller glass.

The preoperational child's failure to show conservation also comes about because of a characteristic of thought known as ***irreversibility.*** That is, the child fails to realize that an action such as pouring water from the tall glass to the squat glass can be reversed, thereby restoring things to their original condition.

If all this sounds rather illogical, that is because it *is* illogical—or, to be precise, preoperational. But if you have any doubts concerning its accuracy, borrow a 3-year-old and try the water experiment for yourself.

After you have tried the experiment with the water, try the following experiment on conservation of number. Make two rows with four pennies in each, about half an inch apart. As the 3-year-old child is watching, move the pennies in the second row to about an inch apart, as in Figure 9.4. Then ask the child which row has more pennies. What do you think the child will say? Why?

**CLASS INCLUSION** ***Class inclusion*** is another task that requires children to focus on two aspects of a situation at once. Class inclusion means that one category or class of things includes several other subclasses. For example, the class "animals" includes the subclasses of dogs, cats, horses, and so on.

In one of Piaget's class-inclusion tasks, the child is shown several objects from two subclasses of a larger class (see Figure 9.5). For example, a 4-year-old child is shown pictures of four cats and six dogs. She is asked whether there are more dogs or more animals. Now, this child knows what dogs and cats are. She also knows they are both types of animals. What do you think she will say? You may be surprised to learn that preoperational children typically answer that there are more dogs than animals (Piaget, 1963). In other words, they fail to show class inclusion.

Why do children make this error of logic? According to Piaget, the preoperational child cannot think about the two subclasses and the larger class at the same time and so, cannot readily compare them. Put another way, the child views

***Centration*** Focusing on one dimension of a situation while ignoring others.

***Irreversibility*** Failure to realize that actions can be reversed.

***Class inclusion*** The principle that one category or class of things includes several subclasses.

FIGURE 9.4

**CONSERVATION OF NUMBER.** *In this demonstration, we begin with two rows of pennies spread out equally (left). Then one row of pennies is spread out even more (right). We then asked the child, "Do the two rows still have the same number of pennies"? Do you think that a preoperational child will conserve the number of pennies or focus on the length of the row?*

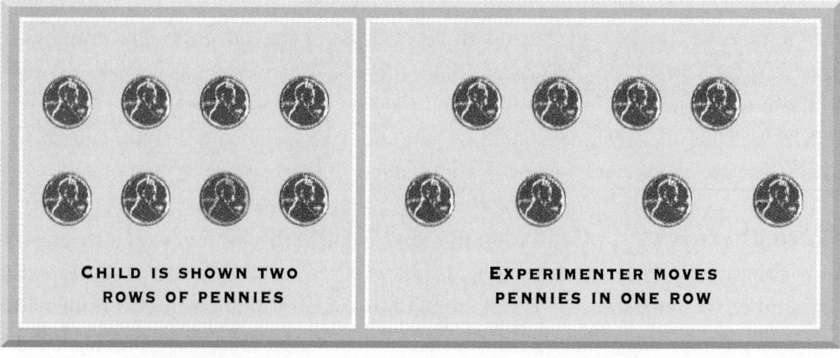

FIGURE 9.5

***Class Inclusion.*** *In one of Piaget's class-inclusion tasks, the child is shown several objects from two subclasses of a larger class. For example, a 4-year-old is shown pictures of four cats and six dogs. She is asked whether there are more dogs or more animals. What do you think she will say?*

dogs as dogs *or* as animals, but finds it difficult to see them as *both* dogs and animals simultaneously (Reyna, 1991). Another view is that young children fail to show class inclusion because their attention is too limited to focus on all aspects of the problem at once (Howe & Rabinowitz, 1991).

## *Evaluation of Piaget*

Piaget was an astute observer of the cognitive abilities of young children. But more recent research questions the accuracy of his age estimates concerning children's failures (or apparent failures) to display certain cognitive skills. As in the case of Piaget's estimates of infant capabilities, the reasons for his underestimation are partly a result of the testing methods used. Let us examine some of these newer testing methods and their results.

**Newer Research on Egocentrism** Margaret Donaldson (1979) argues that the difficulty young children have with the three-mountains test may not be due to egocentrism. Instead, she attributes much of their problem to the ***demand characteristics*** of the three-mountains test—to the demands that this particular experimental approach makes on the young child.

Donaldson believes that the three-mountains test presents a lifeless scene devoid of people and human motives. By contrast, she has found that when children are asked to place a doll of a little boy behind tabletop screens, so that it cannot be ''seen'' by police dolls, 3½-year-olds succeed in doing so most of the time.

Other tasks designed to test the perspective-taking ability of preoperational children similarly reveal that they can, indeed, make inferences about others' views (Newcombe & Huttenlocher, 1992). These tasks typically involve a single object rather than a complex array. Some allow children to move the objects themselves or to use familiar words to label the perspectives of others (Yaniv & Shatz, 1991). In one study, for example, a doll was seated across the table from two empty chairs. A cardboard screen was placed in front of the doll, blocking the doll's view of one of the chairs. When 3-year-olds were asked to put a toy duck on one of the chairs "so that the doll can see it," they correctly picked the chair in the doll's line of view (Yaniv & Shatz, 1988).

***Demand characteristics*** The demands that a specific experimental approach or task makes on a subject, as opposed to the demands that would be made if the theoretical concepts were tested in a different way.

Developing language skills may also play a role in tests of children's egocentrism and other aspects of cognitive development. Young children may not quite understand what is being asked of them in the three-mountains test, even though they may proceed to select the (wrong) photograph rather quickly. Let us give you an example. One of the authors (S. R.) was interested in knowing whether Allyn, at 2 years 9 months, thought that her mother could see her from another room. "Can Mommy see you now?" he asked. "Sure," said Allyn, "if she wants to." Allyn had interpreted his question as asking whether her mother could have permission to see her, not whether she had the capacity to see Allyn from behind a wall.

To summarize, it seems that children show the seeds of taking on the viewpoints of others earlier than Piaget suggested. One important implication is that they are likely to be concerned about the feelings of others at an earlier age than previously thought.

**NEWER RESEARCH ON CAUSALITY** Newer studies indicate that the young child's understanding of causality is more sophisticated than Piaget believed. Again, much depends on how the task is presented. When 4- to 7-year-olds are asked the kind of open-ended questions that Piaget used (for example, "Where did the ocean come from?"), they give artificialistic responses such as "The ocean comes from sinks." But when asked direct questions ("Do you think people made the oceans?"), most will correctly respond that people do not make natural events such as oceans or flowers, but do make such objects as cups and TVs (Gelman & Kremer, 1991).

Another study also shows that preoperational children correctly reject artificialistic explanations for certain biological events. Children ages 4 to 7 were asked how dogs, flowers, and cans got their color. The children correctly preferred natural mechanisms for the dogs and flowers. (For example, "While the puppy was still growing inside its mother, the mother gave it some very tiny things which made the puppy turn brown.") But children also recognized that people are responsible for producing the color of manufactured items, such as cans (Springer & Keil, 1991). Even children as young as age 3 reason differently about living organisms and inanimate objects. For example, they realize that young animals increase in size over time but that manufactured items, such as cups and television sets, do not (Rosengren et al., 1991).

**NEWER RESEARCH ON CONSERVATION** A major criticism of Piaget's tasks is that they not only require knowledge of conservation, but also language and attention skills that are difficult for young children. For instance, young children have difficulty understanding such relational terms as "more," "less," and "the same," which often are used in conservation tasks (Small, 1990).

In addition, certain demand characteristics of the standard conservation task may give a misleading picture of the child's real knowledge of conservation. Recall experiments in which Piaget and other experimenters fill two identical beakers with the same amount of water and then pour the water from one into a beaker of another shape. Before pouring the water from one beaker into another, the experimenter typically does two things. First, he or she asks the child whether both beakers have the same amount of water. Second, the child is instructed to watch the pouring carefully. A variation on this experiment by Susan Rose and Marion Blank (1974) suggests that this approach gives the experiment demand characteristics that push the child toward the wrong answer.

Rose and Blank simply avoided questioning their young subjects as to whether the amounts in the two beakers were the same before the water was poured from one beaker to another. With this approach, 6-year-olds were significantly more likely to state that the differently shaped glasses did contain the same amount of water. The researchers suggest that initially asking children whether the beakers have the same amount of water can prime them to expect a change. The instruction to watch the pouring process closely can then reinforce the expectation of change. And so, Piaget and other researchers may have been systematically underestimating the age at which children can conserve quantities of water because of the different demand characteristics of their experimental approach. For still another criticism of Piaget's conservation tasks, turn to Focus on Research.

Other recent studies also demonstrate that young children's thought is not as limited as Piaget believed. For example, the development of conservation of number appears to be tied to the development of counting ability in children. One of the key principles underlying counting ability is the ***cardinal word principle.*** This principle states that the last number in a count is special because it indicates how many total items there are. Studies by Karen Wynn (1990, 1992b) indicate that children appear to learn the cardinal word principle at about 3½ years of age, much earlier than Piaget would have predicted. In her 1990 study, 2½- to 3½-year-olds were asked to give a puppet one, two, three, five, and six items from a pile. The younger children gave only one or two items and never used counting to solve the task. But the 3½-year-olds counted the items, showing a clear understanding of the cardinal word principle.

In summary, researchers have taken issue with Piaget's view of the ages at which young children develop certain cognitive skills. As more sensitive tests have been developed, they are revealing that preschoolers have competencies that Piaget believed did not emerge until the school years (Flavell et al., 1993b).

***Cardinal word principle*** The principle that the last number in a count indicates how many total items there are.

**THINKING ABOUT DEVELOPMENT**

Agree or disagree with the following statement and support your answer: "Young children are not capable of thinking logically."

**FOCUS ON RESEARCH**

### RESPONSE ALTERNATION: ANOTHER PROBLEM IN CONSERVATION RESEARCH

The Rose and Blank (1974) study described in the text indicates that in a standard conservation experiment, children are misled by the repetition of the conservation question. The repeated question is perceived by children as a signal that their previous answer was wrong, and so they change it.

But the failure of young children to stick with their first answer when questioned a second time could also be explained by a simple bias against repeating responses. In guessing tasks in which children have to choose between two or more alternatives, they tend to alternate responses. So, when children are asked the same question twice in a consecutive task, they may have a tendency to switch their answer the second time. To test this hypothesis, Ed Elbers and his colleagues (1991) tested 4- to 7-year-olds on a conservation of number problem using wooden blocks. One group was tested in the standard way. Both before and after the row of blocks was spread out, they were asked the same question: "Do the two rows have the same number of blocks?" Most children correctly answered "yes" to the first question, but incorrectly switched to "no" the second time.

A second group (the reverse-question group) was first asked "Does one of the rows contain *more* blocks?" After one row was spread out, the group then was asked the standard question ("Do the two rows have the same number of blocks?"). Most children correctly answered "no" to the first question and "yes" to the second. You can see that when the questions are posed in this order, alternating responses results in better performance. So young children's poor performance on Piaget's standard conservation task may be partly due to their tendency to alternate responses, and not to a failure to understand the principle of conservation.

## THEORY OF MIND

Adults appear to have a commonsense understanding of how the mind works. This understanding, known as a ***theory of mind,*** allows us to explain and predict behavior by referring to mental processes (Flavell et al., 1993a; O'Neill & Gopnik, 1991). For example, we understand that we may acquire knowledge through our senses or through hearsay. We understand the distinction between external and mental events and between how things appear and how they really are. We are able to infer the perceptions, thoughts, and feelings of others. We understand that mental states affect behavior (Flavell et al., 1993b; Montgomery, 1992).

At what ages do children begin to develop these different aspects of a "theory of mind"? As we have seen, Piaget would have predicted that preoperational children are too egocentric and too focused on misleading external appearances to have a "theory of mind." But recent research has shown that even preschool-aged children can accurately predict and explain human action and emotion in terms of mental states. They are beginning to understand where knowledge comes from. And they have a rudimentary ability to distinguish appearance from reality (Bartsch & Wellman, 1993; Moses & Chandler, 1992; Wellman & Banerjee, 1991; Woolley & Wellman, 1993). Let us examine each of these developments in turn.

### *FALSE BELIEFS*

One important indication of the young child's understanding that mental states affect behavior is the ability to understand ***false beliefs.*** This involves children's ability to separate their beliefs from those of another person who has false knowledge of a situation. The concept is illustrated in a study of 3-year-olds by Louis Moses and John Flavell (1990). The children were shown a videotape in which a girl named Cathy found some crayons in a bag. When Cathy left the room briefly, a clown entered the room. The clown removed the crayons from the bag, hid them in a drawer, and put rocks in the bag instead. When Cathy returned, the children were asked whether Cathy thought there were going to be rocks or crayons in the bag. Most of the 3-year-olds incorrectly answered "rocks," demonstrating their difficulty in understanding that the other person's belief would be different than their own (see Figure 9.6). But by the age of 4 to 5 years, children do not have trouble with this concept and correctly answer "crayons" (Flavell, 1993; Flavell et al., 1990). At this age, they also start to understand that beliefs may be held with differing degrees of certainty (Moore et al., 1990).

Another intriguing demonstration of the false belief concept comes from studies of children's ability to deceive others. For example, Beate Sodian and her colleagues (1991) asked children to hide a toy truck driver in one of five cups in a sandbox so that another person could not find it. The child was given the opportunity to deceive the other person by removing real trails in the sand and creating false ones. Once again, 4-year-olds acted in ways that were likely to mislead the other person. Younger children did not.

From the research we have looked at so far, it is tempting to conclude that an understanding of false belief and deception does not emerge until age 4 (Peskin, 1992; Ruffman et al., 1993). But some studies have found that under certain conditions, children at age 3 and even younger may show some knowledge of these concepts (Freeman et al., 1991; Robinson & Mitchell, 1992). One such condition involves asking 3-year-olds a series of very specific questions about

***Theory of mind*** A commonsense understanding of how the mind works.

***False beliefs*** Separating one's beliefs from those of another person who has false knowledge of a situation.

FIGURE 9.6

**False Beliefs.** *When are children able to separate their beliefs from those of someone who has false knowledge of a situation? John Flavell and his colleagues showed preschoolers a videotape in which a girl named Cathy found crayons in a bag (a). When Cathy left the room, a clown entered, removed the crayons from the bag, hid them in a drawer (b), and filled the bag with rocks (c). When asked whether Cathy thought there would be rocks or crayons in the bag, most 3-year-olds said "rocks." but 4-year-olds correctly answered "crayons," showing the ability to understand false beliefs.*

their beliefs and those of the other person (Lewis & Osborne, 1990). Even slight changes in experimental procedures or in the way questions are worded can result in 3-year-olds correctly demonstrating knowledge of false beliefs and deceptive strategies (Hala et al., 1991; Siegel & Beattie, 1991; Sullivan & Winner, 1991). Participating in family conversations about feelings and about causality enhances the ability of 3-year-olds to understand other people's beliefs and feelings (Dunn et al., 1991).

TRUTH OR FICTION REVISITED

*By the age of 4, and in some cases by age 3, children are able to separate their beliefs from those of another person who has false knowledge of a situation.*

**Culture and Development: False Beliefs** Almost all research on the development of the false-belief concept has been carried out with children in industrialized countries. But the same pattern of development was shown in a study of children of the Baka, a pygmy people of Cameroon. Children were invited to move a desirable food from its container to a hiding place in the absence of the adult preparing the food. The children then were asked to predict the reaction of the adult on his return. Most 5-year-olds correctly predicted that the adult would approach the now-empty container and would feel happy before opening it. Only a minority of 3-year-olds responded this way, however (Avis & Harris, 1991).

### *Origins of Knowledge*

Another aspect of "theory of mind" is how we acquire knowledge. Do children understand where their knowledge comes from? If so, how early do they show this ability?

By age 3, most children begin to realize that people gain knowledge about something by looking at it (Pratt & Bryant, 1990). By age 4, children understand

***Appearance–reality distinction*** The difference between real events on the one hand and mental events, fantasies, and misleading appearances on the other hand.

***Mental representations*** The different mental forms that a real object or event can take.

that particular senses provide information about only certain qualities of an object—for example, we come to know an object's color through our eyes, but we learn about its weight by feeling it (O'Neill et al., 1992; Perner, 1991). In one study by Daniela O'Neill and Alison Gopnik (1991), 3-, 4-, and 5-year-olds learned about the contents of a toy tunnel in three different ways. They either saw the contents, were told about them, or felt them. The children then were asked to state what was in the tunnel and also how they *knew* what was in the tunnel. While 4- and 5-year-olds had no trouble identifying the sources of their knowledge, the 3-year-olds did. For example, after feeling but not seeing a ball in the tunnel, a number of 3-year-olds told the experimenter that they could tell it was a *blue* ball. The children apparently did not realize that it was impossible to discover the ball's color just by feeling it.

### The Appearance–Reality Distinction

One of the most important things children must acquire in developing a theory of mind is a clear understanding of the difference between real events, on the one hand, and mental events, fantasies, and misleading appearances, on the other hand (Flavell et al., 1993a). This is known as the ***appearance–reality distinction.***

Piaget's view was that children do not differentiate reality from appearances or mental events until the age of 7 or 8. But more recent studies have found that children's ability to distinguish between the two emerges in the preschool years. Children as young as age 3 can distinguish between pretend actions and real actions, between pictures of objects and the actual objects, and between toy versions of an object and the real object (Woolley & Wellman, 1990). By the age of 4, children make a clear distinction between real items (such as a cup), and imagined items (such as an imagined cup or an imagined monster) (Harris et al., 1991).

Despite these accomplishments, preoperational children still show some difficulties in recognizing the appearance–reality distinction. According to John Flavell and his colleagues (1990), this is because children of this age still have only a limited understanding of ***mental representations.*** That is, they have trouble comprehending that a real object or event can take many forms in our minds. This would account for certain problems in distinguishing between appearance and reality. For example, in a recent study by Marjorie Taylor and Barbara Hort (1990), children ages 3 to 5 were shown a variety of objects that had misleading appearances, such as an eraser that looked like a cookie. Children initially reported that the eraser looked like a cookie. But once they learned that it was actually an eraser, they tended to report that it *looked* like an eraser, ignoring its cookie-like appearance. Apparently, the children could not mentally represent the eraser as both *being* an eraser and *looking like* a cookie.

Three-year-olds also have difficulty with other tasks that require them to think of the same object or event in more than one way. For example, children of this age apparently cannot understand changes in their mental states. In one study (Gopnik & Slaughter, 1991), 3-year-olds were shown a crayon box. They consistently said they thought crayons were inside. The box was opened, revealing birthday candles, not crayons. When the children were asked what they *had* thought was in the box before it was opened, they now said "candles."

Very young children also find it difficult to understand the relationship between a scale model and the larger object or space which it represents (DeLoache, 1991). Perhaps this is because the child cannot conceive that the model can be two things at once: both a representation of something else and an object in its own right.

**Recognition** A memory task in which the individual indicates whether presented information has been experienced previously.

**Recall** A memory task in which the individual must reproduce material from memory without any cues.

## DEVELOPMENT OF MEMORY

We saw in Chapter 6 that even newborns have at least minimal memory skills and that memory improves substantially throughout the first 2 years of life (Kail, 1990). What sorts of memory skills do children possess in early childhood?

### *MEMORY TASKS: RECOGNITION AND RECALL*

Two of the basic tasks used in the study of memory are ***recognition*** and ***recall.*** Recognition is the easiest type of memory task. This is why multiple-choice tests are easier than fill-in-the-blank or essay tests. In a recognition test, one simply indicates whether a presented item has been seen before, or which of a number of items is paired with a stimulus (as in a multiple-choice test). Children are capable of simple recognition during early infancy, as we have seen. They recognize their mother's nursing pads, her voice, and her face. To test recognition memory in a preschooler, you might show the child some objects and then present those objects along with some new ones. The child is then asked which objects you showed her the first time.

Recall is more difficult than recognition. In a recall task, children must reproduce material from memory without any cues. If I ask you to name the capital of Wyoming, that is a test of recall. A recall task for a preschooler might consist of showing her some objects, taking them away, and asking her to name the objects from memory.

When preschoolers are presented lists of objects, pictures, or words to learn, they typically can recognize many more items later on than they can recall (Schneider & Pressley, 1989). In fact, younger preschoolers are almost as good as older ones in recognizing objects they have seen. However, younger preschoolers are not nearly as good as older ones when it comes to recall. In Figure 9.7,

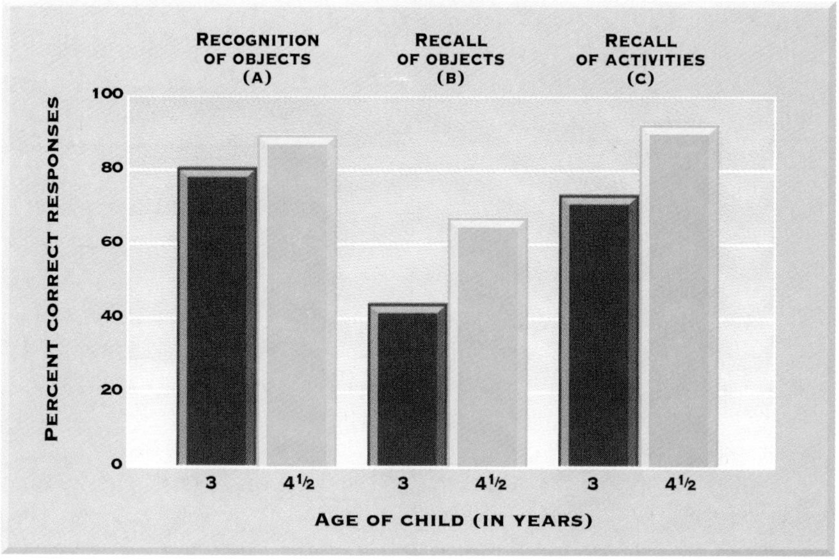

FIGURE 9.7

**RECOGNITION AND RECALL MEMORY.** *Preschoolers can recognize previously seen objects (a) better than they can recall them (b). They also are better at recalling their activities (c) than recalling objects (b). Older preschoolers (green bars) have better memories than younger ones (red bars). (Source: Jones et al., 1988).*

***Scripts*** Abstract generalized accounts of familiar repeated events.

compare the ability of 3- and 4½-year-olds to recognize and recall various objects from a life-size playhouse (Jones et al., 1988). (We will discuss the "activities" part of this figure later.)

### *Memory Competence in Early Childhood*

Until a few years ago, most studies of children's memory were done in laboratory settings. The tasks used had little meaning for the children. Results from these studies appeared to show that the memories of young children are rather deficient compared with those of older children. But parents will often tell you that their children have excellent memories for events in their lives. It turns out that they are right. More recently, psychologists have focused their research on children's memory for events and activities that are meaningful to them. These studies show that young children's memories are indeed impressive (Nelson, 1990, 1993).

For example, children as young as 11½ months of age can remember organized sequences of events they have just experienced (Bauer & Mandler, 1992). Even after a delay of 6 weeks, 16-month-old children can reenact a sequence of events they experienced only one time, such as placing a ball in a cup, covering it with another cup, and shaking the resulting "rattle" (Bauer & Mandler, 1990). By the age of 4 years, children can remember events that occurred at least 1½ years earlier (Fivush & Hammond, 1990).

Katherine Nelson and her colleagues (1990, 1993) have interviewed children ages 2 to 5 to study their memory for recurring events in their lives, such as having dinner, playing with friends, and going to birthday parties (see Figure 9.8). They found that even 3-year-olds can present coherent, orderly accounts of familiar events. Furthermore, young children seem to form ***scripts,*** which are abstract, generalized accounts of these repeated events. For example, in describing what happens during a birthday party, a child might say, "You play games, open presents, and eat cake" (Farrar & Goodman, 1990). Details of particular events often are omitted. However, an unusual experience may be remembered in detail for a year or more (Nelson, 1989a).

Young children begin forming scripts after experiencing an event only once. The script becomes more elaborate with repeated experiences. As might be

FIGURE 9.8

**SCRIPTS OF FAMILIAR EVENTS.** *Children in the preschool years form* scripts, *which are abstract, generalized accounts of repeated events. For example, in describing what happens during a birthday party, a child might say, "You play games, open presents, and eat cake." The script becomes more detailed with repeated experiences.*

expected, older preschool children form detailed scripts more quickly than younger children (Price & Goodman, 1990; Ratner et al., 1990).

Even though children as young as 1 and 2 years of age clearly can remember past events, these memories seldom last into adulthood. Most adults cannot remember significant events in their lives that occurred before the age of 2 or 3 (Howe & Courage, 1993). This memory of specific events—known as ***autobiographical memory***—appears to be linked to the development of language skills, as children begin to talk with their parents and others about past events (Bauer, 1993b; Nelson, 1993; Reese & Fivush, 1993).

***Autobiographical memory*** The memory of specific events.

**TRUTH OR FICTION REVISITED**

*It is true that even 1- and 2-year-olds can remember past events. Not until the age of about 2 or 3, however, do children form memories of specific events that will last into adulthood.*

### *FACTORS INFLUENCING MEMORY*

A number of factors affect the young child's ability to remember. These include what the child is asked to remember, the interest level of the child, the availability of retrieval cues or reminders, and what memory measure we are using. Let us discuss each of these in turn.

**TYPES OF MEMORY** Preschoolers' memories for activities are better than their memories for objects. Return to Figure 9.7 once again. Compare children's accuracy in recalling the *activities* they engaged in while in the playhouse with their accuracy in recalling the *objects* they used. You will see that children were much better at recalling their activities (for example, washing a shirt, chopping ice) than they were at recalling specific objects, such as shirts and icepicks (Jones et al., 1988).

Children also find it easier to remember events that follow a logical order than events that do not occur in a particular order. For instance, 3- and 5-year-olds have a better memory for the activities involved in making pretend cookies out of Play-Doh (you put the ingredients in the bowl, then mix the ingredients, then roll out the dough, and so on) than they do for the activities involved in sand play, which can occur in any order (Fivush et al., 1992).

**INTEREST LEVEL** Interest level and motivation also contribute to memory, even among young children. In one study, for example, 3-year-old boys were more interested in playing with toys like cars and rockets, while 3-year-old girls were more interested in playing with dolls, dishes, and teddy bears. Later, the children showed better recognition and recall for the toys in which they were interested (Renninger, 1990). Even by this age, gender-role expectations may exert their influence on cognitive development.

**RETRIEVAL CUES** While young children remember a great deal, they depend more than older children on cues provided by adults to help them retrieve their memories. Consider the following interchange between a mother and her 2-year-old child:

*Mother: What did we look for in the grass and in the bushes?*
*Child: Easter bunny.*
*Mother: Did we hide candy eggs outside in the grass?*
*Child: (nods)*
*Mother: Remember looking for them? Who found two? Your brother?*
*Child: Yes, brother (Hudson, 1990, p. 186).*

Young children whose mothers elaborate on the child's experiences and ask questions that encourage the child to contribute information to the narrative remember an episode better than children whose mothers simply provide reminders (Nelson, 1990). Parental assistance is more important under some conditions than others. For example, when 4-year-olds were internally motivated to remember items needed to prepare their own sack lunches, they did equally well with or without maternal coaching. But when the task was simply to recall a series of items, they did better with maternal assistance (Rogoff & Mistry, 1990).

**TYPES OF MEASUREMENT** Children's memory is often assessed by asking them to verbally report what they remember. But verbal reports, especially from very young children, no doubt underestimate how much children actually remember (Mandler, 1990). In one longitudinal study, children's memory for certain events was tested at age 2½ and again at age 4. Most of the information recalled at 4 had not been mentioned at 2½, indicating that when they were younger, the children remembered much more than they reported (Fivush & Hammond, 1990).

What measures might be more accurate than verbal report? One study found that when young children were allowed to use dolls to reenact an event, their recall was much better than when they gave a verbal report of the event (Goodman et al., 1990).

## *MEMORY STRATEGIES*

When adults and older children are trying to remember things, they use strategies to help their memory. One common strategy is mental repetition or ***rehearsal.*** If you are trying to remember a new friend's phone number, for example, you

***Rehearsal*** Repetition.

FIGURE 9.9

***HELPING YOUNG CHILDREN REMEMBER.*** *Young children depend on cues provided by adults to help them remember. Adults can help by elaborating on the child's experiences and asking questions that encourage the child to contribute information.*

might repeat it several times. Another strategy is to organize things to be remembered into categories. Many students outline textbook chapters to prepare for an exam. This is a way of organizing information in a meaningful way, which makes it easier to learn and remember (Kail, 1990). Similarly, if you are going to buy some things at the grocery store, you might mentally group together items that belong to the same category: dairy items, produce, household cleaners, and so on.

But preschool children generally do not appear to employ memory strategies on their own initiative. The majority of young children do not spontaneously engage in rehearsal until around 5 years of age (Small, 1990). They also rarely group objects into related categories to help them remember (Kail, 1990). By about 5, many children have learned to verbalize information silently to themselves—counting in their heads, for example, instead of aloud. This strategy improves their ability to remember visual information (Adler, 1993c).

***Thinking About Development***

Agree or disagree with the following statement and support your answer: "The best way to remember information is to repeat it over and over again."

***Truth or Fiction Revisited***

*Three-year-old children generally do not spontaneously use rehearsal to help them remember things. This strategy first emerges at about the age of 5.*

But even very young children are capable of using some simple and concrete memory aids to help them remember. They engage in behaviors such as looking, pointing, and touching when trying to remember. For example, in a study by Judith DeLoache and her colleagues (1985), 18- to 24-month-olds watched the experimenter hide a Big Bird doll under a pillow. They then were given attractive toys to play with and after a short period of time, were asked to find the hidden object. During the play interval, the children frequently looked or pointed at the hiding place, or repeated the name of the hidden object. These behaviors suggest the beginning of memory strategy.

Young children also can be trained to successfully use strategies they might not use spontaneously. For example, 6-year-old children who are trained to rehearse show a marked improvement in their ability to recall items on a memory test (Small, 1990). Similarly, requiring preschoolers to sort objects into categories enhances their memory of the material (Lange & Pierce, 1992; Schneider & Pressley, 1989). Even 3- and 4-year-olds will use rehearsal and labeling strategies if they are explicitly told to try to remember something (Fabricius & Cavalier, 1989; Weissberg & Paris, 1986).

The preschooler's use of memory strategies is not nearly as sophisticated as that of the school-age child. As we shall see in Chapter 12, the use of memory strategies and the child's understanding of how memory works advances greatly in middle childhood.

## Factors in Cognitive Development

Many factors influence the cognitive development of children. Some of the most important include social and family factors such as family income, the parents' educational level, family size, parents' mental health, and the presence of stressful family events such as divorce, job loss, or illness (Sameroff et al., 1993). In this section, we examine the role of three key factors in the young child's cognitive development: the home environment provided by the parents, preschool education, and television.

### THE EFFECT OF THE HOME ENVIRONMENT

Bettye Caldwell has developed a measure for evaluating children's home environments labeled, appropriately enough, *HOME*—an acronym for Home Observation for the Measurement of the Environment. With this method, researchers directly observe parent–child interaction in the home. The HOME inventory contains six subscales, as shown in Table 9.2.

HOME inventory items are better predictors of young children's later IQ scores than social class, mother's IQ, or infant IQ scores (Bradley, 1989; Luster & Dubow, 1992). In a longitudinal study, Caldwell and her colleagues observed children from poor and working-class families over a period of years, starting at 6 months of age. The HOME inventory was used at the early ages, and standard IQ tests were given at ages 3 and 4. The children of mothers who were emotionally and verbally responsive, who were involved with their children, and who provided appropriate play materials and a variety of daily experiences during the early years showed advanced social and language development even at 6 months of age (Parks & Bradley, 1991). These children also attained higher IQ scores at ages 3 and 4 and higher achievement-test scores at age 7 (Bradley, 1989).

**CULTURE AND DEVELOPMENT: THE HOME ENVIRONMENT** Many other studies support the view that the early environment of the child is linked to IQ scores and academic achievement in a variety of cultures, as well as in various ethnic groups in the United States (Duncan et al., 1993; Moore & Snyder, 1991; Wachs et al., 1993). For example, Marc Bornstein and Catherine Tamis-LeMonda

**TABLE 9.2**

***SCALES OF THE HOME INVENTORY***

| SCALES | SAMPLE ITEM |
|---|---|
| EMOTIONAL AND VERBAL RESPONSIVENESS OF MOTHER | MOTHER SPONTANEOUSLY VOCALIZES TO CHILD DURING VISIT.<br>MOTHER RESPONDS TO CHILD'S VOCALIZATIONS WITH VOCAL OR VERBAL RESPONSE. |
| AVOIDANCE OF RESTRICTION AND PUNISHMENT | MOTHER DOES NOT SHOUT AT CHILD.<br>MOTHER DOES NOT INTERFERE WITH CHILD'S ACTIONS OR RESTRICT CHILD'S MOVEMENTS MORE THAN THREE TIMES DURING VISIT. |
| ORGANIZATION OF THE PHYSICAL ENVIRONMENT | CHILD'S PLAY ENVIRONMENT SEEMS TO BE SAFE AND FREE FROM HAZARDS. |
| PROVISION OF APPROPRIATE PLAY MATERIALS | CHILD HAS A PUSH OR A PULL TOY.<br>CHILD HAS ONE OR MORE TOYS OR PIECES OF EQUIPMENT THAT PROMOTE MUSCLE ACTIVITY.<br>FAMILY PROVIDES APPROPRIATE LEARNING EQUIPMENT. |
| MATERNAL INVOLVEMENT WITH CHILD | MOTHER STRUCTURES CHILD'S PLAY PERIODS.<br>MOTHER TENDS TO KEEP CHILD WITHIN VISUAL RANGE AND LOOKS AT THE CHILD FREQUENTLY. |
| OPPORTUNITIES FOR VARIETY IN DAILY STIMULATION | CHILD GETS OUT OF THE HOUSE AT LEAST FOUR TIMES WEEKLY.<br>MOTHER READS STORIES TO CHILD AT LEAST THREE TIMES WEEKLY. |

FIGURE 9.10

***The Home Environment.*** *The home environment of the young child is linked to intellectual development and later academic achievement. Key aspects of the home environment include the parents' involvement and encouragement of the child, the availability of toys and learning materials, and the variety of experiences to which the child is exposed.*

(1989) studied the responsiveness of Japanese and American mothers toward their babies during the infants' first 6 months of life. They noted how often mothers responded to their infants' vocalizations or other behaviors by talking, touching, picking up, patting, feeding, and so forth. Maternal responsiveness was positively linked to Japanese children's IQ scores at the ages of 2½ and to American children's scores at age 4.

Similar results were found in a collaborative project involving six different longitudinal studies and three ethnic groups in the United States (Bradley et al., 1989). In this project, three aspects of the home environment during the first 3 years of life were related to higher IQ scores at age 3 for white, African-American, and Mexican-American children. These sources of stimulation were the availability of toys and learning materials, the parents' involvement and encouragement of the child, and the variety of experiences to which the child was exposed.

**Scaffolding and the Zone of Proximal Development** We have seen that parental responsiveness and interaction with the child is a key ingredient in the child's cognitive development. One important component of this social interaction is a process call ***scaffolding.*** A scaffold is a temporary structure used for holding workers during building construction. Similarly, scaffolding refers to temporary support provided by a parent or teacher to a child who is learning to perform a task. The amount of guidance provided by the adult decreases as the child becomes more skilled and capable of carrying out the task without help (Maccoby, 1992).

A related concept is the ***zone of proximal development*** proposed by Lev Vygotsky (1978). The zone refers to the gap between what the child is capable of doing now and what she or he could do with help from others. Adults or older children can best guide the child through this zone by gearing their assistance to the child's current capabilities (Flavell et al., 1993a).

The concepts of scaffolding and the zone of proximal development are illustrated in a study in which 3- and 5-year-old children had to sort doll furniture into the rooms in which they belonged (Freund, 1990). Children who were

***Scaffolding*** Temporary support provided by an adult to a child who is learning to perform a task.

***Zone of proximal development*** The gap between what the child is capable of doing now and what she or he could do with help from others.

FIGURE 9.11

***HEAD START.*** *Preschoolers enrolled in Head Start programs have made dramatic increases both in readiness for elementary school and IQ scores. Head Start and other similar programs also can have long-term effects on educational and employment outcomes.*

allowed to interact with their mothers performed at a higher level than children who worked alone. Furthermore, mothers adjusted the amount of help they gave to fit the child's level of competence. They gave younger children more detailed, concrete suggestions than they gave older children. When the experimenters made the task more difficult, mothers gave more help to children of both ages.

### *THE EFFECT OF EARLY CHILDHOOD EDUCATION*

How important are academic experiences in early childhood? Do they facilitate cognitive development? Some educators believe that preschool education enables children to get an early start on school achievement. Others have cautioned against the dangers of academic pressure on children (Rescorla, 1991a). Let us take a closer look at these issues.

**PRESCHOOL EDUCATION FOR ECONOMICALLY DISADVANTAGED CHILDREN** Children growing up in poverty generally perform less well on standardized intelligence tests, and they are at greater risk for school failure (Seitz, 1990). As a result, a number of preschool programs were begun in the 1960s and 1970s to enhance the cognitive development and academic skills of poor children to increase their readiness for elementary school. Some, such as the federally funded Head Start program, also provide health care to children and social services to their families (DeParle, 1993). Children in these programs typically are exposed to letters and words, numbers, books, exercises in drawing, pegs and pegboards, puzzles, and toy animals and dolls, along with other materials and activities that middle-class children can usually take for granted. Many programs encourage parental involvement in the program itself.

Studies of Head Start and other intervention programs provide convincing evidence that environmental enrichment can significantly enhance the cognitive development of economically disadvantaged children (Zigler & Styfco, 1994; Weikart & Schweinhart, 1991). The initial effects often are quite dramatic. In one study, known as the Milwaukee Project, poor children of low-IQ mothers were provided with enriched day care from the age of 6 months. By the late preschool years, their IQ scores averaged about 121, compared with an average of 95 for children from similar backgrounds who did not receive day care (Garber, 1988). In addition to positively influencing IQ scores, Head Start and other programs also lead to gains in school readiness tests and achievement tests (Haskins, 1989; Lee et al., 1990). Those programs that involve and educate the parents may be particularly beneficial for children (Wasik et al., 1990; Seitz, 1990).

*TRUTH OR FICTION REVISITED*

*It is true that children's levels of intelligence are influenced by early learning experiences. Programs such as Head Start have improved children's performances on intelligence tests.*

One source of concern has been that the gains of the preschoolers tended to evaporate during the elementary school years. By the end of the second or third grade, the performance of children in these programs dropped back to the equivalent of those who had not had early enrichment experiences (Haskins, 1989). However, more recent evaluations of the programs suggest more promising outcomes. For one thing, some of the early results that indicated no lasting effects of early intervention apparently were due to faulty methodology. In some cases, Head Start children were compared to control group children who were from less disadvantaged backgrounds. Such comparisons tend to underestimate the effects of Head Start. When the intellectual competence of graduates of Head Start programs is compared to that of carefully matched control children, the children from Head Start do appear to maintain gains on measures of school success at least through first grade (Lee et al., 1990). Graduates of at least one program, the Carolina Abecedarian Project, continued to show enhanced performance in reading and mathematics through the age of 15 (Campbell & Ramey, 1993).

Furthermore, there is now good evidence that preschool intervention programs can have major long-term effects on important life outcomes for poor children, even if initial IQ gains fade out (Seitz, 1990). During the elementary and high school years, graduates of preschool programs are less likely to have been left back or placed in classes for slow learners. They are more likely to graduate from high school, go on to college, and earn higher incomes. They are less likely to be delinquent, unemployed, or on welfare (Schweinhart & Weikart, 1993; Sigel, 1991; Zigler & Styfco, 1993).

One of the tragic contributors to the perpetuation of the cycle of poverty is the incidence of pregnancy among unwed teenage girls. Pregnancy in these cases usually means that formal education comes to an end, so that the children born to unwed teenagers are destined to be reared by poorly educated mothers. Some researchers have found that girls from preschool education programs are less likely to become unwed mothers (Schweinhart & Weikart, 1993). Others have found that girls who attended preschool intervention programs became pregnant as frequently as matched controls, but were more likely to return to school after giving birth (Haskins, 1989).

Evidence is mounting that the long-term benefits of preschool intervention programs are greatest when the intervention continues into the early elementary school grades (Farran, 1990). One such effort, for example, is the Maryland-based Success for All program, which runs from preschool through third grade. It combines academic tutoring with a family support team that emphasizes parental involvement (Madden et al., 1991). First- through third-graders in the program outperform control children in reading achievement. Similar results have been found for Chicago's Child–Parent Centers, which also enroll children from preschool through at least third grade and employ some of the same methods as Success for All. Children in the program have higher reading scores, are more likely to graduate from high school, and are less likely to be held back a grade than children who have only attended preschool or who have no preschool experience (Chira, 1992b; Reynolds, 1993).

> ***Thinking About Development***
>
> Agree or disagree with the following statement and support your answer: "The effects of Head Start programs are illusory. You can't really boost children's IQs."

**Preschool Education for Middle-Class Children: Too Much Pressure?** According to some educators, academic environments in the preschool years will benefit advantaged as well as disadvantaged children (Rescorla, 1991a; Storfer, 1990). Others argue that formal academic instruction and strong pressures to achieve, especially on the part of middle-class parents, may have a harmful effect on children's learning and social–emotional development (Elkind, 1990, 1991; Sigel, 1991).

A recent series of studies by Kathy Hirsch-Pasek, Marion Hyson, and Leslie Rescorla examined the effects of strong academic pressures on preschool children. They studied middle-class children attending a variety of preschools, ranging from those with a highly academic orientation (for example, class periods of formal instruction in math, computers, and French) through those that were more

FIGURE 9.12

**TOO MUCH PRESSURE?** *According to some educators, academic instruction in the preschool years benefits both advantaged and disadvantaged children. Others argue that formal academic instruction and strong pressures to achieve, especially by middle-class parents, may have a harmful effect on children's learning and social–emotional development.*

child-oriented and less academic (strong free-play emphasis, no direct instruction). Not surprisingly, those mothers who placed a strong value on early academics sent their children to the academically oriented schools (Rescorla, 1991b). They also enrolled their children in music, art, and sports lessons outside of school and were very directive and controlling when interacting with their child (Hyson, 1991). What is the effect on the child of this "hothouse" approach? Maternal academic expectations had a positive but short-lived effect. That is, higher maternal expectations were linked to an increase in academic skills in preschool. However, by kindergarten the other children had caught up. Furthermore, the children of the mothers with high expectations were less creative, showed more anxiety when performing tasks, and tended to think less positively about school (Hirsh-Pasek, 1991; Hirsh-Pasek et al., 1990).

TRUTH OR FICTION REVISITED

*A highly academic preschool education actually seems to provide only temporary academic advantages to children. Moreover, children exposed to such a "hothouse" approach are often less creative and more anxious about academic tasks than other children.*

## TELEVISION

How many people do you know who do not have a television set? Probably very few, for more than 98 percent of all U.S. households contain at least one television set (Comstock & Paik, 1991). American children spend more time watching television than they do in school. By the time they turn 3, the average child already watches between 2 and 3 hours of television a day, and some watch considerably more than this (Huston et al., 1992).

Television clearly has great potential for teaching a variety of cognitive skills, social behaviors, and attitudes. In Chapter 10, we will examine the effects of television on children's social behaviors and attitudes. Here, we will focus on television's impact on cognitive development in early childhood.

**EDUCATIONAL TELEVISION** By far the most successful of the television programs designed to educate children is "Sesame Street" (see Figure 9.13). Begun in 1969, its goal is to promote intellectual growth of preschoolers, particularly those from disadvantaged backgrounds. "Sesame Street" is viewed regularly by an estimated 50 to 60 percent of all children between the ages of 2 and 3, including large numbers of children from ethnic minority and lower income households (Comstock & Paik, 1991).

Several large-scale evaluations of the effects of "Sesame Street" have concluded that regular viewing of the program increases children's learning of numbers, letters, and cognitive skills such as sorting and classification (Ball & Bogatz, 1970; Bogatz & Ball, 1971; Cook et al., 1975). These effects are found for African-American and white children, girls and boys, and urban, suburban, and rural children.

Longitudinal research by Mabel Rice and her colleagues (1990) shows that viewing "Sesame Street" between the ages of 3 and 5 also leads to improved vocabulary at age 5. Viewing animated cartoons does not benefit vocabulary development. Follow-up studies have found that children learn the most from

FIGURE 9.13

***"SESAME STREET."*** *"Sesame Street" is viewed regularly by an estimated 50–60 percent of U.S. children between 2 and 3 years of age. Research shows that regular viewing of the program improves children's cognitive and language skills.*

segments that give them time to respond, clap, or sing along; from segments that are repeated in a show and throughout the season; and from those skits that they find more entertaining (Chira, 1989).

What about the effects of television on other aspects of cognitive behavior in the young child? There is some evidence that television watching can affect impulse control. One study (Desmond et al., 1990) found that heavy TV viewing is associated with greater restlessness in children. Other research, however, indicates that exposure to such educational programs as ''Sesame Street,'' ''Electric Company,'' and ''Mister Rogers' Neighborhood'' may actually increase impulse control and concentration among preschoolers (Comstock & Paik, 1991).

It has been suggested that television may stifle imagination (Singer, 1991; Singer & Singer, 1990). But at least among preschoolers, television appears to have little or no effect on children's imaginativeness (Comstock & Paik, 1991).

**TELEVISION COMMERCIALS** Critics are concerned that the cognitive limitations of young children make them particularly susceptible to commercial messages, which can be potentially misleading and even harmful. Children below the age of about 7 or 8 do not understand the selling intent of advertising, and they often are unable to tell the difference between commercials and program content (Freiberg, 1991a; Kutner, 1992c). Exposure to commercials does not make the child a sophisticated consumer. In fact, children who are heavy TV viewers are more likely than light viewers to believe commercial claims (Huston et al., 1992).

TRUTH OR FICTION REVISITED

*It is true that preschoolers often cannot differentiate between commercials and television programs themselves. Commercials appear to have powerful impacts on the preferences of preschoolers.*

Television advertising that encourages children to choose nutritionally inadequate foods—such as sugared breakfast cereals, candy, and fast foods—has been heavily criticized (Burros, 1991). Critics point out that advertisements for heavily sugared foods have an adverse effect on children's nutritional beliefs and diets (Liebert & Sprafkin, 1988). Young children do not understand that sugary foods are detrimental to health nor do they understand disclaimers in ads that, for example, state that sugared cereals should be part of a balanced breakfast (Tinsley, 1992). In response to these concerns, the U.S. Congress recently passed legislation limiting advertising on children's television shows (Condry et al., 1993; Kunkel, 1993).

Given that television can make both positive and negative contributions to the child's cognitive and social development, what's a parent to do? Simply removing the television set from the home eliminates the good with the bad. There are a number of things parents can do to help plan their children's television use, taking advantage of its positive offerings and reducing its negative effects (Antilla, 1993; Huston et al., 1992). Developing Today offers a list of suggestions for parents.

## LANGUAGE DEVELOPMENT

Children's language skills grow enormously during the preschool years. By the fourth year, children are asking adults and each other questions, taking turns talking, and engaging in lengthy conversations. Some of the milestones of language development during early childhood are shown in Table 9.3. Let us now examine these developments.

**TABLE 9.3**

***DEVELOPMENT OF LANGUAGE SKILLS IN EARLY CHILDHOOD***

| AGE | CHARACTERISTICS | TYPICAL SENTENCES |
|---|---|---|
| 2 1/2 YEARS | RAPID INCREASE IN VOCABULARY WITH NEW ADDITIONS EACH DAY | |
| | NO BABBLING | |
| | INTELLIGIBILITY STILL NOT VERY GOOD | |
| | USES 2-3 WORDS IN SENTENCES | |
| | USES PLURALS | TWO CARS |
| | USES POSSESSIVE | ADAM'S BALL |
| | USES PAST TENSE | IT BROKE |
| | USES SOME PREPOSITIONS | ANTHONY IN BED |
| 3 YEARS | VOCABULARY OF SOME 1,000 WORDS | |
| | SPEECH NEARS 100 PERCENT INTELLIGIBILITY | |
| | FAULTY ARTICULATIONS OF *l* AND *r* FREQUENT | |
| | USES 3-4 WORDS IN SENTENCES | |
| | USES YES-NO QUESTIONS | WILL I GO? |
| | USES *wh* QUESTIONS | WHERE IS THE DOGGY? |
| | USES NEGATIVES | I NOT EAT YUCKY PEAS. |
| | EMBEDS ONE SENTENCE WITHIN ANOTHER | THAT'S THE CAR MOMMY BUYED ME. |
| 4 YEARS | VOCABULARY OF 1,500-1,600 WORDS | |
| | SPEECH FLUENT | |
| | ARTICULATION GOOD EXCEPT FOR *sh*, *z*, *ch*, AND *j* | |
| | USES 5-6 WORDS IN SENTENCES | |
| | COORDINATES TWO SENTENCES | I WENT TO ANDI'S AND I HAD COOKIES. |

SOURCE: DUMTSCHIN, 1988; LOWREY, 1986; WHITEHURST, 1982.

## Development of Vocabulary

As we noted in Chapter 6, the development of vocabulary proceeds at an extraordinary pace during the preschool years, with children learning an average of nine new words per day (Rice, 1989). But how can this be possible when each new word has so many potential meanings? Consider the following example. A toddler observes a small black dog running through the park. His older sister points to

### Developing Today

#### Helping Children Use Television Wisely: Suggestions for Parents

Regulating Time with TV

- Keep a time chart with the child of his or her activities, including TV viewing, homework, and play with friends. Discuss with the child what to eliminate and what to put in its place.
- Set a weekly viewing limit. Have the child select programs from television schedules at the beginning of the week. Parents can assign points to programs and give the child a point total to spend weekly. Programs that a parent does not want the child to watch can cost more in points.
- Rule out TV at certain times, such as before breakfast or on school nights.
- Make a list of alternative activities—riding a bicycle, reading a book, working on a hobby. Before watching TV, the child must choose and do something from the list.
- Encourage the entire family to choose a program before turning the TV set on and to turn the set off when the show they planned to watch is over.
- Remember that you set an example for your child. If you watch a lot of TV, chances are your child will also.

Coping with Violence

- Watch at least one episode of the programs the child watches to know how violent they are.
- When viewing TV together, discuss the violence with the child. Talk about why the violence happened and how painful it is. Ask the child how conflict can be resolved without violence.
- Explain to the child how violence on TV shows is faked.
- Encourage children to watch programs with characters who cooperate, help, and care for each other. These programs have been shown to influence children in a positive way.

Applying Television to Real Life

- Ask children to compare what they see on the screen with people, places, and events they know firsthand, have read about, or have studied in school.
- Encourage children to read newspapers, listen to the radio, talk to adults about their work, or meet people from different ethnic or social backgrounds.
- Tell children what is real and what is make-believe on TV. Explain how television uses stunt people, camera zooms, dream sequences, and animation to create fantasy.
- Explain to the child your family's values with regard to sex, alcohol, and drugs.

Understanding Advertising

- Tell children that the purpose of advertising is to sell products to as many viewers as possible.
- Put advertising disclaimers into words children understand; for example, "partial assembly required" means "you have to put it together before you can play with it."
- On shopping trips, let children see the toys that look big, fast, and exciting on the screen, but that look disappointingly small and slow close up.
- Teach the child a few facts about nutrition and then let him or her use them. For example, if the youngster can read package labels, allow the child to choose the breakfast cereal from those in which sugar is not one of the first ingredients listed.

SOURCE: *Huston et al., 1992, pp. 102, 103.*

FIGURE 9.14

***LANGUAGE DEVELOPMENT.*** *By the fourth year, children are asking adults and each other questions, taking turns talking, and engaging in lengthy conversations.*

the animal and says "doggy." The word *doggy* could mean this particular dog, or all dogs, or all animals. It could refer to one part of the dog (for example, its tail) or to its behavior (running, barking) or to its characteristics (small, black) (Waxman & Kosowski, 1990). Does the child consider all these possibilities before determining what *doggy* actually means?

Studies have generally shown that word learning, in fact, does not occur gradually but is better characterized as a ***fast-mapping*** process in which the child quickly attaches a new word to its appropriate concept (Behrend, 1990; Waxman, 1990). The key to fast mapping seems to be that children are equipped with early cognitive biases or constraints that lead them to prefer certain meanings over others (Woodward & Markman, 1991).

One bias that children have is assuming that words refer to whole objects and not to their component parts or to their characteristics, such as color, size, or texture (Golinkoff et al., 1992; Hall, 1991). This is known as the ***whole-object assumption.*** In the example given at the beginning of the section, this bias would lead the young child to assume that "doggy" refers to the dog rather than to its tail, its color, or its barking.

Another bias about word meanings that children seem to hold is that objects have only one label. Therefore, novel terms must refer to unfamiliar objects and not to familiar objects that already have labels. This is the ***contrast*** or ***mutual exclusivity assumption*** (Woodward & Markman, 1991). How might this bias help children figure out the meaning of a new word? Suppose a child is shown two objects, one of which has a known label ("doggy") and one of which is an unknown object. Let us further suppose that an adult now says "Look at the lemur." If the child assumes that "doggy" and "lemur" each can refer to only one object, the child would correctly figure out that "lemur" refers to the other object and is not just another name for "doggy." Several studies have found evidence of this bias in children, which facilitates their word learning (Au & Glusman, 1990; Merriman & Schuster, 1991; Waxman & Senghas, 1992).

***Fast mapping*** A process of quickly determining a word's meaning, which facilitates children's vocabulary development.

***Whole-object assumption*** The assumption that words refer to whole objects, and not their component parts or characteristics.

***Contrast (or mutual exclusivity) assumption*** The assumption that objects have only one label.

FIGURE 9.15

**Vocabulary Development.** *When this adult points to the goat and says "goat," the child assumes that "goat" refers to the whole animal, rather than to its horns, fur, size, or color. This bias, known as the* whole object assumption, *helps children acquire a large vocabulary in a relatively short period of time.*

## *Development of Grammar: Toward More Complex Language*

Somewhat like the naming explosion in the second year, during the third year there is a "grammar explosion" (deVilliers & deVilliers, 1992). Children's sentence structure expands to include the missing words in telegraphic speech. During the third year, children usually add to their vocabulary an impressive array of articles (*a, an, the*), conjunctions (*and, but, or*), possessive adjectives (*your, her*), pronouns (*she, him, one*), and prepositions (*in, on, over, around, under,* and *through*). Usually between the ages of 3 and 4, children show knowledge of rules for combining phrases and clauses into complex sentences. An early example of a complex sentence is "You goed and Mommy goed, too."

**Overregularization** One of the more intriguing language developments, termed ***overregularization,*** is based on the fact that children acquire grammatical rules as they learn language. At very young ages they tend to apply these rules rather strictly, even in cases that call for exceptions (Marcus et al., 1992; Stemberger, 1993). Consider the formation of the past tense and of plurals in English. We add *d* or *ed* to regular verbs and *s* to regular nouns. Thus, *walk* becomes *walked* and *doggy* becomes *doggies.* But then there are irregular verbs and irregular nouns. For example, *sit* becomes *sat,* and *go* becomes *went. Sheep* remains *sheep* (plural) and *child* becomes *children.*

At first children learn a small number of these irregular verbs by imitating their parents. Two-year-olds tend to form them correctly temporarily. Then they become aware of the syntactic rules for forming the past tense and plurals in English. As a result, they tend to make charming errors (Mervis & Johnson, 1991; Mervis et al., 1992). Some 3- to 5-year-olds, for example, are more likely to say "Mommy sitted down" than "Mommy sat down." They are likely to talk about the "sheeps" they "seed" on the farm, and about all the "childs" they ran into at the playground. This tendency to regularize the irregular is what is meant by overregularization.

***Overregularization*** The application of regular grammatical rules for forming inflections (for example, past tense and plurals) to irregular verbs and nouns.

**TABLE 9.4**

***SOME EXAMPLES OF ALLYN'S SPEECH DURING THE THIRD YEAR***

| |
|---|
| (OBJECTING TO SOMETHING SAID TO HER) "NO, THAT IS NOT A GOOD TALK TO SAY. I DON'T LIKE THAT." |
| (DESCRIBING HER YOUNGER SISTER) "JORDAN IS VERY LAUGHY TODAY." |
| (ON THE SECOND FLOOR OF HER HOME) "THIS IS NOT HOME. THIS IS UPSTAIRS." |
| (OBJECTING TO HER FATHER'S LEAVING) "STAY HERE FOR A COUPLE OF WHILES." |
| (DIRECTING HER FATHER TO TURN UP THE STEREO) "MAKE IT A BIG LOUDER, NOT A SMALL LOUDER." |
| "I SEE TWO POLICEMANS." |
| "I GOED ON THE CHOO-CHOO." |
| "I GIVED IT TO MOMMY." |
| (REQUESTING A NICKEL) "GIVE ME ANOTHER MONEY." |
| (EXPLAINING THAT SHE AND MOMMY ARE FINISHED SINGING A SONG) "WE SINGED IT ALL UP." |
| (REQUESTING AN EMPTY CUP) "GIVE ME THAT. I NEED IT TO DRINK NOTHING." |
| "THAT CAR IS BLUE, JUST LIKE US'S." |
| (WHEN SHE WANTS HER FATHER TO HOLD HER) "I WANT YOU TO PICK UP ME." |
| (DIRECTING HER FATHER TO TURN ON THE STEREO) "PUSH THE BUTTON AND MAKE IT TOO LOUD." (A MINUTE LATER) "MAKE IT MORE LOUDER." |
| (REFUSING TO ANSWER A QUESTION) "I DON'T WANT YOU TO ASK THAT TO ME." |
| (CONFESSING WHAT SHE DID WITH SEVERAL COINS) "I TAKED THOSE MONEY AND PUT IT ON THE SHELF." |

Some parents recognize that their children were forming the past tense of irregular verbs correctly and that they then began to make errors. The thing to remember is that overregularization does represent an advance in the development of syntax. Overregularization reflects accurate knowledge of grammar—not faulty language development. In another year or two, *mouses* will be boringly transformed into *mice,* and Mommy will no longer have *sitted* down. Parents might as well enjoy overregularization while they can.

## TRUTH OR FICTION REVISITED

*Ironically, it is true that 3-year-olds say "Daddy goed away" instead of "Daddy went away" because they* do *understand rules of grammar. They are overregularizing the verb* to go *by applying general rules for forming the past tense to an irregular verb.*

In a classic experiment designed to show that preschool children are not just clever mimics in their formation of plurals but have actually grasped rules of grammar, Berko (1958) showed children pictures of nonexistent animals, as in

FIGURE 9.16

**WUGS.** *Many bright, sophisticated college students have not heard of "wugs." Here are several wugs—actually, make-believe animals used in a study to learn whether preschool children can use rules of grammar to form the plurals of unfamiliar nouns.*

Figure 9.16. She first showed them a single animal and said, "This is a wug." Then she showed them a picture of two animals and said, "Now there are two of them. There are two ______," asking the children to finish the sentence. Ninety-one percent of the children said "wugs," correctly pluralizing the bogus word.

**QUESTIONS** Children's first questions are telegraphic and characterized by a rising pitch (which signifies a question mark in English) at the end. "More milky?" for example, can be translated into "May I have more milk?", "Would you like more milk?", or "Is there more milk?", depending on the context. It is usually toward the latter part of the third year that the *wh* questions appear. Consistent with the child's general cognitive development, certain *wh* questions (*what, who,* and *where*) appear earlier than others (*why, when, which,* and *how*) (Bloom et al., 1982). *Why* is usually too philosophical for the 2-year-old, and *how* too involved. Two-year-olds are also likely to be now-oriented, so that *when,* too, is of less than immediate concern. By the fourth year, most children are spontaneously producing *why, when,* and *how* questions. These *wh* words are initially tacked on to the beginnings of sentences. "Where Mommy go?" can stand for "Where is Mommy going?", "Where did Mommy go?", or "Where will Mommy go?", and its meaning must be derived from context. Later on, the child will add auxiliary verbs *is, did,* and *will* to indicate whether the question concerns the present, past, or future.

**PASSIVE SENTENCES** Passive sentences, such as "The food is eaten by the dog," are difficult for 2- and 3-year-olds to understand and are almost never produced by them. In a fascinating study of children's comprehension (Strohner & Nelson, 1974), 2- to 5-year-olds used puppets and toys to act out a number of sentences that were read to them. Two- and 3-year-olds in the study made errors in acting out passive sentences (for example, "The car was hit by the truck") 70 percent of the time. Older children had less difficulty interpreting the meanings of passive sentences correctly. However, most children usually do not produce passive sentences spontaneously even at the ages of 5 and 6.

## PRAGMATICS

***Pragmatics*** in language development refers to the practical aspects of communications. Children are showing pragmatism when they adjust their speech to fit the social situation. For example, children show greater formality in their choice of words and syntax when they are role-playing high-status figures, such as teachers or physicians, in their games. They also say "please" more often when making requests of high-status people (Owens, 1990). Children also show pragmatism in their adoption of motherese when they are addressing a younger child.

***Pragmatics*** The practical aspects of communication, such as adaptation of language to fit the social context.

FIGURE 9.17

**PRAGMATICS.** *Young children show pragmatism when they adjust their speech to fit the social situation.*

Pragmatism provides another example of the ways in which cognitive and language development are intertwined. As we saw earlier in the chapter, preschoolers tend to be egocentric; that is, they show some difficulty in taking the viewpoints of other people. A 2-year-old telling another child "Gimme my book," without specifying which book, is not just assuming that the other child knows what she herself knows. She is also overestimating the clearness of her communication and how well she is understood (Beal & Flavell, 1983). Once children can perceive the world through the eyes of others, however, they advance in their abilities to make themselves understood to others. Now the child recognizes that the other child will require a description of the book or of its location to carry out the request. Between the ages of 3 and 5, egocentric speech gradually disappears and there is rapid development of pragmatic skills. The child's conversation shows increasing sensitivity to the listener, as, for example, in allowing turn-taking (Baker & Cantwell, 1991).

## *THEORETICAL INTERLUDE: THE RELATIONSHIP BETWEEN LANGUAGE AND COGNITION*

Language and cognitive development are strongly interwoven. For example, the child gradually gains the capacity to discriminate between animals on the basis of distinct features, such as size, patterns of movement, and the sounds they make. At the same time, the child also is acquiring words that represent broader categories, such as *mammal* and *animal.*

But which comes first? Does the child first develop concepts and then acquire the language to describe them? Or does the child's increasing language ability lead to the development of new concepts?

**DOES COGNITIVE DEVELOPMENT PRECEDE LANGUAGE DEVELOPMENT?** Jean Piaget (1976) believed that cognitive development precedes language development. He argued that children must first understand concepts before they can use words that describe the concepts. In Chapter 6, we saw that object permanence emerges toward the end of the first year. Piaget believed that words that relate to the disappearance and appearance of people and objects (such as *allgone* and *bye-bye*) are used only after the emergence of object permanence.

From Piaget's perspective, children learn words in order to describe classes or categories that they have already created (Nelson, 1982). Children can learn the word *doggy* because they have already perceived the characteristics that distinguish dogs from other things.

Some recent studies support the notion that cognitive concepts may precede language. For example, the vocabulary explosion that occurs at about 18 months of age is related to the child's ability to group a set of objects into two categories, such as "dolls" and "cars" (Gopnik & Meltzoff, 1987, 1992). Both developments may reflect the child's understanding that objects belong in categories. Other studies (Brownell, 1988; Ogura, 1991) show that at the same time children make the transition from one- to two-word sentences, they also begin to string together sequences of play activities (such as placing a doll in bed, covering it with a blanket, and rocking it). These transitions seem to indicate a basic change from "oneness" to "twoness" that is occurring in the child's cognitive development (Bates et al., 1987).

**DOES LANGUAGE DEVELOPMENT PRECEDE COGNITIVE DEVELOPMENT?** While many theorists argue that cognitive development precedes language development, others reverse the causal relationship and claim that children create cognitive classes in order to understand things that are labeled by words (Clark, 1983). When children hear the word *dog,* they try to understand it by searching for characteristics that separate dogs from other things.

**AN INTERACTIONIST VIEW** Today, most cognitive psychologists find something of value in each of these cognitive views (Gopnik & Choi, 1990; Greenberg & Kuczaj, 1982). In the early stages of language development, concepts often precede words, so that many of the infant's words describe classes that have already developed. Later on, however, language is not merely the servant of thought; language influences thought.

Similar ideas were advanced by the Russian psychologist Lev Vygotsky more than half a century ago. Vygotsky believed that during most of the first year, vocalizations and thought are separate. But usually during the second year, thought and speech—cognition and language—combine forces. "Speech begins to serve intellect and thoughts begin to be spoken" (Vygotsky, 1962, p. 43). Usually during the second year, children discover that objects have labels. Learning labels becomes more active, more self-directed. At some point, children ask what new words mean. Learning new words clearly fosters the creation of new categories and classes. An interaction develops in which classes are filled with labels for new things, and labels nourish the blossoming of new classes.

Vygotsky's concept of ***inner speech*** is a key feature of his position. At first, according to Vygotsky, children's thoughts are spoken aloud. You can overhear the 3-year-old giving herself instructions as she plays with toys. At this age her vocalizations may serve to regulate her behavior. But language gradually becomes internalized. What was spoken aloud at 4 and 5 becomes an internal dialogue by 6 or 7. This internal dialogue, or *inner speech,* is the ultimate binding of language and thought. Inner speech is essential to the development of planning and self-regulation and seems to facilitate children's learning (Bivens & Berk, 1990). Vygotsky's ideas about the self-regulative function of language have inspired psychological treatment approaches for children with self-control problems. For example, hyperactive children can be taught to use self-directed speech to increase self-control (Crain, 1992).

***Inner speech*** Lev Vygotsky's concept of the ultimate binding of language and thought. Inner speech originates in vocalizations that may regulate the child's behavior and become internalized by age 6 or 7.

And so, language is inextricably bound not only to thought but also to aspects of personality and social behavior in the young child. It is to these areas of development that we turn in Chapter 10.

## Summary

1. Piaget theorized that preoperational thought characterized the ages of 2–7 years. Preoperational thought is symbolic, as evidenced by language, drawings, and symbolic play. However, preoperational thought is relatively inflexible and leads to egocentrism; precausal ideas about causality (for example, transductive reasoning, animism, and artificialism); confusion of mental and physical events; inability to focus on more than one dimension at a time when solving problems; and failure to show conservation and class inclusion.

2. Critics of Piaget have shown that the demand characteristics of his experimental methods led him to underestimate the cognitive abilities of many children below the age of 7.

3. A theory of mind is a commonsense understanding of how the mind works. Preschool children begin to develop a theory of mind, as shown by their ability to understand false beliefs, deception, the origins of knowledge, and some aspects of the appearance–reality distinction.

4. Recognition memory tasks are easier than recall tasks for both young children and adults. Young children's memory for events and meaningful activities is impressive. They can remember events in an orderly sequence even after a single experience. Children form scripts, which are abstract accounts of repeated familiar activities.

5. Several factors affect young children's ability to remember. Their memory for activities is better than their memory for objects. They show better memory for things that interest them. Young children are more reliant than older ones on memory cues provided by adults. Preschool children generally do not employ memory strategies on their own initiative, but they can be trained to use strategies such as rehearsal.

6. The early home environment of the child is linked to later social and cognitive development. Children whose parents are emotionally and verbally responsive, and who provide appropriate play materials and varied experiences during the early years, attain higher IQ and achievement-test scores.

7. Adults can help children master difficult tasks by providing support known as *scaffolding*. Such support can guide children through the zone of proximal development, which is the gap between the child's current level of skill and the level that can be achieved with help.

8. Head Start and other preschool intervention programs have long-term effects on important life outcomes for poor children, even though initial gains in IQ fade during the early school years.

9. Middle-class children who attend academically oriented preschools and whose mothers put pressure on them to achieve do not do any better in school, like school less, are less creative, and are more anxious than children under less academic pressure.

10. "Sesame Street" is the most widely watched and successful educational television program for children. Regular watching of "Sesame Street" improves various cognitive skills. Children below the age of 7 or 8 do not understand the selling intent of television commericals, making them particularly susceptible to misleading and potentially harmful advertising messages.

11. Vocabulary development in early childhood does not occur gradually but is a fast-mapping process in which children quickly figure out a word's meaning. This process is aided by certain cognitive biases or assumptions, including the whole-object assumption (that is, words refer to whole objects, not their component parts or characteristics) and the contrast or mutual exclusivity assumption (that is, objects have only one label).

12. Children in the second and third years overregularize inflections, such as word endings, in forming the past tense of irregular verbs and in forming the plurals of irregular nouns. These errors are made because children *are* applying grammatical rules, not because of a lack of knowledge of them.

13. As development progresses, children attain the capacities to produce articles, conjunctions, adjectives, questions, and passive sentences. They also become more sensitive to the practical aspects of communication—the pragmatics—of language.

14. Many theorists argue that cognitive development precedes language development. However, a number of cognitive theorists, such as Lev Vygotsky, have pointed out that language learning sometimes precedes and promotes the development of cognitive structure.

CHAPTER

10

# EARLY CHILDHOOD: SOCIAL AND PERSONALITY DEVELOPMENT

## CHAPTER OUTLINE

## TRUTH OR FICTION?

______ *Trying to reason with children is the least effective way of fostering self-control.*

______ *Parents who make strong demands on their children for mature behavior are most likely to foster motivation to achieve.*

______ *Firstborn children are more highly motivated to achieve than later-born children.*

______ *Children who play by themselves are more likely to develop social problems.*

______ *Aggressive boys and girls are likely to be aggressive as adults.*

______ *Children who are physically punished are more likely to be aggressive.*

______ *Children mechanically imitate the aggressive behavior they observe on television and in films.*

______ *Preschoolers are most likely to fear social disapproval.*

______ *Boys and girls typically think their own gender is superior.*

______ *A 2½-year-old may know that she is a girl but still think that she can grow up to be a daddy.*

*Jeremy and Jessica, both 2½ years old, are standing at the water table in the preschool classroom. Jessica is filling a plastic container with water and spilling it out, watching the water splash down the drain. Jeremy watches and then goes to get another container. He, too, begins to fill his container with water and spill it out. The two children stand side by side, both emptying and refilling their plastic pails, glancing at each other and exchanging a few words. They continue playing like this for several minutes until Jessica drops her pail and runs off to ride the tricycle. Soon after, Jeremy, too, loses interest in this activity and finds something else to do.*

*Meanwhile, 4½-year-olds Melissa and Mike are building in the block corner, making the huge rambling structure that they have decided is a spaceship. They are talking animatedly as they work, discussing who should be the captain of the ship and who should be the space alien. Mike and Melissa take turns adding blocks. They continue to build, working together, and talking as they play, engrossed in what they are doing.*

(ADAPTED FROM CAMPBELL, 1990)

These two episodes illustrate some of the dramatic changes that occur in social development during the early years. Very young preschoolers often spend time watching and imitating each other but not interacting very much. Older preschoolers are more likely to take turns, work cooperatively toward a goal, and share. They often engage in fantasy play that involves adopting adult roles.

In this chapter, we will examine some of the changes that occur in social and personality development in early childhood. We start by examining the important role that parents, siblings, and peers play in this process. We then turn to the social behaviors themselves and examine changes in play, in positive social behaviors such as helping and sharing, and in the negative social behavior of aggression. We next examine personality and emotional development, starting with the development of self-concept, moving on to Erikson's stage of initiative and guilt, and exploring the changing nature of children's fears. Finally, we discuss the development of gender roles and gender differences in behavior.

## INFLUENCES ON DEVELOPMENT: PARENTS, SIBLINGS, AND PEERS

Young children usually spend most of their time within the family. Most parents attempt to foster certain behavior patterns in their children. They want their children to develop a sense of responsibility and conform to family routines. They want them to develop into well-adjusted individuals. They want them to acquire a variety of social skills. In other words, they want to ensure healthy social and personality development in their children. How do parents go about trying to achieve these goals? What part do siblings play in this process? And how do a child's peers influence social and personality development? Let us start by examining the influence of parents.

### *DIMENSIONS OF CHILD REARING*

Parents have different approaches to rearing their children. Investigators of parental patterns of child rearing have found it useful to classify them according to two broad dimensions: warmth–coldness and restrictiveness–permissiveness

(Baumrind, 1989, 1991a, b). Warm parents can be either restrictive or permissive. So can cold parents.

**Warmth–Coldness** Warm parents are affectionate toward their children. They tend to hug and kiss them and to smile at them frequently. Warm parents are caring and supportive of their children. They generally behave in ways that communicate their enjoyment in being with them.

Cold parents may not enjoy being with their children and may have few feelings of affection for them. They are likely to complain about their children's behavior, saying that they are naughty or have "minds of their own." Warm parents may also say that their children have "minds of their own," but they are frequently proud of and entertained by their children's stubborn behavior. Even when they are irked by it, they usually focus on attempting to change it, instead of rejecting the children outright.

It requires no stretch of the imagination to conclude that warmth is superior to coldness in rearing children (Dix, 1991). Children of parents who are accepting and warm are more likely to develop internalized moral standards of conduct or conscience (Grusec & Lytton, 1988; MacDonald, 1992). Parental warmth also is related to healthy social and emotional adjustment in children (MacDonald, 1992; Miller et al., 1993).

**Restrictiveness–Permissiveness** Parents must generally decide how restrictive they will be toward many of their children's behavior patterns. Consider just a brief list: making excessive noise when other people are sleeping or are trying to converse, playing with dangerous objects, damaging property, keeping their rooms neat, aggression, nudity, and masturbation.

Parents who are highly restrictive tend to impose many rules and to watch their children closely. Parents who are restrictive about one thing also tend to be restrictive about others.

The effects of restrictiveness on children's behavior depend on how "restrictiveness" is defined. If it is defined as consistent control and firm enforcememt of rules, it can have positive consequences for the child, particularly when combined with strong support for the child and feelings of affection (Grusec & Lytton, 1988; Putallaz & Heflin, 1990). This parenting style, known as the *authoritative style,* is described in more detail a bit later. But "restrictiveness" defined as physical punishment, interference, or intrusiveness can have negative effects, such as disobedience, lack of compliance, and lower levels of cognitive performance (Olson et al., 1992; Westerman, 1990).

Permissive parents impose few if any rules and supervise their children less closely. They allow their children to do what is "natural"—to make noise, treat the objects in their play spaces carelessly (although they may also extensively child-proof their homes to prevent their children from getting hurt and to protect the furniture), and to experiment or play with their own bodies. They may also allow their children to show a good deal of aggression, intervening only when another child appears to be in serious danger—if then. Parents may be permissive for different reasons. Some parents believe that children need the freedom to express their natural urges. Others may be disinterested in their children and uninvolved.

### *Ways in Which Parents Enforce Restrictions*

Regardless of their general approaches to child rearing, most if not all parents are restrictive now and then, even if only when they are teaching their children

***Inductive*** Characteristic of disciplinary methods, such as reasoning, that attempt to foster an understanding of the principles behind parental demands.

not to run into the street or to touch the stove. However, parents use different techniques in restricting their children's behavior. In this section we describe the methods of *induction, power assertion,* and *withdrawal of love.*

**INDUCTIVE TECHNIQUES** ***Inductive*** methods attempt to provide children with knowledge that will enable them to generate desirable behavior patterns in similar situations. The major inductive technique is "reasoning," or explaining why one sort of behavior is good and another is not (see Figure 10.1). Reasoning with a 1- or 2-year-old can be primitive. "Don't do that–it hurts!" qualifies as reasoning when children are very young. After all, "it hurts!" is an explanation, however brief.

There is some evidence that the inductive approach helps the child develop internalized moral standards of conduct or conscience (Grusec & Lytton, 1988). Induction also appears to promote positive social behaviors such as helping and sharing (Eisenberg & Miller, 1990; Hart et al., 1992).

**TRUTH OR FICTION REVISITED**

*Reasoning with children—that is, using inductive methods to enforce restrictions—actually seems to help foster development of internalized moral standards and prosocial behaviors.*

**POWER-ASSERTIVE METHODS** Other parents use power or coercion. Power-assertive methods include physical punishment and deprivation of privileges. Parents who use power assertion often justify physical punishments with sayings such as "Spare the rod, and spoil the child." Power-assertive parents also tend to yell at their children, rather than reason with them.

Power-assertive parents sometimes argue that their approach is necessary precisely because their children are noncompliant. In many cases it is unclear

**FIGURE 10.1**

***INDUCTIVE REASONING.*** *Inductive methods for enforcing restrictions attempt to teach children the principles they should use in guiding their own behavior. This father is using the inductive technique of reasoning.*

**TABLE 10.1**

***BAUMRIND'S PATTERNS OF PARENTING***

| PARENTAL STYLE | PARENTAL BEHAVIOR PATTERNS | |
|---|---|---|
| | RESTRICTIVENESS AND CONTROL | WARMTH AND RESPONSIVENESS |
| AUTHORITATIVE | HIGH | HIGH |
| AUTHORITARIAN | HIGH | LOW |
| PERMISSIVE-INDULGENT | LOW | HIGH |
| REJECTING-NEGLECTING | LOW | LOW |

ACCORDING TO BAUMRIND, THE CHILDREN OF AUTHORITATIVE PARENTS SHOW THE GREATEST COMPETENCE, WHILE THE CHILDREN OF REJECTING-NEGLECTING PARENTS ARE THE LEAST COMPETENT.

which came first—power-assertive methods or children's noncompliance. However, power assertion and noncompliance can clearly escalate into a (literally) vicious cycle.

Power assertion is associated with greater defiance (Crockenberg & Litman, 1990), lower acceptance by peers (Hart et al., 1990), poorer academic performance (Wentzel et al., 1991), and higher rates of antisocial behavior and interpersonal problems (DeBaryshe et al., 1993; Kochanska, 1992). The more parents use power-assertive techniques, the less children appear to develop internalized standards of moral conduct. The combination of a high use of punishment and rejection is often linked to aggression and delinquency (Grusec & Lytton, 1988; Lewis, 1991b).

**WITHDRAWAL OF LOVE** Still other parents attempt to control their children by threatening them with withdrawal of love. They tend to isolate or ignore their children when they misbehave. Since most children have strong needs for approval and for physical contact with their parents, loss of love can be more threatening than physical punishment. Frequent use of love withdrawal seems to facilitate compliance with adult standards, but it also may create feelings of guilt and anxiety (Grusec & Lytton, 1988).

## *BAUMRIND'S STUDIES OF PARENTING STYLES*

Diana Baumrind has undertaken research to determine the relationship between parenting styles and the development of competent behavior in young children. Baumrind (1989, 1991b) focuses on the two dimensions of child rearing we have just examined: warmth–coldness and restrictiveness–permissiveness. She developed a classification of four parenting styles based on whether parents are high or low on each of the two dimensions, as seen in Table 10.1.

**AUTHORITATIVE PARENTS** The parents of the most competent children are rated as high on both dimensions of behavior (see Table 10.1). They make strong efforts to control their children (that is, are highly restrictive) and they make strong maturity demands. However, they also reason with their children and show strong support and feelings of love. Baumrind labels these parents ***authoritative*** to suggest that they know very clearly what they want, but are also loving and respectful of their children's point of view.

***Authoritative*** A child-rearing style in which parents are restrictive and demanding, yet communicative and warm.

Compared to other children, children of authoritative parents tend to show self-reliance and independence, high self-esteem, high levels of activity and exploratory behavior, and social competence. They are highly motivated to achieve and do well in school (Baumrind, 1989, 1991b; Dumas & La Frenière, 1993).

## TRUTH OR FICTION REVISITED

*It is true that parents who make strong demands on their children for mature behavior are most likely to foster motivation to achieve. Strong demands in combination with parental warmth and encouragement are especially effective.*

**AUTHORITARIAN PARENTS** ***Authoritarian*** parents tend to look upon obedience as a virtue to be pursued for its own sake. Authoritarian parents believe in strict guidelines for determining what is right and wrong. They demand that their children accept these guidelines without question. Like authoritative parents, they are controlling. Unlike authoritative parents, their enforcement methods rely on coercion. Moreover, authoritarian parents communicate poorly with their children. They do not respect their children's points of view, and they are cold and rejecting.

In Baumrind's research, sons of authoritarian parents were relatively hostile and resistive and girls were low in independence and dominance (Baumrind, 1989). Other researchers have found children of authoritarian parents to be less competent socially and academically than children of authoritative parents. Children of authoritarian parents also tend to be conflicted and irritable. They are less friendly and spontaneous in their social interactions (DeKovic & Janssens, 1992; Maccoby & Martin, 1983). As adolescents, they are conforming and obedient but have lower self-reliance and self-esteem (Buri et al., 1988; Lamborn et al., 1991).

**PERMISSIVE PARENTS** Baumrind found two types of parents who are permissive, as opposed to restrictive. One type may be labeled "permissive–indulgent" and the other "rejecting–neglecting." ***Permissive–indulgent*** parents are rated low in their attempts to control their children and in their demands for mature behavior. They are easygoing and unconventional. Their brand of permissiveness is accompanied by high nurturance (warmth and support).

***Rejecting–neglecting*** parents also are rated low in their demands for mature behavior and their attempt to control their children. But unlike the indulgent parents, they are low in support and responsiveness.

It is perhaps not surprising that the neglectful parenting style is associated with the poorest child outcomes. By and large, the children of neglectful parents are the least competent, responsible and mature, and the most prone to problem behaviors. Children of permissive–indulgent parents, like those of neglectful parents, show less competence in school and more deviant behavior (for example, misconduct and substance abuse) than children of more restrictive, controlling parents. But children from permissive–indulgent homes, unlike those from neglectful homes, are fairly high in social competence and self-confidence (Baumrind, 1991a; Lamborn et al., 1991).

***Authoritarian*** A child-rearing style in which parents demand submission and obedience from their children but are not very communicative and warm.

***Permissive–indulgent*** A child-rearing style in which parents are not controlling and restrictive but are warm.

***Rejecting–neglecting*** A child-rearing style in which parents are neither restrictive and controlling nor supportive and responsive.

### *Effects of the Situation and the Child on Parenting Styles*

In our discussion of parenting styles, we have focused thus far on the influence of the parent on the child. But the parenting style that parents use also depends partly on the situation and on the characteristics of the child.

For example, parents are more likely to use power-assertive techniques for dealing with aggressive behavior than social withdrawal behavior (Mills & Rubin, 1990). Parents prefer power-assertive techniques over inductive techniques when they believe that children understand the rules they have violated, are capable of acting more appropriately, and are responsible for their bad behavior (Dix et al., 1989). Stressful life events, marital discord, and depression in the mother are additional factors that contribute to the mother's use of power-assertive techniques (Campbell et al., 1991).

Remember from Chapter 7 that children's behaviors and temperamental characteristics also influence adult behaviors. In one intriguing experiment (Anderson et al., 1986), mothers of normal boys and mothers of boys with behavior problems interacted with boys of both types. Both groups of mothers were more negative and controlling when dealing with the conduct-disordered boys. This indicates the importance of the child's behavior in eliciting certain types of responses from parents.

In conclusion, the research of Baumrind and others does not prove that certain child-rearing patterns *cause* the outcomes described. On the other hand, Baumrind's research suggests that we can make an effort to avoid some of the pitfalls of being authoritarian or overly permissive. Some recommended techniques that parents can use to help control and guide their children's behavior are listed in Developing Today.

## *Developing Today*

### Controlling and Guiding Children's Behavior

**Some "Do's" and "Don'ts" for Parents**

*Do's*

- Reward good behavior with praises, smiles, hugs.
- Give clear, simple, realistic rules appropriate to the child's age.
- Enforce rules with reasonable consequences.
- Ignore annoying behavior such as whining and tantrums.
- Child-proof the house, putting dangerous and breakable items out of reach. Then establish limits.
- Be consistent.

*Don'ts*

- Pay attention only to a child's misbehavior.
- Issue too many rules or enforce them haphazardly.
- Try to control behavior solely in the child's domain, such as thumbsucking, which can lead to frustrating power struggles.
- Nag, lecture, shame, or induce guilt.
- Yell or spank.
- Be overly permissive.

Sources: *Windell, 1991; Schmitt, 1991.*

## CULTURE AND DEVELOPMENT: PATTERNS OF CHILD REARING

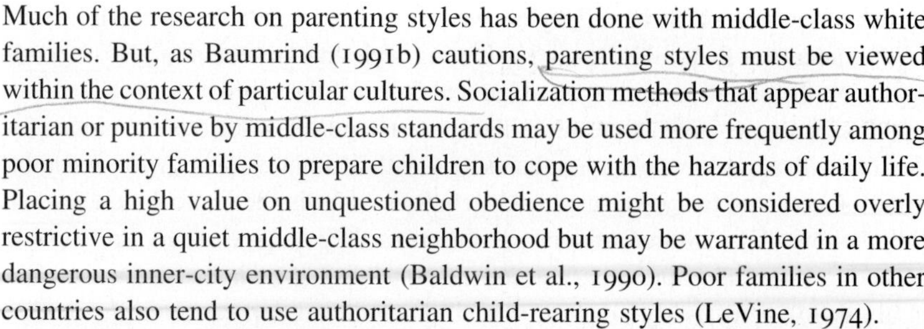

Much of the research on parenting styles has been done with middle-class white families. But, as Baumrind (1991b) cautions, parenting styles must be viewed within the context of particular cultures. Socialization methods that appear authoritarian or punitive by middle-class standards may be used more frequently among poor minority families to prepare children to cope with the hazards of daily life. Placing a high value on unquestioned obedience might be considered overly restrictive in a quiet middle-class neighborhood but may be warranted in a more dangerous inner-city environment (Baldwin et al., 1990). Poor families in other countries also tend to use authoritarian child-rearing styles (LeVine, 1974).

Do different cultural values influence parental child-rearing techniques?

What about middle-class families in other parts of the world? How do their parenting styles compare with those of middle-class U.S. parents? An interesting study by Kobayashi-Winata and Power (1989) compared child-rearing practices of middle-class Japanese and American parents whose children ranged in age from 4 to 7 years old. In both groups of families, the most compliant children had parents who provided opportunities for appropriate behavior and who used relatively little punishment. Japanese and American parents did differ, however, in the relative use of various child-rearing practices. American parents were more likely to rely on external punishments such as sending children to their room, whereas Japanese parents more often used verbal commands, reprimands, and explanations. These differences in disciplinary practices may reflect differences in cultural values. Japanese parents emphasize conformity and acceptance of group goals, whereas American parents are more likely to emphasize independence and individualism. It may be that verbal methods are more effective in ensuring group cooperation.

Other studies reveal additional differences in the child-rearing techniques of American and Japanese parents that appear to foster the American emphasis on early socialization and independence and the Japanese focus on group harmony and dependence on others. For example, in one study, U.S. mothers of preschoolers expected their children to follow more rules but also were more likely to listen to their children's opinions. Japanese mothers, in contrast, made many fewer demands on their children and were more indulgent (Power et al., 1992).

| Culture | Parental Value | Child-Rearing Practices |
|---|---|---|
| American Middle-Class | Early socialization<br>Independence<br>Individualism | Expect child to follow more rules<br>Listen to child's opinion<br>External punishment (e.g., send child to room) |
| Japanese Middle-Class | Group harmony<br>Dependence on others<br>Conformity | Fewer demands<br>More indulgent<br>Verbal commands<br>Reprimands and explanations |

**FIGURE 10.2**

***Child-Rearing Techniques in Japan.*** *Japanese parents use more verbal commands, reprimands, and explanations than American parents.*

### *Influence of Siblings*

Of U.S. families with children, about 80 percent have at least two (Dunn, 1985). In many cases, children spend more time with their siblings in the early years than they spend with their parents (Crouter & McHale, 1989).

Siblings make a unique contribution to one another's social, emotional, and cognitive development (Azmitia & Hesser, 1993; Graham-Bermann, 1991; Wachs et al., 1993). They serve many functions, including physical care giving, providing emotional support and nurturance, offering advice and direction, serving as role models, providing social interaction that helps develop social skills, and making demands and imposing restrictions (Dunn, 1992b; Stocker & Dunn, 1990).

In the early years of childhood, when siblings spend a great deal of time together, their interactions often are emotionally loaded and marked by both positive aspects (cooperation, teaching, nurturance) and negative aspects (conflict, control, competition) (Dunn et al., 1990). By and large, older siblings are more nurturant and dominating than younger siblings (Buhrmester & Furman, 1990). Younger siblings are more likely to imitate older siblings (Abramovitch et al., 1986; Hartup, 1989) and are more likely to accept their direction (Shantz & Hobart, 1989).

However, older siblings may also imitate younger siblings, especially when parents remark ''how cute'' the baby is being in front of the older child. At the age of 2 years 5 months, S. R.'s daughter Allyn would pretend that she could not talk every once in a while, just like her 5-month-old sister Jordan.

In many cultures, older girls are expected to care for younger siblings (Whiting & Edwards, 1988; Zukow, 1989). Younger siblings frequently turn to older sisters when the mother is unavailable (see Figure 10.3).

As siblings move from early childhood through middle childhood and into adolescence, the nature of their relationship changes in at least two important ways (Buhrmester, 1992; Buhrmester & Furman, 1990). First, as siblings grow more competent and as their developmental statuses become similar, their relationship becomes more egalitarian. In other words, as later-born siblings grow older and become more self-sufficient, they need and accept less nurturance and direction from older siblings. Second, sibling relationships become less intense as children grow older. The exercise of power and the amount of conflict declines. The extent of warmth and closeness diminishes somewhat as well, although the attachment between siblings remains fairly strong throughout adolescence.

Other factors also affect the development of sibling relationships. For example, there is more conflict between siblings in families in which the parents treat the children very differently (Brody et al., 1992a, b; Dunn, 1992a). Conflict between siblings also is greater when the relationship between the parents or between the parents and children is not harmonious (Brody et al., 1992a, b; Volling & Belsky, 1992). It should also come as no surprise that children who have a difficult temperament have more trouble getting along with their siblings (Dunn, 1993).

**Adjusting to the Birth of a Sibling** The birth of a sister or brother is often a source of stress for young children because of changes in family relationships and the environment (Gottlieb & Mendelson, 1990). When a new baby comes into the home, the mother pays relatively more attention to it and spends much less time in playful activities with the older child (Dunn, 1985). No wonder that the child may feel displaced and resentful of the affection lavished on the newborn. These feelings are illustrated by the comments of a 3-year-old

FIGURE 10.3

**Siblings.** *Siblings make a unique contribution to one another's social, emotional, and cognitive development. In many cultures, older girls are expected to care for younger siblings.*

***Regression*** A return to behaviors characteristic of earlier stages of development.

***Sibling rivalry*** Jealousy or rivalry among brothers and sisters.

who worried that his new sister would take all his mother's love and not leave enough for him (Campbell, 1990).

Children show a mixture of negative and positive reactions to the birth of a sibling. These include ***regression*** to babyish behaviors, such as increased clinging, crying, and toilet accidents. Anger and naughtiness may increase as well. But the same children will often show increased independence and maturity, insisting on feeding or dressing themselves, and helping to take care of the baby (Dunn, 1985; Kutner, 1989; Teti, 1992).

What can parents do to help a young child cope with the arrival of a new baby? For one thing, they can prepare the child by explaining in advance what is to come. In one study, preschoolers who attended a sibling preparation class with their mothers showed fewer signs of ***sibling rivalry*** (Fortier et al., 1991). Parental support is extremely important as well. Children show less distress following the birth of a sibling when the parents give them lots of affection, encouragement, and praise and spend time doing things with them (Gottlieb & Mendelson, 1990).

**THE EFFECTS OF BIRTH ORDER** Many differences in personality and achievement have been observed among firstborns and only children as compared with later-born children (Falbo, 1992; Falbo & Poston, 1993; Hoffman, 1991). On the positive side (from the standpoint of two highly achievement-oriented adults), firstborns and only children are more highly motivated to achieve, perform better academically, are more cooperative, helpful, and adult-oriented, and are less aggressive. On the negative side, firstborns and only children show greater anxiety and are less self-reliant.

*Firstborn children do tend to be more highly motivated to achieve than later-born children. They are also generally more cooperative and helpful, but more anxious.*

Later-born children frequently learn that they must act aggressively to earn the attention of their parents and older siblings. They also tend to accept that they do not come first. Perhaps for that reason, their self-concepts tend to be lower than those of firstborns or of only children. The social skills they acquire from dealing with and accommodating to the desires of their older siblings seems to translate into their greater popularity with peers.

Differences in personality and achievement among firstborns and later-borns may be linked to contrasting styles in parenting (Dunn & Kendrick, 1982; Dunn et al., 1986; McCabe et al., 1992). Firstborns start life with experience as only children. For a year or more, they receive the singular attention of both parents. They are held more, spoken to more, stimulated more. All in all, they spend more time with their parents than later-borns do. Even after other children come along, parents still tend to relate to the first child more than to later-borns. Parents continue to make demands and to orient their speech toward levels that are appropriate for the firstborn. Parents have greater expectations for firstborn children. They impose tougher restrictions on them and make greater demands of them. They are also more highly involved in their activities (Hoffman, 1991).

By and large, parents are more relaxed and flexible with later-borns (Dunn, 1985). Children are quite aware of the greater permissiveness often given to later-borns. Andi, the adult daughter of one of the authors (C. E.), to this day chides her mother for finally allowing sugared cereal in the house only after her younger brother, Adam, requested it. Why are parents more indulgent with laterborns? They have probably gained some self-confidence in child rearing. They see that the firstborn is turning out all right. Parents may interpret the first child's success as a sign of their own competence and may, therefore, assume that laterborns will also turn out all right.

**Peers** Children of the same age. (More generally, people of similar background and social standing.)

## PEER RELATIONSHIPS

The importance of ***peers*** in the development of the young child is widely recognized (Putallaz & Dunn, 1990; Rubin & Coplan, 1992). As children move into the preschool years, they spend more time in the company of other children. The peer interactions of children serve many functions. Children learn a variety of social skills in the peer group—sharing, helping, taking turns, dealing with conflict. They learn how to lead and to follow. Physical and cognitive skills develop through peer interactions. Finally, peers are a source of emotional support (Grusec & Lytton, 1988; Parker & Gottman, 1989). In this section, we look at the development of peer relationships in the preschool years.

**DEVELOPMENT OF PEER RELATIONSHIPS** Infants first show positive interest in one another at about 6 months. If they are placed on the floor facing one another, they will smile, occasionally imitate each other, and often touch one another. Social interaction increases over the next few months, but during the first year, contacts between infants tend to be brief (Hartup, 1992b; Howes, 1987). In the second year, children show increased interest in each other and interact by playing with each other's play materials. But they still show relatively little social interaction. By about 2 years of age, however, children are readily imitating each other's play actions and engaging in social games such as follow the leader (Brownell, 1990; Eckerman & Stein, 1990; Hanna & Meltzoff, 1993). Also by the age of 2, children have established preferences for playing with two or three particular playmates (Strayer et al., 1990).

**FRIENDSHIPS** The preferences shown by toddlers for certain other children as playmates is an early sign of friendship (Collins & Gunnar, 1990). Friendship goes beyond casual interaction with peers (see Figure 10.4). It is characterized

FIGURE 10.4

**FRIENDSHIP.** *Friendship takes on different meanings as children develop. Preschoolers focus on sharing toys and activities. Five- to 7-year-olds report that friends are children with whom they have "fun." Sharing confidences becomes important in late childhood and in adolescence.*

by shared, positive interactions and feelings of attachment (Grusec & Lytton, 1988; Park et al., 1993). Even early friendships are fairly stable. Howes (1988) found that 1- to 6-year-olds tended to maintain their friendships from one year to the next, some for as long as 3 years.

Preschool children behave somewhat differently toward their friends than toward ordinary playmates. Friends, as compared with nonfriends, show higher levels of interaction, helpful behavior, smiling and laughing, and more frequent cooperation and collaboration (Collins & Gunnar, 1990; Costin & Jones, 1992; Rubin & Coplan, 1992). Conflicts between young friends are less intense and are resolved more readily than conflicts between nonfriends (Hartup, 1992a).

What are children's conceptions of friendships? When preschoolers are asked what they like about their friends, they typically mention the play materials and activities that they share (Hartup, 1993). Five- to 7-year-olds usually report that their friends are the children they do things with, the children with whom they have "fun" (Berndt & Perry, 1986). As we shall see in Chapter 13, it is not until late childhood and adolescence that the friends' traits and notions of trust, communication, and intimacy become important aspects of friendship.

## SOCIAL BEHAVIORS

During the early childhood years, children make tremendous strides in the development of social skills and behavior. Their play activities increasingly involve other children. They learn how to share, cooperate, and comfort others. But young children, like adults, are complex beings. They can be aggressive at times, as well as loving and helpful. We turn now to the development of social behaviors in the early years.

### *PLAY*

Play is an activity with many characteristics. It is meaningful, pleasurable, voluntary, and internally motivated (Fromberg, 1990). Play is fun! But play also serves many important functions in the life of the young child (Christie & Wardle, 1992; Lewis, 1993; Sutton-Smith, 1993). Play helps children develop motor skills and coordination. It contributes to social development, as children learn to share play materials, take turns, and try on new roles through dramatic play. It supports the development of such cognitive qualities as curiosity, exploration, symbolic thinking, and problem solving. And play may help children learn to deal with conflict and anxiety (Fisher, 1992; Johnson 1990).

**PARTEN'S TYPES OF PLAY** In classic research on children's play, Mildred Parten (1932) observed the development of five types of play among 2- to 5-year-old nursery school children.

First is ***solitary play,*** in which children play with toys by themselves, independently of the children around them. Solitary players do not appear influenced by children around them. They make no effort to approach them.

Second is ***onlooker play,*** in which children observe other children who are at play. Onlookers frequently talk to the children they are observing and may make suggestions, but they do not overtly join in. Solitary play and onlooker play are both considered types of ***nonsocial play***—that is, play in which children do not interact. Nonsocial play occurs more often in 2- and 3-year-olds than in older preschoolers.

***Solitary play*** Play that is independent from that of nearby children and in which no effort is made to approach other children.

***Onlooker play*** Play during which children observe other children at play but do not enter into their play themselves.

***Nonsocial play*** Forms of play (solitary play or onlooker play) in which play is not influenced by the play of nearby children.

**TRUTH OR FICTION REVISITED**

*It is not necessarily true that children who play by themselves are more likely to develop social problems. The issue is at what age children play by themselves. Solitary play is quite normal for 2-year-olds, for example.*

Third is ***parallel play,*** in which children play with toys similar to those of surrounding children. However, they treat the toys as they choose and do not directly interact with other children.

Fourth is ***associative play,*** in which children interact and share toys. However, they do not seem to share group goals. Although they interact, individuals still treat toys as they choose. The association with the other children appears to be more important than the nature of the activity. They seem to enjoy each other's company.

Fifth is ***cooperative play,*** in which children interact to achieve common, group goals. The play of each child is subordinated to the purposes of the group. One or two group members direct the activities of others. There is also a division of labor, with different children taking different roles. Children may pretend to be members of a family, animals, space monsters, and all sorts of creatures.

Parallel play, associative play, and cooperative play are types of ***social play.*** In each case children are influenced by other children as they are playing. Parten found that associative and cooperative play become common at age 5. More recent research continues to show that they are more likely to be found among older and more experienced preschoolers (Howes & Matheson, 1992b). Also, girls are somewhat more likely than boys to engage in social play (Zheng & Colombo, 1989).

But there are exceptions to these age trends in social play. Nonsocial play can involve educational activities that foster cognitive development. In fact, many 4- and 5-year-olds spend a good deal of time in parallel constructive play. For

***Parallel play*** Play in which children use toys similar to those of nearby children but approach their toys in their own ways. No effort is made to interact with others.

***Associative play*** Play with other children in which toys are shared but there is no common goal or division of labor.

***Cooperative play*** Organized play in which children cooperate to meet common goals. There is a division of labor, and children take on specific roles as group members.

***Social play*** Play in which children interact with and are influenced by the play of others. Examples include parallel play, associative play, and cooperative play.

**FIGURE 10.5**

***ASSOCIATIVE PLAY.*** *Associative play is a form of social play in which children interact and share toys.*

***Dramatic play*** Play in which children enact social roles, which is made possible by the attainment of symbolic thought. A form of *pretend play.*

instance, they may work on puzzles or build with blocks near other children. Parallel constructive players are frequently perceived by teachers to be socially skillful and are popular with their peers (Coplan et al., 1994; Rubin, 1982). Some toddlers are also more capable of social play than one might expect, given their age. Two-year-olds with older siblings or with a great deal of group experience may engage in advanced forms of social play.

**DRAMATIC PLAY** In Chapter 9, we saw that children in the second year of life begin to engage in symbolic or pretend play. From the ages of 2 to 5, pretend play becomes increasingly social, involving recognizable characters such as doctor or teacher and themes such as playing house or cops and robbers. This is a type of cooperative play known as ***dramatic play.***

Catherine Garvey (1990) examined the emergence of dramatic play in 3- to 5-year-olds in a nursery school setting. Even 3-year-olds engaged in dramatic play sequences, but the themes of the older children were more realistic, integrated, and complex. Children assumed a variety of roles in their dramatic play. Of great importance for children of all ages were family roles, such as mommy, daddy, and baby. Older children were more likely than younger ones to adopt character roles such as doctor, nurse, bus driver, or teacher.

Much theorizing has been done about the function of dramatic play. It has been suggested that dramatic play fosters social and emotional development (Nicolopoulou, 1991; Smilansky, 1990). For one thing, social interactions during dramatic play are longer, more positive, and more complex than interactions that occur during nondramatic play (Doyle et al., 1992). In addition, dramatic play allows children to experiment with different social roles and obtain feedback from peers. Enacting the roles of other people may help them learn to take the perspective of others and to develop empathy. Finding solutions to make-believe problems may help children find ways to solve problems in the real world. On an emotional level, it has been suggested that dramatic play allows children to express their fears and their fantasies (Parker & Gottman, 1989; Singer & Singer, 1990).

FIGURE 10.6

***GIRLS ENJOYING A GAME OF BASEBALL.*** *Although preferences for gender-typed toys are well established by the age of 3, girls are more likely to stray from the stereotypes, as in this photograph of girls playing the masculine-typed game baseball.*

**GENDER DIFFERENCES IN PLAY** In Chapter 7, we saw that boys and girls begin to show gender-stereotyped preferences for toys and activities early in the second year. Although preferences for gender-typed toys are well developed by the ages of 15 to 36 months, girls are more likely to stray from the stereotypes (Bussey & Bandura, 1992; Frey & Ruble, 1992; Lobel & Menashri, 1993). Girls request as gifts and play with ''boys' toys'' such as cars and trucks more frequently than boys choose ''girls' toys'' such as dolls (Etaugh & Liss, 1992). These cross-role activities may reflect the greater prestige of ''masculine'' activities and traits in U.S. culture. Therefore, a boy's playing with ''girls' toys'' might be seen as his taking on an inferior role. A girl's playing with ''boys' toys'' might be interpreted as an understandable desire for power or esteem. In addition, studies show that children find ''boys' toys'' more appealing and interesting than ''girls' toys'' (Rosenblum, 1991).

Girls and boys differ not only in toy preferences but also in their choice of play environments and activities. During the preschool and early elementary school years, boys prefer vigorous physical outdoor activities such as climbing, playing with large vehicles, and rough-and-tumble play (discussed in Chapter 8). In middle childhood, boys spend more time than girls in large play groups of five or more children and spend more time in competitive play (Crombie & Desjardins, 1993; Van Brunschot et al., 1993). Girls are more likely to engage in arts and crafts activities and domestic play. Their activities are more closely directed and more structured by adults than are boys' activities (Maccoby, 1993b; Pellegrini, 1990; Pomerleau et al., 1990). Girls spend more time than boys playing with just one other child or with a small group of children (Crombie & Desjardins, 1993; Van Brunschot et al., 1993).

Why do children show these early preferences for gender-stereotyped toys and activities? Although one cannot rule out the possibility of biological factors, such as boys' slightly greater strength and activity levels and girls' slightly greater physical maturity and coordination, note that these differences are just that—slight. On the other hand, we have already seen in Chapter 7 that parents and other adults treat girls and boys very differently from birth onwards. They consistently provide gender-stereotyped toys and room furnishings and encourage gender-typing in children's play activities and even household chores (Etaugh & Liss, 1992; Lytton & Romney, 1991; Pomerleau et al., 1990).

Children who attempt to "cross the line" by exhibiting an interest in toys or activities considered appropriate for the other gender are often teased, ridiculed, rejected, or simply ignored by their parents, teachers and other adults, and peers (Etaugh & Liss, 1992). Boys are more likely to be criticized than girls for showing such behavior (Fagot & Hagan, 1991; Garvey, 1990).

Another well-documented gender difference in play is that girls prefer the company of girls, whereas boys prefer to play with boys. This phenomenon is found in a wide variety of cultures and ethnic groups (Fishbein & Imai, 1992; Whiting & Edwards, 1988), and it appears early in life. Children begin to prefer same-gender playmates by age 2, with girls developing this preference somewhat earlier than boys (Fagot, 1990; Legault & Strayer, 1990; Strayer, 1990). The tendency to associate with peers of the same gender becomes even stronger during middle childhood (Bukowski et al., 1993a; Crombie & Desjardins, 1993). Perhaps you remember a period during your childhood when you and your friends found members of the other gender absolutely loathesome and wanted nothing to do with them.

During middle childhood, contact with members of the other gender is strongly discouraged by peers. For example, a recent study of white, African-American, Hispanic, and Native-American 10- and 11-year-olds found that those who crossed the "gender boundary" were especially unpopular with their peers (Sroufe et al., 1993). Even so, there are certain circumstances under which contact with the other gender is acceptable, as shown in Table 10.2.

Why do children choose to associate with peers of their own gender? Eleanor Maccoby (1990b) believes that two factors are important. One is that boys' play is more oriented toward dominance, aggression, and rough play. The second is that boys are not very responsive to girls' polite suggestions. Maccoby suggests that girls avoid boys because they want to protect themselves from boys' aggression, and because they find it unpleasant to interact with unresponsive people. Additionally, boys may avoid the company of girls because girls are perceived as inferior (Caplan & Larkin, 1991). Another view is that children simply like

**FIGURE 10.7**

***PREFERENCE FOR PEERS OF ONE'S OWN GENDER.*** *During early and middle childhood, children prefer the company of peers of their own gender. Why?*

TABLE 10.2

**KNOWING THE RULES: UNDER WHAT CIRCUMSTANCES IS IT PERMISSIBLE TO HAVE CONTACT WITH THE OTHER GENDER IN MIDDLE CHILDHOOD?**

| | |
|---|---|
| RULE | THE CONTACT IS ACCIDENTAL. |
| EXAMPLE | YOU'RE NOT LOOKING WHERE YOU ARE GOING, AND YOU BUMP INTO SOMEONE. |
| RULE | THE CONTACT IS INCIDENTAL. |
| EXAMPLE | YOU GO TO GET SOME LEMONADE AND WAIT WHILE TWO CHILDREN OF THE OTHER GENDER GET SOME. (THERE SHOULD BE NO CONVERSATION.) |
| RULE | THE CONTACT IS IN THE GUISE OF SOME CLEAR AND NECESSARY PURPOSE. |
| EXAMPLE | YOU MAY SAY "PASS THE LEMONADE" TO PERSONS OF THE OTHER GENDER AT THE NEXT TABLE. NO INTEREST IN THEM IS EXPRESSED. |
| RULE | AN ADULT COMPELS YOU TO HAVE CONTACT. |
| EXAMPLE | "GO GET THAT MAP FROM X AND Y AND BRING IT TO ME." |
| RULE | YOU ARE ACCOMPANIED BY SOMEONE OF YOUR OWN GENDER. |
| EXAMPLE | TWO GIRLS MAY TALK TO TWO BOYS THOUGH PHYSICAL CLOSENESS WITH YOUR OWN PARTNER MUST BE MAINTAINED AND INTIMACY WITH THE OTHERS IS DISALLOWED. |
| RULE | THE INTERACTION OR CONTACT IS ACCOMPANIED BY DISAVOWAL. |
| EXAMPLE | YOU SAY SOMEONE IS UGLY OR HURL SOME OTHER INSULT OR (MORE COMMONLY FOR BOYS) PUSH OR THROW SOMETHING AT THEM AS YOU PASS BY. |

SOURCE: SROUFE ET AL., 1993.

peers of their own gender more than peers of the other gender (Bukowski et al., 1993a).

Still another possibility is that preference for peers of one's own gender is related to preference for toys that are stereotyped as appropriate for one's gender (Etaugh & Liss, 1992). That is, children who prefer dolls to transportation toys may prefer to associate with children who share their preference.

## PROSOCIAL BEHAVIOR

**THINKING ABOUT DEVELOPMENT**

Agree or disagree with the following statement and support your answer: "Children are basically prosocial. They engage in antisocial behavior only when their natural prosocial tendencies have been thwarted."

***Prosocial behavior,*** sometimes known as *altruism,* is behavior intended to benefit another without expectation of reward. Prosocial behavior includes helping and comforting others in distress, sharing, and cooperating (Eisenberg, 1992).

Even in the first year of life, children begin to share. They spontaneously offer food and objects to others (Hay & Murray, 1982). In the second year of life, children continue to share objects and they also begin to comfort distressed companions and help others with tasks and chores (Hay et al., 1991; Zahn-Waxler, et al., 1992).

By the preschool and early school years, children frequently engage in prosocial behavior. Some types of prosocial behaviors occur more often than others. One study observed 4- and 7-year-olds at home and found that helping occurred more often than sharing, affection, and reassuring (Grusec, 1991).

The development of prosocial behavior is linked to the development of other capabilities in the young child, such as empathy and perspective-taking. Let us now examine these.

***Prosocial behavior*** Behavior intended to benefit another without expectation of reward.

***Empathy*** Ability to share another person's feelings.

**EMPATHY** ***Empathy*** is the ability to understand and share another person's feelings. Children respond emotionally from a very early age when others are in distress (Caplan & Hay, 1989; Eisenberg, 1989). During infancy, children frequently begin to cry when they hear other children crying (Eisenberg, 1992). However, this early agitated response may be largely reflexive. Crying, like other strong stimuli, can be aversive, and infants generally react to aversive stimulation by crying. Even so, this early unlearned behavior pattern might contribute to the development of empathy.

Empathy appears to promote prosocial behavior, and this link is evident by the second year of life (Eisenberg & Miller, 1990; Kalliopuska, 1991; Strayer & Schroeder, 1989). During the second year, as we noted earlier, many children approach other children and adults who are in distress and attempt to help them. They may try to hug a crying child or tell the child not to cry.

There is some evidence that girls show more empathy than boys and that this difference increases with age (Eisenberg, 1992; Gross & Ballif, 1991; Lips, 1993). Research indicates that the difference may arise because girls are socialized to be more attuned to others' emotions than boys are (Eisenberg et al., 1989).

**Perspective-Taking** Various cognitive abilities, such as being able to take another person's perspective, should be related to knowing when someone is in need or distress (Carlo et al., 1991). Perspective-taking skills improve with age, as we saw in Chapter 9, and so do prosocial skills. Among children of the same age, those with better developed perspective-taking ability also show more prosocial behavior (Bengtsson & Johnson, 1992; Eisenberg & Miller, 1990).

**Influences on Prosocial Behavior** Prosocial behavior is influenced by rewards and punishments. Observations of nursery school children show that the peers of children who are cooperative, friendly, and generous respond more positively to them than they do to children whose behavior is self-centered (Hartup, 1983). Children who are rewarded in this way for acting prosocially are likely to continue these behaviors (Eisenberg, 1992).

Some children at early ages are made responsible for doing household chores and caring for younger siblings. They are taught helping and nurturance skills, and their performances are selectively reinforced by other children and adults. Whiting and Edwards (1988) reported that children given such tasks are more likely to show prosocial behaviors than children who are not.

There is evidence that children can acquire sharing behavior by observing models who help and share. For example, children who watch shows such as "Mister Rogers' Neighborhood," which model prosocial behavior, show increased social interaction, sharing behavior, cooperation, and use of positive reinforcement with other children (Hearold, 1986; Comstock & Paik, 1991; Huston et al., 1992). In one experiment in sharing, 29- to 36-month-olds were more likely to share toys with playmates who first shared toys with them (Levitt et al., 1985). That is, the children appeared to model the sharing behavior of their peers.

It also appears that children's prosocial behavior is influenced by the kinds of interactions they have with their parents. For example, prosocial behavior and empathy are enhanced in children who are securely attached to their parents (Kestenbaum et al., 1989) and whose mothers show a high degree of empathy (Fabes et al., 1990).

Parenting styles also affect the development of prosocial behavior. Prosocial behavior is fostered when parents use inductive techniques such as explaining how behavior affects others ("You made Josh cry. It's not nice to hit"). Parents of prosocial children are more likely to expect mature behavior from their children. They are less likely to use power-assertive techniques of discipline (Bar-Tal, 1990; Eisenberg, 1992).

FIGURE 10.8

***AGGRESSION.*** *Aggressive behavior in childhood is predictive of a variety of social and emotional difficulties in adulthood. What causes some children to be more aggressive than others?*

### *AGGRESSION*

Children, like adults, are complex beings. Not only can they be loving and altruistic. They can also be aggressive. Aggression refers to behavior intended to cause pain or hurt to another person.

**DEVELOPMENTAL PATTERNS** Aggression, like other behaviors, seems to follow certain developmental patterns. For one thing, the aggression of preschoolers is frequently instrumental or possession-oriented (Parke & Slaby, 1983). That is, young children tend to use aggression to obtain the toys and things they want, such as a favored seat at the dinner table or in the family car. But older preschoolers are more likely than younger ones to resolve their conflicts over toys by sharing rather than fighting (Caplan et al., 1991).

By 6 or 7, aggression becomes hostile and person-oriented. Children taunt and criticize each other and call each other names as well as attack physically. Person-oriented aggression may emerge because of cognitive development (Ferguson & Rule, 1980). At 6 or 7 children are more capable of processing information about the motives and intentions of other people. As a result, they are less likely to stand by idly when another child intends to hurt or ridicule them.

Other evidence for the role of information processing is that aggressive boys are more likely than nonaggressive boys to incorrectly interpret the behavior of other children as potentially harmful (Dodge, 1993b; Hudley & Graham, 1993; Quiggle et al., 1992). This bias may make the aggressive child quick to respond aggressively in social situations.

Aggressive behavior appears to be remarkably stable and predictive of a wide variety of social and emotional difficulties in adulthood (Kellam & Rebok, 1992; National Research Council, 1993). A longitudinal study of more than 600 children found that aggressive 8-year-olds tended to remain more aggressive than their peers 22 years later, at age 30 (Eron et al., 1991). Aggressive children of both genders were more likely to have criminal convictions as adults, to abuse their spouses, and to drive while drunk. Boys were more likely to show aggression than girls from childhood through adulthood, a finding that has been well-documented in many cultures (Koot & Verhulst, 1992; Lips, 1993).

TRUTH OR FICTION REVISITED

*It is true that aggressive boys and girls are likely to be aggressive as adults. They are more likely to be convicted of crimes, abuse their spouses, and drive when drunk.*

**THEORETICAL INTERLUDE: DEVELOPMENT OF AGGRESSION** What causes aggression in children? What causes some children to be more aggressive than others? Aggression in childhood appears to result from a complex interplay of biological factors and environmental factors such as reinforcement and modeling.

***Biological Factors*** Some evidence exists that genetic factors may be involved in at least certain extreme forms of aggression such as criminality and antisocial behavior (Brennan et al., 1991; Plomin & McClearn, 1993). For example, a longitudinal study of over 14,000 adoptees in Denmark found that biological sons of criminal fathers had elevated crime rates even when adopted at birth and raised by noncriminal parents (Mednick et al., 1987).

Another biologically based factor that may indirectly influence the development of aggression is a child's temperament. Children who are impulsive, uninhibited, and relatively fearless may be more likely to elicit punitive, aggressive reactions from parents (Bates et al., 1991; National Research Council, 1993). Such parental reactions, as we shall see below, may contribute to the development of aggression.

***Reinforcement*** Social-learning explanations of aggression focus on the role of environmental factors such as reinforcement and modeling. Children, like adults, are most likely to be aggressive when they are frustrated in their attempts to gain something they want, such as the attention of a parent, or a particular toy. Aggressive behavior is reinforced by removing sources of frustration. When children repeatedly push, shove, and hit in order to grab toys or break into line, other children usually let them have their way (Cole et al., 1991). The child who is thus rewarded for acting aggressively is likely to continue to use aggressive means.

Peers may also help maintain aggressive behavior patterns by valuing and encouraging aggression (Perry et al., 1990). Aggressive children are more likely to hang around with each other and support each other's aggressive behavior (Cairns & Cairns, 1991). These children have often been rejected by their less aggressive peers, which further decreases their opportunity to learn appropriate social skills (Coie & Koeppl, 1990; Rubin, 1990).

Parents as well as peers may provide reinforcement for aggression, sometimes quite inadvertently. Gerald Patterson and his colleagues (1991) have examined families in which children are reinforced for displaying ***coercive behavior.*** Coercive behavior includes such aggressive acts as noncompliance, talking back, temper tantrums, hitting, and so on. In these families, parents may respond to a child's misbehavior by nagging or scolding. The child reacts coercively and the parent often gives in, thus rewarding the coercive (that is, aggressive) behavior. Such interactions can lead to increasingly disruptive child behavior (Duncan, 1991).

***Coercive behavior*** Aggressive acts such as noncompliance, talking back, temper tantrums, and hitting.

***Modeling*** Children learn not only from the effects of their own behavior, but also from observing the behavior of others. They may model the aggressive behavior of their peers or parents. Children are more apt to imitate what their parents do than to heed what they say. If adults say they disapprove of aggression, but smash furniture or hit each other when frustrated, children are likely to develop the notion that this is the way to handle frustration.

Children who are physically punished are more likely to behave aggressively themselves (American Psychological Association, 1993; Schwartz, 1993; Weiss et al., 1992). Physically aggressive parents serve as models for aggression and also increase their children's anger. Once aggressive patterns of interaction become established, the cycle can be truly vicious.

**TRUTH OR FICTION REVISITED**

*It is true that children who are physically punished are more likely to be aggressive. Their punishers model aggression and give the children the idea that it is appropriate to respond to stress by aggressive means.*

***Media Influences*** Real people are not the only models of aggressive behavior in children's lives. A classic study by Bandura, Ross, and Ross (1963) suggests the powerful influence of televised models on children's aggressive

FIGURE 10.9

***A Classic Experiment in the Imitation of Aggressive Models.*** *Research by Albert Bandura and his colleagues has shown that children frequently imitate the aggressive behavior they observe. In the top row, an adult model strikes a clown doll. The lower rows show a boy and a girl imitating the aggressive behavior.*

behavior. One group of preschool children observed a film of an adult model hitting and kicking an inflated Bobo doll, while a control group saw an aggression-free film. The experimental and control children were then left alone in a room with the same doll, as hidden observers recorded their behavior. The children who had observed the aggressive model showed significantly more aggressive behavior toward the doll themselves (see Figure 10.9). Many children imitated bizarre attack behaviors devised for the model in this experiment—behaviors that they would not have thought up themselves.

The children exposed to the aggressive model also showed aggressive behavior patterns that had not been modeled. Observing the model, therefore, not only led to imitation of modeled behavior patterns, it also apparently ***disinhibited*** previously learned aggressive responses. The results were similar whether children observed human or cartoon models on film.

Television is a fertile source of aggressive models throughout much of the world (Clermont, 1990). Surprisingly, a great deal of aggression is shown on children's shows. More than 82 percent of the children's programs shown on the three major U.S. broadcast networks, and 77 percent of those shown on cable TV in the United States, contain violence (Gerbner, 1993). The Saturday morning cartoons are by far the most violent programs on television, with about 20 to 25 acts of violence per hour (Huston et al., 1992).

Extensive research over the past 30 years shows that exposure to televised violence increases aggressive behavior in children (Comstock & Paik, 1991; Huston et al., 1992; National Research Council, 1993). This relationship has been found for girls and boys of different ages, social classes, ethnic groups, and cultures (Huston et al., 1992; Liebert & Sprafkin, 1988). Moreover, the effects can be long lasting. One longitudinal study found that children who watched a lot of TV violence at age 8 were more likely to engage in criminal behaviors at age 30 (Eron et al., 1991).

***Disinhibited*** Stimulated a response that had been suppressed (inhibited) by showing a model engaging in that response without aversive consequences.

Certain factors increase the likelihood that televised violence will increase aggression in children. Seeing the perpetrator of the violence go unpunished increases the chances that the child will act aggressively. If the violence occurs in a setting familiar to the child, aggression is more likely to occur. For example, a televised episode in which siblings are fighting is more apt to trigger aggression than an episode depicting space aliens zapping each other with ray guns. Viewers who are in a state of anger or frustration are more likely to be influenced by TV violence. Finally, those children who are more aggressive to begin with are more affected by television violence (Comstock & Paik, 1991). There seems to be a circular relationship between viewing TV violence and aggressive behavior (Eron, 1987). TV violence contributes to aggressive behavior, and aggressive children are more likely to watch violent television. Aggressive children are less popular than nonaggressive children, and Eron theorizes that aggressive children watch more television because their peer relationships are less fulfilling.

**THINKING ABOUT DEVELOPMENT**

Does violence on television and in films cause aggression in young viewers?

**TRUTH OR FICTION REVISITED**

*It is not true that children mechanically imitate the aggressive behavior they observe on television and in films. Many children may acquire aggressive skills and become somewhat habituated to violence from watching television. However, most children do not imitate the aggressive acts they observe.*

**TREATMENT OF CHILDHOOD AGGRESSION** A variety of treatments have been developed to help overly aggressive children. Some are designed to modify the behaviors of parents in relation to their aggressive children (Forehand & Long, 1991; Forgatch, 1991; Hawkins et al., 1991). These programs typically involve teaching parents a variety of skills such as

1. Providing positive reinforcement for good behavior
2. Applying a mild consequence such as "time-out" (removal to a boring place for 5 minutes) for misbehavior
3. Issuing clear, simple rules
4. Providing close supervision for their children
5. Learning problem-solving strategies

Notice the similarity between this list and the guidelines for parents presented in Developing Today.

Other programs are designed to address the problem of the school bully (Lore & Schultz, 1993). In one large-scale intervention study, teachers, school administrators, and parents were provided with specific procedures to follow when bullying incidents occurred. Over a 2-year period, the incidence of bullying decreased by 50 percent (Olweus, 1991).

Still other programs focus on the children themselves, teaching them a variety of social and cognitive skills and social problem-solving activities (Pepler & Rubin, 1991; Hudley & Graham, 1993; Selman et al., 1992). Many of these programs have met with at least some success in reducing aggressive behaviors of children.

## PERSONALITY AND EMOTIONAL DEVELOPMENT

In the early childhood years, children's personalities start becoming more defined. Their sense of self—who they are and how they feel about themselves—continues to develop and becomes more complex. They begin to acquire a sense of their own abilities and their increasing mastery of the environment. As they move out into the world, they also face new experiences that may cause them to feel fearful and anxious. Let us now explore some of these facets of personality and emotional development.

### THE SELF

As we saw in Chapter 7, the sense of self, or the ***self-concept,*** emerges gradually during infancy. Infants and toddlers visually begin to recognize themselves and differentiate from other individuals such as their parents.

In the preschool years, children continue to develop their sense of self. Almost as soon as they begin to speak, they describe themselves in terms of certain categories, such as age groupings (baby, child, adult) and gender (girl, boy). These self-definitions that refer to concrete external traits have been called the ***categorical self*** (Damon & Hart, 1992; Lewis & Brooks-Gunn, 1979).

Children as young as age 3 are able to describe themselves in terms of behaviors and internal states that appear to occur frequently and are fairly stable over time (Eder, 1989, 1990). For example, in response to the question "Tell me how you feel when you're scared," young children frequently respond, "Usually like running away" (Eder, 1989). Or, in answer to the question "Tell me how you've usually been with grown-ups?" a typical response might be, "I mostly been good with grown-ups." Thus, even preschoolers seem to understand they have stable characteristics that endure over time.

One aspect of the self-concept is ***self-esteem,*** the value or worth that people attach to themselves. Children who have a good opinion of themselves during the preschool years show secure attachment and have mothers who are sensitive to their needs (Cassidy, 1988; Mueller & Tingley, 1990). These children also are more likely to engage in prosocial behavior (Cauley & Tyler, 1989).

By the age of 4, children begin to make evaluative judgments about two different aspects of themselves (Harter, 1990a; Harter & Pike, 1984). One is their cognitive and physical competence (for example, being good at puzzles, counting, swinging, tying shoes), and the second is their social acceptance by peers and parents (for example, having lots of friends, being read to by mom). But preschoolers do not yet make a clear distinction between different areas of competence. For example, a child of this age is not likely to report being good in school but poor in physical skills. One is either "good at doing things" or one is not (Harter & Pike, 1984).

During middle childhood, as we shall see in Chapter 13, personality traits become increasingly important in children's self-definitions. They also are able to make judgments about their self-worth in many different areas of competence, behavioral conduct, appearance, and social relations.

***Self-concept*** One's impression of oneself; self-awareness.

***Categorical self*** Definitions of the self that refer to concrete external traits.

***Self-esteem*** The sense of value, or worth, that people attach to themselves.

### INITIATIVE VERSUS GUILT

As preschool children continue to develop a separate sense of themselves, they increasingly move out into the world and take the initiative in learning new skills. You will recall from Chapter 2 that Erikson refers to these early childhood years as the stage of initiative versus guilt.

Children in this stage strive to achieve independence from their parents and master adult behaviors. They are curious, try new things, and test themselves. These qualities are illustrated in the following account of a day in the life of a 5-year-old:

> *In a single day, he decided to see how high he could build his blocks, invented a game that consisted of seeing who could jump the highest on his parents' bed, and led the family to a new movie containing a great deal of action and violence (Crain, 1992, p. 254).*

During these years, children learn that not all of their plans, dreams, and fantasies can be realized. Adults prohibit children from doing certain things, and children begin to internalize these adult rules. Fear of violating the rules may cause the child to feel guilty and may curtail efforts to master new skills. Parents can help children develop and maintain a healthy sense of initiative by encouraging their attempts to learn and explore and by not being unduly critical and punitive.

FIGURE 10.10

***INITIATIVE.*** *In the preschool years, children increasingly move out into the world and take the initiative in learning new skills. This girl shows off her newly acquired mastery of the jungle gym.*

## FEARS

We have just seen that in Erikson's view, fear of violating parental prohibitions can be a powerful force in the life of a young child. What other sorts of fears do children have in the early years?

Both the frequency and the content of fears change as children move from infancy into the preschool years. The number of fears seems to peak between 2½ and 4 years and then tapers off (Miller et al., 1990b).

The preschool period is marked by a decline in fears of loud noises, falling, sudden movement, and strangers. Preschool children are most likely to have fears that revolve around animals, imaginary creatures, the dark, and personal safety (Finch & McIntosh, 1990; Ollendick & King, 1991; Wenar, 1990). The fantasies of young children frequently involve stories they are told, as well as TV and film images. Frightening images of imaginary creatures can persevere. Many young children are reluctant to have the lights turned off at night because of fear that these creatures may harm them in the dark. In a sense, fears of imaginary creatures also involve personal safety.

**TRUTH OR FICTION REVISITED**

*Preschoolers are actually more likely to fear animals, the dark, and other objects and situations that concern physical safety.*

But there are also real objects and situations that cause many children to fear for their personal safety: lightning, thunder and other loud noises, the dark, high places, sharp objects and being cut, blood, people who are unfamiliar or who act strangely, stinging and crawling insects, other animals, and on and on. Some of these objects are also frightening because of their aversiveness, even when they are not direct threats. Children may not expect to be hurt by thunder or worms, but they may still view them as awful.

During middle childhood, children's fears become more realistic. They become less fearful of imaginary creatures, but fears of bodily harm and injury remain fairly common. Children grow more fearful of failure and criticism in school and in social relationships (Finch & McIntosh, 1990; Ollendick & King, 1991; Wenar, 1990).

Girls report more fears and higher levels of anxiety than boys (Ollendick et al., 1989, 1991b). Whether these findings reflect actual differences in fears and anxieties or differences in the willingness of girls and boys to report "weaknesses" is a matter of debate (Finch & McIntosh, 1990).

**HELPING CHILDREN COPE WITH FEARS** A number of methods have been developed to help children cope with irrational, debilitating fears (Izard, 1991; King & Gullore, 1990). Professionals who work with children today are most likely to use such behavior-modification methods as *systematic desensitization, operant conditioning,* and *participant modeling* (Vitulano & Tebes, 1991). Each of them is based on the principles of learning discussed in Chapter 2.

***Systematic desensitization*** **Systematic desensitization** A process in which one loses fear of anxiety-evoking objects by gradual exposure to them.

***Systematic desensitization*** ***Systematic desensitization*** is based on principles of classical conditioning. In systematic desensitization, children are exposed gradually to the sources of their fears while they are engaging in behavior that is incompatible with feelings of fear. Fear includes bodily responses such as rapid heart rate and respiration rate. By doing things that reduce the heart and respiration rates, children are doing something that is incompatible with fear.

In a classic study, Mary Cover Jones (1924) used systematic desensitization to eliminate a fear of rabbits in a 2-year-old boy named Peter. Jones arranged for a rabbit to be gradually brought closer to Peter while the boy engaged in some of his favorite activities, such as munching merrily away on candy and cookies. Peter, to be sure, cast a wary eye in the rabbit's direction, but he continued to eat. Jones suspected that if she brought the rabbit too close too quickly, the cookies left on Peter's plate and those already eaten might have decorated the walls. But gradually the animal could be brought nearer without upsetting the boy. Eventually, Peter could eat and touch the rabbit at the same time. (No, we don't know how much weight and how many cavities Peter acquired while overcoming his fear of rabbits.)

A favorite systematic desensitization technique with adults involves the progressive relaxation of muscle groups throughout the body. This technique has also been used with older children, but other techniques may be more effective with younger children, such as giving the child a treat (as Jones did), playing with a game or favorite toy, or asking the child to talk about a favorite book or TV hero (Vitulano & Tebes, 1991).

In systematic desensitization, the parent or helping professional brings the child gradually into closer contact with the feared object or situation, while the child remains relaxed. An excellent way to bring a child into gradual contact with a large mature dog, for instance, is to give the child a puppy. Also, children will frequently do things in the company of their parents that they would be afraid to do alone. Therefore, it may be helpful to desensitize a child to a new situation, such as a day-care center, by initially attending with the child. Then the parent can depart progressively earlier.

***Operant Techniques*** Operant techniques are based on principles of operant conditioning. In operant conditioning, children are guided into desirable behaviors, then reinforced for engaging in them. Reinforcement increases the frequency of desired behavior. Behavior modification in the classroom is an example of the use of operant techniques. In this method, good (desired) behavior is reinforced and misbehavior is ignored.

Parents and other adults use operant techniques all the time. They may teach children how to draw letters of the alphabet by guiding their hand and saying "Good!" when the desired result is obtained. When children fear touching a dog, parents frequently take their hands and guide them physically in petting the animal. Then they say something reinforcing, such as "Look at that big girl/boy petting that doggy!" or "Isn't the puppy nice and soft?" In one study that demonstrates the effectiveness of operant techniques, two young girls with nighttime fears were successfully treated by praising them for sleeping in their own beds at night (Ollendick et al., 1991a).

***Participant Modeling*** ***Participant modeling*** is based on principles of observational learning. In participant modeling, children first observe models (ideally, children similar in age) engage in the behavior that evokes fear. Then they imitate the behavior of the models. Models may be live or filmed.

Observing the models is thought to have a number of positive effects. First, it shows children how to act in the situations or interact with the objects that evoke fear. Second, it communicates the idea that the object or situation is not so dreadful. Third, observing others engage in feared activities without negative results may extinguish some of the observer's own fear. Fourth, it may help motivate children to try to engage in the observed activities themselves.

FIGURE 10.11

***Can Chocolate Chip Cookies Countercondition Fears?*** *Yes, they taste good, but do they have the capacity to countercondition fears? In the 1920s, Mary Cover Jones helped a boy overcome his fear of rabbits by having him munch away as the animal was brought closer.*

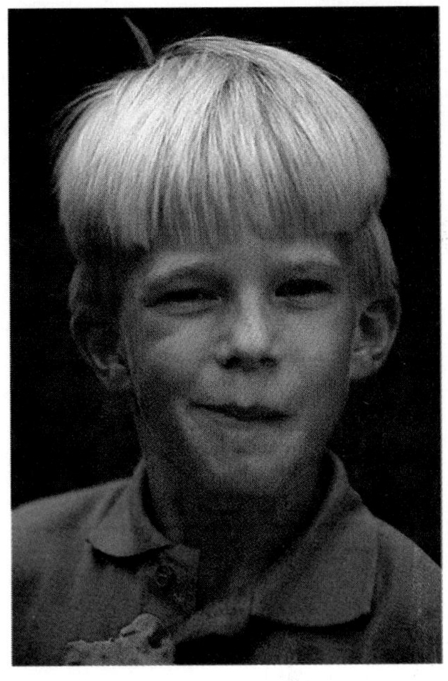

***Participant modeling*** A process in which one loses fear of anxiety-evoking objects by first observing models interact with them and then imitating the models.

FIGURE 10.12

**PARTICIPANT MODELING.** *Participant modeling helps children overcome fears through principles of observational learning. In these photos, children with a fear of snakes observe, then imitate, models who are unafraid. Parents often try to convince children that something tastes good by eating it in front of them and saying ''Mmm!''*

In an often-cited experiment on participant modeling, Albert Bandura and his colleagues (1969) found that participant modeling was as effective as systematic desensitization for people who are afraid of snakes. It also worked more rapidly than systematic desensitization. Figure 10.12 shows a number of children and adults in the Bandura study study who observed and then imitated the behavior of models who were unafraid of snakes.

Filmed models can exert a powerful effect on children, and one implication is that television could have significant potential in reducing such commonly occurring fears as going to the dentist, entering school, and so on (Crain, 1992). Some programs, such as ''Sesame Street,'' have included segments that portray children coping with the potentially stressful experiences of handling animals, making new friends, and going to a new school, among others.

## DEVELOPMENT OF GENDER ROLES AND GENDER DIFFERENCES

Two children were treated at Johns Hopkins University Hospital for the same problem. But the treatments and the outcomes were vastly different. Each child was genetically female, and each had the internal sex organs of a female. But because of excessive prenatal exposure to male sex hormones, each had developed external sex organs that resembled a male's (Money & Ehrhardt, 1972).

The problem was identified in one child (let's call her Nora) early. The masculinized sex organs were surgically removed when she was 2. Like many girls, Nora was tomboyish during childhood, but she was feminine in appearance and had a female ***gender identity.***

***Gender identity*** Knowledge that one is a female or a male. (The first stage in the cognitive-developmental theory of the assumption of gender roles.)

The other child (let's call him Edward) was at first mistaken for a genetic male with stunted external sex organs. The error was discovered at the age of 3½. But by then Edward had a firm male gender identity. Surgery further masculinized the appearance of his sex organs. During childhood he preferred typical masculine toys and activities and was accepted as one of the boys.

Nora and Edward both had ***androgenital syndrome.*** In this hormonal disorder, prenatal exposure to androgens masculinizes the sex organs of genetic females. In the case of Nora, the child was assigned to the female gender and reared as a girl. The other child, Edward, was labeled male and reared as a boy. Each child acquired the gender identity of the assigned gender.

The situation encountered by Nora and Edward is rare. Still, it raises questions about what it means to be a girl or boy in our society. Let us explore this issue further by discussing masculine and feminine gender-role stereotypes and their development. Then we shall review research on gender differences and explore their origins. Finally, we shall examine the concept of psychological androgyny, which involves the combination of both feminine and masculine traits in the same individual.

## *Development of Gender Roles and Stereotypes*

"Why Can't a Woman Be More Like a Man?" You may recall this song from the musical *My Fair Lady*. In the song, Henry Higgins laments that women are emotional and fickle, whereas men are logical and dependable. The "emotional woman" is a ***stereotype***—a fixed, oversimplified, and often distorted idea about a group of people. The "logical male" is also a stereotype, although a more generous one.

Cultural stereotypes of males and females involve broad expectations of behavior we call ***gender roles.*** In our culture, the feminine gender-role stereotype includes such traits as dependence, gentleness, helpfulness, kindness, warmth, emotionality, submissiveness, and home-orientation. The masculine gender-role stereotype includes aggressiveness, self-confidence, independence, competitiveness, and competence in business, math, and science (Ruble, 1988).

Gender-role stereotypes appear to develop through a series of stages. First, children learn to label the genders. Around 2 to 2½ years of age, they become quite accurate in identifying pictures of girls and boys (Etaugh & Duits, 1990; Etaugh et al., 1989; Fagot & Leinbach, 1993). By age 3, they display knowledge of gender stereotypes for toys, clothing, work, and activities (Fagot et al., 1992; Huston & O'Brien, 1985; Perry et al., 1984; Weinraub et al., 1984). For example, children of this age generally agree that boys play with cars and trucks, help their fathers, and tend to hit others. They also agree that girls play with dolls, help their mothers, and don't hit others.

Children become increasingly traditional in their stereotyping of activities, occupational roles, and personality traits between the ages of 3 and about 9 or 10 (Martin, 1993; Martin et al., 1990; Serbin et al., 1993). For example, traits such as "cruel" and "repairs broken things" are viewed as masculine, while "often are afraid" and "cooks and bakes" are seen in feminine.

Stereotyping then levels off or declines slightly over the next couple of years (Biernat, 1991; Ruble, 1988). Older children and adolescents apparently become somewhat more flexible in their perceptions of males and females. They retain the broad stereotypes but also perceive similarities between the genders and recognize that there are individual differences. They are more capable of recognizing the arbitrary aspects of gender categories, and they are more willing to try new behaviors that are typical of the other gender (Katz & Walsh, 1991).

Children and adolescents also show some chauvinism. That is, they perceive their own gender in a somewhat better light. For example, girls perceive other

***Androgenital syndrome*** A disorder in which genetic females become masculinized as a result of prenatal exposure to male hormones.

***Stereotype*** A fixed, conventional idea about a group.

***Gender roles*** Complex clusters of behaviors that are considered stereotypical of females and males.

girls as nicer, harder workers, and less selfish than boys. Boys, on the other hand, think *they* are nicer, harder workers, and less selfish than girls (Etaugh et al., 1984).

*It is true that boys and girls typically think that their own gender is superior.*

## GENDER DIFFERENCES: VIVE LA DIFFÉRENCE OR VIVE LA SIMILARITÉ?

Clearly, females and males are anatomically different. And according to the gender-role stereotypes we have just examined, people believe that they also differ in their behaviors, personality characteristics, and abilities. But just how different are females and males?

We saw in Chapter 7 that gender differences in infancy are small and rather inconsistent. In this chapter, we have reviewed gender differences during early childhood. You will recall that young girls and boys display some differences in their choices of toys and play activities. Boys engage in more rough-and-tumble play and also are more aggressive. Girls tend to show more empathy and to report more fears. In Chapter 15, we shall see that girls show greater verbal ability than boys, whereas boys show greater visual-spatial ability than girls. Girls excel in certain areas of mathematics, while boys excel in others. What are the origins of these gender differences in behavior? Different theoretical accounts have been proposed. We turn to these now.

## THEORETICAL INTERLUDE: VIEWS ON THE DEVELOPMENT OF GENDER DIFFERENCES IN BEHAVIOR

Like mother, like daughter; like father, like son—at least often, if not always. Why is it that little girls (often) grow up to behave according to the cultural stereotypes of what it means to be female? Why is it that little boys (often) grow up to behave like male stereotypes? Let us have a look at various explanations of the development of gender differences.

**BIOLOGICAL INFLUENCES** Some researchers have looked for the origins of gender differences in the organization of the brain. We saw in Chapter 8 that the hemispheres of the brain are specialized to perform certain functions. In most people, the left hemisphere is more involved in language skills, whereas the right hemisphere is specialized to carry out visual-spatial tasks. Testosterone in the brain of the male fetus spurs greater growth of the right hemisphere and slows the rate of growth of the left hemisphere (Geschwind & Galaburda, 1987). The difference may be connected with males' (slight) superiority on spatial-relations tasks and females' (slight) superiority on verbal tasks.

Might the greater frequency of aggressive behavior and rough-and-tumble play in boys also be linked to prenatal brain organization? Some researchers theorize that prenatal hormones masculinize or feminize the brain by creating predispositions that are consistent with gender-role stereotypes (Jacklin, 1989; Money, 1987). John Money suggests that predispositions may be created prenatally, but argues that social learning plays a stronger role in the development of gender identity, personality traits, and preferences. He claims that social learning is even powerful enough to counteract many prenatal predispositions.

**THINKING ABOUT DEVELOPMENT**

Agree or disagree with the following statement and support your answer: "Boys are naturally more aggressive than girls."

There is very little experimental research on prenatal hormone influences in children. Ethical considerations prevent us from experimentally manipulating prenatal levels of sex hormones in people. But now and then sex hormones are manipulated for other reasons, and we can observe the results. Many women, for example, have taken androgens to help maintain their pregnancies. Anke Ehrhardt and Susan Baker (1978) were able to study the effects of such prenatal androgens on 17 children ages 4 to 26.

Compared with sisters who had not been exposed to prenatal androgens, androgenized girls were more active during play and more likely to perceive themselves to be tomboys. They were less vain about their appearance than their unaffected sisters. They did not enjoy caring for babies or show much interest in playing with dolls or eventually marrying. The boys whose mothers had received male hormones engaged more often in outdoor sports and rough-and-tumble play than their brothers.

There are some methodological problems in the Ehrhardt and Baker report and in other, more recent studies that have found that androgenized girls show increased play with "boys' toys" (Berenbaum & Hines, 1992). First is the selection factor. The mothers in the Ehrhardt and Baker study, for example, were not assigned at random to androgens, but were a group with a history of miscarriages. This history might somehow have been responsible for the behaviors shown by their children. Second, the samples in these studies are small, rendering the evidence almost anecdotal. Third, the prenatal androgen levels may require that the children receive the steroid cortisone for the rest of their lives. Cortisone has a number of side effects, among them an increased level of activity. Thus, play styles among the children could reflect the cortisone therapy as well as prenatal androgen levels. Finally, girls exposed to androgens typically are born with genitalia that are masculinized to some degree. As a result, parents may treat these girls in a more masculine fashion.

Let us now consider psychological views of the development of gender differences.

**PSYCHOANALYTIC THEORY** Sigmund Freud explained the acquisition of gender roles in terms of the concept of ***identification.*** In psychoanalytic theory, identification is the process of incorporating within ourselves our perceptions of the behaviors, thoughts, and feelings of other people. Freud believed that gender identity remains flexible until the resolution of the Oedipus and Electra complexes at about the age of 5 or 6 (see Chapter 2). These complexes are resolved by the child's abandoning incestuous wishes for the parent of the other gender and identifying with the parent of the same gender. Through identification with the same-gender parent, the child develops gender-typed behaviors. But, as we saw earlier in this chapter, children display stereotypical gender-typed behaviors earlier than Freud predicted.

**SOCIAL-LEARNING THEORY** Social-learning theorists explain the development of gender-typed behavior in terms of the processes of observational learning, identification, and socialization. Children learn much of what is considered masculine or feminine by observing and imitating models of the same gender

***Identification*** A process in which one person becomes like another through broad imitation and incorporation of the other person's personality traits.

(see Figure 10.13). These models may be their parents, as well as other adults, children, and even television characters (Jacklin, 1989; Lott & Maluso, 1991), as discussed in Focus on Research.

The importance of observational learning is shown in an experiment conducted by Kay Bussey and Albert Bandura (1984). In this study, children learned how behaviors are gender-typed by observing the relative frequencies with which women and men performed them. While children of ages 2 to 5 observed them, female and male adult role models exhibited different behavior patterns, such as choosing a blue or a green hat, marching or walking across a room, and repeating different words. Then the children were given a chance to imitate the models. Girls were twice as likely to imitate the woman's behavior as the man's, and boys were twice as likely to imitate the man's behaviors as the woman's.

Social learning theorists view identification as a broad, continuous learning process in which children are influenced by rewards and punishments to imitate adults of the same gender—particularly the parent of the same gender (Lips, 1993). In identification, as opposed to imitation, children do not simply imitate a certain behavior pattern. They also try to become broadly like the model.

Socialization also plays a role in gender-typing. Parents, teachers, other adults—even other children—inform children about how they are expected to behave. As we saw earlier in this chapter, they reward children for behavior they consider gender-appropriate. They punish (or fail to reinforce) children for behavior they consider inappropriate. As noted in Chapter 7 and in this chapter's discussion of gender differences in play, parents and others encourage children to engage in behavior consistent with gender-role stereotypes.

Boys are encouraged to be independent, while girls are more likely to be restricted and given assistance. For example, boys are allowed to roam farther from home at an earlier age and are more likely to be left unsupervised after school (Block, 1983). Parents and other adults also have lower expectations for and attach less importance to the academic achievements and accomplishments of girls than of boys (Roggman et al., 1991; Ruble, 1988).

Fathers are more likely than mothers to communicate norms for gender-typed behaviors to their children (Lytton & Romney, 1991; Power, 1985). Mothers share fathers' cultural expectations concerning gender-appropriate behavior pat-

FIGURE 10.13

***ACQUIRING GENDER ROLES.*** *What psychological factors contribute to the acquisition of gender roles? Psychoanalytic theory focuses on the concept of identification. Social-learning theory focuses on imitation of the behavior patterns of same-gender adults and reinforcement by parents and peers.*

## FOCUS ON RESEARCH

### *NONEDUCATIONAL TELEVISION CAN BE EDUCATIONAL, INDEED, OR, "I'M POPEYE, THE SAILOR WOMAN"?*

What do Popeye, the Pink Panther, Bugs Bunny, and the Teenage Mutant Ninja Turtles have in common—aside from hefty bank accounts? They're all male. Almost every study of children's television shows done in the last 20 years has found that several shows have all-male casts and that among shows with characters of both genders, males outnumber females at least two or three to one (Comstock & Paik, 1991; Huston et al., 1992).

Children who watch television are learning more than how to rescue Olive Oyl and trap roadrunners. Television—and other popular media such as books, magazines, radio, and film—portray females and males in traditional gender roles (DeBell, 1993; Kortenhaus & Demarest, 1993; Signorielli, 1990). Female television characters are portrayed as less active than males and more likely to follow the directions of others (especially males). Females' activities have less impact than those of males. Male characters are more likely to conceive and carry out plans and to be aggressive, dominant, and authoritative. These gender role images have not changed much over the past 20 or so years (DeBell, 1993; Signorielli, 1989).

Television commercials also support gender-role stereotypes. Even though women and men now appear equally often in prime-time commercials, women are more likely to be seen inside the home, advertising domestic products. Men continue to provide 90 percent of the narratives (known as "voice-overs") in commercials, conveying the idea that men are more authoritative and knowledgeable (Bretl & Cantor, 1988; DeBell, 1993; Lovdal, 1989).

Perhaps not surprisingly, children who spend more hours watching television are more likely to show stereotyped concepts of masculine and feminine behavior (Comstock & Paik, 1991; Huston et al., 1992). There is also disconcerting experimental evidence that television portrayals of gender-role stereotypes affect young viewers. Children shown cartoons in which characters adhere to traditional gender-role stereotypes are more likely than children shown nontraditional behavior to describe men and women according to these stereotypes (Davidson et al., 1979). But the Davidson study also showed signs of hope. Five- and 6-year-olds who observed girls in nontraditional roles, such as building a clubhouse, held stereotyped attitudes less strongly afterward.

There is also some evidence that the impact of TV on children's stereotypes can be minimized by rearing children with nontraditional gender-role attitudes. In one study, third-graders were classified as either high, medium, or low stereotyped on the basis of their preferences for "masculine" or "feminine" activities (List et al., 1983). The children were then divided into groups and either shown a film of a woman in a traditional role (wife and mother) or a nontraditional role (physician and army officer). Children who were highly stereotyped later remembered less about the film in which the woman played the doctor and officer. However, children low in gender-role stereotyping recalled more about both films.

Television has a powerful potential to hurt but an equally powerful potential to help. Perhaps awareness of the potential of the medium will encourage producers to eliminate sexism from a greater percentage of shows.

terns, but are usually less demanding that children show gender-typed behavior. Fathers tend to encourage their sons to develop instrumental behavior (that is, behavior that gets things done or accomplishes something) and their daughters to develop warm, nurturant, behavior (Block, 1979). Fathers are likely to cuddle their daughters gently. By contrast, they are likely to toss their sons into the air and use hearty language with them, such as "How're yuh doin', Tiger?" and "Hey you, get your keister over here" (Jacklin et al., 1984; Power & Parke, 1982). Being a nontraditionalist, one of the authors (S. R.) liked to toss his young daughters into the air, which raised objections from relatives who criticized him for being too rough. This, of course, led him to modify his behavior. He learned to toss his daughters into the air when the relatives were not present.

Not all families raise their children alike, of course, nor do they hold identical views regarding gender stereotypes. While many families adhere to traditional gender-role concepts, others are less traditional and make an effort to treat their daughters and sons equally and minimize gender-typing. One recent study found

***Gender identity*** Knowledge that one is a female or a male.

that in families in which parents actively discouraged gender-typing, preschoolers displayed less stereotyping in their activities and interests, even though they were just as aware of conventional gender roles as children in more traditional families (Weisner & Wilson-Mitchell, 1990). Another study found that elementary school children showed less stereotyping in their activity preferences if their mothers frequently engaged in traditionally "masculine" household and child-care tasks such as doing yard work, washing the car, taking children to ball games, or assembling toys (Serbin et al., 1993).

One change in family life today is that more children are spending part of their childhood in a single-parent home (see Chapter 13). Children from single-parent homes generally are less traditional in their gender-typing. This may come about for at least two reasons. First, the single parent typically engages in tasks normally carried out by both parents (for example, going to work, doing household repairs, caring for the children, cooking and cleaning) and so provides a less strongly gender-typed model. Second, the absent parent is usually the father who, as we have seen, is usually the parent most concerned with gender-typing of the children (Katz, 1987).

Another change in family life today is the increasing participation of mothers in the labor force (see Chapter 13). More daughters today have mothers who serve as career-minded role models. More boys are exposed to fathers who take a larger role than men used to in child care and household responsibilities. Not surprisingly, many studies show that maternal employment is associated with less stereotyped gender-role concepts for girls and boys (Etaugh, 1993; Hoffman, 1989). The daughters of employed women also have higher educational and career aspirations than daughters of nonemployed women, and they are more likely to choose careers that are nontraditional for women.

Social-learning theory has helped outline the ways in which rewards, punishments, and modeling foster gender-typed behavior. But *how* do rewards and punishment influence behavior? Do reinforcers mechanically increase the frequency of behavior, or, as suggested by cognitive theories, do they provide us with concepts that in turn guide our behavior? Let us consider two cognitive approaches to gender-typing that shed light on these matters: cognitive-developmental theory and gender-schema theory.

**COGNITIVE-DEVELOPMENTAL THEORY** Lawrence Kohlberg (1966) proposed a cognitive-developmental view of gender-typing. According to this perspective, gender-typing is not the product of environmental influences that mechanically stamp in gender-appropriate behavior. Rather, children themselves play an active role. They form concepts about gender and then fit their behavior to their gender concepts. These developments occur in stages and are entwined with general cognitive development.

According to Kohlberg, gender-typing involves the emergence of three concepts: *gender identity, gender stability,* and *gender constancy.* The first step in gender-typing is attaining ***gender identity.*** Gender identity is the knowledge that

FIGURE 10.14

**GENDER ROLES AND MATERNAL EMPLOYMENT.** *When both parents are employed, they provide their children with less stereotyped views of the male and female roles.*

one is male or female. Gender identity appears to originate in gender assignment, or the process in which other people label the child a girl or boy. Gender assignment is a response to the child's anatomic sex that usually occurs at birth. Gender assignment is so important to parents that they usually want to know "Is it a girl or a boy?" before they begin to count fingers and toes.

Most children acquire a firm gender identity by the age of 36 months (Money, 1977). At 2 years of age, most children can verbally state whether they are boys or girls. At age 2½, they can classify pictures of themselves properly according to gender (Thompson, 1975). By the age of 3, many children also have acquired the capacity to discriminate anatomic gender differences (Bem, 1989).

At around the age of 4 or 5, most children develop the concept of ***gender stability,*** according to Kohlberg. They recognize that people retain their genders for a lifetime. Girls no longer believe they can grow up to be daddies, and boys no longer think they can become mommies.

**TRUTH OR FICTION REVISITED**

*It is true that a 2½-year-old may know that she is a girl but still think that she can grow up to be a daddy. Children do not recognize that they will retain their genders until the concept of gender stability emerges at about the age of 4 or 5.*

By 5 to 7 years of age, Kohlberg believes that most children develop the more sophisticated concept of ***gender constancy.*** Children with gender constancy recognize that gender does not change, even if people modify their dress or behavior. So, gender remains constant even when appearances change. A woman who cuts her hair short remains a woman. A man who dons an apron and cooks dinner remains a man.

We could relabel gender constancy as "conservation of gender," highlighting the theoretical debt to Jean Piaget. Indeed, researchers have found that the development of gender constancy is related to the general development of conservation, as described in Chapter 9 (Serbin & Sprafkin, 1986). For this reason, it seems that conservation concepts may lay the cognitive groundwork for gender constancy. More intelligent children also develop gender constancy earlier, further suggestive of the cognitive nature of the task.

According to cognitive-developmental theory, once children have established concepts of gender stability and constancy, they will be motivated to behave in ways that are consistent with their genders (Bauer, 1993a). For example, once girls understand that they will remain female, they will show a preference for "feminine" activities. As shown by the Bussey and Bandura (1984) study described earlier, children do appear to actively seek information about which behavior patterns are "masculine" and which are "feminine." They are then significantly more likely to imitate the "gender appropriate" patterns.

Interestingly, Ullian (1981) found that 6-year-old children who have developed gender stability but not gender constancy tend to adhere rather rigidly to gender-typed behavior patterns. It is as if they think that behaving in inappropriate ways could actually change their genders. By the age of 8, children are more willing to engage in behaviors associated with the other gender. Perhaps the achievement of gender constancy makes children secure in the knowledge that they will remain as they were (Maccoby, 1990b).

In a similar vein, Smetana and Letourneau (1984) found that girls with gender stability more often chose girl playmates than did girls who had developed

***Gender stability*** The concept that one's gender is a permanent feature.

***Gender constancy*** The concept that one's gender remains the same despite superficial changes in appearance or behavior.

gender identity only. The researchers theorize that female companionship helps confirm their female self-concepts prior to the certainty of gender constancy. Once they have attained gender constancy, girls know that playing with boys will not alter their gender. For this reason, they become less rigid in use of gender as a factor in choice of playmates.

Cross-cultural studies in the United States, Samoa, Nepal, Belize, and Kenya (Munroe et al., 1984) have found that the concepts of gender identity, gender stability, and gender constancy emerge in the order predicted by Kohlberg (Leonard & Archer, 1989; Munroe et al., 1984). Children may achieve gender constancy earlier than Kohlberg stated, however. Many 3- and 4-year-olds show at least some understanding of gender constancy (Bem, 1989; Leonard & Archer, 1989).

Kohlberg's theory also has difficulty accounting for the age at which gender-typed play emerges. Many children prefer gender-typed toys such as cars and dolls by the age of 2 (Caldera et al., 1989). At this age, children are likely to have a sense of gender identity, but gender stability and gender constancy remain at least a year or two away (Ruble, 1988). Therefore, gender identity alone seems to provide a child with sufficient motivation to assume gender-typed behavior patterns (Martin & Little, 1990). Kohlberg's theory also does not explain why the concept of gender plays such a prominent role in children's classification of people and behavior (Bem, 1983; Jacklin & McBride-Chang, 1991). Another cognitive view, gender-schema theory, attempts to address these concerns.

**GENDER-SCHEMA THEORY: AN INFORMATION-PROCESSING VIEW** ***Gender-schema theory*** proposes that children use gender as one way of organizing their perceptions of the world (Bem, 1985; Bigler & Liben, 1992; Signorella et al., 1993). A gender schema is a cluster of mental representations about male and female physical qualities, behaviors, and personality traits. According to gender-schema theory, gender gains prominence as a schema for organizing experience because of society's emphasis on it. As a result, even young children begin to mentally group people of the same gender according to the traits that represent that gender.

As in social-learning theory, children learn ''appropriate'' behavior by observation. Children's cognitive processing of information also contributes to their gender-typing, however.

Consider the dimension of *strength–weakness.* Children learn that strength is linked to the male gender-role stereotype and weakness to the female stereotype. They also learn that some dimensions, such as strength–weakness, are more relevant to one gender than the other—in this case, to males. Bill will learn that the strength he displays in weight training or wrestling affects the way others perceive him. But most girls do not find this trait to be important to others, unless they are competing in gymnastics, tennis, swimming, or other sports. Even so, boys are expected to compete in these sports and girls are not. Jane is likely to find that her gentleness and neatness are more important in the eyes of others than her strength.

Children thus learn to judge themselves according to the traits that are considered relevant to their genders. In doing so, their self-concepts become blended with the gender schema of their culture. The gender schema provides standards for comparison. Children whose self-concepts are consistent with their society's gender schema are likely to have higher self-esteem than children whose self-concepts are not (Cramer & Skidd, 1992).

***Gender-schema theory*** The view that one's knowledge of the gender schema in one's society (the behavior patterns that are considered appropriate for men and women) guides one's assumption of gender-typed preferences and behavior patterns.

From the viewpoint of gender-schema theory, gender identity is sufficient to inspire ''gender appropriate'' behavior. Thus, gender-typed behavior is believed to emerge earlier than would be proposed by cognitive-developmental theory. As soon as children understand the labels "girl" and "boy," they actively seek information concerning gender-typed traits and strive to live up to them. Bill may fight back when provoked because boys are expected to do so. Jane may be gentle and kind because that is expected of girls. Bill and Jane's self-esteem will depend in part on how they measure up to the gender schema.

Studies indicate that children do possess information according to a gender schema. For example, boys show better memory for "masculine" toys, activities, and occupations, while girls show better memory for "feminine" toys, activities, and occupations (Bauer, 1993a; Bigler & Liben, 1990; Liben & Signorella, 1993).

In sum, brain organization and sex hormones may contribute to gender-typed behavior. However, there is also evidence that the effects of social learning may be strong enough to counteract most prenatal biological influences. But social-learning theory may pay insufficient attention to children's active roles as seekers of gender-related information. Cognitive-developmental and gender-schema theories integrate the strengths of social-learning theory with the ways in which children process information so as to blend their self-concepts with the gender schema of their culture.

## *Psychological Androgyny*

Most of us think of masculinity and femininity as opposite poles of a continuum (Ruble, 1988). We assume that the more masculine people are, the less feminine they are and vice versa. A boy who shows the "feminine" traits of nurturance, tenderness, and emotionality might be considered less masculine than other boys. Girls who are competitive and assertive are seen not only as more masculine than other girls, but also as less feminine.

Today, many psychologists assert that masculinity and femininity are independent personality dimensions. That is, people (male or female) who score high on measures of masculine traits need not score low on feminine traits. People with both stereotypical feminine and masculine traits are said to show ***psychological androgyny.*** People high in masculine traits *only* are typed as masculine. People high in feminine traits *only* are typed as feminine. People who show neither strong feminine nor masculine traits are termed "undifferentiated."

Some psychologists suggest that it is worthwhile to promote psychological androgyny in children, because they will then possess both the feminine and masculine traits that are valued in our culture (Hyde et al., 1991). There is a good deal of evidence that androgynous children and adults are relatively well adjusted apparently because they can summon a wider range of traits to meet the challenges of their worlds. For example, compared with their masculine, feminine, or undifferentiated peers, androgynous children and adolescents have better social relations and superior adjustment (Wells, 1980), higher self-esteem (Alpert-Gillis & Connell, 1989; Lamke, 1982a, b), and higher levels of ego identity—that is, a sense of who they are and what they stand for (Schiedel & Marcia, 1985; Turiel, 1984).

But some studies have reported little or no differences between androgynous and masculine individuals. Several studies, for example, have found that androgynous and masculine individuals are equally high in self-esteem (Ruble, 1988). These results and others support the idea that it is the masculine component of androgyny that is most strongly related to the psychosocial well-being of children, adolescents, and adults (Boldizar, 1991; Spence, 1991). This finding suggests that it is more acceptable for females in our society to adopt masculine traits than for males to adopt feminine traits (Markstrom-Adams, 1991). Thus, androgyny is not necessarily the most desirable gender-role orientation.

***Psychological androgyny*** Possession of both stereotypical feminine and masculine traits.

Some feminist scholars criticize the concept of psychological androgyny, because it is defined as the possession of both masculine and feminine personality traits. However, the definition relies upon the presumed reality of masculine and feminine gender-role stereotypes. Feminists would prefer to see the stereotypes recognized as culturally induced and then dissolved or de-emphasized (Lips, 1993; Matlin, 1993).

The changes in physical, cognitive, social, and personality development reviewed in the last three chapters lay the groundwork for the next major period in development: the middle childhood years. We will explore those years in the next three chapters, starting with physical development in Chapter 11.

## Summary


1. Parental approaches to child rearing may be classified according to the independent dimensions of warmth–coldness and restrictiveness–permissiveness. Parents usually attempt to enforce restrictions by inductive, power-assertive, or withdrawal of love techniques. Induction relies on reasoning. Power-assertion relies on physical rewards and punishments. Withdrawal of love involves isolating or ignoring children when they misbehave.

2. Diana Baumrind classifies parenting styles as either authoritative (high restrictiveness, high warmth), authoritarian (high restrictiveness, low warmth), permissive–indulgent (low restrictiveness, high warmth) and rejecting–neglecting (low restrictiveness, low warmth). Authoritative parents are more likely to have competent children. Parenting styles depend partly on the situation, the characteristics of the child, and the cultural context.

3. Siblings provide care giving, nurturance, advice, role models, and social interaction for children. Parental support can help children adjust to the birth of a sibling.

4. Firstborn children tend to be more achievement-oriented, get higher grades, and are more cooperative and helpful than later-borns. However, they are also usually more anxious. Later-born children tend to acquire superior social skills and to be more popular with peers.

5. Early friendships are fairly stable and are based on shared play materials and activities.

6. Play contributes to social and emotional development. Parten noted several types of play, including solitary, onlooker, parallel, associative, and cooperative play. Dramatic play is cooperative play in which children take on and enact various social roles.

7. Preferences for gender-typed toys are well-developed by 15 to 36 months. Children prefer to play with peers of their own gender. Pressure to engage in gender-typed activities is exerted by parents, teachers, and peers.

8. Children begin to share as early as the first year. Most children show concern for others who are in distress during the second year. Such prosocial behavior is fostered when parents explain how the child's behavior affects others.

9. Aggressiveness tends to remain stable from middle childhood to adulthood. Boys generally are more aggressive than girls. Genetic factors may be involved in extreme forms of aggression such as criminality. Difficult tempera-

ment also may contribute indirectly to aggression. From a social-learning perspective, children acquire aggressive responses through operant conditioning and observational learning.

10. Preschool childern often describe themselves in terms of external traits such as age and gender. This is called the *categorical self.* Children with high self-esteem (feelings of positive worth) tend to show secure attachment and prosocial behavior.

11. According to Erik Erikson, the main developmental task of the early childhood years is taking the initiative in mastering new skills. Fear of violating adult prohibitions, however, may cause the child to feel guilty.

12. Preschool children often have fears of animals, imaginary creatures, the dark, and concerns about personal safety, whereas older children may develop social- and school-related fears. Techniques for helping children cope with fears include systematic desensitization, operant conditioning, and participant modeling.

13. A gender role is a cluster of stereotypes attributed to females or males. Children by the age of about 3 have developed gender stereotypes for toys, clothing, work, and activities. Children's stereotypes are most rigid at about the ages of 9 and 10. Adolescents are less rigid in their stereotypes.

14. Biological influences may partly explain a number of gender differences. But social learning may outweigh possible biological influences on gender differences in cognitive functioning and personality.

15. According to psychoanalytic theory, gender-typing stems from resolution of the conflicts of the phallic stage. Social-learning theory explains gender-typing in terms of observational learning and socialization. Cognitive-developmental theory views gender-typing in terms of the emergence of the cognitive concepts of gender identity, gender stability, and gender constancy. Gender-schema theory includes elements from social-learning theory and cognitive-developmental theory. Gender-schema theory proposes that children use the gender schema of their society to organize their perceptions and that children attempt to blend their self-concepts with the gender schema.

16. Children who show both masculine and feminine traits are labeled "psychologically androgynous." Psychologically androgynous children may be better adjusted than stereotypically masculine boys and feminine girls, because they can summon a wider range of traits and skills to meet the challenges of their situations.

# Middle Childhood

Middle childhood is a time of steady growth and increasing competence. Change is less dramatic during these years than during either the preceding infancy and preschool years or the adolescent period that will follow.

Children begin elementary school, and school life assumes great importance. The child is more self-sufficient now, and the companionship of peers is highly valued. Physical growth progresses at an even pace, and children become much more skilled at motor activities. Thinking is more logical, although still focused more on tangible objects than on abstract ideas.

For many children, middle childhood is a calm, happy time, although some face challenges imposed by social, economic, or family stresses.

Physical, cognitive, social, and personality development in middle childhood are the topics of Chapters 11, 12, and 13.

# MIDDLE CHILDHOOD:

## PHYSICAL DEVELOPMENT

## Chapter Outline

## Truth or Fiction?

_____ *Boys begin to surpass girls in height and weight at about age 11 or 12.*

_____ *Most children outgrow "baby fat."*

_____ *Recent studies indicate that heredity plays almost no role in the development of obesity.*

_____ *Children who spend more time watching television are likely to become heavy.*

_____ *During the middle childhood years, boys begin to outperform girls in motor activities.*

_____ *With the recent emphasis on fitness, U.S. children have become more fit.*

_____ *Hyperactivity is caused by chemical food additives.*

_____ *The activity levels of many hyperactive children have been lowered by stimulants.*

_____ *Some children who are intelligent and provided with stimulating home environments cannot learn how to read or do simple math problems.*

_____ *Mainstreaming is a more effective educational approach for disabled students than special-needs classes.*

*Jessica is a 6-year-old attending her first day of school. During recess, she runs to the climbing apparatus in the schoolyard and climbs to the top. As she reaches the top, she announces to the other children, "I'm coming down." She then walks to the parallel bars, goes halfway across, lets go, and tries again.*

*Steve and Mike are 8-year-olds. They are riding their bikes up and down the street. Steve tries riding with no hands on the handlebars. Mike starts riding fast, standing up on the pedals. Steve shouts, "Boy, you're going to break your neck!"*

(ADAPTED FROM ROWEN, 1973)

Middle childhood is a time for learning many new motor skills. Success in both gross and fine motor skills reflects children's increasing physical maturity, their opportunities to learn, and personality factors such as their persistence and self-confidence. Competence in motor skills enhances children's self-esteem and their acceptance by their peers.

In this chapter, we will examine physical and motor development during middle childhood. We will also discuss children with certain disabilities.

## GROWTH PATTERNS

Gains in height and weight are fairly steady throughout middle childhood. But notable variations in growth patterns also occur from child to child.

### *HEIGHT AND WEIGHT*

**Growth spurt** A period during which growth advances at a dramatically rapid rate as compared with other periods.

Following the growth trends begun in early childhood, boys and girls continue to gain a little over 2 inches in height per year during the middle childhood years. This pattern of gradual gains does not vary significantly until children reach the adolescent ***growth spurt*** (see Figure 11.1). The average gain in weight

FIGURE 11.1

**GROWTH CURVES FOR HEIGHT AND WEIGHT.** *Gains in height and weight are fairly steady during middle childhood. Boys continue to be slightly heavier and taller than girls through 9 or 10 years of age. Girls then begin their adolescent growth spurt and surpass boys in height and weight until about age 13 or 14. (Source: Department of Health and Human Services).*

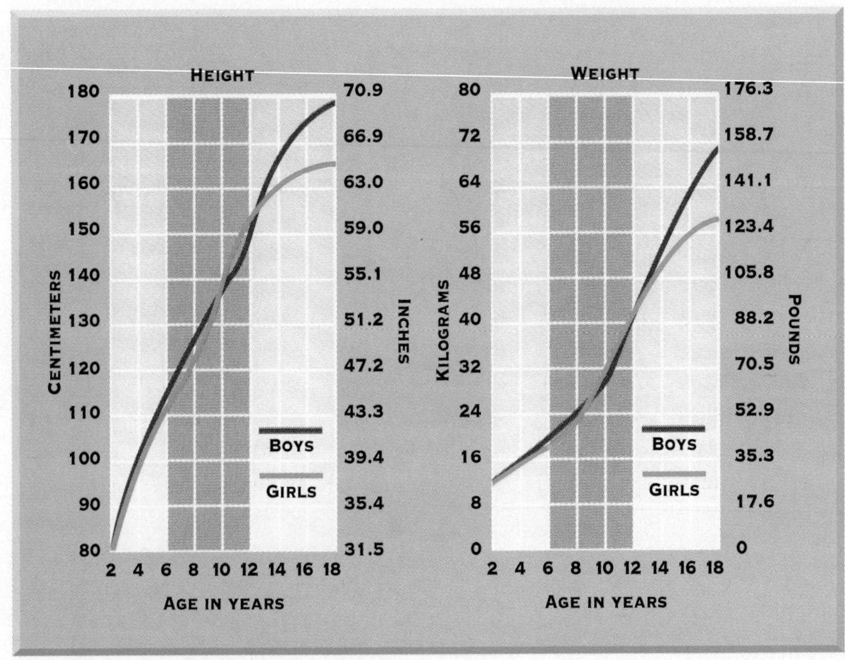

between the ages of 6 and 12 is about 5 to 7 pounds a year. During these years, children continue to become less stocky and more slender (Meredith, 1987).

Most deviations from these average height and weight figures are quite normal. Individual differences are more marked in middle childhood than they were earlier. For example, most 3-year-olds are within 8 to 10 pounds and 4 inches of each other. But by the age of 10, children's weights may vary by as much as 30 to 35 pounds, and their heights may vary by as much as 6 inches.

**Gender and Physical Growth** You can also see from Figure 11.1 that boys continue to be slightly heavier and taller than girls through the ages of 9 or 10. Girls then begin their adolescent growth spurt and surpass boys in height and weight until about age 13 or 14. At that time, boys are approaching the peak of their adolescent growth spurt, and they become taller and heavier than girls (Malina, 1990).

**Truth or Fiction Revisited**

*Boys are slightly taller and heavier than girls in the early years of middle childhood. But after the age of 9 or 10, girls begin their adolescent growth spurt and become taller and heavier than boys for a few years.*

The steady gain in height and weight during middle childhood is paralleled by an increase in muscular strength for both girls and boys (Malina, 1990). The relative proportion of muscle and fatty tissue is about the same for boys and girls in early middle childhood. But this begins to change at around age 11, as males develop relatively more muscle tissue and females develop more fatty tissue (Michael, 1990).

**Nutrition and Growth** In middle childhood, average body weight doubles. Children also expend a good deal of energy as they engage in physical activity and play. To fuel this growth and activity, children need to eat more than they did in the preschool years. The average 4- to 6-year-old needs about 1,800 calories per day. But the average 7- to 10-year-old requires 2,000 calories a day (Ekvall, 1993a).

**Culture and Development: Physical Growth** A number of factors, including nutrition and disease, affect the growth of children. Studies of children in different parts of the world have found that children in urban areas are taller than those living in rural areas and that middle-class children are taller than lower income children (Meredith, 1978, 1982, 1984; Tanner, 1989). Malnutrition and disease appear to play a large role in these differences in physical growth. By the age of 4, poor Asian and African children are as much as 7 inches shorter and 13 pounds lighter than children of the same age in Europe and the United States. The importance of malnutrition and disease is demonstrated by studies that find only small growth differences among economically advantaged children of different ethnic groups (Hendrick, 1990).

But ethnic origin plays a role as well. For example, Asian children tend to be somewhat shorter than European and African children growing up in comparable environments. In the United States, African-American children tend to grow slightly more rapidly than white children (Eveleth & Tanner, 1990).

Do patterns of physical growth differ for children in different cultural groups?

**Differences in Physical Growth**

- Children in urban areas are taller than those living in rural areas.
- Middle-class children are taller than lower income children.
- By age 4, poor Asian and African children are shorter and lighter than U.S. and European children.
- Economically advantaged children of different ethnic groups show small growth differences.
- Asian children are somewhat shorter than European and U.S. children growing up in comparable environments.
- African-American children grow slightly more rapidly than white U.S. children.

## CHILDHOOD OBESITY

***Obesity*** A disorder characterized by excessive accumulation of fat.

***Obesity*** is a disorder characterized by the excessive accumulation of fat. Most authorities define obesity as a body weight in excess of 20 percent of the norm. If we use this criterion, about 15 to 25 percent of American children are obese (Lucas, 1991; Niedbala & Ekvall, 1993). In spite of the current emphasis on fitness and health in our society, the prevalence of obesity has increased in recent years among all races and both genders (Jackson, 1992; Muecke et al., 1992). In the past 20 years, for example, obesity increased 54 percent among children aged 6–11 years, and 39 percent among those aged 12–17 (D.V. Harris, 1991).

Parents (and children) frequently assume that heavy children will "outgrow" their "baby fat"—especially once they hit the growth spurt of adolescence. Not so. Most overweight children become overweight adults (Lucas, 1991; Tiwary & Holguin, 1992). By contrast, only about 40 percent of normal-weight boys and 20 percent of normal-weight girls become obese adults.

### TRUTH OR FICTION REVISITED

*Children do not necessarily outgrow baby fat at all. The majority of obese children become obese adults.*

Obese children, despite the stereotype, are usually far from jolly. Preschool children show negative attitudes toward overweight people (Fritz & Wetherbee, 1982). During childhood, heavy children are often socially rejected by their peers (Jackson, 1992). They usually perform poorly in athletic activities, which is a source of much prestige for other children (Smoll & Schultz, 1990). As obese children approach adolescence, they become even less popular, because they are less likely to be found attractive by peers of the other gender. It is no surprise, then, that obese children tend to like their bodies less than children of normal weight. Moreover, overweight adolescents are more likely to be depressed and anxious than their peers of normal weight (Brack et al., 1991; Rosen et al., 1990).

Overweight in adolescence may have social and economic consequences in young adulthood, especially for females. Women who were overweight as teens are less likely to marry than women of normal weight. They have lower incomes and complete fewer years of school. Similar but weaker trends are found for men (Gortmaker et al., 1993).

Being overweight in adolescence also can lead to chronic illness and earlier death in adulthood, even for those teens who later lose weight. One recent study reported that overweight boys were more likely than boys of normal weight to die of heart disease, strokes, and cancer before the age of 70 (Must et al., 1992). Women who were overweight as teens had more difficulty with tasks such as climbing stairs, lifting, and walking by the time they became 70.

**THEORETICAL INTERLUDE: CAUSES OF OBESITY** Obesity runs in families. Two recent studies provide convincing evidence that heredity plays a major role in obesity. One study found that some people inherit a tendency to burn up extra calories, while others inherit a tendency to turn their extra calories into fat (Bouchard et al., 1990). A second study showed that identical twins had the same body weight in adulthood whether they had been reared together or apart (Stunkard, 1990). In other words, childhood experiences appeared to have little effect on adult weight.

## Truth or Fiction Revisited

*While environmental factors do contribute to the development of obesity, research suggests that heredity plays a major role.*

Obesity has also been related to the amount of fat cells or ***adipose tissue*** we have, and we may have some tendency to inherit different numbers of fat cells. Hunger may be related to the amount of fat stored in these cells. As time passes after a meal, the blood-sugar level drops. Fat is then drawn from fat cells to provide further nourishment, causing them to shrivel. At some point, referred to as the *set point,* the hypothalamus is signaled of the fat deficiency in these cells, triggering the hunger drive.

Children with more fat cells than other children will feel food deprived sooner, even though they may be equal in weight. This might be because more signals are being sent to the brain. Obese people and formerly obese people tend to have more adipose tissue than people of normal weight (Braitman et al., 1985). As a result, childhood obesity may cause the adult dieter to feel persistent hunger, even after leveling off at a new desired weight.

Moreover, obese people may be more sensitive than normal-weight individuals to external sources of stimulation, such as the aroma of food, the sight of others eating, even the clock. That is, obese children may be more likely than others to feel hungry just because it's lunchtime or dinnertime. This high sensitivity to external sources of stimulation has also been found among rats in whom a part of the hypothalamus has been destroyed. For this reason, it has been suggested that some obese children are suffering from faulty regulation of hunger because of problems in the hypothalamus (Schachter, 1971). However, this view has been challenged by Judith Rodin (1981), who found that people in all weight categories, not only the obese, may be external eaters. Thus, the link between obesity and responsiveness to external cues is not as powerful as had been thought.

Evidence that genetic and physiological factors are involved in obesity does not necessarily mean that environment plays no role (Grilo & Pogue–Geile,

***Adipose tissue*** Fat.

FIGURE 11.2

**OBESITY.** *Obesity runs in families. Both genetic and environmental factors appear to be involved.*

**THINKING ABOUT DEVELOPMENT**

Agree or disagree with the following statement and support your answer: "Children who are overweight simply eat too much."

1991). Obese parents may create a home environment that encourages weight gain. For example, they may be models of poor exercise habits, may encourage overeating, and may keep the wrong kinds of food around (Rosenthal, 1990a).

Television watching also appears to play a role in the development of obesity. A large-scale longitudinal study showed that children who watched television for 25 or more hours per week during the middle childhood years were more likely to become obese as adolescents (Dietz, 1990; Dietz & Gortmaker, 1985). The influence of TV watching is at least threefold. First, children tend to consume snacks while watching. Second, television bombards children with commercials for fattening foods, such as candy and potato chips. Third, watching television is sedentary. We burn fewer calories sitting than engaging in strenuous physical activity. Moreover, children who are heavy TV viewers are less physically active overall (Wong et al., 1992). Overweight children burn even fewer calories than normal-weight children when watching television, which further contributes to their obesity (Brody, 1993b).

**TRUTH OR FICTION REVISITED**

*It is true that children who watch a great deal of television are likely to be heavier than children who watch less television. Factors that may contribute to their greater weight include inactivity, snacking while watching, and exposure to commercials for fattening foods.*

Overeating may occur in response to severe stresses, such as those due to bickering in the home, parental divorce, or the birth of a sibling. There also is evidence that dieting efforts are impeded by negative emotional states such as depression (Lucas, 1991).

For some suggestions on how parents can help their children (and themselves) lose weight, see Developing Today.

## MOTOR DEVELOPMENT

The school years are marked by increases in the child's speed, strength, agility, and balance (Cratty, 1986). These developments, in turn, lead to more skillful performance of motor activities.

### *GROSS MOTOR SKILLS*

Throughout middle childhood, children show steady improvement in their ability to perform various gross motor skills (Cratty, 1986; Laszlo, 1990). School-age children are usually eager to participate in group games and athletic activities that require the movement of large muscles, such as catching and throwing balls. As seen in Table 11.1, children are hopping, jumping, and climbing by age 6 or so, and by 6 or 7, they are usually capable of pedaling and balancing on a bicycle. By the ages of 8 to 10, children are showing the balance, coordination, and strength that allows them to engage in gymnastics and team sports (see Figure 11.3).

## Developing Today

### HELPING CHILDREN LOSE WEIGHT

Today's parents not only want to be slimmer themselves, they are also more aware of the health benefits their children gain by avoiding obesity. However, losing weight is one of the most difficult problems in self-control for children and adults alike.

Long-term, insight-oriented psychotherapy has not been shown to be of much use in helping children lose weight. However, behavioral methods show promise (S. W. Ekvall et al., 1993b; Epstein et al., 1984; Israel et al., 1984; Lucas, 1991). These methods include: (a) improving nutritional knowledge, (b) reducing calories, (c) exercise, and (d) behavior modification. The behavioral methods involve tracking the child's calorie intake and weight, keeping the child away from temptations, setting a good example, and the systematic use of praise and other rewards (Epstein et al., 1985, 1990; Foster et al., 1985; Israel et al., 1985). The most successful weight-loss programs for children combine exercise, decreased caloric intake, behavior modification, and emotional support from parents (Niedbala & Ekvall, 1993). Here are a number of suggestions gleaned from the literature:

*Teach children about their nutritional needs—calories, protein, vitamins, minerals, fiber, food groups, and so on.* Indicate which foods may be eaten in nearly unlimited quantities (for example, green vegetables) and which foods should be eaten only sparingly (cakes, cookies, soft drinks sweetened with sugar, and so on).

*Do not insist that the entire family sit down at the same time for a large meal.* Allow your child to eat only when hungry. This will break the tyranny of the clock—the expectation that he or she must be hungry because it's noon or 6 p.m.

*Substitute low-calorie foods for high-calorie foods.* There's no way around it: Calories translate into pounds.

*Don't push your child to "finish the plate."* Children should be allowed to stop eating when they are no longer hungry. There is no moral or nutritional value to stuffing.

*Prepare low-calorie snacks for your child to eat throughout the day.* In this way, children do not become extremely deprived and feel desperate for food. Desperation can prompt binging.

*Do not cook, eat, or display fattening foods when the child is at home.* The sight and aroma of tantalizing foods can be more than children can bear.

*Involve the child in more activities.* When children are kept busy, they are less likely to think about food.

*Do not take your child food shopping, or, if you do, try to avoid the market aisles with ice cream, cake, and candy.* If fattening food is left at the supermarket, it does not wind up in the child's stomach.

*Ask relatives and friends not to offer fattening treats when you visit.* Be insistent—stand up to the grandparent who insists that high-calorie foods "can't hurt."

*Don't allow snacking in front of the TV set, while playing, reading, or engaging in any other activity.* Allowing children to snack while watching TV makes eating a mindless habit.

*Involve the child in calorie-burning exercise.* Check with the pediatrician about possible risks, but try to involve the child in activities such as swimming or prolonged bicycle riding. Exercise will burn calories, increase the child's feelings of competence and self-esteem, improve cardiovascular condition, and, possibly, promote lifetime exercise habits.

*Reward the child for taking steps in the right direction, such as eating less or exercising more.* Praise and approval are powerful rewards, but children also respond to tangible rewards such as going on a special trip or getting a new toy.

*Don't assume it's a catastrophe if the child slips and goes on a binge.* Don't rant and rave. Don't get overly upset. Talk over what triggered the binge with the child so that similar problems may be averted in the future. Remind the child (and yourself) that tomorrow is another day and another start.

*If you and your children are overweight, lose weight together.* Follow-up studies show that it is more effective for overweight children and their parents to diet and exercise together than for the children to go it alone (Epstein et al., 1990).

During these years, the muscles are growing stronger, and the pathways that connect the cerebellum to the cortex are becoming increasingly myelinated. Experience also plays an indispensable role in refining many sensorimotor abilities, especially at championship levels, but there are also individual differences that seem inborn. Some people, for example, have better visual acuity or better depth perception than others. For reasons such as these, they will have an edge in playing the outfield or hitting a golf ball.

FIGURE 11.3

**GROSS MOTOR SKILLS.** *By the ages of 8 to 10, children are showing the balance, coordination, and strength that allows them to engage in team sports such as soccer.*

***Reaction time*** The amount of time required to respond to a stimulus.

One of the most important factors in athletic performance is ***reaction time,*** or the amount of time required to respond to a stimulus. Reaction time is basic to the child's timing of a swing of the bat to meet the ball. Reaction time is basic to adjusting to a fly ball or hitting a tennis ball. Reaction time is also involved in children's responses to cars and other (sometimes deadly) obstacles when they are riding their bicycles or running down the street.

Reaction time gradually improves (that is, *decreases*) from early childhood to about age 18 (Bard et al., 1990; Cratty, 1986; Kail, 1991). Reaction time begins to increase again in the adult years. Even so, 75-year-olds still outperform children. Baseball and volleyball may be "child's play," but, everything else being equal, adults will respond to the ball more quickly.

## *FINE MOTOR SKILLS*

By 6 to 7 years, children can usually tie their shoelaces and hold their pencils as adults do (see Table 11.2). The abilities to fasten buttons, zip zippers, brush

TABLE 11.1

***DEVELOPMENT OF GROSS MOTOR SKILLS DURING MIDDLE CHILDHOOD***

| AGE | SKILLS |
|---|---|
| 6 YEARS | HOPS, JUMPS, CLIMBS |
| 7 YEARS | BALANCES ON AND PEDALS A BICYCLE |
| 8 YEARS | HAS GOOD BODY BALANCE |
| 9 YEARS | ENGAGES IN VIGOROUS BODILY ACTIVITIES, ESPECIALLY TEAM SPORTS SUCH AS BASEBALL, FOOTBALL, VOLLEYBALL, AND BASKETBALL |
| 10 YEARS | BALANCES ON ONE FOOT FOR 15 SECONDS; CATCHES A FLY BALL |
| 12 YEARS | DISPLAYS SOME AWKWARDNESS AS A RESULT OF ASYNCHRONOUS BONE AND MUSCLE GROWTH |

THE AGES PRESENTED IN THE TABLE ARE AVERAGES; THERE ARE WIDE INDIVIDUAL VARIATIONS.
SOURCE: ADAPTED FROM SAHLER & MCANARNEY, 1981.

**TABLE 11.2**

***Development of Fine Motor Skills During Middle Childhood***

| Age | Skills |
|---|---|
| 6-7 years | Ties shoelaces<br>Throws ball by using wrist and finger release<br>Holds pencil with fingertips<br>Follows simple mazes<br>May be able to hit a ball with a bat |
| 8-9 years | Spaces words when writing<br>Writes and prints accurately and neatly<br>Copies a diamond shape correctly<br>Swings a hammer well<br>Sews and knits<br>Shows good hand-eye coordination |

There are wide variations in the timing of the acquisition of the fine motor skills shown in this table.
Source: Adapted from Gesell, 1972.

teeth, wash themselves, and coordinate a knife and fork all develop during the early school years and improve during childhood (Cratty, 1986).

### *Gender and Motor Skills*

Throughout the middle years, boys and girls perform similarly in most motor activities. Boys show slightly greater overall strength and, in particular, more forearm strength, which aids them in swinging a bat or throwing a ball (Butterfield & Loovis, 1993).

*During middle childhood, girls and boys perform similarly in most motor activities.*

Girls, on the other hand, show somewhat greater limb coordination and overall flexibility, which is valuable in dancing, balancing, and gymnastics (Cratty, 1986). Girls with a certain type of physique seem particularly well-suited to gymnastics. Those who are short, lean, and small boned make the best gymnasts, according to Olympic coaches, because they displace gravity most effectively. This may explain why female gymnasts are considered old for the sport by the time they reach their late teens. By then, they have often grown taller and their body contours have filled out (Adler & Starr, 1992; Press, 1992).

At puberty, gender differences in motor performance favoring boys become progressively greater (Smoll & Schultz, 1990). What factors might account for the development of gender differences in physical performance? Thomas and French (1985), after reviewing the available research, concluded that the slight gender differences in motor performance prior to puberty are not large enough to be attributed to biological variables. (The one exception may be throwing, a skill in which boys excel from an early age.) Thomas and French point out that boys are more likely than girls to receive encouragement, support, and opportunities for participation in sports. We saw in Chapter 7 that even during the preschool years, parents emphasize gross motor behavior in boys more than

FIGURE 11.4

***GENDER AND MOTOR SKILLS.*** *Girls and boys are similar in their motor abilities in middle childhood. Boys have somewhat greater forearm strength, which helps the young football player on the opposite page throw the ball. Girls, like this gymnast, show somewhat greater limb coordination and overall flexibility.*

in girls. By middle childhood, boys are involved in more competitive games than girls and in games of longer duration. They also engage in more vigorous activity than girls (Riddoch et al., 1991; Reynolds et al., 1990).

At puberty, when boys begin to excel in such areas as running, the long jump, sit-ups, and grip strength, boys' greater size and strength confer a certain biological advantage. But some environmental factors that operated in middle childhood may exert even greater importance in puberty. "Tomboy" behaviors of girls are less socially accepted in adolescence than they were in middle childhood. Girls may, therefore, become less interested in participating in athletic activities and may be less motivated to do well in the ones in which they do engage (Thomas & French, 1985). Recent research shows that by the age of 12 and 13, girls are less likely than boys to perceive themselves as competent and interested in physical exercise and activity (Ferguson et al., 1989; Whitehead & Corbin, 1991).

## *EXERCISE AND FITNESS*

The health benefits of exercise for both adults and children are well known. Exercise reduces the risk of heart disease, stroke, diabetes, and certain forms of cancer (Brody, 1991a, 1993b). Exercise confers psychological benefits as well. For example, physically active adolescents have better self-image and better coping skills than those who are physically inactive (Covey & Feltz, 1991; Reynolds et al., 1990).

U.S. adults are becoming more conscientious about exercising and staying fit. But curiously, children in the United States are less fit than ever. A study of the fitness of U.S. children in grades 1 through 12 found a decline over a 10-year period in strength, flexibility, and cardiovascular endurance (Brody, 1990b). Nearly two-thirds of American children fail to meet the standards set by the President's Council on Physical Fitness (D.V. Harris, 1991).

What are some possible reasons for this decline in fitness? One obvious culprit, discussed earlier in this chapter in the section on obesity, is television watching. High school students who watch relatively little television (less than

2 hours a day) are more physically fit than those who watch more than 4 hours per day (Tucker, 1986, 1987).

## TRUTH OR FICTION REVISITED

*Despite the recent emphasis on fitness among adults, children have actually become less fit over the past decade or so. Contributing factors may include TV watching and cutbacks in school physical-education programs.*

Cutbacks in school-based physical education programs may also play a role. Only about one-third of children in grades 1 through 12 have daily physical education classes (Brody, 1990c; "Healthy People 2000," 1991). One study found that children in physical education classes spent nearly half their time not moving at all (Parcel et al., 1987). Only 6 minutes out of 35, on the average, were devoted to fitness-oriented activities.

Cardiac and muscular fitness, both in childhood and adulthood, is developed by participation in continuous exercise such as running, walking quickly, swimming laps, bicycling, or jumping rope for intervals of several minutes at a time (Michael, 1990). Unfortunately, schools and parents tend to focus on sports such as baseball and football, which are less apt to promote fitness (Brody, 1990b).

As you might expect, children who engage in exercise and are physically fit have more positive attitudes toward physical activity and are more likely to perceive its benefits (Brustad, 1991; Desmond et al., 1990; Ferguson et al., 1989). Children with high levels of physical activity are more likely to have parents who encourage their children to exercise and who actively exercise themselves (Stucky-Ropp & DiLorenzo, 1992). How, then, can more children be motivated to engage in regular physical activity? Here are some suggestions for parents (Bjorklund & Bjorklund, 1989; Brody, 1990b, c).

- ✦ Find time for family outdoor activities that promote fitness: walking, swimming, bicycling, skating (see Figure 11.5).
- ✦ Reduce television viewing.

- ✦ Encourage outdoor play during daylight hours after school.
- ✦ Do not assume that your child gets sufficient exercise by participating in a team sport. Many team sports involve long periods of inactivity.

A further comment about competitive team sports is worth noting. Organized sports for children have become enormously popular in recent years. An estimated 35 million children between the ages of 6 and 18 participate annually in at least one organized sport (Seefeldt et al., 1991). But unfortunately, many children ultimately lose their enthusiasm for sports and drop out. Sports participation declines steadily after the age of 10 (Seefeldt et al., 1991). Why does this occur? Sometimes children are pushed too hard, too early, or too quickly by parents or coaches. This may result in feelings of frustration and inferiority, not to mention physical injury (Brody, 1990c; Kolata, 1992b). Hence, a few more guidelines for parents are in order here:

- ✦ Do not put excessive performance demands on your children. Let them progress at their own pace.
- ✦ Focus on the fun and health benefits of physical activity and sports, not on winning.

## CHILDREN WITH DISABILITIES

Certain disabilities of childhood are most apt to be noticed in the middle childhood years, when the child enters school. The school setting requires that a child sit still, pay attention, and master a number of academic skills. But some children have difficulty with one or more of these demands. In this section, we focus on children with two types of disabilities: attention-deficit hyperactivity disorder and learning disabilities.

FIGURE 11.5

***EXERCISE AND FITNESS.*** *One way parents can motivate their children to engage in regular physical activity is to find time for family outdoor activities that promote fitness, such as bicycling.*

### ATTENTION-DEFICIT HYPERACTIVITY DISORDER (ADHD)

*Scott, age 7, is extremely restless and distractible in class. Every few minutes, he is out of his seat, exploring something on a bookshelf or looking out the window. When in his seat, he swings his legs back and forth, drums his fingers on the table, shifts around, and keeps up a high level of movement. He speaks rapidly, and his ideas are poorly organized, although his intelligence is normal. During recess, Scott is aggressive and violates many of the playground rules. Scott's behavior at home is similar to his behavior in school. He is unable to concentrate on any activity for more than a few minutes. Scott is suffering from attention-deficit hyperactivity disorder. (Adapted from Halgin & Whitbourne, 1993, p. 335)*

Many parents feel that their children do not pay enough attention to them—that they tend to run around as the whim strikes and to do things in their own way. Some inattention, especially at early ages, is to be expected. But in ***attention-deficit hyperactivity disorder*** (ADHD), the child shows developmentally inappropriate or excessive inattention, impulsivity, and ***hyperactivity*** (Gillis et al., 1992; Platzman et al., 1992; White & Sprague, 1992). A more complete list of problems is shown in Table 11.3. The degree of hyperactive behavior is crucial, since many normal children are labeled overactive and fidgety from time to time. In fact, if talking too much were the sole criterion for ADHD, the label would have applied to many of us.

The onset of ADHD occurs by age 7 (Frick & Lahey, 1991). The behavior pattern must have persisted for at least 6 months for the diagnosis to apply. The hyperactivity and restlessness of children with ADHD impair their ability to function in school (August et al., 1992; Hinshaw, 1992). They simply cannot sit still (see Figure 11.6). They also have difficulty getting along with others (Alessandri, 1992a; Landau & Moore, 1991; Whalen & Henker, 1992). Their disruptive and noncompliant behavior often elicits punishment from parents (Barkley et al., 1991b; Buhrmester et al., 1992).

***Attention-deficit hyperactivity disorder*** (ADHD) A behavior disorder characterized by excessive inattention, impulsiveness, and hyperactivity.

***Hyperactivity*** Excessive restlessness and overactivity. Not to be confused with misbehavior or with normal high activity levels that occur during childhood. One of the primary characteristics of attention-deficit hyperactivity disorder (ADHD).

**TABLE 11.3**

**SYMPTOMS OF ATTENTION-DEFICIT HYPERACTIVITY DISORDER (ADHD)**

| | |
|---|---|
| LACK OF ATTENTION | FREQUENTLY FAILS TO FINISH PROJECTS<br>DOES NOT SEEM TO PAY ATTENTION<br>IS READILY DISTRACTED<br>CANNOT SUSTAIN CONCENTRATION ON SCHOOLWORK OR RELATED TASKS<br>DOES NOT SUSTAIN INTEREST IN PLAY ACTIVITIES |
| IMPULSIVITY | FREQUENTLY ACTS WITHOUT THINKING<br>SHIFTS FROM ACTIVITY TO ACTIVITY<br>CANNOT ORGANIZE TASKS OR WORK<br>REQUIRES CONSTANT SUPERVISION<br>OFTEN CALLS OUT IN CLASS<br>DOES NOT WAIT FOR TURN IN LINE, GAMES, AND SO ON |
| HYPERACTIVITY | CONSTANTLY RUNS AROUND OR CLIMBS ON THINGS<br>CANNOT SIT STILL; FIDGETS CONSTANTLY<br>DOES NOT REMAIN IN SEAT IN CLASS<br>SHOWS EXCESSIVE MOTOR ACTIVITY WHEN ASLEEP<br>IS CONSTANTLY ON THE GO, RUNNING LIKE A MOTOR<br>TALKS EXCESSIVELY |

CHILDREN WHO ARE DIAGNOSED WITH ADHD DISPLAY MANY OF THE BEHAVIORS LISTED IN THIS TABLE. THEIR ACADEMIC FUNCTIONING, AND SOMETIMES THEIR SOCIAL FUNCTIONING, SUFFER AS A RESULT.

SOURCE: ADAPTED FROM AMERICAN PSYCHIATRIC ASSOCIATION, 1987.

FIGURE 11.6

***ATTENTION-DEFICIT HYPERACTIVITY DISORDER.*** *Hyperactive children are continually on the go, as if their ''motors'' are constantly running. Hyperactivity as an abnormal syndrome is not to be confused with the normal high energy levels of children.*

Sad to say, ADHD is not rare. It is diagnosed in about 1 to 5 percent of school-aged children and is one of the most common causes of childhood referrals to mental-health clinics (S.W. Ekvall et al., 1993a; Weiss, 1991). ADHD is about three to six times more common in boys than in girls (Barkley, 1990; Bhatia et al., 1991).

**THEORETICAL INTERLUDE: CAUSES OF ADHD** Many theorists focus on possible physical causes. For one thing, ADHD tends to run in families (Frick et al., 1991a; Gillis et al., 1992; Mannuzza et al., 1991). At least some children with ADHD appear to have an inherited defect in the body's thyroid hormone system (Hauser et al., 1993). Some studies have found ADHD is more prevalent in children who have suffered from encephalitis (Anderson & Cohen, 1991). Recordings of brain waves frequently show abnormalities as well (Hechtman, 1991).

Evidence such as this has led some investigators to suggest that ADHD children suffer from ''minimal brain damage'' or ''minimal brain dysfunction.'' These labels, of course, do not add much to efforts to locate and remedy possible damage.

More recent research, however, has found that ADHD is related to a metabolic disorder in the brain. Alan Zametkin and his colleagues (1990) found that individuals with ADHD have reduced activity in those areas of the brain that control attention and movement.

One other physical hypothesis that has been proposed is that the chemical additives in processed food are largely responsible for hyperactivity. However, experimental studies of the so-called Feingold diet, which removes such additives from children's food, have not supported this hypothesis (S.W. Ekvall et al., 1993a; Hynd et al., 1991; Hynd & Hooper, 1992).

**TRUTH OR FICTION REVISITED**

*It has not been demonstrated that hyperactivity is caused by chemical food additives. (Nonetheless, it has not been shown that such additives are good for children either.)*

**TREATMENT AND OUTCOME** The most widespread treatment for ADHD is medical—the use of ***stimulants*** such as Ritalin and Dexadrine. It may seem ironic that stimulants would be used with children who are already overly active. The rationale is that the activity of the hyperactive child stems from inability of the cerebral cortex to inhibit more primitive areas of the brain. The drugs, in theory, act to stimulate the cortex and facilitate cortical control of primitive areas.

Children with ADHD who are given stimulants show increased attention span (Handen et al., 1992; de Sonneville et al., 1991), improved cognitive and academic performance (Carlson et al., 1992; DuPaul & Rapport, 1993; Klorman et al., 1992), reduced activity level (Klorman et al., 1990), and a reduction in disruptive, annoying, and aggressive behaviors (Gadow et al., 1990; Granger et al., 1993). The use of stimulants is controversial, however. Some critics argue that stimulants suppress gains in height and weight, do not contribute to academic gains, and lose effectiveness over time (Henker & Whalen, 1989; Green, 1991). Another concern is that stimulants are overused or misused in an attempt to control normal high activity levels of children at home or in the classroom. Supporters of stimulant treatment argue that many ADHD children are helped by medication. They counter that the suppression of growth appears to be related to the dosage and the specific drug chosen (Weiss, 1991).

**TRUTH OR FICTION REVISITED**

*The activity levels of many hyperactive children have, in fact, been lowered by stimulants. The stimulants theoretically foster cerebral control over more primitive areas of the brain.*

Another approach that shows some promise is cognitive behavioral therapy (Baer & Nietzel, 1991; Bloomquist et al., 1991; Fehlings et al., 1991). This approach attempts to increase the child's self-control and problem-solving abilities through modeling, role playing, and self-instruction. Operant conditioning methods have also been used with some success, both in decreasing hyperactivity and in improving academic performance (Abramowitz & O'Leary, 1991; Vitulano & Tebes, 1991). It appears that a combination of behavior therapy and stimulants

***Stimulants*** Drugs that increase the activity of the nervous system.

***Dyslexia*** A reading disorder characterized by problems such as letter reversals, mirror reading, slow reading, and reduced comprehension (from the Greek roots *dys-*, meaning "bad," and *lexikon,* meaning "of words").

***Learning disabilities*** A group of disorders characterized by inadequate development of specific academic, language, and speech skills.

may be the most effective approach to treating ADHD children (Whalen & Henker, 1991; Weiss, 1990).

Even so, many children do not outgrow ADHD. Follow-up studies show that at least two-thirds of children with ADHD continue to exhibit one or more of the core symptoms in adolescence and adulthood (Barkley et al., 1991a; Gagnon et al., 1993; McGee et al., 1991). Problems in attention, conduct, hyperactivity, and learning frequently continue. ADHD children are at risk for later development of antisocial and criminal behavior (Lambeir et al., 1991). Most are employed, although their final educational and work record achievements are lower than those of matched normal controls (Mannuzza et al., 1993; Weiss, 1991).

## LEARNING DISABILITIES

Nelson Rockefeller served as vice-president of the United States under Gerald Ford. He was intelligent and well educated. Yet despite the best of tutors, he could never master reading. Rockefeller suffered from ***dyslexia.***

Dyslexia is one type of ***learning disability.*** The term "learning disability" refers to a group of disorders characterized by inadequate development of specific academic, language, and speech skills, as shown in Table 11.4 (Adelman & Taylor, 1993; Farnham–Diggory, 1992; Silver, 1991). Learning-disabled children may show problems in math, writing, or reading. Some have difficulties in articulating sounds of speech or in understanding spoken language. Others have problems in motor coordination. Children are considered to have a learning disability when they are performing below the level expected for their age and IQ and when there is no evidence of other handicaps such as vision or hearing problems, mental retardation, or socioeconomic disadvantage (Cantwell & Baker, 1991a).

### TRUTH OR FICTION REVISITED

*Some children who are intelligent and provided with stimulating home environments cannot learn how to read or do simple math problems. Such children are said to have learning disabilities.*

### THINKING ABOUT DEVELOPMENT

Agree or disagree with the following statement and support your answer: "Learning disabilities must be understood within a particular cultural context."

Children with learning disabilities frequently display other problems as well. They are more likely than other children to have attention-deficit hyperactivity disorder (Cantwell & Baker, 1991a). They do not communicate as well with their peers (Lapadat, 1991), have poorer social skills (Vaughn et al., 1990; Wiener & Harris, 1993), show more behavior problems in the classroom (Bender & Smith, 1990), and are more likely to experience emotional problems (Feagans & Haldane, 1991).

For most learning-disabled children, the disorder will persist through life. But with early recognition and appropriate special education intervention, most individuals can overcome or learn to compensate for their learning disability (Andrews & Conte, 1993; Silver, 1991).

To illustrate some of the theoretical and treatment issues involved in learning disabilities, let us return to dyslexia, the learning disability we mentioned at the beginning of our discussion. Dyslexia, you will recall, involves difficulty in learning to read. As with other learning disabilities, dyslexia is puzzling because

**TABLE 11.4**

***TYPES OF LEARNING DISABILITIES***

| DISABILITY | BRIEF DESCRIPTION |
| --- | --- |
| **ACADEMIC SKILLS DISORDERS** | |
| DEVELOPMENTAL ARITHMETIC DISORDER (DYSCALCULIA) | DEFICIENCIES IN ARITHMETIC SKILLS, SUCH AS PROBLEMS IN UNDERSTANDING BASIC MATHEMATICAL TERMS OR OPERATIONS SUCH AS ADDITION OR SUBTRACTION, IN DECODING MATHEMATICAL SYMBOLS (+,=, ETC.), OR IN LEARNING MULTIPLICATION TABLES. |
| DEVELOPMENTAL EXPRESSIVE WRITING DISORDER | GROSSLY DEFICIENT WRITING SKILLS. THE IMPAIRMENT IN WRITING ABILITY MAY BE CHARACTERIZED BY ERRORS IN SPELLING, GRAMMAR, OR PUNCTUATION, OR BY DIFFICULTY IN COMPOSING SENTENCES AND PARAGRAPHS. |
| DEVELOPMENTAL READING DISORDER (DYSLEXIA) | POORLY DEVELOPED SKILLS IN RECOGNIZING WORDS AND COMPREHENDING WRITTEN TEXT. READING DISABLED CHILDREN MAY READ LABORIOUSLY AND DISTORT, OMIT, OR SUBSTITUTE WORDS WHEN READING ALOUD. DYSLEXIC CHILDREN HAVE TROUBLE DECODING LETTERS. DYSLEXIC CHILDREN MAY PERCEIVE LETTERS UPSIDE-DOWN (*w* FOR *m*) OR IN REVERSED IMAGES (*b* FOR *d*). |
| **LANGUAGE AND SPEECH DISORDERS** | |
| DEVELOPMENTAL ARTICULATION DISORDER | DIFFICULTY ARTICULATING THE SOUNDS OF SPEECH, ALTHOUGH THERE IS NO APPARENT NEUROLOGICAL IMPAIRMENT OR DEFECT IN THE ORAL SPEECH MECHANISM. CHILDREN WITH THE DISORDER MAY OMIT, SUBSTITUTE, OR MISPRONOUNCE CERTAIN SOUNDS–ESPECIALLY *ch*, *f*, *l*, *r*, *sh*, AND *th* SOUNDS, WHICH ARE USUALLY ARTICULATED PROPERLY BY THE EARLY SCHOOL YEARS. SPEECH THERAPY IS OFTEN HELPFUL. MILDER CASES OFTEN RESOLVE THEMSELVES. |
| DEVELOPMENTAL EXPRESSIVE LANGUAGE DISORDER | IMPAIRMENTS IN THE SPOKEN LANGUAGE SUCH AS SLOW VOCABULARY DEVELOPMENT, FREQUENT ERRORS IN USAGE, AND PROBLEMS WITH GRAMMAR. AFFECTED CHILDREN MAY ALSO HAVE AN ARTICULATION DISORDER COMPOUNDING THEIR SPEECH PROBLEMS. |
| DEVELOPMENTAL RECEPTIVE LANGUAGE DISORDER | DIFFICULTIES UNDERSTANDING THE SPOKEN LANGUAGE. IN MILD CASES, CHILDREN HAVE DIFFICULTY UNDERSTANDING CERTAIN WORD TYPES (SUCH AS WORDS EXPRESSING DIFFERENCES IN QUANTITY–*large*, *big*, OR *huge*) OR CERTAIN SENTENCE TYPES (SUCH AS SENTENCES THAT BEGIN WITH THE WORD *unlike*). MORE SEVERE CASES ARE MARKED BY DIFFICULTIES UNDERSTANDING SIMPLE WORDS OR SENTENCES. |

there is every indication that the child ought to be able to read. Frequently, dyslexic children are at least average in intelligence and from a middle-class background. Their vision and hearing check out as perfectly normal. However, problems in developing reading skills persist (American Academy of Pediatrics, 1992; Rack et al., 1992).

Dyslexia affects an estimated 5 to 10 percent of American children (Kolata, 1992a). It is at least five times as common among boys as girls (Halpern, 1992). Researchers have identified a number of frequently occurring characteristics of dyslexic children and these are listed in Table 11.5.

Until recently, it was assumed that while the symptoms of dyslexia could respond to proper treatment, the disorder could not be cured (Silver, 1991). But recent research by Sally Shaywitz and her colleagues (1992) found that most of the children considered dyslexic in the first grade were no longer dyslexic in later grades. And some children who were not dyslexic earlier became so later

**TABLE 11.5**

***Characteristics of Dyslexic Children***

| |
|---|
| USUALLY FIRST RECOGNIZED DURING EARLY SCHOOL YEARS |
| OMISSIONS AND ADDITIONS OF WORDS |
| REVERSAL OR ROTATION OF LETTERS OF THE ALPHABET – CONFUSING *b* WITH *d* AND *p* WITH *q* |
| MIRROR READING AND WRITING – READING AND WRITING WORDS THAT LOOK NORMAL WHEN VIEWED IN A MIRROR, AS IN READING *saw* WHEN PRESENTED WITH THE VISUAL STIMULUS *was* |
| SLOW READING |
| REDUCED READING COMPREHENSION |
| SUBTLE LANGUAGE DIFFICULTIES, SUCH AS IMPAIRED SOUND DISCRIMINATION (ALTHOUGH OVERALL AUDITORY ACUITY IS WITHIN NORMAL LIMITS) |
| AT LEAST SOME IMPAIRMENT IN GENERAL ACADEMIC FUNCTIONING |
| MAY BE EASILY DISTRACTED, OR FAIL TO LISTEN OR TO FINISH THINGS THAT HE OR SHE HAS STARTED |
| MAY BE IMPULSIVE, CALL OUT IN CLASS, FIND IT DIFFICULT TO WAIT IN LINES |
| MORE COMMON AMONG TWINS, PREMATURELY BORN CHILDREN, CHILDREN BORN TO OLDER MOTHERS, AND CHILDREN WHO HAVE SUSTAINED HEAD INJURIES |
| MORE COMMON AMONG BOYS |
| READING, SPEECH, AND LANGUAGE PROBLEMS MORE COMMON IN FAMILY THAN IN GENERAL POPULATION |
| PROBLEM FREQUENTLY CONTINUES INTO ADOLESCENCE AND ADULTHOOD |

on. According to Shaywitz and her colleagues, dyslexia is not a specific condition that you either have or do not have. Rather, like obesity or high blood pressure, it occurs in degrees. Even children with a mild degree of reading disorder may profit from special help.

**Theoretical Interlude: Origins of Dyslexia** The cause of dyslexia and other learning disabilities is a matter of considerable debate and discussion. Current hypotheses focus on possible underlying biological and neurological factors (Rosenberger, 1992; Shaywitz et al., 1992; Williams & Lovegrove, 1992).

One hypothesis centers on the possibility of ''minimal brain damage.'' Dyslexic children, for example, frequently show a number of behaviors found among children with known brain damage. These include a short attention span and difficulty sitting still. And so, it has been speculated that children with dyslexia may also be brain damaged, even though the brain damage is so minimal that it cannot be detected by direct means.

Another hypothesis focuses on the possibility that dyslexia is inherited. In support of this view, it is known that dyslexia runs in families. Children with dyslexia often have relatives who are themselves dyslexic (DeFries et al., 1991; Pauls, 1991).

If a genetic mechanism is involved in dyslexia, what is it that may be inherited? Studies indicate that ''faulty wiring'' in the left hemisphere of the brain which controls language may be involved in dyslexia (Silver, 1991). Recent research also has shown that the left hemispheres of dyslexics are smaller than those of normal readers (Hynd & Hooper, 1992).

Such patterns of abnormal neurological development may be due to genetic factors. Some researchers, however, believe that they may stem from excessive prenatal exposure to the male hormone testosterone. Norman Geshwind and Albert Galaburda (1987) propose that a high level of prenatal testosterone slows growth in the left hemisphere. Males normally are exposed to higher levels of testosterone during pregnancy than females, because their testes secrete it. And, as we have seen, males are much more likely to suffer from dyslexia.

Recent research suggests still another neurological basis for dyslexia. Studies indicate that dyslexia may involve a brain abnormality that slows down one of two major visual pathways in the brain so that visual information is not received in the right sequence (Blakeslee, 1991b; Lehmkuhle et al., 1993; Livingstone et al., 1991). This may result in words seeming to blur, fuse, or jump off the page.

**Remediation** There are several contemporary approaches to helping learning-disabled children (Adelman & Taylor, 1933; Lyon & Moats, 1988):

***The Psychoeducational Approach*** This approach capitalizes on children's strengths and preferences rather than aiming to correct assumed, underlying cognitive deficiencies. For example, a child who retains auditory information better than visual information might be taught verbally by means of tape recordings rather than written materials.

***The Behavioral Approach*** The behavioral approach assumes that academic learning is a complex form of behavior that is built on a hierarchy of basic skills, or "enabling behaviors." To read effectively, one must first learn to recognize letters, then attach sounds to letters, then combine letters and sounds into words, and so on. The child is tested to determine where deficiencies lie in the hierarchies of skills. An individualized program of instruction and reinforcement is designed to help the child acquire the skills necessary to perform more complex academic tasks. Typically, parents and schools try to help learning-disabled students by imposing a good deal of structure and rigid rules. But recent research shows that these children may do better in school when teachers and parents provide less control and more reinforcement (Kutner, 1992a).

***The Medical Approach*** This approach assumes that learning disabilities are symptoms of biologically based problems in cognitive processing. Proponents suggest that remediation should be directed at the underlying pathology rather than the learning disability itself. If the child has a visual defect that makes it difficult to follow a line of text, treatment should aim to remediate the visual deficit, perhaps through visual-tracking exercises. Improvement in reading ability ought to follow. One of the more controversial approaches to treating dyslexia

FIGURE 11.7

**Writing Samples of a Dyslexic Child.** *Dyslexic children have trouble perceiving letters in their correct orientation. They may perceive letters upside-down (confusing* w *with* m*) or reversed (confusing* b *with* d*). This perceptual difficulty may lead to rotations or reversals in their writing, as shown here.*

involves providing dyslexic individuals with colored lenses that filter out the light of certain wavelengths (Scheiman et al., 1991; Ward, 1991). Use of this technique, developed by Helen Irlen, has shown promising results in improving the reading performance of dyslexic children (O'Connor et al., 1990; Robinson & Conway, 1990).

***The Neuropsychological Approach*** This approach assumes that learning disabilities reflect underlying deficits in processing information that involve the cerebral cortex. Remediation involves presentation of instructional material to the more efficient or intact neural systems. Inefficient or damaged parts of the brain are bypassed.

***The Linguistic Approach*** Language deficiencies can give rise to problems in reading, spelling, and verbal expression. Adherents of this approach focus on language deficiencies. Language skills are taught sequentially, helping the student to grasp the structure and use of words (Wagner & Torgesen, 1987).

***The Cognitive Approach*** This approach focuses on the ways in which children organize their thoughts when they learn academic material. Children are helped to learn by recognizing the nature of the learning task, applying effective problem-solving strategies to complete them, and monitoring the success of these strategies. Children having problems with arithmetic may be guided to break a math problem down into its component tasks, think through the steps necessary to complete each task, and evaluate performance at each step so that appropriate adjustments can be made. This systematic approach to problem solving can be applied to diverse academic tasks. For example, dyslexic children have trouble breaking words into their constituent sounds. They benefit from tutoring that focuses on this skill (Kolata, 1992a).

To date, research appears most supportive of the behavioral approach to remediation (Koorland, 1986). The linguistic approach has received some support but not enough to support widespread use in treating children with reading and spelling deficiencies (Lyon & Moats, 1988). The cognitive model, too, has received some support, but many learning-disabled children have not developed enough basic knowledge in their problem areas to systematically apply it to problems (Lyon & Moats, 1988). Evidence for the psychoeducational, medical, and neurological approaches is less persuasive (Lyon & Moats, 1988). But it may be that no one approach is best suited to all learning-disabled children.

## EDUCATING CHILDREN WITH DISABILITIES

Special educational programs have been created to meet the needs of schoolchildren with mild to moderate disabilities (Center et al., 1991; Farnham–Diggory, 1992; Hebbeler et al, 1991). These disabilities include learning disabilities, emotional disturbance, mild mental retardation, and physical disabilities such as blindness, deafness, or paralysis. However, placing disabled children in separate classes can also stigmatize them and segregate them from other children. Special-needs classes also negatively influence teacher expectations. Neither the teacher nor the students themselves come to expect very much. This negative expectation becomes a ***self-fulfilling prophecy,*** and the exceptional students' achievements suffer.

***Mainstreaming*** is intended to counter the negative effects of special-needs classes. In mainstreaming, disabled children are placed in regular classrooms that have been adapted to their needs (Salisbury, 1991; Sanche & Dahl, 1991; Wong et al., 1991). Today, the majority of students with mild disabilities spend 40 percent or more of their school day in regular classrooms (Cannon et al., 1992).

***Self-fulfilling prophecy*** An expectation that is confirmed because of the behavior of those who hold the expectation.

***Mainstreaming*** The practice of placing disabled children in classrooms with nondisabled children.

FIGURE 11.8

***MAINSTREAMING.*** *Today, the majority of students with mild disabilities spend part of their school day in regular classrooms. The goals of mainstreaming include providing broader educational opportunities for disabled students and fostering interactions with nondisabled children.*

The mainstreaming of disabled children seems consistent with democratic ideals and the desire to provide every child with an equal opportunity to learn. Mainstreaming also permits disabled and nondisabled children to socialize and interact on a number of levels (see Figure 11.8).

The goals of mainstreaming include inspiring disabled students to greater achievements, providing disabled students with better educational opportunities, and fostering normal social interactions between disabled and nondisabled students, so that the disabled will have a better chance of fitting into society as adults.

While the goals of mainstreaming are laudable, observations of the results are mixed. There is some suggestion that disabled children may achieve more when they are mainsteamed (Truesdell & Abramson, 1992). But other studies suggest that many disabled children do not fare well in regular classrooms (Brady et al., 1988; Chira, 1993a). Rather than inspiring them to greater achievements, regular classrooms can be overwhelming for many disabled students. When low-performing students are taught with all students, their failure may become more obvious (Chalfant, 1989). In fact, higher performing disabled students appear to gain more from regular classes, whereas lower performing students gain more from segregated classes (Cole et al., 1991).

Nor is it clear that placement in regular classrooms spurs socializing with disabled students. Nondisabled students often choose not to socialize with disabled students in these classes (Honig & McCarron, 1988). Ironically, disabled students sometimes become further isolated and stigmatized. However, efforts to improve the social skills of children with disabilities have met with some success (Hundert & Houghton, 1992; York et al, 1992). These efforts generally appear to be more effective with children who are mainstreamed into regular classes than they are with those who are in special classes (McIntosh et al., 1991).

Recent research indicates that structured teaching techniques and appropriate resource support are associated with successful mainstream placement of disabled children (Center et al., 1991). But we need to learn more about what types of teacher training and what types of preparation for nondisabled students will ease the way of the disabled child in the regular classroom. We also need to find out what sorts of supplementary educational experiences are needed to round out the educational and social experiences of mainstreamed children (Murphy &

Hicks-Stewart, 1991; Simmons et al., 1991). Until we have this information, the results of mainstreaming may remain mixed.

*Disabled students may achieve more when they are mainstreamed. But some disabled children do not fare well in regular classrooms.*

Our examination of educational programs for children with disabilities leads us next into an investigation of cognitive development in middle childhood and the conditions that influence it. It is to this topic that we turn in Chapter 12.

## Summary

1. Throughout middle childhood, boys and girls tend to gain 2 to 3 inches and 4 to 6 pounds per year.

2. The adolescent growth spurt begins in girls at a little over 10 years of age and about 2 years later in boys. Girls surpass boys in height and weight from about 10 to 13 years of age. Boys surpass girls in height and weight after the age of 13 or 14.

3. Around the world, middle-class children and those living in urban areas are taller than lower income children and those living in rural areas. Malnutrition and disease play a large role in these growth differences.

4. Obesity has increased among children in recent years. Heredity appears to play a major role in obesity, but environmental factors also are important. Behavioral methods show promise in helping children lose weight.

5. In middle childhood, children make incremental gains in their gross motor and fine motor skills.

6. Boys and girls are usually not too far apart in motor development during these years, but girls tend to be somewhat more flexible, and boys tend to be slightly stronger. At puberty, gender differences favoring boys become greater. These differences appear to be due to both biological and environmental factors.

7. American children have declined in physical fitness in recent years. Possible reasons include television watching and cutbacks in school-based physical education programs.

8. Attention-deficit hyperactivity disorder (ADHD) is most often found in boys and is characterized by lack of attention, impulsivity, and hyperactivity. Hyperactivity is characterized by running around, fidgeting, not remaining seated, and while asleep, excessive motor activity. ADHD is thought to reflect neurological problems and has been treated by stimulants (which facilitate cortical control over primitive areas of the brain) and behavior therapy.

9. Learning disabilities are characterized by inadequate development of specific academic language and speech skills in the absence of other handicaps such as vision or hearing problems, mental retardation, or socioeconomic disadvantage.

10. One type of learning disability is dyslexia. Different theories have attempted to link dyslexia to neurological problems or to faulty learning. Possible neurological problems include minimal brain damage, problems in the "wiring" of the left hemisphere of the cerebral cortex, and an abnormality in one of the two major visual pathways in the brain. However, the status of the research into the causes of dyslexia suggests that it would be premature to draw conclusions.

11. Approaches to helping learning-disabled children include the psychoeducational, behavioral, medical, neuropsychological, linguistic, and cognitive approaches.

12. Mainstreaming is intended to inspire disabled students to greater achievements, provide them with the best educational opportunities, and encourage social interactions with nondisabled students. Unfortunately, some disabled students feel overwhelmed in regular classrooms and also tend to be avoided by nondisabled students.

# MIDDLE CHILDHOOD:
## COGNITIVE DEVELOPMENT

## CHAPTER OUTLINE

## TRUTH OR FICTION?

_____ *The sequences of cognitive development vary from child to child.*

_____ *Children cannot memorize the alphabet until they can keep 26 pieces of information in mind at once.*

_____ *Musical ability is a kind of intelligence.*

_____ *Knowing what problem to tackle is an aspect of intelligence.*

_____ *"IQ" is an abbreviation for intelligence.*

_____ *Two children can answer exactly the same items on an intelligence test correctly, yet one can be above average in intelligence and the other below average.*

_____ *Highly intelligent children are creative.*

_____ *The IQ scores of adopted children correlate more highly with the IQ scores of their adoptive parents than with the IQ scores of their biological parents.*

_____ *Some African-American children can switch back and forth between Black English and standard English.*

_____ *Bilingual children encounter more academic problems than children who know only one language.*

id you hear the one about the judge who pounded her gavel and yelled, "Order! Order in the court!"? "A hamburger and french fries, Your Honor," responded the defendant.

Or how about this one? "I saw a man-eating lion at the zoo." "Big deal! I saw a man eating snails at a restaurant."

Or how about, "Make me a glass of chocolate milk!"? "Poof! You're a glass of chocolate milk."

These children's jokes are based on ambiguities in the meanings of words and phrases. The joke about order in the court will be found funny by most children when they are about 7 and can recognize that the word *order* has more than one meaning. The jokes about the man-eating lion and chocolate milk will strike most children as funny about the age of 11, when they can understand ambiguities in grammatical structure.

Children make enormous strides in their cognitive development during the middle childhood years. Their thought processes and language become more logical and more complex.

In this chapter, we follow the course of cognitive development in middle childhood. First, we examine Piaget's cognitive developmental view. We then consider the information-processing approach that has been stimulated by our experience with that high-tech phenomenon, the computer. We next examine the development of intelligence, various ways of measuring it, and the roles of heredity and environment in shaping it. Finally, we turn to the development of language.

## PIAGET: THE CONCRETE-OPERATIONAL STAGE

According to Piaget, the typical child is entering the stage of ***concrete operations*** by the age of 7. In the stage of concrete operations, which lasts until about the age of 12, children show the beginnings of the capacity for adult logic. However, their thought processes, or operations, generally involve tangible objects rather than abstract ideas. This is why we refer to their thinking as "concrete."

The thinking of the concrete-operational child is characterized by ***reversibility*** and flexibility. Consider adding the numbers 2 and 3 to get 5. This is an example of an operation. The operation is reversible in that the child can then subtract 2 from 5 to get 3. There is flexibility in that the child can also subtract 3 from 5 to get the number 2. To the concrete-operational child, adding and subtracting are not simply rote activities. The concrete-operational child recognizes that there are certain relationships among numbers—that operations can be carried out according to certain rules. It is this understanding that lends concrete-operational thought its flexibility and reversibility.

Concrete-operational children are less *egocentric*. Their abilities to take on the roles of others and view the world, and themselves, from other peoples' perspectives are greatly expanded. They recognize that people see things in different ways due to different situations and different sets of values.

As compared with preoperational children, who can focus on only one dimension of a problem at a time, concrete-operational children can engage in ***decentration.*** That is, they can focus simultaneously on multiple dimensions or aspects of a problem. Decentration has implications for conservation and other intellectual undertakings.

***Concrete operations*** The third stage in Piaget's scheme, characterized by flexible, reversible thought concerning tangible objects and events.

***Reversibility*** According to Piaget, recognition that processes can be undone, leaving things as they were before. Reversibility is a factor in conservation of the properties of substances.

***Decentration*** Simultaneous focusing (centering) on more than one aspect or dimension of a problem or situation.

### CONSERVATION

Concrete-operational children show understanding of the laws of conservation. The 7-year-old girl in Figure 12.1 would say that the flattened ball still has the same amount of clay. If asked why, she might reply, "Because you can roll it up again like the other one"—an answer that shows reversibility.

The concrete-operational girl is also aware of the principle that objects can have several properties or dimensions. Things that are tall can also be heavy or light. Things that are red can also be round or square, or thick or thin. Knowledge of this principle allows her to *decenter* and avoid focusing on only the diameter of the clay pancake. By paying simultaneous attention to both the height and the width of the clay, she recognizes that the loss in height compensates for the gain in width.

Researchers have found that children do not develop conservation in all kinds of tasks simultaneously (Kreitler & Kreitler, 1989). For example, conservation of mass usually develops first, followed by conservation of weight and conservation of volume. Piaget referred to the sequential development of concrete operations as ***horizontal décalage.*** As Piaget theorized, the cognitive gains of the concrete-operational stage are so tied to specific events that achievement in one area does not automatically transfer to achievement in another.

***Horizontal décalage*** (day-kah-lahzh) The sequential unfolding of the ability to master different kinds of cognitive tasks within the same stage.

***Transitivity*** The principle that if A is greater than B in a property, and B is greater than C, then A is greater than C.

### TRANSITIVITY

We have asked you some tough questions in this book, but here is a real ogre: If your parents are older than you are, and you are older than your children, are your parents older than your children? The answer, of course, is yes. But how did you arrive at this answer? If you said yes simply on the basis of knowing that your parents are older than your children (for example, 58 and 56, compared with 5 and 3), your answer was not based on concrete-operational thought. Concrete-operational thought requires awareness of the principle of ***transitivity:*** If A exceeds B in some property (say age or height), and B exceeds C, then A must also exceed C.

FIGURE 12.1

**CONSERVATION OF MASS.** *This concrete-operational girl has rolled two clay balls. In the photo on the left, she agrees that both have the same amount (mass) of clay. In the photo on the right, she (gleefully) flattens one clay ball. When asked whether the two pieces still have the same amount of clay, she says yes. Since she is in the concrete operations stage, she recognizes that despite the change in shape, the mass of the clay has been conserved.*

***Seriation*** Placing objects in an order or series according to a property or trait.

***Seriation*** is the placing of objects in a series, or order, according to some property or trait, such as lining up one's family members according to age, height, or weight. Seriation is made possible when one has knowledge of transitivity. Let us consider some examples with preoperational and concrete-operational children.

Piaget frequently assessed children's abilities at seriation by asking them to place 10 sticks in order of size. Four- to 5-year-old children usually place the sticks in a random sequence, or in small groups, as in small, medium, or large. Six- to 7-year-old children, who are in transition between the preoperational and concrete-operational stages, may arrive at proper sequences. However, they usually do so by trial and error, rearranging their series a number of times. In other words, they are capable of comparing two sticks and deciding that one is longer than the other, but their overall perspective seems limited to the pair they are comparing at the time and does not seem to encompass the entire array.

But consider the approach of 7- and 8-year-olds who are capable of concrete operations. They go about the task systematically, usually without error. In the case of the 10 sticks, they look over the array, then select either the longest or shortest and place it at the point from which they will build their series. Then they select the next longest (or shortest) and continue in this fashion until the task is complete.

Knowledge of the principle of transitivity allows concrete-operational children to go about their task unerringly. They realize that if stick A is longer than stick B, and stick B is longer than stick C, then stick A is also longer than stick C. After putting stick C in place, they need not double-check in hope that it will be shorter than stick A; they *know* that it will be.

Concrete-operational children also have the decentration capacity to allow them to seriate in two dimensions at once. Consider a seriation task used by Piaget and his longtime colleague Bärbel Inhelder (see Figure 12.2). In this test, children are given 49 leaves and asked to classify them according to size and

FIGURE 12.2

**A GRID FOR DEMONSTRATING THE DEVELOPMENT OF SERIATION.** *To classify these 49 leaves, children must be able to focus on two dimensions at once: size and brightness. They must also recognize that if quantity A exceeds quantity B, and quantity B exceeds quantity C, then quantity A must also exceed quantity C. This relationship is called the* principle of transitivity.

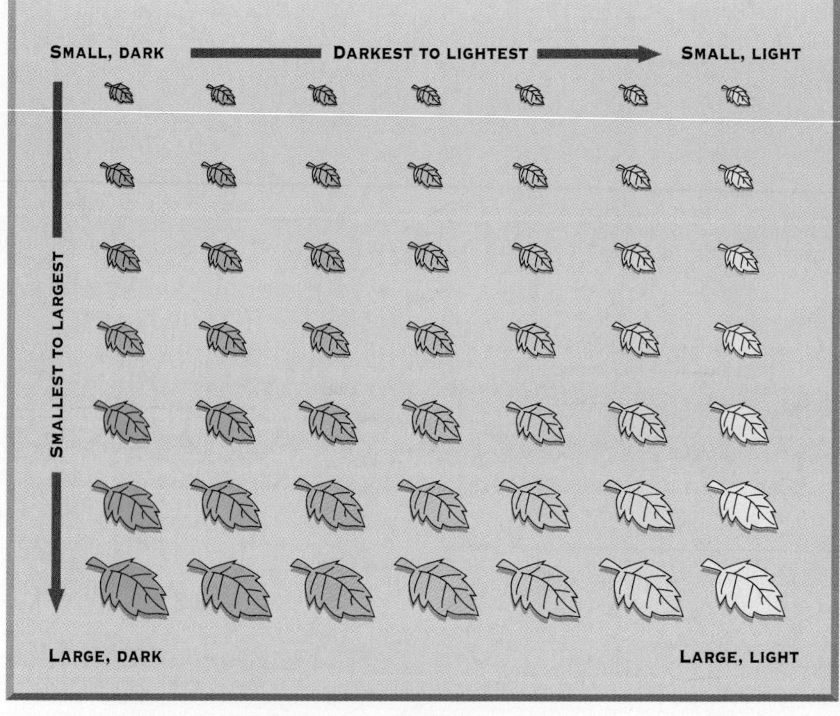

brightness (from small to large and from dark to light). As the grid is completed from left to right, the leaves become lighter. As it is filled in from top to bottom, the leaves become larger. Preoperational 6-year-olds can usually order the leaves according to size or brightness, but not both simultaneously. But concrete-operational children of age 7 or 8 can work with both dimensions at once and fill in the grid properly.

As with other dimensions of cognitive development, a number of researchers have argued that children develop seriation ability earlier than Piaget believed and that Piaget's results reflected the demand characteristics of his experiments (Blevins-Knabe, 1987; Small, 1990). This may be so, but the *sequence* of developments in seriation and transitivity seems to have been captured fairly well by Piaget.

***Class inclusion*** The principle that one category or class of things includes several subclasses.

## *Class Inclusion*

Another example of an operation is ***class inclusion.*** Remember from Chapter 9 that class inclusion involves the ability to recognize that one class of things (A) includes several other subclasses (B1 and B2). In the example in Chapter 9, a 4-year-old was shown pictures of four cats and six dogs. When asked whether there were more dogs or more animals, she said more dogs. This preoperational child could not focus on the two subclasses (dogs, cats) and the larger subclass (animals) at the same time.

Concrete-operational children, however, can focus on two dimensions (in this case, classes and subclasses) at the same time. Therefore, they are more likely to answer the question about the dogs and the animals correctly (Chapman & McBride, 1992). But their thought remains concrete in that they will give you the correct answer if you ask them about dogs and animals (or daffodils and flowers), but not if you attempt to phrase the question in terms of abstract symbols, such as *A, B1,* and *B2.*

As with other areas of cognitive development, researchers have taken issue with Piaget's views of the ages at which class-inclusion skills develop, and they have argued that language continues to pose hazards for the children being tested. One review of the literature on class inclusion suggests that many children cannot answer standard class-inclusion questions correctly until they are 10 years old, or even older (Winer, 1980).

## *Culture and Development: Concrete Operations*

As we saw in Chapter 2, Piaget's theory stresses the prominence of maturation in cognitive development. In support of Piaget's view, studies have found that children in many different cultures proceed through the stages of cognitive development in the order he predicted (Dasen, 1977; Mwamwenda, 1992). But the rate at which children move through stages, and the level of performance that they ultimately attain, appears to depend on children's experiences within a particular culture. For example, one study gave conservation tasks to rural Mexican children. Half of the children came from families that made pottery for a living, and half came from families that did not (Price-Williams et al., 1969). The pottery-makers' children, who had extensive experience working with clay, displayed knowledge of conservation earlier than children from families that did not make pottery.

Formal schooling is another experience that shapes performance on cognitive tasks (Cole, 1992; Rogoff, 1990). For example, school experiences give children practice in categorizing objects, memorizing lists of unrelated items, and engaging in logical problem solving (Rogoff, 1990). An extensive review of studies of cognitive development in African children highlights the important role of environmental factors such as formal education and urbanization (Mwamwenda, 1992). The performance of educated children on concrete-operations tasks was found to be superior to that of uneducated children. Educated African children acquired Piagetian concepts at roughly the same chronological age as Western children. Children without formal schooling typically acquired the concepts about 2 years later than educated children. The performance of urban African children was superior to that of rural children. Mwamwenda (1992) suggests that urban areas, with their blend of different cultures, languages, and life-styles, create an enriched environment that enhances children's cognitive development.

## *APPLICATIONS OF PIAGET'S THEORY TO EDUCATION*

Piaget's theory has several applications to the educational process (Crain, 1992; Davis, 1991). He pointed out some of these himself. First, Piaget felt that learning is a process of active discovery. Therefore, teachers should not simply try to impose knowledge on the child but should find materials to interest and stimulate the child. Second, instruction should be geared to the child's level of development. When teaching a concrete-operational child about fractions, for example, the teacher should not simply lecture but should allow the child to divide concrete objects into parts. Third, Piaget believed that learning to take into account the perspectives of others was a key ingredient in the development of both cognition and morality. Accordingly, he felt that teachers should promote group discussions and interactions among their students.

## *EVALUATION OF PIAGET'S THEORY*

Although Piaget's theory has led many psychologists to recast their concepts of children, it has also met with criticism on several grounds. Some of these criticisms were pointed out in Chapters 6 and 9, but let us review them again here.

**WAS PIAGET'S TIMING ACCURATE?** Some researchers have shown that Piaget underestimated children's abilities. In regard to egocentricity, as we saw in Chapter 9, researchers who present preschool children with different task demands arrive at different impressions of how egocentric they are. We have also seen how modified task demands suggest that children are capable of conservation and other concrete-operational tasks earlier than Piaget believed.

**IS COGNITIVE DEVELOPMENT REALLY DISCONTINUOUS?** Perhaps the most potentially damaging of the criticisms leveled at Piaget is that cognitive skills appear to develop more independently and continuously than Piaget thought—not in general stages.

For example, children's cognitive skills at a given age show *horizontal* inconsistencies. As noted in the discussion of horizontal décalage, conservation does not arrive all at once. Instead, children develop conservation for mass, weight, and volume at different ages. The onset of conservation may be more *continuous* than cognitive-development theory suggests. If this is so, the onset of conservation could be viewed in terms of the gradual accumulation of problem-solving abilities, instead of in terms of changing cognitive structures (Flavell et al., 1993b).

**Are the Sequences of Development Invariant?** Here we can probably offer a reasonably assured "yes." While the notion of horizontal décalage is inconsistent with some of Piaget's ideas, it may not refute the heart of Piaget's concepts. The sequence of cognitive change—even within horizontal décalage—appears to remain invariant. We think it is fair to say that the sequences of development are more essential to Piaget's theory than their timing.

*It is not true that the sequences of cognitive development vary from child to child. The sequences appear to be invariant.*

**What About the Effects of Training?** Another criticism of Piaget is the extent to which education can accelerate children's cognitive development. As noted, Piaget's stages are not completely age bound. He allowed that some children develop different capacities earlier than others. Piaget also acknowledged that training could foster cognitive advances—although in minor and meaningless increments. This is why Piaget paid little attention to what he called the "American question," that is, how education could be tailored to accelerate cognitive development. But several studies have found that children as young as 4 and 5 years of age can develop conservation as a result of demonstrations, instruction, and practice (Gelman & Baillargeon, 1983). The achieving of a stage several years prior to Piaget's expectations is not a minor or meaningless discrepancy. Such a difference creates problems for Piaget's concept of the timing of cognitive development.

In sum, Piaget's theoretical edifice has been rocked, but it has not been dashed to rubble. Although research continues to wear away at his timing and at his views on the futility of attempting to speed up cognitive development, his observations on the sequences of development appear to remain relatively inviolate.

## Information-Processing Approaches to Cognitive Development

Whereas Piaget looked upon children as budding scientists, psychologists who favor the ***information-processing*** approach view children (and adults) as akin to computer systems. Children, like computers, attain information (input) from the environment, store it, retrieve, and manipulate it, then respond to it overtly (output). One goal of the information-processing approach is to learn how children store, retrieve, and manipulate information—how their "mental programs" develop. Information-processing theorists also study the development of children's strategies for processing information (Harnishfeger & Bjorklund, 1990; Klahr, 1992).

Although there may be something to be gained from thinking of children in terms of computers, children, of course, are not computers. Children are self-aware and capable of creativity and intuition.

***Information processing*** The view in which cognitive processes are compared to the functions of computers. The theory deals with the input, storage, retrieval, manipulation, and output of information. The focus is on the development of children's strategies for solving problems—their "mental programs."

## DEVELOPMENT OF SELECTIVE ATTENTION

***Memory*** The processes by which we store and retrieve information.

One important cognitive process is the ability to pay attention to relevant features of a task. The ability to focus one's attention and screen out distractions advances steadily through middle childhood (Miller et al., 1990a). Preoperational children engaged in problem solving tend to focus (or center) their attention on one element of the problem at a time—a major reason that they lack conservation. Concrete-operational children, by contrast, can attend to multiple aspects of the problem at once, permitting them to conserve number, volume, and so on.

An experiment by Strutt and colleagues (1975) illustrates how selective attention and the ability to ignore distraction develop during middle childhood. The researchers asked children between 6 and 12 years of age to sort a deck of cards as quickly as possible on the basis of the figures depicted on each card (for example, circle versus square). In one condition, only the relevant dimension (that is, form) was shown on each card. In another condition, a dimension not relevant to the sorting also was present (for example, the presence of a horizontal or vertical line in the figure). In a third condition, *two* irrelevant dimensions were present (for example, the presence of a star above or below the figure, in addition to a horizontal or vertical line in the figure). As seen in Figure 12.3, the irrelevant information interfered with sorting ability for all age groups, but older children were much less affected than younger children.

## DEVELOPMENTS IN THE STORAGE AND RETRIEVAL OF INFORMATION

Psychologists use the familiar term ***memory*** to refer to the processes of storing and retrieving information. Psychologists divide memory functioning into three major processes or structures: *sensory memory, short-term memory,* and *long-term memory.*

**SENSORY MEMORY** When we look at an object and then blink our eyes, the visual impression of the object lasts for a fraction of a second in what is

FIGURE 12.3

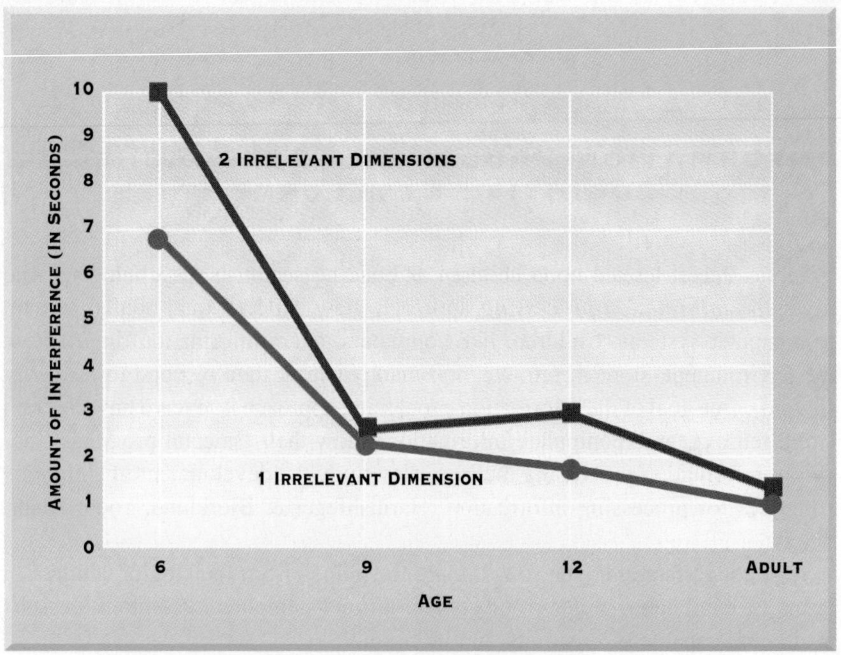


**DEVELOPMENT OF THE ABILITY TO IGNORE DISTRACTION.** *Strutt and his colleagues (1975) demonstrated how the ability to ignore distraction develops during middle childhood. They asked children to sort a deck of cards as quickly as possible on the basis of figures shown on each card. In one condition, no irrelevent dimension was present. In a second condition, one irrelevant dimension was present, and in a third condition, two irrelevant dimensions were present. The effect of irrelevant dimensions on sorting speed was determined by subtracting the speed of the sort in the no-irrelevant-dimension condition from the speed of the other two conditions. As shown here, irrelevant information interfered with sorting ability for all age groups, but older children were less affected than younger ones. (Source: Strutt et al., 1975).*

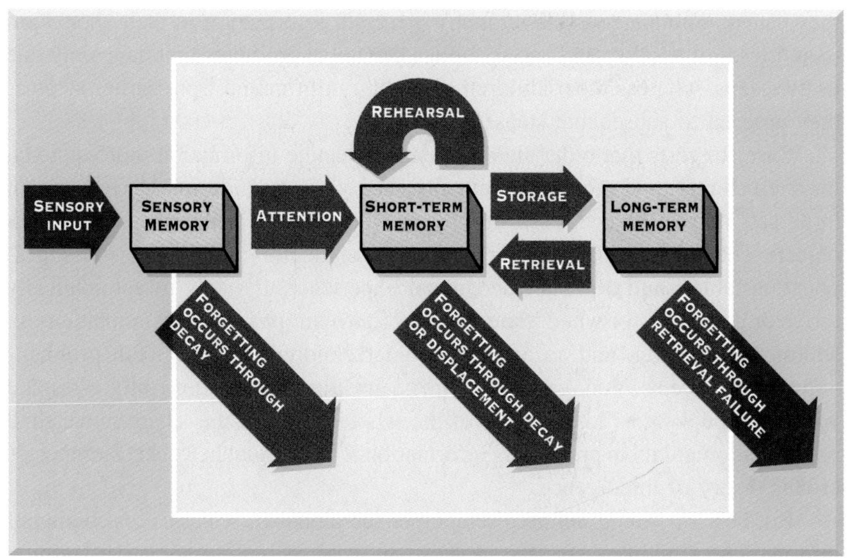


FIGURE 12.4

***The Structure of Memory.*** *Psychologists divide memory into three processes or structures. Sensory information enters the registers of sensory memory, where memory traces are held briefly before decaying. If we attend to the information, much of it is transferred to short-term memory, where it may decay or be displaced if it is not transferred to long-term memory. We usually use rehearsal to transfer memories to long-term memory. Once in long-term memory, memories may be retrieved through appropriate search strategies. But if information is organized poorly or we cannot find cues to retrieve it, it may be lost.*

called ***sensory memory,*** or the ***sensory register.*** Then the "trace" of the stimulus decays (Figure 12.4).

**Short-Term Memory** When children focus their attention on a stimulus in the sensory register, it will tend to be retained in ***short-term memory*** for up to 30 seconds or so after the trace of the stimulus decays. Ability to maintain information in short-term memory depends on cognitive strategies as well as basic capacity to continue to perceive a vanished stimulus.

Auditory stimuli can be maintained longer in short-term memory than can visual stimuli (Keele, 1973). For this reason, one strategy for promoting memory is to ***encode*** visual stimuli as sounds, or auditory stimulation. Then the sounds can be repeated out loud or mentally. That is, the sounds can be ***rehearsed.***

Encoding visual material is an example of a cognitive *strategy* that enhances the ability to recall that material. Older children are more successful than younger children at recalling information, both because of improvements in the basic capacities of their short-term memories and because of their sophistication in employing strategies for enhancing memory.

***Capacity of Short-Term Memory*** The basic capacity of the short-term memory may be described in terms of the number of "bits" or chunks of information that may be kept in memory at once. To remember a new phone number, for example, one must keep seven chunks of information in short-term memory simultaneously—that is, one must rehearse them consecutively.

The average adult can keep about seven chunks of information—plus or minus two—in short-term memory at a time (Miller, 1956). As measured by the ability to recall digits, the typical 5- to 6-year-old can work on two chunks of information at a time. The ability to recall series of digits improves throughout middle childhood, and 15-year-olds, like adults, can keep about seven chunks of information in short-term memory at the same time (Pascual–Leone, 1970).

***Case's View*** Robbie Case has advanced an information-processing view that focuses on children's capacity for memory and their use of cognitive strategies, such as the way in which they focus their attention (Case, 1985, 1992). He notes, for example, that certain Piagetian tasks require several cognitive strategies instead of one and that young children frequently fail at such tasks because

***Sensory memory*** The structure of memory first encountered by sensory input. Information is maintained in sensory memory only for a fraction of a second.

***Sensory register*** Another term for sensory memory.

***Short-term memory*** The structure of memory that can hold a sensory stimulus for up to 30 seconds after the trace decays.

***Encode*** To transform sensory input into a form that is more readily processed.

***Rehearsed*** Repeated.

***Rote learning*** Learning by repetition.

***Long-term memory*** The memory structure capable of relatively permanent storage of information.

they cannot simultaneously hold many pieces of information in their short-term memories. Put another way, preschoolers can solve problems that have only one or two steps, whereas older children can retain information from earlier steps as they proceed to subsequent steps.

Case suggests that older children learn to handle information more quickly, more efficiently, and more automatically. The younger child may have to count three sets of two objects each one by one in order to arrive at a total of six objects. The older child, with a larger short-term memory, familiarity with multiplication tables, and a greater perceptual experience, is likely to automatically arrive at a total of six when three groups of two are perceived. Automaticity in adding, multiplying, and so on allows older children to solve math problems with several steps. Younger children, meanwhile, become lengthily occupied with individual steps, losing sight of the whole. Later in this chapter, we shall see that automaticity in processing information is an element in Robert Sternberg's (1988) theory of intelligence.

But how do young children remember the alphabet, which is 26 chunks of information? Children learn the alphabet by ***rote***—simple associative learning based on repetition. After the alphabet is repeated many, many times, *M* triggers the letter *N*, *N* triggers *O*, and so on. The typical 3-year-old who has learned the alphabet by rote will not be able to answer the question "What letter comes after *N*?" However, if you recite "*H, I, J, K, L, M, N*" with the child and then pause, the child is likely to say, "*O, P*." The 3-year-old probably will not realize that he or she can find the answer by using the cognitive strategy of reciting the alphabet, but many 5- or 6-year-olds will.

**TRUTH OR FICTION REVISITED**

*Children (and adults) can memorize alphabets without keeping 26 pieces of information in mind at once. They manage the task by means of rote repetition.*

**LONG-TERM MEMORY** Think of ***long-term memory*** as a vast storehouse of information containing names, dates, places, what Johnny did to you in second grade, what Susan said about you when you were 12. Long-term memories may last days, years, or, for practical purposes, a lifetime.

There is no known limit to the amount of information that can be stored in long-term memory. From time to time it may seem that we have forgotten, or lost, a long-term memory, such as the names of elementary or high school classmates. But it is more likely that we simply cannot find the proper cues to help us retrieve the information. It is "lost" in the same way as when we misplace an object but know that it is still in the house. It remains there somewhere for the finding.

How is information transferred from short-term to long-term memory? Rehearsal is one method. Older children are more likely to rehearse than are younger children (Small, 1990). But pure rehearsal, with no attempt to make information meaningful by linking it to past learning, is no guarantee the information will be stored permanently.

A more effective method than simple rehearsal is to purposefully relate new material to well-known information. Relating new material to well-known

**THINKING ABOUT DEVELOPMENT**

Agree or disagree with the following statement and support your answer: "You never forget how to ride a bicycle."

material is known as an ***elaborative strategy*** (Small, 1990). English teachers encourage children to use new vocabulary words in sentences to help them remember them. This is an example of an elaborative strategy. In this way, children are building extended ***semantic codes*** that will help them retrieve their meanings in the future.

***Elaborative strategy*** A method for increasing retention of new information by relating it to well-known information.

***Semantic code*** A code based on the meaning of information.

Before proceeding to the next section, here's a question for you. Which of the following words is spelled correctly: *retreival* or *retrieval?* The spellings sound alike, so an acoustic code for reconstructing the correct spelling would not be of help. But a semantic code, such as the spelling rule ''*i* before *e* except after *c*,'' would allow you to reconstruct the correct spelling: retr*ie*val. This is why children are taught rules and principles. Of course,whether these rules are retrieved in the appropriate situation is another issue.

**Organization in Long-Term Memory** As children's knowledge of concepts advances, the storehouse of their long-term memory becomes gradually organized according to categories. Preschoolers tend to organize their memories by grouping objects that share the same function (Lucariello & Nelson, 1985). ''Toast'' may be grouped with ''peanut butter sandwich,'' because they are both edible. Only during the early elementary school years are toast and peanut butter likely to be joined into a single category with the term *food* applied to both.

David Bjorklund and Melanie de Marchena (1984) found that as children advanced from the first grade to the seventh grade, they became as likely to remember the names of animals that are linked categorically (for example, dog and rabbit) as associatively (for example, dog and cat). This finding suggests that the seventh-grade children were more likely to include dogs and rabbits (and cats) in the same category (''animals''), whereas the first graders were more likely to link dogs and cats just on the basis of their usually going together around the house.

When items are correctly categorized in long-term memory, children and adults are also more likely to recall accurate information about them (Schneider & Bjorklund, 1992). For instance, do you ''remember'' whether whales breathe underwater? If you did not know that whales are mammals, or knew nothing about mammals, a correct answer might depend on some remote instance of rote learning. You might recall some details from a documentary on whales, for example. But if you did know that whales are mammals, you would be able to ''remember'' (or reconstruct the fact) that whales do not breathe underwater because mammals breathe air.

If children have incorrectly classified whales as fish, they might search their ''memories'' and construct the incorrect answer that whales do breathe underwater. Correct categorization, in sum, expands children's knowledge and allows them to retrieve information more readily. As they develop, children's knowledge becomes increasingly organized to form complex hierarchies of concepts.

But it has also been shown that when the knowledge of children in a particular area surpasses that of adults, the children show superior capacity to store and retrieve related information. For example, studies have found that chess experts were superior to novice chess players at remembering where chess pieces had been placed on the board (Chi, 1978; Opwis et al., 1990). This may not surprise you, until you learn that in these studies, the experts were 8-to-12-year-old children, while the novices were adults. The point is that enhanced knowledge of relationships between concepts improves memory functioning, so that children can outperform adults in those areas in which they have received special training.

## DEVELOPMENT OF RECALL MEMORY

***Metacognition*** Awareness of and control of one's cognitive abilities, as shown by the intentional use of cognitive strategies in solving problems.

***Metamemory*** Knowledge of the functions and processes involved in one's storage and retrieval of information (memory), as shown by use of cognitive strategies to retain information.

Recall memory involves retrieval of information from memory, as you may recall from Chapter 9 (pardon the pun!). As children develop, their capacity for recalling information increases (Henry & Millar, 1991). Their memory improvement appears to be linked to their ability to quickly process (that is, scan and categorize) the stimulus cues (Case, 1985).

In one experiment on how categorizing information helps children remember, pictures of typical objects that fell into four categories (furniture, clothing, tools, fruit) were placed on a table before second- and fourth-graders (Hasselhorn, 1992). The children were allowed 3 minutes to arrange the pictures as they wished and to remember as many of them as they could. Fourth-graders were more likely to categorize the pictures than second-graders. The tendency to categorize the pictures was directly related to the capacity to recall them.

When the materials to be remembered fall easily into categories, children are more likely to develop effective memory strategies, which they then transfer to other memory tasks that are less well-organized (Best, 1993). These findings suggest that highly structured school settings may induce children to develop task strategies on their own that they can then apply to other less structured materials or settings.

## DEVELOPMENT OF METACOGNITION AND METAMEMORY

***Metacognition*** refers to children's awareness and purposeful control of their cognitive abilities. The ability to formulate problems, awareness of the cognitive processes required to solve a problem, the activation of cognitive rules and strategies, keeping one's attention focused on the problem, and checking one's answers—all these are evidence of the emergence of metacognition.

When a sixth-grader decides which homework assignments to do first, memorizes the state capitals for tomorrow's test, and then tests herself to see which ones she needs to study some more, she is engaging in metacognition. Clearly, metacognition has important applications in the field of education. Research suggests that teaching students metacognitive skills improves their performance in reading and other areas (Flavell et al., 1993b).

***Metamemory*** is one type of metacognition. It more specifically refers to children's awareness of the functioning of their memory processes. Older children show greater insight into how their memories work (Hashimoto, 1991; Kail, 1990). One important reason that older children store and retrieve information more effectively than younger children is the greater sophistication of their metamemory (Kail, 1990; Small, 1990).

For example, young elementary school students frequently announce that they have memorized educational materials before they have actually done so. Older elementary school students are more likely to assess accurately the extent of their knowledge (Paris & Winograd, 1990).

Older children also show more knowledge of strategies that can be used to facilitate memory. For example, as we saw in Chapter 9, preschoolers will usually use rehearsal if someone else suggests that they do, but not until about the ages of 6 or 7 do children use rehearsal without being instructed to do so (Flavell et al., 1993b). As elementary school children become older, they also become better at adapting their rehearsal strategies to fit the characteristics of the task at hand (McGilly & Siegler, 1990).

### THINKING ABOUT DEVELOPMENT

Agree or disagree with the following statement and support your answer: "The memory is like a muscle. The more we practice using it, the better it becomes."

As children develop, they also are more likely to use selective rehearsal to remember important information. That is, they more efficiently exclude the meaningless mass of perceptions milling about them by confining rehearsal to that which they are attempting to remember. This selectivity in rehearsal is found significantly more often among 15- and 18-year-olds than among 11-year-olds (Bray et al., 1985).

If you are trying to remember a new phone number, you would know to rehearse it several times or to write it down before setting out to do a series of math problems. However, 5-year-olds, asked whether it would make a difference if they jotted the number down before or after doing the math problems, do not reliably report that doing the problems first would matter. Ten-year-olds, however, are aware that new mental activities (the math problems) can interfere with old ones (trying to remember the telephone number) and usually suggest jotting the number down before attempting the math problems.

Your metamemory is advanced to the point, of course, where you recognize that it would be poor judgment to read this book while watching *Wheel of Fortune* or fantasizing about your next vacation, isn't it?

We have seen that children's memory improves throughout middle childhood. But how good is the memory of children for eyewitnessed or experienced events? For a discussion of this controversial issue, turn to Focus on Research.

## INTELLIGENCE

At an early age, we gain impressions of how intelligent we are as compared with other family members and schoolmates. We think of some people as having more ***intelligence*** than others. We associate intelligence with academic success, advancement on the job, and appropriate social behavior.

Despite our sense of familiarity with the concept of intelligence, intelligence cannot be seen, touched, or measured physically. For this reason, intelligence is subject to various interpretations. Theories about intelligence are some of the most controversial issues in psychology today.

### *THEORIES OF INTELLIGENCE*

Psychologists generally distinguish between ***achievement*** and intelligence. Achievement is what a child has learned, the knowledge and skills that have been gained by experience. Achievement involves specific content areas such as English, history, and math. Educators and psychologists use achievement tests to measure what children have learned in academic areas. The strong relationship between achievement and experience seems obvious. We are not surprised to find that a student who has taken Spanish, but not French, does better on a Spanish achievement test than on a French achievement test.

The meaning of *intelligence* is more difficult to pin down (Weinberg, 1989). Most psychologists would agree that intelligence somehow provides the cognitive basis for academic achievement. Intelligence is usually perceived as a measure of a child's underlying *competence* or *learning ability,* whereas achievement involves a child's acquired competencies or *performance*. Most psychologists also would agree that many of the competencies underlying intelligence manifest themselves during middle childhood, when the child is first exposed to the rigors of formal schooling. Psychologists disagree, however, about the nature and origins

***Intelligence*** A complex and controversial concept, defined by David Wechsler as the "capacity . . . to understand the world [and the] resourcefulness to cope with its challenges" (from the Latin *inter,* meaning "among," and *legere,* meaning "to choose." Intelligence implies the capacity to make adaptive choices).

***Achievement*** That which is attained by one's efforts and presumed to be made possible by one's abilities.

FOCUS ON RESEARCH

## CHILDREN'S EYEWITNESS TESTIMONY

Nowadays, more children than ever before are called upon to provide legal testimony about events they have seen or experienced. These events often involve instances of alleged child abuse (Goodman et al., 1992; Penrod, 1993; Yuille & Wells, 1991). But just how reliable is the eyewitness testimony of children?

As we saw in Chapter 9, even preschoolers are able to recall and describe personally experienced events, even though the account may be somewhat sketchy and lacking in detail (Ceci & Bruck, 1993; McCarthy, 1993). Consequently, the child witness typically is asked questions to provide additional information. Such questions are often leading questions, which suggest an answer to the witness. For example, the question "What happened at school?" is not a leading question, but the question "Did your teacher touch you?" is (Kail, 1990).

Are children's recollections susceptible to being distorted by such leading questions? By the age of 10 or 11, children are no more suggestible than adults. The results for children below that age are inconsistent, however (Saywitz, 1990). Several studies find that the recall of these younger children is more likely to be influenced by misleading information, but some have found that younger children are no more susceptible than older children (Ceci & Bruck, 1993; Loftus, 1992; Loftus et al., 1992). Most of this research has studied children's memory for routine or nonstressful stimuli (such as words or pictures). But children in court typically are testifying about stressful and traumatic events, such as molestation. Is a child's memory for such events better or worse than memory for routine occurrences? It is difficult to study this question since it is unethical to deliberately expose children to stressful conditions in experiments. Instead, we have to study children's memory of naturally occurring stressful situations, such as receiving an inoculation or having blood drawn. Again, the results are somewhat mixed. Some research finds that the memory of preschool and school-age children is impaired when they are anxious or frightened (Peters, 1991). But other studies indicate that stress does not affect children's memories (Goodman & Clarke-Stewart, 1991). In fact, very high levels of stress may actually improve children's memory (Goodman et al., 1991).

One hotly debated question is the following: Can children be led into making false reports of abuse? There is no simple answer to this question, as illustrated by a study carried out by Gail Goodman and her colleagues (Goodman & Clarke-Stewart, 1991). They interviewed 5- and 7-year-old girls following a routine medical checkup that included genital and anal exams for half of the girls. Most of the children who experienced genital and anal touching failed to mention it when simply asked what happened during the exam. But when asked specific leading questions ("Did the doctor touch you there?"), 31 of 36 girls mentioned the experience. Of the 36 girls who did not have genital and anal exams, none reported any such experience when asked what happened during the exam. When asked the leading questions, 3 falsely reported being touched in these areas. Goodman and Clarke-Stewart (1991) point out that these results illustrate the dilemma faced by sexual abuse investigators. Their study indicates that children may not reveal genital contact until specifically asked, but that asking may influence some children to give a false report.

Furthermore, recent research by Stephen Ceci (1993) indicates that repeated questioning over periods of several weeks may lead young children to make up events that never happened to them. In one study, preschoolers were questioned each week for 11 weeks about events that either had or had not happened to them. By the 11th week, 58 percent of the children reported at least one false event as true.

What, then, are investigators of alleged child abuse to do? Ceci (1993) recommends that interviewers avoid repeated leading or suggestive questions to minimize influencing the child's response.

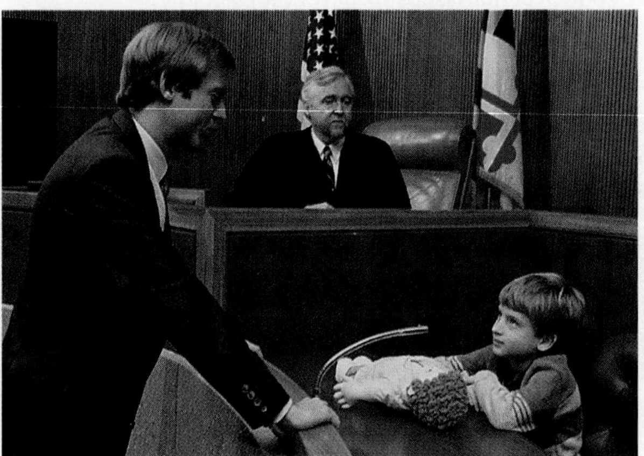

**FIGURE 12.5 HOW RELIABLE IS CHILDREN'S EYEWITNESS TESTIMONY?** *This question remains hotly debated. By age 10 or 11, children are no more suggestible than adults. The findings for younger children are inconsistent, however. Repeated questioning of young children may influence them to give false reports.*

of a child's underlying competence or learning ability. Let us look at three approaches to understanding intelligence.

**Factor** A condition or quality that brings about a result—in this case, "intelligent" behavior. A cluster of related items, such as those found on an intelligence or personality test.

**FACTOR THEORIES** Many investigators have viewed intelligence as consisting of one or more major mental abilities, or ***factors.*** Alfred Binet, for example, the Frenchman who developed intelligence testing methods at the turn of the century, believed that intelligence consists of several related factors. Other investigators have argued that intelligence consists of one, two, or hundreds of factors.

In 1904, British psychologist Charles Spearman suggested that the various behaviors we consider intelligent have a common, underlying factor. He labeled this factor *g,* for "general intelligence." He felt that *g* represented broad reasoning and problem-solving abilities. He supported this view by noting that people who excel in one area generally show the capacity to excel in others. But he also noted that even the most capable people seem more capable in some areas—perhaps in music or business or poetry—than in others. For this reason, he also suggested that *s,* or specific capacities, account for a number of individual abilities.

This view seems to make sense. Most of us know children who are good at math but poor in English and vice versa. Nonetheless, some link seems to connect different mental abilities, even if it is not so strong as the links among the items that define specific factors. The data still show that the person with excellent reasoning ability is likely to have a larger than average vocabulary and better than average numerical ability. There are few, if any, people who surpass 99 percent of the population in one mental ability, yet are surpassed by 80 or 90 percent of the population in others.

**MULTIPLE INTELLIGENCES** To psychologist Howard Gardner (1983, 1993), intelligence—or intelligences—reflect much more than logical and problem-solving abilities. Gardner labels several different kinds of intelligence (see Figure 12.6). Two are familiar: verbal ability and logical–mathematical reasoning. The others are spatial intelligence, bodily–kinesthetic intelligence (as shown by dancers and gymnasts), musical intelligence, interpersonal intelligence (as shown

**FIGURE 12.6**

***MULTIPLE INTELLIGENCES.*** *Psychologist Howard Gardner argues that there are many intelligences, not just one, including bodily talents as expressed through dancing or gymnastics. Each "intelligence" is an inborn talent that must be developed through educational experiences, if it is to be expressed.*

***Triarchic*** Governed by three. Descriptive of Sternberg's view that intellectual functioning occurs on three levels: contextual, experiential, and componential.

***Contextual level*** Those aspects of intelligent behavior that permit people to adapt to their environment.

by empathy and ability to relate to others), and personal knowledge (self-insight). Occasionally, individuals show great "intelligence" in one area—as the young Mozart with the piano, or the island girl who can navigate her small boat to hundreds of islands by observing the changing patterns of the stars—without notable abilities in others.

## TRUTH OR FICTION REVISITED

*We must hedge on whether musical ability is a kind of intelligence. Gardner considers it to be, but many psychologists consider musical ability to be a special talent rather than an "intelligence."*

**A TRIARCHIC MODEL OF INTELLIGENCE** Robert Sternberg (1988) has constructed a ***triarchic,*** or three-level, model of intelligence (See Figure 12.7). The three levels are *contextual, experiential,* and *componential*. Individual differences are found at each level.

The ***contextual level*** concerns the environmental setting. It is assumed that intelligent behavior permits people to adapt to the demands of their environments. For example, keeping a job by changing one's behavior to meet the requirements of one's employer is adaptive. But if the employer is making unreasonable demands, reshaping the environment (by changing the employer's attitudes) or selecting an alternate environment (finding a more suitable job) is also adaptive. Rochelle, a child who is street smart and knows how to manipulate the environment, is displaying contextual intelligence.

FIGURE 12.7

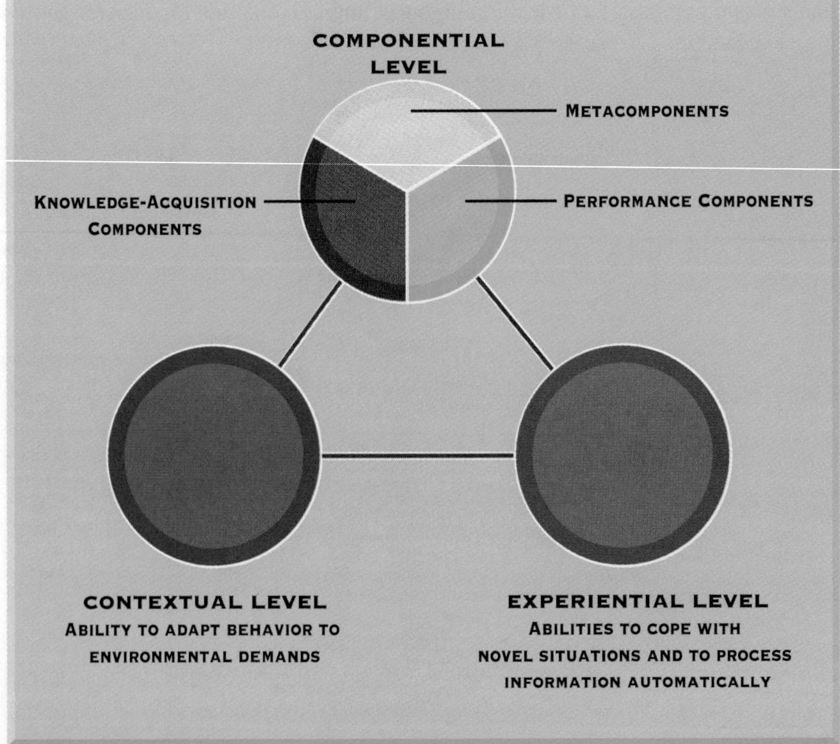


***STERNBERG'S TRIARCHIC MODEL OF INTELLIGENCE.*** *Robert Sternberg views intelligence as consisting of contextual, experiential, and componential levels. The componential level consists of metacomponents, performance components, and knowledge-acquisition components.*

On the ***experiential level,*** intelligent behavior is defined by the abilities to cope with novel situations and to process information automatically. The ability to relate novel situations to familiar situations quickly (that is, to perceive their similarities and differences) fosters adaptation. Nora doesn't have the best IQ test scores, but she is a creative thinker who has a knack for looking at problems in new ways. She is an example of a child with a great deal of experiential intelligence.

The ***componential level*** of intelligence consists of three internal processes: *knowledge-acquisition components* (that is, acquiring new information); *performance components* (comparing pieces of information and generating a solution); and *metacomponents* (being aware of and monitoring one's own intellectual processes). Metacomponents are involved in deciding what problem to solve, selecting appropriate strategies and formulas, and changing performance in the light of knowledge of results. Jeff, who has high IQ test scores and is a strong analytical thinker, is showing componential intelligence.

Sternberg's model is quite complex, but it does a promising job of capturing what most investigators mean by intellectual functioning.

*According to Sternberg, knowing what problem to tackle is an aspect of intelligence. Sternberg refers to this aspect of intelligence as a metacomponent of intelligence.*

## MEASUREMENT OF INTELLIGENCE

There may be disagreements about the nature of intelligence, but thousands of intelligence tests are administered by psychologists and educators every day.

The Stanford–Binet Intelligence Scale (SBIS) and the Wechsler scales for preschool children, school-age children, and adults are the most widely used and well-respected intelligence tests. The SBIS and Wechsler scales yield scores called ***intelligence quotients,*** or IQs. Each of them has been carefully developed and revised over the years. Each of them has been used to make vital decisions about the academic careers of children. In many cases, children whose test scores fall below or above certain scores are placed in special classes for the retarded or the gifted.

*"IQ" is not an abbreviation for intelligence. It stands for intelligence* quotient *and refers to a score on an intelligence test.* Intelligence, *by contrast, is a hypothetical concept.*

It must be noted just as emphatically that each test has been accused of discriminating against racial minorities such as African-American and Hispanic children, the foreign-born, and the children of the socially and economically disadvantaged. Because of the controversy surrounding IQ tests, probably no

***Experiential level*** Those aspects of intelligence that permit people to cope with novel situations and process information automatically.

***Componential level*** The level of intelligence that consists of metacomponents, performance components, and knowledge-acquisition components.

***Intelligence quotient*** (1) Originally, a ratio obtained by dividing a child's score (or "mental age") on an intelligence test by his or her chronological age. (2) Generally, a score on an intelligence test.

single test should be used to make important decisions about a child. Decisions about children should be made only after a battery of tests is given by a qualified psychologist, in consultation with parents and teachers.

**THE STANFORD–BINET INTELLIGENCE SCALE** The SBIS originated through the work of Frenchmen Alfred Binet and Theodore Simon early in this century. The French public school system sought an instrument that could identify children who were unlikely to profit from the regular classroom setting, so that they could receive special attention. The Binet–Simon scale came into use in 1905. Since that time, it has undergone revision and refinement.

As noted earlier, Binet believed that intelligence involves a number of factors, including reasoning, comprehension, and judgment. Despite his view that many factors are involved in intellectual functioning, Binet constructed his test to yield a single overall score so that it could be more easily used by the school system.

Binet also assumed that intelligence increased with age. Therefore, older children should get more items right than younger children. Thus, Binet included a series of age-graded questions and he arranged them in order of difficulty, from easier to harder. Items were ordered so that they were answered correctly by about 60 percent of the children at a given age level. It was also required that they be answered correctly by significantly fewer children who were one year younger and by a significantly greater number of children who were one year older.

The Binet–Simon scale yielded a score called a ***mental age,*** or **MA.** The MA shows the intellectual level at which a child is functioning. A child with an MA of 6 is functioning, intellectually, like the average child aged 6. In taking the test, children earned months of credit for each correct answer. Their MA was determined by adding the years and months of credit they attained.

Louis Terman adapted the Binet–Simon scale for use with American children. Because Terman carried out his work at Stanford University, he renamed the test the Stanford–Binet Intelligence Scale (SBIS). The first version of the SBIS was published in 1916. The SBIS yielded an intelligence quotient, or IQ, rather than an MA. American educators soon developed interest in learning the IQs of their pupils. The SBIS today may be used with children from the age of 2 onward up to adults. Items at the youngest age levels include placing blocks correctly in a three-holed form board, stating what we do with common objects, naming parts of the body, and repeating a series of two numbers. At older age levels, children are asked to define advanced vocabulary words and are asked questions that require more complex verbal reasoning, as in explaining how objects are alike or different. The current edition of the Stanford–Binet (Thorndike et al., 1985) assesses performance in four distinct areas: verbal reasoning, quantitative reasoning, abstract/visual reasoning, and short-term memory.

The ***IQ*** states the relationship between a child's mental age and actual or ***chronological age,*** or **CA.** Use of this ratio reflects the fact that the same MA score has different implications for children of different ages. That is, an MA of 8 is an above-average score for a 6-year-old, but an MA of 8 is below average for a 10-year-old.

The IQ is computed by the formula IQ = (Mental Age/Chronological Age) × 100, or

$$IQ = \frac{MA}{CA} \times 100$$

According to this formula, you can readily see that a child with an MA of 6 and a CA of 6 would have an IQ of 100. Children who can handle intellectual problems as well as older children will have IQs above 100. For instance, an

***Mental age (MA)*** The accumulated months of credit that a person earns on the Stanford–Binet Intelligence Scale.

***IQ*** Intelligence quotient.

***Chronological age (CA)*** A person's age.

8-year-old who does as well on the SBIS as the average 10-year-old will attain an IQ of 125. Children who do not answer as many items correctly as other children of their age will attain MAs that are lower than their CAs. Consequently, their IQ scores will be below 100.

Today, IQ scores on the SBIS are derived by seeing how children's and adults' performances deviate from those of other people of the same age. People who get more items correct than average attain IQ scores above 100, and people who answer fewer items correctly attain scores below 100.

**TRUTH OR FICTION REVISITED**

*It is true that two children can answer exactly the same items on an intelligence test correctly, yet one can be above average in intelligence and the other below average. The younger of the two children would be the more intelligent.*

**THE WECHSLER SCALES** David Wechsler (1975) developed a series of scales for use with school-age children (Wechsler Intelligence Scale for Children), younger children (Wechsler Preschool and Primary Scale of Intelligence), and adults (Wechsler Adult Intelligence Scale). These tests, abbreviated WISC, WPPSI, and WAIS, respectively, have been revised in recent years. The current version of the WISC is referred to as the WISC-III, for example.

The Wechsler scales group test questions into a number of separate subtests (such as those shown in Table 12.1). Each subtest measures a different type of intellectual task. For this reason, the test shows how well a person does on one

**TABLE 12.1**

***SUBTESTS FROM THE WECHSLER INTELLIGENCE SCALE FOR CHILDREN***

| VERBAL SUBTESTS | PERFORMANCE SUBTESTS |
|---|---|
| 1. INFORMATION: "WHAT IS THE CAPITAL OF THE U.S.?" "WHO WAS SHAKESPEARE?" | 1. PICTURE COMPLETION: POINTING TO THE MISSING PART OF A PICTURE. |
| 2. COMPREHENSION: "WHY DO WE HAVE ZIP CODES?" "WHAT DOES 'A STITCH IN TIME SAVES NINE' MEAN?" | 2. PICTURE ARRANGEMENT: ARRANGING CARTOON PICTURES SO THAT THEY TELL A MEANINGFUL STORY. |
| 3. ARITHMETIC: "IF 3 CANDY BARS COST 25 CENTS, HOW MUCH WILL 18 CANDY BARS COST?" | 3. BLOCK DESIGN: USING MULTICOLORED BLOCKS TO COPY PICTURES OF GEOMETRIC DESIGNS. |
| 4. SIMILARITIES: "HOW ARE PEANUT BUTTER AND JELLY ALIKE?" "HOW ARE GOOD AND BAD ALIKE?" | 4. OBJECT ASSEMBLY: PUTTING PIECES OF A PUZZLE TOGETHER SO THAT THEY FORM A MEANINGFUL OBJECT. |
| 5. VOCABULARY: "WHAT DOES 'CANAL' MEAN?" | 5. CODING: RAPID SCANNING FOR AND DRAWING OF SYMBOLS THAT ARE ASSOCIATED WITH NUMBERS. |
| 6. DIGIT SPAN: REPEATING SERIES OF NUMBERS, PRESENTED ORALLY BY THE EXAMINER, FORWARD AND BACKWARD. | 6. MAZES: USING A PENCIL TO TRACE THE CORRECT ROUTE FROM A STARTING POINT TO HOME. |

ITEMS FOR VERBAL SUBTESTS 1-5 ARE SIMILAR BUT NOT IDENTICAL TO ITEMS ON THE WISC-III.

type of task (such as defining words) as compared with another (such as using blocks to construct geometric designs). In this way, the Wechsler scales help reveal children's relative strengths and weaknesses, as well as provide measures of overall intellectual functioning.

As you can see in Table 12.1, Wechsler described some of his scales as measuring verbal tasks, and others as assessing performance tasks. In general, verbal subtests require knowledge of verbal concepts, whereas performance subtests (see Figures 12.8 and 12.9) require familiarity with spatial-relations concepts. Wechsler's scales permit the computation of verbal and performance IQs. It is not unusual for nontechnically oriented college students to attain higher verbal than performance IQs.

Table 12.2 indicates the labels that Wechsler assigned to various IQ scores and the approximate percentages of the population who attain IQ scores at those levels. As you can see, most children's IQ scores cluster around the average. Only about 5 percent of the population have IQ scores of above 130 or below 70.

## *INTELLECTUAL DEVELOPMENT IN CHILDHOOD*

Rapid advances in intellectual functioning occur during childhood. Within a few years, children gain the abilities to symbolize experiences and manipulate symbols to solve increasingly complex problems. Their vocabularies leap, and their senten-

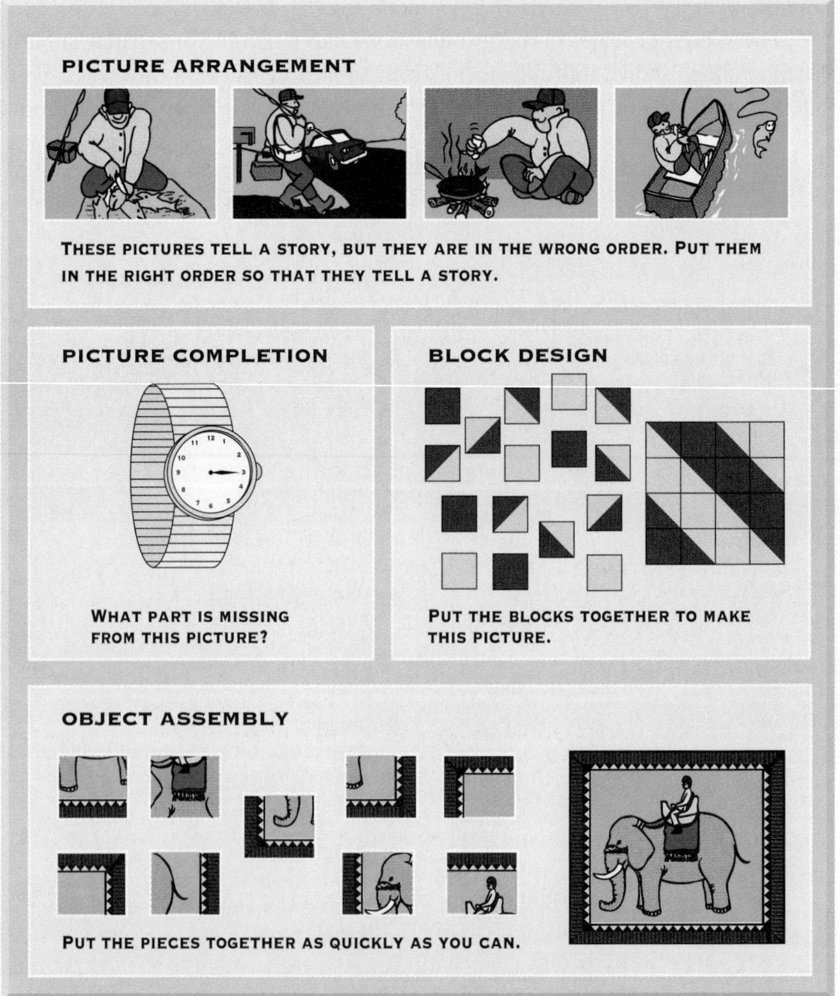


FIGURE 12.8

**PERFORMANCE ITEMS OF AN INTELLIGENCE TEST.** *This figure shows a number of items that resemble those found in the Wechsler Intelligence Scale for Children. (Source: The Psychological Corporation).*

**TABLE 12.2**

***VARIATIONS IN IQ SCORES***

| RANGE OF SCORES | PERCENTAGE OF POPULATION | BRIEF DESCRIPTION OF INTELLECTUAL FUNCTIONING* |
|---|---|---|
| 130 AND ABOVE | 2 | VERY SUPERIOR |
| 120-129 | 7 | SUPERIOR |
| 110-119 | 16 | BRIGHT NORMAL |
| 100-109 | 25 | HIGH AVERAGE |
| 90-99 | 25 | LOW AVERAGE |
| 80-89 | 16 | DULL NORMAL |
| 70-79 | 7 | BORDERLINE DEFICIENT |
| BELOW 70 | 2 | INTELLECTUALLY DEFICIENT |

*ACCORDING TO DAVID WECHSLER.

ces become more complex. Their thought processes become increasingly logical and abstract, and they gain the capacity to focus on two or more aspects of a problem at once.

There seem to be at least two major spurts in intellectual growth. The first occurs at about the age of 6. As noted by Rebok (1987), this spurt coincides with entry into a school system and also with the shift from preoperational to concrete-operational thought. The school experience may begin to help crystallize intellectual functioning at this time. The second spurt occurs at about age 10 or 11, and possible influences are harder to pin down. Rebok suggests that this spurt may reflect general physical and psychological changes linked to approaching puberty or, perhaps, the shift from concrete-operational thought to the formal operational thought of adolescence (discussed in Chapter 15).

Although there are spurts, once they reach middle childhood, children appear to undergo relatively more stable patterns of gains in intellectual functioning (Schuerger & Witt, 1989; Turkheimer & Gottesman, 1991). As a result, intelligence tests gain greater predictive power at about this time. In a classic study by Marjorie Honzik and associates (1948), intelligence test scores taken at the age of 9 correlated +.90 with scores at the age of 10 and +.76 with scores at the age of 18. More recent studies confirm these general findings.

Despite the increased predictive power of intelligence tests during middle childhood, individual differences exist. In the Fels Longitudinal Study (see Figure 12.10), two groups of children (1 and 3) made reasonably consistent gains in intelligence-test scores between the ages of 10 and 17, whereas three groups showed declines. Group 4, who had shown the most intellectual promise at age 10, went on to show the most precipitous decline, although they still wound up in the highest 2–3 percent of the population (McCall et al., 1973). Many factors can influence changes in intelligence test scores, including changes in the child's home environment, social and economic circumstances, and educational experiences (Storfer, 1990).

Although intelligence-test scores change throughout childhood, some children show reasonably consistent patterns of below- or above-average performance. In the following section, we discuss children who show consistent patterns of extreme scores—low and high.

**FIGURE 12.9**

***TAKING THE WECHSLER.*** *A number of Wechsler performance subtests, such as the block design subtest shown in this photo, tap spatial relations abilities.*

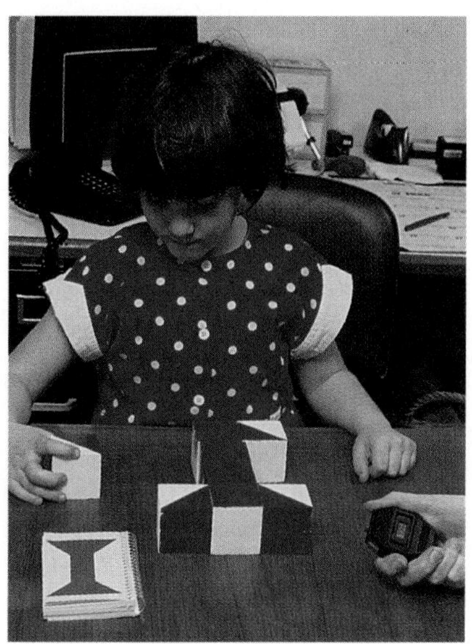

FIGURE 12.10

***FIVE PATTERNS OF CHANGE IN IQ SCORES FOR CHILDREN IN THE FELS LONGITUDINAL STUDY.*** *In the Fels Longitudinal Study, IQ scores remained stable between the ages of 2½ and 17 for only one of five groups—group number 1. (Source: McCall et al., 1973).*

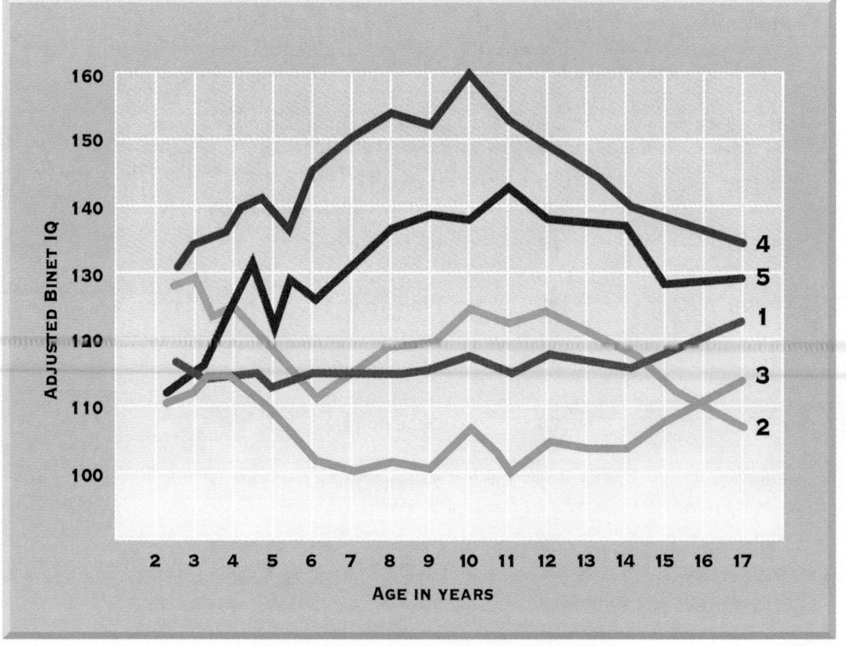


## *DIFFERENCES IN INTELLIGENCE*

The average IQ score in the United States is very close to 100, and about 50 percent of U.S. children attain IQ scores in the broad average range from 90 to 110. Nearly 95 percent attain scores between 70 and 130. But what of the other 5 percent? Children who attain IQ scores below 70 are generally labeled "mentally retarded." Children who attain scores of 130 or above are usually labeled "gifted." Both of these labels—these extreme individual differences—lead to certain expectations of children. Both can place heavy burdens on children and their parents.

There are also social-class, racial, and ethnic differences in IQ. Individual differences may tax our school systems and create the need for educational innovation, but racial and cultural differences have stimulated social and political strife. In this section, we consider mental retardation, gifted and creative children, and social-class, racial, and ethnic differences in IQ.

**MENTAL RETARDATION** Mental retardation is typically assessed through a combination of children's IQ scores and observations of the adaptiveness of their behavior (Michaelson, 1993b; Tanguay & Russell, 1991). IQ scores, when used alone, are not highly predictive of how well the child can function.

Most of the children (more than 80 percent) who are retarded are mildly retarded. Mildly retarded children, as the term implies, are the most capable of adjusting to the demands of educational institutions and, eventually, to society at large. Many mildly retarded children are ***mainstreamed*** in regular classrooms, as opposed to being placed in special-needs classes, as we saw in Chapter 11.

Children with Down syndrome are most likely to fall within the moderately retarded range. Moderately retarded children can learn to speak, dress, feed, and clean themselves, and, eventually, to engage in useful work under supportive conditions, as in the sheltered workshop. However, they usually do not acquire skills in reading and arithmetic. Severely and profoundly retarded children may not acquire speech and self-help skills and remain highly dependent on others for survival throughout their lives.

***Mainstreamed*** Placed in educational settings (for example, schools and classrooms) with normal children.

What causes retardation? As noted in earlier chapters, some of the causes of retardation are biological. Retardation, for example, can stem from chromosomal abnormalities, such as Down syndrome; genetic disorders, such as phenylketonuria (PKU); and brain damage (Tanguay & Russell, 1991). Brain damage may have many origins, including accidents during childhood and problems during pregnancy. For example, maternal alcohol abuse, malnutrition, or diseases during pregnancy can lead to retardation in the unborn child.

There is also ***cultural–familial retardation,*** in which the child is biologically normal but does not develop age-appropriate behaviors at the normal pace because of social isolation of one kind or another. For example, the later-born children of impoverished families may have little opportunity to interact with adults or play with stimulating toys. As a result, they may not develop sophisticated language skills or the motivation to acquire the kinds of knowledge that are valued in a technologically oriented society.

***Cultural–familial retardation*** Substandard intellectual performance that is presumed to stem from lack of opportunity to acquire the knowledge and skills considered important within a cultural setting.

Naturally, we wish to encourage all children to develop to the maximum of their capacities—including retarded children. As a rule of thumb, we should keep in mind that IQs are nothing but scores on tests. They are not perfectly reliable, meaning that they can and do change somewhat from testing to testing. Thus, it is more important to focus on children's current levels of achievement in the academic and self-help skills that we wish to impart so that we can try to build these skills gradually and coherently, step by step.

In the case of children with cultural–familial retardation, there is every reason to believe that they can change dramatically when we intervene by providing enriched learning experiences, especially at early ages. In Chapter 9, we saw how Head Start programs, for example, have enabled children at cultural–familial risk to function at above-average levels.

**Gifted Children** Giftedness involves more than excellence on the tasks provided by standard intelligence tests. In determining who is gifted, most educators include children who have outstanding abilities, are capable of high performance in a specific academic area, such as language or mathematics, or who show creativity, leadership, distinction in the visual or performing arts, or bodily talents, as in gymnastics and dancing (DeAngelis, 1992; Heller et al., 1993).

**Figure 12.11**

***A Musical Prodigy.*** *A gifted child may have outstanding abilities, be capable of high performance in a specific academic area, such as language or mathematics, or show creativity, leadership, distinction in the visual or performing arts, or bodily talents, as in gymnastics and dancing.*

This view of giftedness exceeds the realm of intellectual ability alone and is consistent with Gardner's (1983, 1993) view, mentioned earlier, that there are multiple intelligences, not one. According to this view, one could compose magnificent symphonies or make advances in mathematical theory while remaining average in, say, language skills.

Much of our knowledge of the progress of children who are gifted in overall intellectual functioning stems from Terman's classic longitudinal studies of genius (Oden, 1968; Janos, 1987). In 1921, Terman began to track the progress of some 1,500 California schoolchildren who had attained IQ scores of 135 or above. The average score was 150, which places these children in a very superior group. As adults, the group was extremely successful, compared with the general population, in terms of level of education (nearly 10 percent had earned doctoral degrees), socioeconomic status, and creativity (the group had published more than 90 books and many more shorter pieces). Boys were much more likely than girls to climb the corporate ladder or distinguish themselves in science, literature, or the arts. But we must keep in mind that the Terman study began in the 1920s, when it was generally agreed that the woman's place was in the home. As a result, more than two-thirds of the girls became full-time homemakers or office workers (Lips, 1993). Some of the women later expressed regret that they had not fulfilled their potential. But both the women and men in the study were well-adjusted, with mental illness and suicide rates below the national average. Other, more recent studies are also positive, showing that gifted children tend to be well-adjusted socially and emotionally (Feldhusen, 1989).

**FACILITATING DEVELOPMENT OF THE GIFTED CHILD** Gifted children have more books in their homes and an expanded number of learning opportunities compared with other children. Parents of young gifted children spend more time in reading, play, and stimulating outings with them than do other parents (Fowler et al., 1993; Robinson, 1992). Gifted adults who excel in science, sports, or the arts recall that their parents provided a home environment that was both challenging and nurturing (Tannenbaum, 1992). Responsive, sensitive parenting, but not pushing, appears to facilitate development of the gifted child (Robinson, 1992).

And what of the role of the schools? Educational programs for gifted students typically involve either providing an enriched curriculum or accelerating the student. Acceleration may involve covering all of the normal curriculum but in a shorter period of time (Mills, 1992). The most frequent form of acceleration, however, is skipping a grade.

Some educators are concerned that skipping may cause social and emotional problems (Southern & Jones, 1991). But reviews of the research conclude that skipping and other forms of acceleration are not harmful. In fact, many studies find that acceleration is beneficial to the social and emotional development of gifted children, as well as to their academic progress (Benbow, 1991; Noble et al., 1992).

**CREATIVITY** ***Creativity*** can be one aspect of giftedness, as we mentioned above. Many psychologists view creativity as the ability to make unusual, original associations to the elements of problems, so that new solutions may be generated (Perkins, 1990). According to Amabile (1989), an essential aspect of a creative response is the apparent leap from the elements of the problem to the novel solution. Table 12.3 presents some items from a test of creativity.

***Creativity*** The ability to generate novel solutions to problems. A trait characterized by flexibility, ingenuity, and originality.

***Convergent thinking*** A thought process that attempts to narrow in on the single best solution to a problem.

Creativity demands divergent thinking rather than convergent thinking (Guilford & Hoepfner, 1971). In ***convergent thinking,*** thought is limited to present facts as the problem-solver tries to narrow thinking to find the best solution. In

**TABLE 12.3**

***THE REMOTE ASSOCIATES TEST***

ONE ASPECT OF CREATIVITY IS THE ABILITY TO ASSOCIATE FREELY TO ALL ASPECTS OF A PROBLEM. CREATIVE PEOPLE TAKE FAR-FLUNG IDEAS AND PIECE THEM TOGETHER IN NOVEL COMBINATIONS. FOLLOWING ARE ITEMS FROM THE REMOTE ASSOCIATES TEST, WHICH MEASURES ABILITY TO FIND WORDS THAT ARE DISTINCTLY RELATED TO STIMULUS WORDS. FOR EACH SET OF THREE WORDS, TRY TO THINK OF A FOURTH WORD THAT IS RELATED TO ALL THREE WORDS. FOR EXAMPLE, THE WORDS *rough, resistance,* AND *beer* SUGGEST THE WORD *draft* BECAUSE OF THE PHRASES *rough draft, draft resistance,* AND *draft beer*. THE ANSWERS ARE GIVEN BELOW.

| | | | |
|---|---|---|---|
| 1. | CHARMING | STUDENT | VALIANT |
| 2. | FOOD | CATCHER | HOT |
| 3. | HEARTED | FEET | BITTER |
| 4. | DARK | SHOT | SUN |
| 5. | CANADIAN | GOLF | SANDWICH |
| 6. | TUG | GRAVY | SHOW |
| 7. | ATTORNEY | SELF | SPENDING |
| 8. | ARM | COAL | PEACH |
| 9. | TYPE | GHOST | STORY |

ANSWERS: PRINCE, DOG, COLD, GLASSES, CLUB, BOAT, DEFENSE, PIT, WRITER.

***divergent thinking,*** one associates more freely and fluently to the various elements of a problem.

Tests that measure intelligence—as defined traditionally—are not useful in measuring creativity. Intelligence-test questions require convergent thinking, not creative thinking, to focus in on the single right answer. On intelligence tests, ingenious responses that differ from the designated answers are marked wrong. Tests of creativity, by contrast, are oriented toward determining how flexible and fluent one's thinking can be. Such tests include items such as suggesting improvements or unusual uses for a familiar toy or object, naming things that belong in the same class, producing words similar in meaning, and writing different endings for a story (Meador, 1992; Perkins, 1990).

What factors contribute to creativity? For one thing, intelligence and creativity sometimes, but not always, go hand in hand (Runco, 1992; Sawyers & Mehrotra, 1989). For example, a Canadian study found that highly intelligent boys and girls aged 9 to 11 were, as a group, more creative than less intelligent children (Kershner & Ledger, 1985). Still, not all of the gifted children were more creative than their less intelligent peers. It also sometimes happens that people of only moderate intelligence excel in some aspects of creativity, especially in fields like music and art (Gardner, 1993).

***TRUTH OR FICTION REVISITED***

*It is not necessarily true that highly intelligent children are creative. Creativity correlates only moderately with intelligence.*

Guilford (1959) reported that creative people show the cognitive characteristics of flexibility, fluency in generating words and ideas, and originality. Creative people tend to be independent and nonconformist (Runco, 1992). But independence and nonconformity do not necessarily make a person creative. Unfortunately, creative children are often at odds with their teachers because of their

***Divergent thinking*** A thought process that attempts to generate multiple solutions to problems. Free and fluent association to the elements of a problem.

independence. Faced with the task of managing large classes, teachers often prefer quiet, submissive, "good" children.

**GENDER AND CREATIVITY** Throughout history, most of the well-known artists, musicians, and scientists have been men. Does this mean that women are less creative than men? Maccoby and Jacklin's (1974) review of studies on this topic found that females showed more creativity than males on tests requiring verbal fluency. Gender differences generally did not appear on nonverbal tests of creativity, however. Since then, cross-cultural research has continued to confirm Maccoby and Jacklin's findings. For example, the Canadian study discussed earlier (Kershner & Ledger, 1985) reported higher verbal creativity scores for girls. Other studies in India (Kelgeri et al., 1989) and the United States (Chusmir & Koberg, 1986) have not found gender differences in creativity. Hillary Lips (1993) concludes, therefore, that the relative shortage of eminent women cannot be explained by gender differences in creative ability.

What, then, is the explanation? Many factors appear to be involved. For one thing, the fulfillment of creative potential depends on appropriate experience. Women historically have been denied preparation and opportunities in most fields (Abra & Valentine-French, 1991). Also, traits like independence and nonconformity, which are often associated with creativity, have been discouraged more frequently in girls than boys (Lips, 1993). These traits are inconsistent with the passive and compliant social roles traditionally ascribed to females. Because of changing societal attitudes towards women, the number of women in the creative arts and sciences is growing rapidly today. In the past, the creativity of many girls may have been nipped in the bud.

**CULTURE AND DEVELOPMENT: IQ SCORES AND ACHIEVEMENT** Retardation and giftedness are examples of the differences found *within* every racial and cultural group. However, there is also a body of research suggestive of differences *between* social, racial, and ethnic groups (Taylor & Richards, 1991).

For example, lower-class U.S. children attain IQ scores some 10–15 points lower than those of middle- and upper-class children. African-American children tend to attain IQ scores some 15–20 points lower than their white age-mates (Storfer, 1990). As groups, Hispanic and Native-American children also score significantly below norms of whites. For the first 18 months, white and African-American infants tend to score about the same on infant scales of intelligence. Differences in IQ appear when children enter school, and they appear to increase throughout childhood. Several studies of IQ and academic achievement have confounded the factors of social class and race because disproportionate numbers of African Americans, Hispanics, and Native Americans are found among the lower socioeconomic classes (Patterson et al., 1990).

**THINKING ABOUT DEVELOPMENT**

Are there *real* social-class, racial, and ethnic differences in intelligence?

Research has also discovered differences between Asian and white children. Asian Americans, for example, frequently outscore white Americans on the math test of the Scholastic Aptitude Test. Students in China (Taiwan) and Japan also outscore Americans on standardized achievement tests in math and science (Chen & Stevenson, 1993; Lapointe et al., 1992; Stevenson et al., 1993). Asian Americans also are more likely to get good grades in school (Farkas et al., 1990), to complete high school, and to graduate from college than are white, Hispanic, and African Americans (Sue & Okazaki, 1990). Asian Americans are vastly overrepresented in competitive colleges and universities. In 1990, they made up only 2.4 percent of the American population but accounted for 17 percent of Harvard University's undergraduates, 18 percent of MIT's, and 27 percent of Berkeley's (Butterfield, 1990). Forty percent of the winners in the 1993 Westing-

FIGURE 12.12

***Who's Smart?*** *Asian children and Asian-American children frequently outscore other American children on intelligence tests. Can we attribute the difference to genetic factors or to Asian parents' emphasis on acquiring the kinds of cognitive skills that enable children to fare well on such tests and in school?*

house Science Talent Search for high school students were Asian Americans ("Chicago Student Wins," 1993).

Lynn (1991) argues that the greater intellectual accomplishments of Asians are at least in part genetically determined. Others argue that it has *not* been shown that Asian Americans possess greater basic competence than other Americans (Sue & Okazaki, 1990; Yatani, 1992). Harold Stevenson and his colleagues (Stevenson et al., 1985; Uttal et al., 1988), for example, gave 10 cognitive tasks along with reading and math achievement tests to first- and fifth-graders from the United States, Taiwan, and Japan. Although the Asian children attained higher achievement scores than the Americans, their performance on the cognitive tasks was comparable.

The superior achievements of Asian children may reflect different values in the home, school, or the culture at large rather than differences in underlying competence. Sue and Okazaki (1990) argue that Asian Americans have been discriminated against in careers that do not require advanced education, so they place relatively greater emphasis on the value of education. Asian and American attitudes about the determinants of achievement also are quite different. Americans believe that academic achievement depends more on a child's innate ability, whereas Asians believe effort and hard work will lead to success (N. Caplan et al., 1992; Okagaki & Sternberg, 1993; Stevenson & Stigler, 1992).

Environmental factors such as intensive educational practices in the school and at home may motivate Asian children to achieve more than their American and European peers (Hess & Azuma, 1991; Sue & Okazaki, 1990). Compared with Chinese or Japanese schools, American schools spend less time on academic activities, give less emphasis to homework, and impart less information (Uttal et al., 1988). Chinese, Japanese, and Asian-American parents also emphasize academic achievement more than white American parents. For example, Chinese, Japanese, and Asian-American parents hold higher standards for their children's achievements and are more likely to stress the importance of hard work (Chen & Stevenson, 1993; Stevenson et al., 1993). The emphasis on succeeding through hard work is illustrated by the increasing popularity of cram schools, or *juku,* which prepare Japanese children for entrance exams to private schools and colleges. More than half of all Japanese school children are enrolled in these schools, which meet after the regular school day is over (Weisman, 1992).

How do Asian and U.S. attitudes toward achievement differ?

| Asian | U.S. |
|---|---|
| Achievement depends more on hard work | Achievement depends more on innate ability |
| Schools spend more time on academics and homework | Schools spend less time on academics and homework |
| Mothers hold higher standards for children's achievements | Mothers hold lower standards for children's achievements |

## THE TESTING CONTROVERSY

***Cultural bias*** A factor hypothesized to be present in intelligence tests that provides an advantage for test-takers from certain cultural or ethnic backgrounds, but that does not reflect true intelligence.

***Culture-free*** Descriptive of a test in which cultural biases have been removed. On such a test, test-takers from different cultural backgrounds would have an equal opportunity to earn scores that reflect their true abilities.

*I was almost one of the testing casualties. At 15 I earned an IQ test score of 82, three points above the track of the special education class. Based on this score, my counselor suggested that I take up bricklaying because I was "good with my hands." My low IQ, however, did not allow me to see that as desirable. (Williams, 1974, p. 32)*

This testimony, offered by African-American psychologist Robert Williams, echoes the sentiments of many psychologists. A survey of psychologists and educational specialists found that most consider intelligence tests somewhat biased against African Americans and members of lower social classes (Snyderman & Rothman, 1990). Some states such as California have outlawed the use of IQ tests as the sole standard for placing children in special education classes (Turkington, 1992).

On the other hand, critics point out that intelligence tests measure traits that are required in modern, high-technology societies (Anastasi, 1988). The vocabulary and arithmetic subtests on the Wechsler scales, for example, clearly reflect achievement in language skills and computational ability. It is generally assumed that the broad types of achievement measured by these tests reflect intelligence, but they might also reflect cultural familiarity with the concepts required to answer test questions correctly. In particular, the tests seem to reflect middle-class white culture in the United States (Allen & Majidi-Ahi, 1991; Miller-Jones, 1989).

If scoring well on intelligence tests requires a certain type of cultural experience, the tests are said to have a ***cultural bias.*** Children reared to speak Black English in African-American neighborhoods could be at a disadvantage, not because of differences in intelligence, but because of cultural differences (Helms, 1992). For this reason, psychologists have tried to construct ***culture-free*** or culture-fair intelligence tests.

Some tests do not rely on expressive language at all. For example, Cattell's Culture-Fair Intelligence Test (1949) evaluates reasoning ability through the child's comprehension of the rules that govern a progression of geometric designs, as shown in Figure 12.14.

FIGURE 12.13

***THE TESTING CONTROVERSY.*** *A number of critics of intelligence tests argue that the tests are geared to middle-class white children who tend to share interests and learning opportunities not available to all children. These critics have further argued that different norms or different tests should be developed for children from different racial and ethnic backgrounds.*

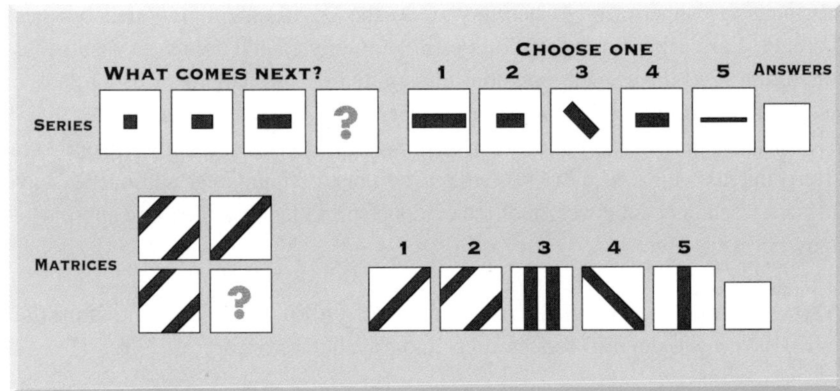


FIGURE 12.14

***SAMPLE ITEMS FROM CATTELL'S CULTURE-FAIR INTELLIGENCE TEST.*** *Culture-fair tests attempt to exclude items that discriminate on the basis of cultural background rather than intelligence.*

Unfortunately, culture-free tests have not lived up to their promise. First, middle-class children still outperform lower-class children on them (Anastasi, 1988). Middle-class children, for example, are more likely to have basic familiarity with materials such as blocks and pencils and paper. They are more likely than disadvantaged children to have arranged blocks into various designs (practice relevant to the Cattell test). Second, culture-free tests do not predict academic success as well as other intellegence tests, and scholastic aptitude remains the central concern of educators.

There may really be no such thing as a culture-fair or culture-free intelligence test (Humphreys, 1992). Motivation to do well, for example, might also be a cultural factor. Because of life-style differences, children from low-income families in the United States sometimes may not have the same motivation as middle-class children to do well on tests (Zigler & Seitz, 1982). And, as noted above, even basic familiarity with test-relevant materials such as pencils and paper is a cultural factor.

Some of the controversy over using intelligence tests in the public schools might be diffused if they were viewed as broad achievement tests—which, of course, they are—rather than direct measures of intelligence (Elliott, 1988). It would be clearly understood that they measure a child's performance in certain areas on a given day. The focus might be on using follow-up techniques, perhaps behavioral observations or interviews, to more fully outline a child's academic strengths and weaknesses, including factors like motivation and adjustment, and to determine the best strategies to help enhance the child's academic performance (Moses, 1991). Then testing would promote equal opportunity instead of excluding some children from privileges. It is irresponsible to make major decisions about children's lives on the basis of an isolated test score attained in an impersonal group-testing situation.

**THINKING ABOUT DEVELOPMENT**

Agree or disagree with the following statement and support your answer: "It is not possible to construct a truly culture-free intelligence test."

## THEORETICAL INTERLUDE: THE DETERMINANTS OF INTELLIGENCE

What do psychologists know about the ***determinants*** of intelligence? What are the roles of heredity and the environment? In our review of the literature, we shall see that there seems to be evidence for both genetic and environmental influences on IQ. Moreover, many of the same studies—in particular, kinship studies and studies of adopted children—appear to provide evidence for both genetic and environmental influences.

Consider the problems in attempting to decide whether a child's performance on an intelligence test is mainly influenced by nature or nurture—that is, by genetic or environmental factors. If a superior child has superior parents, do we

***Determinants*** Factors that define or set limits.

attribute the superiority to heredity or to the environment provided by these parents? Similarly, if a dull child lives in an impoverished home, do we attribute the dullness to the genetic potential transmitted by the parents or to the lack of intellectual stimulation in the environment?

No research strategy for attempting to ferret out genetic and environmental determinants of IQ is flawless. Still, a number of ingenious approaches have been devised. The total weight of the evidence provided through these approaches may be instructive.

**STRATEGIES FOR STUDYING GENETIC INFLUENCES** The following strategies have been devised for research into genetic factors:

- Kinship studies: Correlating the IQ scores of twins, other siblings, and parents and children who have lived together and apart. Strong positive correlations between the IQ scores of closely related children, such as monozygotic (identical) twins, who have been reared apart could be taken as evidence of genetic influences.
- Studies of adopted children: Correlating the IQ scores of adopted children with those of their biological and adoptive parents. If the IQ scores of adopted children correlate more highly with those of their biological than their adoptive parents, we have another argument for genetic influences.

***Intelligence and Family Relationship (Kinship)*** If heredity is involved in human intelligence, closely related people ought to have more similar IQs than distantly related or unrelated people, even when they are reared separately. Figure 12.15 shows the results of 111 studies of IQ and heredity in human beings (Bouchard & McGue, 1981). The IQ scores of identical (MZ) twins are more alike than the scores for any other pairs, even when the twins have been reared apart. The average correlation for MZ twins reared together is .85; for those reared apart, it is .67. Correlations between the IQ scores of fraternal (DZ) twins, siblings, and parents and children are generally comparable, as is their degree of genetic relationship. The correlations tend to vary from the middle +.40s to the upper +.50s. Correlations between the IQ scores of children and their natural parents (.48) are higher than those between children and adoptive parents (.18).

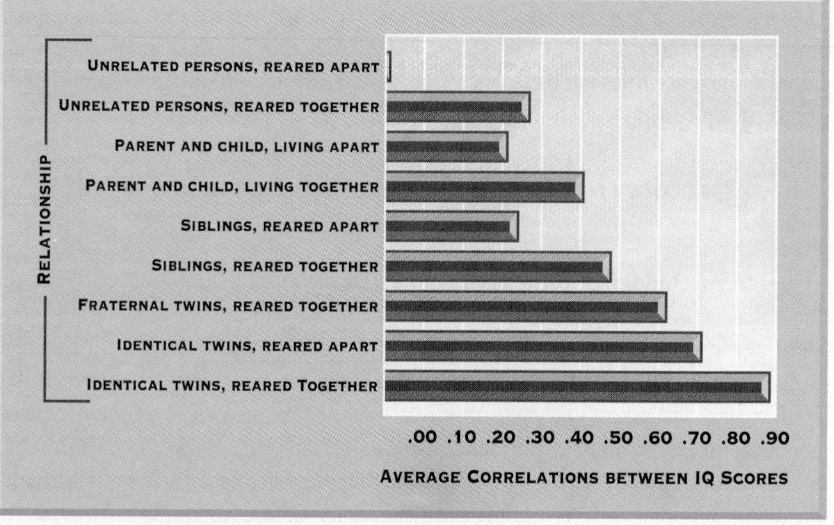


FIGURE 12.15

**FINDINGS OF STUDIES OF THE RELATIONSHIP BETWEEN IQ SCORES AND HEREDITY.** *The data are a composite of 111 studies. By and large, correlations grow stronger for persons who are more closely related. Persons reared together or living together have more similar IQ scores than persons reared or living apart. Such findings support both genetic and environmental hypotheses of the origins of intelligence. (Source: Bouchard & McGue, 1981).*

**TRUTH OR FICTION REVISITED**

*Actually, the IQ scores of adopted children correlate more highly with the IQ scores of their* biological *parents than with the IQ scores of their adoptive parents. This kind of evidence supports the view that heredity plays an important role in the development of intelligence.*

All in all, studies suggest that genes account for about 50 percent of the differences in intelligence in children (Bouchard et al., 1990; Emde et al., 1992). In other words, about half of the variations (the technical term is *variance*) in IQ scores among people can be accounted for by heredity. This is *not* the same as saying that you inherited about half of your intelligence; the implication of such a statement would be that you got the other half of your intelligence somewhere else. It means, rather, that about half of the difference between your IQ score and the IQ scores of other people can be explained in terms of genetic factors. Even this view of the inheritance of intelligence may be too broad to be highly accurate. Research also suggests that the role of heredity is greater for verbal ability than for cognitive skills such as spatial-relations ability and memory (Thompson et al., 1991a).

Let us return to Figure 12.15 for a moment. Note that genetic pairs (like MZ twins) reared together show higher correlations between IQ scores than similar genetic pairs (like other MZ twins) who were reared apart. This finding holds for MZ twins, siblings, parents, children, and unrelated people. *For this reason, the same group of studies that suggests that heredity plays a role in determining IQ scores also suggests that environment plays a role.*

***Studies of the Intelligence of Adopted Children*** When children are separated from their biological parents at early ages, one can argue that strong relationships between their IQ scores and those of their natural parents reflect genetic influences. Strong relationships between their IQs and those of their adoptive parents, on the other hand, might reflect environmental influences. Several projects involving adopted children in Colorado, Texas, and Minnesota (Coon et al., 1990; Scarr, 1993; Turkheimer, 1991) have found a stronger relationship between the IQ scores of adopted children and those of their biological parents than with the IQ scores of their adoptive parents.

These studies thus also point to a genetic influence on intelligence. We shall see in a moment that environment also has an impact, however.

**STRATEGIES FOR STUDYING ENVIRONMENTAL INFLUENCES** Studies of environmental influences on IQ employ several research strategies:

- Discovering situational factors that affect IQ scores. If children's motivation to do well, their familiarity with testing materials, their nourishment, and their comfort in the testing situation can be shown to affect IQ scores, environmental influences play a role.
- Exploring children's abilities to rebound from early deprivation. If children who have spent some of their early lives in impoverished circumstances can make dramatic gains in IQ when stimulated later on, it would appear that IQ is subject to environmental influences.

- Exploring the effects of positive early environments. If good parent–child relations, early language stimulation, and preschool programs are linked to gains in IQ, we have more evidence for the role of environmental influences.

***Situational Influences on Intelligence*** In some cases, we need look no further than the testing situation to explain some of the discrepancy between the IQ scores of middle-class children and those of children from economically disadvantaged backgrounds. In one study (Zigler et al., 1982), the examiner simply made children as comfortable as possible during the test. Rather than being cold and impartial, the examiner was warm and friendly, and care was taken to see that the children understood the directions. As a result, the children's test anxiety was markedly reduced and their IQ scores were six points higher than those for a control group treated in a more indifferent manner. Disadvantaged children made relatively greater gains from the procedure. By doing nothing more than making testing conditions more optimal for all children, we may narrow the IQ gap between low-income and middle-class children.

***Rebounding from Early Deprivation*** In Chapter 7, we discussed a longitudinal study of retarded orphanage children that provided striking evidence children can recover from early deprivation. These 19-month-old children were placed with surrogate mothers in the orphanage who provided a great deal of intellectual and social stimulation. Four years later, the children had made dramatic gains in IQ scores.

***The Effects of Early Home and School Environments*** In Chapter 9, we saw that children whose parents are emotionally and verbally responsive, and who provide appropriate play materials and varied experiences during the early years, attain higher IQ and achievement-test scores. Remember, too, that graduates of Head Start and other preschool programs show significant gains in later educational outcomes.

***Back to the Kinship Studies and Studies of Adopted Children*** As noted earlier, these suggest a genetic influence on intelligence. But the same studies also suggest a role for environmental influences. For example, an analysis of a large number of twin and kinship studies shows that the older twins and other siblings become, the less alike they are on various measures of intelligence and personality (McCartney et al., 1990). This appears to be due to increasing exposure to different environments and experiences outside the family.

Studies of adopted children also indicate the importance of environment. African-American children who were adopted during the first year by white parents who were above average in income and education showed IQ scores some 15 to 25 points higher than those attained by African-American children reared by their natural parents (Scarr & Weinberg, 1976). The adopted children's average IQ scores, about 106, remained somewhat below those of their adoptive parents' natural children—117 (Scarr & Weinberg, 1977). Even so, the adoptive early environment closed a good deal of the IQ gap.

**ON THE DETERMINANTS OF INTELLIGENCE: A CONCLUDING NOTE** Many psychologists believe that heredity and environment interact to influence intelligence (Cardon et al., 1992; Scarr, 1992). Experts usually see genetic influences as providing the reaction range for the complex pattern of verbal and reasoning abilities and problem-solving skills that we interpret to be signs of intelligence. An impoverished environment may prevent some children from living up to their potential. An enriched environment may encourage others to realize their potential, minimizing possible differences in heredity.

Perhaps we need not be concerned with how much of a person's IQ is due to heredity and how much is due to environmental influences. Psychology has traditionally supported the dignity of the individual. It might be more appropriate for us to try to identify children of *all* races whose environments place them at high risk for failure and to do what we can to enrich them.

## LANGUAGE

Children's ability to understand and use language becomes increasingly sophisticated in middle childhood. They learn to read as well. Many children are exposed to varieties of linguistic experience other than standard English, and this experience has important ramifications for language development. In this chapter, we will examine each of these topics.

### *Vocabulary and Grammar*

By the age of 6, the child's vocabulary has expanded to 10,000 words, give or take a few thousand. By 7 to 9, most children realize that words can have different meanings, and they become entertained by riddles and jokes that require semantic sophistication. (Remember the jokes at the beginning of the chapter?) By the age of 8 or 9, children are able to form "tag questions," in which the question is tagged onto the end of a declarative sentence (Dennis et al., 1982). "You want more ice cream, don't you?" and "You're sick, aren't you?" are examples of tag questions.

Children also make subtle advances in articulation and in the capacity to use complex grammar. For example, we saw in Chapter 9 that preschool-age children have difficulty in understanding passive sentences such as "The truck was hit by the car." But children in the middle years have less difficulty interpreting the meanings of passive sentences correctly (Whitehurst, 1982).

During these years, children develop the ability to use connectives, as illustrated by the sentence "I'll eat my spinach but I don't want to." They also learn to form indirect object–direct object constructions (for example, "She showed her sister the toy").

### *Reading Skills*

In many ways, reading is a key to unlocking the benefits our society has to offer. Good readers find endless pleasure in literature, reading and rereading favorite poetic passages countless times. Reading makes textbook learning possible. Reading also permits us to identify subway stops, to consider the contents of food packages, to assemble barbecue grills and children's swing sets, and to learn how to use a microcomputer.

**The Integration of Auditory and Visual Information** Reading is a complex process that depends on perceptual, cognitive, and linguistic processes (Siegel, 1993). It relies on skills in the integration of visual and auditory information. Accurate awareness of the sounds in the child's language is an extremely important factor in subsequent reading achievement (Bruck, 1993; Stanovich, 1993).

***Word-recognition method*** A method for learning to read in which children come to recognize words through repeated exposure to them.

***Phonetic method*** (fo-NET-tick) A method for learning to read in which children decode the sounds of words based on their knowledge of the sounds of letters and letter combinations.

Reading also requires the ability to make basic visual discriminations (Rack et al., 1993). In reading, for example, children must "mind their *p*'s and *q*'s." That is, in order to recognize letters, children must be able to perceive the visual differences between letters such as *b* and *d*, or *p* and *q*.

During the preschool years, neurological maturation and experience combine to allow most children to make visual discriminations between different letters with relative ease. Those children who can recognize and name the letters of the alphabet by kindergarten age are better readers in the early school grades (Siegler, 1986).

How do children acquire familiarity with their own written languages? More and more today, U.S. children are being exposed to TV programs such as "Sesame Street," but these are relatively recent educational innovations. Children are also exposed to books, street signs, names of stores and restaurants, and to writing on packages, especially at the supermarket. Some children, of course, have more books in the home than others do. Children from affluent homes where books and other sources of stimulation are plentiful learn to read more readily than children from impoverished homes. But regardless of income level, reading storybooks with parents in the preschool years helps prepare a child for reading (Crain-Thoreson & Dale, 1992; Scarborough, 1993). And children who read at home during the school years show better reading skills in school and more positive attitudes toward reading (Rowe, 1991).

**METHODS OF TEACHING READING** When they read, children integrate visual and auditory information (associate what they see with sounds), whether they are reading by the *word-recognition method* or by the *phonetic method.* If they are using the ***word-recognition method,*** they must be able to associate visual stimuli such as *cat* and *Robert* with the sound combinations that produce the spoken words "cat" and "Robert." This capacity is usually acquired by *rote learning,* or extensive repetition.

In the ***phonetic method,*** children first learn to associate written letters and letter combinations (such as *ph* or *sh*) with the sounds they are meant to indicate. Then they sound out words from left to right, decoding them. The phonetic method has the obvious advantage of giving children skills that they can use to

FIGURE 12.16

***READING.*** *Children who read at home during the school years, like this boy, show better reading skills in school and more positive attitudes toward reading.*

FIGURE 12.17

***Black English in the Classroom.*** *Black English is spoken by segments of the African-American community. The major differences between Black English and standard English lie in the use of verbs. Many linguists note that the grammatical rules of Black English differ from those of standard English, but Black English has consistent rules, and they allow for the expression of thoughts as complex as those permitted by standard English.*

decode (read) new words. However, some children learn more rapidly at early ages through the word-recognition method. The phonetic method can also slow them down when it comes to familiar words. Most children and adults, in fact, tend to read familiar words by the word-recognition method (regardless of the method of their original training) and to make some effort to sound out new words.

A controversy that we cannot resolve here rages over which method is superior (Rayner, 1993). Some words in English can be read only by the word-recognition method—consider the numbers *one* and *two.* This method is useful when it comes to words such as *danger, stop, poison,* and the child's name, for it helps provide children with a basic ***sight vocabulary.*** But decoding skills must be acquired at some point if children are to be able to read new words on their own.

***Sight vocabulary*** Words that are immediately recognized on the basis of familiarity with their overall shapes, rather than decoded.

### *Culture and Development: Linguistic Experience*

Some U.S. children are exposed to nonstandard English. Others are exposed to English plus a second language. Let us explore their linguistic experiences.

**Black English** Segments of the African-American community speak a form of English called Black English (see Figure 12.17). Black English has taken hold most strongly in working-class African-American neighborhoods. A study in which an audiotape of standard English was played to low-income African-American children who were asked to repeat what they had heard provides an example of Black English. The taped sentence was "I asked him if he did it, and he said he didn't do it." One 5-year-old African-American girl recast the sentence in Black English as follows: "I asks him if he did it, and he says he didn't did it, but I knows he did" (Anastasiow & Hanes, 1976, p. 3).

As the example suggests, the major differences between Black English and standard English lie in the use of verbs. Tenses are formed differently in Black English. Consider the verb *to be.* In Black English, "He be gone" indicates the standard "He has been gone for a long while," and "He gone" signifies what is "He is gone right now" in standard English.

***Dialect*** The variety of a spoken language particular to a region, community, or social group. Dialects of a language tend to be understandable to persons who speak another dialect of the language without special training, whereas other languages are not.

Some observers have felt that standard English verbs are used haphazardly in Black English, as if the bare bones of English are being adapted and downgraded. As a consequence, school systems have, in some instances, reacted to Black English with disfavor. However, many linguists have argued that Black English is just one ***dialect*** of English (Taylor, 1990). The grammatical rules of Black English differ from those of standard English. Yet the rules of Black English are consistent, and they allow for the expression of thoughts that are as complex as those permitted by standard English. In other words, Black English is different, but not inferior.

Let us consider a couple of examples of rules in Black English—rules involving use of the verb *to be*. In standard English, *be* is part of the infinitive form of the verb used in the formation of the future tense, as in "I'll be angry tomorrow." Thus "I be angry" is incorrect. In Black English, *be* is used to denote a continuing state of being. "I am angry" would be perfectly good standard English *and* Black English. But the Black English sentence "I be angry" means in standard English, "I have been angry for a while" and is good Black English.

Black English also *omits* the verb *to be* in some cases (Rebok, 1987), usually when standard English would use a contraction. For example, "She's the one I'm talking about" could be translated as "She the one I talking about." Omitting the verb in Black English is no more careless than contracting it in standard English. Contraction follows a rule of standard English; omission in the example follows a rule of Black English. The Black English sentence is no simpler than the standard one.

Some African-American children can switch readily from standard English to Black English (Brice-Heath, 1988). That is, they tailor their language to their social situations. They use standard English in a conference with their teacher or in a job interview, but they use Black English in the neighborhood. Their facility in doing so is a fine example of their use of the pragmatics of speech.

Other children do not show facility in switching back and forth. For them, the ever-present frowns of standard-English-speaking teachers become an academic burden.

*TRUTH OR FICTION REVISITED*

*Some African-American children can, in fact, switch back and forth between Black English and standard English. This is an example of pragmatism in language usage.*

Standard English is spoken by the majority. For this reason, African-American children who want to succeed usually find it to their advantage to use standard English—at least in college, on the job, and in similar social situations. However, if the educators who instruct African-American children realize that Black English is just as complex and rule-governed as standard English, they will treat Black-English-speaking children with greater respect—even as they help provide African-American children with the mainstream linguistic alternative.

In the next section, we shall learn more about how showing children respect helps them acquire a second language in school.

**Bilingualism** Most people throughout the world speak two or more languages (Paulston, 1988). Most countries have minority populations whose languages differ from the national tongue. Nearly all Europeans are taught English and the languages of neighboring nations. Consider the Netherlands. Dutch is the native tongue, but all elementary school children are also taught French, German, and English and are expected to become fluent in each of them.

For about 32 million Americans, English is a second language (Barringer, 1993). Spanish, Russian, Chinese, or Arabic is spoken in the home and, perhaps, the neighborhood. Some of these children receive no training in English until they enter school. Table 12.4 provides a snapshot of the 25 languages most commonly spoken in the home in the United States in the 1990s. Much of the 38-percent jump in the numbers of speakers of foreign languages is due to waves of immigration from Latin America and Asia.

A few decades ago, it was widely believed that children reared in ***bilingual*** homes were retarded in their cognitive and language development (Hakuta & Garcia, 1989). However, the U.S. Bureau of the Census reports that more than 75 percent of Americans who first spoke another language in the home also speak English "well" or "very well" (Barringer, 1993). Recent analysis of

***Bilingual*** Using or capable of using two languages with nearly equal or equal facility.

**Table 12.4**

***Bilingualism, U.S.A.***

| Language spoken in the home | Total number of speakers, age 5 and above | | Change (percent) |
|---|---|---|---|
| | 1990 | 1980 | |
| Spanish | 17,339,000 | 11,549,000 | 50 |
| French[1] | 1,703,000 | 1,572,000 | 8 |
| German | 1,547,000 | 1,607,000 | -4 |
| Italian | 1,309,000 | 1,633,000 | -20 |
| Chinese | 1,249,000 | 632,000 | 98 |
| Tagalog[2] | 843,000 | 452,000 | 87 |
| Polish | 723,000 | 826,000 | -12 |
| Korean | 626,000 | 276,000 | 127 |
| Vietnamese | 507,000 | 203,000 | 150 |
| Portuguese | 430,000 | 361,000 | 19 |
| Japanese | 428,000 | 342,000 | 25 |
| Greek | 388,000 | 410,000 | -5 |
| Arabic | 355,000 | 227,000 | 57 |
| Hindi, Urdu | 331,000 | 130,000 | 155 |
| Russian | 242,000 | 175,000 | 39 |
| Yiddish | 213,000 | 320,000 | -34 |
| Thai | 206,000 | 89,000 | 132 |
| Persian | 202,000 | 109,000 | 85 |
| French Creole[3] | 188,000 | 25,000 | 654 |
| Armenian | 150,000 | 102,000 | 46 |
| Navajo[4] | 149,000 | 123,000 | 21 |
| Hungarian | 148,000 | 180,000 | -18 |
| Hebrew | 144,000 | 99,000 | 46 |
| Dutch | 143,000 | 146,000 | -3 |
| Mon-Khmer[5] | 127,000 | 16,000 | 676 |
| Total | 31,845,000 | 23,060,000 | 38% |

Source: U.S. Bureau of the Census (1993).
[1]Spoken commonly in the home in New Hampshire, Maine, and Louisiana.
[2]Main language of the Philippines.
[3]Mainly spoken by Haitians.
[4]Native-American language.
[5]Cambodian language.

older studies in bilingualism shows that the families observed were often low in socioeconomic status and level of education. Lack of education, not bilingualism, was the problem. Today, most linguists consider it advantageous for children to be bilingual (Bialystok, 1988; Diaz, 1985). For one thing, knowledge of more than one language expands children's awareness of different cultures and broadens their perspectives. The evidence suggests that bilingual children perform as well as or better than monolingual children on intelligence tests and related tests of cognitive and linguistic functioning (Hakuta & Garcia, 1989; Padilla et al., 1991; Umbel et al., 1992).

## TRUTH OR FICTION REVISITED

*Bilingual children do* not *encounter more academic problems than children who know only one language. Bilingualism can be advantageous for children who know both languages well.*

Despite the positive aspects of bilingualism, many U.S. children who speak a different language in the home have problems learning English in school. Early in the century, the educational approach to teaching English to non-English-speaking children was simple: sink or swim. Children were taught in English from the outset. It was incumbent upon them to catch on as best they could. Most children swam. Some sank.

A more formal term for the sink-or-swim method is ***total immersion.*** Total immersion has a checkered history. There are, of course, many successes with total immersion, but there are also more failures than the U.S. educational system is willing to tolerate. For this reason, bilingual education has been adopted in many school systems (Celis, 1991a).

**BILINGUAL EDUCATION** Bilingual-education legislation requires that non-English-speaking children be given the chance to study in their own language in order to smooth the transition to U.S. life. The purpose of federal bilingual programs is to help foreign-speaking children use their native tongue to learn English rapidly, then switch to a regular school program. Yet, the degree of English differs markedly from program to program.

So-called transitional programs move their students into regular English-speaking classes as soon as possible. Under a second technique, called the maintenance method, rapid mastery of English is still the goal. But students continue to study their own language and culture (Berger, 1993).

Iris Rotberg (1982) suggests that bilingual education has been most successful when four criteria have been met: (1) The child begins with mastery of the language spoken in the home, providing a secure linguistic base. (2) The bilingual program focuses specifically on teaching English and does not just start teaching other subjects in English, even at a low level. (3) The child's parents understand and support the goals and methods of the program. (4) Teachers, parents, and other members of the community have mutual respect for each other and for each others' languages.

When instruction in a second language is carried out carefully, there is little evidence to suggest that it interferes with the first language. In fact, high-quality

***Total immersion*** A method of language instruction in which a person is placed in an environment in which only the language to be learned is used.

**FIGURE 12.18**

***BILINGUALISM.*** *Most people throughout the world speak two or more languages, and most countries have minority populations whose languages differ from the national tongue. It was once thought that children reared in bilingual homes were retarded in their cognitive and language development, but today most linguists consider it advantageous for children to be bilingual. Knowledge of more than one language certainly expands children's awareness of diverse cultures and broadens their perspectives.*

bilingual education programs appear to enhance academic achievement and language proficiency in both languages (Padilla et al., 1991).

All in all, it seems that following Rotberg's principles will accomplish more than just teaching children English. The principles will also help ensure that bilingual children will be proud of the ethnic heritage they bring with them into the mainstream culture. Children may attain the language skills necessary to forge ahead in today's workplace and participate in political and social processes, while they retain a sense of ethnic identity and self-esteem. The development of self-esteem and other aspects of social and personality development is the focus of the next chapter.

## Summary

1. Piaget theorized that children engage in concrete mental operations between the ages of 7 and 12. As a consequence, they are less egocentric and they show conservation, transitivity, and class inclusion.

2. Piaget's views have been criticized on three major grounds: (1) The timing of development may have been inaccurate. (2) Cognitive development may be more continuous than Piaget theorized. (3) Cognitive development may be accelerated by training to a greater extent than Piaget thought possible. However, Piaget's observations of the sequences of development appear correct.

3. Information-processing theorists view cognitive development in terms that are derived from computer technology: for example, storing and retrieving information and using "mental programs" to solve problems. As children develop, their attention becomes selective and they screen out distractions. Their

concepts become structured into complex hierarchies, which facilitates their recall memory. Case theorizes that children become more capable of solving problems because of improvements in short-term memory, in application of cognitive strategies, and in automaticity in solving problems.

4. In middle childhood, children become aware of and learn to control their cognitive performance and their memory processes. The first of these is known as *metacognition* and the second is called *metamemory.*

5. Achievement is what a person has learned. Intelligence is presumed to be the learning ability that underlies achievement.

6. Spearman's factor theory of intelligence proposes that a common factor, *g,* underlies all intelligent behavior, while specific *s* factors account for specific abilities and talents. Gardner's theory of multiple intelligences proposes that such special talents as musical and bodily–kinesthetic abilities are factors of intelligence. Sternberg's triarchic theory of intelligence proposes contextual, experiential, and componential levels of intelligence.

7. Intelligence tests yield scores called *intelligence quotients,* or IQs. The major individual intelligence tests are the Stanford–Binet Intelligence Scale (SBIS) and the Wechsler scales.

8. In middle childhood, IQ scores begin to show moderate-to-high correlations with those attained at the ages of 10 to 18.

9. About 5 percent of children have IQ scores below 70 and above 130. Children with scores below 70 and with various problems in adaptation are usually considered mentally retarded. Retardation can have a number of biological causes, but also often reflects cultural-familial factors.

10. Gifted children are identified not only on the basis of high IQ scores, but also by exceptional talents. The Terman "studies of genius" found that children with IQs of 135 and above went on, as a group, to excel in their careers. Gifted children also tend to be well-adjusted socially and emotionally.

11. Creativity is the ability to generate novel solutions to problems. Creative children show divergent thinking ability by associating freely to the elements of a problem. There is a correlation between intelligence and creativity, but above-average intelligence is not a guarantee of creativity.

12. Social-class, racial, and ethnic differences in performance on intelligence tests have been found. Many critics assert that intelligence tests are culturally biased in favor of middle-class children. As a consequence, efforts have been made to develop culture-fair or culture-free tests. However, these efforts have met with limited success.

13. Evidence concerning genetic influences on intelligence focuses on kinship studies and studies of adopted children. Evidence concerning environmental influences tends to focus on (1) effects of the early environment, including the home environment, parenting styles, and preschool programs; (2) kinship studies, emphasizing the differences in IQ between close relatives when reared together or apart; and (3) studies of adopted children. Many developmentalists believe that genetic and environmental factors interact to determine intelligence.

14. As language development progresses, children's vocabulary grows and they develop the ability to produce tag questions, passive sentences, and connectives.

15. The process of reading requires integrating auditory and visual stimulation and making visual discriminations—for example, perceiving the difference between the written letters *b* and *d*. Reading is taught by the word-recognition and the phonetic methods.

16. Black English is a dialect that follows consistent rules of grammar.

17. Bilingual children do not necessarily suffer language or academic problems when they are adequately educated.

# MIDDLE CHILDHOOD: SOCIAL AND PERSONALITY DEVELOPMENT

## Chapter Outline



## Truth or Fiction?

_____ *During middle childhood, children define themselves only in terms of superficial traits, such as their appearance, activities, and living situations.*

_____ *Children with high self-esteem tend to have strict parents.*

_____ *Aggressive children tend to be looked up to by their peers.*

_____ *In middle childhood, children's friendships are almost exclusively with children of the same gender.*

_____ *About half of divorced fathers do not keep up with their child-support payments.*

_____ *The daughters of employed women are more achievement-oriented and set themselves higher career goals than the daughters of nonemployed women.*

_____ *Class size is not of particular importance in education.*

_____ *Teachers who have high expectations of students frequently elicit greater achievements from them.*

_____ *Teachers are less likely to accept calling out from boys than from girls.*

_____ *There is no connection between conduct disorders in middle childhood and antisocial behavior in adulthood.*

_____ *Misbehavior in middle childhood can reflect feelings of depression.*

_____ *Children with school phobia should not be placed back in school until the origins of the problem are uncovered and resolved.*

*A college student taking a child development course had the following conversation with a 9-year-old girl named Karen:*

STUDENT: *Karen, how was school today?*
KAREN: *Oh, it was all right. I don't like it a lot.*
STUDENT: *How come?*
KAREN: *Sara and Becky won't talk to me. I told Sara I thought her dress was very pretty, and she pushed me out of the way. That made me so mad.*
STUDENT: *That wasn't nice of them.*
KAREN: *No one is nice except for Amy. At least she talks to me.*

*Here is part of a conversation between a different college student and her 9-year-old cousin Sue:*

SUE: *My girl friend Heather in school has the same glasses as you. My girl friend, no, not my girl friend—my friend—my friend picked them up yesterday from the doctor, and she wore them today.*
STUDENT: *What do you mean—not your girl friend, but your friend? Is there a difference?*
SUE: *Yeah, my friend. 'Cause Wendy is my girl friend.*
STUDENT: *But what's the difference between Heather your friend, and Wendy, your girl friend?*
SUE: *Well, Wendy is my best friend, so she's my girl friend. Heather isn't my best friend, so she's just a friend.*
(ADAPTED FROM ROWEN, 1973)

In the years from 6 to 12, the child's social world expands. As illustrated by the remarks of these 9-year-old girls, peers take on a much greater importance than before, and friendships become deeper. Entry into school exposes the child to the influence of teachers, as well as to a new peer group. Relationships with parents change as children develop greater independence. Some children will face adjustments resulting from the divorce and remarriage of parents. During these years, major advances occur in children's ability to understand themselves. Their knowledge of social relationships and their skill in developing such relationships increases as well (Collins, 1984a). Some children, unfortunately, develop problems during these years, although some are better able than others to cope with life's stresses.

In this chapter, we will discuss each of these areas. We first examine some major theories of social and personality development in the middle years. We then examine the development of self-concept and of relationships with peers and parents. We turn next to the influences of the changing family and the school. Finally, we look at some of the social and emotional problems that may arise in the middle years of childhood.

## PERSONALITY

What are some of the important features of personality development during the middle childhood years? The major theories have had less to say about this age group than the other periods of childhood and adolescence (Collins, 1984b). Nevertheless, certain common threads emerge, as we shall see. These include the development of skills, the importance of interpersonal relationships, and the expansion of self-understanding. Let us examine these developments.

## *Theoretical Interlude: Theories of Social and Personality Development in the Middle Years*

**Psychoanalytic Theory** According to Freud, children in the middle years are in the ***latency stage.*** As we saw in Chapter 2, Freud believed that sexual feelings remain repressed and unconscious during this period. Children use this period to focus on developing intellectual, social, and other culturally valued skills.

Erikson, like Freud, sees the major developmental task of middle childhood as the acquisition of cognitive and social skills. Erikson labels this stage ***industry versus inferiority.*** To the extent that children are able to master the various tasks and challenges of the middle years, they develop a sense of industry or competence. But if a child has difficulties in school or with peer relationships, a sense of inferiority may result.

***Latency stage*** In psychoanalytic theory, the fourth stage of psychosexual development, characterized by repression of sexual impulses and development of skills.

***Industry versus inferiority*** The fourth stage of psychosocial development in Erikson's theory, occurring in middle childhood. Mastery of tasks leads to a sense of industry, while failure produces feelings of inferiority.

**Social-Learning Theory** Social-learning theory focuses on the continued importance of rewards and modeling in middle childhood. During these years, children depend less on external rewards and punishments and increasingly regulate their own behavior (Crain, 1992).

How do children acquire moral and social standards for judging their own behavior? According to Bandura (1989), one mechanism involves direct reward and punishment. For example, parents may praise a child when she shares her toys with her younger brother. In time, she incorporates the importance of sharing into her own value system.

Another mechanism for acquiring self-evaluative standards is through modeling. Children in the middle years are exposed to an increasing variety of models. Not only parents, but teachers, other adults, peers, and symbolic models (such as TV characters or the heroine in a story) can serve as influential models (Bandura, 1989).

**Cognitive-Developmental Theory and Social Cognition** Cognitive-developmental theory stresses the importance of the child's growing cognitive capacities. In Chapter 12, we examined Piaget's description of the concreteoperational skills that emerge in middle childhood. You will recall that a major

**Figure 13.1**

**Development of Skills.** *According to both Freud and Erikson, the major developmental task of middle childhood is the acquisition of cognitive, social, and other culturally valued skills.*

***Social cognition*** Development of children's understanding of the relationship between the self and others.

milestone of the concrete-operations stage is a decline in egocentrism and an expansion of the capacity to view the world and oneself from other people's perspectives. This cognitive advance not only enhances the child's intellectual functioning, but also has a major impact on the child's social development.

***Social cognition*** refers to the development of children's knowledge about the social world. It focuses on the child's understanding of the relationship between the self and others (Small, 1990).

One key factor in the development of social understanding is the ability to take the role or perspective of another person. Robert Selman and his colleagues (Selman, 1980, 1989; Selman & Schultz, 1989) devised a method to study the development of perspective-taking skills in childhood. They presented children with a social dilemma like the following:

> *Holly is an 8-year-old girl who likes to climb trees. She is the best tree climber in the neighborhood. One day while climbing down from a tall tree, she falls off the bottom branch but does not hurt herself. Her father sees her fall. He is upset and asks her to promise not to climb trees any more. Holly promises. Later that day, Holly and her friends meet Sean. Sean's kitten is caught up in a tree and can't get down. Something has to be done right away, or the kitten may fall. Holly is the only one who climbs trees well enough to reach the kitten and get it down, but she remembers her promise to her father. (Selman, 1980, p. 36)*

Children then were asked a series of questions designed to test their ability to take the role of another person. (For example, "How will Holly's father feel if he finds out she climbed the tree?") Based on children's responses to these questions, Selman and his colleagues described five levels of perspective-taking skills in childhood (Selman, 1976):

- ✦ *Level 0* (about 3 to 6 years of age). Children are still egocentric and do not realize that other people have perspectives different from their own. A child of this age will typically say that Holly will save the kitten because she likes kittens and that her father will be happy because he likes kittens too. The child assumes that everyone feels as she does.
- ✦ *Level 1* (about 5 to 9 years of age). Children understand that people in different situations or having different information may have different perspectives. But the child still assumes that only one perspective is "right." At this age, a child might say that Holly's father would be angry if he didn't know why she climbed the tree. But if she told him why, he would understand. The child recognizes that the father's perspective may differ from Holly's because of lack of information. But once he has the information, he will assume the "right" (that is, Holly's) perspective.
- ✦ *Level 2* (about 7 to 12 years of age). The child understands that people may think or feel differently because they have different values or ideas. The child also recognizes that others are capable of understanding the child's own perspective. Therefore, the child is better able to anticipate reactions of others. The typical child of this age might say that Holly knows that her father will understand why she climbed the tree and that he therefore won't punish her.
- ✦ *Level 3* (about 10 to 15 years of age). The child finally realizes that she and another person can both consider each other's point of view

at the same time. The child may say something like this: Holly's father will think that Holly shouldn't have climbed the tree. But now that he has heard her side of the story, he would feel that she was doing what she thought was right. Holly realizes that her father will consider how she felt.

- *Level 4* (about 12 years and older). The child realizes that mutual perspective-taking doesn't always lead to agreement. The perspectives of the larger social group also must be considered. A child of this age might say that society expects children to obey their parents and, therefore, that Holly should realize why her father might punish her.

More recent research indicates that children in the middle years show the developmental progression in perspective-taking proposed by Selman (Dixon & Moore, 1990; Fox, 1991). Also, as you might expect, children with better perspective-taking skills tend to be more skilled at peer relations (LeMare & Rubin, 1987).

### THE SELF-CONCEPT

In early childhood, children's self-concepts, or self-definitions, focus on concrete external traits, such as appearance, activities, and living situations. But as children undergo the cognitive developments of middle childhood, their more abstract internal traits, or personality characteristics, begin to play a role in their self-definition. Social relationships and group memberships also take on significance (Damon, 1991; Damon & Hart, 1992).

**TRUTH OR FICTION REVISITED**

*It is not true that children in middle childhood define themselves only in terms of superficial traits, such as their appearance, activities, and living situations. They also begin to consider personality characteristics.*

An investigative method called the Twenty Statements Test bears out this progression and also highlights the relationships between the self-concept and general cognitive development. In this method, children are given a sheet of paper with the question "Who am I?" and 20 spaces in which to write answers. Consider the answers offered by a 9-year-old boy and an 11-year-old girl:

> Nine-year-old boy: *My name is Bruce C. I have brown eyes. I have brown hair. I have brown eyebrows. I'm 9 years old. I LOVE? sports. I have 7 people in my family. I have great? eye site. I have lots! of friends. I live on 1923 Pinecrest Drive. I'm going on 10 in September. I'm a boy. I have a uncle that is almost 7 feet tall. My school is Pinecrest. My teacher is Mrs. V. I play hockey! I'm also the smartest boy in the class. I LOVE! food. I love fresh air. I LOVE school.*
>
> Eleven-year-old girl: *My name is A. I'm a human being. I'm a girl. I'm a truthful person. I'm not pretty. I do so-so in my studies. I'm a very good cellist. I'm a very good pianist. I'm a little bit tall for my age. I like several boys. I like several girls. I'm old fashioned. I play tennis. I am a very good musician. I try to be helpful. I'm always ready to be friends with anybody. Mostly I'm good, but I lose my temper. I'm not well liked by some girls and boys. I don't know if boys like me or not. (Montemayor & Eisen, 1977, pp. 317–318)*

Only the 9-year-old lists his age and address, discusses his family, and focuses on physical traits, such as eye color, in his self-definition. The 9-year-old mentions his likes, which may be considered rudimentary psychological traits, but they are tied to the concrete, as would be expected of a concrete-operational child.

The 9- and 11-year-olds both list their competencies. The 11-year-old's struggle to bolster her self-esteem—her insistence on her musical abilities despite her qualms about her attractiveness—shows a greater concern with internal traits, psychological characteristics, and social relationships.

**SELF-ESTEEM** One of the most critical aspects of self-concept is ***self-esteem,*** the value or worth that people attach to themselves. A positive self-image seems to be important for healthy psychological adjustment in children and adults (Adler et al., 1992).

As children enter middle childhood, their self-concepts become more differentiated and they are able to evaluate their self-worth in many different areas. You will remember from Chapter 10 that preschoolers do not yet make a clear distinction between different areas of competence. They are either ''good at doing things'' or not. At one time, it was assumed that prior to age 8, children could differentiate only between two broad facets of self-concept. One involved general competence and the other, social acceptance (Harter & Pike, 1984). It was also believed that an overall, or general, self-concept did not emerge until the age of 8. But more recent research indicates that even as early as 5 to 7 years of age, children are able to make judgments about their performance in seven different areas: physical ability, physical appearance, peer relationships, parent relationships, reading, mathematics, and general school performance. They also display an overall, or general, self-concept (Eccles et al., 1993a; Marsh et al., 1991).

Children's self-esteem declines throughout middle childhood, reaching a low point at about age 12 or 13 and then increasing during middle and late adolescence (Harter, 1990b, c; Pomerantz et al., 1993). What accounts for the decline in self-esteem? Young children are egocentric, as we have seen, and their initial self-concepts may be unrealistic. As children become older, they incorporate more external information into their self-concepts as they compare themselves with other children. For most children, this results in a more realistic and critical self-appraisal and a decline in self-esteem.

Does one gender have a more favorable self-image than the other? The answer depends on the area. Girls tend to have more positive reading and general academic self-concepts than boys, whereas boys tend to have more positive self-concepts in math, physical ability, and physical appearance (Marsh et al., 1991; Eccles et al., 1993a). Why do girls and boys differ in their self-concepts? Socialization and the presence of gender stereotypes appear to have an impact on the way females and males react to their own achievements. For example, girls predict that they will do better on tasks that are labeled "feminine" and boys predict better performance for themselves when tasks are labeled "masculine" (Lips, 1993).

A classic study by Stanley Coopersmith (1967) and more recent research by Diana Baumrind (1991a, b) suggest that authoritative parenting contributes to high self-esteem in children. In other words, children with a favorable self-image tend to have parents who are strict, involved, and loving. Children with low self-esteem are more likely to have authoritarian or rejecting–neglecting parents.

***Self-esteem*** The sense of value or worth that people attach to themselves.

## Truth or Fiction Revisited

*It is true that children with high self-esteem tend to have parents who are strict but also involved and loving.*

High self-esteem in children is related to their closeness to their parents, especially as found in father–son and mother–daughter relationships (Dickstein & Posner, 1978; Elrod & Crase, 1980). Close relationships between the parents themselves also is associated with positive self-concepts in their children (Bishop & Ingersoll, 1989).

Peers also play an important role in children's self-esteem. As we shall see later in the chapter, social acceptance by one's peers is related to children's self-perceived competence in a variety of domains—academic, social, athletic, physical attractiveness, and behavioral conduct (Cole, 1991b). Parents and classmates have an equally strong impact on children's sense of self-worth in the middle years. Close friends and teachers have somewhat less influence in shaping self-esteem than parents and classmates, although they too play a role (Harter, 1987).

### Thinking About Development

Agree or disagree with the following statement and support your answer: "Success breeds success."

Self-esteem, once established, seems to endure. One longitudinal study, for example, found that children's self-esteem remained stable from the ages of 7 to 11 years (Hoglund & Bell, 1991). Most children will encounter failure, but high self-esteem may contribute to a continuing belief that they can master adversity. Low self-esteem may become a self-fulfilling prophecy: Children with low self-esteem may not carve out much to boast about in life.

**Learned Helplessness** One outcome of low self-esteem in the academic area is known as ***learned helplessness.*** This refers to the belief that one is unable to control one's environment (Borkowski et al., 1990). Helpless children tend to give up following failure, whereas mastery-oriented children increase

***Learned helplessness*** The belief that one is unable to control one's environment.

**Figure 13.2**

***Authoritative Parenting and Self-Esteem.*** *Parents of children with high self-esteem tend to make demands and impose restrictions but are also warmly encouraging.*

their efforts or change strategies. One reason for this is that helpless children believe that success is due more to ability than to effort and that they have little ability in a particular area. Consequently, persisting in the face of failure seems futile to them (Carr et al., 1991). These children typically perform more poorly in school and on standardized tests of intelligence and achievement (Chapman et al., 1990).

**GENDER AND LEARNED HELPLESSNESS** Girls exhibit more learned helplessness than boys (Boggiano & Barrett, 1991). One area in which this gender difference emerges is mathematics (Stipek & Gralinski, 1991). Jacquelynne Eccles and her colleagues have been carrying out longitudinal studies of elementary and high school aged children (Eccles et al., 1991; Jacobs, 1991). They have found that even when girls are performing as well as boys in math and science, they have less confidence of their aptitude in these areas. Why is this? Parents' expectations that their children will do well (or poorly) in a given area influences both the children's own view of their abilities and their actual performance. Parents tend to hold the stereotyped view that girls have less math ability than boys. This is true regardless of their own daughter's actual mathematical performance. These lowered parental expectations appear to influence girls' estimates of their own abilities. Girls may ultimately shy away from math-related activities and therefore not develop their math skills to the extent that boys do (Eccles et al., 1991). This is a good example of the self-fulfilling prophecy that we talked about in Chapter 11.

## PEER RELATIONSHIPS

Families exert the most powerful influences on children during the child's first few years. But as children move into middle childhood, their activities and interests become directed progressively further away from home. Peers take on an increasing importance. Let us explore the ways in which peers socialize one another. Then we shall examine factors in peer acceptance and rejection. Finally, we shall see how friendships develop.

### *PEERS AS SOCIALIZATION INFLUENCES*

Peer relationships are a major part of growing up. Peers exert powerful socialization influences and pressures to conform. As involved and authoritative as they may be, parents can only provide their children with experience in relating to adults. Children also profit from experience in relating to peers. Peers, like adults, have various needs and interests, various competencies, and social skills. Not only do they belong to a different generation from parents, they also differ as individuals. For all these reasons, peer experiences broaden children.

Peers guide children and afford practice in sharing and cooperation, in relating to leaders, and in coping with aggressive impulses, including their own. Peers, like parents, help children learn what types of impulses—affectionate, aggressive, and so on—they can safely express, and with whom. Children who are at odds with their parents can turn to peers as sounding boards. With peers they can compare feelings and experiences they would not bring up in the home. When children share troubling ideas and experiences with peers, they often learn that their friends have similar concerns. They realize that they are normal and not alone (Corsaro & Eder, 1990; Zarbatany et al., 1990).

### *Peer Acceptance and Rejection*

Acceptance or rejection by peers is of major importance, because problems with peers are a harbinger of later social and emotional maladjustment (Coie & Cillesen, 1993; McCendie & Schneider, 1993). What are the characteristics of popular and rejected children?

On a physical level, popular children tend to be attractive and relatively mature for their age, although physical attractiveness seems to be more important for girls than boys (Jackson, 1992; Langlois, 1985). Socially speaking, popular children are friendly, nurturant, cooperative, helpful, and skilled in social interaction (Denham & Holt, 1993; Newcomb et al., 1993; Tryon & Keane, 1991). Popular children also tend to be lavish in their dispensing of praise and approval (Landau & Milich, 1990). Popular children have higher self-esteem than other children (Boivin & Begin, 1989; East et al., 1992). They also tend either to do well in school or to excel in valued activities such as sports (Wentzel, 1991).

Later-born children are more likely to be popular than firstborns, probably because they generally develop superior skills in relating to peers (Hartup, 1983). This trend holds despite the fact that school achievement is a factor in popularity (Cornell, 1990) and that firstborns tend to earn higher grades than later-borns.

Children who show behavioral and learning problems, who are aggressive, and who disrupt group activities by bickering or deviant behavior are more likely to be rejected by their peers (Coie & Cillesen, 1993; Eisenberg et al., 1993; LaFreniere et al., 1992; Olson, 1992). Shy, socially withdrawn children also are likely to be unpopular with their peers (Bierman et al., 1993; Rubin, 1993; Volling et al., 1993).

*Aggressive children actually tend to be rejected by their peers.*

Although pressure to conform to group norms and standards can be powerful indeed, most children who are rejected do not shape up their behavior. Instead, they tend to remain alone, lonely, and on the fringes of the group (Cassidy & Asher, 1992; Crick & Ladd, 1993; Parker & Asher, 1993). In some cases, they join deviant subcultures whose values and goals differ from the mainstream. Fortunately, training in social skills seems to have the capacity to increase children's popularity with peers (Coie & Koeppl, 1990).

### *Culture and Development: Peer Acceptance and Rejection*

Most of the research on peer acceptance and rejection has been carried out in Western cultures. But behaviors that peers view as acceptable or unacceptable in Western societies may not always be evaluated in the same way in non-Western cultures.

This point was strikingly illustrated in a study of peer relationships among 8- and 10-year-old Chinese and Canadian children (Chen et al., 1992). Sociability and leadership behaviors led to peer acceptance, while aggression led to peer

FIGURE 13.3

***Peer Rejection.*** *Children who are rejected by their peers may show later social and emotional problems. However, teaching children social skills can increase their popularity with peers.*

rejection in both groups of children. Shy, socially isolated children were rejected by the Canadian children, consistent with other studies done in North America (Hymel et al., 1990). But shy, socially withdrawn children were *more* likely than others to be accepted and sought out by the Chinese children.

Shy, socially inhibited behavior apparently is viewed in Western cultures as reflecting social immaturity, fearfulness, and deviance. In Chinese culture, however, cautious and inhibited behavior in children is highly praised and encouraged. It is no wonder that children who show these behaviors are thus more likely to be accepted by their peers (Chen et al., 1992).

## Development of Friendships

In the early years of middle childhood, friendships are based on geographical closeness or proximity. Friendships are relatively superficial—quickly formed, quickly broken. What matters are shared activities and who has the swing set or sandbox. Five- to 7-year-olds usually report that their friends are the children they do things with, the children with whom they have "fun" (Berndt & Perry, 1986; Damon, 1977; Epstein, 1989). There is little reference to friends' traits.

Between the ages of 8 and 11, children show increased recognition of the importance of friends meeting each others' needs and possessing desirable traits (Damon, 1977; Epstein, 1989). Children at these ages are more likely to say that friends are nice to one another and share interests as well as things. During these years, children increasingly pick friends who are similar to themselves in behavior and personality. A sense of loyalty, mutual understanding, and a willingness to disclose personal information characterize friendships in middle childhood and adolescence (Clark & Bittle, 1992; Hartup, 1993).

Robert Selman (1980) has described five stages in children's changing concepts of friendship (see Table 13.1). You will recognize that these stages correspond to the five levels of perspective-taking skills in childhood discussed near the beginning of this chapter.

Friends behave differently with each other than with nonfriends. School-age friends are more verbal, attentive, expressive, relaxed, and mutually responsive to each other during play than are children who are only acquaintances (Field et al., 1992). Cooperation occurs more readily between friends than between nonfriends, as might be expected. But intense competition may also occur among friends, especially among boys (Hartup, 1989). When conflicts occur between friends, they tend to be less intense and are resolved in ways that maintain positive social interaction (Hartup, 1993; Laursen, 1993).

Children in middle childhood typically will tell you that they have more than one "best" friend (Berndt et al., 1989). One study found that 9-year-olds reported having an average of four best friends (Lewis & Feiring, 1989). Best friends tend to be more similar to each other than other friends (Epstein, 1989).

In middle childhood, girls and boys do not differ in the number of best friends they report (Benenson, 1990; Krappmann et al., 1993). Boys tend to play in larger groups than girls, however. By middle childhood, children's friendships are almost exclusively with others of the same gender, continuing the trend of gender segregation that began in the early years (Hartup, 1993; Krappmann et al., 1993).

**TRUTH OR FICTION REVISITED**

*It is true that children's friendships are almost exclusively with children of the same gender in middle childhood.*

**TABLE 13.1**

***SELMAN'S FIVE STAGES IN CHILDREN'S CONCEPTS OF FRIENDSHIP***

| STAGE | NAME | APPROXIMATE AGE | DESCRIPTION |
|---|---|---|---|
| 0 | MOMENTARY PHYSICAL INTERACTION | 3-6 | CHILDREN ARE STILL EGOCENTRIC AND UNABLE TO TAKE ANOTHER'S VIEWPOINT. THUS, THEIR CONCEPT OF A FRIEND IS SOMEONE WHO LIKES TO PLAY WITH THE SAME THINGS THEY DO AND WHO LIVES CLOSE BY. |
| 1 | ONE-WAY ASSISTANCE | 5-9 | THE CHILD REALIZES THAT SHE AND HER FRIENDS MAY HAVE DIFFERENT THOUGHTS AND FEELINGS, BUT THE CHILD PUTS HER OWN DESIRES FIRST. SHE VIEWS A FRIEND AS SOMEONE WHO DOES WHAT SHE WANTS. |
| 2 | FAIR-WEATHER COOPERATION | 7-12 | FRIENDS ARE VIEWED AS DOING THINGS FOR EACH OTHER. BUT THE FOCUS STILL IS ON EACH FRIEND'S SELF-INTEREST, RATHER THAN ON THE RELATIONSHIP. |
| 3 | INTIMATE AND MUTUAL SHARING | 10-15 | THE FOCUS IS ON THE RELATIONSHIP ITSELF, RATHER THAN ON EACH INDIVIDUAL SEPARATELY. THE FUNCTION OF FRIENDSHIP IS SEEN AS MUTUAL SUPPORT OVER A LONG PERIOD OF TIME, RATHER THAN A CONCERN FOR IMMEDIATE ACTIVITY OR SELF-INTEREST. |
| 4 | AUTONOMOUS INTERDEPENDENCE | 12 AND OLDER | CHILDREN UNDERSTAND THAT FRIENDSHIPS GROW AND CHANGE AS PEOPLE CHANGE. THEY REALIZE THAT ONE MAY HAVE DIFFERENT FRIENDS TO SATISFY DIFFERENT NEEDS. |

SOURCE: SELMAN, 1980.

FIGURE 13.4

***FRIENDSHIP.*** *A sense of loyalty, mutual understanding, and a willingness to disclose personal information characterize friendships in the later years of middle childhood.*

## THE FAMILY

In middle childhood, the family continues to play a key role in socializing the child, even though peers, teachers, and others outside the family begin to play a greater role than before (Maccoby, 1984a). In this section, we examine developments in parent–child relationships during the middle years. We will also look at the effects of living in different types of family environments. We will focus on three aspects of family diversity. The first deals with families in different ethnic groups. The second concerns the experience of living in families with varying marital arrangements: original two parents, single parent, stepparent. The third area of family diversity deals with the effects of having a mother who is or is not in the labor force.

### *PARENT–CHILD RELATIONSHIPS*

Parent–child interactions focus on some new concerns during the middle childhood years. These include school-related matters, assignment of chores, and peer activities (DeLuccie & Davis, 1991; Maccoby, 1984a).

During the middle years, parents do less monitoring of children's activities and provide less direct feedback than they did in the preschool years. In middle childhood, children do more monitoring of their own behavior. While the parents still retain control over the child, there is a gradual transferring of control from parent to child, a process known as ***coregulation*** (Maccoby, 1984b). Children no longer need to be constantly reminded of do's and don'ts as they begin to internalize the standards of their parents.

***Coregulation*** A gradual transferring of control from parent to child, beginning in middle childhood.

Children and parents spend less time together in middle childhood than in the preschool years. But as in the early childhood years, children spend more time with their mothers than with their fathers (Russell & Russell, 1987). Mothers' interactions with their school-age children continue to revolve around care giving and household tasks, while fathers are more involved in recreational activities, especially with sons (Collins & Russell, 1991).

In the later years of middle childhood (ages 10 to 12), children evaluate their parents more critically than they do in the early years (Reid et al., 1990). This shift in perception may reflect the child's growing social cognitive capacity to perceive relationships in more complex ways (Selman, 1989). But throughout middle childhood, children rate their parents as their best source of emotional support, rating them even more highly than friends (Reid et al., 1990).

### *Culture and Development: The Diversity of the Family*

Families in different ethnic groups vary on a number of dimensions, including their size and the composition of the household. Large and extended families are more prevalent among ethnic minorities than among whites (Spencer et al., 1990). For example, nearly 30 percent of Hispanic families have five or more members, compared with 19 percent of African-American families and 14 percent of white families (U.S. Bureau of the Census, 1992). African Americans, Hispanics, and Native Americans have large, close-knit kinship networks consisting of grandparents, aunts, uncles, and cousins (Lynch & Hanson, 1992; MacPhee et al., 1993; R.D. Taylor et al., 1993). These extended kin often assume substantial parenting responsibilities. Such support is especially beneficial in single-parent families, which are more prevalent among ethnic minorities than among whites. In 1991, for example, 79 percent of white children lived with two parents, as compared with 66 percent of Hispanic children and 36 percent of African-American children (U.S. Bureau of the Census, 1992).

Children may live with a single parent because their mother never married or because a parent died. The most common cause, however, is divorce or separation of the parents. Let us turn now to examine the effects of divorce on children.

FIGURE 13.5

***Parent–Child Relationships.*** *Children and parents spend less time together in middle childhood than in the preschool years. As in early childhood, children spend more time with their mothers than with their fathers. Throughout middle childhood, children rate their parents as their best source of emotional support.*

## CHILDREN OF DIVORCE

Currently, more than 1 million children a year experience the divorce of their parents (Kantrowitz, 1992). Nearly 40 percent of white children and 75 percent of African-American children in the United States who are born to married parents will spend at least part of their childhoods in single-parent families resulting from divorce (Amato & Keith, 1991).

Divorce requires many adjustments for children, as well as for parents. Change itself is stressful, and divorce involves a multitude of changes (Guttmann, 1993; Wallerstein & Blakeslee, 1990). Divorce turns the children's world topsy-turvy. The simple things that had been taken for granted are no longer simple: Eating meals and going on trips with both parents, curling up with either parent to read a book or watch television, kissing both parents at bedtime come to an end.

Divorced parents must support two households, not one. And so, children of divorce often suffer downward movement in socioeconomic status (Barber & Eccles, 1992). If the downward movement is not severe, it may require minor adjustments and loss of but a few privileges. But following divorce, children are twice as likely to be living in poverty than they were before the breakup (DeParle, 1991). In severe cases, the downward trend can mean moving from a house into a cramped apartment or from a more desirable to a less desirable neighborhood. With moving may come a change of schools, and the children may have to begin relating to children who share unfamiliar backgrounds and values. Divorce in families in which the mother had stayed in the home may suddenly require her to rejoin the work force and place her children in day care. Such women typically suffer the stresses of task overload, as well as the other problems divorce entails (Chase-Lansdale & Hetherington, 1990; Etaugh, 1990).

About 88 percent of the children of divorce live with their mothers (Seligmann, 1992). Fathers usually see their children frequently during the first months after the divorce, but visitation often drops precipitously later on. One study by Frank Furstenberg and Kathleen Mullins Harris found that nearly half the children whose fathers did not live with them had not seen their fathers at all in the previous year (Lewin, 1990). And half of that group had not seen their fathers for the past 5 years. Also, about half of fathers do not keep up with their child-support payments, exacerbating the family's downward trend in socioeconomic status (DePar1e, 1992; Waldman, 1992).

**TRUTH OR FICTION REVISITED**

*It is true that about half of divorced fathers do not keep up with their child-support payments. For this reason, among others, the children of divorce frequently show downward movement in socioeconomic status.*

**EFFECTS OF DIVORCE** Given all this outer and inner turmoil, it is not surprising that many children of divorce show behavioral and emotional problems in the first few years following divorce. Common reactions include problems in academic achievement and school adjustment, conduct problems, poorer psychological adjustment, lower self-esteem, and problems in relationships with parents and peers (Featherstone et al., 1992; Hetherington et al., 1991, 1992; Wallerstein, 1991).

Researchers attribute children's problems not only to the divorce, but also to a decline in the quality of child rearing that frequently follows (Grych & Fincham, 1992). In a longitudinal study by E. Mavis Hetherington and her colleagues (Hetherington, 1987, 1989; Hetherington et al., 1989), the adjustment of children who were 4 years old at the time of the divorce was assessed at 2 months, 1 year, 2 years, and 6 years following divorce. They found that the organization of family life tends to deteriorate following divorce. The family is more likely to eat their meals pick-up style, as opposed to sitting down together. Children are less likely to get to school on time or to get to sleep at a regular hour. Divorced mothers have a more difficult time setting limits and enforcing restrictions on sons' behavior. The Hetherington group, as well as others (Emery, 1988), found that divorced parents, on the whole, are significantly less likely to show the authoritative behaviors that foster instrumental competence. They make fewer demands for mature behavior, decline in communication ability, and show less nurturance and warmth. Moreover, their disciplinary methods become inconsistent. And divorced parents who show the poorest parenting skills are more likely to have poorly adjusted children (Capaldi & Patterson, 1991).

**Factors in Adjusting to Divorce** Within 2 or 3 years following divorce, many parents and children are adapting fairly well (Hetherington, 1989; Hetherington et al., 1989). But children differ widely in their reactions to divorce. Some children emerge from divorce as extremely competent and well-functioning individuals, while others continue to suffer for many years following the divorce (Aro & Palosaari, 1992; Barber & Eccles, 1992; Furstenberg & Cherlin, 1991). Which children are most likely to emerge unscathed, and which ones are most likely to struggle?

For one thing, boys seem to have a harder time than girls coping with divorce and they take a longer time to recover (Doherty & Needle, 1991; Furstenberg, 1990). In the Hetherington study, boys from divorced homes showed more conduct problems and more difficulties in peer relations and school achievement than boys from nondivorced homes. These difficulties sometimes continued up to 6 years following divorce. Girls, on the other hand, were functioning well within 2 years after divorce (Hetherington 1989; Hetherington et al., 1989).

Girls, however, may show certain delayed effects of divorce in late adolescence or adulthood, particularly in the realm of sexual activity and marriage (Furstenberg, 1990). Research indicates that young women from divorced families may have a harder time forming emotional commitments (Wallerstein, 1991). They are more likely to be promiscuous and to marry early (Chase-Lansdale & Hetherington, 1990). And young women whose parents divorced are more likely to get divorced themselves (Kantrowitz, 1992). This greater tendency to divorce does not necessarily mean that children from divorced families are less stable or less committed to the institution of marriage, as is sometimes assumed. An alternative explanation is that children's exposure to divorce makes them aware that terminating an unhappy marriage is a viable alternative to staying in it (Barber & Eccles, 1992).

Does a child's age at the time of the divorce make a difference in how well the child adapts? The picture is unclear (Guttmann, 1993). Some studies find that preschoolers have the hardest time adjusting (Allison & Furstenberg, 1989). Others, however, indicate that children in the elementary and high school years are affected most (Amato & Keith, 1991).

A clearer picture emerges for the roles of child temperament and parenting style. Let us consider the three clusters of children identified by Hetherington (1989) 6 years after their parents' divorce. One group, labeled "aggressive and insecure," consisted largely of boys. They were impulsive, aggressive, and socially withdrawn. These children had been temperamentally difficult since early childhood. Their parents tended to use neglecting or authoritarian parenting styles. The other two clusters consisted of competent children who were functioning well. These children had high self-esteem, few behavior problems, got along well with peers and teachers, and did well in school. They had a caring relationship with at least one supportive adult, often a parent but sometimes another relative, teacher, or neighbor. One of the two clusters, called opportunistic-competent, consisted equally of girls and boys. These children were manipulative and opportunistic, often playing one parent against the other. Their families tended to be high in conflict. The caring-competent cluster consisted mostly of girls. They were very prosocial in their behavior and often looked after younger siblings. Their mothers were warm and supportive and encouraged mature independent behavior. In other words, their mothers showed an authoritative parenting style, which, as we have seen, fosters competence in children.

Studies of school-aged children suggest that boys adjust somewhat better when their fathers have custody of them but that girls do somewhat better with their mothers (Camara & Resnick, 1989; Zill, 1988). However, traits such as authoritativeness and warmth seem to be more important than the custodian's gender in promoting children's adjustment. It also comes down to an individual issue: Which parent truly wants the children and has the emotional resources to cope with their needs?

Regardless of which parent has custody, children's adjustment to divorce is facilitated when parents maintain their commitment to the children and set aside their own disputes long enough to agree on child-rearing practices (Forehand et al., 1991b; Maccoby, 1993a; Portes et al., 1992). It is helpful for divorced parents to encourage each other to continue to play roles in their children's lives and to avoid saying negative things about each other in front of the children.

**SHOULD CONFLICTED PARENTS STAY TOGETHER FOR THE SAKE OF THE CHILDREN?** It is good for divorced parents to cooperate in rearing their children. Is it also better for the children for parents to remain together despite their conflicts?

It is well-documented that marital conflict is associated with a wide range of behavior and adjustment problems for children ranging from toddlerhood through adolescence (Black & Pedro-Carroll, 1993; Depner et al., 1992; Fincham & Osborne, 1993; Grych & Fincham, 1990). Boys appear to be affected more than girls.

One longitudinal study of 17,000 British families looked at children over a period of years, both before and after their parents divorced (Cherlin et al., 1991). The researchers found that many of the problems children have after divorce are present *before* the divorce and appear to be due more to marital discord than to the divorce. Among children whose parents subsequently divorced, half of the problems of boys and a smaller percentage of girls' problems had been evident before the divorce. Findings were similar for a smaller U.S. sample.

But are children still better off living in a two-parent family with high conflict than in a single-parent family? The answer may be no, particularly if divorce results in a lessening of hostilities between the parents. Research has found that children living in two-parent families characterized by high levels of parental conflict are more poorly adjusted than those living in divorced families with low

FIGURE 13.6

***Should Conflicted Parents Stay Together for the Sake of the Children?*** *Marital conflict is associated with a wide range of behavioral and adjustment problems in children and adolescents. When parents cannot get along, divorce followed by cooperative child rearing may be the best alternative.*

conflict (Barber & Eccles, 1992; Hetherington et al., 1989). When parents cannot get along, divorce followed by cooperative child rearing may be the best alternative.

Given that many children begin to adjust reasonably well by 2 or 3 years following divorce, the assumption that divorce irreparably harms children seems to be unwarranted. Some researchers believe that the challenges of growing up in a divorced family may provide certain positive benefits as well. Children may develop an enhanced sense of independence and competence and may learn how to cope successfully with stress (Barber & Eccles, 1992).

**Stepparent Families** About 75 percent of divorced women and 80 percent of divorced men get remarried, usually within 5 years of their divorces (Darden & Zimmerman, 1992; Glick, 1989). Thirty-five percent of American children can expect to spend some part of their lives in a stepfamily. And so, the effects of stepparenting are also an important issue in U.S. family life.

How well do children adjust to their parent's remarriage? Even 7 to 10 years after the marriage, children feel less close to their stepparents than to their biological parents. The closer the relationship between the child and the biological parents, the harder it is for the child to accept a stepparent (Emery, 1988; Kutner, 1991b). Younger children respond more positively to a stepparent, but adolescents often are angry, confused, and resentful of the "intruder" (Emery, 1988; Hetherington et al., 1992; Kutner, 1991a).

Girls and boys react differently to their parents' remarriage. Boys adapt better to a new stepmother or stepfather than girls do (Brand et al., 1988; Kurdek et al., 1992). Remarriage generally appears to be more beneficial for boys than for girls. Since mothers have custody of their children in 88 percent of divorces, let us consider the situation in which the custodial mother remarries. Stepfathers may ease the strained relationship between divorced mothers and sons and may serve as male role models and companions (Emery, 1988). Close relationships between boys and stepfathers are associated with fewer behavioral problems and increased social competence (Vuchinich et al., 1991). Girls, however, often become closer to their mothers following divorce, and the stepfather may be viewed as a threat to that relationship.

## MATERNAL EMPLOYMENT

The past half century has witnessed one of the most dramatic social changes in the history of the United States. Mothers are entering the labor force in record-breaking numbers. In 1991, 67 percent of married mothers of children under age 18 were employed, as were 73 percent of divorced, separated, or widowed mothers (U.S. Bureau of the Census, 1992). Life-styles have changed significantly for American families as more women combine maternal and occupational roles. It is no longer the norm for mothers to spend their days at home taking care of their children. The traditional role of mothering is changing, and in its place is emerging a new tradition of American motherhood (Frankel, 1993).

**CULTURE AND DEVELOPMENT: THE DIVERSITY OF EMPLOYED MOTHERS** Employed mothers constitutue a heterogeneous group of women. During the past 20 years, more and more women in two-parent families have gone to work because two incomes are needed to support the family. For single mothers, financial considerations are even more critical. They must work to avoid poverty (Stegelin & Frankel, 1993).

Employment experiences also differ for mothers in different ethnic groups. Historically, married African-American mothers have been more likely to be employed outside the home than married white mothers. The employment rate for single African-American mothers, on the other hand, is lower than that for single white mothers (McLoyd, 1993). This is partly because single African-American mothers are younger and less well-educated. The extended family is a major source of support for employed African-American mothers, especially with respect to child care (Weitzman & Fitzgerald, 1993).

Hispanic employed mothers represent a diverse group, including women of Mexican, Puerto Rican, Central and South American, and Cuban origin. Among Hispanic women, Cubans have the highest employment rate and Puerto Ricans the lowest (Ries & Stone, 1992). Like African-American women, employed Hispanic mothers often rely on an extended family system of support (Weitzman & Fitzgerald, 1993). Obstacles faced by employed Hispanic mothers may include a language barrier, more traditional gender-role expectations within Hispanic cultures, and lower levels of educational attainment (Bonilla-Santiago, 1990).

Asian-American mothers also constitute a diverse group, including women of Chinese, Japanese, Korean, Filipino, and Asian Indian descent. Many of these women have achieved high levels of education (Weitzman & Fitzgerald, 1993). A number of Asian-American women work in small family-operated businesses (Lott, 1990). But many, like other ethnic minority women, are segregated into low-paying, female-dominated occupations.

**EFFECTS OF MATERNAL EMPLOYMENT ON CHILDREN** What are the effects of maternal employment on children? Must mother be available for round-the-clock love and attention?

Psychologists have not found evidence that maternal employment is detrimental (Etaugh, 1990, 1993; Gottfried, et al., 1994). Children of employed women do not differ from those of full-time homemakers in their social, emotional, or intellectual development. In fact, maternal employment may benefit school-age children by fostering greater independence and encouraging responsibility and competence (Alessandri, 1992b; Hoffman, 1989). Children of working women are more helpful with the housework (Bartko & McHale, 1991). The daughters of employed women are more achievement-oriented and set themselves higher career goals than the daughters of nonemployed women (Richards & Duckett,

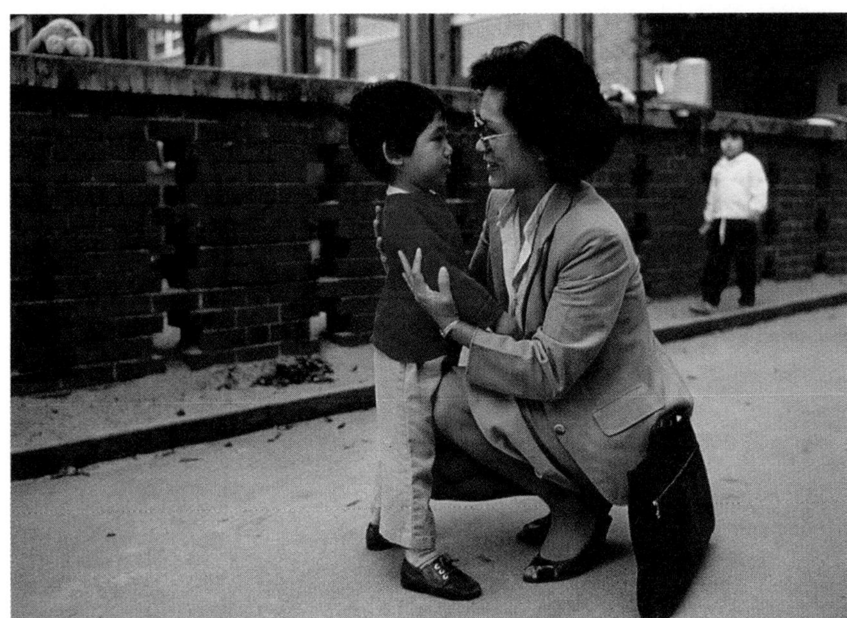

FIGURE 13.7

**MATERNAL EMPLOYMENT.** *Maternal employment may benefit school-age children by fostering greater independence and encouraging responsibility and competence.*

1991). Adolescent sons and daughters whose mothers are employed show better personality and social adjustment and have better family relations and better interpersonal relationships at school (Lerner & Hess, 1991). Children with employed mothers view their mothers as more competent and hold fewer stereotypical gender-role attitudes (Etaugh, 1993).

Employed mothers and their husbands are more egalitarian in their distribution of chores in the home, as well as in the breadwinning role. The fathers spend more time with the children than in single-earner families (Gottfried et al., 1994). When mothers choose to work outside the home and find their work fulfilling, they are happier with their lives (Hoffman, 1989; Zaslow et al., 1991). Perhaps the employed mothers' feelings of competence and high self-esteem transfer into more positive relationships with their children. In any case, mothers who are satisfied with their lives—whether employed or not—have better adjusted children than mothers who are less satisfied (Etaugh, 1990, 1993).

TRUTH OR FICTION REVISITED

*It is true that the daughters of employed women are more achievement-oriented and set themselves higher career goals than the daughters of nonemployed women.*

## THE SCHOOL

The school exerts a powerful impact on many aspects of the child's development. Schools, like parents, set limits on behavior, make demands for mature behavior, attempt to communicate, and are oriented toward nurturing positive physical, social, and cognitive development. The schools, like parents, have a direct influence on children's IQ scores, achievement motivation, and career aspirations (Ceci, 1991; Linney & Seidman, 1989; Stipek, 1992). Like the family, schools influence social and moral development (Battistich et al., 1991b; Thorkildsen, 1993).

In this section, we consider children's transition to school and then examine the effects of the school environment and of teachers.

## *School Entry*

An increasing number of children attend preschool. About 40 percent have had some type of formal prekindergarten experience (Love et al., 1992). But most children first experience full-time schooling when they enter kindergarten or first grade. Children must master many new tasks when they start school. They will have to meet new academic challenges, learn new school and teacher expectations, and fit into a new peer group (Ladd & Price, 1987; Pianta & Steinberg, 1992). They must learn to accept extended separation from parents and develop increased attention, self-control, and self-help skills (Love et al., 1992).

What happens to children during the transition from home or preschool to elementary school may be critical for the eventual success or failure of their educational experience. This is particularly true for low-income children. Families of children living in poverty may be less able to supply both the material and emotional supports that help the child adjust successfully to school (Campbell & Bryant 1993; McLoyd, 1990).

How well prepared are children to enter school? The National Association for the Education of Young Children (1990) points out that any discussions of school readiness must consider at least three critical factors:

- The diversity and inequity of children's early life experiences
- Individual differences in young children's development and learning
- The degree to which schools establish reasonable and appropriate expectations of children's capabilities when they enter school

FIGURE 13.8

***School Readiness.*** *Children differ in their readiness to enter school. Unfortunately, many children enter school less well-prepared than the boy in this cartoon.*

Unfortunately, some children enter school less well prepared than others. In one survey, 7,000 U.S. kindergarten teachers reported that more than one-third of their students began school unprepared to learn (Chira, 1991). Nearly half felt that children entered school less ready to learn than children 5 years earlier. Most said children often lacked the language skills needed to succeed. This report and others (National Association for the Education of Young Children, 1990; Willer & Bredekamp, 1990) conclude that poor health care and nutrition and lack of adequate stimulation and support by parents place many children at risk for academic failure even before they enter school.

But a recent study by the U.S. Department of Education concludes that the schools themselves could do a better job of easing the transition to kindergarten (Love et al., 1992). The researchers surveyed schools in 1,003 school districts and also visited eight schools. The average school reported that between 10 and 20 percent of incoming kindergartners had difficulty adjusting to kindergarten. Adjusting to the academic demands of school was reported to be the area of greatest difficulty. Low-income children had a more difficult time adjusting than other children, particularly in the area of academics. Sad to say, children who enter school with deficits in language and math skills generally continue to show deficits in these areas during at least the first 2 years of school (Morrison et al., 1993).

Children's adjustment to kindergarten can be made easier when schools provide transition activities to build continuity between kindergarten and the child's previous experiences at home or in preschool. But most schools do not provide such activities, according to the U.S. Department of Education study. Only 21 percent of the school districts surveyed reported a wide range of transition activities. About half the schools arranged formal school visits by parents. But only 10 percent had systematic communication between kindergarten teachers and the child's previous care givers or teachers.

### *Culture and Development: The Child's Transition to School*

A study by Alexander and Entwistle (1988) highlights some differences in the transition to full-time schooling for African-American and white children from working-class families. They found that both groups of students started first grade with similar achievement-test scores in verbal skills and mathematics computation. But by the end of the first year, the performance of the African-American children had fallen behind that of the white children, and the gap increased in second grade. The African-American children also received lower marks on their report cards. These results indicate that the transition to full-time schooling may be more problematic for African-American children than for white children.

Why might this be? Alexander and Entwistle note that poverty, the stresses of single parenting, and a personal history of academic difficulty are more prevalent in the African-American community. These conditions make it more difficult for parents to provide effective support for their children's academic efforts. Studies have shown that African-American parents value schooling highly and want to encourage high levels of accomplishment for their children, but they may lack the experience, knowledge base, and personal resources to follow through effectively (Alexander & Entwistle, 1988). These findings highlight the need for schools that service a high proportion of low-income children to create school transition activities involving parents (Love et al., 1992).

## *THE SCHOOL ENVIRONMENT*

What are the characteristics of a good school? Research summaries (Linney & Seidman, 1989; van de Grift, 1990; Wang et al., 1990, 1993) indicate that an effective school has the following characteristics:

- an active, energetic principal
- an atmosphere that is orderly but not oppressive
- teachers who participate in decision making
- teachers who have high expectations that children will learn
- a curriculum that emphasizes academics
- frequent assessment of student performance
- student participation in setting goals, making classroom decisions, and engaging in cooperative learning activities with other students

Certain aspects of the school environment are important as well. One key factor is class size. Smaller classes permit students to receive more individual attention and to express their ideas more often (Finn & Achilles, 1990). Several studies have found that smaller classes lead to increased achievement in mathematics and reading in the early primary grades (Robinson & Wittebols, 1986; Slavin, 1989). Smaller classes are particularly useful in teaching the three R's to elementary school students at risk for academic failure (Finn & Achilles, 1990; van de Grift, 1990). Small schools have their advantages as well. Recent research shows that students in high schools limited to about 400 students have fewer behavioral problems, better attendance and graduation rates, and, sometimes, higher test scores and grades than students in larger schools (Chira, 1993b).

**TRUTH OR FICTION REVISITED**

*It has actually been shown that smaller class size is connected to greater achievement, especially among students considered at risk for academic failure.*

## *TEACHERS*

The influence of the schools is mainly due to teachers. Teachers, like parents, set limits, make demands, communicate values, and foster development. Teacher–student relationships are more limited than parent–child relationships, but teachers still have the opportunity to serve as powerful role models and dispensers of reinforcement. After all, children spend several hours each weekday in the presence of teachers.

**TEACHER INFLUENCES ON STUDENT PERFORMANCE** Jere Brophy (1986) has summarized a large number of studies that indicate many different aspects of teacher behavior are related to student achievement. Achievement is enhanced when teachers expect students to master the curriculum, allocate most of the

FIGURE 13.9

**CLASS SIZE.** *Smaller classes permit students to receive more individual attention and express their ideas more often.*

available time to academic activities, and manage the classroom environment effectively. Students learn more in classes when actively instructed or supervised by teachers than when working on their own. The most effective teachers ask a lot of questions, give personalized feedback, and provide ample opportunities for drill and practice, as opposed to straight lecturing.

Student achievement also is linked to the emotional climate of the classroom. Students do not do as well when teachers rely heavily on criticism, ridicule, threats, or punishment. Achievement is high in classrooms with a pleasant, friendly atmosphere, but not in classrooms marked by extreme teacher warmth.

**TEACHER EXPECTATIONS** There is a saying that "You find what you're looking for." In Greek mythology, the amorous sculptor Pygmalion breathed life into a beautiful statue he had carved. Similarly, in the musical *My Fair Lady,* which is a reworking of the Pygmalion legend, Henry Higgins fashions a great lady from the working-class Eliza Doolittle.

Teachers also try to bring out positive traits that they believe dwell within their students. A classic experiment by Robert Rosenthal and Lenore Jacobson suggests that teacher expectations can become ***self-fulfilling prophecies*** (see Chapter 11). As reported in their book, *Pygmalion in the Classroom,* Rosenthal and Jacobson (1968) first gave students a battery of psychological tests. Then they informed teachers that a handful of the students, although average in performance to date, were late bloomers. The tests clearly suggested that they were about to blossom forth intellectually in the current school year.

Now, the fact is that the tests had indicated nothing in particular about the "chosen" children. These children had been selected at random. The purpose of the experiment was to determine whether modifying teacher expectations could enhance student performance. As it happened, the identified children made significant gains in intelligence-test scores. But in subsequent research, results have been mixed. Some studies have shown the ***Pygmalion effect*** (another name for the self-fulfilling prophecy). Others have not (Jussim, 1989, 1991). A review of 18 such experiments found that the Pygmalion effect was most pronounced when the procedure for informing teachers of the potential in the target student had greatest credibility (Raudenbusch, 1984). An appropriate conclusion would be

***Self-fulfilling prophecy; Pygmalion effect*** An expectation that is confirmed because of the behavior of those who hold the expectation.

that teacher expectations often, but not always, influence students' achievement motivation, self-esteem, expectations for success, and actual achievement (Brophy, 1983).

**TRUTH OR FICTION REVISITED**

*It is true that teachers who have high expectations of students frequently elicit greater achievements from them. This is the so-called Pygmalion effect.*

These findings have serious implications for children from ethnic minority and low-income families. There is some indication that teachers expect less academically from children in these groups (Entwistle, 1990). Teachers with lower expectations for certain children may spend less time encouraging and interacting with them.

What are some of the ways that teachers can help motivate *all* students to do their best? Woolfolk (1987, pp. 332–333) suggests the following:

- Make the classroom and the lesson interesting and inviting
- Assure that students can fulfill their needs for affiliation and belonging
- Make the classroom a safe and pleasant place
- Recognize that students' backgrounds can give rise to diverse patterns of needs
- Help students take appropriate responsibility for their successes and failures
- Encourage students to perceive the links between their own efforts and their achievements
- Help students set attainable, short-term goals

**SEXISM IN THE CLASSROOM** Although girls were systematically excluded from formal education for centuries, today we might not expect to find ***sexism*** among teachers. Teachers, after all, are generally well-educated. They are also trained to be fair-minded and sensitive to the needs of their young charges in today's changing society.

However, we may not have heard the last of sexism in our schools. According to a recent review of more than 1,000 publications about girls and education, girls are treated unequally by their teachers, their male peers, the school curriculum, and standardized tests (American Association of University Women, 1992). Among the conclusions of the reviewers were these (Chira, 1992a):

- Teachers pay less attention to girls than boys.
- Girls are subjected to increasing ***sexual harassment***—unwelcome verbal or physical conduct of a sexual nature—from male classmates. Many teachers continue to tolerate such behavior.
- School textbooks still stereotype or ignore women. Girls learn almost nothing in school about such pressing problems as discrimination, sexual abuse, and discrimination.

***Sexism*** Discrimination or bias against people based on their gender.

***Sexual harassment*** Unwelcome verbal or physical conduct of a sexual nature.

- ✦ Some standardized tests, such as the SAT, are biased against girls, hurting their chances of getting into college and getting scholarships.

In one of the most widely cited studies mentioned in the review, Myra and David Sadker (1985) observed students in fourth-, sixth-, and eighth-grade classes in four states and in the District of Columbia. Teachers and students were white and African American, urban, suburban, and rural. In almost all cases, findings were depressingly similar. Boys generally dominated classroom communication, whether the subject was math (a traditionally "masculine" area) or language arts (a traditionally "feminine" area). Boys, in fact, were eight times more likely than girls to call out answers without raising their hands. So far, it could be said, we have evidence of a gender difference, but not of sexism. However, teachers were less than impartial in responding to boys and girls when they called out. Teachers, male and female, were significantly more likely to accept calling out from boys. Girls were significantly more likely, as the song goes, to receive "teachers' dirty looks"—or to be reminded that they should raise their hands and wait to be called upon. Boys, it appears, are expected to be impetuous, but girls are reprimanded for "unladylike behavior." Sad to say, teachers generally were unaware, until they saw tapes of themselves, that they were treating girls and boys differently.

**TRUTH OR FICTION REVISITED**

*Teachers are actually more likely to accept calling out from boys than from girls. Teachers are apparently more willing to accept misbehavior from boys.*

Other studies show that elementary and secondary teachers give more active teaching attention to boys than to girls. They call on boys more often, ask them more questions, talk to and listen to them more, give them lengthier directions, and praise and criticize them more often (Kelly, 1988; Sadker & Sadker, 1994; Stipek, 1992).

**FIGURE 13.10**

**SEXISM IN THE CLASSROOM.** *Teachers give more active teaching attention to boys than to girls. They call on boys more often, ask them more questions, talk to and listen to them more, give them lengthier directions, and praise and criticize them more often.*

The irony is that our educational system has been responsible for lifting many generations of the downtrodden into the mainstream of U.S. life. Unfortunately, the system may be doing more to encourage development of academic skills in boys than girls.

## SOCIAL AND EMOTIONAL PROBLEMS

Sad to say, somewhere between 17 percent and 22 percent of the children in this country suffer from emotional or behavioral problems that require mental health treatment (Kazdin, 1993b). Yet, from 70 percent to 80 percent of these children may not be getting appropriate mental health services (Tuma, 1989). What are some of the more common psychological problems of middle childhood? In previous chapters, we examined ADHD and learning disabilities. Now we focus on conduct disorders, depression, and school phobia. We also examine some cultural differences in children's behavioral and emotional problems. Finally, we look at characteristics of children who seem to be better able than others to cope with life's stresses. These are the so-called resilient children.

### CONDUCT DISORDERS

*David is a 16-year-old high school dropout. He has just been arrested for the third time in 2 years for stealing video equipment and computers from people's homes. Acting alone, David was caught in each case when he tried to sell the stolen items. In describing his actions in each crime, David expressed defiance and showed a lack of remorse. In fact, he bragged about how often he had gotten away with similar crimes. (Adapted from Halgin & Whitbourne, 1993, p. 335)*

***Conduct disorders*** Disorders marked by persistent breaking of the rules and violations of the rights of others.

Children like David who show ***conduct disorders*** persistently break rules or violate the rights of others (see Figure 13.11). They exhibit behaviors such as lying, stealing, fire setting, truancy, cruelty to animals, and fighting (Frick

FIGURE 13.11

**CONDUCT DISORDERS.** *Children with conduct disorders persistently break rules and violate the rights of others. They exhibit behaviors such as lying, stealing, fire setting, truancy, cruelty to animals, and fighting.*

et al., 1991b). To receive this label, children must have engaged in the troublesome behavior pattern for at least 6 months (Martin & Hoffman, 1990). Conduct disorders typically emerge by 8 years of age (Routh, 1990). They are much more prevalent among boys than girls, by a ratio of about 4 or 5 to 1 (Robins, 1991).

Children with conduct disorders are often involved in sexual activity prior to puberty and often engage in smoking, drinking, and the abuse of various other substances (Capaldi & Dishion, 1993). They typically have a low tolerance for frustration and may have temper flare-ups. They usually blame other people for the scrapes they get into. They believe that they are misperceived and treated unfairly. Their academic accomplishments are usually below grade level, but their intelligence is usually at least average (Lewis, 1991a). Many children with conduct disorders also are diagnosed as having ADHD (Loeber et al., 1992; Pihl & Peterson, 1991).

Conduct disorders show a good deal of stability. One longitudinal study found that children who show conduct disorders in kindergarten through third grade have more contacts with police through adolescence (Spivack et al., 1986). Longitudinal data from the Berkeley Guidance study show that children who had temper tantrums at ages 8 to 10 were more likely to have erratic work lives and get divorced as adults (Caspi et al., 1987). Children with conduct disorders also are more likely to display antisocial behavior and substance abuse as adults (Robins & Price, 1991; Windle, 1991).

**TRUTH OR FICTION REVISITED**

*Actually, children who show conduct disorders in middle childhood are more likely to display antisocial behavior in adulthood.*

**ORIGINS OF CONDUCT DISORDERS** There may be a genetic component in conduct disorders, because they are more likely to be found among the biological parents than the adoptive parents of adopted children with such problems (Lytton, 1990a, b). But the presence of sociopathic models in the family, inconsistent discipline, parents' insensitivity to the child's behavior, and family stress can also contribute to antisocial behavior (Dodge, 1990b; Kazdin, 1992; Vuchinich et al., 1992). Conduct disorders in children also sometimes appear to be direct reflections of marital problems (Grych & Fincham, 1990).

**TREATMENT OF CONDUCT DISORDERS** The treatment of conduct disorders is challenging and less than satisfactory. No one approach has been shown to be particularly effective (Kazdin, 1987). Psychotherapy has not been reliably shown to help. It may be that placing children with conduct disorders in programs or settings with concrete rules and clear rewards for obeying them offers the greatest promise (Colyar, 1991; Lewis, 1991a). Such programs may use operant conditioning. Some of them use a ***token economy.***

Other approaches include teaching aggressive children various methods for coping with feelings of anger that will not violate the rights of others. One promising method combines cognitive and behavioral techniques to teach children how to use problem-solving skills to manage interpersonal situations (Kazdin et al., 1992). Cognitively based treatments have been found to reduce aggressive and antisocial behavior among children at home and in the classroom (Kazdin, 1993b).

***Token economy*** A behavior-modification technique in which persons receive tokens for desirable behavior that can later be exchanged for desired objects and privileges.

Sometimes, the child's parents are integrated into the treatment (Coie & Koeppl, 1990; Dodge, 1993a; Kazdin et al., 1992). Scott Henggeler and his colleagues (Brunk et al., 1987; Henggeler, 1989) have developed an even broader family–ecological approach based on Bronfenbrenner's (1979) ecological theory. Henggeler, like Bronfenbrenner, sees the child as embedded within several systems. He focuses on the reciprocal relationships between the juvenile offender and the systems with which the child interacts. The techniques employed are not unique. Rather, the family–ecological approach attempts to identify as many of the determinants of conduct disorders as possible and to change the child's interactions with as many systems as needed.

Again, we are reminded that children are not islands unto themselves. They influence and are influenced by others. Reciprocal influences need to be studied more carefully if we are to make the most effective interventions.

### CHILDHOOD DEPRESSION

*Kristin, an 11-year-old, feels that "nothing is working out for me." For the past year, she has been failing in school, although she previously had been a B student. She has trouble sleeping, feels tired all the time, and has started refusing to go to school. She cries easily and thinks her peers are making fun of her because she is "ugly and stupid." Her mother recently found a note written by Kristin that said she wanted to jump in front of a car "to end my misery." (Adapted from Weller & Weller, 1991, p. 655)*

**THINKING ABOUT DEVELOPMENT**

Agree or disagree with the following statement and support your answer: "Children have no reason to feel anxious or depressed."

Depressed children (and adults) like Kristin may feel sad, blue, and down in the dumps. They may complain of poor appetite, insomnia, lack of energy and inactivity, loss of self-esteem, difficulty concentrating, loss of interest in other people and activities they usually enjoy, crying, feelings of hopelessness and helplessness, and thoughts of suicide (Kazdin, 1990, 1993a).

But many depressed children do not report, and are not aware of, feelings of sadness. Part of the problem is cognitive-developmental. Children do not

FIGURE 13.12

***DEPRESSION.*** *Depression has complex psychological and, in some cases, biological origins. Adults can help depressed children by involving them in enjoyable activities, encouraging the development of competencies, offering praise when appropriate, and pointing out when children are being too hard on themselves.*

usually recognize depression in themselves until the age of 7 or so. The capacity for concrete operations apparently contributes to children's abilities to perceive internal feeling states (Glasberg & Aboud, 1982).

When children cannot report their feelings, depression is inferred from behavior. Depressed children in middle childhood engage in less social activity and have poorer social skills than nondepressed peers (Kennedy et al., 1989; Rehm & Carter, 1990). In some cases, childhood depression is masked by apparently unrelated behaviors. Conduct disorders, physical complaints, academic problems, and anxiety sometimes are associated with depression (Brady & Kendall, 1992; Cantwell & Baker, 1991b; Panak & Garber, 1992). But it is not clear whether depression causes these problems or whether the problems cause the depression.

**TRUTH OR FICTION REVISITED**

*It is true that misbehavior and other behavioral problems can reflect (and mask) depression in middle childhood.*

We still do not have a very good idea of how many children are depressed, although estimates run about 2 percent of school-age children and 5 to 7 percent of adolescents (Angold & Rutter, 1992; Petersen et al., 1993). While depression occurs equally often in girls and boys during childhood, higher rates are found in females starting in adolescence (Angold & Rutter, 1992; Koenig et al., in press; Petersen et al., 1993). Depressed children frequently continue to have depressive episodes as adults (Cantwell, 1990; Miller et al., 1990a).

**ORIGINS OF DEPRESSION** The origins of depression are complex and varied. Both psychological and biological explanations have been proposed. Psychoanalysts, for example, have suggested that depressed children have typically been severely threatened with parental loss of love for their shortcomings. They tend to repress rather than express feelings of anger. The net result is that they turn their anger inward upon themselves, experiencing it as misery and self-hatred (Weller & Weller, 1991).

Some social-learning theorists focus on relationships between competencies (knowledge and skills) and feelings of self-esteem in explaining depression. Children who gain academic, social, and other competencies also usually have high feelings of self-esteem. Perceived low levels of competence are linked to helplessness, low self-esteem, and depression in children and adolescents (Rehm & Carter, 1990; Weisz et al., 1987). Children who have not developed competencies because of lack of training opportunities, inconsistent parental reinforcement, and so on may also develop feelings of helplessness and hopelessness. Some children do have competencies, but excessive parental expectations might prevent them from crediting themselves for them. For this reason, overly anxious, perfectionistic children are also frequently depressed. They cannot meet their own high standards.

Our perceived reasons for our shortcomings—our ***attributional styles***—can also contribute to feelings of helplessness and hopelessness (Johnson, 1993; Rehm & Carter, 1990). Consider the case of two children who do poorly on a math test. John thinks, "I'm a jerk! I'm just no good in math! I'll never learn." Jim thinks, "That test was tougher than I thought it would be. I'll have to work harder next time." John is perceiving the problem as global (he's "a jerk") and

***Attributional style*** The way in which one is disposed toward interpreting outcomes (successes or failures), as in tending to place blame or responsibility on oneself or external factors.

***Serotonin*** A neurotransmitter that is implicated in behavior disorders such as schizophrenia and depression.

***Norepinephrine*** A neurotransmitter that is implicated in depression. Also called noradrenalin.

stable (he'll ''never learn''). Jim perceives the problem as specific (related to the type of math test the teacher makes up) and unstable (he can change the results by working harder). Depressed children tend to explain negative events in terms of internal, stable, and global causes (Blumberg & Izard, 1985). As a result, they, like John, are more likely than Jim to be depressed.

There is also evidence for genetic factors in depression. Children of depressed parents are at greater risk for depression and other disorders (Dodge, 1990a; Gallimore & Kurdek, 1992; Radke-Yarrow et al., 1992). The concordance rate for depression is about 75 percent for identical twins compared with only 19 percent for fraternal twins (Weller & Weller, 1991). On a neurological level, there is evidence that persistent depression is associated with low utilization of the neurotransmitters ***serotonin*** and ***norepinephrine.***

**TREATMENT OF DEPRESSION** Parents and teachers can do a good deal to alleviate relatively mild feelings of depression among children. They can involve children in enjoyable activities, encourage the step-by-step development of instrumental competencies, offer praise when appropriate, and point out when children are being too hard on themselves. But if feelings of depression persist, treatment is called for.

An approach that combines both biological and psychological intervention often is used. Such an approach includes individual or family psychotherapy, social skills training, and medical management (Weller & Weller, 1991). Antidepressant drugs have shown some usefulness with children (Burke and Puig-Antich, 1990).

## *SCHOOL PHOBIA*

Children with school phobia are emotionally upset at the prospect of going to school. Their upset may take the form of crying, clinging to the parent, and expressing a desire to stay home (see Figure 13.13). Or it may manifest itself in complaints of physical ailments such as headaches and stomach aches. The school-phobic child stays at home with the knowledge of the parent, unlike the

FIGURE 13.13

**SCHOOL PHOBIA.** *A number of comprehensive treatment programs have been developed to help children, like this boy, overcome school phobia. The primary goal of treatment is to get the child back in school as soon as possible.*

truant child who attempts to conceal school absence. The child with school phobia does not show antisocial behaviors such as stealing or lying. School-phobic children often are overly dependent on their parents. Frequently they show symptoms of depression (Berg, 1991; King et al., 1988). An estimated 5 percent of elementary school children and 2 percent of adolescents show school phobia (Brody, 1991b). Girls and boys appear to be equally affected (Berg, 1991).

**Origins of School Phobia** In some cases, school phobia appears to be a form of ***separation-anxiety disorder.*** Separation-anxiety disorder is an extreme form of otherwise normal separation anxiety (discussed in Chapter 7). It is characterized by anxiety about separating from parents and often takes the form of refusal to go to school (Livingston, 1991). But separation anxiety does not appear to be behind all instances of school phobia. Some children avoid school because they perceive it as an unpleasant, unsatisfying, or hostile environment (Pilkington & Piersel, 1991). For example, some children are afraid of doing poorly in school or of being asked to answer questions in class. High parental expectation to perform may contribute to such fears. Other children are fearful of school because of unpleasant and difficult relationships with classmates.

**Treatment of School Phobia** The primary goal is to get the child back in school as soon possible, since many of the symptoms disappear once the child is attending regularly (Berg, 1991). Here are some things parents can do (Brody, 1991b):

- Don't give in to the child's demands to stay home. Tell her she'll feel better once she gets to school and that she can rest there if she needs to.
- Discuss the problem with the child's teacher, principal, and school nurse.
- If there is a specific school-related problem, such as a strict teacher, try to prepare the child to handle the situation.
- Reward the child for attending school.

**Truth or Fiction Revisited**

*Most developmentalists actually suggest that children with school phobia be placed back in school immediately to prevent it from growing worse.*

What if these measures don't work? A variety of therapeutic approaches have been tried (Bernstein & Borchardt, 1991; King et al., 1988; Livingston, 1991). Some focus on using classical conditioning techniques such as systematic desensitization to reduce the child's fear. (You may remember from Chapter 10 that Mary Cover Jones used this method to reduce Peter's fear of rabbits.) Other treatments use operant-conditioning approaches such as rewarding the child for school attendance. Sometimes antidepressant medication has been used in conjunction with the behavioral methods with some success (King et al., 1988; Livingston, 1991).

Comprehensive treatment programs involving a variety of techniques may prove to be most effective. In one approach, both cognitive and behavior methods

***Separation-anxiety disorder*** An extreme form of otherwise normal separation anxiety that is characterized by anxiety about separating from parents and often takes the form of refusal to go to school.

were used to treat school phobia in seven children (Kearney & Silverman, 1990). The techniques used included systematic desensitization, modeling, cognitive restructuring, and shaping and rewarding of school-attending behaviors. Six of the seven children were attending school full-time after treatment and when followed up 6 months later.

## *Culture and Development: Social and Emotional Problems*

The social and emotional problems that children develop are influenced by the cultural context in which they grow up. The child-rearing beliefs, values, and practices of a culture may affect the problems that children show. Cultural attitudes also may influence which child behaviors adults define as problems, as we saw in Chapter 7.

Consider a recent study of parent reports of problem behaviors among Embu children in Kenya, children in Thailand, and African-American and white children in the United States (Weisz et al, 1993). The U.S. white children were rated higher than Thai and Embu youth on problems of undercontrol, such as arguing, disobedience, and cruelty to others. African-American youth fell between the white and Thai children in the ratings. Embu children, by contrast, were rated much higher than the other cultural groups on problems of overcontrol, such as fears, guilt feelings, and various bodily aches and pains. The researchers suggest that these differences in the frequency of problem behaviors may be related to the strict emphasis on obedience and compliance among the Embu, as opposed to the greater independence and emotional expression permitted and often encouraged in the United States.

## *The Resilient Child*

All children experience some stresses in their lives. Some children are exposed to a minimal amount of stress; others, unfortunately, face a much heavier burden. The cumulation of such events as parental discord and/or divorce, parent's loss of a job, living in poverty, being abused or neglected, or having a parent with psychiatric problems places children at high risk for emotional and behavioral maladjustment (Minde, 1991; Reese & Roosa, 1991; Windle, 1992b).

But some children are more resilient than others. That is, they adapt successfully and thrive in the face of the most stressful life events (Kazdin, 1993a; Masten et al., 1990). Consider, for example, the results of a longitudinal study of a multiracial group of children born on the island of Kauai, Hawaii, in 1955 (Werner, 1989, 1990; Werner & Smith, 1992). One-third of the infants were considered at risk because they had experienced stressful births and were reared in poverty conditions in a family marked either by marital discord and divorce or by parental mental illness or alcoholism. While two out of three of these high-risk children later developed behavioral or emotional problems, one-third overcame their stressful childhoods to become competent, confident, and caring young adults.

How are these resilient children different from those who are more vulnerable to stress? Two key factors appear to be the child's personality and the availability of social support.

**Personality Characteristics** At 1 year of age, resilient children are securely attached to their mothers. At the age of 2, they are independent and easygoing, with a high tolerance for frustration, even when they are being abused or neglected. By age 3½, these children are cheerful, persistent, flexible, and good at seeking out help from adults. In middle childhood, they are able to distance themselves from turmoil and are confident and independent (Goleman, 1987). They also have a greater sense of ***self-efficacy,*** that is, greater confidence in their ability to exercise control over their environment and to succeed (Bandura, 1991; Kliewer & Sandler, 1992). What we have described here sounds very much like the temperamentally easy child discussed in Chapter 7 (Werner & Smith, 1992). According to Michael Rutter (1990b), the easy child not only is less likely to be the target of negative behavior from parents, but also is better able to cope with problems when they arise.

***Self-efficacy*** Confidence in one's ability to exercise control over the environment and to succeed.

**SOCIAL SUPPORT** Support from others—parents, grandparents, siblings, peers, or teachers—improves the ability of children (and adults) to cope with life's stresses (DuBois et al., 1992; Ohannessian et al., 1993; Werner & Smith, 1992). One example comes from E. Mavis Hetherington's longitudinal study of divorce and remarriage, which we discussed earlier. You will remember that one of the important characteristics of the children who adjusted well following their parents' divorce was having a relationship with a caring adult whether a parent, other relative, teacher, or neighbor (Hetherington, 1989).

**CULTURE AND DEVELOPMENT: SOCIAL SUPPORT SYSTEMS** Social support systems are particularly important for children who live in poverty and who therefore are at greater risk for adverse developmental outcomes. Ethnic minority children are especially likely to be poor. While 16.9 percent of white U.S. children live in poverty, 39.9 percent of Hispanic and 46.6 percent of African-American children do so (U.S. Bureau of the Census, 1993). Many minority children have extended families that include grandparents and other relatives who either live with them or nearby. Members of extended families provide considerable economic, social, and emotional support for children in the family (Harrison et al., 1990; Levitt et al., 1993; MacPhee et al., 1993; R.D. Taylor et al., 1993). Grandmothers, in particular, play a key role in the parenting of children. In the words of one resident of a low-income African-American community, "If it wasn't for grandmom, the kids wouldn't survive . . . If it wasn't for a lot of the grandmothers, a whole lot of kids wouldn't be able to eat or sleep neither" (Anderson, 1990, p. 90). The involvement of the grandmother and other extended-family members in one-parent families has been shown to facilitate the mother's participation in self-improvement activities, increase the quality of child care, and reduce negative effects of single parenting (Cebello & Olson, 1993; Oyserman et al., 1993; Tolson & Wilson, 1990). For example, one recent study of African-American adolescents and their single mothers found that emotional support from family members reduced mother–adolescent conflict and increased the self-esteem of the youngster (Wadsworth & McLoyd, 1993). Therapists who work with troubled African-American children have found family therapy to be particularly useful, given the importance of the extended family in the African-American community (Allen & Majidi-Ahi, 1991; Gibbs, 1991).

In this chapter and the two preceding it, we have seen that middle childhood is a time of steady growth and change. We have further seen that this period of a child's life isn't as smooth or latent as is often assumed. But most children are able to successfully navigate the challenges of middle childhood, as well as those of the adolescent years that follow. It is time now to leave middle childhood. We are on the threshold of the next major period of development: adolescence.

What percentage of American children live in poverty and are therefore at greater risk for adverse developmental outcomes?

| Ethnic Group | Percent |
|---|---|
| African American | 46.6 |
| Hispanic | 39.9 |
| White | 16.9 |

FIGURE 13.14

***SOCIAL SUPPORT.*** *Support from others—parents, grandparents, siblings, peers, or teachers—helps children cope with life's stresses. Extended family members—such as this grandmother—provide considerable economic, social, and moral support for children who live in poverty.*

## Summary

1. According to Freud, children in the middle years are in the latency stage. Sexual feelings are repressed as children focus on developing cognitive and social skills. Erikson also sees the main developmental task of middle childhood as the mastery of academic and social skills.

2. According to social-learning theory, children in the middle years depend less on external rewards and punishments and increasingly regulate their own behavior.

3. Social cognition refers to the child's understanding of the relationship between oneself and others. A key element in social cognition is the ability to take another's perspective.

4. Children's self-concepts initially focus on concrete, external traits. Later in middle childhood, children define themselves in terms of abstract concepts such as beliefs and motives.

5. Positive self-esteem is important for healthy psychological adjustment and is influenced by the evaluations of parents and peers. In middle childhood, self-concepts become more differentiated, and self-esteem declines. Learned helplessness is the belief that one is unable to control one's environment. It is more prevalent in girls, particularly in areas such as mathematics, and is influenced by parental expectations.

6. Peers become progressively more important as children develop. Attractive, sociable children are most likely to be popular with peers. Aggressive and socially withdrawn children tend to be rejected.

7. In middle childhood, children's conceptions of friendship change from a focus on momentary interactions and common activities to a focus on intimacy, loyalty, and mutual sharing.

8. In middle childhood, parent–child interactions focus on new concerns: school, peers, and chores. Parents do less monitoring of children's activities and more control is transferred to the child. This process is known as *coregulation.*

9. Children of divorced parents generally experience turmoil and downward movement in socioeconomic status. But most children appear to adjust within about 2 years. Gender, temperament, and parenting style influence how well children adapt to divorce. Parents who cooperate in child rearing after a divorce minimize the effects of divorce on their children. Marital conflict is more detrimental to children than living in a single-parent family with low conflict. Children's reactions to stepparents depend on many factors, including gender and closeness to biological parents.

10. Children of employed women do not differ from those of full-time homemakers in their social, emotional, or intellectual development. Maternal employment may benefit school-age children by fostering independence, responsibility, and competence.

11. Schools influence children's IQ scores, achievement, motivation, and career aspirations. Children's readiness to enter school depends on their early life experiences and individual differences in development. Adjustment to kindergarten is made easier when schools provide transition activities between kindergarten and the child's home or preschool experiences.

12. Small classes lead to greater student participation and achievement. Student achievement also is enhanced when teachers emphasize academics, actively instruct, provide feedback, and create a positive classroom climate. Teachers' expectations often influence students' achievement. This is known as the *self-fulfilling prophecy* or *Pygmalion effect.*

13. Teachers give more active teaching attention to boys than girls. They praise and criticize boys more and are more likely to tolerate calling out from boys.

14. Children with conduct disorders are in frequent conflict with society. Physical aggression, stealing, drug abuse, and sexual behavior are common among children with conduct disorders.

15. Childhood depression is characterized by feelings of sadness and hopelessness, low self-esteem, social withdrawal, and inactivity. Children with school phobia are upset at the prospect of going to school. The social and emotional problems that children develop are influenced by the culture in which they grow up.

16. Some children are better able than others to cope with stressful life events. These resilient children tend to have easy temperaments, a sense of self-efficacy, and a good system of social supports.

# ADOLESCENCE

PERHAPS NO OTHER PERIOD OF LIFE IS AS EXCITING—AND AS BEWILDERING—as adolescence. Except for infancy, more changes occur during adolescence than during any other time of life.

In our society, adolescents are ''neither fish nor fowl,'' as the saying goes—neither children nor adults. Adolescents may be old enough to reproduce and are as large as their parents, yet they are required to remain in school through age 16, they may not be allowed to get drivers' licenses until they are 16 or 17, and they cannot attend R-rated films unless accompanied by an adult. Given the restrictions placed on adolescents, their growing yearning for independence, and a sex drive heightened by high levels of sex hormones, it is not surprising that adolescents occasionally are in conflict with their parents.

The capacity to think abstractly and hypothetically emerges during the teenage years. This ability gives rise to a stream of seemingly endless ''Who am I?'' questions, as adolescents search for a sense of identity and ponder the possible directions their adult lives may take.

In Chapters 14, 15, and 16, we explore physical, cognitive, social, and personality development in adolescence.

CHAPTER

14

# ADOLESCENCE:

## PHYSICAL DEVELOPMENT

## Chapter Outline



## Truth or Fiction?

*______ U.S. adolescents are growing taller than their parents.*

*______ Nocturnal emissions in boys accompany "wet dreams."*

*______ Girls are capable of becoming pregnant after they have their first menstrual periods.*

*______ Girls who mature early have higher self-esteem than those who mature late.*

*______ African-American adolescent girls tend to be more satisfied with their bodies than white American girls.*

*______ Homicide is the leading cause of death among male adolescents in the United States.*

*______ You can never be too rich or too thin.*

*______ Some college women control their weight by going on cycles of binge eating followed by self-induced vomiting.*

*______ Substance use and abuse is on the rise among high school and college students.*

*______ Adolescents who are not gay and who do not shoot up drugs need not be concerned about contracting AIDS.*

*______ Some public school districts provide students with condoms to help prevent the spread of AIDS.*

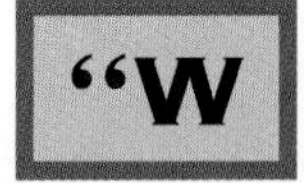

hy is my chest getting bumpy?"
*"Why is my voice acting so funny?"*
*"Why do I get pimples?"*
*"Why am I getting hairy?"*
*"Why is mine not like his?"*
*"What's happening to me?"*

(ADAPTED FROM MAYLE, 1975)

Adolescence often is considered a unique period because of the many changes that occur during this time. Biological change is greater than at any other time except infancy. Height and weight increase markedly, body shape changes, and the capacity to reproduce emerges. The development of abstract thinking ability leads to changes in the self-concept and in conceptions of morality. Partly as a result of these cognitive advances, relationships with peers and parents undergo changes as well (Buchanan et al., 1992; Montemayor et al., 1990).

Adolescence represents a transitional period between childhood and adulthood, a coming of age. In the 19th century, children in the United States assumed adult responsibilities early. Adolescence as a distinct stage of development between childhood and adulthood began to emerge when the demands of an increasingly complex society required a longer period of education and delayed entry into the labor force. It is no longer easy for U.S. adolescents to know when they have made the transition to adulthood. In many preindustrial societies, the transition is marked by clear rites of passage, such as circumcision for boys or special ceremonies surrounding the first menstrual period for girls. But Western societies do not provide such clear rites of passage into adulthood, with the exception of the Jewish tradition of the bar mitzvah for boys and the bat mitzvah for girls. One legally becomes an adult at different ages, depending on whether one is buying a drink, driving a car, voting, or marrying (Atwater, 1992).

In this chapter, we focus on the biological and physical changes of adolescence, leaving coverage of cognitive and social developments for the last two chapters. We start by looking at some theoretical views of adolescence. Next we examine the many changes that occur during puberty. Finally, we look at the health and health problems of adolescents.

## THEORETICAL INTERLUDE: VIEWS OF ADOLESCENT DEVELOPMENT

It is often claimed that adolescence is characterized by wildly fluctuating, unpredictable mood swings and by serious conflicts and rebellion against one's parents (Brooks-Gunn, 1991b; Offer & Church, 1991a). Parents of teens, as well as psychologists, may be quick to endorse this claim. Let us explore some of these theoretical views about the nature of adolescent development and see if there is any basis for them.

**THINKING ABOUT DEVELOPMENT**

Is adolescence a period of "sturm und drang"—storm and stress? If so, why?

### *STORM AND STRESS?*

The idea that adolescence is an important and separate developmental stage was first proposed by G. Stanley Hall (1904), an early American psychologist. Hall believed that adolescence is marked by intense turmoil. He used the term "sturm und drang'' (or ''storm and stress'') to refer to the conflicts and stresses experienced during this stage. According to Hall, adolescents swing back and forth between happiness and sadness, overconfidence and self-doubt, dependence and independence. Hall believed that adolescent mood swings and conflicts with parents are a necessary part of growing up. He felt that children have to rebel against their parents and their parents' values in order to make the transition to adulthood (Offer & Church, 1991b).

## Psychoanalytic Views

Sigmund Freud (1964) placed relatively little emphasis on adolescence, since he believed that the first 5 years of life are the most critical. According to Freud, as you may recall from Chapter 2, we enter the ***genital stage*** of psychosexual development at puberty. Hormonal changes trigger the reemergence of sexual urges, which were repressed during the latency stage. Sexual feelings initially are aimed toward the parent of the other gender, as they were during the genital stage, but they become transferred, or displaced, onto other adults or adolescents of the other gender.

Anna Freud (1969), Sigmund's daughter, saw adolescence as a turbulent period resulting from an increase in the sex drive. These sexual feelings are assumed to cause anxiety and uncertainty. Conflict arises as the ego and superego try to keep these surging sexual impulses in check and redirect them from the parents to more acceptable outlets. The result is unpredictable behavior, defiance of parents, confusion, and mood swings. Anna Freud, like G. Stanley Hall, believed that adolescent turmoil not only is common but actually necessary for normal development. Other psychoanalysts often share this view (Blos, 1988).

## Current Views

Recent research has challenged the view that ''storm and stress'' is either normal or beneficial for adolescents (Buchanan et al., 1992; Larson, 1991). Neither violent mood swings nor deep-rooted parental conflicts appear to be inevitable. Those teens who encounter several life changes at the same time, such as starting puberty, changing schools, breaking up with a boyfriend or girlfriend, and so on, are more likely than other teens to experience emotional distress (Larson & Ham, 1993). But most teenagers report feeling happy with their lives and only a few (perhaps 20 percent) develop some sort of emotional disturbance (Offer & Church, 1991a; Rutter, 1990a).

Teenagers do appear to experience wider and more frequent daily emotional fluctuations than adults. But they are no more moody than younger children. One study, for example, found that fifth-graders showed as much variability in their moods as ninth-graders (Larson, 1991).

It is also true that adolescence often is accompanied by increased conflict between children and parents and by increased emotional distance between them (Paikoff & Brooks-Gunn, 1991a; Smetana et al., 1991b; Steinberg, 1990b). These conflicts seem to be greatest in early adolescence. They usually do not involve serious issues, however, but instead are characterized by bickering and squabbling about everyday matters such as chores, personal appearance, and curfews. Indeed, adolescents generally do not feel that they have major problems with their parents (Offer & Church, 1991b).

So, most adolescents do not seem to undergo a period of ''storm and stress.'' Some adolescents do experience problems, and we shall take a closer look at

***Genital stage*** In psychoanalytic theory, the fifth and final stage of psychosexual development in which gratification is attained through sexual intercourse with an individual of the other gender.

FIGURE 14.1

***Storm and Stress?*** *Recent research has challenged the view that ''storm and stress'' is either normal or beneficial for adolescents. Neither violent mood swings nor deep-rooted parental conflicts appear to be inevitable, and most teenagers report feeling happy with their lives.*

them later in the chapter. Nevertheless, all adolescents are faced with the challenge of adapting to the numerous biological, cognitive, and social changes in their lives. Let us now begin to explore these changes, starting with the biological changes of puberty.

## PUBERTY

***Puberty*** is defined as a stage of development characterized by reaching sexual maturity and the ability to reproduce. The onset of adolescence coincides with the advent of puberty. Puberty, however, is a biological concept, whereas adolescence is a psychosocial concept with biological correlates.

Puberty is controlled by a complex ***feedback loop*** involving the ***hypothalamus, pituitary gland,*** gonads—ovaries in females and testes in males—and hormones (Kulin, 1991a; Susman & Dorn, 1991). The hypothalamus sends signals to the pituitary gland, which, in turn, releases hormones that control physical growth and the functioning of the gonads. The gonads respond to pituitary hormones by increasing their production of sex hormones (androgens and estrogens). The sex hormones further stimulate the hypothalamus, thus perpetuating the feedback loop.

The sex hormones also trigger the development of both the primary and secondary sex characteristics. The ***primary sex characteristics*** are the structures that make reproduction possible. In girls, these structures are the ovaries, vagina, uterus, and Fallopian tubes. In boys, they are the penis, testes, prostate gland, and seminal vesicles. The ***secondary sex characteristics*** are physical indicators of sexual maturation that do not involve the reproductive structures, such as breast development, deepening of the voice, and the appearance of facial, pubic, and ***axillary*** (underarm) hair. Let us now explore the physical changes of puberty, starting with the growth spurt and then examining other pubertal changes in boys and girls involving the primary and secondary sex characteristics.

***Puberty*** The biological stage of development characterized by changes that lead to reproductive capacity. Puberty signals the beginning of adolescence.

***Feedback loop*** A system in which the hypothalamus, pituitary gland, and gonads regulate each other's functioning through a series of hormonal messages.

***Hypothalamus*** A pea-sized structure that is located above the pituitary gland in the brain and is involved in the regulation of body temperature, motivation (for example, hunger, thirst, sex), and emotion.

***Pituitary gland*** The body's ''master gland,'' which is located in the lower central part of the brain and secretes many hormones essential to development, such as oxytocin, prolactin, and growth hormone.

***Primary sex characteristics*** The structures that make reproduction possible.

***Secondary sex characteristics*** Physical indicators of sexual maturation that do not involve the reproductive structures.

***Axillary*** Underarm.

## Growth Spurt

The stable growth patterns in height and weight that characterize early and middle childhood come to an abrupt end with the adolescent growth spurt. Girls start to spurt in height sooner than boys, at an average age of a little over 10. Boys start to spurt about 2 years later, at an average age of about 12 (Malina, 1991a). Girls and boys reach their periods of ***peak growth*** in height about 2 years after the growth spurt begins, at about 12 and 14 years, respectively (see Figure 14.2). The spurt in height for both girls and boys continues for about another 2 years at a gradually declining pace. Boys grow more than girls do during their spurt, averaging nearly 4 inches per year during the fastest year of the spurt compared with slightly over 3 inches per year for girls. Overall, boys add an average of 14½ inches to their height during the spurt, and girls add a little over 13 inches (Tanner, 1991a).

***Peak growth*** A period of growth during which the rate of growth is at its maximum.

Adolescents begin to spurt in weight about half a year after they begin to spurt in height. The period of peak growth in weight occurs about a year and a half after the onset of the spurt. As is the case with height, the growth spurt in weight then continues for a little more than 2 years for both girls and boys. As you can see in Figure 14.3, girls are taller and heavier than boys from about ages 9 or 10 until about age 13 or 14 since their growth spurt occurs earlier. Once boys begin their growth spurt, they catch up with girls and eventually become taller and heavier (Malina, 1990).

Since the spurt in weight lags behind the spurt in height, many adolescents are relatively slender as compared with their preadolescent and post-adolescent statures (Meredith, 1987). However, adolescents tend to eat enormous quantities of food to fuel their growth spurts. Active 14- and 15-year-old boys may consume 5,000 to 6,000 calories a day without becoming obese. If they were to eat this much 20 years later, they might gain upwards of 100 pounds per year. Little wonder that adults fighting the dismal battle of the bulge stare at adolescents in amazement as they wolf down french fries and shakes at the fast-food counter and later go out for pizza!

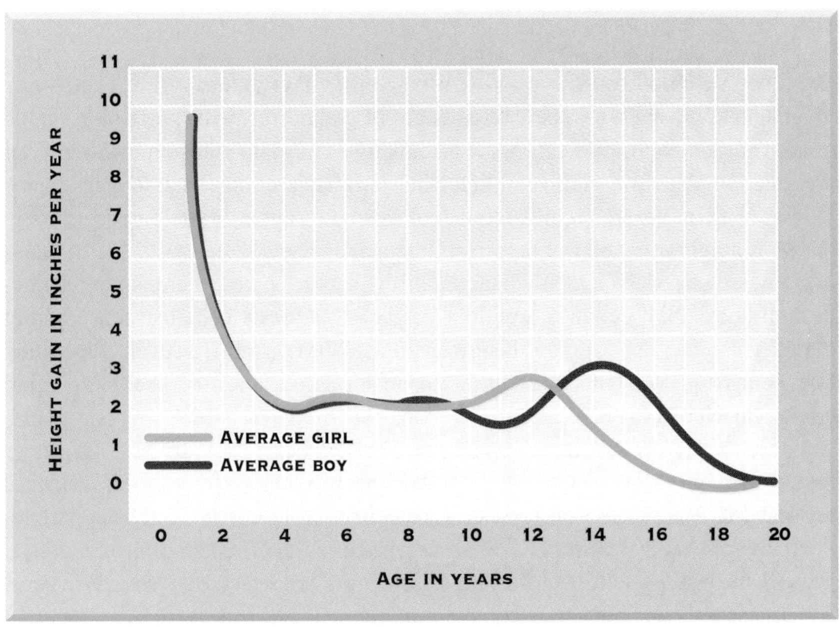


**FIGURE 14.2**

**Spurts in Growth.** *Girls begin the adolescent growth spurt nearly 2 years earlier than boys. Girls and boys reach their periods of peak growth about 2 years after the spurt begins, at about 12 and 14 years, respectively.*

FIGURE 14.3

**GROWTH CURVES FOR HEIGHT AND WEIGHT.** *Girls are taller and heavier than boys from about age 9 or 10 until about age 13 or 14 since their growth spurt occurs earlier. Once boys begin their growth spurt, they catch up with girls and eventually become taller and heavier. (Source: Department of Health and Human Services).*

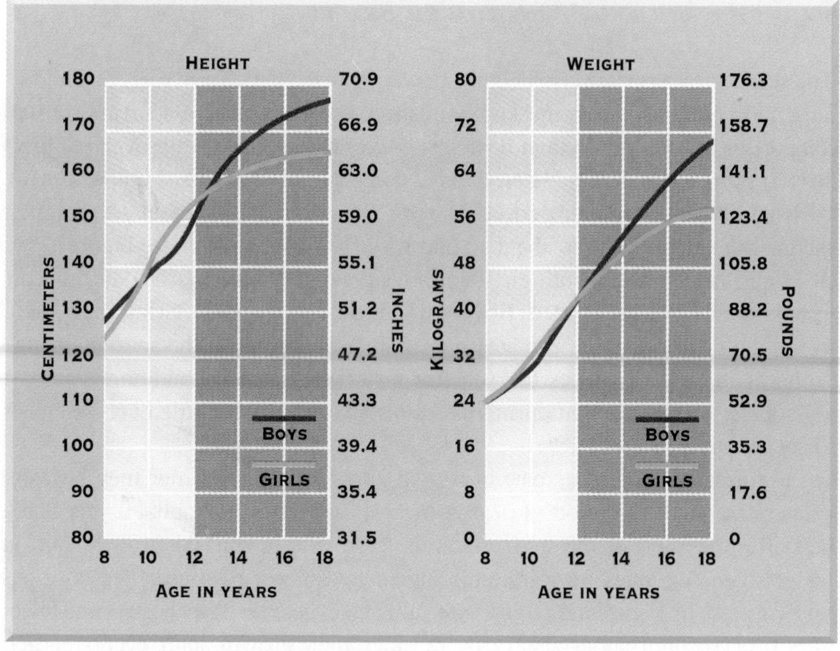


Girls' and boys' body shapes begin to differ in adolescence. For one thing, boys' shoulders become broader than those of girls, while the hip dimensions of both genders do not differ much. So, girls have relatively broader hips compared with their shoulders, whereas the opposite is true for boys. You've also noticed that a girl's body shape is more rounded than that of a boy. This is due to the fact that during puberty, girls gain almost twice as much fatty tissue as boys do, while boys gain twice as much muscle tissue as girls (Malina, 1991b). Thus, a larger proportion of a male's body weight is composed of his muscle mass, whereas a relatively larger part of a female's body weight is composed of fatty tissue.

**INDIVIDUAL DIFFERENCES IN GROWTH-SPURT PATTERNS** The figures given above are averages. Few of us begin or end our growth spurts right on the mark. Children who spurt earlier are also likely to wind up with somewhat shorter legs and longer torsos, while children who spurt late are somewhat longer-legged. However, there are no significant differences between early and late spurters in the total height attained at maturity (Tanner, 1991a).

Regardless of the age at which the growth spurt begins, there is a moderate-to-high correlation between a child's height at the onset of adolescence and at maturity (Tanner, 1989). Are there exceptions? Of course. However, everything else being equal, a tall child has a reasonable expectation of becoming a tall adult, and vice versa.

***Asynchronous growth*** Imbalanced growth, such as that which occurs during the early part of adolescence and causes many adolescents to appear gawky.

**ASYNCHRONOUS GROWTH** Adolescents are often referred to as awkward and gawky. A major reason for this is ***asynchronous growth***—different parts of the body grow at different rates. In an exception to the principle of proximodistal growth, the hands and feet mature before the arms and legs do. As a consequence, adolescent girls and boys may complain of big hands or feet. And, in an apparent reversal of the cephalocaudal growth trend, legs reach their peak growth before the shoulders and chest. This means that boys stop growing out of their pants about a year before they stop growing out of their jackets (Tanner, 1989).

**Secular trend** An historical trend toward increasing adult height and earlier puberty.

**SECULAR TREND IN GROWTH** Children in the 20th century have grown dramatically more rapidly and wound up taller than children from earlier times (Meredith, 1987). This historical trend toward increasing adult height, which also has been accompanied by an earlier onset of puberty, is known as the ***secular trend.*** Figure 14.4 shows that Swedish boys and girls grew more rapidly in 1938 and 1968 than they did in 1883 and ended up several centimeters taller. At the age of 15, the boys were more than 6 inches taller and the girls were more than 3 inches taller, on the average, than their counterparts from the previous century (Tanner, 1989). The occurrence of a secular trend in height and also in weight has been documented in nearly all European countries and the United States.

However, it turns out that children from middle- and upper-class families in industrialized countries have now stopped growing taller, whereas their poorer counterparts continue to make gains in height from generation to generation (Tanner, 1989). Why?

## TRUTH OR FICTION REVISITED

*U.S. adolescents are no longer generally growing taller than their parents. However, there is still some tendency in families of low socioeconomic status for children to grow taller than their parents.*

Nutrition apparently plays an important role in the rate of growth and size at maturity. U.S. government surveys have shown that children from middle- and upper-class families are taller and heavier than their age-mates from lower-class families. This in and of itself would not be very convincing. It could, for

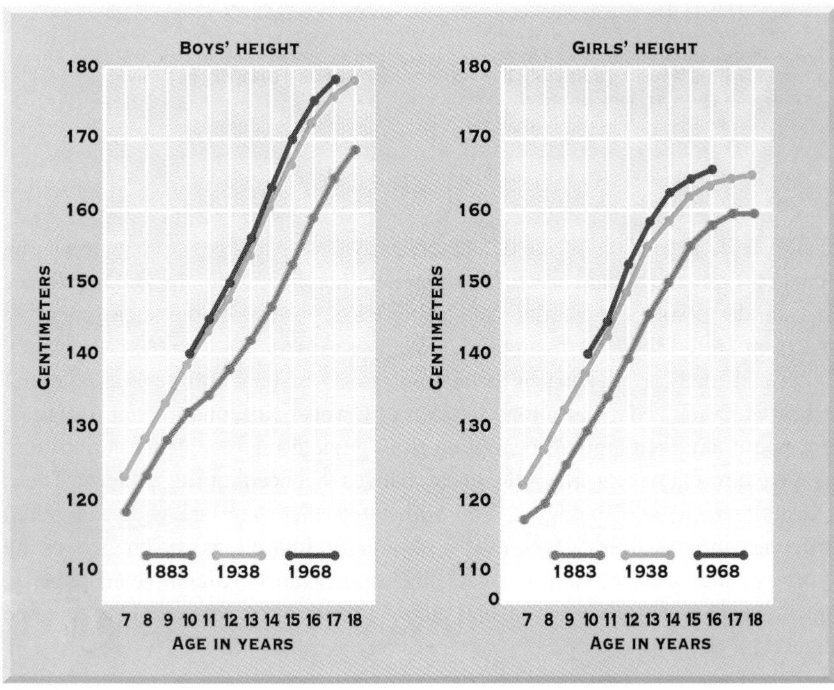


FIGURE 14.4

***ARE WE STILL GROWING TALLER THAN OUR PARENTS?*** *Twentieth-century children have grown more rapidly and grown taller than children in preceding centuries. However, it seems that children from affluent families are no longer growing taller than their parents. But children from the lower part of the socioeconomic spectrum are still doing so. (Source: Tanner, 1989).*

**TABLE 14.1**

***STAGES OF PUBERTAL DEVELOPMENT***

| STAGES OF PUBERTAL DEVELOPMENT IN FEMALES | |
|---|---|
| BEGINNING SOMETIME BETWEEN AGES 8 AND 11 | PITUITARY HORMONES STIMULATE OVARIES TO INCREASE PRODUCTION OF ESTROGEN.<br>INTERNAL REPRODUCTIVE ORGANS BEGIN TO GROW. |
| BEGINNING SOMETIME BETWEEN AGES 9 AND 15 | FIRST THE AREOLA (THE DARKER AREA AROUND THE NIPPLE) AND THEN THE BREASTS INCREASE IN SIZE AND BECOME MORE ROUNDED.<br>PUBIC HAIR BECOMES DARKER AND COARSER.<br>GROWTH IN HEIGHT CONTINUES.<br>BODY FAT CONTINUES TO ROUND BODY CONTOURS.<br>A NORMAL VAGINAL DISCHARGE BECOMES NOTICEABLE.<br>SWEAT AND OIL GLANDS INCREASE IN ACTIVITY, AND ACNE MAY APPEAR.<br>INTERNAL AND EXTERNAL REPRODUCTIVE ORGANS AND GENITALS GROW, WHICH MAKES THE VAGINA LONGER AND THE LABIA MORE PRONOUNCED. |
| BEGINNING SOMETIME BETWEEN AGES 10 AND 16 | AREOLA AND NIPPLES GROW, OFTEN FORMING A SECOND MOUND STICKING OUT FROM THE ROUNDED BREAST MOUND.<br>PUBIC HAIR BEGINS TO GROW IN A TRIANGULAR SHAPE AND TO COVER THE CENTER OF THE MONS.<br>UNDERARM HAIR APPEARS.<br>MENARCHE OCCURS.<br>INTERNAL REPRODUCTIVE ORGANS CONTINUE TO DEVELOP.<br>OVARIES MAY BEGIN TO RELEASE MATURE EGGS CAPABLE OF BEING FERTILIZED.<br>GROWTH IN HEIGHT SLOWS. |
| BEGINNING SOMETIME BETWEEN AGES 12 AND 19 | BREASTS NEAR ADULT SIZE AND SHAPE.<br>PUBIC HAIR FULLY COVERS THE MONS AND SPREADS TO THE TOP OF THIGHS.<br>THE VOICE MAY DEEPEN SLIGHTLY (BUT NOT AS MUCH AS IN MALES).<br>MENSTRUAL CYCLES GRADUALLY BECOME MORE REGULAR.<br>SOME FURTHER CHANGES IN BODY SHAPE MAY OCCUR INTO THE YOUNG WOMAN'S EARLY TWENTIES. |

NOTE: THIS TABLE IS A GENERAL GUIDELINE. CHANGES MAY NORMALLY APPEAR SOONER OR LATER THAN SHOWN, AND NOT ALWAYS IN THE INDICATED SEQUENCE.
SOURCE: COPYRIGHT © 1990 BY THE KINSEY INSTITUTE FOR RESEARCH IN SEX, GENDER, AND REPRODUCTION. FROM THE KINSEY INSTITUTE NEW REPORT ON SEX. REPRINTED WITH PERMISSION FROM ST. MARTIN'S PRESS, NEW YORK, NY.

example, be argued that genetic factors provide advantages that increase the chances for financial gain as well as for greater height and weight. But remember that children from the middle- and upper-class portion of the socioeconomic spectrum are no longer growing taller. Perhaps Americans who have had nutritional and medical advantages have simply reached their full genetic potential in height. Continued gains among families of lower socioeconomic status suggest that poorer children are still benefiting from gradual improvements in nutrition.

We now examine some of the other changes that occur during puberty. These are summarized in Table 14.1. You will notice that there are wide individual differences in the timing of the events of puberty. In a group of teenagers of the same age and gender, you may well find some who have completed puberty, others who haven't even started, and others who are somewhere in between (see Figure 14.5).

| Stages of pubertal development in Males | |
|---|---|
| Beginning sometime between ages 9 and 15 | Testicles begin to grow.<br>Skin of the scrotum becomes redder and coarser.<br>A few straight pubic hairs appear at the base of the penis.<br>Muscle mass develops and boy begins to grow taller.<br>The areola grows larger and darker. |
| Beginning sometime between ages 11 and 16 | The penis begins to grow longer.<br>The testicles and scrotum continue to grow.<br>Pubic hair becomes coarser, more curled, and spreads to cover area between the legs.<br>The body gains in height.<br>The shoulders broaden.<br>The hips narrow.<br>The larynx enlarges, resulting in a deepening of the voice.<br>Sparse facial and underarm hair appears. |
| Beginning sometime between ages 11 and 17 | The penis begins to increase in circumference as well as in length (though more slowly).<br>The testicles continue to increase in size.<br>The texture of the pubic hair is more like an adult's.<br>Growth of facial and underarm hair increases.<br>Shaving may begin.<br>First ejaculation occurs.<br>In nearly half of all boys, gynecomastia (breast enlargement) occurs, which then decreases in a year or two.<br>Increased skin oils may produce acne. |
| Beginning sometime between ages 14 and 18 | The body nears final adult height and the genitals achieve adult shape and size, with pubic hair spreading to the thighs and slightly upward toward the belly.<br>Chest hair appears.<br>Facial hair reaches full growth.<br>Shaving becomes more frequent.<br>For some young men, further increases in height, body hair, and muscle growth and strength continue into their early twenties. |

## *Pubertal Changes in Boys*

At puberty, the pituitary gland stimulates the testes to increase their output of testosterone, leading to further development of the male genitals. The first visible sign of puberty is accelerated growth of the testes, which begins at an average age of about 11½, although a range of ages of plus or minus 2 years is considered perfectly normal. Testicular growth further accelerates testosterone production and other pubertal changes. The penis begins a spurt of accelerated growth about a year later, and still later, pubic hair begins a growth spurt.

Underarm, or axillary, hair appears at about age 15. Facial hair is at first a fuzz on the upper lip. An actual beard does not develop for another 2 to 3 years—only half of American boys shave (of necessity) by 17. The beard and chest hair continue to develop past the age of 20.

***Larynx*** (LAR-inks) The part of the throat that contains the vocal cords.

***Castrate*** To remove the testes, preventing production of sperm and testosterone.

At 14 or 15, the voice deepens because of growth of the "voice box," or ***larynx,*** and the lengthening of the vocal cords. The developmental process is gradual, and adolescent boys sometimes encounter an embarrassing cracking of the voice. Because women were not allowed to sing in the opera during most of pre-19th-century Europe, many boys with promising voices were ***castrated*** so they could assume women's roles later on. So-called *castrati* were used in the pope's choir until early in the last century. At that time nothing was known of hormones, so it was not understood that castration prevented the appearance of secondary sex characteristics in boys by depriving them of testosterone.

Testosterone also triggers the development of acne, which afflicts between 75 percent and 90 percent of adolescents (Lowrey, 1986). Severe acne is manifested by multiple pimples and blackheads on the face, chest, and back. Although

FIGURE 14.5

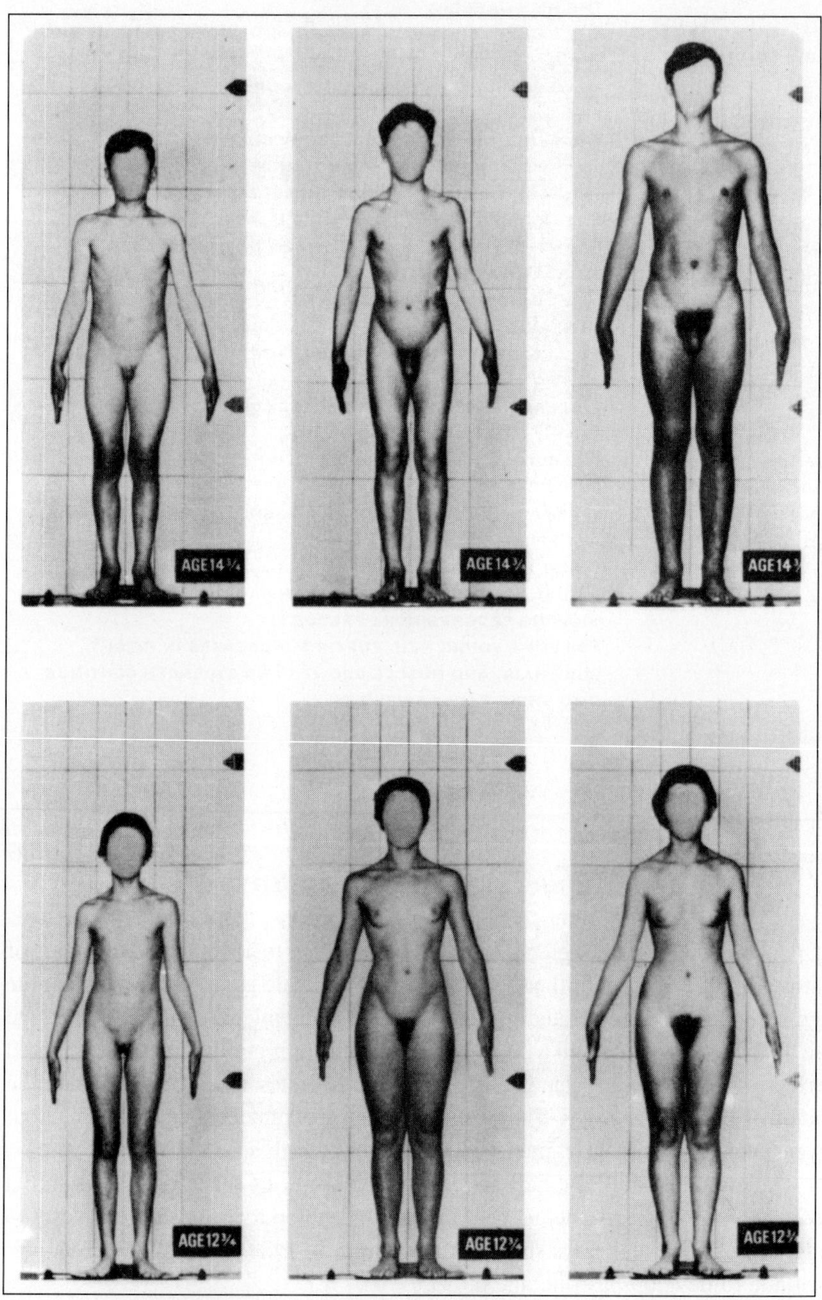


***VARIATIONS IN PUBERTAL DEVELOPMENT.*** *There are wide individual differences in the timing of the events of puberty. In a group of teenagers of the same age and gender, you may find some who have completed puberty, others who haven't even started, and others who are somewhere in between.*

boys are more prone to acne than girls, we cannot say that girls suffer less from it. In our society, a smooth complexion has a higher value for girls than boys, and girls with cases of acne that boys would consider mild may suffer terribly.

Males are capable of producing erections in early infancy (and some male babies are born with erections), but the phenomenon is not a frequent one until age 13 or 14. Many junior high school boys worry that they will be caught with erections when walking between classes or when asked to stand before the class. The organs that produce ***semen*** grow rapidly, and boys typically ejaculate seminal fluid by age 13 or 14—about 1½ years after the penis begins its growth spurt (Kulin, 1991b)—although here, too, there is much individual variation. About a year later they begin to have ***nocturnal emissions,*** also called "wet dreams" because of the myth that emissions accompany erotic dreams. However, nocturnal emissions and erotic dreams need not coincide at all. Mature sperm are found in ejaculatory emissions by about the age of 15. And so ejaculation is not adequate evidence of reproductive capacity. Ejaculatory ability in boys usually precedes the presence of mature sperm by at least a year. Girls also typically menstruate before they can reproduce.

***Semen*** The fluid that contains sperm.

***Nocturnal emission*** Emission of seminal fluid while asleep.

***Gynecomastia*** (gone-uh-co-MAST-tee-uh) Temporary enlargement of the breasts in adolescent males.

***Epiphyseal closure*** (ep-pee-FEES-ee-al) The process by which the cartilage that separates the long end (epiphysis) of a bone from the main part of the bone turns to bone.

***Mammary glands*** Glands that secrete milk.

**TRUTH OR FICTION REVISITED**

*It is not true that nocturnal emissions in boys accompany "wet dreams." Nocturnal emissions can occur when boys are dreaming about nonerotic themes or when they are not dreaming at all.*

Nearly half of all boys experience temporary enlargement of the breasts, or ***gynecomastia.*** This condition probably stems from the small amount of female sex hormones secreted by the testes (Eil, 1991).

At 20 or 21, men stop growing taller because testosterone causes ***epiphyseal closure,*** preventing the long bones from making further gains in length. And so, puberty draws to a close.

### PUBERTAL CHANGES IN GIRLS

In girls, the pituitary gland signals the ovaries to vastly increase estrogen production at puberty. Estrogen may stimulate the growth of breast tissue ("breast buds") as early as the ages of 8 or 9, but the breasts usually begin to enlarge during the 10th year. The development of fatty tissue and ducts elevates the areas of the breasts surrounding the nipples and causes the nipples themselves to protrude. The breasts typically reach full size in about 3 years, but the ***mammary glands*** do not mature fully until childbirth.

Estrogen also promotes the growth of the fatty and supporting tissue in the hips and buttocks, which, along with the widening of the pelvis, causes the hips to become rounded. Growth of fatty deposits and connective tissue varies considerably. For this reason, some girls develop pronounced breasts, whereas others may have relatively large hips.

Small amounts of androgens produced by girls' adrenal glands, along with estrogen, stimulate the growth of pubic and axillary hair, beginning at about the age of 11. Excessive androgen production can darken or increase the amount of facial hair.

***Labia*** The major and minor lips of the female's genitalia.

***Clitoris*** A female sex organ that is highly sensitive to sexual stimulation but not directly involved in reproduction.

***Menarche*** (men-NARK-ee) The onset of menstruation.

While estrogen causes the ***labia,*** vagina, and uterus to develop during puberty, androgens cause the ***clitoris*** to develop. The vaginal lining varies in thickness according to the amount of estrogen in the bloodstream.

Estrogen typically brakes the female growth spurt some years before testosterone brakes that of males. Girls deficient in estrogen during their late teens may grow quite tall, but most girls reach their heights because of normal, genetically determined variations.

**MENARCHE** *Menarche* (first menstruation) commonly occurs between the ages of 11 and 14. But it is quite normal for menarche to occur as early as age 9 or as late as age 16 (Golub, 1992). In the middle 1800s, European girls first menstruated at about the age of 17, as shown in Figure 14.6. But during the past century and a half, the processes of puberty have occurred at progressively earlier ages in Western nations, an example of the secular trend in development. By the 1960s, the average age of menarche in the United States had plummeted to its current figure of 12½ (Frisch, 1991; Tanner, 1991b). What accounts for the earlier age of puberty? One view is that body weight may trigger pubertal changes. As mentioned earlier, today's children are larger probably because of improved nutrition and health care. The average body weight for triggering menarche depends on one's height. For females ranging from 5 feet to 5½ feet tall, the average triggering weight is between 97 and 114 pounds (Frisch, 1991). No single theory of the onset of puberty has found wide acceptance. In any event, the average age of the advent of puberty appears to have leveled off in recent years. The precipitous drop suggested in Figure 14.6 seems to have come to an end.

**HORMONAL REGULATION OF THE MENSTRUAL CYCLE** While testosterone levels remain fairly stable in boys, estrogen and progesterone levels vary markedly and regulate the menstrual cycle. Following menstruation—the sloughing off of the endometrium—estrogen levels increase, leading once more

**FIGURE 14.6**

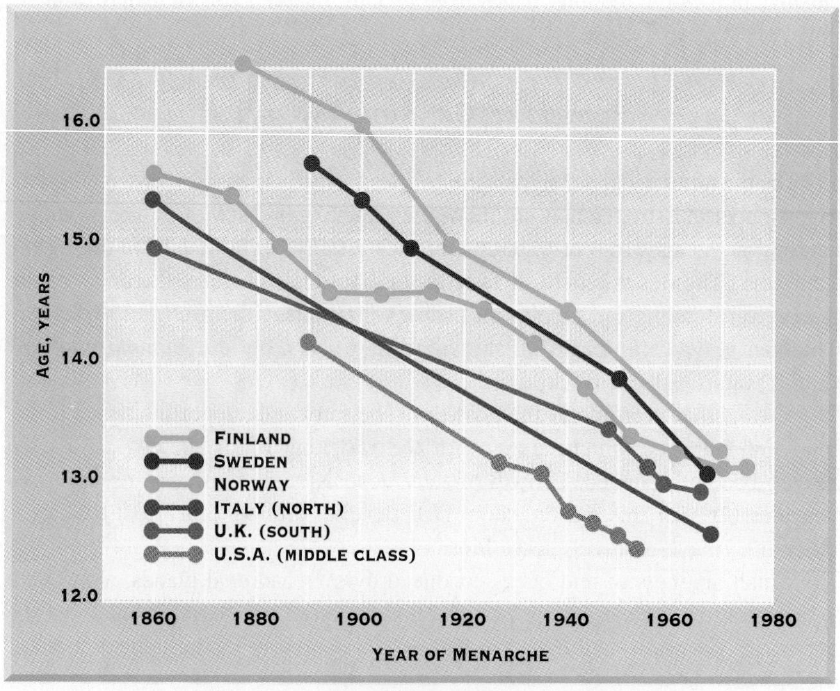


**THE DECLINE IN AGE AT MENARCHE.** *The age at menarche has been declining since the mid-1800s among girls in Western nations, apparently because of improved nutrition and health care. Menarche may be triggered by the accumulation of a critical percentage of body fat. (Source: Tanner, 1989).*

to the growth of endometrial tissue. Once girls have begun to ovulate, which usually occurs about 12 to 18 months after menarche, the surge of estrogen also causes an ovum to ripen. The ripe ovum is released by the ovary when estrogen reaches peak blood levels. Then the inner lining of the uterus thickens in response to the secretion of progesterone. In this way, it gains the capacity to support an embryo if fertilization should occur. If the ovum is not fertilized, estrogen and progesterone levels drop suddenly, triggering menstruation once again.

The average menstrual cycle is 28 days, but variation between girls and in the same girl is common. Girls' cycles are often irregular for a few years after menarche but later tend to assume patterns that are reasonably regular. The majority of menstrual cycles during the first 2 years or so after menarche occur without ovulation having taken place. But keep in mind that in any given individual cycle, an ovum may be produced, making pregnancy possible (Golub, 1992). So it is possible to become pregnant shortly after the onset of menarche.

**TRUTH OR FICTION REVISITED**

*The* majority *of menstrual cycles during the first 2 years after menarche occur without the release of an ovum. However, it is important to remember that in a normal individual cycle, an ovum* may *be produced, making pregnancy possible.*

**Psychological Impact of Menarche** In different times, in different places, menarche has had different meanings. The Manus of New Guinea greet menarche with elaborate ceremony (Golub, 1992). The other girls of the village sleep in the menstruating girl's hut. They feast and have parties.

In the West, menstruation has historically received a mixed response (Golub, 1992). The menstrual flow itself has generally been seen, erroneously, as polluting, and menstruating women have been stereotyped as irrational. Menarche itself has generally been perceived as the event in which a girl suddenly develops into a woman, but because of taboos and the unjustified prejudice against menstruating women, girls usually matured in ignorance of menarche.

Things are changing. In the United States, most of the negative stereotypes about menstruation are diminishing, but menstruation is still not considered an appropriate topic for "polite conversation" (Grief & Ulman, 1982). In one study, a minority of 9- to 12-year-old girls in suburban Midwest schools still clung to certain "taboos" and negative feelings: 36 percent of them believed that menstruating women should not go swimming; 16 percent believed that strenuous sports should be avoided; and 10 percent still saw menstruation as dirty or unclean (Williams, 1983). On the positive side, 64 percent of the 9- to 12-year-old girls in the Williams (1983) study agreed that "Menstruation is exciting because it means a girl is growing up" (p. 146). Also, most premenarcheal girls hope that they will "get their periods" when their age-mates do (Petersen, 1983), just as they hope that their breasts will develop at the same time.

About 90 to 95 percent of girls receive advance information about menstruation, usually from their mothers, sisters, and girlfriends (Brooks-Gunn and Ruble, 1983). Early information about menstruation appears to foster more positive feelings toward it (Brooks-Gunn, 1991c; Golub, 1992).

## *EARLY AND LATE MATURERS*

One of the authors (S. R.) remembers Al from his high school days. When Al entered the ninth grade, he was all of 14, but he was also about 6 feet 3 inches tall, with broad shoulders and arms thick with muscle. His face was cut from rock, and his beard was already dark. Al paraded down the hallways with an entourage of male and female admirers. When there were shrieks of anticipation, you could bet that Al was coming around the corner. Al was given a wide berth in the boys' room. He would have to lean back when he combed his waxed hair up and back—otherwise his head would be too high for the mirror. At that age, S. R. and his friends liked to tell themselves that Al was not all that bright. (This stereotype is unfounded, as we shall see.) Nevertheless, S. R. and his friends were extremely envious of Al.

Al had matured early, and he had experienced the positive aspects of maturing early. What causes some children to mature earlier or later than others? Genetic, dietary, and health factors all seem to influence the timing of puberty. And one controversial new theory suggests that childhood stress may trigger early puberty in girls (see Focus on Research). Early or late maturation can play an important role in the self-esteem and adjustment of adolescent males and females.

**EARLY AND LATE MATURATION IN BOYS** Studies are somewhat mixed in their findings about boys who mature early, but the weight of the evidence suggests that the effects of early maturation are generally positive (Alsaker,

### FOCUS ON RESEARCH

### *IS EARLY PUBERTY LINKED TO CHILDHOOD STRESS?*

We have seen that heredity, diet, and health influence the timing of puberty. We also have discussed the historical secular trend toward an average earlier age of menarche over the past 100 years. More recently, Jay Belsky and his colleagues (Belsky et al., 1991a, b) have proposed that early puberty also may be linked to childhood stress.

Belsky and his co-workers were struck by the fact that girls from father-absent homes or from homes where parents fought frequently experienced earlier menarche than girls from homes with little conflict or no divorce (Steinberg, 1988, 1989; Surbey, 1990). A study of girls in New Zealand (Moffitt et al., 1992) confirmed these findings. Half of the girls who reached menarche at age 12 or earlier lived in homes where the father was absent, most of them due to divorce. Only a quarter of girls with a late onset of menarche (age 14 or later) had an absent father. And, the more family conflict, the earlier the onset of menarche.

Belsky and his colleagues account for these findings by proposing that evolution induces people who grow up in stressful conditions to reproduce early to ensure that their genes survive into the next generation (Goleman, 1991). There is, in fact, some evidence that external factors such as stress and social contact affect hormone levels and may either delay menstruation or cause it to occur early (Hood, 1991; Paikoff et al., 1991). The influence of the environment on hormones is illustrated by the fact that college women who spend a lot of time together, such as roommates or close friends, gradually develop similar menstrual cycles (Golub, 1992).

Belsky's theory has its share of critics (Hinde, 1991; Maccoby, 1991a), including Terrie Moffitt, one of Belsky's own colleagues. Moffitt (Moffitt et al., 1992) proposes a simpler explanation for the relationship between parental conflict, divorce, and early puberty in daughters. She notes that because of genetic factors, girls tend to reach puberty at about the same age as their mothers did (Brooks-Gunn, 1991a). So, the mother of an early maturing girl most likely was an early maturer herself. As we shall see, early maturing girls engage in sexual intercourse at a younger age (Stattin & Magnusson, 1990). They marry and give birth earlier as well. But early marriages are more likely to end in divorce (Lamb & Teti, 1991). Thus, girls whose parents divorce may reach puberty early *not* because of parental conflict and divorce, but simply because their own mothers were early maturers.

FIGURE 14.7

**EARLY AND LATE MATURATION IN BOYS.** *The effects of early maturation in boys are generally positive. Late-maturing boys may feel conspicuous because they are among the last of their peers to lose their childhood appearance. By then, almost all the girls and most of the boys will have begun the physical changes of puberty.*

1992). Late-maturing boys may feel conspicuous because they are among the last of their peers to lose their childhood appearance. Remember that almost all the girls and most of the boys will already have begun the physical changes of puberty (Nottlemann et al., 1990).

Classic research on a cohort of children who participated in the Berkeley Growth Study found that early-maturing boys are more popular than their late-maturing peers and are more likely to be leaders in school (Jones, 1957; Mussen & Jones, 1957). Early-maturing boys are also more poised, relaxed, and good-natured. Their edge in sports and the admiration of their peers heightens their sense of self-worth. Some studies have suggested that the stereotype of the mature, tough-looking boy as dumb is just that—a stereotype. Early-maturing boys may actually be somewhat ahead of their peers intellectually (Tanner, 1982). However, these differences are slight, and, where they exist, they tend to evaporate by adulthood (Jones, 1957).

On the negative side, early maturation may hit some boys before they are psychologically prepared to live up to the expectations of those who admire their new bodies. Coaches may expect too much of them in sports, and peers may want them to fight their battles for them. Sexual opportunities may create demands before they know how to respond to them. Some early maturers may therefore worry about living up to the expectations of others (Kutner, 1993a).

Late maturers have the advantage of avoiding this early pressure. They are not rushed into maturity. On the other hand, late-maturing boys often feel dominated by early-maturing boys. They have been found to be more dependent and insecure. Although they are smaller and weaker than early maturers, they may be more rebellious and more likely to get into fights—perhaps in an effort to prove themselves to be adult (Livson & Peskin, 1980).

But there are many individual differences. While some late maturers appear to fight their physical status and get into trouble, others adjust to their physical development status and find acceptance through academic achievement, music, clubs, and other nonathletic extracurricular activities. Late-maturing boys also show more flexibility and social sensitivity and a greater sense of humor than their early-maturing counterparts. The benefits of early maturation appear to be greatest among lower-income adolescents, because physical prowess is valued more highly among these youngsters than among middle- or upper-income adolescents. Middle- and upper-income adolescents also are likely to place more value on the types of achievements—academic and so on—available to late-maturing boys (Rutter, 1980).

**EARLY AND LATE MATURATION IN GIRLS** The situation is somewhat reversed for girls. Whereas early maturation poses distinct advantages for boys, the picture is mixed for girls. Adolescents tend to be concerned if they are different from their peers. So early-maturing girls may feel awkward, because they are among the first of their peers to begin the physical changes of puberty. They outgrow not only their late-maturing female counterparts, but also their male age-mates. With their tallness and their developing breasts, they quickly become very conspicuous. Boys their own age may tease early-maturing girls about their breasts and their height. Tall girls of dating age frequently find that shorter boys are reluctant to approach them or be seen with them. Occasionally, tall girls walk with a slight hunch, as if trying to minimize their height.

Girls who mature early feel less positive about their puberty experience (Dubas et al., 1991) and have a poorer body image than those who mature later (Alsaker, 1992; Brooks-Gunn, 1991a). These negative feelings are more pronounced for girls who are still in elementary school, where they are more conspicuous, and are less pronounced if they are in high school, where others are catching up (Nottelmann & Welsh, 1986). Because they are taller and heavier than other girls their age, early maturers do not conform to the current cultural emphasis on thinness (Jackson, 1992). This may account for their more negative feelings about their bodies.

TRUTH OR FICTION REVISITED

*It is not true that girls who mature early have higher self-esteem than those who mature late—at least not at first. Prior to high school, early-maturing girls may be conspicuous and the butt of teasing.*

Early maturation in girls is associated with a variety of other problems. Early-maturing girls show lower academic success and have conduct problems in school (Simmons & Blyth, 1987; Stattin & Magnusson, 1990). They have a higher incidence of emotional disturbance, including depression (Brooks-Gunn, 1991b). They are more likely to be involved in violations of societal norms: ignoring parents' prohibitions, staying out late without permission, being truant from school, smoking, drinking, and shoplifting. They also engage in sexual intercourse at an earlier age (Caspi et al., 1993; Flannery et al., 1993; Stattin & Magnusson, 1990). These behaviors may result from the tendency of early-maturing girls to associate with older peers.

A number of studies show that the parents of early-maturing girls may increase their vigilance and restrictiveness (Holmbeck & Hill, 1991; Lynch, 1991). Increased restrictiveness, in turn, can lead to new child–parent conflicts.

We must also keep in mind, however, that not all early-maturing girls develop difficulties. Rather, early maturation appears to accentuate behavioral problems among girls who already have experienced adjustment difficulties earlier in childhood (Caspi & Moffitt, 1991).

Although early-maturing girls are less poised, sociable, and expressive than their late-maturing counterparts during the latter part of middle childhood (Jones, 1958), they appear to adjust by the time they reach high school (Livson & Peskin, 1980). Once in high school, they do not stand out so much, and their size may earn them admiration rather than curiosity. At this time, early-maturing girls may also take on the roles of cosmetic and sexual advisers to later-maturing agemates. Perhaps the task of coping with the problems posed by early maturation also helps them develop coping mechanisms that they use to their advantage in later years.

What are the long-term consequences of early maturation in girls? A longitudinal study of Swedish girls (Stattin & Magnusson, 1990) found that the earliest developed females had completed less education than other women. They were slightly more likely to have committed a criminal offense, but were no more likely to consume alcohol. Overall, they appeared to be as well adjusted socially as other women.

**Body image** Perception of one's physical attractiveness and one's feelings about one's body.

## *Body Image*

***Body image*** refers to how physically attractive we perceive ourselves to be and how we feel about our body. Adolescents are quite concerned about their physical appearance, particularly in early adolescence when the rapid physical changes of puberty are occurring (Duke-Duncan, 1991). By the age of 18, girls and boys are more satisfied with their bodies than they were in the earlier teen years (Rauste-von Wright, 1989).

**Body Image: A Gender Gap** High school and college age females in our society are much more preoccupied with body weight and slimness than males of the same age. Compared with adolescent boys, adolescent girls have a less positive body image, are more dissatisfied with their weight, and are more likely to be dieting (Koff et al., 1990; Paxton et al., 1991; Richards et al., 1990). Somewhere between 50 percent and 80 percent of white adolescent girls have been or are currently dieting (Attie et al., 1990). And, as we shall see later in the chapter, girls are more likely to suffer from eating disorders.

College women generally see themselves as significantly heavier than the figure they believe is most attractive to males and females and heavier, still, than the "ideal" female figure (Cohn & Adlers, 1992; Lamb et al., 1993; Rozin & Fallon, 1988). College men actually prefer an average-size female body to a thin one (Furnham et al., 1990). It appears that a thin ideal of female body attractiveness is held by females but not by males (Jackson, 1992).

Adolescents who have a more positive body image have higher self-esteem (Allgood-Merten et al., 1990; Thornton & Ryckman, 1991). Girls' feelings about themselves are even more closely linked to their physical appearance than is the case for boys (Kutner, 1992b; Williams, 1992). For example, girls who are concerned about their weight tend to have lower self-esteem than girls who do not have this concern. But concern about weight is not related to self-esteem in boys.

FIGURE 14.8

**Body Image.** *Adolescent females in our society are much more preoccupied with body weight and slimness than are adolescent males.*

**Culture and Development: Body Image** Research on body image in various racial and ethnic groups indicates that adolescent females of color are more satisfied with their bodies and are less concerned about weight loss and dieting than are white female adolescents (Jackson, 1992; Root, 1990). Thomas and James (1988), for example, found that unlike most white females, a majority of African-American females do not believe it is necessary to be thin to be attractive. Why might this be? Thomas and James suggest these possibilities: (a) African-American females may believe that African-American males do not equate attractiveness with thinness; and (b) African-American females may reject the white ideal of thinness or may believe that it is less attainable for them because of racial differences in physical makeup.

**TRUTH OR FICTION REVISITED**

*It is true that African-American adolescent girls tend to be more satisfied with their bodies than white American girls. African-American girls appear to be less likely to subscribe to the widespread cultural belief that the ideal female figure is very thin.*

Everything is relative, however. Even though women of color may be more satisfied with their bodies than white women, concerns about weight and dieting still are found frequently in various racial and ethnic groups, including those of African Americans (Hsu, 1987), Hispanics (Hiebert et al., 1988), and Native Americans (Rosen et al., 1988). In one study, for example, three-quarters of a group of Chippewa women were found to be dieting, and many of them were engaging in unhealthy dieting behaviors (Rosen et al., 1988).

## HEALTH IN ADOLESCENCE

How healthy are adolescents in the United States? The good news is that most adolescents are healthy. Few of them are chronically ill or miss school (Kovar, 1991; Orr & Pless, 1991). They make fewer visits to physicians and occupy fewer hospital beds than any other age group (Dryfoos, 1990).

The bad news, according to a recent report by the U.S. Congress Office of Technology Assessment, is that about one out of five of the nation's adolescents has at least one serious health problem (Dougherty, 1993). American teenagers may be less healthy than their parents were at the same age. The reason is not an increase in the incidence of infectious diseases or other physical illnesses. Rather, the causes are external and rooted in life-style and risky behavior: excessive drinking, substance abuse, reckless driving, violence, disordered eating behavior, and unprotected sexual activity leading to sexually transmitted diseases and pregnancy (Arnett, 1992; Hechinger, 1992; Takanishi, 1993). While risk taking sometimes is viewed as a normal part of adolescent development, risk-taking behaviors can be detrimental to the adolescent's health and well-being (Furby & Beyth-Marom, 1992; Maggs & Galambos, 1993). Let us look at some of the health risks of adolescence. We will start by examining causes of death in adolescence. We then turn to three of the major health problems faced by teens: eating disorders, substance use and abuse, and sexually transmitted diseases.

### *CAUSES OF DEATH*

Death rates are low in adolescence, although they are higher for older adolescents than for younger ones. For example, in 1985, 32 out of every 100,000 12- to

14-year-olds died, compared to 66 out of every 100,000 15- to 17-year-olds (Kovar, 1991). Death rates are nearly twice as great for male adolescents as for female adolescents (Millstein & Litt, 1990). A major reason for this is that males are more likely to engage in risk-taking behaviors that result in death due to accidents, suicide, or homicide (Matheny, 1991; Millstein & Litt, 1990). These three causes of death account for 75 percent of all adolescent deaths.

Sixty percent of adolescent deaths are due to accidents, and most of these involve motor vehicles (Irwin & Millstein, 1991). Alcohol often is involved in accidental deaths. Alcohol-related motor vehicle accidents are the leading cause of death for 15- to 24-year-olds. Alcohol frequently is implicated in other causes of accidental death or injury, including drowning and falling (Irwin & Millstein, 1991; Slap, 1991).

The suicide rate for teenagers has increased dramatically in recent years (Brody, 1992b; Lore & Schultz, 1993). It is the second leading cause of death for white adolescents, and the third leading cause for African-American adolescents (Gibbs, 1991). We take a closer look at suicide in Chapter 16.

**Culture and Development: Death by Homicide** Homicide is the second leading cause of death among 15- to 24-year-olds (Lore & Schultz, 1993). But it is the leading cause of death in 15- to 19-year-old African-American males. By contrast, accidents are the major cause of death for white teens (Hammond & Yung, 1993; Center for the Study of Social Policy, 1993). Young African-American males between the ages of 15 and 19 are nearly 10 times as likely as young white males to be murdered. Females are not exempt from this pattern. African-American females aged 15 to 19 are more than five times as likely as their white counterparts to be victims of homicide (Hammond & Yung, 1993). The figures for Hispanic youth are lower than those for African Americans but much higher than those for white youngsters (Jenkins & Bell, 1992).

Youths who are poor and who live in urban areas of high population density have the greatest risk of death by homicide (Fingerhut et al., 1992). Consider, for example, the fact that gang killings in Los Angeles hit a record high in 1992, accounting for 430 of the city's 1,100 murders. The increasing death toll is partly a result of the rising number of multivictim drive-by shootings. One of the most

FIGURE 14.9

**Accidental Death.** *Sixty percent of adolescent deaths are due to accidents, most of them involving motor vehicles. Alcohol often is involved in accidental deaths.*

***Osteoporosis*** A condition involving progressive loss of bone tissue.

***Menopause*** The cessation of menstruation, typically occurring between ages 48 and 52.

chilling trends is the falling age of the gang members involved in the shootings. According to Danny Hernandez, founder of a youth center in Los Angeles, "It used to be 17 or 18. Now it's 10-, 11- or 12-year-olds doing the triggering. And now they spray the areas" (Lacayo, 1993, p. 31).

## TRUTH OR FICTION REVISITED

*Homicide is actually the leading cause of death among African-American male adolescents but the second leading cause of death among 15- to 24-year-old U.S. males overall.*

## NUTRITION AND EATING DISORDERS

**NUTRITIONAL NEEDS** Physical growth occurs more rapidly in the adolescent years than at any other time after birth, with the exception of the first year of life (McCoy & Kenney, 1991). To fuel this growth, the average girl needs to consume about 2,200 calories per day, while the average boy needs about 3,000 calories (Ekvall, 1993b). The nutritional needs of adolescents vary according to their stage of pubertal development. For example, at the peak of their growth spurt, adolescents use twice as much calcium, iron, zinc, magnesium, and nitrogen as they do during the other years of adolescence (Williams & Worthington, 1988). Calcium intake is particularly important for females to build up their bone density and help prevent a serious condition known as ***osteoporosis*** later in life. Osteoporosis, a progressive loss of bone, affects millions of women, particularly after ***menopause*** (Brody, 1993f). But most teenagers—both girls and boys—do not consume enough calcium. Adolescents also are likely to obtain less vitamin A, thiamin, and iron and more fat, sugar, protein, and sodium than recommended (Beard, 1991; Freedland & Dwyer, 1991; Williams & Worthington, 1988).

**FIGURE 14.10**

**DEATH BY HOMICIDE.** *Homicide is the second leading cause of death among 15- to 24-year-olds, but the leading cause of death among 15- to 19-year-old African-American males. Poor youths who live in densely populated urban areas are at greater risk of death by homicide.*

FIGURE 14.11

**NUTRITIONAL NEEDS OF ADOLESCENTS.** *Teenagers require lots of calories to fuel the adolescent growth spurt. They may consume large amounts of fast food and junk food, which is high in calories and fat but not always very nutritious.*

One reason for adolescents' nutritional deficiencies is their often irregular eating patterns. Breakfast frequently is skipped, especially by females who are "watching their weight." Teenagers are more likely to miss meals or eat away from home than they were in the childhood years. They may consume large amounts of fast food and junk food, which is high in fat and calories but not very nutritious (Wardlaw & Insel, 1993; Williams & Worthington, 1988).

**EATING DISORDERS: ANOREXIA NERVOSA AND BULIMIA NERVOSA** Plumpness has been valued in many preliterate societies, and Western paintings of former centuries suggest that there was a time when (literally) well-rounded women were the ideal (Gordon, 1990; O'Neill & Gopnick, 1991). But in contemporary Western culture, slenderness is valued, especially for females (Brenner & Cunningham, 1992; Nagel & Jones, 1992). Obesity is clearly out of fashion, and pediatricians are recommending that children stay slender to avoid obesity in adulthood.

In our discussion of body image, we saw that adolescent girls are more dissatisfied with their weight than adolescent boys and are more likely to be dieting. Is there anything wrong with dieting, you may ask? After all, there is a saying that you can never be too rich or too thin. Excess money may be pleasant enough, but one certainly can be too thin, as in the case of ***anorexia nervosa.*** Anorexia nervosa is a life-threatening eating disorder characterized by intense fear of being overweight, severe weight loss, and refusal to eat enough to reach or maintain a healthful body weight.

***Anorexia nervosa*** (an-or-reks-ee-uh) An eating disorder characterized by irrational fear of weight gain, distorted body image, and severe weight loss.

*TRUTH OR FICTION REVISITED*

*Perhaps you can never be too rich, but you can definitely be too thin—as evidenced by the poor health of anorexic adolescents.*

***Amenorrhea*** (ay-men-or-REE-uh) Lack of menstruation.

By and large, anorexia is a disorder that afflicts girls and young women. The incidence of anorexia has increased dramatically since 1970. Current estimates indicate that about 1 in 500 adolescent girls suffers from anorexia (Whitaker et al., 1990). Anorexic females outnumber anorexic males by estimates of about 9:1 to 20:1 (V. Ekvall et al., 1993; Hamlett & Curry, 1990). The onset of anorexia is most often between the ages of 12 and 18, although females have become anorexic in prepuberty and in old age (Gowers et al., 1991; Woolston, 1991). While most anorexics are white females from the middle and upper classes, the incidence of anorexia also is increasing among minority and lower-income females (Balentine et al., 1991; Phelps & Bajorek, 1991; Root, 1990).

Anorexic girls may drop 25 percent or more of their body weight in a year. Dramatic weight loss is accompanied by ***amenorrhea*** (lack of menstruation) and general health declines (Johnson & Whitaker, 1992; Litt, 1991). Between 5 and 15 percent of anorexic girls die, most from suicide or cardiac arrest (Begley, 1987; Fisher & Brone, 1991).

In the typical pattern, girls notice some weight gain after menarche and decide that it must come off. However, dieting—and, often, exercise—continue at a fever pitch. They go on long after girls reach normal body weights, even after family and others have told them that they are losing too much. Anorexic girls almost always adamantly deny that they are wasting away. They may point to their fierce exercise regimens as proof. While others perceive them as "skin and bones," they frequently sit before the mirror and see themselves as they were. Penner and his colleagues (1991) studied women who averaged 31 percent below their ideal body weight according to Metropolitan Life Insurance Company charts. The women estimated the size of parts of their bodies to be 31 percent larger than they actually were. Clearly, the body images of anorexic women are distorted. Indeed, dissatisfaction with one's body is one of the hallmarks of both anorexia and *bulimia,* a related eating disorder (Dacey et al., 1991; Leon et al., 1993).

FIGURE 14.12

***ANOREXIA NERVOSA.*** *Singer Karen Carpenter is shown here with her brother 4 months before her death. She died from cardiovascular disease, which may have been linked with her eating disorder. Karen and her brother had sold some 60 million records.*

Although the thought of eating can be odious to anorexic girls, now and then they may feel quite hungry. Many anorexics become obsessed with food and are constantly around it. They may engross themselves in cookbooks, take on the family shopping chores, and prepare elaborate dinners for others.

The following description of Alma portrays a graphic picture of an anorexic adolescent:

> *When she came for consultation, she looked like a walking skeleton, scantily dressed in shorts and a halter, with her legs sticking out like broomsticks, every rib showing, and her shoulder blades standing up like little wings. Most striking was the face—hollow like that of a shriveled-up old woman with a wasting disease, sunken eyes, a sharply pointed nose on which the juncture between bone and cartilage was visible. When she spoke or smiled—and she was quite cheerful—one could see every movement of the muscles around her mouth and eyes, like an animated anatomical representation of the skull. Alma insisted that she looked fine and that there was nothing wrong with her being so skinny.*
>
> *At 15 Alma had been healthy and well-developed, had menstruated at age 12, was five feet six inches tall, and weighed 125 pounds. At that time her mother urged her to change to a school with higher academic standing, a change she resisted. Her father suggested that she should watch her weight, an idea that she took up with great eagerness, and she began a rigid diet. She lost rapidly and her menses ceased. That she could be thin gave her a sense of pride, power, and accomplishment. Alma also began a frantic exercise program, would swim by the mile, play tennis for hours, or do calisthenics to the point of exhaustion. Whatever low point her weight reached, Alma feared that she might become "too fat" if she regained as little as an ounce. There were many efforts to make her gain weight, which she would lose immediately, and she had been below 70 pounds most of the time. There was also a marked change in her character and behavior. Formerly sweet, obedient, and considerate, she became more and more demanding, obstinate, irritable, and arrogant. There was constant arguing, not only about what she should eat but about all other activities as well. (Bruch, 1978, pp. 1–2)*

Anorexia is often associated with recurrent cycles of binge eating and purging called ***bulimia nervosa.*** Purging includes self-induced vomiting, fasting or strict dieting, excessive use of laxatives or diuretics, and vigorous exercise (Leon, 1991; Lucas, 1991). As with anorexia, there is overconcern about body shape and weight. The disorder usually begins in adolescence or early adulthood, and, like anorexia, it afflicts many more women than men. Bulimia is more common than anorexia. Bulimia has become epidemic in high schools and on college campuses, where 4 to 8 percent of females have a history of the disorder (Dacey et al., 1990; Heatherton & Baumeister, 1991).

***Bulimia nervosa*** (boo-LEE-me-uh) An eating disorder characterized by cycles of binge eating and vomiting as a means of controlling weight gain.

**TRUTH OR FICTION REVISITED**

*It is true that some college women do control their weight by going on cycles of binge eating followed by self-induced vomiting. They are said to have bulimia nervosa.*

**THEORETICAL INTERLUDE: ORIGINS OF EATING DISORDERS** Biological, psychological, and cultural factors appear to be involved in both anorexia and bulimia (V. Ekvall et al., 1993). Let us first consider biological factors. Anorexia is much more likely to occur in both members of a monozygotic twin pair than in both members of a dizygotic twin pair. This suggests a genetic predisposition toward anorexia (Lucas, 1991). Also, anorexics show disturbances in the functioning of the hypothalamus and the pituitary gland (Hauger et al., 1991), possibly indicating that the disorder has a biological basis. Furthermore, recent research has shown that binge eating is triggered in bulimic women by low levels of the neurotransmitter serotonin (''Chemical Linked,'' 1993).

Other theories focus on possible psychological origins. The frequent link between anorexia and puberty has led some theorists to suggest that anorexia may represent an effort by the girl to remain prepubescent. Anorexia allows the girl to avoid growing up, separating from the family, and assuming adult responsibilities. Weight loss also prevents rounding of the breasts and hips, suggesting that anorexic girls are conflicted about their sexuality and the possibility of pregnancy (Jackson, 1992).

Still other theorists believe that adolescents who develop anorexia are budding ''superwomen'' who have an intense desire to excel in activities and relationships. The external stresses of adolescence, such as pubertal weight gain, dating, and, perhaps, greater competition in school may trigger eating disorders in an attempt to achieve control in at least one area (DeAngelis, 1990; Thornton et al., 1991). Alternatively, the intense focus on eating and dieting that is characteristic of eating disorders may serve as an escape from feeling that one is not living up to the high standards and expectations held by oneself and others (Heatherton & Baumeister, 1991).

These views receive some support when we look at a psychological profile of adolescents with eating disorders. They tend to have low self-esteem, greater difficulty separating from their parents, high anxiety, a high need for approval from others, and high standards of physical attractiveness and thinness (Phelps & Bajorek, 1991; Rhodes & Kroger, 1992).

Self-starvation also has a brutal effect on parents and might be used as a weapon when family relationships become disturbed (Lucas, 1991). Several studies have found that families of anorexics and bulimics are characterized by high levels of conflict and criticism, overemphasis on achievement, and low levels of emotional support (Kenny, 1992; Phelps & Bajorek, 1991; Pike & Rodin, 1991). Young women with eating disorders also are more likely to have a history of childhood physical or sexual abuse (Kashubeck & Walsh, 1992; Miller et al., 1993).

Finally, the cultural idealization of the slender female creates a climate that sets the stage for development of eating disorders among susceptible individuals (DeAngelis, 1990).

**TREATMENT** Eating disorders are difficult to treat. Treatment is most successful when started early in the illness (Brody, 1990a; Connolly & Corbett-Dick, 1990). Even then, the chances of full recovery are not high. David Herzog and his colleagues (1988) reviewed 40 follow-up studies of individuals treated for anorexia and bulimia. After several years, one-third had recovered, another third showed some improvement, and another third were still ill. Relapse rates tend to be high (Herzog et al., 1991). This suggests that we must remain cautious concerning the long-term outlook, even for anorexics who apparently have successfully completed therapy.

Individual psychotherapy is only moderately successful (Fisher & Brone, 1991). Frequently, the patient is placed in a hospital setting, given drugs to heighten hunger and inhibit vomiting, and denied privileges unless she gains weight (Lucas, 1991). ***Family therapy,*** which focuses on problems in family interaction rather than the disorders of one member, may be of some use (Ravenscroft, 1991). In a series of encouraging reports (Minuchin et al., 1978), more than 80 percent of the girls whose families were seen in therapy had retained weight gains in follow-ups ranging from a few months to a few years.

***Family therapy*** A form of therapy in which the family unit is treated and taught to relate to one another more productively.

***Substance abuse*** A persistent pattern of use of a substance characterized by frequent intoxication and impairment of physical, social, or emotional well-being.

***Substance dependence*** A persistent pattern of use of a substance that is accompanied by physiological addiction.

## *Substance Use and Abuse*

We live in a drug-oriented society. We use drugs not only to cope with medical problems, but also with daily tensions, run-of-the-mill depression, even boredom. Drugs are used properly when they are required to maintain or restore health, but we use drugs for many other reasons. Many prepubertal children and adolescents use drugs for the same reasons that adults do. But they also use drugs because their friends do or because their parents tell them not to. They use drugs to experience pleasure, to deaden pain, and to earn prestige among their peers.

It is important to make a distinction between the use and abuse of drugs. Many adolescents occasionally experiment with drugs such as alcohol or marijuana. Some researchers have suggested that occasional experimental drug use among adolescents is a normal part of establishing independence and autonomy from parents (Baumrind, 1991a; Schinke et al., 1991).

But where does drug use end and drug abuse begin? The borderline is not always clear, and even professionals do not always agree on definitions (Helzer & Schuckit, 1990; McWhirter et al., 1993). Many psychologists define ***substance abuse*** as persistent use of the substance despite the fact that it impairs one's social, academic, or physical well-being. Children and adolescents who miss classes or cut school because they are high on drugs or sleeping off their effects, fit the pattern. Sad to say, there are some students who smoke marijuana or gulp an alcoholic beverage between classes and stay high for the day.

***Substance dependence*** is more severe than substance abuse, although the borderline can be confusing here as well (Helzer & Schuckit, 1990). Dependence

### *Thinking About Development*

Agree or disagree with the following statement and support your answer: "Adolescents cannot be held responsible for their behavior when they have been drinking."

**Figure 14.13**

**Substance Use and Abuse.** *It is important to distinguish between the use and abuse of substances. Many adolescents occasionally experiment with substances such as alcohol and marijuana. But where does substance use end and substance abuse begin?*

***Tolerance*** Habituation to a drug such that increasingly higher doses are needed to achieve similar effects.

***Abstinence syndrome*** A characteristic cluster of symptoms that results from sudden decreases in the level of usage of a substance.

***Amphetamine*** A kind of stimulant drug.

has behavioral and physiological aspects. Behaviorally, dependence is often characterized by loss of control over the substance, as in organizing one's life around getting it and using it. Physiologically, dependence is typified by *tolerance,* withdrawal symptoms, or both. ***Tolerance*** is the body's habituation to a substance so that with regular usage, higher doses are required to achieve similar effects. There are characteristic withdrawal symptoms, or an ***abstinence syndrome,*** when the level of usage suddenly drops off. The abstinence syndrome for alcohol includes anxiety, tremors, restlessness, weakness, rapid pulse, and high blood pressure. Many adolescents who begin to use substances such as alcohol for the pleasure of it wind up using them to escape the withdrawal symptoms of the abstinence syndrome.

Adolescents who abuse substances may be using drugs as self-medication in an attempt to cope with or escape from emotional distress (Hussong & Chassin, 1993; Kaminer, 1991). Adolescents who are anxious about their prospects for developing vocational and educational skills, who have difficulties socializing, or who are in a stressful family situation may be drawn to the calming effects of alcohol, marijuana, tranquilizers, and sedatives. Those with low self-confidence and self-esteem may be drawn to the ego-bolstering effects of drugs such as ***amphetamines*** and cocaine. One recent study, for example, found that adolescents who used drugs frequently were more likely than infrequent users to say that they used drugs to cope with or escape from problems (Novacek et al., 1991). Unfortunately, this coping strategy provides only temporary relief, does not solve the adolescent's problems, and often creates new ones.

**CONSEQUENCES OF SUBSTANCE USE AND ABUSE** The effects of substance use and abuse include more than possible physical and psychological addiction. Death by overdose, short- and long-term health problems, motor vehicle accidents, and loss of motivation and productivity are some of the possible consequences of heavy drug use (Rauch & Huba, 1991). Other problems associated with drug use include criminal activity and reduced job and marital stability (Dryfoos, 1990; Newcomb & Bentler, 1989). Although it is not always clear whether drug use causes problem behaviors or results from them, it is clear that involvement with drugs has the potential to produce devastating consequences.

FIGURE 14.14

***PERCENTAGE OF HIGH SCHOOL SENIORS WHO SAID THEY USED VARIOUS DRUGS WITHIN THE PAST YEAR.*** *Since the early 1980s, the use of illicit drugs has been declining among high school seniors. (Source: Johnston et al., 1993a).*

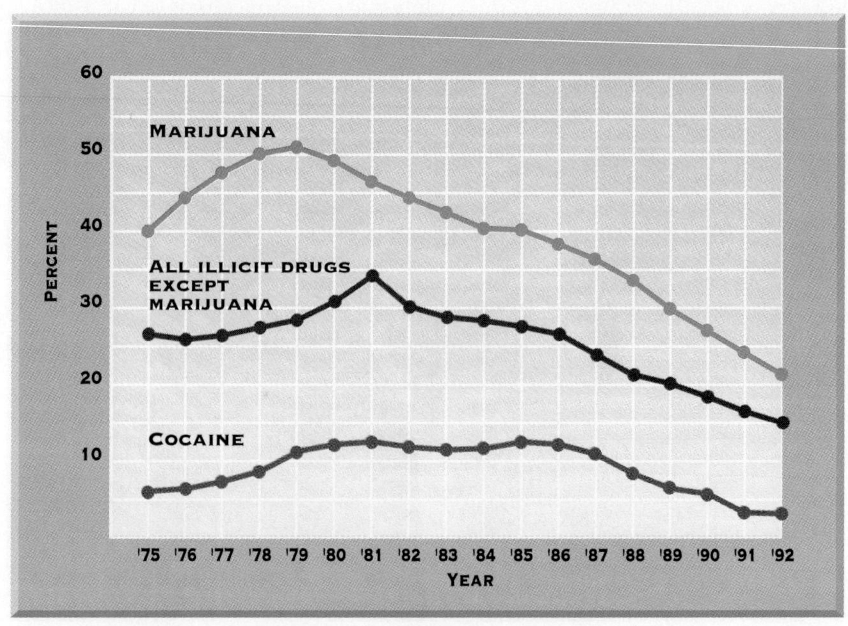

**TABLE 14.2**

**PERCENTAGE OF HIGH SCHOOL SENIORS REPORTING DRUG USE, 1982 AND 1992**

| DRUG | CLASS OF 1982 | CLASS OF 1992 | | |
|---|---|---|---|---|
| | LIFETIME | LIFETIME | PAST YEAR | PAST MONTH |
| MARIJUANA AND HASHISH | 58.7 | 32.6 | 21.9 | 11.9 |
| INHALANTS | 12.8 | 16.6 | 6.2 | 2.3 |
| HALLUCINOGENS | 12.5 | 9.2 | 5.9 | 2.1 |
| LSD | 9.6 | 8.6 | 5.6 | 2.0 |
| PCP | 6.0 | 2.4 | 1.4 | .6 |
| COCAINE | 16.0 | 6.1 | 3.1 | 1.3 |
| CRACK | NO INFORMATION | 2.6 | 1.5 | .6 |
| HEROIN | 1.2 | 1.2 | .6 | .3 |
| OTHER OPIATES | 9.6 | 6.1 | 3.3 | 1.2 |
| STIMULANTS | 27.9 | 13.9 | 7.1 | 2.8 |
| SEDATIVES | 15.2 | 6.1 | 2.9 | 1.2 |
| BARBITURATES | 10.3 | 5.5 | 2.8 | 1.1 |
| METHAQUALONE | 10.7 | 1.6 | .6 | .4 |
| TRANQUILIZERS | 14.0 | 6.0 | 2.8 | 1.0 |
| STEROIDS | NO INFORMATION | 2.1 | 1.1 | .6 |
| ALCOHOL | 92.8 | 87.5 | 76.8 | 51.3 |
| CIGARETTES | 70.1 | 61.8 | NO INFORMATION | 27.8 |

SOURCE: JOHNSTON ET AL., 1993A.

**PATTERNS OF SUBSTANCE USE AND ABUSE AMONG ADOLESCENTS** Much of what we know about changing patterns of substance use and abuse among adolescents comes from an annual survey of high school seniors and college students begun in 1975 at the University of Michigan (Johnston et al., 1993a, b). This survey has found that since the early 1980s, use of most ***illicit*** drugs has been declining among high school seniors and college students (see Figure 14.14). The incidence of marijuana use appears to have peaked in the late 1970s and has been dropping steadily among high school students ever since. Still, as of 1992, one-third of high school seniors had tried marijuana, and 12 percent had used it within the last month (see Table 14.2). A similar decline in marijuana use among college students showed signs of leveling off in 1992 (Johnston et al., 1993b).

In 1992, about 8 percent of college students and 6 percent of high school seniors reported that they had tried the stimulant cocaine at some time in their lives. Even fewer (under 3 percent) had tried the potent cocaine derivative "crack." The use of cocaine and crack began to decline in the mid-1980s when young people started to perceive them as dangerous drugs.

Use of stimulants other than cocaine (such as amphetamines, stay-awake pills, and diet pills) has declined since 1982. As of 1992, about 14 percent of high school seniors had tried stimulants. About 6 percent had tried ***sedatives,*** 6 percent had tried tranquilizers, and 9 percent had used ***hallucinogens*** such as LSD. Unlike most other illicit drugs, use of LSD has risen somewhat in the past

***Illicit*** Illegal.

***Sedatives*** Drugs that soothe or quiet restlessness or agitation.

***Hallucinogens*** Drugs that give rise to hallucinations.

***Licit*** Legal.

few years among both high school and college students (Johnston et al., 1993a, b; Newcomb & Bentler, 1991b).

TRUTH OR FICTION REVISITED

*Actually, substance use and abuse appear to be declining for the most part among high school and college students. However, use of LSD has risen somewhat in the past few years.*

Steroid use has been documented among adolescents, especially among male athletes, although its use is declining. Somewhere between 1 and 2 percent of high school males admit to having used steroids in the prior year (Johnston et al., 1993a). Steroids, which build muscle mass, typically are used in an effort to improve athletic performance, although some users also want to improve their physical appearance (Yesalis, 1991).

While the decline in most drug use among high school seniors and college students is encouraging, the bad news is that drug use is on the rise among the nation's junior high school students. Two recent studies involving sixth and eighth graders found increases in their use of marijuana, cocaine, crack, LSD, stimulants, and inhalants (''Drug Use by Students,'' 1992; Johnston et al., 1993a). We must also keep in mind that rates of drug use are higher among school dropouts and incarcerated youth than among the high school and college population (Hein, 1991; Johnston et al., 1992). Another discouraging note is that the United States has the highest rate of drug use among industrialized countries (Newcomb & Bentler, 1989).

Also, the use of ***licit*** (that is, legal) drugs has remained quite high. By far, the most commonly used of the licit drugs is alcohol. About 70 percent of children have had their first experience with alcohol prior to high school (Johnston et al., 1993a). Alcohol consumption is surprisingly high, even in the first grade. In one recent study, boys in the first, fourth, and seventh grades were asked if they had ever secretly taken a sip of beer, wine, or liquor. About 8 percent of first-graders admitted that they had done so (VanKammen et al., 1991).

Following a drop-off in popularity during the 1960s, alcohol has reasserted its dominance among the drugs used on college campuses and in high schools. As of 1992, 88 percent of U.S. high school seniors had tried alcohol, and 51 percent reported using it within the past 30 days (Johnston et al., 1993a). Of great concern is the widespread occurrence of binge drinking, in which five or more drinks in a row are consumed. About 28 percent of all high school seniors and 43 percent of college students surveyed in 1992 said they had engaged in binge drinking at least once in the past 2 weeks (Johnston et al., 1993a; Presley & Meilman, 1992). The outcome can be tragic, as in the case of a college junior who died after drinking 23 shots of liquor in an hour during a contest with a friend (Celis, 1991b).

The other commonly used licit drug is tobacco. Nearly two-thirds of all high school seniors in 1992 had smoked a cigarette at one time or another, and about 28 percent had smoked within the last month. This figure has scarcely changed since 1981, despite all the publicity about the harmful effects of smoking (Johnston et al., 1993a).

**GENDER DIFFERENCES IN SUBSTANCE USE** In both adolescence and adulthood, males are more likely than females to use most illicit drugs. Males also are likely to use these substances more heavily than females (Johnston et al., 1992; Newcomb & Bentler, 1992). A possible explanation for this gender difference is that tighter social constraints are usually placed on females. But there are a few exceptions to the pattern of greater substance use by males. In both high school and college, for example, females use stimulants and tranquilizers as much as or slightly more than do males.

Recently, gender differences in the use of illicit substances have been declining as a result of a greater drop in use among males. But gender differences in the use of alcohol remain substantial (Newcomb & Bentler, 1992). For example, in 1992 more than half of all college males but only one-third of college females reported having five or more drinks in a row in the past month (Johnston et al., 1993b).

Female teenagers are now somewhat more likely to smoke than are male teenagers (Newcomb & Bentler, 1992). This statistic disguises two trends in smoking patterns: the incidence of smoking has dropped off in males in recent years but has increased in females (Clayton, 1991; Paludi, 1992).

**Factors Associated with Substance Use** Which adolescents are most likely to become involved with drugs? Let us explore some of the factors associated with substance use.

***Peers*** Associating with peers who use drugs and who tolerate drug use is one of the strongest predictors of adolescent drug use and abuse (Buckhalt et al., 1993; Flannery et al., in press; Stanton & Silva, 1992). Children are highly vulnerable to peer pressure in the early teen years (Brown, 1990). If children of this age group are closely involved with a group that uses drugs, they may experience enormous pressure to do so themselves. Adolescents who are extensively involved with their peers, especially to the exclusion of their families, are at greater risk for drug use (Cohen et al., 1991).

***Family*** Children whose parents use drugs such as alcohol, tobacco, tranquilizers, and stimulants are more likely to turn to drugs themselves (Chassin & Barrera, 1993; Cohen et al., 1991; Johnston et al., 1992). Modeling increases children's awareness of drugs and conveys the unfortunate message that use of drugs is appropriate to relieve the stresses and strains of daily life (Newcomb & Bentler, 1991a). Adolescents whose parents and siblings have more tolerant

FIGURE 14.15

**Smoking.** *The incidence of smoking has dropped off in adolescent males in recent years but has increased in adolescent females. As a consequence, female teenagers are now more likely than male teenagers to light up.*

attitudes toward deviant, unconventional, and non-law-abiding behaviors also are more likely to use drugs. Poor parent–child relationships and family discord are contributing factors as well (Campo & Rohner, 1992; Cohen et al., 1991; Thorlindsson & Vilhjalmsson, 1991).

Parenting style also plays a role. Having open lines of communication with a parent helps to inhibit drug use (Kafka & Linden, 1991). More generally, the authoritative pattern of child rearing appears to protect children from problem drug use (Baumrind, 1991a, b). As you may recall, this style of parenting is characterized by high parental involvement, the setting of strict limits, demands for mature behavior, democratic discussion of values and goals, and warmth and encouragement. Heavy drug use is most likely to occur in families with either permissive or neglecting–rejecting parenting styles.

It is becoming increasingly apparent that to understand the nature of family influences on adolescent substance abuse, we must also consider how the behaviors of children influence parental behaviors. Recent research, for example, indicates that childhood problem behaviors, such as hyperactivity, aggression, and refusing adult requests, cause mothers to feel more distress. Mothers who are more distressed show less effective parental coping behaviors, which, in turn, can lead to increased levels of adolescent problem behaviors such as marijuana use, alcohol problems, and delinquency (Conger et al., 1993b; Windle, 1992a).

***Other Factors*** Adolescent drug users often experience school problems. They do poorly in school, and their academic motivation is low (Andrews et al., 1991; Wills et al., 1991, Zucker & Fitzgerald, 1991). Certain psychological characteristics are associated with drug use. These include impulsiveness, rebelliousness, and low self-esteem (Brook et al., 1992; Cambor & Millman, 1991; Schulenberg et al., 1993). Adolescent drug users are more likely to suffer from depression and anxiety (Massey et al., 1992; Thorlindsson & Vilhjalmsson, 1991; Walter et al., 1991b). Problem behaviors such as aggression, delinquency, early sexual behavior, and premarital pregnancy also are associated with teenage drug involvement (Brook et al., 1992; Cohen et al., 1991; Dembo et al., 1991).

Frequent drug users often show signs of maladjustment in childhood. As youngsters, they are more likely to engage in antisocial behavior (Dishion & Ray, 1991; Robins & McEvoy, 1990). They have problems getting along with other children, are insecure, undependable, and show many indications of emotional distress (Shedler & Block, 1990). Boys who later become alcoholics show a variety of interpersonal deficits, including being less considerate and more indifferent to mothers and siblings (Zucker & Fitzgerald, 1991). The fact that these signs of maladjustment often emerge before the beginning of drug use alerts us to the difficulty of separating cause and effect when we examine factors associated with adolescent drug use (Dryfoos, 1990). For example, does drug use cause school failure, or does failing in school cause a youngster to turn to drugs? Does substance abuse lead to depression and anxiety, or do individuals take up drugs to deal with these painful emotional states?

***Possible Genetic Factors*** We have discussed psychological and social factors associated with drug use, but genetic factors may also be involved. There is growing evidence of a genetic predisposition toward developing problems with alcohol (Hawkins et al., 1992; Wilson & Crowe, 1991). Research shows that a specific gene defect often is found among alcoholics (Adler, 1991). Moreover, children of alcoholics who are reared by adoptive parents are more likely to develop alcohol-related problems than are the natural children of the adoptive parents. Also, the likelihood of alcohol problems occurring in both members of a twin pair is higher for identical than for fraternal twins (Brody, 1993a; McGue et al., 1992).

**Culture and Development: Substance Use** Patterns of adolescent drug use vary among different racial and ethnic groups. Native Americans exhibit the greatest overall rate of substance use, and Asian Americans have the lowest rate (Johnston et al., 1992; McKenry, 1991). What about African Americans, Hispanics, and whites? Different studies give different answers. A national survey of older adolescents indicated that African Americans and Hispanics had equal or higher rates of use than whites (Brunswick, 1991; McKenry, 1991; Sigelman et al., 1992). Poverty, unemployment, discrimination, deviant role models, and escape from the harsh realities of life in the inner city or on the reservation have been offered as explanations for the higher incidence of drug use among ethnic minorities, particularly among those who are economically and socially disadvantaged (Brunswick, 1991; McKenry, 1991; Pumariega et al., 1992).

The University of Michigan annual survey of high school seniors presents a very different picture, however. After Native Americans, whites have the next highest rates of use for most drugs. Hispanics generally are next and African Americans are second to lowest, with Asian Americans being lowest of all. How can one account for the disparity in findings of the national survey of adolescents and the surveys of high school seniors?

Differences in dropout rates appear to be the key. As we have seen, drug use is higher among high school dropouts. Hispanics and African Americans have higher dropout rates than whites (Johnston et al., 1992). Those African-American and Hispanic youth who are involved with drugs will be more likely to drop out and so will not be included in a survey of high school seniors. This point was illustrated in a study (Chavez & Swain, 1992) that compared drug usage rates of Mexican-American and white 8th- and 12th-graders. Mexican-American 8th-graders had higher use rates than whites, but the pattern was reversed among 12th-grade students. These results appear to reflect the higher dropout rate of drug-using Mexican-American youth.

Not only frequency of use but patterns of drug use differ according to racial and ethnic group. For example, as compared with white adolescents, African Americans start using drugs at an earlier age, use a greater number of drugs, and use drugs more frequently (McKenry, 1991). Another example of different patterns of drug use is that while Hispanic adolescents are less likely to consume alcohol than whites, those who do drink are heavier users (Bettes et al., 1990).

Having pointed out some differences in drug use among racial and ethnic groups, we also should note that there are certain similarities. For instance, a study of African-American, Mexican-American, and white juvenile delinquents found that frequent use of alcohol, tobacco, marijuana, and other illicit drugs was related to delinquent behavior in all three groups (Watts & Wright, 1990). Another example comes from a study of substance use among Hispanic and white adolescents. In both groups, substance users were more influenced by their peers than were abstainers (Coombs et al., 1991).

**Prevention** Prevention has become a buzzword in our society. No longer are we as willing as we once were to sit back and deal with the consequences of illness or problem behavior when they strike. Now the focus has shifted to ways in which we can change our daily lives to avert medical and behavior problems, including drug abuse.

Various programs to prevent drug abuse have sprung into being for use with elementary school children as well as for adolescents and adults (M. Caplan et al., 1992; Dabrowski et al., 1992; Rollin et al., 1992). Most of these programs are aimed at preventing the use of the so-called gateway drugs—cigarettes, alcohol, and marijuana—that typically are tried before other illicit drugs

(Newcomb & Bentler, 1989). Unfortunately, the results of prevention programs are mixed (Bangert-Downs, 1988; Logan, 1991; Walter et al., 1991b). Sometimes they help; other times they don't. Attempts to use scare tactics and provide information about the effects of drugs sometimes backfire, with drug use among children actually increasing after they have been exposed to program materials (Kazdin, 1993b; Newcomb & Bentler, 1989).

The peer-influence approach is based on the assumption that peer pressure is an important factor in drug use. This approach focuses on building refusal skills ("Just say no") and social skills. The peer-influence approach has been shown to be more effective than other models, particularly in terms of increasing knowledge about drugs (Dryfoos, 1990; Kreutter et al., 1991). This approach also helps reduce drug use or prevent the initiation of drug use for the average teenager (Ellickson & Bell, 1990; Hawkins et al., 1992). Programs led by older peers appear to be more successful than those led by adults, such as teachers (Hawkins et al., 1992; Perry, 1991).

The peer-influence approach is much less successful among adolescents who are most at risk for drug abuse. For this group, alternative strategies are more effective. These programs build competence by providing job training, community

**FIGURE 14.16**

***SCARE TACTICS.*** *Attempts to use scare tactics to prevent drug use, such as in this ad, sometimes backfire. The peer influence approach appears to be more effective than other prevention models.*

and leisure activities, remedial education, and counseling (Hawkins et al., 1992; Walter et al., 1991a).

**Treatment** When prevention efforts fail, treatment becomes the next step. A number of inpatient and outpatient substance abuse treatment programs for adolescents have been created in the past few years (Cambor & Millman, 1991; McWhirter et al., 1993; Schinke et al., 1991). Surprisingly little is known about the effectiveness of these programs. There is some evidence that programs that involve the family are more successful. Still, relapse rates are quite high, ranging from 35 percent to 70 percent (Newcomb & Bentler, 1989).

Which adolescents are most likely to profit from treatment? Positive outcomes are associated with being female, younger, white, having fewer legal difficulties, being less addicted, being enrolled in school, and spending more time in treatment (Knapp et al., 1991; Newcomb & Bentler, 1989; Schinke et al., 1991).

## *Sexually Transmitted Diseases*

*A boyfriend of mine got very angry with me when he wanted to have sex without a condom and I wouldn't let him. He was quite promiscuous, and how should I know how clean those other women were? We both wanted to be tested for AIDS, but we didn't because we were too scared. If one of us did have AIDS, we really wouldn't know what to do.*

*—Maureen, 19, Florida (Rathus & Boughn, 1993)*

Teenagers are at high risk for ***sexually transmitted diseases*** (STDs). Sexually active adolescents have higher rates of STDs than any other age group (Millstein, 1990; Rotheram-Borus & Koopman, 1991b). Each year, an estimated 2.5 million adolescents—one out of every seven—contracts a sexually transmitted disease (Dryfoos, 1990; Krener, 1991). Chlamydia (an infection of the vagina or urinary tract that may result in sterility) is the most commonly occurring STD in adolescents, followed by gonorrhea, genital warts, genital herpes, syphilis, and acquired immunodeficiency syndrome (AIDS) (Dryfoos, 1990). These and other STDs are described in Table 14.3.

**Risk Factors** As we noted earlier in this chapter, adolescents often engage in various risk-taking behaviors that have harmful consequences for their health and well-being. What behaviors place adolescents at greater risk for contracting STDs?

First, and perhaps most obvious, is sexual activity itself. Someone who doesn't engage in sexual intercourse is not likely to contract a sexually transmitted disease. Over the past 30 years, the age at first sexual experience has been dropping (Gardner & Wilcox, 1993). The average age of first sexual intercourse is 16, but in some inner city areas, it is 12 (Boyer & Hein, 1991b). By the age of 19, between 70 percent and 90 percent of adolescents have initiated sexual intercourse (Dryfoos, 1990).

A second high-risk behavior for contracting STDs is having sex with multiple partners. Increasing numbers of teenage girls have multiple sex partners (Lewin, 1992b). Currently, about one in five high school students engages in sex with four or more different partners (Kantrowitz, 1992).

A third factor that increases the chance of contracting STDs is failure to use condoms. In two recent surveys, two-thirds of sexually active adolescents reported not using condoms or using them only inconsistently (DiClemente et al., 1992;

***Sexually transmitted disease*** A disease spread through sexual contact (formerly known as venereal disease).

## TABLE 14.3

*Causes, Modes of Transmission, Symptoms, Diagnosis, and Treatment of Major Sexually Transmitted Diseases (STDs)*

| STD and Pathogen | Modes of Transmission | Symptoms | Diagnosis | Treatment |
|---|---|---|---|---|
| Acquired immune deficiency syndrome (AIDS): Human immunodeficiency virus (HIV) | HIV is transmitted by sexual contact, direct infusion of contaminated blood, from mother to fetus during pregnancy, or from mother to child through childbirth or breast-feeding. | Infected people may initially be asymptomatic or develop mild flu-like symptoms that may then disappear for many years prior to the development of full-blown AIDS. Full-blown AIDS is symptomized by fever, weight loss, fatigue, diarrhea, and opportunistic infections such as rare forms of cancer (Kaposi's sarcoma) and pneumonia (PCP). | A blood test (ELISA) detects HIV antibodies in the bloodstream. The Western blot blood test may be used to confirm positive ELISA results. Diagnosis is usually made on the basis of HIV antibodies, presence of indicator (opportunistic) diseases, and depletion of $T_4$ cells. | There is no cure for AIDS. The drug zidovudine apparently slows the progress of the disease. Patients may profit from proper nutrition, exercise, counseling, and stress-management techniques. |
| Bacterial vaginosis: Gardnerella vaginalis bacterium and others | Can arise by overgrowth of organisms in vagina, allergic reactions, etc.; transmitted by sexual contact. | In women, thin, foul-smelling vaginal discharge, irritation of genitals and mild pain during urination. In men, inflammation of penile foreskin and glans, urethritis, and cystitis. May be asymptomatic in both genders. | Culture and examination of bacterium. | Oral treatment with metronidazole (brand name: Flagyl). |
| Candidiasis (moniliasis, thrush, "yeast infection"): Candida albicans, a yeastlike fungus | Can arise by overgrowth of fungus in vagina; transmitted by sharing a washcloth with an infected person. | In women, vulval itching; white, cheesy, foul-smelling discharge; soreness or swelling of vaginal vulval tissues. In men, itching and burning on urination or a reddening of the penis. | Diagnosis usually made on basis of symptoms. | Vaginal suppositories, creams, or tablets containing miconazole, clotrimazole, or teraconazole. |
| Chlamydia and nongonococcal urethritis (NGU): Chlamydia trachomatis bacterium; NGU in men may also be caused by Ureaplasma urealycticum bacterium and other pathogens. | Transmitted by vaginal, oral, or anal sexual activity; to the eye by touching one's eyes after touching the genitals of an infected partner or by passing through the birth canal of an infected mother. | In women, frequent and painful urination, lower abdominal pain and inflammation, and vaginal discharge (but most women are symptom free). In men, symptoms are similar to but milder than those of gonorrhea–burning or painful urination, slight penile discharge (some men are also asymptomatic). Sore throat may indicate infection from oral–genital contact. | The Abbott Testpack analyzes a cervical smear in women. | Antibiotics: doxycycline, tetracycline, or erythromycin. |
| Gonorrhea ("clap", "drip"): Gonococcus bacterium (Neisseria gonorrhoeae) | Transmitted by vaginal, oral, or anal sexual activity or from mother to newborn during delivery. | In men, yellowish, thick penile discharge, burning urination. In women, increased vaginal discharge, burning urination, irregular menstrual bleeding (most women show no early symptoms) | Clinical inspection, culture of sample discharge. | Antibiotics: penicillin, ceftriaxone, spectinomycin. |

CONTINUED

Walter et al., 1991a). About one quarter to one-third do not use any contraceptives at all (DiClemente, 1990; DiClemente et al., 1992).

***AIDS (Acquired immune deficiency syndrome)*** A fatal, usually sexually transmitted disease that is caused by a virus and cripples the body's immune system, rendering the victim vulnerable to opportunistic diseases.

**AIDS** Of all the sexually transmitted diseases, ***AIDS*** is the most devastating. Other STDs are either treatable or not life threatening. But AIDS ultimately results in death, and a cure is not yet in sight. AIDS is now the sixth leading cause of death among 15- to 24-year olds (Kantrowitz, 1992). First identified in 1981, the HIV virus that causes AIDS is spreading rapidly around the world

| STD and Pathogen | Modes of Transmission | Symptoms | Diagnosis | Treatment |
|---|---|---|---|---|
| Genital herpes: Herpes simplex virus-type 2 (HSV-2) | Almost always by means of vaginal, oral, or anal sexual activity; most contagious during active outbreaks of the disease. | Painful, reddish bumps around the genitals, thigh, or buttocks; in women, may also be in the vagina or on the cervix. Bumps become blisters or sores that fill with pus and break, shedding viral particles. Other possible symptoms: burning urination, fever, aches and pains, swollen glands; in women, vaginal discharge. | Clinical inspection of sores; culture and examintion of fluid drawn from the base of a genital sore. | The antiviral drug acyclovir (brand name: Zovirax) may provide relief and prompt healing over, but is not a cure. |
| Genital warts (venereal warts): Human papilloma virus (HPV) | Transmission is by sexual and other forms of contact, as with infected towels or clothing. Women are especially vulnerable, particularly women who have multiple sex partners. | Appearance of painless warts, often resembling cauliflowers, on the penis, foreskin, scrotum, or internal urethra in men and on the vulva, labia, wall of the vagina, or cervix in women. May occur around the anus and in rectum of both genders. | Clinical inspection. (Because HPV is connected with cervical cancer, regular Pap smears are also advised.) | Methods of removal include cryotherapy (freezing), podophyllin, burning, surgical removal. |
| Pubic lice ("crabs"): Pthirus pubis | Transmission is by sexual contact or by contact with an infested towel, sheet, or toilet seat. | Intense itching in pubic area and other hairy regions to which lice can attach. | Clinical examination. | Lindane (brand name: Kwell)–a prescription drug; nonprescription medications containing pyrethrins or piperonyl butoxide (brand names: A200, RID, Triple X). |
| Syphilis: Treponema pallidum | Transmitted by vaginal, oral, or anal sexual activity or by touching an infectious chancre. | In primary stage, a hard, round painless chancre or sore appears at site of infection within 2 to 4 weeks. May progress through secondary, latent, and tertiary stages if left untreated. | Primary-stage syphilis is diagnosed by clinical examination; or fluid from a chancre is examined in a darkfield test. Secondary-stage syphilis is diagnosed by blood test (the VDRL). | Penicillin, or doxycycline, tetracycline, or erythromycin. |
| Trichomoniasis ("trich"): Trichomonas vaginalis—a protozoan (one-celled animal) | Almost always transmitted sexually. | In women, foamy, yellowish, odorous, vaginal discharge; itching or burning sensation in vulva. Many women are asymptomatic. In men, usually asymptomatic, but mild urethritis is possible. | Microscopic examination of a smear of vaginal secretions, or of culture of the sample (latter method preferred). | Metronidazole (Flagyl). |

and may infect 30 million to 40 million people by the year 2000 (Altman, 1993a). As of 1993, 946 cases of AIDS were reported in American teenagers ("The Children," 1993). This may not sound like a lot. But more than 20 percent of all individuals with AIDS in this country are in their 20s. Since HIV has a long incubation period ranging from 2 to 10 years, it is likely that many of these young adults became infected when they were teenagers (Gardner & Wilcox, 1993).

What factors put adolescents at risk for contracting AIDS? First, those behaviors that increase the risk of STDs in general also enhance the likelihood of getting AIDS. These behaviors include early and unprotected sexual activity with multiple partners. Young gay males, and homeless and runaway youths have elevated risk for AIDS because they are more likely to engage in unprotected sex with several partners (Gelman, 1993; Millstein, 1990; Rotheram-Borus & Koopman, 1991a). Injecting drugs is another risk factor for AIDS. Sexual partners of people who inject drugs are vulnerable as well (Millstein, 1990; Rotheram-Borus & Koopman, 1991a). Engaging in anal intercourse heightens the risk of infection (Rathus & Boughn, 1993). Also at risk are hemophiliacs and other individuals who received contaminated blood from transfusions prior to 1985, when donated blood was not yet tested for the presence of the HIV virus (Boyer & Hein, 1991a; Navarro, 1993b).

## TRUTH OR FICTION REVISITED

*Actually, many kinds of behavior place one at risk of contracting AIDS and other STDs. Therefore, adolescents who are not gay and who do not shoot up drugs do need to think about AIDS and other STDs—to consider the diseases' modes of transmission and their own behavior patterns.*

Studies regarding knowledge, attitudes, and beliefs about AIDS find that even children in the early school years are aware of AIDS (Fassler et al., 1991; Sigelman et al., 1993). General knowledge of AIDS is even greater among adolescents (Rotheram-Borus & Koopman, 1991b). For example, one national survey found that between 88 and 98 percent of high school students knew that AIDS is transmitted through sexual intercourse (Krener, 1991). But most adolescents are not modifying their sexual practices or methods of contraception as a result of fear of the disease (Kelly et al., 1993; Moore & Burling, 1991; Stiffman et al., 1992). Fewer than half of sexually active high school students are protecting themselves against AIDS by using condoms.

### THINKING ABOUT DEVELOPMENT

Agree or disagree with the following statement and support your answer: "One's behavior, and not one's group membership, places one at risk of AIDS."

**WOMEN AND AIDS** Women now account for about 17 percent of AIDS cases in the United States but nearly one-third of cases worldwide (Cowley, 1993; Kent, 1991). A United Nations study in Europe, Africa, and Southeast Asia has found that sexually active teenage girls have higher rates of HIV infection than older women or young men ("U.N. Finds," 1993). A number of erroneous assumptions about AIDS have had a disproportionately negative impact on women. They include the notions that AIDS is primarily a disease of gay men and people who inject drugs and that it is difficult to contract AIDS through heterosexual intercourse. However, the primary mode of AIDS transmission worldwide is heterosexual intercourse (Altman, 1993a). Larger numbers of Americans also are contracting AIDS through heterosexual intercourse (Altman, 1994). Among American women, heterosexual intercourse has now replaced intravenous drug use as the major source of AIDS infection (Altman, 1993b). The case of Lily highlights the point that one's behavior, not one's group, places one at risk for AIDS:

*Lily was not supposed to get AIDS. She was heiress to a cosmetics fortune and had graduated from a prestigious Eastern college. At age 24, she was diagnosed as having AIDS.*

*"No one believed it" she said. "I was never a male homosexual. I never shot up crack. My boyfriends didn't shoot up either. There was just Matthew . . ." At 17, in her senior year in high school, she had had a brief affair with Matthew. Later she learned that Matthew was bisexual. Five years ago, Matthew died from AIDS.*

*Lily's family was fully supportive, emotionally and, of course, financially. Lily had been to the best clinics. She was on a regimen of antiviral drugs that had shown some ability to slow the progress of AIDS. There were times when she thought she might get over her illness.*

*But then she added, tears welling, "Everyone loves you and wishes they could trade places with you, but they can't. You're suddenly older than everyone around you and you're going to die alone." (Adapted from Rathus & Nevid, 1991, p. 175)*

Lily died in 1992.

**Culture and Development: Sexually Transmitted Diseases** Ethnic minority adolescents have higher rates of sexually transmitted diseases than white adolescents (DiClemente, 1990; Donovan, 1993). For example, the incidence of gonorrhea among 15- to 19-year-olds is 15 times higher in African-American females than in white females. African-American females also have the highest rates of pelvic inflammatory disease, syphilis, and chlamydia (Boyer & Hein, 1991b). Rates for Hispanic youth usually fall between the rates for African-American and white teens (Millstein, 1990). A disproportionate number of minority adolescents have AIDS or are HIV-positive (Boyer & Hein, 1991a; Krener, 1991). More than half of adolescents with AIDS are African American or Hispanic, with the African-American rate twice the Hispanic rate.

In the case of AIDS, patterns of transmission also differ for ethnic minority and white individuals. Homosexual and bisexual activity accounts for more than 75 percent of AIDS cases among whites but only for 40 percent of cases among Hispanics and 36 percent of cases among African Americans. Needle sharing and heterosexual contact account for more than half the cases among minorities but for less than 20 percent of the cases among whites (Millstein, 1990).

What accounts for these racial and ethnic differences in sexually transmitted diseases? Factors related to poverty and substance abuse certainly play a role. Injecting drugs, a risk factor for AIDS, is more prevalent among minorities, particularly those who live in the inner city (Leary, 1993a). Females who have sex with males who inject drugs enhance their own risk as well (Millstein, 1990). Early sexuality increases the risk of getting a sexually transmitted disease, and sexual activity begins earlier among African Americans than among whites (Donovan, 1993). Sixty percent of African-American male teens have had sex by age 16, but white male teens don't reach that figure until age 18. A similar pattern is found for females; 60 percent of African-American females have had intercourse by age 18, while white females hit the 60 percent mark at age 19 (Brooks-Gunn & Furstenberg, 1989).

Differences in attitudes and knowledge also may be involved. Compared with white adolescents, minority adolescents believe they are less susceptible to AIDS. This may be due to their belief that AIDS is primarily a disease of white homosexual men (DiClemente, 1990). Also, Hispanic and African-American teens are less knowledgeable than white teens about the use of condoms to lower the risk of AIDS infection (Boyer & Hein, 1991a).

What are racial and ethnic differences in patterns of transmission of AIDS?

| Racial/ Ethnic Group | Pattern of Transmission: Homosexual and Bisexual Activity | Pattern of Transmission: Heterosexual Contact and Needle Sharing |
|---|---|---|
| African American | 36 percent | More than 50 percent |
| Hispanic | 40 percent | More than 50 percent |
| White | More than 75 percent | Less than 20 percent |

**FIGURE 14.17**

***SAFER SEX.*** *Despite AIDS prevention programs encouraging sexually active people to practice safer sex, many young people, including many college students, continue to engage in unprotected sex.*

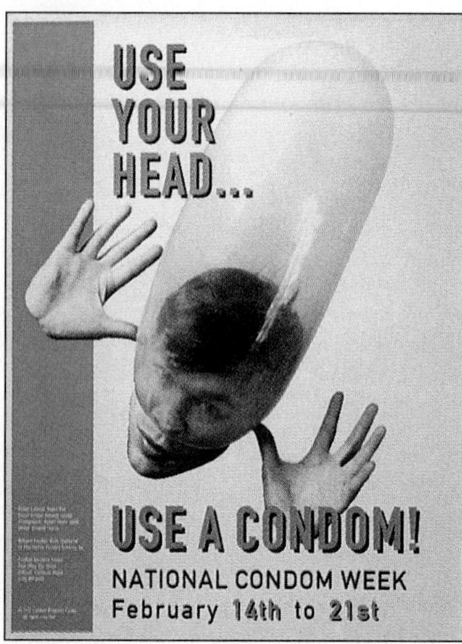


**PREVENTION** Prevention and education strategies are the primary weapons against STDs. This is essential in the case of AIDS, for which no treatment is available. As of 1991, 32 states and the District of Columbia had mandatory AIDS education in the schools, and all but two of the remaining states recommended such education (National Guidelines Task Force, 1991). Unfortunately, many school-based AIDS education programs are limited in scope and focus. Some consist of only a 1-hour presentation (Boyer & Hein, 1991a).

What should be the goals of a school-based program designed to prevent STDs? Increasing knowledge certainly is important. Adolescents need to learn about the transmission, symptoms, and consequences of STDs. They need to learn about "safer sex" techniques, including abstinence, and, if they are sexually active, the use of condoms (Boyer & Hein, 1991b; Rotheram-Borus & Koopman, 1991b). (See Developing Today for a discussion of safer sex and other techniques for preventing AIDS and other STDs.)

But knowledge is not enough to change behavior, as we have seen. Other goals of educational programs should include enhancing the adolescent's sense of control over the prevention of AIDS and modifying sexual and drug behaviors associated with acquiring the disease (Boyer & Hein, 1991a). As with programs designed to prevent substance abuse, the development of effective decision-making and social skills may be critical in programs designed to prevent STDs (DiClemente, 1990; Lewis et al., 1990).

In an effort to prevent AIDS, as well as teenage pregnancy, some school districts now distribute condoms to students (Levy, 1993). This practice has aroused considerable controversy. Some oppose giving contraceptives on religious and moral grounds. Opponents also argue that providing condoms encourages teenagers to become sexually active. Advocates of condom distribution programs argue that while abstinence may be desirable, the fact remains that many teens are sexually active. Given this reality, they contend, the schools should help protect sexually active teens from AIDS and unwanted pregnancies. In a recent nationwide survey, 57 percent of women and men ages 18 to 75 agreed that high schools should make condoms available to students to stop the spread of AIDS (Clements, 1993). Support was highest among African Americans and Hispanics (70 percent) and those 18 to 34 years old (67 percent). What is your opinion on this issue?

**TRUTH OR FICTION REVISITED**

*Some public school districts do provide students with condoms to help prevent the spread of AIDS. The districts of New York City and Los Angeles are examples.*

***THINKING ABOUT DEVELOPMENT***

Agree or disagree with the following statement and support your answer: "Safe sex is the answer to the AIDS epidemic."

Finally, we must keep in mind that even the best school-based programs, unless started early enough, will not reach the 25 percent or so of students who drop out during the high school years. These students often are those who already are at high risk for developing AIDS and other sexually transmitted diseases because of involvement in sexual activity and drug use (Boyer & Hein, 1991a; Wilcox, 1990). Broader, community-based efforts are needed to reach these youth.

The ability of teenagers to deal with the physical changes of adolescence and to engage in health-promoting behaviors depends in part on their growing cognitive abilities. We examine development in that area in Chapter 15.

## Developing Today

### PREVENTING AIDS: IT'S MORE THAN SAFE(R) SEX

As shown by the remarks of one young woman, it can be clumsy to try to protect oneself from sexually transmitted diseases such as AIDS:

> *It's one thing to talk about "being responsible about STD" and a much harder thing to do it at the very moment. It's hard to imagine murmuring into someone's ear at a time of passion, "Would you mind slipping on this condom or using this cream just in case one of us has STD?" Yet it seems awkward to bring it up beforehand, if it's not yet clear between us that we want to make love with one another. (Boston Women's Health Book Collective, 1992, pp. 311–312)*

Because of the difficulties in discussing STDs with sex partners, some people admit they just wing it (Wallis, 1987). They assume that a partner does not have an STD or they hope for the best—even in the age of AIDS. Seventy-two percent of the single people aged 18 to 44 responding to a 1993 *New York Times*/CBS News survey reported that they had become more cautious about sex because of concern about AIDS, however (Kagay, 1993). The most common methods of behavior modification were use of condoms, limiting the number of sex partners, and abstaining from sex.

What can we do to prevent the transmission of HIV and STDs? A number of things.

1. *Refuse to deny the prevalence and harmful nature of AIDS.* Many people try to put AIDS and other STDs out of their minds and wing it when it comes to sex. The first, and perhaps most important, step in protecting oneself against AIDS is thus psychological: keeping it in mind—refusing to play the dangerous game that involves pretending (at least for the moment) that it does not exist. The other measures involve modifying our behavior.
2. *Remain abstinent.* One way of curtailing the sexual transmission of HIV and other pathogens is sexual abstinence. Just what does abstinence mean? Does it mean avoiding sexual intercourse (yes) or any form of sexual activity with another person (not necessarily)? Light kissing (without exchanging saliva), hugging, and petting to orgasm (without coming into contact with semen or vaginal secretions) are generally considered safe, although readers may argue about which of these behaviors is consistent with the definition of abstinence.
3. *Engage in a monogamous relationship with someone who is not infected.* Sexual activity within a monogamous relationship with an uninfected person is safe. The questions here are how certain one can be that one's partner is indeed uninfected and monogamous.

For those who are unwilling to abstain from sexual relationships or to limit themselves to a monogamous relationship, some things can be done that make sex safer—though not perfectly safe:

4. *Be selective.* Engage in sexual activity only with people you know well who do not belong to the high-risk groups for AIDS.
5. *Inspect one's partner's genitals.* People who have been infected by HIV often have other STDs. Visually examining one's partner's genitals for blisters, discharges, chancres, rashes, warts, and lice while engaged in foreplay may yield warning signs of such diseases. An unpleasant odor is also a warning sign.
6. *Wash one's own genitals before and after contact.* Washing beforehand helps protect one's partner, and washing promptly afterward with soap and water helps remove some pathogens. Urinating afterward might be of some help, particularly to men, since the acidity of urine can kill some pathogens in the urethra.
7. *Use spermicides.* Spermicides are marketed as birth-control devices, but many creams, foams, and jellies kill HIV and other pathogens as well as sperm. Check with a pharmacist.
8. *Use condoms.* Latex condoms (but not condoms made from animal membrane) protect the man from vaginal (or other) body fluids and protect the woman from having infected semen enter the vagina. Condoms are particularly effective in preventing gonorrhea, syphilis, and AIDS (Koop, 1988). Combining condoms with spermicides is even more effective.
9. *Consult a physician about medication.* It can be useful to use antibiotics after unprotected sex to guard against bacterial infections, but routine use of antibiotics may do nothing more than make them less effective when they are really needed. Medication will not shield one from herpes or AIDS but may decrease their symptoms or slow their progress.
10. *Have regular medical checkups.* These include blood tests. In this way, one can learn about and treat disorders whose symptoms had gone unnoticed. But again, this method is of little avail against herpes and AIDS.
11. *When in doubt, stop.* If one is not sure that sex is safe, one can stop and mull things over or seek expert advice (Rathus, 1993).

## Summary

1. According to Sigmund Freud, hormonal changes trigger the reemergence of sexual urges during the genital stage. Anna Freud believed that these renewed sexual feelings lead to mood swings and defiance of parents. Both she and G. Stanley Hall felt that adolescent turmoil (''storm and stress'') is necessary for normal development, but recent research has challenged this view.

2. Puberty is a stage of development characterized by reaching sexual maturity and the ability to reproduce. The primary sex characteristics are the structures that make reproduction possible. The secondary sex characteristics are indicators of sexual maturation not involving reproduction, such as breast development and pubic hair.

3. The growth spurt in height begins about 2 years earlier for girls (age 10) than for boys (age 12). The spurt in weight begins about a year and a half after the spurt in height. The adolescent growth spurt has been occurring earlier in this century than in the past. This so-called secular trend may be due to better nutrition.

4. The increase in testosterone secretion in boys leads to a number of pubertal changes, including growth of the testes and penis; the appearance of axillary, pubic, and facial hair; muscle development; deepening of the voice; ejaculation; and acne.

5. The increase in estrogen secretion in girls leads to a number of pubertal changes, including development of the breasts, labia, vagina, and uterus and the growth of fatty tissue.

6. Menarche (first menstruation), like the growth spurt, is occurring at younger ages now than in the past. The menstrual cycle is regulated by hormone levels. In our society, girls receive mixed messages about menarche. Negative stereotypes about menstruation to some degree remain, but menarche is generally perceived as the point at which girls become young women.

7. Early maturation appears more advantageous for boys than late maturation. The reverse pattern holds for girls. But by the high school years, early maturing girls usually are as well-adjusted as late-maturing girls.

8. Adolescents are quite concerned about their physical appearance. Adolescent girls, compared with boys, have a less positive body image, are more dissatisfied with their weight, and are more likely to be dieting.

9. Adolescents generally are healthy. But they may engage in behaviors that can lead to injury or death. The major causes of adolescent death are accidents, homicide, and suicide. Death rates are higher for males than females in all these categories.

10. Calcium, iron, zinc, magnesium, and nitrogen are important for normal growth in adolescence. Many teenagers do not consume sufficient quantities of these nutrients.

11. Anorexia nervosa is characterized by dramatic weight loss and intense fear of being overweight. Bulimia nervosa, a more common eating disorder, is characterized by cycles of binging and purging. Anorexia and bulimia are most often found in adolescent girls. Biological, psychological, and cultural factors appear to be involved in these disorders.

12. Many adolescents occasionally use drugs. Some show problematic patterns of usage labelled "substance abuse" and "substance dependence."

13. Since the early 1980s, substance use has decreased among older adolescents, but it may be increasing among younger adolescents. Marijuana is the most frequently used illicit drug. Use of the licit drugs alcohol and tobacco is much higher. Males are more likely than females to use most illicit drugs and alcohol.

14. Factors associated with substance use include having peers and parents who use drugs, having poor relationships with parents, and having permissive (as opposed to authoritative) parents. Adolescent drug users have a variety of academic, psychological, and social problems, some of which may be present in early childhood. Genetic factors also may be involved. Patterns of drug use vary among different racial and ethnic groups.

15. Results of drug prevention and treatment programs are mixed. The outcome depends partly on the characteristics of the adolescents involved.

16. Sexually active adolescents are at high risk for sexually transmitted diseases (STDs). Risk factors for contracting STDs include early and unprotected sexual activity with multiple partners. Minority adolescents are at greater risk than whites. Many women (and men) contract AIDS through heterosexual intercourse.

CHAPTER

15

# ADOLESCENCE:

## COGNITIVE DEVELOPMENT

## Chapter Outline



## Truth or Fiction?

______ *Many adolescents see themselves as being onstage.*

______ *Many adolescents think of themselves as being invulnerable.*

______ *Adolescent boys outperform adolescent girls in mathematics.*

______ *Five-year-old children generally think that people who accidentally harm others ought not to be punished.*

______ *People who have arrived at the highest level of moral development follow their own ethical principles and may disobey the laws of the land.*

______ *Girls lag behind boys in their moral development.*

______ *The transition from elementary school is more difficult for boys than for girls.*

______ *Increasing numbers of adolescents are dropping out of high school.*

______ *Only one woman in two will join the work force.*

______ *Most adolescents who work do so to help support their families or to put money away for college.*

*I am a college student of extremely modest means. Some crazy psychologist interested in something called "formal operational thought" has just promised to pay me $20 if I can make a coherent logical argument for the proposition that the federal government should under no circumstances ever give or lend more to needy college students. Now what could people who believe* that *possibly say by way of supporting argument? Well, I suppose they* could *offer this line of reasoning . . .*

(ADAPTED FROM FLAVELL ET AL., 1993B, P. 140)

The adolescent thinker approaches problems very differently from the elementary school child. The child sticks to the facts, to concrete reality. Speculating about abstract possibilities and what might be, is very difficult. The adolescent, on the other hand, is able to deal with the abstract and the hypothetical. As shown in the above example, adolescents realize that one does not have to believe in the truth or justice of something in order to argue for it (Flavell et al., 1993b).

In this chapter, we will examine cognitive development in adolescence. We open the chapter with a discussion of intellectual development in adolescence, including Piaget's stage of formal operations, adolescent egocentrism, and gender differences in cognitive development. We then turn to an exploration of moral development, focusing on the views of Piaget, Kohlberg, and Gilligan. We conclude with a look at some areas that are strongly tied to cognitive development: school, vocational development, and work experience.

## INTELLECTUAL DEVELOPMENT

The growing intellectual capabilities of adolescents change the way they approach the world. The cognitive changes of adolescence influence how adolescents view themselves, their families and friends, and how they deal with broader social and moral questions. Let us begin our examination of intellectual development in adolescence with Piaget's stage of formal operations.

### *PIAGET'S STAGE OF FORMAL OPERATIONS*

The stage of ***formal operations*** is the final one in Piaget's scheme—the stage of cognitive maturity. For many children in Western societies, formal operational thought begins at about the time of puberty—the age of 11 or 12. However, not all children enter this stage at this time of puberty, and some people never reach it.

The major achievements of the stage of formal operations involve classification, logical thought, and the ability to hypothesize. Central features are the ability to think about ideas as well as objects and to group and classify ideas—symbols, statements, entire theories. The flexibility and reversibility of operations, when applied to statements and theories, allow adolescents to follow arguments from premises to conclusions and back again.

There are several features of formal operational thought that give the adolescent a generally greater capacity to manipulate and appreciate the outer environment and the world of the imagination: hypothetical thinking, the ability to use symbols to stand for symbols, and deductive reasoning.

***Formal operations*** The fourth stage in Piaget's cognitive-developmental theory, characterized by the capacity for flexible, reversible operations concerning abstract ideas and concepts, such as symbols, statements, and theories.

FIGURE 15.1

***FORMAL OPERATIONS.*** *The ability to deal with the abstract and the hypothetical and the capacity to engage in deductive reasoning are the key features of formal operational thought. These characteristics allow adolescents to engage in scientific reasoning.*

**HYPOTHETICAL THINKING** It is in formal-operational thought that children—by now, adolescents—discover the concept of "what might be" rather than "what is." Adolescents can project themselves into situations that transcend their immediate experience, and, for this reason, they may become wrapped up in lengthy fantasies. Many adolescents can explore endless corridors of the mind, perceiving what would happen as one decision leads to another choice point, and then still another decision is made. Adolescents become aware that situations can have different outcomes. They can think ahead, systematically trying out various possibilities in their minds.

In a sense, it is during the stage of formal operations that people tend to emerge as theoretical scientists—even though they may think of themselves as having little or no interest in science. Adolescents may conduct daily experiments to determine whether their hypotheses are correct. We are not talking about experiments carried out in the laboratory with calipers or Bunsen burners. It is more common for adolescents to experiment with different tones of voice, different ways of carrying themselves, and different ways of treating others to see which sorts of behavior are most effective for them.

Adolescents, who can look ahead to multiple outcomes, may also see varieties of possibilities for themselves. Some become acutely aware that they have the capacity, to a large extent, to create or fashion themselves according to their own images of what they are capable of becoming. In terms of career decisions, the wealth of possible directions leads some adolescents to experience anxiety about whether they will pick the one career that really "is" them, and to experience a sense of loss about the fact that they probably will have the opportunity to choose only one.

This capacity to look ahead, to fashion futures, also frequently leads to ***utopian*** thinking. Just as adolescents can foresee many possibilities for themselves, they can also imagine different outcomes for suffering humanity. "What if" thinking enables adolescents to fashion schemes for putting an end to hunger, disease, and international strife.

The ability to form hypotheses and to test them enables formal-operational children to use more systematic ways of solving problems. Contrast the ways in which children at different ages set about solving a typical problem posed by Inhelder and Piaget (1959) in Focus on Research.

***Utopian*** Having to do with an idealistically perfect vision of society.

## FOCUS ON RESEARCH

### THE PUZZLE AND THE PENDULUM

If you hang a weight from a string and set it swinging back and forth, you have a pendulum. Bärbel Inhelder and Jean Piaget (1959) used a pendulum to explore ways in which children of different ages go about solving problems.

The researchers showed the children several pendulums, with different lengths of string and with different weights at their ends, as in Figure 15.2. They attached the strings to rods and sent the weights swinging. They dropped the weights from various heights and pushed them with different amounts of force. The question they posed—the puzzle—was, what determines how fast the pendulum will swing back and forth?

The researchers had varied four factors: the amount of weight, the length of the string, the height from which the weight was released, and the force with which the weight was pushed. The answer lies either in one of these factors or in some combination of them. That is, the answer could involve one factor, two factors, three factors, or all factors. It could be expressed as 1, 2, 3, or 4; or 1 and 2, 1 and 3, 1 and 4; 2 and 3, and so on.

One could try to solve this problem by deducing the answer from principles of physics, and physicists would probably prefer to use a deductive approach. However, one can also arrive at an empirical solution by trying out each possible combination of factors. Since most children (and most adults) are not physicists, they usually take the empirical approach.

Of the children tested by Inhelder and Piaget, those between the ages of 8 and 13 could not arrive at the correct answer. The fault lay largely in their approach, which was only partly systematic. They made some effort to account for the different factors, but did not control carefully for every single possibility. For example, one child compared a pendulum with a light weight and a short string to a pendulum with a heavy weight and a long string. They swung at different speeds, and so the child concluded that both factors, weight and length, were involved. After narrowing the problem to the two factors, the child did not attempt to control for weight by switching weights while holding the length constant.

The 14- and 15-year-olds generally set about solving the problem more systematically. First, they sat back and reflected for a while before beginning to manipulate the factors. Then, in contrast to the younger children, who haphazardly varied two or more factors at a time, the older children attempted systematically to exclude each factor. They used what we call the process of elimination when we take multiple-choice tests. Not all of the 14- and 15-year-olds solved the problem, but the researchers concluded that, as a group, their approach was more advanced and more likely to succeed.

According to Inhelder and Piaget, the approach of the 14- and 15-year-olds was characteristic of formal operational thought. The approach of the 8- to 13-year-olds was characteristic of concrete-operational thought. As with so many other aspects of Piaget's views and his experimental methods, we have to be somewhat flexible about the age estimates at which children are assumed to be capable of solving this problem. Robert Siegler and his associates (1973), for example, were able to train 10-year-olds to approach the problem in a way that allowed them to isolate the crucial factor of the length of the string. Here, too, is evidence that education and training can make a difference in the development of cognitive skills.

**FIGURE 15.2 THE PENDULUM PROBLEM.** *What determines how fast the pendulum will swing back and forth? The amount of weight? The length of the string? The height from which the weight is released? The force with which the weight is pushed? Or a combination of the above? Formal operational children attempt systematically to exclude each factor.*

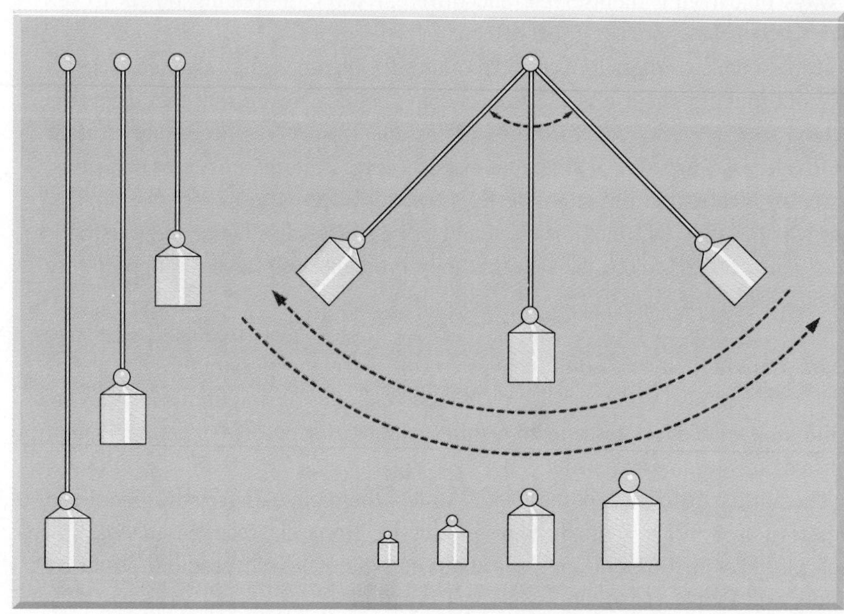

**Sophisticated Use of Symbols** Elementary schoolchildren can understand what is meant by abstract symbols such as 1 and 2. They can also perform operations in which numbers are manipulated—added, subtracted, and so on. But now consider *X*, that unknown (and, sometimes, evasive) quantity in algebra. *X* may be a familiar letter of the alphabet, but its designation as a symbol for an unknown quantity is a formal abstract operation. One symbol (an *X*) is being made to stand for something just as abstract (the unknown). Children through the age of 11 or 12 or so usually cannot fully understand this concept, even if they can be taught the mechanics as solving for *X* in simple equations. But older, formal-operational children show a sophisticated grasp of the nature of symbols that allows them to grasp intuitively what is meant by *X*. Formal-operational children, or adolescents, can perform mental operations with symbols that stand for nothing in their own experience.

This also means that formal-operational children may be ready for geometry. In geometry they learn proofs for relationships between points, lines, and perfect figures (such as circles and squares) that have no existence in the real world. Geometrical knowledge will ultimately allow them to engage in engineering and architecture—to engage, that is, in formal operations (manipulation of geometric symbols) in such a way that they derive solutions to problems with real materials and objects.

Formal-operational individuals can also understand, appreciate, and sometimes produce ***metaphors.*** Metaphors are figures of speech in which words or phrases that ordinarily signify one thing are applied to another. We find endless examples of metaphor in literature, but consider for a moment how everyday figures of speech enhance and transform our experience: *squeezing* out a living, *basking in the sunshine* of fame or glory, *hanging by a thread, jumping* to conclusions, and so on.

Consider the sentence "The ship plowed through the water." A plow is an instrument that furrows the soil. Portraying a ship as plowing through water suggests a comparison between the ship and the plow and creates an image of cutting through and turning up water, as the plow does to the soil. Metaphors play with words as symbols. Words are poetically assimilated to new schemes (as plowing is assimilated to our understanding of the movements of ships). But accommodation also occurs as the schemes are transformed in the process; the plowing metaphor transforms our image of the ship. The adaptation of words as metaphors requires the mental flexibility to associate words with situations that are perceived as having some property in common (for example, the common movements of the ship and plow).

***Metaphor*** A figure of speech that amplifies meaning and dramatizes description by adopting imagery from another situation.

***Syllogism*** A type of reasoning in which two statements or premises are set forth and a logical conclusion is drawn from them.

**Deductive Reasoning** Formal-operational individuals can reason deductively, or draw conclusions, about specific objects or people once they have been classified accurately. Consider this frequently cited ***syllogism:*** "All human beings are mortal. Socrates is a human being. Therefore Socrates is mortal." Formal-operational people can follow the logical process in this syllogism. First, a statement is made about a class or group of objects ("All human beings are mortal"). Second, a particular object or event (in this case, Socrates) is assigned to that class—that is, "Socrates is a human being." Finally, it is concluded, or deduced, that what is true for the class (human beings) is also true for the particular object or event (Socrates)—that is, "Socrates is mortal."

The moral judgments of many adolescents and adults are based on formal-operational thought. That is, they derive their judgments about what is right and wrong in specific situations by reasoning deductively from general moral principles. Their capacity for decentration also allows them to take a broad view of the situation. That is, they can focus on many aspects of a situation at once in arriving at their judgments and solving moral dilemmas.

The new logical abilities of adolescents may lead them to adamantly press for acceptance of their political and social ideas without recognition of the practical problems that are often considered by adults. Consider this syllogism: "It is wrong to hurt people. Industry A occasionally hurts people (perhaps through pollution or economic pressures). Therefore, Industry A must be severely punished or dismantled." This thinking is logical. But it is idealistic, in that it does not take into account practical considerations. For example, there could be thousands of layoffs if the industry were precipitously dismantled. The industry may also be supplying a vital need, and other arrangements may have to be made before production can be discontinued.

Adolescents' new intellectual powers often present them with what seem to be crystal-clear solutions to the world's problems, and they may become intolerant of the relative stodginess of their parents. Their own brilliant images of how to reform the world cause them to be unsympathetic to their parents' earthbound pursuit of a livelihood and other mundane matters. It is, of course, something of a pity that adolescents eventually become weighed down by the *ifs, ands,* and *buts* of the real world. Taking the broader view seems gray, indeed, by comparison.

**REEVALUATION OF PIAGET'S THEORY** Piaget's account of formal operations has received quite a bit of support. There appears to be little question that unique changes do occur in the nature of reasoning between preadolescence and adolescence (Overton & Byrnes, 1991). For example, research strongly supports Piaget's view that the capacity to reason deductively in a systematic way does not emerge until adolescence (Overton, 1991).

But critics have pointed out some limitations in Piaget's views about formal operations (Keating, 1991; Kuhn, 1991). For one thing, formal-operational thought does not appear to be a universal step in cognitive development. The ability to solve abstract problems, such as those found in algebra and the pendulum problem, is much more likely to be developed in technologically oriented Western societies or in major cities than in rural areas or less well-developed nations (Keating & Clark, 1980; Super, 1980). Moreover, formal-operational thought

FIGURE 15.3

***ADOLESCENT IDEALISM.*** *Adolescents' new intellectual powers may lead them to press for acceptance of their political and social ideas without recognition of the practical problems that are often considered by adults.*

may occur later than Piaget thought, if at all. For example, many early adolescents (ages 13 to 16) still perform better on concrete problems than on abstract ones (Markovitz & Vachon, 1990). And reviews of the literature (Keating, 1991; Leadbeater, 1991) suggest that formal-operational thought is found only among 40–60 percent of first-year college students. Also, the same individual may do well on one type of formal-operational task and poorly on another (Niaz, 1991). We are more likely to use formal-operational thought in the academic areas on which we focus. Some of us are formal operational in math or science, but not in the study of literature, and vice versa. Piaget (1972) himself admitted that although formal reasoning is within the grasp of adolescents, they may not always demonstrate it because they lack familiarity with the contents of a particular task (Small, 1990).

**_Imaginary audience_** The belief that others around us are as concerned with our thoughts and behaviors as we are; one aspect of adolescent egocentrism.

**_Personal fable_** The belief that our feelings and ideas are special and unique and that we are invulnerable; one aspect of adolescent egocentrism.

### *Adolescent Egocentrism*

The thought of preschoolers is characterized by egocentrism, or the inability to take another's point of view. Adolescent thought also is marked by a kind of egocentrism, according to David Elkind (1967, 1985). Teenagers have the ability to understand the thoughts of others. But they still have trouble differentiating between those objects that are of concern to others and those that are of concern to themselves. This form of egocentrism manifests itself in two ways: the ***imaginary audience*** and the ***personal fable.***

**Imaginary Audience** The imaginary audience concept is the belief that others around us are as concerned with our thoughts and behaviors as we are. As a result, adolescents believe that they are the center of attention and that others are preoccupied with the adolescent's appearance and behavior (Lapsley, 1991; Milstead et al., 1993). It is as though adolescents feel they are on stage, with all eyes focused upon them.

The intense desire for privacy that often emerges during adolescence may be a by-product of the imaginary audience concept. This concept also helps explain why adolescents are extremely self-conscious about their appearance, worrying about every facial blemish and spending long hours on grooming behavior. Self-consciousness seems to peak during the eighth grade and decline throughout adolescence. Girls are somewhat more self-conscious than boys (Elkind & Bowen, 1979).

**_Truth or Fiction Revisited_**

*It is true that adolescents generally see themselves as being onstage. This self-perception may account for the adolescent's intense desire for privacy.*

**Personal Fable** The other aspect of adolescent egocentrism is the personal fable. This is the belief that our feelings and ideas are special and unique and that we are invulnerable. The personal fable may underlie a number of typical adolescent behaviors, such as showing off and risk taking (Arnett, 1992; Lapsley, 1990, 1991; Milstead et al., 1993). Some adolescents adopt an attitude of "It can't happen to me" as they embark upon such activities as risky sexual activity or drug abuse. Recent research suggests that adolescents are more likely than their parents to minimize how risky an activity is (Adler, 1993b). Another

FIGURE 15.4

***IMAGINARY AUDIENCE.*** *Adolescents often feel that other people are constantly scrutinizing their appearance and behavior. This may explain why adolescents worry about every facial blemish and spend long hours on grooming behavior.*

manifestation of the personal fable is the notion that no one has ever experienced or could possibly know the particular feeling you are now experiencing, such as being in love. Perhaps this is the basis for the age-old teenage lament, "You just don't understand me!"

*TRUTH OR FICTION* ***REVISITED***

*Many adolescents do, in fact, think of themselves as being invulnerable. This self-perception is an aspect of the so-called personal fable.*

## GENDER DIFFERENCES IN COGNITIVE ABILITIES

While females and males do not differ in overall intelligence, gender differences do appear in certain cognitive abilities starting in childhood (Halpern, 1992). Females are somewhat superior to males in verbal ability. Males, on the other hand, seem somewhat superior in visual-spatial ability. The picture for mathematics ability is more complex, with females excelling in some areas and males excelling in others. Let us examine each of these gender differences.

**VERBAL ABILITY** Verbal abilities include a large number of language skills, such as reading, spelling, grammar, oral comprehension, and word fluency. As noted above, females have better verbal abilities than males on average (Halpern, 1992). These differences show up early. Girls seem to acquire language faster than boys. They make more prelinguistic vocalizations, utter their first word sooner, and develop larger vocabularies. Later in childhood, the differences are smaller and more inconsistent (Hyde & Linn, 1988). U.S. boys are more likely than girls to be dyslexic (Halpern, 1992). They also are more likely to have other reading problems, such as reading below grade level. In high school, girls continue to perform better than boys in reading and writing skills (Mullis et al., 1991).

Why do females excel in verbal abilities? As we saw in Chapter 7, parents talk more to their infant daughters than to their infant sons. This may lead to girls' verbal precocity. Because of this early language advantage, girls may rely more on verbal skills to interact with people, thus furthering their abilities in this area (Halpern, 1992). Cultural factors may play a role in gender differences in reading, since these differences disappear or are reversed in other cultures (Matlin, 1993). Reading is stereotyped as a feminine activity in the United States and Canada, and girls surpass boys in reading skills in these countries. Boys score higher than girls on most tests of reading in Nigeria and England, where boys have traditionally been expected to outperform girls in academic pursuits, including reading.

**Visual-Spatial Ability** Visual-spatial ability refers to the ability to visualize objects or shapes and to mentally manipulate and rotate them. As you can imagine, this ability is important in such fields as art, architecture, and engineering. Boys begin to outperform girls on many types of visual-spatial tasks starting at age 8 or 9 and the difference persists into adulthood (Halpern, 1992; Kerns & Berenbaum, 1991; Law et al., 1993). The gender difference is greatest on ***mental rotation*** tasks (see Figure 15.5), which require imagining how objects will look if rotated in space (Linn & Hyde, 1991). Somewhat smaller differences are found on tests of ***spatial perception,*** which involve the ability to identify the horizontal or vertical in spite of distracting information (Liben, 1991). For example, individuals may be shown a partially filled glass and asked to anticipate the position of the water when the glass is tilted at various positions (see Figure 15.5). No gender differences are found on ***spatial visualization*** tasks (see Figure 15.5), such as finding simple shapes hidden within larger, complex shapes (Linn & Petersen, 1986).

***Mental rotation*** The ability to imagine how objects will look if rotated in space.

***Spatial perception*** The ability to identify the horizontal or vertical in spite of distracting information.

***Spatial visualization*** The ability to find simple shapes hidden within larger, complex shapes.

What is the basis for the gender difference in visual-spatial skills? A number of biological and environmental explanations have been offered. One biological theory that has received some attention is that visual-spatial ability is influenced by sex-linked recessive genes on the X chromosome. But this theory has not been supported by research (Halpern, 1992).

There also are some interesting suggestions that the timing of puberty is linked to development of visual-spatial skills. Researchers have found that late maturers, whether boys or girls, perform better than early maturers on tests of visual-spatial ability (Dubas, 1991). And so late maturation would seem to favor development of visual-spatial skills. Since boys usually mature later than girls (see Chapter 14), this could account for their superiority in visual-spatial skills.

Other research links sex hormone levels to visual-spatial performance (Hines, 1990; Kimura, 1992). For example, low levels of androgen during the prenatal period have been linked to better performance on visual-spatial and arithmetic tasks among 4- and 6-year-old girls (Finegan et al., 1992; Jacklin et al., 1988). Similarly, a recent study (Kimura & Hampson, 1992) found that women performed better on visual-spatial tasks when their estrogen levels were low than when estrogen levels were high. (By contrast, they were better on tasks involving verbal skills or motor coordination when estrogen levels were high than when they were low.)

A number of environmental theories also have been proposed to account for the gender difference in visual-spatial skills. One theory is based on the assumption that just as reading is considered feminine in our culture, visual-spatial activities are stereotyped as masculine. (Just think of such visual-spatial activities as throwing a football, basketball, or baseball, or building model planes and cars.) If we further assume that individuals perform better on cognitive tasks that

FIGURE 15.5

***Examples of Tests Used to Measure Visual-Spatial Ability.*** *No gender differences are found on spatial visualization tasks (A). Boys do somewhat better than girls on tasks measuring spatial perception (B). The gender difference is greatest on mental rotation tasks (C). What are some possible reasons for these differences. (Source: Matlin, 1993).*

**A. SPATIAL VISUALIZATION**

**EMBEDDED-FIGURE TEST.** STUDY THE FIGURE ON THE LEFT. THEN COVER IT UP AND TRY TO FIND WHERE IT IS HIDDEN IN THE FIGURE ON THE RIGHT. THE LEFT-HAND FIGURE MAY NEED TO BE SHIFTED IN ORDER TO LOCATE IT IN THE RIGHT-HAND FIGURE.

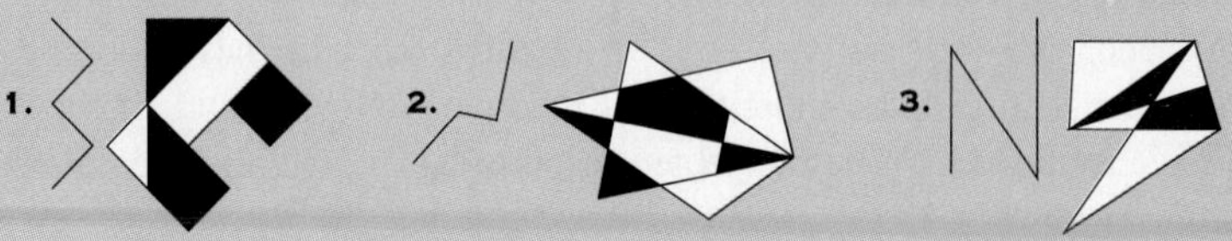


**B. SPATIAL PERCEPTION**

**WATER-LEVEL TEST.** EXAMINE THE GLASS OF WATER ON THE LEFT. NOW IMAGINE THAT IT IS SLIGHTLY TILTED, AS ON THE RIGHT. DRAW IN A LINE TO INDICATE THE LOCATION OF THE WATER LEVEL.

**C. MENTAL ROTATION**

**MENTAL-ROTATION TEST.** IF YOU MENTALLY ROTATE THE FIGURE ON THE LEFT, WHICH OF THE FIVE FIGURES ON THE RIGHT WOULD YOU OBTAIN?

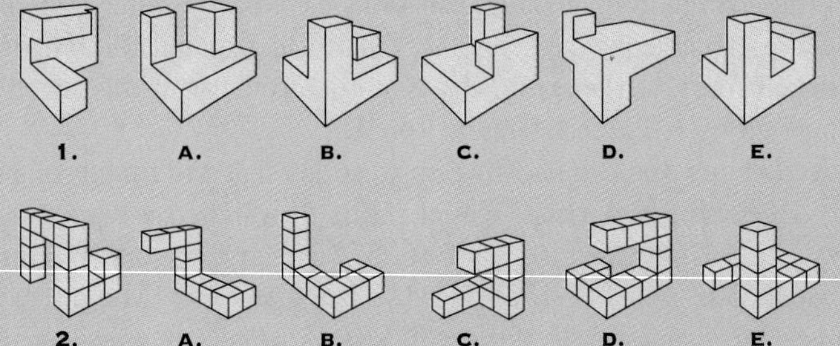


THE ANSWERS TO THESE THREE TESTS APPEAR BELOW.

ANSWERS: A. 1: ORIENT THE PATTERN AS IF IT WERE A TILTED CAPITAL M, WITH THE LEFT PORTION ALONG THE TOP OF THE WHITE TRIANGLE. 2: THIS PATTERN FITS ALONG THE RIGHT SIDES OF THE TWO BLACK TRIANGLES ON THE LEFT. 3: ROTATE THIS FIGURE ABOUT 100° TO THE RIGHT, SO THAT IT FORMS A Z, WITH THE TOP LINE COINCIDING WITH THE TOP LINE OF THE TOP WHITE TRIANGLE. B. THE LINE SHOULD BE HORIZONTAL, NOT TILTED. C. 1: C; 2: D.

match their self-image, then females and males with more masculine self-concepts should perform better on visual-spatial tasks (Halpern, 1992). There is some support for this view (Krasnoff et al., 1989; Newcombe & Dubas, 1992). For example, college women and men whose self-descriptions include many stereotypical masculine traits or few stereotypical feminine traits perform better on visual-spatial tasks (Signorella & Frieze, 1989).

Another related environmental theory is that gender stereotypes also influence the amount and type of spatial experiences children obtain. Gender-stereotyped "boys' toys," such as blocks, Legos, and Erector sets, provide more practice with spatial skills than gender-stereotyped "girls' toys." Boys also are more likely to engage in sports activities, which involve moving balls and other objects through space (Graber & Petersen, 1991). And boys are allowed to travel farther from home than girls are, providing greater opportunities for exploring the unfamiliar (Halpern, 1992). Several studies have found that participation in such spatially related activities is associated with better performance on visual-spatial tasks (Baenninger & Newcombe, 1989; Newcombe & Dubas, 1992; Serbin et al., 1990). Further evidence of the importance of experience in developing visual-spatial skills comes from studies showing that visual-spatial ability can be improved with appropriate training (Baenninger & Newcombe, 1989; Law et al., 1993). In one study, for example, female introductory psychology students given just 3 hours of training in various visual-spatial skills, such as rotating geometric figures, showed no performance deficit in these skills when compared with men (Stericker & LeVesconte, 1982).

**Mathematical Ability** Until recently, reviewers of the research on gender differences in mathematical ability concluded that males outperform females and that these differences first appear early in adolescence (Halpern, 1992). But a review by Janet Hyde and her colleagues (1990a) of 100 studies involving more than 3 million individuals reveals that the picture is more complex. They found a slight superiority for girls in computational skills in the elementary and middle school years. Boys began to perform better in problem solving in high school and college. There were no gender differences in understanding math concepts at any age. Gender differences were smallest and favored females in studies that sampled from the general population. Among groups of more highly selected individuals, such as college students or mathematically precocious youth, differences were larger and favored males. Consider, for example, performance on the mathematics portion of the Scholastic Aptitude Test (SAT). The mean score is 500. Twice as many boys as girls attain scores over 500. But 13 times as many boys as girls attain scores over 700 (Lubinski & Benbow, 1992).

**TRUTH OR FICTION REVISITED**

*The statement that "adolescent boys outperform adolescent girls in mathematics" is too broad to be accurate. Boys show some superiority in problem solving but not in computational skills. Moreover, gender differences favor girls in samples drawn from the general population.*

Gender differences in mathematical ability are most often explained in terms of differences in the socialization of girls and boys. According to this view, there are many reasons why boys are likely to feel more at home with math:

- Fathers are more likely than mothers to help children with math homework (Sherman, 1983; Raymond & Benbow, 1986).
- Advanced math courses are more likely to be taught by men (Fox, 1982).

- Teachers often show higher expectations for boys than for girls in math courses (Fennema, 1990; Halpern, 1992).
- Teachers of math courses spend more time instructing and interacting with boys than girls (AAUW, 1992; Koehler, 1990; Leder, 1990b).
- Girls receive less encouragement and support than boys from parents and peers for studying math (Clewell, 1991; Eccles, 1993).
- Toys may convey the message that math is not for girls. For example, Mattel recently marketed a Barbie doll that says "Math is hard!" (Tilghman, 1993).
- As early as first grade, parents in the United States, China, and Japan believe that boys are better at math than girls (Lummis & Stevenson, 1990).
- Parents are more likely to buy math and science books for boys than for girls (Eccles, 1993).

Given these typical experiences with math, we should not be surprised that

- By junior high, boys view themselves as more competent in math than girls do, even when they receive identical grades (Cramer & Oshima, 1992; Leder, 1990a; Wigfield & Eccles, 1992).
- By junior high, students perceive math as part of the male domain (Hyde et al., 1990b; Tocci & Engelhard, 1991).
- By junior high, boys are more likely than girls to perceive math as useful (Meece et al., 1982).
- Boys are more likely to have positive feelings about math. Girls are more likely to have math anxiety (Hyde et al., 1990b).
- High school and college women take fewer math courses than males, even when they show superior math ability (Eccles, 1985; Fox et al., 1985; Kimball, 1989).
- College women with math anxiety tend to avoid choosing careers in science, even when they are mathematically gifted (Chipman et al., 1992).

FIGURE 15.6

***Why Do Some Girls Avoid Math?*** *Teachers and parents sometimes convey the message that math is not for girls. For example, math teachers spend more time instructing and interacting with boys than with girls.*

**A Cautionary Note** In sum, it does appear that within our culture, girls show greater verbal ability than boys, whereas boys show greater visual-spatial ability than girls. Girls excel in certain areas of mathematics, while boys excel in others. However, two factors should caution us not to attach too much importance to these gender differences. First, in most cases they are very small (Caplan & Caplan, 1994; Halpern, 1992). Boys and girls are much more similar in their cognitive abilities than they are different. In recent years, the size of the gender difference in verbal, visual-spatial, and mathematical abilities has become even smaller (Feingold, 1993; Hyde et al., 1990b; Hyde & Linn, 1988).

Second, these gender differences are *group* differences. Variation in these skills is larger within, than between, the sexes. Despite group differences, millions of females exceed the average male in math and visual-spatial skills. Millions of males outdistance the average female in writing and spelling abilities. Females have produced their Madame Curies and males their Shakespeares.

***Thinking About Development***

Are there real gender differences in cognitive abilities?

## Moral Development

Moral development in childhood and adolescence is a complex issue, with both cognitive and behavioral aspects (Wolff, 1991). On a cognitive level, moral development concerns whether children and adolescents can deduce judgments of right and wrong from social principles. In this section, we examine the contributions of Jean Piaget and Lawrence Kohlberg to our understanding of the cognitive aspects of moral development.

Piaget and Kohlberg argued that moral reasoning undergoes a universal and invariant cognitive-developmental pattern. The moral considerations that children weigh at a given age are likely to reflect the values of the social and cultural settings in which they are being reared. However, moral reasoning is also theorized to reflect the orderly unfolding of cognitive processes. Patterns of moral reasoning are related to the individual's overall cognitive development. Let us describe and evaluate the contributions of each of these theorists.

### *Piaget's Theory*

> *In a sense, child morality throws light on adult morality. If we want to form men and women, nothing will fit us so well for the task as to study the laws that govern their formation. (Jean Piaget, 1932, p. 9)*

For years, Piaget observed children playing games like marbles and making judgments on the seriousness of the wrongdoing of characters in stories. On the basis of these observations, he concluded that children's moral judgments develop in two major overlapping stages: the stages of moral realism and autonomous morality (1932).

**The Stage of Moral Realism** The earlier stage is usually referred to as the stage of ***moral realism,*** or of ***objective morality.*** During this stage, which emerges at about the age of 5, children consider behavior to be correct when it conforms to authority, or to the rules of the game. When asked why something should be done in a certain way, the 5-year-old may answer "Because that's the way to do it," or "Because my Mommy says so."

At the age of 5 or so, children perceive rules as somehow embedded in the structure of the universe. Rules, to them, reflect ultimate reality. Hence, the term

***Moral realism*** According to Piaget, the stage during which children judge acts as moral when they conform to authority or to the rules of the game. Morality at this stage is perceived as embedded in the structure of the universe.

***Objective morality*** The perception of morality as objective, that is, as existing outside the cognitive functioning of people; a characteristic of Piaget's stage of moral realism.

***Immanent justice*** The view that retribution for wrongdoing is a direct consequence of the wrongdoing, reflective of the belief that morality is embedded within the structure of the universe.

*moral realism.* Rules and right and wrong are seen as unchanging and absolute. They are not seen as deriving from people to meet group needs. Realism may reflect the egocentrism of the preoperational child, who frequently assumes that thoughts and mental representations are exact equivalents of external reality.

Another consequence of viewing rules as embedded in the fabric of the world is ***immanent justice,*** or automatic retribution. Punishment is perceived as structurally connected to wrongdoing. Therefore, punishment is inevitable. Five- or 6-year-old children who lie or steal usually believe that they will be found out or at least punished for their acts. If they become ill or trip and scrape their knees, they may assume that this outcome represents punishment for a recent transgression.

Preoperational children also tend to focus on only one dimension at a time. They judge the wrongness of an act only in terms of the amount of damage done,

FIGURE 15.7

***Moral Realism.*** *How "bad" would this girl be if she dropped something on the floor and it broke? Would your answer differ if the girl were (a) trying to help her mother or (b) sneaking a treat against her mother's wishes? Children in the stage of moral realism tend to focus on the amount of damage done in making their judgments. Children in the stage of autonomous morality also consider the motives of the wrongdoer.*

not in terms of the intentions of the wrongdoer. Children in the stage of moral realism are tough jurors indeed. They do not let off the person who harms by accident. As an illustration, consider children's response to Piaget's story about the broken cups. Piaget told children a story in which one child breaks 15 cups accidentally and another child breaks one cup deliberately. Which child is naughtiest? Which should be punished most? Children in the stage of moral realism typically say that the child who did the most damage is the naughtiest and should be punished most. The amount of damage is more important than the child's intentions (Piaget, 1932).

***Autonomous morality*** The second stage in Piaget's cognitive-developmental theory of moral development. In this stage, children base moral judgments on the intentions of the wrongdoer, as well as on the amount of damage done. Social rules are viewed as agreements that can be changed.

**TRUTH OR FICTION REVISITED**

*It is not true that 5-year-old children generally think that people who accidentally harm others ought not to be punished. Most 5-year-olds mete out punishments according to the amount of damage done by a wrongdoer.*

**THE STAGE OF AUTONOMOUS MORALITY** Piaget found that when children reach the ages of 9 to 11, they begin to show ***autonomous morality.*** Their moral judgments tend to become more *autonomous,* or self-governed. The tendency to interpret social rules strictly declines. Children come to view these rules as arbitrary agreements that can be changed. Children no longer automatically view obedience to authority figures as right. They realize that circumstances can require breaking the rules.

Children who show autonomous morality are capable of flexible operational thought. They show decentration in their ability to focus simultaneously on multiple dimensions. And so, they consider not only social rules, but also the motives of the wrongdoer and the demands of the situation.

Children in this stage also show a greater capacity to take the point of view of others, to empathize with them. Decentration and increased empathy prompt children to weigh the intentions of the wrongdoer more heavily than the amount of damage done. The child who broke one cup deliberately may be seen as deserving of more punishment than the child who broke 15 cups accidentally. Children now become capable of considering mitigating circumstances. Accidents are less likely to be considered crimes.

Piaget assumed that autonomous morality usually develops as a result of cooperative peer relationships. But he also believed that parents help foster autonomous morality when they attempt to establish more egalitarian relationships with their children and explain the rationales for social rules.

**THOERETICAL INTERLUDE: EVALUATION OF PIAGET'S THEORY OF MORAL DEVELOPMENT** Many researchers agree that children's moral development proceeds from a stage of moral realism to one of autonomous morality (Hoffman, 1988; Karniol, 1980; Shultz, 1980). A number have found that very young children do make moral judgments on the basis of the consequences of an act, rather than on the intentions of the wrongdoer (Brandt & Strattner-Gregory, 1980).

Still, there are some problems with Piaget's views. One is that many more issues than the amount of damage done and the intentions of the transgressor influence children's moral judgments (Rest, 1983; Smetana, 1985). These include the ultimate outcomes of the acts, whether the object of wrongdoing was an object or a person, whether the effects of the act were physical or psychological, and so on.

Another criticism centers on Piaget's age estimates and on the demand characteristics of his research methods. A number of studies suggest, for example, that most children show autonomous morality prior to the age of 9. Piaget's experimental stories, such as the story of the cups, require that children remember the intentions of two people and the outcomes of two acts. Young children cannot process all this information simultaneously. But when the situations are described one at a time or when intentions are more clearly outlined, many 5- and 6-year-olds consider the intentions of the wrongdoer in passing their moral judgments (Feldman et al., 1976; Nelson, 1980; Surber, 1977).

One study asked children of ages 5, 8, 9, and 11 to judge the wrongness of lies. All age groups considered both the amount of damage done by the lie and the intentions of the liar (Peterson et al., 1983). Lies that did no harm were judged less serious than harmful lies, but selfishly motivated lies were judged as worse than unintended lies and lies that were intended to please the listener. However, the 11-year-olds explained the wrongness of lying in terms of violation of trust and fairness in relationships. Younger children referred to the likelihood of being caught and punished. So, in this study there were clear cognitive developments. Younger children judged social behavior in terms of rewards and punishments, and older children relied on abstract ethical principles that govern social relationships. But these developmental changes were not reflected in a clear transition from moral realism to autonomous morality.

## *Kohlberg's Theory*

Lawrence Kohlberg (1981, 1985) advanced the cognitive-developmental theory of moral development by elaborating on the kinds of information children use, as well as on the complexities of moral reasoning. Before we describe Kohlberg's views, read the following tale used by Kohlberg in his research, and answer the questions that follow.

> *In Europe a woman was near death from a special kind of cancer. There was one drug that the doctors thought might save her. It was a form of radium that a druggist in the same town had recently discovered. The drug was expensive to make, but the druggist was charging 10 times what the drug cost him to make. He paid $200 for the radium and charged $2,000 for a small dose of the drug. The sick woman's husband, Heinz, went to everyone he knew to borrow the money, but he could only get together about $1,000 which was half of what it cost. He told the druggist that his wife was dying and asked him to sell it cheaper or let him pay later. But the druggist said: "No, I discovered the drug and I'm going to make money from it." So Heinz got desperate and broke into the man's store to steal the drug for his wife. (Kohlberg, 1969)*

What do you think? Should Heinz have tried to steal the drug? Was he right or wrong? As you can see from Table 15.1, the issue is more complicated than a simple yes or no. Heinz is caught up in a moral dilemma in which a legal or social rule (in this case, laws against stealing) is pitted against a strong human need (Heinz's desire to save his wife). According to Kohlberg's theory, children and adults arrive at yes or no answers for different reasons. These reasons can be classified according to the level of moral development they reflect.

**TABLE 15.1**

***Kohlberg's Levels and Stages of Moral Development***

| Stage of Development | Examples of Moral Reasoning that Support Heinz's Stealing the Drug | Examples of Moral Reasoning that Oppose Heinz's Stealing the Drug |
|---|---|---|
| **Level I: Preconventional** | | |
| Stage 1: Judgments guided by obedience and the prospect of punishment (the consequences of the behavior.) | It isn't wrong to take the drug. After all, Heinz tried to pay the druggist for it, and it's only worth $200, not $2,000. | It's wrong to take the drug because taking things without paying is against the law; Heinz will get caught and go to jail. |
| Stage 2: Naively egoistic, instrumental orientation (Things are right when they satisfy people's needs.) | Heinz ought to take the drug because his wife really needs it. He can always pay the druggist back. | Heinz shouldn't take the drug. If he gets caught and winds up in jail, it won't do his wife any good. |
| **Level II: Conventional** | | |
| Stage 3: Good-boy orientation (That which helps others and is socially approved is right.) | Stealing is a crime, so it's bad, but Heinz should take the drug to save his wife or else people would blame him for letting her die. | Stealing is a crime. Heinz shouldn't just take the drug, because his family will be dishonored and they will blame him. |
| Stage 4: Law-and-order orientation (Doing one's duty and showing respect for authority are right.) | Heinz must take the drug to do his duty to save his wife. Eventually, he has to pay the druggist for it, however. | If everybody took the law into his or her hands, civilization would fall apart, so Heinz shouldn't steal the drug. |
| **Level III: Postconventional** | | |
| Stage 5: Contractual, legalistic orientation (It is moral to weigh pressing human needs against society's need to maintain the social order.) | This situation is complicated because society has a right to maintain law and order, but Heinz has to take the drug to save his wife. | I can see why Heinz feels he has to take the drug, but laws exist for the benefit of society as a whole and can't simply be cast aside. |
| Stage 6: Universal ethical principles orientation (People must act in accord with universal ethical principles and their own conscience, even if they must break the law in doing so.) | This is a case in which the law comes into conflict with the principle of the sanctity of human life. Heinz must take the drug because his wife's life is more important than the law. | If Heinz, in his own conscience, believes that stealing the drug is worse than letting his wife die, he should not take it. People have to make sacrifices to do what they believe is right. |

Children (and adults) are faced with many moral dilemmas. Consider two issues concerning cheating that children frequently face in school. When children fear failing a test, they may be tempted to cheat. Different children may decide not to cheat for very different reasons. One child may simply fear getting caught. A second child may decide that it is more important to live up to her moral

FIGURE 15.8

**CHEATING.** *When children fear failing a test, they may be tempted to cheat. Different children may decide to cheat–or not to cheat–for a variety of reasons that reflect each child's level of moral development.*

principles than to get the highest possible grade. In each case, the child's decision is not to cheat. However, the cognitive processes behind each decision reflect different levels of reasoning.

Other children may observe a classmate cheating and decide to inform the teacher—again, for different reasons. A child with a grudge against the cheater may tell the teacher so that the cheater will be punished. A second child may tell the teacher to prevent the cheater from getting a high grade and making other students' grades—including the informant's—look bad by comparison. A third may tell the teacher because she believes that reporting cheating is the normal thing to do. A fourth may hate the idea of squealing, but may still inform on the cheater because of concern that the social system could break down if cheating is tolerated by peers.

As a stage theorist, Kohlberg argued that the developmental stages of moral reasoning follow an invariant sequence. Children progress at different rates, and not all children (or adults) reach the highest stage. But children must experience stage 1 before they enter stage 2, and so on. According to Kohlberg, there are three levels of moral development and two stages within each level.

Let us return to Heinz and see how responses to the questions we have posed can reflect different levels and stages of moral development.

**THE PRECONVENTIONAL LEVEL** In the ***preconventional level,*** children base their moral judgments on the consequences of their behavior. For instance, stage 1 is oriented toward obedience and punishment. Good behavior is obedient and allows one to avoid punishment. According to stage 1 reasoning, Heinz could be urged to steal the drug because he did ask to pay for it first. But he could also be urged not to steal the drug so that he will not be sent to jail (see Table 15.1).

In stage 2, good behavior allows people to satisfy their own needs and, perhaps, the needs of others. A stage 2 reason for stealing the drug is that Heinz's wife needs it. Therefore, stealing the drug—the only way of attaining it—is not wrong. A stage 2 reason for not stealing the drug would be that Heinz's wife might die even if he does so. Thus, he might wind up in jail needlessly.

***Preconventional level*** According to Kohlberg, a period during which moral judgments are based largely on expectations of rewards or punishments.

In a study of U.S. children aged 7 through 16, Kohlberg (1963) found that stage 1 and 2 types of moral judgments were offered most frequently by 7- and

10-year-olds. There was a steep falling off of stage 1 and 2 judgments after age 10.

**Conventional level** According to Kohlberg, a period during which moral judgments largely reflect social rules and conventions.

**The Conventional Level** In the ***conventional level*** of moral reasoning, right and wrong are judged by conformity to conventional (family, religious, societal) standards of right and wrong. According to the stage 3 "good-boy/good-girl orientation," it is good to meet the needs and expectations of others. Moral behavior is what is "normal"—what the majority does. From the stage 3 perspective, Heinz should steal the drug, because that is what a "good husband" would do. It is "natural" or "normal" to try to help one's wife. Or, Heinz should not steal the drug because "good people do not steal." Stage 3 judgments also focus on the role of sympathy—on the importance of doing what will make someone else feel good or better.

In stage 4, moral judgments are based on rules that maintain the social order. Showing respect for authority and one's duty are valued highly. From this perspective, one could argue that Heinz must steal the drug, because it is his duty to save his wife. He would pay the druggist when he could. Or one could argue that Heinz should not steal the drug, because he would be breaking the law. He might also be contributing to the breakdown of the social order. Many people do not develop beyond the conventional level.

Kohlberg (1963) found that stage 3 and 4 types of judgments are all but absent among 7-year-olds. However, they are reported by about 20 percent of 10-year-olds and higher percentages of 13- and 16-year-olds. Stage 3 and 4 moral judgments are the types of judgments made most frequently by 13- and 16-year-olds.

Reviews of the research show that juvenile delinquents are less advanced in their moral reasoning than nondelinquents (Nelson et al., 1990; Smetana, 1990). Higher percentages of juvenile delinquents engage in stage 2 moral reasoning than do their nondelinquent counterparts. Nondelinquents are more likely to show moral reasoning typical of stages 3 and 4. Stage 2 reasoning (viewing what is right and wrong in terms of satisfying personal needs) is also characteristic of offenders who engage in crimes such as robbery (Thornton & Reid, 1982).

FIGURE 15.9

***Moral Reasoning Among Juvenile Delinquents.*** *Juvenile delinquents are less advanced in their moral reasoning than nondelinquents. Juvenile delinquents are less likely to show the type of moral reasoning characteristic of the conventional level.*

***Postconventional level*** According to Kohlberg, a period during which moral judgments are derived from moral principles and people look to themselves to set moral standards.

***Reciprocity*** The principle that actions have mutual effects and that people depend upon one another to treat each other morally.

**THE POSTCONVENTIONAL LEVEL** In the ***postconventional level,*** moral reasoning is based on the person's own moral standards. In each instance, moral judgments are derived from personal values, not from conventional standards or authority figures. In stage 5's contractual, legalistic orientation, it is recognized that laws stem from agreed-upon procedures and that many rights have great value and should not be violated. But under exceptional circumstances, laws cannot bind the individual. A stage 5 reason for stealing the drug might be that it is the right thing to do, even though it is illegal. Conversely, it could be argued that if everyone in need broke the law, the legal system and the social contract would be destroyed.

Stage 6 thinking relies on supposed universal ethical principles such as those of human life, individual dignity, justice, and ***reciprocity.*** Behavior that is consistent with these principles is considered right. If a law is seen as unjust or contradicts the right of the individual, it is wrong to obey it. Postconventional people look to their consciences as the highest moral authority. This point has created confusion. To some it suggests that it is right to break the law when it is convenient. But Kohlberg meant that postconventional people feel obligated to do what they believe is right, even if it counters social rules or laws or requires personal sacrifice.

**TRUTH OR FICTION REVISITED**

*It is true, according to Lawrence Kohlberg's theory of moral development, that people who have arrived at the highest level of moral development follow their own ethical principles and may disobey the laws of the land. Kohlberg's views have caused a good deal of controversy and are sometimes misunderstood.*

Consider examples from recent history in which many have faced large-scale moral dilemmas that required personal sacrifice. During the 1960s, many U.S. citizens broke local laws in their civil-rights demonstrations. In most cases these local laws were later overturned by the Supreme Court as discriminatory. During the 1960s and 1970s, many young men who believed that U.S. military involvement in Vietnam was wrong were faced with a dilemma when they were drafted into the armed forces. If they allowed themselves to be inducted, they would be supporting what they saw as an immoral cause. But by refusing induction, they were breaking the law. In the 1980s, other U.S. citizens broke the law in their efforts to prevent the construction of plants for generating nuclear energy. However, they also believed that it would be wrong for them to stand idly by while the country—from their perspective—was building machines that could lead to its own destruction. For these citizens, belief in their cause compelled them to break laws, even though they risked losing their families, careers, social status, and freedom. In the 1990s, environmental issues have emerged as a major concern. Individuals have engaged in demonstrations—sometimes illegally—to protest such activities as deforestation, wildlife extinction, and air pollution.

Of course, it can be argued, and correctly, that not all of the demonstrators and law-breakers in the civil rights, anti-Vietnam War, anti-nuclear, and environmental crusades have acted from such a principled perspective. Certainly some demonstrators broke the law to avoid the disapproval of their own peer groups. A few college students have admitted to participating in demonstrations to find dates. And a few young men refused induction into the armed forces to avoid exposure to the dangers of Vietnam, despite claims of higher moral concerns. Nevertheless, many did break the law because of their interpretation of moral principles and were operating at Kohlberg's stage 6. College students at the postconventional level were more likely than peers at the conventional level of morality to participate in the campus demonstrations and civil disobedience of the 1960s (Haan et al., 1968).

Return to the case of Heinz. It could be argued from stage 6's perspective that the principle of preserving life takes precedence over laws prohibiting stealing. Therefore, it is morally necessary for Heinz to steal the drug, even if he must go to jail. Note that it could also be asserted, from the principled orientation, that if Heinz finds the social contract or the law to be the highest principle, he must remain within the law, despite the consequences.

Stage 5 and 6 moral judgments were virtually absent among the 7- and 10-year-olds in Kohlberg's (1963) sample of U.S. children. They increased in frequency during the early and middle teens. By age 16, stage 5 reasoning was shown by about 20 percent and stage 6 reasoning by about 5 percent of adolescents. However, stage 3 and 4 judgments were made more frequently at all ages, 7 through 16, studied by Kohlberg and other investigators (Colby et al., 1983; Rest, 1983). (See Figure 15.10.)

**Gender and Moral Development** One of the more controversial notions in the history of child development is that males show higher levels of moral development than females. From his psychoanalytic perspective, Freud assumed that males would have stronger superegos than females because of the wrenching Oedipus complex, the fear of castration, and the male's consequent identification with authority figures and social codes. But Freud's views on the Oedipus complex were speculative, and his views on women reflected the ignorance and prejudice of his times.

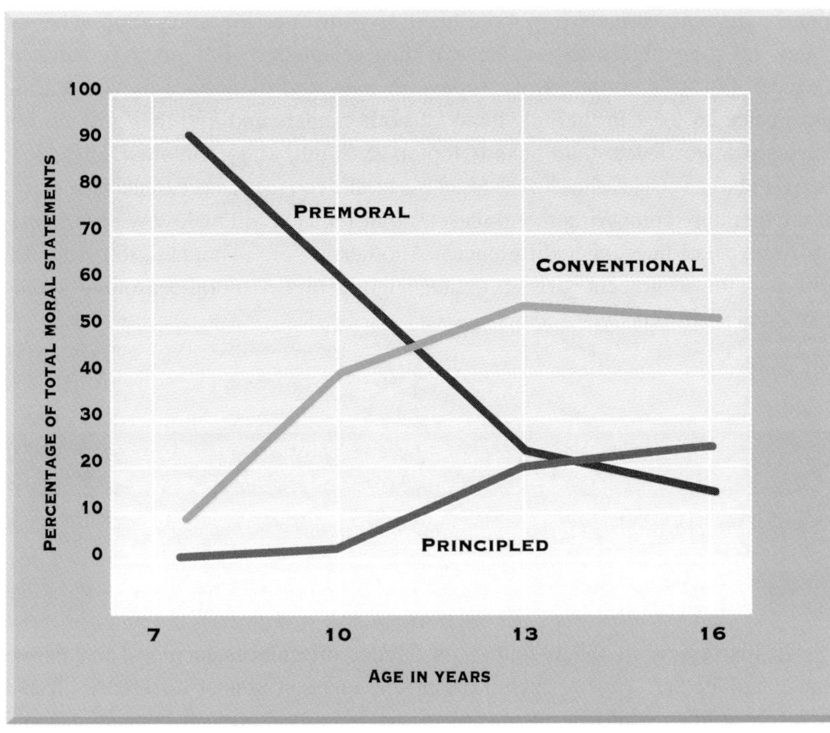


FIGURE 15.10

***Age and Type of Moral Judgment.*** *The incidence of preconventional (premoral) reasoning declines from greater than 90 percent of moral statements at age 7 to under 20 percent of moral statements at age 16. Conventional moral statements increase with age between 7 and 13, but then level off to account for 50–60 percent of moral statements at ages 13 and 16. Postconventional (principled) moral statements are all but absent at ages 7 and 10, but account for about 20–25 percent of moral statements at ages 13 and 16. (Source: Kohlberg, 1963).*

**THINKING ABOUT DEVELOPMENT**

Agree or disagree with the following statement and support your answer: ''Moral judgments based on a 'justice' orientation are more advanced than moral judgments based on a 'caring' orientation.''

However, in more recent years, some cognitively oriented researchers have claimed to find that males reason at higher levels of moral development than females in terms of responses to Heinz's dilemma. For example, Kohlberg and Kramer (1969) reported that the average stage of moral development for men was stage 4, which emphasizes justice, law, and order. The average stage for women was reported to be stage 3, which emphasizes caring and concern for others.

Carol Gilligan (1977, 1982; Gilligan & Attanucci, 1988) argues that this gender difference reflects different patterns of socialization for boys and girls. Gilligan makes her point through two examples of responses to Heinz's dilemma. Eleven-year-old Jake views the dilemma as a math problem. He sets up an equation showing that life has greater value than property. Heinz is thus obligated to steal the drug. Eleven-year-old Amy, on the other hand, notes that stealing the drug and letting Heinz's wife die would both be wrong. Amy searches for alternatives, such as getting a loan, stating that it would profit Heinz's wife little if he went to jail and were no longer around to help her.

According to Gilligan, Amy is showing a pattern of reasoning that is as sophisticated as Jake's. Still, Amy would be rated as showing a lower level of moral development. Gilligan asserts that Amy, like other girls, has been socialized into focusing on the needs of others and foregoing simplistic judgments of right and wrong. As a consequence, Amy is more likely to appear to show stage 3 reasoning, which focuses in part on empathy for others and caring (Gilligan, 1977). Jake, by contrast, has been socialized into making judgments based on logic. To him, clear-cut conclusions are to be derived from a set of premises. Amy was aware of the logical considerations that struck Jake, of course. However, she processed them as one source of information—not as the sole acceptable source. It is ironic that Amy's empathy, a trait that has ''defined the 'goodness' of women,'' marks Amy ''as deficient in moral development'' (Gilligan, 1982, p. 18). Prior to his death in 1987, Kohlberg (1985) had begun efforts to correct the sexism in his scoring system.

For all their differences, both Kohlberg and Gilligan agree that in making moral judgments, females are more likely to show a caring orientation, whereas males are more likely to assume a justice orientation. But other researchers disagree with this notion. Most studies, in fact, find that concerns with caring and justice co-exist in the judgments of both genders and find that girls do not reason at lower levels than boys (Clopton & Sorell, 1993; Galotti et al., 1991; Garrod et al., 1991; Kahn, 1992; Smetana et al., 1991a). Two extensive reviews of the literature comparing moral reasoning of females and males (Walker, 1984, 1991) revealed no gender differences. Another review (Thoma, 1986) found a tendency for adolescent girls to obtain slightly higher moral reasoning scores than adolescent boys.

**TRUTH OR FICTION REVISITED**

*It is not true that girls lag behind boys in their moral development.*

In his review of the literature on gender differences in moral reasoning, Lawrence Walker (1991) concludes that the apparent gender differences found in a few studies could be attributed to gender differences in educational and occupational achievement—at least among adult subjects. That is, subjects who showed the highest levels of moral reasoning had had more education and higher levels of occupational attainment.

How does culture influence the development of moral reasoning?

| Aspect of Moral Reasoning | Culture |
|---|---|
| Postconventional reasoning | More common in the United States than in villages in Mexico, Taiwan, Turkey, Bahamas<br><br>More common in urban middle-class than in folk cultures |
| Self-versus-other orientation | U.S. and Israel city children more self-oriented and less other-oriented than Israeli kibbutz children |
| Caring-versus-justice orientation | Middle-class Hindu children more care-oriented and less justice-oriented than middle-class U.S. children |

**Culture and Development: Moral Development** Cultural background is a powerful shaper of moral reasoning. Kohlberg found postconventional thinking among a minority of U.S. adolescents, but it was all but absent among adolescents in villages in Mexico, Taiwan, Turkey (Kohlberg, 1969), and the Bahamas (White et al., 1978). A review of 45 studies of moral development carried out in 27 countries concluded that postconventional reasoning is more likely to be found in urban cultural groups and middle-class populations, but is rarely seen in traditional folk cultures (Snarey, 1985).

Another cross-cultural study indicates that the moral reasoning of children from Western industrialized countries such as West Germany, Poland, and Italy is quite similar to that of American children from urban areas (Boehnke et al., 1989). On the other hand, the moral reasoning of American children and Israeli city children is more self-oriented and less oriented to the needs of others than the reasoning of Israeli kibbutz children (Eisenberg et al., 1990). These differences are consistent with the differences in the children's social environments. The kibbutz, discussed in Chapter 7, is a collective farm community that emphasizes cooperative relationships and a communal philosophy.

A similar pattern has been found in comparisons of middle-class American and Hindu Indian children and adults. Hindu Indians are more likely to show a caring orientation in making moral judgments, whereas Americans more often demonstrate a justice orientation. These findings are consistent with the greater emphasis Hindu Indian culture puts on the importance of taking responsibility for others (Miller, 1994; Miller & Bersoff, 1992).

**Situational Influences on Moral Development** People who are capable of a certain level of moral reasoning do not always use it (Hoffman, 1980; Weiss, 1982; Krebs et al., 1991). Situational factors apparently play an important role in whether moral judgments will be based on conventional or postconventional principles. A study by Tapp and Levine (1972), for example, suggests that it is easier to talk about higher levels of moral development in theoretical discussions than it is to apply them to one's own life. The investigators asked children and adolescents two questions: (a) "Why should people follow rules?" and (b) "Why do *you* follow rules?" Answers to the first were more advanced. For example, children were more likely to say that people should follow rules to maintain the social order than they were to offer this reason for their own behavior. In their own lives, they admitted that their behavior was more likely to be governed by expectations of reward or punishment.

Similar results were obtained in a study in which teenagers and their parents told how they had handled recent real-life moral dilemmas (Krebs et al., 1991). They also responded to Kohlberg's standard moral dilemmas. Both the adolescents and their parents scored an average of one stage lower on the real-life conflicts than they did on Kohlberg's tests.

A study by Sobesky (1983) also suggests the power of situational influences. High school and college students who were told it was certain Heinz would go to prison for stealing the drug were significantly less likely to use principled thinking and suggest that Heinz should help his wife. Once the consequences were made so clear and certain, many of these students seemed compelled by the situation into making stage 1 moral judgments that were controlled by fear of punishment. Other students, who were told that the drug would definitely save

Heinz's wife, were significantly more likely to suggest that Heinz steal the drug and to justify their decision with principled reasoning.

**Moral Behavior and Moral Reasoning: Is There a Relationship?** Is there a relationship between moral cognitive development and moral behavior? Are children whose moral development is more mature less likely to commit immoral acts? Is there a correspondence between children's behavior and their moral judgments? The answer seems to be yes, for many studies have found relationships between level of moral development and moral behavior (Turiel, 1991).

Preadolescents whose moral reasoning is at stage 2 engage in cheating and other conduct problems in the classroom more frequently than age-mates whose moral reasoning is at higher stages (Bear, 1989; Richards et al., 1992). Among adolescents, those with higher levels of moral reasoning are more likely to exhibit moral behavior, including altruism and other prosocial behaviors (Eisenberg et al., 1991; Eisenberg, 1992).

Experiments also have been conducted in the hope of advancing moral reasoning as a way of decreasing immoral behavior. A number of studies have found that group discussion of moral dilemmas elevates delinquents' level of moral reasoning (Smetana, 1990). Is moral behavior affected as well? In one encouraging study, discussions of moral dilemmas both improved moral reasoning and decreased behaviors such as school tardiness, behavior referrals, and police/court contacts among high-risk behavior-disordered adolescents (Arbuthnot & Gordon, 1986).

**Theoretical Interlude: Evaluation of Kohlberg's Theory of Moral Development** There is evidence that the moral judgments of children develop toward higher stages in sequence (Walker & Taylor, 1991a), even though most children do not reach postconventional thought. Postconventional thought, when it is found, first occurs during adolescence.

Why doesn't postconventional moral reasoning appear until age 13 or so? A number of studies (Tomlinson-Keasey & Keasey, 1974; Kuhn et al., 1977) suggest that formal-operational thinking is a prerequisite condition. That is, postconventional reasoning appears to require the capacities to understand abstract moral principles and to empathize with the attitudes and emotional responses of other people. However, the appearance of formal-operational thought does not guarantee that postconventional moral judgments will follow.

Consistent with Kohlberg's theory, children do not appear to skip stages as they progress (Kohlberg & Kramer, 1969; Kuhn, 1976; White et al., 1978). Children exposed to examples of moral reasoning above and below that of their own stage generally prefer the higher level of reasoning (Rest, 1983). Thus, the thrust of moral development is from lower to higher stages, even if children can be sidetracked by social influences.

One longitudinal study did find that one's level of moral reasoning can slip backward in response to changed circumstances. James Rest and his colleagues (Rest & Narvaez, 1991) observed young adults who went on to college after high school. They showed increasingly higher levels of moral development over the course of the next 10 years. However, high school graduates who did not attend college showed increases in moral development over the next 2 years, and then their development tended to fall back to levels similar to those at time of graduation. Rest suggests a number of explanations for the advances of the college students, including socialization into the (more principled) values likely to be held by college students, the learning of moral philosophies, and general intellectual stimulation. The educational thrust of high school may have fueled the development of non-college-attending graduates for another 2 years or so. But then, perhaps, they were socialized into groups with more of a law-and-order orientation. Or, perhaps, decreased intellectual stimulation dulled the incentive to examine moral issues.

Kohlberg believed that the stages of moral development are universal, following the unfolding of innate sequences. However, he seems to have underestimated the influence of social, cultural, and educational institutions (Tappan & Packer, 1991). Let us consider the role of education. Higher education tends to foster higher levels of moral reasoning (Rest & Thoma, 1985). A number of programs designed to enhance moral development have been developed for schoolchildren. These programs involve student discussion of moral dilemmas and are designed to help students become aware of their own values and the values of others (Battistich et al., 1991a; Lickona, 1991). Typically, about half the students in a class show some advancement in moral reasoning as a result of participating in these programs (Lickona, 1991).

Kohlberg also appears to have underestimated the role that parents play in their children's moral development (Walker, 1993). One recent study, for example, found that the moral development of children and adolescents was enhanced when parents displayed a higher level of moral reasoning and when parents used a highly interactive style when discussing moral dilemmas with the child (Walker & Taylor, 1991b). Moreover, it has been found that the use of inductive disciplinary methods, including discussions of the feelings of others, advances moral reasoning (Hoffman, 1984, 1988). Mothers seem to be particularly influential in fostering advanced moral reasoning, because they, more so than fathers, look for children's motives and discuss the feelings of victims (Hoffman, 1982). (Are there any who still view women's moral development as inferior to men's?)

There is also cross-cultural evidence concerning the importance of the ***macrosystem.*** The fact that postconventional thinking is all but absent in nonindustrialized societies—and infrequent even in the United States—suggests that postconventional reasoning may reflect Kohlberg's personal ideals and not a natural, universal stage of development. Stage 6 reasoning is based on the acceptance of supposedly universal ethical principles. The principles of justice, equality,

***Macrosystem*** In ecological theory, the basic institutions and ideologies that influence the child, such as the American ideals of freedom of expression and equality under the law.

FIGURE 15.11

**PARENTS INFLUENCE THEIR CHILDREN'S MORAL DEVELOPMENT.** *Parents help advance their children's moral development when they discuss moral dilemmas with them.*

integrity, and reverence for human life may have a high appeal to you. But you were reared in a culture that idealizes them and that elevates them to a higher moral status than social customs and conventions such as dress codes and food rituals (Damon, 1988). Abstract principles like justice and welfare are not universally revered, however. They are more reflective of Western cultural influences than of the cognitive development of the child. In some cultures, for instance, violation of social customs is considered a much more serious moral offense than some forms of violent and sexist behavior. For example, some Hindu Brahmin children consider wife beating a far less serious moral transgression than a widow eating fish. American children, on the other hand, condemn wife beating but find fish-eating by widows quite acceptable (Schweder et al., 1987). In his later years, Kohlberg (1985) dropped stage 6 reasoning from his theory in recognition of these problems.

## THE ADOLESCENT IN SCHOOL

No discussion of cognitive development in adolescence would be complete without mentioning the importance of school experiences. Of course, schools do much more than foster intellectual development. They also play a key role in the social growth of the adolescent (Fenzel & Blyth, 1991). In Chapter 13, we examined the young child's transition to school. In this section, we explore the transition from elementary school to middle, junior high, or high school. We also discuss students who drop out of school and possible strategies to encourage students to complete high school.

### *MAKING THE TRANSITION FROM ELEMENTARY SCHOOL*

All students make at least one and sometimes two transitions to a new school before they complete high school. Think back to your own school days. Did you spend the years from kindergarten to eighth grade in one building and then move on to high school? Did you instead attend elementary school through sixth grade and then go to junior high for grades 7–9 before starting high school? Or did you complete grades K through 4 or 5 in one school, then attend a middle school for grades 5 or 6 to 8, and then move on to high school for grades 9–12? (This has become the most common pattern in recent years.)

The transition to middle, junior high, or high school generally involves a shift from a smaller, neighborhood elementary school with self-contained classrooms to a larger, more impersonal setting with many more students and with different teachers for different classes (Entwisle, 1990; Fenzel et al., 1991). These changes may not fit very well with the developmental needs of early adolescents. For example, adolescents express a desire for increased autonomy, yet teachers in junior high typically allow less student input and exert more behavioral control than teachers in elementary school (Eccles, 1991b; Eccles et al., 1993b). Moreover, in the shift to the new school, students move from being the ''top dog'' (that is, the oldest and most experienced students) to the ''bottom dog'' (Simmons, 1987). These changes aren't the only ones facing the early adolescent. Many youngsters also are going through the early stages of pubertal development at about the same time they move to a new school.

How well do students adjust to the transition to a new school? Much of the research has examined children's experiences as they move from elementary school to junior high school. The transition to the new school setting often is

FIGURE 15.12

***The Transition from Elementary School.*** *The transition to junior high or high school is not always easy. Some children experience a decline in grades and lowered self-esteem. School-based programs can ease the transition.*

accompanied by a decline in grades and in participation in school activities. Students may also experience a drop in self-esteem and an increase in psychological distress (Eccles, 1991b; Flanagan & Eccles, 1993; Seidman et al., in press).

Girls appear to be more vulnerable to the junior high transition than boys. In one study, for example, girls who switched to a junior high for seventh grade showed a decrease in self-esteem, whereas girls who stayed in their kindergarten through eighth-grade school did not. Boys' self-esteem did not change when they switched to junior high (Simmons & Blyth, 1987). Why are girls more vulnerable than boys to the transition to junior high school? Children who experience several life changes at the same time seem to have a harder time adjusting to a new school (Flanagan & Eccles, 1993; Simmons & Blyth, 1987). Remember that girls start puberty sooner than boys, on average, and start dating sooner. Both of these life changes often coincide with the girl's entry into junior high school. Boys will not experience those changes until later. This may explain why the shift to junior high is more problematic for girls.

## Truth or Fiction Revisited

*Actually, the transition from elementary school appears to be more difficult for girls than for boys. The difference may reflect that fact that girls are more likely to be undergoing puberty and beginning to date at about this time.*

But the transition to a new school need not be stressful. Elementary and middle schools can take steps to ease the transition to high school. For example, one longitudinal study followed the progress of students who received a 2-year social decision-making and problem-solving program in elementary school. When followed up in high school 4 to 6 years later, these students showed higher levels of prosocial behavior and lower levels of antisocial, self-destructive, and socially disordered behavior than did students who had not been exposed to this program (Elias et al., 1991). Recently, some middle schools have tried to create a more intimate, caring atmosphere. West Baltimore Middle School, for instance, has created smaller schools within the school building, housing each grade in a separate wing. It also has scheduled daily advisory periods when students can talk with a teacher or counselor (Celis, 1992). Other school districts have created bridge programs to carry students through the summer between middle school and high school by introducing them to the new school culture and new style of learning, and strengthening their academic skills (Suro, 1992).

## DROPPING OUT OF SCHOOL

Completing high school is one of the most critical developmental tasks facing adolescents (Eccles, 1991a). The consequences of dropping out can be grim indeed. High school dropouts are more likely to be unemployed (McWhirter et al., 1993). They make lower salaries. Recent research, in fact, shows that each year of education, from grade school through graduate school, adds 16 percent to an individual's lifetime earnings (Passell, 1992). (This is a good incentive for you not only to complete college, but to think about graduate work!) Dropouts also are more likely to show a variety of problem behaviors, including delinquency, criminal behavior, and substance abuse (Dryfoos, 1990). However, it is sometimes difficult to disentangle the consequences of dropping out from its causes (Bachman, 1991). A pattern of delinquent behavior, for example, often precedes as well as follows dropping out.

**STUDENTS WHO DROP OUT** It is difficult to estimate accurately the magnitude of the school dropout problem, since states use different reporting systems, and most do not keep track of those who quit after eighth grade. The good news is that high school dropout rates declined during the 1980s and early 1990s for all ethnic groups (''High School Dropout Rate Down,'' 1993). Even so, some estimates indicate that nearly one in three students still do not complete high school (Tabor, 1992).

*Actually, high school dropout rates have been declining in recent years.*

Who is most at risk for dropping out? Excessive school absence and reading below grade level are two of the earliest and strongest predictors of later school dropout (Weitzman & Siegel, 1992). Other risk factors include low academic achievement, low self-esteem, difficulty getting along with teachers, dissatisfaction with school, substance abuse, being too old for grade level, and being male. Adolescents who adopt adult roles early, such as marrying at a young age, becoming a teen parent, or working long hours, also are more likely to drop out (Goertz et al., 1991; Loughrey & Harris, 1990). Certain demographic factors play a role as well. Students from low-income households, large urban areas, and the West and South are at greater risk (Duncan, 1993; Entwistle, 1990; National Center for Education Statistics, 1992). But not all dropouts come from low-income families. Middle-class youth who feel bored with school, alienated, or strongly pressured to succeed also are at risk (Tabor, 1992).

FIGURE 15.13

**DROPPING OUT.** *The consequences of dropping out of school can be harsh. High school dropouts earn less and are more likely to be unemployed. A variety of programs have been developed to help prevent school dropouts.*

**CULTURE AND DEVELOPMENT: DROPPING OUT** The dropout rates for ethnic groups vary considerably: 35 percent for Hispanics, 14 percent for African Americans, and 9 percent for whites (National Center for Education Statistics, 1992). The higher dropout rate for ethnic minority children is linked to the lower socioeconomic status of their families. Children from lower-income households have higher dropout rates. Ethnic minority families, on average, have lower income levels than white families. When minority and white children of similar income levels are compared, ethnic differences in school dropout rates are greatly reduced (Dryfoos, 1990; National Center for Education Statistics, 1992). And when African-American and white students with similar test scores and high school grades are compared, African Americans are somewhat more likely than whites to finish high school, go to college, and complete a college degree (Entwisle, 1990).

**PREVENTING SCHOOL DROPOUT** A wide variety of programs has been developed to prevent school dropout. Some of the more successful programs have certain common characteristics (Dryfoos, 1990; McCall, 1991; Tabor, 1992):

- Early preschool intervention. Examples are early childhood compensatory education, such as Head Start, which was discussed in Chapter 9
- Identification and monitoring of high-risk students throughout the school years
- Intensive programs with small class size, individualized instruction, and counseling
- Strong vocational components that link learning and community work experiences
- Involvement of adults from families or community organizations
- Positive school climate, which makes students feel like part of a community
- Clear and reasonable educational goals, student accountability for behavior, and motivational systems that involve penalties and rewards

These intervention efforts (with the exception of the early preschool intervention programs) usually are not employed until students are on the verge of dropping out. And few programs are designed to handle students who have already dropped out. More needs to be done to identify and help students at an early age who are at risk of dropping out (Weitzman & Siegel, 1992).

## VOCATIONAL DEVELOPMENT AND WORK EXPERIENCE

Deciding what job or career you wish to pursue after you complete school is one of the most important choices you will make in your life. How do adolescents make vocational choices? Does one's gender influence career choice? What is the role of part-time work during the teen years? In this section, we will address each of these issues.

### *VOCATIONAL DEVELOPMENT*

When you were little, what did you want to be when you grew up? One of the authors (C. E.) remembers vividly wanting to be a shoeshine man. Later, she thought about being a writer. Finally, in college, she decided to become a psychologist (She still likes to write, but not shine shoes!). This course of vocational development is fairly typical. Children's career aspirations often are not very practical at first, but become increasingly realistic as they get older (Ginsberg, 1972). In early adolescence, ideas about the type of work one wants to do may become more firmly established, or ***crystallized,*** but a particular occupation often is not chosen until the college years or later (Super, 1984, 1985).

Many factors influence one's choice of a career, including one's abilities and personality characteristics (Holland, 1985; Osipow, 1990). Let's consider two individuals. Michele has excellent mathematical and mechanical abilities. She is practical and somewhat materialistic. Mark has excellent artistic ability, is expressive and creative. Which one do you think is more likely to choose a career as a computer engineer? Which is more likely to become a graphic designer? Life experiences, job opportunities, parental expectations, and economic factors play an important role as well. Perhaps Michele's family owns a small business. In high school and college, she works there on weekends and vacations. Her parents make it clear that when they retire, they want Michele to run the business. Perhaps she will choose this as her career instead of becoming a computer engineer. Mark wants to become a graphic designer, but his family can't afford to send him to college. His girlfriend becomes pregnant. Mark takes the best job he can find—cashier in a discount store—to help support his new family.

**GENDER AND VOCATIONAL DEVELOPMENT** Women's labor force participation rates are approaching those of men (U.S. Bureau of the Census, 1993). Most young women now expect to be employed following the completion of their education. And the more education a woman has, the more likely she is to be employed (Baber & Monaghan, 1988; Greene, 1990).

*Occupational Gender-typing* Women and men still tend to choose different types of occupations. Even very young children show a high degree of ***occupational gender-typing,*** dividing the workplace into "women's jobs" and "men's jobs." For example, Gettys and Cann (1981) showed 2- and 3-year-olds female and male dolls and asked them to point to the one that held a particular

***Crystallization*** A stage of vocational development when career goals become more firmly established.

***Occupational gender-typing*** Judgments that certain occupations are more appropriate for one gender than the other.

## TRUTH OR FICTION REVISITED

*Actually, the great majority of women work, including the majority of mothers with young children.*

job. Seventy-seven percent of the children thought that the female doll was the teacher. By contrast, only 23 percent pointed to the female doll as a construction worker.

By and large, girls are less restricted in their occupational stereotypes than boys are. In one recent study, seventh and eighth graders were given a list of jobs and were asked to indicate whether each should be performed by a woman or a man, or whether it could be performed by either. Girls were more likely than boys to choose "either" (Jessell & Beymer, 1992).

Girls also are less rigid in their own career aspirations (Kresevich, 1993). One longitudinal study assessed children's career aspirations when they were between 8 and 13 years old and again 5 years later when they were between 13 and 18 years old (Sandberg et al., 1991). Boys chose traditionally male-dominated careers (athlete, pilot, architect, doctor) at both points in time and almost never chose female-dominated fields. By contrast, more than one-quarter of the girls in the first phase and close to one-half during the second phase aspired to male-dominated occupations.

FIGURE 15.14

**A FEMALE ARCHITECTURAL ENGINEER.** *More women today are pursuing careers traditionally dominated by males. The number of men pursuing traditionally female-dominated careers also has increased but not to the same extent. What might account for this?*

Why are females more interested in traditionally male-dominated careers than males are in female-dominated careers? One answer which may occur to you immediately is that male-dominated occupations are typically higher paid. Traditionally male occupations also are considered more prestigious than female-dominated careers. Finally, as we noted earlier when discussing gender differences in play activities, females are given greater latitude than males in expressing gender-atypical behavior (Sandberg et al., 1991).

In recent years, the educational and occupational plans of women and men have become increasingly similar. This is due largely to the greater importance young women are placing on attaining high-status jobs (Fiorentine, 1988). These heightened career aspirations are reflected in the increasing numbers of college women earning college degrees both overall and in traditionally masculine areas (Vetter, 1992). Currently, more than half of all bachelor's degrees are earned by women. In 1991, women earned 15 percent of the bachelor's degrees in engineering, up from less than 1 percent in 1971. The percentage of bachelor's degrees earned by women in 1991 in some other traditionally male-dominated fields is equally revealing: architecture, 40.8 percent; business, 47.2 percent; biological sciences, 50.9 percent; and physical sciences, 31.6 percent (see Figure 15.15). In the same year, women also earned 43 percent of the law degrees and 36 percent of the medical degrees. Pharmacy and veterinary medicine are no longer "men's fields": In 1991, women received 61.8 percent of the degrees in pharmacy and 57.2 percent of those in veterinary medicine ("Earned Degrees," 1993).

FIGURE 15.15

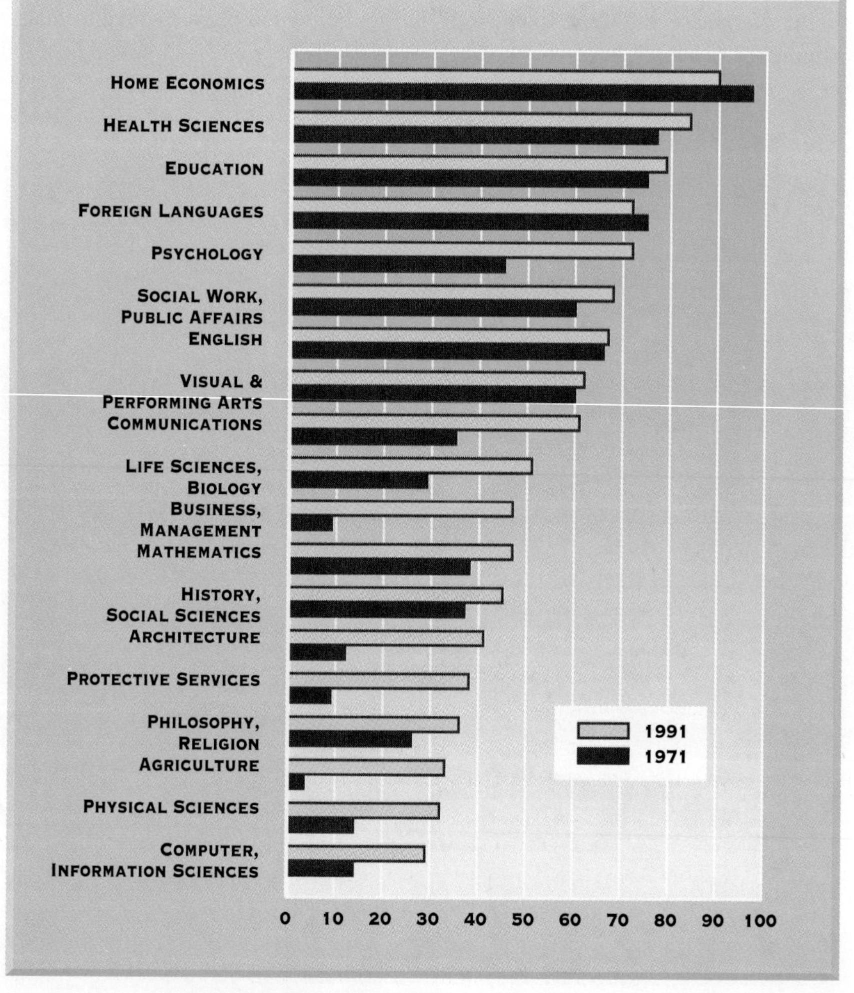


**PERCENT OF BACHELOR'S DEGREES AWARDED TO WOMEN IN 1971 AND 1991.** *More college women are earning degrees in traditionally masculine fields. Still, their numbers remain relatively low in such areas as engineering and computer science. Why? What can we do about it? (Source: "Earned Degrees," 1993; U.S. Bureau of the Census, 1992).*

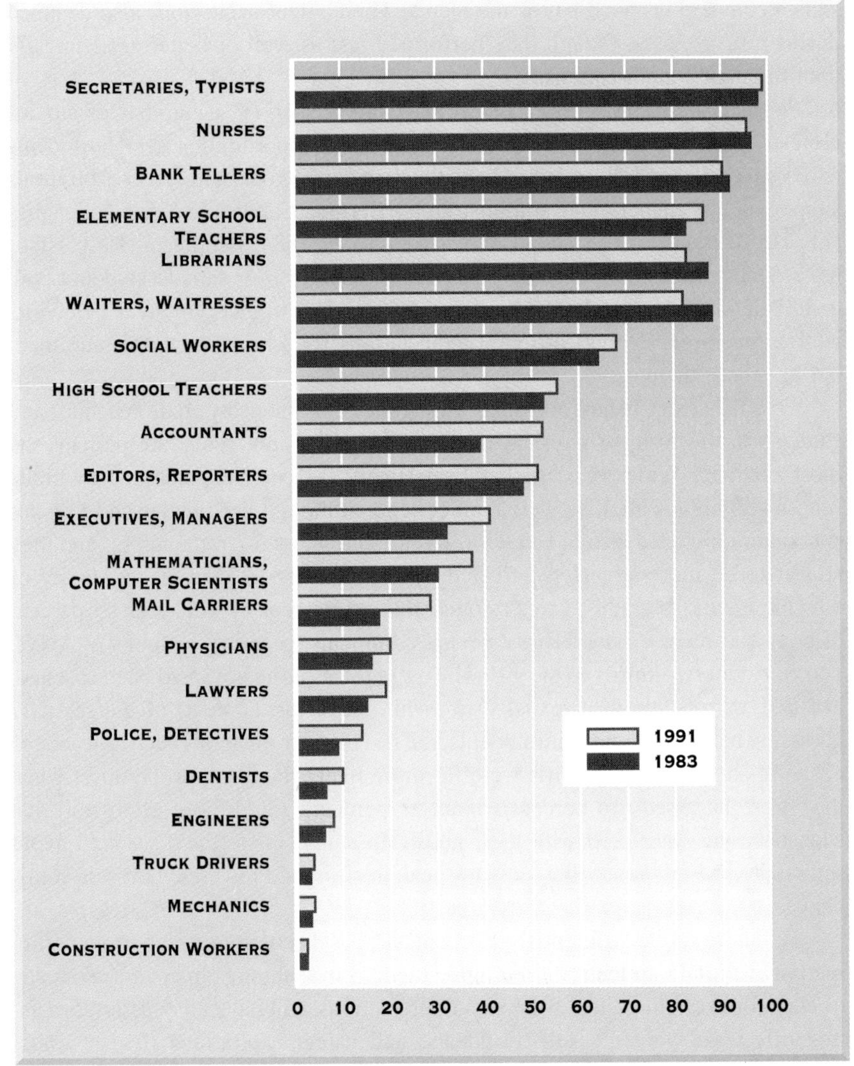


**FIGURE 15.16**

***PERCENTAGE OF WOMEN WORKERS IN VARIOUS FIELDS, 1983 AND 1991.*** *Although more women are working in occupations previously dominated by men, most women are still employed in traditionally female jobs. (Source: U.S. Bureau of the Census, 1992).*

Even though more women are entering so-called nontraditional fields, the career plans of both female and male adolescents still are gender-typed to a large degree (Barber & Eccles, 1992; Jozefowicz et al., 1993). Many women still enter fields traditionally dominated by women, as shown in Figure 15.16. Women in the labor force currently hold two-thirds of the technical, sales and administrative support positions, as they did in 1983. Women have made some inroads into executive, administrative, and managerial occupations, increasing their share from 32 percent in 1983 to 41 percent in 1991. But during these same years, they expanded their representation only slightly in traditionally male fields such as engineering, going from 6 percent to 8 percent (Ottinger & Sikula, 1993).

***The "Chilly Climate"*** Some disturbing trends have emerged in recent research on the career aspirations of girls and young women. During college and graduate school, female students who are well-qualified and highly motivated sometimes show a drop in self-esteem and career aspirations. One longitudinal study found that the educational aspirations of a group of mathematically gifted females declined during the college years and that they were more likely than gifted males to abandon science as a possible career (Benbow & Arjmond, 1990). Another study tracked Illinois high school valedictorians into their college years ("Female Valedictorians," 1988). After just 1 year of college, the women's

***Chilly climate*** Behaviors and activities both inside and outside the classroom that express different expectations for female students or that single them out or ignore them.

self-esteem had dropped below the men's. Their career aspirations also declined during college, even though they performed just as well or better academically than the male valedictorians.

What is happening here? As we saw in Chapter 13, a number of studies indicate that women students do not have the same opportunities as male students to develop self-confidence and to have their academic goals and career aspirations supported by teachers and administrators. Bernice Sandler and her colleagues (Ehrhart & Sandler, 1987; Hall & Sandler, 1982, 1984; Sandler & Hall, 1986) have documented the existence of a ***"chilly climate"*** for female students both inside the classroom and elsewhere on campus. This climate involves behaviors and attitudes that express different expectations for women or that single them out or ignore them.

Overtly sexist behaviors, such as sexual harassment by male teachers and students in the form of physical touching or verbal comments, are perhaps the most obvious. Widespread sexual harassment has been documented in grade school and high school, as well as in college. Although both males and females encounter unwanted sexual behavior, females are most often the target, and they appear to be more adversely affected by the experience. One recent survey of 1,632 students in grades 8 to 11 found that 76 percent of girls and 56 percent of boys had received unwelcome sexual comments, gestures, or looks (AAUW, 1993). About two-thirds of the girls and 42 percent of the boys had been touched, grabbed, or pinched in a sexual way. While most (80 percent) of the sexually harassing behavior came from students, the rest came from adults such as teachers, coaches, and custodians. Girls were far more likely than boys to be upset when they were harassed (70 percent versus 24 percent). Girls more often said that such behavior interfered with their ability to study, made them want to avoid school, decreased their willingness to speak in class, and lowered their self-confidence.

But more subtle differential treatment, such as discouraging classroom participation by female students, discouraging them from seeking help or advice outside of class, or excluding them from social interactions, can have an equally devastating effect on women's self-confidence and career aspirations (Brush, 1991; Healy, 1992; Tilghman, 1993). Consider the following comments from female college students:

> *Students in one of my classes did a tally and found that the male professors called on men more often than on women students. What male students have to say or contribute is viewed as having more importance than what female students have to contribute in class.*
>
> *Have I been overtly discriminated against? Possibly, no. Have I been encouraged, helped, congratulated, received recognition, gotten a friendly hello, a solicitous "Can I help you out?" The answer is no. Being a woman here just makes you be tougher, work harder, and hope if you get a 4.0 GPA someone will say "You're good" . . .*
>
> *A professor repeatedly cuts off women while in the middle of answering in class. He rarely does this to men.*
>
> *If a woman doesn't understand something, she is dismissed. If a male doesn't understand, he gets further attention.*

## Developing Today

### Ways to Encourage Women in Class and Outside the Classroom

**In Class**

- On the first day, tell the class you expect all students to participate equally, not on a daily basis, but over the course of the semester. Say that you will be calling on students, and then ask students who are uncomfortable with this to come see you after class. Tell them you will work with them on their contributions to the class. One way to help a student who comes to you is to share the questions you will use in the class, and ask the student to rehearse the answers with you.
- Call all students by name, and refer to students' contributions by name.
- Call on women directly, even if they don't raise their hands.
- Call on women and men in roughly the same proportions as their ratio in the classroom.
- After asking a question, wait 5 or 10 seconds for hands to go up. The average wait time after asking a question is 1 second. Count one thousand, two thousand, three thousand to help you endure the silence. Recognize that women often wait longer than men to raise their hands, because they are thinking about what to say.
- Coach women as well as men with comments and questions such as: "Tell me more," or "Why do you think that is?" Coaching conveys your belief that the student is bright enough to say more.
- Watch for women's nonverbal clues, such as leaning forward, and then engage them by saying something like, "Can you start us off?" or "Would you like to add to this?"
- When a student deserves it, offer praise. ("I like what you said," or at least, "That's an interesting idea.")
- Keep a teaching diary, especially at the beginning of the semester. Record in it which students are contributing and which are not. Make a point of encouraging the silent students.
- Use the same tone when talking to women students as when talking to men. Don't be impatient or condescending.
- Avoid the so-called generic "he" or "mankind." When you say "he or she," you communicate your awareness of women's concerns.

**Outside the Classroom**

- Meet with female students to discuss academic and career goals.
- Encourage female students to pursue traditionally masculine majors and subspecialities when these areas reflect the particular student's interests and abilities.
- Consider female as well as male students when choosing classroom, teaching, and research assistants.
- Ensure that female and male assistants have equally independent responsibility for their classes and equal opportunities to pursue their own research.
- Make a special effort to consider women for teaching and research assistantships in traditionally masculine fields.
- Offer to write letters of recommendation for female students.
- Consider female as well as male students when making nominations for fellowships, awards, and prizes.
- Include female graduate students in the informal interactions that can be important in communicating support and acceptance as a colleague—for example, by inviting women, as well as men, to share authorships or attend professional conferences. If you are male and uncomfortable inviting a female for lunch or other informal occasion, invite two or three women at a time.
- Provide women with informal as well as formal feedback on the quality of their work.

Sources: *Hall & Sandler, 1982; Sandler & Hoffman, 1992.*

*One woman earned high grades in a traditionally male field. Her professor announced to a mostly male class that this was a most unusual achievement "for a woman". (Hall & Sandler, 1982)*

How can faculty members create a climate that encourages women's full participation in and outside the classroom? See Developing Today for some suggestions.

***Careers and Family*** Young women's increasing interest in pursuing careers has not diminished the value they place on their role in the family. Raising a family continues to be an important goal for female college students (Baber & Monaghan, 1988; Fiorentine, 1988). Employed mothers are now the norm in the United States. Nearly three-quarters of married mothers of school-age children (ages 6–17 years) are in the labor force. More than half of all married women with infants are employed as well. Employment rates are even higher for divorced mothers (U.S. Bureau of the Census, 1993). Women who desire to combine both employment and family roles are faced with the challenge of juggling many sets of responsibilities (Crosby, 1991). How do they cope? Some working couples have fewer children or have them later (Etaugh, 1990). Employed parents are faced with working a "second shift," the housework and child care they do before they go to work and after they return home (Hochschild, 1989). Husbands of women who are employed full-time participate more in housework than do husbands of other women. Nevertheless, women still do most of the child-care and household chores, whether they are employed or not (Etaugh, 1990; Perry-Jenkins et al., 1992). In anticipation of juggling these multiple roles, more high school and college women than men plan to temporarily interrupt their careers for a few years to rear children, followed by a return to full-time work or education (Greene, 1990). Studies report that about 30 percent of college women plan to work full-time when their children are infants and preschoolers (Baber & Monaghan, 1988; O'Connell et al., 1989). Those women pursuing nontraditional careers, such as engineering, are somewhat more likely to seek full-time employment when their children are small.

**CULTURE AND DEVELOPMENT: VOCATIONAL DEVELOPMENT** Vocational development is influenced not only by all the factors we have considered so far, but also by the broader cultural context. Vocational development in the United States and in other Western industrialized countries is quite different than in other areas of the world. The opportunity to choose one's occupation is something we take for granted, but choice is either a luxury or not present at all in many societies. In the People's Republic of China, for instance, individuals are assigned to work on the basis of their abilities and where they are needed, not on the basis of their preferences (Vondracek, 1991).

In most preindustrial societies, girls and boys begin to assume the traditional female and male work roles in their society at an early age, often working alongside their parents and learning from them (Morelli et al., 1992b). Among the Netsilik Eskimo, for example, the boy becomes his father's helper by the age of 10 or 11. He accompanies his father on hunting and fishing trips and helps push and pull the sledge during migrations. The girl begins to participate in her mother's activities at 7 or 8 years of age. She soon learns to perform various household and child-care tasks. Sewing and working with animal skins are learned somewhat later. After the age of 11 or 12, she works very closely with her mother on common tasks (Schlegel & Barry, 1991).

In preindustrial societies, exposure to adult economic activities begins as early as the preschool years. A recent study by Gilda Morelli and her colleagues (1993) compared preschool children's involvement in work activities in three different cultural groups: Efe foragers living in a rain forest in Zaire, Mayan Indians from a rural Guatemalan town, and U.S. middle-class children from Boston and Salt Lake City. Compared with U.S. children, Efe forager and Mayan children spent more time observing and participating in adult economic activities. Even when these children were not working, their play often involved work-related themes, such as pretending to cook or shoot animals. Children learned about adult work by observing and doing, rather than by receiving instruction from adults. By contrast, adults in the U.S. communities were more likely to instruct their children about the physical or social world and were more likely to play with their children.

## Adolescent Work Experience

*Kimberly, age 16, has a job at a fast-food restaurant located in the suburb of a Midwestern city. She has already saved $1,000 toward a car and a stereo by working at the restaurant after school and on weekends. Kimberly is worried because her state legislature is considering regulations that would cut back the number of hours she is allowed to work.*

We noted earlier that life experiences help shape vocational development. One life experience increasingly common among teens in this country is holding a job. In this section, we look at the effects of adolescent employment.

**Prevalence of Adolescent Employment** When you were in high school, did you have a job after school or on weekends? Chances are that you did. About half of all high school sophomores, two-thirds of juniors, and almost three-quarters of seniors have a job during the school year (Freiberg, 1991b). Girls and boys are equally likely to be employed, but boys work more hours. The average male high school senior, for example, works about 21 hours a week, whereas the average female senior works 18 hours (Mortimer, 1991).

At least 4 million adolescents between the ages of 14 to 18 are legally employed. But perhaps another 2 million are working illegally. Some of these teens are paid in cash so their employers can avoid paying taxes or minimum wages. Others work too many hours, work late hours on school nights, or work at hazardous jobs. Some are under 14 and are too young to be legally employed except on farms (Kolata, 1992c).

FIGURE 15.17

**Teenagers and Work.** *Part-time employment during adolescence has both advantages and disadvantages. What are they?*

How do employment rates differ for adolescents in different cultural groups?

EMPLOYMENT RATES

FIFTY TO 75 PERCENT OF U.S. TEENS WORK DURING THE SCHOOL YEAR COMPARED WITH 20 PERCENT OF EUROPEAN AND JAPANESE TEENS.

IN THE UNITED STATES, MIDDLE-INCOME TEENS ARE MORE LIKELY TO WORK THAN LOWER-INCOME TEENS, BUT LOWER-INCOME TEENS WORK LONGER HOURS.

WHITE TEENS ARE TWICE AS LIKELY TO BE EMPLOYED AS ARE AFRICAN-AMERICAN TEENS.

**CULTURE AND DEVELOPMENT: ADOLESCENT EMPLOYMENT** Part-time employment among teenagers is much more common in this country than in other industrialized countries (Mortimer, 1991). For example, it is estimated that only about 20 percent of European and Japanese adolescents work during the school year (Freiberg, 1991b; Waldman & Springen, 1992).

Within the United States, there are both ethnic and social-class differences in adolescent employment rates. White teenagers are twice as likely to be employed as minority teenagers, for example. In past years, teenagers from poorer households were more likely to work in order to help support the family. Nowadays, adolescent employment is more common among middle-class youth. This change may be partly related to the fact that middle-class families are more likely to live near locations, such as suburban shopping malls, that are a fertile source of jobs for teenagers. Lower-income adolescents who are employed work longer hours than middle-class teens, however (Fine et al., 1990; Mortimer, 1991).

**PROS AND CONS OF ADOLESCENT EMPLOYMENT** The potential benefits of adolescent employment are many: developing responsibility, self-reliance, and discipline; learning to appreciate the value of money and education; acquiring positive work habits and values; and enhancing occupational aspirations.

Recently, however, critics have begun to question the benefits of teenage employment. For one thing, the meaning of adolescent work seems to have changed. Most teens no longer work to help support their families. Instead, most use their income for personal purchases, such as clothing, tapes, sports equipment, stereos, TVs, and car payments (Bachman et al., 1987; Fine et al., 1990; Goldstein, 1991). The proportion of earnings devoted to future college expenses or to family expenses is quite small. In one survey of high school seniors, just 10 percent said they were saving most of their earnings for college and only 6 percent said they used most of it to help with family living expenses (Waldman & Springen, 1992).

*Most adolescents who work actually do so to enable them to make personal purchases, such as cars and stereos.*

In addition, most employed adolescents are in service and retail jobs that have low pay, high turnover, little authority, and little chance for advancement. They typically perform simple, repetitive tasks requiring no special skills, minimal supervision, and little interdependence with other workers (Mortimer, 1991). Some question how effective such jobs are in producing the potential benefits of work we discussed earlier.

Furthermore, research indicates that the effects of teenage employment may be detrimental, particularly for those students who work long hours. For example, one study examined the effects of school-year jobs in an ethnically and socioeconomically diverse sample of about 4,000 15–18 year olds attending rural, suburban, and urban high schools in California and Wisconsin (Steinberg & Dornbusch, 1991). Compared with classmates who did not work or who worked only a few hours each week, students who worked longer hours earned lower grades, spent less time on homework, paid less attention in class, reported more mind-wandering in class, cut classes more, and participated less in extracurricular activities.

Students who worked more hours also reported higher rates of drug and alcohol use, more delinquent behavior, lower self-esteem, and higher levels of psychological and psychosomatic distress, such as anxiety, depression, fatigue, insomnia, headaches, and stomachaches. Those who worked longer hours also spent less time in family activities, were monitored less by their parents, and were granted more autonomy over day-to-day decisions. The negative effects of employment generally cut across all ethnic, socioeconomic, and age groups, with one exception: School grades were affected for white and Asian-American students, but not for African-American or Hispanic students. Student workers did not show advantages over nonworkers on any measure.

Research from this study and others (Fine et al., 1990; Mortimer et al., 1993; Steitz & Owen, 1992) indicates that the detrimental effects of adolescent employment are associated with how much, not whether, a student works (Steinberg & Dornbusch, 1991). But how much work is too much? The answer seems to depend on which measure we are looking at. For example, school grades and time spent on homework drop sharply for students who work more than 20 hours a week. But drug and alcohol use increases once a student exceeds only 10 hours of weekly employment.

A cautionary note is in order in interpreting these findings. It is possible that the link between long hours of employment and reduced student achievement could come about because students who are less academically able or interested in school may choose to work longer hours (Fine et al., 1990). And those who already use drugs and alcohol may be more likely to work long hours in order to earn extra money to buy these substances. Two recent studies have examined these issues (Bachman & Schulenberg, 1993; Steinberg et al., 1993). Both found evidence that high school students who work—particularly those who work more than 20 hours a week—are poorer students to begin with. Their grades are lower, they have been held back at least once in school, and they do not plan to complete college. One of the studies (Bachman & Schulenberg, 1993) also found that adolescents who work were more involved than their peers in alcohol, cigarette, and illicit drug use *before* they entered the work force.

But the studies also showed that working long hours produced even further disengagement from school and contributed to increased drug use, delinquent behavior, aggression, and arguments with parents. Students who were employed for many hours also had less sleep, were less likely to eat breakfast or exercise, and had less leisure time.

Probably the most prudent course of action at this point is for parents, educators, and policymakers to continue monitoring the number of hours adolescents work. Some states already have begun to tighten their regulations on the number of hours teenagers can work during the school year ("Washington State Plans," 1992).

Throughout this chapter, we have seen that the intellectual, moral, and vocational development of adolescents is influenced by parents and peers. Adolescents' relationships with family and friends, along with other aspects of their social and personality development, is the topic of the final chapter.

## Summary

1. Piaget theorized that at about the age of 12 or so, many children enter the stage of formal operations, in which they can manipulate abstract concepts and ideas with the flexibility and reversibility they showed earlier in regard

to concrete objects and events. Formal-operational thought allows hypothetical thinking, systematic problem solving, sophisticated use of symbols, and deductive thinking.

2. Formal-operational thought may evolve only in technologically advanced societies, but even in the United States, only about half of first-year college students demonstrate it.

3. Adolescent egocentrism is an exaggerated concern with one's own importance. It takes two forms: the imaginary audience and the personal fable. The imaginary audience is the belief that others are as concerned with our looks and behavior as we are. The personal fable is the belief that our feelings and ideas are unique and that we are invulnerable.

4. While females and males do not differ in overall intelligence, girls show greater verbal ability than boys, whereas boys show greater visual-spatial ability than girls. Girls excel in some areas of mathematics ability, and boys excel in others. These differences are group differences, and they are very small.

5. Moral development has cognitive and behavioral aspects. Cognitive-developmental theorists focus on the orderly unfolding of sequences in moral reasoning.

6. According to Jean Piaget, the egocentrism of preoperational children encourages moral realism. Young children believe that social rules are absolutes and that punishment automatically follows transgressions. Preoperational children also tend to focus on only one dimension at a time. Their judgments of a transgressor, for example, do not take into account the intentions of the transgressor but only the amount of damage done.

7. According to Piaget, more advanced moral judgments are based on operational thinking, and children first show autonomous morality at about the ages of 9 to 11. (Other researchers find autonomous morality at younger ages.) Operational children are more flexible in their thinking. They understand that social rules are conventions constructed by people to meet social needs. Increased capacity for empathy and ability to focus on more than one dimension simultaneously encourage older children to weigh the intentions of transgressors more than the amount of damage done.

8. Lawrence Kohlberg's cognitive theory hypothesizes three levels of moral development—preconventional, conventional, and postconventional—and two stages within each level. Preconventional morality is characterized by the expectation of punishments or rewards. Conventional morality is largely based on the need to attain the approval of others and to maintain the social order. Postconventional morality is found among a minority of individuals. It is characterized by the derivation of moral judgments from one's own moral principles.

9. In Kohlberg's theory, females frequently show lower levels of moral reasoning than males. His research indicated that males tend to adhere to logical deduction of judgments from moral principles, whereas females' judgments tend to focus more on caring and empathy for others. Carol Gilligan argues that both types of reasoning are equally complex. Most studies find that females do not reason at lower levels and that concerns with caring and justice co-exist in the judgments of both genders.

10. While the sequence of Kohlberg's stages is largely invariant, stage 6 reasoning has been shown not to be universal. Moral development may also

be more subject to educational and cultural influences than Kohlberg allowed. Situational factors also affect moral development. Moral behavior and moral development are often related.

11. The transition to middle, junior high, or high school may not fit well with the developmental needs of early adolescents. The transition to junior high often is accompanied by a decline in grades, a drop in self-confidence, and an increase in psychological distress. Girls are more vulnerable than boys to the transition.

12. High school dropouts are more likely to be unemployed, earn low salaries, and show various problem behaviors. Risk factors for dropping out include school absence, poor school performance, low self-esteem, dissatisfaction with school, substance abuse, and early adoption of adult roles. Males from low-income urban households are at increased risk.

13. Children's career aspirations become more realistic and more crystallized as they get older. Factors influencing career choice include one's abilities, personality characteristics, life experiences, job opportunities, parental expectations, and economic factors.

14. Labor force participation rates of women have increased enormously. Occupational gender-typing is present even in young children but is less pronounced in girls. Although more women are entering traditionally male fields, most women and men still are concentrated in fields dominated by their own gender. During the college years, many bright, motivated women experience a "chilly" classroom and campus climate and show a drop in self-esteem and career aspirations. Employed women continue to value family roles. They face the challenge of combining job responsibilities, child care, and housework.

15. Vocational development is influenced by the broader cultural context. It is different in Western industrialized countries than in other areas of the world.

16. The majority of high school students have a part-time job during the school year. There are gender, ethnic, and social class differences in adolescent employment patterns.

17. Although the potential benefits of adolescent employment are many, concerns exist as well. Effects of employment may be detrimental, particularly for students who work long hours.

CHAPTER

16

# ADOLESCENCE:

## SOCIAL AND PERSONALITY DEVELOPMENT

## *Chapter Outline*

## *Truth or Fiction?*

_____ *It is common for adolescents to slavishly imitate their peers' clothing, speech, hairstyles, and ideals.*

_____ *Adolescent males are more concerned about occupational choices than adolescent females are.*

_____ *Children's self-esteem blossoms as they enter adolescence.*

_____ *Minority adolescents have poorer self-concepts than white adolescents.*

_____ *Adolescents are in a constant state of rebellion against their parents.*

_____ *Adolescents have fewer friends than younger children, limiting their friendships to one or two confidants.*

_____ *Parents and peers tend to exert conflicting influences on adolescents.*

_____ *Adolescents who have a close relationship with their parents are less likely to engage in sexual activity at an early age.*

_____ *About 1 million U.S. teenagers become pregnant each year.*

_____ *Only a minority of U.S. adolescents engage in acts of juvenile delinquency.*

_____ *Suicide has become the second leading cause of death among older teenagers.*

*What am I like as a person? Complicated! I'm sensitive, friendly and outgoing, though I can also be shy, self-conscious, and even obnoxious. I'd* like *to be friendly and tolerant all of the time. That's the kind of person I* want *to be, and I'm disappointed when I'm not. I'm responsible, even studious every now and then, but on the other hand I'm a goof-off too, because if you're too studious, you won't be popular. I'm a pretty cheerful person, especially with my friends, where I can even get rowdy. But I'm usually pretty stressed-out at home, or sarcastic, since my parents are always on my case. They expect me to get all A's. It's not fair! I worry about how I probably* should *get better grades. But I'd be mortified in the eyes of my friends. Sometimes I feel phony, especially around boys. Say I think some guy might be interested in asking me out. I try to act different, like Madonna. I'll be flirtatious and fun-loving. And then everybody else is looking at me like they think I'm totally weird! Then I get self-conscious and embarrassed and become radically introverted, and I don't know who I really am! But I don't really care what they think anyway. I just want to know what my close friends think. I can be my true self with my close friends. I can't be my real self with my parents. They don't understand me. They treat me like I'm still a kid. That gets confusing, though. I mean, which am I, a kid or an adult? It's scary, too, because I don't have any idea what I want to be when I grow up. I mean, I have lots of* ideas. *My friend Sheryl and I talk about whether we'll be teachers, or lawyers, veterinarians, maybe mothers. I know I* don't *want to be a waitress or a secretary. But how do you decide all of this? I mean, I think about it a lot, but I can't resolve it.*

(ADAPTED FROM HARTER, 1990C, PP. 352–353)

This self-description from a 15-year-old girl illustrates one of the most important developments of the adolescent years: the search for an answer to the question "Who am I?" Notice how this 15-year-old is struggling to reconcile her seemingly contradictory traits and behaviors to determine which is the "real me." She is preoccupied not only with her present self, but also with what she wishes to become in the future. What were *your* concerns at this age?

In this chapter, we begin our exploration of social and personality development in adolescence by examining the formation of one's identity and the related changes in self-concept and self-esteem. We next turn to adolescents' relationships with their parents and their peers. We look at the emergence of sexual behaviors and attitudes, including teenage pregnancy. We conclude with a discussion of two serious problems that may occur in adolescence: juvenile delinquency and suicide.

## IDENTITY AND SELF-CONCEPT

Adolescence is a particularly important period in the lifelong process of defining who we are. In this section, we will start by examining Erik Erikson's influential theory of identity development in adolescence. We then turn to James Marcia's expansion of Erikson's theory and explore his four identity statuses. Next, we consider gender and cultural perspectives on identity development. Finally, we look at the development of self-concept and self-esteem during adolescence.

### *Theoretical Interlude: Erikson's View of Identity Development*

Erikson's fifth stage of psychosocial development is called identity versus identity diffusion. The primary task of this stage is for adolescents to develop ***ego identity:*** a sense of who they are and what they stand for. Individuals are faced with making choices about their future occupation, their ideological view of the world (including political and religious beliefs), their sexual orientation, and their gender-role behaviors. The ability to engage in formal-operational thinking helps adolescents make these choices. Since thought is no longer tied to concrete experience, adolescents can weigh the possibilities available to them even though they may not have directly experienced any of these options (Kahlbaugh & Haviland, 1991).

An important aspect of identity development is what Erikson (1968) referred to as a ***psychological moratorium.*** This may be described as a time-out period during which adolescents experiment with different roles, values, beliefs, and relationships. During this moratorium period, adolescents often experience an ***identity crisis.*** Erikson defined the identity crisis as a turning point in development during which one examines one's values and makes decisions about life roles. Which college should I choose? Which career? Should I become sexually active or not? If so, with whom? Adolescents may feel overwhelmed by the many options before them and by the need to make choices that inevitably will reduce their future alternatives (Crain, 1992).

In their search for identity, adolescents may join "in" groups, slavishly imitating their peers' clothing, speech, hairstyles, and ideals. They may become intolerant of others outside the group (Erikson, 1963). Those who successfully resolve their identity crisis develop a strong sense of who they are and what they stand for. Those who fail to resolve the crisis may continue to be intolerant of others who are different and may continue to blindly follow others.

**Truth or Fiction Revisited**

*It is indeed common for adolescents to slavishly imitate their peers' clothing, speech, hairstyles, and ideals. This tendency is apparently related to their quest for identity.*

**Four Identity Statuses** Building upon Erikson's approach, James Marcia (1980, 1991, 1993) has identified four identity statuses. These represent the four possible combinations of the dimensions of *exploration* and *commitment,* which Erikson believed were critical for the development of identity. ***Exploration*** involves active questioning and searching among alternatives in the quest to establish goals, values, or beliefs. ***Commitment*** is a stable investment in one's goals, values, or beliefs (Archer & Waterman, 1990). The four identity statuses are shown in Table 16.1.

***Identity diffusion*** is the least developmentally advanced status. This category includes individuals who do not have commitments and who are not in the process of trying to form them (Patterson et al., 1992). This stage often is characteristic of children before they reach high school and in the early high school years. Older adolescents who remain diffused may drift through life in a carefree,

***Ego identity*** According to Erikson, one's sense of who one is and what one stands for.

***Psychological moratorium*** A time-out period when adolescents experiment with different roles, values, beliefs, and relationships.

***Identity crisis*** A turning point in development during which one examines one's values and makes decisions about life roles.

***Exploration*** Active questioning and searching among alternatives in the quest to establish goals, values, or beliefs.

***Commitment*** A stable investment in one's goals, values, or beliefs.

***Identity diffusion*** An identity status that characterizes those who have no commitments and who are not in the process of exploring alternatives.

FIGURE 16.1

***IDENTITY CRISIS.*** *In their search for identity, adolescents may join "in" groups, imitating their peers' clothing, speech, hairstyles, and ideals.*

uninvolved way or may be unhappy and lonely (Kroger, 1989). Some individuals in the diffusion status are apathetic and adopt an ''I don't care'' attitude. Others are angry, alienated, and rebellious and may reject socially approved goals, values, and beliefs (Archer & Waterman, 1990; Marcia, 1991).

In the ***foreclosure*** status, individuals have made commitments without ever seriously considering alternatives. These commitments usually are established early in life and often are based on identification with parents, teachers, or other authority figures who have made a strong impression on the child. For example, a college student may unquestioningly prepare for a career that has been chosen for him by his parents. In other cases, the adolescent may uncritically adopt the life-style of a religious cult or extremist political group (Waterman & Archer, 1990). Foreclosed individuals tend to be more authoritarian and inflexible than individuals in other identity statuses (Berzonsky et al., 1993; Marcia, 1991).

***Foreclosure*** An identity status that characterizes those who have made commitments without considering alternatives.

***Moratorium*** An identity status that characterizes those who are actively exploring alternatives in an attempt to form an identity.

***Identity achievement*** An identity status that characterizes those who have explored alternatives and have developed commitments.

The ***moratorium*** identity status refers to a person who is actively exploring alternatives in an attempt to make choices with regard to occupation, ideological beliefs, and so on (Patterson et al., 1992). Individuals in the moratorium status often are anxious, intense, and have ambivalent feelings toward their parents as they struggle to work toward commitment (Kroger, 1989; Marcia, 1991).

The ***identity achievement*** status includes those who have experienced a period of exploration and have developed relatively firm commitments. Individuals who have achieved a clear sense of identity show a number of strengths. They have a sense of personal well-being in the form of high self-esteem and self-acceptance. They are cognitively flexible and show high levels of moral

TABLE 16.1

***MARCIA'S FOUR IDENTITY STATUSES***

| | | Exploration | |
|---|---|---|---|
| | | Yes | No |
| Commitment | Yes | Identity Achievement | Foreclosure |
| | No | Moratorium | Diffusion |

reasoning. They are able to set goals and work toward achieving them (Berzonsky et al., 1993; Marcia, 1991; Waterman, 1992).

**Development of Identity Statuses** Before the high school years, children show little interest in questions related to identity. Most of them are either in the identity diffusion or foreclosure statuses. During the high school and college years, adolescents increasingly move from the diffusion and foreclosure statuses to the moratorium and achievement statuses (Kroger, 1989; Waterman & Archer, 1990). The greatest gains in identity formation occur during the college years (Waterman, 1985). In college, individuals are exposed to a broad spectrum of life-styles, belief systems, and career choices. These experiences can serve as a catalyst for consideration of a variety of identity issues. Are you one of the many college students who have changed majors once or twice (or more)? If so, you have most likely experienced the moratorium identity status, which is quite common among college students. You should be comforted by the results of numerous studies that show that college seniors have a stronger sense of personal identity than first-year students. Furthermore, the identity commitments of seniors are more likely to result from successfully resolving the identity crises experienced during the moratorium phase (Waterman & Archer, 1990).

## *Gender and Identity Development*

Erikson's view of identity development has been criticized for portraying a primarily male model. In Erikson's theory, the stage of identity development includes embracing a philosophy of life and commitment to a career. It is only in the next stage that the capacity to form intimate relationships with others develops. Erikson himself admitted that this sequence more accurately described the traditional development of males. In his later writings (Erikson, 1968, 1975), he suggested that the development of identity in women differed from that of men in the following ways: First, the development of interpersonal relationships is more important to women's identity than are occupational and ideological issues. Second, women do not complete identity development until after marriage and childbearing. In other words, a woman's identity is not formed apart from her roles as wife and mother. Third, whereas men normally experience identity development before intimacy development, women can resolve both identity and intimacy concerns at the same time (Patterson et al., 1992).

Is the development of identity in women and men as different as Erikson supposed? Let us look at the evidence. Numerous studies have demonstrated that females approach identity formation in a manner that is comparable to and sometimes more sophisticated than that of males (Archer, 1992). In other words, as in so many other areas we have examined in this book, the similarities between females and males are much greater than the differences. In one study, for example, both men and women claimed that the interpersonal area was the most important to them (Bilsker et al., 1988). Other studies (Archer, 1985, 1992) have found that adolescent females and males are equally concerned about occupational choices. Females, however, are more likely to integrate occupational and family plans than males are. For example, Archer (1985) asked high school students questions regarding their vocational plans and their family plans. The vast majority of male students saw no relationship or potential conflict between their vocational choices and their plans to marry and have children. But the majority of female students saw interconnections between their career goals and family goals and expressed a desire to integrate both into their daily lives. Archer (1991) suggests that this gender difference exists because females continue to assume primary responsibility for child rearing, even though the majority of women now are employed outside the home. She poses the following interesting question: If society begins to hold males as accountable as females for family responsibilities, will males also begin to integrate their vocational and family goals?

### TRUTH OR FICTION REVISITED

*Actually, adolescent males and females are about equally concerned about occupational choices.*

What about the timing of identity development in women and men? Both begin the process of identity formation during adolescence. Those women who have uninterrupted careers tend to complete the task of identity achievement in late adolescence. Women who are full-time homemakers or who defer employment until their children are in school are more likely to develop a strong sense of personal identity after their children reach school age (Patterson et al., 1992).

Finally, men appear to develop identity before intimacy, as Erickson suggested. Some women also develop identity before intimacy, whereas others achieve intimacy before identity or achieve them concurrently (Schiedel & Marcia, 1985).

### CULTURE AND DEVELOPMENT: IDENTITY DEVELOPMENT

The development of identity is a crucial task for all adolescents. This task is even more complicated and challenging for ethnic minority adolescents (Cross, 1991; Spencer et al., 1990; Spencer & Markstrom-Adams, 1990). Unlike adolescents who belong to the dominant culture, minority youth are faced with two sets of cultural values: those of their own ethnic group and those of the majority

FIGURE 16.2

**ETHNIC IDENTITY.** *Minority adolescents are faced with two sets of cultural values: those of their own ethnic group and those of the majority culture. The values of the two cultures may conflict, presenting the minority adolescent with the challenging task of reconciling and incorporating elements of both into his or her self-identity.*

culture (Markstrom-Adams, 1991; Phinney & Rosenthal, 1992). The values of the two cultures may conflict, presenting the minority adolescent with the challenging task of reconciling and incorporating elements of both into his or her self-identity.

Another problem in forging a sense of identity is that minority youth often experience prejudice and discrimination. Furthermore, their cultural heroes may be ignored. School textbooks usually make no more than a passing reference to historically important individuals from minority groups (O'Connor, 1989). A relative scarcity of successful role models can also be a problem, particularly for youth living in conditions of poverty (Spencer et al., 1990). Identifying too strongly with the dominant culture may lead to rejection by the minority group. On the other hand, rejecting the dominant culture's values for those of the minority group may limit opportunities for advancement in the larger society (Phinney & Rosenthal, 1992). Biracial adolescents—those with parents from two different racial or ethnic groups—must wrestle not only with all these issues but also with issues relating to their dual cultural heritage (Gibbs & Hines, 1992; Johnson, 1992; Miller, 1992).

Several of the factors we have discussed so far may limit the options available to minority adolescents as they develop their sense of ego identity. To the extent that minority youth have fewer options regarding educational and career opportunities, we might expect that they would be less involved in exploration of identity issues. If one cannot foresee a viable future, why explore (Shorter-Gooden, 1992)? And, in fact, some studies have found that minority adolescents—Hispanics, Asian Americans, African Americans, and Native Americans—tend to foreclose earlier on identity issues than their white peers (Spencer, 1991; Streitmatter, 1988).

But other studies have found that many minority teenagers are engaged in the identity-searching process, rather than experiencing identity foreclosure (Watson & Protinsky, 1991). Minority adolescents often develop strategies for handling the demands of living within both a minority and majority culture, as illustrated in the following comment:

> *Being invited to someone's house, I have to change my ways of how I act at home, because of culture differences. I would have to follow what they do . . . I am used to it now, switching off between the two. It is not difficult. (Phinney & Rosenthal, 1992)*

What are the stages in developing an ***ethnic identity***—that is, a sense of belonging to an ethnic group? Jean Phinney (1989, 1990) has proposed a three-stage model. The first stage is an ***unexamined ethnic identity.*** It is similar to Marcia's ego-identity statuses of diffusion or foreclosure. In some cases, the early adolescent simply hasn't given much thought to ethnic identity issues (diffusion). In other instances, the young adolescent may have adopted an identity either with the dominant group or with the minority group based on societal or parental values, but without exploring or thinking about the issues involved. This represents a foreclosed status. In the second stage, the adolescent embarks upon an ***ethnic identity search.*** This stage, similar to Marcia's moratorium stage, may be based on a significant experience or incident that makes the adolescent aware of her ethnicity. During this stage, the adolescent may explore her ethnic culture, intensely participating in cultural events, reading, and talking to others. In the third stage, individuals have an ***achieved ethnic identity.*** This involves a clear, confident acceptance of oneself as a member of one's ethnic group.

As minority youth move through adolescence, they are increasingly likely to explore their own ethnicity and to acquire an achieved ethnic identity status.

***Ethnic identity*** A sense of belonging to an ethnic group.

***Unexamined ethnic identity*** The first stage of ethnic identity development; similar to the diffusion or foreclosure identity statuses.

***Ethnic identity search*** The second stage of ethnic identity development; similar to the moratorium identity status.

***Achieved ethnic identity*** The final stage of ethnic identity development; similar to the identity achievement status.

For example, only about one-third of African-American 8th-graders were found to show evidence of ethnic identity search, as compared with half of African-American 10th-graders (Phinney, 1989; Phinney & Tarver, 1988). A recent longitudinal study (Phinney & Chavira, 1992) found movement from lower to higher stages of ethnic identity between 16 and 19 years of age. And college undergraduates show higher levels of ethnic identity achievement than do 11th- or 12th-graders (Phinney, 1992).

One way parents can facilitate adolescent ethnic identity is to be sensitive to cultural diversity. A recent study found that Asian-American, African-American, and Mexican-American adolescents who scored high on a measure of ethnic identity had parents who were more likely to state they had tried to prepare their child for living in a culturally diverse society (Phinney & Nakayama, 1991).

## *SELF-CONCEPT*

The adolescent preoccupation with developing a sense of identity is part of a broader process of redefining the way adolescents view themselves. In Chapter 13 we saw that prior to adolescence, children describe themselves primarily in terms of their physical characteristics and their actions. As they approach adolescence, children begin to incorporate psychological characteristics and social relationships into their self-descriptions. Young adolescents frequently describe themselves as having distinct and enduring personality traits (Damon, 1991).

The self-concept also becomes more differentiated. That is, adolescents add more categories to their self-description. Also, self-descriptions begin to vary according to the social role in which adolescents find themselves. For example, like the 15-year-old at the beginning of the chapter, adolescents may describe themselves as being anxious or sarcastic with parents, but as caring, talkative, and cheerful with friends. These seeming contradictions and conflicts in self-description reach their peak at about age 14 and then begin to decline in later adolescence (Harter & Monsour, 1992). The more advanced formal-operational skills of the older adolescent allow her to integrate the many apparently contradictory elements of the self. For example, the older adolescent might say "I'm very adaptable. When I'm around my friends, who think that what I say is important, I'm very talkative; but around my family, I'm quiet because they're not interested enough to really listen to me" (Damon, 1991, p. 988).

## *SELF-ESTEEM*

***Self-esteem*** appears to be at its lowest in early adolescence, at about age 12 or 13 (Harter, 1990a). That is, self-esteem tends to decline as the child progresses from middle childhood into early adolescence. What might account for this drop in self-esteem? The growing cognitive maturity of young adolescents makes them increasingly and painfully aware of the disparity between their ideal self and their real self. The sense of discrepancy between the real and ideal self is especially great in the area of physical appearance (Damon, 1991). Physical appearance contributes more to the development of self-esteem during adolescence than any other characteristic (Harter, 1990b, c).

After hitting a low point at around age 12 or 13, self-esteem gradually improves throughout adolescence (Mullis et al., 1992). It may be that adolescents adjust their notions of the ideal self to better reflect reality. Also, as adolescents increasingly develop competence in areas of importance to themselves, their parents, and their peers, they may gradually become less critical of themselves (Harter, 1990b, c).

***Self-esteem*** The sense of value or worth that people attach to themselves.

## TRUTH OR FICTION REVISITED

*Self-esteem actually declines as children enter adolescence. Perhaps adolescents are more aware than children in middle childhood of the discrepancies between their actual selves and their ideal selves.*

For most adolescents, low self-esteem produces a fairly temporary sense of emotional discomfort (Damon, 1991). But for some, low self-esteem is associated with serious psychological and behavioral consequences. For example, low self-esteem is often found in teenagers who are depressed or suicidal (Harter & Marold, 1991; Patton, 1991).

Emotional support from parents and peers is very important in the development of self-esteem during adolescence. Adolescents who feel that they are highly regarded by family and friends are more likely to have positive feelings about themselves than are those who feel they are lacking such support (Harter, 1990b; Harter et al, 1993). In early adolescence, support from parents and from peers are equally important. By late adolescence, peer support carries more weight (Damon, 1991).

**GENDER AND SELF-ESTEEM** Girls generally show lower self-esteem than boys during adolescence (Block & Robins, 1993; Harper & Marshall, 1991). A national survey of 3,000 children in grades 4–10 indicates that the gender gap in self-esteem increases between the grade school and high school years (American Association of University Women, 1991). At 8 and 9 years of age, 60 percent of the girls and 67 percent of the boys were confident, assertive, and happy with themselves. But by the ages of 16 and 17, only 29 percent of girls, compared with 46 percent of boys, retained their positive self-esteem. More African-American girls maintained high self-esteem than white or Hispanic girls.

Why is the drop in self-esteem greater for girls? One factor may be the physical changes of adolescence, which are central to the development of self-esteem in adolescence. Although physical appearance is a concern for both girls and boys, it is especially important for girls, as we saw in Chapter 14.

FIGURE 16.3

**SELF-ESTEEM.** *Emotional support from both parents and peers contributes to the development of self-esteem during adolescence.*

Others attribute the drop in girls' self-esteem to the negative messages that girls receive in school, a topic we discussed in Chapter 13. In the words of one report, "Students sit in classes that day in and day out deliver the message that women's lives count far less than men's?" (American Association of University Women, 1992, p. 67).

Carol Gilligan and her colleagues (Brown & Gilligan, 1992; Gilligan et al., 1990) offer a related explanation, based on their interviews of girls as they make the transition from the elementary grades into junior high and high school. They report that as girls move into adolescence, they become aware of the conflict between the positive way they see themselves and society's view of females. Many girls respond by "losing their voices," that is, by submerging their own feelings and accepting the negative view of women conveyed by adult authorities (Lips, 1993).

Why are African-American girls more likely to maintain their confidence in high school than other girls? One factor, researchers suggest, is that African-American girls are surrounded by strong women they admire. Another factor may be that African-American parents often teach their children that there is nothing wrong with them, only with the way the world treats them (Daley, 1991).

**CULTURE AND DEVELOPMENT: SELF-ESTEEM** Erik Erikson (1968) believes that minority adolescents are likely to form poor self-concepts because they internalize society's negative views of minority groups. But recent studies have consistently found that the self-concepts and self-esteem of minority youth are as positive as or more positive than those of white youth (Gibbs, 1989). One study, for example, examined the self-concepts of African-American, Hispanic, and white eighth-graders. Eleven different aspects of self-concept were measured. These included four academic aspects (including verbal and mathematical self-concepts) and seven nonacademic aspects (including physical ability, physical appearance, and relationships with parents and with members of the same and the other sex). African-American students had higher self-concept ratings than did white and Hispanic students on all four academically related self-concept scales, as well as in six of the seven nonacademic scales (Widaman et al., 1992).

**TRUTH OR FICTION REVISITED**

*Recent research evidence actually shows that the self-concepts of minority adolescents are as positive or more positive than those of white adolescents.*

Other research has examined the relationship between self-esteem and the stages of developing ethnic identity. Jean Phinney and her colleagues interviewed Hispanic, Asian-American, African-American, and white students attending high school and college. Those who showed higher stages of ethnic identity also had higher self-esteem (Phinney, 1989; Phinney & Alipuria, 1990; Phinney et al., 1992). The association between self-esteem and ethnic identity was stronger for the minority youth than for the white students. These studies and others suggest that having a positive self-concept is related to the extent to which adolescents have learned to understand and accept their ethnicity (Phinney, 1990; Phinney & Rosenthal, 1992).

## Relationships with Parents and Peers

Adolescents coping with the task of establishing a sense of identity and direction in their lives are heavily influenced by both their parents and peers. How do relationships with one's parents and peers change during the course of the teenage years?

### *Parent–Adolescent Relationships*

The "storm and stress" view of adolescence that we examined in Chapter 14 portrays adolescents as being in a state of constant rebellion against their parents. We now know that this picture is far from accurate. Adolescence is indeed a time of transition and change in the relationship between parents and teenagers. But these changes need not be negative and, in fact, may be quite positive (Collins, 1990; Steinberg, 1991).

**Changes in Parent–Adolescent Interactions** During adolescence, children spend much less time with their parents than they did during childhood. In one recent study, for example, children ranging in age from 9 to 15 years carried electronic pagers for one week and reported what they were doing each time they were signaled by the pagers (Larson & Richards, 1991). There was a dramatic decline in the amount of time spent with family as children got older. The 15-year-olds spent half as much time with their families as the 9-year-olds. For older boys, the time with family was replaced by time spent alone, whereas older girls spent more time alone and with friends.

Adolescents continue to interact more with their mothers than with their fathers, continuing the pattern begun in childhood. Teenagers engage in more conflicts with their mothers, but they also view their mothers as being more supportive, as knowing them better, and as being more likely to accept the teenager's opinions (Collins & Russell, 1991; Noller & Callan, 1990). No wonder that teenagers are more likely to seek and follow advice from their mothers than their fathers (Greene & Grimsley, 1990).

The decrease in time spent with family may reflect the adolescent's striving to become more independent from parents. A certain degree of distancing from parents may be adaptive for adolescents as they engage in the tasks of forming relationships outside the family and entering adulthood (Galambos, 1992). But greater independence does not mean that adolescents become emotionally detached from their mothers and fathers. Adolescents continue to maintain a great deal of love, loyalty, and respect for their parents (Montemayor & Flannery, 1991). And adolescents who feel close to their parents are more likely to show greater self-reliance and independence, higher self-esteem, better school performance, and fewer psychological and social problems (Davey, 1993; Forehand et al., 1991a; Papini & Roggman, 1992; Steinberg, 1991).

The relationship between parents and teens is not always rosy, of course. Early adolescence, in particular, is a period characterized by an increase in bickering and disagreements and by a decrease in shared activities and in expressions of affection (Montemayor et al., 1993; Smetana et al., 1991b).

Conflict is greatest during the time the adolescent is going through the changes of puberty, but it declines in later adolescence (Collins & Russell, 1991). Conflicts typically center around the everyday details of family life such as chores, homework, curfews, personal appearance, finances, and dating (Galambos

& Almeida, 1992; Smetana et al., 1991b; Steinberg, 1990a). Conflicts may arise in these areas because adolescents believe that personal issues—such as choice of clothes and friends—that were previously controlled by parents should now come under the control of the adolescent (Smetana et al., 1991b). But parents, especially mothers, continue to believe that they should retain control in most areas. And so conflicts arise. On the other hand, many studies have confirmed that parents and adolescents are quite similar in their values and beliefs regarding basic social, political, religious, and economic issues (Paikoff & Collins, 1991). Disagreements in these areas are relatively few. Even though the notion of a generation gap between adolescents and their parents may persist as a popular stereotype, there is little evidence to support it.

### TRUTH OR FICTION REVISITED

*Actually, most adolescents are not in rebellion against their parents. Studies show that most adolescents tend to share their parents' values and beliefs.*

And so, it appears that adolescence is a time when teenagers and their parents establish a balance between adolescent independence and continued family connectedness. While some conflict is inevitable, it usually is not severe (Montemayor & Flannery, 1991). Although parent–child relationships change during the transition from childhood to adolescence, the change is gradual and is not marked by feelings of alienation. Most adolescents feel that they are close to and get along well with their parents (Galambos, 1992). Adolescents do not reject their parents' values, although they develop a less idealized view of their parents (Silverberg

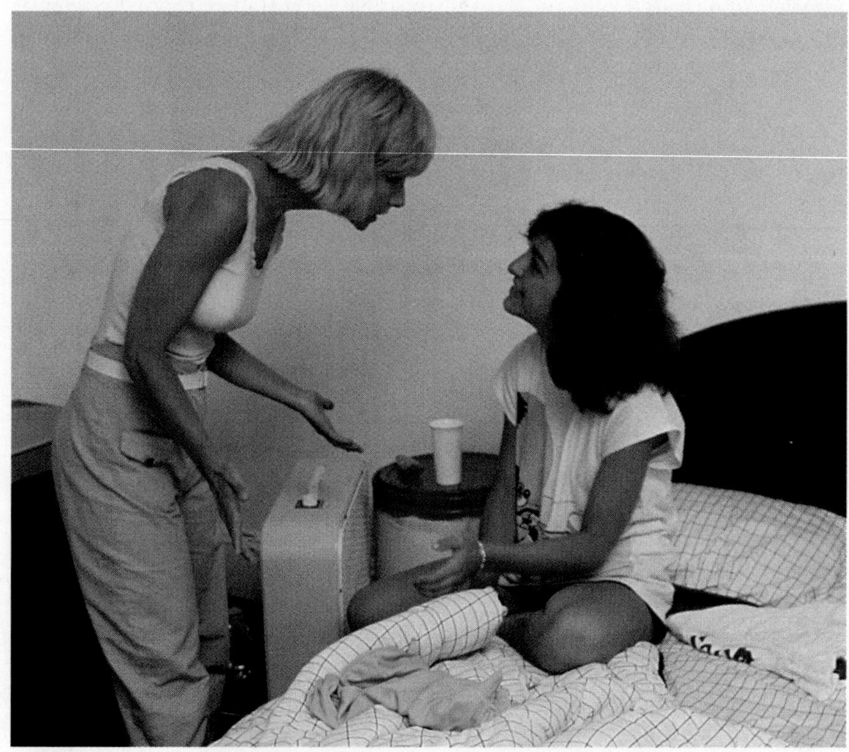

FIGURE 16.4

***PARENT–ADOLESCENT RELATIONSHIPS.*** *Conflicts between teenagers and their parents center around the everyday details of family life. Parents and adolescents share similar values, however. Most adolescents continue to feel close to their parents, even as they strive for independence from them.*

et al., 1992). A very small proportion of families—perhaps 5 to 10 percent—do suffer severe strains during a child's adolescence (Steinberg, 1991). But this is not normal, and professional help should be sought in these instances.

**Parenting Styles** In Chapter 10, we saw that children's development is affected by the degree to which their parents show warmth and set limits on the child's behavior. Differences in parenting styles continue to influence the development of adolescents as well (Baumrind, 1991a, b; Lamborn et al., 1991). Authoritative parents are warm and permit their adolescents to express their opinions, and yet, they also set limits on their behavior. Adolescents from authoritative homes show more competent behavior than any other group of teenagers. They are more self-reliant, do better in school, have better mental health, and show the lowest incidence of psychological problems and misconduct, including drug use. Permissive parents are high in warmth but low in control. Their adolescents are nearly as competent and well-adjusted as those from authoritative homes, but they are more likely to show deviant behavior such as school misconduct and drug use. Authoritarian parents are high in restrictiveness and control but low in warmth. Their adolescents do reasonably well in school, and they show a low incidence of deviant behavior. But they are more likely to be withdrawn, anxious, and depressed, and have low self-confidence (see Figure 16.5). Neglecting–rejecting parents, who are low in both control and warmth, have adolescents who are the least competent and have the most problems in all areas.

**Culture and Development: Parenting Styles** Are parenting styles related to adolescent behaviors in the same way across different ethnic groups? Lamborn and her colleagues (1991) found that authoritative parenting was related to healthy psychological and social adolescent development and that rejecting–neglecting parenting was associated with the poorest outcomes in four different ethnic groups: African Americans, Asian Americans, Hispanics, and whites. Still another study examined the relationship between parenting styles and the school grades of white, African-American, Hispanic, and Asian-American adolescents (Dornbusch et al., 1987). This study also found that students with

FIGURE 16.5

***Parenting Styles.*** *Authoritarian parents, like the father shown here, are highly restrictive and controlling but not very warm. Their adolescent children do reasonably well in school and show a low incidence of deviant behavior but are also more apt to be withdrawn, anxious, and depressed, and have low self-esteem.*

authoritative parents generally received higher grades than students with authoritarian and permissive parents. So an authoritative parenting style seems to be the most beneficial for adolescents across different ethnic groups.

But there are some exceptions to this pattern. For example, in the study by Dornbusch and colleagues (1987), Asian-American students had the best school performance, yet their parents were among the least authoritative and among the most authoritarian. Even though African-American and Hispanic parents were more authoritative than Asian-American parents, their children did not perform as well in school. How can these puzzling findings be explained? A closer look revealed that white students seemed to benefit more from authoritative parenting than did African-American or Asian-American students (Steinberg et al., 1992). Put another way, African-American and Asian-American youngsters with authoritative parents performed no better than those with authoritarian parents. Why is this? A critical factor appeared to be the influence of peers. When peer groups encouraged academic achievement, students generally did well in school even when exposed to the negative effects of an authoritarian parenting style. When peers did not encourage academic achievement, students did more poorly in school, even if their parents had a more beneficial authoritative style. White students, for example, benefited because their parents generally were authoritative and their peers supported achievement as well. Asian-American students also had the benefit of strong peer support for academic excellence. This apparently offset the negative consequences of having authoritarian parents. Hispanic students suffered from a combination of generally authoritarian parenting and low peer support for academic achievement. African-American students also reported that their peers were not very supportive of academic success. This absence of strong peer support may have undermined the positive influence of authoritative parenting. Clearly, the effect of parenting style on adolescents' behavior is not quite the same for all ethnic groups and must be viewed within a broad social context that includes peer attitudes and behaviors.

## *Relationships with Peers*

The transition from childhood to adolescence is accompanied by a shift in the relative importance of parents and peers. Although relationships with parents generally remain positive in adolescence, the role of peers as a source of activities, influence, and support increases markedly during the teen years. For example, parents are perceived as the most frequent providers of social and emotional support by fourth-graders. But by seventh grade, friends of the same gender are seen to be as supportive as parents. And by 10th grade, same-gender friends are viewed as providing more support than parents (Furman & Buhrmester, 1992). Let us examine more closely the role of friends and the peer group during adolescence.

**Friendships in Adolescence** Friendships occupy an increasingly important place in the lives of adolescents. Adolescents have more friends than younger children do (Feiring & Lewis, 1991). Most adolescents have one or two "best friends" and several good friends. Teenagers see their friends frequently, usually several hours a day (Hartup, 1993). And when teenagers are not with their friends, you can often find them talking with each other on the phone. In fact, one of the authors (S. R.) frequently warned his children that he would take them in for major surgery—telephonectomy—unless they got the phones out of their ears by themselves. The warning went unheard (because his children were on the phone). He therefore solved the problem by having a separate line installed for the children and investing heavily in the local telephone company.

**TRUTH OR FICTION REVISITED**

*Adolescents actually have more friends than younger children do, even though not all of them are close confidants.*

Friendships in adolescence differ in important ways from the friendships of childhood. For one thing, adolescents are much more likely to stress the importance of intimate self-disclosure and mutual understanding in their friendships. For example, one eighth-grade girl described her best friend this way: "I can tell her things and she helps me talk. And she doesn't laugh at me if I do something weird—she accepts me for who I am." (Berndt & Perry, 1990, p. 269). Second, adolescents stress loyalty and faithfulness as important aspects of friendship more than younger children do. For example, they may say that a friend will "stick up for you in a fight" and won't "talk about you behind your back" (Berndt & Perry, 1990). Finally, adolescents are more likely than younger children to share equally with friends and to compete less with them.

Adolescents and their friends are similar in many respects. They typically are the same age and the same race. They almost always are the same gender. Even though romantic attachments increase during the teen years, most adolescents still choose members of their own gender as best friends (Hartup, 1993). Friends are likely to share certain behavioral similarities. They often are alike in their school attitudes, educational aspirations, and school achievement. Friends also tend to have similar attitudes about drinking, drug use, and sexual activity (Hartup, 1993; Youniss & Haynie, 1992).

Why are friends similar? Two possibilities exist (Hartup, 1993). First, individuals who are alike to begin with may choose each other as friends. Second, friends become more similar over time as they influence each other and share common experiences. Of course, both of these factors may be at work simultaneously.

Friendship is important in developing a positive self-concept and good psychological adjustment. Adolescents who have a close friend have higher self-esteem than adolescents who do not. Teenagers who have intimate friendships also are more likely to show advanced stages of identity development and have better psychological and social adjustment (Berndt, 1992; Bukowski et al., 1993b). These relationships have been found for both white and African-American youth (Savin-Williams & Berndt, 1990).

**GENDER DIFFERENCES IN ADOLESCENT FRIENDSHIPS** Intimacy and closeness appear to be more central to the friendships of girls than boys both in childhood and in adolescence (Berndt & Perry, 1990; Clark-Lempers et al., 1991; Manke, 1993). Both female and male adolescents describe girls' friendships as more intimate than boys' friendships (Hartup, 1993). Girls spend more time with their friends than do boys (Wong & Csikszentmihalyi, 1991). Adolescent girls view close friendships as more important than adolescent boys do, and they report putting more effort into improving the depth and quality of the relationship (Moore & Boldero, 1991). Adolescent and adult females also are more likely than males to disclose secrets, personal problems, thoughts, and feelings to their friends (Dolgin et al., 1991; Papini et al., 1990; Dindia & Allen, 1992).

Friendship networks among girls are smaller and more exclusive than friendship networks among boys (Crombie & Desjardins, 1993). That is, girls tend to have one or two close friends, whereas boys tend to congregate in larger, less intimate groups. The activities of girls' and boys' friendship networks differ as

FIGURE 16.6

**FRIENDSHIP.** *Intimate self-disclosure and mutual understanding are key elements of friendships during adolescence, especially among girls.*

well. Girls are more likely to engage in unstructured activities such as talking and listening to music. Boys, on the other hand, are more likely to engage in organized group activities, games, and sports (Youniss & Haynie, 1992).

### CULTURE AND DEVELOPMENT: ADOLESCENT FRIENDSHIPS

> *I always notice one thing when I walk through the commons at my high school: The whites are on one side of the room, and the blacks are on the other. When I have to walk through the "black" side to get to class, the black students just quietly ignore me and look in the other direction, and I do the same. But there's one who sometimes catches my eye, and I can't help feel awkward when I see him. He was a close friend from childhood. Ten years ago, we played catch in our backyards, went bike riding, and slept over at one another's houses. By the fifth grade, we went to movies and amusement parks and bunked together at summer camp. We're both juniors now at the same high school. We usually don't say anything when we see each other, except maybe a polite "Hi." Since entering high school, we haven't shared a single class or sport. It's as if fate has kept us apart, though, more likely, it's peer pressure. (Adapted from Jarvis, 1993, p. 14)*

Do friendship patterns differ among African-American and white adolescents?

| | AFRICAN AMERICANS | WHITES |
|---|---|---|
| SCHOOL FRIEND OF OTHER RACE | 82 PERCENT | 87 PERCENT |
| CLOSE OTHER-RACE FRIEND SEEN OUTSIDE SCHOOL | 42 PERCENT | 23 PERCENT |
| PEER INTIMACY AND SUPPORT | SAME FOR FEMALES AND MALES | GREATER FOR FEMALES THAN MALES |

Children are more likely to choose friends of their own ethnic group than from another ethnic group. This pattern becomes increasingly strong in adolescence (Hartup, 1993). Minority adolescents become aware of the differences between their culture and the majority culture. Peers from their own ethnic group provide a sense of sisterhood or brotherhood that reduces feelings of isolation from the dominant culture (Spencer et al., 1990).

Under what conditions do adolescents choose and socialize with friends of another ethnic group? One study compared friendship patterns of African-American and white adolescents attending an integrated junior high school (DuBois & Hirsch, 1990). More than 80 percent of the students of both races reported having a school friend of the other race, but only 28 percent of the students saw such a friend frequently outside of school. African-American youths were almost twice as likely as white youths to see a friend of another race outside of school. Children who lived in integrated as opposed to segregated neighborhoods were more likely to see a friend of another race outside the school setting.

Gender differences relating to peer intimacy and support were found for white students but not for African-American students. White girls reported talking more with friends about personal problems and reported that their friends were more available for help than did white boys. These findings are consistent with the gender differences discussed earlier in this chapter (Hartup, 1993; Youniss & Haynie, 1992). But African-American girls and boys reported the same degree of intimacy and support in their friendships. How can these differences be explained? The researchers suggest that the African-American students may have faced a number of race-related stressors in their school, which was integrated but predominantly white. To cope more effectively, both girls and boys may have relied heavily on the support of their peers.

**Peer Groups** In addition to their close friendships, most adolescents also belong to one or more larger peer groups. Brown (1990) has identified two types of adolescent peer groups: *cliques* and *crowds*. ***Cliques*** are groups of 5 to 10 individuals who hang around together and who share activities and confidences. ***Crowds*** are larger groups of individuals who may or may not spend much time together and who are identified by the particular activities or attitudes of the group. Crowds are usually given labels by other adolescents. Think back on your high school days. You probably recall that different groups of individuals were given such labels as ''jocks,'' ''brains,'' ''druggies,'' ''nerds,'' and so on. The most negatively labeled groups (''druggies,'' ''rejects,'' and so on) show higher levels of alcohol and drug use, delinquency, and depression than other groups (Downs & Rose, 1991).

***Clique*** A group of 5 to 10 individuals who hang around together and who share activities and confidences.

***Crowd*** A large, loosely organized group of people who may or may not spend much time together and who are identified by the activities of the group.

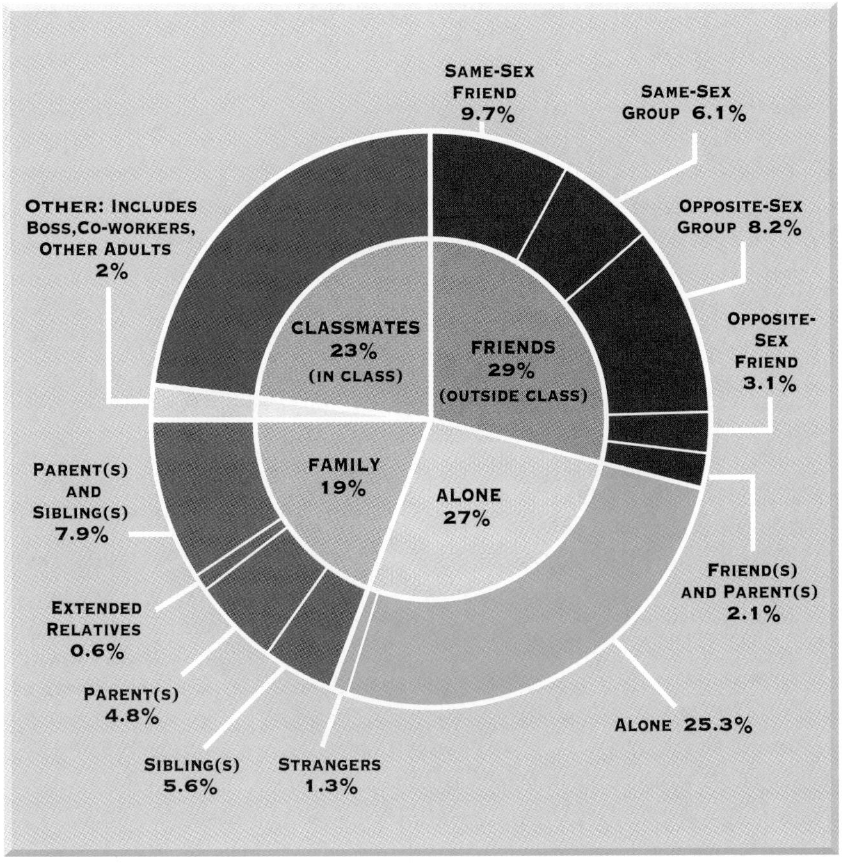

**Figure 16.7**

***With Whom Do Adolescents Spend Their Time?*** *High school students spend over half of their waking hours with peers, either inside or outside the classroom. They spend only about 15 percent of their time with parents and other adults. In this figure and the next one, 1 percentage point is equivalent to approximately 1 hour per week. (Source: Csikszentmihalyi & Larson, 1984).*

Adolescent peer groups differ from childhood peer groups in a number of ways. For one thing, the time spent with peers increases. In the United States, teenagers spend an average of 20 hours per week with peers, compared with the 2 to 3 hours reported in Japan and Russia (Savin-Williams & Berndt, 1990). As you saw in Figure 16.7, high school students spend more than half of their time with peers and only about 15 percent of their time with parents or other adults (Csikszentmihalyi & Larson, 1984).

A second difference between adolescent and childhood peer groups is that adolescent peer groups function with less adult guidance or control (Brown, 1990). Childhood peer groups stay closer to home, under the watchful eye of parents. Adolescent peer groups are more likely to congregate away from home in settings with less adult supervision (the school, for example) or with no supervision at all (shopping malls, for example) (see Figure 16.8).

A third change in adolescent peer groups is the addition of peers of the other gender. This sharply contrasts with the gender segregation of childhood peer groups (Brown, 1990). Association with peers of the other gender leads in some cases to dating and romantic relationships.

**Dating and Romantic Relationships** Romantic relationships begin to appear during early and middle adolescence, and the majority of adolescents start dating by the time they graduate from high school (Savin-Williams & Berndt, 1990). The development of dating typically takes the following sequence: putting oneself in situations where peers of the other gender probably will be present (for example, hanging out in the mall), going to group activities where peers of the other gender definitely will be present (for example, school dances), participating in group dating (for example, joining a mixed-gender group at the movies), and finally, traditional two-person dating (Padgham & Blyth, 1991).

**FIGURE 16.8**

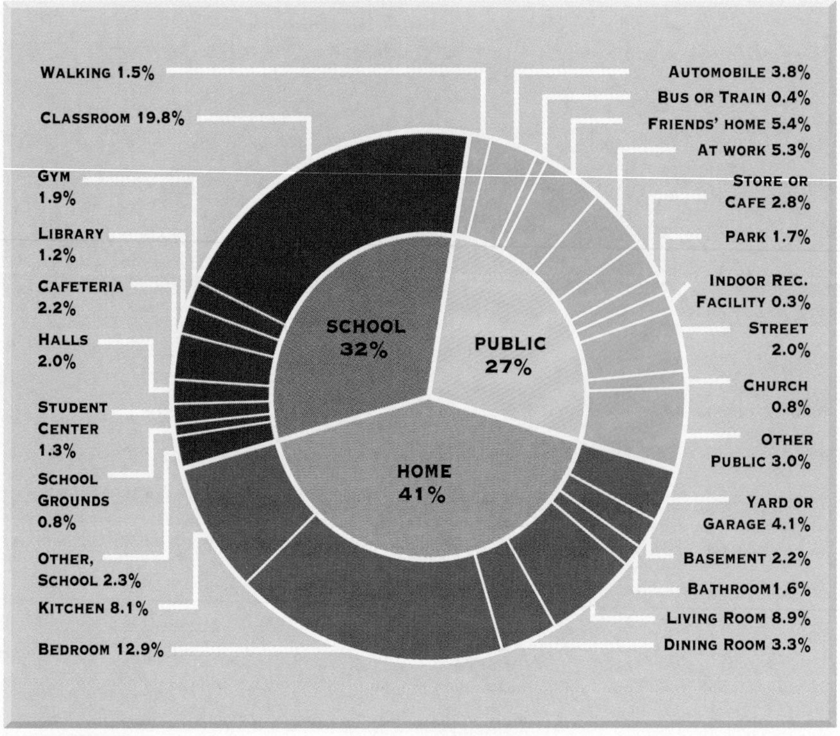


***Where Do Adolescents Spend Their Time?*** *Adolescents spend more time than younger children in settings away from home where there is less adult supervision or none at all. (Source: Csikszentmihalyi & Larson, 1984).*

Dating serves a number of important functions. First and foremost, people date to have fun. High school students rate time spent with a person of the other gender as the time when they are happiest (Csikszentmihalyi & Larson, 1984). Dating, especially in early adolescence, also serves to enhance prestige with one's peers. Dating gives adolescents additional experiences in learning to relate positively to different people. Finally, dating provides preparation for adult courtship activities (Padgham & Blyth, 1991).

Dating relationships tend to be casual and short-lived in early adolescence. In late adolescence, relationships tend to become more stable and committed (Furman & Wehner, in press). It is therefore not surprising that 18-year-olds are more likely than 15-year-olds to mention love, trust, and commitment when describing their romantic relationships (Feiring, 1993).

**Peer Influence** Parents often worry that their teenage children will fall in with the wrong crowd and be persuaded by their peers to engage in behaviors that are self-destructive or go against the parents' wishes (Brown et al., 1993). How much influence do peers have on each other? Does peer pressure cause adolescents to adopt behaviors and attitudes of which their parents disapprove? Peer pressure actually is fairly weak in early adolescence. It peaks during mid-adolescence and declines in late adolescence, after about age 17 (Brown et al., 1993; Youniss & Haynie, 1992).

Why do peers increase in influence during adolescence? One suggestion is that peers provide a standard by which adolescents measure their behavior as they begin to develop independence from the family (Foster-Clark & Blyth, 1991). Another reason is that peers provide social, emotional, and practical support in times of trouble (Kirchler et al., 1991; Pombeni et al., 1990).

It was once the conventional wisdom that peer influence and parental influence were in conflict, with peers exerting pressure on adolescents to engage in negative behaviors such as alcohol and drug use. But recent research paints a much different picture. For one thing, we have seen that adolescents often maintain close and warm relationships with their parents. Parents and peers usually are complementary rather than competing influences on teenagers (Brown et al., 1993; Youniss & Haynie, 1992).

**TRUTH OR FICTION REVISITED**

*Parents and peers actually tend to exert complementary rather than competing influences on adolescents.*

Parents and peers also seem to exert influence in somewhat different domains. Adolescents are more likely to conform to peer standards in matters pertaining to style and taste, such as clothing, hairstyles, speech patterns, and music (Camarena, 1991). They are much more likely to agree with their parents on many serious issues, such as moral principles and future educational and career goals (Savin-Williams & Berndt, 1990).

Adolescents influence each other both positively and negatively. Brown and his colleagues found that peer pressure to finish high school and achieve academically were stronger than pressures to engage in areas of misconduct, such as drug use, sexual activity, and minor delinquency (Brown, 1990). Moreover,

FIGURE 16.9

***PEER INFLUENCE.*** *Peers reinforce behavior patterns that may have existed before the individual joined the group. This is true for positive behaviors such as academic achievement as well as for negative behaviors such as drug use.*

teenagers were much less inclined to follow peer pressure to engage in antisocial activity than in neutral activity.

It is true that adolescents who smoke, drink, use drugs, and engage in sexual activity often have friends who also engage in these behaviors. But we must keep in mind that adolescents tend to choose friends and peers who are similar to them to begin with. Peers reinforce behavior patterns and predispositions that may have existed before the individual joined the group. This is true for positive behaviors, such as academic achievement, as well as for negative behaviors, such as drug use (Brown, 1990).

A number of other factors affect the susceptibility of adolescents to peer influence. One of these is gender. Girls appear to be slightly more concerned with peer acceptance than boys, but boys are more likely than girls to conform to pressures to engage in misconduct (Camarena, 1991; Foster-Clark & Blyth, 1991). Parenting style also is related to susceptibility to peer pressure. Authoritative parenting appears to discourage negative peer influence, while authoritarian and permissive parenting seems to encourage it (Fuligni & Eccles, 1993; Foster-Clark & Blyth, 1991).

## SEXUALITY

*My first sexual experience occurred in a car after the high school junior prom. We were both virgins, very uncertain but very much in love. We had been going together since eighth grade. The experience was somewhat painful. I remember wondering if I would look different to my mother the next day. I guess I didn't because nothing was said. (Adapted from Morrison et al., 1980, p. 108)*

In an episode of the TV series "Growing Pains," an adolescent was referred to as a "hormone with feet." Adolescents wrestle with issues of how and when to express their awakening sexuality. To complicate matters, adults in Western society often send mixed messages to adolescents concerning the how's, why's, and when's of teenage sexual behavior. For example, teens (and adults) are bombarded by sexual messages in TV and radio commercials, print advertising, and virtually every other form of promotion (Rathus et al., 1993). In this section, we consider patterns of sexual behavior in adolescence and some of the factors that influence these behaviors. We then turn to a problematic aspect of adolescent sexuality: teenage pregnancy. We will examine the consequences of teenage pregnancy and look at ways of preventing pregnancy and supporting adolescent parents.

***Masturbation*** Sexual self-stimulation.

***Homosexuality*** An erotic orientation to members of one's own gender.

### *Patterns of Sexual Behavior*

Sexual activity in adolescence can take many forms. In this section, we consider masturbation, homosexuality, heterosexuality, and contraceptive use.

**Masturbation** ***Masturbation,*** or sexual self-stimulation, is the most common source of orgasm in adolescents of both genders (Katchadourian, 1990). Masturbation appears to occur more frequently among boys than girls. In one national survey of 1,067 teenagers, for example, 46 percent of males and 24 percent of females reported that they had masturbated (Coles & Stokes, 1985). Among college students, the figures are even higher: 92 percent of males and 72 percent of females (Kelley & Byrne, 1992). Whether males really masturbate more than females or whether they simply are more willing to report that they do is still an unanswered question. Today, masturbation is more acceptable among adolescents and adults than it was in the past. There is no evidence that masturbation causes any physical harm. Educators view masturbation as a safe sexual outlet that can help individuals learn about their own sexuality. But feelings of shame and guilt still often are attached to this behavior (Katchadourian, 1990). For example, even though masturbation is a more common sexual activity than sexual intercourse among college students, masturbation is perceived more negatively (Kelley & Byrne, 1992).

**Homosexuality** ***Homosexuality*** is an erotic orientation to members of one's own gender. But homosexual activity during adolescence is not necessarily evidence of a permanent homosexual orientation. Many adolescents who have homosexual experiences in adolescence do not continue this activity in adulthood (Rathus et al., 1993). What is the incidence of homosexual activity in adolescence? Accurate figures are hard to come by because negative attitudes toward homosexuality discourage some people from reporting this behavior. About 5 percent of the adolescents in the Coles and Stokes (1985) national survey reported homosexual experiences. A more recent survey of sexually active men aged 20–39 found that only 2 percent had engaged in any same-gender sexual activity during the past 10 years, and only 1 percent reported being exclusively homosexual during that period (Billy et al., 1993).

Gay and lesbian adolescents often face special problems. The process of "coming out"—that is, accepting one's homosexual orientation and declaring it to others—may be a long and painful struggle (Zera, 1992). Homosexual adolescents may be ostracized and rejected by family and friends. Depression and suicide rates are higher among homosexual youth than among other adolescents. They often engage in substance abuse, run away from home, and do poorly in school (Remafedi, 1991; Savin-Williams, 1991; Youngstrom, 1992b). And males who engage in anal intercourse without condoms are at greater risk for AIDS, as we saw in Chapter 14.

**_Thinking About Development_**

Agree or disagree with the following statement and support your answer: "Homosexuality is a sexual preference."

The origins of homosexuality are complex and controversial. A number of psychological and biological theories have been proposed. Freudian theory links male homosexuality with being reared by a strong, dominating mother and a hostile, detached father. But many heterosexuals have been reared in this type of family constellation. Also, many gay males have had excellent relationships with both parents. So Freudian theory has little support. A learning point of view would suggest that early sexual activity with members of one's own gender could influence sexual orientation. But many gay males and lesbians are aware of their orientation before they have engaged in sexual activity, so this theory also seems flawed.

Biological theories concentrate on genetic or hormonal factors. A recent study found that 48 percent of identical twin sisters of lesbians also were homosexual, compared with only 16 percent of fraternal twins and 6 percent of genetically unrelated adopted sisters (Bailey et al., 1993). The same pattern of results emerged in a similar survey of gay men and their siblings (Bailey & Pillard, 1991). In that study, 52 percent of identical twins of gay men also were gay but only 22 percent of fraternal twins and 11 percent of adopted brothers of gay men were also gay (Bailey & Pillard, 1991). Another recent report linked male homosexuality to a small region on the X chromosome (Hamer et al., 1993). Other research has shown that an area of the hypothalamus believed to control sexual activity is less than half the size in gay men that it is in heterosexual men (LeVay, 1991).

Do these findings indicate that homosexuality is more a matter of genetics than experience? Possibly. But it is also possible that sexual orientation could affect brain structure (Gelman, 1992). You will recall from Chapter 5 that not only does the brain influence behavior, but experience also affects the development of the brain. Another biological possibility is that sexual orientation is determined by the effects of sex hormones. For example, some gay men may be more sensitive than heterosexual men to the small amount of estrogen that all males produce (Gladue, 1988).

Most scientists today subscribe to the view that the causes of homosexuality are many and complex. Interaction among genetic, hormonal, and environmental factors probably is involved (Gelman, 1992).

**HETEROSEXUALITY** Since the late 1960s, adolescents have become sexually active in greater numbers and at younger ages (Gardner & Wilcox, 1993; Katchadourian, 1990). Males tend to become sexually active at younger ages than females and African-American youth become active earlier than whites and Hispanics (Dryfoos, 1990). By age 15, about 20 percent of all boys and 5 percent of all girls report having had intercourse. Among African-American males and females, the figures are higher: 40 percent and 10 percent, respectively. By age 17, two-thirds of white and Hispanic males are sexually active, compared with nearly 90 percent of African-American males. By age 19, nearly 85 percent of white and Hispanic males and almost all African-American males report sexual experience. Among 17-year-old females, 40 percent of whites and Hispanics and 60 percent of African Americans are sexually active. By 19 years of age, 70 percent of white and Hispanic females and 85 percent of African-American females have had sex.

**CONTRACEPTIVE USE** Despite the fact that more teenagers are engaging in sexual activity, many of them do not use birth control. More than half of all adolescents do not use contraceptives the first time they have sexual relations (Hofferth, 1990). Unfortunately, a substantial number of teens use contraceptives only sporadically or not at all. About one-third of sexually active 15-year-old

FIGURE 16.10

**SEXUAL ACTIVITY.** *Since the late 1960s, adolescents have become sexually active in greater numbers and at younger ages.*

females and about one-sixth of sexually active older teens and college-age females say they have never used contraceptives (Green et al., 1992).

Who is most likely to use contraceptives regularly? The older teenagers are when they begin sexual activity, the more likely they are to use contraceptives (Treboux & Busch-Rossnagel, 1991). Other factors associated with contraceptive use include: being in a committed relationship, having high educational achievement and aspirations, having knowledge about sex and contraception, having good communication and a supportive relationship with parents, and having high self-esteem and feelings of control over one's life (Brooks-Gunn & Furstenberg, 1989; Green et al., 1992). Not surprisingly, the same factors that are associated with a higher level of contraceptive use also are associated with a decreased likelihood of becoming pregnant (Barnett et al., 1991; McIntyre et al., 1991).

### *Determinants of Early Sexual Behavior*

Most teenagers do not plan their first sexual experience. Rather, it is something that they perceive as simply happening to them (Brooks-Gunn & Furstenberg, 1989). Why do some teenagers initiate sexual activity at an early age, while others wait until later? Let us consider some of the determinants of early sexual behavior.

**Effects of Puberty** The hormonal changes of puberty probably are partly responsible for the onset of sexual activity. In boys, levels of testosterone are associated with sexual behavior. In girls, however, testosterone levels are linked to sexual interests but not sexual behavior. This suggests that social factors may play a greater role in regulating sexual behavior in girls than in boys (Brooks-Gunn & Furstenberg, 1989; Katchadourian, 1990).

The physical changes associated with puberty also may serve as a trigger for the onset of sexual activity (Zabin, 1991). For example, the development of secondary sex characteristics such as breasts in girls and muscles and deep voices in boys may make them more sexually attractive to others (Katchadourian, 1990). As we saw in Chapter 14, early-maturing girls are more likely to have older friends, which may draw them into early sexual relationships (Brooks-Gunn & Furstenberg, 1989).

**Parental Influences** Teenagers who have close relationships with their parents are less likely to have sex at an early age. Adolescents who communicate well with their parents also delay the onset of sexual activity (Brooks-Gunn & Furstenberg, 1989; Katchadourian, 1990; Mueller & Powers, 1990). If these youngsters do have sexual intercourse, they are more likely to use birth control and to have fewer sexual partners (Koch, 1991). Among African-American males, parental strictness also is associated with more consistent use of condoms and fewer sexual partners (Jemmott & Jemmott, 1992).

***Truth or Fiction Revisited***

*It is true that adolescents who have a close relationship with their parents are less likely to engage in sexual activity at an early age. Parents are generally more cautious in their behavior than adolescents, and perhaps this closeness allows the parents to more effectively communicate their standards for behavior and their rationales.*

The double standard of sexuality in our society—acceptable for boys but not girls—seems to influence the way in which parent communication affects sexual behavior in teenagers. In one study, for example, discussing sexual topics with parents was linked with delayed sexual activity in high school girls but with earlier sexual activity and with contraceptive use in boys (Treboux & Busch-Rossnagel, 1990). The message for daughters appears to be "Don't do it," whereas the message for sons is "It's okay to do it as long as you take precautions."

**Peer Influences** Peers also play an important role in determining the sexual behavior of adolescents. One of the most powerful predictors of sexual activity for both female and male adolescents is the sexual activity of their best friends (DiBiasio & Benda, 1992).

When 1,000 teenagers were asked why they had not waited to have sexual intercourse until they were older, the top reason given was peer pressure, cited by 34 percent of girls and 26 percent of boys (Kelley & Byrne, 1992). "Pressure from boys" was mentioned by 17 percent of girls. Other reasons given were that "everyone does it" (14 percent of girls, 10 percent of boys), curiosity (14 percent of girls, 16 percent of boys), sexual gratification (5 percent of girls, 10 percent of boys) and love (11 percent of girls, 6 percent of boys).

Peers, especially those of the same gender, also serve as the primary source of sex education for adolescents. The second most popular source is books or magazines, followed by parents (especially mother) and school (Koch, 1991).

**Culture and Development: Early Sexual Behavior** Sexual activity occurs earlier among African-American teenagers than among other adolescents (Dryfoos, 1990). What might account for this difference? One explanation is that early sexual behavior and teen pregnancy carry less stigma among African Americans (Bingham et al., 1990; Marsiglio & Scanzoni, 1990). Another factor may be social-class differences. When African-American and white teenagers of the same socioeconomic class are compared, much of the racial difference in early sexual activity disappears. In other words, young people from low-income families, regardless of ethnicity, are more likely to engage in sex at early ages (Dryfoos, 1990). In the environments in which low-income youth live, exposure to overcrowding, inappropriate role models, and inadequate opportunities to obtain education about sexual development all may contribute to early sexual activity (Jenkins & Westney, 1991; Marsiglio & Scanzoni, 1990). Of course, not all low-income African-American youth engage in early sexual activity, Who is most likely to delay? Females who are more career-motivated, who have a father at home and a mother who graduated from high school, who are more influenced by family values, and who have more conservative attitudes about teenage sex are least likely to initiate sex at an early age (Handler, 1990; Keith et al., 1991).

### Teenage Pregnancy

Nearly 10 percent of American adolescent girls—about 1 million—become pregnant each year (Children's Defense Fund, 1992b; McWhirter et al., 1993). This rate is higher than that for teens in other Western nations (see Focus on Research). Nearly half of all pregnant teens will get an abortion. More than 90 percent of the others will have their babies out of wedlock and choose to raise them rather than give them up for adoption (Coates & Van Widenfelt, 1991; Furstenberg et al., 1989; Lewin, 1992b). The proportion of babies born to unwed mothers has risen sharply in recent years. By the early 1990s, more than two-thirds of teenage mothers were unmarried, compared with less than one-third in 1970 (Children's Defense Fund, 1992b). The great majority of pregnancies among unmarried teens—nine out of ten—were unplanned (Alan Guttmacher Institute, 1991). Teenage pregnancy rates are higher among lower-class and ethnic minority groups (Testa, 1992).

**Truth or Fiction Revisited**

*It is true that about 1 million U.S. teenagers become pregnant each year. The U.S. rate of teenage pregnancy is higher than that of other industrialized nations.*

Why is teenage pregnancy on the rise? One factor is a loosening of traditional taboos against adolescent sexuality (Hechtman, 1989). Some teenage girls become pregnant as a way of eliciting a commitment from their partner or rebelling against their parents. But most become pregnant because they misunderstand reproduction and contraception or miscalculate the odds of conception. Even

FOCUS ON RESEARCH

### THE PUZZLING TEEN-PREGNANCY EPIDEMIC

The teenage pregnancy rate is higher in the United States than in almost all other Western countries, including England, France, Canada, Sweden, and the Netherlands. How can this be explained? A study by the Alan Guttmacher Institute explored possible reasons (Forrest, 1990). One possibility is that American adolescents start having sex at an earlier age than those in other Western countries. But this turned out not to be so. Another possibility is that public assistance benefits for teens with children are greater in the United States, thereby encouraging pregnancy. Wrong again! Support for unwed mothers appears to be greater in other Western nations than in the United States.

What is the culprit, then? The major difference seems to be that American teens are less likely to use contraceptives than their peers in other countries. This answer leads to a further question: Why is contraceptive use lower among U.S. teenagers? The researchers concluded that compared with adults in the United States, European adults are more open in dealing with sexual topics and are more likely to accept the fact that many teens will be sexually active. As a result, contraceptive services are much more widely available to European adolescents. American adolescents appear to be exposed to mixed messages about sex and birth control. On the one hand, sexual themes often are prominent in advertising, entertainment, and the media. On the other hand, birth control information often is not discussed explicitly by parents, schools, or the media, and contraceptive methods are not easily accessible (Furstenberg et al., 1989).

One reason for denying teenagers access to contraceptive information and devices is a concern that access will encourage teens to become sexually active. However, research evidence supports the effectiveness of school programs that teach young teenagers social skills that enable them to resist peer and social pressures to become sexually active (Howard & McCabe, 1990). Researchers of the Guttmacher Institute study suggest that open communication about sexuality and easy availabilty of birth control devices can help lower pregnancy rates among teens who are already sexually active (Forrest, 1990). The relationships among teenage pregnancy, age, peer pressures, and the availability of contraceptive information and devices are complex, and no simple answer to the problem is in the offing.

those who are well-informed about contraception often do not use it consistently (Hechtman, 1989; Oakley et al., 1991).

**CONSEQUENCES OF TEENAGE PREGNANCY** The medical, social, and economic costs of unplanned teenage pregnancies can be devastating to mothers and their children. Teen mothers are more likely to have medical complications during pregnancy and to have prolonged labor. Their babies are more likely to be born prematurely and to have low birth weight. It appears that these medical problems are largely due not to the young age of the mother, but to the inadequate prenatal care and poor nutrition often experienced by teenage mothers living in conditions of poverty (Coates & Van Widenfelt, 1991; Dryfoos, 1990; Ketterlinus & Lamb, 1991; Wegman, 1992).

Teenage parenthood creates a number of economic and social disadvantages for young mothers as well (White & DeBlassie, 1992). They are less likely to graduate from high school or attend college. Their lack of educational achievement makes it more difficult for them to obtain adequate employment. They have a lower standard of living and are more likely to require public assistance. Their marriages are more likely to be unstable, and they often have more children than they intended (Coates & Van Widenfelt, 1991; Furstenberg, 1991; Center for the Study of Social Policy, 1993). Few receive consistent financial or emotional help from the fathers, who generally are unable to support themselves, let alone a family (Klein, 1993). Among teenage girls who become pregnant, more than 31 percent will become pregnant again within 2 years (Alan Guttmacher Institute, 1991).

While the most attention has been directed toward teenage mothers, young fathers bear an equal responsibility for teenage pregnancies. The consequences of parenthood for adolescent fathers are similar to those for adolescent mothers.

FIGURE 16.11

***Teenage Pregnancy.*** *Nearly 1 in 10 American teenage girls becomes pregnant each year. Most of these pregnancies are unplanned. Teenagers seldom realize that the medical, social, and economic costs of teenage pregnancy can be devastating to the mother, father, and child.*

Teen fathers tend to have lower educational achievement than their peers, and they enter the work force at an earlier age. Their marriages are more unstable, and they tend to have more children (Neville & Parke, 1991).

Children born to teen mothers also are at a disadvantage. As early as the preschool years, they show lower levels of cognitive functioning and more behavioral and emotional problems. Boys appear to be more affected than girls. By adolescence, offspring of teenage mothers are doing more poorly in school and they are more likely to become teenage parents themselves (Brooks-Gunn & Chase-Lansdale 1991; Coates & Van Widenfelt, 1991; Osofsky, et al. 1992).

Again, these problems seem to result not from the mother's age but from the socially and economically deprived environments in which teen mothers and their children often live. Teenage mothers also may be less knowledgeable about child rearing than older mothers and may provide their babies with fewer opportunities for stimulation (Brooks-Gunn & Chase-Lansdale, 1991; Lamb & Ketterlinus, 1991; Sommer et al., 1993).

Some teenage mothers and their children fare better than others. A study of teenage mothers in Baltimore who were followed over a 20-year period found that many of these women returned to school, left public assistance, and found stable employment (Furstenberg et al., 1992). Such positive changes in the lives of teenage mothers are associated with more favorable development in their children (Dubow & Luster, 1990).

**Support for Pregnant Teenagers** A number of programs have been designed in recent years to promote positive social, economic, health, and developmental outcomes for pregnant teenagers and their children (Paikoff & Brooks-Gunn, 1991b). Programs for pregnant teenagers often include prenatal care services. Teen mothers who receive prenatal care during pregnancy are more likely to have healthy babies than those who do not have such care (Coates & Van Widenfelt, 1991; Furstenberg et al., 1989).

Supportive services for teenage parents include family planning services, child-care services, and education about parenting skills, work skills, and life options. Some of these programs have been moderately successful in improving the lives of adolescent parents. Teens who participate in such programs have fewer children in the long run (Seitz & Apfel, 1993). They are less likely to drop out of high school and more likely to become economically self-sufficient. Their babies develop better as well (Coates & Van Widenfelt, 1991). In one study by Tiffany Field and her colleagues (Field, 1991a), 80 low-income teenage mothers received training in stimulating and caring for their infants. In addition, half of these mothers were trained and employed as teachers' aides in an infant nursery. Compared with a control group, the babies of the mothers who received training showed superior growth and motor development during the first 2 years of life. The mothers themselves were more likely to return to school or work and were less likely to become pregnant again. This was especially true for the mothers who were trained as teachers' aides. Sad to say, the positive effects on both infants and mothers were short-lived and were no longer apparent by the time the children had reached grade school.

The effects of other support programs for teenage parents also tend to be more short-term than long-term (Coates & Van Widenfelt, 1991). This does not mean that support services to pregnant teenagers have no value. In the Baltimore study we looked at earlier, teen mothers who received continuing educational and family planning services were more likely in the long term to be economically self-sufficient and to have fewer children (Furstenberg et al., 1989). But many experts believe that a better approach to teen pregnancy is to try to prevent it in the first place.

**Preventing Teenage Pregnancy** The past 20 years have seen a dramatic increase in programs to help prevent teenage pregnancies. The prevention efforts include educating teens about sexuality and contraception and providing contraceptive and family planning services. Let us look at each of these approaches.

An overwhelming majority of American parents—more than 90 percent—want their children to have sex education in the public schools (National Guidelines Task Force, 1991). Carrying out such education is another matter, since opinions differ on what should be taught, and when, and by whom (Lawson, 1991). Twenty-two states now require sex education, and 24 others encourage it. But most schools devote only a few hours to the teaching of sex education, and few programs are comprehensive. Sex education rarely is introduced before seventh or eighth grade. In junior high school, the topics typically covered include pubertal changes, reproduction, dating, and sexually transmitted diseases. Material on contraception often is not included until high school, when it may be too late to prevent many teen pregnancies (Brooks-Gunn & Furstenberg, 1989; Katchadourian, 1990).

A new set of comprehensive guidelines for sex education has been developed by the Sex Information and Education Council of the United States and distributed to school systems throughout the country (National Guidelines Task Force, 1991). The guidelines recommend teaching human sexuality in the context of family relationships and respect for others. Among the many topics covered are puberty, abstinence, masturbation, reproduction, contraception, abortion, dating, love, sexual abuse, sexually transmitted diseases, homosexuality, and parenting. Development of personal skills such as identifying values, taking responsibility for one's behavior, making effective decisions, and communicating with others also is emphasized. The material on each topic is geared for children at four different developmental levels: ages 5 to 8, 9 to 12, 12 to 15, and 15 to 18. It is too early to tell how effective this program will be, but it does appear to contain many of the characteristics that are found in the more successful programs (see Developing Today).

## *Developing Today*

### CHARACTERISTICS OF EFFECTIVE SEX EDUCATION PROGRAMS

Many experts agree that the goal of sex education programs should be to encourage responsible behavior concerning sexual intercourse, use of contraception, and prevention of pregnancy and sexually transmitted diseases. To reach this goal, experts recommend that sex education programs have the following features (Dryfoos, 1990):

- Early intervention: no later than the middle school years.
- Inclusion of parents if possible.
- Wide-ranging, school-based sex and family life education curriculum that includes development of social and life-planning skills.
- Communitywide programs linking schools with outside organizations that offer sex education, health services, individual and group counseling, and family planning.
- Access to birth control and counseling services that ensure the confidentiality of the teenager. Many teens will not use such services if parental notification or permission is required.

How successful are sex education programs? The better programs increase students' knowledge about sexuality. Despite fears that sex education will increase sexual activity in teenagers, that concern appears to be unfounded. In fact, some programs seem to delay the onset of sexual activity (Dryfoos, 1990). Among teenagers who already are sexually active, sex education is associated with the increased use of effective contraception by both females and males (Barth et al., 1992; Koch, 1991; Ku et al., 1992; Moran & Corley, 1991). And some sex education programs appear to reduce teen pregnancy rates (Dryfoos, 1990; Katchadourian, 1990).

FIGURE 16.12

**CONTRACEPTION CLINIC.** *A young woman receives counseling about the use of birth control pills. Should schools provide contraceptive services to sexually active students? Should parents have a say in whether their children receive such services?*

***Juvenile delinquency*** Illegal activities committed by a child or adolescent.

***Status offenses*** Offenses considered illegal only when performed by minors, such as truancy and underage drinking.

School-based clinics that distribute contraceptives and contraceptive information to students have been established recently in some school districts, usually amid some controversy, as we saw in Chapter 14 (Levy, 1993; "Where the Norplant Debate," 1993). In high schools that have such clinics, birthrates often drop significantly. In one such program in St. Paul, Minnesota, not only did the birthrate drop, but contraceptive use continued to be high over a 2-year period (Brooks-Gunn & Furstenberg, 1989). One of the best-known programs is in Baltimore, where pregnancy rates dropped 30 percent in inner-city high schools that distributed contraceptives and contraceptive information but rose nearly 60 percent in schools that did not (Lewin, 1991).

## PROBLEMS

Despite many physical, cognitive, social, and emotional changes of adolescence, most teenagers do not experience major problems. In Chapters 14 and 15, we examined some of the problems that may emerge during adolescence. These include eating disorders, substance abuse, sexually transmitted diseases, and dropping out of school. In this section, we focus on two additional serious problems of adolescence: juvenile delinquency and suicide.

### *JUVENILE DELINQUENCY*

Did you ever commit a delinquent act in your teen years? If you said "yes," then you are like most adolescents. In one large-scale study, for example, four out of five 11- to 17-year-olds reported that they had at some time engaged in a delinquent behavior (Dryfoos, 1990).

The term ***juvenile delinquency*** covers a broad range of illegal activities committed by a child or adolescent. At the most extreme end, it includes serious behaviors such as homicide, rape, and robbery, which are considered criminal acts regardless of the age of the offender. Other less serious offenses, such as truancy, underage drinking, running away from home, and sexual promiscuity, are considered illegal only when performed by minors. Hence, these are known as ***status offenses*** (Henggeler, 1989).

Antisocial and criminal behavior show a dramatic increase in many societies during adolescence and then taper off during adulthood (Kennedy, 1991; Lore & Schultz, 1993). For example, 43 percent of serious crimes in the United States in 1990 were committed by individuals under the age of 21, and 28 percent were committed by teens under the age of 18 (Federal Bureau of Investigation, 1991).

Many delinquent acts do not result in arrest or conviction. And when adolescents are arrested, their cases may be disposed of informally, such as by referral to a mental health agency, without the juvenile being formally declared delinquent in a juvenile court (Kennedy, 1991).

**TRUTH OR FICTION REVISITED**

*Actually, about 80 percent of U.S. adolescents report that they have engaged in acts of juvenile delinquency. Many of these acts are minor, and they do not necessarily result in arrest or conviction.*

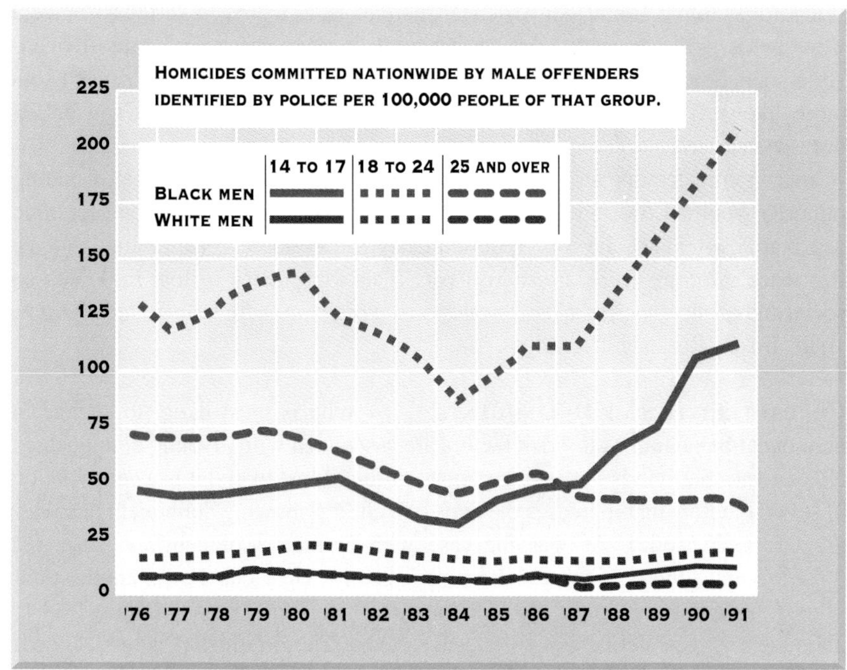


SOURCE: JAMES A. FOX AND GLENN PIERCE, NORTHEASTERN UNIVERSITY.

FIGURE 16.13

***HOMICIDE RATES FOR YOUNG MALES.*** *One of the most alarming trends in recent years is the dramatic increase in murder and other violent crimes committed by teenage males. What might be causing this trend?*

**GENDER DIFFERENCES IN DELINQUENCY** Boys are much more likely than girls to engage in most delinquent behaviors. About four boys are arrested for every girl, but the gender difference is as much as 8 to 1 for serious crimes (Kennedy, 1991; Siegel & Senna, 1991). Boys are more apt to commit crimes of violence, whereas girls are more likely to commit status offenses such as truancy or running away (Dryfoos, 1990). One of the most alarming trends in recent years is the dramatic increase in murder and other violent crimes committed by teenage males, both white and African American (see Figure 16.13). Many social scientists believe that the rise in violence is related to an increase in the sale and possession of illicit drugs, as well as the easy availability of guns (Eckholm, 1993; Federal Bureau of Investigation, 1992).

Violence among adolescent girls appears to be on the rise as well, particularly in poor urban neighborhoods where girls increasingly are joining gangs. In Massachusetts, for example, the number of teenage girls arrested for violent crimes increased 38 percent from 1987 to 1991 (Leslie, 1993).

Even though the delinquent behavior of female adolescents is less frequent and severe than that of males, girls are more likely than boys to be arrested for being runaways. One obvious explanation for this fact is that girls may actually be more likely than boys to run away from home. But another possibility is that the juvenile justice system may have a double standard in this area, viewing female runaways as a more serious problem and therefore treating them more harshly (Siegel & Senna, 1991).

**CULTURE AND DEVELOPMENT: DELINQUENCY** African-American adolescents are more likely to be arrested than white adolescents. For example, African-American youths constitute about 15 percent of the adolescent population in the United States but about 23 percent of the juvenile arrests and about 50 percent of those arrested for violent crimes (Dryfoos, 1990). Yet self-reports of delinquent behavior are not much different for African-American and white youth (Huizinga & Elliott, 1987). How can this discrepancy be explained?

Several researchers have suggested that the overrepresentation of African-American youth in the juvenile justice system is a product of racial bias. One study, for example, found that African-American teens who were serious offenders were twice as likely to be arrested as white serious offenders. And African-American adolescents who had committed nonserious offenses were seven times more likely to be arrested than white nonserious offenders (Huizinga & Elliott, 1987).

Economic factors also may help explain higher delinquency rates among minority youth. Low family income, poor housing, and other socioeconomic deprivations increase the risk of delinquency for all adolescents (Denno, 1990). But since minority teens are more likely than white teens to live in depressed social and economic circumstances, they are at higher risk for delinquency (Gibbs, 1989; Busch-Rossnagel & Zayas, 1991).

**CHARACTERISTICS OF DELINQUENTS** Who is most likely to engage in delinquent behavior? Many risk factors are associated with juvenile delinquency. No one variable stands out as being most critical. Most likely, it is a combination of several factors that increases the odds of a child's showing delinquent behavior (Zigler et al., 1992). As was the case with predictors of substance use, the direction and timing of these factors isn't always clear-cut. For example, poor school performance is related to delinquency. But does school failure lead to delinquency, or is delinquency the cause of the school failure (Dryfoos, 1990)?

Having said all that, what risk factors are associated with delinquency? Children who show aggressive, antisocial, and hyperactive behavior at an early age are more likely to show delinquent behavior in adolescence (Brook et al., 1993; Loeber et al., 1993; Patterson & Yoerger, 1993). Delinquency also is associated with having a lower verbal IQ, immature moral reasoning, low self-esteem, feelings of alienation, and impulsivity (Denno, 1990; Henggeler, 1989; Krueger et al., 1993; White et al., 1989). Other personal factors include poor school performance, little interest in school or religion, early substance use, early sexuality, and having delinquent friends (Denno, 1990; Dryfoos, 1990; Henggeler, 1989; Zigler et al., 1992).

Family factors also are powerful predictors of delinquent behavior. The families of juvenile delinquents often are characterized by lax and ineffective discipline, low levels of affection, and high levels of family conflict, physical abuse, severe parental punishment, and neglect (Dryfoos, 1990; Kopera-Frye et al., 1993; Widom, 1991). The parents and siblings of juvenile delinquents frequently have engaged in antisocial, deviant, or criminal behavior themselves (Mednick et al., 1990; Rowe et al., 1992). For example, one nationwide study found that more than half of all juvenile delinquents imprisoned in state institutions had immediate family members who also had been incarcerated (Butterfield, 1992). This finding has sparked a lively debate about the possible role of genetic factors in criminal behavior. One point of view is that while most factors that increase the risk of delinquency are environmental, some children may be genetically more vulnerable than others. For example, hyperactivity, one of the risk factors for delinquency, may have a genetic basis (Zigler et al., 1992). But most experts believe that delinquency and criminality are largely the outcome of a long and complex chain of psychological and social events and that genetic factors play at most a limited and indirect role (Goleman, 1992a).

**PREVENTION AND TREATMENT OF DELINQUENCY** Over the years, many different approaches have been tried in an effort to prevent delinquent behavior from starting or to reduce delinquent behavior once it appears (Dryfoos, 1990; Henggeler, 1989; Kennedy, 1991; Zigler et al., 1992). What are some of these approaches, and how effective are they?

FIGURE 16.14

***Juvenile Delinquency.*** *Many risk factors are associated with juvenile delinquency. Can you name some of them?*

One type of approach focuses on the individual adolescent offender. Such programs may provide training in moral reasoning (see Chapter 15), social skills training, problem-solving skills training, or a combination of these. In some cases, these programs have the positive effect of reducing subsequent antisocial or delinquent behavior during short-term follow-ups of 6 months to a year. But long-term outcomes are not as promising (Kennedy, 1991; Guerra & Slaby, 1990; Mann & Borduin, 1991). A problem with such approaches is that they focus on individual offenders rather than on the larger social systems in which juvenile delinquents are embedded (Henggeler, 1989).

Another approach tries to deal with various social systems, such as the family, peer groups, school, or community. Examples of such interventions are family therapy approaches; school-based strategies involving teams of students, parents, teachers, and staff; and various community and neighborhood-based programs. These broader, multisystem approaches appear to be more successful in reducing problem behaviors and improving family relations of delinquent adolescents (American Psychological Association, 1993; Dryfoos, 1990; Mann & Borduin, 1991).

One other promising approach starts with the very young child and is aimed at promoting a host of positive child outcomes, not just delinquency prevention. This approach consists of the early childhood intervention programs, such as Head Start, which we examined in Chapter 9. The preschoolers who participated in several of these programs have been tracked longitudinally through adolescence. These follow-ups show several encouraging outcomes, including reductions in aggressive and delinquent behavior (Dryfoos, 1990; Zigler et al., 1992).

### THINKING ABOUT DEVELOPMENT

Agree or disagree with the following statement and support your answer: "You have to be insane to want to take your own life."

## *Suicide*

Adults may assume their adolescent children have everything to live for. Yet increasing numbers of adolescents are taking their own lives. Suicide has become the second leading cause of death among older teenagers (Brody, 1992b). Since 1960, the suicide rate has more than tripled for young people ages 5 to 19 (see Figure 16.15). Currently, about 1 U.S. adolescent in 10,000 commits suicide

TRUTH OR FICTION REVISITED

*Suicide has, in fact, become the second leading cause of death among older teenagers.*

(Berman & Jobes, 1991; Garland & Zigler, 1993). About 6 to 13 percent have attempted suicide at least once (Ackerman, 1993; Meehan et al., 1992). What prompts young people to take their own lives? Who is most at risk of attempting or committing suicide?

**RISK FACTORS IN SUICIDE** Most suicides among adolescents and adults are linked to feelings of depression and hopelessness (Cole, 1991a; King et al., 1990; Myers et al., 1991; Petersen et al., 1993; Tombs, 1991). Teenagers who attempt or commit suicide also are more likely to be substance abusers (Adcock et al., 1991; Berman & Jobes, 1991). Conduct disorders, aggressiveness, delinquent behavior, and impulsivity are found more frequently among suicidal than among nonsuicidal adolescents (Andrews & Lewinsohn, 1992; Borst et al., 1991; King et al., 1990, 1992). But some suicidal teenagers are highly achieving, rigid perfectionists who have set impossibly high expectations for themselves (Brody, 1992c).

Adolescent suicide attempts are more frequent following stressful life events, especially "exit events" (Adams et al., 1992; Violato & Grossi, 1991). Exit events entail loss of social support, as in the death of a parent or friend, breaking up with a boyfriend or girlfriend, or a family member's leaving home. Other major stresses that may precede suicidal behavior include concerns over sexuality, achievement pressures, problems at home, and problems with friends (Berman & Jobes, 1991; Freiberg, 1991c). It is not always a stressful event itself that precipitates suicide but the adolescent's anxiety or fear of being "found out" about something, such as failing a course or getting arrested (Brody, 1992b). Adolescents and adults who consider suicide have also been found to be less capable of solving problems—particularly interpersonal problems—than nonsuicidal people (Berman & Jobes, 1991; Rotheram-Borus et al., 1990; Schotte et al., 1990). Young people contemplating suicide are thus less likely to find productive ways of changing the stressful situation.

Suicide, like many other psychological problems, tends to run in families. Nearly one in four suicide attempters reports that a family member has committed

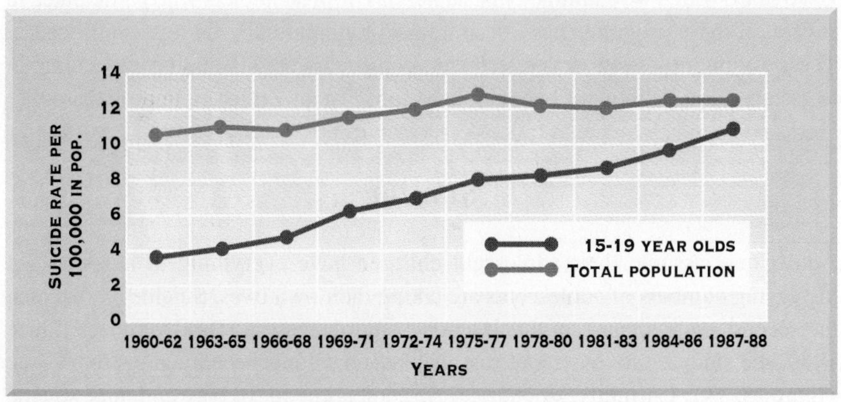


FIGURE 16.15

**SUICIDE RATES IN THE UNITED STATES.** *This figure shows suicide rates per 100,000 people in the United States since 1960. The suicide rate among adolescents has grown dramatically, while it has increased only slightly in the general population. (Source: Garland & Zigler, 1993).*

suicide (Sorensen & Rutter, 1991). Mental disorders among family members also appear to make their contribution (Sorensen & Rutter, 1991; Wilson, 1991). The causal connections are not clear, however. Do suicide attempters inherit disorders that can lead to suicide? Does the family environment subject several family members to feelings of hopelessness? Does the suicide of a family member give one the idea of committing suicide? Perhaps these possibilities and others—such as poor problem-solving ability—form a complex web of contributing factors.

Are there differences in suicidal behavior among teens of different ethnic groups?

| Ethnic Group | Attempted Suicide | Suicidal Thoughts |
|---|---|---|
| Native American | 17 percent | 27 percent |
| Hispanic | 12 percent | 30 percent |
| White | 8 percent | 28 percent |
| African American | 6.5 percent | 20 percent |

**Culture and Development: Suicide** Rates of suicide and suicide attempts vary among different ethnic groups. One in every six Native-American teenagers (17 percent) has attempted suicide—a rate higher than that of other U.S. teenagers (Blum et al., 1992). Twenty-seven percent of Native-American youth also have thought about suicide. Among Hispanic high school students, 12 percent have attempted suicide and 30 percent have thought about it (Centers for Disease Control, 1991). Whites are next, with 8 percent attempting and 28 percent contemplating suicide. African-American teens are least likely to attempt suicide (6.5 percent) or to think about it (20 percent). Actual suicide rates for African Americans are only about 60 percent of those for white Americans at all ages, despite the fact that African Americans are more likely to live in poverty and suffer from discrimination (U.S. Bureau of the Census, 1993). How can this puzzling fact be explained? One possibility is that some suicidal African-American males may engage in risk-taking behaviors that lead to early death by homicide or accident. Another possibility is that cultural factors such as the support offered by extended families and the important role of religion may have a protective effect (Holden, 1992).

**Gender Differences in Suicide** About three times as many adolescent females as males attempt suicide, but about four times as many males succeed (Berman & Jobes, 1991; Garland & Zigler, 1993). In part, males are more likely to succeed because they choose quicker acting and more lethal means. Young males are more likely to shoot or hang themselves, whereas females more often use drugs or poisons (Berman & Jobes, 1991; Garland & Zigler, 1993). While the risk factors for suicide are similar for the two sexes, the relative importance of these factors differs for females and males. Thus, the likelihood of a teenage girl committing suicide is greatest if she suffers from major depression. But the best predictor of suicide for teenage boys is a prior suicide attempt (Pfeffer, 1991). Developing Today describes some of the warning signs of suicide and some things you can do if you notice these signs in a friend or family member.

## A Look Back

It happens that the last topic in this book is suicide, but we do not want to end on a depressing note. Let us remember that the majority of children and adolescents do not encounter the problems discussed in various chapters of this book.

We have charted the course of development from the moment of conception through adolescence. We leave the adolescent poised on the threshold of adulthood. Although our book ends here, development does not. We continue to grow and change throughout our lifetimes. But that is a topic for another book.

For now, let us briefly look back on the path we have traveled so far. Childhood is in many ways the most exciting time of life, a time of continual discovery. As the philosopher Nietzsche so aptly put it, "The child sees everything which has to be experienced and learned as a doorway."

## *Developing Today*

### *WARNING SIGNS OF SUICIDE*

The great majority of young people who commit suicide send out a variety of signals about their impending act (Berman & Jobes, 1991). Sad to say, these signals often are overlooked or are not taken seriously. Here are some of the clues that may alert concerned adults and peers that a teenager may be at risk for suicide (Berman & Jobes, 1991; Brody, 1992b, c; Gould, 1991):

- Changes in eating and sleeping patterns
- Difficulty concentrating on school work
- A sharp decline in school performance and attendance
- Loss of interest in previously enjoyed activities
- Giving away prized possessions
- Complaints about physical problems when no organic basis can be found
- Withdrawal from social relationships
- Personality or mood changes
- Talking or writing about death or dying
- Abuse of drugs or alcohol
- An attempted suicide
- Availability of a handgun
- A precipitating event such as an argument with parents, a broken romantic relationship, academic difficulties, or trouble with the law
- Knowing or hearing about another teenager who has commited suicide (which can lead to so-called "cluster" suicides)

Here are some things you can do if you notice one or more of these warning signs:

- Make an immediate appointment for the person with a helping professional, and make sure the appointment is kept. Or suggest that the person go *with* you to obtain professional help *now*. The emergency room of a general hospital, the campus counseling center or infirmary, or the campus or local police will do. Some campuses have suicide hot lines you can call. Some cities have suicide prevention centers with hot lines that people can use anonymously.
- Draw the person out. Edwin Shneidman, cofounder of the Los Angeles Suicide Prevention Center, suggests asking questions such as "What's going on?" "Where do you hurt?" "What would you like to see happen?" (1985, p. 11). Questions such as these may encourage people to express frustrated psychological needs and provide some relief. They also give you time to assess the danger and think.
- Be empathetic. Show that you understand how upset the person is. Do *not* say, "Don't be silly" or "You're crazy." Do *not* insist on contact with specific people, such as parents or a spouse. Conflict with these people may have led to the suicidal thinking.
- Suggest that measures other than suicide might be found to solve the problem, even if they are not evident at the time. Shneidman (1985) suggests that suicidal people can typically see only two solutions to their problems—either death or a magical resolution of their problems. Therapists thus attempt to remove the mental blinders of suicidal people.
- Ask how the person intends to commit suicide. People with concrete plans and the weapon are at greater risk. Ask if you might hold on to the weapon for a while. Sometimes the person says yes.
- Extract a promise that the person will not commit suicide before seeing you again. Arrange a concrete time and place to meet. Get professional help as soon as you are apart.

**FIGURE 16.16 A SUICIDE-PREVENTION HOT LINE.** *At suicide-prevention centers, trained staff stand by hot lines around the clock. If someone you know is threatening suicide, consult a professional as soon as possible.*

We hope that we have encouraged you to understand the development of children in light of the richness of their diverse backgrounds. Understanding is an essential element in developing respect for all children. Respect is vital to establishing a commitment to ensure that children grow up happy, well-educated, and productive.

The children of the world are the future of the world. In the words of the Children's Defense Fund (1992b, p. vii), let us "leave no child behind."

## *Summary*

1. In Erik Erikson's fifth stage of psychosocial development, the primary task is to develop ego identity, a sense of who one is and what one stands for. James Marcia, building on Erikson's approach, has identified four identity statuses that represent the possible combinations of exploration and commitment. These are identity diffusion (no exploration, no commitment), foreclosure (commitment but no exploration), moratorium (exploration but no commitment), and identity achievement (exploration and commitment).

2. Erikson believed that identity development differed for females and males, but research shows that the similarities are greater than the differences.

3. Minority youth have the challenging task of incorporating elements of both their own culture and the dominant culture into their self-identity.

4. Adolescents incorporate psychological characteristics and social relationships into their self-concepts. The self-concept also becomes both more differentiated and more integrated.

5. Self-esteem is at its lowest at around age 12 or 13 and then gradually improves throughout adolescence. Self-concepts of minority youth are as positive or more positive than those of white youth and are related to a sense of ethnic identity.

6. Adolescents spend less time with their parents than they did during childhood. Conflicts over everyday matters increase, but adolescents and parents share similar values and beliefs.

7. As in childhood, authoritative parenting is associated with higher levels of adolescent competence, psychological adjustment, and school performance.

8. Peer influence and support increase during adolescence. Friendships are characterized by an increasing sense of intimacy, loyalty, and sharing. Most adolescents also belong to larger peer groups called *cliques* and *crowds.* Adolescents spend more time with peers than with parents. Romantic and dating relationships emerge.

9. Peer pressure peaks during mid-adolescence and then declines. Adolescents are most influenced by peers in matters of style and taste. They are more likely to agree with their parents on more serious issues.

10. Masturbation is a common sexual activity in adolescence. Homosexual activity in adolescence does not necessarily indicate a permanent homosexual orientation. The origins of homosexuality are complex and controversial. Interaction among genetic, hormonal, and environmental factors probably is involved.

11. Adolescents are becoming sexually active in greater numbers and at younger ages. Many teens use contraceptives only sporadically or not at all.

12. Early onset of sexual behavior is associated with a number of factors, including pubertal changes, a poor relationship with one's parents, and sexual activity among one's friends and peers.

13. The teenage pregnancy rate in the United States is higher than in other Western nations. Nearly half of all pregnant U.S. teens have an abortion, and most of the others will have their babies out of wedlock and raise them. The medical, social, and economic costs of teen pregnancy are considerable for the mothers, fathers, and children.

14. Sex education programs can delay the onset of sexual activity, increase contraceptive use, and reduce teen pregnancy rates.

15. Juvenile delinquency includes both serious offenses, which are considered criminal regardless of the offender's age, and status offenses, which are considered illegal only when performed by a minor. Antisocial and criminal behavior increases dramatically during adolescence and then tapers off. Delinquency appears to be largely the outcome of a long and complex chain of psychological and social events, with genetic factors playing at most a limited and indirect role.

16. The teenage suicide rate has increased dramatically in recent years. Most suicides are linked to feelings of depression and are most frequent following stressful life events that entail loss of social support.

# Glossary

**Abstinence syndrome** A characteristic cluster of symptoms that results from sudden decreases in the level of usage of a substance.

**Accommodation** According to Piaget, the modification of existing schemes in order to incorporate new events or knowledge. See *Assimilation.*

**Achievement** That which is attained by one's efforts and presumed to be made possible by one's abilities.

**Achieved ethnic identity** The final stage of ethnic identity development; similar to the identity achievement status.

**Acquired immune deficiency syndrome (AIDS)** A fatal, usually sexually transmitted disease that is caused by a virus and cripples the body's immune system, rendering the victim vulnerable to opportunistic diseases.

**Active** Influencing or acting upon the environment.

**Adaptation** According to Piaget, the interaction between the organism and the environment. It consists of two processes: assimilation and accommodation.

**Adipose tissue** Fat.

**Adolescence** The stage bounded by the advent of puberty at the lower end and the capacity to take on adult responsibilities at the upper end. Puberty is a biological concept, while adolescence is a psychological concept.

**Adrenalin** A hormone that generally arouses the body, increasing the heart and respiratory rates.

**Age of viability** The age at which a fetus can sustain independent life.

**AIDS** See *Acquired immune deficiency syndrome.*

**Allele** A member of a pair of genes.

**Alpha-fetoprotein assay** A blood test that assesses the mother's blood level of alpha-fetoprotein, a substance that is linked with neural tube defects in the fetus.

**Ambivalent/resistant attachment** A type of insecure attachment characterized by severe distress at the leave-taking of, and ambivalent behavior at reunions with, an attachment figure.

**Amenorrhea** Lack of menstruation.

**American Sign Language (ASL)** The communication of meaning through the use of symbols that are formed by moving the hands and arms. The language used by some deaf people.

**Amniocentesis** A procedure for drawing and examining fetal cells sloughed off into amniotic fluid to determine the presence of various disorders in the fetus.

**Amniotic fluid** Fluid within the amniotic sac that suspends and protects the fetus.

**Amniotic sac** The sac containing the fetus.

**Amphetamine** A kind of stimulant drug.

**Amplitude** Height. The higher the amplitude of sound waves, the louder they are.

**Anal-expulsive** In psychoanalytic theory, descriptive of behaviors and traits characterized by unregulated self-expression, such as messiness.

**Anal-retentive** In psychoanalytic theory, descriptive of behaviors and traits characterized by expression of self-control or holding in.

**Anal stage** In psychoanalytic theory, the second stage of psychosexual development, in which gratification is attained through anal activities, such as elimination of wastes.

**Androgenital syndrome** A disorder in which a genetic female becomes masculinized as a result of prenatal exposure to male androgens.

**Androgens** Male sex hormones.

**Anesthetics** Agents that produce partial or total loss of the sense of pain.

**Animism** According to Piaget, the attribution of life and intentionality as a way of explaining the behavior of inanimate objects. Characteristic of preoperational thought.

**Anorexia nervosa** An eating disorder seen mostly among adolescent females and characterized by irrational fear of weight gain, distorted body image, and severe weight loss.

**Anoxia** Oxygen deprivation.

**Apgar scale** A measure of a newborn's health that assesses appearance, pulse, grimace, activity level, and respiratory effort.

**Aphasia** A disruption in the ability to understand or produce language.

**Apnea** Temporary suspension of breathing.

**Appearance–reality distinction** The difference between real events on the one hand and mental events, fantasies, and misleading appearances on the other hand.

**Artificialism** According to Piaget, the belief that environmental features were made by people. Characteristic of preoperational thought.

**Artificial insemination** Injection of sperm into the uterus to fertilize an ovum.

**Assimilation** According to Piaget, the incorporation of new events or knowledge into existing schemes. See *Accommodation.*

**Associative play** Play with other children in which toys are shared, but there is no common goal or division of labor.

**Astigmatism** A visual disorder caused by abnormal curvature of the lens, so that images are indistinct or distorted.

**Asynchronous growth** Imbalanced growth, such as that which occurs during the early part of adolescence and causes many adolescents to appear gawky.

**Attachment** An affectionate bond between individuals characterized by a seeking of closeness or contact and a showing of distress upon separation.

**Attachment-in-the-making-phase** The second phase in the development of attachment, occurring at 3 or 4 months of age and characterized by a preference for familiar figures.

**Attention-deficit hyperactivity disorder (ADHD)** A behavior disorder characterized by excessive inattention, impulsiveness, and hyperactivity.

**Attributional style** The way in which one is disposed toward interpreting outcomes (successes or failures), as in tending to place blame or responsibility on oneself or on external factors.

**Authoritarian** A child-rearing style in which parents demand obedience from their children but are not very communicative or warm.

**Authoritative** A child-rearing style in which parents are restrictive and demanding, yet also are communicative and warm.

**Autism** A developmental disorder characterized by failure to relate to others, communication problems, intolerance of change, and ritualistic behavior.

**Autobiographical memory** The memory of specific events.

**Autonomous morality** The second stage in Piaget's cognitive-developmental theory of moral development. In this stage, children base moral judgments on the intentions of the wrongdoer as well as on the amount of damage done. Social rules are viewed as agreements that can be changed.

**Autonomy versus shame and doubt** Erikson's second stage of psychosocial development, during which the child develops (or does not develop) the capacity to exercise self-control and independence.

**Autosome** Either member of a pair of chromosomes (with the exception of sex chromosomes).

**Autostimulation theory** The view that REM sleep in infants fosters development of the brain by stimulating neural activity.

**Avoidance learning** A form of learning in which organisms learn to engage in responses that prevent aversive (painful) stimulation.

**Avoidant attachment** A type of insecure attachment characterized by apparent indifference to the leave-takings of, and reunions with, an attachment figure.

**Axillary** Of the underarm, as in axillary hair or axillary odor.

**Axon** A long, thin part of the neuron that transmits impulses to other neurons through small structures called *axon terminals.*

**Babbling** The child's first vocalizations that have the sounds of speech.

**Babinski reflex** A reflex in which infants fan their toes when the undersides of their feet are stroked.

**Baby biography** A meticulous account of the development of a baby that attends to the sequences and timing of changes.

**Bed-wetting** Failure to control the bladder during the night, resulting in urinating while in bed. See *Enuresis.*

**Behaviorism** The school of psychology founded by John B. Watson that focuses on observable behavior and investigates relationships between stimuli and responses.

**Behavior genetics** The study of the genetic transmission of structures and traits that give rise to behavior.

**Behavior modification** The systematic application of principles of learning to eliminate behavior problems or encourage desired behaviors.

**Bilingual** Using or being capable of using two languages with nearly equal or equal facility.

**Blastocyst** A stage within the germinal period of prenatal development in which the zygote has the form of a sphere of cells surrounding a cavity of fluid.

**Body image** Perception of one's physical attractiveness, and feelings about one's body.

**Bonding** The process of forming bonds of attachment between parents and children.

**Braxton-Hicks contractions** The first contractions of childbirth, which are usually painless.

**Brazelton Neonatal Behavioral Assessment Scale** A measure of a newborn's motor behavior, response to stress, adaptive behavior, and control over physiological states.

**Breech position** A problematic position for childbirth in which the fetus enters the birth canal buttocks first.

**Broca's aphasia** A form of aphasia caused by damage to Broca's area of the cerebral cortex and characterized by slow, laborious speech.

**Bulimia nervosa** An eating disorder most prevalent among women and characterized by cycles of binge eating and vomiting as a means of controlling weight gain.

**Caesarean section** A method of childbirth in which the baby is delivered through a surgical incision in the abdomen.

**Canalization** The tendency of growth rates to return to genetically determined patterns after undergoing environmentally induced changes.

**Cardinal word principle** The principle that the last number in a count indicates how many total items there are.

**Carrier** A person who carries and transmits recessive genetic characteristics but does not exhibit them.

**Case study** A carefully drawn biography of the life of an individual.

**Castration** Removal of the testes, preventing production of sperm and the hormone testosterone.

**Categorical self** Definitions of the self that refer to concrete external traits.

**Centration** In Piaget's theory, focusing on one dimension of a situation while ignoring others. See *Decentration.*

**Cephalocaudal** One of the principles of development, according to which development proceeds from the upper part (head) of the child to the lower extremities.

**Cerebellum** A structure of the hindbrain that is involved in muscle coordination and balance.

**Cerebrum** The large mass of the forebrain, which consists of two hemispheres.

**Child** A person undergoing the period of development from infancy through puberty.

**Chilly climate** Behaviors and activities both inside and outside the classroom that express different expectations for female students or that single them out or ignore them.

**Chronological age (CA)** A child's age in years and months, which was historically compared to the child's mental-age score on the Stanford–Binet Intelligence Scale to derive an IQ score.

**Chorionic villus sampling** A method for the prenatal detection of genetic abnormalities that samples the membrane enveloping the amniotic sac and fetus.

**Chromosome** A rod-like structure composed of genes that is found within the nuclei of cells.

**Class inclusion** In Piaget's theory, the principle that one category or class of things includes several subclasses.

**Classical conditioning** A simple form of learning in which a previously neutral stimulus comes to elicit the response usually brought forth by a second stimulus by being paired repeatedly with the second stimulus.

**Clear-cut attachment phase** The third phase in the development of attachment, occurring at 6 or 7 months of age and characterized by intensified dependence on the primary care giver.

**Clique** A group of 5 to 10 individuals who hang around together and who share activities and confidences. See *Crowd.*

**Clitoris** A female sex organ that is highly sensitive to sexual stimulation but not directly involved in reproduction.

**Coercive behavior** Aggressive acts such as noncompliance, talking back, temper tantrums, and hitting.

**Cognitive** Concerning mental activities and functions, such as thought, language, intelligence, dreams, and fantasies.

**Cognitive-developmental theory** A stage theory of development that holds that the child's abilities to mentally represent the world and solve problems unfold as a result of the interaction between the maturation of neurological structures and experience.

**Cohort effect** Similarities in behavior among a group of peers that stem from the fact that they are of approximately the same age. (A possible source of misleading information in *Cross-sectional research.*)

**Commitment** A stable investment in one's goals, values, or beliefs.

**Componential level** In triarchic theory, the level of intelligence that consists of metacomponents, performance components, and knowledge-acquisition components.

**Conception** The process by which a sperm cell joins with an ovum to begin a new life.

**Concordance** Agreement.

**Concrete operations** The third stage in Piaget's cognitive-developmental theory, characterized by flexible, reversible thought concerning tangible (as opposed to abstract) objects and events.

**Conditioned response (CR)** A learned response to a previously neutral (conditioned) stimulus.

**Conditioned stimulus (CS)** A previously neutral stimulus that elicits a (conditioned) response, because it has been paired repeatedly with another stimulus that already elicited that response.

**Conduct disorders** Disorders marked by persistent breaking of the rules and violations of the rights of others.

**Cones** Cone-shaped receptors of light that transmit sensations of color.

**Congenital** Present at birth. Usually used to refer to children's disorders that can be attributed to conditions in the prenatal environment.

**Conscious** Self-aware.

**Conservation** In Piaget's theory, a type of operational thought in which it is recognized that properties of substances such as weight and mass remain the same (are conserved) even though superficial characteristics such as their shapes or arrangement are changed.

**Contact comfort** The pleasure derived from physical contact with another; according to the Harlows, a need or drive for physical contact with another that provides a basis for the formation of attachment.

**Contextual level** In triarchic theory, those aspects of intelligent behavior that permit people to adjust to their environments or to seek or create new environments.

**Continuous reinforcement** Reinforcement of every correct response. See *Intermittent reinforcement.*

**Contrast (or mutual exclusivity) assumption** The assumption that objects have only one label.

**Control subjects** Participants in an experiment who do not receive the experimental treatment but for whom all other conditions are comparable to those of experimental subjects. See *Experimental subjects.*

**Conventional level** According to Kohlberg, a period during which moral judgments largely reflect social rules and conventions.

**Convergence** The inward movement of the eyes as they focus on an object that is drawing nearer.

**Convergent thinking** A thought process that attempts to narrow in on the single best solution to a problem. See *Divergent thinking.*

**Cooing** Prelinguistic, articulated vowel-like sounds.

**Cooperative play** Organized play in which children cooperate to meet common goals. There is division of labor, and children take on specific roles as group members.

**Coregulation** A gradual transferring of control from parent to child that begins in middle childhood.

**Corpus callosum** The thick bundle of nerve fibers that connects the left and right hemispheres of the brain.

**Correlated** Associated; linked.

**Correlation coefficient** A number ranging from +1.00 to −1.00 that expresses the direction (positive or negative) and strength of the relationship between two variables.

**Correlational method** A method in which researchers determine whether one behavior or trait being studied is related to, or correlated with, another.

**Creativity** The ability to generate novel solutions to problems. A trait characterized by flexibility, ingenuity, and originality.

**Critical period** A period of time during which a developing organism is particularly sensitive to certain sources of stimulation; in ethological theory, a period of development during which a releasing stimulus can elicit a fixed-action pattern. See *Sensitive period.*

**Critical thinking** A type of thinking that helps students sort out evidence from opinion and truth from fiction.

**Cross-cultural study** A comparison of two or more cultures.

**Cross-modal transfer** The ability to recognize that an object experienced in one sensory modality is the same as an identical object experienced in a different modality.

**Cross-sectional research** A method of studying developmental processes in which measures are taken of children of different age groups at the same point in time. See *Longitudinal research.*

**Cross-sequential research** A method of studying development that combines the longitudinal and cross-sectional methods by following individuals of different ages for abbreviated periods of time.

**Crowd** A large, loosely organized group of people who may or may not spend much time together and who are identified by the activities of the group. See *Clique.*

**Crystallization** A stage of vocational development in which career goals become more firmly established.

**Cultural bias** A factor hypothesized to be present in intelligence tests that provides an advantage for test-takers from certain cultural or ethnic backgrounds but that does not reflect true intelligence.

**Cultural–familial retardation** Substandard intellectual performance that is presumed to stem from lack of opportunity to acquire knowledge and strategies for solving problems considered important within a cultural setting.

**Culture-free** Descriptive of a test in which cultural biases have been removed. On such a test, test-takers from different cultural backgrounds would have an equal opportunity to earn scores that reflect their true abilities.

**Cystic fibrosis** A fatal genetic disorder in which mucus obstructs the lungs and pancreas.

**Dendrite** A rootlike part of a neuron that receives impulses from other neurons.

**Deoxyribonucleic acid (DNA)** Genetic material found in the nuclei of cells that takes the form of a double helix composed of phosphates, sugars, and bases.

**Dependent variable** A measure of an assumed effect of an independent variable. See *Independent variable.*

**DES** See *Diethylstilbestrol.*

**Design stage** A stage in the development of children's drawings, immediately following the shape stage, in which children begin to combine shapes.

**Determinants** Factors that define or set limits, such as the determinants of intelligence.

**Development** The processes by which organisms unfold features and traits, grow, and become more complex and specialized in structure and function.

**Dialect** The variety of a spoken language particular to a region, community, or social group. Dialects of a language tend to be understandable to persons who speak another dialect of the language without special training, whereas other languages are not.

**Diethylstilbestrol (DES)** A powerful estrogen that was prescribed for women threatening miscarriage but which has been linked to cancer in the reproductive organs of their children.

**Differentiation** The processes by which behavior patterns and physical structures become more specialized as they develop.

**Dilate** To make wider or larger.

**Discrete** Separate and distinct; made up of distinct parts.

**Disinhibition** In social-learning theory, stimulation of a response that has been suppressed by showing a model engaging in that response without aversive consequences.

**Disorganized–disoriented attachment** A type of insecure attachment characterized by dazed and contradictory behaviors toward an attachment figure.

**Displacement** In psychoanalytic theory, a defense mechanism in which ideas or impulses are transferred from threatening or unsuitable objects onto less threatening objects.

**Divergent thinking** A thought process that attempts to generate multiple solutions to problems. Free and fluent associations to the elements of a problem. See *Convergent thinking.*

**Dizygotic (DZ) twins** Twins who develop from two different zygotes and who are thus no more closely related than other siblings. Fraternal twins. See *Monozygotic twins.*

**Dominant trait** A trait that is expressed. See *Recessive trait.*

**Donor IVF** The transfer of a donor's ovum, fertilized in a laboratory dish, to the uterus of another woman.

**Down syndrome** A chromosomal abnormality characterized by mental retardation and caused by an extra chromosome in the 21st pair.

**Dramatic play** Play in which children enact social roles, which is made possible by the attainment of symbolic thought. A form of *Pretend play.*

**Dyslexia** A reading disorder characterized by problems such as letter reversals, mirror reading, slow reading, and reduced comprehension.

**Debriefing** Receiving information about a just-completed research procedure in an effort to mitigate possible harmful effects of that procedure.

**Decentration** In Piaget's theory, simultaneous focusing (centering) on more than one aspect or dimension of a problem or situation, such that flexible, reversible thought is possible. See *Centration.*

**Deep structure** The underlying meaning of a sentence. See *Surface structure.*

**Defense mechanism** In psychoanalytic theory, an unconscious function of the ego that protects it from anxiety-evoking ideas by distorting them or ejecting them from consciousness.

**Deferred imitation** The imitation of people and events that occurred hours, days, or weeks ago.

**Demand characteristics** The demands made on a research participant by a specific experimental approach or task. The implication is that the theoretical inferences drawn from the study might have been different if tasks with different demand characteristics had been used.

**Early childhood** The period of development from ages 2 to 5; the preschool years.

**Echolalia** The automatic repetition of sounds or words.

**Ecological theory** Urie Bronfenbrenner's approach to understanding child development, which focuses on the reciprocal influences among children and the settings that comprise their environment.

**Ecology** The branch of biology that deals with the relationships between living organisms and their environment.

**Ectoderm** The outermost cell layer of the newly formed embryo from which the skin and nervous system develop.

**Efface** Rub out or wipe out; become thin.

**Ego** According to psychoanalytic theory, the psychic structure that develops following the id. The ego is characterized by self-awareness, planning, and the delay of gratification.

**Egocentrism** Inability to perceive the world from another person's point of view. Characteristic of preoperational thought.

**Ego identity** According to Erikson, one's sense of who one is and what one stands for.

**Elaborative strategy** A strategy for increasing retention of new information by relating it to well-known information.

**Electra complex** A conflict of the phallic stage of psychosexual development in which the girl longs for her father and resents her mother.

**Electroencephalograph (EEG)** An instrument that measures electrical activity of the brain.

**Elicit** Bring forth; evoke.

**Embryonic disk** The platelike inner part of the blastocyst that differentiates into the ectoderm, mesoderm, and endoderm of the embryo.

**Embryonic stage** The stage of prenatal development that lasts from implantation through the eighth week and is characterized by the differentiation of the major organ systems.

**Embryonic transplant** The transfer of an embryo from the uterus of one woman to the uterus of another.

**Emotion** A state of feeling that has physiological, situational, and cognitive components.

**Emotional regulation** Techniques for controlling one's emotional states.

**Empathy** The ability to share another person's feelings or emotions.

**Empirical** Based on observation and experimentation.

**Empiricism** The view that experience determines the ways in which children perceive the world. Contrast with *Nativism.*

**Encoding** The transformation of sensory input into a form that is more readily processed.

**Encopresis** Failure to control the bowels once the normal age for bowel control has been reached. Also called *soiling.*

**Endoderm** The inner layer of the embryo from which the lungs and digestive system develop.

**Endometriosis** A condition caused by inflammation of endometrial tissue that is sloughed off into the abdominal cavity rather than out of the body during menstruation and characterized by abdominal pain and, sometimes, infertility.

**Endometrium** The inner lining of the uterus, which is normally sloughed off during menstruation.

**Enuresis** Failure to control the bladder (urination) once the normal age for control has been reached.

**Epiphyseal closure** The process by which the cartilage that separates the long end (epiphysis) of a bone from the main part of the bone turns to bone, thus preventing further gains in length.

**Episiotomy** A surgical incision in the perineum that widens the vaginal opening, preventing random tearing during childbirth.

**Equilibration** In Piaget's theory, the creation of an equilibrium, or balance, between assimilation and accommodation, thereby facilitating acquisition of knowledge.

**Erogenous zone** An area of the body that is sensitive to sexual sensations.

**Eros** In psychoanalytic theory, the basic instinct to preserve and perpetuate life.

**Ethnic groups** Groups of people distinguished by culture, heritage, race, language, and common history.

**Ethnic identity** A sense of belonging to an ethnic group.

**Ethnic identity search** The second stage of ethnic identity development; similar to the moratorium identity status.

**Ethologist** A scientist who studies the behavior patterns characteristic of various species.

**Exosystem** In ecological theory, community institutions and settings that indirectly influence the child, such as the school board and the parents' workplaces.

**Experiential level** In triarchic theory, those aspects of intelligence that permit people to cope with novel situations and process information automatically.

**Experiment** A method of scientific investigation that seeks to discover cause-and-effect relationships by introducing independent variables and observing their effects on dependent variables.

**Experimental subjects** Participants receiving a treatment in an experiment. See *Control subjects.*

**Exploration** In Erikson's theory, active questioning and searching among alternatives in the quest to establish goals, values, or beliefs.

**Expressive language style** The child's use of language primarily as a means for engaging in social interaction. See *Referential language style.*

**Expressive vocabulary** The sum total of the words that one can use in the production of language. See *Receptive vocabulary.*

**Extinction** A decrease and eventual disappearance of a response in the absence of reinforcement.

**Extrinsic** External.

**Factor** A condition or quality that brings about a result. A cluster of related items, such as those found on an intelligence or personality test.

**Failure to thrive (FTT)** A disorder of impaired growth in infancy and early childhood.

**Fallopian tube** A tube in the woman's abdomen through which ova travel from an ovary to the uterus.

**False beliefs** Separating one's beliefs from those of another person who has false knowledge of a situation.

**Family therapy** A form of therapy in which the family unit is treated and members are taught to relate to one another more productively.

**Fast mapping** A process of quickly determining a word's meaning, which facilitates children's vocabulary development.

**Feedback loop** A system in which the hypothalamus, pituitary gland, and gonads regulate each other's functioning through a series of hormonal messages.

**Fetal alcohol effect (FAE)** A cluster of symptoms less severe than those of FAS shown by children of women who drink during pregnancy. See *Fetal alcohol syndrome.*

**Fetal alcohol syndrome (FAS)** A cluster of symptoms, including mental retardation and characteristic facial features, found among the babies of women who drink heavily during pregnancy. See *Fetal alcohol effect.*

**Fetal monitoring** The use of instruments to track the heart rate and oxygen levels of the fetus during childbirth.

**Fetal stage** The stage of development that lasts from the beginning of the ninth week of pregnancy through birth and is characterized by gains in size and weight and the maturation of the organ systems.

**Fetoscopy** Surgical insertion of a narrow tube into the uterus in order to examine the fetus.

**Fine motor skills** Skills employing the small muscles used in manipulation, such as those in the fingers.

**Fixation** In psychoanalytic theory, arrested psychosexual development. Attachment to objects characteristic of an earlier stage.

**Fixed action pattern (FAP)** An instinct. A stereotyped form of behavior that is characteristic of a species and triggered by a releasing stimulus.

**Forceps** A curved instrument that fits around the head of a baby and permits it to be pulled through the birth canal as a way of facilitating childbirth.

**Foreclosure** In Marcia's theory, an identity status that characterizes those who have made commitments without considering alternatives.

**Formal handling** A series of activities used by parents in Africa and in cultures of African origin to stimulate sitting and walking in their infants.

**Formal operations** The fourth stage in Piaget's cognitive-developmental theory, characterized by the capacity for flexible, reversible operations concerning abstract ideas and concepts, such as symbols, statements, and theories.

**Gender** The state of being female or male.

**Gender constancy** The concept that one's gender remains the same despite superficial changes in appearance or behavior. The third stage in the cognitive-developmental theory of gender-role development.

**Gender identity** Knowledge that one is a female or a male. The first stage in the cognitive-developmental theory of gender-role development.

**Gender roles** Complex clusters of behaviors that are considered stereotypical of females and males.

**Gender-schema theory** A cognitive theory of gender-typing that holds that one's knowledge of the gender schema in one's society (the behavior patterns that are considered appropriate for men and women) guides one's assumptions of gender-typed preferences and behavior patterns.

**Gender stability** The concept that one's gender is a permanent feature. The second stage in the cognitive-developmental theory of gender-role development.

**Gene** The basic unit of heredity. Genes are composed of deoxyribonucleic acid (DNA). See *Chromosome.*

**General anesthesia** The process of eliminating pain by putting people to sleep, such as during childbirth. See *Local anesthesia.*

**Generativity versus stagnation** Erikson's seventh stage of psychosocial development; the middle years during which persons find (or fail to find) fulfillment in expressing creativity and in guiding and encouraging the younger generation.

**Genetic counseling** Advice concerning the probabilities that a couple's children will show genetic abnormalities.

**Genetics** The branch of biology that studies heredity.

**Genital stage** In psychoanalytic theory, the fifth and final stage of psychosexual development in which gratification is attained through sexual intercourse with an individual of the other gender.

**Genotype** The genetic form or constitution of a person as determined by heredity. See *Phenotype.*

**Germ cells** Ova and sperm. The cells from which new organisms are developed.

**Germinal stage** The period of development between conception and implantation of the embryo in the uterine wall. Also called *period of the ovum.*

**Gestation period** The period of carrying young from conception until birth.

**Goodness of fit** Consonance between the parents' expectations of or demands on the child and the child's temperamental characteristics.

**Grasping reflex** A reflex in which infants grasp objects that are pressed against the palms.

**Gross motor skills** Skills employing the large muscles used in locomotion.

**Growth** The processes by which organisms increase in size, weight, strength, and other traits as they develop.

**Growth spurt** A period during which growth advances at a dramatically rapid rate as compared with other periods.

**Gynecomastia** Temporary enlargement of the breasts in adolescent males.

**Habituation** Paying less attention to a repeated stimulus.

**Handedness** The tendency to prefer using the left or right hand in writing and other activities.

**Hallucinogens** Drugs that give rise to hallucinations.

**Hemophilia** A genetic disorder in which the blood does not clot properly.

**Heredity** The transmission of traits and characteristics from parent to child by means of genes.

**Heterozygous** Having two different alleles for a trait, as in showing brown eyes although one also has recessive blue alleles in the nuclei of one's cells. See *Homozygous.*

**Holophrase** A single word used by a child to express complex meanings.

**Homosexuality** An erotic orientation to members of one's own gender.

**Homozygous** Having two identical alleles for a trait, as in showing brown eyes and *not* having recessive blue alleles in the nuclei of one's cells. See *Heterozygous.*

**Horizontal décalage** The sequential unfolding of the ability to master different kinds of cognitive tasks within the same stage. For example, children master different kinds of conservation tasks in an orderly sequence, rather than simultaneously.

**Hue** Color.

**Huntington's disease** A fatal genetic neurological disorder whose onset is in middle age.

**Hyperactivity** Excessive restlessness and overactivity. Not to be confused with misbehavior or with normal high activity levels that occur during childhood. One of the primary characteristics of attention-deficit hyperactivity disorder (ADHD).

**Hypothalamus** A pea-sized structure that is located above the pituitary gland in the brain and is involved in the regulation of body temperature, motivation (for example, hunger, thirst, sex), and emotion.

**Hypothesis** An assumption about behavior that is tested by empirical research.

**Id** In psychoanalytic theory, the psychic structure that is present at birth. The id represents physiological drives and is fully unconscious.

**Identification** A process in which one person becomes like another through broad imitation and incorporation of the other person's personality traits. In psychoanalytic theory, identification is viewed as largely unconscious. In social-learning theory, the focus is on the role of observational learning.

**Identity achievement** In Marcia's theory, an identity status that characterizes those who have explored alternatives and have developed commitments.

**Identity crisis** According to Erikson, a turning point in development during which one examines one's values and makes decisions about life roles.

**Identity diffusion** In Marcia's and Erikson's theories, an identity status that characterizes those who have no commitments and who are not in the process of exploring alternatives.

**Identity versus identity diffusion** Erikson's fifth stage of psychosocial development; the adolescent years during which individuals are challenged to develop a sense of who they are and what they stand for. Failure to do so results in *identity diffusion.*

**Illicit** Illegal.

**Imaginary audience** The belief that others around us are as concerned with our thoughts and behaviors as we are; one aspect of adolescent egocentrism.

**Immanent justice** The view that retribution for wrongdoing is a direct consequence of the wrongdoing, reflective of the belief that morality is embedded within the structure of the universe.

**Imprinting** The process by which some animals exhibit the fixed-action pattern (FAP) of attachment in response to a releasing stimulus. The FAP occurs during a critical period and is difficult to modify.

**In vitro fertilization** Fertilization of an ovum in a laboratory dish.

**Incest taboo** The cultural prohibition against marrying or having sexual relations with a close blood relative.

**Incubator** A heated, protective container for premature babies.

**Independent variable** In a scientific study, a condition that is manipulated (changed) so that its effect may be observed. See *Dependent variable.*

**Indiscriminate attachment** The display of attachment behaviors toward any person.

**Inductive disciplinary method** A method for restricting behavior, such as reasoning, that attempts to foster understanding of the principles underlying parental demands.

**Industry versus inferiority** The fourth stage of psychosocial development in Erikson's theory, occurring in middle childhood. Mastery of tasks leads to a sense of industry, while failure produces feelings of inferiority.

**Infancy** Babyhood. The period of very early childhood, characterized by lack of complex speech; the first 2 years after birth.

**Information-processing theory** The view in which cognitive processes are compared to the functions of computers. The theory deals with the input, storage, retrieval, manipulation, and output of information. The focus is on the development of children's strategies for solving problems—their "mental programs."

**Initial-preattachment phase** The first phase in the formation of bonds of attachment, lasting from birth to about 3 months of age and characterized by indiscriminate attachment.

**Initiative versus guilt** Erikson's third stage of psychosocial development, during which the child tests new skills and initiates new activities. If the child's initiatives are punished, feelings of guilt may develop.

**Inner speech** Lev Vygotsky's concept of the ultimate binding of language and thought. Inner speech originates in vocalizations that may regulate the child's behavior and become internalized by age 6 or 7.

**INSOMNIA** One or more of a number of sleep problems—difficulty falling asleep, difficulty remaining asleep, and waking early.

**INTEGRITY VERSUS DESPAIR** Erikson's eighth stage of psychosocial development; the later years during which adults look back on their lives and experience either a sense of satisfaction (integrity) or regret (despair).

**INTELLIGENCE** A complex and controversial concept defined by David Wechsler as the "capacity . . . to understand the world [and the] resourcefulness to cope with its challenges." Intelligence implies learning ability and the capacity to make the right choice in a given academic or social situation.

**INTELLIGENCE QUOTIENT (IQ)** (1) Originally, a ratio obtained by dividing a child's score (or "mental age") on an intelligence test by his or her chronological age. (2) Generally, a score on an intelligence test.

**INTENSITY** The strength of a stimulus, as in the brightness of a light.

**INTERMITTENT REINFORCEMENT** Reinforcement of some, but not all, correct responses. Contrast with *Continuous reinforcement.*

**INTERVIEW** A method for gathering information in which the subject responds verbally to the researcher's questions.

**INTIMACY VERSUS ISOLATION** Erikson's sixth stage of psychosocial development; the young adult years during which persons commit themselves to intimate relationships with others or else develop feelings of isolation.

**INTONATION** In language, the use of pitches of varying levels to help communicate meaning.

**INTRINSIC** Internal.

**IQ** See *Intelligence quotient.*

**IRREVERSIBILITY** Failure to realize that actions can be reversed.

**JUVENILE DELINQUENCY** Illegal activities committed by a child or adolescent.

**KIBBUTZ** An Israeli farming community in which children are reared in group settings.

**KLINEFELTER'S SYNDROME** A chromosomal disorder found among males that is caused by an extra X sex chromosome and characterized by infertility and mild mental retardation.

**LABIA** The major and minor lips of the female's genitalia.

**LAMAZE METHOD** A childbirth method in which women are educated about childbirth, learn to relax and breath in patterns that conserve energy and lessen pain, and have a coach (usually the father) present during childbirth. Also termed *prepared childbirth.*

**LANGUAGE ACQUISITION DEVICE (LAD)** In the psycholinguistic theory of language development, neural "prewiring" that facilitates the child's learning of grammar.

**LANUGO** Fine, downy hair that covers much of the body of the newborn, especially preterm babies.

**LARYNX** The part of the throat that contains the vocal cords.

**LATENCY STAGE** In psychoanalytic theory, the fourth stage of psychosexual development, characterized by repression of sexual impulses and development of skills.

**LATENT** Hidden.

**LEARNED HELPLESSNESS** The belief that one is unable to control one's environment.

**LEARNING DISABILITIES** A group of disorders characterized by inadequate development of specific academic, language, and speech skills.

**LEBOYER METHOD** A childbirth method that focuses on gently easing the neonate into the world. Also termed *gentle childbirth.*

**LIBIDO** In psychoanalytic theory, the energy of eros; the sexual instinct.

**LICIT** Legal.

**LIFE CRISIS** According to Erik Erikson, an internal conflict that characterizes each stage of psychosocial development. Positive resolution of life crises sets the stage for positive resolution of subsequent life crises.

**LOCAL ANESTHESIA** The process of reducing pain in a specific area of the body, as during childbirth. See *General anesthesia.*

**LOCOMOTION** Movement from one place to another.

**LONGITUDINAL RESEARCH** A method of investigating developmental processes in which repeated measures are taken of the same group of children at various times throughout their development. See *Cross-sectional research.*

**LONG-TERM MEMORY** The memory structure capable of relatively permanent storage of information.

**MACROSYSTEM** In ecological theory, the basic institutions and ideologies that influence the child, such as the American ideals of freedom of expression and equality under the law.

**MAINSTREAMING** The practice of placing disabled children in classrooms with nondisabled children.

**MAMMARY GLANDS** Glands that secrete milk.

**MASTURBATION** Sexual self-stimulation.

**MATERNITY BLUES** A condition characterized by crying, feelings of sadness, anxiety and tension, irritability, and anger that half or more of women experience within a few days after childbirth.

**MATURATION** The unfolding of genetically determined traits, structures, and functions.

**MATURATIONAL THEORY** Arnold Gesell's view that holds that development is self-regulated by the unfolding of natural plans (that is, heredity) and processes.

**MEAN LENGTH OF UTTERANCE** The average number of morphemes used in an utterance. A rough measure of the sophistication of the child's use of language.

**MEDULLA** An oblong-shaped structure of the hindbrain that is involved in heartbeat and respiration.

**MEIOSIS** The type of cell division in which germ cells are formed. Each pair of chromosomes in the parent cell splits, so that one member of each pair moves to a new cell. As a result, each new cell has 23 chromosomes.

**MEMORY** The processes by which we store and retrieve information.

**MENARCHE** The onset of menstruation.

**MENOPAUSE** The cessation of menstruation, typically occurring between ages 48 and 52.

**MENTAL AGE (MA)** The accumulated months of credit that a child earns on the Stanford–Binet Intelligence Scale.

**MENTAL REPRESENTATIONS** The different mental forms that a real object or event can take.

**MENTAL ROTATION** A type of visual-spatial ability characterized by the ability to imagine how objects will look if rotated in space.

**MESODERM** The central layer of the embryo from which the bones and muscles develop.

**MESOSYSTEM** In ecological theory, the interlocking settings that influence the child, such as the interaction of the school and the larger community when children are taken on field trips.

**METACOGNITION** Awareness of and control of one's cognitive abilities, as shown by the intentional use of cognitive strategies in solving problems.

**METAMEMORY** Knowledge of the functions and processes involved in one's storage and retrieval of information (memory), as shown by intentional use of cognitive strategies to retain information.

**METAPELET** A child-rearing professional in a kibbutz.

**METAPHOR** A figure of speech that amplifies meaning and dramatizes description by adopting imagery from another situation.

**MICROSYSTEM** In ecological theory, the immediate settings with which the child interacts, such as the home, the school, and his or her peers.

**MIDDLE CHILDHOOD** The period of development from ages 6 to 12; the elementary school years.

**MIDWIFE** An individual (nonphysician) who is trained to help women in childbirth.

**MITOSIS** The form of cell division in which each chromosome splits lengthwise to double in number. Half of each chromosome combines with chemicals to retake its original form and then each moves to the new cell.

**MODEL** In social-learning theory, a person who engages in behavior that is imitated by another.

**MONOZYGOTIC (MZ) TWINS** Twins that derive from a single zygote that has divided into two separate zygotes and that thus carry the same genetic code. Identical twins. See *Dizygotic twins.*

**Moral realism** According to Piaget, the stage during which children judge acts as moral when they conform to authority or to the rules of the game. Morality at this stage is perceived as embedded in the structure of the universe.

**Moratorium** According to Marcia, an identity status that characterizes those who are actively exploring alternatives in an attempt to form an identity.

**Moro reflex** A reflex in which infants arch their backs and fling out their arms and legs and draw them back toward the chest in response to a sudden change in position.

**Morpheme** The smallest unit of meaning in a language.

**Motility** Self-propulsion. A measure of the viability of sperm cells.

**Motor development** The development of the capacity for movement, particularly as made possible by maturation of the nervous system and the muscles.

**Multifactorial problems** Problems that stem from the interaction of heredity and environmental factors.

**Multiple sclerosis** A disease in which myelin is replaced by hard, fibrous tissue that impedes the transmission of neural impulses.

**Muscular dystrophy** A chronic disease characterized by a progressive wasting away of the muscles.

**Mutation** A sudden variation in an inheritable characteristic, as by an accident that affects the composition of genes.

**Mutism** The inability or refusal to speak.

**Myelin sheath** A fatty, whitish substance that encases and insulates the axons of neurons, permitting more rapid transmission of neural impulses.

**Myelination** The process by which axons of neurons are coated with myelin.

**Nativism** The view that children have inborn predispositions to perceive the world in certain ways. See *Empiricism.*

**Natural childbirth** A method of childbirth in which women use no anesthesia and are educated about childbirth and strategies for coping with discomfort.

**Natural experiment** Comparison of naturally occurring groups that differ along some dimension of interest, such as children who were exposed prenatally to drugs versus those who were not.

**Naturalistic observation** A method of scientific observation in which children (and others) are observed in their natural environments.

**Nature** The processes within an organism that guide the organism to develop structures and traits according to its genetic code.

**Negative correlation** A relationship between two variables in which one variable increases as the other variable decreases.

**Negative reinforcer** A reinforcer that, when removed, increases the frequency of a response. See *Positive reinforcer.*

**Neonate** A newborn child.

**Nerve** A bundle of axons from many neurons.

**Neural** Of the nervous system.

**Neural tube** A hollowed-out area in the blastocyst from which the nervous system develops.

**Neuron** A nerve cell.

**Neuroticism** A personality trait characterized by anxiety and emotional instability.

**Neurotransmitter** A chemical substance that transmits neural impulses from one neuron to another.

**Nightmares** Frightening dreams that occur during REM sleep, often in the morning hours.

**Night terrors** Frightening, dreamlike experiences that occur during the deepest stage of NREM sleep, shortly after the child has gone to sleep.

**Nocturnal emission** Emission of seminal fluid while asleep.

**Non-rapid-eye-movemement (NREM) sleep** Periods of sleep during which we are unlikely to dream. See *Rapid-eye-movement sleep.*

**Nonsocial play** Forms of play (such as solitary play and onlooker play) in which play is not influenced by the play of nearby children.

**Norepinephrine** A neurotransmitter that is implicated in depression. Also called *noradrenalin.*

**Nurture** The processes external to an organism that provide nourishment as it develops according to its genetic code or cause it to swerve from its genetically programmed course. Environmental factors that influence development. See *Nature.*

**Obesity** A disorder characterized by excessive accumulation of fat.

**Objective morality** The perception of morality as objective, or as existing outside the cognitive functioning of people; a characteristic of Piaget's stage of moral realism.

**Object permanence** Recognition that objects continue to exist even when they are not seen.

**Observational learning** In social-learning theory, the acquisition of expectations and skills by means of observing others. In observational learning, skills can be acquired without their being emitted and reinforced.

**Occupational gender-typing** Judgments that certain occupations are more appropriate for one gender than the other.

**Oedipus complex** In psychoanalytic theory, a conflict of the phallic stage of psychosexual development in which the boy wishes to possess his mother sexually and perceives his father as a rival.

**Onlooker play** Play during which children observe other children at play but do not enter into their play themselves.

**Operant conditioning** A simple form of learning in which an organism learns to engage in behavior that is reinforced. See *Classical conditioning.*

**Operations** In Piaget's theory, flexible, reversible mental manipulations of objects such that objects can be mentally transformed and then returned to their original states.

**Oral rehydration therapy** A treatment involving administration of a salt and sugar solution to a child who is dehydrated from diarrhea.

**Oral stage** In psychoanalytic theory, the first stage of psychosexual development, during which gratification is attained primarily through oral activities, such as sucking and biting.

**Osteoporosis** A condition involving progressive loss of bone tissue.

**Ovary** A female reproductive organ located in the abdomen that produces female reproductive cells, or ova.

**Overextension** A normal aspect of language development in which words are used in situations in which their meanings become extended, or inappropriate, as in an infant's extension of the label "doggy" to several types of four-legged animals.

**Overregularization** A normal aspect of language development in which the child applies regular grammatical rules for forming inflections (for example, past tense and plurals) to irregular verbs and nouns.

**Ovulation** The releasing of an ovum from an ovary.

**Ovum** A female reproductive cell. Plural: ova.

**Oxytocin** A pituitary hormone that stimulates labor contractions.

**Pacifier** An artifical nipple or a teething ring that is used to soothe babies.

**Parallel play** Play in which children use toys similar to those of nearby children but approach their toys in their own ways. No effort is made to interact with others.

**Participant modeling** A process in which one loses fear of anxiety-evoking objects by first observing models interact with them and then imitating the models.

**Passive** As a developmental concept, influenced or acted upon by environmental stimuli as opposed to acting upon the environment. See *Active.*

**Peak growth** A period of growth during which the growth rate is at its maximum.

**Peer** A child of the same age. More generally, a person of similar background and social standing.

**Pelvic inflammatory disease (PID)** Any of a number of diseases that infect the abdominal region, impairing fertility.

**Penis envy** In psychoanalytic theory, jealousy of the male sex organ attributed to girls in the phallic stage.

**Perceptual constancy** The tendency to perceive objects as the same although sensations produced by them differ when, for example, they shift in position or distance. See *Shape constancy* and *Size constancy.*

**PERINEUM** The area between the female's genital region and the anus.

**PERMISSIVE–INDULGENT** A child-rearing style in which parents are not controlling and restrictive and are warm.

**PERSONAL FABLE** The belief that our feelings and ideas are special and unique and that we are invulnerable; one aspect of adolescent egocentrism.

**PERSONALITY** Each individual's distinctive ways of responding to people and events.

**PHALLIC STAGE** In psychoanalytic theory, the third stage of psychosexual development, characterized by a shift of libido to the phallic region.

**PHENOTYPE** The actual form or constitution of a person as determined by the interaction of genetic and environmental factors.

**PHENYLKETONURIA (PKU)** A genetic abnormality in which a child cannot metabolize phenylalanine, which consequently builds up in the body and causes mental retardation. If treated with a special diet, retardation is prevented.

**PHONETIC METHOD** A method for learning to read in which children decode the sounds of words based on their knowledge of the sounds of letters and letter combinations.

**PICTORIAL STAGE** A stage in drawing attained between ages 4 and 5 in which designs begin to resemble recognizable objects.

**PINCER GRASP** The use of the opposing thumb to grasp objects.

**PITCH** The highness or lowness of a sound, as determined by the frequency of sound waves.

**PITUITARY GLAND** The body's "master gland," which is located in the lower central part of the brain and secretes many hormones essential to development, such as oxytocin, prolactin, and growth hormone.

**PKU** See *Phenylketonuria.*

**PLACEMENT STAGE** An early stage in drawing in which 2-year-olds place their scribbles in various locations on the page (such as in the middle or near a border).

**PLACENTA** An organ connected to the uterine wall and the fetus by the umbilical cord. The placenta serves as a relay station between mother and fetus for exchange of nutrients and wastes.

**PLASTICITY OF THE BRAIN** The tendency of new parts of the brain to take up the functions of injured parts of the brain.

**POLYGENIC** Descriptive of traits that result from many genes.

**POSITIVE CORRELATION** A relationship between variables in which one variable increases as the other variable also increases.

**POSITIVE REINFORCER** A reinforcer that, when applied, increases the frequency of a response. See *Negative reinforcer.*

**POSTCONVENTIONAL LEVEL** According to Kohlberg, a period during which moral judgments are derived from moral principles and people look to themselves to set moral standards.

**POSTPARTUM DEPRESSION** Severe, prolonged depression that afflicts 10 percent of women after childbirth and is characterized by sadness, apathy, feelings of worthlessness, difficulty concentrating, and physical symptoms. More severe than *Maternity blues.*

**POSTPARTUM PERIOD** The period that immediately follows childbirth.

**POST-TRAUMATIC STRESS DISORDER** A disorder that follows a psychologically distressing event that is outside the range of normal human experience. It is characterized by symptoms such as intense fear, avoidance of stimuli associated with the event, and reliving of the event.

**PRAGMATICS** The practical aspects of communication, such as adaptation of language to fit the social context.

**PRECAUSAL THINKING** In cognitive-developmental theory, a type of thought in which natural cause-and-effect relationships are attributed to will and other preoperational concepts.

**PRECONSCIOUS** In psychoanalytic theory, descriptive of ideas and feelings of which one is not currently aware but that can be brought into awareness by focusing one's attention. See *Unconscious.*

**PRECONVENTIONAL LEVEL** According to Kohlberg, a period during which moral judgments are based largely on expectations of rewards or punishments.

**PRELINGUISTIC VOCALIZATIONS** Vocalizations such as crying, cooing, and babbling that occur prior to the development of language.

**PREMATURE** Born before the full term of gestation. See *Preterm.*

**PRENATAL PERIOD** The period of development from conception to birth. See *Germinal stage, Embryonic stage,* and *Fetal stage.*

**PREOPERATIONAL STAGE** The second stage in Piaget's cognitive-developmental theory, characterized by inflexible and irreversible mental manipulation of symbols.

**PRETEND PLAY** See *Symbolic play.*

**PRETERM** Born prior to completion of 37 weeks of gestation. See *Premature.*

**PRIMARY CIRCULAR REACTIONS** In Piaget's theory, a substage in the sensorimotor period, during which infants repeat actions that first occurred by chance and that focus on the infant's own body.

**PRIMARY REINFORCER** An unlearned reinforcer, such as food, warmth, or pain. See *Secondary reinforcer.*

**PRIMARY SEX CHARACTERISTICS** The structures that make reproduction possible.

**PRIMATES** An order of mammals that includes humans, apes, and monkeys.

**PROGESTIN** A hormone that is used to maintain pregnancy but that can cause masculinization of the fetus.

**PROGRAMMED LEARNING** A learning method in which complex tasks are broken down into simple steps. The proper performance of each step is reinforced, while incorrect responses are not reinforced.

**PROSOCIAL BEHAVIOR** Behavior intended to benefit another without expectation of reward.

**PROSTAGLANDINS** Hormones that stimulate uterine contractions.

**PROXIMODISTAL DEVELOPMENT** One of the principles of development, according to which development proceeds from the inner part (or axis) of the body outward.

**PSYCHIC STRUCTURE** In psychoanalytic theory, a hypothesized mental structure, such as the ego, that helps explain different aspects of behavior.

**PSYCHOANALYTIC THEORY** The school of psychology, founded by Sigmund Freud, that emphasizes the importance of unconscious, primitive motives and conflicts as determinants of behavior and personality development.

**PSYCHODYNAMIC** Descriptive of Freud's view that various forces move through the personality and determine behavior.

**PSYCHOLINGUISTIC THEORY** The view that language acquisition involves an interaction between environmental influences and an inborn tendency to learn language. The emphasis is on the inborn tendency.

**PSYCHOLOGICAL ANDROGYNY** Possession of both stereotypical feminine and masculine traits.

**PSYCHOLOGICAL MORATORIUM** In Erikson's theory, a time-out period when adolescents experiment with different roles, values, beliefs, and relationships.

**PSYCHOLOGICAL TRAIT** An aspect of personality that is inferred from behavior and is assumed to account for behavioral consistency.

**PSYCHOSEXUAL DEVELOPMENT** In psychoanalytic theory, the process by which libidinal energy is expressed through different erogenous zones during five stages of development.

**PSYCHOSOCIAL DEVELOPMENT** Erikson's eight-stage theory of development, which, in contrast to Freud's theory of development, focuses on social relationships and the conscious assumption of various life roles.

**PUBERTY** The biological stage of development characterized by changes that lead to reproductive capacity. Puberty signals the beginning of adolescence.

**PUNISHMENT** An aversive or unpleasant stimulus that suppresses the behavior it follows. Contrast with *Negative reinforcement.*

**PUPILLARY REFLEX** The reflexive tendency of the pupils of the eyes to narrow or widen in response to the intensity of light.

**PYGMALION EFFECT** The process by which one's expectations about the abilities of another person influence the performance of that person.

**QUALITATIVE CHANGES** Changes in type or kind.

**QUANTITATIVE CHANGES** Changes in amount.

**QUESTIONNAIRE** A method for gathering information in which the subject responds in writing to a set of written questions.

**RAPID-EYE-MOVEMENT (REM) SLEEP** A period of sleep during which the eyes move back and forth rapidly beneath closed lids, suggestive of dreaming.

**Rationalization** In psychoanalytic theory, a defense mechanism in which the individual finds self-deceptive justifications for unacceptable ideas or behaviors.

**Reaction range** The variability in the expression of inherited traits as they are influenced by environmental factors.

**Reaction time** The amount of time required to respond to a stimulus.

**Recall** A memory task in which the individual must reproduce material from memory without any cues.

**Receptive vocabulary** The extent of one's knowledge of the meanings of words that are communicated to one by others. See *Expressive vocabulary.*

**Recessive trait** A trait (such as blue eyes) that is not expressed when the gene or genes involved have been paired with dominant genes (such as those determining brown eye color). Recessive traits are transmitted to future generations and expressed if they are paired with other recessive genes. See *Dominant trait.*

**Reciprocal** Done, felt, or given in return. Referring to a mutual exhange in which each side influences the other.

**Reciprocal determinism** Mutual interplay among the child's behavior, cognitive characteristics, and environment.

**Reciprocity** The principle that actions have mutual effects and that people depend upon one another to treat each other morally.

**Recognition** A memory task in which the individual indicates whether presented information has been experienced previously.

**Referential language style** The child's use of language primarily as a means for labeling objects. See *Expressive language style.*

**Reflex** An unlearned, stereotypical response to an environmental stimulus.

**Regression** In psychoanalytical theory, a defense mechanism in which the individual, under stress, returns to behavior patterns characteristic of earlier stages of development.

**Rehearsal** In information processing, the mental repetition of information to facilitate long-term storage.

**Reinforcement** Any stimulus or change in the environment that follows a behavior and increases the frequency of that behavior.

**Rejecting–neglecting** A child-rearing style in which parents are neither restrictive and controlling nor supportive and responsive.

**Releasing stimulus** A stimulus that elicits a fixed-action pattern.

**Repression** In psychoanalytic theory, a major defense mechanism that is hypothesized to protect the individual from anxiety by ejecting anxiety-evoking ideas from awareness.

**Respiratory distress syndrome** A cluster of breathing problems, including weak and irregular breathing, to which preterm babies are especially prone.

**Retrolintal fibroplasia** A type of blindness caused by excessive oxygen, as may be found in an incubator.

**Reversibility** According to Piaget, recognition that processes can be undone, leaving things as they were before. Reversibility is a factor in conservation of the properties of substances.

**Rh incompatibliity** A condition in which antibodies produced by a pregnant woman are transmitted to the fetus and may cause brain damage or death to the fetus.

**Risk factors** Variables such as ethnicity and social class that do not directly cause problems but are associated with them.

**Rods** Rod-shaped receptors for light that are sensitive to the intensity of light only. Rods permit black-and-white vision.

**Rooting reflex** A reflex in which infants turn their mouths and heads in the direction of a tactile stimulus that strokes the cheek or the corner of the mouth.

**Rote learning** Learning by repetition.

**Rough-and-tumble play** Play fighting and chasing.

**Rubella** A viral infection that can cause retardation and heart disease in the embryo. Also called *German measles.*

**Saturation** In visual perception, the richness or purity of a color.

**Scaffolding** Temporary support that is provided by an adult to a child who is learning to perform a task.

**Scheme** According to Piaget, an action pattern or mental structure that is involved in the acquisition and organization of knowledge.

**Scripts** Abstract, generalized accounts of familiar, repeated events.

**Secondary circular reactions** In Piaget's theory, a substage in the sensorimotor period during which the infant repeats actions that produce an effect on the environment.

**Secondary reinforcer** A reinforcer, such as money or social approval, whose effectiveness is based on association with established reinforcers. See *Primary reinforcer.*

**Secondary sex characteristics** Physical indicators of sexual maturation, such as depth of voice and breast development, that do not involve the reproductive structures.

**Secular trend** An historical trend toward increasing adult height and earlier puberty.

**Secure attachment** A type of attachment characterized by mild distress at leave-takings, a seeking of nearness to an attachment figure, and the ability to be readily soothed by the figure.

**Sedatives** Drugs that soothe or quiet restlessness or agitation.

**Self-concept** One's impression of oneself; self-awareness.

**Self-efficacy** Confidence in one's ability to exercise control over the environment and to succeed.

**Self-esteem** The sense of value, or worth, that people attach to themselves.

**Self-fulfilling prophecy** An expectation that is confirmed because of the behavior of those who hold the expectation.

**Semantic code** In information processing, a code based on the meaning of information.

**Semen** The fluid that contains sperm.

**Sensitive period** In language development, the period from about 18 months of age to puberty, when the child is thought to be especially capable of learning language because of plasticity of the brain.

**Sensory memory** The structure of memory first encountered by sensory input. Information is maintained in sensory memory for only a fraction of a second. See *Sensory register.*

**Sensory register** Another term for *Sensory memory.*

**Separation anxiety** Fear of being separated from a target of attachment—usually a primary care giver.

**Separation-anxiety disorder** An extreme form of otherwise normal separation anxiety that is characterized by anxiety about separating from parents and often takes the form of refusal to go to school.

**Separation-individuation** The child's increasing sense of becoming separate from and independent of the mother.

**Seriation** Placing objects in an order or series according to a property or trait.

**Serotonin** A neurotransmitter that is implicated in behavior disorders such as schizophrenia and depression.

**Sex chromosome** A chromosome in the shape of a Y (male) or X (female) that determines the sex of the child.

**Sexism** Discrimination or bias against people based on their gender.

**Sex-linked genetic abnormalities** Abnormalities that stem from genes that are found on the X chromosome. They are more likely to be shown by male offspring (who do not have an opposing gene from a second X chromosome) than by female offspring.

**Sexual harassment** Unwelcome verbal or physical conduct of a sexual nature.

**Sexually transmitted disease (STD)** A disease spread through sexual contact.

**Shape constancy** The tendency to perceive objects as being the same shape although the shapes of their retinal images may differ when the objects are viewed from different positions.

**Shape stage** A stage in drawing, attained by age 3, in which children draw basic shapes such as circles, squares, triangles, crosses, Xs, and odd shapes.

**Shaping** An operant-conditioning procedure for gradually building complex behavior patterns by means of reinforcing successive approximations of the target behavior.

**Short-term memory** The structure of memory that can hold a sensory stimulus for up to 30 seconds after the trace decays.

**Sibling rivalry** Jealousy or rivalry among brothers and sisters.

**Sickle-cell anemia** A genetic disorder that decreases the blood's capacity to carry oxygen.

**Sight vocabulary** Words that are immediately recognized on the basis of familiarity with their overall shapes, rather than decoded.

**Size constancy** The tendency to perceive objects as being the same size, although the sizes of their retinal images may differ as a result of distance.

**Small for dates** Descriptive of neonates who are unusually small for their age.

**Social-learning theory** A cognitively oriented learning theory that emphasizes observational learning in determining behavior.

**Social cognition** Development of children's understanding of the relationship between the self and others.

**Social play** Play in which children interact with and are influenced by the play of others. Examples include parallel play, associative play, and cooperative play.

**Social referencing** Using another person's reaction to a situation to form one's own assessment of it.

**Social smile** A smile that occurs in response to a human voice or face.

**Socialization** A process in which children are encouraged to adopt socially desirable behavior patterns by means of guidance, rewards and punishments, and exposure to role models.

**Solitary play** Play that is independent from that of nearby children and in which no effort is made to approach other children.

**Somnambulism** Sleepwalking.

**Sonogram** A procedure for using ultrasonic sound waves to create a picture of an embryo or fetus. See *Ultrasound.*

**Spatial perception** A type of visual-spatial ability characterized by the ability to identify the horizontal or vertical in spite of distracting information.

**Spatial visualization** A type of visual-spatial ability characterized by the ability to find simple shapes hidden within larger, complex shapes.

**Spina bifida** A neural tube defect that causes abnormalities of the brain and spine.

**Spontaneous abortion** Unpremeditated, accidental abortion.

**Stage** A distinct period of development that differs qualitatively from other periods. Stages follow one another in an orderly sequence.

**Stage theory** A theory of development characterized by hypothesizing the existence of stages.

**Standardized test** A test of some ability or characteristic in which an individual's score is compared to the scores of a group of similar individuals.

**States** Levels of sleep and wakefulness in infants.

**Status offenses** Offenses considered illegal only when performed by minors, such as truancy and underage drinking.

**Stepping reflex** A reflex in which infants take steps when held under the arms and leaned forward so that their feet press against the ground.

**Stereotype** A fixed, conventional idea about a group.

**Stillbirth** The birth of a dead fetus.

**Stimulants** Drugs that increase the activity of the nervous system.

**Stimulus** A change in the environment that leads to a change in behavior.

**Stranger anxiety** A fear of unfamiliar people that emerges between 6 and 9 months of age.

**Subjects** Participants in a scientific study. Many psychologists consider this term dehumanizing and no longer use it in reference to human participants.

**Substance abuse** A persistent pattern of use of a substance characterized by frequent intoxication and impairment of physical, social, or emotional well-being.

**Substance dependence** A persistent pattern of use of a substance that is accompanied by physiological addiction.

**Successive approximations** An operant conditioning procedure that rewards a series of behaviors that become progressively more like the target behavior.

**Sudden Infant Death Syndrome (SIDS)** The death, while sleeping, of apparently healthy babies who stop breathing for unknown medical reasons. Also called crib death.

**Superego** In psychoanalytic theory, the last psychic structure to develop. The superego functions as a conscience: It sets forth high standards for behavior and floods the ego with feelings of guilt and shame when it falls short.

**Surface structure** The superficial construction of a sentence, as determined, for example, by word order. See *Deep structure.*

**Surfactants** Substances that lubricate the walls of the air sacs in the lungs.

**Surrogate mother** A woman who is artificially inseminated and carries to term a child who is then given to another woman, typically the spouse of the man who donated the sperm used in insemination.

**Syllogism** A pattern of reasoning in which two statements or premises are set forth and a logical conclusion is drawn from them.

**Symbolic play** Play in which children make believe that objects and toys are other than what they are. Also called *Pretend play.*

**Syntax** The rules in a language for placing words in proper order to form meaningful sentences.

**Syphilis** A sexually transmitted disease that, in advanced stages, can attack major organ systems.

**Systematic desensitization** A process in which one loses fear of anxiety-evoking objects by gradual exposure to them.

**Tabula rasa** A Latin phrase meaning "blank slate," referring to the view that children are born without ethical, cultural, or vocational preferences and that such preferences are shaped by the environment.

**Tay-Sachs disease** A fatal genetic neurological disorder.

**Telegraphic speech** Speech in which only the essential words are used, such as in children's one- and two-word utterances.

**Temperament** Individual differences in styles of reaction that are present very early in life.

**Teratogens** Environmental influences or agents that can damage the embryo or fetus.

**Term** A set period of time, such as the normal duration of the gestation period.

**Tertiary circular reactions** In Piaget's theory, a substage of the sensorimotor period in which the infant purposefully adapts established schemes to new situations.

**Thalidomide** A sedative used in the 1960s that has been linked to birth defects, especially deformed or absent limbs.

**Theory** A formulation of relationships underlying observed events. A theory involves assumptions and logically derived explanations and predictions.

**Theory of mind** A commonsense understanding of how the mind works.

**Time lag** A method of studying developmental processes in which measures are taken of children of the same age group at different times.

**Time out** A behavior-modification technique in which a child who misbehaves is temporarily placed in a drab, restrictive environment in which reinforcement is unavailable.

**Toddler** A child who walks with short, uncertain steps. Toddlerhood lasts from about 18 to 30 months of age.

**Token economy** A behavior-modification technique in which persons receive tokens for desirable behavior that can later be exchanged for desired objects and privileges.

**Tolerance** Habituation to a drug such that increasingly higher doses are needed to achieve similar effects.

**Tonic-neck reflex** A reflex in which infants turn their head to one side, extend the arm and leg on that side, and flex the limbs on the opposite side. Also known as the "fencing position."

**Total immersion** A method of language instruction in which a person is placed in an environment in which only the language to be learned is used.

**Toxemia** A life-threatening disease that can afflict pregnant women and is characterized by high blood pressure.

**Track** Visually follow.

**Transductive reasoning** A type of preoperational thought in which the child reasons from the specific to the specific.

**Transition** In childbirth, the initial movement of the head of the fetus into the birth canal.

**Transitional object** A soft, cuddly object often carried to bed by a child to ease the separation from parents.

**Transitivity** Recognition that if A is greater than B in a property, and B is greater than C, then A is greater than C.

**Transverse position** A problematic position for childbirth in which the fetus lies crosswise across the opening to the birth canal.

**Tranquilizer** A drug that reduces feelings of anxiety and tension.

**Treatment** In an experiment, a condition received by participants so that its effects may be observed.

**Triarchic theory** Sternberg's view that intellectual functioning occurs on three levels: contextual, experiential, and componential.

**Trophoblast** The outer part of the blastocyst from which the amniotic sac, placenta, and umbilical cord develop.

**Trust versus mistrust** The first of Erikson's stages of psychosocial development, during which the child comes to develop (or not develop) a basic sense of trust in others.

**Turner's syndrome** A chromosomal disorder found among females that is caused by having a single X sex chromosome and characterized by infertility.

**Ultrasound** Sound waves too high in pitch to be sensed by the human ear. See *Sonogram.*

**Umbilical cord** A tube that connects the fetus to the placenta.

**Unconditioned response (UCR)** An unlearned response to an unconditioned stimulus.

**Unconditioned stimulus (UCS)** A stimulus that elicits an unlearned response.

**Unconscious** In psychoanalytic theory, descriptive of ideas and feelings that are not available to awareness under ordinary means, such as by simple focusing of attention. See *Preconscious.*

**Unexamined ethnic identity** The first stage of ethnic identity development; similar to the diffusion or foreclosure identity statuses.

**Uterus** The hollow organ within females in which the embryo and fetus develop.

**Utopian** Having to do with an idealistically perfect vision of society.

**Vacuum extraction tube** An instrument that uses suction to pull the baby through the birth canal as a way of facilitating childbirth.

**Variable** In research, a quantity that can vary from child to child, or from occasion to occasion, such as height, weight, intelligence, and attention span.

**Vernix** An oily, white substance that coats the skin of the neonate, especially in preterm babies.

**Visual accommodation** The automatic adjustments made by the lenses of the eyes to bring objects into focus.

**Visual acuity** Keenness or sharpness of vision.

**Visual-recognition memory** An infant's ability to discriminate previously seen objects from novel objects. An experimental measure of infant intelligence.

**Voluntarily** Intentionally.

**Wernicke's Aphasia** A type of aphasia caused by damage to Wernicke's area of the cerebral cortex and characterized by impaired comprehension of speech and difficulty in producing the right word.

**Whole-object assumption** The assumption that words refer to whole objects and not their component parts or characteristics.

**Womb simulator** An artificial environment used primarily with preterm babies that mimics some of the features of the uterus, particularly temperature, sounds, and rocking movements.

**Word-recognition method** A method for learning to read in which children come to recognize words through repeated exposure to them.

**Zone of proximal development** The gap between what the child is capable of doing now and what she or he could do with help from others.

**Zygote** A fertilized egg cell or ovum.

# REFERENCES


AAP Task Force on Infant Positioning and SIDS. (1992). Positioning and SIDS. *Pediatrics, 89,* 1120–1126.

Abbott, S. (1992). Holding on and pushing away: Comparative perspectives on an Eastern Kentucky child-rearing practice. *Ethos, 20,* 33–65.

Abel, E. L., & Sokol, R. J. (1988). Marijuana and cocaine use during pregnancy. In J. R. Niebyl (Ed.), *Drug use in pregnancy* (2nd ed.). Philadelphia: Lea & Febiger.

Abra, J., & Valentine–French, S. (1991). Gender differences in creative achievement: A survey of explanations. *Genetic, Social and General Psychological Monographs, 117,* 233–284.

Abramovitch, R., Corter, C., Pepler, D. J., & Stanhope, L. (1986). Sibling and peer interaction: A final follow-up and a comparison. *Child Development, 57,* 217–229.

Abramowitz, A. J., & O'Leary, S. G. (1991). Behavioral interventions for the classroom: Implications for students with ADHD. *School Psychology Review, 20,* 220–234.

Abravanel, E., & DeYong, N. G. (1991). Does object modeling elicit imitative-like gestures from young infants? *Journal of Experimental Child Psychology, 52,* 22–40.

Acebo, C., & Thomas, E. B. (1992). Crying as social behavior. *Infant Mental Health Journal, 13,* 67–82.

Achenbach, T. M., Howell, C. T., Aoki, M. F., & Rauh, V. A. (1993). Nine-year outcome of the Vermont intervention program for low birth weight infants. *Pediatrics, 91,* 45–55.

Achenbach, T. M., Phares, V., Howell, C. T., Rauh, V. A., & Nurcombe, B. (1990). Seven-year outcome of the Vermont intervention program for low-birthweight infants. *Child Development, 61,* 1672–1681.

Ackerman, G. L. (1993). A congressional view of youth suicide. *American Psychologist, 48,* 183–184.

Adams, D. M., Overholser, J. C., & Spirito, A. (1992, August). *Life stress related to adolescent suicide attempts.* Paper presented at the meeting of the American Psychological Association, Washington, DC.

Adcock, A. G., Nagy, S., & Simpson, J. A. (1991). Selected risk factors in adolescent suicide attempts. *Adolescence, 104,* 817–827.

Adelman, H. W., & Taylor, L. (1993). *Learning problems and learning disabilities: Moving forward.* Pacific Groves, CA: Brooks–Cole.

Adler, J., & Starr, M. (1992, August 10). Flying high now. *Newsweek,* pp. 20–21.

Adler, J., Wingert, P., Wright, L., Houston, P., Manly, H., Cohen, A. D. (1992, February 17). Hey, I'm terrific! *Newsweek,* pp. 46–51.

Adler, T. (1991, December). Scientists debate gene, alcoholism link. *APA Monitor,* p. 14.

Adler, T. (1993a, January). EEGs differ widely for those with different temperaments. *APA Monitor,* p. 7.

Adler, T. (1993b, April). Sense of invulnerability doesn't drive teen risks. *APA Monitor,* p. 15.

Adler, T. (1993c, June). Kids' memory improves if they talk to themselves. *APA Monitor,* p. 8.

Ainsworth, M. D. S. (1967). *Infancy in Uganda: Infant care and the growth of love.* Baltimore: Johns Hopkins University Press.

Ainsworth, M. D. S. (1989). Attachments beyond infancy. *American Psychologist, 44,* 709–716.

Ainsworth, M. D. S., Bell, S. M., & Stayton, D. J. (1974). Infant–mother attachment and social development: Socialization as a product of reciprocal responsiveness to signals. In M. P. M. Richards (Ed.), *The integration of the child into a social world.* London: Cambridge University Press.

Ainsworth, M. D. S., Blehar, M. C., Waters, E., & Wall, S. (1978). *Patterns of attachment: A psychological study of the Strange Situation.* Hillsdale, NJ: Erlbaum.

Ainsworth, M. D. S., & Bowlby, J. (1991). An ethological approach to personality development. *American Psychologist, 46,* 331–341.

Akhtar, N., Dunham, F., & Dunham, P. J. (1991). Directive interactions and early vocabulary development: The role of joint attentional focus. *Journal of Child Language, 18,* 41–49.

Alan Guttmacher Institute. (1991). *Facts in brief.* New York: Author.

Alessandri, S. M. (1992a). Attention, play, and social behavior in ADHD preschoolers. *Journal of Abnormal Child Psychology, 20,* 289–302.

Alessandri, S. M. (1992b). Effects of maternal work status in single-parent families on children's perception of self and family and school achievement. *Journal of Experimental Child Psychology, 54,* 417–433.

Alexander, K. L., & Entwisle, D. R. (1988). Achievement in the first 2 years of school: Patterns and processes. *Monographs of the Society for Research in Child Development, 53*(2, Serial No. 218).

Allen, L., & Majidi–Ahi, S. (1991). Black American children. In J. T. Gibbs, L. N. Huang & Associates (Eds.), *Children of color: Psychological interventions with minority youth.* San Francisco: Jossey–Bass.

Allen, M. C., & Alexander, G. R. (1990). Gross motor milestones in preterm infants: Correction for degree of prematurity. *Journal of Pediatrics, 116,* 955–959.

Allgood–Merten, B., Lewinsohn, P. M., & Hops, H. (1990). Sex differences and adolescent depression. *Journal of Abnormal Psychology, 99,* 55–63.

Allison, P. D., & Furstenberg, F. F. (1989). How marital dissolution affects children: Variations by age and sex. *Developmental Psychology, 25,* 540–549.

Alpert–Gillis, L. J., & Connell, J. P. (1989) Gender and sex-role influences on children's self-esteem. *Journal of Personality, 57,* 97–114.

Alsaker, F. D. (1992). Pubertal timing, overweight, and psychological adjustment. *Journal of Early Adolescence, 12,* 396–419.

Altepeter, T. S., & Walker, C. E. (1992). Prevention of physical abuse of children through parent training. In D. J. Willis, E. W. Holden, & M. Rosenberg (Eds.), *Prevention of child maltreatment.* New York: Wiley.

Altman, L. K. (1993a, June 6). At AIDS talks, science faces a daunting maze. *New York Times,* p. 4.

Altman, L. K. (1993b, July 23). AIDS cases linked to sex are on the rise for women. *New York Times,* p. A6.

Altman, L. K. (1994, March 11). Cases of AIDS increase among heterosexuals. *New York Times,* p. A8.

Amabile, T. (1989). *Growing up creative.* New York: Crown.

Amato, P. R., & Keith B. (1991). Parental divorce and the well-being of children: A meta-analysis. *Psychological Bulletin, 110,* 26–46.

American Academy of Pediatrics. (1992). Learning disabilities, dyslexia, and vision. *Pediatrics, 90,* 124–126.

American Association of University Women. (1991). *Shortchanging girls, shortchanging America.* Washington, DC: AAUW Educational Foundation.

American Association of University Women. (1992). *How schools shortchange women: The AAUW report.* Washington, DC: AAUW Educational Foundation.

American Association of University Women. (1993). *Hostile hallways.* Washington, DC: AAUW Educational Foundation.

American Psychiatric Association. (1987). *Diagnostic and statistical manual of the mental disorders* (3rd ed., rev.). Washington, DC: American Psychiatric Press.

American Psychological Association. (1992). Ethical principles of psychologists and code of conduct. *American Psychologist, 47,* 1597–1611.

American Psychological Association. (1993). *Violence and youth.* Washington, DC: Author.

Anastasi, A. (1988). *Psychological testing* (6th ed). New York: Macmillan.

Anastasiow, N. J., & Hanes, M. L. (1976). *Language patterns of poverty children.* Springfield, IL: Charles C. Thomas.

Anders, T. F., Halpern, L. F., & Hua, J. (1992). Sleeping through the night: A developmental perspective. *Pediatrics, 90,* 554–560.

Anderson, E. (1990). *Streetwise: Race, class, and change in an urban community.* Chicago: University of Chicago Press.

Anderson, G. C. (1993, March). *Risk in mother–infant separation postbirth.* Paper presented at the meeting of the Society for Research in Child Development, New Orleans, LA.

Anderson, G. M., & Cohen, D. J. (1991). The neurology of childhood neuropsychiatric disorders. In M. Lewis (Ed.), *Child and adolescent psychiatry: A comprehensive textbook.* Baltimore: Williams & Wilkins.

Anderson, R. L., & Golbus, M. S. (1989). Chemical teratogens. In M. I. Evans, J. C. Fletcher, A. O. Dixler, & J. D. Schulman (Eds.), *Fetal diagnosis and therapy: Science, ethics and the law.* Philadelphia: Lippincott.

Anderson, S. R., Christian, W. P., & Luce, S. C. (1986). Transitional residential programming for autistic individuals. *Behavior Therapist, 9,* 205–211.

Andersson, B. (1992). Effects of day-care on cognitive and socioemotional competence of thirteen-year-old Swedish schoolchildren. *Child Development, 63,* 20–36.

Andrews, J., & Conte, R. (1993, March). *Enhancing the social cognition of learning disabled children through a cognitive strategies approach.* Paper presented at the meeting of the Society for Research in Child Development, New Orleans, LA.

Andrews, J., Smolkowski, K., Hops, H., Tildesley, E., Ary, D., & Harris, J. (1991, August). *Adolescent substance use and academic achievement and motivation.* Paper presented at the meeting of the American Psychological Association, San Francisco.

Andrews, J. A., & Lewinsohn, P. M. (1992). Suicidal attempts among older adolescents: Prevalence and co-occurrence with psychiatric disorders. *Journal of American Academy of Child and Adolescent Psychiatry, 31,* 655–662.

Angier, N. (1992a, January 30). Odor receptors discovered in sperm cells. *New York Times,* p. A19.

Angier, N. (1992b, April 14). With direct injections, gene therapy takes a step into a new age. *New York Times,* p. B6.

Angier, N. (1993, March 24). Team pinpoints genetic cause of Huntington's. *New York Times,* pp. A1, C19.

Angold, A., & Rutter, M. (1992). Effects of age and pubertal status on depression in a large clinical sample. *Development and Psychopathology, 4,* 5–28.

Anisfeld, E., Casper, V., Kozyce, M., & Cunningham, N. (1990). Does infant carrying promote attachment? An experimental study of the effects of increased physical contact on the development of attachment. *Child Development, 61,* 1617–1627.

Anisfeld, M. (1991). Review: Neonatal imitation. *Developmental Review, 11,* 60–97.

Annas, G. J. (1993, Spring). Who's afraid of the human genome? *National Forum,* pp. 35–37.

Antilla, S. (1993, January 10). Bringing up a TV-wise child. *New York Times,* pp. A4, 34–35.

Antonarakis, S. E., and the Down Syndrome Collaborative Group. (1991). Parental origin of the extra chromosome in trisomy 21 as indicted by analysis of DNA polymorphisms. *New England Journal of Medicine, 324,* 872–876.

Apgar, V. (1953). A proposal for a new method of evaluation in the newborn infant. *Anesthesia and Analgesia, 52,* 260–267.

Arbuthnot, J., & Gorden, D. A. (1986). Behavioral and cognitive effects of a moral reasoning development intervention for high-risk behavior-disordered adolescents. *Journal of Consulting and Clinical Psychology, 54,* 206–216.

Archer, S. L. (1985). Career and/or family: The identity process for adolescent girls. *Youth and Society, 16,* 289–314.

Archer, S. L. (1991). Gender differences in identity development. In R. M. Lerner, A. C. Petersen, & J. Brooks-Gunn (Eds.), *Encyclopedia of adolescence.* New York: Garland.

Archer, S. L. (1992). A feminist's approach to identity research. In G. R. Adams, T. P. Gullotta, & R. Montemayor (Eds.), *Adolescent identity formation.* Newbury Park, CA: Sage.

Archer, S. L. & Waterman, A. S. (1990). Varieties of identity diffusions and foreclosures: An exploration of subcategories of the identity statuses. *Journal of Adolescent Research, 5,* 96–111.

Arendt, R. E., Singer, L. T., & Minnes, S. (1993, March). *Development of cocaine-exposed infants.* Paper presented at the meeting of the Society for Research in Child Development, New Orleans, LA.

Aries, P. (1962). *Centuries of childhood.* New York: Knopf.

Armstrong, B. G., McDonald, A. D., & Sloan, M. (1992). Cigarette, alcohol, and coffee consumption and spontaneous abortion. *American Journal of Public Health, 82,* 85–87.

Arnett, J. (1992). Reckless behavior in adolescence: A developmental perspective. *Developmental Review, 12,* 339–373.

Aro, H. M., & Palosaari, U. K. (1992). Parental divorce, adolescence, and transition to young adulthood: A follow-up study. *American Journal of Orthopsychiatry, 62,* 421–429.

Asendorpf, J. B. (1993). Beyond temperament: A two-factorial coping model of the development of inhibition during childhood. In K. H. Rubin & J. B. Asendorpf (Eds.), *Social withdrawal, inhibition, and shyness in childhood.* Hillsdale, NJ: Erlbaum.

Asendorpf, J. B., & Baudonnière, P. (1993). Self-awareness and other-awareness: Mirror self-recognition and synchronic imitation among unfamiliar peers. *Developmental Psychology, 29,* 88–95.

Aslin, R. N. (1987). Visual and auditory development in infancy. In J. D. Osofsky (Ed.), *Handbook of infant development* (2nd ed.). New York: Wiley.

Aslin, R. N., Pisoni, D. B., & Juscyk, P. W. (1983). Auditory development and speech perception in infancy. In P. H. Mussen (Ed.), *Handbook of child psychology: Vol. 2. Infancy and experimental psychobiology.* New York: Wiley.

Astley, S. J., Clarren, S. K., Little, R. E., Sampson, P. D., & Daling, J. R. (1992). Analysis of facial shape in children gestationally exposed to marijuana, alcohol, and/or cocaine. *Pediatrics, 89,* 67–77.

Attie, I., Brooks-Gunn, J., & Petersen, A. C. (1990). A developmental perspective in eating disorders and eating problems. In M. Lewis & S. M. Miller (Eds.), *Handbook of developmental psychopathology.* New York: Plenum.

Atwater, E. (1992). *Adolescence* (3rd ed.). Englewood Cliffs, NJ: Prentice Hall.

Au, T. K., & Glusman, M. (1990). The principle of mutual exclusivity in word learning: To honor or not to honor? *Child Development, 61,* 1474–1490.

August, G. J., Ostrander, R., & Bloomquist, M. J. (1992). Attention deficit hyperactivity disorder: An epidemiological screening method. *American Journal of Orthopsychiatry, 62,* 387–396.

Autti-Rämö, I., Korkman, M., Hilakivi-Clarke, L., Lehtonen, M., Halmesmaki, E., & Granstrom, M. L. (1992). Mental development of 2-year-old children exposed to alcohol in utero. *Journal of Pediatrics, 120,* 740–746.

Avery, M. E., & Merritt, T. A. (1991). Surfactant-replacement therapy. *New England Journal of Medicine, 324,* 910–912.

Avis, J., & Harris, P. L. (1991). Belief-desire reasoning among Baka children: Evidence for a universal conception of mind. *Child Development, 62,* 460–467.

Azmitia, M., & Hesser, J. (1993). Why siblings are important agents of cognitive development: A comparison of siblings and peers. *Child Development, 64,* 430–444.

Baber, K. M., & Monaghan, P. (1988). College women's career and motherhood expectations: New options, old dilemmas. *Sex Roles, 19,* 189–203.

Bachman, J. G. (1991). School dropouts. In R. M. Lerner, A. C. Petersen, & J. Brooks-Gunn (Eds.), *Encyclopedia of adolescence.* New York: Garland.

Bachman, J. G., Johnston, L. D., & O'Malley, D. M. (1987). *Monitoring the future: Questionnaire responses from the nation's high school seniors: 1986.* Ann Arbor, MI: Survey Research Center, Institute for Social Research.

Bachman, J. G., & Schulenberg, J. (1993). How part-time work intensity relates to drug use, problem behavior, time use, and satisfaction among high school seniors: Are these consequences or merely correlates? *Developmental Psychology, 29,* 220–235.

Baenninger, M., & Newcombe, N. (1989). The role of experience in spatial test performance: A meta-analysis. *Sex Roles, 20,* 327–344.

Baer, R. A., & Nietzel, M. T. (1991). Cognitive and behavioral treatment of impulsivity in children: A meta-analytic review of the outcome literature. *Journal of Clinical Child Psychology, 20,* 400–412.

Baghurst, P. A., McMichael, A. J., Wigg, N. R., Vimpani, G. V., Robertson, E. F., Roberts, R. J., & Tong, S. (1992). Environmental exposure to lead and children's intelligence at the age of seven years. *New England Journal of Medicine, 327,* 1279–1284.

Bailey, J. M., & Pillard, R. C. (1991). A genetic study of male sexual orientation. *Archives of General Psychiatry, 48,* 1089–1096.

Bailey, J. M., Pillard, R. C., Neale, M. C., & Agyei, Y. (1993). Heritable factors influence sexual orientation in women. *Archives of General Psychiatry, 50,* 217–223.

Baillargeon, R. (1987). Object permanence in 3½- and 4½-month-old infants. *Developmental Psychology, 23,* 655–664.

Baillargeon, R. (1991). Reasoning about the height and location of a hidden object in 4½- and 6½-month-old infants. *Cognition, 38,* 13–42.

Baillargeon, R. (1993). The object concept revisited: New directions in the investigation of infants' physical knowledge. In C. E. Granrud (Ed.), *Visual perception and cognition in infancy.* Hillsdale, NJ: Erlbaum.

Baillargeon, R., Graber, M., DeVos, J., & Black, J. (1990). Why do young infants fail to search for hidden objects? *Cognition, 36,* 255–284.

Bakan, P. (1990). Nonright-handedness and the continuum of reproductive casualty. In S. Coren (Ed.), *Left-handedness: Behavior implications and anomalies.* Amsterdam: North–Holland.

Baker, L., & Cantwell, D. P. (1991). The development of speech and language. In M. Lewis (Ed.), *Child and adolescent psychiatry: A comprehensive textbook.* Baltimore: Williams & Wilkins.

Baldwin, A. L., Baldwin, C., & Cole, R. E. (1990). Stress-resistant families and stress-resistant children. In J. Rolf, A. Masten, D. Cicchetti, K. Nuechterlein & S. Weintraub (Eds.)., *Risk and protective factors in the development of psychopathology.* Cambridge: Cambridge University Press.

Balentine, M., Stitt, K., Bonner, J., & Clark, L. (1991). Self-reported eating disorders of black, low-income adolescents: Behavior, body weight perceptions, and methods of dieting. *Journal of School Health, 61,* 392–396.

Ball, S., & Bogatz, G. A. (1970). *The first year of "Sesame Street": An evaluation.* Princeton, NJ: Educational Testing Service.

Bamford, F. N., Bannister, R. P., Benjamen, C. M., Hiller, V. F., Ward, B. S., & Moore, W. M. O. (1990). Sleep in the first year of life. *Developmental Medicine and Child Neurology, 32,* 718–724.

Bandura, A. (1989). Social cognitive theory. In R. Vasta (Ed.), *Annals of child development* (Vol. 6). Greenwich, CT: JAI Press.

Bandura, A. (1991). Human agency: The rhetoric and the reality. *American Psychologist, 46,* 157–162.

Bandura, A., Blanchard, E. B., & Ritter, B. (1969). The relative efficacy of desensitization and modeling approaches for inducing behavioral, affective, and cognitive changes. *Journal of Personality and Social Psychology, 13,* 173–199.

Bandura, A., Ross, S. A., & Ross, D. (1963). Imitation of film-mediated aggressive models. *Journal of Abnormal and Social Psychology, 66,* 3–11.

Bangert–Downs, R. (1988). The effects of school-based substance education: A meta-analysis. *Journal of Drug Education, 18,* 243–264.

Banks, M. S., & Salapatek, P. (1983). Infant visual perception. In P. H. Mussen (Ed.), *Handbook of child psychology: Vol. 2. Infancy and experimental psychobiology.* New York: Wiley.

Banks, M. S., & Shannon, E. (1993). Spatial and chromatic visual efficiency in human neonates. In C. E. Granrud (Ed.), *Visual perception and cognition in infancy.* Hillsdale, NJ: Erlbaum.

Barabas, G. (1990). Physical disorders. In M. Lewis & S. M. Miller (Eds.), *Handbook of developmental pathology.* New York: Plenum.

Barber, B. L., & Eccles, J. S. (1992). Long-term influence of divorce and single parenting on adolescent family and work-related values, behaviors, and aspirations. *Psychological Bulletin, 111,* 108–126.

Bard, C., Hay, L., & Fleury, M. (1990). Timing and accuracy of visually directed movements in children: Control of direction and amplitude components. *Journal of Experimental Child Psychology, 50,* 102–118.

Barkley, R. A. (1990). Attention deficit disorders: History, definition, and diagnosis. In M. Lewis & S. M. Miller (Eds.), *Handbook of developmental psychopathology.* New York: Plenum.

Barkley, R. A., Anastopoulos, A. D., Guevremont, D. C., & Fletcher, K. E. (1991a). Adolescents with ADHD: Patterns of behavioral adjustment, academic functioning and treatment utilization. *Journal of the American Academy of Child and Adolescent Psychiatry, 30,* 752–761.

Barkley, R. A., Fischer, M., Edelbrock, C., & Smallish, L. (1991b). The adolescent outcome of hyperactive children diagnosed by research criteria—III. Mother-child interactions, family conflicts and maternal psychopathology. *Journal of Child Psychology and Psychiatry, 32,* 233–255.

Barnard, K. E., & Bee, H. L. (1983). The impact of temporally patterned stimulation on the development of preterm infants. *Child Development, 54,* 1156–1167.

Barnett, J. K., Papini, D. R., & Gbur, E. (1991). Familial correlates of sexually active pregnant and nonpregnant adolescents. *Adolescence, 26,* 457–472.

Baron–Cohen, S., & Bolton, P. (1993). *Autism.* New York: Oxford.

Barr, H. M., Streissguth, A. P., Darby, B. L., & Sampson, P. D. (1990). Prenatal exposure to alcohol, caffeine, tobacco, and aspirin: Effects on fine and gross motor performance in 4-year-old children. *Developmental Psychology, 26,* 339–348.

Barr, R. G., Rotman, A., Yaremko, J., Leduc, D., & Francoeur, T. E. (1992). The crying of infants with colic: A controlled empirical description. *Pediatrics, 90,* 14–21.

Barratt, M. S., Negayama, K., & Minami, T. (1993). The social environments of early infancy in Japan and the United States. *Early Development and Parenting, 2,* 51–64.

Barrett, D. E., Radke–Yarrow, M., & Klein, R. E. (1982). Chronic malnutrition and child behavior: Effects of early caloric supplementation on social and emotional functioning at school age. *Developmental Psychology, 18,* 541–556.

Barrett, M., Harris, M., & Chasin, J. (1991). Early lexical development and maternal speech: A comparison of children's initial and subsequent uses of words. *Journal of Child Language, 18,* 21–40.

Barringer, F. (1993, April 28). Immigration in 80's made English a foreign language for millions. *New York Times,* pp. A1, 10.

Barros, F. C., Huttly, S. R. A., Victora, C. G., Kirkwood, B. R., & Vaughan, J. P. (1992). Comparison of the causes and consequences of prematurity and intrauterine growth retardation: A longitudinal study in Southern Brazil. *Pediatrics, 90,* 238–244.

Bar–Tal, D. (1990). Prosocial behavior. In R. M. Thomas (Ed.), *The encyclopedia of human development and education: Theory, research, and studies.* Oxford: Pergamon.

Bartsch, K., & Wellman, H. M. (1993, March). *Before belief: Children's early psychological theory.* Paper presented at the meeting of the Society for Research in Child Development, New Orleans, LA.

Barth, R. P., Fetro, J. V., Leland, N., & Volkan, K. (1992). Preventing adolescent pregnancy with social and cognitive skills. *Journal of Adolescent Research, 7,* 208–232.

Bartko, W. T., & McHale, S. M. (1991). The household labor of children from dual- versus single-earner families. In S. V. Lerner & N. L. Galambos (Eds.), *Employed mothers and their children.* New York: Garland.

Bates, E., O'Connell, B., & Shore, C. (1987). Language and communication in infancy. In J. D. Osofsky (Ed.), *Handbook of infant development* (2nd ed.). New York: Wiley.

Bates, E., Thal, D., & Janowsky, J. S. (1992). Early language development and its neural correlates. *Handbook of Neuropsychology, 7,* 69–110.

Bates, J. E., Bayles, K., Bennett, D. S., Ridge, B., & Brown, M. M. (1991). Origins of externalizing behavior problems at eight years of age. In D. J. Pepler & K. H. Rubin (Eds.), *The development and treatment of childhood aggression.* Hillsdale, NJ: Erlbaum.

Battistich, V., Schaps, E., Solomon, D., & Watson, M. (1991b). The role of the school in prosocial development. In H. E. Fitzgerald, B. M. Lester, & M. W. Yogman (Eds.), *Theory and research in behavioral pediatrics* (Vol. 5). New York: Plenum.

Battistich, V., Watson, M., Solomon, D., Schaps, E., & Solomon, J. (1991a). The Child Development Project: A comprehensive program for the development of prosocial character. In W. M. Kurtines & J. L. Gewirtz (Eds.), *Handbook of moral behavior and development* (Vol. 3). Hillsdale, NJ: Erlbaum.

Bauer, P. J. (1993a). Memory for gender-consistent and gender-inconsistent event sequences by twenty-five-month-old children. *Child Development, 64,* 285–297.

Bauer, P. J. (1993b). Identifying subsystems of autobiographical memory: Commentary on Nelson. In C.A. Nelson (Ed.), *Minnesota symposia on child psychology: Vol. 26. Memory and affect in development.* Hillsdale, NJ: Erlbaum.

Bauer, P. J., & Mandler, J. M. (1990). Remembering what happened next: Very young children's recall of event sequences. In R. Fivush & J. A. Hudson (Eds.), *Knowing and remembering in young children.* Cambridge: Cambridge University Press.

Bauer, P. J., & Mandler, J. M. (1992). Putting the horse before the cart: The use of temporal order in recall of events by one-year-old children. *Developmental Psychology, 28,* 441–452.

Bauer, W. D., & Twentyman, C. T. (1985). Abusing, neglectful, and comparison mothers' responses to child-related and non-child-related stressors. *Journal of Consulting and Clinical Psychology, 53,* 335–343.

Bauerfeld, S. L., & Lachenmeyer, J. R. (1992). Prenatal nutritional status and intellectual development. In B. B. Lahey & A. E. Kazdin (Eds.), *Advances in clinical child psychology* (Vol. 14). New York: Plenum.

Baumrind, D. (1989). Rearing competent children. In W. Damon (Ed.), *Child development today and tomorrow.* San Francisco: Jossey–Bass.

Baumrind, D. (1991a). The influence of parenting style on adolescent competence and substance use. *Journal of Early Adolescence, 11,* 56–95.

Baumrind, D. (1991b). Parenting styles and adolescent development. In J. Brooks–Gunn, R. Lerner, & A. C. Petersen (Eds.), *Encyclopedia of adolescence.* New York: Garland.

Baydar, N., & Brooks–Gunn, J. (1991). Effects of maternal employment and child-care arrangements on preschoolers' cognitive and behavioral outcomes: Evidence from the Children of the National Longitudinal Survey of Youth. *Developmental Psychology, 27,* 932–945.

Bayley, N. (1993). *Bayley Scales of Infant Development.* New York: The Psychological Corporation.

Beal, C. R., & Flavell, J. H. (1983). Young speakers' evaluation of their listeners' comprehensions in a referential communication task. *Child Development, 54,* 148–153.

Bear, G. G. (1989). Sociomoral reasoning and antisocial behaviors among normal sixth graders. *Merrill–Palmer Quarterly, 35,* 181–196.

Beard, J. L. (1991). Iron deficiency anemia in adolescence. In R. M. Lerner, A. C. Petersen, & J. Brooks–Gunn (Eds.), *Encyclopedia of adolescence.* New York: Garland.

Beckwith, L., Rodning, C., & Cohen, S. (1992). Preterm children at early adolescence and continuity and discontinuity in maternal responsiveness from infancy. *Child Development, 63,* 1198–1208.

Beeson, J. H. (1989). Controversies surrounding antepartum Rh immune globulin prophylaxis. In M. I. Evans, J. C. Fletcher, A. O. Dixler, & J. D. Schulman (Eds.), *Fetal diagnosis and therapy: Science, ethics and the law.* Philadelphia: Lippincott.

Begley, S. (1987, March). When food is the enemy. *Newsweek on Campus,* pp. 18–19.

Begley, S. (1993, February 22). Cures from the womb. *Newsweek,* pp. 49–51.

Behrend, D. A. (1990). The development of verb concepts: Children's use of verbs to label familiar and novel events. *Child Development, 61,* 681–696.

Beilin, H., & Pearlman, E. G. (1991). Children's iconic realism: Object versus property realism. In H. W. Reese (Ed.), *Advances in child development and behavior* (Vol. 23). San Diego, CA: Academic Press.

Belkin, L. (1992, March 25). Births beyond hospitals fill an urban need. *New York Times,* pp. A1, 15.

Bellinger, D., Leviton, A., Waternaux, C., Needleman, H., & Rabinowitz, M. (1987). Longitudinal analysis of prenatal and postnatal lead exposure and early cognitive development. *New England Journal of Medicine, 316,* 1037–1043.

Bellinger, D., Sloman, J., Leviton, A., Rabinowitz, M., Needleman, H. L., & Waternaux, C. (1991). Low-level lead exposure and children's cognitive function in the preschool years. *Pediatrics, 87,* 219–227.

Bellinger, D. C., Stiles, K. M., & Needleman, H. L. (1992). Low-level lead exposure, intelligence and academic achievement: A long-term follow-up study. *Pediatrics, 90,* 855–861.

Belsky, J. (1990a). Developmental risks associated with infant day care: Attachment insecurity, noncompliance and aggression? In S. Cherazi (Ed.), *Psychosocial issues in day care.* New York: American Psychiatric Press.

Belsky, J. (1990b). The "effects" of infant day care reconsidered. In N. Fox & G. G. Fein (Eds.), *Infant day care: The current debate.* Norwood, NJ: Ablex.

Belsky, J., & Eggebeen, D. (1991). Early and extensive maternal employment and young children's socioemotional development: Children of the National Longitudinal Survey of Youth. *Journal of Marriage and the Family, 53,* 1083–1098.

Belsky, J., & Pensky, E. (1988). Marital change across the transition to parenthood. *Marriage and Family Review, 12,* 133–156.

Belsky, J., & Rovine, M. (1988). Nonmaternal care in the first year of life and infant–parent attachment security. *Child Development, 59,* 157–167.

Belsky, J., Rovine, M., & Fish, M. (1989). The developing family system. In M. R. Gunnar & E. Thelen (Eds.), *Systems and development* (Vol. 22). Hillsdale, NJ: Erlbaum.

Belsky, J., Steinberg, L., & Draper, P. (1991a). Childhood experience, interpersonal development, and reproductive strategy: An evolutionary theory of socialization. *Child Development, 62,* 647–670.

Belsky, J., Steinberg, L., & Draper, P. (1991b). Further reflections on an evolutionary theory of socialization. *Child Development, 62,* 682–685.

Bem, S. L. (1983). Gender schema theory and its implications for child development: Raising gender-aschematic children in a gender-schematic society. *Signs, 8,* 598–616.

Bem, S. L. (1985). Androgyny and gender schema theory: A conceptual and empirical integration. In T. B. Sonderegger (Ed.), *Nebraska symposium on motivation, 1984: Psychology and gender.* Lincoln: University of Nebraska Press.

Bem, S. L. (1989). Genital knowledge and gender constancy in preschool children. *Child Development, 60,* 649–662.

Benbow, C. P. (1991). Meeting the needs of gifted students through use of acceleration. In M. C. Wang, M. C. Reynolds, & H. J. Walberg (Eds.), *Handbook of special education: Research and practice.* Oxford, England: Pergamon.

Benbow, C. P., & Arjmond, O. (1990). Predictors of high academic achievement in mathematics and science by mathematically talented students: A longitudinal study. *Journal of Educational Psychology, 82,* 430–441.

Bender, W. N., & Smith, J. K. (1990). Classroom behavior of children and adolescents with learning disabilities: A meta-analysis. *Journal of Learning Disabilities, 23,* 298–305.

Benenson, J. F. (1990). Gender differences in social networks. *Journal of Early Adolescence, 10,* 472–495.

Bengtsson, H., & Johnson, L. (1992). Perspective taking, empathy, and prosocial behavior in late childhood. *Child Study Journal, 22,* 11–22.

Benin, M., & Chong, Y. (1993). Child care concerns of employed mothers. In J. Frankel (Ed.), *The employed mother and the family context.* New York: Springer.

Berenbaum, S. A., & Hines, M. (1992). Early androgens are related to childhood sex-typed toy preferences. *Psychological Science, 3,* 203–206.

Berezin, N. (1980). *The gentle birth book: A practical guide to Leboyer family-centered delivery.* New York: Pocket Books.

Berg, I. (1991). School avoidance, school phobia, and truancy. In M. Lewis (Ed.), *Child and adolescent psychiatry: A comprehensive textbook.* Baltimore: Williams & Wilkins.

Berg, W. K., & Berg, K. M. (1987). Psychophysiological development in infancy: State, startle, and attention. In J. D. Osofsky (Ed.), *Handbook of infant development* (2nd ed.). New York: Wiley.

Berger, J. (1993, January 4). New York's bilingual bureaucracy assailed as non-English programs cover more pupils. *New York Times,* p. A13.

Berkell, D. E. (1992). Instructional planning: Goals and practice. In D. E. Berkell (Ed.), *Autism.* Hillsdale, NJ: Erlbaum.

Berko, J. (1958). The child's learning of English morphology. *Word, 14,* 150–177.

Berkowitz, G.S. (1988). Smoking and pregnancy. In J. R. Niebyl (Ed.), *Drug use in pregnancy* (2nd ed.). Philadelphia: Lea & Febiger.

Berkowitz, G. S., Skovron, M. L., Lapinski, R. H., & Berkowitz, R. L. (1990). Delayed childbearing and the outcome of pregnancy. *New England Journal of Medicine, 322,* 659–664.

Berman, A. L., & Jobes, D. A. (1991). *Adolescent suicide: Assessment and intervention.* Washington, DC: American Psychological Association.

Berman, B. D., Winkleby, M., Chesterman, E., & Boyce, W. T. (1992). After-school child care and self-esteem in school-age children. *Pediatrics, 89,* 654–659.

Bernard, J., & Sontag, L. W. (1947). Fetal reactivity to sound. *Journal of Genetic Psychology, 70,* 205–210.

Berndt, T. J. (1992). Friendship and friends' influence in adolescence. *Current Directions in Psychological Science, 1,* 156–159.

Berndt, T. J., Cheung, P. C., Lau, S., Hau, K., & Lew, W. J. F. (1993). Perceptions of parenting in mainland China, Taiwan, and Hong Kong: Sex differences and societal differences. *Developmental Psychology, 29,* 156–164.

Berndt, T. J., Miller, K. E., & Park, K. E. (1989). Adolescents' perceptions of friends and parents' influence on aspects of their school adjustment. *Journal of Early Adolescence, 9,* 419–435.

Berndt, T. J., & Perry, T. B. (1986). Children's perceptions of friendships as supportive relationships. *Developmental Psychology,* 640–648.

Berndt, T. J., & Perry, T. B. (1990). Distinctive features and effects of early adolescent friendships. In R. Montemayor, G. R. Adams, & T.P. Gullotta (Eds.), *From childhood to adolescence: A transitional period?* Newbury Park, CA: Sage.

Bernstein, G. A., & Borchardt, C. M. (1991). Anxiety disorders of childhood and adolescence: A critical review. *Journal of the American Academy of Child and Adolescent Psychiatry, 30,* 519–532.

Bertenthal, B. I., & Campos, J. J. (1990). A systems approach to the organizing effects of self-produced locomotion during infancy. In C. Rovee–Collier & L. Lipsitt (Eds.), *Advances in infancy research* (Vol. 6). Norwood, NJ: Ablex.

Berzonsky, M. C., Kuk, L. S., & Storer, C. J. (1993, March). *Identity development, autonomy, and personal effectiveness.* Paper presented at the meeting of the Society for Research in Child Development, New Orleans, LA.

Best, D. L. (1993). Inducing children to generate mnemonic organizational strategies: An examination of long-term retention and materials. *Developmental Psychology, 29,* 324–336.

Betancourt, H., & López, S. R. (1993). The study of culture, ethnicity, and race in American psychology. *American Psychologist, 48,* 629–637.

Bettes, B. A., Dusenbury, L., Kernep, J., James–Oritz, S., & Botvin, G. J. (1990). Ethnicity and psychosocial factors in alcohol and tobacco use in adolescence. *Child Development, 61,* 557–565.

Bhatia, M. S., Nigam, V. R., Bohra, N., & Malik, S. C. (1991). Attention deficit disorder with hyperactivity among paediatric outpatients. *Journal of Child Psychology and Psychiatry, 32,* 297–306.

Bialystock, E. (1988). Aspects of linguistic awareness in reading comprehension. *Applied Linguistic Research, 18,* 369–387.

Bierman, K. L., Smoot, D. L., & Aumiller, K. (1993). Characteristics of aggressive-rejected, aggressive (nonrejected), and rejected (nonaggressive) boys. *Child Development, 64,* 139–151.

Biernat, M. (1991). A multicomponent, developmental analysis of sex typing. *Sex Roles, 24,* 567–586.

Bigler, R. S., & Liben, L. S. (1990). The role of attitudes and interventions in gender-schematic processing. *Child Development, 61,* 1440–1452.

Bigler, R. S., & Liben, L. S. (1992). Cognitive mechanisms in children's gender stereotyping: Theoretical and educational implications of a cognitive-based intervention. *Child Development, 63,* 1351–1363.

Billy, J. O. G., Tanfer, K., Grady, W. R., & Klepinger, D. H. (1993). The sexual behavior of men in the United States. *Family Planning Perspectives, 25,* 52–60.

Bilsker, D., Schiedel, D., & Marcia, J. E. (1988). Sex differences in identity status. *Sex Roles, 18,* 231–236.

Bing, E. D. (1983). *Dear Elizabeth Bing: We've had our baby.* New York: Pocket Books.

Bingham, C. R., Miller, B. C., & Adams, G. R. (1990). Correlates of age at first sexual intercourse in a national sample of young women. *Journal of Adolescent Research, 5,* 18–33.

Birch, L. L. (1990). Development of food acceptance patterns. *Developmental Psychology, 26,* 515–519.

Bishop, J. E. (1993, Spring). Unnatural selection. *National Forum,* pp. 27–29.

Bishop, S. M., & Ingersoll, G. M. (1989). Effects of marital conflict and family structure on the self-concepts of pre- and early adolescents. *Journal of Youth and Adolescence, 18,* 25–38.

Bithoney, W. G., McJunkin, J., Michalek, J., Snyder, J., Egan, H., & Epstein, D. (1991). The effect of a multidisciplininary team approach on weight gain in nonorganic failure-to-thrive children. *Developmental and Behavioral Pediatrics, 12,* 254–258.

Bivens, J. A., & Berk, L. E. (1990). A longitudinal study of the development of elementary school children's private speech. *Merrill–Palmer Quarterly, 36,* 443–463.

Bjorklund, D. F., & Bjorklund, B. R. (1989, June). Physically fit families. *Parents' Magazine,* p. 215.

Bjorklund, D. F., & de Marchena, M. R. (1984). Developmental shifts in the basis of organization in memory: The role of associative versus categorical relatedness in children's free recall. *Child Development, 55,* 952–962.

Black, A. E., & Pedro–Carroll, J. (1993). The role of parent–child relationships in mediating the effects of marital disruption. *Journal of the American Academy of Child and Adolescent Psychiatry,* 32, 1019–1027.

Blackman, J. A. (1991). Update on AIDS, CMV and herpes in young children: Health, developmental and educational issues. *Advances in Developmental and Behavioral Pediatrics, 9,* 33–58.

Blakeslee, S. (1989, February 14). Crib death: Suspicion turns to the brain. *New York Times,* pp. C1, 3.

Blakeslee, S. (1991a, September 10). Brain yields new clues on its organization for language. *New York Times,* pp. B5, 6.

Blakeslee, S. (1991b, September 15). Study ties dyslexia to brain flow affecting vision and other senses. *New York Times,* pp. L1, 15.

Blass, E. M., & Smith, B. A. (1992). Differential effects of sucrose, fructose, glucose, and lactose on crying in 1- to 3-day-old human infants: Qualitative and quantitative considerations. *Developmental Psychology, 28,* 804–810.

Blevins–Knabe, B. (1987). Development of the ability to insert into a series. *Journal of Genetic Psychology, 148,* 427–441.

Block, J., & Robins, R. W. (1993). A longitudinal study of consistency and change in self-esteem from early adolescence to early adulthood. *Child Development, 64,* 909–923.

Block, J. H. (1979, August). *Personality development in males and females: The influence of differential socialization.* Paper presented at the meeting of the American Psychological Association, New York.

Block, J. H. (1983). Differential premises arising from differential socialization of the sexes: Some conjectures. *Child Development, 54,* 1335–1354.

Bloom, L. (1993, Winter). Word learning. *SRCD Newsletter,* pp. 1, 9, 13.

Bloom, L., Merkin, S., & Wootten, J. (1982). *Wh*-questions: Linguistic factors that contribute to the sequence of acquisition. *Child Development, 53,* 1084–1092.

Bloomquist, M. L., August, G. J., & Ostrander, R. (1991). Effects of a school-based cognitive-behavioral intervention for ADHD children. *Journal of Abnormal Child Psychology, 19,* 591–605.

Blos, P. (1988). The inner world of the adolescent. In A. H. Esman, S. C. Feinstein, & S. Lebovici (Eds.), *International Annals of Adolescent Psychiatry, 1,* 11–23.

Blum, R. W., Harmon, B., Harris, L., Bergeisen, L., & Resnick, M. D. (1992). American Indian—Alaska native youth health. *Journal of the American Medical Association, 267,* 1637–1644.

Blumberg, S. H., & Izard, C. E. (1985). Affective and cognitive characteristics of depression in 10- and 11-year-old children. *Journal of Personality and Social Psychology, 49,* 194–202.

Boccia, M., & Campos, J. J. (1989). Maternal emotional signals, social referencing, and infants' reactions to strangers. In N. Eisenberg (Ed.), *New directions for child development: No. 44. Empathy and related emotional responses.* San Francisco: Jossey–Bass.

Boehnke, K., Silbreisen, R. K., Eisenberg, N., Reykowski, J., & Palmonari, A. (1989). The development of prosocial motivation: A cross-national study. *Journal of Cross-Cultural Psychology, 20,* 219–243.

Bogatz, G. A., & Ball, S. (1971). *The second year of "Sesame Street": A continuing evaluation* (Vols. 1 & 2). Princeton, NJ: Educational Testing Service.

Boggiano, A. K., & Barrett, M. (1991). Strategies to motivate helpless and mastery-oriented children: The effect of gender-based expectancies. *Sex Roles, 25,* 487–510.

Bohannon, J. N., III, & Stanowicz, L. (1988). The issue of negative evidence: Adult responses to children's language errors. *Developmental Psychology, 24,* 684–689.

Boismier, J. D. (1977). Visual stimulation and wake–sleep behavior in human neonates. *Developmental Psychology, 10,* 219–227.

Boivin, M., & Begin, G. (1989). Peer status and self-perception among early elementary school children: The case of the rejected children. *Child Development, 60,* 591–596.

Boldizar, J. P. (1991). Assessing sex typing and androgyny in children: The Children's Sex Role Inventory. *Developmental Psychology, 27,* 505–515.

Bonilla–Santiago, G. (1990). A portrait of Hispanic women in the United States. In S. E. Rix (Ed.), *The American woman: 1990–91.* New York: Norton.

Borden, M. C., & Ollendick, T. H. (1992). The development and differentiation of social subtypes in autism. In B. B. Lahey & A. E. Kazdin (Eds.), *Advances in clinical child psychology* (Vol. 14). New York: Plenum.

Borkowski, J. G., Carr, M., Rellinger, E., & Pressley, M. (1990). Self-regulated cognition: Interdependence of metacognition, attributions, and self-esteem. In B. F. Jones & L. Idol (Eds.), *Dimensions of thinking and cognitive instruction.* Hillsdale, NJ: Erlbaum.

Bornstein, M. H. (1992). Perceptual development in infancy, childhood, and old age. In M. H. Bornstein & M. E. Lamb (Eds.), *Developmental psychology: An advanced textbook* (3rd ed.). Hillsdale, NJ: Erlbaum.

Bornstein, M. H., & Lamb, M. E. (1992). *Development in infancy: An introduction* (3rd ed.). New York: McGraw–Hill.

Bornstein, M. H., Tal, J., Rahn, C., Galperín, C. Z., Pêcheux, M., Lamour, M., Toda, S., Azuma, H., Ogino, M., & Tamis–LeMonda, C. S. (1992a). Functional analysis of the contents of maternal speech to infants of 5 and 13 months in four cultures: Argentina, France, Japan, and the United States. *Developmental Psychology, 28,* 593–603.

Bornstein, M. H., & Tamis–LeMonda, C. S. (1989). Maternal responsiveness and cognitive development in children. In M. H. Bornstein (Ed.), *New directions for child development: No. 43. Maternal responsiveness: Characteristics and consequences.* San Francisco: Jossey–Bass.

Bornstein, M. H., Tamis–LeMonda, C. S., Tal, J., Ludemann, P., Toda, S., Rahn, C. W., Pêcheux, M., Azuma, H., & Vardi, D. (1992b). Maternal responsiveness to infants in three societies: The United States, France, and Japan. *Child Development, 63,* 808–821.

Borst, S. R., Noarn, G. G., & Bartok, J. A. (1991). Adolescent suicidality: A clinical-developmental approach. *Journal of the American Academy of Child and Adolescent Psychiatry, 30,* 796–803.

Boston Women's Health Book Collective (1992). *The new our bodies, ourselves.* New York: Simon & Schuster.

Bouchard, C., Tremblay, A., Despries, J. P., Nadeau, A., Lupien, P. J., Theriault, G., Dussault, J., Moorjani, S., Pinault, S., & Fournier, G. (1990). The response to long-term overfeeding in identical twins. *New England Journal of Medicine, 322,* 1477–1482.

Bouchard, T. J., Lykken, D. T., McGue, M., Segal, N. L., & Tellegen, A. (1990). Sources of human psychological differences: The Minnesota study of twins reared apart. *Science, 250,* 223–228.

Bouchard, T. J., & McGue, M. (1981). Familial studies of intelligence: A review. *Science, 212,* 1055–1059.

Bower, T. G. R. (1974). *Development in infancy.* San Francisco: W. H. Freeman.

Bowlby, J. (1988). *A secure base.* New York: Basic Books.

Boyer, C. B., & Hein, K. (1991a). AIDS and HIV infection in adolescents: The role of education and antibody testing. In R. M. Lerner, A. C. Petersen, & J. Brooks–Gunn (Eds.), *Encyclopedia of adolescence.* New York: Garland.

Boyer, C. B., & Hein, K. (1991b). Sexually transmitted diseases in adolescence. In R. M. Lerner, A. C. Petersen, & J. Brooks–Gunn (Eds.), *Encyclopedia of adolescence.* New York, NY: Garland.

Brack, C. J., Brack, G., & Orr, D. P. (1991, August). *Relationships between behaviors, emotions and health behaviors in early adolescents.* Paper presented at the meeting of the American Psychological Association, San Francisco.

Brackbill, Y., McManus, K., & Woodward, L. (1985). *Medication in maternity: Infant exposure and maternal information.* Ann Arbor: University of Michigan Press.

Bradley, B. S., & Gobbart, S. K. (1989). Determinants of gender-typed play in toddlers. *Journal of Genetic Psychology, 150,* 453–455.

Bradley, R. H. (1989). HOME measurement of maternal responsiveness. In M. H. Bornstein (Ed.), *New directions for child development: No 43. Maternal responsiveness: Characteristics and consequences.* San Francisco: Jossey–Bass.

Bradley, R. H., Caldwell, B. M., Rock, S. L., Ramey, C. T., Barnard, K. E., Gray, C., Hammond, M. A., Mitchell, S., Gottfried, A. W., Siegel, L., & Johnson, D. L. (1989). Home environment and cognitive development in the first 3 years of life: A collaborative study involving six sites and three ethnic groups in North America. *Developmental Psychology, 25,* 217–235.

Brady, E. V., & Kendall, P. C. (1992). Comorbidity of anxiety and depression in children and adolescents. *Psychological Bulletin, 111,* 244–255.

Brady, M. P., Swank, P. R., Taylor, R. D., & Freiberg, H. J. (1988). Teacher–student interactions in middle school mainstreamed classes: Differences with special and regular students. *Journal of Educational Research, 81,* 332–340.

Braine, M. D. S. (1976). Children's first word combinations. *Monographs of the Society for Research in Child Development, 41*(1, Serial No. 164).

Braitman, L. E., Adlin, E. V., & Stanton, J. L., Jr. (1985). Obesity and caloric intake. *Journal of Chronic Diseases, 38,* 727–732.

Brand, E., Clingempeel, W. G., & Bowen–Woodward, K. (1988). Family relationships and children's psychological adjustment in stepmother and stepfather families. In E. M. Hetherington & J. D. Arasteh (Eds.), *Impact of divorce, single parenting and stepparenting on children.* Hillsdale, NJ: Erlbaum.

Brandt, M. M., & Strattner–Gregory, M. J. (1980). Effect of highlighting intention on intentionality and restitutive justice. *Developmental Psychology, 16,* 147–148.

Braungart, J. M., Plomin, R., DeFries, J. C., & Fulker, D. W. (1992). Genetic influence on tester-rated infant temperament as assessed by Bayley's infant behavior record: Nonadoptive and adoptive siblings and twins. *Developmental Psychology, 28,* 40–47.

Bray, N. W., Hersh, R. E., & Turner, L. A. (1985). Selective remembering during adolescence. *Developmental Psychology, 21,* 290–294.

Brazelton, T. B. (1990a). Forward: Observations of the neonate. In C. Rovee–Collier & L. P. Lipsitt (Eds.), *Advances in infancy research* (Vol. 6). Norwood, NJ: Ablex.

Brazelton, T. B. (1990b). Saving the bathwater. *Child Development, 61,* 1661–1671.

Brazelton, T. B., Nugent, J. K., & Lester, B. M. (1987). Neonatal behavior assessment scale. In J. D. Osofsky (Ed.), *Handbook of infant development* (2nd ed.). New York: Wiley.

Brennan, P., Mednik, S., & Kandel, E. (1991). Congenital determinants of violent and property offending. In D. J. Pepler & K. H. Rubin (Eds.), *The development and treatment of childhood aggression.* Hillsdale, NJ: Erlbaum.

Brenner, J. B., & Cunningham, J. G. (1992). Gender differences in eating attitudes, body concept, and self-esteem among models. *Sex Roles, 27,* 413–437.

Bretherton, I., Golby, B., & Halvorsen, C. (1993, March). *Fathers as attachment and caregiving figures.* Paper presented at the meeting of the Society for Research in Child Development, New Orleans, LA.

Bretherton, I., Stolberg, U., & Kreye, M. (1981). Engaging strangers in proximal interaction: Infants' social initiative. *Developmental Psychology, 17,* 746–755.

Bretl, D. J., & Cantor, J. (1988). The portrayal of men and women in U.S. television commercials: A recent content analysis and trends over 15 years. *Sex Roles, 18,* 595–609.

Brice–Heath, S. (1988). Language socialization. In D. T. Slaughter (Ed.), *New directions for child development, No. 42. Black children and poverty: A developmental perspective.* San Francisco: Jossey–Bass.

Bridges, K. (1932). Emotional development in early infancy. *Child Development, 3,* 324–341.

British study finds leukemia risk in children of A-plant workers (1990, February 18). *New York Times,* p. A27.

Broberg, A. G. (1993). Inhibition and children's experiences of out-of-home care. In K. H. Rubin & J. B. Asendorpf (Eds.), *Social withdrawal, inhibition, and shyness in childhood.* Hillsdale, NJ: Erlbaum.

Brody, G. H., Stoneman, Z., & McCoy, J. K. (1992a). Associations of maternal and paternal direct and differential behavior with sibling relationships: Contemporaneous and longitudinal analyses. *Child Development, 63,* 82–92.

Brody, G. H., Stoneman, Z., McCoy, J. K., & Forehand, R. (1992b). Contemporaneous and longitudinal associations of sibling conflict with family relationship assessments and family discussions about sibling problems. *Child Development, 63,* 391–400.

Brody, J. E. (1990a, February 22). Bulimia and anorexia, insidious eating disorders that are best treated when detected early. *New York Times,* p. B9.

Brody, J. E. (1990b, May 24). Preventing children from joining yet another unfit generation. *New York Times,* p. B14.

Brody, J. E. (1990c, May 31). Children in sports: Tailoring activities to their abilities and needs will avoid pitfalls. *New York Times,* p. B8.

Brody, J. E. (1990d, November 1). Prenatal sonography: A diagnostic tool that can provide vital data in managing pregnancy. *New York Times,* p. B8.

Brody, J. E. (1991a, January 31). In pursuit of the best possible odds of preventing or minimizing the perils of major diseases. *New York Times,* p. B6.

Brody, J. E. (1991b, September 4). Averting a crisis when the offspring show symptoms of school phobia. *New York Times,* p. B7.

Brody, J. E. (1992a, January 29). Silence on fecal incontinence is harmful; from 1 to 2 percent of children over 4 have the problem. *New York Times,* p. B8.

Brody, J. E. (1992b, June 16). Suicide myths cloud efforts to save children. *New York Times,* pp. B5, 6.

Brody, J. E. (1992c, June 17). Psychotherapists warn parents not to dismiss their children's statements about suicide. *New York Times,* p. B8.

Brody, J. E. (1992d, November 18). Lead is public enemy no. 1 for American children. *New York Times,* p. B8.

Brody, J. E. (1993a, January 5). Gene link seen in drug abuse and depression. *New York Times,* p. B6.

Brody, J. E. (1993b, February 3). The trend toward inactivity continues with the unkindest cut of all: Children's fitness. *New York Times,* p. B7.

Brody, J. E. (1993c, February 18). The adult years are bringing new afflictions for 'DES babies', men as well as women. *New York Times,* p. B7.

Brody, J. E. (1993d, April 28). Modern certified midwives are leading a revolution in high-quality obstetric care. *New York Times,* p. B7.

Brody, J. E. (1993e, August 11). Skipping vaccinations puts children at risk. *New York Times,* p. C11.

Brody, J. E. (1993f, August 18). The time to head off osteoporosis, the nemesis of many older women, is in the teen-age years. *New York Times,* p. B7.

Brody, J. E. (1994, March 1). Folic acid emerges as a nutritional star. *New York Times,* pp. B7, 9.

Brody, L. R., Zelazo, P. R., & Chaika, H. (1984). Habituation–dishabituation to speech in the neonate. *Developmental Psychology, 20,* 114–119.

Broman, S. H. (1983). Obstetric medications. In C. C. Brown (Ed.), *Childhood learning disabilities and prenatal risk.* Skillman, NJ: Johnson & Johnson.

Bronfenbrenner, U. (1973). The dream of the kibbutz. In *Readings in human development.* Guilford, CT: Dushkin.

Bronfenbrenner, U. (1977). Toward an experimental ecology of human development. *American Psychologist, 32,* 513–531.

Bronfenbrenner, U. (1979). *The ecology of human development: Experiments by nature and design.* Cambridge, MA: Harvard University Press.

Bronfenbrenner, U. (1989). Ecological systems theory. In R. Vasta (Ed.), *Annals of child development* (Vol. 6). Greenwich, CT: JAI Press.

Bronson, G. W. (1990). Changes in infants' visual scanning across the 2- to 14-week age period. *Journal of Experimental Child Psychology, 49,* 101–125.

Bronson, G. W. (1991). Infant differences in rate of visual encoding. *Child Development, 62,* 44–54.

Bronstein, P., & Quina, K. (Eds.). (1988). *Teaching a psychology of people: Resources for gender and sociocultural awareness.* Washington, DC: American Psychological Association.

Brook, J. S., Whiteman, M., Cohen, P., & Tanaka, J. S. (1992). Childhood precursors of adolescent drug use: A longitudinal analysis. *Genetic, Social and General Psychology Monographs, 118,* 197–213.

Brook, J. S., Whiteman, M. M., & Finch, S. (1993). Childhood aggression, adolescent delinquency, and drug use: A longitudinal study. *Journal of Genetic Psychology, 153,* 369–383.

Brooks–Gunn, J. (1991a). Antecedents of maturational timing variations in adolescent girls. In R. M. Lerner, A. C. Petersen, & J. Brooks–Gunn (Eds.), *Encyclopedia of adolescence.* New York: Garland.

Brooks–Gunn, J. (1991b). Consequences of maturational timing variations in adolescent girls. In R. M. Lerner, A. C. Petersen, & J. Brooks–Gunn (Eds.), *Encyclopedia of adolescence.* New York: Garland.

Brooks–Gunn, J. (1991c). How stressful is the transition to adolescence for girls? In M. E. Colten & S. Gore (Eds.), *Adolescent stress: Causes and consequences.* New York: Aldine deGruyter.

Brooks–Gunn, J., & Chase–Lansdale, P. L. (1991). Adolescent childbearing: Effects on children. In R. M. Lerner, A. C. Petersen, & J. Brooks–Gunn (Eds.), *Encyclopedia of adolescence.* New York: Garland.

Brooks–Gunn, J., & Furstenberg, F. F. (1989). Adolescent sexual behavior. *American Psychologist, 44,* 249–257.

Brooks–Gunn, J., Klebanov, P. K., Liaw, F., & Spiker, D. (1993). Enhancing the development of low-birthweight, premature infants: Changes in cognition and behavior over the first three years. *Child Development, 64,* 736–768.

Brooks–Gunn, J., & Ruble, D. N. (1983). The experience of menarche from a developmental perspective. In J. Brooks–Gunn & A. C. Petersen (Eds.), *Girls at puberty.* New York: Plenum.

Brophy, J. (1986). Teacher influences on student achievement. *American Psychologist, 41,* 1069–1077.

Brophy, J. E. (1983). Research on the self-fulfilling prophecy and teacher expectations. *Journal of Educational Psychology, 75,* 631–661.

Brown, A. M. (1990). Development of visual sensitivity to light and color vision in human infants: A critical review. *Vision Research, 30,* 1159–1188.

Brown, B. B., Mounts, N., Lamborn, S. D., & Steinberg, L. (1993). Parenting practices and peer group affiliation in adolescence. *Child Development, 64,* 467–482.

Brown, L. M., & Gilligan, C. (1992). *Meeting at the crossroads: Women's psychology and girls' development.* Cambridge, MA: Harvard University Press.

Brown, R. (1973). *A first language: The early stages.* Cambridge, MA: Harvard University Press.

Brown, R. (1977). Introduction. In C. A. Snow & C. Ferguson (Eds.), *Talking to children.* New York: Cambridge University Press.

Brown, S. A., & Grimes, D. E. (1993). *Nurse practitioners and certified midwives: A meta-analysis of studies on nurses in primary care roles.* Washington, DC: American Nurses Publishing.

Brownell, C. A. (1988). Combinatorial skills: Converging developments over the second year. *Child Development, 59,* 675–685.

Brownell, C. A. (1990). Peer social skills in toddlers: Competencies and constraints illustrated by same-age and mixed-age interaction. *Child Development, 61,* 838–848.

Brownell, C. A., & Carriger, M. S. (1990). Changes in cooperation and self-other differentiation during the second year. *Child Development, 61,* 1164–1174.

Bruch, H. (1978). *The golden cage: The enigma of anorexia nervosa.* Cambridge, MA: Harvard University Press.

Bruck, M. (1993). Word recognition and component phonological processing skills of adults with childhood diagnosis of dyslexia. *Developmental Review, 13,* 258–268.

Brunk, M., Henggeler, S. W., & Whelan, J. P. (1987). Comparison of multisystemic therapy and parent training in the brief treatment of child abuse and neglect. *Journal of Consulting and Clinical Psychology, 55,* 171–178.

Brunswick, A. F. (1991). Health and substance use in adolescence: Ethnic and gender perspectives. In R. M. Lerner, A. C. Petersen, & J. Brooks–Gunn (Eds.), *Encyclopedia of adolescence.* New York: Garland.

Brush, S. G. (1991). Women in science and engineering. *American Scientist, 79,* 404–419.

Brustad, R. J. (1991). Children's perspectives on exercise and physical activity: Measurement issues and concerns. *Journal of School Health, 61,* 228–230.

Bryden, M. P., MacRae, L., & Steenhuis, R. E. (1991). Hand preference in school children. *Developmental Neuropsychology, 7,* 477–486.

Buchanan, C. M., Eccles, J. S., & Becker, J. B. (1992). Are adolescents the victims of raging hormones? Evidence for activational effects of hormones on moods and behavior at adolescence. *Psychological Bulletin, 111,* 62–107.

Buckhalt, J. A., Moracco, J. C., & Kiedinger, R. E. (1993, August). *Risk factors associated with substance use in adolescents.* Paper presented at the meeting of the American Psychological Association, Toronto.

Budd, K. S., McGraw, T. E., Farbisz, R., Murphy, T. B., Hawkins, D., Heilman, N., & Werle, M. (1992). Psychosocial concomitants of children's feeding disorders. *Journal of Pediatric Psychology, 17,* 81–94.

Bugental, D. B., Blue, J., & Cruzcosa, M. (1989). Perceived control over caregiving outcomes: Implications for child abuse. *Developmental Psychology, 25,* 532–539.

Bugental, D. B., Blue, J., & Lewis, J. (1990). Caregiver beliefs and dysphoric affect directed to difficult children. *Developmental Psychology, 26,* 631–638.

Buhrmester, D. (1992). The developmental courses of sibling and peer relationships. In F. Boar & J. Dunn (Eds.), *Children's sibling relationships: Developmental and clinical issues.* Hillsdale, NJ: Erlbaum.

Buhrmeister, D., Camparo, L., Christensen, A., Gonzalez, L. S., & Hinshaw, S. P. (1992). Mothers and fathers interacting in dyads and triads with normal and hyperactive sons. *Developmental Psychology, 28,* 500–509.

Buhrmester, D., & Furman, W. (1990). Perceptions of sibling relationships during middle childhood and adolescence. *Child Development, 61,* 1387–1398.

Bukowski, W. M., Gauze, C., Hoza, B., & Newcomb, A. F. (1993a). Differences and consistency between same-sex and other-sex peer relationships during early adolescence. *Developmental Psychology, 29,* 255–263.

Bukowski, W. M., Hoza, B., & Boivin, M. (1993b). Popularity, friendship and emotional adjustment during early adolescence. In B. Laursen (Ed.), *New directions in child development: No. 60. Close friendships in adolescence.* San Francisco: Jossey–Bass.

Bullock, M., & Lütkenhaus, P. (1990). Who am I? Self-understanding in toddlers. *Merrill–Palmer Quarterly, 36,* 217–238.

Buri, J. R., Louiselle, P. A., Misukanis, T. M., & Mueller, R. A. (1988). Effects of parental authoritarianism and authoritativeness of self-esteem. *Personality and Social Psychology Bulletin, 14,* 271–282.

Burke, P., & Puig–Antich, J. (1990). Psychobiology of childhood depression. In M. Lewis & S. M. Miller (Eds.), *Handbook of developmental psychopathology* (pp. 327–339). New York: Plenum.

Burros, M. (1991, June 12). A push is on to fight television ads that some call harmful to children's nutrition. *New York Times,* p. B8.

Busch–Rossnagel, N. A., & Zayas, L. H. (1991). Hispanic adolescents. In R. M. Lerner, A. C. Petersen, & J. Brooks–Gunn (Eds.), *Encyclopedia of adolescence.* New York: Garland.

Bushnell, E. W. (1993, June). *A dual-processing approach to cross-modal matching: Implications for development.* Paper presented at the Society for Research in Child Development, New Orleans, LA.

Bushnell, I. W. R., Sai, F., & Mullin, J. T. (1989). Neonatal recognition of the mother's face. *British Journal of Developmental Psychology, 7,* 3–15.

Bussey, K., & Bandura, A. (1984). Influence of gender constancy and social power on sex-linked modeling. *Journal of Personality and Social Psychology, 47,* 1292–1302.

Bussey, K., & Bandura, A. (1992). Self-regulatory mechanisms governing gender development. *Child Development, 63,* 1236–1250.

Butterfield, F. (1990, January). Why they excel. *Parade,* pp. 4–5.

Butterfield, F. (1992, January 1). Studies find a family link to criminality. *New York Times,* pp. A1, 8.

Butterfield, S.A., & Loovis, E. M. (1993). Influence of age, sex, balance, and sport participation on development of throwing by children in grades K–8. *Perceptual and Motor Skills, 76,* 459–464.

Butterworth, G. (1990). Self-perception in infancy. In D. Cicchetti & M. Beeghly (Eds.), *The self in transition.* Chicago: University of Chicago Press.

Byrne, J., Ellsworth, C., Bowering, E., & Vincer, M. (1993). Language development in low birth weight infants: The first two years of life. *Developmental and Behavioral Pediatrics, 14,* 21–27.

Caesarean delivery is found to lessen AIDS risk at birth. (1993, July 9). *New York Times,* p. A10.

Cairns, R. B., & Cairns, B. D. (1991). Social cognition and social networks: A developmental perspective. In D. J. Pepler & K. H. Rubin (Eds.), *The development and treatment of childhood aggression.* Hillsdale, NJ: Erlbaum.

Caldera, Y. M., Huston, A. C., & O'Brien, M. (1989). Social interactions and play patterns of parents and toddlers with feminine, masculine, and neutral toys. *Child Development, 60,* 70–76.

Camara, K. A., & Resnick, G. (1989). Styles of conflict and cooperation between divorced parents: Effects on child behavior and adjustment. *American Journal of Orthopsychiatry, 59,* 560–575.

Camarena, P. M. (1991). Conformity in adolescence. In R. M. Lerner, A. C. Petersen, & J. Brooks–Gunn (Eds.), *Encyclopedia of adolescence.* New York: Garland.

Cambor, R. L., & Millman, R. B. (1991). Alcohol and drug abuse in adolescents. In M. Lewis (Ed.), *Child and adolescent psychiatry: A comprehensive textbook.* Baltimore: Williams & Wilkins.

Campbell, F. A., & Bryant, D. M. (1993, March). *Growing into a wider world: Transition from Head Start to kindergarten in Chapel Hill–Carrboro.* Paper presented at the meeting of the Society for Research in Child Development, New Orleans, LA.

Campbell, F. A., & Ramey, C. T. (1993, March). *Mid-adolescent outcomes for high-risk students: An examination of the continuing effects of early intervention.* Paper presented at the meeting of the Society for Research in Child Development, New Orleans, LA.

Campbell, S. B. (1990). *Behavior problems in preschool children: Clinical and developmental issues.* New York: Guilford.

Campbell, S. B., & Cohn, J. F. (1991). Prevalence and correlates of postpartum depression in first-time mothers. *Journal of Abnormal Psychology, 100,* 594–599.

Campbell, S. B., Cohn, J. F., Flanagan, C., Popper, S., & Meyers, T. (1992). Course and correlates of postpartum depression during the transition to parenthood. *Development and Psychopathology, 4,* 29–47.

Campbell, S. B., Cohn, J. F., Meyers, T. A., Ross, S., & Flanagan, C. (1993, March). *Chronicity of maternal depression and mother–infant interaction.* Paper presented at the meeting of the Society for Research in Child Development, New Orleans, LA.

Campbell, S. B., Pierce, E. W., March, C. L., & Ewing, L. J. (1991). Noncompliant behavior, overactivity, and family stress as predictors of negative maternal control with preschool children. *Development and Psychopathology, 3,* 175–190.

Campo, A. T., & Rohner, R. P. (1992). Relationships between perceived parental acceptance–rejection, psychological adjustment, and substance abuse among young adults. *Child Abuse and Neglect, 16,* 429–440.

Campos, J. J., Hiatt, S., Ramsey, D., Henderson, C., & Svejda, M. (1978). The emergence of fear on the visual cliff. In M. Lewis & L. Rosenblum (Eds.), *The origins of affect.* New York: Plenum.

Campos, J. J., Langer, A., & Krowitz, A. (1970). Cardiac responses on the visual cliff in prelocomotor human infants. *Science, 170,* 196–197.

Camras, L. A., Campos, J. J., Oster, H., Miyake, K., & Bradshaw, D. (1992). Japanese and American infants' responses to arm restraint. *Developmental Psychology, 28,* 578–583.

Camras, L. A., & Sachs, V. B. (1991). Social referencing and caretaker expressive behavior in a day care setting. *Infant Behavior and Development, 14,* 27–36.

Camras, L. A., Sullivan, J., & Michel, G. (1993, Fall). Do infants express discrete emotions?: Adult judgments of facial, vocal, and body actions. *Journal of Nonverbal Behavior, 17,* 171–186.

Cannon, G. S. Idol, L., & West, J. F. (1992). Educating students with mild handicaps in general classrooms: Essential teaching practices for general and special educators. *Journal of Learning Disabilities, 25,* 300–317.

Cantwell, D. P. (1990). Depression across the early life span. In M. Lewis & S. M. Miller (Eds.), *Handbook of developmental psychopathology.* New York: Plenum.

Cantwell, D. P., & Baker, L. (1991a). Association between attention deficit-hyperactivity disorder and learning disorders. *Journal of Learning Disabilities, 24,* 88–95.

Cantwell, D. P., & Baker, L. (1991b). Manifestations of depressive affect in adolescence. *Journal of Youth and Adolescence, 20,* 121–133.

Capaldi, D. M., & Dishion, T. J. (1993, March). *The relation of conduct problems and depressive symptoms to growth in substance use in adolescent boys.* Paper presented at the meeting of the Society for Research in Child Development, New Orleans, LA.

Capaldi, M. D., & Patterson, G. R. (1991). Relation of parental transitions to boys' adjustment problems: I. A linear hypothesis. II. Mothers at risk for transitions and unskilled parenting. *Developmental Psychology, 22,* 489–504.

Caplan, M., Vespo, J., Pedersen, J., & Hale, D. F. (1991). Conflict and its resolution in small groups of one-and-two-year-olds. *Child Development, 62,* 1513–1524.

Caplan, M., Weissberg, R. P. Grober, J. S., Sivo, P. J., Grady, K., & Jacoby, C. (1992). Social competence promotion with inner-city and suburban young adolescents: Effects on social adjustment and alcohol use. *Journal of Consulting and Clinical Psychology, 60,* 56–63.

Caplan, M. Z., & Hay, D. F. (1989). Preschoolers' responses to peers' distress and beliefs about bystander intervention. *Journal of Child Psychology and Psychiatry, 30,* 231–242.

Caplan, N., Choy, M. H., & Whitmore, J. K. (1992). Indochinese refugee families and academic achievement. *Scientific American,* 36–42.

Caplan, P. J., & Caplan, J. B. (1994). *Thinking critically about research on sex and gender.* New York: HarperCollins.

Caplan, P. J., & Larkin, J. (1991). The anatomy of dominance and self-protection. *American Psychologist, 46,* 536.

Capute, A. J., Shapiro, B. K., Palmer, F. B., Ross, A., & Wachtel, R. C. (1985). Normal gross motor development: The influences of race, sex and socioeconomic status. *Developmental Medicine and Child Neurology, 27,* 635–643.

Cardon, L. R., Fulker, D. W., DeFries, J. C., & Plomin, R. (1992). Continuity and change in general cognitive ability from 1 to 7 years of age. *Developmental Psychology, 28,* 64–73.

Carlo, G., Knight, G. P., Eisenberg, N., & Rotenberg, K. (1991). Cognitive processes and prosocial behaviors among children: The role of affective attributions and reconciliations. *Developmental Psychology, 27,* 456–461.

Carlson, C. L., Pelham, W. E., Jr., Milich, R., & Dixon, J. (1992). Single and combined effects of methylphenidate and behavior therapy on the classroom performance of children with attention-deficit hyperactivity disorder. *Journal of Abnormal Child Psychology, 20,* 213–232.

Caron, A. J., Caron, R. F., & Carlson, V. R. (1979). Infant perception of the invariant shape of objects varying in slant. *Child Development, 50,* 716–721.

Carr, M., Borkowski, J. G., & Maxwell, S. E. (1991). Motivational components of underachievement. *Developmental Psychology, 27,* 108–118.

Carson, J., Burks, V., & Parke, R. D. (1993). Parent–child physical play: Determinants and consequences. In K. MacDonald (Ed.), *Parent–child play: Descriptions and implications.* Albany, NY: SUNY Press.

Carson, S. (1988). Sex selection: The ultimate in family planning. *Fertility and Sterility, 50,* 16–19.

Caruso, G. L. (1992, September). Patterns of maternal employment and child care for a sample of two-year-olds. *Journal of Family Issues, 13,* 297–311.

Casaer, P. (1993). Old and new facts about perinatal brain development. *Journal of Child Psychology and Psychiatry, 34,* 101–109.

Case, R. (1985). *Intellectual development: Birth to adulthood.* New York: Academic Press.

Case, R. (1992). *The mind's staircase: Exploring the conceptual underpinnings of children's thought and knowledge.* Hillsdale, NJ: Erlbaum.

Caspi, A., Elder, G. H., Jr., & Bem, D. J. (1987). Moving against the world: Life-course patterns of explosive children. *Developmental Psychology, 23,* 308–313.

Caspi, A., Lynam, D., Moffitt, T. E., & Silva, P. A. (1993). Unraveling girls' delinquency: Biological, dispositional, and contextual contributions to adolescent misbehavior. *Developmental Psychology, 29,* 19–30.

Caspi, A., & Moffitt, T. E. (1991). Individual differences are accentuated during periods of social change: The sample case of girls at puberty. *Journal of Personality and Social Psychology, 61,* 157–168.

Cassidy, J. (1988). Child–mother attachment and the self in six-year-olds. *Child Development, 59,* 121–134.

Cassidy, J., & Asher, S. R. (1992). Loneliness and peer relations in young children. *Child Development, 63,* 350–365.

Cassill, K. (1982). *Twins reared apart.* New York: Atheneum.

Cattell, R. B. (1949). *The culture-free intelligence test.* Champaign, IL: Institute for Personality and Ability Testing.

Caughy, M. O., DiPietro, J. A., & Strobino, D. M. (in press). Daycare participation as a protective factor in the cognitive development of low-income children. *Child Development.*

Cauley, K., & Tyler, B. (1989). The relationship of self-concept to prosocial behavior in

children. *Early Childhood Research Quarterly, 4,* 51–60.
Cebello, R., & Olson, S. L. (1993, March). *The role of alternative caregivers in the lives of children from poor, single-parent families.* Paper presented at the meeting of the Society for Research in Child Development, New Orleans, LA.
Ceci, S. J. (1991). How much does schooling influence general intelligence and its cognitive components? A reassessment of the evidence. *Developmental Psychology, 21,* 703–722.
Ceci, S. J. (1993, August). *Cognitive and social factors in children's testimony.* Master lecture presented at the meeting of the American Psychological Association, Toronto.
Ceci, S. J., & Bruck, M. (1993). Suggestibility of the child witness: A historical review and synthesis. *Psychological Bulletin, 113,* 403–439.
Celis, W. (1991a, November 27). Bilingual teaching: A new focus on both tongues. *New York Times,* p. A11.
Celis, W. (1991b, December 31). As fewer students drink, abuse of alcohol persists. *New York Times,* pp. A1, 8.
Celis, W. (1992, June 10). Educators focus on the forgotten years: The middle grades. *New York Times,* p. B8.
Center for the Study of Social Policy. (1993). *Kids count data book.* Washington, DC: Author.
Center, Y., Ward, J., & Ferguson, C. (1991). Towards an index to evaluate the integration of children with disabilities into regular classes. *Educational Psychology, 11,* 77–95.
Centers for Disease Control. (1991). Attempted suicide among high school students—United States, 1990. *Morbidity and Mortality Weekly Report, 40,* 633–635.
Centers for Disease Control. (1993). Infant mortality—United States, 1990. *Morbidity and Mortality Weekly Report, 42,* 161–165.
Cernoch, J., & Porter, R. (1985). Recognition of maternal axillary odors by infants. *Child Development, 56,* 1593–1598.
Chalfant, J. C. (1989). Learning disabilities: Policy issues and promising approaches. *American Psychologist, 44,* 392–398.
Chapman, M., & McBride, M. C. (1992). Beyond competence and performance: Children's class inclusion strategies, superordinate class cues, and verbal justifications. *Developmental Psychology, 28,* 319–327.
Chapman, M., Skinner, E. A., & Baltes, P. B. (1990). Interpreting correlations between children's perceived control and cognitive performance: Control, agency, or means–ends beliefs? *Developmental Psychology, 26,* 246–253.
Chase–Lansdale, P. L., & Hetherington, E. M. (1990). The impact of divorce on life-span development: Short- and long-term effects. In P. B. Baltes, D. L. Featherman, & R. M. Lerner (Eds.), *Life-span development and behavior.* Hillsdale, NJ: Erlbaum.
Chasnoff, I. J., Griffith, D.R., Freier, C., & Murray, J. (1992). Cocaine/polydrug use in pregnancy: Two-year follow-up. *Pediatrics, 89,* 284–289.
Chassin, L., & Barrera, M., Jr. (1993, March). *Substance use escalation and substance use restraint among adolescent children of alcoholics.* Paper presented at the meeting of the Society for Research in Child Development, New Orleans, LA.
Chavez, E. L., & Swain, R. C. (1992). An epidemiological comparison of Mexican-American and white non-Hispanic 8th- and 12th-grade students' substance use. *American Journal of Public Health, 82,* 445–447.
Chemical linked to binge eating. (1993, May 28). *New York Times,* p. A12.
Chen, C., & Stevenson, H. W. (1993, March). *Motivation and mathematics achievement of Asian-American high school students.* Paper presented at the meeting of the Society for Research in Child Development, New Orleans, LA.
Chen, X., Rubin, K. H., & Sun, Y. (1992). Social reputation and peer relationships in Chinese and Canadian children: A cross-cultural study. *Child Development, 63,* 1336–1343.
Cherlin, A. J., Furstenberg, F. F., Chase–Lansdale, P. L., Kierna, K. E., Robins, P. K., Morrison, D. R., & Teitler, J. O. (1991). Longitudinal studies of effects of divorce on children in Great Britain and the United States. *Science, 252,* 1386–1389.
Chess, S., & Thomas, A. (1984). *Origins and evolution of behavior disorders: From infancy to early adult life.* New York: Brunner/Mazel.
Chess, S., & Thomas, A. (1991). Temperament. In M. Lewis (Ed.), *Child and adolescent psychiatry: A comprehensive textbook.* Baltimore: Williams & Wilkins.
Chi, M. T. H. (1978). Knowledge structures and memory development. In R. S. Siegler (Ed.), *Children's thinking: What develops?* Hillsdale, NJ: Erlbaum.
Chicago student wins top science prize. (1993, March 9). *New York Times,* p. A9.
Child safety seats. (1992, January). *Consumer Reports,* pp. 16–20.
The children of the shadows: Shaping young lives (1993, April 4). *New York Times,* p. 17.
Children's Defense Fund (1992a). *The health of America's children 1992.* Washington, DC: Author.
Children's Defense Fund (1992b). *The state of America's children 1992.* Washington, DC: Author.
Chilmonczyk, B. A., Salmun, L. M., Megathlin, K. N., Neveux, L. M., Palomaki, G. E., Knight, G. J., Pulkkinen, A. J., & Haddow, J. E. (1993). Association between exposure to environmental tobacco smoke and exacerbations of asthma in children. *New England Journal of Medicine, 328,* 1665–1669.
Chipman, S. F., Krantz, D. H., & Silver, R. (1992). Mathematics anxiety and science careers among able college women. *Psychological Science, 3,* 292–295.
Chira, S., (1989, November 15). "Sesame Street" at 20: Taking stock of learning. *New York Times,* p. B13.
Chira, S. (1991, December 8). Report says too many aren't ready for school. *New York Times,* p. B18.
Chira, S. (1992a, February 12). Bias against girls is found rife in schools, with lasting damage. *New York Times,* pp. A1, B6.
Chira, S. (1992b, March 4). New Head Start studies raise question on help: Should fewer get more? *New York Times,* p. B9.
Chira, S. (1993a, May 19). When disabled students enter regular classrooms. *New York Times,* pp. A1, B8.
Chira, S. (1993b, July 14). Is small better? Educators now say yes for high school. *New York Times,* pp. A1, 10.
Chira, S. (1993c, July 20). Student poll finds wide use of guns. *New York Times,* p. A6.
Chisholm, J. S. (1983). *Navajo infancy.* New York: Aldine de Gruyter.
Chomsky, N. (1988). *Language and problems of knowledge.* Cambridge, MA: MIT Press.
Chomsky, N. (1990). On the nature, use and acquisition of language. In W. G. Lycan (Ed.), *Mind and cognition.* Oxford: Blackwell.
Christie, J. F., & Wardle, F. (1992, March). How much time is needed for play? *Young Children,* 28–32.
Christophersen, E. R. (1989). Injury control. *American Psychologist, 44,* 237–241.
Chusmir, L. H., & Koberg, C. S. (1986). Creativity differences among managers. *Journal of Vocational Behavior, 29,* 240–253.
Cicchetti, D., & Barnett, D. (1991). Attachment organization in maltreated preschoolers. *Development and Psychopathology, 3,* 397–411.
Cicchetti, D., & Beeghly, M. (Eds.). (1990). *Children with Down syndrome: A developmental perspective.* Cambridge: Cambridge University Press.
Clark, E. V. (1973). What's in a word? On the child's acquisition of semantics in his first language. In E. Moore (Ed.), *Cognitive development and the acquisition of language.* New York: Academic Press.
Clark, E. V. (1975). Knowledge, context, and strategy in the acquisition of meaning. In D. P. Date (Ed.), *Georgetown University roundtable on language and linguistics.* Washington, DC: Georgetown University Press.
Clark, M. L., & Bittle, M. L. (1992). Friendship expectations and the evaluation of present friendships in middle childhood and early adolescence. *Child Study Journal, 22,* 115–135.
Clark, R. (1983). *Family life and school achievement: Why poor black children succeed or fail.* Chicago: University of Chicago Press.
Clark–Lempers, D. S., Lempers, J. D., & Ho, C. (1991). Early, middle, and late adolescents' perceptions of their relationships with significant others. *Journal of Adolescent Research, 6,* 296–315.

Clarke–Stewart, K. A. (1990). The 'effects' of infant day care reconsidered: Risks for parents, children, and researchers. In N. Fox & G. G. Fein (Eds.), *Infant day care: The current debate.* Norwood, NJ: Ablex.

Clarke–Stewart, K. A. (1989). Infant day care: Maligned or malignant? *American Psychologist, 44,* 266–273.

Clarke–Stewart, K. A. (1991). A home is not a school: The effects of child care on children's development. *Journal of Social Issues, 47,* 105–123.

Clarkson, M. G., Clifton, R. K., & Morrongiello, B.A. (1985). The effects of sound duration on newborns' head orientation. *Journal of Experimental Child Psychology, 39,* 20–36.

Clayton, S. (1991). Gender differences in psychosocial determinants of adolescent smoking. *Journal of School Health, 61,* 115–120.

Clements, M. (1993, May 16). What's wrong with our schools? *Parade,* pp. 4–5.

Clermont, C. M. (1990). Television and development. In R. M. Thomas (Ed.), *The encyclopedia of human development and education: Theory, research, and studies.* Oxford: Pergamon.

Clewell, B. C. (1991). Increase in minority and female participation in math and science: The importance of the middle school years. In R. M. Lerner, A. C. Petersen, & J. Brooks–Gunn (Eds.), *Encyclopedia of adolescence.* New York: Garland.

Clopton, N. A., & Sorell, G. T. (1993). Gender differences in moral reasoning. *Psychology of Women Quarterly, 17,* 85–101.

Cnattingius, S., Forman, M. R., Berendes, H. W., & Isotalo, L. (1992). Delayed childbearing and risk of adverse perinatal outcome. *Journal of the American Medical Association, 268,* 886–890.

Coates, D. C., & Van Widenfelt, B. (1991). Pregnancy in adolescence. In R. M. Lerner, A. C. Petersen, & J. Brooks–Gunn (Eds.), *Encyclopedia of adolescence.* New York: Garland.

Cocaine-using fathers linked to birth defects. (1991, October 15). *New York Times,* p. C5.

Cochi, S. L., Edmonds, L. E., Dyer, K., Greaves, W. L., Marks, J. S., Rovira, E. Z., Preblud, S. R., & Orenstein, W. A. (1989). Congenital rubella syndrome in the United States 1970–1985: On the verge of elimination. *American Journal of Epidemiology, 129,* 349–361.

Cohen, L. B., DeLoache, J. S., & Strauss, M. S. (1979). Infant visual perception. In J. D. Osofsky (Ed.), *Handbook of infant development.* New York: Wiley.

Cohen, P., Brook, J. S., & Kandel, D. B. (1991). Predictors and correlates of adolescent drug use. In R. M. Lerner, A. C. Petersen, & J. Brooks–Gunn (Eds.), *Encyclopedia of adolescence.* New York: Garland.

Cohn, L. D. & Adlers, N. E. (1992). Female and male perceptions of ideal body shapes: Distorted views among Caucasian college students. *Psychology of Women Quarterly, 16,* 69–79.

Coie, J. D., & Cillessen, A. H. N. (1993). Peer rejection: Origins and effects on children's development. *Current Directions in Psychological Science, 2,* 89–92.

Coie, J. D., Dodge, K. A., Terry, R., & Wright, V. (1991). The role of aggression in peer relations: An analysis of aggression episodes in boys' play groups. *Child Development, 62,* 812–826.

Coie, J. D., & Koeppl, G. K. (1990). Adapting intervention to the problems of aggressive and disruptive rejected children. In S. R. Asher & J. D. Coie (Eds.), *Peer rejection in childhood.* Cambridge: Cambridge University Press.

Colby, A., Kohlberg, L. Gibbs, J., & Lieberman, M. (1983). A longitudinal study of moral judgment. *Monographs of the Society for Research in Child Development, 48*(4, Serial No. 200).

Cole, D. A. (1991a). Adolescent suicide. In R. M. Lerner, A. C. Petersen, & J. Brooks–Gunn (Eds.), *Encyclopedia of adolescence.* New York: Garland.

Cole, D. A. (1991b). Change in self-perceived competence as a function of peer and teacher evaluation. *Developmental Psychology, 27,* 682–688.

Cole, K. N., Mills, P. E., Dale, P. S., & Jenkins, J. R. (1991). Effects of preschool integration for children with disabilities. *Exceptional Children, 58,* 36–45.

Cole, M. (1992). Culture in development. In M. H. Bornstein & M. E. Lamb (Eds.), *Developmental psychology: An advanced textbook* (3rd ed.). Hillsdale, NJ: Erlbaum.

Coles, C. D., Platzman, K. A., Smith, I. E., James, M. E., & Falek, A. (1992). Effects of cocaine and alcohol use in pregnancy on neonatal growth and neurobehavioral status. *Neurotoxicology and Teratology, 14,* 23–33.

Coles, R., & Stokes, G. (1985). *Sex and the American teenager.* New York: Harper & Row.

Coley, J. D. (1993, March). *Parental feedback to child labeling as input to conceptual development.* Paper presented at the meeting of the Society for Research in Child Development, New Orleans, LA.

Collins, W. A. (1984a). Conclusion: The status of basic research on middle childhood. In W. A. Collins (Ed.), *Development during middle childhood: The years from six to twelve.* Washington, DC: National Academy Press.

Collins, W. A. (1984b). Introduction. In W. A. Collins (Ed.), *Development during middle childhood: The years from six to twelve.* Washington, DC: National Academy Press.

Collins, W. A. (1990). Parent–child relationships in the transition to adolescence: Continuity and change in interaction, affect, and cognition. In R. Montemayor, G. R. Adams, & T. P. Gullotta (Eds.), *From childhood to adolescence: A transitional period.* Newbury Park, CA: Sage.

Collins, W. A., & Gunnar, M. R. (1990). Social and personality development. *Annual Review of Psychology, 41,* 387–416.

Collins, W. A., & Russell, G. (1991). Mother–child and father–child relationships in middle childhood and adolescence: A developmental analysis. *Developmental Review, 11,* 99–136.

Colombo, J. (1993). *Infant cognition.* Newbury Park, CA: Sage.

Colombo, J., Moss, M., & Horowitz, F. D. (1989). Neonatal state profiles: Reliability and short-term predictions of neurobehavioral status. *Child Development, 60,* 1102–1110.

Colyar, D. E. (1991). Residential care and treatment of youths with conduct disorders: Conclusions of a conference of childcare workers. *Child and Youth Care Forum, 20,* 195–204.

Comstock, G., & Paik, H. (1991). *Television and the American child.* San Diego: Academic Press.

Condon, W. S., & Sander, L. W. (1974). Synchrony demonstrated between movements of the neonate and adult speech. *Child Development, 45,* 456–462.

Condry, J., Scheibe, C., Bahrt, A., & Potts, K. (1993, March). *Children's television before and after the Children's Television Act of 1990.* Paper presented at the meeting of the Society for Research on Child Development, New Orleans, LA.

Conel, J. L. (1959). *The postnatal development of the human cerebral cortex.* Cambridge, MA: Harvard University Press.

Conger, R. D., Conger, K. J., Elder, G. H., Jr., Lorenz, F. O., Simons, R. L., & Whitbeck, L. B. (1993a). Family economic stress and adjustment of early adolescent girls. *Developmental Psychology, 29,* 206–219.

Conger, R. D., Rueter, M. R., & Conger, K. J. (1993b, March). *Adolescent vulnerability to alcohol use and abuse: The role of family stress, older sibs, and ineffective parenting.* Paper presented at the meeting of the Society for Research in Child Development, New Orleans, LA.

Connolly, C., & Corbett–Dick, P. (1990). Eating disorders: A framework for school nursing initiatives. *Journal of School Health, 60,* 401–405.

Cook, T. D., Appleton, H., Conner, R., Shaffer, A., Tamkin, G., Weber, J. J. (1975). *"Sesame Street" revisited: A study in evaluation research.* New York: Russell Sage Foundation.

Coombs, R. H., Paulson, M. J., & Richardson, M. A. (1991). Peer vs. parental influence in substance use among Hispanic and Anglo children and adolescents. *Journal of Youth and Adolescence, 20,* 73–88.

Coon, H., Carey, G., Corley, R., & Fulker, D. W. (1992). Identifying children in the Colorado adoption project at risk for conduct disorder. *Journal of the American Academy of Child and Adolescent Psychiatry, 31,* 503–511.

Coon, H., Fulker, D. W., & DeFries, J. C. (1990). Home environment and cognitive ability of 7-year-old children in the Colorado adoption project: Genetic and environmental etiologies. *Developmental Psychology, 26,* 459–468.

Coons, S., & Guilleminault, C. (1982). Development of sleep–wake patterns and non-rapid-eye-movement sleep stages during the first six months of life in normal infants. *Pediatrics, 69,* 793–798.

Cooper, R. P., & Aslin, R. N. (1990). Preference for infant-directed speech in the first month after birth. *Child Development, 61,* 1584–1595.

Coopersmith, S. (1967). *The antecedents of self-esteem.* San Francisco: W. H. Freeman.

Coplan, R. J., Rubin, K. H., Fox, N. A., Calkins, S. D., & Stewart, S. L. (1994). Being alone, playing alone, and acting alone: Distinguishing among reticence, and passive-, and active-solitude in young children. *Child Development, 65,* 129–137.

Coren, S. (1990). (Ed.). *Left-handedness: Behavioral implications and anomalies.* Amsterdam: North–Holland.

Coren, S. (1992). *The left-hander syndrome.* New York: Free Press.

Coren, S., & Halpern, D. F. (1991). Left-handedness: A marker for decreased survival fitness. *Psychological Bulletin, 109,* 90–106.

Coren, S., & Searleman, A. (1990). Birth stress and left-handedness: The rare trait marker model. In S. Coren (Ed.), *Left-handedness: Behavior implications and anomalies.* Amsterdam: North–Holland.

Cornell, D. G. (1990). High ability students who are unpopular with their peers. *Gifted Child Quarterly, 34,* 155–160.

Corsaro, W. A., & Eder, D. (1990). Children's peer cultures. *Annual Review of Sociology, 16,* 197–220.

Cossette, L., Malcuit, G., & Pomerleau, A. (1991). Sex differences in motor activity during early infancy. *Infant Behavior and Development, 14,* 175–186.

Costin, S. E., & Jones, D. C. (1992). Friendship as a facilitator of emotional responsiveness and prosocial interventions among young children. *Developmental Psychology, 28,* 941–947.

Courage, M. L., & Adams, R. J. (1993, March). *Infant peripheral vision: The development of spatial resolution in the early months of life.* Paper presented at the meeting of the Society for Research in Child Development, New Orleans, LA.

Covey, L. A., & Feltz, D. L. (1991). Physical activity and adolescent female psychological development. *Journal of Youth and Adolescence, 20,* 463–474.

Cowan, C. P. (1992). *When partners become parents.* New York: Basic Books.

Cowan, P. A. (1978). *Piaget with feeling.* New York: Holt, Rinehart and Winston.

Cowley, G. (1993, June 21). What if a cure is far off? *Newsweek,* p. 70.

Cox, M. J., Owen, M. T., Henderson, V. K., & Margand, N. A. (1992). Prediction of infant–father and infant–mother attachment. *Developmental Psychology, 28,* 474–483.

Cox, R. D., & Schopler, E. (1991). Social skills training for children. In M. Lewis (Ed.), *Child and adolescent psychiatry.* Baltimore: Williams & Wilkins.

Crain, W. C. (1992). *Theories of development: Concepts and applications* (3rd ed.). Englewood Cliffs, NJ: Prentice Hall.

Crain–Thoreson, C., & Dale, P. S. (1992). Do early talkers become early readers? Linguistic precocity, preschool language, and emergent literacy. *Developmental Psychology, 28,* 421–429.

Cramer, J., & Oshima, T. C. (1992). Do gifted females attribute their math performance differently than other students? *Journal for the Education of the Gifted, 16,* 18–35.

Cramer, P., & Skidd, J. E. (1992). Correlates of self-worth in preschoolers: The role of gender-stereotyped styles of behavior. *Sex Roles, 26,* 369–390.

Cratty, B. (1986). *Perceptual and motor development in infants and children* (3rd ed.). Englewood Cliffs, NJ: Prentice Hall.

Crick, N. R., & Ladd, G. W. (1993). Children's perceptions of their peer experiences: Attributions, loneliness, social, anxiety, and social avoidance. *Developmental Psychology, 29,* 244–254.

Crittenden, P. M., & Ainsworth, M. D. S. (1989). Child maltreatment and attachment theory. In D. Cicchetti & V. Carlson (Eds.), *Child maltreatment: Theory and research on the causes and consequences of child abuse and neglect.* Cambridge: Cambridge University Press.

Crnic, K. A., Ragozin, A. S., Greenberg, M. T., Robinson, M. N., & Basham, R. B. (1983). Social interaction and developmental competence of preterm and full-term infants during the first year of life. *Child Development, 54,* 1199–1210.

Crockenberg, S., & Litman, C. (1990). Autonomy as competence in 2-year-olds: Maternal correlates of child defiance, compliance, and self-assertion. *Developmental Psychology, 26,* 961–971.

Crockenberg, S. B., & Smith, P. (1982). Antecedents of mother-infant interaction and infant irritability in the first three months of life. *Infant Behavior and Development, 5,* 105–119.

Crombie, G., & Desjardins, M. J. (1993, March). *Predictors of gender: The relative importance of children's play, games, and personality characteristics.* Paper presented at the meeting of the Society for Research in Child Development, New Orleans, LA.

Crook, C. K., & Lipsitt, L. P. (1976). Neonatal nutritive sucking: Effects of taste stimulation upon sucking rhythm and heart rate. *Child Development, 47,* 518–522.

Crosby, F. J. (1991). *Juggling.* New York: Free Press.

Cross, W. (1991). *Shades of identity.* Philadelphia: Temple University Press.

Crouter, A., & McHale, S. (1989, April). *Childrearing in dual- and single-earner families: Implications for the development of school-age children.* Paper presented at the meeting of the Society for Research in Child Development, Kansas City, MO.

Crowe, H. P., & Zeskind, P. S. (1992). Psychophysiological and perceptual response to infant cries varying in pitch: Comparison of adults with low and high scores on the child abuse potential inventory. *Child Abuse and Neglect, 16,* 19–29.

Crowell, J. A., & Waters, E. (1990). Separation anxiety. In M. Lewis and S. M. Miller (Eds.), *Handbook of developmental psychopathology.* New York: Plenum.

Csikszentmihalyi, M., & Larson, R. (1984). *Being adolescent.* New York: Basic Books.

Cummings, M. R. (1991). *Human heredity: Principles and issues* (2nd ed.). St. Paul, MN: West.

Cunningham, F. G., & Gilstrap, L. C. (1991). Maternal serum alpha-fetoprotein screening. *New England Journal of Medicine, 325,* 55–57.

Curtiss, S. (1977). *Genie: A psycholinguistic study of a modern-day "wild child".* New York: Academic Press.

Cutrona, C. E., & Troutman, B. R. (1986). Social support, infant temperament, and parenting self-efficacy: A mediational model of postpartum depression. *Child Development, 57,* 1507–1518.

Dabrowski, R. M., Emshoff, J. G., Lewis, M. D. & Maguire, M. A. (1992, August). *Examining the effectiveness of a substance abuse prevention program for adolescents.* Paper presented at the meeting of the American Psychological Association, Washington, DC.

Dacey, C. M., Nelson, W. M., & Aikman, K. G. (1990). Prevalency rate and personality comparisons of bulimic and normal adolescents. *Child Psychiatry and Human Development, 20,* 243–251.

Dacey, C. M., Nelson, W. M., Clark, V. F., & Aikinan, K. G. (1991). Bulimia and body image dissatisfaction in adolescence. *Child Psychiatry and Human Development, 21,* 179–183.

Daley, S. (1991, January 19). Girls' self-esteem is lost on way to adolescence, new study finds. *New York Times,* pp. B1, 6.

Damon, W. (1977). *The social world of the child.* San Francisco: Jossey–Bass.

Damon, W. (1988). *The moral child.* New York: The Free Press.

Damon, W. (1991). Adolescent self-concept. In R. M. Lerner, A. C. Petersen, & J. Brooks–Gunn (Eds.), *Encyclopedia of adolescence.* New York: Garland.

Damon, W., & Hart, D. (1992). Self-understanding and its role in social and moral development. In M. H. Bornstein & M. E. Lamb (Eds.), *Developmental psychology: An advanced textbook.* Hillsdale, NJ: Erlbaum.

Danner, F., Noland, F., McFadden, M., Dewalt, K., & Kotchen, J. M. (1991). Description of the physical activity of young children using movement sensor and observation methods. *Pediatric Exercise Science, 3,* 11–20.

Darden, E. C., & Zimmerman, T. S. (1992). Blended families: A decade review, 1979 to 1990. *Family Therapy, 19,* 25–31.

Dasen, P. R. (Ed.). (1977). *Piagetian psychology: Cross-cultural contributions.* New York: Gardner.

Davey, L. F. (1993, March). *Developmental implications of shared and divergent perceptions in the parent–adolescent relationship.* Paper presented at the meeting of the Society for Research in Child Development, New Orleans, LA.

Davidson, E. C., Jr., & Fukushima, T. (1992). The racial disparity in infant mortality. *New England Journal of Medicine, 327,* 1022–1024.

Davidson, E. S., Yasuna, A., & Tower, A. (1979). The effects of television cartoons on sex-role stereotyping in young girls. *Child Development, 50,* 597–600.

Davidson, L. M., & Baum, A. (1990). Posttraumatic stress in children following natural and human-made trauma. In M. Lewis & S. M. Miller (Eds.), *Handbook of developmental psychopathology.* New York: Plenum.

Davis, A. (1991). Piaget, teachers and education: Into the 1990's. In P. Light, S. Sheldon, & M. Woodhead (Eds.), *Learning to think.* New York: Rutledge.

DeAngelis, T. (1990, December). Who is susceptible to bulimia, and why? *APA Monitor,* p. 8.

DeAngelis, T. (1992, April). Conference explores issues of giftedness. *APA Monitor,* pp. 42–43.

DeAngelis, T. (1993, July). Science meets practice on PKU studies' findings. *APA Monitor,* pp. 16–17.

DeBaryshe, B. D., Patterson, G. R., & Capaldi, D. M. (1993). A performance model for academic achievement in early adolescent boys. *Developmental Psychology, 29,* 795–804.

DeBell, C. (1993, August). *Occupational gender-role stereotyping in television commercials: A nine-year longitudinal study.* Paper presented at the meeting of the American Psychological Association, Toronto.

de Boysson–Bardies, B., Halle, P., Sogart, L., & Durand, C. (1989). A crosslinguistic investigation of vowel formants in babbling. *Journal of Child Language, 16,* 1–17.

DeBruyne, L. K., & Rolfes, S. R. (1989). *Life cycle nutrition: Conception through adolescence.* St. Paul, MN: West.

DeCasper, A. J., & Fifer, W. P. (1980). Of human bonding: Newborns prefer their mothers' voices. *Science, 208,* 1174–1176.

DeCasper, A. J., & Prescott, P. A. (1984). Human newborns' perception of male voices: Preference, discrimination, and reinforcing value. *Developmental Psychobiology, 17,* 481–491.

DeCasper, A. J., & Spence, M. J. (1986). Prenatal maternal speech influences newborns' perception of speech sounds. *Infant Behavior and Development, 9,* 133–150.

DeCasper, A. J., & Spence, M. J. (1991). Auditorially mediated behavior during the perinatal period: A cognitive view. In M. J. Weiss & P. R. Zelazo (Eds.), *Infant attention,* 142–176. Norwood, NJ: Ablex.

Declercq, E. R. (1992). The transformation of American midwifery: 1975 to 1988. *American Journal of Public Health, 82,* 680–684.

de Cubas, M. M., & Field, T. (1993). Children of methadone-dependent women: Developmental outcomes. *American Journal of Orthopsychiatry,* 63, 266–276.

DeFries, J. C., Olson, R. K., Pennington, B. F., & Smith, S. D. (1991). Colorado reading project: Past, present, and future. *Learning Disabilities, 2,* 37–46.

DeKovic, M., & Janssens, J. (1992). Parents' child-rearing style and child's sociometric status. *Developmental Psychology, 28,* 925–932.

DeLoache, J. S. (1991). Symbolic functioning in very young children: Understanding of pictures and models. *Child Development, 62,* 736–752.

DeLoache, J. S., Cassidy, D. J., & Brown, A. L. (1985). Precursors of mnemonic strategies in very young children's memory. *Child Development, 56,* 125–137.

DeLuccie, M. F., & Davis, A. J. (1991). Father–child relationships from the preschool years through mid-adolescence. *Journal of Genetic Psychology, 152,* 225–238.

Dembo, R., Williams, L., Schmeidler, J., Wish, E. D., Getreu, A., & Berry, E. (1991). Juvenile crime and drug abuse: A prospective study of high risk youth. *Journal of Addictive Diseases, 11,* 5–31.

DeMulder, E. K., & Radke–Yarrow, M. (1991). Attachment with affectively ill and well mothers: Concurrent behavioral correlates. *Development and Psychopathology, 3,* 227–242.

Denham, S. A., & Holt, R. W. (1993). Preschoolers' likability as cause or consequence of their social behavior. *Developmental Psychology, 29,* 271–275.

Denmark, F., Russo, N. F., Frieze, I. H., & Sechzer, J. A. (1988). Guidelines for avoiding sexism in psychological research. *American Psychologist, 43,* 582–585.

Dennis, M., Sugar, J., & Whitaker, H. A. (1982). The acquisition of tag questions. *Child Development, 53,* 1254–1257.

Dennis, W. (1960). Causes of retardation among institutional children: Iran. *Journal of Genetic Psychology, 96,* 47–59.

Dennis, W., & Dennis, M. G. (1940). The effect of cradling practices upon the onset of walking in Hopi children. *Journal of Genetic Psychology, 56,* 77–86.

Dennis, W., & Sayegh, Y. (1965). The effect of supplementary experiences upon the behavioral development of infants in institutions. *Child Development, 36,* 81–90.

Denno, D. W. (1990). *Biology and violence: From birth to adulthood.* Cambridge: Cambridge University Press.

DeParle, J. (1991, March 2). Child poverty twice as likely after family splits, study says. *New York Times,* p. 8.

DeParle, J. (1992, May 13). Radical overhaul proposed in system of child support. *New York Times,* p. A8.

DeParle, J. (1993, March 19). Sharp criticism for Head Start, even by friends. *New York Times,* pp. A1, 11.

Depner, C. E., Leino, E. V., & Chun, A. (1992). Interparental conflict and child adjustment. *Family and Conciliation Courts Review, 30,* 323–341.

Desmond, R. J., Singer, J. L., & Singer, D. G. (1990). Family mediation: Parental communication patterns and the influences of television on children. In J. Bryant (Ed.), *Television and the American family.* Hillsdale, NJ: Erlbaum.

de Sonneville, L. M. J., Njiokiktjien, C., & Hilhorst, R. C. (1991). Methylphenidate-induced changes in ADDH information processors. *Journal of Child Psychology and Psychiatry, 32,* 285–295.

deVilliers, P. A., & deVilliers, J. G. (1992). Language development. In M. H. Bornstein & M. E. Lamb (Eds.), *Developmental psychology: An advanced textbook* (3rd ed.). Hillsdale, NJ: Erlbaum.

Diamond, J. M., Kataria, S., & Messer, S. C. (1989). Latchkey children: A pilot study investigating behavior and academic achievement. *Child and Youth Care Quarterly, 18,* 131–140.

Diaz, R. M. (1985). Bilingual cognitive development: Addressing three gaps in current research. *Child Development, 56,* 1376–1388.

DiBlasio, F. A., & Benda, B. B. (1992). Gender differences in theories of adolescent sexual activity. *Sex Roles, 27,* 221–239.

Dick–Read, G. (1944). *Childbirth without fear: The principles and practices of natural childbirth.* New York: Harper & Bros.

Dickstein, E., & Posner, J. M. (1978). Self-esteem and relationship with parents. *Journal of Genetic Psychology, 133,* 273–276.

Dickstein, S., & Parke, R. D. (1988). Social referencing in infancy: A glance at fathers and marriage. *Child Development, 59,* 506–511.

DiClemente, R. J. (1990). The emergence of adolescents as a risk group for human immunodeficiency virus infection. *Journal of Adolescent Research, 5,* 7–17.

DiClemente, R. J., Durbin, M., Siegel, D., Krasnovsky, F., Lazarus, N., & Comacho, T. (1992). Determinants of condom use among junior high school students in a minority, inner-city school district. *Pediatrics, 89,* 197–202.

Dietz, W. H. (1990). You are what you eat—what you eat is what you are. *Journal of Adolescent Health Care, 11,* 76–81.

Dietz, W. H., Jr., & Gortmaker, S. L. (1985). Do we fatten our children at the television set? Obesity and television viewing in children and adolescents. *Pediatrics, 75,* 807–812.

Dindia, K., & Allen, M. (1992). Sex differences in self-disclosure: A meta-analysis. *Psychological Bulletin, 112,* 106–124.

Dishion, T. J., & Ray, J. (1991, August). The development and ecology of substance use in adolescent boys. In T. Wills (Chair), *Adolescent substance use: Current theoretical models.* Symposium conducted at the meeting of the American Psychological Association, San Francisco.

Dix, T. (1991). The affective organization of parenting: Adaptive and maladaptative processes. *Psychological Bulletin, 110,* 3–25.

Dix, T., Ruble, D. N., & Zambarino, R. J. (1989). Mother's implicit theories of discipline: Child effects, parental effects and the attribution process. *Child Development, 60,* 1373–1392.

Dixon, J. A., & Moore, C. F. (1990). The development of perspective taking: Understanding differences in information and weighting. *Child Development, 61,* 1502–1513.

Dodge, K. A. (1990a). Developmental psychopathology in children of depressed mothers. *Developmental Psychology, 26,* 3–6.

Dodge, K. A. (1990b). Nature versus nurture in childhood conduct disorder: It is time to ask a different question. *Developmental Psychology, 26,* 698–701.

Dodge, K. A. (1993a, March). *Effects of intervention on children at high risk for conduct problems.* Paper presented at the meeting of the Society for Research in Child Development, New Orleans, LA.

Dodge, K. A. (1993b, March). *Social information processing and peer rejection factors in the development of behavior problems in children.* Paper presented at the meeting of the Society for Research in Child Development, New Orleans, LA.

Dodwell, P. C., Humphrey, G. K., & Muir, D. W. (1987). Shape and pattern perception. In P. Salapatek & L. Cohen (Eds.), *Handbook of infant perception: Vol. 2. From perception to cognition.* Orlando, FL: Academic Press.

Doherty, W. J., & Needle, R. H. (1991). Psychological adjustment and substance use among adolescents before and after a parental divorce. *Child Development, 62,* 328–337.

Dolgin, K. G., Meyer, L., & Schwartz, J. (1991). Effects of gender, target's gender, topic, and self-esteem on disclosure to best and middling friends. *Sex Roles, 25,* 311–329.

Donaldson, M. (1979). *Children's minds.* New York: Norton.

Donovan, P. (1993). *Testing positive.* New York: Alan Guttmacher Institute.

Dooker, M. (1980, July/August). Lamaze method of childbirth. *Nursing Research,* pp. 220–224.

Dornbusch, S. M., Ritter, P. L., Leiderman, P. H., Roberts, D. F., & Fraleigh, M. J. (1987). The relation of parenting style to adolescent school performance. *Child Development, 58,* 1244–1257.

Dougherty, D. M. (1993). Adolescent health. *American Psychologist, 48,* 193–201.

Downs, W. R., & Rose, S. R. (1991). The relationship of adolescent peer groups to the incidence of psychosocial problems. *Adolescence, 26,* 473–492.

Doyle, A., Ceschin, F., Tessier, O., & Doehring, P. (1991). The relation of age and social class factors in children's social pretend play to cognitive and symbolic ability. *International Journal of Behavioral Development, 14,* 395–410.

Doyle, A. B., Doehring, P., Tessier, O., & De Lorimier, S. (1992). Transitions in children's play: A sequential analysis of states preceding and following social pretense. *Developmental Psychology, 28,* 137–144.

Draper, W. (1990). Father's role in development. In R. M. Thomas (Ed.), *The encyclopedia of human development and education: Theory, research and studies.* Oxford: Pergamon.

Drotar, D. (1991). The family context of nonorganic failure to thrive. *American Journal of Orthopsychiatry, 61,* 23–34.

Drotar, D., & Sturm, L. (1992). Personality development, problem solving, and behavior problems among preschool children with early histories of nonorganic failure-to-thrive: A controlled study. *Developmental and Behavioral Pediatrics, 13,* 266–273.

Drug use by students rising, survey finds. (1992, October 19). *New York Times,* p. A8.

Dryfoos, J. G. (1990). *Adolescents at risk: Prevalence and prevention.* New York: Oxford.

Dubas, J. S. (1991). Cognitive abilities and physical maturation. In R. M. Lerner, A. C. Petersen, & J. Brooks-Gunn (Eds.), *Encyclopedia of adolescence.* New York: Garland.

Dubas, J. S., Graber, J. A., & Petersen, A. C. (1991). A longitudinal investigation of adolescents' changing perception of pubertal timing. *Developmental Psychology, 27,* 580–586.

DuBois, D. L., Felner, R. D., Brand, S., Adan, A. M., & Evans, E. G. (1992). A prospective study of life stress, social support, and adaptation in early adolescence. *Child Development, 63,* 542–557.

DuBois, D. L., & Hirsch, B. J. (1990). School and neighborhood friendship patterns of blacks and whites in early adolescence. *Child Development, 61,* 524–536.

Dubow, E. F., & Luster, T. (1990). Adjustment of children born to teenage mothers: The contribution of risk and protective factors, *Journal of Marriage and the Family, 52,* 393–404.

Duke-Duncan, P. (1991). Body image. In R. M. Lerner, A. C. Petersen, & J. Brooks-Gunn (Eds.), *Encyclopedia of adolescence.* New York: Garland.

Dumas, J. E., & La Frenière, P. J. (1993). Mother–child relationships as sources of support or stress: A comparison of competent, average, aggressive, and anxious dyads. *Child Development, 64,* 1732–1754.

Dumtschin, J. U. (1988, March). Recognize language development and delay in early childhood. *Young Children,* 16–24.

Duncan, G. J. (1993, March). *Families and neighbors as sources of disadvantage in the schooling decisions of white and black adolescents.* Paper presented at the meeting of the Society for Research in Child Development, New Orleans, LA.

Duncan, G. J., Brooks-Gunn, J., & Klebanov, P. K. (1993, March). *Economic deprivation and early-childhood development.* Paper presented at the meeting of the Society for Research in Child Development, New Orleans, LA.

Duncan, S. (1991). Convention and conflict in the child's interaction with others. *Developmental Review, 11,* 337–366.

Dunham, P., & Dunham, F. (1992). Lexical development during middle infancy: A mutually driven infant–caregiver process. *Developmental Psychology, 28,* 414–420.

Dunn, J. (1985). *Sisters and brothers.* Cambridge, MA: Harvard University Press.

Dunn, J. (1992a). Siblings and development. *Current Directions in Psychological Science, 1,* 6–9.

Dunn, J. (1992b). Sisters and brothers: Current issues in developmental research. In F. Boer & J. Dunn (Eds.), *Children's sibling relationships: Developmental and clinical issues.* Hillsdale, NJ: Erlbaum.

Dunn, J. (1993). *Young children's close relationships: Beyond attachment.* Newbury Park, CA: Sage.

Dunn, J., Brown, J., Slomkowski, C., Tesla, C., & Youngblade, L. (1991). Young children's understanding of other people's feelings and beliefs: Individual differences and their antecedents. *Child Development, 62,* 1352–1366.

Dunn, J., & Kendrick, C. (1982). Siblings and their mothers: Developing relationships within the family. In M. E. Lamb & B. Sutton-Smith (Eds.), *Sibling relationships.* Hillsdale, NJ: Erlbaum.

Dunn, J., Plomin, R., & Daniels, D. (1986). Consistency and change in mothers' behavior toward young siblings. *Child Development, 57,* 348–356.

Dunn, J., Stocker, C. & Plomin, R. (1990). Assessing the relationship between young siblings: A research note. *Journal of Child Psychology and Psychiatry, 31,* 983–991.

DuPaul, G. J., & Rapport, M. D. (1993). Does methylphenidate normalize the classroom performances of children with attention deficit disorder? *Journal of the American Academy of Child and Adolescent Psychiatry, 32,* 190–198.

Durand, A. M. (1992). The safety of home birth: The farm study. *American Journal of Public Health, 82,* 450–453.

Durand, V. M. (1992). New directions in educational programming for students with autism. In D. E. Berkell (Ed.), *Autism.* Hillsdale, NJ: Erlbaum.

Earned degrees. (1992, May 13). *The Chronicle of Higher Education,* p. A37.

Earned degrees. (1993, June 2). *The Chronicle of Higher Education,* pp. A25, 26.

East, P. L., Lerner, R. M., Lerner, J. V., Soni, R. T., Ohannessian, C. M., & Jacobson, L. P. (1992). Early adolescent-peer group fit, peer relations, and psychosocial competence: A short-term longitudinal study. *Journal of Early Adolescence, 12,* 132–152.

Easterbrooks, M. A., & Goldberg, W. A. (1984). Toddler development in the family: Impact of father involvement and parenting characteristics. *Child Development, 55,* 740–752.

Eaton, W. O., & Saudino, K. J. (1992). Prenatal activity level as a temperament dimension? Individual differences and developmental functions in fetal movement. *Infant Behavior and Development, 15,* 57–70.

Eaton, W. O., & Yu, A. P. (1989). Are sex differences in child motor activity a function of sex differences in maturational status? *Child Development, 60,* 1005–1011.

Eccles, J. S. (1985). Sex differences in achievement patterns. In T. Sonderegger (Ed.), *Nebraska symposium on motivation.* Lincoln: University of Nebraska Press.

Eccles, J. S. (1991a). Academic achievement. In R. M. Lerner, A. C. Petersen, & J. Brooks–Gunn (Eds.), *Encyclopedia of adolescence.* New York: Garland.

Eccles, J. S. (1991b). Changes in motivation and self-perceptions. In R. M. Lerner, A. C. Petersen, & J. Brooks–Gunn (Eds.), *Encyclopedia of adolescence.* New York: Garland.

Eccles, J. S. (1993, March). *Parents as gender-role socializers during middle childhood and adolescence.* Paper presented at the meeting of the Society for Research on Child Development, New Orleans, LA.

Eccles, J. S., Jacobs, J., Harold, R., Yoon, K. S., Aberbach, A., & Doan, C. F. (1991, August). *Expectancy effects are alive and well on the home front: Influences on, and consequences of, parents' beliefs regarding their daughters' and sons' abilities and interests.* Paper presented at the meeting of the American Psychological Association, San Francisco.

Eccles, J. S., Midgley, C., Wigfield, A., Buchanan, C. M., Reuman, D., Flanagan, C., & Mac Iver, D. (1993b). Development during adolescence. *American Psychologist, 48,* 90–101.

Eccles, J. S., Wigfield, A., Harold, R. D., & Blumenfeld, P. (1993a). Age and gender differences in children's self- and task perceptions during elementary school. *Child Development, 64,* 830–847.

Eckenrode, J., Laird, M., & Doris, J. (1993). School performance and disciplinary problems among abused and neglected children. *Developmental Psychology, 29,* 53–62.

Eckerman, C. O., & Oehler, J. M. (1992). Very-low-birthweight newborns and parents as early social partners. In S. L. Friedman & M. D. Sigman (Eds.), *The psychological development of low birthweight infants.* Norwood, NJ: Ablex.

Eckerman, C. O., & Stein, M. R. (1990). How imitation begets imitation and toddlers' generation of games. *Developmental Psychology, 26,* 370–378.

Eckholm, E. (1993, January 31). Teen-age gangs are inflicting lethal violence on small cities. *New York Times,* pp. A1, 16.

Eder, R. A. (1989). The emergent personologist: The structure and content of 3½-, 5½-, and 7½-year-olds' concepts of themselves and other persons. *Child Development, 60,* 1218–1228.

Eder, R. A. (1990). Uncovering young children's psychological selves: Individual and developmental differences. *Child Development, 61,* 849–863.

Egeland, B., & Farber, E. A. (1984). Infant–mother attachment: Factors related to its development and changes over time. *Child Development, 55,* 753–771.

Egeland, B., Jacobvitz, D., & Sroufe, L. A. (1988). Breaking the cycle of abuse. *Child Development, 59,* 1080–1088.

Egeland, B., & Sroufe, L. A. (1981). Attachment and early maltreatment. *Child Development, 52,* 44–52.

Ehrhardt, A., & Baker, S. W. (1978). Fetal androgens, human central nervous system differentiation and behavioral sex differences. In R. Friedman, R. M. Richart, & R.L. Vande Wiele (Eds.), *Sex differences in behavior.* Huntington, NY: Krieger.

Ehrhart, J. K., & Sandler, B. R. (1987). *Looking for more than a few good women in traditionally male fields.* Washington, DC: Association of American Colleges.

Eiger, M. S., & Olds, S.W. (1986). *The complete book of breast-feeding,* (2nd ed.). New York: Bantam Books.

Eil, C. (1991). Gynecomastia. In R. M. Lerner, A. C. Petersen, & J. Brooks–Gunn (Eds.), *Encyclopedia of adolescence.* New York: Garland.

Eimas, P. D., Sigueland, E. R. Juscyk, P., & Vigorito, J. (1971). Speech perception in infants. *Science, 171,* 303–306.

Eisenberg, N. (1989). Editor's notes. In N. Eisenberg (Ed.), *New directions for child development: No. 44. Empathy and related emotional responses.* San Francisco: Jossey–Bass.

Eisenberg, N. (1992). *The caring child.* Cambridge, MA: Harvard University Press.

Eisenberg, N., Fabes, R. A., Bernzweig, J., Karbon, M., Poulin, R., & Hanish, L. (1993). The relations of emotionality and regulation to preschoolers' social skills and sociometric status. *Child Development, 64,* 1418–1438.

Eisenberg, N., Fabes, R. A., Schaller, M., & Miller, P. A. (1989). Sympathy and personal distress: Development, gender differences, and interrelations of indexes. In N. Eisenberg (Ed.), *New directions for child development: No. 44. Empathy and related emotional responses.* San Francisco: Jossey–Bass.

Eisenberg, N., Hertz–Lazarowitz, R., & Fuchs, I. (1990). Prosocial moral judgment in Israeli kubbutz and city children: A longitudinal study. *Merrill–Palmer Quarterly, 36,* 273–285.

Eisenberg, N., & Miller, P. (1990). The development of prosocial behavior versus nonprosocial behavior in children. In M. Lewis & S. M. Miller (Eds.), *Handbook of developmental psychopathology.* New York: Plenum.

Eisenberg, N., Miller, P. A., Shell, R., McNalley, S., & Shea, C. (1991). Prosocial development in adolescence: A longitudinal study. *Developmental Psychology, 27,* 849–857.

Eisner, E. W. (1990). The role of art and play in children's cognitive development. In E. Klugman & S. Smilansky (Eds.), *Children's play and learning: Perspectives and policy implications.* New York: Teachers College Press.

Ekvall, S.W. (1993a). Nutritional assessment and early intervention. In S. W. Ekvall (Ed.), *Pediatric nutrition in chronic diseases and developmental disorders: Prevention, assessment,and treatment.* New York: Oxford.

Ekvall, S. W. (Ed.). (1993b). *Pediatric nutrition in chronic diseases and developmental disorders: Prevention, assessment, and treatment.* New York: Oxford.

Ekvall, S. W. (1993c). Prenatal growth in pregnancy. In S. W. Ekvall (Ed.), *Pediatric nutrition in chronic diseases and developmental disorders: Prevention, assessment, and treatment.* New York: Oxford.

Ekvall, S. W., Bandini, L., & Ekvall, V. (1993b). Obesity. In S. W. Ekvall (Ed.), *Pediatric nutrition in chronic diseases and developmental disorders: Prevention, assessment, and treatment.* New York: Oxford.

Ekvall, S. W., Ekvall, V., & Mayes, S. D. (1993a). Attention deficit hyperactivity disorder. In S. W. Ekvall (Ed.), *Pediatric nutrition in chronic diseases and developmental disorders: Prevention, assessment, and treatment.* New York; Oxford.

Ekvall, V., Ekvall, S. W., & Farrell, M. (1993). Anorexia nervosa and bulimia. In S. W. Ekvall (Ed.), *Pediatric nutrition in chronic diseases and developmental disorders: Prevention, assessment, and treatment.* New York: Oxford.

Elbers, E., Wiegersma, S., Brand, N., & Vroon, P. A. (1991). Response alternation as an artifact in conservation research. *Journal of Genetic Psychology, 152,* 47–56.

Elias, M. J., Gara, M. A., Schuyler, T. F., Brandon–Muller, L. R., & Sayette, M. A. (1991). The promotion of social competence: Longitudinal study of a preventative school-based program. *American Journal of Orthopsychiatry, 61,* 409–417.

Elkind, D. (1967). Egocentrism in adolescence. *Child Development, 38,* 1025–1034.

Elkind, D. (1985). Egocentrism redux. *Developmental Review, 5,* 218–226.

Elkind, D. (1990). Academic pressures—too much, too soon: The demise of play. In E. Klugman & S. Smilansky (Eds.), *Children's play and learning: Perspectives and policy.* New York: Teachers College Press.

Elkind, D. (1991). Early childhood education. In M. Lewis (Ed.), *Child and adolescent psychiatry: A comprehensive textbook.* Baltimore: Williams & Wilkins.

Elkind, D., & Bowen, R. (1979). Imaginary audience behavior in children and adolescents. *Developmental Psychology, 15,* 38–44.

Ellickson, P. L., & Bell, R. M. (1990). Drug prevention in junior high: A multi-site longitudinal test. *Science, 16,* 1299–1305.

Elliott, R. (1988). Tests, abilities, race, and conflict. *Intelligence, 12,* 333–350.

Elrod, M. M., & Crase, S. J. (1980). Sex differences in self-esteem and parental behavior. *Psychological Reports, 46,* 719–727.

Emde, R. N. (1992). Individual meaning and increasing complexity: Contributions of Sigmund Freud and René Spitz to developmental psychology. *Developmental Psychology, 28,* 347–359.

Emde, R. N., Gaensbauer, T. J., & Harmon, R. J. (1976). *Emotional expression in infancy: A biobehavioral study.* New York: International Universities Press.

Emde, R. N., Harmon, R. J., Metcalf, D., Koenig, K. L., & Wagonfeld, S. (1971). Stress and neonatal sleep. *Psychosomatic Medicine, 33,* 491–497.

Emde, R. N., Plomin, R., Robinson, J., Corley, R., DeFries, J., Fulker, D. W. Reznick, J. S., Campos, J., Kagan, J., & Zahn-Waxler, C. (1992). Temperament, emotion, and cognition at fourteen months: The MacArthur Longitudinal Twin Study. *Child Development, 63,* 1437–1455.

Emery, R. E. (1988). *Marriage, divorce, and children's adjustment.* Newbury Park, CA: Sage.

Emery, R. E. (1989). Family violence. *American Psychologist, 44,* 321–328.

Engen, T., & Lipsitt, L. P. (1965). Decrement and recovery of responses to olfactory stimuli in the human neonate. *Journal of Comparative and Physiological Psychology, 59,* 312–316.

Entwistle, D. R. (1990). Schools and the adolescent. In S. S. Feldman & G. R. Elliott (Eds.), *At the threshold: The developing adolescent.* Cambridge, MA: Harvard University Press.

Epstein, J. L. (1989). The selection of friends: Changes across the grades and in different school environments. In T. J. Berndt & G. W. Ladd (Eds.), *Peer relationships in child development.* New York: Wiley.

Epstein, L. H., Valoski, A., Wing, R. P., & McCurley, J. (1990). Ten-year follow up of behavioral, family-based treatment for obese children. *Journal of the American Medical Association, 264,* 2519–2523.

Epstein, L. H., Wing, R. R., Woodall, K., Penner, B. C., Kress, M. J., & Koeske, R. (1985). Effects of family-based behavioral treatment on obese 5- to 8-year-old children. *Behavior Therapy, 116,* 205–212.

Epstein, L. H., Woodall, K., Goreczny, A. J., Wing, R. R., & Robertson, R. J. (1984). The modification of activity patterns and energy expenditure in obese young girls. *Behavior Therapy, 15,* 101–108.

Erikson, E. H. (1963). *Childhood and society.* New York: Norton.

Erikson, E. H. (1968). *Identity, youth and crisis.* New York: Norton.

Erikson, E. H. (1975). *Life history and the historical moment.* New York: Norton.

Erikson, E. H. (1983). Cited in Hall, E. (1983, June). A conversation with Erik Erikson. *Psychology Today,* pp. 22–30.

Erickson, J. D., & Bjerkedal, T. (1981). Down's syndrome associated with father's age in Norway. *Journal of Medical Genetics, 18,* 22–28.

Eron, L. D. (1987). The development of aggressive behavior from the perspective of a developing behaviorism. *American Psychologist, 42,* 435–442.

Eron, L. D., Huesmann, L. R., & Zelli, A. (1991). The role of parental variables in the learning of aggression. In D. J. Pepler & K. H. Rubin (Eds.), *The development and treatment of childhood aggression.* Hillsdale, NJ: Erlbaum.

Escobar, G. J., Littenberg, B., & Petitti, D. B. (1991). Outcome among surviving very low birthweight infants: A meta-analysis. *Archives of Disease in Childhood, 66,* 204–211.

Espinosa, M. P., Sigman, M. D., Neumann, C. G., Bwibo, N. O., & McDonald, M. A. (1992). Playground behaviors of school-age children in relation to nutrition, schooling, and family characteristics. *Developmental Psychology, 28,* 1188–1195.

Etaugh, C. (1983). Introduction: The influence of environmental factors on sex differences in children's play. In M. B. Liss (Ed.), *Social and cognitive skills: Sex roles and children's play.* New York: Academic Press.

Etaugh, C. (1990). Women's lives: Images and realities. In M. A. Paludi & G. Steuernagel (Eds.), *Foundations for a feminist restructuring of the academic disciplines.* New York: Harrington Park Press.

Etaugh, C. (1993). Maternal employment: Effects on children. In J. Frankel (Ed.), *The employed mother and the family context.* New York: Springer.

Etaugh, C., & Duits, T. (1990). Development of gender discrimination: Role of stereotypic and counterstereotypic gender cues. *Sex Roles, 23,* 215–222.

Etaugh, C., Grinnell, K., & Etaugh, A. (1989). Development of gender labeling: Effect of age of pictured children. *Sex Roles, 21,* 769–773.

Etaugh, C., Levine, D., & Mennella, A. (1984). Development of sex biases in children: 40 years later. *Sex Roles, 10,* 911–922.

Etaugh, C., & Liss, M. B. (1992). Home, school and playroom: Training grounds for adult gender roles. *Sex Roles, 26,* 129–147.

Evans, H. J. (1981). Abnormalities and cigarette smoking. *Lancet, 1,* 627–634.

Evans, M. I., Quigg, M. H., Koppitch, F. C., & Schulman, J. C. (1989). Prenatal diagnosis of chromosomal and Mendelian disorders. In M. I. Evans, J. C. Fletcher, A. O. Dixler, & J. D. Schulman (Eds.), *Fetal diagnosis and therapy: Science, ethics and the law.* Philadelphia: Lippincott.

Eveleth, P. B., & Tanner, J. M. (1990). *Worldwide variation in human growth* (2nd ed.). Cambridge: Cambridge University Press.

Ewigman, B. G., Crane, J. P., Frigoletto, F. D., LeFevre, M. L., Bain, R. P., McNellis, D., & The RADIUS Study Group (1993, September 16). Effect of prenatal ultrasound screening on perinatal outcome. *New England Journal of Medicine, 329,* 821–827.

Eyer, D. E. (1993). *Mother–infant bonding: A scientific fiction.* New Haven, CT: Yale University Press.

Fabes, R. A., Eisenberg, N., & Miller, P. A. (1990). Maternal correlates of children's vicarious emotional responsiveness. *Developmental Psychology, 26,* 639–648.

Fabricius, W. V., & Cavalier, L. (1989). The role of causal theories about memory in young children's memory strategy choice. *Child Development, 60,* 298–308.

Fagan, J. F., & Detterman, D. K. (1992). The Fagan test of infant intelligence: A technical summary. *Journal of Applied Developmental Psychology, 13,* 173–193.

Fagot, B. I. (1990). A longitudinal study of gender segregation: Infancy to preschool. In F. F. Strayer (Ed.), *Social interaction and behavioral development during early childhood.* Montreal: La Maison D'Ethologie de Montreal.

Fagot, B. I., & Hagan, R. (1991). Observations of parent reactions to sex-stereotyped behaviors: Age and sex effects. *Child Development, 62,* 617–628.

Fagot, B. I., & Kavanagh, K. (1993). Parenting during the second year: Effects of children's age, sex, and attachment classification. *Child Development, 64,* 258–271.

Fagot, B. I., & Leinbach, M. D. (1993). Gender-role development in young children: From discrimination to labeling. *Developmental Review, 13,* 205–224.

Fagot, B. I., Leinbach, M. D., & O'Boyle, M. D. (1992). Gender labeling, gender stereotyping, and parenting behaviors. *Developmental Psychology, 28,* 225–230.

Falbo, T. (1992). Social norms and the one-child family: Clinical and policy implications. In F. Boer & J Dunn (Eds.), *Children's sibling relationships: Developmental and clinical issues.* Hillsdale, NJ: Erlbaum.

Falbo, T., & Poston, D. L., Jr. (1993).The academic, personality and physical outcomes of only children in China. *Child Development, 64,* 18–35.

Famularo, R., Kinscherff, R., & Fenton, T. (1992). Parental substance abuse and the nature of child maltreatment. *Child Abuse and Neglect, 16,* 475–483.

Fantz, R. L. (1961). The origin of form perception. *Scientific American, 204,* 66–72.

Fantz, R. L., Fagan, J. F., III, & Miranda, S. B. (1975). Early visual selectivity. In L. B. Cohen & P. Salapatek (Eds.), *Infant perception: From sensation to cognition* (Vol. 1). New York: Academic Press.

Farkas, G., Sheehan, D., & Grobe, R. P. (1990). Coursework mastery and school success: Gender, ethnicity, and poverty groups within an urban school district. *American Educational Research Journal, 27,* 807–827.

Farnham–Diggory, S. (1992). *The learning-disabled child.* Cambridge, MA: Harvard University Press.

Farran, D. C. (1990). Effects of intervention with disadvantaged and disabled children: A decade review. In S. J. Meisels & J. P. Shonkoff (Eds.), *Handbook of early childhood intervention.* Cambridge: Cambridge University Press.

Farrar, M. J. (1992). Negative evidence and grammatical morpheme acquisition. *Developmental Psychology, 28,* 90–98.

Farrar, M. J., & Goodman, G. S. (1990). Developmental differences in the relation between scripts and episodic memory: Do they exist? In R. Fivush & J. A. Hudson (Eds.), *Knowing and remembering in young children.* Cambridge: Cambridge University Press.

Fassler, D., McQueen, K., Duncan, P., & Copeland, L. (1991). Children's perceptions of AIDS. *Journal of the American Academy of Child and Adolescent Psychology, 29,* 459–462.

Feagans, L. V., & Haldane, D. (1991). Adolescents with learning disabilities. In R. M. Lerner, A. C. Petersen, & J. Brooks–Gunn (Eds.), *Encyclopedia of adolescence.* New York: Garland.

Featherstone, D. R., Cundick, B. P., & Jensen, L. C. (1992). Differences in school behavior and achievement between children from intact, reconstituted, and single-parent families. *Adolescence, 27,* 1–12.

Federal Bureau of Investigation. (1991, August). *Uniform crime reports for the United States.* Washington, DC: U.S. Department of Justice.

Federal Bureau of Investigation. (1992, August). *Uniform crime reports for the United States.* Washington, DC: U.S. Department of Justice.

Fehlings, D. L., Roberts, W., Humphries, T., & Dawe, G. (1991). Attention deficit hyperactivity disorder: Does cognitive behavioral therapy improve home behavior? *Developmental and Behavioral Pediatrics, 12,* 223–228.

Feingold, A. (1993). Cognitive gender differences: A developmental perspective. *Sex Roles, 29,* 91–112.

Feinman, S., & Lewis, M. (1983). Social referencing at 10 months: A second-order effect on infants' responses to strangers. *Child Development, 54,* 878–887.

Feiring, C. (1993, March). *Developing concepts of romance from 15 to 18 years.* Paper presented at the meeting of the Society for Research in Child Development, New Orleans, LA.

Feiring, C., & Lewis, M. (1991). The transition from middle to early adolescence: Sex differences in the social network and perceived self-competence. *Sex Roles, 24,* 489–509.

Feldhusen, J. F. (1989, March). Synthesis of research on gifted youth. *Educational Leadership,* pp. 6–11.

Feldman, N. S., Klosson, E. C., Parsons, J. E., Rholes, W. S., & Ruble, D. N. (1976). Order of information presentation and children's moral judgments. *Child Development, 47,* 556–559.

Female valedictorians stymied by multiple roles. (1988, Winter). *On Campus with Women, 17*(3), pp. 8–9.

Fennema, E. (1990). Teachers' beliefs and gender differences in mathematics. In E. Fennema & G. C. Leder (Eds.), *Mathematics and gender.* New York: Teachers College Press.

Fenzel, L. M., & Blyth, D. A. (1991). Schooling. In R. M. Lerner, A. C. Petersen, & J. Brooks–Gunn (Eds.), *Encyclopedia of adolescence.* New York: Garland.

Ferguson, K. J., Yesalis, C. E., Pomrehn, P. R., & Kirkpatrick, M. B. (1989). Attitudes, knowledge, and beliefs as predictions of exercise intent and behavior in schoolchildren. *Journal of School Health, 59,* 112–115.

Ferguson, T. J., & Rule, B. G. (1980). Effects of inferential sex, outcome severity and basis of responsibility on children's evaluations of aggressive acts. *Developmental Psychology, 16,* 141–146.

Fernald, A. (1991). Prosody in speech to children: Prelinguistic and linguistic functions. In R. Vasta (Ed.), *Annals of child development* (Vol. 8). London: Kingsley.

Fernald, A. (1992). Meaningful melodies in mother's speech to infants. In H. Papousek, U. Jürgens, & M. Papousek (Eds.), *Nonverbal vocal communication: Comparative and developmental aspects.* Cambridge: Cambridge University Press.

Fernald, A., & Mazzie, C. (1991). Prosody and focus in speech to infants and adults. *Developmental Psychology, 27,* 209–221.

Fernald, A., & Morikawa, H. (1993). Common themes and cultural variations in Japanese and American mothers' speech to infants. *Child Development, 64,* 637–656.

Field, T. M. (1980). Interactions of high risk infants: Quantitative and qualitative differences. In D. B. Sawin, R. C. Hawkins, L. P. Walker, & J. H. Penticuff (Eds.), *Exceptional infant: Vol. 4. Psychosocial risks in infant environmental transactions.* New York: Brunner/Mazel.

Field, T. (1990). *Infancy: The developing child.* Cambridge, MA: Harvard University Press.

Field, T. (1991a). Adolescent mothers and their young children. In R. M. Lerner, A. C. Petersen, & J. Brooks–Gunn (Eds.), *Encyclopedia of adolescence.* New York: Garland.

Field, T. M. (1991b). Quality infant day-care and grade school behavior and performance. *Child Development, 62,* 863–870.

Field, T. M. (1991c). Young children's adaptations to repeated separations from their mothers. *Child Development, 62,* 539–547.

Field, T. (1992a). Infants of depressed mothers. *Development and Psychopathology, 4,* 49–66.

Field, T. (1992b, May). *Massaging high-risk infants.* Paper presented at the International Conference on Infant Studies, Miami Beach, FL.

Field, T. M., Gewirtz, J. L., Cohen, D., Garcia, R., Greenberg, R., & Collins, K. (1984). Leave-takings and reunions of infants, toddlers, preschoolers, and their parents. *Child Development, 55,* 628–635.

Field, T. M., Greenwald, P., Morran, C., Healy, B., Foster, T., Guthertz, M., & Front, P. (1992). Behavior state matching during interactions of preadolescent friends versus acquaintances. *Developmental Psychology, 28,* 242–250.

Fielder, A. R., Dobson, V., Moseley, M. J., & Mayer, D. L. (1992). Preferential looking—clinical lessons. *Ophthalmic Paediatrics and Genetics, 13,* 101–110.

Finch, A. J., & McIntosh, J. A. (1990). Assessment of anxieties and fears in children. In A. LaGreca (Ed.), *Through the eyes of a child.* Boston: Allyn & Bacon.

Fincham, F. D., & Osborne, L. N. (1993). Marital conflict and children: Retrospect and prospect. *Clinical Psychology Review, 13,* 75–88.

Fine, G., Mortimer, J., & Roberts, D. (1990). Leisure, work, and mass media. In S. Feldman & G. Elliot (Eds.), *At the threshold: The developing adolescent.* Cambridge, MA: Harvard University Press.

Finegan, J. K., Niccols, G. A., & Sitarenios, G. (1992). Relations between prenatal testosterone levels and cognitive abilities at 4 years. *Developmental Psychology, 28,* 1075–1089.

Fingerhut, L., Ingram, D., & Feldman, J. (1992). Firearm and nonfirearm homicide among persons 15 through 19 years of age. *Journal of the American Medical Association, 267,* 3048–3053.

Finkelhor, D., & Dziuba-Leatherman, J. (1994). Victimization of children. *American Psychologist, 49,* 173–183.

Finn, J. D., & Achilles, C. M. (1990). Answers and questions about class size: A statewide experience. *American Educational Research Journal, 27,* 557–577.

Fiorentine, R. (1988). Increasing similarity in the values and life plans of male and female college students? Evidence and implications. *Sex Roles, 18,* 143–158.

Fishbein, H. D., & Imai, S. (1992, August). *Preschoolers select playmates on the basis of sex and race.* Paper presented at the meeting of the American Psychological Association, Washington, DC.

Fisher, C. B., & Brone, R. J. (1991). Eating disorders in adolescence. In R. M. Lerner, A. C. Petersen, & J. Brooks–Gunn (Eds.), *Encyclopedia of adolescence.* New York: Garland.

Fisher, E. P. (1992). The impact of play on development: A meta-analysis. *Play and Culture, 5,* 159–181.

Fitzgerald, H. E., & Brackbill, Y. (1976). Classical conditioning in infancy: Development and constraints. *Psychological Bulletin, 83,* 353–376.

Fitzgerald, H. E., Harris, L. J., Barnes, C. L., Wang, X., Cornwell, K., Kamptner, N. L.,

Dagenbach, D., & Carlson, D. (1991). The organization of lateralized behavior during infancy. In H. E. Fitzgerald, B. M. Lester, & M. W. Yogman (Eds.), *Theory and research in behavioral pediatrics.* New York: Plenum.

Fivush, R. (1993). Emotional content of parent–child conversations about the past. In C. A. Nelson (Ed.), *Minnesota symposia on child psychology: Vol. 26. Memory and affect in development.* Hillsdale, NJ: Erlbaum.

Fivush, R., & Hammond, N. R. (1990). Autobiographical memory across the preschool years: Toward reconceptualizing childhood amnesia. In R. Fivush & J. A. Hudson (Eds.), *Knowing and remembering in young children.* Cambridge: Cambridge University Press.

Fivush, R., Kuebli, J., & Clubb, P. A. (1992). The structure of events and event representations: A developmental analysis. *Child Development, 63,* 188–201.

Flanagan, C. A., & Eccles, J. S. (1993). Changes in parents' work status and adolescents' adjustment at school. *Child Development, 64,* 246–257.

Flannery, D. J., Rowe, D. C., & Gulley, B. L. (1993). Impact of pubertal status, timing, and age on adolescent sexual experience and delinquency. *Journal of Adolescent Research, 8,* 21–40.

Flannery, D. J., Vazsonyi, A. T., Torquati, J., & Fridrich, A. (in press). Ethnic and gender differences in risk for early adolescent substance use. *Journal of Youth and Adolescence.*

Flavell, J. H. (1993). Young children's understanding of thinking and consciousness. *Current Directions in Psychological Science, 2,* 40–43.

Flavell, J. H., Flavell, E. R., Green, F. L., & Moses, L. J. (1990). Young children's understanding of fact beliefs versus value beliefs. *Child Development, 61,* 915–928.

Flavell, J. H., Green, F. L., & Flavell, E. R. (1993a). Children's understanding of the stream of consciousness. *Child Development, 64,* 387–398.

Flavell, J. H., Miller, P. H., & Miller, S. A. (1993b). *Cognitive development* (3rd ed.). Englewood Cliffs, NJ: Prentice Hall.

Fleisher, L. C. (1987). What about the children? The dilemma of prematernal liability. In M. I. Evans, J. C. Fletcher, A. O. Dixler, & J. D. Schulman (Eds.), *Fetal diagnosis and therapy: Science, ethics and the law.* Philadelphia: Lippincott.

Fleming, A. S. (1989, Spring). Maternal responsiveness in human and animal mothers. In M. H. Bornstein (Ed.), *New directions for child development: No. 43. Maternal responsiveness: Characteristics and consequences.* San Francisco: Jossey–Bass.

Fleming, A. S., Klein, E., & Corter, C. (1992). The effects of a social support group on depression, maternal attitudes and behavior in new mothers. *Journal of Child Psychology & Psychiatry, 33,* 685–698.

Forehand, R., & Long, N. (1991). Prevention of aggression and other behavior problems in the early adolescent years. In D. J. Pepler & K. H. Rubin (Eds.), *The development and treatment of childhood aggression.* Hillsdale, NJ: Erlbaum.

Forehand, R., Wierson, M., Thomas, A. M., Armistead, L., Kempton, T., & Neighbors, B. (1991a). The role of family stressors and parent relationships on adolescent functioning. *Journal of the American Academy of Child and Adolescent Psychiatry, 30,* 316–322.

Forehand, R., Wierson, M., Thomas, A. M., Fauber, R., Armistead, L., Kempton, T., & Long, N. (1991b). A short-term longitudinal examination of young adolescent functioning following divorce: The role of family factors. *Journal of Abnormal Child Psychology, 19,* 97–111.

Forgatch, M. S. (1991). The clinical science vortex: A developing theory of antisocial behavior. In D. J. Pepler & K. H. Rubin (Eds.), *The development and treatment of childhood aggression.* Hillsdale, NJ: Erlbaum.

Forrest, J. D. (1990). Cultural influences on adolescents' reproductive behavior. In J. Bancroft & J. M. Reinisch (Eds.), *Adolescence and puberty.* New York: Oxford.

Fortier, J. C., Carson, V. B., Will, S., & Shubkagel, B. L. (1991). Adjustment to a newborn: Sibling preparation makes a difference. *Journal of Obstetric, Gynecologic, and Neonatal Nursing, 20,* 73–79.

Foster, G. D., Wadden, T. A., & Brownell, K. D. (1985). Peer-led program for the treatment and prevention of obesity in the schools. *Journal of Consulting and Clinical Psychology, 53,* 538–540.

Foster–Clark, F. S., & Blyth, D. A. (1991). Peer relations and influences. In R. M. Lerner, A. C. Petersen, & J. Brooks–Gunn (Eds.), *Encyclopedia of adolescence.* New York: Garland.

Fowler, W., Ogston, K., Roberts–Fiati, G., & Swenson, A. (1993, February). *The long term development of giftedness and high competencies in children enriched in language during infancy.* Paper presented at the Esther Katz Rosen Symposium on the Psychological Development of Gifted Children, University of Kansas.

Fox, L. H. (1982). *Sex differences among the mathematically gifted.* Paper presented at the meeting of the American Association for the Advancement of Science, Washington, DC.

Fox, L. H., Brody, L., & Tobin, D. (1985). The impact of early intervention programs upon course-taking and attitudes in high school. In S. F. Chipman, L. R. Brush, & D. M. Wilson (Eds.), *Women and mathematics: Balancing the equation.* London: Erlbaum.

Fox, N. A. (1991). If it's not left, it's right. *American Psychologist, 46,* 863–872.

Fox, N. A. (1992). The role of temperament in attachment in normal and high-risk infants. In C. W. Greenbaum & J. G. Auerbach (Eds.), *Longitudinal studies of children at psychological risk: Cross-national perspectives.* Norwood, NJ: Ablex.

Fox, N. A., Kimmerly, N. L., & Schafer, W. D. (1991). Attachment to mother/attachment to father: A meta-analysis. *Child Development, 62,* 210–225.

Fox, R. (1991). Developing awareness of mind reflected in children's narrative writing. *British Journal of Developmental Psychology, 9,* 281–298.

Foxx, R. M., & Azrin, N. H. (1973). *Toilet training the retarded: A rapid program for day and night time independent toileting.* Champaign, IL: Research Press.

Frank, R. G., Bouman, D. E., Cain, K., & Watts, C. (1992). Primary prevention of catastrophic injury. *American Psychologist, 47,* 1045–1049.

Frankel, J. (1993). Introduction. In J. Frankel (Ed.), *The employed mother and the family context.* New York: Springer.

Frankel, K. A., & Bates, J. E. (1990). Mother–toddler problem solving: Antecedents in attachment, home behavior, and temperament. *Child Development, 61,* 810–819.

Frankenburg, W. K., Dodds, J., Archer, P., Shapiro, H., & Bresnick, B. (1992). The Denver II: A major revision and restandardization of the Denver Developmental Screening Test. *Pediatrics, 89,* 91–97.

Freedland, J., & Dwyer, J. (1991). Nutrition in adolescent girls. In R. M. Lerner, A. C. Petersen, & J. Brooks–Gunn (Eds.), *Encyclopedia of adolescence.* New York: Garland.

Freeman, M. S., Spence, M. J., and Oliphant, C. M. (1993, June). *Newborns prefer their mothers' low-pass filtered voices over other female filtered voices.* Paper presented at the meeting of the American Psychological Society, Chicago.

Freeman, N. H., Lewis, C., & Doherty, M. J. (1991). Preschoolers' grasp of a desire for knowledge in false-belief prediction: Practical intelligence and verbal report. *British Journal of Developmental Psychology, 9,* 139–157.

Freilberg, P. (1991a, January). Bills aiding children passed by Congress. *APA Monitor,* p. 22.

Freilberg, P. (1991b, June). Teens' long work hours detrimental, study says. *APA Monitor,* pp. 19–20.

Freilberg, P. (1991c, June). More long-term problems seen for abused kids. *APA Monitor,* pp. 18–19.

Freud, A. (1969). Adolescence as a developmental disturbance. In G. Kaplan & S. Leborici (Eds.), *Adolescence: Psychosocial perspectives.* New York: Basic Books.

Freud, S. (1964). New introductory lectures. In *Standard edition of the complete psychological works of Sigmund Freud,* (Vol. 22). London: Hogarth. (Original work published 1933).

Freund, C. S. (1990). Maternal regulation of children's problem-solving behavior and its impact on children's performance. *Child Development, 61,* 113–126.

Frey, K. S., & Ruble, D. N. (1992). Gender constancy and the "cost" of sex-typed behavior: A test of the conflict hypothesis. *Developmental Psychology, 28,* 714–721.

Frick, P. J., & Lahey, B. B. (1991). The nature and characteristics of attention-deficit hyperactivity disorder. *School Psychology Review, 20,* 163–173.

Frick, P. J., Lahey, B. B., Christ, M. G., Loeber, R., & Green, S. (1991a). History of childhood behavior problems in biological relatives of boys with attention-deficit hyperactivity disorder and conduct disorder. *Journal of Clinical Child Psychology, 20,* 445–451.

Frick, P. J., Lahey, B. B., Loeber, R., Stouthamer–Laeber, M., Green, S., Hart, E. L., & Christ, M. A. G. (1991b). Oppositional defiant disorder and conduct disorder in boys: Patterns of behavioral covariation. *Journal of Clinical Child Psychology, 20,* 202–208.

Fried, P. A., O'Connell, C. M., & Watkinson, B. (1992, December). 60- and 72-month follow-up of children prenatally exposed to marijuana, cigarettes, and alcohol: Cognitive and language assessment. *Journal of Developmental and Behavioral Pediatrics, 13,* 383–391.

Frisch, R. E. (1991). Puberty and body fat. In R. M. Lerner, A. C. Petersen, & J. Brooks–Gunn (Eds.), *Encyclopedia of adolescence.* New York: Garland.

Fritz, J., & Wetherbee, S. (1982). Preschoolers' beliefs regarding the obese individual. *Canadian Home Economics Journal, 33,* 193–196.

Frodi, A. M. (1985). When empathy fails: Infant crying and child abuse. In B. M. Lester & C. F. Z. Boukydis (Eds.), *Infant crying.* New York: Plenum.

Frodi, A., & Senchak, M. (1990). Verbal and behavioral responsiveness to the cries of atypical infants. *Child Development, 61,* 76–84.

Fromberg, D. (1990). Play issues in early childhood education. In C. Seefeldt (Ed.), *Continuing issues in early childhood education.* Columbus, OH: Merrill.

Fuligni, A. J., & Eccles, J. S. (1993). Perceived parent–child relationships and early adolescents' orientation toward peers. *Developmental Psychology, 29,* 622–632.

Furby, L., & Beyth–Marom, R. (1992). Risk taking in adolescence: A decision-making perspective. *Developmental Review, 12,* 1–44.

Furman, W., & Buhrmester, D. (1992). Age and sex differences in perceptions of networks of personal relationships. *Child Development, 63,* 103–115.

Furman, W., Rahe, D., & Hartup, W. W. (1979). Social rehabilitation of low-interactive preschool children by peer intervention. *Child Development, 50,* 915–922.

Furman, W., & Wehner, E. A. (in press). Romantic views: Toward a theory of adolescent romantic relationships. In R. Montemayor (Ed.), *Advances in adolescent development: Vol. 6. Relationships in adolescence.* Beverly Hills, CA: Sage.

Furnham, A., Hester, C., & Weir, C. (1990). Sex differences in the preferences for specific female body shapes. *Sex Roles, 22,* 743–754.

Furstenberg, F. F., Jr. (1990). Divorce and the American family. *Annual Review of Sociology, 16,* 379–403.

Furstenberg, F. F., Jr., (1991). Pregnancy and childbearing: Effects on teen mothers. In R. M. Lerner, A. C. Petersen, & J. Brooks–Gunn (Eds.), *Encyclopedia of adolescence.* New York: Garland.

Furstenberg, F. F., Jr., Brooks–Gunn, J., & Chase–Lansdale, L. (1989). Teenaged pregnancy and childbearing. *American Psychologist, 44,* 313–320.

Furstenberg, F. F., Jr., & Cherlin, A. J. (1991). *Divided families: What happens to children when parents part?* Cambridge, MA: Harvard University Press.

Furstenberg, F. F., Hughes, M. E., & Brooks–Gunn, J. (1992). The next generation: The children of teenage mothers grow up. In M. K. Rosenheim & M. F. Testa (Eds.), *Early parenthood and coming of age in the 1990s.* New Brunswick, NJ: Rutgers University Press.

Gadow, K. D., Nolan, E. E., Sverd, J., Sprafkin, J., & Paolicell, L. (1990). Methylphenidate in aggressive-hyperactive boys: I. Effects on peer aggression in public school settings. *Journal of the American Academy of Child and Adolescent Psychiatry, 29,* 710–718.

Gagnon, C., Tremblay, R. E., Craig, W., & Zhou, R. M. (1993, March). *Kindergarten predictors of boys' stable disruptive behavior at the end of elementary school.* Paper presented at the meeting of the Society for Research in Child Development, New Orleans, LA.

Galambos, N. L. (1992). Parent–adolescent relations. *Current Directions in Psychological Science, 1,* 146–149.

Galambos, N. L., & Almeida, D. M. (1992). Does parent–adolescent conflict increase in early adolescence? *Journal of Marriage and the Family, 54,* 737–747.

Galambos, N. L., & Maggs, J. L. (1991). Out-of-school care of young adolescents and self-reported behavior. *Developmental Psychology, 27,* 644–655.

Galler, J. A. (1989). A follow-up study of the influence of early malnutrition on development: Behavior at home and at school. *Journal of the American Academy of Child and Adolescent Psychiatry, 28,* 254–261.

Galler, J. R., Ramsey, F. C., Morley, D. S., Archer, E., & Salt, P. (1990). The long-term effects of early kwashiorkor compared with marasmus IV. Performance on the national high school entrance examination. *Pediatric Research, 28,* 235–239.

Gallimore, M., & Kurdek, L. A. (1992). Parent depression and parent authoritative discipline as correlates of young adolescents' depression. *Journal of Early Adolescence, 12,* 187–196.

Galotti, K. M., Kozberg, S. F., & Farmer, M. C. (1991). Gender and developmental differences in adolescents' conception of moral reasoning. *Journal of Youth and Adolescence, 20,* 13–30.

Ganchrow, J. R., Steiner, J. E., & Daher, M. (1983). Neonatal facial expressions in response to different qualities and intensities of gustatory stimuli. *Infant Behavior and Development, 6,* 189–200.

Garbarino, J. (1982). *Children and families in the social environment.* New York: Aldine deGruyter.

Garbarino, J. (1992). *Children in danger: Coping with the consequences of community violence.* San Francisco: Jossey–Bass.

Garbarino, J., Dubrow, N., & Kostelny, K. (1991). *No place to be a child: Growing up in a war zone.* Lexington, MA: Lexington Books.

Garber, H. L. (1988). *The Milwaukee Project: Preventing mental retardation in children at risk.* Washington, DC: American Association on Mental Retardation.

Garcia-Coll, C. T. (1990). Developmental outcome of minority infants: A process-oriented look into our beginnings. *Child Development, 61,* 270–289.

Garcia-Coll, C. T., Halpern, L. F., Vohr, B. R., Seifer, R., & Oh, W. (1992). Stability and correlates of change of early temperament in preterm and full-term infants. *Infant Behavior and Development, 15,* 137–153.

Gardner, H. (1982). *Art, mind, and brain: A cognitive approach to creativity.* New York: Basic Books.

Gardner, H. (1983). *Frames of mind: The theory of multiple intelligences.* New York: Basic Books.

Gardner, H. (1993). *Multiple intelligences.* New York: Basic Books.

Gardner, W., & Wilcox, B. L. (1993). Political intervention in scientific peer review: Research on adolescent sexual behavior. *American Psychologist, 48,* 972–983.

Gargan, E. A. (1991, December 13). Ultrasonic tests skew ratio of births in India. *New York Times,* p. A12.

Garland, A. F., & Zigler, E. (1993). Adolescent suicide prevention. *American Psychologist, 48,* 169–182.

Gärling, A., & Gärling, T. (1993). Mothers' supervision and perception of young children's risk of unintentional injury in the home. *Journal of Pediatric Psychology, 18,* 105–114.

Garner, P. W., & Landry, S. H. (1992). Preterm infants' affective responses in independent versus toy-centered play with their mothers. *Infant Mental Health Journal, 13,* 219–230.

Garrod, A., Beal, C., & Shin, P. (1991). The development of moral orientation in elementary school children. *Sex Roles, 22,* 13–27.

Garvey, C. (1990). *Developing child.* Cambridge, MA: Harvard University Press.

Gath, A. (1992). The brothers and sisters of mentally retarded children. In F. Boer &

J. Dunn (Eds.), *Children's sibling relationships: Developmental and clinical issues.* Hillsdale, NJ: Erlbaum.

Gelles, R. J., & Conte, J. R. (1990). Domestic violence and sexual abuse of children: A review of research in the eighties. *Journal of Marriage and the Family, 52,* 1045–1058.

Gelman, D. (1992, February 24). Born or bred? *Newsweek,* pp. 46–53.

Gelman, D. (1993, January 11). The young and the reckless. *Newsweek,* pp. 60–61.

Gelman, R. (1978). Cognitive development. *Annual Review of Psychology, 29,* 297–332.

Gelman, R., & Baillargeon, R. (1983). A review of some Piagetian concepts. In P. H. Mussen (Ed.), *Handbook of child psychology: Vol. 3. Cognitive development.* New York: Wiley.

Gelman, S. A., & Kremer, K. E. (1991). Understanding natural cause: Children's explanations of how objects and their properties originate. *Child Development, 62,* 396–414.

Gerbner, G. (1993). *Violence in cable-originated television programs: A report to the National Cable Television Association.* University Park: University of Pennsylvania, Annenberg School for Communication.

Geschwind, N., & Galaburda, A. M. (1987). *Cerebral lateralization: Biological mechanisms, associations, and pathology.* Cambridge, MA: MIT Press.

Gesell, A. (1928). *Infancy and human growth.* New York: Macmillan.

Gesell, A. (1929). Maturation and infant behavior patterns. *Psychological Review, 36,* 307–319.

Gesell, A. (1972). *The embryology of behavior.* Westport, CT: Greenwood.

Gettys, L. D., & Cann, A. (1981). Children's perceptions of occupational sex stereotypes. *Sex Roles, 7,* 301–308.

Gewirtz, J. L., & Peláez–Nogueras, M. (1992). B. F. Skinner's legacy to human infant behavior and development. *American Psychologist, 47,* 1411–1422.

Gibbs, J. T. (1989). Black American adolescents. In J. T. Gibbs & L. N. Huang (Eds.), *Children of color: Psychological interventions with minority youth.* San Francisco: Jossey–Bass.

Gibbs, J. T. (1991). Toward an integration of Kohlberg's and Hoffman's theories of morality. In W. M. Kurtines & J. L. Gewirtz (Eds.), *Handbook of moral behavior and development* (Vol. 1). Hillsdale, NJ: Erlbaum.

Gibbs, J. T., & Hines, A. M. (1992). Negotiating ethnic identity: Issues for black–white biracial adolescents. In M. P. P. Root (Ed.), *Racially mixed people in America.* Newbury Park, CA: Sage.

Gibran, K. (1970). *The prophet.* New York: Knopf.

Gibson, E. J. (1969). *Principles of perceptual learning and development.* New York: Appleton–Century–Crofts.

Gibson, E. J. (1991). *An odyssey in learning and perception.* Cambridge, MA: MIT Press.

Gibson, E. J., & Walk, R. D. (1960). The visual cliff. *Scientific American, 202,* 64–71.

Gilbert, S. (1993, April 25). Waiting game. *New York Times Magazine,* pp. 70–72, 92.

Gilbert–Barness, E., & Barness, L. A. (1992). Cause of death: SIDS or something else? *Contemporary Pediatrics, 9,* 13–29.

Gilligan, C. (1977). In a different voice: Women's conceptions of self and morality. *Harvard Educational Review, 47,* 481–517.

Gilligan, C. (1982). *In a different voice.* Cambridge, MA: Harvard University Press.

Gilligan, C., & Attanucci, J. (1988). Two moral orientations: Gender differences and similarities. *Merrill–Palmer Quarterly, 34,* 223–237.

Gilligan, C., Lyons, P., & Hanmer, T. J. (Eds.). (1990). *Making connections: The relational worlds of adolescent girls at Emma Willard School.* Cambridge, MA: Harvard University Press.

Gillis, J. J., Gilger, J. W., Pennington, B. F., & DeFries, J. C. (1992). Attention deficit disorder in reading-disabled twins: Evidence for a genetic etiology. *Journal of Abnormal Child Psychology, 20,* 303–315.

Ginsberg, E. (1972). Toward a theory of occupational choice: A restatement. *Vocational Guidance Quarterly, 20,* 169–176.

Giovannoni, J. (1989). Definitional issues in child maltreatment. In D. Cicchetti & V. Carlson (Eds.), *Child maltreatment: Theory and research on the causes and consequences of child abuse and neglect.* Cambridge: Cambridge University Press.

Gitlin, M. J., & Pasnay, R. O. (1989). Psychiatric syndromes linked to reproductive function in women: A review of current knowledge. *American Journal of Psychiatry, 146,* 1413–1422.

Gladue, B. A. (1988). Hormones in relationship to homosexual/bisexual/heterosexual gender orientation. In J. M. A. Sitsen (Ed.), *Handbook of Sexology* (Vol. 6). Amsterdam: Elsevier.

Glasberg, R., & Aboud, F. (1982). Keeping one's distance from sadness: Children's self-reports of emotional experience. *Developmental Psychology, 18,* 287–293.

Glass, R. H., & Ericsson, R. (1982). *Getting pregnant in the 1980s.* Berkeley: University of California Press.

Gleitman, L. R., & Wanner, E. (1988). Current issues in language learning. In M. H. Bornstein & M. E. Lamb (Eds.), *Developmental psychology: An advanced textbook* (2nd ed.). Hillsdale, NJ: Erlbaum.

Glick, P. C. (1989). The family life cycle and social change. *Family Relations, 38,* 123–129.

Glik, D. C., Greaves, P. E., Kronenfeld, J. J., & Jackson, K. L. (1993). Safety hazards in households with young children. *Journal of Pediatric Psychology, 18,* 115–131.

Goedert, J. J., Duliège, A., Amos, C. I., Felton, S., Biggar, R. J., & The International Registry of HIV-Exposed Twins (1991). High risk of HIV-1 infection for first-born twins. *Lancet, 338,* 1471–1475.

Goertz, M. E., Ekstrom, R. B., & Rock, D. (1991). High school dropouts: Issues of race and sex. In R. M. Lerner, A. C. Petersen, & J. Brooks–Gunn (Eds.), *Encyclopedia of adolescence.* New York: Garland.

Goldberg, S. (1983). Parent–infant bonding: Another look. *Child Development, 54,* 1355–1382.

Goldberg, S., Lojkasek, M., Gartner, G., & Corter, C. (1989). Maternal responsiveness and social development in preterm infants. In M. H. Bornstein (Ed.), *New directions for child development: No. 43. Maternal responsiveness: Characteristics and consequences.* San Francisco: Jossey–Bass.

Goldfield, B. A., & Reznick, J. S. (1990). Early lexical acquisition: Rate, content and the vocabulary spurt. *Journal of Child Language, 17,* 171–183.

Goldsmith, H. H., Buss, A. H., Plomin, R., Rothbart, M. K., Thomas, A., Chess, S., Hinde, R. A., & McCall, R. B. (1987). Roundtable: What is temperament? Four approaches. *Child Development, 58,* 505–529.

Goldson, E. (1992). The longitudinal study of very low birthweight infants and its implications for interdisciplinary research and public policy. In C. W. Greenbaum & J. G. Auerbach (Eds.), *Longitudinal studies of children at psychological risk: Cross-national perspectives.* Norwood, NJ: Ablex.

Goldstein, M. B. (1991, August). *The impacts of teenage employment: Teachers' perceptions versus student realities.* Paper presented at the meeting of the American Psychological Association, San Francisco.

Goleman, D. (1987, October 13). Thriving despite hardship: Key childhood traits identified. *New York Times,* pp. C1, 11.

Goleman, D. (1991, July 30). Theory links early puberty to childhood stress. *New York Times,* pp. B5, 6.

Goleman, D. (1992a, September 15). New storm brews on whether crime has roots in genes. *New York Times,* pp. B5, B8.

Goleman, D. (1992b, December 6). Attending to the children of all the world's war zones. *New York Times,* p. E7.

Goleman, D. (1993, July 13). New treatments for autism arouse hope and skepticism. *New York Times,* pp. B5, 7.

Golinkoff, R., Hirsh–Pasek, K., Bailey, L., & Wenger, N. (1992). Young children and adults use lexical principles to learn new nouns. *Developmental Psychology, 28,* 99–108.

Golub, S. (1992). *Periods: From menarche to menopause.* Newbury Park, CA: Sage.

Goodchilds, J. D. (Ed.). (1991). *Psychological perspectives on human diversity in America.* Washington, DC: American Psychological Association.

Goodman, G. S., & Clarke–Stewart, A. (1991). Suggestibility in children's testimony: Implications for sexual abuse investigations. In J. Doris (Ed.), *The suggestibility of children's recollections.* Washington, DC: American Psychological Association.

Goodman, G. S., Hirschman, J. E., Hepps, D., & Rudy, L. (1991). Children's memory for stressful events. *Merrill–Palmer Quarterly, 37,* 109–157.

Goodman, G. S., Rudy, L., Bottoms, B. L., & Aman, C. (1990). Children's concerns and memory: Issues of ecological validity in the study of children's eyewitness testimony. In R. Fivush & J. A. Hudson (Eds.), *Knowing and remembering in young children.* Cambridge: Cambridge University Press.

Goodman, G. S., Taub, E. P., Jones, D. P. H., England, P., Port, L. K., Rudy, L., & Prado, L. (1992). Testifying in criminal court. *Monographs of the Society for Research in Child Development, 57* (5, Serial No. 229).

Goodsitt, J. V., Morse, P. A., Ver Hoeve, J. N., & Cowan, N. (1984). Infant speech recognition in multisyllabic contexts. *Child Development, 55,* 903–910.

Gopnik, A., & Choi, S. (1990). Do linguistic differences lead to cognitive differences? A cross-linguistic study of semantic and cognitive development. *First Language, 10,* 199–215.

Gopnik, A., & Meltzoff, A. N. (1987). The development of categorization in the second year and its relation to other cognitive and linguistic developments. *Child Development, 58,* 1523–1531.

Gopnik, A., & Meltzoff, A. N. (1992). Categorization and naming: Basic-level sorting in eighteen-month-olds and its relation to language. *Child Development, 63,* 1091–1103.

Gopnik, A., & Slaughter, V. (1991). Young children's understanding of changes in their mental states. *Child Development, 62,* 98–110.

Gordon, C. T., State, R. C., Nelson, J. E., Hamburger, S. D., & Rapoport, J. L. (1993). A double-blind comparison of clomipramine, despiramine, and placebo in treatment of autistic disorder. *Archives of General Psychiatry, 50,* 441–447.

Gordon, D. E. (1990). Formal operational thinking: The role of cognitive-developmental processes in adolescent decision-making about pregnancy and contraception. *American Journal of Orthopsychiatry, 60,* 346–356.

Gortmaker, S. L., Must, A., Perrin, J. M., Sobol., A. M., & Dietz, W. H. (1993). Social and economic consequences of overweight in adolescence and young adulthood. *New England Journal of Medicine, 329,* 1008–1012.

Gottfried, A. E., Bathurst, K., & Gottfried, A. W. (1994). Role of maternal and dual-earner employment in children's development: A longitudinal study. In A. E. Gottfried & A. W. Gottfried (Eds.), *Redefining families: Implications for children's development.* New York: Plenum.

Gottlieb, G. (1991). The experimental canalization of behavioral development: Theory. *Developmental Psychology, 27,* 4–13.

Gottlieb, L. N., & Mendelson, M. J. (1990). Parental support and firstborn girls' adaptation to the birth of a sibling. *Journal of Applied Developmental Psychology, 11,* 29–48.

Gould, M. D. (1991). Cluster suicides. In R. M. Lerner, A. C. Petersen, & J. Brooks–Gunn (Eds.), *Encyclopedia of adolescence.* New York: Garland.

Gowers, S. G., Crisp, A. H., Joughlin, N., & Bhat, A. (1991). Premenarcheal anorexia nervosa. *Journal for Child Psychology and Psychiatry, 32,* 515–524.

Graber, J. A., & Petersen, A. C. (1991). Cognitive changes at adolescence: Biological perspectives. In K. R. Gibson & A. C. Petersen (Eds.), *Brain maturation and cognitive development.* New York: Aldine de-Gruyter.

Graham, P. J. (1991). Psychiatric aspects of pediatric disorders. In M. Lewis (Ed.), *Child and adolescent psychiatry: A comprehensive textbook.* Baltimore: Williams & Wilkins.

Graham–Bermann, S. A. (1991). Siblings in dyads: Relationships among perceptions and behavior. *Journal of Genetic Psychology, 152,* 207–216.

Granger, D. A., Webster, T., Ikeda, S., & Kauneckis, D. (1993, March). *Methylphenidate effects on hyperactive children's social behavior: A meta-analysis.* Paper presented at the meeting of the Society for Research in Child Development, New Orleans, LA.

Granrud, C. E. (1987). Size constancy in newborn human infants. *Investigative Ophthalmology and Visual Science, 28*(Suppl.), 5.

Grant, J. P. (1993). *The state of the world's children.* New York: UNICEF and Oxford University Press.

Grant, J. P. (1994). *The state of the world's children.* New York: UNICEF and Oxford University Press.

Greco, C., Rovee–Collier, C., Hayne, H., Griesler, P., & Early, L. (1986). Ontogeny of early event memory: II. Encoding and retrieval by 2- and 3-month-olds. *Infant Behavior and Development, 9,* 461–472.

Green, J. A., Jones, L. E., & Gustafson, G.E. (1987). Perception of cries by parents and nonparents: Relation to cry acoustics. *Developmental Psychology, 23,* 370–382.

Green, V., Johnson, S., & Kaplan, D. (1992). Predictors of adolescent female decision making regarding contraceptive usage. *Adolescence, 27,* 613–632.

Green, W. H. (1991). Principles of psychopharmacotherapy and specific drug treatments. In M. Lewis (Ed.), *Child and adolescent psychiatry: A comprehensive textbook.* Baltimore: Williams & Wilkins.

Greenberg, J., & Kuczaj, S. A., II. (1982). Towards a theory of substantive word-meaning acquisition. In S. A. Kucaj, II (Ed.), *Language development: Vol. 1. Syntax and semantics.* Hillsdale, NJ: Erlbaum.

Greene, A. L. (1990). Great expectations: Constructions of the life course during adolescence. *Journal of Youth and Adolescence, 19,* 289–306.

Greene, A. L., & Grimsley, M. D. (1990). Age and gender differences in adolescents' preferences for parental advice: Mum's the word. *Journal of Adolescent Research, 5,* 396–413.

Greenfield, P. M., & Cocking, R. R. (Eds.). (1994). *Cross-cultural roots of minority children development.* Hillsdale, NJ: Erlbaum.

Greenough, B. S. (1993, April 5). Breaking the genetic code. *Newsweek,* pp. 10–11.

Greenough, W. T. (1991). Experience as a component of normal development: Evolutionary considerations. *Developmental Psychology, 27,* 14–17.

Greenough, W. T., Black, J. E., & Wallace, C.S. (1987). Experience and brain development. *Child Development, 58,* 539–559.

Greensher, J. (1991). Environmental risks in the industrialized countries. In M. Manciaux & C. J. Romer (Eds.), *Accidents in childhood and adolescence.* Geneva: World Health Organization.

Greenwood, C. R., Carta, J. J., Hart, B., Kamps, D., Terry, B., Arreaga–Mayer, C., Atwater, J., Walker, D., Risley, T., & Delquadri, J. C. (1992). Out of the laboratory and into the community. *American Psychologist, 47,* 1464–1474.

Grief, E. B., & Ulman, K. J. (1982). The psychological impact of menarche on early adolescent females: A review of the literature. *Child Development, 53,* 1413–1430.

Grilo, C. M., & Pogue–Geile, M. F. (1991). The nature of environmental influences on weight and obesity: A behavior genetic analysis. *Psychological Bulletin, 110,* 520–537.

Gross, A. L., & Ballif, B. (1991). Children's understanding of emotion from facial expressions and situations: A review. *Developmental Review, 11,* 368–398.

Gross, S. J., Slagle, T. A., D'Eugenio, D. B., & Mettelman, B. B. (1992). Impact of a matched term control group on interpretation of developmental performance in preterm infants. *Pediatrics, 90,* 681–687.

Grossmann, K., & Grossmann, K. E. (1991). Newborn behavior, the quality of early parenting and later toddler–parent relationships in a group of German infants. In J. K. Nugent, B. M. Lester, & T. B. Brazelton (Eds.), *The cultural context of infancy* (Vol. 2). Norwood, NJ: Ablex.

Groves, B. M., Zuckerman, B., Marans, S., & Cohen, D. J. (1993, January 13). Silent victims: Children who witness violence. *Journal of the American Medical Association, 269,* 262–264.

Grusec, J. E. (1991). Socializing concern for others in the home. *Developmental Psychology, 27,* 338–342.

Grusec, J. E. (1992). Social learning theory and developmental psychology: The legacies of Robert Sears and Albert Bandura. *Developmental Psychology, 28,* 776–786.

Grusec, J. E., & Lytton, H. (1988). *Social development: History, theory and research.* New York: Springer–Verlag.

Gruson, L. (1993, February 16). A mother's gift: Bearing her grandchild. *New York Times,* pp. B1, 4.

Grych, J. H., & Fincham, F. D. (1990). Marital conflict and children's adjustment: A cognitive–contextual framework. *Psychological Bulletin, 108,* 267–290.

Grych, J. H., & Fincham, F. D. (1992). Interventions for children of divorce: Toward greater integration of research and action. *Psychological Bulletin, 111,* 434–454.

Gualtieri, T., & Hicks, R. E. (1985). An immunoreactive theory of selective male affliction. *Behavioral and Brain Sciences, 8,* 427–441.

Guerra, N. G., & Slaby, R. G. (1990). Cognitive mediators of aggression in adolescent offenders: Intervention. *Developmental Psychology, 26,* 269–277.

Guilford, J. P. (1959). Traits of creativity. In H. H. Anderson (Ed.), *Creativity and its cultivation.* New York: Harper & Row.

Guilford, J. P., & Hoepfner, R. (1971). *The analysis of intelligence.* New York: McGraw–Hill.

Gustafson, G. E., & Harris, K. L. (1990). Women's responses to young infants' cries. *Developmental Psychology, 26,* 144–152.

Guttmann, J. (1993). *Divorce in psychosocial perspective: Theory and research.* Hillsdale, NJ: Erlbaum.

Haan, N., Smith, M. B., & Block, J. (1968). Moral reasoning of young adults: Political–social behavior, family background and personality correlates. *Journal of Personality and Social Psychology, 10,* 183–201.

Habib, M., Touze, F., & Galaburda, A. M. (1990). Intrauterine factors in sinistrality: A review. In S. Coren (Ed.), *Left-handedness: Behavior implications and anomalies.* Amsterdam: North–Holland.

Hack, M., Breslau, N., & Aram, D. (1992). The effect of very low birth weight and social risk on neurocognitive abilities at school age. *Journal of Developmental & Behavioral Pediatrics, 13,* 412–420.

Hainline, L., & Abramov, I. (1992). Assessing visual development: Is infant vision good enough. In C. Rovee–Collier & L. P. Lipsitt (Eds.), *Advances in infancy research* (Vol. 7). Norwood, NJ: Ablex.

Haith, M. M. (1966). The response of the human newborn to visual movement. *Journal of Experimental Child Psychology, 3,* 235–243.

Haith, M. M. (1979). Visual cognition in early infancy. In R. B. Kearsly & I. E. Sigel (Eds.), *Infants at risk: Assessment of cognitive functioning.* Hillsdale, NJ: Erlbaum.

Haith, M. M. (1986). Sensory and perceptual processes in early infancy. *Journal of Pediatrics, 109,* 158–171.

Haith, M. M. (1990). Progress in the understanding of sensory and perceptual processes in early infancy. *Merrill–Palmer Quarterly, 36,* 1–26.

Hakuta, K., & Garcia, E. E. (1989). Bilingualism and education. *American Psychologist, 44,* 374–379.

Hala, S., Chandler, M., & Fritz, A. S. (1991). Fledgling theories of mind: Deception as a marker of three-year-olds' understanding of false belief. *Child Development, 62,* 83–97.

Hale, C., & Windecker, E. (1993, March). *Influence of parent–child interaction during reading on preschoolers' cognitive abilities.* Paper presented at the meeting of the Society on Research in Child Development, New Orleans, LA.

Halgin, R. P., & Whitbourne, S. K. (1993). *Abnormal psychology.* Fort Worth, TX: Harcourt Brace Jovanovich.

Hall, D. G. (1991). Acquiring proper nouns for familiar and unfamiliar animate objects: Two-year-olds' word-learning biases. *Child Development, 62,* 1142–1154.

Hall, E. (1983, June). A conversation with Erik Erikson. *Psychology Today,* pp. 22–30.

Hall, G. S. (1904). *Adolescence: Its psychology and its relation to physiology, anthropology, sociology, sex, crime, religion and education.* Englewood Cliffs, NJ: Prentice Hall.

Hall, J. G., Sybert, V. P., Williamson, R. A., Fisher, N. L., & Reed, S. D. (1982). Turner's syndrome. *West Journal of Medicine, 137,* 32–44.

Hall, R. M., & Sandler, B. R. (1982). *The classroom climate: A chilly one for women?* Project on the Status and Education of Women. Washington, DC: Association of American Colleges.

Hall, R. M., & Sandler, B. R. (1984). *Out of the classroom: A chilly campus climate for women?* Project on the Status and Education of Women. Washington, DC: Association of American Colleges.

Halpern, D. (1992). *Sex differences in cognitive abilities* (2nd ed.). Hillsdale, NJ: Erlbaum.

Hamamy, H. A., Al–Hakkak, Z. S., & Al–Taha, S. (1990). Consanguinity and the genetic control of Down syndrome. *Clinical Genetics, 37,* 24–29.

Hamer, D. H., Hu, S., Magnuson, V. L., Hu, N., & Pattatucci, A. M. L. (1993). A linkage between DNA markers on the X chromosome and male sexual orientation. *Science, 261,* 321–327.

Hamlett, K. W., & Curry, J. F. (1990). Anorexia nervosa in adolescent males: A review and case study. *Child Psychiatry and Human Development, 21,* 79–94.

Hammond, W. R., & Yung, B. (1993). Psychology's role in the public health response to assaultive violence among young African-American men. *American Psychologist, 48,* 142–154.

Hamod, K. A., & Khouzami, V. A. (1988). Antibiotics in pregnancy. In J. R. Niebyl (Ed.), *Drug use in pregnancy* (2nd ed.). Philadelphia: Lea & Febiger.

Hampson, J. (1989, April). *Elements of style: Maternal and child contributions to expressive and referential styles of language acquisition.* Paper presented at the meeting of the Society for Research in Child Development, Kansas City, MO.

Handen, B. L., Breaux, A. M., Janofsky, J., McAuliffe, S., Feldman, H., & Gosling, A. (1992). Effects and noneffects of methylphenidate in children with mental retardation and ADHD. *Journal of American Academy of Child and Adolescent Psychiatry, 31,* 455–461.

Handford, H. A., Mattison, R. E., & Kales, A.(1991). Sleep disturbances and disorders. In M. Lewis (Ed.), *Child and adolescent psychiatry: A comprehensive textbook.* Baltimore: Williams & Wilkins.

Handleman, J. S. (1992). Assessment for curriculum planning. In D. E. Berkell (Ed.), *Autism.* Hillsdale, NJ: Erlbaum.

Handler, A. (1990). The correlates of the initiation of sexual intercourse among young urban black females. *Journal of Youth and Adolescence, 19,* 159–169.

Handyside, A. H., Lesko, J. G., Tarín, J. J., Winston, R. M. L., & Hughes, M. R. (1992). Birth of a normal girl after in vitro fertilization and preimplantation diagnostic testing for cystic fibrosis. *New England Journal of Medicine, 327,* 905–909.

Hanna, E. (1993, March). *Sex differences in play and imitation in toddlers.* Paper presented at the meeting of the Society for Research in Child Development, New Orleans, LA.

Hanna, E., & Meltzoff, A. N. (1993). Peer imitation by toddlers in laboratory, home, and day care contexts: Implications for social learning and memory. *Developmental Psychology, 29,* 701–710.

Hans, S. L., Henson, L. C., & Jeremy, R. J. (1992). The development of infants exposed in utero to opioid drugs. In C. W. Greenbaum & J. G. Auerbach (Eds.), *Longitudinal studies of children at psychological risk: Cross-national perspectives.* Norwood, NJ: Ablex.

Harding, J. J. (1989). Postpartum psychiatric disorders: A review. *Comprehensive Psychiatry, 30,* 109–112.

Harlow, H. F., & Harlow, M. K. (1966). Learning to love. *American Scientist, 54,* 244–272.

Harlow, H. F., Harlow, M. K., & Suomi, S. J. (1971). From thought to therapy: Lessons from a primate laboratory. *American Scientist, 59,* 538–549.

Harnishfeger, K. K., & Bjorklund, D. F. (1990). Strategic and nonstrategic factors in gifted children's free recall. *Contemporary Educational Psychology, 15,* 346–363.

Harper, J. F., & Marshall, E. (1991). Adolescents' problems and their relationship to self-esteem. *Adolescence, 26,* 799–807.

Harris, D. L., Brown, E., Marriott, C., Whittall, S., & Harmer, S. (1991). Monsters, ghosts and witches: Testing the limits of the fantasy–reality distinction in young children. *British Journal of Developmental Psychology, 9,* 105–123.

Harris, D. V. (1991). Exercise and fitness during adolescence. In R. M. Lerner, A. C. Petersen, & J. Brooks–Gunn (Eds.), *Encyclopedia of adolescence.* New York: Garland.

Harris, J. (1990). *Early language development.* New York: Routledge.

Harris, L. J. (1990). Cultural influences on handedness: Historical and contemporary theory and evidence. In S. Coren (Ed.), *Left-handedness: Behavior implications and anomalies.* Amsterdam: North–Holland.

Harris, L. J. (1991). The human infant in studies of lateralization of function: A historical perspective. In H. E. Fitzgerald, B. M. Lester, & M. W. Yogman (Eds.), *Theory and research in behavioral pediatrics.* New York: Plenum.

Harris, P. L. (1987). The development of search. In P. Salapatek & L. Cohen (Eds.), *Handbook of infant perception: Vol. 2. From perception to cognition.* New York: Academic Press.

Harris, P. L., & Kavanaugh, R. D. (1993). Young children's understanding of pretense. *Monographs of the Society for Research in Child Development, 58*(1, Serial No. 231).

Harrison, A. O., Wilson, M. N., Pine, C. J., Chan, S. Q., & Buriel, R. (1990). Family ecologies of ethnic minority children. *Child Development, 61,* 347–362.

Harrison, M. R., Adzick, N. S., Longaker, M. T., Goldberg, J. D., Rosen, M. A., Filly, R. A., Evans, M. I., & Golbus, M. S. (1990). Successful repair in utero of a fetal diaphragmatic hernia after removal of herniated viscera from the left thorax. *New England Journal of Medicine, 322,* 1582–1584.

Hart, B. (1991). Input frequency and children's first words. *First Language, 11,* 289–300.

Hart, C. H., DeWolf, D. M., Wozniak, P., & Burts, D. C. (1992). Maternal and paternal disciplinary styles: Relations with preschoolers' playground behavioral orientations and peer status. *Child Development, 63,* 879–892.

Hart, C. H., Ladd, G. W., & Burleson, B. R. (1990). Children's expectations of the outcomes of social strategies: Relations with sociometric status and maternal disciplinary styles. *Child Development, 61,* 127–138.

Hart, S. N., & Brassard, M. R. (1987). A major threat to children's mental health. *American Psychologist, 42,* 160–165.

Harter, S. (1987). The determinants and mediational role of global self-worth in children. In N. Eisenberg (Ed.), *Contemporary topics in developmental psychology.* New York: Wiley.

Harter, S. (1990a). Issues in the assessment of the self-concept of children and adolescents. In A. LaGreca (Ed.), *Through the eyes of a child.* Boston: Allyn & Bacon.

Harter, S. (1990b). Processes underlying adolescent self-concept formation. In R. Montemayor, G. R. Adams, T. P. Gullotta (Eds.), *From childhood to adolescence: A transitional period?* Newbury Park, CA: Sage.

Harter, S. (1990c). Self and identity development. In S. S. Feldman & G. R. Elliott (Eds.), *At the threshold: The developing adolescent.* Cambridge, MA: Harvard University Press.

Harter, S., & Marold, D. B. (1991). A model of the determinants and mediational role of self-worth: Implications for adolescent depression and suicidal ideation. In J. Strauss & G. R. Goethals (Eds.), *The self: Interdisciplinary approaches.* New York: Springer–Verlag.

Harter, S., Marold, D. B., & Whitesell, N. R. (1993, March). *A model of conditional parent support and adolescent false self behavior.* Presented at the meeting of the Society for Research in Child Development, New Orleans, LA.

Harter, S., & Monsour, A. (1992). Developmental analysis of conflict caused by opposing attributes in the adolescent self-portrait. *Developmental Psychology, 28,* 251–260.

Harter, S., & Pike, R. (1984). The pictorial scale of perceived competence and social acceptance for young children. *Child Development, 55,* 1969–1982.

Hartup, W. W. (1983). The peer system. In P. H. Mussen (Ed.), *Handbook of child psychology: Vol. 4. Socialization, personality, and social development.* New York: Wiley.

Hartup, W. W. (1989). Behavioral manifestations of children's friendships. In T. J. Berndt & G. W. Ladd (Eds.), *Peer relationships in child development.* New York: Wiley.

Hartup, W. W. (1992a). Conflict and friendship relations. In C. U. Shantz & W. W. Hartup (Eds.), *Conflict in child and adolescent development.* Cambridge, MA: Cambridge University Press.

Hartup, W. W. (1992b). Friendships and their developmental significance. In H. McGurk (Ed.), *Childhood social development.* Hove, United Kingdom: Erlbaum.

Hartup, W. W. (1993). Adolescents and their friends. In B. Laursen (Ed.), *New directions in child development: No. 60. Close friendships in adolescence.* San Francisco: Jossey–Bass.

Hashimoto, N. (1991). Memory development in early childhood: Encoding process in a spatial task. *Journal of Genetic Psychology, 152,* 101–117.

Haskins, R. (1989). Beyond metaphor: The efficacy of early childhood education. *American Psychologist, 44,* 274–282.

Hasselhorn, M. (1992). Task dependency and the role of typicality and metamemory in the development of an organizational strategy. *Child Development, 63,* 202–214.

Hauger, R. L., Irwin, M., & Richter, R. (1991). Developmental aspects of psychoneuro-endocrinology. In M. Lewis (Ed.), *Child and adolescent psychiatry: A comprehensive textbook.* Baltimore: Williams & Wilkins.

Hauser, P., Zametkin, A. J., Martinez, P., Vitiello, B., Matochik, J. A., Mixson, A. J., & Weintraub, B. D. (1993). Attention deficit-hyperactivity disorder in people with generalized resistance to thyroid hormone. *New England Journal of Medicine, 328,* 997–1001.

Havard, J. (1991). The role of legislation. In M. Manciaux & C. J. Romer (Eds.), *Accidents in childhood and adolescence.* Geneva: World Health Organization.

Hawkins, C., & Williams, T. I. (1992). Nightmares, life events and behaviour problems in preschool children. *Child: Care, Health and Development, 18,* 117–128.

Hawkins, J. D., Catalano, R. F., & Miller, J. Y. (1992). Risk and protective factors for alcohol and other drug problems in adolescence and early adulthood: Implications for substance abuse prevention. *Psychological Bulletin, 112,* 64–105.

Hawkins, J. D., Von Cleve, E., & Catalano, R. F., Jr. (1991). Reducing early childhood aggression: Results of a primary prevention program. *Journal of the American Academy of Child and Adolescent Psychiatry, 30,* 208–217.

Hawley, T. L. (1993, March). *Maternal cocaine addiction: Correlates and consequences.* Paper presented at the meeting of the Society for Research in Child Development, New Orleans, LA.

Hawley, T. L., Halle, T., Drasin, R., & Thomas, N. (1993, March). *Children of the crack epidemic: The cognitive, language, and emotional development of preschool children of addicted mothers.* Paper presented at the meeting of the Society for Research in Child Development, New Orleans, LA.

Hay, D. F., Caplan, M., Castle, J., & Stimson, C. A. (1991). Does sharing become increasingly "rational" in the second year of life? *Developmental Psychology, 27,* 987–993.

Hay, D. F., & Murray, P. (1982). Giving and requesting: Social facilitation of infants' offers to adults. *Infant Behavior and Development, 5,* 301–310.

Hayes, D. C., Palmer, J. L., & Zaslow, M. S. (Eds.). (1990). *Who cares for America's children?: Child care policy for the 1990s.* Washington, DC: National Academy Press.

Healthy People 2000: National health promotion and disease prevention objectives. (1990). Washington, DC: U.S. Public Health Service.

Healthy People 2000: National health promotion and disease prevention objectives and healthy schools. (1991). *Journal of School Health, 61,* 298–311.

Healy, B. (1992). Women in science: From panes to ceilings. *Science, 255,* 1333.

Hearold, S. (1986). A synthesis of 1043 effects of television on social behavior. In G. Comstock (Ed.), *Public communications and behavior* (Vol 1). New York: Academic Press.

Heath, A. C., Kessler, R. C., Neale, M. C., Eaves, L. J., & Kendler, K. S. (1992). Evidence for genetic influences on personality from self-reports and informant ratings. *Journal of Personality and Social Psychology, 63,* 85–96.

Heatherton, T. F., & Baumeister, R. F. (1991). Binge eating as escape from self-awareness. *Psychological Bulletin, 110,* 86–108.

Hebbeler, K. M., Smith, B. J., & Black, T. L. (1991). Federal early childhood special education policy: A model for the improvement of services for children with disabilities. *Exceptional Children, 58,* 104–112.

Hechinger, F. M. (1992). *Fateful choices: Healthy youth for the 21st century.* New York: Hill & Wang.

Hechtman, L. (1989). Teenage mothers and their children: Risks and problems: A review. *Canadian Journal of Psychiatry, 34,* 569–575.

Hechtman, L. (1991). Developmental, neurobiological and psychosocial aspects of hyperactivity, impulsivity, and inattention. In M. Lewis (Ed.), *Child and adolescent psychiatry: A comprehensive textbook.* Baltimore: Williams & Wilkins.

Hein, K. (1991). Developmental pharmacology. In R. M. Lerner, A. C. Petersen, & J. Brooks–Gunn (Eds.), *Encyclopedia of adolescence.* New York: Garland.

Heller, K. A., Mönks, F. J., & Passow, A. H. (Eds.) (1993). *International handbook of research and development of giftedness and talent.* New York: Pergamon.

Helms, J. E. (1992, September). Why is there no study of cultural equivalence in standardized cognitive ability testing? *American Psychologist, 47,* 1083–1101.

Helzer, J. E., & Schuckit, M. A. (1990, August/September). Substance use disorders. In American Psychiatric Association, *DSM-IV Update.* Washington, DC: American Psychiatric Association.

Hendrick, J. B. (1990). Early childhood. In R. M. Thomas (Ed.), *The encyclopedia of human development and education: Theory, research, and studies.* Oxford: Pergamon.

Henggeler, S. W. (1989). *Delinquency in adolescence.* Newbury Park, CA: Sage.

Henggeler, S. W., Rodick, J. D., Borduin, C. M., Hanson, C. L., Watson, S. M., & Urey, J. R. (1986). Multisystemic treatment of juvenile offenders: Effects on adolescent behavior and family interaction. *Developmental Psychology, 22,* 132–141.

Henker, B., & Whalen, C. K. (1989). Hyperactivity and attention deficits. *American Psychologist, 44,* 216–223.

Henry, L. A., & Millar, S. (1991). Memory span increase with age: A test of two hypotheses. *Journal of Experimental Child Psychology, 51,* 459–484.

Hertzig, M. E., & Shapiro, T. (1990). Autism and pervasive developmental disorders. In M. Lewis & S. M. Miller (Eds.), *Handbook of developmental psychopathology.* New York: Plenum.

Herzog, D. B., Keller, M. B., & Laron, P. W. (1988). Outcome in anorexia nervosa and bulimia nervosa. *Journal of Nervous and Mental Diseases, 176,* 131–143.

Herzog, D. B., Keller, M. B., Laron, P. W., & Bradburn, I. S. (1991). Bulimia nervosa in adolescence. *Developmental and Behavioral Pediatrics, 12,* 191–195.

Hess, R. D., & Azuma, H. (1991). Cultural support for schooling: Contrasts between Japan and the United States. *Educational Researcher, 20,* 2–8.

Hetherington, E. M. (1987). Family relations six years after divorce. In K. Pasley & M. Ihinger–Tallman (Eds.), *Remarriage and stepparenting: Current theory and research.* New York: Guilford.

Hetherington, E. M. (1989). Coping with family transition: Winners, losers, and survivors. *Child Development, 60,* 1–14.

Hetherington, E. M., Anderson, E. R., & Hagan, M. S. (1991). Divorce: Effects on adolescents. In R. M. Lerner, A. C. Petersen, & J. Brooks–Gunn (Eds.), *Encyclopedia of adolescence.* New York: Garland.

Hetherington, E. M., Clingempeel, W. G., Anderson, E. R., Deal, J. E., Hagan, M. S., Hollier, E. A., & Lindner, M. S. (1992). Coping with marital transitions. *Monographs of the Society for Research in Child Development, 57*(2-3, Serial No. 227).

Hetherington, E. M., Stanley–Hagan, M., & Anderson, E. R. (1989). Marital transitions: A child's perspective. *American Psychologist, 44,* 303–312.

Hiebert, K. A., Felice, M. E., Wingard, D. M., Munoz, R., & Ferguson, J. M. (1988). Comparison of outcome in Hispanic and Caucasian patients with anorexia nervosa. *International Journal of Eating Disorders, 7,* 693–696.

Higgins, A. T., & Turnure, J. E. (1984). Distractibility and concentration of attention in children's development. *Child Development, 55,* 1799–1810.

High school dropout rates down. (1993, June 21). *Higher Education and National Affairs, 42*(12), p. 3.

Higley, J. D., Lande, J. S., & Suomi, S. J. (1989). Day care and the promotion of emotional development: Lessons from a monkey laboratory. In J. S. Lande, S. Scarr, & N. Gunzenhauser (Eds.), *Caring for children: Challenge to America.* Hillsdale, NJ: Erlbaum.

Hilgard, E. R. (1993). Which psychologists prominent in the second half of this century made lasting contributions to psychological theory? *Psychological Science, 4,* 70–80.

Hilts, P. J. (1991, October 3). Study finds a decline in breastfeeding. *New York Times,* p. A8.

Hinde, R. A. (1991). When is an evolutionary approach useful? *Child Development, 62,* 671–675.

Hindley, C. B., Filliozat, A. M., Klackenberg, G., Nicolet–Neister, D., & Sand, E. A. (1966). Differences in age of walking for five European longitudinal samples. *Human Biology, 38,* 364–379.

Hines, M. (1982). Prenatal gonadal hormones and sex differences in human behavior. *Psychological Bulletin, 92,* 56–80.

Hines, M. (1990). Gonadal hormones and human cognitive development. In J. Balthazart (Ed.), *Hormones, brain and behavior in vertebrates: Vol. 1. Sexual differentiation, neuroanatomical aspects, neurotransmitters and neuropeptides.* Basel: Karger.

Hinshaw, S. P. (1992). Externalizing behavior problems and academic underachievement in childhood and adolescence: Causal relationships and underlying mechanisms. *Psychological Bulletin, 111,* 127–155.

Hirshberg, L. M., & Svejda, M. (1990). When infants look to their parents: I. Infants' social referencing of mothers compared to fathers. *Child Development, 61,* 1175–1186.

Hirsh–Pasek, K. (1991). Pressure or challenge in preschool? How academic environments affect children. In L. Rescorla, M. C. Hyson, & K. Hirsh–Pasek (Eds.), *New directions in child development: No. 53. Academic instruction in early childhood: Challenge or pressure?* San Francisco: Jossey–Bass.

Hirst–Pasek, K., Hyson, M. C., & Rescorla, L. (1990). Academic environments in preschool: Do they pressure or challenge young children. *Early Education and Development, 1,* 401–423.

Hobbins, J. C. (1991). Diagnosis and management of neural-tube defects today. *New England Journal of Medicine, 324,* 690–691.

Hochschild, A. (1989). *The second shift.* New York: Viking Penguin.

Hodges, J., & Tizard, B. (1989). Social and family relationships of ex-institutional adolescents. *Journal of Child Psychology and Psychiatry, 30,* 77–97.

Hofferth, S. L. (1990). Trends in adolescent sexual activity, contraception, and pregnancy in the United States. In J. Bancroft & J. M. Reinisch (Eds.), *Adolescence and puberty.* New York: Oxford.

Hofferth, S. L., Brayfield, A., Deich, S., & Holcomb, P. (1991). *National child care survey, 1990.* Washington, DC: Urban Institute Press.

Hofferth, S. L., & Phillips, D. A. (1991). Child care policy research. *Journal of Social Issues, 47,* 1–13.

Hoff–Ginsberg, E. (1986). Function and structure in maternal speech: Their relation to the child's development of syntax. *Developmental Psychology, 22,* 155–163.

Hoff–Ginsberg, E. (1990). Maternal speech and the child's development of syntax: A further look. *Journal of Child Language, 17,* 85–99.

Hoff–Ginsberg, E. (1991). Mother–child conversation in different social classes and communicative settings. *Child Development, 62,* 782–796.

Hoffman, L. W. (1989). Effects of maternal employment in the two-parent family. *American Psychologist, 44,* 283–292.

Hoffman, L. W. (1991). The influence of the family environment on personality: Accounting for sibling differences. *Psychological Bulletin, 110,* 187–203.

Hoffman, M. L. (1980). Moral development in adolescence. In J. Adelson, (Ed.), *Handbook of adolescent psychology.* New York: Wiley.

Hoffman, M. L. (1982). The role of the father in internal moralization. In M. E. Lamb (Ed.), *The role of the father in child development.* New York: Wiley.

Hoffman, M. L. (1984). Empathy, its limitations, and its role in a comprehensive moral theory. In W. M. Kurtines & J. L. Gewirtz (Eds.), *Morality, moral behavior and moral development.* New York: Wiley.

Hoffman, M. L. (1988). Moral development. In M. H. Bernstein & M. E. Lamb (Eds.), *Developmental psychology: An advanced textbook* (2nd ed.). Hillsdale, NJ: Erlbaum.

Hoglund, C. L., & Bell, T. S. (1991, August). *Longitudinal study of self-esteem in children from 7–11 years.* Paper presented at the meeting of the American Psychological Association, San Francisco.

Holden, C. (1992). A new discipline probes suicide's multiple causes. *Science, 256,* 1761–1762.

Holland, J. L. (1985). *Making vocational choices: A theory of vocational personalities and work environments* (2nd ed.). Englewood Cliffs, NJ: Prentice Hall.

Hollenbeck, A. R., Gewirtz, J. K., & Sebris, S. L. (1984). Labor and delivery medication influences parent–infant interaction in the first postpartum month. *Infant Behavior and Development, 7,* 201–209.

Holmbeck, G. N., & Hill, J. P. (1991). Conflictive engagement, positive affect, and menarche in families with seventh-grade girls. *Child Development, 62,* 1030–1048.

Honig, A. S., & McCarron, P. A. (1988). Prosocial behaviors of handicapped and typical peers in an integrated preschool. *Early Child Development and Care, 33,* 113–125.

Honig, A. S., & Park, K. (1993, March). *Preschool aggression and cognition: Effects of infant care.* Paper presented at the meeting of the Society for Research in Child Development, New Orleans, LA.

Honzik, M. P., Macfarlane, J. W., & Allen, L. (1948). The stability of mental test performance between two and eighteen years. *Journal of Experimental Education, 17,* 309–324.

Hood, K. E. (1991). Menstrual cycle. In R. M. Lerner, A. C. Petersen, & J. Brooks–Gunn (Eds.), *Encyclopedia of adolescence.* New York: Garland.

Hoosain, R. (1991). Cerebral lateralization of bilingual functions after handedness switch in childhood. *Journal of Genetic Psychology, 152,* 263–268.

Hopkins, B. (1991). Facilitating early motor development: An intracultural study of West Indian mothers and their infants living in Britain. In J. K. Nugent, B. M. Lester, & T. B. Brazelton (Eds.), *The cultural context of infancy* (Vol. 2). Norwood, NJ: Ablex.

Hopkins, B., & Westra, T. (1990). Motor development, maternal expectations, and the role of handling. *Infant Behavior and Development, 13,* 117–122.

Hopkins, E. (1992, March 15). Tales from the baby factory. *New York Times Magazine,* pp. 40–41, 78, 80, 82, 84, 90.

Horney, K. (1967). *Feminine psychology.* New York: Norton.

Horowitz, F. D. (1992). John B. Watson's legacy: Learning and environment. *Developmental Psychology, 28,* 360–367.

Hossain, Z., & Roopnarine, J. L. (in press). African-American fathers involvement with infants: Relationship to their functioning style, support, education, and income. *Infant Behavior and Development.*

Howard, M., & McCabe, J. B. (1990). Helping teenagers postpone sexual involvement. *Family Planning Perspectives, 22,* 21–26.

Howe, M. L., & Courage, M. L. (1993). On resolving the enigma of infantile amnesia. *Psychological Bulletin, 113,* 305–326.

Howe, M. L., & Rabinowitz, F. M. (1991). Gist another panacea? Or just the illusion of inclusion. *Developmental Review, 11,* 305–316.

Howes, C. (1987). Social competence with peers in young children: Developmental sequences. *Developmental Review, 7,* 252–272.

Howes, C. (1988). Peer interaction of young children. *Monographs of the Society for Research in Child Development, 53*(1, Serial No. 217).

Howes, C. (1990). Can the age of entry into child care and the quality of child care predict adjustment in kindergarten? *Developmental Psychology, 26,* 292–303.

Howes, C., & Matheson, C. C. (1992a). Contextual constraints on the concordance of mother–child and teacher–child relationships. In R. C. Pianta (Ed.), *New directions for child development: No. 57. Beyond the parent: The role of other adults in children's lives.* San Francisco, Jossey–Bass.

Howes, C., & Matheson, C. C. (1992b). Sequences in the development of competent play with peers: Social and social pretend play. *Developmental Psychology, 28,* 961–974.

Howes, C., Phillips, D. A., & Whitebook, M. (1992). Thresholds of quality: Implications for the social development of children in center-based child care. *Child Development, 63,* 449–460.

Howlin, P., & Yule, W. (1990). Taxonomy of major disorders in childhood. In M. Lewis & S. M. Miller (Eds.), *Handbook of developmental psychopathology.* New York: Plenum.

Hoy, E. A., Sykes, D. H., Bill, J. M., Halliday, H. L., McClure, B. G., & McC. Reid, M. (1992). The social competence of very-low-birthweight children: Teacher, peer, and self-perceptions. *Journal of Abnormal Child Psychology, 20,* 123–150.

Hsu, L. K. G. (1987). Are the eating disorders becoming more common in blacks? *International Journal of Eating Disorders, 6,* 113–124.

Hu, S. M. (1988). The Chinese family: Continuity and change. In B. Birns & D. F. Hay (Eds.), *The different faces of motherhood.* New York: Plenum.

Huber, A., & Ekvall, S. W. (1993). The fetal alcohol syndrome. In S. W. Ekvall (Ed.), *Pediatric nutrition in chronic diseases and developmental disorders: Prevention, assessment, and treatment.* New York: Oxford.

Hudley, C., & Graham, S. (1993). An attributional intervention to reduce peer-directed aggression among African-American boys. *Child Development, 64,* 124–138.

Hudson, J. A. (1990). The emergence of autobiographical memory in mother–child conversation. In R. Fivush & J. A. Hudson (Eds.), *Knowing and remembering in young children.* Cambridge: Cambridge University Press.

Huizinga, D., & Elliott, D. S. (1987). Juvenile offenders: Prevalence, offender incidence, and arrest rates by race. *Crime & Delinquency, 33,* 206–223.

Humphreys, L. G. (1992). Commentary: What both critics and users of ability tests need to know. *Psychological Science, 3,* 271–274.

Hundert, J., & Houghton, A. (1992). Promoting social interaction of children with disabilities in integrated preschools: A failure to generalize. *Exceptional Children, 58,* 311–398.

Hunt, C. E. (1990). Sudden infant death syndrome and apnea of infancy. *Seminars in Respiratory Medicine, 11,* 165–175.

Hunt, C. E. (1992). Sudden infant death syndrome. In R. C. Beckermann, R. T. Brouillette, & C. E. Hunt (Eds.), *Respiratory control disorders in infants and children.* Baltimore: Williams and Wilkins.

Hunt, M., & Berry, H. (1993). Phenylketonuria. In S. W. Ekvall (Ed.), *Pediatric nutrition in chronic diseases and developmental disorders: Prevention, assessment, and treatment.* New York: Oxford.

Huntington, L., Hans, S. L., & Zeskind, P. S. (1990). The relations among cry characteristics, demographic variables, and developmental test scores in infants prenatally exposed to methadone. *Infant Behavior and Development, 13,* 535–538.

Hussong, A. M., & Chassin, L. (1993, March). *The stress-negative affect model of adolescent alcohol use: Disaggregating negative affect.* Paper presented at the meeting of the Society for Research in Child Development, New Orleans, LA.

Huston, A. C., Donnerstein, E., Fairchild, H., Feshbach, N. D., Katz, P. A., Murray, J. P., Rubinstein, E. A., Wilcox, B. L., & Zuckerman, D. (1992). *Big world, small screen: The role of television in American society.* Lincoln: University of Nebraska Press.

Huston, A. C., & O'Brien, M. (1985). Activity level and sex-stereotyped toy choice in toddler boys and girls. *Journal of Genetic Psychology, 146,* 527–533.

Hutcheson, J., Black, M., & Starr, R. (1993). Developmental changes in interactional characteristics of mothers and their children with failure to thrive. *Journal of Pediatric Psychology, 18,* 453–466.

Hutt, C. (1978). Biological bases of psychological sex differences. *American Journal of Diseases of Children, 132,* 170–177.

Huttenlocher, J., Haight, W., Bryk, A., Seltzer, M., & Lyons, T. (1991). Early vocabulary growth: Relation to language input and gender. *Developmental Psychology, 27,* 236–248.

Hyde, J. S., Fennema, E., & Lamon, S. J. (1990a). Gender differences in mathematics performance: A meta-analysis. *Psychological Bulletin, 107,* 139–155.

Hyde, J. S., Fennema, E., Ryan, M., Frost, L. A., & Hopp, C. (1990b). Gender comparisons of mathematics attitudes and affect: A meta-analysis, *Psychology of Women Quarterly, 14,* 299–324.

Hyde, J. S., Krajnik, M., & Skuldt–Niederberger, K. (1991). Androgyny across the life span: A replication and longitudinal follow-up. *Developmental Psychology, 27,* 516–519.

Hyde, J. S., & Linn, M. C. (1988). Gender differences in verbal ability: A meta-analysis. *Psychological Bulletin, 104,* 53–69.

Hymel, S., Rubin, K. H., Rowden, L., & LeMare, L. (1990). Children's peer relationships: Longitudinal prediction of internalizing and externalizing problems from middle to late childhood. *Child Development, 61,* 2004–2021.

Hynd, G. W., Hern, K. L., Voeller, K. K., & Marshall, R. M. (1991). Neurobiological basis of attention-deficit hyperactivity disorder. *School Psychology Review, 20,* 174–186.

Hynd, G. W., & Hooper, S. R. (1992). *Neurological basis of childhood psychopathology.* Newbury Park, CA: Sage.

Hyson, M. C. (1991). Building the hothouse: How mothers construct academic environments. In L. Rescorla, M.C. Hyson, & K. Hirsh–Pasek (Eds.), *New directions in child development: No. 53. Academic instruction in early childhood: Challenge or pressure?* New York: Jossey–Bass.

Inhelder, B., & Paiget, J. (1959). *The early growth of logic in the child: Classification and seriation.* New York: Harper & Row.

Irwin, C. E., & Millstein, S. G. (1991). Risk taking behaviors during adolescence. In R. M. Lerner, A. C. Petersen, & J. Brooks–Gunn (Eds.), *Encyclopedia of adolescence.* New York: Garland.

Isabella, R. A. (1993). Origins of attachment: Maternal interactive behavior across the first year. *Child Development, 64,* 605–621.

Israel, A. C., Stolmaker, L., & Andrian, C. A. G. (1985). The effects of training parents in general child management skills on a behavioral weight loss program for children. *Behavior Therapy, 16,* 169–180.

Israel, A. C., Stolmaker, L., Sharp, J. P., Silverman, W. K., & Simon, L. G. (1984). An evaluation of two methods of parental involvement in treating obese children. *Behavior Therapy, 15,* 266–272.

Is there lead in your water? (1993, February). *Consumer Reports,* pp. 73–78.

Izard, C. E. (1983). *Maximally discriminative facial movement scoring system.* Newark, DE: University of Delaware Instructional Resources Center.

Izard, C. E. (1991). *The psychology of emotions.* New York: Plenum.

Izard, C. E. (1992). Basic emotions, relations among emotions, and emotion–cognition relations. *Psychological Review, 99,* 561–565.

Izard, C. E., Haynes, O. M., Chisholm, G., & Baak, K. (1991). Emotional determinants of infant–mother attachment. *Child Development, 62,* 906–917.

Izard, C. E., Hembree, E. A., & Huebner, R. R. (1987). Infants' emotion expressions to acute pain: Developmental change and stability of individual differences. *Developmental Psychology, 23,* 105–113.

Izard, C. E., & Malatesta, C. Z. (1987). Perspectives on emotional development. I. Differential emotions theory of early emotional development. In J. D. Osofsky (Ed.), *Handbook of infant development* (2nd ed.). New York: Wiley.

Jacklin, C. N. (1989). Female and male: Issues of gender. *American Psychologist, 44,* 127–133.

Jacklin, C. N., DiPietro, J. A., & Maccoby, E. E. (1984). Sex-typing behavior and sex-typing pressure in child–parent interaction. *Sex Roles, 13,* 413–425.

Jacklin, C. N., & McBride–Chang, C. (1991). The effects of feminist scholarship on developmental psychology. *Psychology of Women Quarterly, 15,* 549–556.

Jacklin, C. N., Wilcox, K. T., & Maccoby, E. E. (1988). Neonatal sex-steroid hormones and cognitive abilities at six years. *Developmental Psychobiology, 21,* 567–574.

Jackson, L. A. (1992). *Physical appearance and gender: Sociobiological and sociocultural perspectives.* Albany, NY: SUNY Press.

Jacobs, J. E. (1991). Influence of gender stereotypes on parent and child mathematics attitudes. *Journal of Educational Psychology, 83,* 518–527.

Jacobson, J. L., & Jacobson, S. W. (1990). Methodological issues in human behavioral teratology. In C. Rovee–Collier & L. P. Lipsitt (Eds.), *Advances in infancy research* (Vol. 6). Norwood, NJ: Ablex.

Jacobson, J. L., Jacobson, S. W., Padgett, R. J., Brumitt, G.A., & Billings, R. L. (1992). Effects of prenatal PCB exposure on cognitive processing efficiency and sustained attention. *Developmental Psychology, 28,* 297–306.

Jacobson, S. W. (1979). Matching behavior in the young infant. *Child Development, 50,* 425–430.

Jacobson, S. W., & Frye, K. F. (1991). Effect of maternal social support on attachment: Experimental evidence. *Child Development, 62,* 572–582.

James, W. (1890). *The principles of psychology.* New York: Holt.

Jancin, B. (1988). Prenatal gender selection appears to be gaining acceptance. *Obstetrical and Gynecological News, 23,* 30.

Janos, P. M. (1987). A fifty-year follow-up of Terman's youngest college students and IQ-matched agemates. *Gifted Child Quarterly, 31,* 55–58.

Jarvis, B. (1993, May 3). Against the great divide. *Newsweek,* p. 14.

Jason, J. (1991). Breast-feeding in 1991. *New England Journal of Medicine, 325,* 1036–1038.

Jemmott, L. S., & Jemmott, J. B., III. (1992). Family structure, parental strictness, and sexual behavior among inner-city black male adolescents. *Journal of Adolescent Research, 7,* 192–207.

Jenkins, E. J., & Bell, C. C. (1992). Adolescent violence: Can it be curbed? *Adolescent Medicine, 3,* 71–86.

Jenkins, R. R., & Westney, O. E. (1991). Initiation of sexual behavior in black adolescents. In R. M. Lerner, A. C. Petersen, & J. Brooks–Gunn (Eds.), *Encyclopedia of adolescence.* New York: Garland.

Jensen, J. K., & Neff, D. L. (1993). Development of basic auditory discrimination in preschool children. *Psychological Science, 4,* 104–107.

Jessell, J. C., & Beymer, L. (1992). The effects of job title vs. job description on occupational sex typing. *Sex Roles, 27,* 73–83.

Johnson, C. M. (1991). Infant and toddler sleep: A telephone survey of parents in one community. *Developmental and Behavioral Pediatrics, 12,* 108–114.

Johnson, D. J. (1992). Developmental pathways: Toward an ecological theoretical formulation of race identity in black–white biracial children. In M. P. P. Root (Ed.), *Racially mixed people in America.* Newbury Park, CA: Sage.

Johnson, E. A. (1993, March). *The relationship of self-blame and responsibility attributions and motivations, for schoolwork and conduct, to self-worth and self-perceptions.* Paper presented at the meeting of the Society for Research in Child Development, New Orleans, LA.

Johnson, J. (1990). The role of play in cognitive development. In E. Klugman & S. Smilansky (Eds.), *Children's play and learning.* New York: Teachers College Press.

Johnson, J., & Whitaker, A. H. (1992). Adolescent smoking, weight changes, and binge–purge behavior: Associations with secondary amenorrhea. *American Journal of Public Health, 82,* 47–54.

Johnson, M. H., Dziurawiec, S., Bartrip, J., & Morton, J. (1992). The effects of movement of internal features on infants' preferences for face-like stimuli. *Infant Behavior and Development, 15,* 129–136.

Johnson, T. D., & Moely, B. E. (1993, March). *The psychosocial impact of encopresis on children and their families.* Paper presented at the meeting of the Society for Research in Child Development, New Orleans, LA.

Johnson, W., Emde, R. N., Pannabecker, B., Stenberg, C., & Davis, M. (1982). Maternal perception of infant emotion from birth to 18 months. *Infant Behavior and Development, 5,* 313–322.

Johnston, L. D., O'Malley, P. M., & Bachman, J. G. (1992). *Smoking, drinking, and illicit drug use among American secondary school students, college students and young adults, 1975–1991.* Rockville, MD: National Institute on Drug Abuse.

Johnston, L. D., O'Malley, P. M., & Bachman, J. G. (1993a). *National survey results on drug use from the Monitoring the Future Study, 1975–1992: Vol. 1. Secondary school students.* Rockville, MD: National Institute on Drug Abuse.

Johnston, L. D., O'Malley, P. M., & Bachman, J. G. (1993b). *National survey results on drug use from the Monitoring the Future Study, 1975–1992: Vol. 2. College students and young adults.* Rockville, MD: National Institute on Drug Abuse.

Jones, D. C., Swift, D. J., & Johnson, M. A. (1988). Nondeliberate memory for a novel event among preschoolers. *Developmental Psychology, 24,* 641–645.

Jones, D. S., Byers, R. H., Bush, T. J., Oxtoby, M. J., & Rogers, M. F. (1992). Epidemiology of transfusion-associated acquired immunodeficiency syndrome in children in the United States, 1981 through 1989. *Pediatrics, 89,* 123–127.

Jones, J. (1991). Psychological models of race: What have they been and what should they be? In J. Goodchilds (Ed.), *Psychological perspectives on human diversity in America.* Washington, DC: American Psychological Association.

Jones, M. C. (1924). Elimination of children's fears. *Journal of Experimental Psychology, 7,* 381–390.

Jones, M. C. (1957). The late careers of boys who were early- or late-maturing. *Child Development, 28,* 115–128.

Jones, M. C. (1958). The study of socialization patterns at the high school level. *Journal of Genetic Psychology, 93,* 87–111.

Joos, S. K., Pollitt, K. E. Mueller, W. H., & Albright, D. L. (1983). The Bacon Chow study: Maternal nutritional supplementation and infant behavioral development. *Child Development, 54,* 669–676.

Jouen, F., & Lepecq, J. (1990). Early perceptuo-motor development: Posture and locomotion. In C. A. Hauert (Ed.), *Developmental psychology: Cognitive, perceptuo-motor and neuropsychological perspectives.* Amsterdam: North–Holland.

Jozefowicz, D. M., Barber, B. L., & Eccles, J. S. (1993, March). *Adolescent work-related values and beliefs: Gender differences and relation to occupational aspirations.* Paper presented at the meeting of the Society for Research in Child Development, New Orleans, LA.

Jussim, L. (1989). Teacher expectations: Self-fulfilling prophecies, perceptual biases and accuracy. *Journal of Personality and Social Psychology, 87,* 469–480.

Jussim, L. (1991). Social perception and social reality: A reflection-construction model. *Psychological Review, 98,* 54–73.

Kafka, R. R., & Linden, P. (1991). Communication in relationships and adolescent substance use: The influence of parents and friends. *Adolescence, 26,* 587–598.

Kagan, J. (1992). Yesterday's premises, tomorrow's promises. *Developmental Psychology, 28,* 990–997.

Kagan, J., & Klein, R. E. (1973). Cross-cultural perspectives on early development. *American Psychologist, 28,* 947–961.

Kagan, J., & Snidman, N. (1991). Temperamental factors in human development. *American Psychologist, 46,* 856–862.

Kagan, J., Snidman, N., & Arcus, D. (1993). On the temperamental categories of inhibited and unhibited children. In K. H. Rubin & J. B. Asendorpf (Eds.), *Social withdrawal, inhibition, and shyness in childhood.* Hillsdale, NJ: Erlbaum.

Kagan, S. L. (1990). Children's play: The journey from theory to practice. In E. Klugman & S. Smilansky (Eds.), *Children's play and learning: Perspectives and policy implications.* New York: Teachers College Press.

Kagay, M. R. (1993, June 8). Poll finds knowledge about AIDS increasing. *New York Times,* p. B9.

Kahlbaugh, P., & Haviland, J. M. (1991). Formal operational thinking and identity. In R. M. Lerner, A. C. Petersen, & J. Brooks–Gunn (Eds.), *Encyclopedia of adolescence.* New York: Garland.

Kahn, P. H. (1992). Children's obligatory and discretionary moral judgments. *Child Development, 63,* 416–430.

Kail, R. (1990). *The development of memory in children* (3rd ed.). New York: W. H. Freeman.

Kail, R. (1991). Processing time declines exponentially during childhood and adolescence. *Developmental Psychology, 27,* 259–266.

Kalliopuska, M. (1991). Study on the empathy and prosocial behavior of children in three day-care centres. *Psychological Reports, 68,* 375–378.

Kaminer, Y. (1991). the magnitude of concurrent psychiatric disorders in hospitalized substance abusing adolescents. *Child Psychiatry and Human Development, 22,* 89–95.

Kantrowitz, B. (1992, August 3). Teenagers and AIDS. *Newsweek,* pp. 45–50.

Kaplan, S. J. (1991). Physical abuse and neglect. In M. Lewis (Ed.), *Child and adolescent psychiatry: A comprehensive textbook.* Baltimore: Williams & Wilkins.

Karapetsas, A., & Kantas, A. (1991). Visuomotor organization in the child: A neuropsychological approach. *Perceptual and Motor Skills, 72,* 211–217.

Karniol, R. (1980). A conceptual analysis of immanent justice response in children. *Child Development, 51,* 118–130.

Kashubeck, S., & Walsh, B. (1992, August). *Factors associated with eating disorders: An exploratory model.* Paper presented at the meeting of the American Psychological Association, Washington, DC.

Katchadourian, H. (1990). Sexuality. In S. S. Feldman & G. R. Elliott (Eds.), *At the threshold: The developing adolescent.* Cambridge, MA: Harvard University Press.

Katz, P. A. (1987). Variations in family constellations: Effects on gender schemata. In L. S. Liben & M. L. Signorella (Eds.), *New directions for child development: No. 38. Children's gender schemata.* San Francisco: Jossey–Bass.

Katz, P. A., & Walsh, P. V. (1991). Modification of children's gender-stereotyped behavior. *Child Development, 62,* 338–351.

Kaufman, J., & Zigler, E. (1989). The intergenerational transmission of child abuse. In D. Cicchetti & V. Carlson (Eds.), *Child maltreatment: Theory and research on the causes and consequences of child abuse and neglect.* Cambridge: Cambridge University Press.

Kaufman, J., & Zigler, E. (1992). The prevention of child maltreatment: Programming, research, and policy. In D. J. Willis, E. W. Holden, & M. Rosenberg (Eds.), *Prevention of child maltreatment: Developmental and ecological perspectives.* New York: Wiley.

Kazdin, A. E. (1987). *Conduct disorders in childhood and adolescence.* Newbury Park, CA: Sage.

Kazdin, A. E. (1990). Assessment of childhood depression. In A. M. LaGreca (Ed.), *Through the eyes of a child.* Boston: Allyn and Bacon.

Kazdin, A. E. (1992). Overt and covert antisocial behavior: Child and family characteristics among psychiatric inpatient children. *Journal of Child and Family Studies, 1,* 3–20.

Kazdin, A. E. (1993a). Adolescent mental health. *American Psychologist, 48,* 127–141.

Kazdin, A. E. (1993b). Psychotherapy for children and adolescents. *American Psychologist, 48,* 644–657.

Kazdin, A. E., Siegel, T. C., & Bass, D. (1992). Cognitive problem-solving skills training and parent management training in the treatment of antisocial behavior in children. *Journal of Consulting and Clinical Psychology, 60,* 733–747.

Kearney, C. A., & Silverman, W. K. (1990). A preliminary analysis of a functional model of assessment and treatment for school refusal behavior. *Behavior Modification, 14,* 340-366.

Keating, D. P. (1991). Adolescent cognition. In R. M. Lerner, A. C. Petersen, & J. Brooks–Gunn (Eds.), *Encyclopedia of adolescence.* New York: Garland.

Keating, D. P., & Clark, L. V. (1980). Development of physical and social reasoning in adolescents. *Developmental Psychology, 16,* 23–30.

Keele, S. W. (1973). *Attention and human performance.* Santa Monica, CA: Goodyear.

Keith, J. B., McCreary, C., Collins, K., Smith, C. P., & Bernstein, I. (1991). Sexual activity and contraceptive use among low-income urban black adolescent females. *Adolescence, 26,* 769–785.

Kelgeri, Khadi, P. B., & Phadnis (1989). Creativity among urban and rural boys and girls. *Indian Journal of Behaviour, 13,* 10–14.

Kellam, S. G., & Rebok, G. W. (1992). Building developmental and etiological theory through epidemiologically based preventive intervention trials. In J. McCord & R. E. Tremblay (Eds.), *Preventing antisocial behavior: Interventions from birth through adolescence.* New York: Guilford.

Kelley, K., & Byrne, D. (1992). *Human sexuality.* Englewood Cliffs, NJ: Prentice Hall.

Kellman, P. J., & von Hofsten, C. (1992). The world of the moving infant: Perception of motion, stability, and space. In C. Rovee–Collier & L. P. Lipsitt (Eds.), *Advances in infancy research* (Vol. 7). Norwood, NJ: Ablex.

Kellogg, R. (1970). Understanding children's art. In P. Cramer (Ed.), *Readings in developmental psychology today.* Del Mar, CA: CRM.

Kelly, A. (1988). Gender differences in teacher-pupil interactions: A meta-analytic review. *Research in Education, 39,* 1–23.

Kelly, J. A., Murphy, D. A., Sikkema, K. J., & Kalichman, S. C. (1993). Psychological interventions to prevent HIV infection are urgently needed. *American Psychologist, 48,* 1023–1034.

Kelsey, K. (1993). Failure to thrive. In S. W. Ekvall (Ed.), *Pediatric nutrition in chronic diseases and developmental disorders: Prevention. assessment, and treatment.* New York: Oxford.

Kempe, A., Wise, P. H., Barkan, S. E., Sappenfield, W. M., Sachs, B., Gortmaker, S. L., Sobol, A. M., First, L. R., Pursley, D., Rinehart, H., Kotelchuck, M., Cole, F. S., Gunter, N., & Stockbauer, J. W. (1992). Clinical determinants of the racial disparity in very low birth weight. *New England Journal of Medicine, 327,* 969–973.

Kendall–Tackett, K. A., Williams, L. M., & Finkelhor, D. (1993). Impact of sexual abuse on children: A review and synthesis of recent empirical studies. *Psychological Bulletin, 113,* 164–180.

Kennedy, E., Spence, S. H., & Hensley, R. (1989). An examination of the relationship between childhood depression and social competence amongst primary school children. *Journal of Child Psychology & Psychiatry, 30,* 561–573.

Kennedy, R. E. (1991). Delinquency. In R. M. Lerner, A. C. Petersen, & J. Brooks–Gunn (Eds.), *Encyclopedia of adolescence.* New York: Garland.

Kennell, J. H., & Klaus, M. H. (1984). Mother–infant bonding: Weighing the evidence. *Developmental Review, 4,* 275–282.

Kennell, J. H., Klaus, M. H., McGrath, S., Robertson, S., & Hinkley, C. (1991). Continuous emotional support during labor in a U. S. hospital: A randomized clinical trial. *Journal of the American Medical Association, 265,* 2197–2201.

Kennell, J. H., & McGrath, S. (1993, March). *Perinatal effects of labor support.* Paper presented at the meeting of the Society for Research in Child Development, New Orleans, LA.

Kenny, M. E. (1992, August). *Parental attachment, psychological separation and eating disorder symptoms among college women.* Paper presented at the meeting of the American Psychological Association, Washington, DC.

Kent, M. R. (1991). Women and AIDS. *New England Journal of Medicine, 324,* 1442.

Kerns, K. A., & Berenbaum, S. A. (1991). Sex differences in spatial ability in children. *Behavior Genetics, 21,* 383–395.

Kershner, J. R., & Ledger, G. (1985). Effect of sex, intelligence, and style of thinking on creativity: A comparison of gifted and average IQ children. *Journal of Personality and Social Psychology, 48,* 1033–1040.

Kessen, W., Leutzendoff, A. M., & Stoutsenberger, K. (1967). Age, food deprivation, non-nutritive sucking and movement in the human newborn. *Journal of Comparative and Physiological Psychology, 63,* 82–86.

Kestenbaum, R., Farber, E. A., & Sroufe, L. A. (1989). Individual differences in empathy among preschoolers: Relation to attachment history. In N. Eisenberg (Ed.), *New directions for child development: No. 44. Empathy and related emotional responses.* San Francisco: Jossey–Bass.

Ketterlinus, R. D., & Lamb, M. E. (1991). Childbearing adolescent: Obstetric and filial outcomes. In R. M. Lerner, A. C. Petersen, & J. Brooks–Gunn (Eds.), *Encyclopedia of adolescence.* New York: Garland.

Kimball, M. M. (1989). A new perspective on women's math achievement. *Psychological Bulletin, 105,* 198-214.

Kimura, D. (1992). Cognitive function: Sex differences and hormonal influences. *Neuroscience year: Supplement 2 to the Encyclopedia of neuroscience.* Boston: Birkhauser.

Kimura, D., & Hampson, E. (1992). Neural and hormonal mechanisms mediating sex differences in cognition. In P. A. Vernon (Ed.), *Biological approaches to the study of human intelligence.* Norwood, NJ: Ablex.

King, C. A., Raskin, A., Gdowski, C. L., Butkus, M., & Opipari, L. (1990). Psychosocial factors associated with urban adolescent female suicide attempts. *Journal of the American Academy of Child and Adolescent Psychiatry, 29,* 289–294.

King, N. J., & Gullore, E. (1990). Acceptability of fear reduction procedures with children. *Journal of Behavior Therapy and Experimental Psychiatry, 21,* 1–8.

King, N. J., Hamilton, D. I., & Ollendick, T. H. (1988). *Children's phobias: A behavioral perspective.* Chichester, England: Wiley.

King, R. A., Pfeffer, C., Gammon, G. D., & Cohen, D. J. (1992). Suicidality of childhood and adolescence. In B. B. Lahey & A. E. Kazdin (Eds.), *Advances in clinical child psychology* (Vol. 14). New York: Plenum.

Kirchler, E., Pombeni, M. L., & Palmonari, A. (1991). Sweet sixteen . . . Adolescents' problems and the peer group as source of support. *European Journal of Psychology of Education, 6,* 393–410.

Kitchen, W. H., Doyle, L. W., Ford, G. W., Murton, L. J., Keith, C. G., Rickards, A. L., Kelly, E., & Callanan, C. (1991). Changing two-year outcome of infants weighing 500 to 999 grams at birth: A hospital study. *Journal of Pediatrics, 118,* 938–943.

Klahr, D. (1992). Information-processing approaches to cognitive development. In M. H. Bornstein & M. E. Lamb (Eds.), *Developmental psychology: An advanced textbook* (3rd ed.). Hillsdale, NJ: Erlbaum.

Klaus, M., & Kennell, J. (1976). *Maternal-infant bonding.* St. Louis: C. V. Mosby.

Klaus, M. H., & Kennell, J. H. (1978). Parent-to-infant attachment. In J. H. Stevens, Jr., & M. Mathews (Eds.), *Mother/child, father/child relationships.* Washington, DC: National Association for the Education of Young Children.

Klein, J. (1993, June 21). 'Make the daddies pay.' *Newsweek,* p. 33.

Kliewer, W., & Sandler, I. N. (1992). Locus of control and self-esteem as moderators of stressor-symptom relations in children and adolescents. *Journal of Abnormal Child Psychology, 20,* 393–413.

Klimes–Dougan, B. (1993, March). *The emergence of negotiation.* Paper presented at the meeting of the Society for Research in Child Development, New Orleans, LA.

Klinnert, M. C., Emde, R. N., & Butterfield, P. (1986). Social referencing: The infant's use of emotional signals from a friendly adult with mother present. *Developmental Psychology, 22,* 427–432.

Klorman, R., Brumaghim, J. T., Fitzpatrick, P. A., & Borgstedt, A. D. (1990). Clinical effects of a controlled trial of methylphenidate on adolescents with attention deficit disorder. *American Academy of Child and Adolescent Psychiatry, 29,* 702–709.

Klorman, R., Brumaghim, J. T., Fitzpatrick, P. A., & Borgstedt, A. D. (1992). Methylphenidate reduces abnormalities of stimulus classification in adolescents with attention deficit disorder. *Journal of Abnormal Psychology, 101,* 130–138.

Knapp, J. E., Templer, D. I., Cannon, W. G., & Dobson, S. (1991). Variables associated with success in an adolescent drug treatment program. *Adolescence, 26,* 305–317.

Kobayashi–Winata, H., & Power, T. G. (1989). Childrearing and compliance: Japanese and American families in Houston. *Journal of Cross-Cultural Psychology, 20,* 333–356.

Koch, P. B. (1991). Sex education. In R. M. Lerner, A. C. Petersen, & J. Brooks-Gunn (Eds.), *Encyclopedia of adolescence.* New York: Garland.

Kochanska, G. (1992). Children's interpersonal influence with mothers and peers. *Developmental Psychology, 28,* 491–499.

Kochanska, G., & Radke–Yarrow, M. (1992). Inhibition in toddlerhood and the dynamics of the child's interaction with an unfamiliar peer at age five. *Child Development, 63,* 325–335.

Koehler, M. S. (1990). Classrooms, teachers, and gender differences in mathematics. In E. Fennema & G. C. Leder (Eds.), *Mathematics and gender.* New York: Teachers College Press.

Koenig, L. J., Isaacs, A. M., & Schwartz, J. A. J . (in press). Sex differences in adolescent depression and loneliness: Why are boys lonelier if girls are more depressed? *Journal of Research in Personality.*

Koff, E., Rierdan, J., & Stubbs, M. L. (1990). Gender, body image, and self-concept in early adolescence. *Journal of Early Adolescence, 10,* 56–68.

Kohlberg, L. (1963). Moral development and identification. In H. W., Stevenson (Ed.), *Child psychology: 62nd yearbook of the National Society for the Study of Education.* Chicago: University of Chicago Press.

Kohlberg, L. (1966). Cognitive stages and preschool education. *Human Development, 9,* 5–17.

Kohlberg, L. (1969). Stage and sequence: The cognitive-developmental approach to socialization. In D. A. Goslin (Ed.), *Handbook of socialization theory and research.* Chicago: Rand McNally.

Kohlberg, L. (1981). *The meaning and measurement of moral development.* Worcester, MA: Clark University Press.

Kohlberg, L. (1985). *The psychology of moral development.* San Francisco: Harper & Row.

Kohlberg, L., & Kramer, R. (1969). Continuities and discontinuities in childhood and adult moral development. *Human Development,* 12, 93–120.

Kolata, G. (1991, November 10). Young women offer to sell their eggs to infertile couples, *New York Times,* pp. A1, 16.

Kolata, G. (1992a, January 16). Study reports dyslexia isn't always permanent. *New York Times,* p. A13.

Kolata, G. (1992b, April 26). A parents' guide to kids' sports. *New York Times Magazine,* pp. 12–15, 40, 44–46.

Kolata, G. (1992c, June 21). More children are employed, often perilously. *New York Times,* pp. 1, 22.

Kolata, G. (1992d, July 15). As fears about a fetal test grow, many doctors are advising against it. *New York Times,* p. B7.

Kolata, G. (1992e, October 30). Baby's growth rate not fast enough? Just wait. *New York Times,* p. A8.

Kolata, G. (1993, June 6). Miniature scope gives the earliest pictures of a developing embryo. *New York Times,* p. B6.

Konner, M. J. (1977). Infancy among the Kalahari San. In P. H. Leiderman, S. R. Tulkin, & A. Rosenfeld (Eds.), *Culture and infancy: Variations in the human experience.* New York: Academic Press.

Kontos, S. (1993, March). *The ecology of family day care.* Paper presented at the meeting of the Society for Research in Child Development, New Orleans, LA.

Koop, C. E. (1988). *Understanding AIDS* (HHS Publication No. [CDC] HHS-88-8404). Washington, DC: U.S. Government Printing Office.

Koorland, M. A. (1986). Applied behavior analysis and the correction of learning disabilities. In J. K. Togesen, & B. Y. L. Wong (Eds.), *Psychological and educational perspectives on learning disabilities.* Orlando, FL: Academic Press.

Koot, H. M., & Verhulst, F. C. (1992). Prediction of children's referral to mental health and special education services from earlier adjustment. *Journal of Child Psychology & Psychiatry, 33,* 717–729.

Kopera–Frye, K., Ager, J., Saltz, E., Poindexter, J., & Lee, S. (1993, March). *Predictors of adolescent delinquency.* Paper presented at the meeting of the Society for Research in Child Development, New Orleans, LA.

Kopp, C. B. (1989). Regulation of distress and negative emotions: A developmental view. *Developmental Psychology, 25,* 343–354.

Kopp, C. B. (1992, Spring). Emotional distress and control in young children. In N. Eisenberg & R. A. Fabes (Eds.), *New directions for child development: No. 55. Emotion and its regulation in early development.* San Francisco: Jossey–Bass.

Korn, J. H., Davis, R., & Davis, S. F. (1991). Historians' and chairpersons' judgments of eminence among psychologists. *American Psychologist, 46,* 789–792.

Korner, A. F. (1987). Preventive intervention with high-risk newborns: Theoretical, conceptual, and methodological perspectives. In J. D. Osofsky (Ed.), *Handbook of infant development* (2nd ed). New York: Wiley.

Kortenhaus, C. M., & Demarest, J. (1993). Gender role stereotyping in children's literature: An update. *Sex Roles, 28,* 219–231.

Kovar, M. G. (1991). Health of adolescents in the United States: An overview. In R. M. Lerner, A. C. Petersen, & J. Brooks–Gunn (Eds.), *Encyclopedia of adolescence.* New York: Garland.

Krappmann, L., Oswald, H., Weiss, K., & Uhlendorff, H. (1993, March). *Peer relationships of children in middle childhood.* Paper presented at the meeting of the Society for Research in Child Development, New Orleans, LA.

Krasnoff, A. G., Walker, J. T., & Howard, M. (1989). Early sex-linked activities and interests related to spatial abilities. *Personality and Individual Differences, 10,* 81–85.

Krebs, D. L., Vermeulen, S. C. A., Carpendale, J. I., & Denton, K. (1991). In W. M. Kurtines & J. L. Gewirtz (Eds.), *Handbook of moral behavior and development* (Vol. 2). Hillsdale, NJ: Erlbaum.

Kreitler, S., & Kreitler, H. (1989). Horizontal décalage: A problem and its solution. *Cognitive Development, 4,* 89–119.

Krener, P. G. (1991). HIV-spectrum disease. In M. Lewis (Ed.), *Child and adolescent psychiatry: A comprehensive textbook.* Baltimore: Williams & Wilkins.

Kresevich, D. M. (1993, March). *Traditional and non-traditional career choices of elementary aged children.* Paper presented at the meeting of the Society for Research in Child Development, New Orleans, LA.

Kreutter, K. J., Gewirtz, H., Davenny, J. E., & Love, C. (1991). Drug and alcohol prevention project for sixth graders: First-year findings. *Adolescence, 26,* 287–293.

Kristof, N. D. (1991, November 15). Stark data on women: 100 million are missing. *New York Times,* pp. B5, 9.

Kristof, N. D. (1993a, April 25). China's crackdown on births: A stunning, and harsh, success. *New York Times,* pp. 1, 6.

Kristof, N. D. (1993b, July 21). Peasants of China discover new way to weed out girls. *New York Times,* pp. A1, 4.

Kroger, J. (1989). *Identity in adolescence.* New York: Routledge.

Krueger, R. F., Schmutte, P. S., Caspi, A., Moffitt, T. E., Campbell, K., & Silva, P. A. (1993, May). *Delinquency affect and constraint: Personality and illegal behavior in late adolescence.* Paper presented at the meeting of the Midwestern Psychological Association, Chicago.

Ku, L. C., Sonenstein, F. L., & Pleck, J. H. (1992). The association of AIDS education and sex education with sexual behavior and condom use among teenage men. *Family Planning Perspectives, 24,* 100–106.

Kuczaj, S. A., II (1982). On the nature of syntactic development. In S. A. Kuczaj, II (Ed.), *Language development: Vol. 1. Syntax and semantics.* Hillsdale, NJ: Erlbaum.

Kuczynski, L., & Kochanska, G. (1990). Development of children's noncompliance strategies from toddlerhood to age 5. *Developmental Psychology, 26,* 398–408.

Kuhl, P. K. (1987). Perception of speech and sound in early infancy. In P. Salapatek & L. Cohen (Eds.), *Handbook of infant perception: Vol. 2. From perception to cognition.* Orlando, FL: Academic Press.

Kuhl, P. K., Williams, K. A., Lacerda, F., Stevens, K. N., & Lindblom, B. (1992). Linguistic experience alters phonetic perception in infants by 6 months of age. *Science, 255,* 606–608.

Kuhn, D. (1976). Short-term longitudinal evidence for the sequentiality of Kohlberg's early stages of moral development. *Developmental Psychology, 2,* 162–166.

Kuhn, D. (1991). Higher-order reasoning in adolescence. In R. M. Lerner, A. C. Petersen, & J. Brooks–Gunn (Eds.), *Encyclopedia of adolescence.* New York: Garland.

Kuhn, D., Kohlberg, L., Langer, J., & Hanna, N. (1977). The development of formal operations in logical and moral judgment. *Genetic Psychology Monographs, 95,* 97–188.

Kulin, H. E. (1991a). Hypothalamic-pituitary changes of puberty. In R. M. Lerner, A. C. Petersen, & J. Brooks–Gunn (Eds.), *Encyclopedia of adolescence.* New York: Garland.

Kulin, H. E. (1991b). Spermarche. In R. M. Lerner, A. C. Petersen, & J. Brooks–Gunn

(Eds.), *Encyclopedia of adolescence.* New York: Garland.

Kunkel, D. (1993). Policy and the future of children's television. In G. Berry & J. Asamen (Eds.), *Children and television in a changing socio-cultural world.* Newbury Park, CA: Sage.

Kurdek, L. A., Fine, M. A., & Sinclair, R. J. (1992, August). *Parenting transitions and adjustment in young adolescents.* Paper presented at the meeting of the American Psychological Association, Washington, DC.

Kutner, L. (1989, May 30). Helping a child adapt to the new baby in the family. *New York Times,* p. C2.

Kutner, L. (1991a, March 28). Remarriage may bring joy, trepidation and changing roles for stepchildren. *New York Times,* p. B5.

Kutner, L. (1991b, May 9). When you don't like your stepchildren and they aren't enthusiastic about you. *New York Times,* p. B7.

Kutner, L. (1992a, February 27). Encouragement rather than control is often best in helping children with learning disabilities. *New York Times,* p. B6.

Kutner, L. (1992b, March 12). The more subtle shades of body dissatisfaction are just as insidious as anorexia and bulimia. *New York Times,* p. B2.

Kutner, L. (1992c, May 17). When young children watch television, they usually believe everything they see. *New York Times,* p. B4.

Kutner, L. (1993a, February 4). For both boys and girls, early or late puberty can lead to social or emotional problems. *New York Times,* p. B6.

Kutner, L. (1993b, May 6). No no no no lima beans: Picky eaters may just be responding to biology. *New York Times,* p. B5.

Lacayo, R. (1993, April 19). Unhealed wounds. *Time,* pp. 26–31.

Ladd, G. W., & Price, J. M. (1987). Predicting children's social and school adjustment following the transition from preschool to kindergarten. *Child Development, 58,* 1168–1189.

La Frenière, P. J., Dumas, J. E., Capuano, F., & Dubeau, D. (1992). Development and validation of the preschool socioaffective profile. *Psychological Assessment, 4,* 442–450.

Lamaze, F. (1981). *Painless childbirth.* New York: Simon & Schuster.

Lamb, C. S., Jackson, L. A., Cassiday, P. B., & Priest, D. J. (1993). Body figure preferences of men and women: A comparison of two generations. *Sex Roles, 28,* 345–358.

Lamb, M. E. (1981). The development of father–infant relationships. In M. E. Lamb (Ed.), *The role of the father in child development.* New York: Wiley.

Lamb, M. (1987). Predictive implications of individual differences in attachment. *Journal of Consulting and Clinical Psychology, 55,* 817–824.

Lamb, M. E., & Ketterlinus, R. D. (1991). Adolescent parental behavior. In R. M. Lerner, A. C. Petersen, & J. Brooks-Gunn (Eds.), *Encyclopedia of adolescence.* New York: Garland.

Lamb, M. E., Ketterlinus, R. D., & Fracasso, M. P. (1992). Parent-child relationships. In M. H. Bornstein & M. E. Lamb (Eds.), *Developmental psychology: An advanced textbook* (3rd ed.). Hillsdale, NJ: Lawrence Erlbaum.

Lamb, M. E., & Oppenheim, D. (1989). Fatherhood and father-child relationships. In S. H. Cath, A. Gurwitt, & L. Gunsberg (Eds.), *Fathers and their families.* Hillsdale, NJ: Analytic Press.

Lamb, M. E., Sternberg, K. J., & Ketterlinus, R. D. (1992a). Child care in the United States: The modern era. In M. E. Lamb, K. J. Sternberg, C. Hwang, & A. G. Broberg (Eds.), *Child care in context.* Hillsdale, NJ: Erlbaum.

Lamb, M. E., Sternberg, K. J., & Prodromidis, M. (1992b). Nonmaternal care and the security of infant–mother attachment: A reanalysis of the data. *Infant Behavior and Development, 15,* 71–83.

Lamb, M. E., & Teti, D. M. (1991). Adolescent childbirth and marriage: Associations with long-term marital instability. In R. M. Lerner, A. C. Petersen, & J. Brooks–Gunn (Eds.), *Encyclopedia of adolescence.* New York: Garland.

Lambeir, E. J., Bouman, N. H., & Nolen, W. A. (1991). What becomes of hyperactive children? A review of outcome studies on hyperactive children. *Kind en Adolescent, 12,* 209–214.

Lamborn, S. D., Mounts, N. S., Steinberg, L., & Dornbusch, S. M. (1991). Patterns of competence and adjustment among adolescents from authoritative, authoritarian, indulgent and neglectful families. *Child Development, 62,* 1049–1065.

Lamke, L. K. (1982a). Adjustment and sex-role orientation. *Journal of Youth and Adolescence, 11,* 247–259.

Lamke, L. K. (1982b). The impact of sex-role orientation on self-esteem in early adolescence. *Child Development, 53,* 1530–1535.

Lampl, M., Veldhuis, J. D., & Johnson, M. L. (1992). Saltation and stasis: A model of human growth. *Science, 258,* 801–803.

Landau, S., & Milich, R., (1990). Assessment of children's social status and peer relations. In A. M. LaGreca (Ed.), *Through the eyes of a child.* Boston: Allyn and Bacon.

Landau, S., & Moore, L. A. (1991). Social skill deficits in children with attention-deficit hyperactivity disorder. *School Psychology Review, 20,* 235–251.

Landesman, S. (1990). Institutionalization revisited: Expanding views on early and cumulative life experiences. In M. Lewis & S. M. Miller (Eds.), *Handbook of developmental psychopathology.* New York: Plenum.

Lang, P. J., & Melamed, B. B. (1969). Case report: Avoidance conditioning therapy of an infant with chronic ruminative vomiting. *Journal of Abnormal Psychology, 74,* 1–8.

Lange, G., & Pierce, S. H. (1992). Memory-strategy learning and maintenance in preschool children. *Developmental Psychology, 28,* 453–462.

Langlois, J. H. (1985). From the eye of the beholder to behavioral reality: The development of social behaviors and social relations as a function of physical attractiveness. In C. P. Herman (Ed.), *Physical appearance, stigma, and social behavior.* Hillsdale, NJ: Erlbaum.

Langlois, J. H., Ritter, J. M., Roggman, L. A., & Vaughn, L. S. (1991). Facial diversity and infant preferences for attractive faces. *Developmental Psychology, 26,* 153–159.

Langlois, J. H., Roggman, L. A., & Rieser–Danner, L. A. (1990). Infants' differential social responses to attractive and unattractive faces. *Developmental Psychology, 26,* 153–159.

Lapadat, J. C. (1991). Pragmatic language skills of students with language and/or learning disabilities: A quantitative synthesis. *Journal of Learning Disabilities, 24,* 147–157.

Lapointe, A. E., Mead, N. A., & Askew, J. M. (1992). *Learning mathematics: The international assessment of educational progress.* Princeton, NJ: Educational Testing Service.

Lapsley, D. K. (1990). Continuity and discontinuity in adolescent social cognitive development. In R. Montemayor, G. R. Adams, & T. P. Guillotta (Eds.), *From childhood to adolescence: A transitional period?* Newbury Park, CA: Sage.

Lapsley, D. K. (1991). Egocentrism theory and the "new look" at the imaginary audience and personal fable in adolescence. In R. M. Lerner, A. C. Petersen, & J. Brooks–Gunn (Eds.), *Encyclopedia of adolescence.* New York: Garland.

Larson, R. (1991). Adolescent moodiness. In R. M. Lerner, A. C. Petersen, & J. Brooks–Gunn (Eds.), *Encyclopedia of adolescence.* New York: Garland.

Larson, R., & Ham, M. (1993). Stress and "storm and stress" in early adolescence: The relationship of negative events with dysphoric affect. *Developmental Psychology, 29,* 130–140.

Larson, R., & Richards, M. H. (1991). Daily companionship in late childhood and early adolescence: Changing developmental contexts. *Child Development, 62,* 284–300.

Laszlo, J. I. (1990). Child perceptive-motor development: Normal and abnormal development of skilled behavior. In C. A. Hauert (Ed.), *Developmental psychology: Cognitive, perceptive-motor and neuropsychological perspectives.* Amsterdam: North-Holland.

Laurendeau, M., & Pinard, A. (1970). *The development of the concept of space in the child.* New York: International Universities Press.

Laursen, B. (1993). Conflict management among close peers. In B. Laursen (Ed.), *New directions in child development: No. 60. Close friendships in adolescence.* San Francisco: Jossey–Bass.

Law, D. J., Pellegrino, J. W., & Hunt, E. B. (1993). Comparing the tortoise and the hare: Gender differences and experience in dynamic spatial reasoning tasks. *Psychological Science, 4,* 35–40.

Lawson, C. (1991, October 17). A new guide charts a life's lesson plan for sex education. *New York Times,* pp. B1, 4.

Leadbeater, B. (1991). Relativistic thinking in adolescence. In R. M. Lerner, A. C. Petersen, & J. Brooks–Gunn (Eds.), *Encyclopedia of adolescence.* New York: Garland.

Leadbeater, B. J., & Linares, D. (1992). Depressive symptoms in black and Puerto Rican adolescent mothers in the first 3 years postpartum. *Development and Psychopathology, 4,* 451–468.

Leary, W. E. (1992, November 4). For some adults, bed-wetting is far from a distant memory. *New York Times,* p. A19.

Leary, W. E. (1993a, January 12). Spread of AIDS is spurred by racism, U. S. panel says. *New York Times,* p. A10.

Leary, W. E. (1993b, April 28). Sickle-cell screening urged for all newborns. *New York Times,* p. B7.

Leary, W. E. (1993c, September 16). Waste is found in use of prenatal ultrasound. *New York Times,* p. A12.

Leboyer, F. (1975). *Birth without violence.* New York: Knopf.

Leder, G. C. (1990a). Gender differences in mathematics: An overview. In E. Fennema & G. C. Leder (Eds.), *Mathematics and gender.* New York: Teachers College Press.

Leder, G. C. (1990b). Teacher/student interactions in the mathematics classroom: A different perspective. In E. Fennema & G. C. Leder (Eds.), *Mathematics and gender.* New York: Teachers College Press.

Lederberg, A. R., & Mobley, C. E. (1990). The effect of hearing impairment on the quality of attachment and mother–toddler interaction. *Child Development, 61,* 1596–1604.

Lederman, S. A. (1992). Estimating infant mortality from human immunodeficiency virus and other causes in breast-feeding and bottle-feeding populations. *Pediatrics, 89,* 290–296.

Lee, F. R. (1993, March 7). The scythe of AIDS leaves a generation of orphans. *New York Times,* p. 18.

Lee, N. E., Brooks–Gunn, J., Schnur, E., & Liaw, F. R. (1990). Are Head Start effects sustained? A longitudinal follow-up comparison of disadvantaged children attending Head Start, no preschool, and other preschool programs. *Child Development, 61,* 495–507.

Legault, F., & Strayer, F. F. (1990). The emergence of gender-segregation in preschool peer groups. In F. F. Strayer (Ed.), *Social interaction and behavioral development during early childhood.* Montreal: La Maison D'Ethologie de Montreal.

Lehmkuhle, S., Garzia, R. P., Turner, L., Hash, T., & Baro, J. A. (1993). A defective visual pathway in children with reading disability. *New England Journal of Medicine, 328,* 989–996.

Leifer, M. (1980). *Psychological effects of motherhood: A study of first pregnancy.* New York: Praeger.

LeMare, L. J., & Rubin, K. H. (1987). Perspective taking and peer interaction: Structural and developmental analysis. *Child Development, 58,* 306–315.

Lenneberg, E. H. (1967). *Biological foundations of language.* New York: Wiley.

Leon, G. R. (1991). Bulimia nervosa in adolescence. In R. M. Lerner, A. C. Petersen, & J. Brooks–Gunn (Eds.), *Encyclopedia of adolescence.* New York: Garland.

Leon, G. R., Fulkerson, J. A., Perry, C. L., & Cudeck, R. (1993). Personality and behavioral vulnerabilities associated with risk status for eating disorders in adolescent girls. *Journal of Abnormal Psychology, 102,* 438–444.

Leonard, S. P., & Archer, J. (1989). A naturalistic investigation of gender constancy in three- to four-year-old children. *British Journal of Developmental Psychology, 7,* 341–346.

Lerner, G. (1993). *The creation of feminist consciousness.* New York: Oxford University Press.

Lerner, J. V., Hertzog, C., Hooker, K. A., Hassibi, M., & Thomas, A. (1988). A longitudinal study of negative emotional states and adjustment from early childhood through adolescence. *Child Development, 59,* 356–366.

Lerner, J. V., & Hess, L. E. (1991). Maternal employment influences on adolescent development. In R. M. Lerner, A. C. Petersen, & J. Brooks–Gunn (Eds.), *Encyclopedia of adolescence.* New York: Garland.

Lerner, R. M. (1991). Changing organism-context relations as the basic process of development: A developmental contextual perspective. *Developmental Psychology, 27,* 27–32.

Leslie, C. (1993, August 2). Girls will be girls. *Newsweek,* p. 44.

Lester, B. M., Als, H., & Brazelton, T. B. (1982). Regional obstetric anesthesia and newborn behavior: A reanalysis toward synergistic effects. *Child Development, 53,* 687–692.

Lester, B. M., Boukydis, C. F. Z., Garcia-Coll, C. T., Hole, W., & Peucker, M. (1992). Infantile colic: Acoustic cry characteristics, maternal perception of cry, and temperament. *Infant Behavior and Development, 15,* 15–26.

Lester, B. M., Corwin, M. J., Sepkoski, C., Seifer, R., Peucker, M., McLaughlin, S., & Golub, H. L. (1991). Neurobehavioral syndromes in cocaine-exposed newborn infants. *Child Development, 62,* 694–705.

Lester, B. M., & Dreher, M. (1989). Effects of marijuana use during pregnancy on newborn cry. *Child Development, 60,* 765–771.

LeVay, S. (1991, August 30). A difference in hypothalamic structure between heterosexual and homosexual men. *Science, 253,* 1034–1037.

Le Vine, R. A. (1974). Parental goals: A cross-cultural view. In H. J. Leichter (Ed.), *The family as educator.* New York: Teachers College Press.

Levitt, M. J., Guacci–Franco, N., & Levitt, J. L. (1993). Convoys of social support in childhood and early adolescence: Structure and function. *Developmental Psychology, 29,* 811–818.

Levitt, M. J., Weber, R. A., Clark, M. C., & McDonnell, P. (1985). Reciprocity of exchange in toddler sharing behavior. *Developmental Psychology, 21,* 122–123.

Levy, C. J. (1993, July 28). Distribution of condoms to include fifth graders. *New York Times,* p. B10.

Lewin, T. (1990, June 4). Father's vanishing act called common drama. *New York Times,* p. A18.

Lewin, T. (1991, February 8). Studies on teen-age sex cloud condom debate. *New York Times,* p. A10.

Lewin, T. (1992a, November 23). Syphilis among babies climbs with crack use. *New York Times,* p. A9.

Lewin, T. (1992b, December 10). Sex partners on increase among teen-age girls. *New York Times,* p. A14.

Lewis, C., Battistich, V., & Schaps, E. (1990). School-based primary prevention. What is an effective program? In W. Gardner, S. G Millstein, & B. L. Wilcox (Eds.), *New directions for child development: No. 50. Adolescents in the AIDS epidemic.* San Francisco: Jossey–Bass.

Lewis, C., & Osborne, A. (1990). Three-year-olds' problems with false belief: Conceptual deficit or linguistic artifact? *Child Development, 61,* 1514–1519.

Lewis, D. O. (1991a). Conduct disorder. In M. Lewis (Ed.), *Child and adolescent psychiatry: A comprehensive textbook.* Baltimore: Williams & Wilkins.

Lewis, D. O. (1991b). The development of the symptom of violence. In M. Lewis (Ed.), *Child and adolescent psychiatry.* Baltimore: Williams & Wilkins.

Lewis, J. M. (1993). Childhood play in normality, pathology, and therapy. *American Journal of Orthopsychiatry, 63,* 6–15.

Lewis, M. (1990). Social knowledge and social development. *Merrill–Palmer-Quarterly, 36,* 93–116.

Lewis, M. (1991). Ways of knowing: Objective self-awareness or consciousness. *Developmental Review, 11,* 231–243.

Lewis, M., & Brooks–Gunn, J. (1979). *Social cognition and the acquisition of self.* New York: Plenum.

Lewis, M., & Feiring, C. (1989). Early predictors of childhood friendship. In T. J. Berndt & G. W. Ladd (Eds.), *Peer relationships in child development.* New York: Wiley.

Lewis, M., Worobey, J., Ramsay, D. S., & McCormack, M. K. (1992). Prenatal exposure to heavy metals: Effect on childhood cognitive skills and health status. *Pediatrics, 89,* 1010–1015.

Liben, L. S. (1991). The Piagetian water-level task: Looking below the surface. In R. Vasta (Ed.), *Annals of child development* (Vol. 8). London: Kingsley.

Liben, L. S., & Signorella, M. L. (1993). Gender-schematic processing in children: The role of initial interpretations of stimuli. *Developmental Psychology, 29,* 141–149.

Lickona, T. (1991). Moral development in the elementary school classroom. In W. M. Kurtines & J. L. Gewirtz (Eds.), *Handbook of moral behavior and development* (Vol. 3). Hillsdale, NJ: Erlbaum.

Liebert, R. M., & Fischel, J. E. (1990). The elimination disorders: Enuresis and encopresis. In M. Lewis & S. M. Miller (Eds.), *Handbook of developmental pathology.* New York: Plenum.

Liebert, R. M., & Sprafkin, J. (1988). *The early window* (3rd ed.). New York: Pergamon.

Lillard, A. S. (1993). Pretend play skills and the child's theory of mind. *Child Development, 64,* 348–371.

Lin, C. (1989). High-risk situations: The very low birth weight fetus. In M. J. Evans, J. C. Fletcher, A. O. Dixler, & J. D. Schulman (Eds.), *Fetal diagnosis and therapy: Science, ethics and the law.* Philadelphia: Lippincott.

Linn, M. C., & Hyde, J. S. (1991). Trends in cognitive and psychosocial gender differences. In R. M. Lerner, A. C. Petersen, & J. Brooks–Gunn (Eds.), *Encyclopedia of adolescence.* New York: Garland.

Linn, M. C., & Petersen, A. C. (1986). A meta-analysis of gender differences in spatial ability: Implications for mathematics and science achievement. In J. S. Hyde & M. C. Linn (Eds.), *The psychology of gender: Advances through meta-analysis.* Baltimore: Johns Hopkins University Press.

Linn, S., Lieberman, E., Schoenbaum, S. C., Monson, R. R., Stubblefield, P. G., & Ryan, K. J. (1988). Adverse outcomes of pregnancy in women exposed to diethylstilbestrol in pregnancy. *Journal of Reproductive Medicine, 33,* 3–7.

Linney, J. A., & Seidman, E. (1989). The future of schooling. *American Psychologist, 44,* 336–340.

Lips, H. (1993). *Sex and gender: An introduction* (2nd ed.). Mountain View, CA: Mayfield.

Lipsitt, L. P. (1990a). Learning and memory in infants. *Merrill–Palmer Quarterly, 36,* 53–66.

Lipsitt, L. P. (1990b). Learning process in the human newborn. In A. Diamond (Ed.), *The development and neutral bases of higher cognitive functions.* New York: New York Academy of Sciences.

List, J. A., Collins, W. A., & Westby, S. D. (1983). Comprehension and inferences from traditional and nontraditional sex-role portrayals on television. *Child Development, 54,* 1579–1587.

Litt, I. F. (1991). Medical complications of eating disorders. In R. M. Lerner, A. C. Petersen, & J. Brooks–Gunn (Eds.), *Encyclopedia of adolescence.* New York: Garland.

Little, A. H., Lipsitt, L. P., & Rovee–Collier, C. (1984). Classical conditioning and retention of the infants' eyelid response: Effects of age and interstimulus interval. *Journal of Experimental Child Psychology, 37,* 512–524.

Livingston, R. (1991). Anxiety disorders. In M. Lewis (Ed.), *Child and adolescent psychiatry: A comprehensive textbook.* Baltimore: Williams & Wilkins.

Livingstone, M. S., Rosen, G. D., Drislane, F. W., & Galaburda, A. M. (1991). Physiological and anatomical evidence for a magno cellular defect in developmental dyslexia. *Proceedings of the National Academy of Science, 88,* 7943–7947.

Livson, N., & Peskin, H. (1980). Perspectives on adolescence from longitudinal research. In J. Adelson (Ed.), *Handbook of adolescent psychology.* New York: Wiley.

Lobel, M., Dunkel–Schetter, C., & Scrimshaw, S. C. M. (1992). Prenatal maternal stress and prematurity: A prospective study of socio-economically disadvantaged women. *Health Psychology, 11,* 32–40.

Lobel, T. E., & Menashri, J. (1993). Relations of conceptions of gender-role transgressions and gender constancy to gender-typed toy preferences. *Developmental Psychology, 29,* 150–155.

Loeber, R., Green, S. M., Lahey, B. B., Christ, M. A. G., & Frick, P. J., (1992). Developmental sequences in the age of onset of disruptive child behaviors. *Journal of Child and Family Studies, 1,* 21–41.

Loeber, R., Wung, P., Keenan, K., Giroux, B., Stouthamer–Loeber, M., Van Kammen, W. B., & Maughan, B. (1993). Developmental pathways in disruptive child behavior. *Development and Psychopathology, 5,* 101–133.

Loehlin, J. C. (1992). *Genes and environment in personality development.* Newbury Park, CA: Sage.

Loftus, E. F. (1992, August). When a lie becomes memory's truth: Memory distortion after exposure to misinformation. *Current Directions in Psychological Science, 1,* 121–123.

Loftus, E. F., Levidow, B., & Duensing, S. (1992). Who remembers best? Individual differences in memory for events that occurred in a science museum. *Applied Cognitive Psychology, 6,* 93–107.

Logan, B. N. (1991). Adolescent substance abuse prevention: An overview of the literature. *Family Community Health, 13,* 25–36.

Longaker, M. T., Golbus, M. S., Filly, R. A., Rosen, M. A., Chang, S. W., & Harrison, M. R. (1992). Maternal outcome after open fetal surgery. *Journal of the American Medical Association, 265,* 737–741.

Lore, R. K., & Schultz, L. A. (1993). Control of human aggression. *American Psychologist, 48,* 16–25.

Lorenz, K. (1962). *King Solomon's ring.* London: Methuen.

Lorenz, K. (1981). *The foundations of ethology.* New York: Springer–Verlag.

Lott, B., & Maluso, D. (1991, August). *The social learning of gender: A feminist review.* Paper presented at the meeting of the American Psychological Association, San Francisco.

Lott, J. T. (1990). A portrait of Asian and Pacific American women. In S. E. Rix (Ed.), *The American woman: 1990–91.* New York: Norton.

Loughrey, M. E., & Harris, M. B. (1990). A descriptive study of at-risk high school students. *High School Journal, 73,* 187–193.

Lovaas, O. I., Smith, T., & McEachin, J. J. (1989). Clarifying comments on the young autism study: Reply to Schapler, Short, and Mesibov. *Journal of Consulting and Clinical Psychology, 57,* 165–167.

Lovdal, L. T. (1989). Sex role messages in television commercials: An update. *Sex Roles, 21,* 715–724.

Love, J. M., Logue, M. E., Trudeau, J. V., & Thayer, K. (1992). *Transitions to kindergarten in American schools.* Portsmouth, NH: RMC Research Corp.

Lowrey, G. H. (1986). *Growth and development of children.* Chicago: Year Book Medical Publishers.

Lozoff, B. (1989). Nutrition and behavior. *American Psychologist, 44,* 231–236.

Lubinski, D., & Benbow, C. P. (1992). Gender differences in abilities and preferences among the gifted: Implications for the math–science pipeline. *Current Directions in Psychological Science, 1,* 61–66.

Lucariello, J., & Nelson, K. (1985). Slotfiller categories as memory organizers for young children. *Developmental Psychology, 21,* 272–282.

Lucas, A. R. (1991). Eating disorders. In M. Lewis (Ed.), *Child and adolescent psychiatry: A comprehensive textbook.* Baltimore: Williams & Wilkins.

Lummis, M., & Stevenson, H. W. (1990). Gender differences in beliefs and achievement: A cross-cultural study. *Developmental Psychology, 26,* 254–263.

Luster, T., & Dubow, E. (1992). Home environment and maternal intelligence as predictors of verbal intelligence: A comparison of preschool and school-age children. *Merrill–Palmer Quarterly, 38,* 151–173.

Lykken, D. T., McGue, M., Tellegen, A., & Bouchard, T. J. (1992). Genetic traits that may not run in families. *American Psychologist, 47,* 1565–1577.

Lynch, E. W., & Hanson, M. J. (1992). *Developing cross-cultural competence.* Baltimore: Brookes.

Lynch, M. E. (1991). Gender intensification. In R. M. Lerner, A. C. Petersen, & J. Brooks–Gunn (Eds.), *Encyclopedia of adolescence.* New York: Garland.

Lynn, R. (1991). Educational achievements of Asian Americans. *American Psychologist, 46,* 875–876.

Lyon, F. R., & Moats, L. C. (1988). Critical issues in the instruction of the learning disabled. *Journal of Consulting and Clinical Psychology, 56,* 830–835.

Lyons-Ruth, K., Alpern, L., & Repacholi, B. (1993). Disorganized infant attachment classification and maternal psychosocial problems as predictors of hostile–aggressive behavior in the preschool classroom. *Child Development, 64,* 572–585.

Lyons-Ruth, K., Connell, D. B., Grunebaum, H. U., & Botein, S. (1990). Infants at social risk: Maternal depression and family support services as mediators of infant development and security of attachment. *Child Development, 61,* 85–98.

Lytton, H. (1990a). Child and parent effects in boys' conduct disorder: A reinterpretation. *Developmental Psychology, 26,* 683–697.

Lytton, H. (1990b). Child effects—still unwelcome? Response to Dodge and Wahler. *Developmental Psychology, 26,* 702–704.

Lytton, H., & Romney, D. M. (1991). Parents' differential socialization of boys and girls: A meta-analysis. *Psychological Bulletin, 109,* 267–296.

Lyytinen, P. (1991). Developmental trends in children's pretend play. *Child Care, Health, and Development, 17,* 9–25.

Lyytinen, P. (1992, July). *Cross-situational stability of children's pretend play.* Paper presented at the XXV International Congress of Psychology, Brussels.

Maccoby, E. E. (1984a). Middle childhood in the context of the family. In A. Collins (Ed.), *Development during the middle years: The years from six to twelve.* Washington, DC: National Academy of Sciences Press.

Maccoby, E. E. (1984b). Socialization and developmental change. *Child Development, 55,* 317–328.

Maccoby, E. E. (1990a). Gender and relationships: A developmental account. *American Psychologist, 45,* 513–520.

Maccoby, E. E. (1990b). The role of gender identity and gender constancy in sex-differentiated development. In D. Schrader (Ed.), *New directions for child development: No. 47. The legacy of Lawrence Kohlberg.* San Francisco: Jossey–Bass.

Maccoby, E. E. (1991a). Different reproductive strategies in males and females. *Child Development, 62,* 676–681.

Maccoby, E. E. (1991b). Gender and relationships: A reprise. *American Psychologist, 46,* 538–539.

Maccoby, E. E. (1992). The role of parents in the socialization of children: An historical overview. *Developmental Psychology, 28,* 1006–1017.

Maccoby, E. E. (1993a, March). *Coparenting apart: Variations in the forms and outcomes of coparenting after divorce.* Paper presented at the meeting of the Society for Research in Child Development, New Orleans, LA.

Maccoby, E. E. (1993b, March). *Trends and issues in the study of gender role development.* Paper presented at the meeting of the Society for Research in Child Development, New Orleans, LA.

Maccoby, E. E., & Feldman, S. (1972). Mother-attachment and stranger reactions in the third year of life. *Monographs of the Society for Research in Child Development, 37*(1, Serial No. 146).

Macoby, E. E., & Jacklin, C. N. (1974). *The psychology of sex differences.* Stanford, CA: Stanford University Press.

Maccoby, E. E., & Jacklin, C. N. (1987). Gender segregation in childhood. In H. W. Reese (Ed.), *Advances in child development and behavior* (Vol. 20). Orlando, FL: Academic Press.

Maccoby E. E., & Martin, J. A. (1983). Socialization in the context of the family: Parent–child interaction. In P. Mussen (Ed.), *Handbook of child psychology: Vol. 4. Socialization, personality, and social development.* New York: Wiley.

MacDonald, K. (1992). Warmth as a developmental construct: An evolutionary analysis. *Child Development, 63,* 753–773.

Macey, T. J., Harmon, R. J., & Easterbrooks, M. A. (1987). Impact of premature birth on the development of the infant in the family. *Journal of Consulting and Clinical Psychology, 55,* 846–852.

Macfarlane, A. (1977). *The psychology of childbirth.* Cambridge, MA: Harvard University Press.

Macfarlane, A., Harris, P., & Barnes, I. (1976). Central and peripheral vision in early infancy. *Journal of Experimental Child Psychology, 21,* 532–538.

Macfarlane, J. A. (1975). Olfaction in the development of social preferences in the human neonate. In M. A. Hofer (Ed.), *Parent–infant interaction.* Amsterdam: Elsevier.

MacPhee, D., Fritz, J., & Miller–Heyl, J. (1993, March). *Ethnic variations in social support networks.* Paper presented at the meeting of the Society for Research in Child Development, New Orleans, LA.

Madden, N. A., Slavin, R. E., Karweit, N. L., Dolan, L., & Wasik, B. A. (1991, April). Success for all. *Phi Delta Kappan,* pp. 593–599.

Maggs, J., & Galambos, N. (1993, March). *Risky business: Why do adolescents engage in problem behavior anyway?* Paper presented at the meeting of the Society for Research in Child Development, New Orleans, LA.

Mahaffey, K. R. (1992, October 29). Exposure to lead in childhood: The importance of prevention. *New England Journal of Medicine, 327,* 1308–1309.

Mahler, M. S., Pine, F., & Bergman, A. (1975). *The psychological birth of the human infant: Symbiosis and individuation.* New York: Basic Books.

Main, M., & Cassidy, J. (1988). Categories of responses to reunion with the parent at age 6: Predictable from infant attachment classifications and stable over a 1-month period. *Developmental Psychology, 24,* 415–426.

Main, M., & Hesse, E. (1990). Parents' unresolved traumatic experiences related to infant disorganized attachment status: Is frightened and/or frightening parental behavior the linking mechanism? In M. T. Greenberg, D. Cicchetti, & E. M. Cummings (Eds.), *Attachment in the preschool years.* Chicago: University of Chicago Press.

Main, M., & Weston, D. R. (1981). The quality of the toddler's relationship to mother and to father: Related to conflict behavior and the readiness to establish new relationships. *Child Development, 52,* 932–940.

Malatesta, G. Z., Culver, C., Tesman, J. R., & Shepard, B. (1989). The development of emotion expression during the first two years of life. *Monographs of the Society for Research in Child Development, 54*(1-2, Serial No. 219).

Malina, R. M. (1990). Physical growth and performance during the transitional years. In R. Montemayor, G. Adams, & T. Gullotta (Eds.), *From childhood to adolescence: A transition period?* New York: Sage.

Malina, R. M. (1991a). Adolescent growth spurt, II. In R. M. Lerner, A. C. Petersen, & J. Brooks–Gunn (Eds.), *Encyclopedia of adolescence.* New York: Garland.

Malina, R. M. (1991b). Physical growth and performance during the transitional years (9–16). In R. Montemayor, G. R. Adams, & T. P. Gullotta (Eds.), *From childhood to adolescence: A transitional period?* Newbury Park, CA: Sage.

Mandler, J. M. (1990). Recall and its verbal expression. In R. Fivush & J. A. Hudson (Eds.), *Knowing and remembering in young children.* Cambridge: Cambridge University Press.

Mangelsdorf, S. C. (1992). Developmental changes in infant–stranger interaction. *Infant Behavior and Development, 15,* 191–208.

Mangelsdorf, S., Gunnar, M., Kestenbaum, R., Lang, S., & Andreas, D. (1990). Infant proneness-to-distress temperament, maternal personality, and mother–infant attachment: Associations and goodness of fit. *Child Development, 61,* 820–831.

Manke, B. (1993, March). *Dimensions of intimacy during adolescence: Correlates and antecedents.* Paper presented at the Society for Research in Child Development, New Orleans, LA.

Mann, B. J., & Borduin, C. M. (1991). A critical review of psychotherapy outcome studies with adolescents: 1978–1988. *Adolescence, 26,* 505–541.

Mann, N. C., Weller, S. C., & Rauchschwalbe, R. (1992). Bucket-related drownings in the United States, 1984 through 1990. *Pediatrics, 89,* 1068–1071.

Mannuzza, S., Klein, R. G., & Addalli, K. A. (1991). Young adult marital status of hyperactive boys and their brothers: A prospective follow-up. *Journal of the American Academy of Child and Adolescent Psychiatry, 30,* 743–751.

Mannuzza, S., Klein, R. G., Bessler, A., Malloy, P., & LaPadula, M. (1993). Adult outcome of hyperactive boys: Educational achievement, occupational rank, and psychiatric status. *Archives of General Psychiatry, 50,* 565–576.

Maratsos, M. (1983). Some current issues in the study of the acquisition of grammar. In J. H. Flavell & E. M. Markman (Eds.), *Handbook of child psychology: Vol. 3. Cognitive development.* New York: Wiley.

Marcia, J. E. (1980). Identity in adolescence. In J. Adelson (Ed.), *Handbook of adolescent psychology.* New York: Wiley.

Marcia, J. E. (1991). Identity and self-development. In R. M. Lerner, A. C. Petersen, & J. Brooks–Gunn (Eds.), *Encyclopedia of adolescence.* New York: Garland.

Marcia, J. E., Waterman, A. S., Matteson, D. R., Archer, S. L., & Orlofsky, J. L. (1993). *Ego identity: A handbook for psychosocial research.* New York: Springer–Verlag.

Marcus, G. F., Pinker, S., Ullman, M., Hollander, M., Rosen, T. J., & Xu, F. (1992). Overregularization in language acquisition. *Monographs of the Society for Research in Child Development, 57*(4, Serial No. 228).

Marean, G. C., Werner, L. A., & Kuhl, P. K. (1992). Vowel categorization by very young infants. *Developmental Psychology, 28,* 396–405.

Markovitz, H., & Vachon, R. (1990). Conditional reasoning, representation, and level of abstraction. *Developmental Psychology, 26,* 942–951.

Marks, I. M. (1987). The development of normal fear: A review. *Journal of Child Psychology and Psychiatry, 28,* 667–697.

Marks, P. (1993, February 14). Shots are often free but many children miss immunizations. *New York Times,* pp. A1, 17.

Markstrom–Adams, C. (1991). A consideration of intervening factors in adolescent identity formation. In G. R. Adams, T. P. Gullotta, & R. Montemayor (Eds.), *Adolescent identity formation.* Newbury Park, CA: Sage.

Marsh, H. W., Craven, R. G., & Debus, R. (1991). Self-concepts of young children 5 to 8 years of age: Measurement and multidimensional structure. *Journal of Educational Psychology, 83,* 377–392.

Marsiglio, W., & Scanzoni, J. H. (1990). Pregnant and parenting black adolescents: Theoretical and policy perspectives. In A. R. Stiffman & L. E. Davis (Eds.), *Ethnic issues in adolescent mental health.* Newbury Park, CA: Sage.

Martin, B., & Hoffman, J. A. (1990). Conduct disorders. In M. Lewis & S. M. Miller (Eds.), *Handbook of developmental psychopathology.* New York: Plenum.

Martin, C. L. (1990). Attitudes and expectations about children with nontraditional and traditional gender roles. *Sex Roles, 22,* 151–165.

Martin, C. L. (1993). New directions for investigating children's gender knowledge. *Developmental Review, 13,* 184–204.

Martin, C. L., & Little, J. K. (1990). The relation of gender understanding to children's sex-typed preferences and gender stereotypes. *Child Development, 61,* 1427–1439.

Martin, C. L., Wood, C. H., & Little, J. K. (1990). The development of gender stereotype components. *Child Development, 61,* 1891–1904.

Martinez, F. D., Cline, M., & Burrows, B. (1992). Increased incidence of asthma in children of smoking mothers. *Pediatrics, 89,* 21–26.

Martinez, P., & Richters, J. E. (1993, February). The NIMH Community Violence Project: II. Children's distress symptoms associated with violence exposure. *Psychiatry, 56,* 22–35.

Massey, R. F., Walfish, S., & Krone, A. (1992). Cluster analysis of MMPI profiles of adolescents in treatment for substance abuse. *Journal of Adolescent Chemical Dependency, 2,* 23–33.

Masten, A. S., Best, K. M., & Garmezy, N. (1990). Resilience and development: Contributions from the study of children who overcome adversity. *Development and Psychopathology, 2,* 425–444.

Matheny, A. P. (1991). Unintentional injuries: Gender differences in accidents. In R. M. Lerner, A. C. Petersen, & J. Brooks–Gunn (Eds.), *Encyclopedia of adolescence.* New York: Garland.

Mathew, A., & Cook, M. (1990). The control of reaching movements by young infants. *Child Development, 61,* 1238–1257.

Matlin, M. (1993). *The psychology of women* (2nd ed.). New York: Harcourt Brace Jovanovich.

Matthews, J. (1990). Drawing and individual development. In R. M. Thomas (Ed.), *The encyclopedia of human development and education: Theory, research and studies.* Oxford: Pergamon.

Maurer, D. M., & Maurer, C. E. (1976, October). Newborn babies see better than you think. *Psychology Today,* pp. 85–88.

May, K. A., & Perrin, S. P. (1985). Prelude: Pregnancy and birth. In S. M. H. Hanson & F. W. Boett (Eds.), *Dimensions of fatherhood.* Beverly Hills, CA: Sage.

Mayes, L. C. (1991). Infant assessment. In M. L. Lewis (Ed.), *Child and adolescent psychiatry: A comprehensive textbook.* Baltimore: Williams & Wilkins.

Mayes, L. C., & Zigler, E. (1992). An observational study of the affective concomitants of mastery in infants. *Journal of Child Psychology & Psychiatry, 33,* 659–667.

Mayle, P. (1975). *What's happening to me?* Secaucus, NJ: Lyle Stuart.

Maziade, M., Boudreault, M., Cate, R., & Thivierge, J. (1986). Clinical and laboratory observations. *Journal of Pediatrics, 108,* 134–136.

McAdoo, J. L. (1993). The roles of African American fathers: An ecological perspective. *Journal of Contemporary Human Services, 74,* 28–34.

McCabe, A. E., Roberts, B., & Hope, P. (1992, July). *Contextual influences on child language: Gender, birth order, and the speech of others.* Paper presented at the XXV International Congress of Psychology, Brussels.

McCall, R. B. (1991). Underachievers and dropouts. In R. M. Lerner, A. C. Petersen, & J. Brooks–Gunn (Eds.), *Encyclopedia of adolescence.* New York: Garland.

McCall, R. B., Applebaum, M. I., & Hogarty, P. S. (1973). Developmental changes in mental performance. *Monographs of the Society for Research in Child Development, 38*(3, Serial No. 150).

McCall, R. B., & Carriger, M. S. (1993). A meta-analysis of infant habituation and recognition memory performance as predictors of later IQ. *Child Development, 64,* 57–79.

McCarthy, K. (1993, July). Kids' eyewitness recall is focus for conference. *APA Monitor,* pp. 1, 28–29.

McCartney, K., Harris, M. J., & Bernjeri, F. (1990). Growing up and growing apart: A developmental meta-analysis of twin studies. *Psychological Bulletin, 107,* 226–237.

McCauley, E., Kay, T., Ito, J., & Treder, R. (1987). The Turner syndrome: Cognitive deficits, affective discrimination, and behavior problems. *Child Development, 58,* 464–473.

McCendie, R., & Schneider, B. (1993, March). *Problematic peer relations in childhood and adult maladjustment: A quantitative synthesis.* Paper presented at the meeting of the Society for Research in Child Development, New Orleans, LA.

McConnochie, K. M., & Roghmann, K.J. (1992). Immunization opportunities missed among urban poor children. *Pediatrics, 89,* 1019–1026.

McCoy, J. H., & Kenney, M. A. (1991). Nutrient intake of female adolescents. In R. M. Lerner, A. C. Petersen, & J. Brooks–Gunn (Eds.), *Encyclopedia of adolescence.* New York: Garland.

McCune, L. (1993). The development of play as the development of consciousness. In M. H. Bornstein & A. W. O'Reilly (Eds.), *New directions for child development: No 59. The role of play in the development of thought.* San Francisco: Jossey–Bass.

McDonald, A. D., Armstrong, B. G., & Sloan, M. (1992a). Cigarette, alcohol, and coffee consumption and congenital defects. *American Journal of Public Health, 82,* 91–93.

McDonald, A. D., Armstrong, B. G., & Sloan, M. (1992b). Cigarette, alcohol, and coffee consumption and prematurity. *American Journal of Public Health, 82,* 87–90.

McEachin, J. J., Smith, T., & Lovaas, O. I. (1993). Long-term outcome for children with autism who received early intensive behavioral treatment. *Journal of Mental Retardation, 97,* 359–372.

McEwan, M. H., Dihoff, R. E., & Brosvic, G. M. (1991). Early infant crawling experience is reflected in later motor skill development. *Perceptual and Motor Skills, 72,* 75–79.

McFalls, J. A. (1990). The risks of reproductive impairment in the later years of childbearing. *Annual Review of Sociology, 16,* 491–519.

McGee, R., Partridge, F., Williams, S., & Silva, P. (1991). A twelve-year follow-up of preschool hyperactive children. *Journal of the American Academy of Child and Adolescent Psychiatry, 30,* 224–232.

McGilly, K., & Siegler, R. S. (1990). The influence of encoding and strategic knowledge on children's choices among serial recall strategies. *Developmental Psychology, 26,* 931–941.

McGinty, D. J., & Drucker–Colin, R. (1982). Sleep mechanisms: Biology and control of REM sleep. *International Review of Neurobiology, 23,* 391–436.

McGovern, T. V., Furumoto, L., Halpern, D. F., Kimble, G. A., & McKeachie, W. J. (1991). Liberal education, study in depth, and the arts and sciences major–psychology. *American Psychologist, 46,* 598–605.

McGue, M., Pickens, R. W., & Svikis, D. S. (1992). Sex and age effects on the inheritance of alcohol problems: A twin study. *Journal of Abnormal Psychology, 101,* 3–17.

McGuinness, D. (1990). Behavioral tempo in preschool boys and girls. *Learning and Individual Differences, 2,* 315–325.

McIntosh, R., Vaughn, J., & Zaragora, N. (1991). A review of social interventions for students with learning disabilities. *Journal of Learning Disabilities, 24,* 451–458.

McIntyre, A., Saudargas, R. A., & Howard, R. (1991). Attribution of control and teenage pregnancy. *Journal of Applied Developmental Psychology, 12,* 55–61.

McKenry, P. C. (1991). Minority youth and drug use. In R. M. Lerner, A. C. Petersen, & J. Brooks–Gunn (Eds.), *Encyclopedia of adolescence.* New York: Garland.

McKusick, V. A. (1992). *Mendelian inheritance in man: Catalog of autosomal dominant, autosomal recessive and x-linked phenotypes* (10th ed.). Baltimore: Johns Hopkins University Press.

McLaughlin, F. J., Altemeier, W. A., Christensen, M. J., Sherrod, K. B., Dietrich, M. S., & Stern, D. T. (1992). Randomized trial of comprehensive prenatal care for low-income women: Effect on infant birth weight. *Pediatrics, 89,* 128–132.

McLoyd, V. C. (1990). The impact of economic hardship on black families and children: Psychological distress, parenting, and socioemotional development. *Child Development, 61,* 311–346.

McLoyd, V. C. (1993). Employment among African-American mothers in dual-earner families: Antecedents and consequences for family life and child development. In J. Frankel (Ed.), *The employed mother and the family context.* New York: Springer.

McManus, I. C., & Bryden, M. P. (1991). Geschwind's theory of cerebral lateralization: Developing a formal, causal model. *Psychological Bulletin, 110,* 237–253.

McManus, I. C., Sik, G., Cole, D.R., Mellon, A. F., Wong, J., & Kloss, J. (1988). The development of handedness in children. *British Journal of Developmental Psychology, 6,* 257–273.

McWhirter, J. J., McWhirter, B. T., McWhirter, A. M., & McWhirter, E. H. (1993). *At-risk youth: A comprehensive response.* Pacific Grove, CA: Brooks/Cole.

Meador, K. S. (1992). Emerging rainbows: A review of the literature on creativity in preschoolers. *Journal for the Education of the Gifted, 15,* 163–181.

Mednick, B. R., Baker, R. L., & Carothers, L. E. (1990). Patterns of family instability and crime: The association of timing of the family's disruption with subsequent adolescent and young adult criminality. *Journal of Youth and Adolescence, 19,* 201–220.

Mednick, S. A., Moffitt, T. E., & Stack, S. (1987). *The causes of crime: New biological approaches.* Cambridge: Cambridge University Press.

Meece, J. L., Parsons, J. E., Kaczala, C. M., Goff, S. B., & Futterman, R. (1982). Sex differences in math achievement: Toward a model of academic choice. *Psychological Bulletin, 91,* 324–348.

Meehan, P. J., Lamb, J. A., Saltzman, L. E., & O'Carroll, P. W. (1992). Attempted suicide among young adults: Progress toward a meaningful estimate of prevalence. *American Journal of Psychiatry, 149,* 41–44.

Mehregany, D. V. (1991, Winter). The relation of temperament and behavior disorders in a preschool clinical sample. *Child Psychiatry and Human Development, 22,* 129–136.

Melnick, S., Cole, P., Anderson, D., & Herbst, A. (1987). Rates and risks of diethylstilbestrol-related clear-cell adenocarcinoma of the vagina and cervix. *New England Journal of Medicine, 316,* 514–516.

Meltzoff, A. N. (1988). Infant imitation and memory: Nine-month-olds in immediate and deferred tests. *Child Development, 59,* 217–225.

Meltzoff, A. N. (1990). Towards a developmental cognitive science. In A. Diamond (Ed.), *The development and neural bases of higher cognitive functions.* New York: New York Academy of Sciences.

Meltzoff, A. N., & Moore, M. K. (1992). Early imitation within a functional framework: The importance of person identity, movement, and development. *Infant Behavior and Development, 15,* 479–505.

Mennella, J. A., & Beauchamp, G. K. (1991). The transfer of alcohol to human milk: Effects on flavor and the infant's behavior. *New England Journal of Medicine,* 325, 981–985.

Meredith, H. V. (1978). Research between 1960 and 1970 on the standing height of young children in different parts of the world. In H. W. Reese & L. P. Lipsitt (Eds.), *Advances in child development and behavior* (Vol. 12). New York: Academic Press.

Meredith, H. V. (1982). Research between 1950 and 1980 on urban–rural differences in body size and growth rate of children and youths. In H. W. Reese (Ed.), *Advances in child development and behavior* (Vol. 17). New York: Academic Press.

Meredith, H. V. (1984). Body size of infants and children around the world in relation to socioeconomic status. In H. W. Reese (Ed.), *Advances in child development and behavior* (Vol. 18). New York: Academic Press.

Meredith, H. V. (1987). Variation in body stockiness among and within ethnic groups at ages from birth to adulthood. In H. W. Reese (Ed.), *Advances in child development and behavior* (Vol. 20). New York: Academic Press.

Merewood, A. (1991, April). Sperm under siege: More than we ever guessed, having a healthy baby may depend on dad. *Health,* pp. 53–57, 76–77.

Merriman, W. E., & Schuster, J. M. (1991). Young children's disambiguation of object name reference. *Child Development, 62,* 1288–1301.

Mervis, C. B., & Johnson, K. E. (1991). Acquisition of the plural morpheme: A case study. *Developmental Psychology, 27,* 222–235.

Mervis, C. B., Mervis, C. A., Johnson, K. E., & Bertrand, J. (1992). Studying early lexical development: The value of the systematic diary method. In C. Rovee–Collier & L. P. Lipsitt (Eds.), *Advances in infancy research* (Vol. 7). Norwood, NJ: Ablex.

Meyer, S. L., Murphy, C. M., Cascardi, M., & Birns, B. (1991). Gender and relationships: Beyond the peer group. *American Psychologist, 46,* 537.

Michael, E. D. (1990). Physical development and fitness. In R. M. Thomas (Ed.), *The encyclopedia of human development and education: Theory, research and studies.* Oxford: Pergamon.

Michaelson, R. (1993a, April). When disasters hit, children need special help. *APA Monitor,* pp. 30–31.

Michaelson, R. (1993b, May). Tug-of-war is developing over defining retardation. *APA Monitor,* pp. 34–35.

Michel, C. (1989). Radiation embryology. *Experientia, 45,* 69–77.

Mikkelsen, E. J. (1991). Modern approaches to enuresis and encopresis. In M. Lewis (Ed.), *Child and adolescent psychiatry: A comprehensive textbook.* Baltimore: Wiliams & Wilkins.

Miles, S. A., Balden, E., Magpantay, L., Wei, L., Leiblein, A., Hofheinz, D., Toedter, G., Stiehm, E. R., Bryson, Y., and the Southern California Pediatric AIDS Consortium (1993). Rapid serologic testing with immune-complex-dissociated HIV p24 antigen for early detection of HIV infection in neonates. *New England Journal of Medicine, 328,* 297–302.

Millar, W. S. (1972). A study of operant conditioning under delayed reinforcement in early infancy. *Monographs of the Society for Research in Child Development, 37*(2, Serial No. 147).

Millar, W. S. (1990). Span of integration for delayed-reward contingency learning in 6- to 8-month-old infants. In A. Diamond (Ed.), *The development and neural bases of higher cognitive functions.* New York: New York Academy of Sciences.

Miller, A. (1992, June 29). Baby Makers, Inc. *Newsweek,* pp. 38–39.

Miller, D. A. F., McCluskey–Fawcett, K., & Irving, L. M. (1993). The relationship between childhood sexual abuse and subsequent onset of bulimia nervosa. *Child Abuse and Neglect, 17,* 305–314.

Miller, G. A. (1956). The magical number seven, plus or minus two: Some limits on our capacity to process information. *Psychological Review, 63,* 81–97.

Miller, J. G. (1994). Cultural diversity in the morality of caring: Individually-oriented versus duty-based interpersonal moral codes. *Cross-cultural Research, 28,* 3–39.

Miller, J. G., & Bersoff, D. M. (1992). Culture and moral judgment: How are conflicts between justice and interpersonal responsibilities resolved? *Journal of Personality and Social Psychology, 62,* 541–554.

Miller, N. B., Cowan, P. A., Cowan, C. P., Hetherington, E. M., & Clingempeel, W. G. (1993). Externalizing in preschoolers and early adolescents: A cross-study replication of a family model. *Developmental Psychology, 29,* 3–18.

Miller, P. H. (1983). *Theories of developmental psychology.* San Francisco: Freeman.

Miller, R. L. (1992). The human ecology of multiracial identity. In M. P. P. Root (Ed.), *Racially mixed people in America.* Newbury Park, CA: Sage.

Miller, S. M., Birnbaum, A., & Durbin, D. (1990a). Etiologic perspectives on depression in childhood. In M. Lewis & S. M. Miller (Eds.), *Handbook of developmental psychopathology.* New York: Plenum.

Miller, S. M., Boyer, B.A., & Rodoletz, M. (1990b). Anxiety in children: Nature and development. In M. Lewis & S. M. Miller (Eds.), *Handbook of developmental psychopathology.* New York: Plenum.

Miller–Jones, D. (1989). Culture and testing. *American Psychologist, 44,* 360–366.

Mills, C. J. (1992). Academically talented children: The case for early identification and nurturance. *Pediatrics, 89,* 156–157.

Mills, J. L., Graubard, B. I., Harley, E. E., Rhoads, G. G., & Berendes, H. W. (1984). Maternal alcohol consumption and birth weight: How much drinking is safe during pregnancy? *Journal of the American Medical Association, 252,* 1875–1879.

Mills, J. L., Holmes, L. B., Aarons, J. H., Simpson, J. L., Brown, Z. A., Jovanovic–Peterson, L. G., Conley, M. R., Graubard, B. I., Knopp, R. H., & Metzger, B. E. (1993). Moderate caffeine use and the risk of spontaneous abortion and intrauterine growth retardation. *Journal of the American Medical Association, 269,* 593–597.

Mills, R. S. L., & Rubin, K. H. (1990). Parental beliefs about problematic social behaviors in early childhood. *Child Development, 61,* 138–152.

Millstein, S. G. (1990). Risk factors for AIDS among adolescents. In W. Gardner, S. G. Millstein, & B. L. Wilcox (Eds.), *New directions for child development: No. 50. Adolescents in the AIDS epidemic.* San Francisco: Jossey–Bass.

Millstein, S. G., & Litt, I. F. (1990). Adolescent health. In S. S. Feldman & G. R. Elliott (Eds.), *At the threshold: The developing adolescent.* Cambridge, MA: Harvard University Press.

Milstead, M., Lapsley, D., & Hale, C. (1993, March). *A new look at imaginary audience and personal fable.* Paper presented at the meeting of the Society for Research in Child Development, New Orleans, LA.

Minde, K. (1991). The effect of disordered parenting on the development of children. In M. Lewis (Ed.), *Child and adolescent psychiatry: A comprehensive textbook.* Baltimore: Williams & Wilkins.

Minuchin, S., Rosman, B. L., & Baker, L. (1978). *Psychosomatic families.* Cambridge, MA: Harvard University Press.

Miringoff, M. L. (1992). *Index of social health: Monitoring the social well-being of the nation.* Tarrytown, NY: Fordham University Press.

Mitchell, P. R., & Kent, R. D. (1990). Phonetic variation in multisyllable babbling. *Journal of Child Language, 17,* 247–265.

Moffitt, T. E., Caspi, A., Belsky, J., & Silvis, P. A. (1992). Childhood experience and the onset of menarche: A test of a sociobiological model. *Child Development, 63,* 47–58.

Mohan, D., & Romer, C. J. (1991). Accident mortality and morbidity in developing countries. In M. Manciaux & C. J. Romer (Eds.), *Accidents in childhood and adolescence.* Geneva: World Health Organization.

Molfese, D. L., Burger–Judisch, L. M., & Hans, L. L. (1991). Consonant discrimination by newborn infants: Electrophysiological differences. *Developmental Neuropsychology, 7,* 177–195.

Moller, L. C., Hymel, S., & Rubin, K. H. (1992). Sex typing in play and popularity in middle childhood. *Sex Roles, 26,* 331–353.

Money, J. (1977). Human hermaphroditism. In F. A. Beach (Ed.), *Human sexuality in four perspectives.* Baltimore: Johns Hopkins University Press.

Money, J. (1987). Sin, sickness, or status? Homosexual gender identity and psychoneuroendocrinology. *American Psychologist, 42,* 384–399.

Money, J., & Ehrhardt, A. A. (1972). *Man and woman, boy and girl: The differentiation and dimorphism of gender identity from conception to maturity.* Baltimore: Johns Hopkins University Press.

Montemayor, R., Adams, G. R., & Gullotta, T. P. (1990). Introduction. In R. Montemayor, G. R. Adams, & T. P. Gullottla (Eds.), *From childhood to adolescence: A transitional period?* Newbury Park, CA: Sage.

Montemayor, R., Eberly, M., & Flannery, D. J. (1993). Effects of pubertal status and conversation topic on parent and adolescent affective expression. *Journal of Early Adolescence, 13,* 431–447.

Montemayor, R., & Eisen, M. (1977). The development of self-conceptions from childhood to adolescence. *Developmental Psychology, 13,* 314–319.

Montemayor, R., & Flannery, D. J. (1991). Parent–adolescent relations in middle and late adolescence. In R. M. Lerner, A. C. Petersen, & J. Brooks–Gunn (Eds.), *Encyclopedia of adolescence.* New York: Garland.

Montgomery, D. E. (1992). Review: Young children's theory of knowing: The development of a folk epistemology. *Developmental Review, 12,* 410–430.

Moore, C., Pure, K., & Furrow, O. (1990). Children's understanding of the model expression of speaker certainty and uncertainty and its relation to the development of a representational theory of mind. *Child Development, 61,* 722–730.

Moore, K. A., & Snyder, N. O. (1991). Cognitive attainment among firstborn children of adolescent mothers. *American Sociological Review, 56,* 612–624.

Moore, K. L. (1989). *Before we are born* (3rd ed.). Philadelphia: Saunders.

Moore, L. L., Lombardi, D. A., White, M. J., Campbell, J. L., Oliveria, S. A., & Ellison, R. C. (1991). Influence of parents' physical activity levels on activity levels of young children. *Journal of Pediatrics, 118,* 215–219.

Moore, S., & Boldero, J. (1991). Psychosocial development and friendship functions in adolescence. *Sex Roles, 25,* 521–536.

Moore, S. M., & Burling, N. R. (1991). Developmental status and AIDS attitudes in adolescence. *Journal of Genetic Psychology, 152,* 5–16.

Moran, J. R., & Corley, M. D. (1991). Sources of sexual information and sexual attitudes and behaviors of Anglo and Hispanic adolescent males. *Adolescence, 26,* 857–864.

Morelli, G. A., Oppenheim, D., Rogoff, B., & Goldsmith, D. (1992a). Cultural variation in infants' sleeping arrangements: Questions of independence. *Developmental Psychology, 28,* 604–613.

Morelli, G. A., Rogoff, B., & Angelillo, C. (1992b). *Cultural variation in young children's opportunities for involvement in adult activities.* Paper presented at the meeting of the American Anthropology Association, San Francisco.

Morelli, G. A., Rogoff, B., & Angelillo, C. (1993, March). *Cultural variation in children's work and social activities.* Paper presented at the meeting of the Society for Research in Child Development, New Orleans, LA.

Morrison, E. S., Starks, K., Hyndman, C., & Ronzio, N. (1980). *Growing up sexual.* New York: Van Nostrand Reinhold.

Morrison, F. J., Griffith, E. M., & Williamson, G. L. (1993, March). *Two strikes from the start: Individual differences in early literacy.* Paper presented at meeting of the Society for Research in Child Development, New Orleans, LA.

Morrongiello, B. A., & Clifton, R. K. (1984). Effects of sound frequency on behavioral and cardiac orienting in newborn and 5-month-old infants. *Journal of Experimental Child Psychology, 38,* 429–446.

Morrongiello, R. A., Fenwick, K. D., & Chance, G. (1990). Sound localization acuity in very young infants: An observer-based testing procedure. *Developmental Psychology, 26,* 75–84.

Mortimer, J. T. (1991). Employment. In R. M. Lerner, A. C. Petersen, & J. Brooks–Gunn (Eds.), *Encyclopedia of adolescence.* New York: Garland.

Mortimer, J. T., Finch, M. D., Ryu, S., Shanahan, M. J., & Call, K. T. (1993, March). *The effects of work intensity on adolescent mental health, achievement and behavioral adjustment: New evidence from a prospective study.* Paper presented at the meeting of the Society for Research in Child Development, New Orleans, LA.

Morton, J., & Johnson, M. H. (1991). CONSPEC and CONLERN: A two-process theory of infant face recognition. *Psychological Review, 98,* 164–181.

Moses, L. J., & Chandler, M. J. (1992). Traveler's guide to children's theories of mind. *Psychological Inquiry, 3,* 286–301.

Moses, L. J., & Flavell, J. H. (1990). Inferring false beliefs from actions and reactions. *Child Development, 61,* 929–945.

Moses, S. (1991, December). Special-ed assessment plans opposed. *APA Monitor,* pp. 36–37.

Muecke, L., Simons–Morton, B., Hyang, I. W., & Parcel, G. (1992). Is childhood obesity associated with high-fat foods and low physical activity? *Journal of School Health, 62,* 19–23.

Mueller, E., & Tingley, E. (1990). The Bear's Picnic: Children's representations of themselves and their families. In I. Bretherton & M. W. Watson (Eds.), *New directions for child development: No. 48. Children's perspectives on the family.* San Francisco: Jossey–Bass.

Mueller, K. E., & Powers, W. G. (1990). Parent–child sexual discussion: Perceived communicator style and subsequent behavior. *Adolescence, 25,* 469–482.

Muir, D. W., & Hains, S. M. J. (1993). Infant sensitivity to perturbations in adult facial, vocal, tactile, and contingent stimulation during face-to-face interactions. In de Boysson–Bardies, B., de Schonen, S., Jusczyk, P. W., MacNeilage, P. F., & Morton, J. (Eds.), *Changes in speech and face processing in infancy: A glimpse at developmental mechanisms of cognition.* Dordrecht, The Netherlands: Klumer Academic Publishers.

Mullis, A. K., Mullis, R. L., & Normandin, D. (1992). Cross-sectional and longitudinal comparisons of adolescent self-esteem. *Adolescence, 27,* 51–61.

Mullis, I. V. S., Dossey, J. A., Foertsch, M. A., Jones, L. R., & Gentile, C. A. (1991). *Trends in academic progress* (Report No. 21-T-01). Washington DC: National Center for Educational Statistics.

Munroe, R. H., Shimmin, H. S., & Munroe, R. L. (1984). Gender role understanding and sex role preference in four cultures. *Developmental Psychology, 20,* 673–682.

Murphy, L. B. (1983). Issues in the development of emotion in infancy. In R. Plutchik & H. Kellerman (Eds.), *Emotion: Theory, research, and experimentation.* New York: Academic Press.

Murphy, V., & Hicks–Stewart, K. (1991). Learning disabilities and attention deficit-hyperactivity disorder: An interactional perspective. *Journal of Learning Disabilities, 24,* 386–388.

Murray, A. D., Johnson, J., & Peters, J. (1990). Fine-tuning of utterance length to preverbal infants: Effects on later language development. *Journal of Child Language, 17,* 511–525.

Mussen, P. H., & Jones, M. C. (1957). Self-conceptions, motivations, and interpersonal attitudes of late- and early-maturing boys. *Child Development, 28,* 243–256.

Must, A., Jacques, P. F., Dallal, G. E., Bajema, C. J., & Dietz, W. (1992). Long-term morbidity and mortality of overweight adolescents. *New England Journal of Medicine, 327,* 1350–1354.

Mwamwenda, T. S. (1992). Cognitive development in African children. *Genetic, Social, and General Psychology Monographs, 118(1),* 7–72.

Myers, K., McCauley, E., Calderon, R., Mitchell, J., Burke, P., & Schloredt, K. (1991). Risks for suicidality in major depressive disorder. *Journal of the American Academy of Child and Adolescent Psychology, 30,* 86–94.

Nagel, K. L., & Jones, K. H. (1992). Sociological factors in the development of eating disorders. *Adolescence, 27,* 107–113.

National Association for the Education of Young Children. (1990, November). NAEYC position statement on school readiness. *Young Children, 46,* 21–23.

National Center for Children in Poverty. (1990). *Five million children: A statistical profile of our poorest young citizens.* New York: Author.

National Center for Education Statistics. (1992). *Dropout rates in the United States: 1991.* Washington, DC: U.S. Government Printing Office.

National Guidelines Task Force. (1991). *Guidelines for comprehensive sexuality education.* New York: Sex Information and Education Council of the U.S.

National Research Council. (1993). *Understanding and preventing violence.* Washington, DC: National Academy Press.

National Science Foundation. (1991). *Selected data on science and engineering doctorate awards: 1990.* Washington, DC: Author.

Natsopoulos, D., Kiosseoglou, G., & Xeromeritou, A. (1992). Handedness and spatial ability in children: Further support for Geschwind's hypothesis of "pathology of superiority" and for Annett's theory of intelligence. *Genetic, Social, and General Psychology Monographs, 118*(1) 103–126.

Navarro, M. (1993a, March 21). Unexpected lives: Children grow up with the AIDS virus. *New York Times,* p. 20.

Navarro, M. (1993b, May 10). Hemophiliacs demand answers as AIDS toll rises. *New York Times,* pp. A1, 12.

Needleman, H. L., & Jackson, R. J. (1992). Lead toxicity in the 21st century: Will we still be treating it? *Pediatrics, 89,* 678–680.

Nelson, C. A., & Ludemann, P. M. (1989). Past, current and future trends in infant face perception research. *Canadian Journal of Psychology, 43,* 183–198.

Nelson, J. R., Smith, D. J., & Dodd, J. (1990). The moral reasoning of juvenile delinquents: A meta-analysis. *Journal of Abnormal Child Psychology, 18,* 231–239.

Nelson, K. (1973). Structure and strategy in learning to talk. *Monographs for the Society for Research in Child Development, 38*(1-2, Serial No. 149).

Nelson, K. (1981). Individual differences in language development: Implications for development of language. *Developmental Psychology, 17,* 170–187.

Nelson, K. (1982). The syntagmatics and paradigmatics of conceptual development. In S. A. Kuczaj, II (Ed.), *Language development: Vol. 2. Language, thought, and culture.* Hillsdale, NJ: Erlbaum.

Nelson, K. (1989a). Remembering: A functional developmental perspective. In P. R. Solomon, G. R. Goetheys, C. M. Kelley, & B. R. Stephens (Eds.), *Memory: An interdisciplinary approach.* New York: Springer–Verlag.

Nelson, K. (1989b). Strategies for first language teaching. In M. L. Rice & R. L. Schiefelbusch (Eds.), *The teachability of language.* Baltimore: Brookes.

Nelson, K. (1990). Remembering, forgetting, and childhood amnesia. In R. Fivush & J. A. Hudson (Eds.), *Knowing and remembering in young children.* Cambridge: Cambridge University Press.

Nelson, K. (1993). Events, narratives, memory: What develops? In C. A. Nelson (Ed.), *Minnesota symposia on child psychology: Vol. 26. Memory and affect in development.* Hillsdale, NJ: Erlbaum.

Nelson, N., Enkin, M., Saigal, S., Bennett, K., Milner, R., & Sackett, D. (1980). A randomized clinical trial of the Leboyer approach to childbirth. *New England Journal of Medicine, 302,* 655–660.

Nelson, S. A. (1980). Factors influencing young children's use of motives and outcomes as moral criteria. *Child Development, 51,* 823–829.

Netriova, Y., Brezina, M., Hruskovic, I., & Kacenatova, M. (1990). Growth of children living in areas with a contaminated atmosphere. *Ceskoslovensta Pediatrie, 45,* 456–458.

Nevid, J. S., Rathus, S. A., & Greene, B. A. (1994). *Abnormal psychology in a changing world* (2nd ed.). Englewood Cliffs, NJ: Prentice Hall.

Neville, B., & Parke, R. D. (1991). Adolescent fathers. In R. M. Lerner, A. C. Petersen, & J. Brooks-Gunn (Eds.), *Encyclopedia of adolescence.* New York: Garland.

Newacheck, P. W., & Taylor, W. R. (1992). Childhood chronic illness: Prevalence, severity, and impact. *American Journal of Public Health, 82,* 364–371.

Newcomb, A. F., Bukowski, W. M., & Pattee, L. (1993). Children's peer relations: A meta-analytic review of popular, rejected, neglected controversial, and average sociometric status. *Psychological Bulletin, 113,* 99–128.

Newcomb, M., & Bentler, P. (1989). Substance use and abuse among children and teenagers. *American Psychologist, 44,* 242–248.

Newcomb, M. D., & Bentler, P. M. (1991a). Antecedents/predictors of cocaine use among adolescents and young adults. In R. M. Lerner, A. C. Petersen, & J. Brooks-Gunn (Eds.), *Encyclopedia of adolescence.* New York: Garland.

Newcomb, M. D., & Bentler, P. M. (1991b). Hallucinogens. In R. M. Lerner, A. C. Petersen, & J. Brooks-Gunn (Eds.), *Encyclopedia of adolescence.* New York: Garland.

Newcomb, M. D., & Bentler, P. M. (1992, August). *Substance abuse and gender: Accounting for the differences.* Paper presented at the meeting of the American Psychological Association, Washington, DC.

Newcombe, N., & Dubas, J. S. (1992). A longitudinal study of predictors of spatial ability in adolescent females. *Child Development, 63,* 37–46.

Newcombe, N., & Huttenlocher, J. (1992). Children's early ability to solve perspective-taking problems. *Developmental Psychology, 28,* 635–643.

Newport, E. L. (1992, June). *Critical periods and creolization: Effects of maturational state and input on the acquisition of language.* Paper presented at the meeting of American Psychological Society, San Diego, CA.

Niaz, M. (1991). Correlates of formal operational reasoning: A neo-Piagetian analysis. *Journal of Research in Science Teaching, 28,* 19–40.

Nicolopoulou, A. (1991). Play, cognitive development, and the social world. In B. Scales, M. Almy, A. Nicolopoulou, & S. Ervin-Tripp (Eds.), *Play and the social context of development in early care and education.* New York: Teachers College Press.

Niedbala, B., & Ekvall, S. W. (1993). Postnatal growth in infancy. In S. W. Ekvall (Ed.), *Pediatric nutrition in chronic diseases and developmental disorders: Prevention, assessment and treatment.* New York: Oxford.

Niedbala, B., & Tsang, R. (1993). The small for gestational age infant. In S. W. Ekvall (Ed.), *Pediatric nutrition in chronic diseases and developmental disorders: Prevention, assessment, and treatment.* New York: Oxford.

Ninio, A., & Rinotti, N. (1988). Fathers' involvement in the care of their infants and their attributions of cognitive competence in infants. *Child Development, 59,* 652–663.

Noble, B. P. (1993, April 18). Worthy childcare pay scales. *New York Times,* p. F25.

Noble, K. D., Robinson, N. M., & Gunderson, S. A. (1992). All rivers lead to the sea: A follow-up study of gifted young adults. *Roeper Review, 15,* 124–130.

Noller, P., & Callan, V. J. (1990). Adolescents' perceptions of the nature of their communication with parents. *Journal of Youth and Adolescence, 19,* 349–362.

Noppe, I. C., Noppe, L. D., & Hughes, F. P. (1991). Stress as a predictor of the quality of parent–infant interactions. *Journal of Genetic Psychology, 152,* 17–28.

Norbeck, J. S., & Tilden, V. P. (1983). Life stress, social support, and emotional disequilibrium in complications of pregnancy: A prospective multivariate study. *Journal of Health and Social Behavior, 24,* 30–46.

Nottelmann, E. D., Inoff-Germain, G., Susman, E. J., & Chrousos, G. P. (1990). Hormones and behavior at puberty. In J. Bancroft & J. M. Reinisch (Eds.), *Adolescence and puberty.* New York: Oxford.

Nottelmann, E. D., & Welsh, C. J. (1986). The long and the short of physical stature in early adolescence. *Journal of Early Adolescence, 6,* 15–27.

Notzon, F. C. (1990). International differences in the use of obstetric interventions. *Journal of the American Medical Association, 263,* 3286–3291.

Novacek, J., Raskin, R., & Hogan, R. (1991). Why do adolescents use drugs? Age, sex, and user differences. *Journal of Youth and Adolescence, 20,* 475–492.

Nsamenang, A. B. (1992). *Human development in cultural context.* Newbury Park, CA: Sage.

Nugent, J. K., Lester, B. M., & Brazelton, T. B. (Eds.). (1991). *The cultural context of infancy* (Vol. 2). Norwood, NJ: Ablex.

Oakley, D., Sereika, S., & Bogue, E. (1991). Oral contraceptive pill use after an initial visit to a family planning clinic. *Family Planning Perspectives, 23,* 150–154.

Oberfield, R., & Gabriel, H. P. (1991). Prematurity, birth defects, and early death: Impact on the family. In M. Lewis (Ed.), *Child and adolescent psychiatry: A comprehensive textbook.* Baltimore: Williams & Wilkins.

O'Boyle, M. W., & Benbow, C. P. (1990). Handedness and its relationship to ability and talent. In S. Coren (Ed.), *Left-handedness: Behavior implications and anomalies.* Amsterdam: North–Holland.

O'Connell, L., Betz, M., & Kurth, S. (1989). Plans for balancing work and family life: Do women pursuing nontraditional and traditional occupations differ? *Sex Roles, 20,* 35–45.

O'Connor, P. D., Sufo, F., Kendall, L., & Olsen, G. (1990). Reading disabilities and the effects of colored filters. *Journal of Learning disabilities, 23,* 597–603.

O'Connor, T. (1989). Cultural voices and strategies for multicultural education. *Journal of Education, 171,* 57–74.

Oden, M. H. (1968). The fulfillment of promise: 40-year follow-up of the Terman gifted group. *Genetic Psychology Monographs, 77,* 3–93.

Offer, D., & Church, R. B. (1991a). Adolescent turmoil. In R. M. Lerner, A. C. Petersen, & J. Brooks-Gunn (Eds.), *Encyclopedia of adolescence.* New York: Garland.

Offer, D., & Church, R. B. (1991b). Generation gap. In R. M. Lerner, A. C. Petersen, & J. Brooks-Gunn (Eds.), *Encyclopedia of adolescence.* New York: Garland.

Ogura, T. (1991). A longitudinal study of the relationship between early language development and play development. *Journal of Child Language, 18,* 273–294.

Ohannessian, C. M., Lerner, R. M., Lerner, J. V., & von Eye, A. (1993, March). *A longitudinal study of family satisfaction and psychosocial adjustment in early adolescence.* Paper presented at the meeting of the Society for Research in Child Development, New Orleans, LA.

O'Hara, M. W., Schlecte, J. A., Lewis, D. A., & Varner, M. W. (1991). Controlled prospective study of postpartum mood disorders: Psychological, environmental and hormonal variables. *Journal of Abnormal Psychology, 99,* 3–15.

Ohlendorf-Moffat, P. (1991, February). Surgery before birth. *Discover,* pp. 59–65.

Ojemann, G. A. (1991). Cortical organization of language. *Journal of Neuroscience, 11,* 2281–2287.

Okagaki, L., & Sternberg, R. J. (1993). Parental beliefs and children's school performance. *Child Development, 64,* 36–56.

Olds, D. L., & Henderson, C. R. (1989). The prevention of maltreatment. In D. Cicchetti & V. Carlson (Eds.), *Child maltreatment: Theory and research on the causes and consequences of child abuse and neglect.* Cambridge: Cambridge University Press.

O'Leary, D. S. (1990). Neuropsychological development in the child and adolescent: Functional maturation of the central nervous system. In C. A. Hauert (Ed.), *Developmental psychology: Cognitive, perceptuomotor and neuropsychological perspectives.* Amsterdam: North–Holland.

Ollendick, T. H., Hagopian, L. P., & Huntzinger, R. M. (1991a). Cognitive-behavior therapy with nighttime fearful children. *Journal of Behavioral Therapy and Experimental Psychiatry, 22,* 113–121.

Ollendick, T. H., & King, N. J. (1991). Origins of childhood fears: An evaluation of Rachman's theory of teen-acquisition. *Behavior Research and Therapy, 29,* 117–123.

Ollendick, T. H., King, N. J., & Frary, R. B. (1989). Fears in children and adolescents: Reliability and generalizability across gender, age, and nationality. *Behavior Research and Therapy, 27,* 19–26.

Ollendick, T. H., Yule, W., & Ollier, K. (1991b). Fears in British children and their relationship to manifest anxiety and depression. *Journal of Child Psychology and Psychiatry, 32,* 321–331.

Oller, D. K. (1981). Infant vocalizations: Exploration and reflectivity. In R. E. Stark (Ed.), *Language behavior in infancy and early childhood.* New York: Elsevier.

Oller, D. K., & Eilers, R. E. (1988). The role of audition in infant babbling. *Child Development, 59,* 441–449.

Olley, J. G. (1992). Autism: Historical overview, definition, and characteristics. In D. E. Berkell (Ed.), *Autism.* Hillsdale, NJ: Erlbaum.

Olson, H. C., Sampson, P. D., Barr, H., Streissguth, A. P., & Bookstein, F. L. (1992). Prenatal exposure to alcohol and school problems in late childhood: A longitudinal prospective study. *Development and Psychopathology, 4,* 341–359.

Olson, S. L. (1992). Development of conduct problems and peer rejection in preschool children: A social systems analysis. *Journal of Abnormal Child Psychology, 20,* 327–350.

Olson, S. L., Bates, J. E., & Bayles, K. (1990). Early antecedents of childhood impulsivity: The role of parent–child interaction, cognitive competence, and temperament. *Journal of Abnormal Child Psychology, 18,* 317–334.

Olweus, D. (1991). Bully/victim problems among school children: Basic facts and effects of a school-based intervention program. In D. J. Pepler & K. H. Rubin (Eds.), *The development and treatment of childhood aggression.* Hillsdale, NJ: Erlbaum.

Omer, H., & Everly, G. S. (1988). Psychological factors in preterm labor: Critical review and theoretical synthesis. *American Journal of Psychiatry, 145,* 1507–1513.

O'Neill, D. K., Astington, J. W., & Flavell, J. H. (1992). Young children's understanding of the role that sensory experiences play in knowledge acquisition. *Child Development, 63,* 474–490.

O'Neill, D. K., & Gopnik, A. (1991). Young children's ability to identify the sources of their beliefs. *Developmental Psychology, 27,* 390–397.

Opwis, K., Gold, A., Gruber, H., & Schneider, W. (1990). The influence of expert knowledge on memory performance and self-assessment in children and adults. *Zeitschrift-für-Entwick lungspsychologie-und-Pädagogische Psychologie, 22,* 207–224.

Oram, J., & Oshima–Takane, Y. (1993, March). *Parental language functions and attentional types: Relationship to child language.* Paper presented at the meeting of the Society for Research in Child Development, New Orleans, LA.

Orr, D. P., & Pless, I. B. (1991). Chronic illness. In R. M. Lerner, A. C. Petersen, & J. Brooks–Gunn (Eds.), *Encyclopedia of adolescence.* New York: Garland.

Osberg, J. S., & DiScala, C. (1992, March). Morbidity among pediatric motor vehicle crash victims: The effectiveness of seat belts. *American Journal of Public Health, 82,* 422–425.

Osipow, S. (1990). Convergence in theories of career choice and development: Review and prospect. *Journal of Vocational Behavior, 39,* 122–131.

Osofsky, J. D., Eberhart–Wright, A., Ware, L. M., & Hann, D. M. (1992). Children of adolescent mothers: A group at risk for psychopathology. *Infant Mental Health Journal, 13,* 119–131.

Oster, H., Hegley, D., & Nagel, L. (1992). Adult judgments and fine-grained analysis of infant facial expressions: Testing the validity of a priori coding formulas. *Developmental Psychology, 28,* 1115–1131.

Ostertag, P. A., & McNamara, J. R. (1991). "Feminization" of psychology. *Psychology of Women Quarterly, 15,* 349–369.

Ottinger, C., & Sikula, R. (1993). *Women in higher education: Where do we stand?* Washington, DC: American Council on Education.

Overpeck, M. D., Hoffman, H. J., & Prager, K. (1992). The lowest-birth-weight infants and the U.S. infant mortality rate: NCHS 1983 linked birth/infant death data. *American Journal of Public Health, 82,* 441–444.

Overton, W. F. (1991). Reasoning in the adolescent. In R. M. Lerner, A. C. Petersen, & J. Brooks–Gunn (Eds.), *Encyclopedia of adolescence.* New York: Garland.

Overton, W. F., & Byrnes, J. B. (1991). Cognitive development. In R. M. Lerner, A. C. Petersen, & J. Brooks–Gunn (Eds.), *Encyclopedia of adolescence.* New York: Garland.

Owens, R. E. (1990). Development of communication, language, and speech. In G. Shames & E. Wiig (Eds.), *Human communication disorders* (3rd ed.). Columbus, OH: Merrill.

Oyserman, D., Radin, N., & Benn, R. (1993). Dynamics in a three-generational family: Teens, grandparents, and babies. *Developmental Psychology, 29,* 564–572.

Padgham, J. J., & Blyth, D. A. (1991). Dating during adolescence. In R. M. Lerner, A. C. Petersen, & J. Brooks–Gunn (Eds.), *Encyclopedia of adolescence.* New York: Garland.

Padilla, A. M., & Lindholm, K. J. (1992, August). *What do we know about culturally diverse children?* Paper presented at the meeting of the American Psychological Association, Washington, DC.

Padilla, A. M., Lindholm, K. J., Chen, A., Duran, R., Hakuta, K., Lambert, W., & Tucker, G. R. (1991). The English-only movement: Myths, reality and implications for psychology. *American Psychologist, 46,* 120–130.

Paikoff, R. L., & Brooks–Gunn, J. (1991a). Do parent–child relationships change during puberty? *Psychological Bulletin, 110,* 47–66.

Paikoff, R. L., & Brooks–Gunn, J. (1991b). Interventions to prevent pregnancy. In R. M. Lerner, A. C. Petersen, & J. Brooks–Gunn (Eds.), *Encyclopedia of adolescence.* New York: Garland.

Paikoff, R. L., Buchanan, C. M., & Brooks–Gunn, J. (1991). Methodological issues in the study of hormone-behavior links at puberty. In R. M. Lerner, A. C. Petersen, & J. Brooks–Gunn (Eds.), *Encyclopedia of adolescence.* New York: Garland.

Paikoff, R. L., & Collins, A. C. (1991). Editors' notes: Shared views in the family during adolescence. In R. L. Paikoff (Ed.), *New directions for child development: No. 51. Shared views in the family during adolescence.* San Francisco: Jossey–Bass.

Palkovitz, R. (1984). Parental attitudes and fathers' interactions with their 5-month-old infants. *Developmental Psychology, 20,* 1054–1060.

Paludi, M. A. (1992). *The psychology of women.* Dubuque, IA: Brown & Benchmark.

Panak, W. F., & Garber, J. (1992). Role of aggression, rejection, and attributions in the prediction of depression in children. *Development and Psychopathology, 4,* 145–165.

Papini, D. R., Farmer, F. F., Clark, S. M., Micka, J. C., & Barnett, J. K. (1990). Early adolescent age and gender differences in patterns of emotional self-disclosure to parents and friends. *Adolescence, 25,* 959–976.

Papini, D. R., & Roggman, L. A. (1992). Adolescent perceived attachment to parents in relation to competence, depression, and anxiety: A longitudinal study. *Journal of Early Adolescence, 12,* 420–440.

Papousek, M., Papousek, H., & Symmes, D. (1991). The meanings of melodies in motherese in tone and stress languages. *Infant Behavior and Development, 14,* 415–440.

Parcel, G. S., Simons–Morton, B. G., O'Hara, N. M., Baranowski, T., Kolbe, L. T., & Bee, D. E. (1987). School promotion of healthful diet and exercise behavior: An integration of organizational change and social learning theory interventions. *Journal of School Health, 57,* 150–156.

Paris, S. G., & Winograd, P. (1990). How metacognition can promote academic learning and instruction. In B. F. Jones & L. Idol (Eds.), *Dimensions of thinking and cognitive instruction.* Hillsdale, NJ: Erlbaum.

Park, K. A., Lay, K., & Ramsay, L. (1993). Individual differences and developmental changes in preschoolers' friendships. *Developmental Psychology, 29,* 264–270.

Parke, R. D. (1977). Punishment in children: Effects, side effects, and alternate strategies. In H. L. Hom & P. A. Robinson (Eds.), *Psychological processes in early education.* New York: Academic Press.

Parke, R. D., & Slaby, R. G. (1983). The development of aggression. In P. H. Mussen (Ed.), *Handbook of child psychology: Vol. 4. Socialization, personality and social development.* New York: Wiley.

Parke, R. D., & Tinsley, B. J. (1987). Family interaction in infancy. In J. D. Osofsky

(Ed.), *Handbook of infant development.* New York: Wiley.

Parker, J. G., & Asher, S. R. (1993). Friendship and friendship quality in middle childhood: Links with peer group acceptance and feelings of loneliness and social dissatisfaction. *Developmental Psychology, 29,* 611–621.

Parker, J. G., & Gottman, J. M. (1989). Social and emotional development in a relational context. In T. J. Berndt & G. W. Ladd (Eds.), *Peer relationships in child development.* New York: Wiley.

Parker, S. J., Zahr, L. K., Cole, J. G., & Brecht, M. (1992). Outcome after developmental intervention in the neonatal intensive care unit for mothers of preterm infants with low socioeconomic status. *Journal of Pediatrics, 120,* 780–785.

Parks, P., & Bradley, R. (1991). The interaction of home environment features and their relation to infant competence. *Infant Mental Health Journal, 12,* 3–16.

Parmelee, A. H., Jr. (1986). Children's illnesses: Their beneficial effects on behavioral development. *Child Development, 57,* 1–10.

Parten, M. B. (1932). Social participation among preschool children. *Journal of Abnormal and Social Psychology, 27,* 243–269.

Pascual–Leone, J. (1970). Mathematical model for the transition rule in Piaget's developmental stages. *Acta Psychologica, 63,* 301–345.

Passell, P. (1992, August 9). Twins study shows school is a sound investment. *New York Times,* p. A14.

Patterson, C. J., Kupersmidt, J. B., & Vader, N. A. (1990). Income level, gender, ethnicity, and household composition as predictors of children's school-based competence. *Child Development, 61,* 485–494.

Patterson, G. R., Capaldi, D., & Bank, L. (1991). An early starter model for predicting delinquency. In D. J. Pepler & K. H. Rubin (Eds.), *The development and treatment of childhood aggression.* Hillsdale, NJ: Erlbaum.

Patterson, G. R., & Yoerger, K. (1993, March). *Adolescent first arrest: One model or two?* Paper presented at the meeting of the Society for Research in Child Development, New Orleans, LA.

Patterson, S. J., Sochting, I., & Marcia, J. E. (1992). The inner space and beyond: Women and identity. In G. R. Adams, T. P. Gullotta, & R. Montemayor (Eds.), *Adolescent identity formation.* Newbury Park, CA: Sage.

Patton, W. (1991). Relationship between self-image and depression in adolescents. *Psychological Reports, 68,* 867–870.

Pauls, D. L. (1991). Genetic influences on child psychiatric conditions. In M. Lewis, (Ed.), *Child and adolescent psychiatry: A comprehensive textbook.* Baltimore: Williams & Wilkins.

Paulston, C. (Ed.). (1988). *International handbook of bilingualism and bilingual education.* New York: Greenwood.

Paxton, S. J., Wertheim, E. H., Gibbons, K., Szumkler, G. I., Hillier, L., & Petrovich, J. L. (1991). Body image satisfaction, dieting beliefs, and weight loss behaviors in adolescent girls and boys. *Journal of Youth and Adolescence, 20,* 361–379.

Pear, R. (1992, September 13). U.S. orders testing of poor children for lead poisoning. *New York Times,* pp. 1, 18.

Pear, R. (1993, August 16). U.S. to guarantee free immunization for poor children. *New York Times,* p. A1, 9.

Pederson, D. R., & Moran, G. (1993, March). *A categorial description of infant–mother relationships in the home and its relation to Q-sort measures of infant attachment security and maternal sensitivity.* Paper presented at the meeting of the Society for Research in Child Development, New Orleans, LA.

Pellegrini, A. D. (1990). Elementary school children's playground behavior: Implications for childrens social-cognitive development. *Children's Environments Quarterly, 7,* 8–16.

Pellegrini, A. D., & Prelmutter, J. C. (1988, January). Rough-and-tumble play on the elementary school playground. *Young Children,* pp. 14–17.

Pemberton, E. F. (1990). Systematic errors in children's drawings. *Cognitive Development, 5,* 395–404.

Penner, L. A., Thompson, J. K., & Coovert, D. L. (1991). Size overestimation among anorexics: Much ado about very little? *Journal of Abnormal Psychology, 100,* 90–93.

Penner, S. G. (1987). Parental responses to grammatical and ungrammatical child utterances. *Child Development, 58,* 376–384.

Penrod, S (1993). The child witness, the courts, and psychological research. In C. A. Nelson (Ed.), *Minnesota symposia on child psychology: Vol. 26. Memory and affect in development.* Hillsdale, NJ: Erlbaum.

Pepler, D. J., & Rubin, K. H. (Eds.). (1991). *The development and treatment of childhood aggression.* Hillsdale, NJ: Erlbaum.

Perkin, J. E. (1993, Summer). Facing the health-policy challenge of HIV infection. *National Forum, 72*(3), 45–47.

Perkins, D. N. (1990). The nature and nurture of creativity. In B. F. Jones & L. Idol (Eds.), *Dimensions of thinking and cognitive instruction.* Hillsdale, NJ: Erlbaum.

Perner, J. (1991). *Understanding the representational mind.* Cambridge, MA: MIT Press.

Perry, C. L. (1991). Programs for smoking prevention with early adolescents. In R. M. Lerner, A. C. Petersen, & J. Brooks–Gunn (Eds.), *Encyclopedia of adolescence.* New York: Garland.

Perry, D. G., Perry, L. C., & Boldizar, J. P. (1990). Learning of aggression. In M. Lewis & S. M. Miller (Eds.), *Handbook of developmental psychopathology.* New York: Plenum.

Perry, D. G., White, A. S., & Perry, L. C. (1984). Does early sex typing result from children's attempts to match their behavior to sex role stereotypes? *Child Development, 55,* 2114–2121.

Perry–Jenkins, M., Seery, B., & Crouter, A. C. (1992). Linkages between women's provider-role attitudes, psychological well-being, and family relationships. *Psychology of Women Quarterly, 16,* 311–329.

Peskin, J. (1992, January). Ruse and representations: On children's ability to conceal information. *Developmental Psychology, 28,* 84–89.

Peters, D. P. (1991). The influence of stress and arousal on the child witness. In J. Doris (Ed.), *The suggestibility of children's recollections.* Washington, DC: American Psychological Association.

Peters, M. (1990). Phenotype in normal left-handers: An understanding of phenotype is the basis for understanding mechanism and inheritance of handedness. In S. Coren (Ed.), *Left-handedness: Behavior implications and anomalies.* Amsterdam: North–Holland.

Petersen, A. C. (1983). Menarche: Meaning of measures and measuring meaning. In S. Golub (Ed.), *Menarche.* Lexington, MA: Lexington Books.

Petersen, A. C., Compas, B. E., Brooks–Gunn, J., Stemmler, M., Ey, S., & Grant, K. E. (1993). Depression in adolescence. *American Psychologist, 48,* 155–168.

Peterson, C. C., Peterson, J. L., & Seeto, D. (1983). Developmental changes in ideas about lying. *Child Development, 54,* 1529–1535.

Peterson, L., & Roberts, M. C. (1992). Complacency, misdirection, and effective prevention of children's injuries. *American Psychologist, 47,* 1040–1044.

Petittio, L. A., & Marentette, P. F. (1991). Babbling in the manual mode: Evidence for the ontogeny of language. *Science, 251,* 1493–1496.

Pfeffer, C. R. (1991). Attempted suicide in children and adolescents: Causes and management. In M. Lewis (Ed.), *Child and adolescent psychiatry: A comprehensive textbook.* Baltimore: Williams & Wilkins.

Pfeiffer, S. I., & Aylward, G. P. (1990). Outcome for preschoolers of very low birthweight: Sociocultural and environmental influences. *Perceptual and Motor Skills, 70,* 1367–1378.

Phelps, L., & Bajorek, E. (1991). Eating disorders of the adolescent: Current issues in etiology, assessment, and treatment. *School Psychology Review, 20,* 9–22.

Phinney, J. (1989). Stages of ethnic identity in minority group adolescents. *Journal of Early Adolescence, 9,* 34–49.

Phinney, J. (1990). Ethnic identity in adolescents and adults: Review of research. *Psychological Bulletin, 108,* 499–514.

Phinney, J. (1992). The multigroup ethnic identity measure: A new scale for use with adolescents and young adults with diverse groups. *Journal of Adolescent Research, 12,* 156–176.

Phinney, J., & Alipuria, L. (1990). Ethnic identity in older adolescents from four ethnic groups. *Journal of Adolescence, 13,* 171–183.

Phinney, J., & Chavira, P. (1992). Ethnic identity and self-esteem: An exploratory longitudinal study. *Journal of Adolescence, 15,* 1–11.

Phinney, J., DuPont, S., Espinosa, C., Onwughalu, M., Revill, J., & Sanders, K. (1992, March). *Group identity among minority adolescents: Ethnic, American, or bicultural?* Paper presented at the meeting of the Society for Research on Adolescence, Washington, DC.

Phinney, J., & Nakayama, S. (1991, April). *Parental influence on ethnic identity formation in minority adolescents.* Paper presented at the meeting of the Society for Research in Child Development, Seattle.

Phinney, J., & Rosenthal, D. A. (1992). Ethnic identity in adolescence: Process, context, and outcome. In G. R. Adams, T. P. Gullotta, & R. Montemayor (Eds.), *Adolescent identity formation.* Newbury Park, CA: Sage.

Phinney, J., & Tarver, S. (1988). Ethnic identity search and commitment in black and white eight graders. *Journal of Early Adolescence, 8,* 265–277.

Piaget, J. (1932). *The moral judgment of the child.* London: Kegan Paul.

Piaget, J. (1962). *Play, dreams and imitation in childhood.* New York: Norton. (Original work published 1946).

Piaget, J. (1963). *The origins of intelligence in children.* New York: Norton. (Original work published 1936).

Piaget, J. (1967). In D. Elkind (Ed.), *Six psychological studies.* New York: Random House. (Original work published 1964).

Piaget, J. (1972). Intellectual evolution from adolescence to adulthood. *Human Development, 15,* 1–12.

Piaget, J. (1976). *The grasp of consciousness: Action and concept in the young child.* Cambridge, MA: Harvard University Press.

Piaget, J., & Inhelder, B. (1969). *Psychology of the child.* New York: Basic Books.

Pianta, R. C., & Steinberg, M. (1992). Teacher–child relationships and the process of adjusting to school. In R. C. Pianta (Ed.), *New directions for child development: No. 57. Beyond the parent: The role of other adults in children's lives.* San Francisco: Jossey–Bass.

Pick, A. D. (1991). Perception. In R. M. Thomas (Ed.), *The encyclopedia of human development and education: Theory, research, and studies.* Oxford: Pergamon.

Pihl, R. O., & Peterson, J. B. (1991). Attention-deficit hyperactivity disorder, childhood conduct disorder, and alcoholism. *Alcohol Health and Research World, 15,* 25–31.

Pike, K. M., & Rodin, J. (1991). Mothers, daughters, and disordered eating. *Journal of Abnormal Psychology, 100,* 198–204.

Pilkington, C. L., & Piersel, W. C. (1991). School phobia: A critical analysis of the separation anxiety theory and an alternative conceptualization. *Psychology in the Schools, 28,* 290–303.

Platt, O. S., Thorington, B. D., Brambilla, D. J., Milner, P. F., Rosse, W. F., Vichinsky, E., & Kinney, T. R. (1991). Pain in sickle cell disease. *New England Journal of Medicine, 325,* 11–16.

Platzman, K. A., Stoy, M. R., Brown, R. T., Coles, C. D., Smith, I. E., & Falek, A. (1992). Review of observational methods in attention deficit hyperactivity disorder (ADHD): Implications for diagnosis. *School Psychology Quarterly, 7,* 155–177.

Plomin, R., & McClearn, G. E. (1993). *Nature, nurture, and psychology.* Washington, DC: American Psychological Association.

Poest, C. A., Williams, J. R., Witt, D., & Atwood, M. E. (1989). Physical activity patterns of preschool children. *Early Childhood Research Quarterly, 4,* 367–376.

Poets, C. F., & Southall, D. P. (1993). Prone sleeping position and sudden infant death. *New England Journal of Medicine, 329,* 425–426.

Polan, H. J., Kaplan, M. D., Kessler, D. B., Shindledecker, R., Newmark, M., Stern, D. N., & Ward, M. J. (1991). Psychopathology in mothers of children with failure to thrive. *Infant Mental Health Journal, 12,* 55–64.

Pollitt, E., Gorman, K. S., Engle, P., Martorell, R., & Rivera, J. (1993). Early supplementary feeding and cognition: Effect over two decades. *Monographs of the Society for Research in Child Development, 58,* (7, Serial No. 235).

Pombeni, M. L., Kirchler, E., & Palmonari, A. (1990). Identification with peers as a strategy to muddle through the troubles of the adolescent years. *Journal of Adolescence, 13,* 351–369.

Pomerantz, E. M., Frey, K., Greulich, F., & Ruble, D. N. (1993, March). *Explaining the decrease in perceived competence: Grade and gender differences in perceptions of ability as stable.* Paper presented at the meeting of the Society for Research in Child Development. New Orleans, LA.

Pomerleau, A., Bolduc, D., Malcuit, G., & Cossette, L. (1990). Pink or blue: Environmental gender stereotypes in the first two years of life. *Sex Roles, 22,* 359–367.

Ponsonby, A., Dwyer, T., Gibbons, L. E., Cochrane, J. A., & Wang, Y. (1993). Factors potentiating the risk of sudden infant death syndrome associated with the prone position. *New England Journal of Medicine, 329,* 377–382.

Pooler, W. S. (1991). Sex of child preferences among college students. *Sex Roles, 25,* 569–576.

Porac, C., & Buller, T. (1990). Overt attempts to change hand preference: A study of group and individual characteristics. *Canadian Journal of Psychology, 44,* 512–521.

Porter, B. (1993, April 11). I met my daughter at the Wuhan Foundling Hospital. *New York Times Magazine,* pp. 24, 26, 31, 44, 46.

Porter, F. L., Porges, S. W., & Marshall, R. E. (1988). Newborn pain cries and vagal tone: Parallel changes in response to circumcision. *Child Development, 59,* 495–505.

Porter, R. H., Makin, J. W., Davis, L. B., & Christensen, K. M. (1992). Breast-fed infants respond to olfactory cues from their own mother and unfamiliar lactating females. *Infant Behavior and Development, 15,* 85–93.

Portes, P. R., Howell, S. C., Brown, J. H., Eichenberger, S., & Mass, C. A. (1992). Family functions and children's postdivorce adjustment. *American Journal of Orthopsychiatry, 62,* 613–617.

Powell, G. F., & Bettes, B. A. (1992). Infantile depression, nonorganic failure to thrive, and DSM-III-R: A different perspective. *Child Psychiatry and Human Development, 22,* 185–198.

Power, T. G. (1985). Mother- and father-infant play: A developmental analysis. *Child Development, 56,* 1514–1524.

Power, T. G., Gershenhorn, S., & Stafford, D. (1990). Maternal perceptions of infant difficulties: The influence of maternal attitudes and attributions. *Infant Behavior and Development, 13,* 421–437.

Power, T. G., Kobayashi–Winata, H., & Kelley, M. L. (1992). Childrearing patterns in Japan and the United States: A cluster analytic study. *International Journal of Behavioral Development, 15,* 185–205.

Power, T. G., & Parke, R. D. (1982). Play as a context for early learning: Lab and home analysis. In L. M. Laosa & I. E. Sigel (Eds.), *The family as a learning environment.* New York: Plenum.

Powers, M. D. (1992). Early intervention for children with autism. In D. E. Berkell (Ed.), *Autism.* Hillsdale, NJ: Erlbaum.

Powledge, T. M. (1981). Unnatural selection. In H. B. Holmes, B. B. Hoskins, & M. Gross (Eds.), *The custom-made child? Women-centered perspectives.* Clifton, NJ: Humana Press.

Pratt, C., & Bryant, P. (1990). Young children understand that looking leads to knowing (so long as they are looking into a single barrel). *Child Development, 61,* 973–982.

Presley, C. A., & Meilman, P. W. (1992). *Alcohol and drugs on American college campuses.* Carbondale: Southern Illinois University.

Press, Aric (1992, August 10). Old too soon, wise too late? *Newsweek,* pp. 22–25.

Preventive health care for young children: Findings from a 10-country study and directions for United States policy. (1992). *Pediatrics, 89,* 983–998.

Price, D. W. W., & Goodman, G. S. (1990). Visiting the wizard: Children's memory for a recurring event. *Child Development, 61,* 664–680.

Price, R. H. (1992). Psychosocial impact of job loss on individuals and families. *Current Directions in Psychological Science, 1,* 9–11.

Price–Williams, D. R., Gordon, W., & Ramirez, M. (1969). Skill and conservation. *Developmental Psychology, 1,* 769.

Provence, S., & Lipton, R. C. (1962). *Infants in institutions.* New York: International Universities Press.

Pumariega, A. J., Swanson, J. W., Holzer, C. E., Linskey, A. O., & Quintero–Salinas, R. (1992). Cultural context and substance abuse in Hispanic adolescents. *Journal of Child and Family Studies, 1,* 75–92.

Purvis, A. (1990, November 26). The sins of the fathers. *Time,* pp. 90, 92.

Putallaz, M., & Dunn, S. E. (1990). The importance of peer relations. In M. Lewis & S. M. Miller (Eds.), *Handbook of developmental psychopathology.* New York: Plenum.

Putallaz, M., & Heflin, A. H. (1990). Parent–child interaction. In S. R. Asher & J. D. Coie (Eds.), *Peer rejection in childhood.* Cambridge: Cambridge University Press.

Quiggle, N. L., Garber, J., Panak, W. F., & Dodge, K. A. (1992). Social information processing in aggressive and depressed children. *Child Development, 63,* 1305–1320.

Rack, J. P., Hulme, C., & Snowling, M. J. (1993). Learning to read: A theoretical synthesis. In H. W. Reese (Ed.), *Advances in child development and behavior* (Vol. 24). San Diego, CA: Academic Press.

Rack, J. P., Snowling, M. J., & Olson, R. K. (1992). The nonword reading deficit in developmental dyslexia: A review. *Reading Research Quarterly, 27,* 29–53.

Radke–Yarrow, M., Nottelmann, E., Martinez, P., Fox, M. B., & Belmont, B. (1992). Young children of affectively ill parents: A longitudinal study of psychosocial development. *American Academy of Child and Adolescent Psychiatry, 31,* 68–77.

Rakic, P. (1991). Plasticity of cortical development. In S. E. Brauth, W. S. Hall, & R. J. Dooling (Eds.), *Plasticity of development.* Cambridge, MA: MIT Press.

Ramey, C. T., Bryant, D. M., Wasik, B. H., Sparling, J. J., Fendt, K. H., & LaVange, L. M. (1992). Infant health and development program for low birth weight, premature infants: Program elements, family participation, and child intelligence. *Pediatrics, 89,* 454–465.

Rathus, S. A. (1988). *Understanding child development.* New York: Holt, Rinehart and Winston.

Rathus, S. A. (1993). *Psychology* (5th ed.). Fort Worth: Harcourt Brace Jovanovich.

Rathus, S. A., & Boughn, S. (1993). *AIDS: What every student needs to know.* Fort Worth: Harcourt Brace Jovanovich.

Rathus, S. A., & Nevid, J. S. (1991). *Abnormal psychology.* Englewood Cliffs, NJ: Prentice Hall.

Rathus, S. A., Nevid, J. S., & Fichner–Rathus, L. (1993). *Human sexuality.* Fort Worth: Harcourt Brace Jovanovich.

Ratner, H. H., Smith, B. S., & Padgett, R. J. (1990). Children's organization of events and event memories. In R. Fivush & J. A. Hudson (Eds.), *Knowing and remembering in young children.* Cambridge: Cambridge University Press.

Rauch, J. M., & Huba, G. J. (1991). Adolescent drug use. In R. M. Lerner, A. C. Petersen, & J. Brooks–Gunn (Eds.), *Encyclopedia of adolescence.* New York: Garland.

Raudenbusch, S. W. (1984). Magnitude of teacher expectancy effects on pupil IQ as a function of credibility of expectancy induction: A synthesis from 18 experiments. *Journal of Experimental Psychology, 76,* 85–97.

Rauh, V. A., Achenbach, T. M., Nurcombe, B., Howell, C. T., & Teti, D. M. (1988). Minimizing adverse effect of low birthweight: Four-year results of an early intervention program. *Child Development, 59,* 544–553.

Rauste–von Wright, M. (1989). Body image satisfaction in adolescent girls and boys: A longitudinal study. *Journal of Youth and Adolescence, 18,* 71–83.

Ravenscroft, K. (1991). Family therapy. In M. Lewis (Ed.), *Child and adolescent psychiatry: A comprehensive textbook.* Baltimore: Williams & Wilkins.

Raymond, C. L., & Benbow, C. P. (1986). Gender differences in mathematics: A function of parental support and student sex typing? *Developmental Psychology, 22,* 808–819.

Rayner, K. (1993). Reading symposium: An introduction. *Psychological Science, 4,* 280–282.

Rebok, G. W. (1987). *Life-span cognitive development.* New York: Holt, Rinehart and Winston.

Reese, E., & Fivush, R. (1993). Parental styles of talking about the past. *Developmental Psychology, 29,* 596–606.

Reese, F. L., & Roosa, M. W. (1991). Early adolescents' self-reports of major life stressors and mental health risk status. *Journal of Early Adolescence, 11,* 363–378.

Rehm, L. P., & Carter, A. S. (1990). Cognitive components of depression. In M. Lewis & S. M. Miller (Eds.), *Handbook of developmental psychopathology.* New York: Plenum.

Reid, M., Ramey, S. L., & Burchinal, M. (1990). Dialogues with children about their families. In I. Bretherton & M. Watson (Eds.), *New directions for child development: No. 48. Children's perspectives on their families.* San Francisco: Jossey–Bass.

Reinisch, J. M. (1981). Prenatal exposure to synthetic progestins increases potential for aggression in humans. *Science, 21,* 1171–1173.

Reisman, J. E. (1987). Touch, motion, and proprioception. In P. Salapatek & L. Cohen (Eds.), *Handbook of infant perception: Vol. 1. From sensation to perception.* Orlando, FL: Academic Press.

Reissland, N. (1988). Neonatal imitation in the first hour of life: Observations in rural Nepal. *Developmental Psychology, 24,* 464–469.

Remafedi, G. (1991). Adolescent homosexuality. In R. M. Lerner, A. C. Petersen, & J. Brooks–Gunn (Eds.), *Encyclopedia of adolescence.* New York: Garland.

Renninger, K. A. (1990). Children's play interests, representation, and activity, In R. Fivush & J. A. Hudson (Eds.), *Knowing and remembering in young children.* Cambridge: Cambridge University Press.

Rescorla, L. (1991a). Early academics: Introduction to the debate. In L. Rescorla, M. C. Hyson, & K. Hirsh–Pasek (Eds.), *New directions in child development: No. 53. Academic instruction in early childhood: Challenge or pressure?* San Francisco: Jossey–Bass.

Rescorla, L. (1991b). Parent and teacher attitudes about early academics. In L. Rescorla, M. C. Hyson, & K. Hirsh–Pasek (Eds.), *New directions in child development: No. 53. Academic instruction in early childhood: Challenge or pressure?* San Francisco: Jossey–Bass.

Rest, J. R. (1983). Morality. In P. H. Mussen (Ed.), *Handbook of child psychology: Vol. 3. Cognitive development.* New York: Wiley.

Rest, J., & Narvaez, D. (1991). The college experience and moral development. In W. M. Kurtines & J. L. Gewirtz (Eds.), *Handbook of moral behavior and development* (Vol. 2). Hillsdale, NJ: Erlbaum.

Rest, J. R., & Thoma, S. J. (1985). Relation of moral judgment development to formal education. *Developmental Psychology, 21,* 709–714.

Reyna, V. F. (1991). Class inclusion, the conjunction fallacy, and other cognitive illusions. *Developmental Review, 11,* 317–336.

Reynolds, A. J. (1993, March). *Effects of a preschool plus follow-on intervention program for children at risk.* Paper presented at the meeting of the Society for Research in Child Development, New Orleans, LA.

Reynolds, K. D., Killen, J. D., Bryson, S. W., Maron, D. J., Taylor, C. B., Maccoby, N., & Farquhar, J. W. (1990). Psychological predictors of physical activity in adolescents. *Preventive Medicine, 19,* 541–551.

Reznick, J. S., & Goldfield, B. A. (1992). Rapid change in lexical development in comprehension and production. *Developmental Psychology, 28,* 406–413.

Rheingold, H. L., & Cook, K. V. (1975). The contents of boys' and girls' rooms as an index of parents' behavior. *Child Development, 46,* 459–463.

Rheingold, H. L., Gewirtz, J. L., & Ross, H. W. (1959). Social conditioning of vocalizations in the infant. *Journal of Comparative and Physiological Psychology, 52,* 68–73.

Rhodes, B., & Kroger, J. (1992). Parental bonding and separation-individuation difficulties among late adolescent eating disordered women. *Child Psychiatry and Human Development, 22,* 249–263.

Ricciuti, H. N. (1993). Nutrition and mental development. *Current Directions in Psychological Science, 2,* 43–46.

Rice, M. L. (1989). Children's language acquisition. *American Psychologist, 44,* 149–156.

Rice, M. L., Huston, A. C., Truglio, R., & Wright, J. (1990). Words from "Sesame Street": Learning vocabulary while viewing. *Developmental Psychology, 26,* 421–428.

Richards, H. C., Bear, G. G., Stewart, A. L., & Norman, A. D. (1992). Moral reasoning and classroom conduct: Evidence of a curvilinear relationship. *Merrill–Palmer Quarterly, 38,* 176–190.

Richards, M. H., Boxer, A. M., Petersen, A. C., & Albrecht, R. (1990). Relation of weight to body image in pubertal girls and boys from two communities. *Developmental Psychology, 26,* 313–321.

Richards, M. H., & Duckett, E. (1991). Maternal employment and adolescents. In S. V. Lerner & N. L. Galambos (Eds.), *Employed mothers and their children.* New York: Garland.

Richards, T. W., & Nelson, V. L. (1938). Studies in mental development: 2. Analyses of abilities tested at six months by the Gesell schedule. *Journal of Genetic Psychology, 52,* 327–331.

Richters, J. E., & Martinez, P. (1993). The NIMH Community Violence Project: I. Children as victims of and witnesses to violence. *Psychiatry, 56,* 7–35.

Riddoch, C., Mahoney, C., Murphy, N., Boreham, C., & Cran, G. (1991). The physical activity patterns of Northern Irish schoolchildren ages 11–16 years. *Pediatric Exercise Science, 3,* 300–309.

Ries, P., & Stone, A. J. (Eds.). (1992). *The American woman 1992–93: A status report.* New York: Norton.

Rieser, J., Yonas, A., & Wikner, K. (1976). Radial localization of odors by human newborns. *Child Development, 47,* 856–859.

Ritvo, E. R., Freeman, B. J., Mason–Brothers, A., Mo, A., & Ritvo, A. M. (1985). Concordance for the syndrome of autism in 40 pairs of afflicted twins. *American Journal of Psychiatry, 142,* 74–77.

Roberts, R. N., Wasik, B. H., Casto, G., & Ramey, C. T. (1991). Family support in the home: Programs, policy, and social change. *American Psychologist, 46,* 131–137.

Robertson, C. M. T., Hrynchyshyn, G. J., Etches, P. C., & Pain, K. S. (1992). Population-based study of the incidence, complexity, and severity of neurologic disability among survivors weighing 500 through 1250 grams at birth: A comparison of two birth cohorts. *Pediatrics, 90,* 750–755.

Robins, L. N. (1991). Conduct disorder. *Journal of Child Psychology and Psychiatry, 32,* 193–212.

Robins, L. N., & McEvoy, L. (1990). Conduct problems as predictors of abuse. In L. N. Robins & M. Rutter (Eds.), *Straight and devious pathways from childhood to adulthood.* Cambridge: Cambridge University Press.

Robins, L. N., & Price, R. K. (1991). Adult disorders predicted by childhood conduct problems: Results from the NIMH epidemiologic catchment area project. *Psychiatry, 54,* 116–132.

Robinson, E. J., & Mitchell, P. (1992). Children's interpretation of messages from a speaker with a false belief. *Child Development, 62,* 639–652.

Robinson, G. E., & Wittebols, J. H. (1986). Class size research: *A related cluster analysis for decision making.* Arlington, VA: Educational Research Service.

Robinson, L. W., & Conway, R. N. F. (1990). The effects of Irlen colored lenses on students' specific reading skills and their perception of ability: A 12-month validity study. *Journal of Learning Disabilities, 23,* 589–596.

Robinson, N. M. (1992, August). *Development and variation: The challenge of nurturing gifted young children.* Paper presented at the meeting of the American Psychological Association, Washington, DC.

Rodin, J. (1981). Current status of the internal–external hypothesis of obesity: What went wrong? *American Psychologist, 36,* 361–372.

Rodning, C., Beckwith, L., & Howard, J. (1991). Quality of attachment and home environments in children prenatally exposed to PCP and cocaine. *Development and Psychopathology, 3,* 351–366.

Roffwarg, H. P., Muzio, J. N., & Dement, W. C. (1966). Ontogenetic development of the human sleep–dream cycle. *Science, 152,* 604–619.

Roggman, L. A., Kinnaird, J. V., & Carroll, K. A. (1991, August). *Physical attractiveness, sex, and clothing effects on adults' expectations of children.* Paper presented at the meeting of the American Psychological Association, San Francisco.

Rogoff, B. (1990). *Apprenticeship in thinking.* Oxford: Oxford University Press.

Rogoff, B., & Mistry, J. (1990). The social and functional context of children's remembering. In R. Fivush & J. A. Hudson (Eds.), *Knowing and remembering in young children.* Cambridge: Cambridge University Press.

Rogoff, B., & Morelli, G. (1989). Perspectives on children's development from cultural psychology. *American Psychologist, 44,* 343–348.

Rollin, S. A., Rubin, R., Hardy–Blake, B., Marcil, R., Groomes, E., & Ferrullo, U. (1992, August). *A school-based drug education health promotion research project.* Paper presented at the meeting of the American Psychological Association, Washington, DC.

Roopnarine, J. L., Talukder, E., Jain, D., Joshi, P., & Srivastav, P. (1990). Characteristics of holding, patterns of play, and social behaviors between parents and infants in New Delhi, India. *Developmental Psychology, 26,* 667–673.

Root, M. P. P. (1990). Disordered eating in women of color. *Sex Roles, 22,* 525–536.

Rose, S. A., & Blank, M. (1974). The potency of context in children's cognition: An illustration through conservation. *Child Development, 45,* 499–502.

Rose, S. A., Feldman, J.F., Rose, S. L., Wallace, I. F., & McCarton, C. (1992a). Behavior problems at 3 and 6 years: Prevalence and continuity in full-terms and preterms. *Development and Psychopathology, 4,* 361–374.

Rose, S. A., Feldman, J. F., & Wallace, I. F. (1992b). Infant information processing in relation to six-year cognitive outcomes. *Child Development, 63,* 1126–1141.

Rose, S. A., & Orlian, E. K. (1991). Asymmetries in infant cross-model transfer. *Child Development, 62,* 706–718.

Rose, S. A., & Ruff, M. A. (1987). Cross-modal abilities in human infants. In J. Osofky (Ed.), *Handbook of infant development* (2nd ed.). New York: Wiley.

Rosen, J. C., Tacy, B., & Howell, D. (1990). Life stress, psychological symptoms and weight reducing behavior in adolescent girls: A prospective analysis. *International Journal of Eating Disorders, 9,* 17–26.

Rosen, K., & Rothbaum, F. (1993). Quality of parental caregiving and security of attachment. *Developmental Psychology, 29,* 358–367.

Rosen, L. W., Shafer, C. L., Dummer, G. M., Cross, L. K., Deuman, G. W., & Malmberg, S. R. (1988). Prevalence of pathogenic weight-control behaviors among Native American women and girls. *International Journal of Eating Disorders, 7,* 807–811.

Rosen, W. D., Adamson, L. B., & Bakeman, R. (1992). An experimental investigation of infant social referencing: Mothers' messages and gender differences. *Developmental Psychology, 28,* 1172–1178.

Rosenberg, M. S. (1987). New directions for research on the psychological maltreatment of children. *American Psychologist, 42,* 166–171.

Rosenberger, P. B. (1992). Dyslexia—Is it a disease? *New England Journal of Medicine, 326,* 192–193.

Rosenblith, J. F., & Sims–Knight, J. E. (1989). *In the beginning: Development in the first two years of life.* Newbury Park, CA: Sage.

Rosenblum, C. (1991, October 31). Yipes! An eerie metamorphosis is turning girls into turtles. *New York Times,* p. B1.

Rosengren, K. S., Gelman, S. A., Kalish, C. W., & McCormick, M. (1991). As time goes by: Children's early understanding of growth in animals. *Child Development, 62,* 1302–1320.

Rosenstein, D., & Oster, H. (1988). Differential facial responses to four basic tastes. *Child Development, 59,* 1555–1568.

Rosenthal, E. (1990a, January 4). New insights on why some children are fat offer clues on weight loss. *New York Times,* p. B7.

Rosenthal, E. (1990b, February 4). When a pregnant woman drinks. *New York Times Magazine,* pp. 30, 49, 61.

Rosenthal, E. (1991, July 10). Technique for early prenatal test comes under question in studies. *New York Times,* p. B6.

Rosenthal, E. (1992a, May 10). Innovation for premature babies: Snuggling with loving parents. *New York Times,* p. B7.

Rosenthal, E. (1992b, May 26). Cost of high-tech fertility: Too many tiny babies. *New York Times,* pp. B1, 7.

Rosenthal, R., & Jacobson, L. (1968). *Pygmalion in the classroom.* New York: Holt, Rinehart and Winston.

Ross, G., Kagan, J., Zelazo, P., & Kotelchuck, M. (1975). Separation protest in infants in home and laboratory. *Developmental Psychology, 11,* 256–257.

Rossetti, L. M. (1990). *Infant–toddler assessment: An interdisciplinary approach.* Boston: College Hill Press.

Rossiter, B. J. F., & Caskey, C. T. (1993, Spring). Medical consequences of the human genome project. *National Forum,* pp. 12–14.

Rotberg, I. C. (1982). Some legal and research considerations in establishing federal policy in bilingual education. *Harvard Educational Review, 52,* 149–168.

Rothbart, M. K., Ziaie, H., & O'Boyle, C. G. (1992). Self-regulation and emotion in infancy. In N. Eisenberg & R. A. Fabes (Eds.), *New directions for child development: No. 55. Emotion and its regulation in early development.* San Francisco, CA: Jossey–Bass.

Rotheram–Borus, M. J., & Koopman, C. (1991a). AIDS and adolescents. In R. M. Lerner, A. C. Petersen, & J. Brooks–Gunn (Eds.), *Encyclopedia of adolescence.* New York: Garland.

Rotheram–Borus, M. J., & Koopman, C. (1991b). Safer sex and adolescence. In R. M. Lerner, A. C. Petersen, & J. Brooks–Gunn (Eds.), *Encyclopedia of adolescence.* New York: Garland.

Rotheram–Borus, M. J., Trautman, P. D., Dopkins, S. C., & Shrout, P. E. (1990). Cognitive style and pleasant activities among female adolescent suicide attempters. *Journal of Consulting and Clinical Psychology, 58,* 554–561.

Roussounis, S. H., Hubley, P. A., & Dear, P. R. (1993). Five-year follow-up of very low birthweight infants: Neurological and psychological outcome. *Health and Development, 19,* 45–59.

Routh, D. K. (1990). Taxonomy in developmental psychopathology: Consider the source. In M. Lewis & S. M. Miller (Eds.), *Handbook of developmental psychopathology.* New York: Plenum.

Rovee–Collier, C. (1993). The capacity for long-term memory in infancy. *Current Directions in Psychological Science, 2,* 130–135.

Rovee–Collier, C., & Shyi, G. (1992). A functional and cognitive analysis of infant long-term retention. In M. L. Howe, C. J. Brainerd, & V. F. Reyna (Eds.), *Development of long-term retention.* New York: Springer–Verlag.

Rovet, J. F. (1993). The psychoeducational characteristics of children with Turner syndrome. *Journal of Learning Disabilities, 26,* 333–341.

Rowe, D. C., Rodgers, J. L., & Meseck–Bushey, S. (1992). Sibling delinquency and the family environment: Shared and unshared influences. *Child Development, 63,* 59–67.

Rowe, K. J. (1991). The influence of reading activity at home on students' attitudes towards reading, classroom attentiveness and reading achievement: An application of structural equation modeling. *British Journal of Educational Psychology, 61,* 19–35.

Rowen, B. (1973). *The children we see.* New York: Holt, Rinehart & Winston.

Rozin, P. (1990). Development in the food domain. *Developmental Psychology, 26,* 555–562.

Rozin, P., & Fallon, A. (1988). Body image, attitudes to weight, and misperceptions of figure preferences of the opposite sex: A comparison of men and women in two generations. *Journal of Abnormal Psychology, 97,* 342–345.

Rubin, K. H. (1982). Nonsocial play in preschoolers: Necessary evil. *Child Development, 53,* 651–657.

Rubin, K. H. (1993). The Waterloo Longitudinal Project: Correlates and consequences of social withdrawal from childhood to adolescence. In K. H. Rubin & J. B. Asendorpf (Eds.), *Social withdrawal, inhibition, and shyness,* Hillsdale, NJ: Erlbaum.

Rubin, K. H., & Coplan, R. J. (1992). Peer relationships in childhood. In M. H. Bornstein & M. E. Lamb (Eds.), *Developmental psychology: An advanced textbook* (3rd ed.). Hillsdale, NJ: Erlbaum.

Rubin, R. T. (1990). Mood changes during adolescence. In J. Bancroft & J. M. Reinisch (Eds.), *Adolescence and puberty.* New York: Oxford.

Ruble, D. N. (1988). Sex role development. In M. H. Bornstein & M. E. Lamb (Eds.), *Developmental psychology: An advanced textbook* (2nd ed.). Hillsdale, NJ: Erlbaum.

Ruble, D. N., Brooks–Gunn, J., Fleming, A. S., Fitzmaurice, G., Stangor, C., & Deutsch, F. (1990). Transition to motherhood and the self: Measurement, stability, and change. *Journal of Personality and Social Psychology, 58,* 450–463.

Ruff, H. A., Bijur, P. E., Markowitz, M., Ma, Y., & Rosen, J. F. (1993). Declining blood lead levels and cognitive changes in moderately lead-poisoned children. *Journal of the American Medical Association, 269,* 1641–1646.

Ruff, H. A., & Lawson, K. R. (1990). Development of sustained, focused attention in young children during free play. *Developmental Psychology, 26,* 85–93.

Ruffman, T., Olson, D. R., Ash, T., & Keenan, T. (1993). The ABCs of deception: Do young children understand deception in the same way as adults? *Developmental Psychology, 29,* 74–87.

Runco, M. A. (1992). Children's divergent thinking and creative ideation. *Developmental Review, 12,* 233–264.

Russell, G., & Russell, A. (1987). Mother–child and father–child relationships in middle childhood. *Child Development, 58,* 1573–1585.

Rutter, M. (1980). *Changing youth in a changing society: Patterns of adolescent development and disorder.* Cambridge, MA: Harvard University Press.

Rutter, M. (1981). *Maternal deprivation reassessed* (2nd ed.). Middlesex, England: Penguin Books.

Rutter, M. (1990a). Changing patterns of psychiatric disorders during adolescence. In J. Bancroft & J. M. Reinisch (Eds.), *Adolescence and puberty.* New York: Oxford.

Rutter, M. (1990b). Psychosocial resilience and protective mechanisms. In J. Rolf, A. S. Masten, D. Chicchetti, K. H. Nuechterlein, & S. Weintraub, (Eds.), *Risk and protective factors in the development of psychopathology.* New York: Cambridge University Press.

Rutter, M. (1991). Autism: Pathways from syndrome definition to pathogenesis. *Comprehensive Mental Health Care, 1,* 5–26.

Ryan, A. S., Rush, D., Krieger, F. W., & Lewandowski, G. E. (1991). Recent declines in breast-feeding in the United States, 1984 through 1989. *Pediatrics, 88,* 719–727.

Rymer, R. (1993). *Genie: An abused child's flight from silence.* New York: Harper-Collins.

Sadker, M., & Sadker, D. (1985, March). Sexism in the schoolroom of the '80s. *Psychology Today,* pp. 54–57.

Sadker, M., & Sadker, D. (1994). *Failing at fairness: How America's schools cheat girls.* New York: Scribners.

Sagi, A., Van IJzendoorn, M. H., & Koren–Karie, N. (1991). Primary appraisal of the Strange Situation: A cross-cultural analysis of preseparation episodes. *Developmental Psychology, 27,* 587–596.

Sahler, O. J. Z., & McAnarney, E. R. (1981). *The child from three to eighteen.* St. Louis, MO: Mosby.

Salapatek, P. (1975). Pattern perception in early infancy. In L. B. Cohen & P. Salapatek (Eds.), *Infant perception: From sensation to cognition.* New York: Academic Press.

Salisbury, C. L. (1991). Mainstreaming during the early childhood years. *Exceptional Children, 58,* 146–155.

Salive, M. E., Guralnik, J. M., & Glynn, R. J. (1993). Left-handedness and mortality. *American Journal of Public Health, 83,* 265–267.

Salzinger, S., Feldman, R. S., Hammer, M., & Rosario, M. (1993). The effects of physical abuse on children's social relationships. *Child Development, 64,* 169–187.

Sameroff, A. J., Seifer, R., Baldwin, A., & Baldwin, C. (1993). Stability of intelligence from preschool to adolescence: The influence of social and family risk factors. *Child Development, 64,* 80–97.

Sanche, R. P., & Dahl, H. G. (1991). Progress in Saskatchewan toward integration of students with disabilities. *Canadian Journal of Special Education, 7,* 16–31.

Sandberg, D. E., Ehrhardt, A. A., Ince, S. E., & Meyer–Bahlburg, H. F. L. (1991). Gender differences in children's and adolescents' career aspirations: A follow-up study. *Journal of Adolescent Research, 6,* 371–386.

Sandler, B. R., & Hall, R. M. (1986). *The campus climate revisited: Chilly for women, faculty, administrators, and graduate students.* Washington, DC: Association of American Colleges.

Sandler, B. R., & Hoffman, E. (1992). *Teaching faculty members to be better teachers.* Washington, DC: Association of American Colleges.

Saudino, K. J., & Eaton, W. O. (1993, March). *Genetic influences on activity level: II. An analysis of continuity and change from infancy to early childhood.* Paper presented at the meeting of the Society for Research in Child Development, New Orleans, LA.

Savin–Williams, R. C. (1991). Gay and lesbian youth. In R. M. Lerner, A. C. Petersen, & J. Brooks–Gunn (Eds.), *Encyclopedia of adolescence.* New York: Garland.

Savin–Williams, R. C., & Berndt, T. (1990). Friendship and peer relations. In S. S. Feldman & G. R. Elliott (Eds.), *At the threshold: The developing adolescent.* Cambridge, MA: Harvard University Press.

Sawyers, J. K., & Mehrotra, J. (1989). A longitudinal study of original thinking in young children. *Creative Child and Adult Quarterly, 14,* 130–135.

Saywitz, K. (1990). The child as witness: Experimental and clinical considerations. In A. M. LaGreca (Ed.), *Through the eyes of a child.* Boston: Allyn & Bacon.

Scafidi, F. A., Field, T. M., Schanberg, S. M., Bauer, C. R., Tucci, K., Roberts, J., Morrow, D., & Kuhn, C. M. (1990). Massage stimulates growth in preterm infants: A replication. *Infant Behavior and Development, 13,* 167–188.

Scarhorough, H. S. (1993, March). *Fostering literacy through shared parent–child reading: Past results and current direction.* Paper presented at the meeting of the Society for Research in Child Development, New Orleans, LA.

Scarr, S. (1985). An author's frame of mind. (Review of *Frames of mind,* by H. Gardner). *New Ideas in Psychology, 3,* 95–100.

Scarr, S. (1992). Developmental theories for the 1990s: Development and individual differences. *Child Development, 63,* 1–19.

Scarr, S. (1993, March). *IQ correlations among members of transracial adoptive families.* Paper presented at the meeting of the Society for Research in Child Development, New Orleans, LA.

Scarr, S., & Weinberg, R. A. (1976). IQ test performance of black children adopted by white families. *American Psychologist, 31,* 726–739.

Scarr, S., & Weinburg, R. A. (1977). Intellectual similarities within families of both adopted and biological children. *Intelligence, 1,* 170–191.

Schachter, S. (1971). Some extraordinary facts about obese humans and rats. *American Psychologist, 26,* 129–144.

Schaffer, H. R. (Ed.). (1971). *The origins of human social relations.* New York: Academic Press.

Schaffer, H. R., & Emerson, P. E. (1964). The development of social attachments in infancy. *Monographs of the Society for Research in Child Development, 29*(Whole No. 94).

Scheiman, M., Blastey, P., Parisi, M., & Ciner, E. (1991). "Irlen lenses" response. *Journal of Learning Disabilities, 24,* 516–517.

Scheinfeld, A. (1973). *Twins and super-twins.* Baltimore: Penguin Books.

Schiedel, D. G., & Marcia, J. E. (1985). Ego identity, intimacy, sex role orientation, and gender. *Developmental Psychology, 18,* 149–160.

Schinke, S. P., Botrin, G. J., & Orlande, M. A. (1991). *Substance abuse in children and adolescents: Evaluation and intervention.* Newbury Park, CA: Sage.

Schlegel, A., & Barry, H. (1991). *Adolescence: An anthropological inquiry.* New York: Free Press.

Schmeck, H. M. (1990, April 29). Battling the legacy of illness. *New York Times Magazine,* pp. 36, 37, 46, 48, 50.

Schmitt, B. D. (1991). *Your child's health.* New York: Bantam.

Schneider, W., & Bjorklund, D. (1992, April). Expertise, aptitude, and strategic remembering. *Child Development, 63,* 461–473.

Schneider, W., & Pressley, M. (1989). *Memory development between 2 and 20.* New York: Springer–Verlag.

Schneider–Rosen, K., & Cicchetti, D. (1991). Early self-knowledge and emotional development: Visual self-recognition and affective reactions to mirror self-images in maltreated and non-maltreated toddlers. *Developmental Psychology, 27,* 471–478.

Schoendorf, K. C., & Kiely, J. L. (1992). Relationship of sudden infant death syndrome to maternal smoking during and after pregnancy. *Pediatrics, 90,* 905–908.

Scholl, T. O., Hediger, M. L., Khoo, C., Healey, M. F., & Rawson, N. L. (1991). Maternal weight gain, diet and infant birth weight: Correlations during adolescent pregnancy. *Journal of Clinical Epidemiology, 44,* 423–428.

Schotte, D. E., Cools, J., & Payvar, S. (1990). Problem-solving deficits in suicidal patients: Trait vulnerability or state phenomenon? *Journal of Consulting and Clinical Psychology, 58,* 562–564.

Schuerger, J. M., & Witt, A. C. (1989). The temporal stability of individually tested intelligence. *Journal of Clinical Psychology, 45,* 294–302.

Schulenberg, J., Wadsworth, K. N., O'Malley, P. M., Bachman, J. G., Ebata, A. T., & Johnston, L. D. (1993, March). *The impact of personality and social context on trajectories of binge drinking during the transition to young adulthood.* Paper presented at the annual meeting of the Society for Research on Child Development, New Orleans, LA.

Schulman, J. D., & Bustillo, M. (1989). In vitro fertilization: Clinical and research aspects. In M. I. Evans, J. C. Fletcher, A. O. Dixler, & J. D. Schulman (Eds.), *Fetal diagnosis and therapy: Science, ethics and the law.* Philadelphia: Lippincott.

Schultz, S. R. (1990). Nutrition and human development. In R. M. Thomas (Ed.), *The encyclopedia of human development and education: Theory, research, and studies.* Oxford: Pergamon.

Schwartz, D. (1993, March). *Antecedents of aggression and peer victimization: A prospective study.* Paper presented at the meeting of the Society for Research in Child Development, New Orleans, LA.

Schwartz, L. L. (1991). *Alternatives to infertility: Is surrogacy the answer?* New York: Brunner/Mazel.

Schwartz, M. (1990). Left-handedness and prenatal complications. In S. Coren (Ed.), *Left-handedness: Behavior implications and anomalies.* Amsterdam: North–Holland.

Schwartz–Bickenbach, D., Schulte–Hobein, B., Abt, S., Plum, D., & Nau, H. (1987). Smoking and passive smoking during pregnancy and early infancy: Effects on birth weight, lactation period, and cotinine concentrations in mother's milk and infant's urine. *Toxicology Letters, 35,* 73–81.

Schweder, R., Mahapatra, M., & Miller, J. (1987). Culture and moral development. In J. Kagan & S. Lamb (Eds.), *The emergence of morality in young children.* Chicago: University of Chicago Press.

Schweinhart, L. J., & Weikart, D. P. (Eds.) (1993). *Significant benefits: The High/Scope Perry Preschool Study through age 27.* Ypsilanti, MI: High/Scope Press.

Scott, J. R., DiSaia, P. J., Hamn ond, C. B., & Spellacy, W. N. (Eds.). (1990). *Danforth's obstetrics and gynecology* (6th ed.). Philadelphia: Lippincott.

Seefeldt, C. (1990). Assessing young children. In C. Seefeldt (Ed.), *Continuing issues in early childhood education.* Columbus, OH: Merrill.

Seefeldt, V., Ewing, M., & Walk, S. (1991). *An overview of youth sports programs in the United States.* Washington, DC: Carnegie Council on Adolescent Development.

Seidman, E., Allen, L., Aber, J. L., Mitchell, C., & Feinman, J. (in press). The impact of school transitions in early adolescence on the self-system and perceived social context of poor urban youth. *Child Development.*

Seitz, V. (1990). Intervention programs for impoverished children: A comparison of educational and family support models. *Annals of Child Development, 7,* 73–103.

Seitz, V., & Apfel, N. H. (1993, March). *Long-term effects of a school for pregnant students: Repeated childbearing through six years postpartum.* Paper presented at the meeting of the Society for Research in Child Development, New Orleans, LA.

Seligmann, J. (1992, December 14). It's not like Mr. Mom. *Newsweek,* pp. 70–71, 73.

Selman, R. L. (1976). Social-cognitive understanding. In T. Lickona (Ed.), *Moral development and behavior: Theory research and social issues.* New York: Holt, Rinehart & Winston.

Selman, R. (1980). *The growth of interpersonal understanding: Developmental and clinical analysis.* New York: Academic Press.

Selman, R. L. (1989). Fostering intimacy and autonomy. In W. Damon (Ed.), *Child development today and tomorrow.* San Francisco: Jossey–Bass.

Selman, R. L., & Schultz, L. H. (1989). Children's strategies for interpersonal negotiation with peers: An interpretive/empirical approach to the study of social development. In T. J. Berndt & G. W. Ladd (Eds.), *Peer relationships in child development.* New York: Wiley.

Selman, R. L., Schultz, L. H., Nakkula, M., Barr, D., Watts, C., & Richmond, J. B. (1992). Friendship and fighting: A developmental approach to the study of risk and prevention of violence. *Development and Psychopathology, 4,* 529–558.

Sepkoski, C. M. (1985). Maternal obstetric medication and newborn behavior. In J. W. Scanlon (Ed.), *Prenatal anesthesia.* London: Blackwell.

Sepkoski, C. M., Corwin, M. J., Lester, B. M., Gross, S., Peucker, M., & Golub, H. L. (1993, March). *Predicting developmental delay from cry analysis in preterm infants.* Paper presented at the meeting of the Society for Research in Child Development, New Orleans, LA.

Serbin, L. A., Powlishta, K. K., & Gulko, J. (1993). The development of sex typing in middle childhood, *Monographs of the Society for Research in Child Development, 58*(2, Serial No. 232).

Serbin, L. A., & Sprafkin, C. (1986). The salience of gender and the process of sex typing in three- to seven-year-old children. *Child Development, 57,* 1188–1199.

Serbin, L. A., Zelkowitz, P., Doyle, A. B., Gold, D., & Wheaton, B. (1990). The socialization of sex-differentiated skills and academic performance: A mediational model. *Sex Roles, 23,* 613–628.

Shakin, M., Shakin, D., & Sternglanz, S. H. (1985). Infant clothing: Sex labeling for strangers. *Sex Roles, 12,* 955–964.

Shakoor, B., & Chalmers, D. (1991). Covictimization of African-American children who witness violence: Effects on cognitive, emotional, and behavioral development. *Journal of the National Medical Association, 83,* 233–237.

Shannon, M. W., & Graef, J. W. (1992). Lead intoxication in infancy. *Pediatrics, 89,* 87–90.

Shantz, C. U., & Hobart, C. J. (1989). Social conflict and development. In T. J. Berndt, & G. W. Ladd (Eds.), *Peer relationships in child development.* New York: Wiley.

Shapiro, L. (1993, April 19). Rush to judgment. *Newsweek,* pp. 54–60.

Shaywitz, S. E., Escobar, M. D., Shaywitz, B. A., Fletcher, J. M., & Makuch, R. (1992). Evidence that dyslexia may represent the lower tail of a normal distribution of reading ability. *New England Journal of Medicine, 326,* 145–150.

Shea, S., Stein, A. D., Basch, C. E., Contento, I. R., & Zybert, P. (1992). Variability and self-regulation of energy intake in young children in their everyday environment. *Pediatrics, 90,* 542–546.

Shedler, J., & Block. J. (1990). Adolescent drug use and psychological health: A longitudinal inquiry. *American Psychologist, 45,* 612–630.

Sheeber, L. B., & Johnson, J. H. (1992). Child temperament, maternal adjustment, and changes in family life style. *American Journal of Orthopsychiatry, 62,* 178–185.

Sherman, J. A. (1983). Factors predicting girls' and boys' enrollment in college preparatory mathematics. *Psychology of Women Quarterly, 7,* 272–281.

Shettles, L. (1982, June). Predetermining children's sex. *Medical Aspects of Human Sexuality,* p. 172.

Shneidman, E. S. (1985). *Definition of suicide.* New York: Wiley.

Shonkoff, J. P., Hauser–Cram, P., Krauss, M. W., & Upshur, C. C. (1992). Development of infants with disabilities and their families. *Monographs of the Society for Research in Child Development, 57*(6, Serial No. 230).

Shorter–Gooden, K. (1992, February). *Identity development in African-American female adolescents.* Paper presented at the meeting of the Association of Women in Psychology, Long Beach, CA.

Shucard, J. L., & Shucard, D. W. (1990). Auditory evoked potentials and hand preference in 6-month-old infants: Possible gender-related differences in cerebral organization. *Developmental Psychology, 26,* 923–930.

Shultz, T. (1980). Development of the concept of intention. In W. A. Collins (Ed.), *Minnesota symposia on child psychology* (Vol. 13). Hillsdale, NJ: Erlbaum.

Siegel, L. J., & Senna, J. J. (1991). *Juvenile delinquency: Theory, practice and law.* St. Paul, MN: West.

Siegel, L. S. (1992). Infant motor, cognitive, and language behaviors as predictors of achievement at school age. In C. Rovee–Collier & L. P. Lipsitt (Eds.), *Advances in infancy research,* (Vol. 7). Norwood, NJ: Ablex.

Siegel, L. S. (1993). The development of reading. In H. W. Reese (Ed.), *Advances in child development and behavior,* (Vol. 24). Orlando, FL: Academic Press.

Siegel, M. (1987). Are sons and daughters treated more differently by fathers than by mothers? *Developmental Review, 7,* 183–209.

Siegel, M., & Beattie, K. (1991). Where to look first for children's knowledge of false beliefs. *Cognition, 38,* 1–12.

Siegler, R. S. (1986). *Children's thinking.* Englewood Cliffs, NJ: Prentice Hall.

Siegler, R. S., Liebert, D. E., & Liebert, R. M. (1973). Inhelder and Piaget's pendulum problem: Teaching pre-adolescents to act as scientists. *Developmental Psychology, 9,* 97–101.

Sigel, I. E. (1991). Preschool education: For whom and why? In L. Rescorla, M. C. Hyson, & K. Hirsh–Pasek (Eds.), *New directions in child development: No. 53. Academic instruction in early childhood: Challenge or pressure?* San Francisco: Jossey–Bass.

Sigelman, C., Didjurgis, T., Marshall, B., Vargas, F., & Stewart, A. (1992). Views of problem drinking among Native American, Hispanic, and Anglo children. *Child Psychiatry and Human Development, 22,* 265–276.

Sigelman, C., Maddock, A., Epstein, J., & Carpenter, W. (1993). Age differences in understandings of disease causality: AIDS, colds, and cancer. *Child Development, 64,* 272–284.

Sigman, M., McDonald, M. A., Neumann, C., & Bwibo, N. (1991). Prediction of cognitive competence in Kenyan children from toddler nutrition, family characteristics and abilities. *Journal of Child Psychology and Psychiatry, 32,* 307–320.

Sigman, M., & Sena, R. (1993, March). Pretend play in high-risk and developmentally delayed children. In M. H. Bornstein & A. W. O'Reilly (Eds.), *New directions for human development: No. 59. The role of play in the development of thought.* San Francisco: Jossey–Bass.

Signorella, M. L., Bigler, R. S., & Liben, L. S. (1993). Developmental differences in children's gender schemata about others: A meta-analytic review. *Developmental Review, 13,* 147–183.

Signorella, M. L., & Frieze, I. H. (1989). Gender schemas in college students. *Psychology: A Journal of Human Behavior, 26,* 16–23.

Signorielli, N. (1989). Television and conceptions about sex roles: Maintaining conventionality and the status quo. *Sex Roles, 21,* 341–360.

Signorielli, N. (1990). Children, television, and gender roles: Messages and impact. *Journal of Adolescent Health Care, 11,* 50–58.

Silver, L. B. (1991). Developmental learning disorders. In M. Lewis (Ed.), *Child and adolescent psychiatry: A comprehensive textbook.* Baltimore: Williams & Wilkins.

Silverberg, S. B., Tennenbaum, D. L., & Jacob, T. (1992). Adolescence and family interaction. In V. B. VanHasselt and M. Hersen (Eds.), *Handbook of social development.* New York: Plenum.

Silverstein, L. B. (1991). Transforming the debate about child care and maternal employment. *American Psychologist, 10,* 1025–1032.

Simensen, R. J., & Marshall, T. A. (1992, July). *Growth and developmental outcome among VLBW infants (<1,000 g).* Paper presented at the XXV International Congress of Psychology, Brussels.

Simmons, D. C., Fuchs, D., & Fuchs, L. S. (1991). Instructional and curricular requisites of mainstreamed students with learning disabilities. *Journal of Learning Disabilities, 24,* 354–360.

Simmons, R. G. (1987). Social transition and adolescent development. In C. E. Irwin (Ed.), *New directions for child development: No. 37. Adolescent social behavior and health.* San Francisco: Jossey–Bass.

Simmons, R. G., & Blyth, D. A. (1987). *Moving into adolescence: The impact of pubertal change and school context.* Hawthorne, NY: Aldine deGruyter.

Simons, R. L., Lorenz, F. O., Wu, C., & Conqer, R. D. (1993). Social network and marital support as mediators and moderators of the impact of stress and depression on parental behavior. *Developmental Psychology, 29,* 368–381.

Simons, R. L., Whitbeck, L. B., Conger, R. D., & Chyi–In, W. (1991). Intergenerational transmission of harsh parenting. *Developmental Psychology, 27,* 159–171.

Singer, D. G., & Singer, J. L. (1990). *The house of make-believe: Children's play and developing imagination.* Cambridge, MA: Harvard University Press.

Singer, J. L. (1991). Cognitive and affective implications of imaginative play in childhood. In M. Lewis (Ed.), *Child and adolescent psychiatry: A comprehensive textbook.* Baltimore: Williams & Wilkins.

Singer, L., Farkas, K., & Kliegman, R. (1992). Childhood medical and behavioral consequences of maternal cocaine use. *Journal of Pediatric Psychology, 17,* 389–406.

Singer, L. T., Song, L. Y., Hill, B. P., & Jaffee, A. C. (1990). Stress and depression in mothers of failure-to-thrive children. *Journal of Pediatric Psychology, 15,* 711–720.

Skeels, H. M. (1966). Adult status of children with contrasting early life experiences: A follow-up study. *Monographs of the Society for Research in Child Development, 31*(3, Serial No. 105).

Skinner, B. F. (1957). *Verbal behavior.* New York: Appleton.

Skinner, B. F. (1983). *A matter of consequences.* New York: Knopf.

Slap, G. B. (1991). Risk factors for injury during adolescence. In R. M. Lerner, A. C. Petersen & J. Brooks–Gunn (Eds.), *Encyclopedia of adolescence.* New York: Garland.

Slater, A., Mattock, A., & Brown, E. (1990). Size constancy at birth: Newborn infants' responses to retinal and real size. *Journal of Experimental Child Psychology, 49,* 314–322.

Slavin, R. E. (1989). Achievement effects of substantial reductions in class size. In R. E. Slavin (Ed.), *School and classroom organization.* Hillsdale, NJ: Erlbaum.

Slobin, D. I. (1972, July). Children and language: They learn the same way all around the world. *Psychology Today,* pp. 71–74ff.

Slobin, D. I. (1973). Cognitive prerequisites for the development of grammar. In C. A. Ferguson & D. I. Slobin (Eds.), *Studies of child development.* New York: Holt, Rinehart and Winston.

Slobin, D. I. (1983, April). *Crosslinguistic evidence for basic child grammar.* Paper presented at the meeting of the Society for Research in Child Development, Detroit.

Slobin, D. I. (1988). From the garden of Eden to the tower of Babel. In F. S. Kessel (Ed.), *The development of language and language researchers.* Hillsdale, NJ: Erlbaum.

Small, M. Y. (1990). *Cognitive development.* San Diego, CA: Harcourt Brace Jovanovich.

Smetana, J. G. (1985). Children's impressions of moral and conventional transgressors. *Developmental Psychology, 21,* 715–724.

Smetana, J. G. (1990). Morality and conduct disorders. In M. Lewis & S. M. Miller (Eds.), *Handbook of developmental psychopathology.* New York: Plenum.

Smetana, J. G., Killen, M., & Turiel, E. (1991a). Children's reasoning about interpersonal and moral conflicts. *Child Development, 62,* 629–644.

Smetana, J. G., & Letourneau, K. J. (1984). Development of gender constancy and children's sex-typed free play behavior. *Developmental Psychology, 20,* 691–696.

Smetana, J. G., Yau, J., Restrepo, A., & Braeges, J. L. (1991b). Conflict and adaptation in adolescence: Adolescent–parent conflict. In M. E. Colten & S. Gore (Eds.), *Adolescent stress: Causes and consequences.* New York: Aldine deGruyter.

Smilansky, S. (1990). Sociodramatic play: Its relevance to behavior and achievement in school. In E. Klugman & S. Smilansky (Eds.), *Children's play and learning.* New York: Teachers College Press.

Smith, B. A., Fillion, T. J., & Blass, E. M. (1990). Orally mediated sources of calming in 1- to 3-day-old human infants. *Developmental Psychology, 26,* 731–737.

Smith, P. K. (1979). The ontogeny of fear in children. In W. Sluckin (Ed.), *Fears in animals and man.* London: Von Nostrand Reinhold.

Smoll, F. L., & Schultz, R. W. (1990). Quantifying gender differences in physical performance: A developmental perspective. *Developmental Psychology, 26,* 360–369.

Snarey, J. R. (1985). Cross-cultural universality of social-moral development: A critical review of Kohlbergian research. *Psychological Bulletin 97,* 202–232.

Snyderman, M., & Rothman, S. (1990). *The I.Q. controversy.* New Brunswick, NJ: Transaction.

Sobesky, W. E. (1983). The effects of situational factors on moral judgments. *Child Development, 54,* 575–584.

Sodian, B., Taylor, C., Harris, P. L., & Perner, J. (1991). Early deception and the child's theory of mind: False trails and genuine markers. *Child Development, 62,* 468–483.

Sommer, K., Whitman, T. L., Borkowski, J. G., Schellenbach, C., Maxwell, S., & Keogh, D. (1993). Cognitive readiness and adolescent parenting. *Developmental Psychology, 29,* 389–398.

Sontag, L. W. (1966). Implications of fetal behavior and environment for adult personality. *Annals of the New York Academy of Science, 134,* 782–786.

Sontag, L. W., & Richards, T. W. (1938). Studies in fetal behavior: Fetal heart rate as a behavioral indicator. *Child Development Monographs, 3*(4).

Sorce, J. F., Emde, R. N., Campos, J. J., & Klinnert, M. D. (1985). Maternal emotional signaling: Its effect on the visual cliff behavior of 1-year-olds. *Developmental Psychology, 21,* 195–200.

Sorenson, S. B., & Rutter, C. M. (1991). Transgenerational patterns of suicide attempt. *Journal of Consulting and Clinical Psychology, 59,* 861–866.

Southern, T., & Jones, E. D. (1991). *The academic acceleration of gifted children.* New York: Teachers College Press.

Spangler, G. (1990). Mother child and situational correlates of toddler's social competence. *Infant Behavior and Development, 13,* 405–419.

Sparling, J., Lewis, I., Ramey, C. T., Wasik, B. H., Bryant, D. M., & LaVange, L. M. (1991). Partners: A curriculum to help premature low birthweight infants get off to a good start. *Topics in Early Childhood Special Education, 11,* 36–55.

Spelke, E. S., & Owsley, C. (1979). Intermodal exploration and knowledge in infancy. *Infant Behavior and Development, 2,* 13–27.

Spence, J. T. (1991). Do the BSRI and PAQ measure the same or different concepts? *Psychology of Women Quarterly, 15,* 141–165.

Spencer, M. B. (1991). Development of minority identity. In R. M. Lerner, A. C. Petersen, & J. Brooks–Gunn (Eds.), *Encyclopedia of adolescence.* New York: Garland.

Spencer, M. B., Dornbusch, S. M., & Mont–Reynaud, R. (1990). Challenges in studying minority youth. In S. S. Feldman & G. R. Elliott (Eds.), *At the threshold: The developing adolescent.* Cambridge, MA: Harvard University Press.

Spencer, M. B., & Markstrom–Adams, C. (1990). Identity processes among racial and ethnic minority children in America. *Child Development, 61,* 290–310.

Spiker, D. (1990). Early intervention from a developmental perspective. In D. Cicchetti & M. Beeghly (Eds.), *Children with Down syndrome: A developmental perspective.* Cambridge: Cambridge University Press.

Spitz, R. A. (1965). *The first year of life: A psychoanalytic study of normal and deviant object relations.* New York: International Universities Press.

Spivack, G., Marcus, J., & Swift, M. (1986). Early classroom behaviors and later misconduct. *Developmental Psychology, 22,* 124–131.

Spohr, H. L., Willms, J., & Steinhausen, H. C. (1993). Prenatal alcohol exposure and long-term developmental consequences. *Lancet, 341,* 907–910.

Springer, K., & Keil, F. C. (1991). Early differentiation of causal mechanisms appropriate to biological and nonbiological kinds. *Child Development, 62,* 767–781.

Springer, S. P., & Deutsch, G. (1989). *Left brain, right brain (3rd ed.).* New York: Freeman.

Sroufe, L. A. (1979). Socioemotional development. In J. Osofsky (Ed.), *Handbook of infant development.* New York: Wiley.

Sroufe, L. A., Bennett, C., Englund, M., Urban, J., & Shulman, S. (1993). The significance of gender boundaries in preadolescence: Contemporary correlates and antecedents of boundary violation and maintenance. *Child Development, 64,* 455–466.

Sroufe, L. A., Waters, E., & Matas, L. (1974). Contextual determinants of infant affectional response. In M. Lewis & L. Rosenblum (Eds.), *The origins of fear.* New York: Wiley.

Stanovich, K. E. (1993). A model for studies of reading disability. *Developmental Review, 13,* 225–245.

Stanton, W. R., & Silva, P. A. (1992). A longitudinal study of the influence of parents and friends on children's initiation of smoking. *Journal of Applied Developmental Psychology, 13,* 423–434.

Stark, L. J., Owens–Stively, J., Spirito, A., Lewis, A., & Guevremont, D. (1991). Group behavioral treatment of retentive encopresis. *Journal of Pediatric Psychology, 15,* 659–671.

Stattin, H., & Magnusson, D. (1990). *Pubertal maturation in female development.* Hillsdale, NJ: Erlbaum.

Stechler, G., & Halton, A. (1982). Prenatal influences on human development. In B. B. Wolman (Ed.), *Handbook of developmental psychology.* Englewood Cliffs, NJ: Prentice Hall.

Steffenburg, S., Gillberg, C., Hellgren, L., Anderson, L., Gillberg, C., Jakobsson, G., & Bohman, M. (1989). A twin study of autism in Denmark, Finland, Iceland, Norway, and Sweden. *Journal of Child Psychology and Psychiatry, 30,* 405–416.

Stegelin, D. A., & Frankel, J. (1993). Families of lower-income employed mothers. In J. Frankel (Ed.), *The employed mother and the family context.* New York: Springer.

Steinberg, L. (1988). Reciprocal relation between parent–child distance and pubertal maturation. *Developmental Psychology, 24,* 122–128.

Steinberg, L. (1989). Pubertal maturation and parent–adolescent distance: An evolutionary perspective. In G. Adams, R. Montemayor, & T. Gullotta (Eds.), *Advances in adolescent development* (Vol. 1). Beverly Hills, CA: Sage.

Steinberg, L. (1990a). Autonomy, conflict, and harmony in the family relationship. In S. S. Feldman & G. R. Elliott (Eds.), *At the threshold: The developing adolescent.* Cambridge, MA: Harvard University Press.

Steinberg, L. (1990b). Psychological well-being of parents with early adolescent children. *Developmental Psychology, 26,* 658–666.

Steinberg, L. (1991). Parent–adolescent relations. In R. M. Lerner, A. C. Petersen, & J. Brooks–Gunn (Eds.), *Encyclopedia of adolescence.* New York: Garland.

Steinberg, L., & Dornbusch, S. M. (1991). Negative correlates of part-time employment during adolescence: Replication and elaboration. *Developmental Psychology, 27,* 304–313.

Steinberg, L., Fegley, S., & Dornbusch, S. M. (1993). Negative impact of part-time work on adolescent adjustment: Evidence from a longitudinal study. *Developmental Psychology, 29,* 171–180.

Steinberg, L., Lamborn, S. D., Dornbusch, S. M., & Darling, N. (1992). Impact of parenting practices on adolescent achievement: Authoritative parenting, school involvement, and encouragement to succeed. *Child Development, 63,* 1266–1281.

Steiner, J. E. (1979). Facial expressions in response to taste and smell discrimination. In H. W. Reese & L. P. Lipsitt (Eds.), *Advances in child development and behavior (Vol. 13).* New York: Academic Press.

Steitz, J. A., & Owen, T. P. (1992). School activities and work: Effects on adolescent self-esteem. *Adolescence, 27,* 37–50.

Stemberger, J. P. (1993). Vowel dominance in overregularizations. *Journal of Child Language, 20,* 503–522.

Stericker, A., & LeVesconte, S. (1982). Effect of brief training on sex-related differences in visual-spatial skill. *Journal of Personality and Social Psychology, 43,* 1018–1029.

Stern, M., & Karraker, K. H. (1989). Sex stereotyping of infants: A review of gender labeling studies. *Sex Roles, 20,* 501–521.

Sternberg, K. J., Lamb, M. E., Greenbaum, C., Cicchetti, D., Dawud, S., Cortes, R. M., Krispin, O., & Lorey, F. (1993). Effects of domestic violence on children's behavior problems and depression. *Developmental Psychology, 29,* 44–52.

Sternberg, R. J. (1988). *The triarchic mind.* New York: Viking.

Stevenson, H. W., Chen, C., & Lee, S. (1993). Mathematics achievement of Chinese, Japanese, and American children: Ten years later. *Science, 259,* 53–58.

Stevenson, H. W., & Stigler, J. W. (1992). *The learning gap: Why our schools are failing and what we can learn from Japanese and Chinese education.* New York: Summit Books.

Stevenson, H. W., Stigler, J. W., Shin–Ying, L., Lucker, G. W., Kitamura, S., & Hsu, C. (1985). Cognitive performance and academic achievement of Japanese, Chinese, and American children. *Child Development, 56,* 718–734.

Stevenson, J. (1992). Evidence for a genetic etiology in hyperactivity in children. *Behavior Genetics, 22,* 337–344.

Stiffman, A. R., Earls, F., Doré, P., & Cunningham, R. (1992). Changes in acquired immunodeficiency syndrome-related risk behavior after adolescence: Relationships to knowledge and experience concerning human immunodeficiency virus infection. *Pediatrics, 89,* 950–956.

Stipek, D. (1992). The child at school. In M. H. Bornstein & M. E. Lamb (Eds.), *Developmental psychology: An advanced textbook* (3rd ed.). Hillsdale, NJ: Erlbaum.

Stipek, D. J., & Gralinski, J. H. (1991). Gender differences in children's achievement-related beliefs and emotional responses to success and failure in mathematics. *Journal of Educational Psychology, 83,* 361–371.

Stipek, D. J., Gralinski, J. H., & Kopp, C. B. (1990). Self-concept development in the toddler years. *Developmental Psychology, 26,* 972–977.

Stipek, D., Recchia, S., & McClintic, S. (1992). Self-evaluation in young children. *Monographs of the Society for Research in Child Development, 57*(1, Serial No. 226).

Stocker, C., & Dunn, J. (1990). Sibling relationships in childhood: Links with friendships and peer relationships. *British Journal of Developmental Psychology, 8,* 227–244.

Stockman, I. J., & Vaughn–Cooke, F. (1992). Lexical elaboration in children's locative action expression. *Child Development, 63,* 1104–1125.

Stone, W. L., & Caro–Martinez, L. M. (1990). Naturalistic observations of spontaneous communication in autistic children. *Journal of Autism and Developmental Disorders, 20,* 437–453.

Stone, W. L., & Lemanek, K. L. (1990). Parental report of social behaviors in autistic preschoolers. *Journal of Autism and Developmental Disorders, 20,* 513–522.

Storfer, M. D. (1990). *Intelligence and giftedness: The contributions of heredity and early environment.* San Francisco: Jossey–Bass.

Straus, M. A., & Gelles, R. J. (1990). Societal change and change in family violence from 1975 to 1985 as revealed by two national surveys. In M. A. Straus & R. J. Gelles (Eds.), *Physical violence in American families.* New Brunswick, NJ: Transaction.

Straus, M. A., & Smith, C. (1990). Family patterns and child abuse. In M. A. Straus & R. J. Gelles (Eds.), *Physical violence in American families.* New Brunswick, NJ: Transaction.

Strayer, F. F. (1990). The social ecology of toddler play groups and the origins of gender discrimination. In F. F. Strayer (Ed.), *Social interaction and behavioral development during early childhood.* Montreal: La Maison D'Ethologie de Montreal.

Strayer, F. F., Leclere, D., & LaFerte, P. (1990). The nature and development of peer networks in very young children. In F. F. Strayer (Ed.), *Social interaction and behavioral development during early childhood.* Montreal: La Maison D'Ethologie de Montreal.

Strayer, J., & Schroeder, M. (1989). Children's helping strategies: Influences of emotion, empathy and age. In N. Eisenberg (Ed.), *New directions for child development: No. 44. Empathy and related emotional responses.* San Francisco: Jossey–Bass.

Streissguth, A. P., Aase, J. M., Clarren, S. K., Randels, S. P., LaDue, R. A., & Smith, D. F. (1991). Fetal alcohol syndrome in adolescents and adults. *Journal of the American Medical Association, 265,* 1961–1967.

Streissguth, A. P., Barr, H. M., & Sampson, P. D. (1992). Alcohol use during pregnancy and child development: A longitudinal, prospective study of human behavioral teratology. In C. W. Greenbaum & J. G. Auerbach (Eds.), *Longitudinal studies of children at psychological risk: Cross-national perspectives.* Norwood, NJ: Ablex.

Streitmatter, J. L. (1988). Ethnicity as a mediating variable of early adolescent identity development. *Journal of Adolescence, 11,* 335–346.

Strelau, J., & Angleitner, A. (1991). Temperament research: Some divergences and similarities. In J. Strelau & A. Angleitner (Eds.) *Explorations in temperament: International perspectives on theory and measurement.* New York: Plenum.

Strohner, H., & Nelson, K. E. (1974). The young child's development of sentence comprehension: Influence of event probability, nonverbal context, syntactic form, and strategies. *Child Development, 45,* 567–576.

Strutt, G. F., Anderson, D. R., & Well, A. D. (1975). A developmental study of the effects of irrelevant information on speeded classification. *Journal of Experimental Child Psychology, 20,* 127–135.

Stucky–Ropp, R. C., & DiLorenzo, T. M. (1992, August). *Determinants of exercise in children.* Paper presented at the meeting of the American Psychological Association, Washington, DC.

Study finds risk to infant in early prenatal test. (1994, March 12). *New York Times,* p. 6.

Stunkard, A. J., Harris, J. R., Pedersen, N. I., & McClearn, G. E. (1990). The body-mass index of twins who have been reared apart. *New England Journal of Medicine, 322,* 1483–1487.

Sue, S. (1991). Ethnicity and culture in psychological research and practice. In J. D. Goodchilds (Ed.), *Psychological perspectives on human diversity in America.* Washington, DC : American Psychological Association.

Sue, S., & Okazaki, S. (1990). Asian-American educational achievements. *American Psychologist, 45,* 913–920.

Suess, G. J., Grossmann, K. E., & Sroufe, L. A. (1992). Effects of infant attachment to mother and father on quality of adaptation in preschool: From dyadic to individual organisation of self. *International Journal of Behavioral Development, 15,* 43–65.

Sullivan, K., & Winner, E. (1991). When 3-year-olds understand ignorance, false belief and representational change. *British Journal of Developmental Psychology, 9,* 159–171.

Sullivan, S. A., & Birch, L. L. (1990). Pass the sugar, pass the salt: Experience dictates preference. *Developmental Psychology, 26,* 546–551.

Suomi, S. J., Harlow, H. F., & McKinney, W. T. (1972). Monkey psychiatrists. *American Journal of Psychiatry, 128,* 927–932.

Super, C. M. (1980). Cognitive development: Looking across at growing up. In C. M. Super & S. Harkness (Eds.), *New directions for child development: No. 8. Anthropological perspectives on child development.* San Francisco: Jossey–Bass.

Super, C. M., & Harkness, S. (1981). Figure, ground and gestalt: The cultural context of the active individual. In R. M. Lerner & N. A. Busch–Rossnagel (Eds.), *Individuals as producers of their development.* New York: Academic Press.

Super, C. M., Herrena, M. G., & Mora, J. O. (1990). Long-term effects of food supplementation and psychosocial intervention on the physical growth of Colombian infants at risk of malnutrition. *Child Development, 61,* 29–49.

Super, D. E. (1984). Career and life development. In D. Brown & L. Brooks (Eds.), *Career choice and development.* San Francisco: Jossey–Bass.

Super, D. E. (1985). Coming of age in Middletown: Careers in the making. *American Psychologist, 40,* 405–414.

Surber, C. F (1977). Developmental processes in social inference: Averaging of intentions and consequences in moral judgment. *Developmental Psychology, 13,* 654–665.

Surbey, M. (1990). Family composition, stress, and human menarche. In F. Bercovitch & T. Zeigler (Eds.), *The socioendocrinology of primate reproduction.* New York: Liss.

Suro, R. (1992, August 2). Bridging a gap. *New York Times,* Special Report: Education, p. 20.

Suro, R. (1993, January 11). Pollution-weary minorities try civil rights tack. *New York Times,* pp. A1 & B7.

Susman, E. J., & Dorn, L. D. (1991). Hormones and behavior in adolescence. In R. M. Lerner, A. C. Petersen, & J. Brooks–Gunn (Eds.), *Encyclopedia of adolescence.* New York: Garland.

Sutton-Smith, B. (1993). Dilemmas in adult play with children. In K. MacDonald (Ed.), *Parent–child play: Descriptions and implications.* Albany, NY: SUNY Press.

Szapocznik, J., & Kurtines, W. M. (1993). Family psychology and cultural diversity. *American Psychologist, 48,* 400–407.

Szatmari, P., Bartolucci, G., Bremner, R., Bond, S., & Rich, S. (1989). A follow-up study of high-functioning autistic children. *Journal of Autism and Developmental Disorders, 19,* 213–225.

Szilagyi, P. G., Rodewald, L. E., Humiston, S. G., Raubertas, R. F., Cove, L. A., Doane, C. B., Lind, P. H., Tobin, M. S., Roghmann, K. J., & Hall, C. B. (1993). Missed opportunities for childhood vaccinations in office practices and the effect on vaccination status. *Pediatrics, 91,* 1–7.

Tabor, M. B. W. (1992, August 2). Living on the edge. *New York Times,* Special Report: Education, p. 16.

Takahashi, K. (1990). Are the key assumptions of the "Strange Situation" procedure universal? A view from Japanese research. *Human Development, 33,* 23–30.

Takanishi, R. (1993). The opportunities of adolescence: Research, interventions, and policy. *American Psychologist, 48,* 85–87.

Taket, A. R., Manciaux, M., & Romer, C. J. (1991). Mortality and morbidity: The available data and their limitations. In M. Manciaux & C. J. Romer (Eds.), *Accidents in childhood and adolescence.* Geneva: World Health Organization.

Tallandini, M. A., Nicolini, C., & Cristante, F. (1990). Four behavioural patterns in the development of prehension. *Early Child Development and Care, 59,* 29–41.

Tallandini, M. A., & Valentini, P. (1991). Symbolic prototypes in children's drawings of schools. *Journal of Genetic Psychology, 152,* 179–190.

Tamis–LeMonda, C. S., & Bornstein, M. H. (1991). Individual variation, correspondence, stability, and change in mother and toddler play. *Infant Behavior and Development, 14,* 143–162.

Tamis–LeMonda, C. S., & Bornstein, M. H. (1993). Play and its relations to other mental functions in the child. In. M. H. Bornstein. & A. W.. O'Reilly (Eds.), *New directions for child development: No. 59. The role of play in the development of thought.* San Francisco: Jossey–Bass.

Tamis–LeMonda, C. S., Bornstein, M. H., Cyphers, L., Toda, S., & Ogino, M. (1992). Language and play at one year: A comparison of toddlers and mothers in the United States and Japan. *International Journal of Behavioral Development, 15,* 19–42.

Tanguay, P. E., & Russell, A. T. (1991). Mental retardation. In M. Lewis (Ed.), *Child and adolescent psychiatry: A comprehensive textbook.* Baltimore: Williams & Wilkins.

Tannenbaum, A. (1992). Early signs of giftedness: Research and commentary. In P. Klein and A. Tannenbaum (Eds.), *To be young and gifted.* Norwood, NJ: Ablex.

Tanner, J. M. (1982). *Growth at adolescence* (2nd ed.). Oxford: Scientific Publications.

Tanner, J. M. (1989). *Fetus into man: Physical growth from conception to maturity.* Cambridge, MA: Harvard University Press.

Tanner, J. M. (1991a). Adolescent growth spurt, I. In R. M. Lerner, A. C. Petersen, &

J. Brooks–Gunn (Eds.), *Encyclopedia of adolescence.* New York: Garland.

Tanner, J. M. (1991b). Secular trend in age of menarche. In R. M. Lerner, A. C. Petersen, & J. Brooks–Gunn (Eds.), *Encyclopedia of adolescence.* New York: Garland.

Tapp, J. L., & Levine, F. J. (1972). Compliance from kindergarten to college: A speculative research note. *Journal of Adolescence and Youth, 1,* 233–249.

Tappan, M. B., & Packer, M. (1991). Editors' notes. In M. B. Tappan & M. Packer (Eds.), *New directions for child development: No. 54. Narrative and story telling: Implication for understanding moral development.* San Francisco: Jossey–Bass.

Taylor, M., Cartwright, B. S., & Carlson, S. M. (1993). A developmental investigation of children's imaginary companions. *Developmental Psychology, 29,* 276–285.

Taylor, M., & Hort, B. (1990). Can children be trained in making the distinction between appearances and reality? *Cognitive Development, 5,* 89–99.

Taylor, O. L. (1990). Language and communication differences. In G. Shames & E. Wiig (Eds.), *Human communication disorders* (3rd ed.). Columbus, OH: Merrill.

Taylor, R. C., & Richards, S. B. (1991). Patterns of intellectual differences of black, Hispanic and white children. *Psychology in the Schools, 28,* 5–9.

Taylor, R. D., Casten, R., & Flickinger, S. M. (1993). Influence of kinship social support on the parenting experiences and psychosocial adjustment of African-American adolescent. *Developmental Psychology, 29,* 382–388.

Teller, D. Y., & Lindsey, D. T. (1993). Motion nulling techniques and infant color vision. In C. E. Granrud (Ed.), *Visual perception and cognition in infancy.* Hillsdale, NJ: Erlbaum.

Terr, L. C. (1991). Acute responses to external events and posttraumatic stress disorders. In M. Lewis (Ed.), *Child and adolescent psychiatry: A comprehensive textbook.* Baltimore: Williams & Wilkins.

Testa, M. F. (1992). Introduction. In M. K. Rosenheim & M. F. Testa (Eds.), *Early parenthood and coming of age in the 1990s.* New Brunswick, NJ: Rutgers University Press.

Teti, D. M. (1992). Sibling interaction. In V. B. VanHasselt & M. Hersen (Eds.), *Handbook of social development.* New York: Plenum.

Teti, D. M., Gelfand, D. M., & Messinger, D. S. (1992, August). *Attachment security & mothering: Does depression make a difference?* Paper presented at the meeting of the American Psychological Association, Washington, D.C.

Thal, D., & Bates, E. (1990). Continuity and variation in early language development. In J. Colombo & J. Fagen (Eds.), *Individual differences in infancy: Reliability, stability and prediction.* Hillsdale, NJ: Erlbaum.

Thapar, A., Davies, G., Jones, T., & Rivett, M. (1992). Treatment of childhood encopresis: A review. *Child: Care, Health & Development, 18,* 343–353.

Thelen, E. (1990). Dynamical systems and the generation of individual differences. In J. Colombo & J. W. Fagen (Eds.), *Individual differences in infancy: Reliability, stability and prediction.* Hillsdale, NJ: Erlbaum.

Thelen, E., & Adolph, K. E. (1992). Arnold L. Gesell: The paradox of nature and nurture. *Developmental Psychology, 28,* 368–380.

Thelen, E., & Ulrich, B. D. (1991). Hidden skills. *Monographs of the Society for Research in Child Development, 56*(1, Serial No. 223).

Thoma, S. J. (1986). Estimating gender differences in the comprehension and preference of moral issues. *Developmental Review, 6,* 165–180.

Thoman, E. B. (1993). Obligation and option in the premature nursery. *Developmental Review, 13,* 1–30.

Thomas, A., & Chess, S. (1989). Temperament and personality. In G. A. Kohnstamm, J. E. Bates, & M. K. Rothbart (Eds.), *Temperament in childhood.* Chichester, England: Wiley.

Thomas, J. R., & French, K. E. (1985). Gender differences across age in motor performance: A meta-analysis. *Psychological Bulletin, 98,* 260–282.

Thomas, R. M. (1990). Motor development. In R. M. Thomas (Ed.), *The encyclopedia of human development and education: Theory, research, and studies.* Oxford: Pergamon.

Thomas, R. M. (1992). *Comparing theories of child development* (3rd ed.). Belmont, CA: Wadsworth.

Thomas, V. G., & James, M. D. (1988). Body image, dieting tendencies, and sex role traits in urban black women. *Sex Roles, 18,* 523–529.

Thompson, L. A., Detterman, D. K., & Plomin, R. (1991a). Associations between cognitive abilities and scholastic achievement: Genetic overlap but environmental differences. *Psychological Science, 2,* 158–165.

Thompson, L. A., Fagan, J. F., & Fulker, D. W. (1991b). Longitudinal prediction of specific cognitive abilities from infant novelty preference. *Child Development, 62,* 530–538.

Thompson, R. A. (1991a). Attachment theory and research. In M. Lewis (Ed.), *Child and adolescent psychiatry: A comprehensive textbook.* Baltimore: Williams & Wilkins.

Thompson, R. A. (1991b). Infant daycare: Concerns, controversies, choices. In J. V. Lerner & N. L. Galambos (Eds.), *Employed mothers and their children.* New York: Garland.

Thompson, R. A., Lamb, M. E., & Estes, D. (1982). Stability of infant–mother attachment and its relationship to changing life circumstances in an unselected middle-class sample. *Child Development, 53,* 144–148.

Thompson, R. A., & Limber, S. P. (1990). "Social anxiety" in infancy: Stranger and separation reactions. In H. Leitenberg (Ed.), *Handbook of social and evaluation anxiety.* New York: Plenum.

Thompson, S. K. (1975). Gender labels and early sex role development. Child Development, 46, 339–347.

Thomson, M. E., & Kramer, M. S. (1984). Methodologic standards for controlled clinical trials of early contact and maternal–infant behavior. *Pediatrics, 73,* 294–300.

Thorkildsen, T. A. (1993, March). *Morality in the sphere of school.* Paper presented at the meeting of the Society for Research in Child Development, New Orleans, LA.

Thorlindsson, T., & Vilhjalmsson, R. (1991). Factors related to cigarette smoking and alcohol use among adolescents. *Adolescence, 26,* 399–418.

Thorndike, R. L., Hagan, E. P., & Sattler, J. M. (1985). *The Stanford-Binet Intelligence Scale* (4th ed.). Chicago: Riverside.

Thornton, B., Leo, R., & Alberg, K. (1991). Gender role typing, the superwoman ideal, and the potential for eating disorders. *Sex Roles, 25,* 469–484.

Thornton, B., & Ryckman, R. M. (1991). Relationship between physical attractiveness, physical effectiveness, and self-esteem: A cross-sectional analysis among adolescents. *Journal of Adolescence, 14,* 85–98.

Thornton, D., & Reid, R. L. (1982). Moral reasoning and type of criminal offense. *British Journal of Social Psychology, 21,* 231–238.

349,000 Caesareans in '91 called unnecessary (1993, April 23). *New York Times,* p. A16.

Tilghman, S. M. (1993, January 25). Science vs. the female scientist. *New York Times,* p. A11.

Tinsley, B. J. (1992). Multiple influences on the acquisition and socialization of children's health attitudes and behavior: An integrative review. *Child Development, 63,* 1043–1069.

Tiwary, C., & Holguin, A. H. (1992). Prevalence of obesity among children of military dependents at two major medical centers. *American Journal of Public Health, 82,* 354–357.

Tizard, B., Philips, J., & Plewis, I. (1976). Play in preschool centres. *Journal of Child Psychology and Psychiatry, 17,* 265–274.

Tocci, C. M., & Engelhard, G. (1991). Achievement, parental support, and gender differences in attitudes toward mathematics. *Journal of Education Research, 84,* 280–286.

Tolson, T. F. J., & Wilson, M. N. (1990). The impact of two- and three-generational black family structure on perceived family climate. *Child Development, 61,* 416–428.

Tombs, D. A. (1991). Child psychiatric emergencies. In M. Lewis (Ed.), *Child and adolescent psychiatry: A comprehensive textbook.* Baltimore: Williams & Wilkins.

Tomlinson–Keasey, C., & Keasey, C. B. (1974). The mediating role of cognitive development in moral judgment. *Child Development, 45,* 291–298.

Toth, S. L., Manly, J. T., & Cicchetti, D. (1992). Child maltreatment and vulnerability to depression. *Development and Psychopathology, 4,* 97–112.

Treaster, J. B. (1993, February 16). For children of cocaine, fresh reasons for hope. *New York Times,* A1, B12.

Treboux, D., & Busch-Rossnagel, N A. (1990). Social network influences on adolescent sexual attitudes and behaviors. *Journal of Adolescent Research,* 5(2), 175–189.

Treboux, D. A., & Busch-Rossnagel, N. A. (1991). Age differences in adolescent sexual behavior, sexual attitudes and contraceptive use. In R. M. Lerner, A. C. Petersen, & J. Brooks-Gunn (Eds.), *Encyclopedia of adolescence.* New York: Garland.

Trehub, S. E., Schneider, B. A., Thorpe, L. A., & Judge, P. (1991). Observational measures of auditory sensitivity in early infancy. *Developmental Psychology, 27,* 40–49.

Trehub, S. E., Trainor, L. J., & Unyk, A. M. (1993). Music and speech processing in the first year of life. In H. W. Reese (Ed.), *Advances in child development and behavior* (Vol. 24). San Diego, CA: Academic Press.

Trickett, P. K., Aber, J. L., Carlson, V., & Cicchetti, D. (1991). Relationship of socioeconomic status to the etiology and developmental sequelae of physical child abuse. *Developmental Psychology, 27,* 148–158.

Trickett, P. K., & Kuczynski, L. (1986). Children's misbehaviors and parental discipline strategies in abusive and nonabusive families. *Developmental Psychology, 22,* 115–123.

Trickett, P. K., & Putnam, F. W. (1993). Impact of child sexual abuse on females: Toward a developmental, psychobiological integration. *Psychological Science, 4,* 81–87.

Tronick, E. Z. (1989). Emotions and emotional communication in infants. *American Psychologist, 44,* 112–119.

Truesdell, L. A., & Abramson, T. (1992). Academic behavior and grades of mainstreamed students with mild disabilities. *Exceptional Children, 58,* 392–398.

Tryon, A. S., & Keane, S. P. (1991). Popular and aggressive boys' initial social interaction patterns in cooperative and competitive settings. *Journal of Abnormal Child Psychology, 19,* 395–406.

Tsai, L. Y. (1992). Medical treatment in autism. In D. E. Berkell (Ed.), *Autism.* Hillsdale, NJ: Erlbaum.

Tsai, L. Y., & Ghaziuddin, M. (1992). Biomedical research in autism. In D. E. Berkell (Ed.), *Autism.* Hillsdale, NJ: Erlbaum.

Tubman, J. G., Lerner, R. M., Lerner, J. V., & von Eye, A. (1992). Temperament and adjustment in young adulthood: A 15-year longitudinal analysis. *American Journal of Orthopsychiatry, 62,* 564–574.

Tucker, L. A. (1986). The relationships of television viewing to physical fitness and obesity. *Adolescence, 21,* 797–806.

Tucker, L. A. (1987). Television, teenagers and health. *Journal of Youth and Adolescence, 16,* 415–425.

Tuma, J. M. (1989). Mental health services for children. *American Psychologist, 44,* 188–199.

Turiel, D. (1984). Sex role typing and ego identity in Israeli, Oriental, and Western adolescents. *Journal of Personality and Social Psychology, 46,* 440–457.

Turiel, E. (1991). Moral judgment, action, and development. In D. Schrader (Ed.), *New directions for child development: No. 47. The legacy of Lawrence Kohlberg.* San Francisco: Jossey-Bass.

Turkheimer, E. (1991). Individual and group differences in adoption studies of IQ. *Psychological Bulletin, 110,* 392–405.

Turkheimer, E., & Gottesman, I. I. (1991). Individual differences and the canalization of human behavior. *Developmental Psychology, 27,* 18–22.

Turkington, C. (1992, December). Ruling opens door—a crack—to IQ-testing some black kids. *APA Monitor,* pp. 28–29.

Turner, J. S., & Helms, D. B. (1983). *Lifespan development* (2nd ed.). New York: Holt, Rinehart & Winston.

Ullian, D. Z. (1981). The child's construction of gender: Anatomy as destiny. In E. K. Shapiro & E. Weber (Eds.), *Cognitive and affective growth.* Hillsdale, NJ: Erlbaum.

Umbel, V. M., Pearson, B. Z., Fernández, M. C., & Oller, D. K. (1992). Measuring bilingual children's receptive vocabularies. *Child Development, 63,* 1012–1020.

U. N. finds teen-age girls at high risk of AIDS (1993, July 30). *New York Times,* p. A6.

U.S. Bureau of the Census. (1992). *Statistical abstract of the United States: 1992,* 112th ed. Washington, DC: U.S. Government Printing Office.

U.S. Bureau of the Census. (1993). *Statistical abstract of the United States: 1993,* 113th ed. Washington, DC: U.S. Government Printing Office.

U.S. Department of Health and Human Services. (1988). *Study of national incidence and prevalence of child abuse and neglect.* Washington, DC: U.S. Government Printing Office.

U.S. Environmental Protection Agency. (1993). *Respiratory health effects of passive smoking: Lung cancer and other disorders.* Washington, DC: Author.

Uttal, D. H., Lummis, M., & Stevenson, H. W. (1988). Low and high mathematics achievement in Japanese, Chinese, and American elementary-school children. *Developmental Psychology, 24,* 335–342.

Van Brunschot, M., Zarbatany, L., & Strang, K. (1993, March). *Ecological contributions to gender differences in intimacy among peers.* Paper presented at the meeting of the Society for Research in Child Development, New Orleans, LA.

van de Grift, W. (1990). Educational leadership and academic achievement in elementary education. *School Effectiveness and School Improvement, 1,* 26–40.

Vandell, D. L. (1990). Development in twins. In R. Vasta (Ed.), *Annals of child development* (Vol. 7). London: Kingsley.

Vandell, D. L., & Ramanan, J. (1991). Children of the national longitudinal survey of youth: Choices in after-school care and child development. *Developmental Psychology, 27,* 637–643.

Vandell, D. L., & Ramanan, J. (1992). Effects of early and recent maternal employment on children from low-income families. *Child Development, 63,* 938–949.

Van den Bergh, B. R. H. (1990). The influence of maternal emotions during pregnancy on fetal and neonatal behavior. *Pre- and Peri-Natal Psychology, 5,* 119–130.

van IJzendoorn, M. H., & Kroonenberg, P. M. (1988). Cross-cultural patterns of attachment: A meta-analysis of the Strange Situation. *Child Development, 59,* 147–156.

van IJzendoorn, M. H., Sagi, A., & Lambermon, M. W. E. (1992). The multiple caretaker paradox: Data from Holland and Israel. In R. C. Pianta (Ed.), *New directions for child development: No. 57. Beyond the parent: The role of other adults in children's lives.* San Francisco: Jossey-Bass.

Van Kammen, W. B., Loeber, R., & Stouthamer-Lober, M. (1991). Substance use and its relationship to conduct problems and delinquency in young boys. *Journal of Youth and Adolescence, 20,* 399–413.

Vasta, R. (1990). Child abuse. In R. M. Thomas (Ed.), *The encyclopedia of human development and education: Theory, research and studies.* Oxford: Pergamon.

Vaughn, B. E., Stevenson-Hinde, J., Waters, E., Kotsaftis, A., Lefever, G. B., Shouldice, A., Trudel, M., & Belsky, J. (1992). Attachment security and temperament in infancy and early childhood: Some conceptual clarifications. *Developmental Psychology, 28,* 463–473.

Vaughn, S., Hogan, A., Kouzekanani, K., & Shapiro, S. (1990). Peer acceptance, self-perceptions, and social skills of learning disabled students prior to identification. *Journal of Educational Psychology, 82,* 101–106.

Vetter, B. (1992, Fall). Ferment: yes progress: maybe change: slow. *Mosaic, 23*(3), 34–41.

Violato, C., & Grossi, V. (1991, August). *Adolescent suicide and early loss: A stepwise discriminant analysis.* Paper presented at the meeting of the American Psychological Association, San Francisco.

Vitulano, L. A. & Tebes, J. K. (1991). Child and adolescent behavior therapy. In M. Lewis (Ed.), *Child and adolescent psychiatry.* Baltimore: Williams & Wilkins.

Vogel, D. A., Lake, M. A., Evans, S., & Karraker, K. H. (1991). Children's and adult's sex-stereotyped perceptions of infants. *Sex Roles, 24,* 605–616.

Volden, J., & Lord, C. (1991). Neologisms and idiosyncratic language in autistic speakers. *Journal of Autism and Developmental Disorders, 21,* 109–130.

Volkmar, F. R. (1991). Autism and the pervasive developmental disorders. In M. Lewis (Ed.), *Child and adolescent psychiatry.* Baltimore: Williams & Wilkins.

Volling, B. L., & Belsky, J. (1992). The contribution of mother–child and father–child relationships to the quality of sibling interaction: A longitudinal study. *Child Development, 63,* 1209–1222.

Volling, B. L., MacKinnon–Lewis, C., & Dechman, K. (1993, March). *The family correlates of peer rejection and social withdrawal.* Paper presented at the meeting of the Society for Research in Child Development, New Orleans, LA.

Vondracek, F. W. (1991). Vocational development and choice in adolescence. In R. M. Lerner, A. C. Petersen, & J. Brooks–Gunn (Eds.), *Encyclopedia of adolescence.* New York: Garland.

Vorhees, C. V., & Mollnow, E. (1987). Behavioral teratogenesis long-term influences on behavior from early exposure to environmental agents. In J. D. Osofsky (Ed.), *Handbook of infant development* (2nd ed.). New York: Wiley.

Vuchinich, S., Bank, L., & Patterson, G. R. (1992). Parenting, peers, and the stability of antisocial behavior in preadolescent boys. *Developmental Psychology, 28,* 510–521.

Vuchinich, S., Vuchinich, R. A., Hetherington, E. M., & Clingempeel, W. G. (1991). Parent–child interaction and gender differences in early adolescents' adaptation to stepfamilies. *Developmental Psychology, 27,* 618–626.

Vurpillot, E. (1968). The development of scanning strategies and their relation to visual differention. *Journal of Experimental Child Psychology, 6,* 632–650.

Vygotsky, L. S. (1962). *Thought and language.* Cambridge, MA: MIT Press.

Vygotsky, L. (1978). *Mind in society.* Cambridge, MA: Harvard University Press.

Wachs, T. D. (1993). Multidimensional correlates of individual variability in play and exploration. In M. H. Bornstein & A. W. O'Reilly (Eds.), *New directions for child development: No. 59. The role of play in the development of thought.* San Francisco: Jossey–Bass.

Wachs, T. D., Bishry, Z., Sobhy, A., McCabe, G., Galal, O., & Shaheen, F. (1993). Relation of rearing environment to adaptive behavior of Egyptian toddlers. *Child Development, 64,* 586–604.

Wadsworth, K. W., & McLoyd, V. C. (1993, March). *The impact of mother-adolescent self-esteem: Effects of social support.* Paper presented at the meeting of the Society for Research in Child Development, New Orleans, LA.

Wagner, R. K., & Torgesen, J. K. (1987). The nature of phonological processing and its causal role in the acquisition of reading skills. *Psychological Bulletin, 101,* 192–212.

Walden, T. A., & Baxter, A. (1989). The effect of context and age on social referencing. *Child Development, 60,* 1511–1518.

Waldman, S. (1992, May 4). Deadbeat dads. *Newsweek,* pp. 46–51.

Waldman, S., & Springen, K. (1992, November 16). Too old, too fast? *Newsweek,* pp. 80–88.

Walker, L. J. (1982). The sequentiality of Kohlberg's stages of moral development. *Child Development, 53,* 1330–1336.

Walker, L. J. (1984). Sex differences in the development of moral reasoning: A critical review. *Child Development, 55,* 677–691.

Walker, L. J. (1991). Sex differences in moral reasoning. In W. M. Kurtines & J. L. Gewirtz (Eds.), *Handbook of moral behavior and development* (Vol. 2). Hillsdale, NJ: Erlbaum.

Walker, L. J. (1993, March). *Is the family a sphere of moral growth for children?* Paper presented at the meeting of the Society for Research in Child Development, New Orleans, LA.

Walker, L. J., & Taylor, J. H. (1991a). Family interactions and the development of moral reasoning. *Child Development, 62,* 264–283.

Walker, L. J., & Taylor, J. H. (1991b). Stage transitions in moral reasoning: A longitudinal study of development processes. *Developmental Psychology, 27,* 330–337.

Waller, D. K., Lustig, L. S., Cunningham, G. C., Golbus, M. S., & Hook, E. B. (1991). Second-trimester maternal serum alpha-fetoprotein levels and the risk of subsequent fetal death. *New England Journal of Medicine, 325,* 6–10.

Wallerstein, J. S. (1991). The long-term effects of divorce on children: A review. *Journal of the American Academy of Child and Adolescent Psychiatry, 30,* 349–360.

Wallerstein, J. S., & Blakeslee, S. (1990). *Second chances.* New York: Ticknor & Fields.

Wallis, C. (1987, February 16). The big chill: Fear of AIDS. *Time,* pp. 50–56.

Walter, H. J., Vaughan, R. D., & Cohall, A. T. (1991a). Psychosocial influences on acquired immunodeficiency syndrome-risk behaviors among high school students. *Pediatrics, 88,* 846–852.

Walter, H. J., Vaughan, R. D., & Cohall, A. T. (1991b). Risk factors for substance use among high school students: Implications for prevention. *Journal of the American Academy of Child and Adolescent Psychiatry, 130,* 556–562.

Walton, G. E., Bower, N. J. A., & Bower, T. G. R. (1992). Recognition of familiar faces by newborns. *Infant Behavior and Development, 15,* 265–269.

Wang, M. C., Haertel, G. D., & Walberg, H. J. (1990). What influences learning? A content analysis of review literature. *Journal of Educational Research, 84,* 30–43.

Wang, M. C., Haertel, G. D., & Walberg, H. J. (1993). Toward a knowledge base for school learning. *Review of Educational Research, 63,* 249–294.

Ward, B. J. (1991). Irlen lenses. *Journal of Learning Disabilities, 24,* 514–516.

Wardlaw, G. M., & Insel, P. M. (1993). *Perspectives in nutrition.* (2nd ed.). St. Louis, MO: Mosby–Yearbook.

Washington State plans tighter child-labor rules. (1992, August 19). *New York Times,* p. A12.

Wasik, B. H., Ramey, C. T., Bryant, D. M., & Sparling, J. J. (1990). A longitudinal study of two early intervention strategies: Project CARE. *Child Development, 61,* 1682–1696.

Wasserman, A. L. (1984). A prospective study of the impact of home monitoring on the family. *Pediatrics, 74,* 323–329.

Wasserman, G., Graziano, J. H., Factor–Litvak, P., Popovac, D., Morina, N., Musabegovic, A., Vrenezi, N., Capuni–Paracka, S. Lekic, V., Preteni–Redjepi, E., Hadzialjevic, S., Slavkovich, V., Kline, J., Shrout, P., & Stein, Z. (1992). Independent effects of lead exposure and iron deficiency anemia on developmental outcome at age 2 years. *Journal of Pediatrics, 121,* 695–703.

Waterman, A. S. (1985). Identity in the context of adolescent psychology. In A. S. Waterman (Ed.), *Identity in adolescence: Processes and contents.* San Francisco: Jossey–Bass.

Waterman, A. S. (1992). Identity as an aspect of optimal psychological functioning. In G. R. Adams, T. P. Gullotta, & R. Montemayor (Eds.), *Adolescent identity formation.* Newbury Park, CA: Sage.

Waterman, A. S., & Archer, S. L. (1990). A life-span perspective on identity formation: Developments in form, function, and process. In P. B. Baltes, D. L. Featherman, & R. M. Lerner (Eds.), *Life-span development and behavior* (Vol. 10). Hillsdale, NJ: Erlbaum.

Watkins, B., & Bentovim, A. (1992). The sexual abuse of male children and adolescents: A review of current research. *Journal of Child Psychology and Psychiatry, 33,* 197–248.

Watson, J. B. (1924). *Behaviorism.* New York: Norton.

Watson, J. D., & Crick, F. H. C. (1958). Molecular structure of nucleic acids: A structure for deoxyribose nucleic acid. *Nature, 171,* 737–738.

Watson, M. F., & Protinsky, H. (1991, Winter). Identity status of black adolescents: An empirical investigation. *Adolescence, 26,* 963–966.

Watson, M. W., & Getz, K. (1990). Developmental shifts in Oedipal behaviors related to family role understanding. In I. Bretherton & M. W. Watson (Eds.), *New directions for child development: No. 48. Children's perspectives on the family.* San Francisco: Jossey–Bass.

Watts, W. D., & Wright, L. S. (1990). The relationship of alcohol, tobacco, marijuana, and other illegal drug use to delinquency among Mexican-American, black, and white adolescent males. *Adolescence, 25,* 171–181.

Waxman, S. R. (1990). Linguistic biases and the establishment of conceptual hierarchies: Evidence from preschool children. *Cognitive Development, 5,* 123–150.

Waxman, S. R., & Kosowski, T. D. (1990). Nouns mark category relations: Toddlers' and preschoolers' word-learning biases. *Child Development, 61,* 1461–1473.

Waxman, S. R., & Senghas, A. (1992). Relations among word meaning in early lexical development. *Developmental Psychology, 28,* 862–873.

Wechsler, D. (1975). Intelligence defined and undefined: A relativistic appraisal. *American Psychologist, 30,* 135–139.

Wegman, M. E. (1992, December). Annual summary of vital statistics—1991. *Pediatrics, 90,* 835–845.

Weikart, D. P., & Schweinhart, L. J. (1991). Disadvantaged children and curriculum effects. In L. Rescorla, M. C. Hyson, & K. Hirsh–Pasek (Eds.), *New directions in child development: No. 53. Academic instruction in early childhood: Challenge or pressure?* San Francisco: Jossey–Bass.

Weinberg, R. A. (1989). Intelligence and IQ. *American Psychologist, 44,* 98–104.

Weiner, T. S., & Adolph, K. E. (1993, March). *Toddler's perception of slant vs. slope height for descending slopes.* Paper presented at the meeting of the Society for Research in Child Development, New Orleans, LA.

Weinraub, M., Clemens, L. P., Sockloff, A., Ethridge, T., Gracely, E., & Myers, B. (1984). The development of sex role stereotypes in the third year: Relationships to gender labeling, gender identity, sex-typed toy preference, and family characteristics, *Child Development, 55,* 1493–1503.

Weisman, S. R. (1992, April 27). How do Japan's students do it? They cram. *New York Times,* pp. A1, 6.

Weisner, T. S., & Wilson–Mitchell, J. E. (1990). Nonconventional family life-styles and sex typing. *Child Development, 61,* 1915–1933.

Weiss, B., Dodge, K. A., Bates, J. E., & Pettit, G. S. (1992). Some consequences of early harsh discipline: Child aggression and a maladaptive social information processing style. *Child Development, 63,* 1321–1335.

Weiss, G. (1990). Hyperactivity in childhood. *New England Journal of Medicine, 323,* 1413–1415.

Weiss, G. (1991). Attention deficit hyperactivity disorder. In M. Lewis (Ed.), *Child and adolescent psychiatry: A comprehensive textbook.* Baltimore: Williams & Wilkins.

Weiss, R. J. (1982). Understanding moral thought: Effects on moral reasoning and decision-making. *Developmental Psychology, 18,* 852–861.

Weissberg, J. A., & Paris, S. G. (1986). Young children's remembering in different contexts: A reinterpretation of Istomine's study. *Child Development, 57,* 1123–1129.

Weisz, J. R., Sigman, M., Weiss, B., & Mosk, J. (1993). Parent reports of behavioral and emotional problems among children in Kenya, Thailand, and the United States. *Child Development, 64,* 98–109.

Weisz, J. R., Weiss, B., Wasserman, A. A., & Rintoul, B. (1987). Control-related beliefs and depression among clinic-referred children and adolescents. *Journal of Abnormal Psychology, 96,* 58–63.

Weitzman, L. M., & Fitzgerald, L. F. (1993). Employed mothers: Diverse life-styles and labor force profiles. In J. Frankel (Ed.), *The employed mother and the family context.* New York: Springer.

Weitzman, M., Aschengrau, A., Bellinger, D., Jones, R., Hamlin, J. S., & Beiser, A. (1993). Lead-contaminated soil abatement and urban children's blood lead levels. *Journal of the American Medical Association, 269,* 1647–1654.

Weitzman, M., Gortmaker, S., & Sobol, A. (1992). Maternal smoking and behavior problems of children. *Pediatrics, 90,* 342–348.

Weitzman, M., & Siegel, D. M. (1992). What we have not learned from what we know about excessive school absence and school dropout. *Developmental and Behavioral Pediatrics, 13,* 55–58.

Weller, E. B., & Weller, R. A. (1991). Mood disorders. In M. Lewis (Ed.), *Child and adolescent psychiatry: A comprehensive textbook.* Baltimore: Williams & Wilkins.

Wellman, H. M., & Banerjee, M. (1991). Mind and emotion: Children's understanding of the emotional consequences of beliefs and desires. *British Journal of Developmental Psychology, 9,* 191–214.

Wellman, H. M., Cross, D., & Bartsch, K. (1986). Infant search and object permanence: A meta-analysis of the A-not-B error. *Monographs of the Society for Research in Child Development, 5*(3, Serial No. 214).

Wells, K. (1980). Gender-role identity and psychological adjustment in adolescence. *Journal of Youth and Adolescence, 9,* 59–73.

Wen, S. W., Goldenberg, R. L., Cutter, G. R., Hoffman, H. J., Cliver, S. P., Davis, R. O., & DuBard, M. B. (1990, January). Smoking, maternal age, fetal growth, and gestational age at delivery. *American Journal of Obstetrics and Gynecology, 162,* 53–58.

Wenar, C. (1990). Childhood fears and phobias. In M. Lewis & S. M. Miller (Eds.), *Handbook of developmental psychopathology.* New York: Plenum.

Wentzel, K. R. (1991). Relations between social competence and academic achievement in early adolescence. *Child Development, 62,* 1066–1078.

Wentzel, K. R., Feldman, S. S., & Weinberger, D. A. (1991). Parental child rearing and academic achievement in boys: The mediational role of social-emotional adjustment. *Journal of Early Adolescence, 11,* 321–339.

Werker, J. (1989). Becoming a native listener. *American Scientist, 77,* 54–59.

Werner, E. E. (1988). A cross-cultural perspective on infancy. *Journal of Cross-Cultural Psychology, 19,* 96–113.

Werner, E. E. (1989). High-risk children in young adulthood: A longitudinal study from birth to 32 years. *American Journal of Orthopsychiatry, 59,* 72–81.

Werner, E. E. (1990). Protective factors and individual resilience. In S. J. Meisels & J. P. Shonkoff (Eds.), *Handbook of early childhood intervention.* Cambridge: Cambridge University Press.

Werner, E. E., & Smith, R. S. (1992). *Overcoming the odds.* Ithaca, NY: Cornell University Press.

Werner, L. A., & Bargones, J. Y. (1992). Psychoacoustic development of human infants. In C. Rovee–Collier & L. P. Lipsitt (Eds.), *Advances in infancy research* (Vol. 7). Norwood, NJ: Ablex.

Werner, L. A., & Gillenwater, J. M. (1990). Pure-tone sensitivity of 2- to 5-week-old infants. *Infant Behavior and Development, 13,* 355–375.

Werry, J. S. (1991). Brain and behavior. In M. Lewis (Ed.), *Child and adolescent psychiatry: A comprehensive textbook.* Baltimore: Williams & Wilkins.

Westerman, M. A. (1990). Coordination of maternal directives with preschoolers' behavior in compliance-problem and healthy dyads. *Developmental Psychology, 26,* 621–630.

Wetherby, A. M., & Prizant, B. M. (1992). Facilitating language and communication development in autism: Assessment and intervention guidelines. In D. E. Berkell (Ed.), *Autism.* Hillsdale, NJ: Erlbaum.

Wexler, N. (1993, Spring). Presymptomatic testing for Huntington's disease. *National Forum,* pp. 22–26.

Whalen, C. K., & Henker, B. (1991). Therapies for hyperactive children: Comparisons, combinations, and compromises. *Journal of Consulting and Clinical Psychology, 59,* 126–137.

Whalen, C. K., & Henker, B. (1992, October). The social profile of attention-deficit hyperactivity disorder. *Child and Adolescent Psychiatric Clinics of North America, 1,* 395–410.

Where the Norplant debate hits home. (1993, March 7). *New York Times,* p. 17.

Whiffen, V. E., & Gotlib, I. H. (1989). Infants of postpartum depressed mothers: Temperament and cognitive status. *Journal of Abnormal Psychology, 98,* 274–279.

Whitaker, A., Johnson, J., Shaffer, D., Rapoport, J. L., Kalikow, K., Walsh, B. T., Davies, M., Braiman, S., & Dolinsky, A. (1990). Uncommon troubles in young people: Prevalence estimates of selected psychiatric disorders in a nonreferred adolescent population. *Archives of General Psychiatry, 47,* 487–496.

Whitall, J. (1991). The developmental effect of concurrent cognitive and locomotor skills: Time-sharing from a dynamical perspective. *Journal of Experimental Child Psychology, 51,* 245–266.

White, C. B., Bushnell, N., & Regnemer, J. L. (1978). Moral development in Bahamian school children: A three-year examination of Kohlberg's stages of moral development. *Developmental Psychology, 14,* 58–65.

White, D. M., & Sprague, R. L. (1992). The "attention deficit" in children with attention-deficit hyperactivity disorder. In B. B. Lahey & A. E. Kazdin (Eds.), *Advances in clinical child psychology* (Vol. 14). New York: Plenum.

White, J. L., Moffitt, T. E., & Silva, P. A. (1989). A prospective replication of the protective effects of IQ in subjects at high risk for juvenile delinquency. *Journal of Consulting and Clinical Psychology, 57,* 719–724.

White, R. W. (1959). Motivation reconsidered: The concept of competence. *Psychological Review, 66,* 297–333.

White, S. D., & DeBlassie, R. R. (1992). Adolescent sexual behavior. *Adolescence, 27,* 183–191.

Whitehead, J. R., & Corbin, C. B. (1991). Effects of fitness test type, teacher, and gender on exercise intrinsic motivation and physical self-worth. *Journal of School Health, 61,* 11–16.

Whitehurst, G. J. (1982). Language development. In B. B. Wolman (Ed.), *Handbook of developmental psychology.* Englewood Cliffs, NJ: Prentice Hall.

Whitehurst, G. J., Arnold, D. S., Epstein, J. N., Angell, A. L., Smith, M., & Fischel, J. E. (1993, March). *A picture book reading intervention in daycare and home for children from low-income families.* Paper presented at the meeting of the Society for Research in Child Development, New Orleans, LA.

Whitehurst, G. J., & Valdez–Menchaca, M. C. (1988). What is the role of reinforcement in early language acquisition? *Child Development, 59,* 430–440.

Whiting, B. B., & Edwards, C. P. (1988). *Children of different worlds.* Cambridge, MA: Harvard University Press.

Widaman, J. F., MacMillan, D. L., Hemsley, R. E., Little, T. D., & Balow, I. H. (1992). Differences in adolescents' self-concept as a function of academic level, ethnicity, and gender. *American Journal on Mental Retardation, 96,* 387–404.

Wideman, M. V., & Singer, J. F. (1984). The role of psychological mechanisms in preparation for childbirth. *American Psychologist, 34,* 1357–1371.

Widom, C. S. (1991). Childhood victimization: Risk factor for delinquency. In M. E. Colten & S. Gore (Eds.), *Adolescent stress: Causes and consequences.* New York: Aldine deGruyter.

Wiener, J., & Harris, P. J. (1993, March). *Social interaction of children with and without learning disabilities in dyads and small groups.* Paper presented at the meeting of the Society for Research in Child Development, New Orleans, LA.

Wigfield, A., & Eccles, J. S. (1992). The development of achievement task values: A theoretical analysis. *Developmental Review, 12,* 265–310.

Wilcox, A. J., Weinberg, C. R., O'Connor, J. F., Baird, D. D., Schlatterer, J. P., Canfield, R. E., Armstrong, E. G., & Nisula, B. C. (1988). Incidence of early loss in pregnancy. *New England Journal of Medicine, 319,* 189–194.

Wilcox, B. L. (1990). Federal policy and adolescent AIDS. In W. Gardner, S. G. Millstein, & B. L. Wilcox (Eds.), *New directions for child development: No. 50. Adolescents in the AIDS epidemic.* San Francisco: Jossey–Bass.

Willer, B., & Bredekamp, S. (1990, July). Redefining readiness: An essential requisite for educational reform. *Young Children,* 22–24.

Williams, H. (1983). *Perceptual and motor development.* Englewood Cliffs, NJ: Prentice Hall.

Williams, L. (1992, February 6). Girl's self-image is mother of the woman. *New York Times,* pp. A1, 12.

Williams, M. C., & Lovegrove, W. (1992). Sensory and perceptual processing in reading disability. In J. R. Brannan (Ed.), *Advances in psychology: Vol. 86. Applications of parallel processing in vision.* Amsterdam: North–Holland.

Williams, R. L. (1974, May). Scientific racism and IQ: The silent mugging of the black community. *Psychology Today,* p. 32.

Williams, S. R., & Worthington, B. S. (1988). *Nutrition throughout the life cycle.* St. Louis: Mosby.

Willis, D. J., Holden, E. W., & Rosenberg, M. (Eds.). (1992). *Prevention of child maltreatment.* New York: Wiley.

Wills, T. A., Vaccaro, D., & McNamara, G. (1991). *Three domains of competence relate to adolescent substance use.* Washington, DC: National Institute on Drug Abuse.

Wilson, C., Nettelbeck, T., Turnbull, C., & Young, R. (1992). IT, IQ and age: A comparison of developmental functions. *British Journal of Developmental Psychology, 10,* 179–188.

Wilson, G. L. (1991). Comment: Transgenerational patterns of suicide attempt. *Journal of Consulting and Clinical Psychology, 59,* 869–873.

Wilson, J. A. R. (1990a). Brain development and function. In R. M. Thomas (Ed.), *The encyclopedia of human development and education: Theory, research and studies.* Oxford: Pergamon.

Wilson, J. A. R. (1990b). Brain laterality. In R. M. Thomas (Ed.), *The encyclopedia of human development and education: Theory, research and studies.* Oxford: Pergamon.

Wilson, J. R., & Crowe, L. (1991). Genetics of alcoholism. *Alcohol Health and Research World, 15,* 11–17.

Windell, J. (1991). *Discipline: A sourcebook of 50 failsafe techniques for parents.* Indialantic, FL: Collier Books.

Windle, M. (1991). Externalizing disorders (conduct problems). In R. M. Lerner, A. C. Petersen, & J. Brooks–Gunn (Eds.), *Encyclopedia of adolescence.* New York: Garland.

Windle, M. (1992a, August). *Familial influences on adolescent substance abuse.* Paper presented at the meeting of the American Psychological Association, Washington, DC.

Windle, M. (1992b). A longitudinal study of stress buffering for adolescent problem behaviors. *Developmental Psychology, 28,* 522–530.

Winer, G. A. (1980). Class-inclusion reasoning in children: A review of the empirical literature. *Child Development, 51,* 309–328.

Winner, E. (1989). Development in the visual arts. In W. Damon (Ed.), *Child development today and tomorrow.* San Francisco: Jossey–Bass.

Wolf, A., & Lozoff, B. (1989). Object attachment, thumbsucking, and the passage to sleep. *Journal of the American Academy of Child and Adolescent Psychiatry, 28,* 287–292.

Wolff, S. (1991). Moral development. In M. Lewis (Ed.), *Child and adolescent psychiatry: A comprehensive textbook.* Baltimore: Williams & Wilkins.

Wolfner, G. D., & Gelles, R. J. (1993). A profile of violence toward children: A national study. *Child Abuse and Neglect, 17,* 197–212.

Wolock, I., & Horowitz, B. (1984). Child maltreatment as a social problem: The neglect of neglect. *American Journal of Orthopsychiatry, 54,* 530–543.

Women can gain more in pregnancy, panel says. (1990, June 7). *New York Times,* p. 8.

Wong, K. L., Kauffman, J. M., & Lloyd, J. W. (1991). Choices for integration: Selecting teachers for mainstreamed students with emotional or behavioral disorders. *Intervention in School and Clinic, 27,* 108–115.

Wong, M. M., & Csikzentmihalyi, M. (1991). Affiliation motivation and daily experience: Some issues on gender differences. *Journal of Personality and Social Psychology, 60,* 154–164.

Wong, N. D., Hei, T. K., Qaqundah, P. Y., Davidson, D. M., Bassin, S. L., & Gold, K. V. (1992). Television viewing and pediatric hypercholesterolemia. *Pediatrics, 90,* 75–79.

Woodard, J. L., & Fine, M. A. (1991). Long-term effects of self-supervised and adult-supervised child care arrangements on personality traits, emotional adjustment, and cognitive development. *Journal of Applied Developmental Psychology, 12,* 73–85.

Woods, N. S., Eyler, F. D., Behnke, M., & Conlon, M. (1993). Cocaine use during pregnancy: Maternal depressive symptoms and infant neurobehavior over the first month. *Infant Behavior and Development, 16,* 83–98.

Woodward, A. L., & Markman, E. M. (1991). Constraints on learning as default assumptions: Comments on Merriman and Bowman's "The mutuality exclusivity bias in children's word learning." *Developmental Review, 11,* 137–163.

Woodward, K. L. (1993, February 22). A search for limits. *Newsweek,* pp. 52–53.

Woolfolk, A. E. (1987). *Educational psychology* (3rd ed.). Englewood Cliffs, NJ: Prentice Hall.

Woolley, J. D., & Wellman, H. M. (1990). Young children's understanding of realities, nonrealities, and appearances. *Child Development, 61,* 946–961.

Woolley, J. D., & Wellman, H. M. (1993). Origin and truth: Young children's understanding of imaginary mental representations. *Child Development, 64,* 1–17.

Woolston, J. L. (1991). *Eating and growth disorders in infants and children.* Newbury Park, CA: Sage.

Worell, J. (1990). Images of women in psychology. In M. Paludi & G. A. Steuernagel (Eds.), *Foundations for a feminist restructuring of the academic disciplines.* New York: Harrington Park.

WuDunn, S. (1991, February 26). The castaway babies of the Chinese: Heartless feudal practice lives on. *New York Times,* p. A4.

Wuitchik, M., Hesson, K., & Bakal, D. A. (1990, December). Perinatal predictors of pain and distress during labor. *Birth, 17,* 186–191.

Wynn, K. (1990). Children's understanding of counting. *Cognition, 36,* 155–193.

Wynn, K. (1992a, August 27). Addition and subtraction by human infants. *Nature, 358,* pp. 749–750.

Wynn, K. (1992b). Children's acquisition of the number words and the counting system. *Cognitive Psychology, 24,* 220–251.

Yamazaki, J. N., & Schull, W. J. (1990). Perinatal loss and neurological abnormalities among children of the atomic bomb. *Journal of the American Medical Association, 264,* 605–609.

Yaniv, I., & Shatz, M. (1988). Children's understanding of perceptibility. In J. W. Astinton, P. L. Harris, & D. R. Olson (Eds.), *Developing theories of mind.* London: Cambridge University Press.

Yaniv, I., & Shatz, M. (1991). Heuristics of reasoning and analogy in children's visual perspective taking. *Child Development, 61,* 1491–1501.

Yarrow, L. J., & Goodwin, M. S. (1973). The immediate impact of separation: Reactions of infants to a change in mother figures. In L. J. Stone, H. T. Smith, & L. B. Murphy (Eds.), *The competent infant: Research and commentary.* New York: Basic Books.

Yarrow, L. J., Goodwin, M. S., Manheimer, H., & Milowe, I. D. (1971, March). *Infant experiences and cognitive and personality development at ten years.* Paper presented at the meeting of the American Orthopsychiatric Association, Washington, DC.

Yatani, C. (1992, August). *School performance of Asian-American and Asian children: Myth and fact.* Paper presented at the meeting of the American Psychological Association, Washington, DC.

Yates, T. (1991). Theories of cognitive development. In M. Lewis (Ed.), *Child and adolescent psychiatry: A comprehensive textbook.* Baltimore: Williams & Williams.

Yesalis, C. E. (1991). Anabolic steroids, nonmedical use by adolescents. In R. M. Lerner, A. C. Petersen, & J. Brooks–Gunn (Eds.), *Encyclopedia of adolescence.* New York: Garland.

Yirmiya, N., Sigman, M. D., Kasari, C., & Mundy, P. (1992). Empathy and cognition in high-functioning children with autism. *Child Development, 63,* 150–160.

York, J., Vandercook, T., MacDonald, C., Heise–Neff, C., & Caughey, E. (1992). Feedback about integrating middle-school students with severe disabilities in general education classes. *Exceptional Children, 58,* 244–258.

Young, G., & Gagnon, M. (1990). Neonatal laterality, birth stress, familial sinistrality, and left-brain inhibition. *Developmental Neuropsychology, 6,* 127–150.

Youngblade, L. M., & Belsky, J. (1992). Parent–child antecedents of 5-year-olds' close friendships: A longitudinal analysis. *Developmental Psychology, 28,* 700–713.

Youngstrom, N. (1991, September). Drug exposure in home elicits worst behaviors. *APA Monitor,* p. 23.

Youngstrom, N. (1992a, April). Fetal alcohol syndrome carries severe deficits. *APA Monitor,* p. 32.

Youngstrom, N. (1992b, October). Minority youth who are gay: A tough road, but there's hope. *APA Monitor,* pp. 36–37.

Youniss, J., & Haynie, D. L. (1992). Friendship in adolescence. *Developmental and Behavioral Pediatrics, 13,* 59–66.

Yuille, J. C., & Wells, G. (1991). Concerns about the application of research findings: The issue of ecological validity. In J. Doris (Ed.), *The suggestibility of children's recollections.* Washington, DC: American Psychological Association.

Yule, W. (1992). Review: Neurotoxicity of lead. *Child: Care, Health, and Development, 18,* 321–337.

Zabin, L. S. (1991). Early sexual onset. In R. M. Lerner, A. C. Petersen, & J. Brooks–Gunn (Eds.), *Encyclopedia of adolescence.* New York: Garland.

Zahn–Waxler, C., Radke–Yarrow, M., & Wagner, E. (1992). Development of concern for others. *Developmental Psychology, 28,* 126–136.

Zahr, L. K., Parker, S., & Cole, J. (1992). Comparing the effects of neonatal intensive care unit intervention on premature infants at different weights. *Developmental and Behavioral Pediatrics, 13,* 165–172.

Zametkin, A. J., Nordahl, T. E., Gross, M., King, A. C., Semple, W. E., Rumsey, J., Hamburger, S., & Cohen, R. M. (1990). Cerebral glucose metabolism in adults with hyperactivity of childhood onset. *New England Journal of Medicine, 323,* 1361–1366.

Zarbatany, L., Hartmann, D. P., & Rankin, D. B. (1990). The psychological function of pre-adolescent peer activities. *Child Development, 61,* 1067–1080.

Zaslow, M. J. (1991). Variation in child care quality and its implications for children. *Journal of Social Issues, 47,* 125–138.

Zaslow, M. J., Rabinovich, B. A., & Suwalsky, J. T. D. (1991). From maternal employment to child outcomes: Pre-existing group differences and moderating variables. In S. V. Lerner & N. L. Galambos (Eds.), *Employed mothers and their children.* New York: Garland.

Zelazo, N. A., Zelazo, P. R., Cohen, K. M., & Zelazo, P. D. (1993). Specificity of practice effects on elementary neuromotor patterns. *Developmental Psychology, 29,* 686–691.

Zera, D. (1992, Winter). Coming of age in a heterosexist world: The development of gay and lesbian adolescents. *Adolescence, 27,* 849–854.

Zeskind, P. S., & Ramey, C. T. (1981). Preventing intellectual and interactional sequelae of fetal malnutrition: A longitudinal, transactional, and synergistic approach to development. *Child Development, 52,* 213–218.

Zeskind, P. S., & Shingler, L. (1991). Child abusers' perceptual responses to newborn infant cries varying in pitch. *Infant Behavior and Development, 14,* 335–347.

Zheng, S., & Colombo, J. (1989). Sibling configuration and gender differences in preschool social participation. *Journal of Genetic Psychology, 150,* 45–50.

Zigler, E., Abelson, W. D., Trickett, P. K., & Seitz, V. (1982). Is an intervention program necessary in order to improve economically disadvantaged children's IQ scores? *Child Development, 53,* 340–348.

Zigler, E., & Seitz, V. (1982). Social policy and intelligence. In R. Sternberg (Ed.), *Handbook of human intelligence.* New York: Cambridge University Press.

Zigler, E., & Styfco, S. J. (1993). Using research and theory to justify and inform Head Start expansion. *Social Policy Report, 7*(2), 1–21.

Zigler, E., & Styfco, S. J. (1994). Head Start: Criticisms in a constructive context. *American Psychologist, 49,* 127–132.

Zigler, E. Taussig, C., & Black, K. (1992, August). Early childhood intervention: A promising preventive for juvenile delinquency. *American Psychologist, 47,* 997–1006.

Zill, N. (1988). Behavior, achievement, and health problems among children in stepfamilies: Findings from a national survey of child health. In E. M. Hetherington & J. D. Arasteh (Eds.), *Impact of divorce, single-parenting, and stepparenting on children.* Hillsdale, NJ: Erlbaum.

Zucker, R. A., & Fitzgerald, H. E. (1991). Early developmental factors and risk for alcohol problems. *Alcohol Health and Research World, 15,* 18–24.

Zuckerman, B., & Frank, D. A. (1992, February). "Crack kids": Not broken. *Pediatrics, 89,* 337–339.

Zukow, P. G. (Ed.). (1989). *Sibling interaction across cultures.* New York: Springer–Verlag.

# Photo Acknowledgments

**Chapter 1** p. 5: © Michael Heron/Woodfin Camp. p. 9: © Jerry Howard/Positive Images. p. 15: © Museo del Prado, Madrid. All rights reserved. Total or partical reproduction prohibited. p. 16: Reproduced from the collections of the Library of Congress. p. 19: © Comstock. p. 24: © David Austen/Stock, Boston. p. 26: © Bob Daemmrich/Stock, Boston. p. 29: © Bradley University. p. 30: © Jodi Buren. **Chapter 2** p. 41: © George Karger/Life Magazine. p. 42: © National Library of Medicine. p. 45 (from top): © Michael Keller/Uniphoto; © Peter Southwick/Stock, Boston; © Jeff Greenberg/The Picture Cube; © Tim Davis/Photo Researchers; © Billy Barnes/Stock, Boston; © Jefrey Myers/Photo Network; © Tony Freeman/PhotoEdit; © Ulrike Welsch. p. 46: Doonesbury © 1986 G. B. Trudeau. Reprinted with permission of Universal Press Syndicate. All rights reserved. p. 47: Courtesy of Renate Horney. p. 49: © Harvard University Archives. p. 51: © The Ferdinand Hamburger, Jr. Archives of The Johns Hopkins University. p. 53: © Chris Johnson/Stock, Boston. p. 58: © Billy Barnes/PhotoEdit. p. 59: © Stanford University News Service. p. 59: © Tony Freeman/PhotoEdit. p. 61: © 1980 Yves de Braine/Black Star. p. 67: Photo by Chris Hildreth/Cornell University Photography. p. 72: Courtesy of Dr. Kenneth B. Clark. **Chapter 3** p. 85: © Elaine Rebman/Photo Researchers. p. 89: © March of Dimes Birth Defects Foundation. p. 91: © Jason C. Birnholz, M.D., Diagnostic Ultrasound Consultants, Oak Brook, IL. p. 94: © Wide World Photos, Inc. p. 95: © Biophoto Associates/Photo Researchers. p. 97: © Francis Leroy/Biocosmos/Photo Science Library. p. 99: © AP/Wide World Photos. p. 103: © Petit Format/Nestle/Science Source/PR. p. 106: © Petit Format/Nestle/Science Source/PR. p. 107: © Petit Format/Nestle/Science Source/PR. p. 108: © Petit Format/Nestle/Science Source/PR. p. 109: © Petit Format/Nestle/Science Source/PR. p. 118: © 1990 Ted Wood. p. 119: Reprinted by permission of the American Cancer Society. **Chapter 4** p. 129: © David Sams/Texas Inprint. p. 132: © MacDonald Photography/Picture Cube. p. 133: © Tom Tucker/Photo Researchers. p. 134: © 1992 G&J/Black Star. p. 142: © Peter Menzel/Stock, Boston. p. 147: © Dan Bryant. p. 148 (top): © Dan Bryant. p. 148 (bottom): © Dan Bryant. p. 149 (top): © 1992 Praefice/G&J/Black Star. p. 149 (bottom): © 1990 Chris Priest/Custom Medical Stock Photography. p. 150: © 1991 David Weinstein & Assoc/Custom Medical Stock Photography. p. 151: © David H. Linton, courtesy of Ann Linton. p. 152: © Elizabeth Crews. p. 154: © D. S. Rosenstein & H. Oster, "Differential facial responses to four basic tastes in newborns," *Child Development,* 1988, *59.* p. 156: © Anthony DeCasper/Univ of North Carolina. p. 161: © David C. Bitters/The Picture Cube. p. 169: © Four By Five/Super Stock. p. 170: © Robert DeLucia. p. 175: © Pan American Health Organization. p. 176: © Bobbi Carrey/The Picture Cube. p. 182: © Felicia Martinez/PhotoEdit. p. 184 (top): © Elizabeth Crews. p. 184 (bottom): © Tony Freeman/Photo Edit. p. 186: © Joel Gordon 1993. p. 190: © Enricho Ferorelli. **Chapter 6** p. 201: © Elizabeth Crews. © p. 202: © Elizabeth Crews. p. 203: © Sandra Lousada/Woodfin Camp. p. 204: © Elizabeth Crews. p. 205: © Elizabeth Crews. p. 208 (top left): © Doug Goodman/Monkmeyer Press. p. 208 (top right): © Doug Goodman/Monkmeyer Press. p. 208 (bottom row): © George Zimbel/Monkmeyer Press. p. 211: © David Sanders/Arizona Daily Star. p. 212 (top): © courtesy of Carolyn Rovee-Collier. p. 212 (bottom): © From A. N. Meltzoff & M.K. Moore, 1977, "Imitation of facial and manual gestures by human neonates." *Science, 198,* 75–78. p. 214: © Courtesy of The Psychological Corporation. p. 216: © David Sams/Texas Inprint. p. 225: © Spencer Grant/The Picture Cube. p. 227: © For Better or for Worse © 1991 Lynn Johnston Prod. Reprinted with permission of Universal Press Syndicate. All rights reserved. **Chapter 7** p. 235: © Mary D. S. Ainsworth. p. 237: © Karen Kasmauski/Woodfin Camp. p. 239: © Margaret Miller/Photo Researchers. p. 243: © Harlow Primate Laboratory, University of Wisconsin. p. 244: © L. J. Weinstein/Woodfin Camp. p. 245: © Nina Leen/*Life* Magazine—Time, Inc. p. 247: © Harlow Primate Laboratory, University of Wisconsin. p. 250: © Hamblin/Liaison International. p. 253: © Courtesy of the Autism Society of America. p. 255: © Elizabeth Crews. p. 259: © Richard Hutchings/PhotoEdit. p. 262: © Elizabeth Crews. p. 264 (top): © Suzanne Szasz. p. 264 (bottom): © Elizabeth Crews. p. 267: © Elizabeth Crews. p. 270: © George White. **Chapter 8** p. 279: © Elizabeth Zuckerman/PhotoEdit. p. 281 (top left): © Elizabeth Crews. p. 281 (top right): © George White Location Photography. p. 281 (bottom): © Claus Meyer/Black Star. p. 282: © David Woo/Stock, Boston. p. 283: © Andrew Brilliant/The Picture Cube. p. 287: © Frank Siteman/The Picture Cube. p. 288: © 1993; Reprinted courtesy of Bunny Hoest and Parade Magazine. p. 294: © George White. p. 297: © David Schaefer/The Picture Cube. **Chapter 9** p. 305: © Elizabeth Crews. p. 310: © Forsyth/Monkmeyer Press. p. 318: © Tom McCarthy/The Picture Cube. p. 320: © Elizabeth Crews. p. 323: © Mike Kullen/The Picture Cube. p. 324: © Elizabeth Crews/The Image Works. p. 326: © Harry Redl/Black Star. p. 327: © George White Location Photography. p. 330: © Myrleen Ferguson/PhotoEdit. p. 331: © Lawrence Migdale/Stock Boston. p. 334: © Reprinted with special permission of King Features Syndicate. p. 342: © Tom Abbott/Leo de Wys. p. 346: © Elizabeth Crews. p. 347: © Eastcott/Momatiuk/Woodfin Camp. p. 349: © Frances M. Cox/Stock Boston. p. 351: © K. B. Kaplan/Picture Cube. p. 352: © Hugh Rogers/Monkmeyer Press. p. 353: © Reprinted with special permission of North America Syndicate. p. 356: © Elizabeth Crews. p. 358: © Dr. A. Bandura, Stanford University. p. 361: © Elizabeth Crews. p. 363: © 1994 Comstock. p. 364: © Dr. Albert Bandura. p. 368 (left): © Betsy Lee. p. 368 (right): © David Strickler/Monkmeyer. p. 370: © Reprinted with special permission of King Features Syndicate. **Chapter 11** p. 383: © David Young-Wolff/PhotoEdit. p. 386: © Bob Daemmrich. p. 388: © Richard Hutchings/Photo Researchers. p. 389: © George White. p. 390: © Rick Rusing/Leo de Wys. p. 392: © Al Cook. p. 397: © Will & Deni McIntyre/Science Source/PR. p. 399: © Frank Siteman/The Picture Cube. p. 405: © Judy Allen-Newberry. p. 416: © Stacy Pick/Stock, Boston. p. 417: © Samuel Teicher. p. 423: © David Dempster. p. 425: © SuperStock, Inc. p. 429: © Joel Gordon 1990. p. 430: © Lester Sloan/Woodfin Camp. p. 436: © George White. p. 437: © Elizabeth Crews. p. 441: © Mary Kate Denny/PhotoEdit. **Chapter 13** p. 447: © Joel Gordon 1990. p. 451: © Michael Newman/PhotoEdit. p. 454: © Bob Daemmrich/Stock, Boston. p. 456: © Bob Daemmrich. p. 457: © David Young-Wolff/PhotoEdit. p. 461: © Michael Nelson/Photo Network. p. 463: © Charles Gupton/Stock, Boston. p. 464: © 1993; Reprinted courtesy of Bunny Hoest and Parade Magazine. p. 467: © David Grossman. p. 469: © Photo Researchers. p. 470: © Robert Brenner/PhotoEdit. p. 472: © Jean-Claude Lejeune/Stock, Boston. p. 474: © Judy Allen-Newberry. p. 477: © Brent Jones/Stock, Boston. p. 486: © 1991 Robert Fried Photography. p. 492: © J. M. Tanner, M.D. p. 497: © Kevin Beebe/Custom Medical Stock Photography. p. 499: © George White Location Photography. p. 501: © Richard Hutchings/Photo Researchers. p. 502: © Alon Reininger/Woodfin Camp. p. 503: © Jeffrey Myers/Stock, Boston. p. 504: AP/Wide World Photos. p. 507: © Jeff Greenberg/The Picture Cube. p. 511: © John Coletti/Stock, Boston. p. 514: Courtesy of the American Cancer Society. p. 520: Courtesy of the Condom Resource Center. **Chapter 15** p. 527: © Bachman/Photo Network. p. 530: © David Young-Wolff/PhotoEdit. p. 532: © Jeffrey Myers/Stock, Boston. p. 536: © Richard Sobol/Stock, Boston. p. 538: © Richard Frieman/Science Source/Photo Researchers. p. 542: © Richard Hutchings/Photo Researchers. p. 543: © Robert Fried/Stock, Boston. p. 549: © George White. p. 551: © Paul Conklin/PhotoEdit. p. 553: © Telegraph Color Library/FPG. p. 555: © Dan McCoy/Rainbow. p. 561: © John Coletti/The Picture Cube. **Chapter 16** p. 570: © Jodi Buren/Woodfin Camp. p. 572: © Donald Dietz/Stock, Boston. p. 575: © Brent Jones/Stock, Boston. p. 578: © Erika Stone/Peter Arnold, Inc. p. 579: © Richard Hutchings/Photo Researchers. p. 582: © Bob Daemmrich/Stock, Boston. p. 586: © Ron Nelson/Stock, Boston. p. 589: © Jodi Buren/Woodfin Camp. p. 593: © Bob Daemmrich. p. 595: © Jeff Lowenthal/Woodfin Camp. p. 599: © Bob Daemmrich/Stock, Boston. p. 692: © Sybil Shackman/Monkmeyer.

# Text Acknowledgments

Page 4: Excerpt from THE PROPHET by Kahlil Gibran. Copyright 1923 by Kahlil Gibran and renewed 1951 by the Adminstrators C. T. A. of Kahlil Gibran Estate and Mary G. Gibran. Reprinted by permission of Alfred A. Knopf, Inc. Table 1.2, page 13: From *American Psychologist,* Volume 43, by Dr. Florence L. Denmark. Reprinted by permission of Dr. Florence L. Denmark. Page 38: Excerpt, adapted from *Behaviorism,* by John B. Watson is reprinted with the permission of W. W. Norton & Company, Inc. Copyright © 1924 by John B. Watson. Page 67: Excerpt from *American Psychologist,* Volume 40, 1985, by Dr. Sandra Scarr. Reprinted by permission of Dr. Sandra Scarr. Figure 2.15, page 68: Adapted from *The Child* (Fig. 12.1) by Claire B. Kopp and Joanne B. Krakow. Copyright © 1982 by Addison Wesley Publishing Company, Inc. Reprinted by permission. Figure 31.1, page 82: From PSYCHOLOGY, Fifth Edition by Spencer A. Rathus, copyright © 1993 by Holt, Rinehart & Winston, Inc., reprinted by permission of the publisher. Figure 3.2, page 83: From UNDERSTANDING CHILD DEVELOPMENT by Spencer A. Rathus and Peter Favaro, copyright © 1988 by Holt, Rinehart & Winson, Inc., reprinted by permission of the publisher. Figures 3.3 & 3.4, pages 83 & 84: From PSYCHOLOGY, Fifth Edition by Spencer A. Rathus, copyright © 1993 by Holt, Rinehart & Winston, Inc., reprinted by permission of the publisher. Figure 3.7, page 90: From UNDERSTANDING CHILD DEVELOPMENT by Spencer A. Rathus and Peter Favaro, copyright © 1988 by Holt, Rinehart & Winston, Inc., reprinted by permission of the publisher. Figure 3.11, page 96: From Rathus, S. A., Nevid, J. S. and Fichner-Rathus, L., *Human Sexuality.* Copyright 1993 by Allyn & Bacon. Reprinted by permission. Figure 3.15, page 104: From *Before We Were Born,* 4e by K. L. Moore. Copyright © 1993 by K. L. Moore. Reprinted by permission of W. B. Saunders Company. Figure 3.16, page 105: From Rathus, S. A., Nevid, J. S. and Fichner-Rathus, L., *Human Sexuality.* Copyright 1993 by Allyn & Bacon. Reprinted by permission. Figure 3.21, page 113: From *Before We Were Born,* 4e by K. L. Moore. Copyright © 1993 by K. L. Moore. Reprinted by permission of W. B. Saunders Company. Figure 4.1, page 128: From Rathus, S. A., Nevid, J. S. and Fichner-Rathus, L., *Human Sexuality.* Copyright 1993 by Allyn & Bacon. Reprinted by permission. Figure 4.16, page 151: From UNDERSTANDING CHILD DEVELOPMENT by Spencer A. Rathus and Peter Favaro, copyright © 1988 by Holt, Rinehart & Winston, Inc., reprinted by permission of the publisher. Table 4.2, page 157: From *Child Development,* Volume 60, 1989, by J. Colombo, M. Moss, & F. D. Horowitz. Copyright © 1989 by The Society for Research in Child Development. Reprinted by permission of The University of Chicago Press. Figure 4.21, page 158: Adapted from article, "Ontogenetic Development of the Human Sleep—Dream Cycle," from *Science,* Vol. 152, 1966, pages 604–619 by H. P. Roffward, J. N. Muzio, & W. C. Dent. Copyright © 1966 by AAAS. Reprinted by permission of American Association for the Advancement of Science. Figure 5.7 & 5.8, pages 177 & 178: From UNDERSTANDING CHILD DEVELOPMENT by Spencer A. Rathus and Peter Favaro, copyright © 1988 by Holt, Rinehart & Winston, Inc., reprinted by permission of the publisher. Figure 5.9, page 179: From PSYCHOLOGY, Fifth Edition by Spencer A. Rathus, copyright © 1993 by Holt, Rinehart & Winston, Inc., reprinted by permission of the publisher. Figure 5.10, page 179: Reprinted by permission of the publishers from THE POSTNATAL DEVELOPMENT OF THE CEREBRAL CORTEX by J. L. Conel, Cambridge, Mass.: Harvard University Press, Copyright © 1959 by J. L. Conel. Figure 5.12, page 183: From PSYCHOLOGY, Fifth Edition by Spencer A. Rathus, copyright © 1993 by Holt, Rinehart & Winston., Inc., reprinted by permission of the publisher. Figure 5.15, page 185: From *The Cultural Context of Infancy,* Volume 2, by B. Hopkins. Copyright © 1991 by B. Hopkins. Reprinted by permission of Ablex Publishing Corporation. Figure 5.17, page 188: Illustration by Alex Semenoick, Adapted from "The Origin of Form Perception," by Robert L. Fantz. Copyright © 1961 by Scientific American, Inc. All Rights Reserved. Figure 5.18, page 189: From *Infant Perception: From Sensation to Cognition* by P. Salapatek. Copyright © 1975 by P. Salapatek. Reprinted by permission of Academic Press. Figure 5.20, page 193: Adapted from article, "Declining Ability to Discriminate Sounds of Other Languages," from *American Scientist,* Volume 77, 1989, by Janet F. Werker. Reprinted by permission of Scientific Research Society. Pages 200, 202, & 206: Excerpts from *Origin of Intelligence in Children* by Jean Piaget. Copyright © 1963 by Jean Piaget. Reprinted by permission of International Universities Press, Inc. Figure 6.7, page 209: From Baillargeon, et al., 1985 & Baillargeon, 1987. Reprinted by permission of Dr. Renee Baillargeon. Table 6.2, page 213: From *Bayley Scales of Infant Development: 2nd Edition.* Copyright © 1993 by The Psychological Corporation. Reproduced by permission. All Rights Reserved. Table 6.3, page 217: From *Biological Foundations of Language,* by E. H. Lenneberg. Copyright © 1967 by John Wiley & Sons. Reprinted by permission. Figure 6.13, page 221: From UNDERSTANDING CHILD DEVELOPMENT by Spencer A. Rathus and Peter Favaro, copyright © 1988 by Holt, Rinehart & Winston, Inc., reprinted by permission of the publisher. Table 6.4, page 223: From UNDERSTANDING CHILD DEVELOPMENT by Spencer A. Rathus and Peter Favaro, copyright © 1988 by Holt, Rinehart & Winston, Inc., reprinted by permission of the publisher. Figure 6.15, page 229: From PSYCHOLOGY, Fifth Edition by Spencer A. Rathus, copyright © 1993 by Holt, Rinehart & Winston, Inc., reprinted by permission of the publisher. Figure 7.4, page 242: From UNDERSTANDING CHILD DEVELOPMENT by Spencer A. Rathus and Peter Favaro, copyright © 1988 by Holt, Rinehart & Winston, Inc., reprinted by permission of the publisher. Figure 7.14, page 261: From *Maximally Discriminative Facial Movement Scoring System* by Dr. Carroll Izard. Reprinted by permission of the author. Figures 8.7 & 8.8, pages 284 & 285: Reprinted from *Analyzing Children's Art* by Rhoda Kellogg, by permission of Mayfield Publishing Company. Copyright © 1969. 1970 by Rhoda Kellogg. Table 8.3, page 290: From *The New York Times,* February 14, 1993. Copyright © 1993 by The New York Times Company. Reprinted by permission. Page 292: From article, "Lead Poisoning Assessing the Risk," from *The New York Times,* September 13, 1992, by Robert Pear. Copyright © 1992 by The New York Times Company. Reprinted by permission. Figure 9.2, page 307: "The Three Mountains Test," from THE PSYCHOLOGY OF THE CHILD by Jean Piaget and Barbel Inhelder. English language copyright © 1969 by Basic Books, Inc. Reprinted by permission of HarperCollins Publishers, Inc. Figure 9.4, page 31: From UNDERSTANDING CHILD DEVELOPMENT by Spencer A. Rathus and Peter Favaro, copyright © 1988 by Holt, Rinehart & Winston, Inc., reprinted by permission of the publisher. Table 9.3, page 328: Adapted from "Recognize Language Development and Delay in Early Childhood," by J. U. Dumtschin, March 1988, *Young Children,* Volume 43, p. 19. Copyright © 1988 by the National Association of the Education of Young Children. Adapted by permission. Page 329: Reprinted from BIG WORLD, SMALL SCREEN: THE ROLE OF TELEVISION IN AMERICAN SOCIETY, edited by Aletha C. Huston et al, by permission of the University of Nebraska Press. Copyright © 1992 by the University of Nebraska Press. Figure 9.16, page 333: From UNDERSTANDING CHILD DEVELOPMENT by Spencer A. Rathus and Peter Favaro, copyright © 1988 by Holt, Rinehart & Winston, Inc., reprinted by permission of the publisher. Table 10.1, page 343: Reprinted by permission from Richard M. Lerner, Anne C. Petersen, and Jeanne Brooks-Gunn, ed., from *Encyclopedia of Adolescence,* New York: Garland Publishing, Inc., 1991. Table 10.2, page 354: From article, "The Significance of Gender Boundaries in Preadolescence," from *Child Development,* Volume 64, 1993, by Sroufe et al. Copyright © 1993 by The Society of Research in Child Development. Reprinted by permission. Page 365: From *"Why Can't A Woman Be More Like a Man?"* (Alan Jay Lerner, Frederick Loewe). Copyright © 1956 (Renewed) ALAN JAY LERNER & FREDERICK LOEWE. All rights administered by CHAPPELL & CO. Rights Reserved. Used by Permission. Table 11.1, page 386: Adapted from *The Child for Three to Eighteen* by O. Sahler & E. R. McAnarney. Copyright © 1981 by O. Sahler & E. R. McAnarney. Reprinted by permission of Mosby Company. Table 11.2, page 387: "Development of Manipulative Skills," from THE EMBRYOLOGY OF BEHAVIOR by Arnold Gesell. Copyright © 1972 by Arnold Gesell, copyright renewed 1973 by Gerhard A. Gesell, Katherine Gesell Walden. Reprinted by permission of HarperCollins Publishers, Inc. Table 11.3, page 391: Adapted from *Diagnostic and Statistical Manual of Mental Disorders,*

Third Edition, Revised, Washington, D.C., American Psychiatric Association, 1987. Table 11.4, page 395: From PSYCHOLOGY, Fifth Edition by Spencer A. Rathus, copyright © 1993 by Holt, Rinehart & Winston, Inc., reprinted by permission of the publisher. Table 11.5, page 396: From UNDERSTANDING CHILD DEVELOPMENT by Spencer A. Rathus and Peter Favaro, copyright © 1988 by Holt, Rinehart & Winston, Inc., reprinted by permission of the publisher. Figure 12.2, page 406: From UNDERSTANDING CHILD DEVELOPMENT by Spencer A. Rathus and Peter Favaro, copyright © 1988 by Holt, Rinehart & Winston, Inc., reprinted by permission of the publisher. Figure 12.3, page 410: From Strutt, et al., 1975. Reprinted by permission of Dr. George Franklin Strutt. Figures 12.4 & 12.7, pages 411 & 418: From PSYCHOLOGY, Fifth Edition by Spencer A. Rathus, copyright © 1993 by Holt, Rinehart & Winston, Inc., reprinted by permission of the publisher. Table 12.1, page 421: From UNDERSTANDING CHILD DEVELOPMENT by Spencer A. Rathus and Peter Favaro, copyright © 1988 by Holt, Rinehart & Winston, Inc., reprinted by permission of the publisher. Table 12.2, page 423: From PSYCHOLOGY, Fifth Edition by Spencer A. Rathus, copyright © 1993 by Holt, Rinehart & Winston, Inc., reprinted by permission of the publisher. Figure 12.10, page 424: Adapted from article, "Developmental Change in Mental Performance," from *Monographs of Society for Research in Child Development,* Volume 38, 1973, by R. B. McCall, M. I. Applebaum, & P. S. Hogarty. Copyright © 1973 by The Society for Research in Child Development, Inc. Reprinted by permission. Figure 12.15, page 432: Adapted from article, "Familial Studies of Intelligence: A Review," from *Science,* Volume 212, 1981, pages 1055–1059," by T. Bouchard et al. Copyright © 1981 by AAAS. Reprinted by permission of American Association for the Advancement of Science. Table 12.3, page 427: From UNDERSTANDING CHILD DEVELOPMENT by Spencer A. Rathus and Peter Favaro, copyright © 1988 by Holt, Rinehart & Winston, Inc., reprinted by permission of the publisher. Page 437: Excerpt from *Language Patterns of Poverty* by Nicholas J. Anastosiow & Michael L. Hanes. Copyright © 1976 by Nicholas J. Anastosiow & Michael L. Hanes. Reprinted by permission of Charles C. Thomas. Page 449: Excerpt from *Developmental Psychology,* Volume 13, 1977, by Dr. Raymond Montemayor et al. Reprinted by permission of the author. Page 470: Excerpt adapted from ABNORMAL PSYCHOLOGY, THE HUMAN EXPERIENCE OF PSYCHOLOGICAL DISORDERS by Richard P. Halgin and Susan Krauss Whitbourne, copyright © 1993 by Harcourt Brace & Company, reprinted by permission of the publisher. Page 472: Excerpt from *Child and Adolescent Psychiatry: A Comprehensive Textbook* by E. B. Weller & R. A. Weller. Copyright © 1991 by E. B. Weller & R. A. Weller. Reprinted by permission of Williams & Wilkins. Page 484: Excerpt from "WHAT'S HAPPENING TO ME?" by Peter Mayle. Copyright © 1975 by Peter Mayle. Used by arrangement with Carol Publishing Group. A Lyle Stuart Book. Figure 14.2, page 487: From UNDERSTANDING CHILD DEVELOPMENT by Spencer A. Rathus and Peter Favaro, copyright © 1988 by Holt, Rinehart & Winston, Inc., reprinted by permission of the publisher. Figure 14.3, page 488: From the *Vital and Health Statistics Series* of the NCHS. Reprinted by permission of the Department of Health & Human Services. Figures 14.4 & 14.6, pages 489 & 490: Reprinted by permission of the publishers from FETUS INTO MAN by J. M. Tanner, Cambridge, Mass: Harvard University Press, Copyright © 1978 by J. M. Tanner. Table 14.1, page 490: Copyright © 1990, From THE KINSEY INSTITUTE NEW REPORT ON SEX by June M. Reinisch, Ph.D. with Ruth Beasley, M. L. S. Reprinted with permission of St. Martin's Press, Incorporated. Page 508: From paper by Professor Andrea M. Hussong and Professor Laurie Chassin, "The Stress-Negative Affect Model of Adolescent Alcohol Use: Disaggregating Negative Effect." Reprinted by permission of Professor Andrea M. Hussong. Page 515: Excerpt from *Tell Me Like It Is: Straight Talk About Sex* by M. B. Osterhout, A. Formichella, & S. McIntyre. Copyright © 1991 by M. B. Osterhout, A. Formichella, & S. McIntyre. Reprinted by permission of Avon Books. Table 14.3, page 516: From PSYCHOLOGY, Fifth Edition by Spencer A. Rathus, copyright © 1993 by Holt, Rinehart & Winston, Inc., reprinted by permission of the publisher. Pages 518–519: Excerpt from *Handbook of Developmental Psychology* by G. J. Whitehurst, edited by B. B. Wolman. Copyright © 1982 by B. B. Wolman. Reprinted by permission of Prentice-Hall, Inc. Page 521: Excerpt from *The New Our Bodies, Ourselves* by The Boston Women's Health Book Collective. Copyright © 1984, 1992 by The Boston Women's Health Book Collective. Reprinted by permission of Simon & Schuster. Page 526: Excerpt from *Cognitive Development* by J. H. Flavell, P. H. Miller, & S. A. Miller. Copyright © 1993 by J. H. Flavell, P. H. Miller, & S. A. Miller. Reprinted by permission of Prentice-Hall, Inc. Page 528: From UNDERSTANDING CHILD DEVELOPMENT by Spencer A. Rathus and Peter Favaro, copyright © 1988 by Holt, Rinehart & Winston, Inc., reprinted by permission of the publisher. Figure 15.5, page 534: Illustration from *The Psychology of Women,* Second Edition of Margaret W. Matlin, copyright © 1993 by Holt, Rinehart and Winston, Inc., reprinted by permission of the publisher. Table 15.1, page 541: From James R. Rest, "The Hierarchical Nature of Moral Judgment," Journal of Personality, 41:1. Copyright © 1989 by Duke University Press. Reprinted by permission. Figure 15.10, page 545: Adapted from "Moral Development & Identification," by L. Kohlberg, from *Child Psychology: Sixty-Second Yearbook for National Society for Study of Education,* edited by H. W. Stevenson. Copyright © 1963 by National Society for the Study of Education. Reprinted by permission. Page 568: Excerpt adapted with permission of the publishers from AT THE THRESHOLD: THE DEVELOPING ADOLESCENT edited by S. Shirley Feldman and Glen R. Elliott, Cambridge, Mass.: Harvard University Press, Copyright © 1990 by the President and Fellows of Harvard University. Page 573: Excerpt from *Adolescent Identity Formation* by J. S. Phinney & D. A. Rosenthal. Copyright © 1992 by J. S. Phinney & D. A. Rosenthal. Reprinted by permission of Sage Publications, Inc. Page 582: Excerpt from article, "My Turn Column," by Brian Jarvis. From NEWSWEEK, May 3, 1993 and © 1993, Newsweek, Inc. All rights reserved. Reprinted by permission. Figures 16.7 & 16.8, pages 583 & 584: From BEING ADOLESCENT: CONFLICT AND GROWTH IN THE TEENAGE YEARS by Mihaly Csikzentmihalyi. Copyright © 1984 by Basic Books, Inc. Reprinted by permission of HarperCollins Publishers, Inc. Page 586: Excerpt from *Growing Up Sexual* by Eleanor S. Morrison. Copyright © 1980 by Eleanor S. Morrison. Reprinted by permission. Figure 16.13, page 597: From article, "The Killers Get Younger," from *The New York Times,* January 31, 1993, by E. Eckholm. Copyright © 1993 by The New York Times Company. Reprinted by permission.

# Name Index

# Subject Index